DATE DUE

		PRINTED IN U.S.A.	

Literature Criticism from 1400 to 1800

Guide to Gale Literary Criticism Series

For criticism on	You need these Gale series
Authors now living or who died after December 31, 1959	*CONTEMPORARY LITERARY CRITICISM (CLC)*
Authors who died between 1900 and 1959	*TWENTIETH-CENTURY LITERARY CRITICISM (TCLC)*
Authors who died between 1800 and 1899	*NINETEENTH-CENTURY LITERATURE CRITICISM (NCLC)*
Authors who died between 1400 and 1799	*LITERATURE CRITICISM FROM 1400 TO 1800 (LC)* *SHAKESPEAREAN CRITICISM (SC)*
Authors who died before 1400	*CLASSICAL AND MEDIEVAL LITERATURE CRITICISM (CMLC)*
Authors of books for children and young adults	*CHILDREN'S LITERATURE REVIEW (CLR)*
Black writers of the past two hundred years	*BLACK LITERATURE CRITICISM (BLC)*
Short story writers	*SHORT STORY CRITICISM (SSC)*
Poets	*POETRY CRITICISM (PC)*
Dramatists	*DRAMA CRITICISM (DC)*
Major authors from the Renaissance to the present	*WORLD LITERATURE CRITICISM, 1500 TO THE PRESENT (WLC)*

For criticism on visual artists since 1850, see
MODERN ARTS CRITICISM (MAC)

ISSN 0740-2880

Volume 22

Literature Criticism from 1400 to 1800

Excerpts from Criticism of the Works
of Fifteenth-, Sixteenth-, Seventeenth-, and
Eighteenth-Century Novelists, Poets, Playwrights,
Philosophers, and Other Creative Writers,
from the First Published Critical Appraisals
to Current Evaluations

James E. Person, Jr.
Editor

Gale Research Inc. · DETROIT · WASHINGTON, D.C. · LONDON

STAFF

James E. Person, Jr., *Editor*

Michael W. Jones, Jelena O. Krstović, Zoran Miderović, Joseph C. Tardiff, Lawrence J. Trudeau
Associate Editors
Paul J. Buczkowski, Meggin M. Condino, Brian J. St. Germain, *Assistant Editors*

Jeanne A. Gough, *Permissions & Production Manager*
Linda M. Pugliese, *Production Supervisor*
Donna Craft, Paul Lewon, Maureen Puhl, Camille Robinson, Jennifer VanSickle, Sheila Walencewicz, *Editorial Associates*

Sandra C. Davis, *Permissions Supervisor (Text)*
Maria L. Franklin, Josephine M. Keene, Michele M. Lonoconus, Shalice Shah, Denise Singleton, Kimberly F. Smilay,
Permissions Associates
Jennifer A. Arnold, Brandy C. Merritt, *Permissions Assistants*

Margaret A. Chamberlain, *Permissions Supervisor (Pictures)*
Pamela A. Hayes, Keith Reed, *Permissions Associates*
Arlene Johnson, Barbara Wallace, *Permissions Assistants*

Victoria B. Cariappa, *Research Manager*
Maureen Richards, *Research Supervisor*
Robert S. Lazich, Mary Beth McElmeel, Tamara C. Nott, *Editorial Associates*
Kelly Hill, Donna Melnychenko, Stefanie Scarlett, *Editorial Assistants*

Mary Beth Trimper, *Production Manager*
Catherine Kemp, *Production Assistant*

Cynthia Baldwin, *Art Director*
C. J. Jonik, *Desktop Publishers/Typesetters*

Library of Congress Catalog Card Number 84-643570
ISBN 0-8103-7964-3
ISSN 0740-2880

Printed in the United States of America
Published simultaneously in the United Kingdom
by Gale Research International Limited
(An affiliated company of Gale Research Inc.)
10 9 8 7 6 5 4 3 2 1

Contents

Preface   vii

Acknowledgments   xi

Preface

*L*iterature Criticism from 1400 to 1800 (LC) presents criticism of world authors of the fifteenth through eighteenth centuries. The literature of this period reflects a turbulent time of radical change that saw the rise of drama equal in stature to that of classical Greece, the birth of the novel and personal essay forms, the emergence of newspapers and periodicals, and major achievements in poetry and philosophy. Much of modern literature reflects the influence of these centuries. Thus the literature treated in *LC* provides insight into the universal nature of human experience, as well as into the life and thought of the past.

Scope of the Series

LC is designed to serve as an introduction to authors of the fifteenth through eighteenth centuries and to the most significant interpretations of these authors' works. The great poets, dramatists, novelists, essayists, and philosophers of this period are considered classics in every secondary school and college or university curriculum. Because criticism of this literature spans nearly six hundred years, an overwhelming amount of critical material confronts the student. *LC* therefore organizes and reprints the most noteworthy published criticism of authors of these centuries. Readers should note that there is a separate Gale reference series devoted to Shakespearean studies. For though belonging properly to the period covered in *LC*, William Shakespeare has inspired such a tremendous and ever-growing corpus of secondary material that the editors have deemed it best to give his works extensive coverage in a separate series, *Shakespearean Criticism*.

Each author entry in *LC* attempts to present a historical survey of critical response to the author's works. Early criticism is offered to indicate initial responses, later selections document any rise or decline in literary reputations, and retrospective analyses provide students with modern views. The size of each author entry is intended to reflect the author's critical reception in English or foreign criticism in translation. Articles and books that have not been translated into English are therefore excluded. Every attempt has been made to identify and include the seminal essays on each author's work and to include recent commentary providing modern perspectives.

The need for *LC* among students and teachers of literature was suggested by the proven usefulness of Gale's *Contemporary Literary Criticism (CLC)*, *Twentieth-Century Literary Criticism (TCLC)*, and *Nineteenth-Century Literature Criticism (NCLC)*, which excerpt criticism of works by nineteenth- and twentieth-century authors. Because of the different time periods covered, there is no duplication of authors or critical material in any of these literary criticism series. An author may appear more than once in the series because of the great quantity of critical material available and because of the aesthetic demands of the series's *thematic organization*.

Thematic Approach

Beginning with Volume 21, all the authors in each volume of *LC* are organized in a thematic scheme. Such themes include literary movements, literary reaction to political and historical events, significant eras in literary history, and the literature of cultures often overlooked by English-speaking readers. The present volume, for example, focuses upon the Elizabethan dramatists. Future volumes of *LC* will devote substantial space to the English Metaphysical poets and authors of the Spanish Golden Age, among many others.

Organization of the Book

Each entry consists of the following elements: author or thematic heading, introduction, list of principal works (in author entries only), annotated works of criticism (each followed by a bibliographical citation), and a bibliography o further reading. Also, most author entries contain author portraits and others illustrations.

- The **author heading** consists of the author's full name, followed by birth and death dates. If an author wrote consistently under a pseudonym, the pseudonym is used in the author heading, with the real name given in parentheses on the first line of the biographical and critical introduction. Also located here are any name variations under which an author wrote, including transliterated forms for authors whose native languages use nonroman alphabets. Uncertain birth or death dates are indicated by question marks. The **thematic heading** simply states the subject of the entry.

- The **biographical and critical introduction** contains background information designed to introduce the reader to an author and to critical discussion of his or her work. Parenthetical material following many of the introductions provides references to biographical and critical reference series published by Gale in which additional material about the author may be found. The **thematic introduction** briefly defines the subject of the entry and provides social and historical background important to understanding the criticism.

- Most *LC* author entries include portraits of the author. Many entries also contain illustrations of materials pertinent to an author's career, including author holographs, title pages, letters, or representations of important people, places, and events in an author's life.

- The **list of principal works** is chronological by date of first book publication and identifies the genre of each work. In the case of foreign authors whose works have been translated in to English, the title and date of the first English-language edition are given in brackets beneath the foreign-language listing. Unless otherwise indicated, drama are dated by first performance, not first publication.

- **Criticism** is arranged chronologically in each author entry to provide a useful perspective on changes in critical evaluation over the years. For the purpose of easy identification, the critic's name and the composition or publication date or the critical work are given at the beginning of each piece of criticism. Unsigned criticism is preceded by the title of the source in which it appeared. All titles by the author featured in the critical entry are printed in boldface type. Publication information (such as publisher names and book prices) and parenthetical numerical references (such as footnotes or page and line references to specific editions of works) have been deleted at the editors' discretion to provide smoother reading of the text.

- Critical essays are prefaced by **annotations** as an additional aid to students using *LC*. These explanatory notes may provide several types of useful information, including: the reputation of a critic, the importance of a work of criticism, the commentator's individual approach to literary criticism, the intent of the criticism, and the growth of critical controversy or changes in critical trends regarding an author's work. In some cases, these notes cross-reference the work of critics within the entry who agree or disagree with each other.

- A complete **bibliographical citation** of the original essay or book follows each piece of criticism.

- An annotated bibliography of **further reading** appears at the end of each entry and suggests resources for additional study of authors and themes. It also includes essays for which the editors could not obtain reprint rights.

Cumulative Indexes

Each volume of *LC* includes a cumulative **author index** listing all the authors that have appeared in *Contemporary Literary Criticism, Twentieth-Century Literary Criticism, Nineteenth-Century Literature Criticism, Literature Criticism from 1400 to 1800,* and *Classical and Medieval Literature Criticism,* along with cross-references to the Gale series *Short Story Criticism, Poetry Criticism, Children's Literature Review, Authors in the News, Contemporary Authors, Contemporary Authors Autobiography Series, Contemporary Authors Bibliographical Series, Dictionary of Literary Biography, Concise Dictionary of Literary Biography, Something about the Author, Something about the Author Autobiography Series,* and *Yesterday's Authors of Books for Children.* Readers will welcome this cumulative author index as a useful tool for locating an author within the various series. The index, which includes authors' birth and death dates, is particularly valuable for those authors who are identified with a certain period but whose death dates cause them to be placed in another, or for those authors whose careers span two periods. For example, F. Scott Fitzgerald is found in *TCLC,* yet a writer often associated with him, Ernest Hemingway, is found in *CLC.*

Beginning with Volume 12, *LC* includes a cumulative **topic index** that lists all literary themes and topics treated in *LC, NCLC* Topics volumes, *TCLC* Topics volumes, and the *CLC* Yearbook. Each volume of *LC* also includes a cumulative **nationality index** in which authors' names are arranged alphabetically under their respective nationalities and followed by the numbers of the volumes in which they appear.

Each volume of *LC* also includes a cumulative **title index,** an alphabetical listing of the literary works discussed in the series since its inception. Each title listing includes the corresponding volume and page numbers where criticism may be located. Foreign-language titles that have been translated followed by the tiles of the translation—for example, *El ingenioso hidalgo Don Quixote de la Mancha (Don Quixote).* Page numbers following these translated titles refers to all pages on which any form of the titles, either forcign-language or translated, appear. Title of novels, dramas, nonfiction books, and poetry, short story, or essays collections are printed in italics, while individual poems, short stories, and essays are printed in roman type within quotation marks.

A Note to the Reader

When writing papers, students who quote directly from any volume in the Literary Criticism Series may use the following general forms to footnote reprinted criticism. The first example pertains to material drawn from periodicals, the second to material reprinted from books.

T. S. Eliot, "John Donne," *The Nation and the Athenaeum,* 33 (9 June 1923), 321-32; excerpted and reprinted in *Literature Criticism from 1400 to 1800,* Vol. 10, ed. James E. Person, Jr. (Detroit: Gale Research, 1989), pp. 28-9.

Clara G. Stillman, *Samuel Butler: A Mid-Victorian Modern* (Viking Press, 1932); excerpted and reprinted in *Twentieth-Century Literary Criticism,* Vol. 33, ed. Paula Kepos (Detroit: Gale Research, 1989), pp. 43-5.

Suggestions Are Welcome

In response to various suggestion features have been added to *LC* since the series began, including a nationality index, a Literary Criticism Series topic index, thematic entries, a descriptive table of contents, and more extensive illustrations.

Readers who wish to suggest new features, themes or authors to appear in future volumes, or who have other suggestions, are cordially invited to write to the editor.

Acknowledgments

The editors wish to thank the copyright holders of the excerpted criticism included in this volume, the permissions managers of many book and magazine publishing companies for assisting us in securing reprint rights, and Anthony Bogucki for assistance with copyright research. We are also grateful to the staffs of the Detroit Public Library, the Library of Congress, the University of Detroit Library, Wayne State University Purdy/Kresge Library Complex, and the University of Michigan Libraries for making their resources available to us. Following is a list of the copyright holders who have granted us permission to reprint material in this volume of *LC*. Every effort has been made to trace copyright, but if omissions have been made, please let us know.

COPYRIGHTED EXCERPTS IN *LC*, VOLUME 22, WERE REPRINTED FROM THE FOLLOWING PERIODICALS:

Comparative Drama, v. 11, Summer, 1977. © copyright 1977, by the Editors of *Comparative Drama.* Reprinted by permission of AMS Press, Inc.—*ELH,* v. 49, Fall, 1982. Copyright © 1982 by The Johns Hopkins University Press. All rights reserved. Reprinted by permission of the publisher.—*Iowa State Journal of Research,* v. 61, February, 1987. Reprinted by permission of the publisher.—*Mosaic: A Journal for the Comparative Study of Literature and Ideas,* v. IX, Fall, 1975. © *Mosaic* 1975. Acknowledgment of previous publication in herewith made.—*Shakespeare Survey: An Annual Survey of Shakespeare Studies and Production,* v. 42, 1990. © Cambridge University Press, 1990. Reprinted with the permission of Cambridge University Press.—*Studies in English Literature, 1500-1900,* v. VI, Spring, 1966 for "Thomas Dekker: A Partial Reappraisal" by Normand Berlin; v. 25, Spring, 1985 for "The Inverted World of *Bussy D'Ambois*" by Jane Melbourne. © 1966, 1985 William Marsh Rice University. Both reprinted by permission of the publisher and the respective authors./ v. IV, 1964. © 1964 William Marsh Rice University. Reprinted by permission of the publisher.—*Tennessee Studies in Literature,* v. XIII, 1968. Copyright © 1968, by The University of Tennessee Press. Reprinted by permission of The University of Tennessee Press.

COPYRIGHTED EXCERPTS IN *LC*, VOLUME 22, WERE REPRINTED FROM THE FOLLOWING BOOKS:

Archer, William. From *The Old Drama and the New: An Essay in Re-Valuation.* Small, Maynard, 1923. Copyright, 1923 Small, Maynard and Company (Incorporated). Renewed 1950 by Frank Archer.—Barber, C. L. From *Creating Elizabethan Tragedy: The Theater of Marlowe and Kyd.* Edited by Richard P. Wheeler. University of Chicago Press, 1988. © 1988 by The University of Chicago. All rights reserved. Reprinted by permission of the publisher, the editor and the Literary Estate of C. L. Barber.—Barish, Jonas A. From " 'The Spanish Tragedy', or The Pleasures and Perils of Rhetoric," in *Elizabethan Theatre.* Edited by John Russell Brown and Bernard Harris. Arnold, 1966. © Edward Arnold (Publishers) Ltd. 1966. Reprinted by permission of the publisher.—Bowers, Fredson. From *Elizabethan Revenge Tragedy, 1587-1642.* Princeton University Press, 1940. Copyright 1940 by Princeton University Press. Renewed 1968 by Fredson T. Bowers. Reprinted by permission of the publisher.—Brooks, Cleanth. From "The Unity of Marlowe's 'Doctor Faustus'," in *A Shaping Joy: Studies in the Writer's Craft.* Methuen, 1971, Harcourt Brace Jovanovich, 1972. Copyright © 1971 by Cleanth Brooks. Reprinted by permission of Harcourt Brace Jovanovich, Inc. In Canada by Methuen & Co. Ltd.—Champion, Larry S. From *Thomas Dekker and the Traditions of English Drama.* Lang, 1985. © Peter Lang Publishing, Inc., New York 1985. All rights reserved. Reprinted by permission of the publisher.—Daiches, David. From *More Literary Essays.* Oliver & Boyd, 1968. © 1968 by David Daiches. All rights reserved. Reprinted by permission of the author.—Doran, Madeleine. From *Endeavors of Art: A Study of Form in Elizabethan Drama.* University of Wisconsin Press, 1954. Copyright © 1954 The Regents of University of Wisconsin. Renewed 1982 by Madeleine Doran. All rights reserved. Reprinted by permission of the publisher.—Edwards, Philip. From "Thrusting Elysium

George Chapman
1559?-1634

English dramatist, poet, and translator.

INTRODUCTION

Chapman is considered one of the most important classicists of the English Renaissance. Dramatist, poet, and distinguished translator, he embodied the Renaissance ideal of the sophisticated man of letters capable of writing competently in a wide range of genres. He was as much at ease writing non-dramatic poetry as he was writing farcical comedies or philosophical tragedies. Chapman's dramas achieved moderate popular success in his lifetime, though they are now rarely performed. Today Chapman is best known for his tragedy *Bussy D'Ambois*, a representation of the career of the chivalrous Duke of Alençon, as well as for his completion of Christopher Marlowe's poem *Hero and Leander*, though many critics consider his translations of Homer, especially the *Illiads* and the *Odysses*, his most important achievement.

Chapman's life is not well documented. He was born at Hitchin in Hertfordshire, probably around the year 1559, the second son of a prosperous yeoman and copyholder. His mother was the daughter of a royal huntsman at the court of Henry VIII. Very little is known about Chapman's early education, though it is presumed he attended the grammar school at Hitchin. Contemporary accounts also indicate that he attended Oxford beginning in 1574, where he is said to have excelled in Greek and Latin. Following his sojourn at Oxford, Chapman entered in the service of a prominent nobleman, Sir Ralph Sadler, whom he attended from 1583 to 1585. He subsequently served with the military expedition of Sir Francis Vere in the United Provinces, which were then engaged in the Eighty Years War. Chapman returned to England in 1594, establishing residence in London and publishing his first work, *The Shadow of Night: Containing Two Poeticall Hymnes*. Around this time, Chapman entered Sir Walter Raleigh's circle, a literary group devoted to scientific and philosophical speculation, though occasionally dabbling in the occult. Termed "The School of Night" by William Shakespeare for their esoteric ideas, the circle's influence, especially its metaphysical orientation, is evident in Chapman's writings of the 1590s, for example in *Ouid's Banquet of Sence* and his completion of Christopher Marlowe's *Hero and Leander*.

Toward the end of the 1590s Chapman also debuted as a dramatist with a pair of comedies, *The Blind Beggar of Alexandria* and *A Humorous Day's Mirth*, written for the Lord Admiral's Men, a major theatrical company in London. Other comedies followed, written for similar private theatrical companies. By the close of the Elizabethan period, Chapman was widely recognized as a leading drama-

tist and poet, yet the meager income from production of his plays forced him to live in poverty. Increasingly straitened circumstances led to desperate solutions: in 1599, Chapman relinquished his claim to the family estate for a small cash settlement. The following year Chapman was imprisoned for debt, the unwitting victim of a fraudulent money-lender.

With the accession of James I in 1603, Chapman's fortunes suddenly changed when he was given a position in the household of Prince Henry. He continued composing dramas, including his last major comedy, *Eastward Ho*, written in collaboration with Ben Jonson and John Marston. The play's sarcastic political aspersions against policies favored by James I resulted in swift imprisonment for Chapman and Jonson, though both were soon released. Afterward, Chapman turned to tragedy. His best-known works from this period are *Bussy D'Ambois* and the two-part *The Conspiracy and Tragedy of Charles, Duke of Byron*. Chapman's Jacobean career was also notable for his ambitious design to translate into modern English the classical Greek works of Homer. His translation of the first twelve books of the *Iliad* appeared in 1609, prefaced by a dedication to Prince Henry, an enlightened patron of the arts who had endorsed the work with the promise of three hundred pounds and a pension. However, when the young prince died suddenly in 1612, the prince's father failed to fulfill Henry's promise to Chapman. A similar fate befell Chapman's hope in his last patron, Robert Carr, later Earl of Somerset, whose career at court was effectively terminated due to a series of marital scandals. In effect, Chapman remained without a patron for his entire literary career, the financial and professional consequences of which were disastrous. Though he completed a pair of classical tragedies around 1615 (never performed during his lifetime) and a translation of Homer's poetry by 1624, Chapman's last few decades were spent in relative obscurity. Nonetheless, when he died on 12 May 1634, Chapman was honored by the great, including the fashionable architect Inigo Jones, who constructed his funeral monument.

Chapman's approach to literature was similar to that of his famous contemporary Ben Jonson. Like Jonson, Chapman was strongly influenced by the artistic theories of the Italian Renaissance writers, who held that the works of classical antiquity had laid the foundation of true artistic principles. However, while Jonson was specifically concerned with matters of literary style, Chapman was more interested in theoretical and philosophical problems. The Neo-Platonic theories of Marsilio Ficino and Pico della Mirandola, urging that artistic endeavors should aim to represent an ideal realm of truth, formed the basis of Chapman's poetics. The Stoic philosophy enunciated in the works of Seneca and Epictetus also influenced Chapman, particularly with regard to his tragic vision.

Though Chapman is most widely studied for his dramas, like most writers of the English Renaissance he recognized narrative poetry as an important genre of classical literature and imitated such Latin poets as Ovid. His first poem, *The Shadow of Night,* consists of two books, addressed to the figure of Night and the pagan goddess of the Moon, Cynthia. *The Shadow of Night* is written in the form of a complex allegory, exploring different levels of meaning—philosophical, political, and poetic—in an attempt to rationalize man's condition on earth. Perhaps Chapman's most highly regarded poem, *Ouid's Banquet of Sence* depicts Ovid's encounter with Julia, the daughter of the Roman emperor Augustus, who inspires him to write *The Art of Love.* Chapman's next major work, his completion of Christopher Marlowe's first two books of *Hero and Leander,* is viewed by most critics as an austere corrective to Marlowe's sensual imagery. In the final sestiads of *Hero and Leander,* Chapman writes again from an allegorical perspective on the meaning of Ovid's *Metamorphoses.* While some critics link Chapman's poetic canon to seventeenth-century Metaphysical poetry because of his use of dense imagery to illuminate philosophical questions, others maintain that his narrative poems were intended as ironic commentary on the philosophical dilemmas posed by poets during the Augustan Age in Rome.

Chapman's career as a dramatist was divided fairly evenly between comedy and tragedy, with his early years largely devoted to comedies patterned after classical Roman models by Plautus and Terence. Chapman's first play, *The Blind Beggar of Alexandria,* is specifically modeled on the low comic theater of Plautus. It is an irreverent sexual farce wherein the title character succeeds in seducing a series of women through role-playing and manipulation. Certain critics consider the play the first example of the "Comedy of Humours," a type of comedy traditionally attributed to Ben Jonson. Also considered an example of low comedy, *A Humorous Day's Mirth* features a standard disguise plot of great complexity that revolves around the clever romantic intrigues of a courtier named Lemot. *All Fools,* an adaptation of Terence's *Heauton Timoroumenos,* is similarly a romantic farce focusing on the rituals of courtship and marriage. *Eastward Ho* is perhaps Chapman's best known dramatic achievement. Produced in 1604 and intended to capitalize on the success of Thomas Dekker and John Webster's *Westward Ho,* the play explores the social milieu of London's middle class and is considered an excellent example of the city-comedy genre. Chapman's last noncollaborative comedy, *The Gentleman Usher,* is cited by many commentators as his finest work in that genre. Usually described as a tragicomedy, the play is set in an Italian Renaissance court and involves the amorous intrigues of rival courtiers, Medice and Strozza.

Critics agree that Chapman's greatest dramatic achievement was in the tragic genre. In his best-regarded works, he turned for appropriate subjects to recent French history, comprising the reigns of Henry III and Henry IV. His first and most important tragedy, *Bussy D'Ambois,* is based on the life of Louis de Clermont d'Amboise, Seigneur de Bussy, a notorious duelist and adventurer at the court of Henry III. Bussy is cast as a classical hero, echoing Hercules, Prometheus, and other mythical archetypes. Recently, critics have explored the relation of Bussy to the title hero of Christopher Marlowe's *Tamburlaine,* arguing that both personify the Herculean hero type admired by the Italian Humanists. Chapman also wrote a sequel, *The Revenge of Bussy D'Ambois,* considered a far weaker play. None of the characters and events relate to French history as in the original, being entirely the creation of Chapman's imagination. The play's indecisive protagonist, Bussy's avenging brother Clermont, is generally assumed to be patterned after Shakespeare's Hamlet. *The Conspiracy and Tragedy of Charles, Duke of Byron* treats the intrigues and eventual execution of a prominent courtier serving Henry IV. An early performance in 1608 aroused the wrath of the French ambassador, who ordered the arrest of three actors because of a scandalous scene between the king's wife and his mistress. The play was so heavily censored by government authorities that the 1625 reprint bore little resemblance to the original. Chapman's final tragedies, *Caesar and Pompey* and *The Tragedy of Chabot, Admiral of France,* further elaborate on the theme of the stoic hero, but they have received less critical attention. Overall, the verdict on Chapman's dramaturgy is mixed. While many critics note Chapman's competence in plot and characterization, as well as his philosophical depth, others disparage his style as obtuse and overly elaborate.

Chapman's translations of Homer's epic poetry have also received significant critical attention, in his own lifetime and particularly during the Romantic period. The degree to which his translations successfully communicate Homer's language and meaning is now widely disputed because of Chapman's limited knowledge of classical Greek and free interpretation of Homer's original text. Nonetheless, many critics argue that Chapman's achievement as a translator must be assessed in light of his own poetic theories. As Raymond B. Waddington puts it, Chapman "regarded his job as *translation,* making the universal values of Homer comprehensible and therefore relevant to his own time and culture."

PRINCIPAL WORKS

The Shadow of Night: Containing Two Poeticall Hymns (poetry) 1594

Ouid's Banquet of Sence. A Coronet for His Mistresse Philosophie, and His Amorous Zodiacke. With a Translation of a Latine Coppie, Written by a Fryer, Anno Dom. 1400. (poetry) 1595

The Blind Beggar of Alexandria (drama) 1596

A Humorous Day's Mirth (drama) 1597

*Hero and Leander (poetry) 1598

All Fools (drama) 1601

May-Day (drama) 1601-02

The Gentleman Usher (drama) 1602-03

Bussy D'Ambois (drama) 1604

Monsieur D'Olive (drama) 1604-05

The Widow's Tears (drama) 1604-05

†Eastward Ho (drama) 1605

‡The Conspiracy and Tragedy of Charles, Duke of Byron (drama) 1607-08

The Revenge of Bussy D'Ambois (drama) 1610-11

The Illiads of Homer [translator] (poetry) 1611

§Caesar and Pompey (drama) c. 1613

The Tragedy of Chabot, Admiral of France (drama) c. 1613 [published 1639]

Homer's Odysses [translator] (poetry) 1614-15?

The Whole Works of Homer; In His Illiads, and Odysses [translator] (poetry) 1616

The Plays and Poems of George Chapman. 2 vols. (drama and poetry) 1910-13

The Poems of George Chapman (poetry) 1941

Chapman's Homer. 2 vols. [translator] (poetry) 1967

---

*Parts 1 and 2 of this poem were written by Christopher Marlowe c. 1593.

†This drama was written in collaboration with Ben Jonson and John Marston.

‡This work is composed of two separate plays, *Byron's Conspiracy* and *Byron's Tragedy,* that were printed and apparently planned together.

§This work was not published until 1631.

John Dryden   (essay date 1681)

[*Regarded by many scholars as the father of modern English poetry and criticism, Dryden dominated literary life in England during the last four decades of the seventeenth century. Although recognized as a prolific and accomplished Restoration dramatist, Dryden composed a number of satirical poems and critical writings which are acknowledged as his greatest literary achievements. In the following excerpt from a dedicatory epistle to* The Spanish Friar; or, The Double Discovery, *first pub-*lished in 1681, Dryden condemns the author of Bussy d'Ambois *for disregarding the neoclassical conventions of symmetry and decorum.*]

In a play-house, everything contributes to impose upon the judgment; the lights, the scenes, the habits, and, above all, the grace of action, which is commonly the best where there is the most need of it, surprise the audience, and cast a mist upon their understandings; not unlike the cunning of a juggler, who is always staring us in the face, and overwhelming us with gibberish, only that he may gain the opportunity of making the cleaner conveyance of his trick. But these false beauties of the stage are no more lasting than a rainbow; when the actor ceases to shine upon them, when he gilds them no longer with his reflection, they vanish in a twinkling. I have sometimes wondered, in the reading, what was become of those glaring colours which amazed me in **Bussy D'Amboys** upon the theatre; but when I had taken up what I supposed a fallen star, I found I had been cozened with a jelly; nothing but a cold, dull mass, which glittered no longer than it was shooting; a dwarfish thought, dressed up in gigantic words, repetition in abundance, looseness of expression, and gross hyperboles; the sense of one line expanded prodigiously into ten; and, to sum up all, uncorrect English, and a hideous mingle of false poetry and true nonsense; or, at best, a scantling of wit, which lay gasping for life, and groaning beneath a heap of rubbish. A famous modern poet used to sacrifice every year a Statius to Virgil's *Manes;* and I have indignation enough to burn a **D'Amboys** annually to the memory of Jonson. (p. 157)

> *John Dryden, "Nature and Dramatic Art," in his* Dramatic Essays, *J. M. Dent & Sons Ltd., 1912, pp. 156-60.*

Samuel Taylor Coleridge   (letter date 1807)

[*An English poet and critic, Coleridge was central to the English Romantic movement and is considered one of the greatest literary critics in the English language. In the following extract from a letter addressed to William Wordsworth in 1807, Coleridge expresses his approval of Chapman's translations of* The Odyssey *and* The Iliad, *noting that they have "no look, no air of a translation."*]

Chapman I have sent in order that you might read the **Odyssey;** the **Iliad** is fine, but less equal in the translation, as well as less interesting in itself. What is stupidly said of Shakespeare, is really true and appropriate of Chapman; mighty faults counterpoised by mighty beauties. Excepting his quaint epithets which he affects to render literally from the Greek, a language above all others blest in the "happy marriage of sweet words," and which in our language are mere printer's compound epithets—such as quaffed divine *joy-in-the-heart-of-man-infusing* wine, (the undermarked is to be one word, because one sweet mellifluous word expresses it in Homer);—excepting this, it has no look, no air, of a translation. It is as truly an original poem as the *Faery Queene;*—it will give you small idea of Homer, though a far truer one than Pope's epigrams, or Cowper's cumbersome most anti-Homeric Miltonism. For Chapman writes and feels as a poet,—as Homer might have written had he lived in England in the reign of Queen

Elizabeth. In short, it is an exquisite poem, in spite of its frequent and perverse quaintnesses and harshnesses, which are, however, amply repaid by almost unexampled sweetness and beauty of language, all over spirit and feeling. In the main it is an English heroic poem, the tale of which is borrowed from the Greek. The dedication to the *Iliad* is a noble copy of verses, especially those sublime lines beginning,—

> O! 'tis wondrous much
> (Through nothing prisde) that the right vertuous touch
> Of a well written soule, to vertue moves.
> Nor haue we soules to purpose, if their loves
> Of fitting objects be not so inflam'd.
> How much then, were this kingdome's maine soul maim'd,
> To want this great inflamer of all powers
> That move in humane soules! All realmes but yours,
> Are honor'd with him; and hold blest that state
> That have his workes to reade and contemplate.
> In which, humanitie to her height is raisde;
> Which all the world (yet, none enough) hath praisde.
> Seas, earth, and heaven, he did in verse comprize;
> Out sung the Muses, and did equalise
> Their king Apollo; being so farre from cause
> Of princes light thoughts, that their gravest lawes
> May finde stuffe to be fashiond by his lines.
> Through all the pompe of kingdomes still he shines
> And graceth all his gracers. Then let lie
> Your lutes, and viols, and more loftily
> Make the heroiques of your Homer sung,
> To drums and trumpets set his Angels tongue:
> And with the princely sports of haukes you use,
> Behold the kingly flight of his high Muse:
> And see how like the Phœnix she renues
> Her age, and starrie feathers in your sunne;
> Thousands of yeares attending; everie one
> Blowing the holy fire, and throwing in
> Their seasons, kingdomes, nations that have bin
> Subverted in them; lawes, religions, all
> Offerd to change, and greedie funerall;
> Yet still your Homer lasting, living, raigning.—

and likewise the 1st, the 11th, and last but one, of the prefatory sonnets to the *Odyssey*. Could I have foreseen any other speedy opportunity, I should have begged your acceptance of the volume in a somewhat handsomer coat; but as it is, it will better represent the sender,—to quote from myself—

> A man disherited, in form and face,
> By nature and mishap, of outward grace.

Chapman in his moral heroic verse, as in this dedication and the prefatory sonnets to his *Odyssey*, stands above Ben Jonson; there is more dignity, more lustre, and equal strength; but not midway quite between him and the sonnets of Milton. I do not know whether I give him the higher praise, in that he reminds me of Ben Jonson with a sense of his superior excellence, or that he brings Milton to memory notwithstanding his inferiority. His moral poems are not quite out of books like Jonson's, nor yet do

the sentiments so wholly grow up out of his own natural habit and grandeur of thought, as in Milton. The sentiments have been attracted to him by a natural affinity of his intellect, and so combined;—but Jonson has taken them by individual and successive acts of choice.

All this and the preceding is well felt and vigorously, though harshly, expressed, respecting sublime poetry *in genere;* but in reading Homer I look about me, and ask how does all this apply here. For surely never was there plainer writing; there are a thousand charms of sun and moonbeam, ripple, and wave, and stormy billow, but all on the surface. Had Chapman read Proclus and Porphyry?—and did he really believe them,—or even that they believed themselves? They felt the immense power of a Bible, a Shaster, a Koran. There was none in Greece or Rome, and they tried therefore by subtle allegorical accommodations to conjure the poem of Homer into the βιβλιον θεοπαραδοτον of Greek faith.

Chapman's identification of his fate with Homer's, and his complete forgetfulness of the distinction between Christianity and idolatry, under the general feeling of some religion, is very interesting. It is amusing to observe, how familiar Chapman's fancy has become with Homer, his life and its circumstances, though the very existence of any such individual, at least with regard to the *Iliad* and the Hymns, is more than problematic. N. B. The rude engraving in the page was designed by no vulgar hand. It is full of spirit and passion.

I am so dull, that neither in the original nor in any translation could I ever find any wit or wise purpose in this poem. The whole humour seems to lie in the names. The frogs and mice are not frogs or mice, but men, and yet they do nothing that conveys any satire. In the Greek there is much beauty of language, but the joke is very flat. This is always the case in rude ages;—their serious vein is inimitable,—their comic low and low indeed. The psychological cause is easily stated, and copiously exemplifiable. (pp. 230-34)

> *Samuel Taylor Coleridge, in an extract from a letter to William Wordsworth in 1807, in his* Notes and Lectures upon Shakespeare and Some of the Old Poets and Dramatists, *Vol. II, edited by Mrs. H. N. Coleridge, William Pickering, 1849, pp. 230-34.*

Charles Lamb (essay date 1808)

[*An English essayist, critic, and poet, Lamb is credited with initiating the revival of interest in Elizabethan and Restoration drama in nineteenth-century England. His critical comments on the plays of John Webster, Jeremy Taylor, Thomas Heywood, and John Ford, recorded in the form of notes to his anthology,* Specimens of the English Dramatic Poets, Who Lived about the Time of Shakespeare *(1808), demonstrate a refinement of critical method new in his time. In the following excerpt from that work, Lamb censures Chapman's translations of Homer's works, forwarding that "the great obstacle to [their] translations being read is their unconquerable quaintness"; however, Lamb concedes that the passion of the translations continues to render them powerful.*]

Of all the English Play-writers, Chapman perhaps approaches nearest to Shakespeare in the descriptive and didactic, in passages which are less purely dramatic. Dramatic Imitation was not his talent. He could not go out of himself, as Shakespeare could shift at pleasure, to inform and animate other existences, but in himself he had an eye to perceive and a soul to embrace all forms. He would have made a great epic poet, if, indeed, he has not abundantly shown himself to be one; for his **Homer** is not so properly a Translation as the Stories of Achilles and Ulysses re-written. The earnestness and passion which he has put into every part of these poems would be incredible to a reader of mere modern translations. His almost Greek zeal for the honour of his heroes is only paralleled by that fierce spirit of Hebrew bigotry, with which Milton, as if personating one of the Zealots of the old law, clothed himself when he sate down to paint the acts of Samson against the Uncircumcised. The great obstacle to Chapman's Translations being read is their unconquerable quaintness. He pours out in the same breath the most just and natural and the most violent and forced expressions. He seems to grasp whatever words come first to hand during the impetus of inspiration, as if all other must be inadequate to the divine meaning. But passion (the all in all in Poetry) is everywhere present, raising the low, dignifying the mean, and putting sense into the absurd. He makes his readers glow, weep, tremble, take any affection which he pleases, be moved by words, or in spite of them, be disgusted and overcome their disgust. I have often thought that the vulgar misconception of Shakespeare, as of a wild irregular genius "in whom great faults are compensated by great beauties," would be really true applied to Chapman. But there is no scale by which to balance such disproportionate subjects as the faults and beauties of a great genius. To set off the former with any fairness against the latter, the pain which they give us should be in some proportion to the pleasure which we receive from the other. As these transport us to the highest heaven, those should steep us in agonies infernal. (p. 170)

> *Charles Lamb, "Byron's Tragedy," in his* Specimens of English Dramatic Poets, Vol. I, *edited by Israel Gollancz, 1808. Reprint by Johnson Reprint Corporation, 1970, pp. 168-70.*

John Keats   (poem date 1816)

[*Keats is considered a key figure in the English Romantic movement and one of the major poets in the English language. In the following poem, written in 1816, Keats lauds Chapman's poetic rendering of Homer's classical works in English.*]

> Much have I travell'd in the realms of gold,
>   And many goodly states and kingdoms seen;
>   Round many western islands have I been
> Which bards in fealty to Apollo hold.
>
> Oft of one wide expanse had I been told
>   That deep-brow'd Homer ruled as his de-

> mesne;
>   Yet did I never breathe its pure serene
> Till I heard Chapman speak out loud and bold:
> Then felt I like some watcher of the skies
>
> When a new planet swims into his ken;
> Or like stout Cortez when with eagle eyes
>   He star'd at the Pacific—and all his men
> Look'd at each other with a wild surmise—
>   Silent, upon a peak in Darien.

(pp. 85-7)

> *John Keats, "On First Looking into Chapman's Homer," in his* The Poetical Works and Other Writings of John Keats: Poems 1817, Vol. I, *edited by H. Buxton Forman, revised edition, Charles Scribner's Sons, 1938, pp. 85-7.*

William Hazlitt   (lecture date 1819)

[*An English essayist, Hazlitt was one of the most important critics of the Romantic age. In the following excerpt from a lecture delivered in 1819, Hazlitt briefly summarizes Chapman's overall dramatic achievement.*]

Next to Marston, I must put Chapman, whose name is better known as the translator of Homer than as a dramatic writer. He is, like Marston, a philosophic observer, a didactic reasoner: but he has both more gravity in his tragic style, and more levity in his comic vein. His **Bussy D'Ambois,** though not without interest or some fancy, is rather a collection of apophthegms or pointed sayings in the form of a dialogue, than a poem or a tragedy. In his verses the oracles have not ceased. Every other line is an axiom in morals—a libel on mankind, if truth is a libel. He is too stately for a wit, in his serious writings—too formal for a poet. **Bussy d'Ambois** is founded on a French plot and French manners. The character, from which it derives its name, is arrogant and ostentatious to an unheard-of degree, but full of nobleness and lofty spirit. His pride and unmeasured pretensions alone take away from his real merit; and by the quarrels and intrigues in which they involve him, bring about the catastrophe, which has considerable grandeur and imposing effect, in the manner of Seneca. Our author aims at the highest things in poetry, and tries in vain, wanting imagination and passion, to fill up the epic moulds of tragedy with sense and reason alone, so that he often runs into bombast and turgidity—is extravagant and pedantic at one and the same time. From the nature of the plot, which turns upon a love intrigue, much of the philosophy of this piece relates to the character of the sex. Milton says,

> The way of women's will is hard to hit.

But old Chapman professes to have found the clue to it, and winds his uncouth way through all the labyrinth of love. Its deepest recesses 'hide nothing from his view.' The close intrigues of court policy, the subtle workings of the human soul, move before him like a sea dark, deep, and glittering with wrinkles for the smile of beauty. Fulke Greville alone could go beyond him in gravity and mystery. The plays of the latter (*Mustapha* and *Alaham*) are abstruse as the mysteries of old, and his style inexplicable as the riddles of the Sphinx. As an instance of his love for the obscure, the marvellous, and impossible, he calls up 'the ghost of one of the old kings of Ormus,' as prologue to one of his tragedies; a very reverend and inscrutable personage, who, we may be sure, blabs no living secrets. Chapman, in his other pieces, where he lays aside the gravity of the philosopher and poet, discovers an unexpected comic vein, distinguished by equal truth of nature and lively good humour. I cannot say that this character pervades any one of his entire comedies; but the introductory sketch of **Monsieur D'Olive** is the undoubted prototype of that light, flippant, gay, and infinitely delightful class of character, of the professed men of wit and pleasure about town, which we have in such perfection in Wycherley and Congreve, such as Sparkish, Witwoud and Petulant, &c. both in the sentiments and in the style of writing. (pp. 230-31)

His **May-Day** is not so good. **All Fools, The Widow's Tears,** and **Eastward Hoe,** are comedies of great merit, (particularly the last). The first is borrowed a good deal from Terence, and the character of Valerio, an accomplished rake, who passes with his father for a person of the greatest economy and rusticity of manners, is an excellent idea, executed with spirit. **Eastward Hoe** was written in conjunction with Ben Jonson and Marston; and for his share in it, on account of some allusions to the Scotch, just after the accession of James I. our author, with his friends, had nearly lost his ears. Such were the notions of poetical justice in those days! The behaviour of Ben Jonson's mother on this occasion is remarkable. 'On his release from prison, he gave an entertainment to his friends, among whom were Camden and Selden. In the midst of the entertainment, his mother, more an antique Roman than a Briton, drank to him, and shewed him a paper of poison, which she intended to have given him in his liquor, having first taken a portion of it herself, if the sentence for his punishment had been executed.' This play contains the first idea of Hogarth's Idle and Industrious Apprentices. (p. 234)

William Hazlitt, "On Marston, Chapman, Deckar, and Webster," in his The Complete Works of William Hazlitt, Vol. 6, *J. M. Dent and Sons, Ltd., 1931, pp. 223-48.*

James Russell Lowell (lecture date 1887)

[*A celebrated American poet and essayist, Lowell is regarded by literary historians as a major nineteenth-century critic. In the following excerpt from a lecture delivered in 1887, Lowell appraises Chapman's major dramas and his translations of Homer.*]

[Chapman] wrote seven comedies and eight tragedies that have come down to us, and probably others that have perished. Nearly all his comedies are formless and coarse, but with what seems to me a kind of stiff and wilful coarseness, as if he were trying to make his personages speak in what he supposed to be their proper dialect, in which he himself was unpractised, having never learned it in those haunts, familiar to most of his fellow-poets, where it was vernacular. His characters seem, indeed, types, and he frankly

proclaims himself an idealist in the dedication of **The Revenge of Bussy d'Ambois** to Sir Thomas Howard, where he says, "And for the authentical truth of either person or action, who (worth the respecting) will expect it in a Poem whose subject is not truth, but things like truth?" Of his comedies, **All Fools** is by general consent the best. It is less lumpish than the others, and is, on the whole, lively and amusing. In his comedies he indulges himself freely in all that depreciation of woman which had been so long traditional with the sex which has the greatest share in making them what they are. But he thought he was being comic, and there is, on the whole, no more depressing sight than a naturally grave man under that delusion. His notion of love, too, is coarse and animal, or rather the notion he thinks proper to express through his characters. And yet in his comedies there are two passages, one in praise of love, and the other of woman, certainly among the best of their kind. The first is a speech of Valerio in **All Fools:**—

> I tell thee love is Nature's second sun
> Causing a spring of virtues where he shines;
> And as without the sun, the world's great eye,
> All colors, beauties, both of art and nature,
> Are given in vain to men, so without love
> All beauties bred in women are in vain,
> All virtues born in men lie buried;
> For love informs them as the sun doth colors;
> And as the sun, reflecting his warm beams
> Against the earth, begets all fruits and flowers,
> So love, fair shining in the inward man,
> Brings forth in him the honorable fruits
> Of valor, wit, virtue, and haughty thoughts,
> Brave resolution and divine discourse:
> O, 't is the paradise, the heaven of earth!
> And didst thou know the comfort of two hearts
> In one delicious harmony united,
> As to enjoy one joy, think both one thought,
> Live both one life and therein double life, . . .

> Thou wouldst abhor thy tongue for blasphemy.

And now let me read to you a passage in praise of women from **The Gentleman Usher.** It is not great poetry, but it has fine touches of discrimination both in feeling and expression:—

> Let no man value at a little price
> A virtuous woman's counsel; her winged spirit
> Is feathered oftentimes with heavenly words,
> And, like her beauty, ravishing and pure;
> The weaker body still the stronger soul. . . .

> O what a treasure is a virtuous wife,
> Discreet and loving! not one gift on earth
> Makes a man's life so highly bound to heaven;
> She gives him double forces, to endure
> And to enjoy, by being one with him.

Then, after comparing her with power, wealth, music, and delicate diet, which delight but imperfectly,—

> But a true wife both sense and soul delights,
> And mixeth not her good with any ill.
> All store without her leaves a man but poor,
> And with her poverty is exceeding store.

Chapman himself, in a passage of his **Revenge of Bussy d'Ambois,** condemns the very kind of comedy he wrote as a concession to public taste:—

Nay, we must now have nothing brought on
    stages
But puppetry, and pied ridiculous antics;
Men thither come to laugh and feed fool-fat,
Check at all goodness there as being profaned;
When wheresoever goodness comes, she makes
The place still sacred, though with other feet
Never so much 't is scandaled and polluted.
Let me learn anything that fits a man,
In any stables shown, as well as stages.

Of his tragedies, the general judgment has pronounced **Byron's Conspiracy** and **Byron's Tragedy** to be the finest, though they have less genuine poetical ecstasy than his **d'Ambois.** The **Tragedy of Chabot, Admiral of France,** is almost wholly from his hand, as all its editors agree, and as is plain from internal evidence, for Chapman has some marked peculiarities of thought and style which are unmistakable. Because Shirley had some obscure share in it, it is printed with his works, and omitted by the latest editor of Chapman. Yet it is far more characteristic of him than **Alphonsus,** or **Cæsar and Pompey.** The character of Chabot has a nobility less prompt to vaunt itself, less conscious of itself, less obstreperous, I am tempted to say, than is common with Chapman. There is one passage in the play which I will quote, because of the plain allusion in it to the then comparatively recent fate of Lord Bacon. I am not sure whether it has been before remarked or not. The Lord Chancellor of France is impeached of the same crimes with Bacon. He is accused also of treacherous cruelty to Chabot, as Bacon was reproached for ingratitude to Essex. He is sentenced like him to degradation of rank, to a heavy fine, and to imprisonment at the King's pleasure. Like Bacon, again, he twice confesses his guilt before sentence is passed on him, and throws himself on the King's mercy:—

Hear me, great Judges; if you have not lost
For my sake all your charities, I beseech you
Let the King know my heart is full of penitence;
Calm his high-going sea, or in that tempest
I ruin to eternity. O, my lords,
Consider your own places and the helms
You sit at; while with all your providence
You steer, look forth and see devouring quick-
    sands!
My ambition now is punished, and my pride
Of state and greatness falling into nothing;
I, that had never time, through vast employ-
    ments,
To think of Heaven, feel His revengeful wrath
Boiling my blood and scorching up my entrails.
There's doomsday in my conscience, black and
    horrid,
For my abuse of justice; but no stings
Prick with that terror as the wounds I made
Upon the pious Admiral. Some good man
Bear my repentance thither; he is merciful,
And may incline the King to stay his lightning,
Which threatens my confusion, that my free
Resign of title, office, and what else
My pride look'd at, would buy my poor life's
    safety;
Forever banish me the Court, and let
Me waste my life far-off in some mean village.

After the Chancellor's sentence, his secretary says:—

I could have wished him fall on softer ground
For his good parts.

Bacon's monument, in St. Michael's Church at St. Alban's, was erected by *his* secretary, Sir Thomas Meautys. Bacon did not appear at his trial; but there are several striking parallels between his letters of confession and the speech you have just heard.

Another posthumously published tragedy of Chapman's, the **Revenge for Honor,** is, in conception, the most original of them all, and the plot seems to be of his own invention. It has great improbabilities, but as the story is Oriental, we find it easier to forgive them. It is, on the whole, a very striking play, and with more variety of character in it than is common with Chapman.

In general he seems to have been led to the choice of his heroes (and these sustain nearly the whole weight of the play in which they figure) by some half-conscious sympathy of temperament. They are impetuous, have an overweening self-confidence, and an orotund way of expressing it that fitted them perfectly to be the mouth-pieces for an eloquence always vehement and impassioned, sometimes rising to a sublimity of self-assertion. Where it is fine, it is nobly fine, but too often it raves itself into a kind of fury recalling Hamlet's word "robustious," and seems to be shouted through a speaking-trumpet in a gale of wind. He is especially fond of describing battles, and the rush of his narration is then like a charge of cavalry. Of his first tragedy, **Bussy d'Ambois,** Dryden says, with that mixture of sure instinct and hasty judgment which makes his prose so refreshing:

I have sometimes wondered in the reading what has become of those glaring colors which amazed me in **Bussy d'Ambois** upon the theatre; but when I had taken up what I supposed a falling star, I found I had been cozened with a jelly, nothing but a cold dull mass, which glittered no longer than it was shooting; a dwarfish thought dressed up in gigantic words, repetition in abundance, looseness of expression, and gross hyperbole; the sense of one line expanded prodigiously into ten; and, to sum up all, incorrect English, and a hideous mingle of false poetry and true nonsense; or, at best, a scantling of wit which lay gasping for life and groaning beneath a heap of rubbish.

There *is* hyperbole in Chapman, and perhaps Dryden saw it the more readily and disliked it the more that his own tragedies are full of it. But Dryden was always hasty, not for the first time in speaking of Chapman. I am pretty safe in saying that he had probably only run his eye over **Bussy d'Ambois,** and that it did not happen to fall on any of those finely inspired passages which are not only more frequent in it than in any other of Chapman's plays, but of a more purely poetical quality. Dryden was irritated by a consciousness of his own former barbarity of taste, which had led him to prefer Sylvester's translation of Du Bartas. What he says as to the success of **Bussy d'Ambois** on the stage is interesting.

In saying that the sense of "one line is prodigiously expanded into ten," Dryden certainly puts his finger on one of Chapman's faults. He never knew when to stop. But it is not true that the sense is expanded, if by that we are to understand that Chapman watered his thought to make it fill up. There is abundance of thought in him, and of very suggestive thought too, but it is not always in the right place. He is the most sententious of our poets— sententious to a fault, as we feel in his continuation of **Hero and Leander.** In his annotations to the sixteenth book of his translation of the *Iliad,* he seems to have been thinking of himself in speaking of Homer. He says:

> And here have we ruled a case against our plain and smug writers, that, because their own un-wieldiness will not let them rise themselves, would have every man grovel like them. . . . But herein this case is ruled against such men that they affirm these hyperthetical or superlative sort of expressions and illustrations are too bold and bumbasted, and out of that word is spun that which they call our fustian, their plain writing being stuff nothing so substantial, but such gross sowtege or hairpatch as every goose may eat oats through. . . . But the chief end why I extend this annotation is only to entreat your note here of Homer's manner of writing, which, to utter his after-store of matter and variety, is so presse and puts on with so strong a current that it far overruns the most laborious pursuer if he have not a poetical foot and Poesy's quick eye to guide it.

Chapman has indeed a "great after-store of matter" which encumbers him, and does sometimes "far overrun the most laborious pursuer," but many a poetical foot, with Poesy's quick eye to guide it, has loved to follow. He has kindled an enthusiasm of admiration such as no other poet of his day except Shakespeare has been able to kindle. In this very play of **Bussy d'Ambois** there is a single line of which Charles Lamb says that "in all poetry I know nothing like it." When Chapman *is* fine, it is in a way all his own. There is then an incomparable amplitude in his style, as when, to quote a phrase from his translation of Homer, the Lightener Zeus "lets down a great sky out of heaven." There is a quality of northwestern wind in it, which, if sometimes too blusterous, is yet taken into the lungs with an exhilarating expansion. Hyperbole is overshooting the mark. No doubt Chapman sometimes did this, but this excess is less depressing than its opposite, and at least proves vigor in the bowman. His bow was like that of Ulysses, which none could bend but he, and even where the arrow went astray, it sings as it flies, and one feels, to use his own words, as if it were

> the shaft
> Shot at the sun by angry Hercules,
> And into splinters by the thunder broken.

Dryden taxes Chapman with "incorrect English." This is altogether wrong. His English is of the best, and far less licentious than Dryden's own, which was also the best of its kind. Chapman himself says (or makes Montsurry in **Bussy d'Ambois** say for him):—

> Worthiest poets
> Shun common and plebeian forms of speech,
> Every illiberal and affected phrase,
> To clothe their matter, and together tie

Matter and form with art and decency.

And yet I should say that if Chapman's English had any fault, it comes of his fondness for homespun words, and for images which, if not essentially vulgar, become awkwardly so by being forced into company where they feel themselves out of place. For example, in the poem which prefaces his Homer, full of fine thought, fitly uttered in his large way, he suddenly compares the wordlings he is denouncing to "an itching horse leaning to a block or a Maypole." He would have justified himself, I suppose, by Homer's having compared Ajax to an ass, for I think he really half believed that the spirit of Homer had entered into him and replaced his own. So in **Bussy,**—

> Love is a razor cleansing if well used,
> But fetcheth blood still being the least abused.

But I think the incongruity is to be explained as an unconscious reaction (just as we see men of weak character fond of strong language) against a partiality he felt in himself for costly phrases. His fault is not the purple patch upon frieze, but the patch of frieze upon purple. In general, one would say that his style was impetuous like the man himself, and wants the calm which is the most convincing evidence of great power that has no misgivings of itself. I think Chapman figured forth his own ideal in his **Byron:**—

> Give me a spirit that on this life's rough sea
> Loves to have his sails filled with a lusty wind,
> Even till his sail-yards tremble, his masts crack,
> And his rapt ship run on her side so low
> That she drinks water and her keel ploughs air.
> There is no danger to a man that knows
> What life and death is; there's not any law
> Exceeds his knowledge; neither is it lawful
> That he should stoop to any other law.

Professor Minto thinks that the rival poet of whom Shakespeare speaks in his eighty-sixth sonnet was Chapman, and enough confirmation of this theory may be racked out of dates and other circumstances to give it at least some probability. However this may be, the opening line of the sonnet contains as good a characterization of Chapman's style as if it had been meant for him:—

> Was it the proud full sail of his great verse?

I have said that Chapman was generally on friendly terms with his brother poets. But there is a passage in the preface to the translation of the *Iliad* which marks an exception. He says:

> And much less I weigh the frontless detractions of some stupid ignorants, that, no more knowing me than their beastly ends, and I ever (to my knowledge) blest from their sight, whisper behind me vilifyings of my translation, out of the French affirming them, when, both in French and all other languages but his own, our with-all-skill-enriched Poet is so poor and unpleasing that no man can discern from whence flowed his so generally given eminence and admiration.

I know not who was intended, but the passage piques my curiosity. In what is said about language there is a curious parallel with what Ben Jonson says of Shakespeare, and the "generally given eminence and admiration" applies to him also. The "with-all-skill-enriched" reminds me of another peculiarity of Chapman—his fondness for compound words. He seems to have thought that he condensed more meaning into a phrase if he dovetailed all its words together by hyphens. This sometimes makes the verses of his translation of Homer difficult to read musically, if not metrically.

Chapman has been compared with Seneca, but I see no likeness in their manner unless we force an analogy between the rather braggart Hercules of the one and d'Ambois of the other. The most famous passage in Seneca's tragedies is, I suppose, the answer of Medea when asked what remains to her in her desertion and danger: *"Medea superest."* This is as unlike Chapman as he is unlike Marlowe or Webster. His genius never could have compressed itself into so laconic a casket. Here would have been a chance for him to dilate like Teneriffe or Atlas, and he would have done it ample justice. If ever there was a case in which Buffon's saying that the style is the man fitted exactly, it is in that of Chapman. Perhaps I ought to have used the word "mannerism" instead of "style," for Chapman had not that perfect control of his matter which "style" implies. On the contrary, his matter seems sometimes to do what it will with him, which is the characteristic of mannerism. I can think of no better example of both than Sterne, alternately victim of one and master of the other. His mannerism at last becomes irritating affectation, but when he throws it off, his style is perfect in simplicity of rhythm. There is no more masterly page of English prose than that in the *Sentimental Journey* describing the effect of the chorus, "O Cupid, King of Gods and Men," on the people of Abdera.

As a translator, and he translated a great deal besides Homer, Chapman has called forth the most discordant opinions. It is plain from his prefaces and annotations that he had discussed with himself the various theories of translation, and had chosen that which prefers the spirit to the letter. "I dissent," he says, speaking of his translation of the *Iliad,* "from all other translators and interpreters that ever essayed exposition of this miraculous poem, especially where the divine rapture is most exempt from capacity in grammarians merely and grammatical critics, and where the inward sense or soul of the sacred muse is only within eyeshot of a poetical spirit's inspection." This rapture, however, is not to be found in his translation of the *Odyssey,* he being less in sympathy with the quieter beauties of that exquisite poem. Cervantes said long ago that no poet is translatable, and he said truly, for his thoughts will not *sing* in any language but their own. Even where the languages are of common parentage, like English and German, the feat is impossible. Who ever saw a translation of one of Heine's songs into English from which the genius had not utterly vanished? We cannot translate the music; above all, we cannot translate the indefinable associations which have gathered round the poem, giving it more meaning to us, perhaps, than it ever had for the poet himself. In turning it into our own tongue the translator has made it foreign to us for the first time. Why, we do not like to hear any one read aloud a poem that we love, because he translates it into something unfamiliar as he reads. But perhaps it is fair, and this is some-times forgotten, to suppose that a translation is intended only for such as have no knowledge of the original, and to whom it will be a new poem. If that be so, there can be no question that a free reproduction, a transfusion into the moulds of another language, with an absolute deference to its associations, whether of the ear or of the memory, is the true method. There are no more masterly illustrations of this than the versions from the Greek, Persian, and Spanish of the late Mr. Fitzgerald. His translations, however else they may fail, make the same vivid impression on us that an original would. He has aimed at translating the genius, in short, letting all else take care of itself, and has succeeded. Chapman aimed at the same thing, and I think has also succeeded. You all remember Keats's sonnet on first looking in his Homer.

> Then felt I like some watcher of the skies
> When a new planet swims into his ken.

Whether Homer or not, his translation is at least not Milton, as those in blank verse strive without much success to be. If the Greek original had been lost, and we had only Chapman, would it not enable us to divine some of the chief qualities of that original? I think it would; and I think this perhaps the fairest test. Commonly we open a translation as it were the door of a house of mourning. It is the burial-service of our poet that is going on there. But Chapman's poem makes us feel as if Homer late in life had married an English wife, and we were invited to celebrate the coming of age of their only son. The boy, as our country people say, and as Chapman would have said, favors his mother; there is very little Greek in him; and yet a trick of the gait now and then, and certain tones of voice, recall the father. If not so tall as he, and without his dignity, he is a fine stalwart fellow, and looks quite able to make his own way in the world. Yes, in Chapman's poem there is life, there is energy, and the consciousness of them. Did not Dryden say admirably well that it was such a poem as we might fancy Homer to have written before he arrived at years of discretion? Its defect is, I should say, that in it Homer is translated into Chapman rather than into English.

Chapman is a poet for intermittent rather than for consecutive reading. He talks too loud and is too emphatic for continuous society. But when you leave him, you feel that you have been in the company of an original, and hardly know why you should not say a great man. From his works, one may infer an individuality of character in him such as we can attribute to scarce any other of his contemporaries, though originality was far cheaper then than now. A lofty, impetuous man, ready to go off without warning into what he called a "holy fury," but capable of inspiring an almost passionate liking. Had only the best parts of what he wrote come down to us, we should have reckoned him a far greater poet than we can fairly call him. His fragments are truly Cyclopean. (pp. 85-99)

James Russell Lowell, "Chapman," in his The Old English Dramatists, *Houghton, Mifflin and Company, 1892, pp. 78-99.*

William Lyon Phelps (1895)

[An American critic and educator, Phelps was for over forty years a lecturer on English literature at Yale. In the following excerpt, Phelps surveys Chapman's career as a playwright, arguing that, partly because he is so well-respected as a translator, "as a dramatist he has been vastly over-rated."]

The life of Chapman includes practically that whole period of literature known as the Elizabethan drama. He was born before *Gorboduc* and *Gammer Gurton's Needle;* when *Tamburlaine* appeared, he was nearly thirty; he survived Shakspere, Beaumont, Middleton, and Fletcher; every important play of the age was acted during his lifetime. He thus had the opportunity to watch the rise, fruition, and decay of what has been justly called the greatest part of the greatest period of the greatest literature of the world; a tremendous superlative that will be questioned only by those who have not read the material it describes.

Although 1557 is often given as the year of Chapman's birth, we learn, with presumable accuracy, from the circular inscription on his portrait, that he was born in 1559. His birthplace was, in all probability, Hitchin, a town in the northern part of Hertfordshire, thirty-four miles from London. His education was obtained at Oxford, and all indications point to his having also been a student at Cambridge. At Oxford he made something of a reputation as a classical scholar; and our respect for him is not diminished when we are told that he had a contempt for logic and philosophy. The method of teaching metaphysics at that time was almost sure to arouse repugnance, if not rebellion, in any mind endowed with originality or common sense. So Chapman, who is certainly the most metaphysical of all Elizabethan dramatists, must have cultivated that part of his nature with little help from the University curriculum.

From his graduation to the year 1594, we know nothing of his life; we can only conjecture. But it is probable that he spent some time in Continental travel; possibly in France and Italy, almost certainly in Germany, if the familiarity with that tongue displayed in *Alphonsus* is at all significant. In 1594 he published *The Shadow of Night,* "containing two poetical hymns."

It is impossible to ascertain at what exact time he joined the London playwright group, and became a professional writer for the stage. It was probably about 1595 or 1596, for in 1598 he had an established reputation. In that year he is mentioned among the well-known dramatists, in the famous enumeration of Francis Meres. His first extant comedy, *The Blind Beggar of Alexandria,* was produced on February 12, 1596. From every point of view, it is absolutely worthless. In 1599 was published his next comedy, *An Humorous Day's Mirth,* which unfortunately shows scarcely any improvement on the other.

The work on which Chapman's fame principally depends is, of course, his translation of Homer. The first portion of this appeared in 1598: *Seaven Bookes of the Iliades of Homer, Prince of Poets. Translated according to the Greeke in judgement of his best Commentaries.* In translating he used the fourteen syllabled rime, which more nearly expresses the Greek hexameter than any other English measure. In 1611 the complete translation of the *Iliad* was published, and by 1615 the whole of the *Odyssey,* which was written in the heroic couplet. Although many critics have judged Chapman's *Homer* to be the finest English translation ever made, it may more properly be ranked as an original work—a great Elizabethan classic. It has not only immortalised Chapman, but it must stand as one of the noblest monuments of the golden age of English literature.

In 1605 two remarkable plays appeared; Chapman's comic masterpiece, *All Fools,* and the spirited comedy *Eastward Ho,* composed by Chapman, Marston, and Ben Jonson. The three men must have been expert judges of each other's literary faults; for their joint production is singularly free from their individual defects. The play is not marred by Jonson's customary verbosity and pedantry, nor by Marston's disgusting vulgarity, nor by Chapman's obscurity and formlessness. Some remarks in it deemed uncomplimentary to King James caused Chapman and Marston to be sent to prison; whither Jonson, with that touch of *noblesse* that makes us forget all his faults, voluntarily accompanied them. All three were shortly released.

The play *All Fools* has been identified with *The World Runs on Wheels,* which Chapman wrote in 1599, and which was acted the same year. The name was changed to *All Fools but the Fool,* and then to *All Fools.* The influence of Ben Jonson is discernible in two ways; in the complete cynicism which pervades the play, and in the characters, many of whom are simply humour-studies. But—a rare thing in Chapman—we find a real plot; artificial, over-subtle, too ingenious, perhaps, but steadily moving forward to a climax. The play abounds in excellent scenes; and the fun lies fully as much in the situations as in the characters; a skilful combination of two forms of comedy. It impresses one as particularly well adapted for the stage; but it would require a constellation of actors, since nearly every character has more than one good chance.

The Gentleman Usher (1606) has been extravagantly praised by some of Chapman's admirers. It is an entirely different class of work from *All Fools;* that was a realistic satire, this is a romantic poem. But although it contains some beautiful scenes—such as the betrothal of Vincentio and Margaret—it lacks almost every qualification of a good play. In construction it is slipshod and slovenly; the plot is worthless; and the improbabilities do not seem to be presented with any attempt at verisimilitude. Then the characterisation is poor—vague in the extreme; the personages are all shadowy and unreal, so common a fault in Chapman's comedies; it is impossible to grasp or to retain them.

The same year (1606) another comedy, *Monsieur D'Olive,* appeared. This play opens surprisingly well; the first scenes and speeches have the true Elizabethan ring; they are full of life and spirit. But just as the reader's expectations have been raised to a high pitch, the play weakens, wanders aimlessly awhile, and then loses itself in a dreary Sahara of verbosity.

The year 1607 brings us to the first of Chapman's remarkable group of French tragedies—***Bussy D'Ambois.*** Here is an instance of the Elizabethan drama figuring in one of its most important capacities, the nearest analogy to which is the modern newspaper. Chapman selected material that was practically contemporary, arranged it in dramatic form, and presented it to the English groundlings and gallery goddesses. As to the reasons which led him to use this material, we are wholly in the dark; but his dramatic methods in using it are still more difficult to understand. The ordinary motive in arranging foreign matter for the delectation of the pit is clear enough; it was to inflame patriotic feeling, by exhibiting French and Spanish Roman Catholics in most unenviable situations. But Chapman apparently had no such purpose; to be sure he introduces some flattering speeches concerning England and Elizabeth; but, wonderful to relate, the Duke of Guise, whose name to an English Protestant was symbolical of everything particularly fiendish, is represented as something of a hero; and such a portrayal, to a demonstrative audience which had no difficulty in remembering St Bartholomew's Day, is sufficiently remarkable. There is not only no attempt to make political capital, but there is almost too obvious a scorn of public opinion. Furthermore, no pains are taken to insure historical accuracy; in the Byron plays, we find, as we expect to find, the greatest of all French kings, Henry of Navarre, represented as exactly a model of what a sovereign should be; but we are no less surprised in the D'Ambois series to find his wretched predecessor, Henry III., almost equally admirable. Taken together, these four plays are unique in English literature.

Chapman drew his material mainly from De Thou; but in the D'Ambois plays he uses him very little, whereas in the Byron series he follows him fairly closely. The two D'Ambois plays are entirely separate and distinct. The first, published in 1607, contains, as almost every critic has had occasion to remark, the best and the worst of Chapman's work. The hero is after the school of Tamburlaine; a bold, glorious braggart, quick-witted, loud-mouthed (Modesty was not an Elizabethan virtue), sword always loose in scabbard, and whose love choices sublimely overlooked the ordinary obstacle of a husband. In love and war, he is alike invincible; and is finally overcome only by treachery.

Small wonder is it, that with a play containing so much gold and so much dross, critics have varied widely in their estimation of its worth, according as its faults and virtues have been uppermost in their minds. Dryden, and after two hundred years of criticism Dryden is still worth listening to, gives no uncertain sound; in the dedication to *The Spanish Friar* (1681), he says:

> I have sometimes wondered, in the reading, what has become of those glaring colours which amazed me in ***Bussy D'Ambois*** upon the theatre; but when I had taken up what I supposed a fallen star, I found I had been cozened with a jelly; nothing but a cold, dull mass, which glittered no longer than it was shooting; a dwarfish thought, dressed up in gigantic words, repetition in abundance, looseness of expression, and gross hyperboles; the sense of one line expanded prodigiously into ten; and, to sum up all, uncorrect English, and a hideous mingle of false poetry and true nonsense; or, at best, a scantling of wit, which lay gasping for life, and groaning beneath a heap of rubbish. A famous modern poet used to sacrifice every year a Statius to Virgil's manes; and I have indignation enough to burn a ***D'Ambois*** annually to the memory of Jonson.

It is important to remember that these are the words, not only of a truly great critic, but of a man who had seen and judged the play from a seat in the theatre. Skilfully acted before a crowded and enthusiastic house, Dryden had joined heartily in the applause; then, taking up the work in cold blood, and finding it full of fustian and bombast, he felt that he had been deceived under false pretences; for his language in this quotation is certainly that of a man who thinks he has been imposed upon and is determined to give vent to his righteous wrath. His expression, "glittered no longer than it was shooting," evidently means that Bussy was more effective on the stage than in the closet. That a man like Dryden should find such a tragedy better to see than to read, is to our stage notions almost incomprehensible; but his impressions furnish additional proof of the real stage effectiveness of many Elizabethan plays that could not draw to-day.

The Revenge of Bussy D'Ambois, published in 1613, is, from the dramatic point of view, distinctly inferior to its predecessor; but it is crowded with splendid declamation, and full of the richest treasures of thought. It contains passages which make one stop and reflect, and re-read only to ponder again. The hero, Clermont D'Ambois, has little family resemblance to his brother. Bussy is like Tamburlaine, but Clermont suggests Hamlet. He resembles the melancholy Dane not only in his powers of reflection, and in his innate good breeding, but in his constant postponement of revenge.

The D'Ambois plays belong distinctly to the Tragedy of Blood, and in a dim way foreshadow the decay of the drama. The repeated stabbing and torture of Tamyra before the eyes of the audience, the letter written in her blood, the gloomy vault and the presence of ghosts of murdered men, together with all the conventional machinery of the melodrama, are the regular features of that curious development of Blood Tragedies, which began with *The Spanish Tragedy* and *Titus Andronicus,* which affected Shakspere, Marlowe, Middleton, Ford, Tourneur, which reached a grand climax in Webster, and which survives today in cheap sensational theatres. For as truly as the Elizabethan drama descended from the Mysteries, so truly does our present melodrama come from the noisy Tragedy of Blood.

Chapman's tragedies indicate the decay of the drama in their search for the horrible, in their public display of physical anguish, and in their free use of ghosts. The introduction of the supernatural element greatly mars these two plays; for instead of giving colour and atmosphere, as in *Macbeth,* it is here too evidently superfluous. Ghosts are causelessly dragged in, and form not an integral, but wholly an incidental, feature; their entrances and exits are so clumsily managed, that they not only utterly fail to impress us with horror, but make it difficult for us to swallow a guffaw.

Although the D'Ambois plays are most distinctly the characteristic works of their author, and are most essential to a thorough understanding of him, the two Byron dramas are by many considered Chapman's masterpieces of tragedy. In sustained power, they are certainly superior to the D'Ambois pair; for although, as is so often the case in Chapman, action and movement play a subordinate part to poetry and declamation, there is more of the steadily good and less of the absolutely bad than in any other of his dramatic works. There are, perhaps, fewer magnificent outbursts; but there is distinctly less rubbish. These two plays are not by any means separate, like the D'Ambois dramas; they make one tragedy in ten acts, without a break in the thought. Moreover, they are much more nearly contemporary than the chronicles of D'Ambois; the Duke Biron was executed in 1602, and Chapman's two plays, although published in 1608, were written about 1605. The friendship of King Henry for his proud favourite forms one of the most interesting episodes in history; from a bare narrative of the facts, up to the detailed account given by De Thou, any one may see for himself how admirable a subject it is for dramatic treatment. Unfortunately, Chapman has missed most of his opportunities; that wonderful instinct for dramatic situation, which led Webster to construct from a coarse narrative the splendid tragedy of *The Duchess of Malfi,* seems sadly lacking in Chapman. But the character of Byron he has fully grasped, and has given us in him one of the most striking figures of the Elizabethan drama. With a nature originally noble, but gradually tainted with pride and conceit, skilfully worked on by smiling pick-thanks and base newsmongers, his better qualities perceptibly pass into eclipse, and the man's darkened soul stands forth with a certain Satanic grandeur. His magnificent speech after the interview with the magician is a noble succession of mighty lines, ending with a strong climax, in which we may plainly see through the Duke's mask the glowing eyes of Chapman himself.

> Give me a spirit that on this life's rough sea
> Loves t'have his sails fill'd with a lusty wind,
> Even till his sail-yards tremble, his masks crack,
> And his rapt ship run on her side so low
> That she drinks water, and her keel plows air.
> There is no danger to a man that knows
> What life and death is; there's not any law
> Exceeds his knowledge; neither is it lawful
> That he should stoop to any other law.
> He goes before them, and commands them all,
> That to himself is a law rational.

The final death-scene in the *Tragedy* is another, fortunate example of how the clouds and mists that commonly envelop the soul of our great poet break away, and give him complete liberty of expression. The Duke, finally confronted with the actual presence of death, feels his wonted bravado forsaking him; he alternates between piteous supplication and reckless defiance, his soul torn with conflicting passions. There is but one scene similar to this which surpasses it, and that is the agonising cry of Browning's Guido as the executioners descend the stair.

> Life is all!
> I was just stark mad,—let the madman live
> Pressed by as many chains as you please pile!
> Don't open! Hold me from them! I am yours,
> I am the Granduke's—no, I am the Pope's!
> Abate,—Cardinal,—Christ,—Maria,—God, . . .
> Pompilia, will you let them murder me?

But Byron, unlike Guido, after writhing in agony, and vainly casting about for help or delay, finally succumbs in these splendid lines, in which in the last moment the strength of bitterness overcomes the horror of death.

> And so farewell for ever. Nevermore
> Shall any hope of my revival see me.
> Such is the endless exile of dead men.
> Summer succeeds the spring; autumn the summer;
> The frosts of winter, the fall'n leaves of autumn;
> All these and all fruits in them yearly fade,
> And every year return; but cursed man
> Shall never more renew his vanish'd face. . . .
>
> Strike, strike, O strike; fly, fly, commanding soul
> And on thy wings for this thy body's breath,
> Bear the eternal victory of death.

In 1611 Chapman returned to comedy in *May Day,* a play of no value. If he had not written *The Blind Beggar of Alexandria* and *An Humorous Day's Mirth,* we might class this as the worst of his productions. *The Widow's Tears* (1612) is far superior, but still not a real success. It has some genuine force, some dramatic situations, and some powerful speeches; but the interest is not well sustained. Furthermore, it is flavoured by a combination of coarseness and cynicism, which leaves a most disagreeable impression.

From 1613 to 1631 we hear nothing of Chapman's writing for the stage; in Jonson's life there is a similar, but not so lengthy, dramatic hiatus. Chapman was busied with other matters, and apparently let the stage alone. In 1631, however, he published *The Tragedy of Cæsar and Pompey,* to which he prefixed an interesting dedication, whence we learn that the play had never been acted. Chapman evidently thought this a superior literary performance; but it adds scarcely any lustre to his name. The character that seems chiefly to have interested him is Cato, into whose mouth is put many reflective dissertations. There are some finely poetical lines, which Lamb included in his *Specimens.*

Twenty years after Chapman's death, two additional tragedies of his first saw the light. These are *Alphonsus, Emperor of Germany,* and *Revenge for Honour,* both published in 1654. The first is interesting for the knowledge of the German language and customs which it shows; some have accounted for this on the hypothesis that he was assisted by a German writer, but it seems more probable that Chapman had obtained the necessary knowledge by travel in Germany. *Revenge for Honour* is clearly superior to *Alphonsus;* and by the number of feminine endings, it has been generally assigned to a late period in Chapman's life. It is sufficiently sanguinary to claim a place in the Tragedy of Blood.

Three plays, partly written by Chapman, may be included

in a complete list of his dramatic works; the excellent comedy of *Eastward Ho . . . ; The Ball* (1639), by Chapman and Shirley, a comedy in no way remarkable; and one more French tragedy, *Philip Chabot, Admiral of France* (1639), also written by the same two authors. The impossibility, in spite of confident guesses, of discovering what parts were written by Chapman and what by Shirley, make a discussion of the merits of these plays unnecessary, in so short a space as we have at our command.

Just one masque by Chapman is extant. *The Memorable Maske of the two Honorable Houses or Inns of Court; the Middle Temple and Lyncolns Inne.* This was performed at Whitehall, in February 1614. It was given in the most lavish and magnificent style. Chapman must have written other pieces that are now lost, in order to justify Jonson's egotistical compliment, that "next himself, only Fletcher and Chapman could make a masque." (pp. 11-24)

Chapman's fame as a translator of Homer has unduly exalted his merits as a dramatist; he is to-day one of the best-known names in the Elizabethan drama, but an unbiassed study of his work for the stage will show that as a dramatist he has been vastly over-rated. Compare the relative importance of the names of Chapman and Dekker; but is there a single play of the former that we would exchange for *The Honest Whore* or *The Shoemaker's Holiday*? Dekker has suffered from neglect; Chapman has more reputation than his plays will justify. Far be it from one who assumes as a labour of love the task of editing Chapman, to decry his virtues or to be wilfully blind to the inspiration of his splendid verse; but in judging him as a dramatist, we must judge him by those qualities essential to successful dramatic work. In epic, in narrative, in descriptive poetry, he is all and more than we could wish; but only one of his plays, *All Fools,* is well constructed, and many of them are indescribably poor. His formlessness and weakness as a playwright have never been sufficiently estimated; and the infinite verbosity of his plays has caused much needless suffering to patient readers.

In a review of Chapman's fourteen extant dramas—seven comedies and seven tragedies—the quality that seems most prominent is his subtlety of thought. In psychological analysis of character he is weak; but his strength in philosophical reflection is so evident, even to himself, that he can seldom resist a temptation to this indulgence. A comparison of Marlowe's famous apostrophe to beauty, beginning

> If all the pens that ever poets held,

with Chapman's treatment of the same subject, is certainly suggestive.

> And what is beauty? A mere quintessence,
> Whose life is not in being, but in seeming;
> And therefore is not to all eyes the same,
> But like a cozening picture, which one way
> Shows like a crow, another like a swan.

Aspiration is the key-note in Marlowe; in Chapman it is Reflection. And although his genius for meditation often gives us splendid passages, as in *The Revenge of Bussy D'Ambois* and in *Cæsar and Pompey,* it must be confessed that it is as much a defect in his dramas as was Jonson's

pedantry. We should remember in reading Chapman that he did not begin to write for the stage until he was nearly forty years old; by that time the hey-day of the imagination is past; we naturally look, not for spontaneous bursts of glorious poetry, but for more sober thought. The fire of youth, which illumines all Marlowe's dramas, is absent from Chapman's. Furthermore, next to Jonson, he was the most learned of all Elizabethan dramatists; and while his pedantry is by no means so obtrusive as Jonson's, he undoubtedly had much more learning than was sufficient for the composition of a good play. His dramas all show an utter lack of spontaneity; the glory of Marlowe, the freshness of Heywood, the joyousness of Dekker—we search in vain for these qualities in Chapman.

In characterisation he is painfully weak. He never loses himself in his characters, like Shakspere and Middleton; he tries faithfully to do so, but cannot succeed. The splendid speeches in his tragedies have often no reference to the person who speaks them; they are all Chapman's own, and distributed indifferently. In reading his comedies, one always has to keep a finger on the list of *dramatis personæ;* the names mean nothing to us, and we forget them with mournful swiftness. Mr Lowell remarked that the coarseness of his plays was a kind of wilful coarseness, not natural; the people do not talk like genuine low-lived characters, as in the plays of Dekker, but rather as Chapman thought they ought to talk. In the passion of love Chapman is sometimes as bad as Cowley; he masters all the apparatus of passion, carefully works himself into a frenzy, and talks loudly; but we do not hear the language of the heart.

Although Chapman's tragedies must rank as literature much higher than his comedies, he was too self-conscious and too deliberate to fully succeed in tragic art. His statement in the dedication to *The Revenge of Bussy D'Ambois,* that "material instruction, elegant and sententious excitation to virtue, and deflection from her contrary, being the soul, limbs and limits of an authentical tragedy," is sufficient to wreck any play that faithfully follows such doctrine. And with the exception of some notable scenes where Chapman burst his bonds of learning and self-conceit, and spoke out loud and bold, his tragedies often suggest premeditated fury. He feels that he ought to assume the grand style, and so, though not in the least excited himself, he makes his characters attitudinise and saw the air, while in this storm of declamation, passion is calmly sleeping. This is the chief reason why so many of Chapman's characters are not convincing.

But the great difficulty with Chapman's style is his obscurity. He is the only Elizabethan dramatist who is really obscure. Ben Jonson often requires the closest attention; but in the words of Schopenhauer, Chapman wrote lines "to which the mind in vain torments itself to attach any meaning." His obscurity is two-fold: he often needs Falstaff's brand of sherris-sack, which "ascends me into the brain; dries me there all the foolish and dull and crudy vapours which environ it;" and, in the second place, besides his misty intellect, he unfortunately has some impediment in his speech, which makes articulation difficult, if not impossible. He is plainly tongue-tied; many times he begins a passage grandly, and then unexpectedly gets into those "no thoroughfares" that wrought such trouble with Dickens's parliamentary orator. When the mighty spirit of Chapman—for he had a mighty spirit—does get the better of its environment, and finds its true voice, we are swept along resistless on the rushing torrent. At its worst, Chapman's thorny style leads us into a great wood; at its best, it has a deep-sea quality, now a succession of rolling swells, and now infinitely calm, "too full for sound and foam." It is at such times that we fully understand Webster's acknowledgment of how much he had learned from "that full and heightened style of Master Chapman."

Chapman's intellectual kinship to Ben Jonson is sufficiently obvious. The two men stand somewhat apart from their fellows. Both were proud, contemptuous of public opinion, self-conscious, and somewhat burdened with a sense of their own importance; both were scholars and theorists; both satirists, lacking human sympathy; both had strongly-marked personalities, highly respectable and not lovable. Jonson was Chapman's superior in stage-craft and in his lyrical gift; but Jonson never reaches the "proud full sail" of Chapman's noblest verse. (pp. 25-9)

> *William Lyon Phelps, "George Chapman," in* George Chapman, *edited by William Lyon Phelps, T. Fisher Unwin Ltd., 1895, pp. 11-29.*

Algernon Charles Swinburne (essay date 1909)

[*Swinburne was an English poet, dramatist, and critic. Though renowned during his lifetime for his lyric poetry, he is remembered today for his rejection of Victorian mores. In the following excerpt from* The Age of Shakespeare, *Swinburne provides a general overview of Chapman's literary works, praising in particular his originality.*]

George Chapman, translator of Homer, dramatist, and gnomic poet, was born in 1559, and died in 1634. At fifteen, according to Anthony Wood, 'he, being well grounded in school learning, was sent to the university' of Oxford; at thirty-five he published his first poem, *The Shadow of Night.* Between these dates, though no fact has been unearthed concerning his career, it is not improbable that he may have travelled in Germany. At thirty-nine he was reckoned 'among the best of our tragic writers for the stage'; but his only play published at that age was a crude and formless attempt at romantic comedy, which had been acted three years before it passed from the stage to the press; and his first tragedy now extant in print, without name of author, did not solicit the suffrage of a reader till the poet was forty-eight. At thirty-nine he had also published the first instalment of his celebrated translation of the *Iliad,* in a form afterwards much remodelled; at sixty-five he crowned the lofty structure of his labour by the issue of an English version of the 'Hymns' and other minor Homeric poems. The former he dedicated to Robert Devereux, Earl of Essex, the hapless favourite of Elizabeth; the latter to Robert Carr, Earl of Somerset, the infamous minion of James. Six years earlier he had inscribed to Bacon, then Lord Chancellor, a translation of Hesiod's *Works and Days.* His only other versions of classic poems are

from the fifth satire of Juvenal and the *Hero and Leander* which goes under the name of Musæus, the latter dedicated to Inigo Jones. His revised and completed version of the *Iliad* had been inscribed in a noble and memorable poem of dedication to Henry Prince of Wales, after whose death he and his *Odyssey* fell under the patronage of Carr. Of the manner of his death at seventy-five we know nothing more than may be gathered from the note appended to a manuscript fragment, which intimates that the remainder of the poem, a lame and awkward piece of satire on his old friend Jonson, had been 'lost in his sickness.'

Chapman, his first biographer is careful to let us know, 'was a person of most reverend aspect, religious and temperate, qualities rarely meeting in a poet'; he had also certain other merits at least as necessary to the exercise of that profession. He had a singular force and solidity of thought, an admirable ardour of ambitious devotion to the service of poetry, a deep and burning sense at once of the duty implied and of the dignity inherent in his office; a vigour, opulence, and loftiness of phrase, remarkable even in that age of spiritual strength, wealth, and exaltation of thought and style; a robust eloquence, touched not unfrequently with flashes of fancy, and kindled at times into heat of imagination. The main fault of his style is one more commonly found in the prose than in the verse of his time—a quaint and florid obscurity, rigid with elaborate rhetoric and tortuous with labyrinthine illustration; not dark only to the rapid reader through closeness and subtlety of thought, like Donne, whose miscalled obscurity is so often 'all glorious within,' but thick and slab as a witch's gruel with forced and barbarous eccentricities of articulation. As his language in the higher forms of comedy is always pure and clear, and sometimes exquisite in the simplicity of its sincere and natural grace, the stiffness and density of his more ambitious style may perhaps be attributed to some pernicious theory or conceit of the dignity proper to a moral and philosophic poet. Nevertheless, many of the gnomic passages in his tragedies and allegoric poems are of singular weight and beauty; the best of these, indeed, would not discredit the fame of the very greatest poets for sublimity of equal thought and expression: witness the lines chosen by Shelley as the motto for a poem, and fit to have been chosen as the motto for his life.

The romantic and sometimes barbaric grandeur of Chapman's *Homer* remains attested by the praise of Keats, of Coleridge, and of Lamb; it is written at a pitch of strenuous and laborious exaltation, which never flags or breaks down, but never flies with the ease and smoothness of an eagle native to Homeric air. From his occasional poems an expert and careful hand might easily gather a noble anthology of excerpts, chiefly gnomic or meditative, allegoric or descriptive. The most notable examples of his tragic work are comprised in the series of plays taken, and adapted sometimes with singular licence, from the records of such part of French history as lies between the reign of Francis I. and the reign of Henry IV., ranging in date of subject from the trial and death of Admiral Chabot to the treason and execution of Marshal Biron. The two plays bearing as epigraph the name of that famous soldier and conspirator are a storehouse of lofty thought and splendid verse, with scarcely a flash or sparkle of dramatic action.

The one play of Chapman's whose popularity on the stage survived the Restoration is *Bussy d'Ambois* (d'Amboise),—a tragedy not lacking in violence of action or emotion, and abounding even more in sublime or beautiful interludes than in crabbed and bombastic passages. His rarest jewels of thought and verse detachable from the context lie embedded in the tragedy of *Cæsar and Pompey,* whence the finest of them were first extracted by the unerring and unequalled critical genius of Charles Lamb. In most of his tragedies the lofty and labouring spirit of Chapman may be said rather to shine fitfully through parts than steadily to pervade the whole; they show nobly altogether as they stand, but even better by help of excerpts and selections. But the excellence of his best comedies can only be appreciated by a student who reads them fairly and fearlessly through, and, having made some small deductions on the score of occasional pedantry and occasional crudity, finds in *All Fools, Monsieur d'Olive, The Gentleman Usher,* and *The Widow's Tears* a wealth and vigour of humorous invention, a tender and earnest grace of romantic poetry, which may atone alike for these passing blemishes and for the lack of such clear-cut perfection of character and such dramatic progression of interest as we find only in the yet higher poets of our heroic age.

The severest critic of his shortcomings or his errors, if not incompetent to appreciate his achievements and his merits, must recognise in Chapman an original poet, one who held of no man and acknowledged no master, but throughout the whole generation of our greatest men, from the birth of Marlowe wellnigh to the death of Jonson, held on his own hard and haughty way of austere and sublime ambition, not without an occasional pause for kindly and graceful salutation of such younger and still nobler compeers as Jonson and Fletcher. With Shakespeare we should never have guessed that he had come at all in contact, had not the intelligence of Mr. Minto divined or rather discerned him to be the rival poet referred to in Shakespeare's sonnets with a grave note of passionate satire, hitherto as enigmatic as almost all questions connected with those divine and dangerous poems. This conjecture the critic has fortified by such apt collocation and confrontation of passages that we may now reasonably accept it as an ascertained and memorable fact.

The objections which a just and adequate judgment may bring against Chapman's masterwork, his translation of Homer, may be summed up in three epithets: it is romantic, laborious, Elizabethan. The qualities implied by these epithets are the reverse of those which should distinguish a translator of Homer; but setting this apart, and considering the poems as in the main original works, the superstructure of a romantic poet on the submerged foundations of Greek verse, no praise can be too warm or high for the power, the freshness, the indefatigable strength and inextinguishable fire which animate this exalted work, and secure for all time that shall take cognisance of English poetry an honoured place in its highest annals for the memory of Chapman. (pp. 252-58)

Algernon Charles Swinburne, "George Chapman," in his The Age of Shakespeare, *Chatto & Windus, 1909, pp. 252-58.*

William Archer   (essay date 1923)

[*A Scottish dramatist and critic, Archer is best known as one of the earliest and most important translators of Henrik Ibsen's plays and as a drama critic of the London stage during the late nineteenth and early twentieth centuries. In the following excerpt, Archer treats Chapman's dramas, generally dismissing the tragedies, but upholding the dramatic merit of the comedy* All Fools.]

[Summing-up] George Chapman: less of a satirist than Jonson, more of a poet, and, like him, writing dramas, not because he was a dramatist born, but because they were the most remunerative form of literature. His most successful play was *Bussy d'Ambois,* a melodrama of lust, cruelty and murder, seasoned not only with the obligatory ghost, but with a troop of demons, under the command of two of Satan's brigadiers, Behemoth and Cartophylax. . . . It is odd that one of Chapman's comedies, *May Day,* should contain one of the very few satires upon the convention of disguise which occur in Elizabethan literature. "Though it be the stale refuge of miserable poets," says Angelo, "by change of a hat or a cloak to alter the whole state of a comedy, so as the father must not know his own child, forsooth, nor the wife her husband, yet you must not think they do in earnest carry it away so." This comes strangely from the man who, of all others, carried the convention to the most extravagant lengths.

The Revenge of Bussy d'Ambois, a sequel to this popular tragedy of blood, seems also to have been successful. It is a model of impotence in construction. Act I contains nothing except Montsurry's refusal of Clermont d'Ambois's challenge. Acts II, III and IV are devoted to the preparation, execution and final defeat of the plot to get Clermont d'Ambois out of the way—in other words, to an episode which merely retards the essential action of the play. The whole of that action is compressed into Act V, with its murders, its suicide, and its dance of ghosts. Here is the stage-direction:

> Music, and the Ghost of Bussy enters, leading
> the Ghosts of the Guise, Monsieur, Cardinal
> Guise, and Chatillon. They dance about the
> dead body [of Montsurry] and exeunt.

Clermont d'Ambois, who does not know that Guise and the Cardinal have been murdered, expresses mild surprise on seeing them among the ghosts; but spectres are so common at the Court of France (as Chapman sees it) that no one turns a hair on encountering them.

Chapman's other chronicle-plays from French history, *Byron's Conspiracy, Byron's Tragedy* and *The Tragedy of Chabot, Admiral of France,* afford the most amazing testimony to the appetite of Jacobean audiences for sheer laboured declamation, with scarcely a gleam of dramatic life in it. Charles Lamb admits that "dramatic imitation was not his talent," and even Swinburne, speaking of the "small epic" of Byron, says "that such a poem should ever have been 'acted in two plays at the Blackfriars and other public stages' must seem to us one of the strangest records in theatrical history." As we are here concerned with dramatic, not with purely poetic, quality, we need not dwell further on Chapman's tragedies.

In his comedies, on the other hand, critics have discovered much dramatic merit: let us look, then, at *All Fools,* his admitted masterpiece in the lighter vein. It seems to Swinburne "one of the most faultless examples of high comedy to be found in the whole rich field of our Elizabethan drama." Listen to its plot:

Gostanzo and Marc Antonio are two knights of Florence. Gostanzo has a son and a daughter, Valerio and Bellonora; Marc Antonio has two sons, Fortunio and Rinaldo. Gostanzo has made his son, Valerio, the "overseer of his pastures," and considers him a rustic paragon, free from all the vices of the town and far too bashful even to look at a woman. As a matter of fact, Valerio has a very free hand on the dice-box, and has secretly married a lady named Gratiana. In order that Valerio may conveniently enjoy the society of his wife, Rinaldo, who has a genius for "gulling," tells Gostanzo that Fortunio (his elder brother) is secretly married to Gratiana, and suggests that he (Gostanzo) should take the young couple into his house until Marc Antonio is reconciled to the match. Gostanzo despises Marc Antonio's lax method of bringing up his children, and is delighted at the opportunity of crowing over him by contrasting Valerio's submissive virtue with Fortunio's headstrong disobedience. Accordingly he agrees with alacrity to harbour Fortunio and Gratiana; and in securing this end, Rinaldo kills two birds with one stone; for while Valerio and Gratiana can thus be together, Fortunio, nominally the husband of Gratiana, can in fact take advantage of the opportunity to make love to Gostanzo's daughter Bellonora. So far good. A modern play with such an intrigue would be regarded, not as "high comedy," but as extremely conventional farce. The question of nomenclature, however, does not greatly concern me; if *All Fools* were a good play, of whatever order, I should not quarrel as to the precise pigeon-hole in which to place it. But mark what follows. Gostanzo sees Valerio embracing Gratiana, and concludes that he is trying to seduce her from her allegiance to her husband, Fortunio. Unwilling that this should go on, he decrees that Fortunio and Gratiana must leave his house. But the ingenious Rinaldo has another device ready for further "gulling" Gostanzo. Gratiana is to be introduced into Marc Antonio's house on the pretence (as Gostanzo thinks it) that she is the wife, not of Fortunio, but of Valerio; and Gostanzo is to help in this deception (as he believes it) by pretending great wrath against Valerio for his surreptitious marriage.

Human speech does not supply the machinery for making clear this maze of mendacity, this criss-cross of deception and dupery [The critic adds that Chapman borrowed largely from the *Heautontimorumenos* and the *Adelphi* of Terence; and it must be owned that the plot of the former play is sufficiently hard to follow. Terence confesses that in the *Heautontimorumenos* he "doubled" Menander's plot, and Chapman ran together two plays of Terence. No wonder the result was a labyrinth]. The brain reels in the attempt to straighten it out. Nor is the intrigue so developed as to lead to any skilfully-elaborated and diverting situation, such as sometimes excuses, and almost justifies, the incredible complications imagined by French farce-writers. There is a certain rude merit in the character of Gostanzo, a self-satisfied, overbearing, unprincipled blockhead, who thinks that he is duping Marc Antonio, while he himself is being mercilessly duped. But the intrigue (not to put too fine a point on it) is frigid foolishness; nor is it helped by an under-plot turning on the favourite theme of brutal jealousy. It is a little exasperating to find eulogies lavished on such a play, while modern work which has ten times its ingenuity and twenty times its truth, is either ignored or treated with uncomprehending disdain.

The redeeming feature of the piece is the occasional beauty of its verse and the racy vigour of its prose. The Elizabethans somehow caught the language at a fortunate moment; and Chapman, if one of the lesser dramatists, was one of the greater poets of his time. Here, for instance, is a noble anticipation of Coleridge's "All thoughts, all passions, all delights":

> I tell thee Love is Nature's second sunne,
> Causing a spring of vertues where he shines;
> And as without the sunne, the world's great eye,
> All colours, beauties, both of Arte and Nature,
> Are give in vaine to men, so without Love
> All beauties bred in women are in vaine,
> All vertues borne in men lye buried;
> For Love informes them as the sunne doth colours,
> And as the sunne, reflecting his warme beames
> Against the earth, begets all fruites and flowers,
> So Love, fayre shining in the inward man,
> Brings foorth in him the honourable fruites
> Of valour, wit, vertue, and haughty thoughts,
> Brave resolution, and divine discourse.

This is fine verse; but fine verse does not make a great or even a good play. (pp. 88-92)

> *William Archer, "Five Elizabethan Masters—Jonson—Chapman—Marston—Middleton—Massinger," in his* The Old Drama and the New: An Essay in Re-Valuation, *Small, Maynard and Company Publishers, 1923, pp. 78-109.*

Henry W. Wells   (essay date 1939)

[*Wells was an American educator and literary critic who wrote extensively on English-language authors and also explored Chinese, Japanese, and Sanskrit literature. In the following excerpt, Wells examines Chapman's major tragedies in the context of the philosophy and ideals of the English Renaissance, arguing that Chapman and Christopher Marlowe "were leagued closely together by an unsurpassed devotion to neoclassical humanism."*]

Most of the English dramatists of the Renaissance cultivate the regions about the heart, neglecting the more objective fields of contemporary manners and ideas. We wander with them into vague and uncertain realms, to the seacoast of Bohemia or to the Forest of Arden. The Elizabethans scale pinnacles of fancy, the Jacobean playwrights move through stately woods of aristocratic sentiment. Italy, for example, becomes to them more a romantic fiction than a historical actuality. Thus the serious intellectual controversies of the times are seldom reflected on a stage avowedly devoted to recreational pleasure. Plays

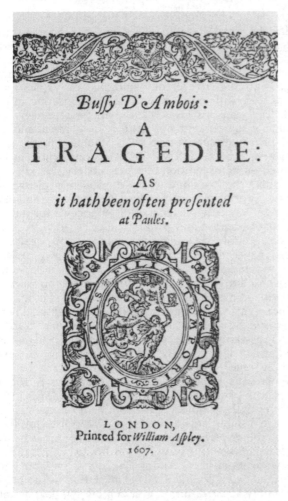

Title page for the 1607 quarto edition of the tragedy
Bussy D'Ambois, *Chapman's most famous play.*

from 1590 to 1642 are more often unphilosophical than not. Contemporary politics are as a rule treated obliquely or neglected altogether, and religion is viewed even more evasively. The theatre as constituted in the period was far from an ideal ground for the free expression of public opinion. Even Edmund Spenser, planning a major poem on both the private and the public virtues, actually failed to reach what he conceived to be his greater theme. Definite restraints were imposed upon literature. The words of Ben Jonson that Shakespeare wrote not for an age but for all time have a peculiar validity. Of course the drama expresses the spirit of the age, but it commonly slurs over many of its graver and more specific problems.

In this regard, as in so many cases, Shakespeare proves typical, his difference from his fellow playwrights lying rather in the magnitude of his genius than in the aims of his art. As usual he touches upon many familiar fields of contemporary thought without allowing his work to be ruled by any spirit other than his own. He is fully aware of the favorite conceptions and values of Renaissance culture without becoming in any marked degree a spokesman for commonly received ideas or a mirror of the customs and manners of the times. He generally assumes these to

be unchallenged and sufficient in themselves without aid from dramatic propaganda. His plays, almost universal in appeal, cannot be shown to be dominated by either the idealistic or the realistic philosophies of his day, by the conduct books, or by the fashions of the hour. Yet the stamp of his age in thought and manners is so frequently to be noted that a few typical instances may be cited here. We are plunged instantly into the high Renaissance by the opening lines of *Love's Labour's Lost* in praise of fame:

> Let fame, that all hunt after in their lives,
> Live register'd upon our brazen tombs,
> And then grace us in the disgrace of death . . .

The entire comedy reflects the stiff, heavily brocaded courtly manners. It comes nearer to exhibiting the taste of a social class than any other of its author's works. Equally in debt to contemporary thought, however, is *The Merchant of Venice,* with its picture of a romantic friendship, a witty and independent woman, and a princely society delighting in carnival gaiety and oratorical exercises. Although the colors of this play have remained fresher than those of *Love's Labour's Lost,* they are scarcely less typical of the times. The idealistic tradition appears in the role of such a gifted prince as Henry V, in the imaginative Romeo, in Brutus, praised by Antony as the ideal man, in Hamlet, the glass of fashion and the mould of form, in the all-accomplished leader, Othello, and in the philosophical Prospero. Courtly taste and morals are well depicted in *Cymbeline* and *The Winter's Tale.* The constituent parts of the ideal king as conceived by the times seem unhappily divided between the poetic Richard II and the coldly scheming Bolingbroke. Doubtless many of Shakespeare's villains, as Iago, evince the acid influence of the realistic school of thought typified in Machiavelli. Yet as a whole the manners and ideas in Shakespeare's plays are not easily dated. And he is more occupied with taste than with philosophy and more concerned with private than with public affairs. Even his portrait of Coriolanus, his most direct excursion into political ideas, shows more regard for the psychology of the individual than for current theories of the state. The most continuous and strenuous assaults of modern scholarship, prying into every conceivable corner left open, have failed to show Shakespeare as primarily a topical writer.

Two dramatists, however, enter with special boldness into the theatre of contemporary thought. Each chants the praises of the Renaissance princely hero or ideal man. What their masterpieces lack in theatrical nicety they make up in spaciousness and splendor of idea. Both were leagued closely together by an unsurpassed devotion to neoclassical humanism. Each was a translator of Greek and Latin poets, one finishing the great poem which the other left incomplete. Chapman is Marlowe's heir, bringing to its logical conclusion his friend's legacy of unfulfilled renown. He is also the complement of Marlowe. In one we see Elizabethan humanism at its radiant dawn; in the other in its zenith and in the smoldering splendor of its decline. Violent death in 1593 left unrealized Marlowe's promise of highly versatile dramatic activity, while Chapman for nearly forty years after essayed a considerable variety of theatrical work, attaining eminence only in four tragedies dealing with contemporary political life.

Tamburlaine, Marlowe's chief contribution to the theme of Renaissance hero-worship, gives rather more of the soul than of the garment of public life; but in much of Chapman's work a more mature and inquisitive mind carries us into the province of historical realism. In the youthful enthusiasm which produced his *Tamburlaine* Marlowe remains untouched by skepticism, while Chapman reveals the hero not only fallen upon evil days but betrayed by what is false within.

Though Marlowe and Chapman represent different stages in the development of Renaissance thought, the consistent evolution cannot well be ignored. Marlowe's Machiavellian satanism, to be sure, differs considerably from the Senecan virtue preached so continually in Chapman's *Revenge of Bussy D'Ambois.* Yet a fiery pride underlies them both. And in Chapman's other notable tragedies the theme still remains the ultra-aggressive personality, treated flatteringly in *The Tragedy of Bussy D'Ambois* and skeptically in the psychological plays, *The Conspiracy and Tragedy of Charles, Duke of Byron.* Behind both playwrights stands a philosophy rising synchronously with the decay of Christian ethics and with the rebirth of the ancient classics. Each depicts the hero as a man intoxicated with the rightness of his own life, acting from the dictation of his own soul and mastered only by the thought of a divine or supernatural force. Their essentially Protestant heroes are aspiring spirits, jealous of their freedom, sensitive of any unwarranted encroachment upon their living, and inclined far more to self-expression than to coöperation with society. Both poets may be viewed as precursors of Carlyle.

In Marlowe there flames up for the first time upon the stage, or for that matter in literature, the soul of the partially barbarous but peculiarly brilliant English spirit as awakened by the social and intellectual urges of the sixteenth century. A new paganism and individualism comes to a sudden blaze of poetical expression. Conventions of the theatre and of poetry no less than limitations of a prosaic realism go down before the overwhelming force of his impassioned thought. Later in his own brief life he was to question on the stage much of the doctrine so naïvely and enthusiastically asserted in *Tamburlaine.* The paganism of Faustus was to be called to account by the ideas of Christianity, and the self-willed and pleasure-loving Edward II was to be shown in the misery of defeat. But for Tamburlaine there could be only victory. A philosophical optimism has seldom shown itself so impetuously. Neither James Thomson, author of *The Seasons,* with his smug faith in eighteenth-century materialism and England's imperial glory, nor Walt Whitman, with his exuberant belief in America's manifest destiny to mould the world's future in soul and matter, quite equals the optimism of the first eminent Elizabethan dramatist. Nor is the childlike innocence of all enthusiastic idealism anywhere more strikingly exhibited. With obvious idolatry for the figure of his own creation, Marlowe evokes Tamburlaine to be the delight, the admiration, and the envy of mankind.

An innovator in art, a rebel in ideas, and in every aspect a creative thinker of unusual force, Marlowe in the earlier stages of his career becomes peculiarly the radical, and

Tamburlaine a glaring symbol of the anti-Christ. A new Lucifer, he proves in more senses than one the scourge of God. Although politically for a while the ally of the Christians against the Turks, he embodies, ethically speaking, all the ideals decried in Christian teaching. Proud, ambitious, wrathful, irreverent, amorous, luxurious, and treacherous, with every breath he commits one of the seven deadly sins. He loves war and not peace, cruelty and not mercy, power and not justice. In political morals, though hardly in subtlety, he rivals Machiavelli. The goddess whom he adores is a woman, Zenocrate, whom he has captured on an expedition of mere robbery. He kills the man whom she loves and whom she has been pledged to marry. In war he mercilessly slays men, women, and children, reserving only the chief of his opponents for the last miseries of disgrace and pangs of physical torture. A tyrant enlarging his kingdom and amassing his wealth by slaughter and pillage, he glories solely in his own ruthless power to rule and to destroy. Over his inferiors he assumes a most absolute command, never seeking their counsel but always dictating their actions. His typical mood is boastful defiance. This "fiery thirster after sovereignty" knows none of the scruples, doubts, compromises, and cautions which necessarily appear in any man grown to full maturity in a world of men. At best this impersonation of Satan faithfully reflects that glorified exterior which belongs more naturally to an Asiatic tyrant than to a European ruler, and so, contrary to Marlowe's intention, no doubt, it adheres to the manners of the continent from which the historical Tamburlaine arose. He is, so to speak, Milton's Satan in minority. For the poet's intention so far as he was a philosopher seems to have been rather to express the aggressive materialism of Tudor England than to embody any distinctively Asiatic ideals. The setting in the pagan East simply assisted him in creating his symbols of anti-Christian thought.

Astonishing remains the only epithet to sum up the effect of the plays depicting Marlowe's epic hero. So daring a sunburst of satanic thought and new-minted poetry England had never seen before nor was destined for a long while to experience again. A humble playwright flung impudent defiance in the face of Christian ethics. In the very extravagance of his poetic madness he verged upon the ridiculous; indeed for a generation after his death English playwrights continued to ridicule his lines, scarcely knowing whether it were better to laugh at them or to admire. It is really touching to find the rationalist Ben Jonson sincerely praising the dead poet whose lines he, with all his fellows, so often subjected to laughter. Utterly simple in the integrity of his art, Marlowe remained in a sense baffling. For his play had almost continuously the qualities of both fustian and pure poetry. From one angle a youthful rant, from another it appeared a profound vision. One could neither convict his god of war of a wholly vulgar brutality nor admire him as a purely renovating spirit. For an explanation of so delicate a blending of the extremes of crudity and subtlety, barbarism and civilization, it becomes necessary for us to go to the too-sudden burst of new vitality that was the Elizabethan age itself.

With the audacity of Milton's resplendent serpent, Tamburlaine and his creator, Marlowe, make the brutal god of war also an inspired artist. The hero is endowed with a gift of gorgeous rhetoric. He and his troops are clad in the most splendid armor and garments. A thunder of clamorous but musical sounds accompanies their movements. The entire play proceeds to the rhythm of some august ritual honoring the god of slaughter. Color adds splendor to the scene. Draperies of various symbolical hues are found upon the tents of the general. His helm is carved and plumed after the manner of Arthur's helmet in *The Faerie Queene.* Through all his campaigns he carries a picture of Zenocrate with him to inspire himself and his army. "But what is beauty, saith my sufferings then?" Had he the services of a Cellini, this satanic sovereign would certainly have employed him to make glorious the face of war and conquest. There is something magnificently superficial in this glowing externality.

The fascination of the art of *Tamburlaine* itself and the force of its ideas lie alike in the poet's certitude. A forthright manner distinguishes Marlowe here both as poet and thinker. Never has an English poet written blank verse with greater fluency of movement. The lithe lines leap out at us with animal grace. The rapidity of the movement remains unclogged by parentheses or qualifications, by elaborations or doubts. Lightning-like flashes of thought are accompanied by the thunder of the rhetoric. Though neither the first nor the second play on Tamburlaine has a semblance of plot, each is composed with a definite beginning, progress, and end. A cumulative series of events terminates in Part One with the marriage of Tamburlaine and Zenocrate celebrated by a period of revelry and truce from war; and in Part Two, with the death of the hero and the transference of his rule to his warlike son. A swiftness and sureness of march-like movement grace all Marlowe's characteristic work, including his two cantos of the narrative poem, *Hero and Leander.* When turning from these introductory cantos by Marlowe to the four by Chapman, the reader passes from the exuberant faith of youth to the complexities of an introverted manhood.

The Renaissance hero, stout in his love of personal freedom and inviolable individuality, in his life of action and lust for fame, appears once more in the person of Chapman's Bussy. Less exuberant in his thinking than Marlowe, however, Chapman depicts an ambitious man who fails to fulfill his own promised renown, a gentleman who enjoys a meteoric rise and fall in the court of France. Shifting the scene from a remote Asiatic court to an almost contemporary Paris, Chapman came as near as practicable to theatrical journalism. As it was, his representation of living persons and political events still green forced the state censor to expurgate the whole second act of *The Tragedy of Byron.* By such means Chapman reduces Marlowe's much idealized picture to a far more realistic scene. Yet much of the earlier spirit remains, translated into a more familiar idiom. While the early glamour of confidence has gone, a more thoughtful and solid structure has been built.

In estimating the place of Chapman's tragedies among the more philosophical dramas of the age, it is best, first, to acknowledge their relation to more typical aspects of the dramatic tradition. *The Tragedy of Bussy D'Ambois* has much in common with the customary Elizabethan drama of romantic passion. Its action centers in the love of Bussy for the wife of Montsurry and in the husband's inevitable revenge. Like so many other theatrical heroes, Bussy is a malcontent fond of chastising the vices of a court with his tongue and sword. The motive of revenge so prominent in *The Revenge of Bussy D'Ambois,* the appearance of the ghosts of murdered men, the sententious quotations and nocturnal atmosphere, all belong to the tradition of the neo-Senecan play as developed during the sixteenth century. All of Chapman's four notable tragedies are based upon French chronicles and hence belong in some measure to the type of chronicle-history play cultivated extensively in England. Moreover, since Chapman had a better knowledge of Greek literature than any English poet of his generation, he naturally preserved more of the classical feeling for tragedy than most of his contemporaries. Nevertheless the soul, and the distinction, of all four of his most notable plays is their philosophical idealism. [Chapman studies the mind and heart of the typical aristocratic leader gifted with the full power and stature demanded by the idealism of the age.] Bussy himself is akin to the impetuous but too rash Achilles; Clermont, his brother, is a Ulysses hardened by stoical doctrine, while Byron represents the decadence of the type fallen before its besetting sins of pride, egoism, and self-infatuation. Each man asserts his own liberty, guarding it jealously; each scorns the vulgar rabble and the corrupted nobles; each pursues the career of arms with a fiery devotion to his own fame. They resemble three generations of a noble family: Bussy, young, arrogant, and supremely adventurous; Clermont, mature, perfect, and admirably self-controlled; Byron, the tragic victim of an excessive aristocratic sensitivity and unlimited pride. Something of Marlowe's youthful and insatiable daring breathes in Bussy; the tragedy of the neurotic cavalier is embodied in Byron; while Clermont is a symbol of the neo-stoical faith as religiously espoused by so many humanists of the age. Chapman's first play excels in the expression of violent emotion, its sequel in an embodiment of a philosophical system, and the tragedy of Byron in its bold portrait of a psychologically fascinating decadence.

Chapman studies the mind and heart of the typical aristocratic leader gifted with the full power and stature demanded by the idealism of the age.

—Henry W. Wells

Unlike most Elizabethan dramatists whose style makes easy and fluent reading, Chapman likes best a knotty, laborious, and intellectual manner, the sign of his philosophical spirit. Dark, mystical, profound, enveloped in clouds of metaphor and simile, he demands the closest attention. Parentheses are long, grammatical constructions are difficult, the thought is involved. Pedantic even in the use of rare words minted from the ancient languages, the great translator of Homer repels the taste that demands smoothness and clarity.

In his lighter moods, as in his comedies, he could write easily and even with some feeling for dramatic characterization. But in his serious vein he is clearly more the epic than the dramatic poet, as his Homeric similes show. His characters speak as a rule in the same heightened and poetic language, highly artificial and highly uncolloquial. Thus his plays stand among the most splendid monuments of Renaissance rhetoric. His tendency to what he calls "virtuous digression" reaches a climax in *The Revenge,* where the sententious style is at its height and action at a minimum. But all his serious plays abound in long and involved speeches, and all have occasional lapses into a brisker movement. *The Tragedy of Bussy D'Ambois* is the most typically Elizabethan, *The Revenge of Bussy D'Ambois* the most profoundly classical of all plays produced during the period, while the plays on Byron with their inclination to a psychological portraiture of the hero resemble a type of analytical biography popular today.

His philosophical bent and neoclassical technique color even his treatment of minor characters. These frequently have small integrity in themselves, but exist to comment upon ideas suggested by the major characters. Thus before Bussy's death Monsieur and Guise converse on the problems of life and death, goodness and immortality. Shortly before the catastrophe in *The Revenge,* Baligny and Renel, two figures unimportant in themselves, speculate on the consequence of luxurious living and the depravity of the King. Similarly in the last act of *The Tragedy of Byron* scenes between such minor persons as Epernon, Soissons, Janin, Vidame, and D'Escures serve merely as the poet's commentary upon Byron's character. This is virtually the technique of the philosophical chorus as used by Aeschylus transferred to the Elizabethan stage.

Chapman simply inverts the moral outlook of Marlowe's *Tamburlaine.* It was not for the grave, "Senecal" dramatist to make a hero of an avowed villain or to glorify Machiavellian theories of politics. Behind all his heroes is the genuine problem of reconciling the highly prized liberty of the individual with the just claims of society. Bussy is presented as too rash and undisciplined, Byron as too ambitious and self-seeking. Only Clermont successfully fights out the battle within his own soul. But if Chapman is theoretically opposed to the devious ways of Machiavellian diplomacy, he shows no small understanding of political intrigue. The plays of Byron in particular become a really subtle study in the relation of internal dissension and international policy. No Elizabethan playwright comes so close as Chapman to a faithful picture of the political spirit of the day. Allusions to contemporary opinions and events are unusually numerous. English statesmen of the times are referred to or mentioned by name. A story is told of the visit paid by the Earl of Oxford to Duke Casimere. There are covert references to Walsingham and Bacon. Of special moment are the debate regarding the Massacre of Saint Bartholomew's Day which Chapman boldly defends and his championship of Philip II, king of Spain and zealous leader of the Inquisition.

Although many lines in the plays indicate that Chapman himself had some sympathy with the Catholic party in Europe, a romantic individualism places this precursor of Carlyle in line with ultra-Protestant thinking. It is to this party that he belongs. When the priest offers consolation to Byron upon the scaffold, the Duke replies with a Senecal argument familiar to all Chapman's readers, that a just man is a microcosm needing no exterior support. To the Archbishop Byron says:

> Horror of death, let me alone in peace,
> And leave my soul to me, whom it concerns;
> You have no charge of it; I feel her free:
> How she doth rouse, and like a falcon stretch
> Her silver wings; as threatening death with
>   death;
> At whom I joyfully will cast her off.

A similar feeling inspires some of the last words of Bussy:

> Prop me, true sword, as thou hast ever done:
> The equal thought I bear of life and death
> Shall make me faint on no side.

In a genuinely dramatic soliloquy Byron exhibits both sides of the allied problem of destiny and free will. Chapman, of course, holds that true personal freedom is attained by conformity to universal laws. Hence he writes satirically, or at least in a purely dramatic vein, when he pictures the Duke infuriated at the prophecy of the astrologer telling him of his evil fortune as written in the stars. In a fit of passion Byron brags that a cup of wine will for him send the heavens reeling in their courses. He boasts that he will kick at fate, that he will risk his life in a giddy drive like a ship listing in a dangerous wind. Here Chapman still satirizes the ungoverned individualist. In the last words of the speech, however, the poet almost certainly returns to his own positive conviction. It is part of the tragic irony that a madman speaks truth:

> There is no danger to a man that knows
> What life and death is; there's not any law
> Exceeds his knowledge; neither is it lawful
> That he should stoop to any other law.
> He goes before them and commands them all,
> That to himself is a law rational.

Chapman's plays make abundant reference to the social and aesthetic life of the nobility of the age. In the Byron plays, for example, much is said of pictures, tapestries, and statues. The daily life of the captain in command is also well indicated. Like Homer, Chapman, the English Cavalier, loves the sea best of all things and gives his affection next to horses. Superb images drawn from horsemanship ennoble all his tragedies. The fine last act of *The Tragedy of Byron* also affords evidence of the fidelity of his pictures. Byron both in his life and in his death, as Chapman explicitly declares, had been said to resemble the ill-fated Earl of Essex. The dramatist had certainly attended some of the important political executions of the day. The great elaboration and vitality of the scene of Byron upon the scaffold afford strong witness to this. Many a gifted, high-strung, and adventurous nobleman of England during Chapman's lifetime lived and died much as his own hero, playing devious politics with ambassadors from foreign countries and in the end paying the full price. For many years the perilous problem of the heir to the throne of England had been similar to that of the heir to the throne of France as Chapman presented it.

How closely the dramatist reflects both contemporary history and taste is unmistakably to be seen in the fourth act of *The Conspiracy of Byron.* The Frenchman had actually paid to Elizabeth the visit here reported and had discussed with the Queen several of the matters here raised. In avoiding the censor's ban Chapman fails to present the Queen upon the stage, but with extraordinary boldness and a complete disregard for English theatrical practice he has their conference reported at length by two minor characters. In the economy of his play the scene is used as a warning to lead Byron back to loyalty to his king. Chapman imagines Elizabeth urging him to be a faithful subject. Thus the scene has not only a choral value but a place in advancing the action of the drama. Of chief interest, however, is the artful reproduction of the elegant diplomatic speech-making and especially of the courtly flattery as practiced during the Renaissance. Elizabeth's own skill and pride in oratory are well depicted in this scene of neo-Ciceronian eloquence. Here is the language of the humanists as spoken in the affairs of state.

Something of the fiery spirit as well as the external aspect of court life appears in Chapman's work. More than any other playwright he reflects the spacious and strenuous public life led by Elizabeth's boldest servants, Essex, Raleigh, and Drake. Bussy is Tamburlaine brought down to earth; Clermont is the same being doubly fortified with the stoical philosophy, and Byron the same being once more, undermined by his own tragic faults. All evince the powerful romantic element in Renaissance thinking. All are touched by the superstitions of the times. Byron consults an astrologer and believes in witchcraft. Bussy is haunted by ghosts. Even Clermont believes in omens and the Socratic daemon. Clermont, to be sure, subjects his will to some degree of discipline, but Bussy and Byron become the victims of their extravagant zeal. All are audacious spirits, battling a hostile world, cherishing an impossible ideal, and destined to shatter their vessels upon rocks.

With all his grave faults as a dramatist Chapman succeeds, then, in embodying his ideas in four really memorable plays, each of which in turn repays special study. Granting its ornate rhetoric, *The Tragedy of Bussy D'Ambois* remains one of the most stirring of the serious dramas of the period. A little too conventional, perhaps, it is none the less thoroughly alive. Although a thoughtful play, it strikes us first as an emotionally exciting one. Only a waning interest in the poetry of the passions caused it to lose its original splendor in the eyes of Dryden and his followers. Here, although uncommon in Chapman's other plays, the lesser characters have considerable value in their own right. Bussy has by no means a monopoly of the eloquent speeches. The domestic scenes between Montsurry and Tamora, for example, possess unusual power. Written in a fine fury of enthusiasm sustained from first to last, the play will at all times presumably be the most admired of Chapman's productions. More successfully than any other, it celebrates the ideal of the Cavalier adventurer. In its first scene is a memorable allusion to Sir Francis Drake.

Its sequel, *The Revenge of Bussy D'Ambois,* belongs obviously in a different category. Nowhere is there an Elizabethan drama more richly sown with aphorisms borrowed from the ancients, nowhere a play of the age so barren of vital action. Clermont is content with the most indefinite view of his position as a revenger. Although he has no clear notion as to whether he should or should not kill Montsurry, he suffers none of Hamlet's qualms of doubtful conscience. Being so admirable a Stoic and, it appears, one of the two virtuous men still living in France, he feels no embarrassment in his own position, no tremblings of uncertainty. He resigns himself to fate, reluctant to rush into a violent revenge, but believing that the just Providence ruling the universe will at some time place him in a favorable position to kill his brother's murderer. His character determines the pace of the play. How slight is the action of this static tragedy may easily be discovered by a summary of its story. Strangely enough, from the beginning Clermont is represented as a friend of Guise, his brother's enemy. With Clermont's consent, however, a challenge after much delay is delivered to Montsurry and declined by him. Clermont's enemies now lay a trap for him which he stoically enters fully aware of the danger. He is imprisoned and thereby debarred from prosecuting revenge. Yet presently he is released from confinement. Three women, more eager than he to reap vengeance, are about to bring the act to a consummation when Clermont arrives just in time to perform his fated task. No sooner has he killed Montsurry than he hears of the death of the friendly Guise, and in fidelity to his loved master he falls upon his sword. The action as a whole is reduced to a minimum, all decisive movement reserved for the last act. Moreover, the teaching of the Stoics, especially of Seneca and Epictetus, whom Chapman chiefly admires, would seem poor material for dramatic art, as it is today unalluring food for the literary appetite. Yet in no respect does Chapman more faithfully reproduce the thought of his times than in finding eloquent poetic and even dramatic expression for this doctrine. More explicit than in the vague allegory of *The Faerie Queene* and more moving than in the utterly untheatrical dramas of the speculative Fulke Greville, Chapman's interpretation of this school of thought is the most striking in Elizabethan literature. That he grasped the meaning of the ancient teaching appears in such a passage as the following:

> Good sir, believe that no particular torture
> Can force me from my glad obedience
> To any thing the high and general Cause,
> To match with his whole fabric, has ordain'd:
> And know ye all (though far from all your aims,
> Yet worth them all, and all men's endless
>   studies)
> That in this one thing, all the discipline
> Of manners and of manhood is contain'd;
> A man to join himself with th' Universe
> In his main sway, and make in all things fit
> One with that All, and go on, round as it;
> Not plucking from the whole his wretched part,
> And into straits, or into nought revert,
> Wishing the complete Universe might be
> Subject to such a rag of it as he;
> But to consider great Necessity,
> All things, as well refract as voluntary,

Reduceth to the prime celestial cause,
Which he that yields to with a man's applause,
And cheek by cheek goes, crossing it no breath,
But, like God's image, follows to the death,
That man is truly wise, and everything,
(Each cause, and every part distinguishing),
In nature, with enough art understands,
And that full glory merits at all hands,
That doth the whole world at all parts adorn,
And appertains to one celestial born.

There remains something still satisfying in this brave fatalistic doctrine of brave men.

The Revenge of Bussy D'Ambois contains more long-drawn-out periods of complicated rhetoric than any other Elizabethan play. It proves the most individual of all its author's works, the most carefully written and toughly labored. A studious reading reveals much more vitality in it than appears upon its forbidding surface. In its sententious language and studied restraint it comes close to the drama of the ancients. Most neoclassical drama resembles the Greek in form but not in spirit; this is like the Greek in spirit though not in form. It still contains some force as poetry.

The plays on Byron move almost as slowly in point of action. Not formless, they are certainly unelastic. They can hardly have been at any time successful on the stage, for Byron is too seldom found in truly theatrical situations. There are no character studies save that of the hero, and only the most embryonic features of an intrigue. In this intellectual drama the emotions are seldom portrayed as powerfully as in *The Tragedy of Bussy D'Ambois,* and of actual doctrine there is far less than in *The Revenge.* What remains is an uncommonly pure vein of poetry much less turgid than in *The Tragedy of Bussy D'Ambois* and much less frigid than in *The Revenge.* The creative feature of this tragedy is its picture of the neurotic and self-deluded nobleman, victim of his own passionate pride, the fall of whom marks the ruin of his ancient family. Although the likeness is more objective and less intimate than the portraiture to which the modern novel has accustomed us, the effect remains none the less vivid. There is nothing in Shakespeare's *Coriolanus,* for example, quite so poignantly real as the spiritual struggle of Byron's last days. The noble idealism of the Renaissance, with its limitless faith in personality, is seen in an hour of trial: the essential meaning of Marlowe's *Tamburlaine* confronted with its own inherent fallacy. In our own age of advancing socialism the limitations of the Renaissance conception stare us in the face. Yet there is not only abiding worth in the ideal but beauty in the tragedy attending its defeat.

Our quest for the cultural philosophy of the upper classes in the Renaissance has led us almost exclusively to two playwrights where in a relatively narrow compass has appeared the spaciousness of their ideal. Some critic might remind us that Hamlet was also an ideal prince, a glass of fashion and a mould of form. The typical revenge plays abound in moral reflections no note of which has been taken here. Nevertheless an impartial view does reveal Marlowe and Chapman as the most powerful and devoted spokesmen of the Renaissance theory. It shows also the breadth of their criticism, an aspect too often neglected by

students stressing the doctrines of Machiavelli as a disturbing background and the revenge play as a type. After all, Marlowe and Chapman mention Spenser as often as Machiavelli and borrow from Castiglione and the idealists no less than from Machiavelli and the so-called realists. They are as much occupied with virtue as with sin. As these playwrights never allow us to forget, the ideal gentleman of the Renaissance is a many-sided, Ulyssean character. (pp. 76-94)

Henry W. Wells, "The Renaissance Ideal," in his Elizabethan and Jacobean Playwrights, *1939. Reprint by Greenwood Press, Publishers, 1975, pp. 76-94.*

C. S. Lewis   (lecture date 1952)

[*Lewis is considered one of the foremost Christian and mythopoeic authors of the twentieth century, as well as a perceptive literary critic. In the following excerpt from a lecture delivered in 1952, Lewis contrasts Christopher Marlowe's two books on* Hero and Leander *with Chapman's four sestiads, arguing that the work must be considered as a "corporate poem."*]

Chapman's four books or sestiads on Hero and Leander are, I believe, very seldom read in conjunction with Marlowe's two. The whole temper of modern criticism, which loves to treat a work of art as the expression of an artist's personality and perhaps values that personality chiefly for its difference from others, is unfavourable to a poem by two authors. It comes naturally to us to treat the total *Hero and Leander* as two separate works. Nor, of course, is there any reason why we should not do so. There are some composite works—for example, the *Romance of the Rose*—which are best dealt with in this way. But there are others such as our composite English *Morte Darthur,* where earlier English work and French work and Malory and Caxton so subtly grow together into 'something of great constancy' that the modern approach is baffled. I am not claiming that *Hero and Leander* is in that class. We know quite well which parts are by which poet, their styles are clearly distinct, there is no 'contamination' (in the textual sense), and pseudo-Musaeus is so far in the background that we can ignore him. Yet I think we shall be richly rewarded if we obey the apparent invitation of the old editions and read the poem, at least sometimes, as a whole. For here, as I shall try to persuade you, collaboration has produced an extremely fortunate result. Each poet has contributed what the other could not have done, and both contributions are necessary to a worthy telling of the story. For the difference in style and outlook here corresponds to the two movements of which that story consists. If we feel young while we read the first two sestiads and feel in the remaining four that youth has died away, our experience is very like Hero's. If Venus dominates Marlowe's narrative and Saturn that of Chapman, the same may be said of the events which each narrates. It is almost, as it ought to be, like passing from a Song of Innocence to a Song of Experience.

Of course, when we speak of 'innocence' in connexion with the first two sestiads we are using the word 'innocence' in a very peculiar sense. We mean not the absence of guilt but the absence of sophistication, the splendour, though a guilty splendour, of unshattered illusions. Marlowe's part of the poem is the most shameless celebration of sensuality which we can find in English literature—unless we extend the category of literature to include such works as the booksellers call 'curious'. It does not even keep within the bounds of what might be called, either in the older or the modern sense, a 'kindly' sensuality. It exults to see

> the gods in sundrie shapes,
> Committing headdie ryots, incest, rapes
> (1, 143),

and the loves of Neptune in Sestiad II are what Saintsbury called 'Greek style'. The point need not be laboured. A critical tradition which can stomach the different, but far worse, depravities of *Tamberlaine,* can well put up with **Hero and Leander.** The question which Marlowe's sestiads invite is not a moral one. They make us anxious to discover, if we can, how Marlowe can write over eight hundred lines of almost unrelieved sensuality without ever becoming mawkish, ridiculous, or disgusting. For I do not believe this is at all easy to do.

Marlowe's success is most easily seen if we compare him with other sixteenth-century specimens of the erotic epyllion. Lodge's *Scillaes Metamorphosis* is hardly good enough: despite its frequent beauties it is too static and too lacrimose. Drayton's *Endimion and Phoebe* suffers from discordant aims and even discordant styles. We shall have to come to *Venus and Adonis.* And I must frankly confess that, in so far as the two works are comparable at all, Marlowe seems to me far superior to Shakespeare in this kind. *Venus and Adonis* reads well in quotation, but I have never read it through without feeling that I am being suffocated. I cannot forgive Shakespeare for telling us how Venus perspired (175), how 'soft and plump' she was, how moist her hand, how Adonis pants in her face, and so forth. I cannot conceive why he made her not only so emphatically older but even so much larger than the unfortunate young man. She is so large that she can throw the horse's rein over one arm and tuck the 'tender boy' under the other. She 'governs him in strength' and knows her own business so badly that she threatens, almost in her first words, to 'smother' him with kisses. The word 'smother', combined with these images of female bulk and strength, is fatal: I am irresistibly reminded of some unfortunate child's efforts to escape the voluminous embraces of an effusive female relative. It is, of course, true that there are touches of reality in Shakespeare's poem which cannot be paralleled in Marlowe's. But I am not sure that reality (in the sense of naturalism) is what a poem of this type demands: at any rate, naturalism such as Shakespeare gives. Shakespeare shows us far too much of Venus' passion as it would appear to a third party, a spectator—embarrassed, disgusted, and even horrified as any spectator of such a scene would necessarily be. No doubt this unwelcome effect comes in because Shakespeare is, in general, a far profounder and more human poet than Marlowe. His very greatness prevents his succeeding in the narrow and specialized world of erotic epyllion. But it suits Marlowe exactly. He does not see beyond the erotic frenzy, but writes from within it. And that, curiously enough, is his poetic salvation.

In reading *Venus and Adonis* we see lust: in reading Marlowe's sestiads we see not lust but what lust thinks it sees. We do not look at the passion itself: we look out from it upon a world transformed by the hard, brittle splendour of erotic vision. Hence all that sickly weight and warmth which makes unrestrained appetite in the real world so unpleasant to the spectator or even, perhaps, in retrospect to the principals themselves, does not appear at all. Instead of Shakespeare's sweating palms and poutings and pantings and duckings and 'lustful language broken' and 'impatience' that 'chokes the pleading tongue' we have a gigantic insolence of hyperbole. The real world, which Shakespeare cannot quite forget, is by Marlowe smashed into bits, and he makes glory out of the ruin. Hero has been offered Apollo's throne. The brightness of her neck makes a collar of pebbles shine like diamonds by reflection. The sun will not burn her hands. The ladies of Sestos, walking in procession, make the street a 'firmament of breathing stars'. In that world there are boys so beautiful that they can never drink in safety from a fountain: the water nymphs would pull them in.

If you compare these hyperboles with one of Shakespeare's you will easily see the difference. His Venus promises Adonis that her hand will 'dissolve or seem to melt' in his. That, of course, is hyperbolical, but it is in touch with fact—with the fact that hands may be hot, moist, and soft. But Marlowe's hyperboles are so towering that they become mythopoeic. They have, none the less, their own wild consistency and co-operate in building up such a world as passion momentarily creates, a topsy-turvy world where beauty is omnipotent and the very laws of nature are her willing captives. This mythopoeic quality is reinforced by Marlowe's use of what may be called the aetiological conceit, as in his passage about Mercury and the fates at the end of I, or his explanation why 'Since Heroes time hath halfe the world beene blacke'. Though the whole two sestiads celebrate the flesh, flesh itself, undisguised, rarely appears in them for long. Leander's beauty is presented half mythically: he is a prize like the golden fleece, his body is as 'straight as *Circes* wand', and the description of him shines with the names of *Nectar, Pelops, Jove,* and the cold *Cinthia.*

With this style there go two other characteristics. One, of course, is the metre—a ringing and often end-stopped couplet, compared with which the stanza of *Venus and Adonis* is unprogressive and the enjambed couplets of *Endymion* invertebrate. I suspect that the masculine quality of the verse, in fruitful tension with the luxury of the matter, plays an important part in making so much pure honey acceptable: it is a beautiful example of Wordsworth's theory of metre. The other is the total absence of tenderness. You must not look in Marlowe for what Dryden called 'the softnesses of love'. You must, indeed, look for love itself only in the narrowest sense. Love here is not 'ful of pittie' but 'deaffe and cruell': his temple is a blaze of grotesques. Leander woos like 'a bold sharpe Sophister'. The male and immortal lover who first tries to ravish him, ends by trying to kill him. Hero is compared to diamonds, and the whole work has something of their hardness and brightness. Marlowe sings a love utterly separated from kindness, *cameraderie,* or friendship. If female spiders, whose grooms (I am told) do 'coldly furnish forth the marriage tables', wrote love-poetry, it would be like Marlowe's. But, however shocking, this treatment is an artistic success. We know from some terrible scenes in Keats's *Endymion* how dangerous it is to attempt the mixture of tenderness and sensuality in verse. Licentious poetry, if it is to remain endurable, must generally be heartless: as it is in Ovid, in Byron, in Marlowe himself. If it attempts pathos or sweetness an abyss opens at the poet's feet. Marlowe never comes near that abyss. His poem, though far from morally pure, has purity of another sort—purity of form and colour and intention. We may feel, as we come to the end of the Second Sestiad, that we have been mad, but we do not feel that we have been choked or contaminated. And yet I believe that the final impression left on an adult's mind is not one of madness or even of splendour, but, oddly enough, of pathos. If we had caught Marlowe striving after that effect in such a poem we should perhaps have turned from him with contempt. But it is not so. What moves us is simply our knowledge that this passionate splendour, so insolent, so defiant, and so 'unconscious of mortality', is 'desperately mortal'.

That it was doomed, for Hero and Leander, to end in misery Marlowe of course knew well. He wrote only the first movement of the story, the ascending movement; how he would have handled the descent we do not know. If he was to do it successfully, he would have had to use powers not found in the first two sestiads: would have had to 'change his notes to tragic'. The necessity of this change, even had he lived, renders tolerable the still greater change, the change to another author, which now meets us at the beginning of the Third Sestiad. If ever one poet were to 'take over' from another, no happier juncture could be found. At the very moment when the theme begins to demand a graver voice, a graver voice succeeds.

In his Dedicatory Epistle Chapman describes himself as drawn 'by strange instigation' to continue Marlowe's work. From a line in the Third Sestiad (195), when he describes himself as 'tendering' Marlowe's 'late desires', some conclude that Marlowe had asked Chapman to finish the poem. But it is not at all clear why this should be called 'strange instigation'. Perhaps Chapman poetically feigned, or (quite as probable) actually believed, that he had been strangely instigated by Marlowe since Marlowe's death. I am certainly inclined to think that when, in the same passage, he sends his own genius ('thou most strangely-intellectuall fire') to 'confer' with Marlowe's 'free soule' in the 'eternall Clime', he is speaking seriously: believing, like Scaliger and others, that a man's *genius* is a personal, immortal creature, distinct from himself. But the question is not of great importance. The poetic impulse which moved Chapman to write is quite clear from his own sestiads as a whole, and especially from the opening lines of the Third. And it was essentially an impulse to continue, to finish. We cannot doubt that he had entered into Marlowe's erotic poetry with the fullest (temporary) sympathy. But, to his graver mind, it cried out for its sequel. As he says

> Joy grauen in sence, like snow in water wasts.
> (III, 35)

It had fallen to Marlowe to tell of joy graven in sense, it fell to him to tell of the wasting. Love, or such love as Hero's and Leander's, is in Chapman's eyes 'a golden bubble full of dreames' (III, 231): he will show how it burst.

I do not think we should regard this as a 'cauld clatter of morality' officiously and unpoetically added to a poem which does not require it. There are several reasons against doing so. The most obvious is the fact, already mentioned, that the myth itself already contained a tragic ending. The second is that the picture of headlong love presented by Marlowe demands some nemesis poetically no less than morally. Every man who sees a bubble swell, will watch it, if he can, till it bursts. A story cannot properly end with the two chief characters dancing on the edge of a cliff: it must go on to tell us either how, by some miracle, they were preserved, or how, far more probably, they fell over. I do not mean that Chapman would have put it to himself quite like that. Conceiving poetry as a kind of philosophy, he would have been content with a purely ethical justification for his sestiads. I mean that even if we banish, as he would not have banished, all moral considerations, our aesthetic interests would still demand a second, downward, movement. Finally, we must remind ourselves that the particular moral content which Chapman put into his part of the poem was not nearly so platitudinous for him as it would have been for a nineteenth-century poet.

Chapman's sestiads are a celebration of marriage in contrast to, and condemnation of, the lawless love between Hero and Leander. We are in danger of taking this as a thing of course. It was not so in Chapman's day. When writers like Lyly and Greene fall into a fit of moralizing they are quite likely not to make a distinction between lawless and wedded love, but to attack love and women altogether in the old ascetic, misogynistic manner which goes back to St Jerome. When Sidney's heroes struggle against love they too are concerned less with the distinction between lawful and unlawful than with the baseness or unmanliness of the passion itself as something contrary to the heroic ideal. In taking the line he does, which is the same as Spenser's, Chapman is therefore doing something not without importance. It may have given him more trouble than it gave Spenser, for there are passages in his plays which suggest that the old conceptions of courtly love still come to life in his mind. His part of *Hero and Leander* is to be taken as the product of serious thought.

It is especially to be noted that his doctrine is no facile warning against enchantments which he could not feel. This is one of those things which a poet can show only by the actual quality of his writing, and Chapman does so. Time and again he writes lines of an extravagant sweetness which Marlowe could not surpass. As this:

> Musick vsherd th'odorous way,
> And wanton Ayre in twentie sweet forms danst
> After her fingers.
> (V, 42)

Or when the Athenian maidens have been carried off by robbers and, at the same hour the stars are coming out,

> the yellow issue of the skie
> Came trouping forth, ielous of crueltie

To their bright fellowes of this vnder heauen.

(V, 171)

When Hymen hands the lily to Eucharis,

> As two cleere Tapers mixe in one their light,
> So did the Lillie and the hand their white.

(V, 221)

A girl's skin is 'softer than soundest sleep'. Leander, dripping from his swim, runs to his sister 'singing like a shower', and as the white foam drops off him

> all the sweetned shore as he did goe,
> Was crownd with odrous roses white as snow.

(III, 81)

I am not saying that the quality in all these is exactly like Marlowe's. Chapman has his own slower movement and his own type of conceit; he is nearer than Marlowe to the metaphysical manner. But they are not less rapturous and exalted than Marlowe's. If Chapman does not permanently abandon himself to 'golden bubbles', it is not because he could not. He knows what he rejects.

This rejection is not in any way that I can discover based on Christian grounds. And this is not to be explained by the fact that the story is Pagan and involves the Pagan deities. That would have presented no difficulties to a medieval or Elizabethan poet if he had wished to christianize it. The gods and goddesses could always be used in a Christian sense, as they are in *Comus* or in *Reason and Sensuality*. If Chapman had wished to theologize, chastity embodied in Diana or divine reason in Minerva would have descended to rebuke Leander. The figure who actually appears to him is someone quite different—the goddess Ceremonie. To a modern Englishman, I suspect, no abstraction will seem less qualified for personification and apotheosis. We do not—at least that class of Englishmen who study literature do not—perform ceremonies gracefully, nor attend them with much enthusiasm, and we doubt whether any ceremony can modify the nature of the act which it accompanies. The Elizabethan sentiment was very different. About ceremonies in the Church there might be some dispute: but even there the Puritans objected to them not so much because they desired a pure, individual inwardness as because they thought that a Divine positive law excluded certain ceremonies. In secular life ceremony reigned undisputed. The chroniclers describe ceremonies at length as if they were equal in importance to the gravest political events. And so perhaps they were. Pageant, masque, tournament, and emblem book taught men to expect a visible and formalized expression of every rank, emotion, attitude, and maxim. One quarrelled, loved, dined, and even played by ceremonial rule. The Ciceronian in Latin and the Euphuist in English made prose a ceremony. The universe itself with its noble and base metals, its sublunary and translunary regions, and the nicely graded hierarchy of planetary intelligences, was a vast ceremony proceeding in all space and all time. It is in ceremony that Shakespeare's 'Degree' and Spenser's 'Concord' are manifested.

Chapman condemns the loves of Hero and Leander not because the pair were ill matched, nor because they lacked the consent of parents, nor because he admires virginity, nor by the Christian law, but only because, being hasty and not waiting for marriage, they had defied *Time* and *Ceremonie*. *Time* must, of course, here be understood as meaning 'the right time', 'timeliness', the Latin *opportunitas*: it is very close to Elyot's virtue of *maturitie* (*Boke named the Gouernour*, I, xxii), and its connexion with Ceremonie becomes plainer if we remember that it is one of the virtues which, in Elyot's scheme, we learn from dancing. Chapman takes great pains to make us understand his point of view. Ceremonie, for him, is what distinguishes a fully human action from an action merely necessary or natural. As he says, no praise goes to the food which 'simply kils our hunger' or the dress that 'clothes but our nakednes'. We reserve praise for 'Beautious apparell and delicious cheere'. Thus unexpectedly the goddess Ceremonie, who forbids lawless *luxuria,* is from another point of view almost the patroness of luxury—the ordered, humane luxury of evening dress, and choice wines, and good cookery. The embraces of Hero and Leander were, after all, only a coarse meal snatched by ravenous hunger 'with ranke desire' (III, 49). Here, as everywhere else, it is the humanised and 'orderd' procedure that 'still giues pleasure freenes to aspire' and

> Vpholds the flowrie bodie of the earth
> In sacred harmonie.

(III, 61)

The whole 'bench of Deities' (the planets) hang in the hair of this goddess. Devotion, Order, State, Reuerence, Societie, and Memorie, are her shadows. Chapman sees her as our defence against utter ruin and brutality: as Shakespeare sees Degree. And, as in the *Dunciad* the enemies are always creeping on, so here we see Confusion, and (close on her heels)

> *Barbarisme,* and *Auarice,*
> That followd eating earth, and excrement
> And humane lims.

(III, 138)

We are told that they would soon storm the palace of the gods 'were *Ceremonie* slaine'. It is tempting to say that Ceremonie is simply Chapman's name for civilization. But that word has long been prostituted, and if we are to use it we must do so with a continual reminder that we mean not town-planning, and plumbing and ready-cooked foods but etiquette, ball-rooms, dinner-parties, judges' robes and wigs, Covent Garden, and coronations in Westminster Abbey. In a word, we must realize that what we should regard as the externals of civilization are, for Chapman, essential and vital. The simplest way of doing this is not to use the word *civilization* at all but to retain his own word *ceremonie*, remembering what he meant by it.

It is early in the third Sestiad that Ceremonie appears to Leander. The remainder of that sestiad and the whole of the next are concerned with Hero's remorse and deterioration—a passage to which I must presently return. Up to the end of the Fourth, Chapman is occupied with his negative theme, the condemnation of lawless, unceremonial, love. In the Fifth we have the positive side, the celebration of the lawful and ceremonial alternative, marriage. The contrast is pointed for us first by the fact that Hero (who has now resolved on a life of consistent hypocrisy) exercises her priestly function by marrying two young lovers and afterwards attending their marriage feast. To this feast, apparently unbidden, there comes a very curious person. She is called a nymph but has rather the characteristics of a sixteenth-century English fairy. She is a 'little Siluane', known as Apollo's 'Dwarfe', a haunter of 'greene *Sestyan* groues', a prophetess. Her name is Teras: that is *monstrum,* portent, prodigy. From that point of view she continues, in a personified form, the sinister omens which have harassed Hero in the preceding sestiad; and her function at the banquet is fulfilled when she left the company and

> the turning of her back
> Made them all shrieke, it lookt so ghastly black.
> (V, 489)

Seen from the front she had been beautiful: in other words, the one omen that had appeared to be good turns out to be bad, and Hero's fate is sealed. But between her pleasing entry and her terrifying exit she has exercised another function. Perched on an altar she has entertained the marriage party with the tale of another marriage, which marriage in its turn (this sestiad is constructed like a Chinese nest of boxes) was between Marriage himself, Hymen, and Eucharis, was in fact the archetypal marriage. Much of it is concerned with mystical explanations of Pagan marriage ceremonies: a sort of learning dear to the Elizabethans. The only thing in it which calls for comment is the part played by the girl Adolesche—Garrulity, or Chatterbox, who had a face

> Thin like an iron wedge, so sharpe and tart,
> As twere of purpose made to cleaue *Loues* hart.
> (V, 299)

This unpleasant young woman hurried off to Athens to spread the news of the love between Hymen and Eucharis, but arrived just as their marriage feast was ending and found no market for her scandal. She sank beneath her disappointment and was promptly metamorphosed into a parrot. The meaning of this little fable is, I suppose, obvious. Adolesche tries to play the part played by the talebearer or *losengier* in an affair of courtly love, but fails because marriage comes in between her and her hopes. Chapman is pointing out that marriage settles the old problem of the *losengier.* From this tale Teras, her terrible back still hidden, turns to sing her Epithalamion: in a sense the heart, though not the climax, of Chapman's story, and perhaps the finest lyric he ever wrote. He never praised Night more deliciously:

> O come soft rest of Cares, come night,
> Come naked vertues only tire,
> The reaped haruest of the light,
> Bound vp in sheaues of sacred fire.

This summary is intended to make clear that Chapman's part of *Hero and Leander* is, as we should expect, a doctrinal and philosophical poem, very seriously meant by the poet. Much invention has gone to the creation of a new mythology which embodies his doctrine. Venus' motive for treating so sternly an offence which she, of all goddesses, might be expected to have pardoned is too trivial and too merely mythological for so grave a story: but with that exception the 'plot' (if one may so call it) is watertight and

enables Chapman to say what he wanted to say. But, of course, all this will be unavailing if the actual texture of the writing fails to please.

It must be admitted that Chapman has his bad moments. The worst is when, in Sestiad VI, 197, Neptune suddenly jumped up and 'for haste his forehead hit Gainst heauens hard Christall'. We might at least have been spared the adjective *hard;* it is for most of us too painfully, and therefore too comically, reminiscent. Of course, what Chapman means is to tell us, in conceited language, that the waves rose heaven-high. The influence at work here is, I have little doubt, that of Du Bartas. Chapman is trying the Bartasian technique which consists in representing things great and superhuman in the most humdrum and anthropomorphic terms. I do not think we should continue to laugh at that technique as our fathers did. The French poet, after all, bequeathed it to our admired Metaphysicals. Marvell's vigilant *patrol* of stars, Donne's liberated soul that 'baits not at the Moone', Herbert's representation of Christ as an innkeeper, are all Bartasian in character. Elsewhere Chapman is more successfully Bartasian. To tell us that the moon rose, he says:

> The Saffron mirror by which *Phoebus* loue,
> Greene *Tellus* decks her, now he held aboue
> The clowdy mountaines.
> (V, 407)

It should be noticed that the lines which I quoted a moment ago from the Epithalamion are really of the same sort:

> The reaped haruest of the light,
> Bound vp in sheaues of sacred fire.

The image, when we work it out, is Bartasian; daylight is mowed like a field at evening and the harvest is tied up into those sheaues which we call stars.

Of course, Chapman is not more conceited than Marlowe had been: he is conceited in a different way. His style admirably exemplifies the transition from the pure Elizabethan manner to that of the Metaphysicals. It can, as earlier quotations have perhaps shown, display on occasion all the old abandonment and sweetness. But in general it is slower, weightier, more difficult. And Chapman, when he first comes on the stage at the opening of Sestiad III, very wisely explains the difference so that, with a little goodwill, one may take it as a change arising from the story itself and not merely from change of authorship.

> More harsh (at lest more hard) more graue and
> hie
> Our subiect runs, and our sterne *Muse* must flie.
> Loues edge is taken off . . .

The last phrase is curiously happy, for it applies not only to the experience of Hero and Leander but to that change in English poetry with which Chapman's succession to Marlowe coincides. The old love for a poetry of pure deliciousness was, indeed, losing its edge. Honey began to pall. That is why a movement either to the more violent and knotty poetry of Donne or to the harder and severer poetry of Milton was necessary. In that way the composite *Hero and Leander* is a kind of bridge. The English Muse herself loses her innocence in the process of telling how Hero lost hers.

The new effect 'more hard, more graue and hie' depends on several changes. The most obvious is that of metre. Marlowe uses some enjambment, but I think he is happiest, most irresistibly himself, when he is most end-stopped: here, as in his plays, the superb single line is his characteristic glory—'The sweet fruition of an earthly crowne', 'To entertaine diuine *Zenocrate*', 'Who euer lov'd, that lov'd not at first sight?' When there is a run-over it seldom adds much music. But Chapman can write true verse paragraphs in couplets, and the pauses are well managed. There is also a far greater intrusion of philosophical and reflective matter: fifteen lines on optics in the Third (235 *et seq.*), nine on the nature of beauty (99 *et seq.*), and eighteen on the properties of numbers (323 *et seq.*) in the Fifth. These will be unwelcome to the modern reader, but the last is relevant to Chapman's intention, and if we cared as much as our ancestors did for Arithmosophy (so to call it), it might please. We can also find in Chapman passages of a saturnine realism which, in their own way, strengthen and, as it were, thicken the poem: the sketch of Adolesche has already been mentioned. You may add the description of women talking at a funeral in the tale of Teras (V, 185 *et seq.*). Yet after all, these detachable passages count for less than that habitual cast—by no means a pale cast—of thought, which mixes with the normal flow of the narrative. A phrase like 'forme-giuing *Cyprias* siluer hand' (V, 314) is typical. *Silver* connects it with the old style of Marlowe: but *forme-giuing* lets in the whole doctrine of the archetypal Uranian Venus and the influence of the third heaven. Chapman is taking his Venus more seriously than Marlowe would have done. When he has to describe a woman yielding to a wholly legitimate love, he says

> The bribde, but incorrupted Garrison
> Sung *Io Hymen.*
>
> (V, 253)

There is a concentration of thought in 'bribde but incorrupted' which it would be hard to find in Spenser, Sidney, or the young Shakespeare. If we could purge the word 'cleverness' of the sneering overtones that it has unfortunately acquired, I should say that Chapman's poetry is almost everywhere cleverer than Marlowe's: his imagination not less stimulated by the senses but more stimulated by ideas. The following describes the moment at which Hero's remorse weakens and a reaction in favour of Leander begins.

> And all this while the red sea of her blood
> Ebd with *Leander:* but now turnd the flood,
> And all her fleete of sprites came swelling in
> With childe of saile, and did hot fight begin
> With those seuere conceits, she too much markt,
> And here *Leanders* beauties were imbarkt.
> He came in swimming painted all with ioyes,
> Such as might sweeten hell: his thought destroyes
> All her destroying thoughts.
>
> (III, 323)

The splendour of the first line and a half has been praised before. What I would rather draw your attention to is the manner in which, throughout, the ideas and images catch fire from one another: how the ebb leads to the flood, and then the flood no longer exists for itself but carries a fleet, and the swelling of its sails leads to 'with childe of saile' and thence to a sea fight, and thence back to Leander, now swimming again; but all this not for ornament, as it might be in a long-tailed epic simile, but closely presenting the movement of Hero's mind.

This passage comes among the lines—there are nearly five hundred of them—which Chapman devotes to Hero in her solitude, in the Third and Fourth Sestiads. This is on the whole the high-light of his poem. The process of her degeneration is well conceived. It begins in blank despair, at first neither hopeful nor desirous of concealment, then passes to a long stillness, then to the reaction which I have just quoted which leads at once to the delusive belief that all will yet (somehow) be well. After that comes the resolution to be a hypocrite. It is, as I say, well conceived: but it is presented not after the fashion of the novelist nor even as Chaucer would have done it. It reaches us through an intricate pattern of conceit, symbol, and myth, much commented on and generalized. The method seems to me highly successful. The first despair is expressed in a tragic conceit which could not be bettered—

> She was a mother straight and bore with paine
> Thoughts that spake straight and wisht their
>   mother slaine.
>
> (III, 227)

The prolonged and static misery which follows is not directly described at all. What we are actually shown is simply Hero's dress and Hero's pose—the robe of black 'Cypres', 'exceeding large', the left hand clasping it at her breast, the bent head, the knees 'Wrapt in vnshapefull foulds'. It is a method proper to painting but equally proper to narrative poetry: we respond to it with our muscular as well as with our visual imagination. In the next sestiad we see her tricked out again in her priestly garments and working with her needle. We are told little about what she felt during this period of false hope, but we are made to feel it for ourselves because every picture her needle makes is truer than her conscious mind will confess—

> These omenous fancies did her soule expresse,
> And euery finger made a Prophetesse.
>
> (IV, 108)

After that comes the ill-omened sacrifice, the resolve to act a part, and the apparition of Venus. Out of Hero's torn robe and torn hair there rises up in the altar fire a new creation, a 'mayd most faire', girdled with snakes and ending in a scorpion's tail. It is Eronusis, Dissimulation. The thing that Hero's mind has conceived now stands before her, like Athene sprung from Jove's head or Sin from Satan's. We are in the world of nightmare. Yet still

> Betwixt all this and *Hero, Hero* held
> *Leanders* picture as a Persian shield.
>
> (IV, 345)

The truth and unexpectedness of this conclusion are surely admirable.

It will be seen that Chapman has his own, highly personal, technique for narrative poetry. It stands about midway between the continuous allegory of Spenser and the phantasmagoric poetry of the moderns. He can mingle at will direct psychological description, full-blown allegory, and emblematic picture. Once we accept it, we do not find ourselves confused. For me at least it has great potency. I do not know that I can find exactly the same sort of power anywhere else.

I must, of course, be careful not to claim too much. Neither Marlowe's nor Chapman's part of **Hero and Leander** is anything like a faultless poem. Here, as always (most inexcusably in his Homer), Chapman is too digressive: he is often obscure, always mannered, sometimes ridiculous. He clogs his lines with consonants. He indulges in that cu-

---

An excerpt from *Chapman's Homer*

In this fire must Hector's triall shine.
    Here must his country, father, friends be in him
      made divine.
    And such a stormy day shall come, in mind and
      soule I know,
    When sacred Troy shall shed her towres for
      teares of overthrow,
    When Priam, all his birth and powre, shall in
      those teares be drownd.
    But neither Troy's postcritie so much my soule
      doth wound—
    Priam, nor Hecuba her selfe, nor all my broth-
      ers' woes
    (Who, though so many and so good, must all be
      food for foes)—
    As thy sad state, when some rude Greeke shall
      leade thee weeping hence,
    These free dayes clouded and a night of captive
      violence
    Loding thy temples, out of which thine eyes
      must never see
    But spin the Greeke wives webs of taske and
      their Fetch-water be
    To Argos, from Messeides, or clear Hyperia's
      spring—
    Which (howsoever thou abhorst) Fate's such a
      shrewish thing
    She will be mistris, whose curst hands, when
      they shall crush out cries
    From thy oppressions (being beheld by other en-
      emies)
    Thus they will nourish thy extremes: 'This dame
      was Hector's wife,
    A man that, at the warres of Troy, did breathe
      the worthiest life
    Of all their armie.' This againe will rub thy fruit-
      full wounds
    To misse the man that to thy bands could give
      such narrow bounds.
    But that day shall not wound mine eyes: the so-
      lide heape of night
    Shall interpose and stop mine eares against thy
      plaints and plight.

George Chapman in Allardyce Nicoll, ed., Chapman's Homer: The Illiad, The Odyssey, and *the* Lesser Homerica, *translated by George Chapman, Princeton University Press, 1956.*

---

rious sort of false rhyme to which Mr Simpson devoted an article. [Percy Simpson, "The Rhyming of Stressed with Unstressed Syllables in Elizabethan Verse," *The Modern Language Review,* vol. XXXVIII (April 1943)]. As for Marlowe's part, it is, after all, a beautiful monstrosity: a thing which, even if no moral objections are felt, can win admission to the mind only in a particular mood. Even in that mood we shall admit, if we are quite honest, that it lasts just a little too long. But heaven forbid that we should never read—and praise—any poems less than perfect. Marlowe's part, with all its limitations, is a very splendid and wonderful expression of accepted sensuality: Chapman's a very grave and moving reply—an antithesis, yet arising naturally, almost inevitably, out of the thesis. My main concern is not to assess the absolute merit of either but to suggest the propriety of reading the composite poem as a whole. I first made that experiment twenty, or it may be nearer thirty, years ago: repeating it the other day, I found my old delight renewed and even deepened. . . . I ask you to admire the lucky accident, if it was no more, which, at that particular moment in the history of poetry, brought together upon that particular story two poets so necessary to one another for enabling us to live through the process which that story embodies. I recommend all who have not done so to read the old book, for once, in the spirit of children to whom a book is an ultimate and who, never thinking even of one author, would not care whether two or twenty-two had written it. (pp. 58-73)

C. S. Lewis, "Hero and Leander," in his Selected Literary Essays, *edited by Walter Hooper, Cambridge at the University Press, 1969, pp. 58-73.*

Peter Ure (essay date 1956)

[*In the following excerpt, Ure considers the aesthetic basis of Chapman's translations of Homer and his major tragedies, arguing that "Chapman is entitled to be judged in the light of his own poetic theory."*]

Between 1594 and 1616 Chapman worked very hard. He translated the *Iliad* and the *Odyssey,* wrote six tragedies and about the same number of comedies, and composed enough original verse to fill nearly four hundred pages in the latest edition. This essay is confined to the translation of Homer and the tragedies, and therefore deals with only about half of his work. There is good reason for this limitation. Most readers are not likely to appreciate his poems unless they have first been attracted by other things in Chapman. The comedies tell us less about Chapman's individual quality than the tragedies, which form a group easily distinguishable from other plays of the time. Chapman considered the translation of Homer to be his greatest work, and the ways in which he modified his original are themselves valuable clues to his artistic purposes. Knowledge of Chapman's mind and art acquired in the study of the tragedies and the Homer will not need to be *radically* revised in the light of the poems and the comedies.

The final, revised version of the Homer, into B. R. Haydon's copy of which Keats looked, appeared in 1616 as *The Whole Works of Homer Prince of Poets in his*

Iliads and Odysseys. It is a thick, unhandsome volume sprinkled with marginal notes and equipped with a slender but pugnacious commentary. Ben Jonson wrote some vigorous *marginalia* in his copy, making fun of the translator for his contumely towards other scholars, but he praised Chapman's later version of Hesiod, and may well have given general approval to the Homer. Pope, Coleridge, and Matthew Arnold all had praise, mingled with blame, for it. The modern reader, unlike Arnold, who censured Chapman for his Elizabethan fantasticality but was perhaps chiefly familiar with the *Iliads,* may be advised to begin with the *Odysseys,* which is written in a kindlier metre than the 'fourteener' of the other epic.

Chapman did play havoc with his original. His knowledge of Greek, exceptional for his time, was still not expert enough to release him from dependence on the great continental Hellenists. Chapman borrows freely from their Latin notes and renderings, and in his own commentary accuses them of bad scholarship. In the process Homer sometimes gets distorted. Transferring the Homeric measure into rhymed fourteeners (in the *Iliads*) or rhymed decasyllabics (in the *Odysseys*) also encouraged deflections. Chapman's love of antitheses, of rhetorical figures, his avoidance of the stock repetitive phrase, his brash anachronisms and colloquialisms, the touches here and there of 'English Senecan' rant are all Elizabethan, not Homeric. Here, from the eleventh book of the *Iliads,* is an example of Chapman's handling of the epic simile, as full of light as Spenser's description of Prince Arthur:

> And as amidst the sky
> We sometimes see an ominous star blaze clear
>   and dreadfully,
> Then run his golden head in clouds, and straight
>   appear again;
> So Hector otherwise did grace the vant-guard,
>   shining plain,
> Then in the rear-guard hid himself, and labour'd
>   everywhere
> To order and encourage all; his armour was so
>   clear,
> And he applied each place so fast, that, like a
>   lightning thrown
> Out of the shield of Jupiter, in every eye he
>   shone.
> And as upon a rich man's crop of barley or of
>   wheat,
> Opposed for swiftness at their work, a sort of
>   reapers sweat,
> Bear down the furrows speedily, and thick their
>   handfuls fall:
> So at the joining of the hosts ran slaughter
>   through them all.

A contrast to this is Anticlea's reply to her son Ulysses in Hell, in language involved, stately, and pathetic:

> 'O son', she answer'd, 'of the race of men
> The most unhappy, our most equal Queen
> Will mock no solid arms with empty shade,
> Nor suffer empty shades again t'invade
> Flesh, bones, and nerves; nor will defraud the
>   fire
> Of his last dues, that, soon as spirits expire
> And leave the white bone, are his native right,
> When, like a dream, the soul assumes her flight.

> The light then of the living with most haste,
> O son, contend to. This thy little taste
> Of this state is enough; and all this life
> Will make a tale fit to be told thy wife.'
>   (*Odysseys,* IX.)

Chapman's contempt for his critics—'Asses at Thistles, bleeding as ye eat', as he called them—sprang from his reverence for the poetic office. Like Drayton, he became the more melancholy and bitter the more he found reason to scourge the bad taste of his contemporaries and appeal from their neglect. The pugnacity so evident in the dedications and commentary to the Homer proceeded from his belief that he alone had been born to interpret aright the Prince of Poets. In some admirable lines in **The Tears of Peace** (1609) he tells how the spiritual form of Homer appeared to him in the green fields of Hitchin, his sacred bosom full of fire; perhaps no English poet enjoyed a like visitation until Blake dined with Isaiah. Such intercourse gave Chapman confidence in his right to clarify and enlarge his author's meaning with insights that no one before him had possessed. For Chapman, Homer is the witness to his faith in poetry, the first great composer of a visionary iconography: 'blind He all things saw':

> He, at Jove's table set, fills out to us
> Cups that repair Age sad and ruinous;
> And gives it built of an eternal stand,
> With his all-sinewy Odyssaean hand . . .
> He doth in men the Gods' affects inflame,
> His fuel Virtue, blown by Praise and Fame.

As this passage shows, Chapman believed that the study of Homer persuaded men to virtue, and this belief helped to introduce into his translation some modifications of the original more radical than any I have yet mentioned. Chapman did not hold, as did some Renaissance scholars, that all Homer was one continued allegory, whose sugared least detail coated a moral pill. But he consistently saw Homer's personages as exemplifications of moral doctrine, as giant forms of justice and fortitude and their opposite vices. Unfortunately for Chapman, Homer had not articulated so clearly the moral roles of his heroes. The noblest of them can cry like children or play ambiguous and sorry parts, unaware that, like Thomas Mann's Joseph, they are participating in a wonderful God-story. Chapman therefore felt impelled to make more plain what he thought Homer's grand design to be:

> the first word of his Iliads, is υηνιν, *wrath:* the first word of his Odysseys, ανδξα, *Man:* contracting in either word his each work's proposition. In one, *Predominant Perturbation;* in the other, *over-ruling Wisdom:* in one, the Body's fervour and fashion of outward Fortitude . . . in the other, the Mind's constant and unconquered Empire.

Thus Chapman's Homer acquires what has been called its 'ethical bias'. By interpolating, adjusting, sharpening, he brings out of Homer's golden haze what he conceives to be the central sun of his moral meaning. Achilles and Hector are transmogrified into warriors more perfect than Homer allowed. Agamemnon is seen as a man thrown from his true course by domineering passions. Their speeches are illuminated with the aphorisms which the

Renaissance inherited from the classical moralists, and of which Homer was innocent. Odysseus becomes 'a moral hero of the Renaissance', as wise as Cato and as pious as Aeneas. Such modifications do not necessarily make the version in its totality untrue to Homer's spirit, although they may outrage anyone seeking Homer's letter. They tell us something important about Chapman's ethical bias in his treatment of human character and his attitude towards poetry.

The bias can be detected in Chapman's tendency to read into human life and history the doctrines of the classical moralists, primarily of Epictetus, secondarily of Plutarch and Seneca. These Stoic writers taught that the hero must master his inward passions, and that the search for sensual gratifications outside himself will lay open the principles of his being defenceless before the storms of war, tyranny, and Fortune. This doctrine had enjoyed a revival in the neo-Stoic movement of the sixteenth century. Many trained themselves, and Chapman amongst them, to perceive Virtue, Justice, and Manhood, not as attributes fastened upon a man by popular suffrage and capable of being stolen from him by ill-luck or enemies, but as aspects of an inward unity, the 'god dwelling in the human body', which Marcus Aurelius honoured. That unity attained, man was fortified within and without. Ignorant of it, he was the helpless prey of his own passions, and became, in his relations with other men, either a persecutor or a victim. These ideas can be traced in systems so far apart in other respects as Giordano Bruno's and Calvin's. The vocabulary of contemporary arts and sciences is flooded with Stoic meanings.

Chapman was much attracted by the doctrine, but he could not escape from the antinomies that the neo-Stoic revival called forth in a milieu so generally busy with intellectual endeavour. If Chapman warmed himself at Stoicism's central fire, he was attracted by other lights as well. Some, like the political theory associated with Machiavelli's name, he did his best to extinguish. But with others, like the great Renaissance attempt to synthesize Christian teaching with Platonic, he attempted to illuminate his own work.

His attitude to poetry, his dominant interest in the business of rendering his vision of life and character in poetic terms, is also implied in his treatment of Homer. We need not be surprised that a poet like Chapman, who is profoundly influenced by a doctrine that seems to us chilly and rigoristic, should also believe that a 'holy fire and hidden heat' burns in the bosom of all true poets from Homer onwards, and should therefore continually strive after large and luminous effects and imaginative portrayals of truth. It has been pointed out that the Stoics, in spite of the passionless objectivity of their doctrines, really aimed at just such an imaginative portrayal of their relations with truth. And Chapman, like other Renaissance artists, was conscious of a prevailing desire to reconcile Minerva, the spirit of a wise inner discipline, with Apollo, the heaven-aspiring genius of poetry. Chapman would have seen no cogency in Blake's argument that the man who is occupied with mental and moral discipline becomes wrapped in a cold and spectral Selfhood that closes his eyes to God

above and within; he is therefore free to embrace and exemplify the Platonic and Ficinian doctrine of poetic inspiration, that 'celestial fire':

> where high Poesy's native habit shines,
> From whose reflections flow eternal lines:
> Philosophy retir'd to darkest caves
> She can discover, and the proud world's braves
> Answer . . .

Pope commented dryly that Chapman must have been 'an enthusiast in poetry', but for Chapman the term (which he does not himself use) would probably have had no colouring of fanatical extravagance. The mind of the heroic enthusiast, wrote Giordano Bruno, himself echoing St Augustine, 'aspires high by plunging into its own depths', for to reach the God within man is one road to God himself. Chapman would have pleaded guilty to such 'misconceit of being inspired', sustained by the example of his Homer, and the belief that there is a correlation between the truth which a poet perceives and the divine authority which bestows upon him the gift of revealing it, in all its force and beauty, to men.

Of the five tragedies written by Chapman between 1603 and 1611, four are drawn from recent French history: *The Tragedy of Bussy d'Ambois,* the double-play of *The Conspiracy and Tragedy of Charles Duke of Byron,* and *The Revenge of Bussy d'Ambois.* The fifth, *Caesar and Pompey,* is Chapman's only Roman play.

All Chapman's tragedies may be described as dramatic studies of the interaction between a great man and his society. There are four main elements at work in this interaction: in the hero, his moral nature (his goodness or badness), and his outward role, as soldier, rebel, or servant to the king; ranged opposite to him in society are two kinds of men, the mouthpieces of Chapman's ideas on social order, or the hypostases of various kinds of social corruption. The plays are built up from the innumerable conflicts and harmonies which arise amongst these elements. This schematization suggests that Chapman's plays, like Marlowe's, tend, if we are thinking of them in terms of the contribution made by characterization to the total play, to be grouped round a single great figure. In the plays that bear their names, it is Bussy and Byron, and, in *The Revenge of Bussy,* Clermont d'Ambois, who hold our interest, while the other personages, ambitious prince, ideal king, political schemer, are more important for what they represent in relation to the protagonist than for what they are themselves.

Two of Chapman's heroes, Bussy and Byron, are great men flawed by their inability to control their inward passions and resist the outward temptations to which this inner disorder exposes them. The others, Clermont d'Ambois, Chabot, and Cato in *Caesar and Pompey,* are meant to be, so far as the exigencies of the plot in each case permit, 'exemplars of calm', men capable of achieving the ενθυμια, inward peace, of Stoic teaching. Pompey oscillates between discipline and disorder, and finally comes to rest in Stoic fortitude. Chapman's subject in the tragedies is still, as in the Homer, μηνιν, *the wrath,* and ανδξα, *the man.*

The Tragedy of Bussy is a good example of the method. When the play begins, France is no longer at war, and the soldier Bussy, poor and neglected, is therefore outside society, his natural habitat of court and camp. This society, represented by Monsieur, now reaches out to grasp Bussy and use him for its secret end, a design upon the crown. Bussy accepts the patronage, but on his own terms. He knows that to be a great man in the opinion of a corrupt society is to spend his life:

> In sights and visitations, that will make
> His eyes as hollow as his mistress' heart.

For himself, he will try to rise in court simply 'by virtue': he is 'a smooth plain ground [that] will never nourish any *politic* seed'. So he behaves rudely to the women of the court as a sign of his refusal to compromise with their corrupt world of political chambering and sexual hypocrisy. Society immediately begins to react to this strange nonconformist. The king is enthralled by Bussy's noble bearing and philosophical speeches; but the king's favourite, the Guise, senses a rival and Monsieur himself finally realizes that he has chosen the wrong man. When the news comes that Bussy is carrying on an intrigue with Tamyra, the wife of the Count Montsurry, the noble politicians see their chance to destroy him. For Bussy's love has taken his nature by storm and muddied the currents of his inward peace; and he is finally overthrown by the conjunction of the enemy passions, which have undermined the virtue within, with the outward machinations of his rivals. We grasp the full measure of his fall from philosophical grace when, in Act IV, in a vain attempt to escape from the jaws of the trap, he adopts the 'policy' which he had formerly repudiated. But he is an amateur at the game of politic murder, and is easily out-manoeuvred by experts like Monsieur and the Guise. His end, none the less, asserts his greatness. As he dies, involved in horror and splendour, we realize how much Chapman's conception of him owes to the ancient idea of the classical hero, that Virtue which the Renaissance moralists allegorized from the myth of Hercules, he who moves continually towards the blazing pyre where mortality will be purged away and godhead assumed.

Byron, too, like Bussy, is related to a classical archetype. In portraying him, Chapman took some suggestions from Plutarch's orations on Alexander the Great. But Byron, although he loudly lays claim to the giant robe of the hero, is flawed by corruptions foreign to Plutarch's Alexander. Choleric, ambitious, haunted by fantastic images of his own splendour, he has never attained inward peace, and therefore certain conspirators find him easier to be played on than a pipe. Their flattery stokes up the fuel in his own heart and turns him finally into a 'rotten exhalation', a meteor destroying itself as it burns up the waste stuff of the kingdom. Chapman makes it clear that Byron's inner corruption contributes as much to his fall as any outward agent, and we are continually enabled to measure its extent by comparing it with King Henry's 'over-ruling Wisdom'. Yet the ancient virtues visit Byron from time to time in glimpses that almost restore his manhood; he never becomes a mere dwarfish thief of honour, and can still be described in terms of virtue or its declination. This allows his death to seem sufficiently tragic as he, too, ascends the fu-

neral pyre of Hercules and prepares to cast off the gross body.

Having written of the exemplars of wrath, Chapman turns to the exemplars of calm. Of these, Chabot is the most consistent, Cato the nearest to a literal interpretation of the Roman ideal of virtue, and the vacillating Pompey the most humanly plausible. They are all Odyssean figures. But Clermont, in *The Revenge of Bussy,* is Chapman's completest study of the Senecal man. He is calm where Bussy and Byron, rage, self-contained where they are ambitious for external goods; and although placed like them in a corrupt society, he is able to judge it more fairly because he is more detached from it than they. Clermont is the most successful issue of previous attempts by other dramatists, including George Buchanan, William Alexander, Marston, Daniel, and Fulke Greville, to dramatize the Stoic Wise Man within a context of political equivocation.

But *The Revenge of Bussy* raises acutely a problem that haunts every investigation into Chapman's merits as a dramatist. How far did Chapman succeed in reconciling his obligations as a writer for the popular public playhouse with his interests in political morality and the relations between greatness and goodness? For such interests are not suitable for our stage unless they are broken down in the crucible of a true dramatic imagination. We have seen that Chapman was able to put things into Homer which are not really there, without making Homer fundamentally the less Homeric. His own explanation of this success is the best: he felt his bosom filled with Homer's fire. But in the drama this sustaining warmth is absent. *The Revenge,* for example, is classifiable as a revenge play in the tradition initiated by Kyd's *The Spanish Tragedy.* In reality, it is four acts of moralizing followed by a fifth in which the dramatist reluctantly sets in motion the traditional machinery of revenge and whining ghost, and—the sharpest incongruity of all—burdens the non-attached Clermont with the Revenger's bloody duty. These are antilogies to which all Clermont's moralizations on his task will not reconcile us.

Is a similar judgement on Chapman's other tragedies unavoidable? Was his imagination not of the kind that makes a successful playwright? It is fair to try to define more precisely some of the elements that go to compose the plays, and leave the final answer to the individual reader's experience.

Chapman did not despise the drama. 'Scenical representation', he wrote, 'is so far from giving just cause of any least diminution, that the personal and exact life it gives to any history, or other such delineation of human actions, adds to them lustre, spirit, and apprehension.' It may well have been the search for a more personal and exact life that caused Chapman to examine so exigently the nature of his protagonists and analyse the virtues and corruptions of their societies. It is not likely that Chapman saw this search as having a purely artistic objective; for the more lustrous and spirited the representation, the more efficiently, in Chapman's theory as well as Sidney's, it would inspire in the beholders that delight which would lead them to 'steal to see the form of goodness ere themselves be aware'.

But however inseparably the motives of artist and moralist combine in Chapman, it remains a fact that he is not content, as Marlowe is in *Tamburlaine,* merely to persuade us that a magnificent existence *is,* and leave us puzzling how, if at all, it fits into the scheme of things. Nor is he willing, as even Jonson sometimes is, to clap an intrusive moral over something profoundly disturbing to Panglossian complacency. Chapman likes to explain as fully as possible what has happened. Thus he provides in several discourses a number of explanations of why Bussy falls and what kind of man he is. Why was he created so hollow within, so vulnerable to Fortune? Are parts of him 'empty' of soul, the vital principle of virtue? Or is he indeed 'fullmann'd', and yet placed by Nature in a world which can only blunt and spoil her splendid instrument? And, restlessly, the characters in the play whom Chapman burdens with these speculations turn to Nature herself and accuse her of a random incompetence in her working. Byron's behaviour is explored in the same way, and the underground issues which are raised by his relationship with king and conspirator debated on the open stage. To the contemporary audience, who remembered the fall of Essex and the execution of the historical Byron at the beginning of the century, and who probably shared Chapman's interest in the behaviour of great men in a changing society, such questions must have seemed sufficiently to the point.

From material of this kind in the plays one can extract a body of opinion and label it Chapman's 'theory of man' or 'political beliefs'. But that will not really tell us what place such things have in a play. It may even lead us—as it has led some critics—to beg the question by assuming that Chapman wanted the drama to be a vehicle for debate and speculation, and did not care whether these helped to bestow upon it a more 'personal and exact life' or not.

It is true that Chapman's questionings shape his dramatic devices. His characters cease to be men in action and become philosophers; they can assume the role of chorus or pause to examine their motives with a queer objectivity. Byron has speeches put into his mouth which transform him from a conspirator into a Chronos or a Muse of History; Cato's relation to Pompey is too bleakly modelled on that of the Epictetian sage to his disciple. These incongruities show that Chapman does not perfectly fuse his underlying moral theme with his men-in-action. In this he differs not only from Shakespeare and Jonson, but even from their inferiors like Heywood (*A Woman Killed with Kindness*) or Middleton (*The Changeling*). His tragedy is often more akin to the old moral play: there are moments in it when the human lineaments dissolve and the blank face of the hypostasis looks through, when the allegorical abstraction blots out the anagogy of art. Thus, there is a curious split running up the character of King Henry in the Byron plays, who is sometimes the Ideal King, a mere abstraction from a handbook for princes, and sometimes simply Henry, raging at the malfeasance of a traitor in a way correspondent with the actualities of history and 'the fury and the mire of human veins'. Such fissures disturb us more in the drama than they do in a vast artefact like *The Faerie Queene.* The shift from mask to face and back again induces a shudder in the action, a momentary lack of focus while the audience adjusts itself from the homily to the warmer contemplation of men in action.

Here it is appropriate to bring into court what is generally taken to be Chapman's rueful comment on his own deficiencies, in the dedication to his second volume of Homer translations (1598):

> But woe is me, what zeal or power soever
> My free soul hath, my body will be never
> Able t'attend: never shall I enjoy
> Th'end of my hapless birth, never employ
> That smother'd fervour that in loathed embers
> Lies swept from light, and no clear hour remembers.
> O had your perfect eye organs to pierce
> Into that chaos whence this stifled verse
> By violence breaks, where glow-worm-like doth shine,
> In night of sorrow, this hid soul of mine,
> And how her genuine forms struggle for birth,
> Under the claws of this foul panther Earth . . . !

This is not really an unexpectedly humble admission that his verse is bad in the sense usually suggested. The 'loathed embers' are the clogging envelope of mortality, not of poetic incompetence, and the whole passage is one of many statements in Chapman's work about the Platonic dualism of soul and body which is an important aspect of his world-view. In Chapman's thought, the large-souled man, whether a Bussy or a poet, is always hampered by this dualism, although some, like Homer, can escape from it. In refusing to himself a Homeric status which he probably would not have granted to any of his contemporaries, Chapman is merely submitting to the burden of the dualism.

Moreover, the passage suggests that some of our discontentments with Chapman's dramatic characters may be resolved if we view the characters not as vitally incomplete, 'left headless for a perfect man' because of some deficiency in their creator's imagination, but as analogues to the artist's struggle as it is here described. Bussy and Byron, Clermont and Pompey, are studies in men striving to achieve their perfect images by hacking from them the 'excess of Humours, perturbations and Affects'. In *The Tears of Peace,* borrowing his similitude from Plotinus, Chapman compares such a struggle to the work of the sculptor who gradually cuts a human figure from an alabaster block. We are reminded that Michelangelo's 'Slaves' and 'Prisoners' are not to be thought of as 'left headless' by their maker once they are conceived as symbols of the birthpangs of giant-forms, 'hid souls' writhing with violence in the stifled night of marble. If the analogy holds, it might be said that Chapman's unfinished men are wiser images of life than the pantomimic integrity with which, in the seventh book of *Paradise Lost,* the creatures burst perfectly formed from the ground, their 'smallest Lineaments exact'.

It is characteristic of Chapman to liken the artist-moralist's task to the sculptor's, for he has, in M. Schoell's phrase: *l'imagination puissamment concrète'.* His dramatic verse is often exquisitely made to express his moralized conceptions of what a man's life may be: either a mist of passion ('wrath'), or a struggle to master it, to hack out the genuine forms of the soul, or a condition of Stoic concord. Its faults are that passion may sometimes slip into incoherence and concord into prosifying. In the speech of the wrathful Montsurry to Tamyra, as he compels her by torture to write a letter to her lover that will lure him into a trap, it is worth observing the vigour and fertility of the language, the complex cross-references to mythology, and the way in which the visual images emerge broken and struggling from the battle with Chapman's unsure syntax:

> Come, Siren, sing, and dash against my rocks
> Thy ruffian galley, rigg'd with quench for lust!
> Sing, and put all the nets into thy voice
> With which thou drew'st into thy strumpet's lap
> The spawn of Venus, and in which ye danced;
> That in thy lap's stead, I may dig his tomb,
> And quit his manhood with a woman's sleight,
> Who never is deceived in her deceit.
> Sing (that is, write), and then take from mine
>   eyes
> The mists that hide the most inscrutable pander
> That ever lapped up an adulterous vomit;
> That I may see the devil, and survive
> To be a devil, and then learn to wive:
> That I may hang him, and then cut him down,
> Then cut him up, and with my soul's beams
>   search
> The cranks and caverns of his brain, and study
> The errant wilderness of a woman's face,
> Where men cannot get out, for all the comets
> That have been lighted at it: though they know
> That adders lie a-sunning in their smiles,
> That basilisks drink their poison from their eyes,
> Yet still they wander there, and are not stay'd
> Till they be fetter'd, nor secure before
> All cares devour them, nor in human consort
> Till they embrace within their wife's two breasts
> All Pelion and Cythaeron with their beasts.
> Why write you not?

In this speech Montsurry's sexualized disgust ('quit his manhood' in l.7 is charged with irony and means 'reward him for his sexual virility') and frenzied desire for violence modulate into a series of confused images which half-invite visualization: the very abrupt transition from the crannies of the brain to the woman's face, perhaps with the suggestion that the face will be found imaged in the lover's dissected brain, and the conception of that face both as a wilderness full of poisonous monsters lit by comets blazing with rotten material and a trap in which men are caught and lost. The playing with paradox in the final lines is found elsewhere as Chapman's means of expressing his view of man's dilemma, 'created sick', as Fulke Greville wrote, 'commanded to be sound', and one way in which he presents the giant form struggling for release from the imprisoning marble of the body:

> . . . wretched world,
> Consisting most of parts that fly each other;
> A firmness breeding all inconstancy,
> A bond of all disjunction; like a man
> Long buried is a man that long hath lived;
> Touch him, he falls to ashes.
>   (*The Tragedy of Byron.*)

In Mr Auden's words, Chapman finds poetic means to express his consciousness of man's 'condition of estrangement from the truth', of the 'ungarnished offended gap between what [men] so questionably are and what [they] are commanded without any question to become' (*The Sea and the Mirror*).

One of Chapman's favoured critical terms, as we have seen, is *lustre*, applied in Renaissance theory, as by Puttenham, to *enargia*, or 'a goodly outward show set upon the matter with words'. For Chapman, its concomitant *energia*, a forcefulness of figurative language that will work inwardly upon the mind, is equally important. Montsurry's speech is both lustrous, set about with verbal ornament, and forceful in the sense of using its figures to reveal to the reader what is *in* the mind of the dramatic character. Chapman strives both to burnish his language outwardly and to give it inward significance. This, after all, is only the linguistic aspect of his philosophy of man, his search for the hero whose inward qualities are not betrayed or diminished by a false outward blaze but who can yet serve, like Cato, as a luminary to other men because he is 'full-mann'd', inwardly solid with virtue and 'soul'. Chapman contrives to present this awareness in such images as the comparison of the worthless man to the hollow colossus, outwardly splendid but within choked with rubbish or ballasted with lead. When he turns not to represent passion but to reflect upon the human situation, he often chooses the form of a visual image, an iconograph or emblem, which is as clear and lustrous as *enargia* requires, but at the same time has a correspondent inward meaning which operates with forceful *energia*. Such a passage as the comparison of religion to a tree growing and withering in the hearts of kings (*Tragedy of Byron*, III. i) has also the calm and elegiac note which distinguishes objective meditation upon truth from the dramatization of the wrathful man. I quote the concluding lines of an elaborate 'mute' emblem:

> The tree that grew from heaven
> Is overrun with moss; the cheerful music
> That heretofore hath sounded out of it
> Begins to cease, and as she casts her leaves,
> By small degrees the kingdoms of the earth
> Decline and wither; and look whensoever
> That the pure sap in her is dried-up quite,
> The lamp of all authority goes out,
> And all the blaze of princes is extinct.

Chapman is entitled to be judged in the light of his own poetic theory. In the heart of this lies a moralized conception of how poetry works and what it does. For Chapman, also, *le mot juste* is, as Professor Bullough has remarked of the Cambridge Platonist Henry More, an intelligible not an aesthetic quantity.

Like Jonson, Chapman thought of himself as living in an age whose very corruption required new discoveries of truth and fitness. Like Blake, he sought intellectual vision; and his reverence for Homer, who appeared to him:

> With eyes turn'd upward, and was outward
>   blind,
> But inward past and future things he saw,

reminds us of More turning inwards to seek knowledge of

truth, and of the visionary logic of the blind Milton: 'So much the rather thou, celestial light, Shine inward'. On one of Chapman's portraits his motto is inscribed: CONSCIVM EVASI DIEM: 'I fled the garish day'. Its corollary is to be found in the line from Ovid that Spenser wrote into *The Shepheardes Calendar,* and which all the poets who belong to Chapman's tradition would have understood: 'Est deus in nobis; agitante calescimus illo', 'There is a God within us, and by his force are we inspired'. (pp. 318-32)

> Peter Ure, "Chapman as Translator and Tragic Playwright," in The Age of Shakespeare, Vol. 2, edited by Boris Ford, Penguin Books, 1956, pp. 318-33.

Robert Ornstein   (essay date 1960)

[*In the following excerpt from his well-regarded study of Jacobean drama, Ornstein explores the philosophical bases of Chapman's late dramas, focusing on the shift in political ideology from the anti-Machiavellism of* Bussy d'Ambois *to the stoic resignation of* Caesar and Pompey.]

Chapman came to tragedy twenty years too late, after the Spenserian dream of chivalry had become something of a

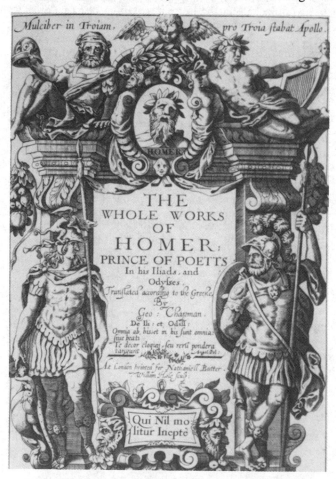

Frontispiece for the 1616 folio edition of Chapman's complete translations of the Iliad *and the* Odyssey.

joke to skeptical Jacobean minds. By training and inclination he was a humanistic scholar, steeped in classical philosophy, and dedicated to the pursuit of the heroic in literature if not in life. As the great translations of Homer testify, he could so immerse himself in the grandeur of antiquity as to appear immune to contemporary anxieties. But his drama, which is more closely attuned to the temper of the age, reveals the vulnerability of his humanistic idealism. His comedy descends rapidly from the superficial satire of *An Humorous Day's Mirth* to the cynical depths of *The Widow's Tears.* His tragedies span the poles of Jacobean disillusion from the bitter scorn of *Bussy D'Ambois* (1604) to the meditative Stoic resignation of *Caesar and Pompey* (1612-13). There are, of course, many echoes of Marlowe and of Elizabethan melodrama in his earliest tragedies, yet even in *Bussy* we can trace a confused attempt to unite Elizabethan convention and Jacobean vision, to dramatize through hackneyed theatrical devices the essential political and moral issues of the time. Only late in his career as a tragedian did Chapman free himself completely from the heritage of Elizabethan revenge melodrama and then the price of victory was dullness. His last plays are upright Moralities, noble in thought and sentiment, but only incidentally or coincidentally dramatic in conception.

It is possible to explain the evolution of Chapman's drama from melodrama to Morality wholly by reference to his subject matter. We can say that he turned away from the Marlovian titan presented in *Bussy D'Ambois* and the Byron tragedies (1607-8) to affairs of state and Stoic philosophy. But it seems to me that Chapman's artistic concerns never changed, that from first tragedy to last he dramatized a personal quest for values in an age when it no longer seemed possible to assent to established political, religious, and moral dogmas. The quest began, to be sure, in confusion, but in play after play he criticized and revised his intellectual position until he arrived at what seemed to him an eternally valid, philosophical solution to the problem of evil. Thus the Stoicism of Chapman's last tragedies, far from being a conventional exposition of Epictetian precepts, is (as we shall see) the journey's end of a long intellectual and artistic pilgrimage.

Scholars have often left the impression that there is little if any serious moral thought in Chapman's early tragedies. Some are content to describe *Bussy D'Ambois* and the Byron plays as Marlovian spectacles or to ascribe the ethics of the tragedies to Chapman's supposed belief in psychological determinism. A counteremphasis long overdue has arrived with Ennis Rees's recent study of the tragedies. Mr. Rees has performed a valuable service by emphasizing the ethical bias of Chapman's art and by demonstrating the parallels of thought in his dramatic and nondramatic works. But Mr. Rees's conception of Chapman as a clear-sighted Christian humanist who confidently lectured to his audiences on the need for learning and the dangers of an active life seems oversimplified if not insensitive to the moods of *Bussy* and the Stoic plays. Indeed Mr. Rees's thesis that the core of Chapman's ethical thought is a traditional Christian doctrine proves embarrassing in the discussion of the *Revenge* and *Caesar and Pompey;* it seems to this reader to obscure rather than to elucidate Chapman's attitudes towards his Stoic heroes.

I think we misinterpret the Stoicism of the tragedies if we assume that the sincere piety expressed in Chapman's poetry is the sunlit reality of his ethical doctrine and his Stoicism the artistic shadows on the wall of the cave. Even if we grant that Chapman's poetry is more personal than his drama, we cannot ignore its public and conventional aspect. And we cannot assume that the essence of his thought lies in any single work or segment of his work, when he seems to use all of his art (his plays as well as his poems) to develop his ideas. Actually we need not oversimplify Chapman's ethical ideas to make them consistent, because there is no contradiction between the sincere piety of **"A Hymne to Our Saviour on the Crosse"** and the Stoicism of the **Revenge** and **Caesar and Pompey.** On the contrary, these are the characteristic dualities of Renaissance humanistic thought; they represent the divided and distinguished worlds native to the humanistic moral speculation of the late sixteenth century.

We find much in the **"Hymne"** that reminds us of the tragedies. It expresses the same skepticism about established religions, the same disgust for the corruption of Churches that one finds in **Bussy.** Like other contemporaries Chapman is driven by the diversity of religious factions to a Protestant faith that is deeply fideistic and, as we might expect, individualistic. He is intellectual in his ethics but anti-intellectual in his religion; like Webster and Marston he is uninterested in and disdainful of theological controversies. In the **"Hymne"** he insists that the Bible reveals with great simplicity the sum of religious truth. He seeks salvation through virtue and simple faith in Christ's redemptive love.

In the **"Hymne"** Chapman sets forth the ultimate goal of a virtuous life, which is to bring man to God and enable him to fulfill his divinely appointed destiny. In **The Teares of Peace,** his most important philosophical poem, he treats quite separately the *practical* humane problem of achieving virtue—a problem which is to be solved by learning rather than piety. In **The Teares of Peace** as in Chapman's tragedies moral issues are viewed philosophically; victory over the passions is to be gained by obedience to reason, not by an act of faith. To be sure, as Chapman moves from the public issues of the Byron tragedies to the more personal concerns of the Stoic plays, his moral philosophy becomes increasingly theological in nature. The Stoicism that was in early plays an instrument of philosophical reason becomes at last profoundly religious in itself. But even when Chapman's divided and distinguished worlds melt into one, we cannot square his ethical position with any particular orthodoxy.

Because Chapman attempted an intellectual drama, we face the continuing problem of distinguishing between his philosophical and his artistic failings. The problem is acute in the interpretation of **Bussy D'Ambois,** a play that seems at first too naïvely moralistic in characterization and design. A keynote of moral fervor is struck in its opening lines as Bussy castigates an effete nobility and sings the praises of virtue. Before long he sets off on a chivalric adventure to reform his society, his lance securely aimed at the dragon of policy. Exactly what policy stands for in **Bussy** is not easy to say, but the term recurs with almost hysterical emphasis, especially in Bussy's diatribes against Monsieur:

> He'll put his plow into me, plow me up;
> But his unsweating thrift is policy,
> And learning-hating policy is ignorant
> To fit his seed-land soil; a smooth plain ground
> Will never nourish any politic seed; . . .
>
> (I.i.123-27)

The meaning of policy would be clearer if the portrait of Monsieur, the arch-Machiavel, were more sharply defined. In some respects he anticipates such later Machiavels as Baligny in the **Revenge,** but he does not have their totally unscrupulous ideology. Ambitious for a throne and armed with the cold, cynical intellect of Kyd's Lorenzo, he nevertheless has firm scruples against killing a king, and so far as we can tell, he is not engaged in illicit intrigue for power. Apart from his attempt to seduce Tamyra and his later machinations against Bussy (which are defensive in intention) he does not show a devil's hand. Still he is accused by Bussy of every diabolical crime popularly attributed to the pseudo-Machiavel. Asked for a candid opinion, Bussy answers Monsieur:

> . . . your political head is the curs'd fount
> Of all the violence, rapine, cruelty,
> Tyranny, and atheism flowing through the
> realm. . . .
>
> you will jest
> With God, and your soul to the Devil tender;
> For lust kiss horror, and with death engender:
> That your foul body is a Lernean fen
> Of all the maladies breeding in all men;
> That you are utterly without a soul; . . .
>
> (III.ii.479-89)

In these lines the thought is conventional but the feeling intense. As in *The Revenger's Tragedy,* the reality of moral passion jars against the unreality—the almost perverse hyperbole—of the portrait of evil. Chapman, it would seem, does not exploit Machiavel for Machiavel's sake. If anything he seems to take the Jew of Malta too seriously and engages the full range of his artistic powers in attacking a monster fabricated of literary clichés.

Taking a larger view, however, we see that Chapman's conception of policy is by no means commonplace. The term is not a collective noun for every imaginable depravity; it stands rather for the decay of social and political order. Far from constructing his play out of anti-Machiavellian clichés, Chapman actually dramatizes the harsh realities of renaissance society which Machiavelli described. Bussy wars against a society fallen from its "original" noblesse, devoid of honor or loyalty. True worth is neglected while unscrupulous courtiers, the hollow colossi of power, grow rich exploiting the poor. The good King Henry is powerless except to complain that his court is a stable. The aristocratic dames disguise their politic whoredoms under pseudo-platonic ideals; the "perfum'd muskcats" waste their time in frivolities and intrigue. Even the bulwarks of morality, law and religion, have been subverted by politicians.

For Chapman, then, *policy* stands for a failure *in the present* of ancient moral values; it represents the triumph of lawless appetite over traditional norms of social and ethical behavior. Where the hyperbole of Elizabethan anti-Machiavellianism was an attempt to exorcise the opportunistic demon from the commonweal, the hyperbole of Chapman's diatribes seems an anguished admission that the medieval communal ideal is no longer cogent—that the Machiavellian assessment of society is, within its limitations, all too accurate. The New Man has arrived in Chapman's tragedy and recreated society in his image. It is Bussy who is an aberration and exception, an isolated virtuous man without a place in the society which destroys him. An ideal protagonist, he embodies man's natural aristocratic virtues in an unnatural world. In contrast to the Guise, who is "great only in faction and in peoples' opinion," Bussy is great in spirit, valor, intellect, and learning. He is also great in aspiration; he knows his own powers and believes he holds the fates fast bound. He is, in a sense, the Marlovian super-man moralized and turned anti-Machiavel. Or more correctly, he is an "anti-Prince," a would-be savior of a decadent society who combats the political opportunism which Machiavelli recommended as the way to moral reformation.

Bussy is doomed, Monsieur explains, because nature itself is devoid of rational purpose:

> Now shall we see that Nature hath no end
> In her great works responsive to their worths;
> That she, that makes so many eyes and souls
> To see and forsee, is stark blind herself;
> And as illiterate men say Latin prayers
> By rote of heart and daily iteration,
> Not knowing what they say, so Nature lays
> A deal of stuff together, and by use,
> Or by the mere necessity of matter,
> Ends such a work, fills it, or leaves it empty
> Of strength or virtue, error or clear truth,
> Not knowing what she does; but usually
> Gives that which we call merit to a man,
> And believe should arrive him on huge riches
> Honour, and happiness, that effects his ruin.
>
> (V.ii.1-15)

But for a brief time Bussy recalls within himself an unfallen world of natural goodness, in which virtue and valor were the rule, not the exception. King Henry, who serves consistently as Chapman's moral chorus, describes Bussy as

> A man so good, that only would uphold
> Man in his native noblesse, from whose fall
> All our dissensions rise; that in himself
> (Without the outward patches of our frailty,
> Riches and honour) knows he comprehends
> Worth with the greatest: kings had never borne
> Such boundless empires over other men,
> Had all maintain'd the spirit and state of
>   D'Ambois;
> Nor had the full impartial hand of Nature
> That all things gave in her original,
> Without these definite terms of Mine and Thine,
> Been turn'd unjustly to the hand of Fortune,
> Had all preserv'd her in her prime, like
>   D'Ambois;
> No envy, no disjunction had dissolv'd,
> Or pluck'd one stick out of the golden faggot
> In which the world of Saturn bound our lives,

> Had all been held together with the nerves,
> The genius, and th' ingenuous soul of
>   D'Ambois.
>
> (III.ii.90-107)

Because there are so many casual poetic allusions to the golden age in Renaissance literature, we may easily overlook the reference in Henry's speech to the centuries-old concept of man's natural freedom and equality. Considering the political climate of Stuart England, it is not surprising that Chapman's reference is couched in classical myth and given to a stage monarch. In an age when the crown claimed absolute and divine authority, the traditional idea of natural equality had become a subversive doctrine. In context, however, Henry's speech is not political. Although Bussy demonstrates his "naturalness" by allegiance to the king, his nobility is intrinsic, it is not measured by the sum of his loyalty. He represents the natural freedom of man in an enslaved world because he is completely and fiercely self-sufficient. An ideal Renaissance courtier, he is also a Stoic, noble in mind and body, who, in theory at least, governs himself by the law of his own reason. There is, in fact, a remarkable parallel between the portrait of Bussy and Seneca's portrait of the "entire" man:

> A man that is entyre ought not to be surmounted with exterior things, he must admire nothing but himselfe, he ought to be confident, disposed against all casualties, a composer of his own life, & see that his resolution be accompanied with science & constancie, that that which he once hath conceived, remayne unaltered, & that no exception accompany his resolution. It is understood likewise although I adde it not, that such a man should be addressed and ordered as hee ought, gracious & magnificent in all his entertaynments, that true reason shall be ingraffed in his senses, and that from thence hee take his principles.

Perhaps only Chapman would have imagined the Marlovian titan and the Senecan "whole man" as a single figure, yet the types are in some ways congruous. Both have heroic proportions; both are laws unto themselves. Moreover the Stoicism of *Bussy* is not a counsel of resignation or a buckler against adversity, it is an intellectual sword aimed against the relativism of policy. Not yet aware of the futility of aspiration, and too much an Elizabethan still to retreat from life's struggle, Chapman seeks to resurrect an aristocratic ideal of active, self-sufficient virtue: his hero must prove his mettle by taking arms against his decadent society. Though scorning to play the sycophant, Bussy must accept Monsieur's aid so that he can rise and set a new fashion of virtue at court.

As soon as Bussy springs into action, however, the moral design of Chapman's play begins to disintegrate. By the last scene, the ideal protagonist has revealed himself to be a headstrong individualist, a killer, and an adulterer. And yet somehow we are to believe that he has never lost his pristine innocence or his exalted motive. He dies as he lives, locked in mortal combat with policy, wreathed in ecstatic poetry, and eulogized by vicious and virtuous alike for his incomparable nobility. We cannot pinpoint the place at which Chapman's moral intention goes awry, because from the beginning there is a contradiction between Bussy's moral character (as expressed in the dialogue) and the actions in which he engages. From the outset, moral design and dramatic fable conflict with one another.

How can we explain Chapman's choice of a fable that brings his play as well as his hero to disaster? An obvious answer would be that in this instance he allowed his melodramatic imagination to overwhelm his moral intent. But if we take a broad enough view of Chapman's tragedies, we may arrive at a quite different explanation: namely, that he consistently lacked the ability to construct plots which would translate his vision of life into vital dramatic terms. All the feverish incidents of *Bussy* do not successfully dramatize the rhetorically announced conflict of Machiavel and anti-Machiavel, because the archpolitician of the play has no policy which Bussy can combat. In other words, there is, in an Aristotelian sense, too little action in *Bussy,* not too much. Moreover, while Chapman brings to the stage a new tragic idea, he depends upon hackneyed devices—incantations, letters written in blood, torture scenes, and ambushes—to provide dramatic excitement. With the exception of Bussy, he peoples his tragedy with stock figures: the satanic Machiavel, the helpful Friar, and the "weak" woman. Other dramatists breathe new life into the stale conventions of revenge tragedy, but when Chapman uses a cliché it remains a cliché still. Because his Jacobean hero wanders through Elizabethan mazes, it is not surprising that both hero and play stumble into confusion.

Of course Chapman attempts to integrate melodrama and moral intention. The different, loosely connected incidents of the plot are designed to illumine Bussy's native virtue as courtier, liege man to the King, duelist, and lover. Restored to rightful elegance by Monsieur, Bussy immediately demonstrates his "noblesse" by courting the Guise's wife in her husband's presence. His deliberate grossness exposes the sham delicacy of the court even as his sophisticated arguments mock platonism. He begins his career as reformer in full stride, more intent on irritating the Guise than in cuckolding him. Before long his daring provokes three courtiers to engage him in a duel. Lest we misinterpret this turn of events, King Henry explains:

> This desperate quarrel sprung out of their envies
> To D'Ambois' sudden bravery, and great spirit.
> 　　　　　　　　　　　　　　　(II.i.1-2)

But when Bussy returns triumphant, having killed two opponents, the King regretfully announces that "these wilful murthers / Are ever past our pardon." Here would seem to be a hopeless impasse! Chapman cannot justify Bussy's actions, nor can he condemn his hero without destroying the moral intention of his play. We discover, however, that the purpose of the duel and of the debate that follows is to clarify the contrast between Bussy and his politic antagonists. Bussy's advocate, Monsieur, argues the way of the world; he justifies revenge when the offense to honor cannot be rectified by law. Henry is not impressed by a code that gives each man the right to kill. Monsieur attempts with even less success to draw a casuistic distinction between murderous minds and just revengers. At last Henry reluctantly pardons Bussy with a warning that he never

presume "to be again so daring." At this ticklish moment Bussy defends himself by explaining his own credo. He announces that he too hates murder, and he asks only the chance to

> 　　make good what God and Nature
> Have given me for my good; since I am free,
> (Offending no just law), let no law make
> By any wrong it does, my life her slave:
> When I am wrong'd, and that law fails to right me,
> Let me be king myself (as man was made),
> And do a justice that exceeds the law;
> If my wrong pass the power of single valour
> To right and expiate; then be you my king,
> And do a right, exceeding law and nature:
> Who to himself is law, no law doth need,
> Offends no law, and is a king indeed.
> 　　　　　　　　　　　　　　　(II.i.194-204)

Here Chapman moves from the immediate issue of revenge to the larger and more significant problem of action in an evil world. Bussy does not sacrifice virtue to honor, and although he assumes that he is a rational law unto himself, he does not exempt himself from conventional codes. He admits that he is naturally free only if he does not offend any just laws. But there do not seem to be any just laws in Bussy's society. Every reference to positive law in the play is pejorative. Sacred law, which should be the "scourge of rapine and exortion," is the protean instrument of policy which makes "poor men offend." Since law is venal, then it follows that the incorruptible rational law of the Stoic takes precedence. Exactly what that Stoic law is, however, Bussy does not make clear. The Stoic concept of right reason, which supposedly objectifies and universalizes moral precept, becomes for Bussy purely subjective and individualistic. Ironically enough Bussy's ethic, though presumably superior to the empty forms of conventional law, is itself mere form without substance.

We can easily believe that Bussy's casuistical speeches in the latter half of the play are, at least in part, improvisations, attempts to retain a moral thread in a fable that is hopelessly ensnared in melodrama. And yet Bussy's moral philosophy (if we may so grace it) is strangely consistent even in its obliquities and even when it provides a rationalization of illicit love. The affair with Tamyra, which is by far the most ambiguous part of the play, introduces Chapman's most bewildering character, the Friar, a politic bawd dedicated to Bussy's cause, who views lust as an appetite that must be satisfied. He is "in voice / A lark of heaven, in heart a mole of earth." By depicting the Friar as a politic bawd, Chapman gives a curious flavor to the Christian sentiments which close the play. Indeed all standards of judgment collapse when the Friar and Montsurrey confront each other over Tamyra's tortured body. Montsurrey defends unmanly cruelty in the name of honor; the Friar drapes the cloak of religion over the filthiness of adultery.

The Friar's deterministic credo serves to extenuate Tamyra's sin. She is one of the "weak dames" who cannot keep a "constant course in virtue," who want desperately to be good but who lack courage and determination. Bussy cannot plead such weakness, nor can he admit sin. Thus he chides Tamyra's troubled conscience after the consummation of their love:

> Sin is a coward, madam, and insults
> But on our weakness, in his truest valour:
> And so our ignorance tames us, that we let
> His shadows fright us: and like empty clouds,
> In which our faulty apprehensions forge
> The forms of dragons, lions, elephants,
> When they hold no proportion, the sly charms
> Of the witch Policy makes him like a monster
> Kept only to show men for servile money:
> That false hag often paints him in her cloth
> Ten times more monstrous than he is in troth:
> In three of us the secret of our meeting
> Is only guarded, . . .
>
> Why should we fear then?
>
> (III.i.20-35)

Bussy seems to denigrate conscience in the same way that Monsieur argues against Tamyra's honor:

> Honour, what's that? Your second maidenhead:
> And what is that? A word: the word is gone,
> The thing remains: . . .
>
> (II.ii.10-12)

But as in the debate over revenge, Monsieur's casuistry is foil to Bussy's "sincerity." The politician does not believe that virtue, honor, or sin exist; the terms merely serve his vicious purposes. Bussy, in contrast, stoically distinguishes between true moral judgments and vulgar opinions. He shares Hamlet's knowledge that there is nothing good and evil in the world but thinking makes it so. He knows that politic religionists terrify the ignorant with superstitious fears of crimes and punishments. His inner law of reason tells him that Tamyra is still "chaste," and he is therefore anxious for secrecy only to preserve her good name against vulgar calumnies.

Together with Bussy's earlier manifesto this speech provides a key to the moral confusion which eventually blankets Chapman's drama. Through his hero's Stoic ethic, Chapman seeks to reaffirm the validity of rational moral absolutes against the slippery, relativistic code of the Machiavel. Yet the Stoic ideal of right reason, so frequently "adapted" in the Renaissance, is here distorted by a skepticism about traditional values which is in itself Machiavellian. Intended as an anti-Prince, Bussy eventually becomes a Stoic version of the Prince, who must transcend conventional law to reform his society.

One cannot imagine that Chapman was oblivious to the moral ambiguities which surround Bussy, Tamyra, and the Friar. For in the last act, he trembles on the edge of condemning all three and of turning his play into a moralistic exemplum of the wages of sin. Early in *Bussy* Chapman does in fact suggest a moralistic interpretation of his hero's fall. After Bussy announces that he will rise by virtue alone, he admits that in politic surroundings "no man riseth by his real merit." He speaks of blind fortune ("time's restless wheel") and hints of the fatality of infinite aspirations. Thus it might seem that the self-sufficient hero loses his freedom of action and betrays his Stoic code by accepting Monsieur's aid. And, to be sure, before he sets out for his fatal appointment, Bussy gloats that he will

flank policy with policy. He relishes adopting the stealthy craft of the Machiavel in his campaign against Montsurry. We can see, though, why Chapman did not—in a sense could not—develop this tragic idea to its logical conclusion. If Bussy is to be condemned, who will condemn him? King Henry, the detached moral chorus, has no place in the Tamyra incident. Monsieur exclaims at Tamyra's looseness, but he is himself a disappointed lecher. Montsurry condemns the Friar's hypocrisy but he is a politic cuckold and cowardly assassin. Moreover if Bussy is condemned for his actions, no moral note can sound in the final chaos; Bussy's fall from virtue will merely confirm and exalt the politician's cynicism about human nature. Bussy's tragedy does not prove that the active life is dangerous to villains like Monsieur and the Guise. It does not convince us that policy is futile because Monsieur exists triumphant. Indeed, an ironic interpretation of Chapman's tragedy reduces it to a confused comedy of vice in which Bussy's pretension to virtue is mocked but Monsieur's outright villainy is unsatirized—in which false virtue is punished but true viciousness is unreproved. Thus the attempt to read *Bussy* as a deliberately ironic, cautionary exemplum makes it seem morally absurd.

Instead of seeking to erase any taint of obliquity from *Bussy,* I think we must assume that Chapman did not successfully achieve his dramatic purpose. And though he muddled his high design, he finally had no alternative than to endow Bussy's death with heroic significance. Unable to end his play on a positive moral note, he had to be content with a negative standard of values by which all actions that conflict with policy assume the name of virtue. The reader is to believe that Bussy maintains his integrity by trading insults with Monsieur (Bussy is a master of invective) in a purely verbal war on policy. And lest the reader think that Bussy dies trapped by adulterous lust, Chapman uses Monsieur and the Guise to impart the "correct" moral interpretation. We learn from them that Bussy falls because he is "young, learned, valiant, virtuous, and full-mann'd." Monsieur explains:

> Yet as the winds sing through a hollow tree
> And (since it lets them pass through) let it stand;
> But a tree solid (since it gives no way
> To their wild rage) they rend up by the root:
> So this whole man
> (That will not wind with every crooked way,
> Trod by the servile world) shall reel and fall
> Before the frantic puffs of blind-born chance,
> That pipes through empty men, and makes them
>   dance.
>
> (V.ii.37-45)

The shock of discovering his mortality at first shakes Bussy's self-confidence. His mood of disillusion soon passes, however, and he dies triumphant, certain that he has achieved immortal fame in his fight against evil.

Tamyra shares Bussy's tragedy because she too cannot wind with the crooked way of the world. Unable to reconcile her love for Bussy with the demands of conscience, she is trapped in a hopeless (and hopelessly rhetorical) dilemma:

> O had I never married but for form,

Never vow'd faith but purpos'd to deceive,
Never made conscience of any sin,
But cloak'd it privately and made it common;
Nor never honour'd been in blood or mind;
Happy had I been then, as others are
Of the like licence; I had then been honour'd;
Liv'd without envy; custom had benumb'd
All sense of scruple and all note of frailty;
My fame had been untouch'd, my heart unbro-
   ken:
But (shunning all) I strike on all offence,
O husband! Dear friend! O my conscience!
                        (V.iv.174-85)

In any other context this lament would seem remarkably obtuse. The pathos of Tamyra's fate is not that she has fallen victim to unlawful desires but that she has too much integrity to assume a hypocritical pose. Like some of Hemingway's heroes she remains "moral" despite her sins simply because she is not totally hardened to them.

Byron's Conspiracy

After the extravagant emotionalism of *Bussy D'Ambois,* the clarity and rationality of Chapman's next tragedy, *Byron's Conspiracy,* seems almost an act of penance, a demonstration that he could study the Marlovian individ-ualist and the Machiavel with some measure of artistic de-corum. Although Chapman again creates a titanic hero, the *Conspiracy* is, in almost all respects, a much smaller play than *Bussy.* The context of action and of philosophi-cal reflection is almost exclusively political. The verse is more subdued and utilitarian; the isolated passages which glow with Promethean fire seem recollections of an emo-tion to which Chapman can no longer uncritically assent. The long, even-tempered, sententious passages already signal a pyrrhic victory of moralizing intellect over dra-matic instinct. Eliminating the clichés of Senecan melo-drama Chapman creates in the *Conspiracy* a static politi-cal Morality whose titanic hero plays an incongruously passive role.

Perhaps we would not notice Byron's passivity if the "in-ward" drama of his temptation and redemption were an adequate substitute for suspenseful external action. But he is too naïve morally and intellectually to be the hero of a sophisticated psychomachia. Instead of being a tragic pro-tagonist he is, I suspect, Chapman's personal scapegoat, a hero sacrificed to expiate the obliquity of *Bussy D'Ambois.* As we shall see, the real drama of the *Conspir-acy* lies not in Byron's struggle against temptation but in Chapman's retrospective analysis of Bussy's confused ethic. In the *Tragedy* Byron's doomed figure does stir the depths of Chapman's imaginative sympathies. In the *Con-spiracy* Byron's majestic aspirations are surrounded by an almost constant mockery that brings the play closer to farce than to tragedy.

In his finer moments Byron, like Bussy, seems to epito-mize a romantic ideal of "noblesse," which as before is clothed in magnificent poetry. "To fear a violent good abuseth goodness," Byron exclaims;

'Tis immortality to die aspiring,
As if a man were taken quick to heaven;
What will not hold perfection, let it burst;

What force hath any cannon, not being charg'd,
Or being not discharg'd? To have stuff and form,
And to lie idle, fearful, and unus'd,
Nor form nor stuff shows; happy Semele,
That died compress'd with glory! Happiness
Denies comparison of less or more,
And not at most, is nothing: like the shaft
Shot at the sun by angry Hercules,
And into shivers by the thunder broken,
Will I be if I burst; and in my heart
This shall be written: 'Yet 'twas high and right'.
                        (I.ii.30-44)

The grandeur of Byron's pronouncement, however, is threaded with ironies. Foreshadowing the fall of his titan, Chapman clearly intimates the irrationality of boundless ambition by comparing it to a futile shaft broken by thun-der (a traditional symbol of retribution). Ironic too is Byron's self-pronounced epitaph, for his rise is neither high nor right. Where Bussy's sole ambition was to set a fashion of virtue, Byron has the more realistic ambition of power and an earthly crown. Where Bussy was the incor-ruptible opponent of policy, Byron is its dupe. And where Bussy was the "complete man" amidst the hollow nobili-ty, Byron is described as a hollow colossus, puffed with "empty hope of much." Thus the superman springs to life from his own ashes only to face a pitiless moral judgment.

In *Bussy* the dichotomy of inner worth and outward "greatness" was blurred by an insistence that the two are compatible in an ideal aristocrat. In the *Conspiracy* the di-chotomy of goodness and greatness set forth in the Pro-logue is unequivocal. Byron admits that he has given hos-tages to policy, and that in a world ruled by Fortune ambi-tion is inevitably tainted. Placed against the decorum of a well-ordered kingdom, the vices of the titanic spirit who "transcends" conventional limitations are clearly etched. We learn that infinite ambition, born of self-infatuation, is *in itself* a mortal flaw because it opposes the larger hier-archical order of the universe. Before his seduction Byron admits that ambition necessitates going out of one's "natu-ral clime of truth," "out of all the bounds / Of justice." Men who do so,

Forsaking all the sure force in themselves
To seek without them that which is not theirs,
The forms of all their comforts are distracted,
The riches of their freedoms forfeited,
Their human noblesse sham'd, . . .
                        (I.ii.157-61)

At the outset Byron is a loyal subject who claims that he will support his politic flatterers in any office except trea-son; but he is easy prey to their sophistries because he lacks the primary attribute of the whole man, intelligence. Savoy can play upon Byron's vanity like a stringed instru-ment and mock him to his face when he roars out of tune:

Nay, nay, we must have no such gall, my lord,
O'erflow our friendly livers; my relation
Only delivers my inflamed zeal
To your religious merits; which, methinks,
Should make your Highness canoniz'd a saint.
                        (III.ii.85-89)

As Byron continues to rage against his king, Savoy's mockery becomes bolder:

It cannot be denied; 'tis all so true
That what seems arrogance, is desert in you.

(III.ii.106-7)

And when Byron denounces the monstrous humours of
his king, Savoy soothes his dupe:

Well, let these contradictions pass, my lord,
Till they be reconcil'd, or put in form,
By power given to your will, and you present
The fashion of a perfect government.

(III.ii.110-13)

The obvious, almost comic, irony that surrounds the portrait of Byron indicates Chapman's new awareness of the
disparity between Stoic apathy and Marlovian aspiration.
Because Byron has the confidence of a self-sufficient man,
he scorns predictions of disaster:

There is no danger to a man that knows
What life and death is; there's not any law
Exceeds his knowledge; neither is it lawful
That he should stoop to any other law.
He goes before them, and commands them all,
That to himself is a law rational.

(III.iii.140-45)

But he asserts his Stoic rationality immediately after assaulting the Astrologer, who foresaw his doom. Boasting
of his inner discipline, Byron is constantly at the mercy of
his humours. As a "Stoic," he scorns opinion; as a soldier
he feeds on the flattery of others and holds "honor"
(which rests on opinion) more precious than life.

Like Bussy, Byron distorts the Stoic concept that life is
opinion to rationalize his "transcendence" of moral law.
Even as Bussy had claimed that "Sin is a coward," Byron
asserts;

There is no truth of any good
To be discern'd on earth: and, by conversion,
Nought therefore simply bad; but as the stuff
Prepar'd for arras pictures is no picture
Till it be form'd, and man hath cast the beams
Of his imaginous fancy through it, . . .

so all things here
Have all their price set down from men's con-
ceits,
Which make all terms and actions good or bad,
And are but pliant and well-colour'd threads
Put into feigned images of truth;
To which to yield and kneel as truth-pure kings,
That pull'd us down with clear truth of their gos-
pel,
Were superstition to be hiss'd to hell.

(III.i.47-62)

There is no question of the casuistry of Byron's moral philosophy. His skepticism is not Bussy's antidote to politic
relativism; it is a product of his seduction by Machiavels,
whose terminology and philosophy he has learned by rote.
Byron's philosophy derives from the cynical Picoté, who
trains his pupil in such weird dialectic as:

Truth is a golden ball, cast in our way,
To make us stript by falsehood.

(II.i.156-57)

Luckily Byron's infection is not mortal and his king is

merciful. With one moving speech Henry reverses Byron's
traitorous career, reclaims him as a loyal subject, and lays
to rest the errant ghost of Bussy D'Ambois. This denouement is so abrupt and unexpected, however, and so completely unprepared for by dialogue or dramatic action,
that it seems merely a convenient way to end a drama that
is more private and intellectual than public and heroic.
The political decorum of the *Conspiracy* seems, in fact,
more of a utilitarian *donnée* than a qualification of the
world view of *Bussy.* The acceptance of legitimate royal
authority provides Chapman with an artistic, not a philosophical, resolution, for the alternative to the politician's
amorality becomes an act of blind submission.

Byron's Tragedy

Superficially at least, **Byron's Tragedy** is a continuation of
the fable tentatively "ended" in the *Conspiracy.* On the
one hand Chapman traces the disintegration of Byron's
unstable greatness; on the other hand he seems to expand
an ideal of royalty in the noble King Henry. But close
study reveals that the *Tragedy* is independent of the *Conspiracy* in theme and characterization. In some respects
it is Chapman's most successful tragedy, too sententious
perhaps yet powerfully conceived and executed. It shows
a far more subtle and mature grasp of political issues than
either of his preceding plays. It presents his most intriguing character, a Byron whose self-delusions, no longer ludicrous, border on the edge of insanity. Byron's career, as
Miss Ellis-Fermor remarks [in her *The Jacobean Drama,*
1947], is a "fine and discriminating study of individualism
becoming egotism, egotism becoming megalomania, and
megalomania breaking down into hysteria." Indeed, the
portrait of Byron is so absorbing that one may easily ignore the political and moral issues raised by the King's
maneuvers even though his council of state is the true
locus of the dramatic action.

During the first half of the play, the moral issue seems all
too obvious; we watch the reckless charge of one Marlovian individualist against the political order. Here is a new
Byron. He is no longer the greathearted loyal soldier misled by sycophantic Machiavels. He now stands alone, a
confirmed traitor who conspires with his country's enemies against his rightful king. He is not duped into believing his king a tyrant; instead he masks an insatiable lust
for power under the common rebel's pretext of reforming
a corrupt kingdom. Byron is not a calculating opportunist,
however, who deliberately invents an excuse for usurpation. His grasp on reality is always tenuous; he believes
whatever he wants to believe about himself, his king, and
his country. His sudden shifts of attention and his illogical
leaps from premise to conclusion suggest a mind enthralled by a powerful, warped imagination. Byron is an
egoist who lies more effectively to himself than to others,
who is so inured to self-deception that he can no longer
distinguish illusion from reality. He moves confidently
into the King's trap armed with the "headless resolution"
of his invincibility. Faced with the damning evidence of
his guilt, he violently protests his innocence. Retreating
further into his fantasy, he recreates the trial scene as a
personal triumph, convinced that he has swayed the implacable judges. And at his execution, he facilely adopts

a religious martyrdom to which he clings with fanatical conviction.

His last plays are upright Moralities, noble in thought and sentiment, but only incidentally or coincidentally dramatic in conception.

—Robert Ornstein

Chaos is Byron's native element. He is the great professional soldier who finds the meaning of life in combat and who literally believes in the stale commonplace that peace rusts men and nations. He seems less concerned with the exercise of power than with the struggle to attain it. He dwells upon a new creation

> Of state and government, and on our Chaos
> Will I sit brooding up another world.
> I, who through all the dangers that can siege
> The life of man have forc'd my glorious way
> To the repairing of my country's ruins,
> Will ruin it again to re-advance it.
> (I.ii.30-35)

Although the truth seems to be that the virtuous Henry has restored order and harmony after the ravages of civil war, Byron announces that

> The world is quite inverted, Virtue thrown
> At Vice's feet, and sensual Peace confounds
> Valour and cowardice, fame and infamy.
> (I.ii.14-16)

With superb illogic Byron sees himself as both Machiavellian savior and anti-Machiavel:

> Dear friend, we must not be more true to kings
> Than kings are to their subjects; there are
>   schools
> Now broken ope in all parts of the world,
> First founded in ingenious Italy,
> Where some conclusions of estate are held
> That for a day preserve a prince, and ever
> Destroy him after; from thence men are taught
> To glide into degrees of height by craft,
> And then lock in themselves by villany:
> But God (who knows kings are not made by art,
> But right of Nature, nor by treachery propp'd,
> But simple virtue) once let fall from heaven
> A branch of that green tree, whose root is yet
> Fast fix'd above the stars; . . .
>
> Religion is a branch, first set and blest
> By Heaven's high finger in the hearts of kings,
> Which whilom grew into a goodly tree;
> Bright angels sat and sung upon the twigs,
> And royal branches for the heads of kings
> Were twisted of them; but since squint-eyed
>   Envy
> And pale Suspicion dash'd the heads of king-
>   doms
> One 'gainst another, two abhorred twins,

> With two foul tails, stern War and Liberty,
> Enter'd the world. The tree that grew from heav-
>   en
> Is overrun with moss; the cheerful music
> That heretofore hath sounded out of it
> Begins to cease; and as she casts her leaves,
> By small degrees the kingdoms of the earth
> Decline and wither; and look, whensoever
> That the pure sap in her is dried-up quite,
> The lamp of all authority goes out,
> And all the blaze of princes is extinct. . . .
>
>   so are kings' revolts
> And playing both ways with religion
> Fore-runners of afflictions imminent,
> Which (like a Chorus) subjects must lament.
> (III.i.1-48)

Note the sinuous weaving of this "idealistic" argument. First justifying the right of rebellion, Byron then associates disloyalty with Machiavellianism. Lingering on the divine origin of monarchy, he loses himself in an embroidered conceit that changes shape as he speaks. Stripped of its poetic ornaments Byron's political philosophy reduces to a simple credo: repay evil with evil, royal policy with politic rebellion; "we must not be more true to kings / Than they are to their subjects."

By the close of **Byron's Tragedy** the aura that once surrounded worldly aspiration in Chapman's drama is considerably dimmed. Byron's hysterical inability to accept imprisonment and execution reveals that

> Strength to aspire is still accompanied
> With weakness to endure.
> (IV.ii.305-6)

Even Byron must admit, in a reflective moment before his death, that

> He is at no end of his actions blest
> Whose ends will make him greatest, and not
>   best.
> (V.iv.144-45)

When he speaks of the "eternal victory of Death" it sounds like an afterthought, for he goes to execution raging, embittered, and whining, obsessed by the vanity of endeavor.

One would think that the ruin of an "atheist," an individualist who challenged the rule of law and legitimacy, would provide a very satisfactory political "lesson." Yet Byron's headlong plunge from greatness does not inspire the usual platitudes about erring or wasted genius. It leaves only uncertainty about man's fate in a world of "dark and stormy night, / Of senseless dreams, terrors, and broken sleeps." Byron's hysterical disintegration calls forth a tragic chorus of noblemen who despairingly comment on the "wearisome Condition of Humanity." Epernon exclaims:

> Oh of what contraries consists a man!
> Of what impossible mixtures! Vice and virtue,
> Corruption, and eternnesse, at one time,
> And in one subject, let together loose!
> We have not any strength but weakens us,
> No greatness but doth crush us into air.
> Our knowledges do light us but to err,
> Our ornaments are burthens, our delights

Are our tormenters, fiends that, rais'd in fears,
At parting shake our roofs about our ears.
(V.iii.189-98)

Soissons similarly bewails the frailty of virtue, and Vidame calls upon "real Goodness," uncertain whether it is "a power / And not a word alone, in human uses," to give Byron religious patience. The prayer is unanswered.

It may be simply an artistic oversight that *Byron's Tragedy* ends on this pessimistic and negative note. Perhaps Chapman, exploiting to the last the drama of Byron's degeneration, simply overlooked the need for a more positive political and moral affirmation. Or perhaps, though he condemned Byron's anarchic ambition, he could not exalt the political order which sacrificed such greatness. *Byron's Conspiracy,* we recall, presented a clear-cut moral conflict between Machiavellian intrigue and legitimate monarchical authority. In the *Tragedy* political blacks and whites merge into grey. The very term *politician* becomes ambiguous because the King's party is more Machiavellian than Byron, who falls because he lacks politic guile. He relies on personal strength and reputation rather than subterfuge. He makes an error, inexcusable in a politician, of implicitly trusting La Fin, who is the King's intelligencer; and he dies proud that D'Auvergne kept faith with him. One might almost say that compared to his opponents Byron is politically "innocent." They ensnare him with spies; they corrupt his allies. They lure him home on specious pretext and trap him where he cannot resist. When La Fin testifies at the trial, Byron exclaims:

> Is it justice
> To tempt and witch a man to break the law,
> And by that witch condemn him?
> (V.ii.156-58)

The Chancellor's pious answer that "witchcraft can never taint an honest mind" does not alter the impression that Byron's trial is a calculated act of state rather than an impartial judicial proceeding.

We see in *Byron's Tragedy* that even the politically virtuous must at times use politic means and that no political motive is untainted by egoism. Henry, a compassionate sovereign, is deeply concerned with his subjects' welfare; but he is also jealous of his place and prerogative and ambitious for his dynasty. Although he would, if possible, reclaim Byron as a loyal servant, he views Byron's death as a pregnant example to other would-be usurpers, especially to Byron's peers, who boycott the trial. Henry's political philosophy, moreover, places a very dangerous emphasis upon the king's personal integrity. Insisting that Byron's execution be perfectly legal, he explains:

> . . . if, because
> We sit above the danger of the laws,
> We likewise lift our arms above their justice,
> And that our heavenly Sovereign bounds not us
> In those religious confines out of which
> Our justice and our true laws are inform'd,
> In vain have we expectance that our subjects
> Should not as well presume to offend their earthly,
> As we our heavenly Sovereign.
> (V.i.49-57)

Henry's sentiment is more comforting than his theory. Placing himself outside the "religious confines" which inform the laws his subjects must obey, he frees himself from the traditional limitations which medieval theorists placed on royal authority. According to Henry a king should be just, not because he is ordained a "living law" but because it would be highly imprudent to be otherwise.

While the King's claim to a supramoral absolutism is implicitly dangerous, the political philosophy of his ministers is explicitly Machiavellian in theory and terminology. Janin, for example, advises Henry to execute Byron by royal decree:

> Princes, you know, are masters of their laws,
> And may resolve them to what forms they
>   please,
> So all conclude in justice; in whose stroke
> There is one sort of manage for the great,
> Another for inferior: the great mother
> Of all productions, grave Necessity,
> Commands the variation; and the profit,
> So certainly foreseen, commends the example.
> (IV.ii.31-38)

According to Janin, the political end justifies the means. When a duke sets himself above the law, the crime is treason. When a king sets himself above the law, the rationalization is divine right.

I do not mean to imply that either the King's party or Byron's trial is portrayed as hypocritical. It was a commonplace of Renaissance political thought (even of writers bitterly opposed to Machiavelli) that to preserve the state the king may deviate from strict morality, and in particular that he need not keep strict faith with traitors. Nevertheless Chapman suggests that to Janin and his colleagues Machiavellian methods are an accepted part of political behavior, not a loathsome ultimate expedient. Whereas in the *Conspiracy* submission to royal authority was the "answer" to Machiavellian temptations, in the *Tragedy* it appears that an absolute royal prerogative is potentially as dangerous as the cynical relativism of the Machiavel.

The Revenge of Bussy D'Ambois (1610-11)

After the narrowly conceived thesis drama of the *Conspiracy,* the larger horizons of *Byron's Tragedy* prepare us for Chapman's return in the *Revenge* to the moral and philosophical themes of *Bussy D'Ambois.* Having clarified his Stoic ethic and his attitude toward Marlovian aspiration, Chapman can now lucidly dramatize the conflict between philosophical hero and corrupt society. Unfortunately, however, he also returns (by popular request, one imagines) to a melodramatic revenge fable, to the ghosts, duels, sinister ambushes, and romantic liaisons of his first tragedy. He is sufficiently in control of his materials to prevent the melodrama from submerging or warping his moral design; but he achieves this only by isolating all didactic intention in the rhetoric and by making it obvious that the moral nature of his hero is utterly opposed to the role circumstances force him to play. Even then he must resort to a crude expedient to make his Senecal man play the part of blood revenger.

In recreating the political milieu of his first tragedy, Chapman discards the somewhat naïve *donnée* of a virtuous king surrounded by an unscrupulous nobility. The inherent link between despotism and policy, faintly suggested in *Byron's Tragedy,* becomes a central theme in the *Revenge.* King and politician are now mutually dependent, fellow conspirators. The King, fearful of opposition, employs the unscrupulous Machiavel to root out seeds of "treason." The Machiavel in turn plays upon royal fears for personal gain and calls opportunism loyalty. Baligny underlines the slipperiness of Janin's political ethic when he assures his monarch:

> Your Highness knows
> I will be honest, and betray for you
> Brother and father: for, I know, my lord,
> Treachery for kings is truest loyalty;
> Nor is to bear the name of treachery,
> But grave, deep policy. All acts that seem
> Ill in particular respects are good
> As they respect your universal rule.
> As in the main sway of the universe
> The supreme Rector's general decrees,
> To guard the mighty globes of earth and heaven,
> Since they make good that guard to preservation
> Of both those in their order and first end,
> No man's particular (as he thinks) wrong
> Must hold him wrong'd; no, not though all
>   men's reasons,
> All law, all conscience, concludes it wrong.
>   (II.i.29-44)

The apologist for absolutism and the Machiavellian relativist agree: the state and the king are above ordinary moral laws.

In contrast to King and Machiavel, Clermont and his friends keep alive moral ideals of political behavior. "Will kings make treason lawful?" the Countess asks,

> Is society
> (To keep which only kings were first ordain'd)
> Less broke in breaking faith 'twixt friend and
>   friend,
> Than 'twixt king and subject? Let them fear.
> Kings' precedents in licence lack no danger.
>   (IV.iii.41-45)

Against policy's claim that it transcends private morality to achieve public "good," Clermont's party insists upon the oneness of communal and private morality. Clermont, they announce, "would not for his kingdom traitor be," for "who hath no faith to men, to God hath none."

It is significant that there are no diabolical bogymen in the *Revenge.* The myth of satanic evil is replaced by a more rational and penetrating analysis of Machiavellian cynicism and of its protean dialectic, which can justify killing a king as well as killing for a king. The ultimate horror of policy, Chapman suggests, is not its rationalization of inhuman acts but its destruction of the fundamental trust upon which society rests. Baligny boasts that he can ruin even the virtuous Clermont because

> 'Tis easy to make good suspected still,
> Where good and God are made but cloaks for ill.
>   (I.i.143-44)

Since policy triumphs by exploiting suspicion and fear, it must continually create real or imagined crises; it cannot admit the existence of the "security" which presumably is the end of its vicious acts. Clermont's sincerity, Baligny remarks,

> we politicians
> Must say, grows out of envy, since it cannot
> Aspire to policy's greatness; and the more
> We work on all respects of kind and virtue,
> The more our service to the King seems great
> In sparing no good that seems bad to him.
>   (I.i.134-39)

In a politic society, any faith in human nature (Clermont's trust in Maillard's word, for example) is suicidal. Having made the exercise of power his ultimate goal, the politician needs no eyes, because he "has no way," or rather his is a "way / Ventur'd in deserts, without guide or path."

In the *Revenge,* Clermont assumes Bussy's anti-Machiavellian role; however, he does not engage in a futile attempt to reform his world. His ambitions are wholly private and philosophical. Where Chapman's earlier heroes supposedly chose between greatness and goodness, now there appears no choice; the only greatness resides in virtue. Thus, in retrospect, Bussy's "noblesse" seems deeply flawed. Because he lacked learning, he was "rapt with outrage oftentimes / Beyond decorum." Bussy, Chapman has now decided, was the Senecal man whose natural virtue was philosophically unrefined, and whom Seneca describes with mixed admiration:

> There are certain passions which never take
> hold-fast but on the strongest spirits: even as the
> most strongest and fruitfullest Coppise grow on
> the land which is least manured, and a Forrest
> flourisheth in a fruitfull soyle. Therefore the
> mindes that by nature are most strongest endure
> Anger and being fierie and hote, suffer nothing
> that is little and feeble; but that vigor is imperfect, as may appear in all things without Art,
> which grow only by the benefit of nature, which
> except they be quickly tamed and tempered, that
> which was disposed to become valour is converted into audaciousnesse and rashnesse. ["Of
> Anger"]

His spirit tamed by philosophy, Clermont personifies, for all his soldierly abilities, moderation and self-discipline. His speeches, which lack the swelling vein and self-intoxicating rapture of Bussy's, have an assurance and dignity not before granted to Chapman's tragic heroes. Clermont is not driven to climb the Everests of power because they exist. Though hardly timid or cowardly he knows

> how dangerous it is
> For any man to press beyond the place
> To which his birth, or means, or knowledge ties
>   him;
> For my part, though of noble birth, my birth-
>   right
> Had little left it, and I know 'tis better
> To live with little, and to keep within
> A man's own strength still, and in man's true
>   end,
> Than run a mix'd course. Good and bad hold
>   never

Anything common; you can never find
Things outward care, but you neglect your
    mind.
God hath the whole world perfect made and
    free,
His part to th' use of th' All; men then that be
Parts of that All, must, as the general sway
Of that importeth, willingly obey
In everything without their power to change.
He that, unpleas'd to hold his place, will range,
Can in no other be contain'd that's fit,
And so resisting th' All, is crush'd with it.
But he, that knowing how divine a frame
The whole world is; and of it all, can name
(Without self-flattery) no part so divine
As he himself, and therefore will confine
Freely his whole powers in his proper part,
Goes on most God-like. He that strives t'invert
The Universal's course with his poor way,
Not only dust-like shivers with the sway
But, crossing God in his great work, all earth
Bears not so cursed and so damn'd a birth.
                                          (III.iv.48-75)

In this final detached comment on the careers of Bussy and Byron, Chapman's idea of natural freedom takes on new meaning. Man, Clermont implies, was created free from external tyrannies but he gains inner liberty only through self-discipline and willing obedience to universal law. In contrast to his brother, Clermont studies to be quiet.

This reaffirmation of universal harmony after the confusions of *Bussy* and the uncertainties of the Byron plays seems a significant turning point in Chapman's intellectual journey. Policy still controls society and state, but, like Hooker, Clermont looks out on a fallen world convinced that beneath its external anarchies is the working of immutable law. Men cursed with Baligny's myopia find it necessary to go with the politic sway of society. A man of Clermont's vision knows that he must join himself "with th' Universe / In his main sway." There is almost a guarded exhilaration in Clermont's recognition of necessity—a confidence that man is capable of heroic *spiritual* aspiration if he can recognize his truly godlike potentialities.

At the same time that Clermont's Stoicism provides, within the context of the play at least, a philosophical solution to the question of evil, it creates an almost insoluble artistic problem. For Clermont's Stoicism makes him an impossible protagonist in a revenge tragedy. He is Guyon in Jacobean dress, flawless, viceless, and nearly impervious to external stimuli. He is insulted with impunity; he faces calamity with a passivity that borders on inertia. And worse still he is a perfect prig, who can do no wrong and is determined the world shall know it. How can this Senecal man undertake so irrational a project as blood revenge? And why, in fact, should he feel impelled to revenge Bussy, who shattered moral decorum and died because of his "foul adulterous guilts"? Though Clermont admits that Bussy's murder was a criminal act, he regrets having pledged vengeance; he would not be "equal" with villains or call revenge "virtuous."

Only an imperative that surmounts Clermont's Stoic rationality and that sanctifies blood revenge can spur him to action. Such an imperative is brought (oh heavy irony!) by Bussy's Ghost, returned from eternal night to demand Christian retribution. Though a blunt sword with which to cut a Gordian knot, the Ghost's speeches are interesting in that they reveal Chapman's awareness of the difference between Christian orthodoxy and Stoic idealism. At one point the Ghost admonishes Clermont:

           . . . you respect not
    (With all your holiness of life and learning)
    More than the present, like illiterate vulgars;
    Your mind (you say) kept in your flesh's bounds,
    Shows that man's will must rul'd be by his
        power:
    When (by true doctrine) you are taught to live
    Rather without the body than within,
    And rather to your God still than yourself;
    To live to Him, is to do all things fitting
    His image, in which, like Himself, we live;
    To be His image is to do those things
    That make us deathless, which by death is only
    Doing those deeds that fit eternity;
    And those deeds are the perfecting that justice
    That makes the world last, which proportion is
    Of punishment and wreak for every wrong,
    As well as for right a reward as strong.
                                          (V.i.79-95)

From this speech we surmise that Bussy remains a confused moralist even though he has found religion beyond the grave. His aspersion of Clermont's Stoicism could be taken more seriously if his Christian ideal of justice was not used to vindicate an unlawful and immoral act. But remembering the Friar's role in *Bussy,* and repeated verbal linkings of religion and policy in Chapman's drama, we need not be surprised that in this instance the Stoic, who repudiates revenge, seems morally superior to the spokesman of a literal-minded and slightly obtuse orthodoxy.

Clermont accepts this heavenly command not inwardly convinced of its validity. He kills Montsurry in a courteous, gentlemanly manner only to learn in his moment of triumph that the Guise has been murdered. Having boasted insufferably of his self-sufficiency, he suddenly decides that life is intolerable without the support and comradeship of the Guise. Complaining that he is "left negligent, / To all the horrors of the vicious time," he exercises his Senecal option of suicide. Perhaps in the abstract Clermont's suicide squares with his Stoic code even though the Stoic sanction of self-destruction is by no means casual. But in the play Clermont's suicide is almost ludicrous. What other dramatist would allow a hero, who has escaped diabolical snares and accomplished his revenge, to kill himself because a relatively minor character has been assassinated? Can we imagine a victorious Hamlet stabbing himself because Horatio has been slain? I suspect that after satisfying the demands of plot and audience by compromising his Stoical protagonist, Chapman ended his play as expeditiously as possible. There are many indications that Chapman was not at ease with his dramatic fable. The climactic duel and the scene in which Monsieur insults Clermont approach absurdity. The verse, particularly in the scenes related to the revenge, frequently descends to a weary reminiscence of Elizabethan theatrical rant. "I savour the rank blood of foes in every corner," snarls Montsurry before he meets Clermont in mortal combat.

The Tragedy of Chabot (1612-13)

The Tragedy of Chabot marks the close of Chapman's interest in policy and political issues. Indeed, even in *Chabot* the machinations of policy though prominent are of peripheral interest; they are an efficient rather than necessary cause of the central dramatic conflict between Chabot and his king. Hardly reconciled to the goals or methods of the politician, Chapman nevertheless accepts his presence as an inevitable fact of political life under the reign of an absolute monarch. Chabot, an ideal magistrate who has risen to high office through merit, is a rare and marvelous exception in his milieu. His rival, Montmorency, who is fundamentally decent though weak, is more typical of Francis' ministers. Montmorency would prefer to satisfy his ambition honestly, but he regretfully agrees to plot Chabot's ruin because one man rises in the King's favor only as another falls.

In his study of Chapman [*The Tragedies of George Chapman*, 1954], Mr. Rees supports Mrs. Solve's contention [in "Stuart Politics in Chapman's *Tragedy of Chabot*," *Univ. of Michigan Publ. Lang. and Lit.*, IV (1928)] that *Chabot* is a topical allegory on one of the most notorious judicial proceedings of Chapman's age: the trial and imprisonment of Somerset for the murder of Sir Thomas Overbury. This topical interpretation seems reasonable enough even if it would have us believe that Chapman returned to the theater after a decade of silence to appeal somewhat obscurely to James's merciful instincts. Yet we should not allow it to divert attention from the larger and far more important political issue which Chapman dramatizes: namely, the conflict between absolutist prerogative and the medieval ideal of the rule of law. While Mrs. Solve identifies Sir Edward Coke with Chapman's Proctor-General, Jacobean history suggests a more fruitful parallel between Coke and Chabot, the two high magistrates who opposed their monarchs' attempts to set themselves above customary procedures of justice.

That *Chabot* is a tract for anxious times is pointed out by Professor Parrott:

> Chapman, like most thinking men of his day, believed in absolute monarchy, but he held that the monarch could be absolute without being arbitrary. . . . The lesson of the tragedy is the necessity for the free play of the individual within the limits of the state organism, or, to put it more concretely, the duty of the absolute monarch to respect the liberty of the loyal subject. [*The Plays and Poems of George Chapman: The Tragedies*, 1910]

But if Chapman "believed" in absolute monarchy it was with grave reservations, for he was increasingly concerned in tragedy with the license granted kings by theories of divine right. In *Chabot* he does not dramatize the possibility that an evil king may turn absolute prerogative into tyranny; he dramatizes the moral dangers *inherent* in absolute government under the best of kings—under a sincere, gracious, and virtuous ruler like Francis.

Because the throne is the direct source of all authorities in the realm, it is the center of unending struggle for royal favor. The state is fortunate when the King chooses his favorites—as he chose Chabot—according to their merits. Nevertheless the very existence of favoritism produces instability, because there are no objective or absolute standards of public service; all depends upon princely whim. Chabot is toppled from his lofty position by an insignificant quarrel which would not have arisen except for Francis' pride. Chabot has no personal interest in rejecting the unlawful bill; he is simply fulfilling the routine obligations of his office. The King is similarly detached from the question. He intervenes at the request of his new favorite, although he is ignorant of the issues involved. Worse still, he is completely unaware that his interference upsets the impartial course of judgment. While he talks a great deal of justice, Francis (like Chapman's monarch, James I) cannot conceive of justice as an ideal above and beyond kingly prerogatives. He is astonished that Chabot should for so petty a cause spurn his gentle request. He does not see that Chabot adheres to a conviction stronger than any personal feeling of gratitude or loyalty.

As Chabot maintains his stand, Francis becomes increasingly irritated. From a minor matter devoid of personal interest, the question inevitably becomes one of the sanctity of royal prerogative, for absolutism makes all issues political. Since the King's authority is theoretically unquestionable, then in practice it cannot be questioned, and the need to safeguard it against encroachments becomes (as it became for the Stuarts) a dominating obsession. It no longer matters why Chabot refuses the King's request. All that matters is that he dares to refuse. Francis is wise enough to accept Chabot's display of personal integrity, but the Queen, jealous of her position (and of Chabot's wife), presses her husband to "act like a king":

> Shall the sacred name of King,
> A word to make your nation bow and tremble,
> Be thus profan'd? Are laws establish'd
> To punish the defacers of your image
> But dully set by the rude hand of others
> Upon your coin, and shall the character
> That doth include the blessing of all France,
> Your name, thus written by your royal hand,
> Design'd for justice and your kingdom's honour,
> Not call up equal anger to reward it?
>
> (II.i.12-21)

The Queen develops an interesting variation of a familiar Stuart principle: no bill, no King.

The central issue in Chapman's drama then is not "What are Chabot's rights as a loyal subject?" but "What is the supreme authority in the state: law or princely prerogative?" Francis' position is clear. He sees himself (as did James I) as a secular god in the commonwealth, from whose divinely ordained power all lesser authorities spring. Thus, while Francis is willing to admit that perhaps in this instance Chabot's judgment is better than his own, he asks:

> Well, sir, grant
> Your force in this; my odds in benefits,
> Paid for your pains, put in the other scale,
> And any equal holder of the balance

Will show my merits hoist up yours to air,
In rule of any doubt or deed betwixt us.

Chabot answers:

You merit not of me for benefits,
More than myself of you for services.
(II.iii.88-95)

To Chabot, the king is a dispenser of justice, not a creator of authority. He believes, as did the medieval theorists, that the rule of law in the commonwealth is a *legal reality* as well as a political ideal.

Chapman allows his hero a remarkable display of integrity. Although it was a commonplace of Renaissance political theorists that no subject was forced to obey a command that broke the laws of nature or God, authorities agreed that in cases of civil law a magistrate should not oppose the king's will. And if he cannot obey, his only recourse is to resign his office. Chabot, we note, refuses either to acquiesce or to resign. He upholds his rights as a magistrate against his king (or more correctly in his king's behalf). On the other hand Chapman sanctions no act of disloyalty. When Chabot's wife speaks too boldly to the Queen, his father intervenes:

Subjects are bound to suffer, not contest
With princes, since their will and acts must be
Accounted one day to a Judge supreme.
(III.i.163-65)

The person and the place of royalty are sacred. The king, though not superior to the law, is not answerable to his subjects for his actions. Thus in *Chabot,* Chapman threads his way between contemporary extremes of absolutism and antimonarchism. At the same time that he criticizes the vagaries of absolutism, he suggests no way by which rule of law can be enforced against absolute prerogative except perhaps by the courage and high purpose of royal ministers. Despite the triumph of justice and Francis' repentance, *Chabot* ends on a melancholy note. Chabot dies of a broken heart and even the Chancellor's trial is tinged with irony, because it is once again apparent that "sovereign" law serves Francis' will. Though more affirmative than *Byron's Tragedy, Chabot* does not offer real hope of political reform, nor is Chabot's political integrity an absolute on which Chapman could rest after the Stoicism of the *Revenge.*

Caesar and Pompey

We have thus far traced the development of Chapman's thought over a period of ten years. We have seen the ambiguities and uncertainties of his earliest tragedies resolved by ethical convictions. We have seen the storm and fury of his early anti-Machiavellianism fade into Stoic resignation and acceptance of political realities. We cannot be sure that *Caesar and Pompey* is Chapman's last play, but it does seem to complete the pattern of his tragedies and to represent the end of a long artistic and intellectual pilgrimage.

Having traced this pilgrimage we can understand why *Caesar and Pompey* seems, despite its turbulent action, a twilight study lost in the shadows of Aurelian meditation. Like *Antony and Cleopatra* (perhaps in imitation of it)

Caesar and Pompey is the tragedy of an antique world well lost. But whereas Shakespeare enhances the historical drama of Plutarch's *Lives,* Chapman reduces it to an impressionistic setting for the inward spiritual drama of Pompey's self-discovery. While empires are being lost and won, while the fate of Roman civilization hangs in perilous balance, Chapman takes pains to assure us that these world-shattering events are insubstantial pageants compared to the making of a single soul. The "Argument" informs us at the very beginning that Caesar's victory is actually meaningless, that he is "(in spite of all his fortune) without his victory victor." Indeed, the inner focus of Chapman's play is evidenced by his willingness to depict an ambiguous Caesar: noble in abilities and temperament, but Machiavellian in ambition; part conspirator, part savior of his country. All that matters to Chapman now is that the conquering Caesar is Fortune's favorite and therefore Fortune's fool, who labors to become the empty colossus of worldly power. Cato and Pompey, in contrast, turn military defeat into spiritual victory. Cato triumphs over adversity; Pompey triumphs over himself as well as the world. Unlike Cato, who is confirmed from the beginning in Stoic virtue, Pompey achieves greatness only by casting it away. He loses an empire to find himself.

The renunciation of power and of worldly aspiration is final in *Caesar and Pompey.* We learn now that high position is intrinsically evil and that goodness can reside only in mediocrity. In one of the most affecting scenes Chapman ever wrote, the defeated Pompey counsels his wife:

O, my Cornelia, let us still be good
And we shall still be great; and greater far
In every solid grace than when the tumour
And bile of rotten observation swell'd us.
Griefs for wants outward are without our cure,
Greatness, not of itself, is never sure.
Before we went upon heaven, rather treading
The virtues of it underfoot in making
The vicious world our heaven, than walking
    there
Even here, as knowing that our home, contemn-
    ing
All forg'd heavens here rais'd, setting hills on
    hills. . . .

we now are like
The two poles propping heaven, on which heav-
    en moves,
And they are fix'd and quiet; being above
All motion far, we rest above the heavens.
(V.i.181-97)

Pathos, which must have seemed to the earlier Chapman an unfitting sentiment in heroic tragedy, surrounds the defeated Pompey as he announces his intention to become the complete man.

I will stand no more
On others' legs, nor build one joy without me.
If ever I be worth a house again
I'll build all inward; not a light shall ope
The common outway; no expense, no art,
No ornament, no door will I use there,
But raise all plain and rudely, like a rampier
Against the false society of men
That still batters

All reason piecemeal, and, for earthy greatness,
All heavenly comforts rarefies to air.
I'll therefore live in dark, and all my light,
Like ancient temples, let in at my top.
                                    (V.i.103-15)

Here is Clermont's philosophy restated without priggery or self-righteousness. Through sheer simplicity of language and homeliness of metaphor, Chapman transforms Clermont's soaring abstract lectures on universal law into an intimate expression of religious and philosophical conviction.

The belief in universal harmony in *Caesar and Pompey* is not, however, a Christian reconciliation with a disordered Creation, nor a metaphysical certainty that Providence will ultimately bring good out of evil. Those who witness Pompey's fall renounce all contention with "this giant world," which "heaven itself / Fails to reform":

A heap 'tis of digested villany:
Virtue in labor with eternal chaos
Press'd to a living death, and rack'd beneath it,
Her throes unpitied, every worthy man
Limb by limb sawn out of her virgin womb,
To live here piecemeal tortur'd.
                                    (V.ii.80-85)

In "eternal chaos" liberty cannot be guaranteed by a political system; it springs only from spiritual self-sufficiency. "Only a just man is a free man"; only a Stoic rises above enslaving circumstances.

It might seem ironic that Pompey's mentor, Cato, achieves "freedom" by committing suicide, except that Cato's suicide is not, like Clermont's, an act of despair. Even as Pompey looks heavenward for inspiration, so Cato looks beyond the grave to the eternal light of the spirit. And whereas Bussy's death once proved that fallen nature works to no end, the liberation of Cato's spirit in death is seen as the triumphant end towards which all nature works. If we measure Cato's speeches against the *Manual* of Epictetus, his knowledge of things unseen—his faith in resurrection and immortality—seems incongruously Christian. If we measure them against the Stoicism of the *Revenge,* the incongruity disappears. For then it is obvious that Chapman's philosophical convictions, even at an earlier stage, bordered on religious faith. The curious scene between Fronto and Ophioneus suggests, moreover, that Chapman's skepticism about the politic aspects of religion had not completely vanished. This touch of "comic relief" reminds us that Cato's Rome has its Jacobean parallel, a disordered world "out of tune," swung this way and that by a thousand rulers and a thousand religions. There is possibly a remembrance of the Friar in *Bussy* in Ophioneus' advice that the malcontented Fronto win his fortune in the priesthood:

And for discharge of the priesthood, what thou want'st in learning thou shalt take out in good-fellowship; thou shalt equivocate with the sophister, prate with the lawyer, scrape with the usurer, drink with the Dutchman, swear with the Frenchman, cheat with the Englishman, brag with the Scot, and turn all this to religion: *Hoc est regnum Deorum gentibus.*
                                    (II.i.111-17)

Perhaps even in his last play Chapman indirectly contrasts the protean forms of established Churches with the immutable certainties of the philosophic mind.

When we consider the extent to which Chapman used the stage for extraliterary purposes, we can understand why his drama was not a formative influence on Jacobean tragedy. Because he had more integrity and independence of purpose than creative sense of the theater, other Jacobeans could respect and admire his plays but learn or borrow little from them. Though a Stoic fortitude in the face of death is often characteristic of Jacobean tragic heroes, and though there are Stoic elements in many other tragedies, no other dramatist followed Chapman's Stoic way. All that can be said is that other Jacobeans also found an ultimate nobility in the strength to endure and an even greater heroism in the acceptance of circumstances than in the rebellion against them.

Dangerous as it would be to identify Chapman with his Stoic heroes, I cannot but feel that he shared their spiritual isolation and their sense of alienation from an unworthy society. Like Milton fallen on evil days he despairs of worldly reformations, and yet he too discovers within himself the paradise which has been elsewhere destroyed. He does not find security, however, through a return to Elizabethan beliefs, nor does he burn his books and renounce his classical learning to embrace salvation. Although in *Byron's Tragedy* knowledge illuminated the way to error, in *Caesar and Pompey* Chapman with Cato follows the light of reason beyond reason itself to the faith that looks through death. (pp. 47-83)

Robert Ornstein, "George Chapman," in his The Moral Vision of Jacobean Tragedy, *1960. Reprint by The University of Wisconsin Press, 1965, pp. 47-83.*

Eugene M. Waith   (essay date 1962)

[*Waith is an American critic and educator who has written extensively on seventeenth-century European drama. In the following excerpt, he analyzes Chapman's portrait of the Herculean hero in* Bussy d'Ambois, *comparing it with Christopher Marlowe's treatment of the hero of* Tamburlaine.]

Chapman's Bussy D'Ambois is less of a demigod than Marlowe's Tamburlaine—more clearly a man with human failings. Nevertheless, Bussy is another Herculean hero. Chapman insists even more than Marlowe on the parallel, translating a passage from *Hercules Oetaeus* for part of one of Bussy's dying speeches and presenting in the lines quoted above a final vision of the hero transfigured like his mythic prototype.

Some of the difference between Tamburlaine and Bussy D'Ambois is due to the sources on which the two playwrights drew. The history of an Oriental conqueror, who had already become almost a myth in Marlowe's day, lent itself to the portrayal of a man surpassing ordinary humanity. French history of the late sixteenth century, to which Chapman turned, was not apt to have in itself any such mythic suggestiveness for an English audience in the first decade of the seventeenth century. Bussy was a much discussed nobleman who died in 1579, when Chapman was twenty. Monsieur, who plays such an important part in the story, was the Duke of Anjou, well known in England as a suitor for the hand of Queen Elizabeth. In fact, the material which Chapman chose for this play looks to be the most improbable basis for a Hercules play. What Chapman saw in the material was a vision shaped by his familiarity with the classics and with the work of Renaissance scholars.

Though certain details are changed, the story of the play is true to history in its main outlines. It is the story of a brilliant adventurer at the court of Henry III, notorious for his daring, his insolence, his duels, his amours. Brought to court by Monsieur, the king's brother, he flirts with the wife of the great Duke of Guise, fights a duel in which he kills both his opponent and one of the seconds, and then launches himself into an affair with Tamyra, the Duchess of Montsurry. It is the discovery of this love-affair which brings about his end, for Monsieur, jealous of Bussy's success where he himself has failed, joins with Guise and the injured husband to set a trap in which Bussy is killed.

For the presentation of such swashbuckling romance the Elizabethan stage was well prepared by Kyd and others, who mixed Seneca with native tradition to produce a popular blend of love and blood and the supernatural. Far from avoiding the theatrical clichés of his day, Chapman exploits them to the hilt. Tamyra is made to be an active intriguer, employing a friar as pander (to the undoubted delight of English theatre-goers). To them alone is known a secret vault, through which Bussy is led, rising with the friar through a trap-door to make an impressive entrance. For the supernatural Chapman introduces conjuring scenes in the great tradition of Greene and Marlowe: spirits rise from the underworld, and in their turn conjure up visions for their masters. For good measure there is also a ghost in the last scenes of the play. Horror is generously provided in the scene where Montsurry stabs Tamyra's arms and finally puts her on the rack in order to compel her to write the letter which will draw Bussy into the trap. The letter is written in blood.

It is amazing that the dominant tone of a play drawn from such sources and utilizing such dramatic conventions should be one of quiet (and at times heavy) seriousness. For this tone the quality of Chapman's verse is partly responsible. Instead of Marlowe's insistent rhythms, his resounding catalogues, and the constructions which sweep the listener on to the conclusion, we have a style which is tough and dense, a learned vocabulary, sentences which are complex and long, reasoning which is hard to follow. At various times both compression and grammatical looseness seem to impede comprehension. Yet once one becomes somewhat accustomed to this difficult style, it attracts much more than it repels. It fascinates with its continual suggestion of further meaning to be unfolded, and in so doing it fulfils its major function. It persuades the reader or the spectator to look beyond the story and its theatrical trappings for the vision which the play embodies.

The Bussy with whom the audience is immediately confronted at the opening of the first scene is dressed as a poor man (an unhistorical touch) and talks more like a philosopher than an adventurer. He talks, in fact, very like Plutarch, from whose ethical writings much of Bussy's first speech is translated. The basis of the entire speech is a contrast between the man who is virtuous and poor and the man whom the world calls great. In the first part of the speech "great" men, the darlings of fortune, are memorably compared to "those colossic statues, / Which, with heroic forms without o'erspread, / Within are nought but mortar, flint, and lead". Their lack of the inner worth possessed by the virtuous man in his poverty seems to suggest to the speaker a yet more general reflection on the insubstantiality of man—"a torch borne in the wind; a dream / But of a shadow . . . " But he is still thinking mainly about the "great" man, for in the second half of his speech he offers himself the somewhat consoling thought that even those who seem outwardly most successful must eventually turn for help to Virtue, just as "great" seamen, after the most glorious of voyages, must call on "a poor, staid fisherman" to pilot them into port. The man who is later to be compared to Hercules is casting himself here in the unheroic role of the poor fisherman, while all the heroic comparisons, qualified though they may be by irony, are reserved for the ambitious man—by implication the politician of the type soon to be exemplified in Monsieur and the Guise. This initial view of Bussy as a despiser of the world becomes especially surprising in retrospect, when we see him in the midst of the "great" men he has described, a favourite at court, behaving in some respects very much like them. Unless the opening speech is taken as the hypocritical scorn of a jealous man, it eventually seems to present a paradox. It is only one of many.

The latter part of the speech exactly depicts the ensuing action. *"Procumbit"* says the Latin stage-direction, and as Bussy lies at one side of the stage, the picture of poor virtue, from the other side the great Monsieur sails on, accompanied by two pages, seeking Bussy as an aid in his ambitious schemes. As he says, "There's but a thread betwixt me and a crown", and though he does not admit that he wants to hasten his brother's death, he wants "resolved spirits" around him. D'Ambois is useful precisely because he is fearless, has nothing to lose, and is angry at the world for the way he has been treated. Monsieur is cynical enough to be sure that an attractive offer will bring him into the world he despises, and by the end of the scene this assurance has been justified. Bussy has accepted Monsieur's money and agreed to come to court: the poor fisherman has been hired to guide the great seaman to his destination.

In accepting Monsieur's offer, however, Bussy loses none of his antipathy to the politic man. He is willing to seize the opportunity because of his belief that "no man riseth by his real merit" but only when time or fortune is favourable to him (I, 1, 134-43). He sees well enough what Monsieur's game is, but determines to outplay his employer by remaining virtuous even at court:

> I am for honest actions, not for great:
> If I may bring up a new fashion,
> And rise in Court for virtue, speed his plow!

(I, 1, 128-30)

The mere acceptance of service in Monsieur's train cannot be taken as proof of corruption, though it would seem to be so if it were not for the commentary of Bussy's speech. Action and speech taken together make quite another point—the extraordinary difficulties attending upon virtuous action in the world. If Bussy continues in the "green retreat" where Monsieur finds him he cannot act at all; in order to act he must enter an arena where virtue is only talked about. The problem, in its abstract formulation, is not unlike that faced by Bussy's contemporary on the stage, Prince Hamlet. It grows out of that venerable topic of debate, the relative merits of the active and the contemplative life.

The activities of Bussy D'Ambois at court have already been referred to. The flirting, the duel, the affair with Tamyra, are characteristic of a wild adventurer such as the historical Bussy apparently was, but Chapman loads all of them with meanings far greater (and far other) than what these activities appear to signify. For instance, Bussy's extravagant attentions to the Duchess of Guise before the eyes of her husband and the rest of the court seem to be mere insolent rudeness. Monsieur in an aside interprets this defiance of the Guise as evidence of heroic self-sufficiency:

> His great heart will not down, 'tis like the sea,
> That partly by his own internal heat,
> Partly the stars' daily and nightly motion,
> Their heat and light, and partly of the place
> The divers frames, but chiefly by the moon,
> Bristled with surges, never will be won,
> (No, not when th' hearts of all those powers are
>   burst)
> To make retreat into his settled home,
> Till he be crown'd with his own quiet foam.
>   (I, 2, 157-65)

The parenthesis and the other qualifying phrases so characteristic of Chapman's style hold the meaning in suspension till the very end, and shape it before our eyes. Even the great natural force of the sea acts partly in response to external force and to geographical circumstance, but once aroused, it alone determines its return to a state of calm. The weight of the meaning is borne chiefly by two images in the latter half of the sentence, "bristled with surges" and "crown'd with his own quiet foam". The second of these, given the utmost force by the previously interrupted flow of the sentence, pushes the entire episode to which it refers into a new realm of meaning. Like the comment of some Renaissance interpreter of one of Hercules' exploits, it turns the attention quite away from what is outward and physical to what is inward and spiritual. What seemed like an irresponsible outburst of restless energy becomes a symbol for majestic self-possession, manifest alike in fury and calm, a law unto itself.

Immediately after this brush with Guise, and partly as a result of it, Bussy avenges an insult by fighting a duel with Barrisor. Not only is this encounter glorified by its presentation in the heightened rhetoric of a Senecan *Nuntius* (II, 1, 35-137), but it is made the occasion of further comments on the nature of Bussy. Monsieur, in pleading for the King's pardon, calls him "a man / In his uprightness, worthy to survive / Millions of such as murther men alive" (II, 1, 177-9). Bussy, when he has received his pardon, asserts the superiority of his virtue to man-made laws:

> since I am free,
> (Offending no just law), let no law make
> By any wrong it does, my life her slave:
> When I am wrong'd, and that law fails to right
>   me,
> Let me be king myself (as man was made),
> And do a justice that exceeds the law . . .
>   (II, 1, 194-9)

The suggestion in this speech that Bussy represents unspoiled man is fully developed in the next act in a remarkable eulogy of Bussy given by King Henry to the Guise, who continues to regard the new favourite as a ruffian and a murderer:

> Cousin Guise, I wonder
> Your honour'd disposition brooks so ill
> A man so good, that only would uphold
> Man in his native noblesse, from whose fall
> All our dissensions rise; that in himself
> (Without the outward patches of our frailty,
> Riches and honour) knows he comprehends
> Worth with the greatest: kings had never borne
> Such boundless empire over other men,
> Had all maintain'd the spirit and state of
>   D'Ambois . . .
>   (III, 2, 88-97)

The speech is too long to be quoted in full. Bussy appears once more as the man of intrinsic virtue, opposed to those whom Fortune has rewarded. He belongs to the Golden Age, when men were free and equal, before crime brought about the development of restrictive legislation. His incomparable assets are greatness of spirit and what Chapman calls "th'ingenious soul", a soul both noble and strong by nature.

While such speeches as these make it clear that the Bussy of Chapman's play is not to be taken as a despicable bully, they raise a difficult problem in interpretation by the lengths to which the praise of the hero is carried. Nothing he could possibly do could fully merit such praise; what he does is far indeed from meriting it. As we go through the play we seem to be moving on two parallel lines, one of which is the adventures of the historical Bussy, the other a progressive revelation of a mythic figure, a Hercules disguised as Bussy. The distance between these lines constitutes the chief problem for the critic. I shall mention some of the solutions which have been offered before I give the one which seems most acceptable to me, but first it is necessary to present the central paradox, Bussy's relations with Tamyra, on which any interpretation must be based.

Tamyra sums up in her own person many of the major thematic contrasts of the play, for Chapman has managed to associate her with all that is most defiantly individualistic in Bussy and also with all the good and the bad in the society which Bussy defies. She is both fatal enchantress and ideal mistress—Acrasia and Gloriana, wrapped up in one person. The affair is initiated in the second act when Monsieur tells Bussy that he is going to lay siege to Tamyra and Bussy announces in a brief soliloquy that his own love has long been vowed to her in his heart, and that he does not fear Monsieur as a rival. Immediately following is a scene in which the contradictions in Tamyra's character are fully displayed. First we see her discussing Bussy with her husband and others, admitting that his conduct in court has been rude, but also defending him:

> For though his great spirit something overflow,
> All faults are still borne, that from greatness
>   grow . . .

She has a reputation for virtue at court, which she defends by saying that she would have been much more severe than the Duchess of Guise if Bussy had made so bold with her, but at this very moment, as it is soon made clear, she is planning to have Bussy brought to her room by the Friar. There is no doubt that she is fully aware of the moral implications of her plan, for on two occasions during this scene she refers to the loss of virtue to which her passion is leading her. Shortly before Bussy arrives she rejects the advances of Monsieur with a show of wifely devotion, sternly refusing a chain of pearl which he offers her. Somewhat later, parting from Bussy after their first assignation, she gives him a chain of pearl as a token of her love.

Her behaviour shows Tamyra to be a deceitful and consciously sinful woman; when Monsieur and, through him, Montsurry find out about her, it is understandable that this is their view of her. It is not, however, the only view that the play presents. Bussy refuses to accept it, blames her for having a Puritan conscience, and asserts the virtue of their love as a corollary of his strength: "Sin is a coward . . . " (III, 1, 20). Like a knight of romance he vows absolute secrecy as well as fealty, and implies that Tamyra is virtuous as long as he can defend her reputation. Surprisingly, this romantic idealization of the affair receives some validation at the end of the play. Montsurry's torture of his wife is so horrible and his hiring of murderers to dispatch Bussy so cowardly that sympathy is thrown to the lovers, and their mutual devotion at the time of Bussy's death is far removed from lust or court intrigue. Against the clear symbolism of Tamyra's blood on the letter which draws Bussy to his destruction is balanced a contrary symbol when Bussy compares the soul and body of man to "two sweet courtly friends . . . / A mistress and a servant" (V, 4, 83-4). In this image, compounded of Platonism and courtly love, the mistress is identified with the hero's immortal part. A moment later, the spectacle of her suffering is the wound which finally breaks his heart (V, 4, 131-4). Tamyra remains acutely conscious of her sin to the end, but the nobility of her attachment to Bussy is equally stressed. In fact, her sense of sin becomes almost a guarantee of the purity of her feelings for her lover, for in one of her last speeches she bitterly observes that if her marriage vows had meant nothing to her she might easily have had the sort of affair which was common at court. Instead, it is her tragedy that, feeling equally her obligations to both men, she has equally betrayed both.

It is not easy to say whether Tamyra is a force for good or evil in Bussy's life. Like Iole, she is the object of passions which the world, but not the hero, regards as guilty; like Deianira, she is the most unwilling agent of the hero's destruction. Her use of the Friar as go-between and her association with night and the powers of darkness add further complexities to the interpretation of her part in the play.

The Friar appears to be a thoroughly hypocritical, scheming person when we first meet him—just a Protestant's idea of a Friar. Escorting Bussy to Tamyra's room in the night, he gives crafty instructions to the would-be lover to seem to have requested the interview for the purpose of explaining to her the reasons of his duel with Barrisor, a former admirer of hers. At the second assignation of the lovers the Friar proves to be an adept at conjuring, raising Behemoth to show them what Monsieur and Montsurry are doing. Yet he is by no means the wicked stereotype he seems. He is always spoken of with reverence; even when his complicity is discovered, Montsurry calls him nothing worse than a "strange creature" (V, 1, 191), and vents his outrage on the general wickedness of the world. The Friar's death is curious. Chapman might easily have shown him punished for his sins by Montsurry's sword. Instead, he dies of shock when he sees Tamyra put to the rack, and his death, as Parrott remarks [in *The Plays and Poems of George Chapman: The Tragedies,* 1910], breaks Tamyra's resolution when torture has not done so. When he reappears as a ghost, he bends his efforts first to the saving of Bussy's life, and then, when these fail, to reconciling Tamyra and Montsurry. His words in the last act are not those of a penitent sinner but of a divine agency. It is he who bids Bussy's spirit "join flames with Hercules", and in the first quarto this valedictory speech ends the play. In the last analysis the irony of Tamyra's using this "holy man" as an "agent for her blood" cuts both ways. The suggestion that religion is being prostituted is certainly there, but for all that, the Friar's constant attendance upon the lovers tends to ennoble their affair. His admiration for both of them and Tamyra's respect and love for him are never undercut. In terms of the parallel actions of the play, it might be said that the Friar as a hypocritical churchman belongs to the adventures of Bussy, while the Friar as supernatural agency belongs to the revelation of Bussy as a mythic figure.

Before the first appearance of Bussy and the Friar in the secret vault Tamyra invokes the night in lines of compelling beauty:

> Now all ye peaceful regents of the night,
> Silently gliding exhalations,
> Languishing winds, and murmuring falls of waters,
> Sadness of heart and ominous secureness,
> Enchantments, dead sleeps, all the friends of rest,
> That ever wrought upon the life of man,
> Extend your utmost strengths, and this charm'd hour
> Fix like the Centre! Make the violent wheels
> Of Time and Fortune stand, and great Existence
> (The Maker's treasury) now not seem to be,
> To all but my approaching friends and me!
>   (II, 2, 108-18)

The conventional equation of light with good and dark with evil makes it quite logical that Tamyra, swayed by what she calls her "dark love" (II, 2, 96), should ask the night to protect her friends and her. Yet how different is this from the invocations of darkness in *Macbeth*! The night to which Macbeth and his Lady pray is "thick" and "seeling", palled "in the dunnest smoke of hell", and has a "bloody and invisible hand". Tamyra's night is a powerful enchanter, capable of arresting the violent motion of Time and Fortune and of establishing a calm like the central point of the revolving earth. The difference between the two is not mainly due to the fact that Macbeth is bent on murder and Tamyra on love; the two conceptions of night are radically different. Chapman's is a vital part of his strange presentation of the hero and heroine and of their involvement in the world of magic. The darkness with which they are associated is so important an element in the play that its significance must be explored before proceeding with the discussion of the characters. Chapman's attitude towards darkness underlies his presentation of the puzzling scenes of conjuration and, more generally, his practice of poetry.

It used to be said that Chapman and Marlowe belonged to a "School of Night", and though the notion of a "school" is no longer widely held there is no doubt that for Chapman, at least, night had a special, mystical attraction. *The Shadow of Night,* composed of two poems, the **"Hymnus in Noctem"** and the **"Hymnus in Cynthiam"**, is a *tour de force* in which night is praised and day disparaged. In the first of these hymns Night, the "Most sacred mother both of Gods and men" (l. 68) is contrasted with "A stepdame Night of minde" (l. 63). The mental night or blindness of man has made a chaos of the corrupt world far worse than the original chaos which existed before creation. Since Day belongs to the created order which has so degenerated, Night becomes the patroness of virtue and truth. She is "deare Night, o goddesse of most worth" (l. 213) as opposed to "haughtie Day" (l. 217), "the whoredome of this painted light" (l. 249), "pale day (with whoredome soked quite)" (l. 329), "Dayes deceiptfull malice" (l. 339), and "shameless Day [who] doth marble us in ill" (l. 369). Hercules is asked to bend his bow against the sun:

> Fall Hercules from heaven in tempestes hurld,
> And cleanse this beastly stable of the world:
> Or bend thy brasen bow against the Sunne,
> As in Tartessus, when thou hadst begunne
> Thy taske of oxen: heat in more extreames
> Then thou wouldst suffer, with his envious
>   beames:
> Now make him leave the world to Night and
>   dreames.
> Never were vertues labours so envy'd
> As in this light: shoote, shoote, and stoope his
>   pride . . .

>   (ll. 255-63)

"Night and dreames." Night is repeatedly associated with the mysterious knowledge which comes in dreams and visions. It is peaceful and strong, a guide to virtuous conduct, a source of poetic inspiration, and a storehouse of learning.

Other writings of Chapman's, both prose and poetry, testify that this praise of night and darkness is not simply a *jeu*

d'esprit or an example of that popular Renaissance exercise, the paradoxical encomium. In **The Tears of Peace,** for example, he speaks of how "the gaudie vulgar light / Burns up my good thoughts, form'd in temperate Night" (ll. 1003-4), and in the dedication of the *Odyssey:*

> *Truth* dwels in Gulphs, whose Deepes hide
>   shades so rich,
> That *Night* sits muffl'd there, in clouds of
>   pitch . . .

>   (*Poems*)

Only the poet who is strong enough can plumb these depths and arrive at the mysteries they contain.

For Chapman the pursuit of knowledge is a heroic and also ecstatic experience and one which he often describes in terms of the penetration of shadowy depths. He opens his dedication of **The Shadow of Night** by saying:

> It is an exceeding rapture of delight in the deepe
> search of knowledge, . . . that maketh men
> manfully indure th'extremes incident to that
> *Herculean* labour . . .

>   (*Poems*)

For the poet in quest of knowledge the darkness not only provides this rapture and attends upon revelation but also determines the manner in which the knowledge is to be transmitted. Style, too, should be somewhat dark. This is explained in the dedication of **Ovid's Banquet of Sense** in words which have often been quoted:

> The prophane multitude I hate, & onelie conse-
> crate my strange Poems to these serching spirits,
> whom learning hath made noble, and nobilitie
> sacred; . . .

> But that Poesie should be as perviall as Oratorie,
> and plainnes her speciall ornament, were the
> plaine way to barbarisme. . . . That, *Enargia,*
> or cleerenes of representation, requird in abso-
> lute Poems is not the perspicuous delivery of a
> lowe invention; but high, and harty invention ex-
> prest in most significant, and unaffected phrase;
> it serves not a skilfull Painters turne, to draw the
> figure of a face onely to make knowne who it rep-
> resents; but hee must lymn, give luster, shad-
> dow, and heightening; which though ignorants
> will esteeme spic'd, and too curious, yet such as
> have the judiciall perspective, will see it hath,
> motion, spirit and life. . . .

> Obscuritie in affection of words, & indigested
> concets, is pedanticall and childish; but where it
> shroudeth it selfe in the hart of his subject, ut-
> terd with fitnes of figure, and expressive Epe-
> thites; with that darknes wil I still labour to be
> shaddowed: rich Minerals are digd out of the
> bowels of the earth, not found in the superficies
> and dust of it . . .

>   (*Poems*)

Though Chapman's vocabulary here is likely to provoke a smile, it has the merit of illustrating the point he is making; it avoids being indecently "perviall". In the *Justification of Andromeda Liberata,* replying to criticism of his obscurity, Chapman goes so far as to say that poetry ought to be ambiguous:

As *Learning*, hath delighted from her Cradle, to hide her selfe from the base and prophane *Vulgare*, her ancient Enemy; under divers vailes of *Hieroglyphickes*, Fables, and the like; So hath she pleased her selfe with no disguise more; then in misteries and allegoricall fictions of *Poesie*. . . . Yet ever held in high Reverence and Aucthority; as supposed to conceale, within the utter barke (as their Eternities approve) some sappe of hidden Truth. . . . Or else recording some memorable Examples for the use of policie and state: ever (I say) enclosing within the Rinde, some fruit of knowledge howsoever darkened; and (by reason of the obscurity) of ambiguous and different construction.

(Poems)

I have quoted at length because the details of Chapman's doctrine of obscurity relate it closely to the tradition . . . that the fictions of the poet *conceal* a truth which would be desecrated by revelation to the ignorant majority, but which the élite may see and delight in. This hieratic point of view was understandably congenial to the Platonists, who were fascinated by the occult and liked to think of the poet as a priest whose divine inspiration (the *furor poeticus*) enabled him to reveal the great mysteries to initiates. Schoell has clearly demonstrated Chapman's familiarity with the writings of Ficino, and it is reasonable to suppose that his theory of style owes a good deal to Ficino and his circle. His hatred of the "prophane multitude", for instance, and his determination to consecrate his poems to those who are worthy of them are not only reminiscences of Horace's "Odi profanum vulgus", but resemble even more closely, in thought and word, passages from Pico della Mirandola's Oration "On the Dignity of Man". To make the occult mysteries public, according to Pico, would be "to give a holy thing to dogs and to cast pearls before swine". Hence, the "Sphinxes carved on the temples of the Egyptians reminded them that mystic doctrines should be kept inviolable from the common herd (*a profana multitudine*) by means of the knots of riddles". Plato and Aristotle figure in the list of those who have hidden their highest learning in riddles, and "so did Orpheus protect the mysteries of his dogmas with the coverings of fables, and conceal them with a poetic veil (*poetico velamento*), so that whoever should read his hymns would suppose there was nothing beneath them beyond idle tales and perfectly unadulterated trifles". Pico returns several times to the deliberate obscurity of poetic fables and to the difficulties which even he, an adept, has had in deciphering them. Edgar Wind, who believes that "a deliberate obliqueness in the use of metaphor" also characterizes a great deal of Renaissance painting, writes:

The enjoyment Pico derived from occult authors was vicarious and poetical; they exercised his imagination in the employment of outlandish metaphors. It never occurred to him, as it did to less speculative minds, that the turgid lore of the dialectical magi might be put to a more nefarious use than for amplifying the Platonic *mystères littéraires*. Black magic, in the sense that it appealed to Agrippa of Nettesheim, he rejected as a vile superstition.

[*Pagan Mysteries in the Renaissance*]

Conti, whose writings Chapman knew well, also speaks of the "occult way of philosophizing", which he says the Greeks took from the Egyptians to avoid publishing "admirable things" to the crowd (*"in vulgus"*); their solution was *"per fabulas philosophari"*. [*Mythologiae*, 1581]

From any of a large number of Renaissance authors Chapman may have derived his belief that the best poetry is deliberately contrived to yield its learning only to initiates. Among the Florentine Platonists he would have found this theory combined with vast admiration for "man in his native noblesse" (sometimes expressed through the myth of Hercules), and with a keen interest in the occult. It is a combination very suggestive of the style and content of **Bussy D'Ambois.** Chapman, though certainly well aware of the "nefarious" uses of black magic, seems also to be aware that incantations, spells and spirits belong to the mysteries which it is man's privilege to penetrate and his duty to preserve inviolate. The darkness of the conjuring scenes, like the darkness of the style, is a means of giving to his hero an added dimension.

In Tamyra's invocation it seems to be assumed that the "peaceful regents of the night" have some of the extraordinary powers referred to in the **"Hymnus in Noctem"**: a mystery surrounds them, they are opposed to Time and Fortune, and their calm is to be made available only to adepts—to Tamyra's friends. These are overtones, barely heard in the scene of the first assignation. In the conjuring scene they are sounded loudly along with other notes which recall the **"Hymnus in Noctem"**. Bussy requests the Friar to use his "deep skill / In the command of good aërial spirits" (IV, 2, 8-9), and the Friar promises to do so "by my power of learned holiness" (l. 45). When Behemoth answers the summons he is shocked by the triviality of the task he is asked to perform:

Why call'dst thou me to this accursed light,
To these light purposes? I am Emperor
Of that inscrutable darkness where are hid
All deepest truths, and secrets never seen,
All which I know, and command legions
Of knowing spirits that can do more than these.

(ll. 66-71)

After he has reluctantly obeyed instructions by revealing the activities of Monsieur and Montsurry, the Friar asks, "What shall become of us?" Behemoth replies:

All I can say,
Being call'd thus late, is brief, and darkly this:
If D'Ambois' mistress dye not her white hand
In his forc'd blood, he shall remain untouch'd;
So, father, shall yourself, but by yourself:
To make this augury plainer, when the voice
Of D'Ambois shall invoke me, I will rise,
Shining in greater light, and show him all
That will betide ye all; meantime be wise,
And curb his valour with your policies.

(ll. 149-57)

Tamyra associates herself with the last piece of advice, urging Bussy to be politic, and Bussy agrees to cover his hate with smiles and fight policy with policy.

We seem to be witnessing in this scene the corruption of the hero by a combination of feminine wile, perverted religion, and the power of hell. Bussy has agreed to imitate what his nature is most opposed to, the politic man, whose appearance always belies his inner reality, as do the outsides of the "colossic statues". At the same time, to anyone familiar with Chapman's interest in the occult, the scene carries a totally different set of suggestions which cannot be dispelled by Behemoth's advocacy of policy just before his disappearance. Up to this time the emphasis is on knowledge. Behemoth and his cohorts are "knowing spirits" from the realm of darkness where truth is hidden, and Bussy, initiated into these mysteries by the Friar, is given the power to summon the spirits himself, and hence to see the "greater light" which comes from the darkness. Behemoth is an awe-inspiring figure but never horrible or repulsive like the cackling witches of *Macbeth*. He has the authority of Marlowe's Mephistophilis, and like him utters some indisputable truths. The Friar bids him to appear *"in forma spiritali, lucente, splendida & amabili"* (l. 58). Never is he presented as explicitly evil.

On the symbolic level, then, both Tamyra, who earlier invoked the "peaceful regents of the night", and Bussy are associated with darkness, to whose mysterious truth the daylight world is violently antagonistic. The opposition set up in the first scene of the play is given further meaning. Bussy's "green retreat" where he "neglects the light" and censures the great men of the world gives way to the secret vault or "Gulf", as it is once called in a stage direction; and to the darkness of Behemoth, from which the inner corruption of the world of great men is plainly seen as "Dayes deceiptfull malice", to use the words of the **"Hymnus in Noctem"**.

The Prince of Darkness appears once more, in response to Bussy's demand. On this occasion the invocation is more impressive than the words spoken by the spirit—it is poetry of great distinction. An unusual feature of the invocation is that Bussy first calls upon Apollo, as god of the sun, though it is clear from the preceding lines that he means to summon Behemoth. Apollo, though given high praise, is made to serve as a foil to Behemoth; the light of day is once again portrayed as inferior to darkness. The passage merits quotation in its entirety:

> Terror of darkness! O thou King of flames!
> That with thy music-footed horse dost strike
> The clear light out of crystal on dark earth,
> And hurl'st instructive fire about the world,
> Wake, wake the drowsy and enchanted night,
> That sleeps with dead eyes in this heavy riddle!
> Or thou great Prince of shades where never sun
> Sticks his far-darted beams, whose eyes are made
> To shine in darkness, and see ever best
> Where men are blindest, open now the heart
> Of thy abashed oracle, that, for fear
> Of some ill it includes, would fain lie hid,
> And rise thou with it in thy greater light.
>
> (V, 3, 41-53)

It is impossible to read this speech as an unequivocal submission to the power of evil. In Chapman's strange terms it expresses the initiate's passionate longing for inner illumination and his courage to face a painful truth. The tone is extraordinarily different from that of the passages in

Doctor Faustus where Marlowe's hero is summoning the powers of darkness. Marlowe constantly maintains the framework of Christian morality in this play (as he does not in *Tamburlaine*), so that the longing for obscure knowledge is clearly seen to be misguided.

> A sound magician is a demi-god:
> Here, tire my brains to get a deity!
>
> (I, 1, 63-4)

The eager zeal of Faustus is quite unlike Bussy's rapt earnestness and anxiety. We scarcely need the Good and Bad Angels' comments to show us what is wrong with the aspirations of Faustus. His own words damn him. He is "glutted" with thoughts of the material benefits he will reap when spirits bring him pearls and "princely delicates", and "fill the public schools with silk" (ll. 79-98). Furthermore, Mephistophilis, as Harry Levin has observed, has somewhat the effect on Faustus that Porfiry has on Raskolnikov, making him accuse and convict himself. Bussy's traffic with Behemoth is never undercut in this way. It is a solemn moment in which salvation is offered and tragically refused: Behemoth warns Bussy not to yield to Tamyra's next summons; Bussy ignores the warning, and walks into the prepared trap.

The reasons for his doing so have an important bearing on the interpretation of his character. Behemoth has no sooner disappeared than Bussy decides that even if he knew Tamyra's summons must lead to death, he would have to obey:

> Should not my powers obey when she commands,
> My motion must be rebel to my will,
> My will to life.
>
> (V, 3, 72-3)

This statement of the bond between them matches Bussy's later comparison of the soul and body of a man to "two sweet courtly friends". When Montsurry comes, disguised as the Friar, bearing the fatal letter, Bussy readily concludes that Behemoth is a "lying spirit", for Behemoth has told him that the Friar is dead. The deception practised by the worldly Montsurry causes distrust of an otherworldly agency. Bussy suffers not for involving himself with the powers of darkness but for not believing in them. The irony is underscored in the revised quarto by the addition of lines in which Bussy says that the "Prince of Spirits may be call'd / The Prince of liars", and Montsurry in his pious disguise answers, "Holy Writ so calls him" (V, 3, 97-8).

In his death Bussy rises to his greatest nobility. Shot in the back after he has killed one of the paid murderers and spared the life of Montsurry, he resigns himself to the inevitable with dignity and shows great fortitude by standing to the end, propped on his sword. The visual image he thus makes is magnificently appropriate to the Herculean allusions which are so abundant in this part of the play. The most striking of them is the passage on fame (V, 4, 98-111), which follows, at times word for word, a chorus in the fourth act of *Hercules Oetaeus*. His final thoughts are for his heroic reputation, for his mistress, for his failure to achieve what he believed himself capable of.

The most important question to be asked is about the nature of this failure, and to answer it is to deal with the problem raised earlier of the discrepancy between Bussy's actions and the extravagant praise of his spirit. Parrott, after pointing out the resemblance between Bussy and Marlowe's heroes, says:

> If we look below the surface for the ground of Bussy's self-confidence, we come at once upon an element in his character which sharply distinguishes him from the Titanic, but simple, heroes of Marlowe. Bussy is not a mere bustling man of action, much less a braggart or *miles gloriosus.* Rather he is the embodiment of an idea which Chapman derived from the Stoics, that of the self-sufficiency, the all-sufficiency, of the virtuous man. Bussy, it is true, is far from virtuous in our modern sense of the word, but he is the very incarnation of *virtus,* as the Romans understood it, "the sum of all the bodily and mental excellences of man".
>
> [*Tragedies,* 1910]

Against this view John Wieler argues that Bussy is at least as far from virtuous in a Stoic sense as in a modern sense of the word, since self-sufficiency meant to the Stoic the ability to control the passions, as Bussy clearly fails to do. Wieler agrees with Theodore Spencer that "The tragedy of Bussy is just this; he is swayed by desires over which he has no control." In general it might be said that critics favourable to Bussy have been willing to overlook his shortcomings, while those who have been most aware of the shortcomings have seen them as the tragic flaw. The most persuasive statement of the theory that Bussy represents a failure of control is that of Ennis Rees, who makes use of Chapman's comparison of Achilles and Ulysses. In the dedication of his translation of the *Odyssey,* Chapman distinguishes between the fortitude of Achilles and the wisdom of Ulysses, and states his preference for the *Odyssey:*

> In one, *Predominant Perturbation;* in the other, *over-ruling Wisedome:* in one, the Bodies fervour and fashion of outward Fortitude, to all possible height of Heroicall Action; in the other, the Minds inward, constant, and unconquerd Empire; unbroken, unalterd, with any most insolent, and tyrannous infliction.
>
> (Poems)

Rees points out the striking division of Chapman's tragedies "into two categories, roughly analogous to the *Iliad* and the *Odyssey*" [*The Tragedies of George Chapman,* 1954]. Bussy and Byron, the hero of the next two tragedies, "correspond to Achilles, a character about whom Chapman was never able to feel quite comfortable"; Clermont, the hero of *The Revenge of Bussy D'Ambois,* Cato, of *Caesar and Pompey,* and Chabot correspond to Ulysses, and have "the poet's ethical sympathy". Emphasizing Chapman's frequently stated preference for the contemplative, as opposed to the active, life, Rees comes to the conclusion that Bussy and Byron are "monstrous characters", "abortions of nature", and "bestial servants of self-love", whose bad ends are used for moral instruction; "Bussy was made to express the frailty and fate of the natural man without true learning and religion."

This distinction, though grounded in Chapman's stated opinions, greatly oversimplifies Chapman's attitude towards Achilles and Ulysses, and towards the two kinds of heroes in his own tragedies. It leads to a serious distortion of the meaning of *Bussy D'Ambois.* Bussy undoubtedly lacks complete control, like Achilles, but also like Achilles he is far from being monstrous or bestial. There is not the slightest indication of irony in the words of the Friar's ghost, already partially quoted, which end the play in the first quarto:

> Farewell, brave relics of a complete man,
> Look up and see thy spirit made a star;
> Join flames with Hercules, and when thou sett'st
> Thy radiant forehead in the firmament,
> Make the vast crystal crack with thy receipt;
> Spread to a world of fire, and the aged sky
> Cheer with new sparks of old humanity.
>
> (V, 4, 147-53)

The praise is anticipated in a scene which shortly precedes Bussy's death. Here Monsieur and Guise, involved as they are in the plot on Bussy's life, discuss him with a detachment which is quite out of character and which tends, therefore, to give their words even more weight. Monsieur says that the death they are about to witness will demonstrate the random operation of Nature, whose most valuable gifts often prove the ruin of a man, just as the stock of ammunition in a warship, the one thing which permits the ship to serve its function, may also blow up and destroy it, while the ship might sail longer, empty and useless. When Guise disagrees with this view of Nature's operations Monsieur returns to his point with another comparison:

> here will be one
> Young, learned, valiant, virtuous, and full mann'd;
> One on whom Nature spent so rich a hand
> That with an ominous eye she wept to see
> So much consum'd her virtuous treasury.
> Yet as the winds sing through a hollow tree
> And (since it lets them pass through) let it stand;
> But a tree solid (since it gives no way
> To their wild rage) they rend up by the root:
> So this whole man
> (That will not wind with every crooked way,
> Trod by the servile world) shall reel and fall
> Before the frantic puffs of blind-born chance,
> That pipes through empty men, and makes them dance.
>
> (V, 2, 32-45)

These two speeches agree with too much else in the play to be disqualified as evidence. From the beginning Bussy is shown to be solid, his inner worth corresponding to his valour. His decision to come to court and "rise by virtue" is not "winding with every crooked way", whether or not it is a wise decision. In spite of some lapses from perfect virtue, his actions at court are not despicable, and at the end he is again the picture of self-control and solidity. When he sees that he is mortally wounded he forgives his murderers and prepares calmly for death. In the first quarto the Friar's ghost tells Tamyra, "He hath the great mind that submits to all / He sees inevitable". Bussy is again like Hercules in submitting to his fate, accepting his limitations. In this very acceptance there is a strength for which the play has already provided an image in the description of the sea retreating "into his settled home, . . . crown'd with his own quiet foam" (I, 2, 164-5).

What is particularly striking is Chapman's failure to blame Bussy for such shortcomings as he is shown to have. The affair with Tamyra undoubtedly leads him into concealment and finally to a decision to counter policy with policy. Parrott, in his insistence on Bussy's *virtus,* may seem to pass too readily over the implications of the affair. Chapman gives the world's opinion of Bussy's conduct its full weight but does not allow this opinion to stand unchallenged. Not only does he plant the suggestions of a far more favourable symbolic interpretation of the episode, but he makes the husband, Montsurry, a far worse man than Bussy—scheming, cowardly, and cruel. The ghost of the Friar, who lauds Bussy so highly, is severe with Montsurry, addressing him as "Son of the earth", and urging a "Christian reconcilement" with Tamyra (V, 4, 154-62). When we last see Montsurry, he is refusing this reconcilement. Not the lover, but the injured husband, appears in an unfavourable light.

The absence of blame for Bussy makes one important difference between Chapman's treatment of him and of Byron, the hero with whom Rees associates him. Though Byron is also an aspiring, impetuous hero at odds with the court, and though at the end he is also compared to Hercules, his faults and virtues are clearly distinguished. Despite his great spirit he is shown as a traitor, whose mistake, as Peter Ure says, is a "deliberate eschewal of virtuous action" [*Studies in Philology* 47 (1950)]. The Chancellor says of him, "A mighty merit and a monstrous crime / Are here concurrent" (**Byron's Tragedy,** V, 2, 277-8), and when he is imprisoned and confronted with death, Byron rages uncontrollably. To the extent that his crimes and weaknesses are blamed, Byron is less like Hercules than is Bussy, but even Byron is presented finally as a paradox:

> Oh of what contraries consists a man!
> Of what impossible mixtures! Vice and virtue,
> Corruption and eternnesse, at one time,
> And in one subject, let together loose!
> We have not any strength but weakens us,
> No greatness but doth crush us into air.
> Our knowledges do light us but to err. . . .
> (V, 3, 189-95)

As one reads Chapman's tragedies it becomes increasingly clear that his preference for one type of man does not imply disapproval for all other types. The lines just quoted from **Byron's Tragedy** reveal a complex attitude toward human nature. Even where the vices and virtues are as clearly separated as they are there, they are seen to be joined fast. In Bussy's case one can hardly speak of vice or corruption. In **The Revenge of Bussy D'Ambois,** written several years later, Clermont D'Ambois is said to have his brother Bussy's valour, but a temper "so much past his, that you cannot move him" (**Revenge,** I, 1, 183). Later, in the same vein, Clermont is said to have not only valour but learning, "Which Bussy, for his valour's season, lack'd; / And so was rapt with outrage oftentimes / Beyond decorum" (II, 1, 88-90). Clermont is Chapman's

"Senecal man", very close to the Stoic ideal, yet the difference between him and his brother is no matter of black and white. He reveres Bussy's memory and revenges his murder, which he considers most unjust. Like Bussy, he is opposed to the Machiavellians, but it requires the appearance of Bussy's ghost to make him take the necessary action of fighting Montsurry. The ghost reproaches Clermont for his "tame spirits", and urges him to imitate God by striking a blow for justice (V, 1, 78-99). The emphasis on virtue expressed in action is characteristic of Chapman, and coming from Bussy's ghost, it suggests that however superior Clermont may be, he has something to learn from his brother. The difference between Bussy and Clermont resembles the difference Tasso makes between Rinaldo and Goffredo. Goffredo is superior in reason, but he has need of Rinaldo in carrying out his enterprise. Rinaldo, without being perfect, is a most admirable hero. In the same way Bussy is admirable, and, though lacking Clermont's learning, is by no means entirely uncontrolled. In the earlier play he is not even entirely unlearned; Monsieur calls him learned, and the scenes with Behemoth suggest symbolically a pursuit of learning if not the acquisition of it.

The comparison of Bussy with Achilles is most instructive. As Donald Smalley has pointed out, Chapman has great respect for Achilles in spite of his preference for Ulysses. Like other Renaissance interpreters, he tends to think of "outward fortitude" as the expression of inward strength of mind, and furthermore shows Achilles as acquiring learning and control. Achilles is markedly different from Ulysses but not his opposite [*Studies in Philology* 36 (1939)]. George Lord has shown that Ulysses, too, has to learn to control himself [*Homeric Renaissance,* 1956]. Though Achilles is characterized by "predominant perturbation" rather than "overruling wisdom", he still rises to the "height of heroical action", which is very high praise from a student of Homer. That Bussy is made to resemble Achilles is no argument that he is held up to censure.

Bussy's failure cannot be equated with moral failing and hence the meaning of his tragedy is not simply what might be suggested by the outlines of his story—that he must pay the penalty for pride, adultery and traffic with the devil. As Chapman dramatizes this story, the failure is rather Bussy's inability to reach his goal. Even so noble a warrior as Bussy cannot avoid a trap baited, however unwillingly, by his lady. The terrible pain expressed in Bussy's last speech is compounded of the bitterness of defeat and anguish for the suffering of Tamyra, who stands before him, still bleeding from Montsurry's torture. He is slain again by "this killing spectacle"; his "sun is turn'd to blood". His lines also reflect the vastness of what he hoped to accomplish:

> O frail condition of strength, valour, virtue,
> In me (like warning fire upon the top
> Of some steep beacon, on a steeper hill)
> Made to express it: like a falling star
> Silently glanc'd, that like a thunderbolt
> Look'd to have stuck and shook the firmament.
> (V, 4, 141-6)

This is the failure of a man like Tamburlaine, who must

die, leaving much unconquered, and of one like Hercules, whose divine mission of purifying the world has not been fulfilled.

Tamburlaine more nearly succeeds in imposing his will on the world; for the forces of tyranny and corruption are less insidiously pervasive than in the world of Chapman's play. The facts of contemporary history have a convincing, circumstantial reality. But, like everything else in this play, they have also an important symbolic value. Guise and Monsieur, the representatives of everything which Bussy opposes, become the embodiments of fate. Behemoth tells Bussy that fate prevents him from giving all the information Bussy seeks.

> BUSSY. Who are Fate's ministers?
> BEHEMOTH. The Guise and Monsieur.
> BUSSY.   A fit pair of shears
> To cut the threads of kings and kingly spirits,
> And consorts fit to sound forth harmony
> Set to the falls of kingdoms!
>
>   (V, 3, 63-7)

In one sense, then, this world of court intrigue which Bussy opposes, yet the only world in which he can act, is his fate. Clermont, too, falls victim to this world in the end. Even his virtues cannot assure victory over such odds.

It is characteristic of Chapman, thinking as he did about poetry, to embody the tragedy of a Herculean hero overcome by fate in a fiction which seemingly tells quite another story. For the more ignorant members of the audience there is a story of bloodshed, intrigue, and supernatural doings in a contemporary court. But the original audience for this play included a large proportion of more knowing spectators, for Chapman wrote **Bussy D'Ambois** for one of the "private houses", where the audience, as Alfred Harbage has said, "was an amalgam of fashionable and academic elements, socially and intellectually self-conscious" [*Shakespeare and the Rival Traditions,* 1952]. These more sophisticated spectators might be expected to share the author's delight in meanings artfully concealed beneath a deceptive surface. The play which resulted from this way of writing cannot be called an unqualified artistic success; the disparities between surface meaning and symbolic meaning, particularly in the conjuring scenes, too often suggest a *tour de force.* However, Chapman's procedure has its merits. Not only are there individual passages of high poetic quality, but the very disparities just referred to make a certain positive contribution to the meaning. Purity of motive and corruption of act are brought out by the ambiguity of every major incident: the decision to go to court is both a capitulation and a defiance, the duel both outrageous and noble, the affair with Tamyra both culpable and ideal, the association with Behemoth both a dabbling with evil and a mystical pursuit of the hidden truth. Together these paradoxes present the moving dilemma of a great-spirited man who attempts to live by a heroic code in a world dominated by Machiavellian policy.

The difference between Marlowe's and Chapman's portrayals of the Herculean hero appears constantly in the imagery of the two plays. The most brilliant images in *Tamburlaine,* such as that of the hero in his chariot,

scourging tyrants, give form and concreteness to the hero's situation. They inevitably interpret that situation, but above all they present it. The poetry of **Bussy D'Ambois** characteristically works towards a different end. Its most brilliant images are those which make some thought about the hero concrete—the sea of his energy, which is both wild and yet contained within bounds—the fire of his spirit, which has the various qualities of a torch borne in the wind, a beacon, a falling star, a thunderbolt, and which, after death, returns to a world of fire. Marlowe's images keep the hero himself before our eyes; Chapman's focus the mind's eye on a problem of the heroic nature. (pp. 88-111)

> *Eugene M. Waith, "Chapman," in his* The Herculean Hero in Marlowe, Chapman, Shakespeare and Dryden, *Columbia University Press, 1962, pp. 88-111.*

Edwin Muir   (essay date 1965)

[*Muir was a distinguished Scottish novelist, poet, critic, and translator. In the following excerpt, he investigates the ethical dimension of Chapman's tragedies, suggesting that "Chapman is not interested in human nature, or in practical morality, or in evil, but in the man of excessive virtue or spirit or pride."*]

Chapman's virtues and faults are both excessive, and are combined in such a way that the faults seem to heighten the virtues, and the virtues to stiffen the faults. He erects his imperfections into principles, and keeps them erect by an act of will. When he succeeds he achieves an elevation beyond what seems possible, and when he fails, collapses into fantastic bathos. His mark is excess, itself a fault which he had seen splendidly displayed in Marlowe, the poet of his time whom he admired most. In Marlowe it is a quality of desire and imagination; in Chapman, of character and will. He is excessive on moral grounds, and because he believes that 'royal man' should be excessive.

> Your mind, you say, kept in your flesh's bounds,
> Shows that man's will must ruled be by his
>   power,
> When by true doctrine, you are taught to live
> Rather without the body, than within,
> And rather to your God still than yourself;
> To live to him, is to do all things fitting
> His image, in which, like himself, we live;
> To be his image, is to do those things
> That make us deathless, which by death is only;
> Doing those deeds that fit eternity;
> And those deeds are the perfecting the justice
> That makes the world last. . . .

Chapman is not interested in human nature, or in practical morality, or in evil, but in the man of excessive virtue or spirit or pride. His tragedies show us one great figure and a crowd of nobodies who succeed somehow in destroying him. We do not believe in their power to do this until it is done, for the conflict is between a man of flesh and blood larger than life and puppets of cardboard. Yet the hero's death is real; so that we involuntarily think of it as self-inflicted or as brought about by some power outside the drama, the acts of the other characters being incapable of accounting for it. The death of Bussy D'Ambois and of Byron have, therefore, a sacrificial quality; we seem to be watching the pursuit and destruction of 'royal man' by an invisible hunter. But we see them simultaneously merely as men who ignore the limitations of human life and are bound to destroy themselves; and their ostensible betrayers, the Montsurrys and La Fins—minuses whose very names seem unreal—can only look on and ratify the foregone verdict. These heroes really exist in another dimension from the rest of the characters, and have a different reality from the action in which they are involved. They wander about, like Chapman himself, enclosed in a dream of greatness and breathing the air of that dream.

It is in these remarkable figures that the dramatic interest resides, for they are conscious of another drama beyond the drama which is shown on the stage, and lift us up into it. In their great speeches they employ a language which is not meant for the other actors; they really talk to themselves, or address an imaginary audience outside the play. Chapman is not interested—except in one or two of his comedies—in character or even in action. He employs action merely to display the soul in one of those supreme crises where action itself seems to become irrelevant, since it has done all that it can do, has come to its end, and can be disregarded. He is concerned solely with the crisis as a thing in itself, for in the crisis the real drama of his heroes is born and they rise into their own world; he therefore tries to reach it without the wearisome labour of working towards it through a methodical arrangement of situations. We can feel his impatience to arrive at those places where the souls of his heroes can expand to their full range, places on the frontier-line between life and death, time and eternity, where all terms seem to become absolute. Consequently a situation which to other tragic figures would bring despair or resignation, merely evokes new potentialities in his heroes, as if it were the opportunity for which they had been waiting. In a sense, therefore, his tragic scenes transcend tragedy, or fail to reach it; for death is merely the final assurance of immortality to his heroes. They always possess this assurance; it is one of their distinguishing marks; but it grows stronger the nearer death comes. In their death the dimension of tragedy expands to include an extra one which is not quite compatible with it, for in dying they conduct us a little distance into their own immortality. They look into that, not backwards at their destruction, except in the elegiac mood in which one may grieve for something that has happened in the past to oneself, or to a friend, or to some legendary figure in a book. The tragedies end in this way because Chapman is concerned with the soul as he conceives it, and with hardly anything else.

This exclusive concern with the soul rather than with the way in which people behave makes him an erratic moralist. His judgments of conduct are sometimes strange and almost incomprehensible, the judgments of a man who is not interested in action, either on the stage or in the ordinary world. The action in a play is the prime means for bringing out the moral character of the actors and the moral significance of the situation. We do not come to know Bussy or Byron morally, as we know Macbeth and Hamlet, for the action has no real effect on them, since

they live in a different world from the other characters, and are a law to themselves.

> There is no danger to a man that knows
> What life and death is; there's not any law
> Exceeds his knowledge; neither is it lawful
> That he should stoop to any other law.
> He goes before them, and commands them all,
> That to himself is a law rational.

In a play, which is a pattern of action and interaction, there must be an implicit standard of judgment applied to all the characters and running through the whole, otherwise its progress is confused and dislocated. Chapman's tragedies are full of such dislocations; sometimes we cannot even guess at the standard by which he judges the action; we find such monstrosities as the scene in the first act of *The Tragedy of Bussy D'Ambois*, where Bussy pays court to the Duchess of Guise in the fustian of a low actor, and insults the Duke so obscurely that one can scarcely make out what he means. It is a scene of fantastic vulgarity, yet it draws this splendid encomium on Bussy from the King's brother:

> His great heart will not down, 'tis like the sea,
> That partly by his own internal heat,
> Partly the stars' daily and nightly motion,
> Their heat and light, and partly of the place,
> The divers frames; but chiefly by the moon,
> Bristled with surges, never will be won,
> (No, not when th' hearts of all those powers are
>   burst)
> To make retreat into his settled home,
> Till he be crowned with his own quiet foam.

There is no proportion between these lines and the conduct which inspires them; and there is little connection in *The Tragedy of Bussy D'Ambois* as a whole: here and there fine dramatic touches which come and go, but leave the characters and the action as they were. When the end does come, after these fits and starts, it comes abruptly, we scarcely know how.

Chapman's figures therefore stick out of the play, or rather burst through it, making havoc of the dramatic machinery and fixing our eyes upon them amid the ruins. Once there, they speak unencumbered in Chapman's own voice, a voice habitually choked by a consciousness of things too great for ordinary utterance and requiring the explosive power of some portent to liberate it. These mouthpieces of Chapman are images of man in his original virtue; there is nothing else quite like them in English literature. The sources from which he might have derived them are obvious enough—his long familiarity with the Homeric heroes, his absorption in Roman history and Senecan tragedy, his knowledge of the lives of some of the Renaissance princes, who attempted so many things which had seemed unthinkable before, and are described by Burckhardt. But the image into which his imagination melted those various conceptions of 'royal man' is striking and original. The French King, speaking of Bussy, gives the most complete idea of it:

> Cousin Guise, I wonder
> Your honour'd disposition brooks so ill
> A man so good, that only would uphold
> Man in his native noblesse, from whose fall

All our dimensions rise; that in himself
(Without the outward patches of our frailty,
Riches and honour) knows he comprehends
Worth with the greatest; kings had never borne
Such boundless empire over other men,
Had all maintain'd the spirit and state of
    D'Ambois;
Nor had the full impartial hand of nature
That all things gave in her original,
Without these definite terms of mine and thine,
Been turn'd unjustly to the hand of Fortune,
Had all preserved her in her prime, like
    D'Ambois;
No envy, no disjunction had dissolved
Or pluck'd one stick out of the golden faggot
In which the world of Saturn bound our lives,
Had all been held together with the nerves,
The genius, and th' ingenuous soul of
    D'Ambois.

The idea that if man had not fallen there would be no kings or subjects, no mine or thine, recurs in the tragedies, and evokes an image which cannot be described either as a new ideal of society or as a new state of being. Bussy D'Ambois and Byron are unfallen men among the fallen, but their virtues are not Adam's; they are not equipped with innocence, but with native noblesse, spirit and state, genius and an ingenuous soul, the virtues of the Renaissance. Bussy is like a cross between Adam and Achilles crossed again by something quite different, the Renaissance man stepping out of the Middle Ages into a new world. There is something legendary in this figure, out of which Chapman might have created the myth of his age if he had possessed greater dramatic power and a less erratic genius. The legendary quality appears more clearly in the description of Byron sitting his horse:

Your Majesty hath miss'd a royal sight:
The Duke Byron, on his brave beast Pastrana,
Who sits him like a full-sail'd argosy,
Danced with a lofty billow, and as snug
Plies to his bearer, both their motions mix'd;
And being consider'd in their site together
They do the best present the state of man
In his first royalty ruling, and of beasts
In their first loyalty serving; one commanding,
And no way being moved; the other serving,
And no way being compell'd; of all the sights
That ever my eyes witness'd; and they make
A doctrinal and witty hieroglyphic
Of a blest kingdom; to express and teach,
Kings to command as they could serve, and sub-
    jects
To serve as if they had power to command.

'A doctrinal and witty hieroglyphic of a blest kingdom': this is the hypothesis on which the real drama of Chapman's heroes is grounded, an action elevated above the ostensible action. This blest kingdom is not set in the past, a mere recollection of the Golden Age, nor in the future, a prophecy of a coming society, but rather in a perpetual present apprehended and to that degree lived in by the hero, the unfallen man. We accept this hero and his drama as real, perhaps because with one part of him man still lives in the world before the Fall, and with another in the world after it, since the Fall—assuming that it stands for anything in human experience—is not a historical event but something which is always happening. Chapman's heroes exist more largely in the world before the Fall than any other figures in tragedy; it is for this reason that they are so clearly conscious of their immortality; for this reason, too, perhaps, that they are so awkward and clumsy in the world of action: we could hardly expect adroitness and expedience from these men existing

In all the free-born powers of royal man.

It is not, then, the world in which they move, but the world we see through their eyes which gives Chapman's heroes their greatness. Their nature demands two things from that world created in their image: freedom and glory, but not power or love. In almost any page of the tragedies we find proofs of Chapman's possession by these qualities:

Hot, shining, swift, light, and aspiring things
Are of immortal and celestial nature. . . .
To fear a violent good, abuseth goodness;
'Tis immortality to die aspiring,
As if a man were taken quick to heaven;
What will not hold perfection, let it burst. . . .
I'll wear those golden spurs upon my heels,
And kick at fate; be free, all worthy spirits,
And stretch yourselves, for greatness and for
    height. . . .

This aspiring life just touching the earth and perpetually mounting into the air is suggested finely in his descriptions of his heroes fighting:

Like bonfires of contributory wood
Every man's look show'd, fed with others' spirit. . . .

D'Ambois (that like a laurel put on fire
Sparkled and spit). . . .

And then like flame and powder they commixt
So spritely, that I wish'd they had been spirits. . . .

He turn'd wild lightning in the lackeys'
    hands. . . .

    their saucy fingers
Flew as too hot off, as he had been fire. . . .

The battles then in two half-moons enclosed
    him,
In which he showed as if he were the light,
And they but earth. . . .

These combats are not kindled and fed by merely human passion; they are like an explosion of the elements into speed and fire, impersonal, non-human, transmuting the fighting heroes into those

Hot, shining, swift, light, and aspiring things

which to Chapman were of immortal and celestial nature. In a well-known passage Clermont D'Ambois, Bussy's brother, says:

And know ye all (though far from all your aims,
Yet worth them all, and all men's endless
    studies)
That in this one thing, all the discipline
Of manners, and of manhood is contain'd;
A man to join himself with th' Universe,

> In his main sway, and make (in all things fit)
> One with that all, and go on, round as it. . . .

Clermont is expounding a high philosophical idea; but there are more ways of joining oneself with the universe than those he lays down, and Chapman's heroes inevitably make for that junction, whether in battle or in speculation or in death. Bussy's last speech calls up a gigantic vision of his memory being taken into the keeping of universal nature:

> The equal thought I bear of life and death
> Shall make me faint on no side; I am up;
> Here like a Roman statue I will stand
> Till death hath made me marble; oh, my fame,
> Live in despite of murder; take thy wings
> And haste thee where the grey-eyed morn per-
>   fumes
> Her rosy chariot with Sabaean spices,
> Fly, where the evening from th' Iberian vales,
> Takes on her swarthy shoulder Hecate,
> Crowned with a grove of oaks; fly where men
>   feel
> The cunning axletree; and those that suffer
> Beneath the chariot of the snowy Bear:
> And tell them all that D'Ambois now is hasting
> To the eternal dwellers. . . .

There is no other last speech like that in Elizabethan drama. 'Oh, my fame, live in despite of murder' recalls Hamlet's wish that his memory might be vindicated; but Hamlet does not confide it to the universe, but to Horatio, mortal like himself:

> If thou didst ever hold me in thy heart,
> Absent thee from felicity awhile,
> And in this harsh world draw thy breath in pain,
> To tell my story.

The difference is great, the difference between an imagination which penetrates deep into human life, and one which is concentrated upon a great idea. The essential thing about Chapman's heroes, as about Marlowe's, is that they are framed of the four elements, not that they are human beings obliged to live somehow with other human beings; they are nearer to earth, water, air and fire than to us as we know ourselves. Marlowe gives the concoction from which Chapman's heroes were drawn:

> Nature that fram'd us of four elements,
> Warring within our breasts for regiment,
> Doth teach us all to have aspiring minds.

For Marlowe's poetry, too, like Chapman's, is inspired by a philosophical idea of man, not by human life as the observer sees it. His idea at first seems to be much the same as Chapman's, but in reality is very different; for though like Chapman he is in love with freedom and glory, he is also in love with their rewards, with

>   the ripest fruit of all
> That perfect bliss and sole felicity,
> The sweet fruition of an earthly crown.

Chapman's heroes have no ambition to achieve an earthly crown. They love freedom and glory disinterestedly as states of the soul, for their own and for the soul's sake. Their aspiring minds reach for a state in which freedom and glory are possessed purely, without admixture, as

things in themselves. Bussy does not try to gain power over others, but merely to live after the pattern of 'royal man'. Byron is drawn into plots against his king, but his hostility is nothing more than that of a man who feels he is a king against another who merely is one. His plots bring him to the scaffold; they also precipitate his spiritual tragedy, for he can no longer enjoy freedom and glory in their purity after he has yielded to private ambition and envy. He is an unfallen man who yields to the persuasions of the fallen and becomes one of them, greater than them still, but no longer different from them. He loses his native noblesse by trying to win the noblesse of this world.

We do not come to know Bussy and Byron morally, for they are never affected by the action, never tested by it; but we do come to know what morality is—or what morality is to Chapman—through their mouths. That morality is a passionate, disinterested devotion to freedom and glory, the

> Doing those deeds that fit eternity.

Chapman carried his idea of freedom and glory to excess, no doubt, but excess was at the root of his virtues.

>   Since I am free,
> (Offending no just law), let no law make
> By any wrong it does, my life her slave:
> When I am wrong'd, and that law fails to right
>   me,
> Let me be king myself (as man was made),
> And do a justice that exceeds the law.

Chapman's conception of morality is partial: in concentrating on greatness it pays little attention to goodness. But it is disinterested; it rises above the very thought of expediency, and takes us into the region of absolute things. (pp. 22-32)

Edwin Muir, " 'Royal Man': Notes on the Tragedies of George Chapman," in his Essays on Literature and Society, *revised edition, Cambridge, Mass.: Harvard University Press, 1965, pp. 22-32.*

Millar MacLure   (essay date 1966)

[*In the following excerpt from his* George Chapman: A Critical Study *(1966), the first book-length study of Chapman in English, MacLure examines the thematic and stylistic development of Chapman's comedies, asserting that "comedy was then . . . the genre of experiment, and in that solvent Chapman examined some of his most cherished opinions."*]

T. L. Beddoes, who should have found Chapman in some ways a kindred spirit, observed that he had the least dramatic talent of any of the Elizabethans, and critics have not generally been kind in their assessment of his powers as a playwright. His tragedies have been taken seriously, as documents if not as play-books, but the comedies are lightly regarded. "Chapman's a sad dul Rogue at Comedy," said an anonymous satirist of the Restoration, starting it off; "exercises in art rather than animate theatre," pronounces Miss Bradbrook, ambiguously; works of secondary importance, according to M. Jacquot; purely con-

Inigo Jones's design for the costume of an Indian torchbearer in Chapman's Masque of the Middle Temple and Lincoln's Inn *(1613).*

ventional, asserts Paul Kreider, who codified the conventions of Elizabethan comedy in terms of Chapman's plays. On the other hand, Swinburne, while finding Chapman "by temperament and inclination . . . rather an epic or tragic than a comic poet," praised the easy and graceful style of the comedies, where Chapman "felt himself no longer bound to talk big or to stalk stiffly," and Parrott, who makes great claims for his poet as an innovator and technician in comedy, also commends Chapman's achievement in the blank verse of comedy as a model for Middleton, Fletcher and others.

Shakespeare and Jonson cast long shadows in this genre, but Chapman is not obscured, for he had a line, or lines of his own, either in the adaptation of the comedy of the schools, or in mixed "romantic" comedy. His development of the character of the *dolosus servus,* the intriguer of Roman comedy, into a Hermes-figure of commanding proportions, has been noted by Parrott, Bradbrook and others. Chapman, like other pious and unsocial contemplatives before and since, was fascinated by *power,* whether in the grandiose tragic hero or in the masters of ceremony at a comic feast of fools. Is power, he wondered, the

gift of Fortune or Virtue? This question, on which Plutarch sums up the thought of the ancient world, troubles the comedies a little and the tragedies much. Not so much noticed is his fascination with the themes of melancholy and entombment (from **An Humorous Day's Mirth** to **The Widow's Tears**), with comedy as the breaking-up of mourning into saturnalia (conventional if you will, but that is not a bad word). He is, as we should expect, Jonsonian in his affiliation: not only in the delineation of humours and his gallery of gulls and boobies (LaBesha, Sir Giles Goosecap, Poggio) but in his generally unsympathetic portrayal of female characters, and the easy savagery of his comments on the cankers of a society of parvenus; he can occasionally rival Jonson in an allusive and athletic piece of prose (e.g. **Widow's Tears,** II, i, 20ff.). Seeming to go ahead without theory—if we except the remarks in the Prologue to **All Fools** and a late humanist profession of contempt for the "puppetry, and pied ridiculous antics" of the popular stage—he created, not a comic "world," neither the crowded parish where Jonson's hungry and obsessed time-servers choke on each other's hyperboles, nor the formal garden where Shakespeare's ladies and gentlemen dance their witty galliards and pavanes, but certainly a set of very interesting divertissements.

Even with such modest expectations, the reader who begins with **The Blind Beggar of Alexandria** will be baffled and irritated, and, if he has learned that Henslowe recorded 22 performances of this piece in 1596-97, and that it was revived in 1601, he will have cause to reflect grimly (as every reader of minor Elizabethan drama must) on the curious tastes of our ancestors—or, if he stops to think further, he may notice in these ridiculous antics a strong resemblance to the quality and in some cases the substance of the fare provided on commercial television. Granted that William Jones's quarto does not represent the play as produced, the romantic plot being almost entirely lost, the title page shows that it was the "variable humours" of the blind beggar, here rescued from oblivion, which were popular. And it is easy to see why, for the piece was obviously designed to remind the spectators continually of Marlowe and especially of Tamburlaine. The central figure, a megalomaniac quick-change artist, appearing as Irus (*Odyssey,* xviii), Count Hermes (note the name) a swaggering ruffian, Leon a usurer and Duke Cleanthes, is "a shepherd's son"; there are echoes like "Why, what is dalliance, says my servant then?"; there is a pompous entrance of barbarous kings "with soldiers and drum and ensign," and so forth. The language is frequently a travesty of Marlowe's style:

> My sweet Acates and Acanthes slain!
> Grief to my heart and sorrow to my soul!
> Then arouse thyself, Cleanthes, and revenge
> Their guiltless blood on these base miscreants.
> Oh, let the canker'd trumpet of the deep
> Be rattled out and ring into their ears
> The dire revenge Cleanthes will inflict
> On these four kings and all their complices.
>
> (sc. ix)

There are other allusions too. In fact this fragment is a kind of index to the catch-words and conventional phrases, the little literary jokes and the general idiom of

the popular theatre of the nineties. Every student (or paro-
dist) of the Elizabethan drama will recognize these—and
many others:

> Leave me awhile, my lords, and wait for me
> At the black fountain. . . .

> And offering stain to Egypt's royal bed. . . .

> Come, gird this pistol closely to my side,
> By which I make men fear my humour still,
> And have slain two or three, as 'twere my
> mood. . . .

> I am Signor Bragadino, the martial Spaniar-
> do. . . .

> Sweet nymph, I love few words; you know my
> intent, my humour is insophistical and plain.
> I am a Spaniard born, my birth speaks for my
> nature, my nature for your grace. . . .

> Die, thou vile wretch, and live, Aspasia. . . .

> Who calls out murther? Lady, was it you?

Did Chapman really think such leaden nuggets as these
could be transmuted into the gold of dramatic rhetoric?
It is impossible to say, but I suspect a certain cynicism.
Parrott's hypothesis, that the printed play represents "a
stage version which was in many respects a perversion of
the original," certainly helps us out of the difficulty, but
not altogether, for though the action may be mangled the
words are there and presumably they have some fairly
close relation to what the dramatist wrote down in the first
place. There are hints, too, of the poet's serious preoccupations and even of some kind of allegory. The master trickster and seducer, who turns his society upside-down, is by
turns a "reverent" seer or "skilled" man, a "wild and frantic" soldier of fortune and swaggerer, a usurer or master
of avarice, and a nobleman; his "transformations" or "humours" thus constitute a microcosm of the social order.
A certain seriousness keeps creeping in: Irus has skill "to
tell the drifts of fate, / Our fortunes, and things hid from
sensual eyes"; he compares himself to Homer, who, blind,
could "best discern / The shapes of everything"; the irony
sharpens his enjoyment of his roles, and he delights in the
game as well as in its rewards. His wooing of Elimine (in
the character of Leon) is not without merit, being sophisti-
cal, ironic, and full of rhetorical bravura:

> And therefore, beauteous lady, make
>   not strange
> To take a friend and add unto the joys
> Of happy wedlock; the end of every act
> Is to increase contentment and renown,
> Both which my love shall amply joy in
>   you.
> ELI. How can renown ensue an act of shame?
> No act hath any shame within itself,
> But in the knowledge and ascription
> Of the base world, from whom this shall
>   be kept,
> As in a labyrinth or brazen tower.
> LEON. But virtue's sole regard must hold me
>   back.
> The virtue of each thing is in the praise,
> And I will rear thy praises to the skies.
> Out of my treasury choose thy choice of

> gold,
> Till thou find some matching thy hair in
>   brightness;
> But that will never be, so choose thou
>   ever.
> Out of my jewelry choose thy choice of
>   diamonds,
> Till thou find some as brightsome as
>   thine eyes;
> But that will never be, so choose thou
>   ever.
> Choose rubies out until thou match thy
>   lips,
> Pearl till thy teeth, and ivory till thy skin
> Be match'd in whiteness, but that will
>   never be;
> Nor ever shall my treasury have end,
> Till on their beauties ladies loathe to
>   spend;
> But that will never be, so choose thou
>   ever.
>   (v, 91-115)

It appears that, in terms of Chapman's private ethical
principles, this comic "lord of the ascendant" (Bradbrook's word) professes "Opinion" to be the world's com-
mander and makes hay while that sun shines. At all
events, the comic world is certainly "outward."

But *The Blind Beggar* is a fragment; *An Humourous
Day's Mirth* (1599), though a bad text, is a whole play.
Whether Chapman in this play "initiated the whole Jonsonian comedy of humours," is an open question; at least
here we find an informing idea and symbol: liberation by
the "word," for the intriguer who reverses everything, and
turns prison into festival, is named Lemot:

> . . . my name signifies word.
> —Well hit, Monsieur *Verbum!*
> —What, are you good at Latin, lady?
> —No, sir, but I know what *verbum* is.
> —Why, 'tis green bum: *ver* is green, and you
>   know
> what bum is, I am sure of that.
> —No, sir, 'tis a verb.
>   (v, 67-74)

Lemot *is* for the green world: for youth against age, for
crowds against solitude, for cakes and ale against sobriety,
for free love against jealousy. He is an active verb too, for
he, as the tale-teller, sets all in motion and dissolves all secrecy.

At the opening of the action, jealousy rules: old Count Labervale jealously guards his young Puritan wife Florilla,
since "pure religion being but mental stuff" she may
"yield unto the motion of her blood"; old Countess Moren
is jealous of her young husband; old Count Foyes jealously
guards his daughter Martia, whom he intends to marry to
the "very fine gull" Labesha, "one that's heir to a great living." By a series of misinformations and crossing plots, by
spreading the word, Lemot shifts the action from the shut-
up homes to the open tavern; at the end, amid general festival, and pardon for misunderstandings, the fair Martia
is betrothed to Dowsecer, Labervale's son by a former
marriage.

The portrait of Florilla is not, *pace* Parrott, of any great interest, being pieced together from the most obvious commonplaces, condemnation of the superstitions of the "times of ignorance," of the vanity of fine clothes (sc. iv), of "idols" (sc. xiv); she has a spiced conscience and is a hypocrite. So much for her, except that her entrance line is very funny indeed:

> What have I done? Put on too many clothes.

Rather, to come to the "rare humours" of the play, we must concentrate upon the triad Dowsecer-Lemot-Labesha: Dowsecer the melancholic scholar whose humour is purged by love; Labesha the "outward" fool who plays at the fashion of being melancholy ("I will in silence live a man forlorn, / Mad, and melancholy as a cat"); and Lemot, "the very imp of desolation," who danced at his parents' funeral, does all his trickery with complete detachment, and remains unmoved by the passions. Lemot is the airy agent of freedom whose activities expose the true soul of Dowsecer and the false front of Labesha. Scholar and fool, inward and outward man, are contrasted formally, even in this loose and confusing action: as Dowsecer is confronted by hose, sword and picture to remind him in his dumps of the active life (sc. vii), so Labesha, having "taken on him the humour of the young Lord Dowsecer," is tempted by "a mess of cream, a spice-cake and a spoon" to purge his humour (sc. xii).

As Lemot's essence is movement, as he is the pipe to make all dance, the ducdame to call all fools into a ring, so Dowsecer's element is stillness; he contemplates, and is contemplated, he sees the true object of his soul's desire, and obtains his reward. He is consequently, except for one scene at the centre of the play (sc. vii), in the background, but not, as Parrott had it, "crowded" into the background; that is where he belongs, for he is Chapman's "shadow."

Premonitions of *Hamlet* abound in this scene, which, in a modern production, would come just before the interval. Trumpets sound, not telling (the King says) "what I am, but what I seem," for he is full of imagined love and is "a king of clouts, a scarecrow, full of cobwebs"; the court comes to observe "the young Lord Dowsecer," who is "rarely learned, and nothing lunatic / As men suppose, / But hateth company and worldly trash." In his way, standing "close," the courtly Lavel places a picture, "a pair of large hose" with a codpiece, and a sword, "to put him by the sight of them in mind of their brave states that use them," for, as the King remarks, "the sense doth still stir up the soul." The melancholic enters, quoting Cicero's *Tusculan Disputations,* marvelling that Cicero could sell for glory "the sweet peace of life," and praising the age of Saturn. The King remarks that "this is no humour, but perfit judgment." Dowsecer, seeing the sword, condemns the "art of murder" of which it is the symbol; his eye falling upon the hose and codpiece, he condemns pomposity in apparel; when he sees the picture of the fair maiden, he speaks sharply of women's painting; confronted by his father, he affects to despise the joys of fatherhood. But Martia's appearance launches him into a neoplatonic (and un-Ovidian) passion:

> What have I seen? How am I burnt to dust
> With a new sun, and made a novel phoenix.
> Is she a woman that objects this sight,

> Able to work the chaos of the world
> Into digestion? Oh, divine aspect!
> The excellent disposer of the mind
> Shines in thy beauty, and thou hast not changed
> My soul to sense, but sense unto my soul;
> And I desire thy pure society,
> But even as angels do to angels fly.

> (vii, 207-16)

At the close of the play, when a maid dressed as "Queen Fortune" draws the posies for all the assembled guests in the tavern, Dowsecer is given a caduceus (Q. "a cats eyes") "or Mercury's rod, of gold set with jacinths and emeralds," and Martia "the two serpents' heads set with diamonds." The hermetic rod of wisdom and healing is appropriate, for Dowsecer is a "holy" figure, inspiring reverence. Chapman seems to attribute to Learning something of the magic with which Shakespeare endows innocence, in his late plays. This impression is sustained when we turn to the portrait of the scholar Clarence in *Sir Giles Goosecap,* which M. Jacquot calls "une image embellie de Chapman lui-meme." Clarence, the hero of a little romance based on *Troilus and Creseide,* and surely the strangest and most unfashionable of all Troilus's avatars, is praised by his friend Momford (Pandarus) for his "dove-like innocence," for "a soul / Where all man's sea of gall and bitterness / Is quite evaporate with her holy flames"; and both his condition and his studies, with his neoplatonic love for Eugenia ("Noblesse"), remind us of the *persona* created in the non-dramatic verse.

His first appearance (I, iv) may be some sort of recollection of Orsino's love-melancholy in *Twelfth Night,* for he enters to music (as does Byron), and later, composing a letter to Eugenia, he invokes the more soulful harmonies of *Ovids Banquet,* and anticipates some of the musical effects in *The Tempest:*

> Sing, good Horatio, while I sigh and write.
> According to my master Plato's mind
> The soul is music, and doth therefore joy
> In accents musical, which he that hates
> With points of discord is together tied,
> And barks at Reason consonant in sense.
> Divine Eugenia bears the ocular form
> Of music and of Reason, and presents
> The soul exempt from flesh in flesh inflam'd.

> (III, ii, 1-9)

In fact this "musical Clarence" (as Momford calls him) works a counterpoint of "sense" and "soul" throughout the piece. Most musical, most melancholy, he begins by choosing love to salve his distressed estate:

> Work on, sweet love; I am not yet resolv'd
> T'exhaust this troubled spring of vanities
> And nurse of perturbations, my poor life;
> And therefore, since in every man that holds
> This being dear, there must be some desire,
> Whose power t'enjoy his object may so mask
> The judging part, that in her radiant eyes
> His estimation of the world may seem
> Upright and worthy, I have chosen love
> To blind my reason with his misty hands
> And make my estimative power believe
> I have a project worthy to employ
> What worth so ever my whole man affords:

Then sit at rest my soul, thou now hast found
The end of thy infusion; in the eyes
Of thy divine Eugenia look for Heaven.

(I, iv, 1-16)

("Troubled spring of vanities" is a good phrase.) His estate is "mean," a "waspish and petulant" star frowns upon him; he is "a thing created for a wilderness," and he is "all liver, and turned lover," loves *passionately* the worthy Eugenia. In this sad state, afflicted with a double melancholy—of the intellectual and of the lover—Momford recommends "confidence":

I tell thee, friend, the eminent confidence of strong spirits is the only witchcraft of this world; spirits wrastling with spirits, as bodies with bodies.

In the triangle of Clarence-Momford-Eugenia, then, will mediates between passion and reason, until sense is turned to soul, reason touched by sense ("Her sensual powers are up, i'faith!"), and in the conclusion Eugenia sees her lover's heart, and they are united in the "knot of [their] eternity."

This is almost technical; the language of these scenes is generally informed with terms from "natural philosophy," of "the strange affections of enchanted number," and what we should now call psychology. For example, we hear a lecture from Momford, in answer to Clarence's assertion that to love a woman is to turn the mind from its proper objects to unsubstantial shadows, to the effect that women's "souls" add fair "forms" to man: "but for women, who could care for forms?" (III, ii, 62 ff.) Clarence's supposed sickness is discussed in terms of the passions, the body and the mind, by the patient and his doctor (V, ii), and here Clarence affirms that the only true "mixture" of souls is in "reason and freedom." The doctor, persuaded finally that Clarence's "passion" is a "high perfection" of his mind, decides that his patient's mind has "so incorporate itself with flesh / And therein rarefied that flesh to spirit" that he has no need of a physician.

Clarence's "field" (as we should say) is astronomy, akin to music, though his studies have a religious end; he broods upon

. . . what Eternesse is,
The world, and time, and generation;
What soul the world's soul is, what the black
   springs
And unreveal'd original of things,
What their perseverance, what is life and death,
And what our certain restauration.

(II, i, 9-14)

A large order, but undertaken not by way of accumulation of knowledge, but of purification. Eugenia, though she is said to be "the best scholar of any woman, but one [i.e. the Queen], in England . . . wise and virtuous," is not exhibited in such a holy light as the melancholy young sage. It is not easy to represent learning (in the ordinary sense) on the stage without the danger of caricature, and though Chapman allows her to misquote Horace once, he does not present a bluestocking. She is simply "Noblesse" (ευγενεια), at first turned "outward" when she respects, as a widow, "the judgment of the world" (II, i, 169). Accepting graciously Momford's trickery in changing the sense of her letter to Clarence in the dictation (IV, i), she suddenly perceives Clarence's "inward wealth and nobleness" and pledges herself to him, since

knowledge is the bond,
The seal, and crown of [their] united minds.

(V, ii, 215-6)

This serious, pedantic, neoplatonic allegory of the Troilus-Cressida story is set down in the midst of a farcical action of gulled knights and witty pages, or rather little or no action and much straining at wit, with a lady of a "drinking humour" for broad effects, apparently, though this scene did not get printed. Yet if the play was composed before 1603, as the reference to Queen Elizabeth suggests, it marks a fairly early experiment in the mixing of romantic and farcical plots and a delight in the set piece of paradox, in this case Clarence's defence of women's painting (IV, iii, 42-72), and prepares us for the same effects in *The Gentleman Usher* and *Monsieur D'Olive*—nothing quite prepares us for *The Widow's Tears.* Before considering these characteristic productions, however, we must glance at Chapman's achievements in the comedy of manners.

All Fools, Chapman's contamination of the *Heautontimoroumenos* and *Adelphi* of Terence, with many original touches, is certainly the best made of his comedies, and the most suavely written, so polished as to be almost impersonal. The sources provided a firmly complicated plot structure, and the humours device a basis for sketching character; to these elements is added another unifying element, the motif of Fortune. The magnificent intriguer Rinaldo, no *servus* but a scholar (I, ii, 85) with a humour of meddling, is a follower of Fortune, "the great commandress of the world" (V, i, 1), hence an opportunist or "occasional" artist, who triumphs over the stern father Gostanzo, a "wretched Machiavellian" as Rinaldo calls him (I, i, 148), a Polonius-like "politician" (also Rinaldo's word) who believes that affairs can be arranged by taking the lowest view of human nature (II, i, 69-85). Fortune is the theme of the "Prologus," and the play opens with a discussion of the different fortunes of the young men: Valerio (son of Gostanzo), who is secretly married to Gratiana, and Fortunio (elder son of Marc. Antonio), who, loving Valerio's sister Bellanora, is denied sight of her by her father. Rinaldo "takes hold on [each] occasion" that will serve to settle their "fortunes"; "blind Chance," the "ape of counsel and advice," brings forth a "rude plot," which his "learning" brings to a "perfect shape" (I, ii, 122-4). (This sounds like a parody of the *forming* power of Learning to make all "circulare," in Chapman's high philosophy.) Rinaldo's "wit" puts "blind Fortune in a string" into Valerio's hand (II, i, 209-10), and Fortune "shifts the chances" of the final scene of recognition, so that Gostanzo, accepting the fact that he has been deceived, as the comic "amnesia" (Frye's word) demands, caps the conclusion with "Marriage is ever made by destiny" (V, ii, 157).

The sub-plot of the jealous husband Cornelio (i.e. he who believes he is a *cornuto*) is deliberately planned as a "rest" or diversion from the main action: to contemplate it serves, Rinaldo says, "to vary / The pleasures of our wits"

(II, i, 213), and it is introduced by his "Well, now let's note . . . ," or "Now we must expect . . . ," or "Now in what taking poor Cornelio is . . . I long to see." Rinaldo stands, as it were, between the main intrigue in which he assists Fortune and the secondary entertainment for which he draws the curtain and which he contemplates with delight. In each action the humour of the victim is his downfall: Gostanzo thinks himself very deep indeed and is an unwitting agent of the device to deceive him (IV, i); Cornelio is the victim of his own jealous suspicions. All who suppose "their wits entire" are "laid flat on earth for gulls."

This is all very neat, nor does the design lack the ornament of eloquence. Not to speak of Gostanzo's superb recollection of his youthful gallantry (II, i, 148-78)—

> I had my congé—plant myself of one leg,
> Draw back the tother with a deep-fetch'd hon-
>   our,
> Then with a bel-regard advant mine eye
> With boldness on her very visnomy—

which is in character, and easily the best chance for an actor in a play rich in such chances, the traditional debate on the nature of woman appears as a flourish on the theme of "all fools," with a paradoxical conclusion set to it. It is introduced in the first scene, where Rinaldo, who has loved and been beloved, scorns womankind as "unconstant shuttlecocks" or proud and wayward sluts; to this Valerio (out of character, for he is a rake and swaggerer) replies with an elevated praise of Love,

> Nature's second sun,
> Causing a spring of virtues where he
>   shines. . . .
> So Love, fair shining in the inward man,
> Brings forth in him the honourable fruits
> Of valour, wit, virtue, and haughty thoughts,
> Brave resolution, and divine discourse.
>   (I, i, 97-8, 107-10)

Love makes the "absolute" man. Set against this we have the page's homily to Cornelio (III, i) on the nature of women, "the light sex," "unfinished creatures," with a large portion of will and a small of wit, and Gostanzo's comical consolation to Cornelio:

> As for your mother, she was wise, a most flip-
> pant tongue she had . . . and she was honest
> enough too. But yet, by your leave, she would
> tickle Dob now and then, as well as the best on
> 'em . . . your father knew it well enough, and
> would he do as you do—think you?—set rascals
> to undermine her, or look to her water, as they
> say? No, when he saw 'twas but her humour . . .
> he . . . would stand talking to his next neigh-
> bour to prolong time, that all things might be rid
> cleanly out of the way before he came, for the
> credit of his wife. This was wisdom now for a
> man's own quiet. [V, ii, 187-202]

Since the women in the play are mere puppets, the hymn to love must carry all one side of the argument, to which is set as epilogue Valerio's long oration in "praise and honour of the most fashionable and autentical HORN" (at the end of the play). This set piece could be and probably was cut; there is an easy transition from V, ii, 230 (Cornelio's

"And now shall the world see I am as wise as my father") to l. 330 (Gostanzo's "Very well done; now take your several wives"), but if "all the world is but a gull, / One man gull to another in all kinds" (II, i, 360-1), then the speech is appropriate enough in a play in which all are fools because all blaspheme "Love's most unmatched ceremonies." Chapman may be covertly insinuating his own high ethics—but this is doubtful, as doubtful as to find Valerio's encounter with "a sort of corporals" sent to arrest him for debt (II, i, 304-35) inspired by Chapman's own troubles.

May Day, a clever adaptation to the English stage of Alessandro Piccolomini's commedia erudita *Alessandro* (from which Chapman also borrowed the names of Gostanzo, Cornelio and Fortunio for *All Fools*) has the very complicated plot of its genre, and its language is rich in parody, allusion and double entendre; the action is boisterous, the pranks of adults seen down the perspective of the Blackfriars as mad children. Apart from such imitations of Jonson, Marston and Shakespeare, and parodies of single lines from popular plays and ballads as have been noted by Parrott, the piece might serve as a source-book for the clichés of Elizabethan comic dialogue. It sounds like parts of "So That's The Way You Like It" in *Beyond the Fringe;* it has all the strenuous anonymity of revue. I cannot follow Parrott in his emphasis upon the character of Lodovico, whom he sees as another of Chapman's "confident" and reckless intriguers; he has one big self-explanatory speech (III, iii, 118-49), in which he boasts of taking Occasion by the forelock, like Rinaldo, and contemns Idleness, being himself "begot in a stirring season," but he does not dominate the play, in which the most conspicuous elements are the practical jokes played on the senile lecher Lorenzo disguised as a chimney-sweep, and the humours of the swaggering captain Quintiliano (a grammarian?), who is modelled on Jonson's Tucca (*Poetaster*) and sounds sometimes also like Falstaff played on a cracked recorder.

Of Chapman's part in *Eastward Ho,* a venture in which Marston was probably the leading spirit, there is little to say. Chapman's contribution seems to have been concentrated in II, iii, in III, and in IV, i: he was concerned, then, with the sub-plot of Sir Petronel Flash and the usurer Security. One would like to think for the sake of his reputation as a comic dramatist that he wrote III, ii (Gertrude taking her coach); the talent which framed *The Old Joiner* would certainly be capable of those effects. But if he could manage the comic delineation of London types, he certainly could not approach Jonson in creating a solid, anti-romantic world which maintains the decorum of comical or savage absurdity, nor, perhaps surprisingly, did he diagram his comic action in morality terms, so that his comedies are not fundamentally *serious*—or rather the seriousness is elevated and "inward," and the laughter is directed outward. He has only one fool who makes us think, and no noble creature who makes us laugh. In consequence, his most interesting comedies are unsophisticated tragicomedies, weak in structure, uncertain of their level, but sometimes striking in their diverse effects. I cannot subscribe to the view that these productions with which we must next be concerned are to be compared with Shakespeare's last plays, even by suppressed implication. There is more indigestion than digestion into a "golden worlde" in these plays. No writer is as consistent as his critics; he hasn't time.

The first of these, **The Gentleman Usher,** is on the face of it an absurd play, a real gallimaufry, weak in construction and faltering in illusion. At the beginning we see a corrupt social order: the old duke Alphonso, abetted by his sinister and illiterate favorite Medice, seeks in marriage the virtuous Margaret, who is loved purely and passionately by his son Vincentio. The latter, who has as friend the noble Strozza, uses the silly gentleman usher Bassiolo as go-between and secretly makes Margaret his betrothed. Strozza, wounded on a boar hunt by a henchman of Medice, becomes suddenly a figure of Christian piety and fortitude, the bearer of magical powers and of a "spirit prophetic"; miraculously recovered, he unmasks Medice, who is really Mendice, once king of the Gypsies. Meanwhile Margaret, who has disfigured her face to foil the amorous pursuit of the old Duke, is miraculously cured by the doctor Benevemus (this from *Arcadia,* the Parthenia story) and all is forgotten and forgiven. The first two acts are largely taken up with the "shows" arranged by the Duke in his wooing of Margaret; the centre of the play with the ridiculous humour of Bassiolo, gulled by Vincentio and Margaret; and the closing scenes with the elevated sentiments of Strozza. As accidents we have the ludicrous Poggio, the foolish nephew of Strozza; Sarpego a pedant; and a drunken old lady, Cortezza, aunt to Margaret. These last flourishes seem to have been left over from **Sir Giles Goosecap;** they serve here merely to disfigure the romance elements, since they do not constitute a genuine sub-plot, but only a series of coarse diversions. Critics in search of Chapman's characteristic sentiments have naturally concentrated on Strozza, who has been compared to Clermont and Cato, in the tragedies.

There is, however, a theme, if we look hard for it, and a theme highly appropriate to romance too: it is the theme of *noblesse,* of the gentle soul and mind, its evidence in virtuous and gracious behaviour, its absence in the base born, and its parody in the apes of gentility. As a character in a play, Medice is a total failure; but he is Strozza's opposite in the matter of noblesse. In the first scene, Strozza, already defined as of a "virtuous spirit" and "hardy mind," describes Medice as a "fustian lord, who in his buckram face / Bewrays a map of baseness," and Vincentio echoes that he is an "unknown minion rais'd to honour's height / Without the help of virtue, or of art," a creature of "base-bred ignorance"; he cannot read or write besides (I, i, 107-27), and he picks his teeth in public. We think that jokes at the expense of the illiterate may be enjoyed only by the semi-literate; Vincentio's and Strozza's scoffs at Medice's uncourtly ignorance may jar upon sentimental ears (Medice seems to have needed a good foster-home, as it is now called). But eloquence is a main mark of noblesse, and the point is made again, at the end, when the Duke, now enlightened, speaks of his favorite's "pretended noblesse," and Strozza underlines this with the authority of his occult powers:

> Set by your princely favour,
> That gave the lustre to his painted state,
> Who ever view'd him but with deep contempt,
> As reading vileness in his very looks?

> And if he prove not son of some base drudge,
> Trimm'd up by Fortune. . . . then that good angel
> That by divine relation spake in me . . . now fails my tongue.
> (V, iv, 194-204)

In the end, Medice confesses the "wrong [he] did to noblesse" and is banished to "live a monster, loath'd of all the world."

So much for this impossible but instructive villain. Poggio inverts noblesse quite literally: a gentleman by connection, he abuses the rhetoric of gentility by his vulgar and mistaken language—Strozza calls him "cousin Hysteron Proteron," the one who gets things backwards, and he is a messenger of fear. Cortezza should be a great lady; she is a drunken, deceived (by Medice) and tattle-tale old bitch. Bassiolo, whose "humours" of correctness (II, ii, 5 ff.) and susceptibility to flattery carry the comic tenor of the play, has pretensions to noblesse: he knows the alphabet of love-letters (III, ii, 392-460), has read the lighter classics and courtesy books (Ovid and Guevara), but he is a hollow man who only reverberates to others' phrases. True noblesse is in Vincentio and Margaret, and, with a difference, in Strozza.

In what Parrott tenderly calls "the highest flight of pure poetry in Chapman's comedies," Vincentio and Margaret "marry before heaven" (IV, ii, 132 ff.), Margaret affirming:

> Are not the laws of God and Nature more
> Than formal laws of men? Are outward rites
> More virtuous then the very substance is
> Of holy nuptials solemnized within
> Or shall laws made to curb the common world,
> That would not be contain'd in form without them,
> Hurt them that are a law unto themselves?

The familiar terms of Chapman's hieratic vocabulary sanctify this match, "far remov'd from custom's popular sects," "sacred," what is called in **All Fools** one of "Love's most unmatched ceremonies." It is not only evidence of noblesse, as with Sidneian overtones the lovers, after Margaret's disfigurement, contend with each other in noble self-abnegation (V, iv, 95-121), but in its proclamation of the "free soul" above law, raised to the lower levels at least of Strozza's transformation. Strozza, wounded, rages against his torment, and threatens suicide, saying that "manliest reason" commands him to take his life into his own power rather than submit to "the torturing delays of slavish Nature" (IV, i, 35 ff.), but from this pagan position he is converted by his wife Cynanche, who "salves with Christian patience pagan sin," reminds him of his "religious noblesse," and counsels patience—turns him in other words from raging Hercules ("I'll break away, and leap into the sea") to suffering Christ.

He accordingly becomes a seer and God's minister and prophet; he is "naught else but soul" since his mind has spread "her impassive powers" through all his suffering body, and expelled its frailty (IV, iii, 45-52). This sounds technical, and M. Jacquot has found passages in Ficino's *Theologica platonica* which might have served as inspiration for the idea, but Cynanche's explanation is clear enough:

> . . . 'tis said afflictions bring to God
> Because they make us like him, drinking up
> Joys that deform us with the lusts of sense,
> And turn our general being into soul.
>
> (IV, i, 63-6)

At any rate, Strozza is raised "to the stars" by his "humility," his "free submission to the hand of Heaven," and sees "things hid from human sight"; he predicts that the arrow-head will fall out of his side on the seventh day, and by his "good angel" (or heavenly familiar) foresees harm to Vincentio (who is wounded by Medice). Against the tyrannous Duke he invokes the doctrine of the free soul:

> And what's a prince? Had all been virtuous men,
> There never had been prince upon the earth,
> And so no subject; all men had been princes:
> A virtuous man is subject to no prince,
> But to his soul and honour, which are laws
> That carry fire and sword within themselves,
> Never corrupted, never out of rule.
>
> (IV, iv, 56-62)

(One is reminded of Achmat in Greville's *Mustapha*: "I first am Natures subject, then my Princes.") It is a perfect human realm, a golden age restored, which is miraculously created in the peripeteia of this play in the triumph of innocence and piety. When Bussy D'Ambois—who is Herculean—utters a similar sentiment,

> Who to himself is law, no law doth need,
> Offends no law, and is a king indeed,

the commonplace book sentence has a different and more complex significance, political and tragic.

Monsieur D'Olive is shorter, somewhat better integrated, and in every way more interesting than *The Gentleman Usher*, though its chief claim to our attention is D'Olive himself, a superb comic creation. Without a scaffolding provided by someone else, Chapman never attempts much of a plot, and the romantic action in this play hardly deserves the name of plot at all. Vandome, returning after three years absence, finds that his mistress Marcellina (mistress in terms of courtly love), injured by the jealousy of her husband Vaumont, has retired from "the common pandress light" and wakes only by night, muffling her beauties in darkness, while Vandome's brother-in-law, St. Anne, watches over the embalmed body of his dead wife and refuses to let her be buried. The hero by persuasion and policy liberates St. Anne from his obsession and attaches his affections to Marcellina's sister Eurione, and tricks Marcellina into the world again. Vandome, then, is the deliverer, by the enchantments of his "divine wit"; "our quick Hermes, our Alcides," Vaumont calls him (IV, i, 95). He speaks himself of his rousing of Marcellina as a "Herculean labour." But as he is at the beginning a noble and innocent soul, a veritable angel to St. Anne, when he tricks Marcellina by convincing her that her husband is unfaithful and mocks her (V, i), he becomes another kind of Hermes, a cheap trickster; the whole tone changes, symbolized by the shift from the elevated language of Vandome's opening tribute to "circular" love and the eloquence of Petrarch's *Secretum* (III, i) to slangy prose and

a reference to "Petrarch in Italian" as a means of "entertaining time" in private courtship with a gallant (V, i, 190-200). This indecorum would be more glaring if Chapman were really interested in delineating character, but he is not. He had two climaxes to arrange: St. Anne is liberated and in love with Eurione by the end of IV, i, and D'Olive, whose preparation for an embassy to the French king, requesting him to command the burial of his niece, wife to St. Anne, makes up the sub-plot, has no further *raison d'être* after the lady is buried. So having to start over again, Chapman borrows the letter-trick from *Twelfth Night* (the cloistered Olivia must have been in his mind anyway) to keep D'Olive in the play, lest "all our audience will forsake us" (IV, ii, 171), and descends to the most obvious intrigue to manage a total denouement, since he has already exhausted the meaning of the romantic action.

As for that meaning, Chapman obviously intended *Monsieur D'Olive* to be in one aspect a little treatise on melancholy and its cure, with two case histories. Both Marcellina and St. Anne are victims of melancholy. Marcellina has allowed "opinion," which is "a vaine, light, crude and imperfect judgement of things drawn from the outward senses, and common report, setling and holding it selfe to be good in the imagination," lodged in the "sensible soul," to overcome her "judgment," that is the exercise of her "rational soul." Before Vandome learns of her "entombment" in melancholy, he praises her "eminent judgment," and, confronting her, exclaims:

> Oh shall it e'er be said
> Such perfect judgment should be drown'd in humour?
>
> (II, i, 75-6)

That she is cured by arousing her *passions*, by a "shoeing-horn," as Vandome calls it, to bring her back into the world of opinion—since she says she aims to prevent her husband's shame in his supposedly unworthy courses (V, i, 246-7)—is surely ironic, especially when we remember Chapman's opinion of "Opinion." "Policy" cynically applied is good enough for a woman; for St. Anne's nobler nature nobler methods are employed. He is "passionate," "feeds his passion" upon his grief, is the victim of "hurtful passions," and, since he is a creature of "blood,"

> fram'd for every shade of virtue
> To ravish into true inamorate fire,
>
> (IV, i, 89-90)

he can be cured not only by the example of Vandome's judgment "suppressing" *his* passion of grief for his deceased sister (III, i, 3-6), but by the "diffusion" or diversion of his passions to another object—in this case Eurione. The authority for this remedy is a series of metaphors from the *Secretum*.

Where Bassiolo's "humour," in *The Gentleman Usher*, is connected with the romance only at the level of action, D'Olive participates in the central theme of this play, for when the gulled courtier is presented to the Duke by the exploiters Rodrigue and Mugeron (II, ii) it appears that he has assumed the pose of the contemplative recluse, and his condition is a parody of the "entombment" of his bet-

ters. He has lived "conceal'd," "his mind in his kingdom,"
and the Duke, entering into the joke, reproaches him:

> . . . what makes wise Nature
> Fashion in men these excellent perfections
> Of haughty courage, great wit, wisdom incredi-
> ble . . .
> But that she aims therein at public good;
> And you in duty thereto, of yourself,
> Ought to have made us tender of your parts,
> And not entomb them, tyrant-like, alive.
>
> (II, ii, 52-9)

If we remember Chapman's own pose of withdrawal to the
inward life, and wonder too if that greater melancholic
Robert Burton sitting in his window in Christ Church
read this play, we will enjoy the more D'Olive's reply. He
murmurs gracefully that "the times before" were not so
favourable as they are now, under so sweet and wise a
prince (James I, with irony?), for "wits of hope" such as
himself, and in those days he accordingly "shrunk [his] despised head in [his] poor shell":

> Faith, sir, I had a poor roof or a pent-house
> To shade me from the sun, and three or four tiles
> To shroud me from the rain . . .
> yet saw all
> That pass'd our State's rough sea, both near and
> far . . .
> our great men
> Like to a mass of clouds that now seem like
> An elephant, and straightways like an ox,
> And then a mouse, or like those changeable
> creatures
> That live in the burdello, now in satin,
> Tomorrow next in stammel;
> When I sat all this while in my poor cell,
> Secure of lightning or the sudden thunder,
> Convers'd with the poor Muses, gave a scholar
> Forty or fifty crowns a year to teach me,
> And prate to me about the predicables,
> When, indeed, my thoughts flew a higher pitch
> Than genus and species.
>
> (II, ii, 83-103)

This is the mad offhanded eloquence of a Lord of Misrule,
a "Christmas Lord," as Mugeron calls him later; in this
he is Falstaffian (though diluted by the antics of fashion
in which he first appears), as also in his description of the
"followers" who seek to attach themselves to his embassy,
three hundred "goldfinches" whom he is "ashamed to
train abroad" (III, ii, 149-200). His account of his powers
of eloquence, in a discussion on the lawful use of tobacco
in a commonwealth (II, ii, 164-280), is easily the finest
piece of rhetoric in Chapman's comedy, particularly in its
narrative part (in verse) where D'Olive describes how a
Puritan weaver (here another smile in the direction of the
author of the *Counterblast to Tobacco*?) condemned "the
gentleman's saint and the soldier's idol," calling it "a rag
of popery." The tone and syntax of this speech are modelled on Hotspur's description of the perfumed gentleman
who came to demand the prisoners, but it suffers not at all
for that, and there are even touches of that happy simplicity which we call Shakespearean, and which it is not easy
to imitate, even in a comic context:

> A little fellow, and yet great in spirit,

> I never shall forget him. . . .

> . . . the colour of his beard
> I scarce remember; but purblind he was
> With the Geneva print. . . .

> . . . but I myself . . .
> Brake phlegm some twice or thrice, then shook
> my ears . . .
> Thus I replied. . . .

D'Olive's supposed reply, in prose, is a panegyric in little,
complete with hyperbolic exordium, *narratio* confirmed
by reason, example, and authority (Giovanni Savonarola's
Practica Canonica de Febribus), and ironic peroration. He
carries this off well, so well that he begins to think himself
a model of presence before the great; " 'tis boldness, boldness does the deed in the Court," he counsels (III, 2, 23),
thus anticipating in the Phrygian mode the theme of confidence which Tharsalio, in *The Widow's Tears*, varies in
the Doric, and his catechism of the little pages in "court
accidence" (IV, ii) must have been especially delightful as
acted by the Revels boys.

The golden thread which runs through all D'Olive's immensely fluent discourse is money: he lives in the world
of those who live by their wits, "few trades but live by
wit," he says. Younger brothers turned poets (like Chapman himself), pandars, soldiers, lawyers—he is himself
"the compound of a poet and lawyer"—all the world lives
by wit, which he of all things admires, being also "prodigal
in wasteful expense," and at the end he repents, a fool's
repentance. Tricked into appearing in his "careless cloak,"
he proclaims that he will no longer be a block for his tormenters to whet their dull wits on, accuses them of presenting him with a set of "threadbare, unbuttoned fellows," to be his followers. "A plague on that phrase, raising of fortunes," he cries. The Duke rescues him, and the
last word of the play is "Good Monsieur D'Olive!"

D'Olive asks for justice, without really expecting it; such
justice as the amused favour of his lord can provide, he receives, with the suggestion that he "reserve [himself] till
fitter times." The lord of misrule has had his splendid—
and uncomfortable—hour. Through his absurdity appears
for a moment a genuine protest; as with Malvolio the joke
has gone too far. "There's as much trust in a common
whore as in one of you" has a broader application than the
attack upon those "good wits" Rodrigue and Mugeron,
and D'Olive is more humane, in the end, than Vandome.

But Chapman's romantic comedy oscillates usually between lofty religiosity and amoral intrigue. Unlike Jonson,
he has no vision of a total social harmony disordered by
folly and vice, and one looks in vain for a spokesman for
the social norm. His last and most powerful comedy, *The
Widow's Tears,* is not the production of a grave moralist
viewing the "swift decadence of his age" (Parrott), but an
"amorality," un-measure for un-measure. The source for
the main plot is the story of the Ephesian matron in the
Satyricon, which has attracted more than one dramatist,
and which certainly offers scope for cynicism, particularly
when, as in this version, the soldier who tries the en-
tombed widow's virtue is her supposedly dead husband in
disguise. But the intrigue of jealousy and far-from-

impregnable chastity is contained, so to speak, within the adventure of Tharsalio, the husband Lysander's younger brother, in wooing and winning the "late governor's admired widow" the Countess Eudora, by an exercise of "Confidence." It is Tharsalio who opens and closes the play, and his spirit infuses it throughout.

The scene is not Ephesus (sacred to Diana), but Cyprus, the island of Venus; the inhabitants swear by Venus, and Tharsalio professes himself her "true servant." The Governor is of mean condition, but raised by bribery of courtiers and "Fortune's injudicious hand" to his "high seat of honour" (V, i, 143-6), while the noble house of Lysander and Tharsalio, the "ancient and most virtue-fam'd" Lysandri, is decayed. In the purely comic milieu of *All Fools,* Rinaldo attaches himself to Fortune; entering the tragic scene, Bussy professes Virtue in a world inverted by Fortune; but Tharsalio ($\theta\alpha\rho\sigma$os—boldness, confidence) in his opening soliloquy, mirror in hand to put a face on his enterprises, renounces Fortune in favour of Confidence:

> Thou blind imperfect goddess, that delights
> (Like a deep-reaching statesman) to converse
> Only with fools, jealous of knowing spirits,
> For fear their piercing judgments might discover
> Thy inward weakness and despise thy power,
> Contemn thee for a goddess; thou that lad'st
> Th'unworthy ass with gold, while worth and
>   merit
> Serve thee for naught, weak Fortune, I renounce
> Thy vain dependence, and convert my duty
> And sacrifices of my sweetest thoughts
> To a more noble deity, sole friend to worth,
> And patroness of all good spirits, Confidence;
> She be my guide, and hers the praise of these
> My worthy undertakings.
>
>   (I, i, 1-14)

"Confidence" (really a personification of his own *virtù,* "spirit" he calls it, virility) is his guide at all times; Love and Fortune are, he believes, her servant deities (I, ii, 178), and she certainly protects him, though in no glorious conflict, since her only opponent is the vowed chastity of widows. Where he is sanguine, his brother is of a melancholy temperament (II, iii, 43), hence subject to jealousy, and *his* "confidence," grievously misplaced, is in his wife's fidelity, in which, as Tharsalio savagely notes,

> he hath invested her in all his state, the ancient
> inheritance of our family . . . so as he dead, and
> she matching (as I am resolved she will) with
> some young prodigal, what must ensue, but her
> post-issue beggared, and our house, already
> sinking, buried quick in ruin. [II, iii, 81-6]

His planting the seed of non-confidence in Lysander is not, then, motiveless malignity, the fruit of a free mischief, but grounded upon hard ambition, like all his actions. He is, says M. Jacquot, "un ambitieux sans rêves et sans foi, et par conséquent sans grandeur." Too much of that "Italian air" drunk in his travels, his sister-in-law Cynthia thinks, has poisoned the very essence of his soul and infected his whole nature; not so, he replies, rather "it hath refined my senses, and made me see with clear eyes, and to judge of objects as they truly are, not as they seem" (I, i, 132-43). A Machiavel too—and also a mean little boy, for when he

is turned back in his first onslaught on the countess, and Lysander mocks him, he takes that moment to revenge his wounded self-esteem by undermining his brother's "confidence" in his Cynthia, thought by her husband heir of the moon-goddess's "bright purity" and "all soul." "That's veney for veney," he exults (I, iii, 132).

When we see Tharsalio "with his glass in his hand" and Lysander entering in turn with *his* glass, and the dialogue begins,

> —Morrow, brother! Not ready yet?
> —No, I have somewhat of the brother in me. I
>   dare say your wife is many times ready, and
>   you not up,

We might almost imagine we were witnessing the first scene of a Restoration comedy of the second class, with two elegant gentlemen exchanging a morning bawdy, but Tharsalio is too savage, too *committed,* for that elegant atmosphere, and he takes his first repulse in a more turbulent fashion:

> Hell and the Furies take this vile encounter!
> Who would imagine this Saturnian peacock
> Could be so barbarous to use a spirit
> Of my erection with such low respect?
> 'Fore heaven, it cuts my gall; but I'll dissemble
>   it.
>
>   (I, iii, 9-13)

He succeeds the second time, after braving Eudora's silly Spartan suitor, by a device which the shocked Parrott calls an example of "physical grossness almost unparalleled in Elizabethan comedy," bribing the bawd Arsace (from $\alpha\rho\alpha\rho\iota\sigma\kappa\omega$, to join together, hence the "joiner," though not of Aldgate this time) to tell Eudora ($\epsilon\nu\delta\omega\rho\sigma$ = generous) that he can satisfy nine women in a night, at which news "her blood went and came of errands betwixt her face and her heart," and she murmurs to herself: "Contentment is the end of all worldly beings." ("Contentment is our heaven, and all our deedes / Bend in that circle," says the poet of the "Coronet.") "Here are your widow-vows, sister," he reports in triumph, being a kiss-and-tell man,

> thus are ye all in your pure naturals; certain
> moral disguises of coyness, which the ignorant
> call modesty, ye borrow of art to cover your
> busk-points; which a blunt and resolute encoun-
> ter, taken under a fortunate aspect [he is not al-
> together consistent] easily disarms you of; and
> then, alas, what are you? Poor naked sinners,
> God wot! Weak paper walls thrust down with a
> finger. This is the way on't, boil their appetites
> to a full height of lust; and then take them down
> in the nick. [III, i, 93-100]

Eudora, like the Player Queen in *Hamlet,* has made infinite protestations of fidelity to her late lord, has protested too much (II, iv, 23-35), and so has Cynthia (II, iii, 79-90), all for "the shadow of popular fame"—"The praise I have had, I would continue." The poison poured in Lysander's ear works, and he feigns death on a journey to test his wife; with Act III the Petronius plot begins, the fall of Eudora providing clinching evidence of female frailty. Since it is useless to demand range or subtlety in Chapman's characterizations of women, the tomb episode must be taken as fabliau, dressed though it is in the hyperbolic rhetoric of Lysander's apostrophe to his still-faithful wife as he contemplates the tomb (IV, ii, 1-4), but the tone changes, as it should, with Cynthia's acceptance of the drink, and the ironic reference to "Dido and Aeneas met in the cave" (IV, iii, 85) as the disguised Lysander enters the vault, underlines the burlesque.

A widow's chastity, then, is a mask for the world's "opinion," and "Opinion" is "the blind goddess of fools, foe to the virtuous," as Lysander ironically counsels Cynthia (V, i, 98-100). She, advised of the plot, determines to "sit out one brunt more," showing neither fear nor shame, evincing, in the end, a boldness worthy of Tharsalio. As in a fabliau, the husband is the victim, and Tharsalio, whose tongue leaves a slime upon everything, is gratified.

Now if the play was to prove a thesis, it might have been closed off just after V, iii, 147, when Cynthia leaves Lysander in the tomb, having revealed to him that she knows his deceit, for the betrothal of Lysander's son Hylus to Laodice, Eudora's daughter, made possible by Tharsalio's success and promised in the masque that attends his nuptials (III, ii, 82-114), and the hurried reconciliation of Cynthia and Lysander through the whispered good offices of Eudora, could have been easily joined on—and perhaps were. The text of the late scenes is often corrupt, and Parrott thinks that Chapman simply burked the conclusion, but the fact remains that with the presentation of the supposed culprits Lysander and his accomplice before the Governor, a final twist is given to the play which no conventional dialogue of reconciliation could possibly have produced.

Nothing in Chapman's earlier comedies encourages us to expect such a sophisticated handling of theme as this final scene seems to hint at. A "Vice," a "wooden dagger . . . gilded over with the title of Governor," presides over the comic resolution. A memory of Dogberry's voice went to his making, and perhaps of Angelo's situation: he accuses Lycus of "a most inconvenient murther" and adds, of the culprit, "I had ever a sympathy in my mind against him"; describing his judicial procedure, he says that he "know[s] no persons. . . . If a suitor . . . thrusts a bribe into my hand, I will pocket his bribe, and proceed"; he tells Eudora that her late husband, "no statesman," "left a foul city behind him," full of vices, and announces an era of reform. Drunkenness, lechery, *jealousy* will be whipped out; "fools shall have wealth, and the learned shall live by their wits." (Such, I take it, would be Chapman's view of conditions in his own time and place.) The Governor continues: "I'll have all young widows spaded for marrying again. . . . To conclude, I will cart pride out o' th'town." But in spite of his assumed role of cleanser of the commonwealth, he is put to a non-plus by the complications of a situation he does not understand, "state points" for which he is not yet trained, and he surrenders it to Tharsalio and Eudora. His role is played.

If we wish, we may find in the Governor's pronouncements a criticism of the pride (another name for "Confidence"), jealousy and lechery which animates the business of the play, with the added irony that this criticism comes

from a fool who can preside only over days of mis-rule. Paradox rules here too. Comedy was then, as it is still, the genre of experiment, and in that solvent Chapman examined some of his most cherished opinions and found, finally, no golden precipitate. The requirements of comedy . . . revealed his capacity of seeing both sides of a case, and his incapacity in forming a synthesis of the elements in his divided imagination. (pp. 83-107)

Millar MacLure, in his George Chapman: A Critical Study, *University of Toronto Press, 1966, 241 p.*

Charlotte Spivack　(essay date 1967)

[*Spivack is an American critic and educator whose writings have covered many aspects of early English drama. In the following excerpt from her comprehensive study of Chapman, Spivack explores metaphysical themes in Chapman's poetry, focusing on* Ovid's Banquet of Sense *and* Hero and Leander.]

Algernon Charles Swinburne, anticipating the twentieth-century critics, spoke of Chapman's "sensual metaphysics." In a contemporary essay on the metaphysical tradition, T. S. Eliot recognized in Chapman what he called "a direct sensuous apprehension of thought, or a recreation of thought into feeling, which is exactly what we find in John Donne." Since then George Williamson, in his study of the Donne tradition, has gone even farther by calling Chapman "the first metaphysical poet." Despite these major critical pronouncements, Chapman has not yet been generally acknowledged for his metaphysical poetry, probably because only a few of his poems can be classified as definitely such. These few poems are of such striking quality, however, as to merit their place in any representative collection of such verse, and their interest is enhanced historically by the fact that they precede those of Donne.

Four of Chapman's major poetic works belong either wholly or partially to the metaphysical school, both for their subject matter and their imagery. *Ovid's Banquet of Sense,* **"A Coronet for My Mistress Philosophy,"** the last four sestiads of *Hero and Leander,* and **"A Hymn to Our Savior on the Cross"** are all concerned with the basic theme of transcending the flesh through the fleshly experience, whether the context is secular, as in the first three, or sacred, as in the last. And all four display the metaphysical conceit, ranging in quality from mere ingenuity to genuine poetic inspiration.

Prefixed to the volume called *Ovid's Banquet of Sense* (which also included the "Coronet" of sonnets as well as some translations) in the form of a letter to Mathew Royden, is a virtual manifesto of the metaphysical approach to poetry. In it the poet declares that these verses are addressed to a select audience: "these searching spirits, whom learning hath made noble, and nobilities sacred." They stress intellectual content over beauty, vigor of expression over form, with an emphasis on "energia, that high and hearty invention exprest in most significant and unaffected phrase." And they are admittedly, even intentionally, difficult: "rich Minerals are digd out of the bowels of the earth, not found in the superficies and dust of it."

Superficially, the *Banquet* is erotic, following the current Ovidian mode, and is akin to Shakespeare's *Venus and Adonis*. In keeping with the amatory vogue, it pictures Ovid celebrating a banquet of all the five senses in the garden of his fictitious mistress Corinna. Although sensual, the sequential vision is actually an enactment of the Platonic ladder of love as celebrated by Baldassare Castiglione, the Italian humanist, and others in the neo-Platonic school of thought, whose main spokesman was Marsilio Ficino, the Florentine academician. The sensual feast is never completed: instead, it yields to the strictly spiritual dessert of the "Coronet," in which Corinna becomes Philosophy.

The heavily erotic atmosphere of the *Banquet* is continually disturbed by hard intellectual conceits that lift the poem inevitably from the merely physical level to the metaphysical. At times the language achieves a striking metaphysical metaphor, as when the sun is described: "Then did Cyrrhus fill his eyes with fire, / Whose ardor curld the foreheads of the trees, / And made his greene-loue burne in his desire" (Section 2). But at times it deviates unhappily from a brilliant anticipation of Andrew Marvell at his best to a sorry harbinger of Richard Crashaw at his worst: "Loues feete are in his eyes" (Section 14). When Corinna sings with lute upon her thigh, the language is not at all the melodious Elizabethan line of Thomas Campion, but strong intellectual stuff, complete with a marginal gloss from Aristotle:

> O that as Intellects themselves transite
> To eache intellegible quallitie,
>   My life might passe into my loues conceit,
> Thus to be form'd in words, her tunes, and breath,
>   And with her kysses, sing it selfe to death.
>
> (Section 24)

When Ovid, sated with Corinna's song, goes on to enjoy her "sovereign odors," the language abandons the momentarily soft Spenserian tone in favor of sharp scientific imagery:

> And as a Taper burning in the darke
> (As if it threatned euery watchfull eye
> That viewing burns it,) makes that eye his marke,
> And hurls guilt Darts at it continually.
>
> (Section 66)

After the banquet of the third sense, Ovid requests a kiss in gratification of the fourth—taste. Corinna's reply is startlingly intellectual:

> Pure love (said she) the purest grace pursues,
> And there is contact, not by application
> Of lips or bodies, but of bodies vertues,
> As in our elementale Nation
>   Stars by theyr powers, which are theyr heat and light
> Do heavenly works, and that which hath probation
>   By vertuall contact hath the noblest plight,
> Both for the lasting and affinitie

It hath with naturall diuinitie.

(Section 92)

But in spite of the coldly Aristotelian prologue, the "Ambrosian kisse" makes him "swoune" with "syrrop to his taste." Then the imagery leaps from syrup to science again:

> And as a Pible cast into a Spring,
> Wee see a sort of trembling cirkles rise,
> One forming other in theyr issuing
> Till over all the Fount they circulize,
>   So this perpetuall-motion-making kisse,
> Is propagate through all my faculties,
>   And makes my breast an endlesse Fount of blisse.
>
> (Section 99)

Emboldened with the kiss, Ovid then makes a bid for complete gratification of feeling. His philosophical justification of the request recalls "The Ecstasie" of Donne and states the very essence of that poem: "Mindes taint no more with bodies touch or tyre, / Then bodies nourish with the mindes desire" (Section 103). But the conclusion of the poem is abrupt and ambiguous. Ovid has just touched Corinna's side, making "her start like sparckles from a fire," when he is interrupted by "the view of other dames." Unlike the reader, who at this point feels only frustration, Ovid somehow becomes so euphoric over this unsensational climax that this prim titillation has qualified him to write the *Art of Love*.

The Platonic significance of the unfinished banquet is clear: sensual gratification is a necessary stepping stone to loftier, intellectual love: "But that a fleshlie engine must unfold / A spirituall notion; birth from Princes sprung / Peasants must nurse, free vertue wait on gold" (Section 111). The Platonic ladder is not, however, completed in *Ovid's Banquet* but the ascent must be completed: "My life that in my flesh a Chaos is / Should to a Golden worlde be thus dygested" (Section 25).

The sequence of ten linked sonnets called **"A Coronet for My Mistress Philosophy"** that follows, rejects the eroticism of the *Banquet* and transcends its "sensual emperie." The interlinking form of the group may have influenced that of Donne's *Coronet of Divine Sonnets*, but it is the striking use of the conceit which establishes this series of poems squarely in the metaphysical tradition. The opening sonnet introduces the subject with such a conceit: "Muses that sing loues sensuall Emperie, / And louers kindling your enraged fires / At *Cupids* bonfires burning in the eye . . . " Then Chapman develops the theme of dualism:

> Blowe with the emptie breath of vaine desires,
> You that prefer the painted Cabinet
>   Before the welthy Iewels it doth store yee,
>   That all your ioyes in dying figures set,
>   And staine the living substance of your glory.
> Abiure those ioyes, abhor their memory,
>   And let my love the honord subiect be
>   Of love, and honors compleate historie;
>   Your eyes were neuer yet, let in to see
> The maiestie and riches of the minde,
> But dwell in darknes; for your God is blinde.

Continuing the theme, the second sonnet focuses first on the conflict and then on the resolution of the struggle between flesh and spirit. The violent torments of sensual love "eate your entrails out with exstasies" and "beate your soules in peeces with a pant," but Philosophy is a benevolent mistress: "But my love is the cordiall of soules, / Teaching by passion what perfection is." The simple statement and homely image echo George Herbert.

Love of Philosophy gives "spirit to flesh" and "soule to spirit." Her beauty is absolute: "Her minde (the beame of God) drawes in the fires / Of her chast eyes, from all earths tempting fewell." The poet deems, therefore, that Philosophy shall become his Muse as well as his mistress, and the cycle ends with a sonnet in praise of the tragic theater of Athens and Rome, which were "the Crownes, and not the base empayre."

Chapman's next contribution to metaphysical poetry was his continuation of Marlowe's *Hero and Leander.* The reader of this entire narrative poem is always struck by the difference in tone between Marlowe's opening two sestiads and Chapman's concluding four. And Chapman frequently, although quite unfairly, suffers in the inevitable comparison simply because Marlowe has set the initial tone with his fine "golden" lyricism—liquid, sensuous, and exquisite. What Chapman is doing is obviously very different, yet it is also first-rate poetry. C. S. Lewis regarded these four sestiads as "the work that I was born to do" for the poet, who had himself applied these words to the mission of his Homeric translation.

Chapman's continuation is a tribute to his friendship with Marlowe, with whom he had drunk from the fountain of the Muses, as he tells us. Yet he was well aware that his draft was headier stuff—"more harsh (at least more hard) more graue and hie"—and he proclaimed the metaphysical springs of his own inspiration:

> Then thou most strangely-intellectual fire,
> That proper to my soule hast power t'inspire
> Her burning faculties, and with the wings
> Of thy unspheared flame visitst the springs
> Of spirits immortall; Now, (as swift as Time
> Doth follow Motion) finde th'eternall Clime
> Of his free soule, whose living subject stood
> Up to the chin in the Pyerean flood,
> And drunke to me halfe this Musean storie,
> Inscribing it to deathles Memorie:
> Confer with it, and make my pledge as deepe,
> That neithers draught be consecrate to sleepe.
> (ll. 183-94)

The moral emphasis of Chapman's continuation is as different as is the language. Whereas Marlowe was concerned mainly with evocation of the lovers' feelings and exaltation of their beauty and their passions, Chapman is, characteristically, concerned with consequences. He does not castigate Leander's sensuality as such but his failure to achieve its spiritualization. Indeed, Leander's metamorphosis was into flesh:

> So to all objects that in compasse came
> Of any sence he had; his sences flame
> Flowd from his parts, with force so virtuall,
> It fir'd with sence things meere insensuall.
> (ll. 87-90)

Leander failed to formalize his physical relationship through proper ritual; he did not sacramentalize the flesh in marriage. He is made aware of this flaw by the goddess Ceremonie—playing rather the same role as Spenser's Concord—who descends to warn the enamored young man of the need to perform the rites of sanctification.

Meanwhile, when Chapman analyzes the conflict in Hero's mind and the painful contradiction between her inward consciousness of guilt and her outward appearance of innocence, he achieves some of his best poetry. Sometimes he chooses a scientific conceit:

> For as a glasse is an inanimate eie,
> And outward formes imbraceth inwardlie:
> So is the eye an animate glasse that showes
> In-formes without us.
> (ll. 235-38)

Sometimes he relies on Classic simplicity and artful sound: "Feare fils the chamber, darknes decks the Bride" (l. 154). The third sestiad ends with an echo of Donne: "Rich, fruitfull loue, that doubling selfe estates / Elixir-like contracts, though separates" (ll. 416-17).

Chapman delays the tragic narrative in the fourth sestiad with an allegorical digression: Venus creates the monster Dissimulation (Eronusis) to "wreak her rites abuses." He further prolongs the story by mythically extending the day in the fifth sestiad, where he recounts another wedding. The artificial interruption of the action is more than justified, however, by the quality of the exquisite Epithalamion Teratos. This lyrical gem is written by a Chapman who is neither the metaphysical poet nor the allegorist nor the satirist but the rare Elizabethan lyricist. The metaphysical poet intrudes only once: "Day is abstracted here, / And varied in a triple sphere" (ll. 451-52). The rest of the poem is Edmund Spenser reborn.

Night finally arrives in the sixth sestiad. As Leander plunges to his fateful swim, the doomed lover calls in vain on Neptune who "for haste his forehead hit / Gainst heauens hard Christall" (ll. 197-98). But the tragic death of the lovers does not separate them for long. The poem ends with an Ovidian metamorphosis, as the kind old god of the sea transforms their bodies into "two sweet birds surnam'd th'Athcanthides" (l. 276).

The continuation of *Hero and Leander,* along with *Ovid's Banquet of Sense* and **"A Coronet For His Mistress Philosophy,"** are the major secular manifestations of Chapman's metaphysical style. His only substantial example of sacred metaphysical verse is his **"Hymn to the Savior on the Cross,"** itself the only original poem in a volume of translations from Petrarch and Virgil. F. L. Schoell long ago noted its affinity with Donne's religious verse, as Eliot later noted the similarity in the secular verse of the two poets. Schoell praised Chapman as "metaphysicien et grave dispensateur de 'theological wit.' " To the contemporary reader the poem is also interesting for its prefiguration of Gerard Manly Hopkins' metaphysical vein. Two of Chapman's homely metaphors in this sincere hymn suggest Hopkins: "All Churches powres, thy writ word doth controule; / And mixt it with the fabulous Alchoran,

/ A man might boult it out, as floure from branne" (ll. 60-62). And the striking physiological metaphor elaborated in these lines:

> All glorie, gratitude, and all auaile,
> Be giuen thy all-deseruing agonie;
> Whose vineger thou Nectar mak'st in me,
> Whose goodnesse freely all my ill turnes good:
> Since thou being crusht, & strained throgh flesh
>   & blood:
> Each nerue and artire needs must tast of thee.
>
>   (ll. 270-75)

The entire poem is not metaphysical, however; and the unevenness of its diction illustrates the difficulty in categorizing Chapman. Written in heroic couplets, as are many of his verses, it also serves to illustrate the second poet named George Chapman, the neo-Classic satirist.

> So in the Church, when controuersie fals,
> It marres her musicke, shakes her batterd wals,
> Grates tender consciences, and weakens faith;
> The bread of life taints, & makes worke for
>   Death;
> Darkens truths light, with her perplext
>   Abysmes,
> And dustlike grinds men into sects and
>   schismes.
>
>   (ll. 81-86)

The final couplet anticipates the age of Dryden and Pope. (pp. 37-44)

> *Charlotte Spivack, in her* George Chapman, *Twayne Publishers, Inc., 1967, 180 p.*

Raymond B. Waddington   (essay date 1974)

[*Waddington is an American critic and educator who has written several studies of English Renaissance poetry, including* The Mind's Empire: Myth and Form in George Chapman's Narrative Poems *(1974). In the following excerpt from that work, Waddington compares Chapman's use of poetic persona and his understanding of the role of the poet with that of John Donne.*]

Jonson once thought "that Done himself for not being understood would perish." He could not have anticipated the phenomenon of twentieth-century taste that for some three decades would elevate Donne's poetry to an enormous popularity, in large part because of its difficulty. One of the side effects of this now-receded Donne boom was to lend a satellite reputation to George Chapman, Donne's older contemporary, who has been described as "perhaps the most complex author of his age." In a famous ricocheting definition T. S. Eliot pronounced [in "The Metaphysical Poets"], "In Chapman especially there is a direct sensuous apprehension of thought, or a recreation of thought into feeling, which is exactly what we find in Donne." Eliot's imprimatur has proved a mixed blessing. While the metaphysical aura has caused Chapman to be read more widely than at any time since the enthusiastic appreciation of the Romantics, it also established a mental set which ensured that much of the reading was a misreading.

Only since Donne's greater light has faded to the point that "now his flasks / Send forth light squibs, no constant

rayes," has it been possible to see that Chapman belongs to an entirely different poetic constellation. The shift in attitude can be measured by a pair of comprehensive Chapman studies: in 1951 Jean Jacquot found it necessary to devote half a dozen pages to the question of "Chapman et Donne"; fifteen years later Donne all but vanishes from the index to Millar MacLure's book [*George Chapman: A Critical Study,* 1966] as MacLure, with a regretful bow to Eliot, concludes that Chapman's verse "is not like anything we have come to understand as 'metaphysical' poetry." Nevertheless, old habits of thought change slowly. One may assent intellectually to the proposition that "The King is dead," while still finding it very difficult to give up lifelong royalist attitudes. We have ceased to find the metaphysical label very pertinent or illuminating for Chapman's poetry; yet, because the preoccupation with style generated by Eliot so drastically narrowed our perception of the poetry, the mental set remains in force, even though we have declared the central premise invalid.

As a case in point, consider a recent article by Charles K. Cannon ["Chapman on the Unity of Style and Meaning," *Journal of English and Germanic Philology,* 68 (1969): 245-64.], which seems representative in its wrongness. According to Cannon, Chapman's "major contribution to poetic theory in the English Renaissance" was the recognition that "sense is immanent in sound; meaning begets the shape of a poem's language and vice versa." Since he can adduce no evidence that Chapman intended to contribute anything of the sort, Cannon is forced to denigrate and explain away Chapman's own critical comments. By focusing upon a post-Renaissance conception of style Cannon understandably fails to perceive any larger poetic structure that Chapman himself might recognize. The **"Hymnvs in Noctem"** is like "a surrealist painting" with symphonic "movements" and "crescendoes," but also manages to suggest "an Hegelian dialectical progression." For Cannon, describing Chapman's "alogical progression through association," Rosemond Tuve might never have lived. Rejecting the idea of Chapman as a metaphysical, Cannon rather pretentiously invokes Joseph Frank's concept of "Spatial Form in Modern Literature" to arrive at the conclusion: "The poet can only express this dark matter in a dark style. Style and meaning become aspects of a unity." By this reading not only is Chapman not a metaphysical, he becomes an anachronistic modern who eschews the rhetoric and logic to which he gives lip service. Ironically, the aesthetic which Frank abstracted from the creative works of Eliot, Pound, Joyce, and Djuna Barnes here substitutes for Eliot's own critical formulation. One brand of twenties impressionism simply replaces another.

In this [essay] I wish to disinter the Donne comparison, but only to prevent the spirit from walking any further. By extending the comparison beyond the largely accidental and superficial stylistic resemblances, I want to emphasize how thoroughly different the two poets are; and, by so doing, to better establish Chapman's own poetic identity. If Chapman can be twinned with any one of his contemporaries, a far better case could be made for Edmund Spenser than for John Donne.

Let us begin with the celebrated obscurity. Donne's obscurity, to summarize the obvious, is the cumulative result of syntactic distortion, logical density, ellipsis and compression, learned allusions, farfetched conceits, harshness in diction and metrics. The style largely derives from satiric tradition, in which such writings are supposed to be rough, "dark," and displeasing; and it receives personal reinforcement from Donne's anxiety not to be mistaken for a professional poet, for someone who sweats to make his verse ingratiating. Donne apparently began his career writing satiric epigrams and verse satires, and the training stuck when he graduated to other kinds of poetry. Rosemond Tuve observed [in *Elizabethan and Metaphysical Imagery,* 1947] that "Donne's 'sonnets' and elegies are many of them virtually short satires, combining the conventions of philosophical dialectic (*genus humile*) with the *energia* and diminishing figures of rhetoric's demonstrative 'dispraise,' and both with the conventionally harsh tone of satire."

In analyzing the imagery of *Hero and Leander,* Tuve isolated two reasons for Chapman's obscurity—his fondness for "introducing an unexpected logical complication into an image" and his frequent assumption of technical learning on the reader's part. He also uses heavily figures of substitution (such as periphrasis and antonomasia); makes a single image carry multiple rhetorical functions; tends to compress rather than amplify or reiterate; and organizes frequently by contraries, antitheses, and paradox. Most of these characteristics could be associated with Donne as easily as with Chapman. Language, therefore, serves as a more clearly differentiating tool. Whereas Donne's diction has a persistent tendency toward "lowness," the satirist's deflating, undercutting "realistic" vision, Chapman's "idealism" nudges his diction in the opposite direction, toward inflation or grandiloquence, the "full and haightned stile" praised by Webster.

But the distance between the two poets becomes fully apparent when we define the ends which the stylistic obscurity is meant to serve, its function as one particular technique in a larger poetic mode. Chapman predominantly wrote allegorical poetry; Donne did not. Consequently Chapman employed "allegorical rhetoric" or—to borrow Edgar Wind's more graceful phrase—"the language of mysteries." Michael Murrin has very helpfully distinguished the differing rhetorical situations presupposed by allegorical and oratorical poets:

> The allegorical poet served the truth which he had received under inspiration, and this truth exercised the primary operative control over his rhetoric. He did not really cater to his audience but tried to preserve his truth intact and communicate it to those capable of understanding it. This requirement forced him to deal with two different audiences: the many who could never accept his revelation and the few who could. He had, therefore, simultaneously to reveal and not to reveal his truth, and for this double purpose he cloaked his truth in the veils of allegory. The many reacted with pleasure to his symbolic tales, and the few knew how to interpret them. [*The Veil of Allegory: Some Notes toward a Theory of Allegorical Rhetoric in the English Renaissance,* (1969)]

Murrin argues that the orator's concern with an immediate audience dictates that he will derive his arguments from the popular beliefs of the audience and strive for clarity of presentation. The allegorist, in contrast, begins with an absolute truth, which creates a presentational dilemma; while he must protect his truth from the unworthy multitude by concealing it, he must conceal in such a way as to reveal it to the few prepared to understand and accept. Accordingly, whereas the orator aims at lucidity of style, the allegorist darkens his by recourse to any one of several accepted devices—riddle, enigma, parable, fable, myth, irony, ambiguity.

The mode of Donne's poetry falls somewhere between the two extremes. His deliberate difficulty and his disdain for the general audience parallel the allegorist's desire to save his message for the few initiates. But Donne's whole manner of truth-telling smacks more of shared commonplaces than of wisdom handed down from above; and a consideration of the Donne circle leads A. Alvarez to believe that the poems were not obscure to its members: "They had too much in common, they used the same shorthand." Donne, it would seem, assumes the oratorical situation but radically narrows his audience to a select coterie.

Consistent with his professed refusal to take poetry seriously, Donne left us no poetics, critical commentaries, or even conversations with a Drummond. With the exception of the forced *Ivstification of Andromeda Liberata,* Chapman's only critical remarks are scattered in the prefaces, dedications, epistles, and commendations which he wrote for specific occasions over the course of his career. The high degree of consistency in theory and attitude permits us to read these serial proclamations as a coherent and fully articulated statement of a poetics. He separates his audience into the many and the few, always expressing contempt for the former and admiration for the latter: "I rest as resolute as *Seneca,* satisfying my selfe if but a few, if one, or if none like it." "The prophane multitude I hate, & onlie consecrate my strange Poems to these serching spirits, whom learning hath made noble, and nobilitie sacred" (*Poems*). Chapman states the obvious with admirable succinctness in an epistle "To the Understander": "You are not every bodie." The elite to whom he looks for understanding are elevated to that position by learning and nobility, with the emphasis on the former; the vulgar, "the base, ignoble, barbarous, giddie multitude" (*Poems*), are characterized by ignorance and passion, addicted to rumor and opinion rather than to learning and judgment. The undertone of satisfaction in Chapman's defense of *Andromeda Liberata* arises not merely from an Elizabethan enjoyment of a good quarrel but from the pleasure, after a twenty-year career, of having been proved *right*—the vulgar rabble by maliciously misinterpreting his poem have demonstrated what he believed all along, that they are incapable of comprehending an allegory.

In his justification Chapman advances the argument, quoting Plato, that poetry inherently is ambiguous: "*Est enim ipsa Natura vniuersa Poesis aenigmatum plena, nec quiuis eam dignoscit.*" The context, however, makes it certain that he is speaking of allegorical or mythological poetry, the "misteries and allegoricall fictions of *Poesie.*" At various times Chapman endorses all the standard justifications for poetic obscurity. He wishes to keep the "base and prophane *Vulgare*" from debasing his truth: "Poesie is the flower of the Sunne, & disdains to open to the eye of a candle. So kings hide their treasures & counsels from the vulgar, *ne euilescant.*" The obscurity exists only in the mind of the reader who is incapable of understanding the truth: "it may perhaps seeme darke to ranke riders or readers that have no more soules than burbolts: but to your comprehension and in it selfe I knew it is not." And, finally, the obscurity enhances the value of the truth by creating obstacles to be overcome by the understanding: "rich Minerals are digd out of the bowels of the earth not found in the superficies and dust of it" (*Poems*). In his commitment to allegorical obscurity, Chapman seems unusually acute in grasping implications of the stylistic opposition to the oratorical mode which this commitment creates. Rather than perspicuity or clarity, which is the stylistic ideal of a Jonson, Chapman maintains "That, *Enargia,* or cleerenes of representation, requird in absolute Poems is not the perspicuous deliuery of a lowe inuention; but high, and harty inuention exprest in most significant, and vnaffected phrase" (*Poems*). He associates the attack upon **Andromeda Liberata** with Demosthenes' slur upon the Delphic Oracle (*Poems*); and he believes that the oratorical standard of audience-oriented poetry runs counter to the true nature of poetry:

> But that Poesie should be as peruiall as Oratorie,
> and plainnes her speciall ornament, were the
> plaine way to barbarisme: and to make the Asse
> runne proude of his eares; to take away strength
> from Lyons, and giue Cammels hornes. [*Poems*]

In fact, if we use Murrin's description as a standard, Chapman's poetics read like a program illustration to the theory of allegorical poetry. It begins and ends with truth. "Nor is this all-comprising *Poesie,* phantastique, or meere fictiue; but the most material, and doctrinall illations of *Truth*" (*Poems*):

> Yet euer held in high Reuerence and Aucthority; as supposed to conceale, within the vtter barke (as their Eternities approue) some sappe of hidden Truth: As either some dimme and obscure prints of diuinity, and the sacred history; Or the grounds of naturall, or rules of morall Philosophie, for the recommending of some vertue, or curing some vice in generall. [*Poems*]

Because Poetry is an epiphany of Truth, Chapman persistently associates her with learning and wisdom; "*Philosophy* retirde to darkest caues / She can discouer" (*Poems*). Although poetry can fulfill any number of particular instructional or doctrinal purposes, the simplest and most accurate description of its function would be that it disseminates the exact pattern or form of truth:

> And, as in a spring,
> The plyant water, mou'd with any thing
> Let fall into it, puts her motion out
> In perfect circles, that moue round about
> The gentle fountaine, one another, raising:
> So Truth, and Poesie worke; so Poesie blazing,
> All subiects falne in her exhaustlesse fount,
> Works most exactly; makes a true account

> Of all things to her high discharges giuen,
> Till all be circular, and round as heauen.
>
> [*Poems*]

The poet receives this truth by inspiration, a *"Diuinus furor"* which Chapman describes as "a perfection directly infused from God" (*Poems,* p. 408). As Chapman explains the process in **The Teares of Peace,** by exacting mental preparation and arduous study the poet readies himself for the silent moment of spiritual illumination which he likens to the Hermetic *gnosis* and to Pythagoras's inner perception of the music of the spheres. Paradoxically, the poet's job is to transform this silent transfiguration into human speech in order to ravish other men with the desire for this truth. Poetry "Erect[s] him past his human Period / And heighten[s] his transition into God" (*Poems,* p. 306). Because of this platonized conception of "diuine infusion," Chapman associates himself with the biblical prophets, who are for him, as was Moses for Pico della Mirandola, poets.

Although Franck L. Scheoll long ago proved Chapman's large and direct indebtedness to the writings of Marsilio Ficino, [in *Études sur l'Humanisme continental en Angleterre a la fin de la Renaissance,* 1926], it remained for Jacquot to demonstrate the pattern to the pieces, the centrality and consistency of Renaissance platonism to Chapman's thought and his poetics. Ficino's massive effort to prove the philosophic harmony of Plato and Christ had, as well, aesthetic and stylistic consequences that were perhaps most explicitly stated by Pico in the *Heptaplus,* his commentary upon the book of Genesis. According to Edgar Wind [*Pagan Mysteries of the Renaissance,* 1958], the "hidden mysteries" concept was disseminated mainly from Plato's fanciful notion that a true philosopher is like one who has undergone a religious initiation and passed beyond the level comprehended by the vulgar populace. Thus inspired by Plato and later systematized by Plotinus, a figurative use of religious terminology and imagery became a staple of philosophic discourse. Armed with this historical precedent, the Renaissance platonists—particularly the Florentine group and their followers—as a matter of course figured their profound truths in poetic myths which were deliberately expressed in exotic styles. We should not be surprised that, when they turned to the Bible, they read with the same vision.

Pico tells us that "Plato himself concealed his doctrines beneath coverings of allegory, veils of myth, mathematical images, and unintelligible signs of fugitive meaning." But Plato was only a "Moses Atticus." Pico believes that Christ chose to use the parable because it is an exclusive mode of discourse: "he proclaimed [the Gospel] to the crowd in parables; and separately, to the few disciples who were permitted to understand the mysteries of the kingdom of heaven openly and without figures. He did not even reveal everything to those few, since they were not fit for everything. . . ." If Plato was an Attic Moses, the converse holds true. Moses was an Hebraic Plato, who learned the secrets of the Egyptians and who wrote Genesis according to the pattern of creation he learned on Sinai, thereby secretly imparting to skilled readers, like Pico, the mysteries of all things. Pico, of course, modeled his own style of writing, described by Wind as "contrived" and "conceited," to conform to the theory: "In attempting to mark the disparity between verbal instrument and mystical object, Pico made his own language sound at once provocative and evasive, as if to veil were implicitly to reveal the sacred fire in an abundance of dense and acrid smoke." The persona selected to speak this "language of mysteries" will be the very antithesis of the orator with his stance of apparent openness and candor. The role assumed by the allegorical rhetor or poet partakes of the biblical prophet, the wise man, the oracle, but usually it goes beyond this to the hierophant and mystagogue. Henry Reynolds speaks of how

> those old wise *AEgyptian* Priests beganne to search out the Misteries of Nature (which was at first the whole worlds only diuinity), they deuized, to the end to retaine among themselves what they had found, lest it should be abused and vilefied by being deliuered to the vulgar, certaine markes they called *Hieroglyphicks* or sacred grauings. And more then thus they deliuered little; or what euer it was, yet alwaies *dissimulanter,* and in Enigma's and mysticall riddles, as their following disciples also did. And this prouizo of theirs those Images of *Sphynx* they placed before all their Temples did insinuate, and which should by riddles and enigmaticall knotts be kept inuiolate from the prophane Multitude. [*Critical Essays of the Seventeenth Century*]

The image of the sphinx before the temple is not a bad one for figuring the rhetorical situation of the allegorical poet—always forbidding, yet tantalizing enough to entice the potential Oedipus who just may solve the meaning of his riddle.

In the poems where Chapman most directly addresses himself to issues of poetic and religious inspiration, **The Shadow of Night** and **The Teares of Peace,** he adapts personae which both Pico and Reynolds would have recognized as appropriate for the stance of the platonic mystagogue. With the first he wraps himself in the mythology of Orpheus, *priscus theologus* as well as *poeticus,* and in the second he suggests an identification with a peculiarly Renaissance Hercules, not the strong man but the wise man, the god of eloquence whom he conflates with Hermes Trismegistus. Wind has remarked the elements of irony and mockery present in Plato's original identification of the philosopher with the heirophant of the mystery cults; and, although the humor was largely missed by the platonic exegetes of the Renaissance, playfulness at least fitfully reappeared in the spirit of *serio ludere.* But the mysteries of which Chapman is custodian permit no such lightness. To approach poetic "skill" with understanding requires an initiation of the spirit: "Now what a supererogation in wit this is, to thinke skil so mightilie pierst with their loues, that she should prostitutely shew them her secrets, when she will scarcely be lookt vpon by others but with inuocation, fasting, watching; yea not without hauing drops of their soules like an heauenly familiar" (**Poems**). And woe betide the reader who approaches Homer with unlaundered mind:

> *Lest with foule hands you touch these holy Rites;*
> *And with preiudicacies too prophane,*

> *Passe Homer, in your other Poets sleights;*
> *Wash here. In this Porch to his numerous*
>   *Phane.*
> *Heare ancient Oracles speake, and tell you whom*
>   *You haue to censure.*

>   [**Poems**]

The entire role of vatic poet and the religious analogy of the inspired prophet/priest who simultaneously protects his sacred trust from the many and imparts it to the fit few, has significant ramifications for the question of poetic form. Put very simply, when the afflatus descends upon the prophet, he loses his human identity, becoming instrumental to the voice of God, no more than a conveyance to the Word which transiently inhabits him. When Ananias questioned Saul's worthiness, the Lord replied, "Go thy way: for his is a chosen vessel unto me" (Acts 9:15); and the Lord touched the mouth of Jeremiah telling him "Behold, I have put my words in thy mouth" (Jer. 1:9). Saul and Jeremiah have far more in common as prophets than they had as private men; they assume a conventionalized role that prepares the audience to expect a certain kind of message, but the message always takes priority in interest over the particular vessel chosen as mouthpiece. The Lord instructed Jeremiah to "speak . . . all the words that I command thee to speak unto them; diminish not a word" (Jer. 26:2). But, just as the personality of the appointed individual is effaced by the conventional figure of the prophet, so that containing vessel inescapably shapes the words which he speaks. Prophetic utterance assumes standard forms which are themselves a reflex of the prophetic persona. Presumably Jeremiah tried to heed very strictly the Lord's admonition to "diminish not a word"; ironically, though, even people who do not have the remotest idea of what Jeremiah prophesied are aware that he gave his name to a conventional literary structure, the jeremiad. To borrow the words of a tiresome latter-day prophet, here the medium really is the message.

What does this mean for the prophetic poet or the allegorical poet? First, I would suggest, it means that for them, as for the public oratorical poet, the question of genre occupies a position of fundamental importance. The selection of a poetic genre as the vessel for his word immediately accomplishes two things for the poet: it supplies him with a formal organizational principle for his matter; and it guarantees at least a generally appropriate level of response from his audience. The concept of poetic genres arises from a vision which orders human experience in a hierarchy. Public poets, whether political or religious, tend to work in the upper range of the hierarchy. Once again the difference between Donne and Chapman may be instructive.

The mode of Donne's poetry is primarily private, aimed at a small audience of intimates or particular individuals; his stylistic level gravitates to the low, for satiric or instructional purposes, and the middle, the vehicle for the familiar epistle. In consequence genre means relatively little to Donne; and with the bulk of his verse ascertaining the correct generic provenance appears to be a less valuable starting point than it is with most Renaissance poets. As Donald Guss observes [*John Donne, Petrarchist,* 1966], "In general, Donne seems to write as courtier rather than *vates,* and to be simply careless of genre." When he does not ignore genre, frequently he stands it on its head, parodies it, or distorts it beyond recognition. There are no sonnets in his *Songs and Sonets.* As innumerable readers have attested, Donne's remarkable simulation of a direct, colloquial, speaking voice overpowers other elements and tends to level out formal distinctions in the poems, which is merely another way of saying that genre does not hold a large place in his poetic strategy. Trying his hand at the epithalamion, the most relentlessly conventional of poetic forms, Donne produced two insipid specimens with which he seems uncomfortable; only by burlesquing the form in the *Epithalamion Made at Lincolnes Inne* was he able to put his usual stamp of identity upon it. Any good poet, however, must be a Gulliver whom the ropes of Lilliputian critics cannot successfully immobilize. The two *Anniversaries* are the conspicuous exception to his antigeneric bent—formal, allegorical, elevated, vatic. The persona of the first is the Mosaic lawgiver (457-66); of the second, a prophet of grace: "Thou art the Proclamation; and I ame / The Trumpet, at whose voice the people came."

Chapman's very strong preoccupation with genre may be most noticeable in his dramatic works; particularly in comedy he seemed to try ceaseless modulations of form to give an audience just the desired perspective upon the story material. We have from him a commedia dell'arte parody of Marlowe, possibly the first humors comedy, a "New" comedy, tragicomedy, satiric comedy, attempts to blend serious platonic love with farce. They are far from uniformly successful; but they evidence a very up-to-date knowledge of comedic theory and practice, both in London and on the continent, and, possibly because comedy was a less serious genre to Chapman, a willingness to venture an almost avant-garde experimentalism. In his nondramatic verse—with a single and deliberate exception, **Ovids Banquet of Sence**—Chapman published nothing that did not have a distinct generic identity, permitting his audience at once to recognize the general type of a poem and from there to ascertain its particular properties. Often a generic precisian, he gives us not plain funeral elegies, but epicedes, epitaphs, and anniversaries.

Whereas Donne's "voice" is primarily confined to poetry appropriate to the middle and low styles, Chapman descends to the middle style in his dedicatory epistles and sonnets, normally inhabiting the top register of epic and heroic poem, religious hymn, public ceremony. He left no pastoral, disclaimed being a satirist (**Poems**), and his invective against Ben Jonson was never published. Chapman works consciously in a public mode. The meditative voice did not affect him; "Goodfriday, 1613. Riding Westward" can cast little light on **"A Hymne to our Sauiour."** His religious poems are private only in the sense that the actions of the hierophant at the altar are, while fully displayed, inscrutable and isolated. Chapman's most private poems are his translations of Petrarch's *Penitential Psalms,* but even these are exercises in a long tradition. His only love poems assume the viewpoint of society rather than of a participant. Genre and voice in this way interact to establish the public, ceremonial character of most of the verse.

Where necessary, conventional genres are tailored to suit the special requirements of the hierophant's role. In *The Teares of Peace* the medieval dream-vision form oddly subsumes the revelation of Pimander to Hermes Trismegistus; and the two hymns which comprise *The Shadow of Night* are not merely religious but Orphic. Henry Reynolds said, paraphrasing Pico's judgment on the *Orphic Hymns:*

> There is nothing of greater efficacy then the hymnes of *Orpheus* in naturall Magick, if the fitting musick, intention of the minde, and other circumstances which are knowne to the wise, bee considered and applyed. And againe,—*that they are no lesse power in naturall magick,* or to the vnderstanding thereof, *then the Psalmes of Dauid* are in the *Caball,* or to vnderstand the *Cabalistick* Science by. [*Critical Essays*]

As we shall see, Chapman exploits fitting music, intention, and "other circumstances" to invest his hymns fully with the aura of Orphic magic.

To complete the running comparison: by and large Donne's poetry is linear, dramatic, a mimesis of particular psychological states. Chapman's poetry is iconic, narrative, and presents universals, as he says himself, *"non Socratem sed Hominem"* (**Poems**). Chapman's true poetic peers are Spenser and Milton, both vatic, public, ceremonious poets as conscious of form and genre as Chapman. The pernicious consequence of the Eliot-Donne-metaphysical syndrome has been the tendency to look upon Chapman primarily as a stylist. The microscopy of style analysis conditioned Chapman's critics not to expect any large organizational principles, such as mode, genre, structure, so they have seldom noticed any. The very title of Havelock Ellis' essay, *George Chapman; With Illustrative Passages* (1934), proclaims a critical assumption; one can detach and appreciate the purple passages without being too concerned about the poems as wholes. The "anthology of passages" approach even has its survivals with MacLure, who is wont to praise a poem as being "not without an occasional felicity." The grounds underlying such judgments have been best articulated by Heninger:

> Chapman's greatest asset was a sensitivity to words comparable to Marlowe's, and he retained much of the energetic forcefulness that enlivens the best Elizabethan poetry. . . . Chapman's inattention to form, in both his poems and plays, is no doubt the major defect that accounts for his failure to please succeeding generations. His most readable works are the translations of Homer and Hesiod, where the form was already provided and he needed to supply only words. Chapman lacked the ability to order his materials into well-organized entities—but throughout his works . . . there are isolated passages of surprising beauty and power. [*A Handbook of Renaissance Meteorology with Particular Reference to Elizabethan and Jacobean Literature,* 1960]

Heninger concludes:

> Chapman never learned to arrange his images so that the completed poem has a well-ordered structure. As a rule, his compositions are long

and formless . . . we might wish that he had learned structural discipline for his poems.

I have no dispute with Heninger's acute discussion of imagery; but the partiality of his examination leads, I believe, to mistaken conclusions about the poems as wholes. On the contrary, Chapman was very keenly attentive to the larger elements of form, structure, overall organization; and in his best works, . . . his imaginativeness and control of them allow him to fashion poems of a high order. Indeed, one could maintain that the frequent unevenness of surface texture or style results from a sometimes too exclusive devotion to form in the larger sense.

We have been considering outer form, i.e., conventional form or genre, as an extension of the persona adopted by the poet. The form of prophetic utterance in this way is as revelatory as the actual content, which of course we know from the Delphic oracles. Milton also was highly conscious of the tradition that we have described. While at school he delivered a speech on Pythagoras, who "followed the example of the poets—or, what is almost the same thing, of the divine oracles—by which no sacred and arcane mystery is ever revealed to vulgar ears without being somehow wrapped up and veiled." Later Milton finely epitomized the desired harmony of form between speaker and speech by remarking that a poet "ought himself to be a true poem." Such an intimate adjustment of the two will not often be achieved by outer form alone, since genre can do no more than establish a basic frame of reference—what kind of thing it is, how it is like other examples.

Chapman works to achieve this refinement by turning to an inner form, shaping the poem to a directly symbolic purpose. *A Hymne to Hymen,* for instance, opens and closes with the same couplet, thus describing the form of a circle. This "circle" symbolizes the temporal progression through the wedding day which goes full circle; Hymen's embrace ("in *Hymens* armes, / His Circkle holds, for all their anguish, charms"); and the union of the lovers ("Two into One, contracting"; "These two, One Twyn are"). More complexly, *"A Coronet for his Mistresse Philosophie"* interweaves ten sonnets with the first line of each sonnet repeating the last line of the preceding one, the whole describing the shape of the coronet, the circle believed to be the perfect geometric form, which Chapman awards to Philosophy. In any lengthy or complicated narrative, however, the technique of symbolic ordering by manipulation of formal units and direct verbal repetitions obviously becomes less tenable, since such patterning will become either mechanically obtrusive or forgettably remote. . . . [Chapman's] significant narrative poems all have in common the use of mythic form as a structuring device. . . .

The mythic narratives function in two general ways: first, as a structure of ideas or meaning. Chapman knows thoroughly the traditional interpretations of the classical myths and the systematic allegorical commentaries of the Renaissance platonists and mythographers. He recognizes a consonance of meaning, a similarity in the core of truth, between the myth and matter he has selected for his narration. Second, acting upon that recognition of essential likeness, he brings it to the fore by selecting, ordering, shaping the raw narrative material in conformity with the typology of the myth. Mythic form, therefore, both describes the structure of the narrative within the conventional mold of genre and points to a transcendent form, the realm of ideas or truth which Chapman believed to be inherent in the myth. Chapman's terms for these two functions of myth within the poem are "body" and "soul." Discussing the moral and ethical truths of Homer's epics, he explains:

> To illustrate both which, in both kinds, with all height of expression, the Poet creates both a Bodie and a Soule in them. Wherein, if the Bodie (being the letter, or historie) seemes fictiue, and beyond Possibilitie to bring into Act: the sence then and Allegorie (which is the soule) is to be sought. [*Poems*]

The body and soul analogy is commonplace, of course, in Renaissance writings, as were most of the critical *topoi* which we have discussed; but the precision with which Chapman argues it and again the consistency with which his various critical statements dovetail in a full platonic poetics suggest that he makes the analogy not because it is familiar but because for him it is true. Chapman, too, would resist the inference that the poet imposes mythic form upon the hapless story by an act of will and ingenuity. He attacks the concept of poetic license, the poet being strictly confined to the laws of eternal truth, and explains poetic creation by the Plotinian concept of the release of indwelling form: using the tools of his learning the poet frees the form and soul of the myth from its imprisonment in the matter of the formless story.

The anthropomorphic analogy of body and soul runs through Chapman's critical commentaries. Here the poem's fictive body offers local habitation for the soul of its truth; but, at the same time, just as the pulse of the human body indicates its state of health, so poetry acts as the "Soules Pulse" (*Poems*). Elsewhere the analogy operates on the cosmic plane: "For, as the Sunne, and Moone, are figures giuen / Of [God's] refulgent Deitie in Heauen: / So, Learning, and her Lightner, Poesie, / In earth present his fierie Maiestie" (*Poems*). The implicit assumption of likeness between the several realms of experience or planes of nature helps to explain how Chapman expected his mythic narratives in all their riddling obscurity to be penetrated by the learned few.

Wind and Murrin have shown how the Renaissance allegorists, artists, and poets preeminently chose to conceal their meaning in the veil of myth, following the model of the hierophants from the mystery religions. This, however, creates the further dilemma of how to make the myth intelligible to the approved audience. Murrin postulates the poet's solution:

> He found an answer to his rhetorical problem in his own subject matter. If the poet expresses the action of the gods in the cosmos and in the human soul, he can at least assume that the educated elite will share the same general theory about the universe as microcosm to macrocosm. It follows then that a *single* theory of the cosmos will serve to explicate the poet's allegories, even on the psychic level, and restrict the kinds of in-

terpretation possible to any given myth. The poet's allegories can serve as a true and precise mode of communication between the few.

In just this way the unvarying correspondence between microcosm, geocosm, and macrocosm acts as a principle of interpretative control in Chapman's allegorized myths. The conception, both of world vision and allegorical principle, is exactly the one which governs the *Heptaplus*. Pico states the theory underlying the entire exposition explicitly at the beginning: "Bound by chains of concord, all these worlds exchange natures as well as names with mutual liberality. From this principle (in case anyone has not yet understood it) flows the science of all allegorical interpretation" [*Heptaplus*]. If the relational pattern is constant, the reader faced with an unknown can interpret meaning confidently by recourse to the corresponding known.

At the risk of seeming deliberately perverse, I will use Donne to illustrate the poetic procedure I have presented as Chapman's. In the *Anniversaries* Donne assumes the persona of biblical prophet, first an Old Testament prophet of law and then a New Testament prophet of grace. The serious funeral occasion and the questions it provokes, the state of the world after the subject's loss and the new life of the subject's soul, dictate choice of the public, conventional, and highly rhetorical outer form; for the inner form of the narratives, Donne takes the platonic myths of the World Body and the World Soul, performing a medical anatomy upon the dead body in the first and describing the ascent of the soul to union with God in the second. The principle of cosmic allegory by which Donne expands from the microcosm of Elizabeth Drury to geocosm and macrocosm serves as interpretative control, keeping the explanations of, e.g., Ben Jonson, Marjorie Nicolson, and Frank Manley at least generally consistent with Donne's own explanation that Elizabeth described "the Idea of a Woman."

Donne's exception will prove to be the rule for Chapman; but the passing similarity described here will, I hope, serve to emphasize the larger differences. Chapman usually draws his myths, whether directly or indirectly, from *The Metamorphoses;* in fact, all the major poems from the 1590s are stimulated by Chapman's dislike for the changing taste in Ovidian poetry, from the mythological to the erotic. Since Donne was a force in the newer vogue for Ovidian eroticism, Thomas Carew's prediction of poetic regression after Donne's death could describe the kind of poetry Chapman had written:

> They will repeale the goodly exil'd traine
> of gods and goddesses, which in thy just raigne
> Were banish'd nobler Poems, now, with these
> The silenc'd tales o'th'Metamorphoses
> Shall stuffe their lines, and swell the windy Page,
> Till Verse refin'd by thee, in this last Age,
> Turne ballad rime, Or those old Idolls bee
> Ador'd againe, with new apostasie.

Chapman's kind of poetry is old-fashioned in comparison to Donne's; but, like many late practitioners of an art, he gains greatly in sophistication because of that. The strategems which the winds of change moved Chapman to deploy result in complexities, tensions, and density that make his best work extremely interesting technically, as well as remarkable poetry. One recurring example of such sophistication would be his skill at typological adaptation of myths. As he explains in the *Ivstification,* poets "haue enlarged, or altred the Allegory, with inuentions and dispositions of their owne, to extend it to their present doctrinall and illustrous purposes" (*Poems*). Understanding Chapman's handling of myth never is merely a matter of having read the same books, although admittedly that helps. Rather, it is necessary to appreciate the flexible systemization of myths that had evolved by Chapman's time, enabling the commentators, emblematists, and poets to adapt freely among typological equivalents, a procedure at which Chapman was a master. (pp. 1-17)

> *Raymond B. Waddington, in his* The Mind's Empire: Myth and Form in George Chapman's Narrative Poems, *The Johns Hopkins University Press, 1974, 221 p.*

Jane Melbourne (essay date 1985)

[*In the following excerpt, Melbourne examines the concept of inversion in* Bussy d'Ambois, *suggesting that the play's "image of a world upside down" derives from Johannes Kepler's invention of modern optics.*]

The purpose of this essay is to examine the idea of inversion in George Chapman's ***Bussy D'Ambois***—to look, first, at its image of the world inverted as a traditional figure that in 1604, when the play was written, was suddenly new because of Kepler's theory of the retinal image; second, at the image as part of a complex of ideas and images supporting Monsieur's reduction of Nature to a sum of forces indifferent to man; and finally, at the inversion of right relationship in the marriage of Tamyra and Montsurry, especially as the inversion culminates in V.i, confirming Monsieur's interpretation of Nature and destroying Bussy.

Many discussions of the play have attempted to define Chapman's conception of Bussy, a difficult task because of dissonance between heroic language and quite ordinary action. Bussy is a malcontent of great gifts but unrewarded merit who is drawn to the French Court by the Monsieur, brother of Henry III, apparently as part of a plan to depose Henry, or worse. At Court, Bussy proceeds to act like the courtiers whose conduct he, as an outsider, had deplored. He provokes great lords by dallying with their wives, kills three courtiers in a duel to avenge an insult to his honor, and becomes the lover of Tamyra, wife of Montsurry. He does, nevertheless, transfer his allegiance to the King and vow to rid the Court of corruption. Before he can act, he is exposed as Tamyra's lover and murdered by her husband. Yet he is hailed as the embodiment of the Golden Age, an identification which he himself, Henry, and even those who oppose him, accept. Given the difficulty of seeing Bussy in the contradiction between plot and language, I propose to look at him by first looking away, toward the secondary and more accessible situation of Tamyra and Montsurry, who, in inverting their duties to each other as wife and husband, deny the possibilities of the play's rhetoric.

Theirs is a central inversion in a play constructed of inversions.

> Fortune, not Reason, rules the state of things,
> Reward goes backwards, Honour on his head.
>
> (I.i.1-2)

Bussy's complaint at his outcast state in the play's first lines is its first image of inversion. Its last occurs near the end of Act V. Montsurry holds a lighted candle and turns it downward as he and Tamyra turn from each other.

> As when the flame is suffer'd to look up
> It keeps his lustre; but, being thus turn'd down
> (His natural course of useful light inverted)
> His own stuff puts it out: so let our love
> Now turn from me, as here I turn from thee,
> And may both points of heaven's straight axle-
> tree
> Conjoin in one, before thyself and me.
>
> (V.iii.258-64)

Donaldson points out that the world upside down had appeared in popular art and literature since classic times as the representation of disordered social and moral values, and was linked as well to a Saturnalian tradition [*The World Upside-Down: Comedy from Jonson to Fielding*, 1970]. By the eighteenth century, as Duchartre and Saulnier document, French engravings of Le Monde Renversé included not only cosmic impossibilities, reversals in the roles of men and animals, and reversals of predictable social and sexual relationships, but also the image of a globe-shaped being balanced on its head with its legs extending skyward [Pierre Louis DuChartre and René Saulnier, *L'Imagerie Populaire: Les Images du Toutes les Provinces Francaises du XV Siecle au Second Empire. Les Complaintes contres. Chansons, Legendes qui ont inspiré les Imagiers*, 1925].

The figure appears in Chapman's earlier poetry and in the work of other writers of his period. Interestingly, from the viewpoint of this [essay], it appears in **"To M. Harriots, accompanying *Achilles Shield* "** (line 113), Chapman's tribute to the contemporary English mathematician and astronomer.

The two fully developed images, however, are in **"A Coronet for his Mistresse Philosophy"** and *Bussy D'Ambois*. In **"A Coronet"** Chapman uses the image conventionally to connote moral and social aberration. Because the world's values are disordered, the world rejects what the poet would give.

> Th' inuersed world that goes vpon her head
> And with her wanton heeles doth kyck the sky,
> My loue disdaynes.
>
> ("A Coronet," 5.5)

It seems useful to place the image among other optical images that appeared in English literature in the 1590s and early 1600s. A number of writers have discussed the use of optical illusions as both metaphor and structural principle. What has been emphasized least, and deserves further study, is that the vogue for optical illusions coincided with a period of great advance in optical theory.

Kepler's theory of the retinal image, published in 1604 in *Ad vitellionem paralipomena,* was a major step in a fundamental change in the manner of knowing. The change was from faith in the constructs of the mind to faith in laws of nature induced from observation. But the change did not happen suddenly, nor was it welcomed by all, certainly not by Chapman, who makes the Monsieur, Bussy's antagonist, spokesman for the new knowledge.

Kepler's theory of lenses in *Dioptrics* (1611) confirmed the scientist's faith in his own observations, but in 1604 the theory of the retinal image, a necessary step in the process toward understanding, made observation seem less reliable than formerly believed, not more so. In a longer view, the revival of interest in the optical tradition of Alhazen (c. 965-1039) during the sixteenth century had raised questions about long-accepted explanations of vision. It became necessary, for instance, to question the validity of applying Euclidean geometry to vision as it was applied in single-point perspective, a breakthrough that had prepared the way for the great accomplishments of Renaissance painting but was itself in part a mathematical defense against classical objections to two-dimensional representation.

The most disturbing feature of the newly revived optical theory, however, was that it led to the conclusion that the image in the eye was inverted. Before Kepler, students of vision had ingeniously avoided reaching a conclusion that so clearly contradicted common experience. But in *Ad vitellionem,* Kepler demonstrated that the image has an existence independent of the observer and is formed as an inverted and reversed picture of the scene observed.

> Therefore vision occurs through a picture of the visible thing [being formed] on the white, concave surface of the retina. And that which is to the right on the outside is portrayed on the left side of the retina; that which is to the left is portrayed on the right; that which is above is portrayed below; and that which is below is portrayed above. . . . Therefore, if it were possible for that picture on the retina to remain after being taken outside into the light, by removing the anterior portion [of the eye] . . . and if there were a man whose vision was sufficiently sharp, he would perceive the very shape of the hemisphere [i.e., the visual field] on the extremely narrow [surface] of the retina.

Natural philosophers before Alhazen had proposed that vision resulted either from some power issuing from the eye (extramission) or from some power of the object to project images of itself to the eye (intromission). Alhazen accepted an improved version of the intromission theory holding that not images, but radiation from points on an illuminated object struck the eye. He took Euclid's geometrical demonstration of a visual pyramid, or cone, from the extramission theory to show a point-to-point correspondence between points in a visual field and points in the eye. Geometry would suggest that if rays from many point sources impact upon the eye, they form cones whose apexes are the points of origin and whose bases are the eye. It would also suggest that rays refracted upon entering the eye are bent toward the perpendicular and converge toward an apex in the eye. However, to allow that the rays achieve an apex and again diverge would lead to the unacceptable conclusion that they communicate a reversed and inverted image.

Alhazen avoided the conclusion, first, by accepting Galen's description of the crystalline humor (crystalline lens), which is located anterior to the center of the eye, as the seat of vision; and, second, by proposing that only one ray from each point in the visual field, the one ray that strikes the eye perpendicularly, enters the eye. Thus he was able to postulate one cone of rays whose base was the visual field and whose apex, if achieved, communicates a point-to-point correspondence to the visual field.

In the West, Roger Bacon, John Pecham, Witelo, and others, building on Alhazen's work, had by the end of the thirteenth century laid out the principles upon which Kepler built. Because of the revival of interest in the tradition during the sixteenth century, Kepler had access to an edition of Alhazen and Witelo published by Friedrich Risner in 1572, and he calls his own work a supplement to Witelo.

The tragedy of [*Bussy d'Ambois*] is that Bussy's rhetoric cannot be sustained, even by Bussy.

—Jane Melbourne

It was, of course, more than a supplement; he made basic corrections in the theory. He objected to the reasoning that excluded from consideration all but the perpendicular ray, making it necessary for him to consider a multiplicity of rays. He identified the retina, not the crystalline humor, as the vision-sensitive part of the eye, following anatomist Felix Platter. Then he reasoned that every point in the visual field produces a cone of diverging rays; the rays that enter the eye intersect in the pupil and then, inverted and reversed, are again refracted to converge toward apexes on the retina. All radiation intercepted from a point on the visual field is returned to a point on the retina, forming a picture.

Kepler was as troubled by the inversion and reversal as Alhazen and others had been. He tried to postulate a second intersection within the eye to realign the image correctly, but could not. Thus he accepted what his geometry demonstrated. "Vision occurs," he said, "when the image of the whole hemisphere of the world that is before the eye . . . is fixed on the reddish white concave surface of the retina" [in David C. Lindberg, *Theories of Vision from Al-Kindi to Kepler*, 1976]. How the mind composes the image, he left to others to explain.

Della Porta had suggested in the middle of the sixteenth century in *Magia Naturalis* that the eye is a miniature camera obscura, and Della Porta had been published in English translation. But in Kepler the suggestion becomes a physical fact rather than an idea to play with.

It seems highly probable that Chapman would have

known about Kepler's 1604 theory, perhaps through friendship with the mathematician and astronomer Thomas Harriot. The *Gesammelte Werke* of Johannes Kepler includes letters from Kepler to Harriot dated 1606, 1607, and 1609. Chapman, like Harriot, was one of a group of intellectuals associated with Sir Walter Ralegh, and in 1598 had addressed a poem to Harriot, published with **Achilles Shield,** in which he refers to Harriot's "perfect eye," which Bartlett glosses as Harriot's telescope.

It is more important in discussing a work of the imagination to establish a milieu in which writer and audience are likely to know and care about an advance in science than to trace the influence of Kepler on Harriot and of Harriot on Chapman. Chapman was of such a milieu. And just as important, he could reasonably expect that a segment of his audience would recognize and respond to a scientific allusion—England ranked second only to Italy in publication of scientific books, most of which were published in English.

Thus, when Chapman uses the image of a world upside down in **Bussy D'Ambois,** the image has the potential for connotations beyond the traditional. It retains the traditional as well in representing social and moral disorder, and in evoking a Saturnian, if not Saturnalian, world. Bussy asks if he must believe backwards and invert the Creed (I.i.100-101) to thrive at Court, which is a "mere mirror of confusion" to the beauty, stateliness, and worth of the Court of Elizabeth (I.ii.27). And Tamyra denies moral responsibility because mutability turns virtue to vice—"every thought in our false clock of life / Oftimes inverts the whole circumference" (III.i.56-57). Structurally, the play overturns the image of the Golden World it evokes. We have seen the petty quarrel in the Court in which Bussy's duel originates before we hear the duel reported as an epic battle by a Nuncius (II.i.25-132). Bussy's defense of himself in heroic terms is balanced against the accusation that his killing of three men in the duel is murder.

In his defense against the charge, Bussy claims the right to make good what God and Nature have given him for his good.

> Let me be King myself (as man was made)
> And do a justice that exceeds the law.
>
> (II.i.198-99)

Henry pardons Bussy, seconds his defense, and expands his definition of Nature.

> Kings had never borne
> Such boundless eminence over other men,
> Had all maintain'd the spirit and state of D'Ambois;
> Nor had the full impartial hand of Nature
> That all things gave in her original,
> Without these definite terms of Mine and Thine,
> Been turn'd unjustly to the hand of Fortune—
> Had all preserv'd her in her prime, like D'Ambois.
>
> (III.ii.95-102)

The Nature of the Golden Age that Henry proclaims is overturned, and so is his definition of man in terms of that

Nature. It is displaced by a Nature which negates man's exalted definition of himself by her indifference to him.

> Now shall we see, that Nature hath no end
> In her great works, responsive to their worths,
> That she who makes so many eyes, and souls,
> To see and foresee, is stark blind herself.
>
> (V.iii.1-4)

Inversion goes beyond traditional connotations. Monsieur replaces an idealized interpretation of Nature with a naturalistic interpretation. He speaks for a Nature which one knows through observation. "Why you shall see it here," as a solid tree is torn up by a storm while winds pass through a hollow one, so a man like Bussy, "young, learned, valiant, virtuous and full-mann'd / . . . shall reel and fall / Before the frantic puffs of purblind Chance" (V.iii.37-47). The Nature Monsieur announces, like Monsieur himself, is deformed, but it prevails.

The central image of the world balanced on its head occurs in the same speech as a reference to Copernican astronomy—"Now is it true, earth moves, and heaven stands still" (V.i.153). More important, the speech is spoken by Montsurry when he fully comprehends his wife's adultery. The Copernican hypothesis is true *because* Tamyra has betrayed him. When Chapman had used the central image in **"A Coronet,"** quoted above, the world was merely personified.

But in **Bussy,** in the tormented imagination of Montsurry, the world and his wife are one.

> The too huge bias of the World hath sway'd
> Her back-part upwards, and with that she braves
> This Hemisphere, that long her mouth hath
>   mock'd:
> The gravity of her religious face
> (Now grown too weighty with her sacrilege
> And here discern'd sophisticate enough)
> Turns to th'Antipodes: and all the forms
> That her illusions have impress'd in her
> Have eaten through her back: and now all see,
> How she is riveted with hypocrisy.
>
> (V.i.155-64)

Hardin Craig sees **Bussy** as presenting for the first time a mechanistic psychology in which man is victim of his own nature ["Ethics in the Jacobean Drama: The Case of Chapman," *The Parrott Presentation Volume,* ed. Hardin Craig, 1935]. He is concerned with the operation of this psychology in Tamyra and Bussy. My point is that in combining a disorienting image from a newly emerging science of physical nature with man's nature, Chapman is obliterating the boundaries between man and nature. I am concerned with the loss of distinctive humanity in Tamyra and Montsurry. In the image, as in much of the poetry of Act V, natural force moves through man in the same manner as it moves through the world external to him. Helpless to withstand the force of Nature within herself, Tamyra was impelled to commit adultery, and Montsurry, equally helpless, is impelled to commit violence upon her.

There are parallels also in their haste to disavow responsibility for their actions. Aware of the mounting power of jealousy within himself Montsurry says

> 'Twas from my troubled blood, and not from
>   me—
> I know not how I fare; a sudden night
> Flows through my entrails, and a headlong
>   Chaos
> Murmurs within me, which I must digest.
>
> (IV.i.153-56)

This is reminiscent of Tamyra's "It is not I, but urgent destiny / That . . . / Enforceth my offense" (III.i.43-46). The emphasis is on blood—for Tamyra, blood as sensual appetite; for Montsurry, blood as revenge. As Tamyra likened her passion to a natural force, most like an earthquake (II.ii.34-49), Montsurry likens his to a disruption of the supernatural order. As she would suspend Time, Fortune, and Existence to satisfy her lust (II.ii.157-66), he locks out the world and would end it to satisfy his revenge.

> O now it nothing fits my cares to speak
> But thunder, or to take into my throat
> The trump of Heaven; with whose determinate
>   blasts
> The winds shall burst, and the enraged seas
> Be drunk up in his sounds; that my hot woes
> (Vented enough) I might convert to vapour,
> Ascending from my infamy unseen;
> Shorten the world, preventing the last breath
> That kills the living, and regenerates death.
>
> (V.i.41-49)

When Montsurry stabs and tortures Tamyra, he is transformed into a monster, but he equates his distortion to hers.

> TAMYRA: with my heart blood
>   Dissolve yourself again, or you
>   will grow
>   Into the image of all Tyranny.
> MONTSURRY: As thou art of Adultery, I will
>   still
>   Prove thee my like in ill, being
>   most a
>   monster.
>
> (V.i.129-33)

The physical torture of Tamyra is the correlative of the psychological torture her adultery has inflicted on him. The similarity between the two, in that they cannot help what they do, is stressed. Each relinquishes control to a natural force. And in relinquishing control, each is less than human. Montsurry insists upon the causality that links them.

> It follows needfully as child and parent;
> The chain-shot of thy lust is yet aloft,
> And it must murder.
>
> (V.i.90-92)

A further similarity is that there is in Montsurry's violence a sensuality, a perverted enjoyment of her lust, turned against himself.

> Come, Siren, sing, and dash against my rocks
> Thy ruffi'n Galley, laden for thy lust:
> Sing, and put all the nets into thy voice,
> With which thou drew'st into thy strumpet's lap
> The spawn of Venus.
>
> (V.i.60-64)

When the Friar is revealed as her pander, Montsurry sums

up the felt corruption of the world by uniting the world and Tamyra in the powerful variation of the figure of a world inverted quoted above (V.i.155-64).

The monstrously inverted world of Montsurry's imagination is the real world of Act V. Passion has usurped governance and the world is a projection of Montsurry and Tamyra themselves. When Bussy comes into Montsurry's world in response to the summons Tamyra has been forced to send to him, he comes into a world of which he is ignorant.

In the first quarto, Monsieur's dialogue (V.iii.1-56), quoted in part above, which equates nature and chance, comes at the beginning of the final scene and makes explicit the interpretation of Nature of which Monsieur is spokesman. Nature has no purpose. What seem to be gifts of Nature are chance gifts, which make the recipient vulnerable. Bussy is to be seen as proof of Monsieur's thesis. The power of the final scene comes largely from the equation in sound and imagery of the violence of Nature to the violence of human passion.

> Not so the sea raves on the Lybian sands,
> Tumbling her billows in each other's neck—
> Not so the surges of the Euxine sea . . .
> Swell being enrag'd, even from their inmost drop.
>
> (V.iii.49-54)

The passage derives from Seneca's *Agamemnon*. The change Chapman makes from his source is to combine with natural force the attributes of persons. The sea tumbles "her billows in each other's neck." The Euxine Sea surges, "being enraged."

In coming into this world, Bussy is an aberration to be destroyed. His valor, seen from the old perspective, is magnificent; viewed against the darker interpretation of the new, it rings as bravado.

> Murder'd? I know not what that Hebrew means:
> That word had ne'er been nam'd had all been D'Ambois.
>
> (V.iii.76-77)

Bussy is shot from offstage, anonymously, so that his death yields him no meaning. In facing death, he questions the Platonic concept of man as a hierarchy, of which the soul, or mind as the essence of soul, is the more excellent, the immortal part.

> is my body then
> But penetrable flesh? And must my mind
> Follow my blood? Can my divine part add
> No aid to th'earthly in extremity?
> Then these divines are but for form, not fact.
>
> (V.iii.125-29)

Unable to hold to his Platonic faith, he seizes upon a Stoic justification—he will stand like a Roman statue until death has made him marble. If his soul will not survive him, his fame will. In words echoing Hercules' dying speech from Seneca's *Hercules Oetaeus*, he bids his fame fly to the four corners of the world of classic myth to tell gods and heroes that Bussy comes to join them (lines 145-55). In the last words of the play, the Friar revives this Stoic hope—"Look up and see thy spirit made a star, /

Join flames with Hercules" (lines 269-70). But it is as if the Ghost had heard the one speech and heard nothing more, had somehow missed Bussy's despair. In the final scene Bussy is stripped of illusion after illusion—his heroic stance, his chivalry, his Platonic faith, his Stoic defiance.

Montsurry's world asserts itself in the bleeding body of Tamyra, and the wholeness of self Bussy has defended from attribution of guilt is pierced by self-accusation. He is the cause of Tamyra's wounds.

> O, my heart is broken.
> Fate, nor these murderers, Monsieur, nor the Guise,
> Have any glory in my death, but this:
> This killing spectacle: this prodigy.
>
> (V.iii.178-81)

He is not above Nature either as soul superior to material process, nor as hero able to defy it. He is linked to Nature in a cause and effect relationship to Tamyra's wounds. He adopts Monsieur's imagery of violent Nature merged with attributes of person and the sweeping rhythm of natural force. Both are intensified because it is he himself who is merged.

> My sun is turn'd to blood 'gainst whose red beams
> Pindus and Ossa (hid in endless snow),
> Laid on my heart and liver, from their veins
> Melt like two hungry torrents, eating rocks,
> Into the Ocean of all human life,
> And make it bitter, only with my blood.
>
> (V.iii.182-87)

"My sun" would seem to be either Tamyra or Bussy's idealized conception of himself. It is Bussy who is violently compressed into Nature. The weight of frozen mountains presses upon him and melts, with his blood. It is an extravagant conceit which matches in despair the extravagance of the illusions he has lost. He dies admitting futility and defeat. He does see himself as a star, a warning beacon made to look

> like a falling star
> Silently glanc'd—that like a thunderbolt
> Look'd to have stuck, and shook the firmament.
>
> (V.iii.190-93)

Only he assumes guilt. Montsurry does not. When the Ghost of the Friar confronts *him* with responsibility for Tamyra's wounds, he points to her guilt instead (lines 206-207). Tamyra asks forgiveness and embraces punishment, but not guilt. She asks remission of sin when she is on the rack (lines 145-46), but finally denies guilt, pointing instead to the successful hypocrisy of others (lines 210-29). Tamyra has inverted her responsibility as wife, not entirely by her act of adultery—Montsurry was quite ready to condone, even to second, the solicitations of the Monsieur—but by desiring the act. Montsurry has inverted his responsibility as husband by breaking the limits of man and husband (line 35) in doing violence upon her. Their final speeches are words of love, tortured and denied, yet though these words are of more depth than any words exchanged between Tamyra and Bussy, reconciliation is not possible. Neither responsibility nor guilt is possible to those who are subjects of forces which act upon them. For *them* Monsieur's Nature is true because they accept it as true.

For Bussy, no such simple equation is possible. The tragedy of the play is that Bussy's rhetoric cannot be sustained, even by Bussy. He is an anachronism, "the brave relicts of a complete man" (line 268), eulogized by a Ghost, in a world in which heroism is not possible. (pp. 381-95)

> *Jane Melbourne, "The Inverted World of* Bussy D'Ambois," *in* Studies in English Literature, 1500-1900, *Vol. 25, No. 2, Spring, 1985, pp. 381-95.*

FURTHER READING

I. General Critical Studies

Presson, Robert K. "Wrestling with This World: A View of George Chapman." *Publications of the Modern Language Association of America* 84, No. 1 (January 1969): 44-50.
    Analyzes Chapman's literary production from a biographical and psychological perspective.

Swinburne, Algernon Charles. *George Chapman: A Critical Essay.* 1875. Reprint. New York: Lemma Publishing Corporation, 1972, 187 p.
    Late Victorian assessment of Chapman's literary achievement.

II. Drama

Acheson, Arthur. *Shakespeare, Chapman and Sir Thomas More.* 1931. Reprint. New York: AMS Press, 1970, 280 p.
    Discloses the circumstances surrounding "the inception of the jealous hostility with which Chapman . . . pursued Shakespeare until the end of his dramatic career."

Aggeler, Geoffrey. "The Unity of Chapman's *The Revenge of Bussy d'Ambois.*" *Pacific Coast Philology* IV (April 1969): 5-18.
    Argues that "the didactic import of the characterization of the hero [Clermont d'Ambois] is comprehensible only with reference to the revenge motif."

Battenhouse, Roy W. "Chapman and the Nature of Man." In *Elizabethan Drama: Modern Essays in Criticism,* edited by Ralph James Kaufmann, pp. 134-52. New York: Oxford University Press, 1961.
    Advances that "like the Florentine Platonists, Chapman is a syncretist of classical and Christian thought."

Bement, Peter. *George Chapman: Action and Contemplation in His Tragedies.* Salzburg Studies in English Literature: Jacobean Drama Studies, edited by James Hogg, vol. 8. Salzburg, Austria: Institut für Englische Sprache und Literatur, 1974, 292 p.
    Explores "Chapman's major tragic themes in the hope that they may provide a key to the total meaning and significance of the plays."

Cope, Jackson I. "George Chapman: Myth as Mask and Magic." In his *The Theater and the Dream: From Metaphor to Form in Renaissance Drama,* pp. 29-76. Baltimore, Md.: John Hopkins University Press, 1973.
    Discusses the development of mythological Platonic themes in *The Gentleman Usher* and *The Widow's Tears.*

Craig, Hardin. "Ethics in the Jacobean Drama: The Case of Chapman." In *The Parrot Presentation Volume,* edited by Hardin Craig, pp. 25-46. Princeton, N. J.: Princeton University Press, 1935.
    Reassessment of Jacobean drama "in terms of Chapman's ethical thought."

Crawley, Derek. *Character in Relation to Action in the Tragedies of George Chapman.* Salzburg Studies in English Literature: Jacobean Drama Studies, edited by James Hogg, vol. 16. Salzburg, Austria: Institut für Englische Sprache und Literatur, 1974, 202 p.
    Thematic analysis of Chapman's major tragedies.

Dean, Paul "Structure in the 'Bussy' Plays of Chapman." *English Studies* 61, No. 2 (April 1980): 119-26.
    Comparative analysis of *Bussy d'Ambois* and *The Revenge of Bussy d'Ambois.*

Florby, Gunilla. *The Painful Passage to Virtue: A Study of George Chapman's "The Tragedy of Bussy d'Ambois" and "The Revenge of Bussy d'Ambois."* Lund: Gleerup, 1982, 265 p.
    Historiographic account and stylistic analysis of Chapman's major tragedies.

Goldstein, Leonard. *George Chapman: Aspects of Decadence in Early Seventeenth-Century Drama.* Vols. I-II. Salzburg Studies in English Literature: Jacobean Drama Studies, edited by James Hogg, vol. 31. Salzburg, Austria: Institut für Englische Sprache und Literatur, 1975, 438 p.
    Relates Chapman's dramaturgy to decadent themes prevalent in seventeenth-century English drama.

Grant, Thomas Mark. *The Comedies of George Chapman: A Study in Development.* Salzburg Studies in English Literature: Jacobean Drama Studies, edited by James Hogg, vol. 5. Salzburg, Austria: Institut für Englische Sprache und Literatur, 1972, 234 p.
    Contends that Chapman's extant comedies "together . . . represent a distinct and substantial pattern of coherent artistic development."

Harris, Julia Hamlet. Introduction to *Eastward Hoe,* by George Chapman, Ben Jonson, and John Marston. Yale Studies in English, edited by Albert S. Cook, Vol. LXXIII. New Haven, Conn.: Yale University Press, 1926, pp. ix-lviii.
    Documents sources, authorship, and stage history of *Eastward Ho.*

Hibbard, G. R. "George Chapman: Tragedy and the Providential View of History." *Shakespeare Survey* 20 (1967): 27-31.
    Purports that "the experience [Chapman's tragedies] embody and explore seems to . . . spring in no small measure from the tension that is created in them by conflicting attitudes to historical material and to history itself."

Ide, Richard S. *Possessed with Greatness: The Heroic Tragedies of Chapman and Shakespeare.* Chapel Hill: The University of North Carolina Press, 1980, 253 p.
    Proposes that the tragedies of William Shakespeare and

Chapman which feature a soldier-hero "share a generic identity."

Jacquot, Jean. "*Bussy d'Ambois* and Chapman's Conception of Tragedy." In *English Studies Today, second series,* edited by G. A. Bonnard, pp. 129-41. Bern: Francke Verlag, 1961.

Insists that a close reading of *Bussy d'Ambois* reveals that "Chapman's tragic art is something more complex than the mechanical application of ethical formulae."

Kennedy, Edward D. "James I and Chapman's Byron Plays." *Journal of English and Germanic Philology* LXIV, No. 4 (October 1965): 677-90.

Argues that in writing the Byron tragedies, "Chapman, while not attempting an allegorical representation of James, was strongly supporting the King's theories and policies."

Perkinson, Richard H. "Nature and the Tragic Hero in Chapman's Bussy Plays." *Modern Language Quarterly* 3 (1942): 263-85.

Maintains that "the problems of Chapman's serious plays are essentially dramatic and revolve about the adaptation of the super-man hero to Jacobean tragedy."

Rees, Ennis. *The Tragedies of George Chapman: Renaissance Ethics in Action.* Cambridge, Mass.: Harvard University Press, 1954, 223 p.

Study of Chapman's tragedies considered as "poetic dramas of unusual quality in which a very definite ethical intention is realized to an unusual degree."

Ribner, Irving. "Character and Theme in Chapman's *Bussy d'Ambois.*" *English Literary History* 26, No. 4 (December 1959): 482-96.

Suggests that "Bussy shares the amplitude which has been a part of the greatest tragic heroes . . . because he is consciously shaped as a dramatic symbol of humanity, faced with a problem which all mankind must face."

Schoenbaum, Samuel. "*The Widow's Tears* and the Other Chapman." *The Huntington Library Quarterly* XXIII, No. 4 (August 1960): 321-38.

Thematic analysis of *The Widow's Tears.*

Smeak, Ethel M. Introduction to *The Widow's Tears,* by George Chapman, pp. xi-xxvi. Lincoln: University of Nebraska Press, 1966.

Historical summary and stylistic assessment of a major comedy by Chapman.

Solve, Norma Dobie. *Stuart Politics in Chapman's "Tragedy of Chabot."* University of Michigan Publications: Language and Literature, vol. IV. Ann Arbor: University of Michigan, 1928, 176 p.

Study of the sources and political setting of *The Tragedy of Chabot, Admiral of France.*

Stagg, Louis Charles. "Characterization through Nature Imagery in the Tragedies of George Chapman." *Ball State University Forum* 9, No. 1 (Winter 1968): 39-43.

Demonstrates the significance of nature imagery in the characterization of Bussy and Clermont D'Ambois, Chabot, and Byron.

Wieler, John William. *George Chapman: The Effect of Stoicism upon His Tragedies.* 1949. Reprint. New York: Octagon Books, 1969, 218 p.

Critical study "devoted entirely to an analysis of the ef-fects of Stoic doctrine upon Chapman's art in tragedy, not only upon the two dramas in which Stoicism is most apparent, but also upon the tragedies comprising the entire canon."

III. Poetry

Battenhouse, Roy. "Chapman's *The Shadow of Night:* An Interpretation." *Studies in Philology* XXXVIII, No. 3 (July 1941): 584-608.

Affirms that the two hymns of *The Shadow of Night* "have a logical plan and a consecutive argument."

Bottrall, Margaret. "George Chapman's Defence of Difficulty in Poetry." *The Criterion* XVI, No. LXV (July 1937): 638-54.

Advances that "by nature and conviction [Chapman] belonged to the company of poets who address themselves to the most highly cultivated among contemporary readers."

Cannon, Charles Kendrick. "Chapman on the Unity of Style and Meaning." *Journal of English and Germanic Philology* LXVIII, No. 2 (April 1969): 245-64.

Discusses Chapman's theory of poetry and analyzes his "Hymnus in Noctem" on the basis of that theory.

Eliot, T. S. "The Metaphysical Poets." In his *Selected Essays,* pp. 241-50. New York: Harcourt, Brace and Co., 1932.

Purports that "In Chapman . . . there is a direct sensuous apprehension of thought, or a recreation of thought into feeling" in the manner of John Donne.

Snare, Gerald. *The Mystification of George Chapman.* Durham, N. C.: Duke University Press, 1989, 186 p.

Reassesses the "body of profound and heady lore . . . presumed to stand behind all of Chapman's [poetic] works."

Waddington, Raymond B. "Visual Rhetoric: Chapman and the Extended Poem." *English Literary Renaissance* 13, No. 1 (Winter 1983): 36-57.

Considers the impact of sixteenth-century printing innovations on the form of Chapman's poetry.

IV. Translations

Bartlett, Phyllis B. "The Heroes of Chapman's Homer." *The Review of English Studies* XVII, No. 67 (July 1941): 257-80.

Affirms that "through the wealth of Elizabethan rhetoric in which [his Homeric] translations are cast . . . Chapman built up his own concept of the Homeric exempla."

———. "Stylistic Devices in Chapman's *Illiads.*" *Publications of the Modern Language Association of America* LVII, No. 3 (September 1942): 661-75.

Observes that "nearly all of the stylistic idiosyncrasies of Chapman's translation, as distinct from the conceptual divergencies of his rendering, accord with his stated principles."

Smalley, Donald. "The Ethical Bias of Chapman's *Homer.*" *Studies in Philology* XXXVI, No. 2 (April 1939): 169-91.

Argues that in his translations "Chapman read into Homer the doctrines which he himself had come to accept as truth."

Additional coverage of Chapman's life and career is contained in the following source published by Gale Research: *Dictionary of Literary Biography*, Vol. 62.

Thomas Dekker

1572?-1632?

(Also Decker, Deckar) English dramatist and essayist.

INTRODUCTION

A prolific author, Dekker wrote, alone or in collaboration, over forty plays, of which seventeen survive. His best-known dramas include *The Shoemaker's Holiday, Old Fortunatus, The Honest Whore,* and *The Witch of Edmonton.* He is also noted for having produced numerous pamphlets, such as *The Wonderful Yeare, The Belman of London, Lanthorne and Candle-Light,* and *A Rod for Run-Awayes,* which provide detailed pictures of the life of Elizabethan and Jacobean London. Admired in his own time for his writings in both comic and tragic veins, Dekker's reputation fell greatly during the eighteenth century but has been rehabilitated by a number of twentieth-century critics who praise Dekker for his romanticism, his ethical concerns, and his considerable, if sometimes uneven, craftsmanship in both drama and prose.

Dekker was born in London, possibly to a Dutch family, as scholars deduce from both his surname and his evident familiarity with Dutch language in *The Shoemaker's Holiday* and other works. Nothing is known of his life until the 1590s, when his name began appearing in theatrical documents. A 1594 entry in The Stationer's Register—a record of works licensed for publication—lists a "Tho: Decker" as the author of a drama entitled *The Jew of Venice,* a work that no longer survives. The next evidence of Dekker's activities dates from 1597, when theater manager Philip Henslowe recorded in his professional diary the hiring of Dekker to write and adapt plays for his company, the Lord Admiral's Men. Subsequent entries in Henslowe's diary indicate that during his tenure with the Lord Admiral's Men, Dekker had a hand in the composition or revision of dozens of plays, at times working with as many as three or four other writers. In the opening years of the seventeenth century, Dekker became involved in "the War of the Theaters," a literary quarrel in which Ben Jonson ridiculed both Dekker and John Marston in several plays, most notably *Poetaster* (1601). Dekker responded by mocking Jonson in *Satiro-Mastix. Or The untrussing of the Humorous Poet.* Dekker wrote steadily for Henslowe until 1603, when the death of Elizabeth I, followed shortly by an outbreak of the plague, resulted in the closing of London's theaters. For the time deprived of the means to support himself by playwriting, Dekker turned to composing prose pamphlets. The epidemic prompted Dekker to publish *The Wonderful Yeare,* a collection of anecdotes, religious meditations, and lamentations for those who died. Surprisingly, in 1604 Dekker was jointly commissioned with Jonson to compose the pageant celebrating the coronation of James I. The two writers remained antipathetic

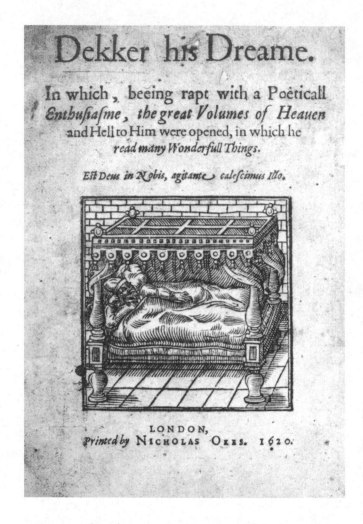

Dekker his Dreame.

In which, beeing rapt with a Poëticall Enthusiasme, the great Volumes of Heauen and Hell to Him were opened, in which he read many Wonderfull Things.

Est Deus in Nobis, agitante calescimus Illo.

LONDON,
Printed by NICHOLAS OKES. 1620.

to one another, however, and each published separately his share in the pageant, which was titled *The Magnificent Entertainment.* With the reopening of the theaters Dekker returned to drama, writing both parts of *The Honest Whore* in 1604-05. About two years later Dekker appears to have stopped writing for the stage, and for the next five years he concentrated exclusively on producing pamphlets. He returned to playwriting in 1611, but this activity was soon terminated as he was imprisoned for debt. He was, however, able to continue composing pamphlets, and he published several while in prison. After his release in 1619, Dekker worked with Samuel Rowley, John Ford, and others, creating such works as *The Virgin Martir* and *The Witch of Edmonton.* Dekker died sometime around 1632.

As a result of the varied conditions and diverse genres in which Dekker wrote, scholars find that his work as a whole is hard to characterize. One of his hallmarks, however, is comic, often raucous, banter. Even his religious play *The Virgin Martir* includes bawdy dialogue, which is given to the pagan antagonists of the title character Dorothea, contrasting their sensuality with her sanctity. Dekker is also often credited with a profound sensitivity to the plight of the poor, the laboring classes, and, particularly, the victims of persecution. Several critics have pointed out that the speeches of jailed prostitutes in Part Two of *The Honest Whore* indict society's indifference to poor women as a major cause of prostitution. In addition, Mother Sawyer, the eponymous witch of Edmonton, is sympathetically portrayed, making a pact with the devil only in response to her neighbors' cruel taunts regarding her ugliness and poverty. *The Shoemaker's Holiday,* perhaps Dekker's most popular work, is commonly regarded as a celebration of working-class life. This comedy depicting the rise of Eyre to the position of Lord Mayor offers several portraits of honorable tradespeople and laborers. Dekker's compassion for the poor and suffering is also reflected in his pamphlets; for example, *The Wonderful Yeare* castigates those of his contemporaries who, fearing contagion, refused to nurse or comfort victims of the plague.

Appraisals of Dekker's works have varied widely over the years. While in the seventeenth century Jonson satirized him as "Demetrius Fannius," an impoverished and incompetent "dresser of plays" in *Poetaster,* William Fennor praised Dekker as "the true heire of Appolo" in his *The Comptor's Commonwealth* (1617), and Edward Phillips lauded him as "a high-flier in wit" in his *Theatrum poetarum anglicanorum* (1675). In the eighteenth century Dekker was generally held in low esteem. For instance, Charles Dibdin, writing in 1795, censured the structure of Dekker's plays and maintained that it was "very probable that [Dekker] could not have been half so well respected as he was," were it not for his famous rivalry with Jonson. Subsequent critics frequently charged Dekker's plays with poor construction, though his reputation rose again in the early nineteenth century, when critics such as William Hazlitt and Charles Lamb praised him for the imaginative situations and believable characterizations in his dramas. Both Lamb and Hazlitt expressed admiration for Dekker's lyrical qualities, as did many later critics. In the Victorian period a number of writers lauded Dekker's compassion for the lower classes while condemning his coarse language and sexual humor. Early twentieth-century opinion continued to reproach Dekker's dramatic technique and considered the quality of his verse uneven and generally inferior to that of his prose.

Significantly, many critics now judge one of Dekker's greatest strengths to be his versatile prose style, which, as demonstrated in his pamphlets as well as his plays, is capable of both dignified formality and lively colloquialism. Recent commentary has increasingly examined Dekker's drama in the context of his overall literary output, with many critics finding a consistent moral view expressed throughout his work. Other modern scholars have challenged the notion that Dekker's plays are poorly integrated, citing thematic patterns, unified plots, consistency of characterization, and other evidence of Dekker's craftsmanship. With such studies has come a heightened appreciation of Dekker as an artist who, as Larry S. Champion has asserted, "genuinely deserves a considerably higher

place in the development and maturation of Elizabethan-Jacobean-Caroline drama than most previous critics have been willing to acknowledge."

PRINCIPAL WORKS

The Jew of Venice (drama) 1594?

The Shoemakers Holiday. Or the Gentle Craft. With the Humorous Life of Simon Eyre, Shoomaker, and Lord Maior of London (drama) 1599

The Pleasant Comedie of Old Fortunatus (drama) 1599

The Pleasant Comodie of Patient Grissill [with Henry Chettle and William Haughton] (drama) 1600

Satiro-Mastix. Or The Untrussing of the Humorous Poet (drama) 1601

The Wonderful Yeare. 1603. Wherein is Shewed the Picture of London, Lying Sicke of the Plague (memoirs) 1603

The Magnificent Entertainment [with Ben Jonson] (pageant) 1604

The Honest Whore, With, The Humours of the Patient Man, and the Longing Wife [with Thomas Middleton] (drama) 1604

West-ward Hoe [with John Webster] (drama) 1604

The Second Part of The Honest Whore, With the Humors of the Patient Man, the Impatient Wife (drama) 1604-05

North-ward Hoe [with Webster] (drama) 1605

The Seuen Deadly Sinnes of London: Drawne in Seuen Seuerall Coaches, through the Seuen Seuerall Gates of the Citie, Bringing the Plague with Them (essays) 1606

The Whore of Babylon (drama) 1605-06

The Belman of London. Bringing to Light the Most Notorious Villanies that Are Now Practiced in the Kingdome (essays) 1608

Lanthorne and Candle-Light. Or the Bell-Mans second Nights Walk. In which Hee brings to Light, a Broode of more strange Villanies, then euer were till this yeare discouered (essays) 1608; enlarged editions published as *O per se O, or a new crier of Lanthorne and Candle-Light* (1612), *Villanies Discouered by Lanthorne and Candle-Light* (1616), and *English Villainies* (1632)

Foure Birds of Noahs Arke: viz. 1. the Dove, 2. the Eagle, 3. the Pelican, 4. the Phoenix (reflections) 1609

The Guls Horne-Booke: Stultorum plena omnia. Al Sauio meza parola, Basta. (essays) 1609

The Roaring Girle, or Moll Cut-purse [with Thomas Middleton] (drama) 1611

If This Be Not a Good Play, the Devil Is in It (drama) 1611

Dekker His Dreame. In which, beeing rapt with a Poeticall Enthusiasme, the great Volumes of Heauen and Hell to Him were opened, in which he read many Wonderfull Things (essays) 1620

The Virgin Martir, A Tragedie [with Philip Massinger] (drama) 1620

A Tragi-Comedy: Called, Match Mee in London (drama) 1621?

The Witch of Edmonton, A known true Story. Composed

into a Tragi-Comedy By divers well-esteemed Poets
[with William Rowley and John Ford] (drama)
1621
A Rod for Run-Awayes: Gods Tokens, of His Fearefull Iudgements, Sundry Wayes Pronounced vpon This City, and on Seuerall Persons, Both Flying from It, and Staying in It (essays) 1625
The Non-Dramatic Works of Thomas Dekker. 5 vols. (memoirs and essays) 1884-86
The Dramatic Works of Thomas Dekker. 5 vols. (drama) 1953-61

Charles Dibdin   (essay date 1800)

[*Dibdin was an English dramatist and theater critic. In this excerpt from a work published in 1800, he reviews some of Dekker's plays and argues that Dekker owes most of his fame to his quarrel with Jonson.*]

Decker . . . for a time in friendship with Jonson, and afterwards most severely satirized by that drawcancer in literature, produced two plays before the reign of James. What was the particular cause of the quarrel cannot now be known, but it is universally agreed that Jonson's envy and rancour, not being able to bear a rival near the throne, was its origin. We may collect a very faithful idea of it from the dispute between Pope and Cibber; which, having originated in rancour on the side of Pope, every stroke he aimed at his adversary recoiled upon himself.

In Jonson's *Poetaster,* the *Dunciad* of that time, Decker, under the title of Crispinus, is most severely handled. This literary hawk, however, so very fond of annoying small birds, had better, in this instance, have soared on without having attempted to pounce upon Decker; for, as it happens with other hawks, that the very sparrows, who are afraid of them on the ground, attack them successfully in the open air; so the light and agile Decker, pegged away at the clumsy and unweildy Jonson, to so good a purpose, that he not only made his feathers fly but he galled him all over.

This he effected by writing a play called the *Satyromastix; or the untrussing the humerous Poet.* Here, under the name of young Horace, he has made Jonson the hero of the piece. The public were charmed with the circumstance, and the play did wonders. Nay this was the foundation of Decker's reputation, whose writings were certainly not of the first rate kind, yet, after his pride had been roused by the favourable turn this controversy took, he made up by assiduity what he wanted in talents, and, having become a good judge of dramatic effect, he enjoyed a considerable degree of reputable success.

Old Fortunatus, which, perhaps, originally roused the hornet Jonson, for, extravagant as the story is the piece has great merit, and *Satyromastix* are all the plays of this author that come under our notice here. He wrote single eight others, several in conjunction with Webster, Day, and other poets, and three or four besides are attributed to him.(pp. 110-11)

. . . . .

Decker, after the death of queen Elizabeth, produced the following pieces. The *Honest Whore,* performed in 1604. The different opinions concerning this play shew how little we know, with any certainty, of the works of authors at that period. A biographer tells us confidently, that neither this play nor the sequel to it is divided into acts; but this is so far from the truth that Dodsley has printed it in his collection of old Plays, where it not only appears in a very regular state, but gives good proof that Decker had considerable merit. The second part, appears to have been a number of scenes thrown together, but it was never digested into a regular play.

Westward Hoe. This play was brought on in 1607. Webster assisted in the writing of it, as he did of *Northward Hoe,* and we are told they had both success, probably more owing to the titles caught from the *Eastward Hoe,* which we have seen so popular in consequence of having involved its authors in such disgrace.

The *Whore of Babylon,* written expressly in compliment to queen Elizabeth, with a view to expose the designs of the Jesuits, and set forth their dangerous plots, from which the queen escaped, was printed in 1607, but it is most probable it never was performed. The queen is represented under the character of Titania, which name Spencer originally gave her, and which was adopted by Shakespear in his *Midsummer Night's Dream.* There were other characters of that time personified, all tending to describe and illustrate the virtues of Elizabeth, a proper tribute to her exalted merit, and a laudable mode of stimulating the loyalty of the people.

If it be not good the Devil's in it. This play is founded on Machiaval's *Marriage of Belphegor,* and is a poor attempt at wit from the title to the last word. The title, indeed, is so contemptible a quibble that as the Devil is actually in the play, so the author gives it under his hand that it is not good; this flimsy stuff has, however, been frequently copied, and once most miserably under the title of a *Comic Opera,* at Drury Lane.

Match me in London. To this play the different writers have given different merits; but, as it is impossible that it should be excellent, poor, tolerable, and good, at the same time, which words I copy, we may fairly take it that it had merit and defects.

These are all the dramatic works the world gives to Decker. He is said, however, to have written, in conjunction with Day, The *Jew of Venice,* not printed, *Guy, Earl of Warwick,* of which various writers have conjectured a good deal but have known nothing, *Gustavus, King of Swithland,* of which the world is nearly as ignorant, and the *Tale of Jocondo and Astolpho,* taken probably from the same stock as La Fontaine's *Joconde,* a circumstance not, however, to be ascertained, this play having been destroyed, together with so many others, by Warburton's servant.

Upon the whole, Decker cannot be ranked with Chapman and Heywood, and it is very probable that he would not have been half so well respected as he was, had not the envy of Jonson, who had he possessed an atom of good sense would have smiled and passed by him, lifted him into a consequence, not only fancied by him but credited by the world. (pp. 257-60)

> *Charles Dibdin, "Chapman, Thomas Heywood, Marloe, and Others," and "Chapman, Heywood, Decker, Marston, and Others," in his* A Complete History of the English Stage, *Vol. III, 1800. Reprint by Garland Publishing, Inc., 1970, pp. 103-13, 247-70.*

John Webster's estimation of the works of Dekker and some of his contemporaries:

Detraction is the sworne friend to ignorance: For mine owne part I have ever truly cherisht my good opinion of other mens worthy Labours, especially of that full and haightned stile of Maister *Chapman:* The labor'd and understanding workes of Maister *Johnson:* The no lesse worthy composures of the both worthily excellent Maister *Beamont,* and Maister *Fletcher:* And lastly (without wrong last to be named) the right happy and copious industry of M. *Shake-speare,* M. *Decker,* and M. *Heywood,* wishing what I write may be read by their light: Protesting, that, in the strength of mine owne judgement, I know them so worthy, that though I rest silent in my owne worke, yet to most of theirs I dare (without flattery) fix that of *Martiall.*

John Webster, in his preface to The White Devil, *1612.*

William Hazlitt   (lecture date 1820)

[*An English essayist, Hazlitt was one of the most important critics of the Romantic age. He contributed significantly to a revival of interest in a number of Elizabethan dramatists, including John Webster and Thomas Heywood. Hazlitt's ideal of criticism was to provide a guide to the work under consideration rather than an ultimate judgment of that work. Moreover, as a journalist writing for the general public, Hazlitt purposely made his criticism palatable to readers by using illustrations, digressions, and repetitions. In this excerpt from a lecture originally published in his* Lectures chiefly on the Dramatic Literature of the Age of Elizabeth *(1820), he praises Dekker's characterizations in* The Honest Whore.]

[Old] honest Deckar's Signior Orlando Friscobaldo I shall never forget! I became only of late acquainted with this . . . worthy character; but the bargain between us is, I trust, for life. We sometimes regret that we had not sooner met with characters like these, that seem to raise, revive, and give a new zest to our being. Vain the complaint! We should never have known their value, if we had not known them always: they are old, very old acquaintance, or we should not recognise them at first sight. We only find in books what is already written within 'the redleaved tables of our hearts.' The pregnant materials are there; 'the pangs, the internal pangs are ready; and poor humanity's afflicted will struggling in vain with ruthless destiny.' But the reading of fine poetry may indeed open the bleeding wounds, or pour balm and consolation into

them, or sometimes even close them up for ever! Let any one who has never known cruel disappointment, nor comfortable hopes, read the first scene between Orlando and Hippolito, in Deckar's play of the **Honest Whore,** and he will see nothing in it. (p. 235)

The execution is, throughout, as exact as the conception is new and masterly. There is the least colour possible used; the pencil drags; the canvas is almost seen through: but then, what precision of outline, what truth and purity of tone, what firmness of hand, what marking of character! The words and answers all along are so true and pertinent, that we seem to see the gestures, and to hear the tone with which they are accompanied. So when Orlando, disguised, says to his daughter, 'You'll forgive me,' and she replies, 'I am not marble, I forgive you;' or again, when she introduces him to her husband, saying simply, 'It is my father,' there needs no stage-direction to supply the relenting tones of voice or cordial frankness of manner with which these words are spoken. It is as if there were some fine art to chisel thought, and to embody the inmost movements of the mind in every-day actions and familiar speech. It has been asked,

> Oh! who can paint a sun-beam to the blind,
> Or make him feel a shadow with his mind?

But this difficulty is here in a manner overcome. Simplicity and extravagance of style, homeliness and quaintness, tragedy and comedy, interchangeably set their hands and seals to this admirable production. We find the simplicity of prose with the graces of poetry. The stalk grows out of the ground; but the flowers spread their flaunting leaves in the air. The mixture of levity in the chief character bespeaks the bitterness from which it seeks relief; it is the idle echo of fixed despair, jealous of observation or pity. The sarcasm quivers on the lip, while the tear stands congealed on the eye-lid. This 'tough senior,' this impracticable old gentleman softens into a little child; this choke-pear melts in the mouth like marmalade. In spite of his resolute professions of misanthropy, he watches over his daughter with kindly solicitude; plays the careful housewife; broods over her lifeless hopes; nurses the decay of her husband's fortune, as he had supported her tottering infancy; saves the high-flying Matheo from the gallows more than once, and is twice a father to them. The story has all the romance of private life, all the pathos of bearing up against silent grief, all the tenderness of concealed affection:— there is much sorrow patiently borne, and then comes peace. Bellafront, in the two parts of this play taken together, is a most interesting character. It is an extreme, and I am afraid almost an ideal case. She gives the play its title, turns out a true penitent, that is, a practical one, and is the model of an exemplary wife. She seems intended to establish the converse of the position, that a *reformed rake makes the best husband,* the only difficulty in proving which, is, I suppose, to meet with the character. The change of her relative position, with regard to Hippolito, who, in the first part, in the sanguine enthusiasm of youthful generosity, has reclaimed her from vice, and in the second part, his own faith and love of virtue having been impaired with the progress of years, tries in vain to lure her back again to her former follies, has an effect the most striking and beautiful. The pleadings on both sides, for and against female faith and constancy, are managed with great polemical skill, assisted by the grace and vividness of poetical illustration. As an instance of the manner in which Bellafront speaks of the miseries of her former situation, 'and she has felt them knowingly,' I might give the lines in which she contrasts the different regard shewn to the modest or the abandoned of her sex.

> I cannot, seeing she's woven of such bad stuff,
> Set colours on a harlot bad enough.
> Nothing did make me when I lov'd them best,
> To loath them more than this: when in the street
> A fair, young, modest damsel, I did meet;
> She seem'd to all a dove, when I pass'd by,
> And I to all a raven: every eye
> That followed her, went with a bashful glance;
> At me each bold and jeering countenance
> Darted forth scorn: to her, as if she had been
> Some tower unvanquished, would they all vail;
> 'Gainst me swoln rumour hoisted every sail.
> She crown'd with reverend praises, pass'd by
>   them;
> I, though with face mask'd, could not 'scape the
>   hem;
> For, as if heav'n had set strange marks on
>   whores,
> Because they should be pointing-stocks to man,
> Drest up in civilest shape, a courtesan,
> Let her walk saint-like, noteless, and unknown,
> Yet she's betray'd by some trick of her own.

Perhaps this sort of appeal to matter of fact and popular opinion, is more convincing than the scholastic subtleties of the Lady in *Comus*. The manner too, in which Infelice, the wife of Hippolito, is made acquainted with her husband's infidelity, is finely dramatic; and in the scene where she convicts him of his injustice by taxing herself with incontinence first, and then turning his most galling reproaches to her into upbraidings against his own conduct, she acquits herself with infinite spirit and address. The contrivance, by which, in the first part, after being supposed dead, she is restored to life, and married to Hippolito, though perhaps a little far-fetched, is affecting and romantic. There is uncommon beauty in the Duke her father's description of her sudden illness. In reply to Infelice's declaration on reviving, 'I'm well,' he says,

> Thou wert not so e'en now. Sickness' pale hand
> Laid hold on thee, ev'n in the deadst of feasting:
> And when a cup, crown'd with thy lover's
>   health,
> Had touch'd thy lips, a sensible cold dew
> Stood on thy cheeks, as if that death had wept
> To see such beauty altered.

Candido, the good-natured man of this play, is a character of inconceivable quaintness and simplicity. His patience and good-humour cannot be disturbed by any thing. The idea (for it is nothing but an idea) is a droll one, and is well supported. He is not only resigned to injuries, but 'turns them,' as Falstaff says of diseases, 'into commodities.' He is a patient Grizzel out of petticoats, or a Petruchio reversed. He is as determined upon winking at affronts, and keeping out of scrapes at all events, as the hero of the *Taming of a Shrew* is bent upon picking quarrels out of straws, and signalizing his manhood without the smallest provocation to do so. The sudden turn of the character of

Candido, on his second marriage, is, however, as amusing as it is unexpected.

Matheo, 'the high-flying' husband of Bellafront, is a masterly portrait, done with equal ease and effect. He is a person almost without virtue or vice, that is, he is in strictness without any moral principle at all. He has no malice against others, and no concern for himself. He is gay, profligate, and unfeeling, governed entirely by the impulse of the moment, and utterly reckless of consequences. His exclamation, when he gets a new suit of velvet, or a lucky run on the dice, 'do we not fly high,' is an answer to all arguments. Punishment or advice has no more effect upon him, than upon the moth that flies into the candle. He is only to be left to his fate. Orlando saves him from it, as we do the moth, by snatching it out of the flame, throwing it out of the window, and shutting down the casement upon it! (pp. 237-40)

William Hazlitt, "Lecture III: On Marston, Chapman, Deckar, Webster," in his The Complete Works of William Hazlitt, Vol. 6, *edited by P. P. Howe, J. M. Dent and Sons, Ltd., 1931, pp. 223-48.*

Charles Lamb on the title character of *The Witch of Edmonton*, 1808:

Mother Sawyer differs from the hags of Middleton or Shakspeare. She is the plain traditional old woman Witch of our ancestors; poor, deformed, and ignorant; the terror of villages, herself amenable to a justice. That should be a hardy sheriff, with the power of the county at his heels, that would lay hands on the Weird Sisters [in *Macbeth*]. They are of another jurisdiction. But upon the common and received opinion the author (or authors) have engrafted strong fancy. There is something frightfully earnest in her invocations to the Familiar.

Charles Lamb, in Lamb as Critic, *edited by Roy Park, University of Nebraska Press, 1980.*

Algernon Charles Swinburne (essay date 1908)

[*Swinburne was an English poet, dramatist, and critic who is particularly remembered today for his rejection of Victorian mores in favor of literature which stressed sensuality and beauty. In this excerpt, he analyzes Dekker's dramas for their poetic qualities, depictions of character, and moral ideals. He also treats the quality of prose in Dekker's pamphlets, focusing on their humor and ethical concerns.*]

Of all English poets, if not of all poets on record, Dekker is perhaps the most difficult to classify. The grace and delicacy, the sweetness and spontaneity of his genius are not more obvious and undeniable than the many defects which impair and the crowning deficiency which degrades it. As long, but so long only, as a man retains some due degree of self-respect and respect for the art he serves or the business he follows, it matters less for his fame in the future than for his prosperity in the present whether he retains or discards any vestige of respect for any other obligation in the world. François Villon, compared with whom all other reckless and disreputable men of genius seem patterns of austere decency and elevated regularity of life, was as conscientious and self-respectful an artist as a Virgil or a Tennyson: he is not a great poet only, but one of the most blameless, the most perfect, the most faultless among his fellows in the first class of writers for all time. If not in that class, yet high in the class immediately beneath it, the world would long since have agreed to enrol the name of Thomas Dekker, had he not wanted that one gift which next to genius is the most indispensable for all aspirants to a station among the masters of creative literature. For he was by nature at once a singer and a maker: he had the gift of native music and the birthright of inborn invention. His song was often sweet as honey; his fancy sometimes as rich and subtle, his imagination as delicate and strong, as that of the very greatest among dramatists or poets. For gentle grace of inspiration and vivid force of realism he is eclipsed at his very best by Shakespeare's self alone. No such combination or alternation of such admirable powers is discernible in any of his otherwise more splendid or sublime compeers. And in one gift, the divine gift of tenderness, he comes nearer to Shakespeare and stands higher above others than in any other quality of kindred genius.

And with all these gifts, if the vulgar verdict of his own day and of later days be not less valid than vulgar, he was a failure. There is a pathetic undertone of patience and resignation not unqualified by manly though submissive regret, which recurs now and then, or seems to recur, in the personal accent of his subdued and dignified appeal to the casual reader, suggestive of a sense that the higher triumphs of art, the brighter prosperities of achievement, were not reserved for him; and yet not unsuggestive of a consciousness that, if this be so, it is not so through want of the primal and essential qualities of a poet. For, as Lamb says, Dekker 'had poetry enough for anything'; at all events, for anything which can be accomplished by a poet endowed in the highest degree with the gifts of graceful and melodious fancy, tender and cordial humour, vivid and pathetic realism, a spontaneous refinement and an exquisite simplicity of expression. With the one great gift of seriousness, of noble ambition, of self-confidence rooted in self-respect, he must have won an indisputable instead of a questionable place among the immortal writers of his age. But this gift had been so absolutely withheld from him by nature or withdrawn from him by circumstance that he has left us not one single work altogether worthy of the powers now revealed and now eclipsed, now suddenly radiant and now utterly extinct, in the various and voluminous array of his writings. Although his earlier plays are in every way superior to his later, there is evidence even in the best of them of the author's infirmity of hand. From the first he shows himself idly or perversely or impotently prone to loosen his hold on character and story alike before his plot can be duly carried out or his conceptions adequately developed. His *pleasant Comedie of The Gentle Craft* [*The Shoemaker's Holiday*], first printed three years before the death of Queen Elizabeth, is one of his brightest and most coherent pieces of work, graceful and lively throughout, if rather thin-spun and slight of structure: but the more serious and romantic part

of the action is more lightly handled than the broad light comedy of the mad and merry Lord Mayor Simon Eyre, a figure in the main original and humorous enough, but somewhat over persistent in ostentation and repetition of jocose catchwords after the fashion of mine host of the Garter [in *The Merry Wives of Windsor*]; a type which Shakespeare knew better than to repeat, but of which his inferiors seem to have been enamoured beyond all reason. In this fresh and pleasant little play there are few or no signs of the author's higher poetic abilities: the style is pure and sweet, simple and spontaneous, without any hint of a quality not required by the subject: but in the other play of Dekker's which bears the same date as this one his finest and rarest gifts of imagination and emotion, feeling and fancy, colour and melody, are as apparent as his ingrained faults of levity and laziness. The famous passage in which Webster couples together the names of 'Mr. Shakespeare, Mr. Dekker, and Mr. Heywood,' seems explicable when we compare the style of **'Old Fortunatus'** with the style of *A Midsummer Night's Dream*. Dekker had as much of the peculiar sweetness, the gentle fancy, the simple melody of Shakespeare in his woodland dress, as Heywood of the homely and noble realism, the heartiness and humour, the sturdy sympathy and joyful pride of Shakespeare in his most English mood of patriotic and historic loyalty. Not that these qualities are wanting in the work of Dekker: he was an ardent and a combative patriot, ever ready to take up the cudgels in prose or rhyme for England and her yeomen against Popery and the world: but it is rather the man than the poet who speaks on these occasions: his singing faculty does not apply itself so naturally to such work as to the wild wood-notes of passion and fancy and pathos which in his happiest moments, even when they remind us of Shakespeare's, provoke no sense of unworthiness or inequality in comparison with these. It is not with the most popular and famous names of his age that the sovereign name of Shakespeare is most properly or most profitably to be compared. His genius has really far less in common with that of Jonson or of Fletcher than with that of Webster or of Dekker. To the last-named poet even Lamb was for once less than just when he said of the 'frantic Lover' in **Old Fortunatus** that 'he talks pure Biron and Romeo; he is almost as poetical as they.' The word 'almost' should be supplanted by the word 'fully'; and the criticism would then be no less adequate than apt. Sidney himself might have applauded the verses which clothe with living music a passion as fervent and as fiery a fancy as his own. Not even in the rapturous melodies of that matchless series of songs and sonnets which glorify the inseparable names of Astrophel and Stella will the fascinated student find a passage more enchanting than this.

Thou art a traitor to that white and red
   Which sitting on her cheeks (being Cupid's
   throne)
Is my heart's sovereign: O, when she is dead,
   This wonder, Beauty, shall be found in none.
Now Agripyne's not mine, I vow to be
In love with nothing but deformity.
O fair Deformity, I muse all eyes
Are not enamoured of thee: thou didst never
Murder men's hearts, or let them pine like wax,

Melting against the sun of thy disdain;
Thou art a faithful nurse to Chastity;
Thy beauty is not like to Agripyne's,
For cares, and age, and sickness, hers deface,
But thine's eternal: O Deformity,
Thy fairness is not like to Agripyne's,
For, dead, her beauty will no beauty have,
But thy face looks most lovely in the grave.

Shakespeare has nothing more exquisite in expression of passionate fancy, more earnest in emotion, more spontaneous in simplicity, more perfect in romantic inspiration. But the poet's besetting sin of laxity, his want of seriousness and steadiness, his idle, shambling, shifty way of writing, had power even then, in the very prime of his promise, to impede his progress and impair his chance of winning the race which he had set himself—and yet which he had hardly set himself—to run. And if these things were done in the green tree, it was only too obvious what would be done in the dry; it must have been clear that this golden-tongued and gentle-hearted poet had not strength of spirit or fervour of ambition enough to put conscience into his work and resolution into his fancies. But even from such headlong recklessness as he had already displayed no reader could have anticipated so singular a defiance of all form and order, all coherence and proportion, as is exhibited in his *Satiromastix.* The controversial part of the play is so utterly alien from the romantic part that it is impossible to regard them as component factors of the same original plot. It seems to me unquestionable that Dekker must have conceived the design, and probable that he must have begun the composition, of a serious play on the subject of William Rufus and Sir Walter Tyrrel, before the appearance of Ben Jonson's *Poetaster* impelled or instigated him to some immediate attempt at rejoinder; and that being in a feverish hurry to retort the blow inflicted on him by a heavier hand than his own he devised—perhaps between jest and earnest—the preposterously incoherent plan of piecing out his farcical and satirical design by patching and stitching it into his unfinished scheme of tragedy. It may be assumed, and it is much to be hoped, that there never existed another poet capable of imagining—much less of perpetrating—an incongruity so monstrous and so perverse. The explanation so happily suggested by a modern critic that William Rufus is meant for Shakespeare, and that 'Lyly is Sir Vaughan ap Rees,' wants only a little further development, on the principle of analogy, to commend itself to every scholar. It is equally obvious that the low-bred and foul-mouthed ruffian Captain Tucca must be meant for Sir Philip Sidney; the vulgar idiot Asinius Bubo for Lord Bacon; the half-witted underling Peter Flash for Sir Walter Raleigh; and the immaculate Celestina, who escapes by stratagem and force of virtue from the villainous designs of Shakespeare, for the lady long since indicated by the perspicacity of a Chalmers as the object of that lawless and desperate passion which found utterance in the sonnets of her unprincipled admirer—Queen Elizabeth. As a previous suggestion of my own, to the effect that George Peele was probably the real author of *Romeo and Juliet,* has had the singular good fortune to be not merely adopted but appropriated—in serious earnest—by a contemporary student, without—as far as I am aware—a syllable of acknowledgment, I cannot but anticipate a similar acceptance in similar quarters for the modest effort at interpretation now submitted to the judgment of the ingenuous reader.

Gifford is not too severe on the palpable incongruities of Dekker's preposterous medley: but his impeachment of Dekker as a more virulent and intemperate controversialist than Jonson is not less preposterous than the structure of this play. The nobly gentle and manly verses in which the less fortunate and distinguished poet disclaims and refutes the imputation of envy or malevolence excited by the favour enjoyed by his rival in high quarters should have sufficed, in common justice, to protect him from such a charge. There is not a word in Jonson's satire expressive of anything but savage and unqualified scorn for his humbler antagonist: and the tribute paid by that antagonist to his genius, the appeal to his better nature which concludes the torrent of recrimination, would have won some word of honourable recognition from any but the most unscrupulous and ungenerous of partisans. That Dekker was unable to hold his own against Jonson when it came to sheer hard hitting—that on the ground or platform of personal satire he was as a light weight pitted against a heavy weight—is of course too plain, from the very first round, to require any further demonstration. But it is not less plain that in delicacy and simplicity and sweetness of inspiration the poet who could write the scene in which the bride takes poison (as she believes) from the hand of her father, in presence of her bridegroom, as a refuge from the passion of the king, was as far above Jonson as Jonson was above him in the robuster qualities of intellect or genius. This most lovely scene, for pathos tempered with fancy and for passion distilled in melody, is comparable only with higher work, of rarer composition and poetry more pure, than Jonson's: it is a very treasure-house of verses like jewels, bright as tears and sweet as flowers. When Dekker writes like this, then truly we seem to see his right hand in the left hand of Shakespeare.

To find the names of Ben Jonson and Thomas Dekker amicably associated in the composition of a joint poem or pageant within the space of a year from the publication of so violent a retort by the latter to so vehement an attack by the former must amuse if it does not astonish the reader least capable of surprise at the boyish readiness to quarrel and the boyish readiness to shake hands which would seem to be implied in so startling a change of relations. In all the huge, costly, wearisome, barbaric and pedantic ceremonial which welcomed into London the Solomon of Scotland, the exhausted student who attempts to follow the ponderous elaboration of report drawn up by these reconciled enemies will remark the solid and sedate merit of Jonson's best couplets with less pleasure than he will receive from the quaint sweetness of Dekker's lyric notes. Admirable as are many of Ben Jonson's songs for their finish of style and fullness of matter, it is impossible for those who know what is or should be the special aim or the distinctive quality of lyric verse to place him in the first class—much less, in the front rank—of lyric poets. He is at his best a good way ahead of such song-writers as Byron; but Dekker at his best belongs to the order of such song-writers as Blake or Shelley. Perhaps the very finest example of his flawless and delicate simplicity of excellence in this field of work may be the well-known song in honour of honest poverty and in praise of honest labour which so gracefully introduces the heroine of a play published in this same year of the accession of James—***Patient Grissel;*** a romantic tragicomedy so attractive for its sweetness and lightness of tone and touch that no reader will question the judgment or condemn the daring of the poets who ventured upon ground where Chaucer had gone before them with such gentle stateliness of step and such winning tenderness of gesture. His deepest note of pathos they have not even attempted to reproduce: but in freshness and straightforwardness, in frankness and simplicity of treatment, the dramatic version is not generally unworthy to be compared with the narrative which it follows afar off. Chettle and Haughton, the associates of Dekker in this enterprise, had each of them something of their colleague's finer qualities; but the best scenes in the play remind me rather of Dekker's best early work than of *Robert Earl of Huntington* or of *Englishmen for my Money.* So much has been said of the evil influence of Italian example upon English character in the age of Elizabeth, and so much has been made of such confessions or imputations as distinguish the clamorous and malevolent penitence of Robert Greene, that it is more than agreeable to find at least one dramatic poet of the time who has the manliness to enter a frank and contemptuous protest against this habit of malignant self-excuse. 'Italy,' says an honest gentleman in this comedy to a lying and impudent gull, 'Italy infects you not, but your own diseased spirits. Italy? Out, you froth, you scum! because your soul is mud, and that you have breathed in Italy, you'll say Italy has defiled you: away, you boar: thou wilt wallow in mire in the sweetest country in the world.'

There are many traces of moral or spiritual weakness and infirmity in the writings of Dekker and the scattered records or indications of his unprosperous though not unlaborious career: but there are manifest and manifold signs of an honest and earnest regard for justice and fair dealing, as well as of an inexhaustible compassion for suffering, an indestructible persistency of pity, which found characteristic expression in the most celebrated of his plays. There is a great gulf between it and the first of Victor Hugo's tragedies: yet the instinct of either poet is the same, as surely as their common motive is the redemption of a fallen woman by the influence of twinborn love and shame. Of all Dekker's works, ***The Honest Whore*** comes nearest to some reasonable degree of unity and harmony in conception and construction; his besetting vice of reckless and sluttish incoherence has here done less than usual to deform the proportions and deface the impression of his design. Indeed, the connection of the two serious plots in the first part is a rare example of dexterous and happy simplicity in composition: the comic underplot of the patient man and shrewish wife is more loosely attached by a slighter thread of relation to these two main stories, but is so amusing in its light and facile play of inventive merriment and harmless mischief as to need no further excuse. Such an excuse, however, might otherwise be found in the plea that it gives occasion for the most beautiful, the most serious, and the most famous passage in all the writings of its author. The first scene of this first part has always appeared to me one of the most effective and impressive on our

stage: the interruption of the mock funeral by the one true mourner whose passion it was intended to deceive into despair is so striking as a mere incident or theatrical device that the noble and simple style in which the graver part of the dialogue is written can be no more than worthy of the subject: whereas in other plays of Dekker's the style is too often beneath the merit of the subject, and the subject as often below the value of the style. The subsequent revival of Infelice from her trance is represented with such vivid and delicate power that the scene, short and simple as it is, is one of the most fascinating in any play of the period. In none of these higher and finer parts of the poem can I trace the touch of any other hand than the principal author's: but the shopkeeping scenes of the underplot have at least as much of Middleton's usual quality as of Dekker's; homely and rough-cast as they are, there is a certain finish or thoroughness about them which is more like the careful realism of the former than the slovenly naturalism of the latter. The coarse commonplaces of the sermon on prostitution by which Bellafront is so readily and surprisingly reclaimed into respectability give sufficient and superfluous proof that Dekker had nothing of the severe and fiery inspiration which makes a great satirist or a great preacher; but when we pass again into a sweeter air than that of the boudoir or the pulpit, it is the unmistakable note of Dekker's most fervent and tender mood of melody which enchants us in such verses as these, spoken by a lover musing on the portrait of a mistress whose coffin has been borne before him to the semblance of a grave.

> Of all the roses grafted on her cheeks,
> Of all the graces dancing in her eyes,
> Of all the music set upon her tongue,
> Of all that was past woman's excellence
> In her white bosom, look, a painted board
> Circumscribes all!

Is there any other literature, we are tempted to ask ourselves, in which the writer of these lines, and of many as sweet and perfect in their inspired simplicity as these, would be rated no higher among his countrymen than Thomas Dekker?

From the indisputable fact of Middleton's partnership in this play Mr. Dyce was induced to assume the very questionable inference of his partnership in the sequel which was licensed for acting five years later. To me this second part seems so thoroughly of one piece and one pattern, so apparently the result of one man's invention and composition, that without more positive evidence I should hesitate to assign a share in it to any colleague of the poet under whose name it first appeared. There are far fewer scenes or passages in this than in the preceding play which suggest or present themselves for quotation or selection: the tender and splendid and pensive touches of pathetic or imaginative poetry which we find in the first part, we shall be disappointed if we seek in the second: its incomparable claim on our attention is the fact that it contains the single character in all the voluminous and miscellaneous works of Dekker which gives its creator an indisputable right to a place of perpetual honour among the imaginative humourists of England, and therefore among the memorable artists and creative workmen of the world. Apart from their claim to remembrance as poets and dramatists of more or less artistic and executive capacity, Dekker and Middleton are each of them worthy to be remembered as the inventor or discoverer of a wholly original, interesting, and natural type of character, as essentially inimitable as it is undeniably unimitated: the savage humour and cynic passion of De Flores, the genial passion and tender humour of Orlando Friscobaldo, are equally lifelike in the truthfulness and completeness of their distinct and vivid presentation. The merit of the play in which the character last named is a leading figure consists mainly or almost wholly in the presentation of the three principal persons: the reclaimed harlot, now the faithful and patient wife of her first seducer; the broken-down, ruffianly, light-hearted and light-headed libertine who has married her; and the devoted old father who watches in the disguise of a servant over the changes of her fortune, the sufferings, risks, and temptations which try the purity of her penitence and confirm the fortitude of her constancy. Of these three characters I cannot but think that any dramatist who ever lived might have felt that he had reason to be proud. It is strange that Charles Lamb, to whom of all critics and all men the pathetic and humorous charm of the old man's personality might most confidently have been expected most cordially to appeal, should have left to Hazlitt and Leigh Hunt the honour of doing justice to so beautiful a creation—the crowning evidence to the greatness of Dekker's gifts, his power of moral imagination and his delicacy of dramatic execution. From the first to the last word of his part the quaint sweet humour of the character is sustained with an instinctive skill which would do honour to a far more careful and a far more famous artist than Dekker. The words with which he receives the false news of his fallen daughter's death; 'Dead? my last and best peace go with her!'—those which he murmurs to himself on seeing her again after seventeen years of estrangement; 'The mother's own face, I ha' not forgot that'—prepare the way for the admirable final scene in which his mask of anger drops off, and his ostentation of obduracy relaxes into tenderness and tears. 'Dost thou beg for him, thou precious man's meat, thou? has he not beaten thee, kicked thee, trod on thee? and dost thou fawn on him like his spaniel? has he not pawned thee to thy petticoat, sold thee to thy smock, made ye leap at a crust? yet wouldst have me save him?—What, dost thou hold him? let go his hand: if thou dost not forsake him, a father's everlasting blessing fall upon both your heads!' The fusion of humour with pathos into perfection of exquisite accuracy in expression which must be recognised at once and remembered for ever by any competent reader of this scene is the highest quality of Dekker as a writer of prose, and is here displayed at its highest: the more poetic or romantic quality of his genius had already begun to fade out when this second part of his finest poem was written. Hazlitt has praised the originality, dexterity, and vivacity of the effect produced by the strategem which Infelice employs for the humiliation of her husband, when by accusing herself of imaginary infidelity under the most incredibly degrading conditions she entraps him into gratuitous fury and turns the tables on him by the production of evidence against himself; and the scene is no doubt theatrically effective: but the grace and delicacy of the character are sacrificed to this comparatively unworthy consideration: the pure, high-minded,

noble-hearted lady, whose loyal and passionate affection was so simply and so attractively displayed in the first part of her story, is so lamentably humiliated by the cunning and daring immodesty of such a device that we hardly feel it so revolting an incongruity as it should have been to see this princess enjoying, in common with her father and her husband, the spectacle of imprisoned harlots on penitential parade in the Bridewell of Milan; a thoroughly Hogarthian scene in the grim and vivid realism of its tragicomic humour.

But if the poetic and realistic merits of these two plays make us understand why Webster should have coupled its author with the author of *Twelfth Night* and *The Merry Wives of Windsor,* the demerits of the two plays next published under his single name are so grave, so gross, so manifold, that the writer seems unworthy to be coupled as a dramatist with a journeyman poet so far superior to him in honest thoroughness and smoothness of workmanship as, even at his very hastiest and crudest, was Thomas Heywood. In style and versification the patriotic and anti-Catholic drama which bears the Protestant and apocalyptic title of **The Whore of Babylon** is still, upon the whole, very tolerably spirited and fluent, with gleams of fugitive poetry and glimpses of animated action; but the construction is ponderous and puerile, the declamation vacuous and vehement. An Æschylus alone could have given us, in a tragedy on the subject of the Salamis of England, a fit companion to the *Persæ;* which, as Shakespeare let the chance pass by him, remains alone for ever in the incomparable glory of its triumphant and sublime perfection. Marlowe perhaps might have made something of it, though the task would have taxed his energies to the utmost, and overtasked the utmost of his skill; Dekker could make nothing. The empress of Babylon is but a poor slipshod ragged prostitute in the hands of this poetic beadle. . . . (pp. 60-80)

The next play which bears his name alone was published five years later than the political or historical sketch or study which we have just dismissed; and which, compared with it, is a tolerable if not a creditable piece of work. It is difficult to abstain from intemperate language in speaking of such a dramatic abortion as that which bears the grotesque and puerile inscription, ***If this be not a good Play, the Devil is in it.*** A worse has seldom discredited the name of any man with a spark of genius in him. Dryden's delectable tragedy of *Amboyna,* Lee's remarkable tragicomedy of *Gloriana,* Pope's elegant comedy of *Three Hours after Marriage,* are scarcely more unworthy of their authors, more futile or more flaccid or more audacious in their headlong and unabashed incompetence. Charity would suggest that it must have been written against time in a debtor's prison, under the influence of such liquor as Catherina Bountinall or Doll Tearsheet would have flung at the tapster's head with an accompaniment of such language as those eloquent and high-spirited ladies, under less offensive provocation, were wont to lavish on the officials of an oppressive law. I have read a good deal of bad verse, but anything like the metre of this play I have never come across in all the range of that excruciating experience. The rare and faint indications that the writer was or had been an humourist and a poet serve only to bring into fuller relief the reckless and shameless incompetence of the general workmanship.

This supernatural and 'superlunatical' attempt at serious farce or farcical morality marks the nadir of Dekker's ability as a dramatist. The diabolic part of the tragicomic business is distinctly inferior to the parallel or similar scenes in the much older play of *Grim the Collier of Croydon,* which is perhaps more likely to have been the writer's immediate model than the original story by Machiavelli. The two remaining plays now extant which bear the single name of Dekker give no sign of his highest powers, but are tolerable examples of journeyman's work in the field of romantic or fanciful comedy. *Match me in London* is the better play of the two, very fairly constructed after its simple fashion, and reasonably well written in a smooth and unambitious style: *The Wonder of a Kingdom* is a light, slight, rough piece of work, in its contrasts of character as crude and boyish as any of the old moralities, and in its action as mere a dance of puppets: but it shows at least that Dekker had regained the faculty of writing decent verse on occasion. The fine passage quoted by Scott in *The Antiquary,* and taken by his editors to be a forgery of his own, will be familiar to many myriads of readers who are never likely to look it up in the original context. Of two masques called *Britannia's Honour* and *London's Tempe* it must suffice to say that the former contains a notable specimen of cockney or canine French which may serve to relieve the conscientious reader's weariness, and the latter a comic song of blacksmiths at work which may pass muster at a pinch as a tolerably quaint and lively piece of rough and ready fancy. But Jonson for the court and Middleton for the city were far better craftsmen in this line than ever was Dekker at his best. (pp. 80-83)

Among his numerous pamphlets, satirical or declamatory, on the manners of his time and the observations of his experience, one alone stands out as distinct from the rest by right of such astonishing superiority in merit of style and interest of matter that I prefer to reserve it for separate and final consideration. But it would require more time and labour than I can afford to give an adequate account of so many effusions or improvisations as served for fuel to boil the scanty and precarious pot of his uncertain and uncomfortable sustenance. *The Wonderful Year* of the death of Elizabeth, the accession of James, and the devastation of London by pestilence, supplied him with matter enough for one of his quaintest and liveliest tracts: in which the historical part has no quality so valuable or remarkable as the grotesque mixture of horror and humour in the anecdotes appended 'like a merry epilogue to a dull play, of purpose to shorten the lives of long winter's nights that lie watching in the dark for us,' with touches of rude and vivid pleasantry not unworthy to remind us, I dare not say of the Decameron, but at least of the *Cent Nouvelles Nouvelles.* In *The Seven Deadly Sins of London*—one of the milder but less brilliant 'Latterday Pamphlets' of a gentler if no less excitable Carlyle—there are touches of earnest eloquence as well as many quaint and fitful illustrations of social history; but there is less of humorous vigour and straightforward realism than in the preceding tract. And yet there are good things to be gathered out of this effusive and vehement lay sermon: this sentence for example is worth recollection:—'He is not slothful that is only lazy, that only wastes his good hours and his silver in luxury and licentious ease:—no, he is the true slothful man, that does no good.' And there is genuine insight as well as honesty and courage in his remonstrance with the self-love and appeal against the self-deceit of his countrymen, so prone to cry out on the cruelty of others, on the bloodthirstiness of Frenchmen and Spaniards, and to overlook the heavy-headed brutality of their own habitual indifference and neglect. Although the cruelty of penal laws be now abrogated, yet the condition of the poorest among us is assuredly not such that we can read without a sense of their present veracity the last words of this sentence:—'Thou set'st up posts to whip them when they are alive: set up an hospital to comfort them being sick, or purchase ground for them to dwell in when they be well; *and that is, when they be dead.'* The next of Dekker's tracts is more of a mere imitation than any of his others: the influence of a more famous pamphleteer and satirist, Tom Nash, is here not only manifest as that of a model, but has taken such possession of his disciple that he is hardly more than a somewhat servile copyist; not without a touch of his master's more serious eloquence, but with less than little of his peculiar energy and humour. That rushing wind of satire, that storm of resonant invective, that inexhaustible volubility of contempt, which rages through the controversial writings of the lesser poet, has sunk to a comparative whisper; the roar of his Homeric or Rabelaisian laughter to a somewhat forced and artificial chuckle. This *News from Hell, brought by the Devil's Carrier,* and containing *The Devil's Answer to Pierce Penniless,* might have miscarried by the way without much more loss than that of such an additional proof as we could have been content to spare of Dekker's incompetence to deal with a subject which he was curiously fond of handling in earnest and in jest. He seems indeed to have fancied himself, if not something of a Dante, something at least of a Quevedo; but his terrors are merely tedious, and his painted devils would not terrify a babe. In this tract, however, there are now and then some fugitive felicities of expression; and this is more than can be said for either the play or the poem in which he has gone, with feebler if not more uneasy steps than Milton's Satan, over the same ground of burning marl. There is some spirit in the prodigal's denunciation of his miserly father: but the best thing in the pamphlet is the description of the soul of a hero bound for paradise, whose name is given only in the revised and enlarged edition which appeared a year later under the title of *A Knight's Conjuring; done in earnest; discovered in jest.* The narrative of 'William Eps his death' is a fine example of that fiery sympathy with soldiers which glows in so many pages of Dekker's verse, and flashes out by fits through the murky confusion of his worst and most formless plays; but the introduction of this hero is as fine a passage of prose as he has left us.

> The foremost of them was a personage of so composed a presence, that Nature and Fortune had done him wrong, if they had not made him a soldier. *In his countenance there was a kind of indignation, fighting with a kind of exalted joy,* which by his very gesture were apparently decipherable; for he was jocund, that his soul went

out of him in so glorious a triumph; but disdain-
fully angry, that she wrought her enlargement
through no more dangers: yet were there bleeding witnesses enow on his breast, which testified,
he did not yield till he was conquered, and was
not conquered, till there was left nothing of a
man in him to be overcome.

That the poet's loyalty and devotion were at least as ardent when offered by his gratitude to sailors as to soldiers
we may see by this description of 'The Seaman' in his next
work.

A progress doth he take from realm to realm,
With goodly water-pageants borne before him;
The safety of the land sits at his helm,
No danger here can touch, but what runs o'er
    him:
But being in heaven's eye still, it doth restore
    him
To livelier spirits; to meet death with ease,
If thou wouldst know thy maker, search the seas.

These homely but hearty lines occur in a small and mainly
metrical tract bearing a title so quaint that I am tempted
to transcribe it at length:—*The Double PP. A Papist in
Arms. Bearing Ten several Shields. Encountered by the
Protestant. At Ten several Weapons. A Jesuit Marching
before them. Cominùs and Eminùs.* There are a few other
vigorous and pointed verses in this little patriotic impromptu, but the greater part of it is merely curious and
eccentric doggrel.

The next of Dekker's tracts or pamphlets was the comparatively well-known *Gull's Horn-book.* This brilliant and
vivid little satire is so rich in simple humour, and in lifelike
photography taken by the sunlight of an honest and kindly
nature, that it stands second only to the author's masterpiece in prose, *The Bachelor's Banquet,* which has waited
so much longer for even the limited recognition implied
by a private reprint. There are so many witty or sensible
or humorous or grotesque excerpts to be selected from this
pamphlet—and not from the parts borrowed or copied
from a foreign satire on the habits of slovenly Holland-
ers—that I take the first which comes under my notice on
reopening the book; a study which sets before us in fascinating relief the professional poeticule of a period in which
as yet clubs, coteries, and newspapers were not—or at the
worst were nothing to speak of.

If you be a Poet, and come into the Ordinary
(though it can be no great glory to be an ordinary Poet) order yourself thus. Observe no man,
doff not cap to that gentleman to-day at dinner,
to whom, not two nights since, you were behold-
en for a supper; but, after a turn or two in the
room, take occasion (pulling out your gloves) to
have some Epigram, or Satire, or Sonnet fastened in one of them, that may (as it were unwittingly to you) offer itself to the Gentlemen: they
will presently desire it: but, without much conjuration from them, and a pretty kind of counterfeit lothness in yourself, do not read it; and,
though it be none of your own, swear you made
it.

This coupling of injunction and prohibition is worthy of
Shakespeare or of Sterne.

Marry, if you chance to get into your hands any
witty thing of another man's, that is somewhat
better, I would counsel you then, if demand be
made who composed it, you may say: ' 'Faith, a
learned Gentleman, a very worthy friend.' And
this seeming to lay it on another man will be
counted either modesty in you, or a sign that you
are not ambitious of praise, *or else that you dare
not take it upon you, for fear of the sharpness it
carries with it.*

The modern poetaster by profession knows a trick worth
any two of these: but it is curious to observe the community of baseness, and the comparative innocence of awk-
wardness and inexperience, which at once connote the
species and denote the specimens of the later and the earlier animalcule.

The *Jests to make you merry,* which in Dr. Grosart's edition are placed after *The Gull's Horn-book,* though dated
two years earlier, will hardly give so much entertainment
to any probable reader in our own time as *The Misery of
a Prison, and a Prisoner,* will give him pain to read of in
the closing pages of the same pamphlet, when he remembers how long—at the lowest computation—its author
had endured the loathsome and hideous misery which he
has described with such bitter and pathetic intensity and
persistency in detail. Well may Dr. Grosart say that 'it
shocks us to-day, though so far off, to think of 1598 to
1616 onwards covering so sorrowful and humiliating trials
for so finely touched a spirit as was Dekker's'; but I think
as well as hope that there is no sort of evidence to that
surely rather improbable as well as deplorable effect. It
may be 'possible,' but it is barely possible, that some 'seven
years' continuous imprisonment' is the explanation of an
ambiguous phrase which is now incapable of any certain
solution, and capable of many an interpretation far less deplorable than this. But in this professedly comic pamphlet
there are passages as tragic, if not as powerful, as any in
the immortal pages of *Pickwick* and *Little Dorrit* which
deal with a later but a too similar phase of prison discipline
and tradition.

The thing that complained was a man:—'Thy
days have gone over thee like the dreams of a
fool, thy nights like the watchings of a madman.—Oh sacred liberty! with how little devotion do men come into thy temples, when they
cannot bestow upon thee too much honour! Thy
embracements are more delicate than those of a
young bride with her lover, and to be divorced
from thee is half to be damned! For what else is
a prison but the very next door to hell? It is a
man's grave, wherein he walks alive: it is a sea
wherein he is always shipwrackt: it is a lodging
built out of the world: it is a wilderness where
all that wander up and down grow wild, and all
that come into it are devoured.'

In Dekker's next pamphlet, his *Dream,* there are perhaps
half a dozen tolerably smooth and vigorous couplets immersed among many more vacuous and vehement in the
intensity of their impotence than any reader and admirer
of his more happily inspired verse could be expected to believe without evidence adduced. Of imagination, faith, or
fancy, the ugly futility of this infernal vision has not—

unless I have sought more than once for it in vain—a single saving trace or compensating shadow.

Two years after he had tried his hand at an imitation of Nash, Dekker issued the first of the pamphlets in which he attempted to take up the succession of Robert Greene as a picaresque writer, or purveyor of guidebooks through the realms of rascaldom. *The Bellman of London, or Rogue's Horn-book,* begins with a very graceful and fanciful description of the quiet beauty and seclusion of a country retreat in which the author had sought refuge from the turmoil and forgetfulness of the vices of the city; and whence he was driven back upon London by disgust at the discovery of villainy as elaborate and roguery as abject in the beggars and thieves of the country as the most squalid recesses of metropolitan vice or crime could supply. The narrative of this accidental discovery is very lively and spirited in its straightforward simplicity, and the subsequent revelations of rascality are sometimes humorous as well as curious: but the demand for such literature must have been singularly persistent to evoke a sequel to this book next year, *Lantern and Candle-light, or the Bellman's Second Night-walk,* in which Dekker continues his account of vagrant and villainous society, its lawless laws and its unmannerly manners; and gives the reader some vivid studies, interspersed with facile rhetoric and interlarded with indignant declamation, of the tricks of horse-dealers and the shifts of gipsies—or 'moon-men' as he calls them; a race which he regarded with a mixture of angry perplexity and passionate disgust. *A Strange Horse-race* between various virtues and vices gives occasion for the display of some allegoric ingenuity and much indefatigable but fatiguing pertinacity in the exposure of the more exalted swindlers of the age—the crafty bankrupts who anticipated the era of the Merdles described by Dickens, but who can hardly have done much immediate injury to a capitalist of the rank of Dekker. Here too there are glimpses of inventive spirit and humorous ingenuity; but the insufferable iteration of jocose demonology and infernal burlesque might tempt the most patient and the most curious of readers to devote the author, with imprecations or invocations as elaborate as his own, to the spiritual potentate whose 'last will and testament' is transcribed into the text of this pamphlet.

In *The Dead Term* such a reader will find himself more or less relieved by the return of his author to a more terrene and realistic sort of allegory. This recriminatory dialogue between the London and the Westminster of 1608 is now and then rather flatulent in its reciprocity of rhetoric, but is enlivened by an occasional breath of genuine eloquence, and redeemed by touches of historic or social interest. The title and motto of the next year's pamphlet—*Work for Armourers, or the Peace is Broken.—God help the Poor, the rich can shift*—were presumably designed to attract the casual reader, by what would now be called a sensational device, to consideration of the social question between rich and poor—or, as he puts it, between the rival queens, Poverty and Money. The forces on either side are drawn out and arrayed with pathetic ingenuity, and the result is indicated with a quaint and grim effect of humorous if indignant resignation. *The Raven's Almanack* of the same year, though portentous in its menace of plague, famine, and civil war, is less noticeable for its moral and religious declamation than for its rather amusing than edifying anecdotes; which, it must again be admitted, in their mixture of jocular sensuality with somewhat ferocious humour, rather remind us of King Louis XI. than of that royal novelist's Italian models or precursors. *A Rod for Runaways* is the title of a tract which must have somewhat perplexed the readers who came to it for practical counsel or suggestion, seeing that the very title-page calls their attention to the fact that, 'if they look back, they may behold many fearful judgments of God, sundry ways pronounced upon this city, and on several persons, both flying from it, and staying in it.' What the medical gentleman to whom this tract was dedicated may have thought of the author's logic and theology, we can only conjecture. But even in this little pamphlet there are anecdotes and details which would repay the notice of a social historian as curious in his research and as studious in his condescension as Macaulay.

A prayerbook written or compiled by a poet of Dekker's rank in Dekker's age would have some interest for the reader of a later generation even if it had not the literary charm which distinguishes the little volume of devotions, [*Four Birds of Noah's Ark*], now reprinted from a single and an imperfect copy. We cannot be too grateful for the good fortune and the generous care to which we are indebted for this revelation of a work of genius so curious and so delightful that the most fanatical of atheists or agnostics, the hardest and the driest of philosophers, might be moved and fascinated by the exquisite simplicity of its beauty. Hardly even in those almost incomparable collects which Macaulay so aptly compared with the sonnets of Milton shall we find sentences or passages more perfect in their union of literary grace with ardent sincerity than here. Quaint as are several of the prayers in the professional particulars of their respective appeals, this quaintness has nothing of irreverence or incongruity: and the subtle simplicity of cadence in the rhythmic movement of the style is so nearly impeccable that we are perplexed to understand how so exquisite an ear as was Dekker's at its best can have been tolerant of such discord or insensible to such collapse as so often disappoints or shocks us in the hastier and cruder passages of his faltering and fluctuating verse. The prayer for a soldier going to battle and his thanksgiving after victory are as noble in the dignity of their devotion as the prayers for a woman in travail and 'for them that visit the sick' are delicate and earnest in their tenderness. The prayer for a prisoner is too beautiful to stand in need of the additional and pathetic interest which it derives from the fact of its author's repeated experience of the misery it expresses with such piteous yet such manful resignation. The style of these faultlessly simple devotions is almost grotesquely set off by the relief of a comparison with the bloated bombast and flatulent pedantry of a prayer by the late Queen Elizabeth which Dekker has transcribed into his text—it is hardly possible to suppose, without perception of the contrast between its hideous jargon and the refined purity of his own melodious English. The prayer for the Council is singularly noble in the eloquence of its patriotism: the prayer for the country is simply magnificent in the austere music of its fervent cadences: the prayer in time of civil war is so passionate in its cry for deliverance from all danger of the miseries then or lately afflicting the continent that it might well have been put up by a loyal patriot in the very heat of the great war which Dekker might have lived to see break out in his own country. The prayer for the evening is so beautiful as to double our regret for the deplorable mutilation which has deprived us of all but the opening of the morning prayer. The feathers fallen from the wings of these *Four Birds of Noah's Ark* would be worth more to the literary ornithologist than whole flocks of such 'tame villatic fowl' as people the ordinary coops and hen-roosts of devotional literature.

One work only of Dekker's too often over-tasked and heavy-laden genius remains to be noticed; it is one which gives him a high place for ever among English humourists. No sooner has the reader run his eye over the first three or four pages than he feels himself, with delight and astonishment, in the company of a writer whose genius is akin at once to Goldsmith's and to Thackeray's; a writer whose style is so pure and vigorous, so lucid and straightforward, that we seem to have already entered upon the best age of English prose. Had Mr. Matthew Arnold, instead of digging in Chapman for preposterous barbarisms and eccentricities of pedantry, chanced to light upon this little treatise; or had he condescended to glance over Daniel's compact and admirable *Defence of Rhyme;* he would have found in writers of the despised Shakespearean epoch much more than a foretaste of those excellent qualities which he imagined to have been first imported into our literature by writers of the age of Dryden. The dialogue of the very first couple introduced with such skilful simplicity of presentation at the opening of Dekker's pamphlet is worthy of Sterne: the visit of the gossip or kinswoman in the second chapter is worthy of Molière; and the humours of the monthly nurse in the third are worthy of Dickens. The lamentations of the lady for the decay of her health and beauty in consequence of her obsequious husband's alleged neglect, 'no more like the woman I was than an apple is like an oyster'; the description of the poor man making her broth with his own hands, jeered at by the maids and trampled underfoot by Mrs. Gamp; the preparations for the christening supper and the preliminary feast of scandal; are full of such bright and rich humour as to recall even the creator of Dogberry and Mrs. Quickly. It is of Shakespeare again that we are reminded in the next chapter, by the description of the equipage to which the husband of 'a woman that hath a charge of children' is reduced when he has to ride to the assizes in sorrier plight than Petruchio rode in to his wedding; the details remind us also of Balzac in the minute and grotesque intensity of their industrious realism: but the scene on his return reminds us rather of Thackeray at the best of his bitterest mood—the terrible painter of Mrs. Mackenzie and Mrs. General Baynes. 'The humour of a woman that marries her inferior by birth' deals with more serious matters in a style not unworthy of Boccaccio; and no comedy of the time—Shakespeare's always excepted—has a scene in it of richer and more original humour than brightens the narrative which relates the woes of the husband who invites his friends to dinner and finds everything under lock and key. Hardly in any of Dekker's plays is the comic dialogue so masterly as here—so vivid and so vigorous in

its lifelike ease and spontaneity. But there is not one of the fifteen chapters, devoted each to the description of some fresh 'humour,' which would not deserve, did space and time allow of it, a separate note of commentary. The book is simply one of the very finest examples of humorous literature, touched now and then with serious and even tragic effect, that can be found in any language; it is generally and comparatively remarkable for its freedom from all real coarseness or brutality, though the inevitable change of manners between Shakespeare's time and our own may make some passages or episodes seem now and then somewhat over particular in plain-speaking or detail. But a healthier, manlier, more thoroughly good-natured and good-humoured book was never written; nor one in which the author's real and respectful regard for womanhood was more perceptible through the veil of a satire more pure from bitterness and more honest in design.

The list of works over which we have now glanced is surely not inconsiderable; and yet the surviving productions of Dekker's genius or necessity are but part of the labours of his life. If he wanted—as undoubtedly he would seem to have wanted—that 'infinite capacity for taking pains' which Carlyle professed to regard as the synonym of genius, he was at least not deficient in that rough and ready diligence which is habitually in harness, and cheerfully or resignedly prepared for the day's work. The names of his lost plays—all generally suggestive of some true dramatic interest, now graver and now lighter—are too numerous to transcribe: but one at least of them must excite unspeakable amazement as well as indiscreet curiosity in every reader of Ariosto or La Fontaine who comes in the course of the catalogue upon such a title as *Jocondo and Astolfo.* How on earth the famous story of Giocondo could possibly be adapted for representation on the public stage of Shakespearean London is a mystery which the execrable cook of the execrable Warburton has left for ever insoluble and inconceivable: for to that female fiend, the object of Sir Walter Scott's antiquarian imprecations, we owe, unless my memory misguides me, the loss of this among other irredeemable treasures.

To do justice upon the faults of this poet is easy for any sciolist: to do justice to his merits is less easy for the most competent scholar and the most appreciative critic. In despite of his rare occasional spurts or outbreaks of self-assertion or of satire, he seems to stand before us a man of gentle, modest, shiftless and careless nature, irritable and placable, eager and unsteady, full of excitable kindliness and deficient in strenuous principle; loving the art which he professionally followed, and enjoying the work which he occasionally neglected. There is no unpoetic note in his best poetry such as there is too often—nay, too constantly—in the severer work and the stronger genius of Ben Jonson. What he might have done under happier auspices, or with a tougher fibre of resolution and perseverance in his character, it is waste of time and thought for his most sympathetic and compassionate admirers to assume or to conjecture: what he has done, with all its shortcomings and infirmities, is enough to secure for him a distinct and honourable place among the humourists and the poets of his country. (pp. 90-109)

Algernon Charles Swinburne, "Thomas Dekker," in his The Age of Shakespeare, 1908. *Reprint by AMS Press Inc., 1965, pp. 60-109.*

Leigh Hunt on Dekker and some of his contemporaries:

I take Webster and Decker to have been the two greatest of the Shakspeare men, for unstudied genius, next after Beaumont and Fletcher; and in some respects they surpassed them. Beaumont and Fletcher have no such terror as Webster, nor any such piece of hearty, good, affecting human clay as Decker's "Old Signior Orland Friscobaldo." Is there any such man even in Shakspeare?—any such exaltation of that most delightful of all things, *bonhomie?* Webster sometimes overdoes his terror; nay, often. He not only riots, he debauches in it; and Decker, full of heart and delicacy as he is, and qualified to teach refinement to the refined, condescends to an astounding coarseness. Beaumont and Fletcher's good company saved them from that, in words. In spirit they are full of it. But Decker never mixes up (at least not as far as I can remember) any such revolting and impossible contradictions in the same character as they do. Neither does he bring a doubt of his virtues by exaggerating them. He believes heartily in what he does believe, and you love him in consequence.

Leigh Hunt, in his Imagination and Fancy, 1844.

Mary Leland Hunt   (essay date 1911)

[*Hunt was an American literary scholar. In this excerpt, she describes the characteristic strengths and weaknesses of Dekker's works.*]

Besides the warmheartedness, the sincerity, the piety and the patriotism with which Dekker is usually with justice credited, he possessed a manly and independent spirit that despised servility and resented injustice, a democratic breadth of sympathy more in accordance with the twentieth than the sixteenth century, a keen and wise interest in matters of good citizenship, and that other modern virtue of a generally optimistic outlook upon life. He loved all sorts of beauty; most of all, the beauty of music, poetry, and religion, and disillusion never came to brush off its bloom. We know less about the habits of the man: he probably did not escape the personal grossness that seems to have prevailed equally among bohemians, citizens, and gentlemen.

Born with the temperament of the idealist and the seeing eye of the realist, endowed with a two-fold gift for poetry and prose, and possessed of unusual wit and humor, Dekker was bound in the nature of the case to scatter his powers. The necessity of rapid production very likely conduced towards the same end, although this seems to me less certain, for ease has seldom been a nurse to literature, and Dekker, like most of his fellow playwrights, wrote primarily to make a living.

Of his non-dramatic work only a few words need to be spoken. A duly weighed appreciation of his lyrics must wait for a collection that shall include all the floating songs; but it may now be said of the best that they have upon them the freshness and spontaneity of the early days, and of the one that Palgrave has made familiar, that it ranks with Shakespere's, but it could not have been written by Shakespere, for it is a song of the people.

Dekker's prose is once more coming into its own. Although the books most popular during his lifetime have the least enduring value, yet all possess interest, for they afford us luminous glimpses into the past and they reflect the personality of the author, upon whom city scenes exercised so potent a fascination, and who loved, pitied, and laughed with and at the people who thronged them. Always clear and idiomatic, he commanded a variety of styles, often swift, gay, exuberant, nearly always picturesque, but at will whimsical, dramatic, ironical, or epigrammatic, and rising at his very best to a noble simplicity that may have had its origin in his susceptibility, moral and aesthetic, to the rhythm of the English Bible. He also possessed an admirable gift as raconteur. Modern prose had not to wait for Dryden.

Any attempt to estimate Dekker's dramatic achievement is at the outset almost paralyzed by the fact that about half the plays he wrote alone and the great majority of those he wrote with others have been lost. We must further remind ourselves that, yielding to a temptation presented to few, he gave up some four years to prose alone and that nearly seven of what should have been his best years were spent in prison. During a career that, thus interrupted, lasted from about 1594 to the end of 1624, he tried his hand, alone or with others, at almost every variety of play except the tragedy of blood, though examples of some species have perished. He was most successful when he set up a new type, as in *The Shoemaker's Holiday,* or greatly modified an old type, as in *Old Fortunatus* or *The Virgin Martyr,* or a prevailing type as in *The Honest Whore.* He retained a taste for allegory and a vital interest in the strife between good and evil, but he showed little subtlety in depicting the inner struggle against temptation. Since the romantic is seldom absent from his plays and since his most beautiful poetry was composed for romantic scenes, we may assume that his permanent sympathies lay in that field; but with a sort of fore-feeling for the direction literature was to take in the distant future, he realized the artistic possibilities in the unsophisticated life of the humble, and he represented it upon the stage with more fidelity to fact, humor, grace, and sympathy than any other Elizabethan. While his conceptions were often large in their scope, they were usually simple and treated with simplicity; and though he used spectacle freely, and surprise not infrequently, he depended for effect rather upon faithfulness to life than upon involved or startling stories. He therefore seldom uses Italian motives; even the pastoral did not attract him. He avoided the violent, the unnatural, the disgusting, the unwholesome; his only intrigue plays were collaborated with others and exhibit none of his gifts except goodnatured satire. He shows a marked preference for the gentler virtues: to his lovers, love is a sacrament—there is no passion except in connection with lust, and his plays offer us no villains worth mentioning; his most heroic figures are gentle in their heroism rather than sublime, and he was but obeying an instinct of his genius when he gave to Dorothea a child angel as attendant and protector and when he made Bellafront climb a slow and painful path to salvation. Whether conditioned by the bent of his own mind or by the composition of the companies he was writing for, he was fond of depicting elderly or old men—Old Fortunatus dominated by hunger and thirst after experience, mad Simon Eyre by a different sort of Elizabethan rapture, Gentili by the passion of hospitality. But after all, Dekker's characters do not readily classify themselves: not all his women are gentle nor all his lovers mad.

Dekker must early have learned to depend upon his humor for a part of his success. At its best it finds expression in the creation of character, and there he showed a modern tendency to temper the humorous with the serious, the pathetic or the strongly likable: it is so with Orlando, with Eyre, his wife, and his band of shoemakers; even with the "high-flying" Matheo, and it is so with his servant-fools. He also drew well simple, rather naïve persons—not clowns, but a knight and his wife or an eligible widow. He had no aptitude for the comedy of humors. His use of dialect—Dutch-English and Welsh-English—is the most convincing on the Elizabethan stage and it is so used as to seem to reveal racial characteristics in the speakers. He kept his early fondness for puns and Lylyisms, and his love of the unexpected often makes his humor flash with wit. What has been called the Hogarthian quality in some of his comedy scenes is perhaps not based wholly upon desire to please the vulgar, for elsewhere a note of grimness or of irony is heard in the speech of that keen observer of life. Against him, however, must be reckoned a limited volcabulary of innuendo and "scrurrility" of the sort not wholly unemployed by the greatest. Though more than annoying, for it gets into one's way, it does not affect an important character or enter into a situation, and no one can remember it.

Dekker's greater faults as a dramatist are well known: the two most serious are a considerable unevenness of execution, although this is not found in all the plays; and a more considerable weakness of structure, though even here one play usually described as incoherent would assume form with proper editing. His own words and the evidence of careful workmanship in other matters forbid us to assume that he had no fitting sense of the dignity of his art. Perhaps the explanation may be sought for in the circumstances of his life and in his temperament: his long collaboration with men of inferior talent during his formative period must have worked him injury, perhaps even his precocity if he actually began writing at twenty-two; his humor, poetry and naturalness probably obscured to himself and to others his generally poor technique; the long interruptions suffered by his dramatic work were also against him. But possibly a genius that was essentially lyrical and bound to attain its most nearly perfect expression in a scene, a mood, sometimes a mood lasting through a whole play, was more capable of producing unity of sentiment or of character than any other unity. As there seems to me some evidence that he did not produce rapidly his greatest work—with the possible exception of his songs—I am inclined to ascribe to temperament that other fault of a descent to slovenly verse so astounding to the reader; for no amount of industry quite answers the stubborn demand for the time and the place and the right mood "all together."

It is often said that Dekker showed no evolution, no development. In the absence of so much of the evidence, late plays as well as early, this is a difficult problem to face. Yet I venture to think that dramatically and psychologically *The Honest Whore* is an advance upon *Old Fortunatus* and *The Shoemaker's Holiday;* that the finest scenes in *The Virgin Martyr* show a more exquisite perception of the power of language to reveal character than any previous play; and that in tragic power *The Witch of Edmonton* surpasses all earlier work.

Dekker's positive contributions to the drama have been partly indicated: power of varied humor, power of pathos and the most delicate sentiment, not even shadowed by sentimentality; power to make the everyday aspects of life seem as attractive as they really are; power to create character,—a power based on sound psychology, for he was, to employ one of his own phrases, "deep read in the volume of a man"; hence we have no violation of human nature, no treacherous friend is made hero or heroine, no nice girl is compelled to marry a newly converted ruffian, no woman falls, repents, and promptly dies without any special reason, as in Heywood's most famous tragedy, and there are few unmotivated conversions. At Dekker's very best he was able to create, also, brief scenes of surpassing beauty, as when he suggests with poignant and haunting phrase a thing so elusive as the charm of a girl's being when she awakes from sleep, or with unmatched purity makes poetry, in diction and melody, a translucent garment for young angelhood and young sainthood. And he had command, not only of fresh, racy, natural prose dialogue, but also of beautiful poetical dialogue, whether to set forth the ardors of hopeless love or the frail and dying beauty of spring.

Many and varied gifts go to the making of a great dramatist, and from the fame of every one of Shakespere's contemporaries large deductions have had to be made: from Dekker's too they must be made. But his best work has remained unhurt by changing tastes and manners. What-

---

A. H. Bullen on Dekker's works:

[Dekker's] sympathy with sinful and sorrowing humanity was genuine and deep; but his poignant feelings sometimes found expression in language which seems to have the air of insincerity. In the fine scenes where Hippolito implores Bellafront to abandon her vicious course of life, and again where he strives to undo the effect of his former teaching, one feels that the arguments and illustrations are enforced with over-heated vehemence. This note of exaggeration is never absent from Dekker's work; he let his fancy have full swing and did not write "with slower pen." But he was the most natural of writers, lovable at all points, full of simplicity and tenderness. The character of Orlando Friscobaldo is drawn in Dekker's cheeriest, sunniest manner.

A. H. Bullen, in his introduction to The Works of Thomas Middleton, *Volume I, 1885.*

ever he wrote is touched with the artistic and spiritual grace of sincerity, and not even the form of the drama can conceal from us the personality of the most poetical and the most lovable of the group that surrounded the master. (pp. 199-204)

> *Mary Leland Hunt, in her* Thomas Dekker: A Study, *The Columbia University Press, 1911, 212 p.*

L. C. Knights   (essay date 1937)

[*Knights was a renowned English Shakespearean scholar and critic. Along with such Cambridge critics as F. R. Leavis and Q. D. Leavis, he sought to establish close reading of texts and an awareness of the social setting of literature as important critical techniques. In this excerpt, he dismisses Dekker's works as mere reflections of popular tastes. He does concede, however, that the writer's plays and pamphlets do embody "a decent traditional morality."*]

To turn from Jonson to Dekker is to be jolted into recognition of the gulf between the higher and the lower ranges of Jacobean dramatic literature. With a few exceptions Dekker's plays are uniformly dull, and the effort of attention they require—the sheer effort to keep one's eyes on the page—is out of all proportion to the reward. They were, however, 'best sellers'—most of them were acted 'with great applause' by the Admiral's (afterwards the Prince's) Men, the Queen's Men or the Children of Paul's—and as an index of contemporary taste and opinion they provide some information that is relevant to [Jacobean studies].

Dekker was one of the neediest of the journeymen of letters at a time when authorship was one of the most precarious trades. He had neither a share in a fellowship of players, nor aristocratic patronage, and he was forced to follow the taste of the moment as closely and as quickly as possible, either in play or pamphlet. It is usual to think of him as primarily a playwright, but his essentially journalistic talent is best brought out if we approach him through his non-dramatic works; many of his plays are little more than dramatized versions of these.

As a journalist Dekker addressed the lower levels of the London reading public. His journalism was not, of course, the newsmongering of a Nathaniel Butter. A representative pamphlet such as *The Wonderful Year* (1603) consists of desultory gossip together with rhetorical accounts of events that were known to everybody, larded with 'tales cut out in sundry fashions, of purpose to shorten the lives of long winter nights'. His accounts of wonders and marvels are all homely and commonplace, and the descriptions are matched by the moralizing. Dekker's purpose was not solely to amuse. The majority of the pamphlets contain accounts of 'an Army of insufferable abuses, detestable vices, most damnable villainies, abominable pollutions, inexplicable mischiefs, sordid iniquinations, horrible and hell-hound-like perpetrated flagitious enormities' [*The Bellman of London*], so 'that thou and all the world shall see their ugliness, for by seeing them, thou mayst avoid them' [*The Seven Deadly Sins of London*]. There is

no need to doubt Dekker's moral purpose in his description of damnable villainies, but the quality of the description is fairly indicated by the tautological introduction that I have quoted. In the pamphlets mainly designed to show up abuses we learn little of the peculiar quality of contemporary social life; or rather, such evidence as they present is incidental.

In *The Seven Deadly Sins of London* (1606) the seven sins are 'Politick Bankruptism', Lying, 'The Nocturnal Triumph', Sloth, Apishness, 'Shaving' and Cruelty. There are the usual puns and forced rhetoric, but what distinguishes the pamphlet is its humanitarianism. In the section on cruelty Dekker denounces parents who drive their children into unwilling marriages, cruel creditors, and unconscionable masters, and he pleads for the provision of hospitals and decent burial grounds. The approach to economic problems is entirely moralistic. In his denunciation of the 'politic bankrupt' he appeals to the Commandments, and shows the sin as a combination of covetousness and theft, whilst the practice of imprisonment for debt is described as both useless and inhuman: 'We are most like to God that made us when we show love one to another, and do most look like the Devil that would destroy us, when we are one another's tormentors'. So too he complains of the members of the London Companies who try to limit their numbers, and who will not allow apprentices, their seven years expired, to become masters,

> as if Trades, that were ordained to be communities, had lost their first privileges, and were now turned Monopolies. . . . Remember, O you rich men, that your servants are your adopted children; they are naturalized into your blood, and if you hurt theirs, you are guilty of letting out your own, than which, what cruelty can be greater?

Dekker, in short, is following the traditions of the Church in regarding 'buying and selling, lending and borrowing, as a simple case of neighbourly or unneighbourly conduct' [R. H. Tawney, *Religion and the Rise of Capitalism*]. It is on these grounds that he judges landlords who rack rents, cheating tradesmen, brewers and bakers who give false measure, fraudulent executors, and usurers,

> who for a little money and a great deal of trash (as fire-shovels, brown paper, motley cloak-bags, etc.) bring young novices into a fool's paradise till they have sealed the mortgage of their lands, and then like pedlars go they (or some familiar spirit for them, raised by the usurer) up and down to cry *Commodities,* which scarce yield the third part of the sum for which they take them up.

A summary of the admirably humane proposals scattered throughout Dekker's pamphlets would suggest that I had done him an injustice. But what I am complaining of is the lack of something that can only be called the artistic conscience. Dekker is never sure of what he wants to do. The moral drive is dissipated by the constant striving after obvious 'effects', by the recurring introduction of irrelevancies, by the failure to maintain a consistent tone, so that although Dekker is never guilty of tickling his readers' palates with descriptions of vice, one often suspects the journalistic intention. One thing at least is proved by the blemishes themselves: Dekker was completely at one with his London audience. He does not draw on popular thought and refine it, like Jonson, his thoughts *are* the thoughts of the average Londoner.

Dekker's social morality is a morality that the average decent citizen would find acceptable. He does not despise or distrust riches so long as they are used conscionably. Virtue itself is rewarded by earthly prosperity—

> England shall ne'er be poor, if England strive
> Rather by virtue than by wealth to thrive.
> [*Old Fortunatus,* V, ii]

The rich should be fair and charitable; the poor should aim at content; the honest workman should maintain himself decently in his calling, and if he rises it must only be within the limits of his own order. One cannot classify this morality as either 'medieval' or 'modern'. Dekker accepts the traditional social ethic, but his Protestant Christianity is that of the seventeenth-century middle class. It is significant that in *A Strange Horse Race* (1613) the first virtue that he mentions is Humility, the second, Thrift. Thrift, running a race with Prodigality, is 'vigilant in his course, subtle in laying his wager, provident in not venturing too much, honest to pay his losses, industrious to get more (twenty sundry ways) if he should happen to be cheated of all'. It is a citizen morality, but it is neither entirely individualistic nor out of touch with tradition.

The plays, like the pamphlets, gave the public—Alleyn's public—what it wanted and what it could digest easily: amusement, naïvely 'dramatic' situations, moral 'sentences' and pictures of contemporary virtues and vices, eked out occasionally by fireworks. Shakespeare took popular elements and transformed them to his own purposes; Dekker gives us an amalgam of all that popular taste demanded. His dramatic satire is usually directed against fairly obvious abuses:

> *1st Devil.* I have with this fist beat upon rich men's hearts, To make 'em harder: and these two thumbs thrust,(In open churches) into brave dames' ears, Damming up attention; whilst the loose eye peersFor fashions of gown-wings, laces, purles, ruffs,Falls, cauls, tires, wires, caps, hats, and muffs and puffs.For so the face be smug, and carcase gay,That's all their pride.
> [*If It Be not Good, the Devil is in It*]

His satire, that is, either deals in generalities, or else it presents particulars drawn from the life of the time without grasping their full significance and implications. It does not penetrate far below the surface.

It is for this reason that Dekker's comedies, although far less 'universal' than Jonson's, tell us comparatively little about the economic and social changes that can be discerned behind *The Alchemist.* There are, of course, scattered references. *Westward Ho!* (1604), in particular, gives some interesting thumbnail sketches. There are needy courtiers and luxurious citizens; there is satire on the buying of knighthoods, and on monopolies; and farmers are described as 'grinding the jaw-bones of the poor'.

But in this play Dekker collaborated with Webster, and I think that it is to Webster that the most effective satire belongs. In *If It be not Good, the Devil is in It* (1610-1612), it is true, there is a straightforward attack on commercial wiles. Pluto sends to earth three devils, one to corrupt a court, another a monastery, and a third is given these instructions:

> Be thou a city-devil. Make thy hands
> Of Harpy's claws, which being on courtiers' lands
> Once fasten'd, ne'er let loose. The Merchant play,
> And on the Burse, see thou thy flag display,
> Of politic bankruptism: train up as many
> To fight under it, as thou canst, for now's not any
> That break, (They'll break their necks first). If beside,
> Thou canst not through the whole city meet with pride,
> Riot, lechery, envy, avarice, and such stuff,
> Bring 'em all in coach'd, the gates are wide enough.
> The spirit of gold instruct thee.

Bartervile, the merchant with whom the city-devil takes service, does not need much instruction. He gets the lands of a gentleman who owes him money by pretending that the hour for repayment is passed; he loses the farm of some royal imposts, but obtains it again because the King needs to borrow money ('Who bids most, he buys it'). He devises a variation on 'Politic bankruptism', and boasts that he has the royal protection:

> *Bartervile.* A merchant, and yet know'st not
> What a protection is? I'll tell thee. . . .
> It is a buckler of a large fair compass,
> Quilted with fox-skins; in the midst
> A pike sticks out, (sometimes of two years long,
> And sometimes longer). And this pike keeps off
> Sergeants and bailiffs, actions, and arrests:
> 'Tis a strong charm 'gainst all the noisome smells
> Of Counters, Jailors, garnishes, and such hells;
> By this, a debtor craz'd, so lusty grows,
> He may walk by, and play with his creditor's nose.
> Under this buckler, here I'll lie and fence.

Above all, he lives solely for his immediate gain:

> *Lurchall.* But pray sir, what is't turns you into a Turk?
> *Bartervile.* That, for which many their Religion,
> Most men their Faith, all change their honesty,
> Profit, (that gilded god) Commodity,
> He that would grow damn'd rich, yet live secure,
> Must keep a case of faces. . . .

Dekker, however, is not often so consistently explicit. Generally he is content to denounce gold, 'the world's saint', in general terms. Old Fortunatus, given the choice of wisdom, strength, health, beauty, long life, and riches, chooses riches:

> My choice is store of gold; the rich are wise.

He that upon his back rich garments wears,
Is wise, though on his head grow Midas' ears.
Gold is the strength, the sinews of the world,
The health, the soul, the beauty most divine,
A mask of gold hides all deformities;
Gold is Heaven's physic, life's restorative,
Oh therefore make me rich.

[*Old Fortunatus,* I,i]

But it is obvious that Dekker's acceptance of citizen thrift and industry is severely qualified by the traditional distrust.

'Twas never merry world with us, since purses and bags were invented, for now men set lime-twigs to catch wealth: and gold, which riseth like the sun out of the East Indies, to shine upon everyone, is like a cony taken napping in a purse-net, and suffers his glistering yellow-face deity to be lapped up in lambskins, as if the innocency of those leather prisons should dispense with the cheveril consciences of the ironhearted gaolers.

[I,ii]

Dekker never manages to work up this theme into an effective play (the effect of a single play is very different from the effect of these assembled extracts); but what we have to notice is that even in giving the public what it wanted, even in praising the citizen virtues, he is far nearer to the medieval moralists than to the new economic rationalists.

Dekker's best known play—a favourite with his contemporary audience—is *The Shoemaker's Holiday.* There is no doubt that its success was largely due to the way in which it appealed to the pride of the citizen-craftsman in his craft and status. It called for no effort of readjustment or reorganization, but—like the long line of patriotic chronicle plays—simply reinforced a prevalent social attitude. In the first place, the citizens had the pleasure of familiar recognition. Simon Eyre, celebrated by Stow as well as by Deloney, was a figure of traditional legend, and the account of the building and naming of the Leadenhall appealed to the taste which produced such things as *If You Know not Me You Know Nobody, With the Building of the Royal Exchange.* Eyre's progress from master craftsman to Sheriff and finally Lord Mayor of London (not, significantly, to a house in the country) represented a dream which a good many apprentices must have cherished. And Eyre's relations with his workmen are presented in the most attractive light. He drinks and jests with them, listens to their advice, and protects them from the tongue of his wife; 'By the Lord of Ludgate', he swears, 'I love my men as my life'. The relationship, although obviously idealized, had . . . a basis in fact, and its presentation would be particularly appreciated since it depicted a state of affairs that was rapidly vanishing as business became more impersonal. Moreover, the pride, the ambition, the prejudices of Eyre and his men are limited by the city. Not only does the Earl of Lincoln oppose the marriage of Lacy, his nephew, to Rose, a citizen's daughter, her father the Lord Mayor 'scorns to call Lacy son-in-law', and Eyre advises her:

A courtier, wash, go by, stand not upon pishery-pashery: those silken fellows are but painted images, outsides, outsides, Rose; their inner linings are torn. No, my fine mouse, marry me with a gentleman grocer like my lord mayor, your father; a grocer is a sweet trade: plums, plums. Had I a son or daughter should marry out of the generation and blood of the shoemakers, he should pack; what, the gentle trade is a living for a man through Europe, through the world.

[III,v]

Rose, it is true, marries Lacy in the end, but Lacy has proved himself a good fellow and has not scorned the gentle craft; besides, romance demanded it. It is the citizen's independence, however, that is most applauded. Even the surly attitude of the shoemakers when they demand the journeyman's wife, Jane, from the wealthy and inoffensive Hammon (V,ii) is presented for approval; and Eyre, though proud of his civic dignities, has none of those ambitions to step outside the limits of his order which were already providing material for the comic dramatists.

Am I not Simon Eyre? Are not these my brave men, brave shoemakers, all gentlemen of the gentle craft? Prince am I none, yet am I nobly born.

[III,i]

It is impossible, however, merely to dismiss Dekker by saying that *The Shoemaker's Holiday* is an appeal to prejudice (in any case its appeal was wider than my account may suggest) or that his work in general is a mere reflection of popular taste. What we have to ask ourselves, with the twentieth-century reading public in mind, is what that taste demanded besides easy amusement. For in spite of Dekker's feeble grasp of tradition, his narrow moral scope, his work does embody, or reflect, however fragmentarily, a decent traditional morality. I am not thinking of the stilted moralism of *The Honest Whore* but of the shrewd, caustic comments on social ambition, wealth and luxury that are scattered throughout his plays. His approval of Eyre does not prevent him from laughing at the naïve assumption of dignity by Eyre's wife, and I have shown something of his attitude towards mere acquisition. But the point is best made by a comparison with a modern novel. There is no need to draw on the fiction that caters for the needs of a class corresponding to 'the original civility of the Red Bull'. The standards behind Arnold Bennett's popular *Imperial Palace* are fairly indicated by extracts such as these:

And he liked her expensive stylishness. The sight of a really smart woman always gave him pleasure. In his restaurant, when he occasionally inspected it as a spy from a corner behind a screen, he always looked first for the fashionable, costly frocks, and the more there were the better he was pleased. . . . Only half an hour ago she had probably been steering a big car at a mile a minute on a dark curving road. And here with delicate hands she was finishing the minute renewal of her delicate face.

. . . . .

Gracie, stared at by a hundred eyes until she sat down, was just as much at her ease as a bride at a wedding. Created by heaven to be a cynosure, rightly convinced that she was the best-dressed woman in the great, glittering, humming room, her spirit floated on waves of admiration as naturally as a goldfish in water. Evelyn, impressed, watched her surreptitiously as she dropped on to the table an inlaid vanity-case which had cost her father a couple of hundred pounds. . . . Surely in the wide world that night there could not be anything to beat her! Idle, luxurious rich, but a master-piece! Maintained in splendour by the highly skilled and expensive labour of others, materially useless to society, she yet justified herself by her mere appearance. And she knew it, and her conscience was clear.

Throughout the book—there is a little, uneasy, irony—the reader is invited to admire, or to accept with complacence, the monstrous material standards symbolized by a modern luxury hotel. Dekker and his audience had another set of values.

> Lord, Lord, to see what good raiment doth.
> . . . O sweet wares! Prunes, almonds, sugar-candy, carrot-roots, turnips, O brave fatting meat!
> [*The Shoemaker's Holiday,* III,i]

Whenever Dekker dwells on luxury there is no doubt of the expected response: here, for example:

> *Birdlime.* O the entertainment my Lord will make you. Sweet wines, lusty diet, perfumed linen, soft beds, O most fortunate gentlewoman!
> [*Westward Ho!* I,i]

Or here, where the devil, disguised as a novice, is told to say grace:

> *Prior.* Stand forth, and render thanks.
> *Rush.* Hum, hum:
>   For our bread, wine, ale and beer,
>   For the piping hot meats here:
>   For broths of sundry tastes and sort,
>   For beef, veal, mutton, lamb, and pork:
>   Green-sauce with calve's head and bacon,
>   Pig and goose, and cramm'd-up capon:
>   For pastries rais'd stiff with curious art,
>   Pie, custard, florentine and tart.
>   Bak'd rumps, fried kidneys, and lamb-stones,
>   Fat sweet-breads, luscious marrowbones,
>   Artichoke, and oyster pies,
>   Butter'd crab, prawns, lobsters' thighs,
>   Thanks be given for flesh and fishes,
>   With this choice of tempting dishes:
>   To which preface, with blithe looks sit ye,
>   Rush bids this Convent, much good do't ye.
>   [*If It be not Good, the Devil is in It*]

It is not merely that Dekker, without Jonson's poise, is nevertheless insistent on 'the rotten strength of proud mortality'—

> And though mine arm should conquer twenty worlds, There's a lean fellow beats all conquerors—
> [*Old Fortunatus,* II,ii; I,i]

he had been taught by religion, by the traditional morality, that there were other standards than those implied by 'the high standard of living' of the Imperial Palace.

And, finally, Dekker's conception of the ordered state is,

in general, the traditional conception that lies behind Ulysses' speech on 'Degree' [in Shakespeare's *Troilus and Cressida*], on the one hand, and the acts of the Elizabethan Privy Council on the other. So far as one can piece together a coherent social attitude behind the plays, it is approval of a scheme in which each man has his proper place, the whole being bound together by justice. The King in *If It be not a Good Play,* planning his reign, gives first place to equity.

> That day, from morn till night, I'll execute
> The office of a judge, and weigh out laws
> With even scales. . . .
> The poor and rich man's cause
> I'll poise alike: it shall be my chief care
> That bribes and wrangling be pitch'd o'er the bar. . . .
> Tuesdays we'll sit to hear the poor man's cries,
> Orphans and widows: our own princely eyes
> Shall their petitions read: our progress then
> Shall be to hospitals which good minded men
> Have built to pious use, for lame, sick, and poor.
> We'll see what's given, what spent, and what flows o'er.
> Churls (with God's money) shall not feast, swill wine,
> And fat their rank guts whilst poor wretches pine.

Dekker praises thrift, industry, and the citizen virtues, but his description of the artisan is significant:

> The rear-ward last advanced up, being led
> By the industrious, thriving Artisan:
> The ways of science needs he well must tread,
> For seven years go to make him up a man.
> And then by all the lawful steps he can,
> Climbs he to wealth. Enough is his he vaunts,
> If though he hoard not much, he feels not wants.
> [*The Double PP*]

Alexander B. Grosart on Dekker's Pamphlets:

Some of the books, as his *Canaan's Calamitie* and *Foure Birdes of Noah's Arke,* almost startle us from their theological and devotional character, much as Thomas Nashe does with his *Teares.* I fear they were produced for a 'piece of bread.' The main *quick* element to-day of them all is their substantively racy English, graphic character and manners painting, capital stories, gleams of swift wit and drollery, and now and again sage and serious apothegms and felicitous phrasings, and in his rugged verse memorable and Milton-like lines in most unlikely places. . . .

Occasionally there are bits of nature-painting which suggest that the Author made escapes to the country, perhaps with "strolling companies." Occasionally, too, there are proofs of his heart being in the right place—*e.g.,* his pleading against the cruelty of baiting a blind bear, his pitifulness for widows, orphans, debtors, and his passion of compassion for the neglected or oppressed poor. His indignation against usurers pulsates with a noble wrath. He was a whole-brained, whole-hearted Englishman.

Alexander B. Grosart, in his introduction to The Non-Dramatic Works of Thomas Dekker, *Volume V, 1886.*

The 'lawful steps' are insisted upon, and Dekker sets his face against the 'doctrineless individualism' represented by the merchant, Bartervile:

> Nature sent man into the world, alone,
> Without all company, but to care for one,
> And that I'll do.
>
> (pp. 228-43)

It is the devil who insists that this is 'True City doctrine, sir'.

> *L. C. Knights, "Dekker, Heywood and Citizen Morality," in his* Drama & Society in the Age of Jonson, *1937. Reprint by Chatto & Windus, 1962, pp. 228-55.*

Thomas Marc Parrott and Robert Hamilton Ball (essay date 1943)

[*American educators Parrott and Ball were respected authorities on Shakespearean and Elizabethan drama. In this excerpt, they review Dekker's major works and describe him as a talented, though uneven, poet and playwright.*]

Dekker's career as an author falls roughly into three periods: his early plays, 1596-1604; his prose period, 1606 to 1610; and his later work in drama and in prose. During the four years from 1598 to 1602 Dekker was one of the busiest of Henslowe's hacks; he was always ready to lend a hand in the hasty preparation of plays for the Admiral's. These dealt with British history in the form of the popular chronicle, with classic story—a lost *Troilus and Cressida*—, with Domestic Tragedy—*Page of Plymouth* in collaboration with Ben Jonson—, and even with the old-fashioned sacred play—a lost *Jephthah* with Anthony Munday. His surviving plays up to 1600-01 are in the field of romantic comedy with at times a dash of the old native realism.

The *Fortunatus* of 1596 does not seem to have been very successful; it was performed only six times and disappeared from the Admiral's repertoire. In November, 1599, Henslowe advanced £5 in earnest of the "whole history of Fortunatus." The "whole history" was, no doubt, a revision combining the original first and second parts. A month later Henslowe paid Dekker £2 more for "the end of Fortunatus for the Court." It was, we know, played at Court on December 27, 1599, and it is in this form that it has come down to us.

It is unfortunate that we do not have the two-part play in its original form. Dekker's amalgamation of the two plays and his further alterations of this "whole part" for the Court performance have quite obscured his original dramatization of the pleasant old story of Fortunatus and his sons with the purse of gold and the wishing cap. Whole sections of the action seem to have disappeared to make way for the Prologue at Court, for the masque-like effects of the Vice and Virtue scenes, and for the long closing scene in which Virtue kneeling before Elizabeth exclaims:

> I am a counterfeit, you are the true.

The result is a badly constructed but delightful play. It is an old-fashioned piece of work for 1599 when Shakespeare was writing his perfect comedies. It harks back to Greene in its dramatization of folk-tale; the prose with its puns, its paradoxes, and its quick-fire repartee suggests Lyly brought up to date for the popular theatre. The special charm of the play lies in its lovely verse.

Even before Dekker began his revision of *Old Fortunatus,* he was at work on what is now his best-known play. On July 15, 1599, Henslowe advanced £3 "to buy a book of Thomas Dickers called the Gentle Craft." This is *The Shoemaker's Holiday,* played at Court on New Year's Day, 1600, and published that same year with the double title, *The Shoemaker's Holiday, or The Gentle Craft.* In this delightful play Dekker turns from the fairy-land of *Fortunatus* to Elizabethan London. The action plays about the figure of a London shoemaker, Simon Eyre, who by a happy combination of industry, good-luck, and high spirits rises to be Lord Mayor, and ordains Shrove Tuesday a holiday for all London prentices. To add variety to so simple a tale of a citizen's progress Dekker interweaves two pretty, romantic love-stories. The first tells how a noble youth loves the Lord Mayor's daughter, woos her in secret, disguised as a Dutch shoemaker in Eyre's shop, weds her, and secures a pardon from the King—just the kind of tale to gratify an audience of London citizens. The second has a touch of pathos: Ralph, one of Eyre's shoemakers, is pressed for the wars in France; his young wife, deceived by a false report of his death, reluctantly consents to wed a London gentleman, but is snatched from him at the altar by the returned Ralph and a group of Eyre's workmen. For once in his life Dekker exercised control over his material and wove all the threads of his plot together into one harmonious pattern.

It is not the story, however, entertaining as it is, that gives this play its perennial charm. It is rather the abounding joy of life in general, of Elizabethan London life in particular, that flows from Dekker's heart and brain to find full and unrestrained expression in the character of Simon Eyre. Shrewd, honest, kindly, and democratic in Elizabethan fashion, Simon's special characteristic is an exuberant flow of speech, larded with tag-ends of proverbs and humorous abuse, and marked by a trick of repetitions that ring like a triple peal of bells. Well matched with him is his wife, Dame Margery, the would-be shrew, controlled and kept in place by Simon's firm hand, but rejoicing in the hood, the periwig, and the mask that mark her rise in social status; the "world's calling is costly," she says, "but it is one of the wonderful works of God."

Behind these figures and those of Eyre's singing, jesting workmen lies the London of Dekker's day. It would be hard to find another Elizabethan play where the background of contemporary life gives so strong a sense of atmosphere, an atmosphere of Old and Merry England at its jolliest. There were other and darker days to come in Dekker's London, and he was to tell of them in later work. Meantime this play of his joyous youth remains his unchallenged masterpiece.

Some time in 1601 Dekker was engaged on a play which, had it been finished as he planned it, would have been, perhaps, the most interesting of all his early work. The theme was the rescue of a bride from the lustful clutches of King William Rufus by her father and the bridegroom, Walter Tirrell, popularly supposed to be the slayer of Rufus in the New Forest. It seems as if Dekker had planned something like Greene's *James IV;* one cannot be quite sure of this, however, for while Dekker was still at work he was induced to take part in the War of the Theatres and to reply in a stage-play to Jonson's *Poetaster.* Working against time to get this reply in rehearsal as soon as possible, Dekker had the unhappy idea of inserting it into his unfinished tragi-comedy. The result is *Satiromastix, or the Untrussing of the Humorous Poet,* one of the most incoherent plays in Elizabethan drama. It must have been effective on the stage, for it was produced not only by the Chamberlain's Company, but by Paul's Boys in their private theatre. It was promptly printed, 1602, and seems to have brought the so-called War to a laughing conclusion.

A change seems to come over the tone of Dekker's plays after *Satiromastix.* So far they had been essentially romantic; even the realistic scenes of *The Shoemaker's Holiday* show a dash of romantic lightness and gayety. His shift to a somewhat sordid realism had, perhaps, a double cause. The theatrical fashion was changing; romantic comedy was yielding on the one hand to tragedy, on the other hand to a realistic and often satirical portrayal of contemporary middle-class life and manners. There is little in Dekker's work to show that he had either desire or capacity for tragic drama; much, on the other hand, to show a keen observation of contemporary life which needed only a push to drive him along the road of realistic comedy. This impulse may well have been given by his association with Middleton. Better born, better bred, a stronger and a harder genius than Dekker, Middleton was well qualified to influence his gentle friend. He and Dekker had worked together on the lost play, *Cæsar's Fall,* in 1602, and his influence on Dekker is plainly visible in a couple of plays: *Westward Ho,* 1604, and *Northward Ho,* 1605, in which Dekker collaborated with Webster. It is not easy to assign particular scenes of these plays to their respective authors; fortunately it matters little, for neither of the plays is a credit to either of the authors. . . . [*Westward Ho* provoked] a dramatic rebuke by Jonson, Chapman, and Marston. *Northward Ho,* in turn, is a reply to *Eastward Ho* with some lighthearted raillery of Chapman. There is little of Dekker's gay humor in these plays, and less of his poetry than in any of his earlier work.

Early in 1604 Henslowe paid Dekker and Middleton for work on *The Honest Whore.* This fascinating play appeared in two parts, the first in 1604, the second, though no doubt written soon after the first, not until 1630. Dekker's name alone appears on both title-pages: Middleton may have contributed a scene or two, but both plays are essentially Dekker's; he has assimilated Middleton's influence and used it here for his own purposes.

Like many popular Elizabethan plays *The Honest Whore* is a story in dramatic form rather than a well-built play. In fact it is three stories running side by side and only brought together at the very end. The first of these is a romantic tale of two young Italian lovers, Hippolito and In-

felice. They are separated by a family feud and only reunited after the lady's recovery from a deathlike swoon caused by a sleeping-potion. Dekker seems to be rearranging the plot of *Romeo and Juliet* to turn it into a tragi-comedy. To this theme he adds the story of Bellafront, the courtesan. She falls in love with Hippolito mourning over the supposed death of his lady, offers herself to him, is moved to repentance by his bitter denunciation of her trade, and resolves to return to her father. In the comic realistic under-plot, an amusing inversion of the patient Griselda theme, a shop-keeper's wife tries in vain to break the patience of her long-suffering husband. She finally hits on the desperate expedient of having him carried to Bedlam as insane. Here all the characters assemble: Hippolito and Infelice secretly married, the repentant wife come to free her patient husband, and, quite surprisingly, Bellafront playing the part of a madwoman. The Duke, Infelice's father, has also come there to see a show of lunatics, a popular Elizabethan indoor sport. There is a general *éclaircissement,* the lovers are pardoned, the wife regains her husband, and by the Duke's command, Bellafront is made an honest woman by marriage to her first seducer, Matheo.

Like most sequels the Second Part falls below the First. The same characters reappear, but now in changed roles. Hippolito, who had converted Bellafront, now seeks to make her his mistress; Bellafront, the former courtesan, becomes the virtuous wife; and the shop-keeper teaches a second wife the duty of obedience. What gives interest and distinction to this sequel is Dekker's extraordinary power of vivid characterization. Bellafront is a more vital character than in Part I; her role is that of a patient Griselda but she plays it with a fine, instinctive loyalty to the husband who abuses her and the father who has disowned her. Matheo, a somewhat shadowy figure in Part I, comes to life here as an Elizabethan gallant of the wildest type, a swaggerer and a gambler, who pawns the clothes off his wife's back, robs pedlars on the highway, and faces the gallows with a cynical jest. A new character in this part is Orlando Friscobaldo, Bellafront's father, who watches over her in the disguise of an old serving-man. His behavior is fantastic, but his speech reveals a warm heart behind his gruff and forbidding exterior. He is a Simon Eyre grown old, but still with Simon's inexhaustible vitality and his kindly sympathy for those in trouble. All in all *The Honest Whore* is the high-water mark of Dekker's work as a popular playwright.

From 1606 to 1610 Dekker devoted himself mainly to the composition of prose pamphlets. One of these, *The Gull's Horn-book,* in modern phrase, *An A. B. C. for Simpletons,* may be specially recommended to students of Elizabethan drama. One chapter in particular, "How a Gallant should behave himself in a Playhouse," offers a striking picture of the indignities which playwrights and actors suffered at the hands of the impudent pretenders to fashion who sat on stools upon the stage.

In 1610 Dekker joined once more with Middleton in *The Roaring Girl,* a play introducing a notorious figure in contemporary London, Mary Frith, alias Moll Cutpurse, a virago who dressed like a man, wore a sword and used it, and consorted with the scum of the city. It is characteristic of Dekker that he presents her as a woman more sinned against than sinning, "a roaring girl," indeed, but an honest one, as ready to help lovers in distress as to browbeat a bully. A pair of plays about this time, 1610-1612, show Dekker experimenting in various styles. The first, *If It be not Good, the Devil is in It,* is a dramatization of the folktale of Friar Rush. By way of variety Dekker next offered his audience a tragi-comedy in the fashionable Beaumont and Fletcher style, *Match Me in London.* This was not Dekker's line and he made a sad mess of it.

On his release from prison in 1619 Dekker returned to the theatre, but there is no extant play of this time which can be identified as his unaided work. On the contrary we find him now working in collaboration with younger playwrights. Where a stronger and more careful hand devised the plot, Dekker was always ready to contribute scenes of lively action. This is particularly clear in *The Virgin Martyr,* 1620, in which he collaborated with Massinger. The theme, the legend of St. Dorothea, was probably chosen by Massinger, of all Elizabethan playwrights the most interested in the doctrine and ritual of the Roman Church. The careful construction is his, as are quite certainly the beginning and the end of the play. Dekker fills in with some boisterous comic scenes in prose and with some exquisite poetry that passes between the Saint and her guardian angel.

In the following year he joined with Ford, just beginning his career as a playwright, and with the actor-dramatist William Rowley, in *The Witch of Edmonton,* 1621. This is an interesting example of the Elizabethan theatre functioning like the newspaper of today in bringing the latest sensation before the public, for it is based on an account of the trial of Elizabeth Sawyer burnt as a witch earlier in the year. But it is much more than the hasty dramatization of a recent happening; it is a real play and a fine one. Along with the story of the witch there runs a domestic tragedy in which a young man murders his wife. This plot is probably Ford's invention, but Dekker intervenes to create the figure of Susan, the murdered wife, one of the simplest and sweetest girls in Elizabethan drama. His great contribution, however, is the character of Mother Sawyer, the wretched old woman hounded by slander and persecution into a compact with the devil. Dekker was enough of his time to believe in witchcraft; he was far beyond his time in the pity that he felt for the witch. Her defense against the charges brought against her is instinct with Dekker's sympathy for the poor and miserable.

Dekker seems to have liked working with Ford, for in 1624 there are records of several plays, most of them lost, of their joint authorship. In one of these, *Keep the Widow Waking,* they joined with Webster and Rowley to huddle up in a month a play that linked the incongruous themes of a scandalous marriage and a recent matricide in London. The only surviving play of this year of collaboration is *The Sun's Darling,* "in the nature of a masque," "often presented at Court and played at the private theatre, the Cockpit, with great applause." This charming dramatic poem—it is a pageant rather than a play—traces the career of Raybright, child of the Sun God, through the four seasons of the year. It is crowded with masquelike ele-

ments, songs, dances, and apparitions of the Sun in splendor. In such a work one cannot expect real dramatic action or strong characterization, but it is pleasant to find in the Dekker scenes of this, his last known work for the stage, a late flowering of his happy humor and his lilting lyric.

It is hard to form a final judgment of Dekker as a dramatist. There is so much in his work to delight us that it is easy to dwell upon his charm and overlook his weakness. On the other hand if one examines his plays closely, it is only too easy to point out his failures. Perhaps if one takes into account the circumstances under which his work was done, one may arrive at a fairly impartial conclusion.

Dekker was a professional Elizabethan playwright. Not only that, but he was from the beginning one of Henslowe's hacks, trained in the journeyman's craft of revision, collaboration, and hasty production. He never quite broke free, as Chapman and others did, from these bonds; to the end of his life we find him collaborating with other men to dramatize swiftly a contemporary sensation. It is hard to believe that under these circumstances he had any real pride in his art. As a professional playwright he naturally was inclined to make use of well-tried effects, sleeping-potions and feigned madness in serious plays, disguise and comic patter in his lighter work. His gravest fault is an amazing carelessness of construction; a crowded and tangled action is often brought to a swift and huddled close. Few of his fellow playwrights had any special reverence for the dramatic unities, but Dekker strays farther than most of them from the important unity of theme. No playwright with an artist's conscience would have shoved his satiric retort to Jonson into the framework of a romantic tragi-comedy.

Yet the merits of Dekker as a dramatist are far from inconsiderable. No one has spoken of him without dwelling on the beauty of his verse, but it has not always been observed how easily and naturally this verse often attains dramatic expression. Song is a natural and fitting decoration of Elizabethan drama, and Dekker's lyrics are among the sweetest in the chorus of Elizabethan song. Nor in praising Dekker's poetry should we overlook his command of a vigorous and racy prose. One of Dekker's characteristics is his keen observation of contemporary life. He knew his London as well as Jonson and loved it better, for there is none of Jonson's lofty scorn of human follies in Dekker's work; a romantic at heart, he tempered his comment on life with a kindly humor. He had a genuine if intermittent power of characterization; many of his characters are mere conventional dramatic types, but the best are vividly realized and strongly presented, the London shopkeeper, the long-suffering wife, and the swaggering gallant, all drawn from the life, creatures less of poetic imagination than of sympathetic observation. He is not a great dramatist, but certainly a delightful poet-playwright. (pp. 107-15)

Thomas Marc Parrott and Robert Hamilton Ball, "The Henslowe Group: Chapman, Dekker, Heywood," in their A Short View of Elizabethan Drama: Together with Some Account of Its Principal Playwrights and the

Conditions Under Which It Was Produced, *1943. Reprint by Charles Scribner's Sons, 1958, pp. 93-125.*

George Saintsbury on *The Honest Whore*:

My own reason for preferring [*The Honest Whore*] to almost all the non-tragical work of the time out of Shakespere, is the wonderful character of Bellafront, both in her unreclaimed and her reclaimed condition. In both she is a very woman—not as conventional satirists and conventional ecomiasts praise or rail at women, but as women are. If her language in her unregenerate days is sometimes coarser than is altogether pleasant, it does not disguise her nature,—the very nature of such a woman misled by giddiness, by curiosity, by love of pleasure, by love of admiration, but in no thorough sense depraved. Her selection of Matheo not as the instrument of her being "made an honest woman," not apparently because she had any love for him left, or had ever had much, but because he was her first seducer, is exactly what, after a sudden convincing of sin, such a woman would have done; and if her patience under the long trial of her husband's thoughtlessness and occasional brutality seem excessive, it will only seem so to one who has been unlucky in his experience. Matheo indeed is a thorough good-for-nothing, and the natural man longs that Bellafront might have been better parted; but Dekker was a very moral person in his own way, and apparently he would not entirely let her—Imogen gone astray as she is—off her penance.

George Saintsbury, in his History of Elizabethan Literature, *1887.*

M. C. Bradbrook   (essay date 1955)

[*Bradbrook is an English literary scholar specializing in Elizabethan studies. In this excerpt, she treats Dekker's works as embodiments of Elizabethan and Jacobean popular tastes.*]

Dekker, the most traditional of Elizabethan writers, was by nature little of a dramatist and practised intermittently. His plays have moments of tenderness, gleams of pathos, but the general effect is too often amorphous and blurred. His work is mingled with that of others and often survives in a poor state. The titles of forty-two of his plays are recorded; seventeen remain of which five are entirely his own—*Old Fortunatus, The Shoemakers' Holiday, The Whore of Babylon, If it be not a good play, the devil is in it* and *Match Me in London.* In plays where he collaborated, the other partner seems generally to have influenced the plot. Dekker tried all the popular forms, and he wrote for the men and the boys' companies over a period of more than thirty years. His drama falls roughly into three divisions: the early popular comedies, including *Old Fortunatus, Patient Grissel* and *The Shoemakers' Holiday;* the citizen comedies written with Middleton and Webster; and after an interval, the final tragic lyric mode of *The Witch of Edmonton,* inconsequently joined with some poor fustian.

Old Fortunatus and *If it be not a good play* are probably compressions of two double plays; the first includes both the life of Fortunatus and those of his sons, and the second gives an account of the adventures of Friar Rush, who had formerly been shown in a double play. Magic hats and purses, devils with magic shows, a golden head which drops coins, and a scene in hell with the torturing of Ravaillac, Guy Fawkes, a Usurer and a Prodigal, provided bait for the groundlings. Mingled with these are adventures for the king, set speeches for the clown: in *Old Fortunatus* there are long declamations, and Fortune, Vice and Virtue appear in the Induction: in *If it be not a good play,* three devils are despatched to earth in the shapes of a courtier, a friar and a usurer, and the play ends with their return to hell, bearing their human spoils to an infernal conclave which is broken up by a boatload of Puritans from Charon's ferry. There is no coherence in the episodes: all is haphazard, and the folk-tales of fabulous good luck allow any kind of augmentation. There is a faint and far-off echo of situations in Marlowe's *Faustus,* but nothing of Marlowe's power to realize an inward state of being or even of Peele's brevity and delicate mockery.

A dramatic poem, which was perhaps not meant for staging, achieved success at the noisy Red Bull. This was *The Whore of Babylon,* full of dumb shows and written in Marlovian blank verse. It tells of the troubles of Queen Elizabeth under the name of Titania the Faerie Queen. She is opposed by the Empress of Rome and wards off the attacks of three kings and of three assassins, Campeius, Paridel (Parry) and Lupus (Lopez). The play concludes with a grand seafight; but Dekker in a preface of unusual spleen reproaches the actors for their noisy additions.

Another history play was hastily adapted by Dekker to provide *Satiromastix,* his contribution to the Poets' War, directed chiefly against Jonson. These two writers, born within a year or two of each other and dying in the same decade, are in opposition throughout their lives. All Jonson's virtues of concentration, order and critical control were lacking in Dekker, while Dekker's virtues of sympathy, tolerance and spontaneity were equally lacking in Jonson. Jonson's work can be judged only as a whole: Dekker's demands to be judged by his happiest efforts. They were at one only in their devotion to London, its history and customs; both delineated the very streets and alleys, and named it over ward by ward. In *The Wonder of a Kingdom,* Dekker wrote a play in celebration of the founding of Dulwich College by his old friend Alleyn. The festival of Simon and Jude, when the Liveries' pageants turned out, is especially dear to Dekker. His foreigners are real denizens of London—the Italian writing master, the Dutch artisan; the cockney 'prentices and their sweethearts are his heroes. Dekker only once satirizes the Puritans, he never shows cheating tradesmen or professional thieves. His rebuke to Jonson, 'Tis the easiest and the basest art to rail', was fairly spoken, for he was free of acerbity himself. Vigour, fidelity and directness in the Dutch manner which his name suggests, were his to command, as well as lively caricature and a journalist's passion for detail. He is like an earlier Dickens who never got past the stage of *The Pickwick Papers. The Shoemakers' Holiday,* based on a popular work by the ballad-writer Deloney, remains his one successful play and the natural antithesis to *Bartholomew Fair.* Both delight in a popular festival of the city; both catch the flavour of a proverb, the smell of a shop. Yet while Jonson's judicial eye noted merely the follies and affectations of his characters, Dekker shows only the happy, the faithful and the generous. Here is the King who frolics among his subjects, the noble who loves a girl of low degree but resigns her to another; the somewhat anæmic pathos of Jane, which pales beside the boisterous excitement of Simon Eyre and the humours of the three 'prentices, softens the revelry and introduces a new note. Although the language is varied, this remains the most consistent of Dekker's works. All his other plays have some incongruity or other. His readiness to reflect the fashions of the hour, coupled with his great facility, was his undoing. His plague-pamphlets and book of prayers show a depth of feeling which in his drama emerges only in short passages. His early clowns echo Lyly, his heroes Marlowe, his magicians Greene, and his masque Nashe. In his last works, **Match Me in London** and **The Wonder of a Kingdom,** he tries the tragi-comedy of Fletcher and Massinger. He has certain stock ingredients, such as a comic Dutchman and a comic Welshman; among his lost plays are treatments of such well-known legends as Constance of Rome, Guy of Warwick and The Faery Knight. Jonson describes him contemptuously:

> O sir, his doublet's a little decayed: he is other-
> wise a very simple honest fellow, one Demetrius,
> a dresser of plays

and at the end of *Poetaster* arrays him in a fool's coat, and cap.

Dekker's happiest characters are traditional: frolicking men or patient women. Simon Eyre and Orlando Friscobaldo are merry, humorous old jesters of boundless high spirits—Hazlitt and Lamb overworked the pathos of Orlando, who is serious only in flashes. The boisterous gaiety of Simon Eyre as he rattles away to his sovereign is typical of Dekker's comic rhetoric.

> Mark this old wench, my king: I danced the
> shaking of the sheets with her six and thirty
> years ago, and yet I hope to get two or three
> young Lord Mayors ere I die. I am lusty still,
> Sim Eyre still. Care and cold lodging bring white
> hairs. My sweet Majesty, let care vanish, cast it
> upon thy nobles, it will make thee always look
> young, like Apollo, and cry Humph!'

This headlong style is speeded up yet more in the speech of Matheo, the prodigal of **The Honest Whore,** who, as he strips his wife's gown off her back and orders her off to her old trade, proclaims himself one of the roarers:

> Must have money, must have a cloak and rapier
> and things. Will you go set your limetwigs and
> get me some birds, some money? . . . You will
> not, then? Must have cash and pictures, do you
> hear, frailty? Shall I walk in a Plymouth cloak,
> that's to say, like a rogue in my doublet and
> hose, and a crab-tree cudgel in my hand, and you
> swim in your satins? Must have money, come!

The blunt style of his father-in-law, old Orlando, matches

this torrent, with only an occasional note of pathos, as when he speaks of his dead wife:

> She's an old dweller in these high countries, yet
> she's not from me: she's here.

Disguised as a servant, Orlando watches and adds to his daughter's trials with the same improbable detachment as Gualter shows to Grissel. Patience in adversity is Dekker's endowment of all his heroines. Patient Grissel, Lady Jane Grey in **Sir Thomas Wiat,** the other Jane of **The Shoemakers' Holiday,** Infelice and Bellafront in *The Honest Whore* and Susan in **The Witch of Edmonton** are all dedicated to it. The accent of constancy is the same in these and other heroines: it is simple and penetrating as that of a ballad.

> Yet good sir, because I will not grieve you,
> With hopes to taste fruit which will never fall,
> In simple truth, this is the sum of all·
> My husband lives, at least I hope he lives:
> Pressed was he to these bitter wars in France.
> Bitter they are to me by wanting him.
> I have but one heart and that heart's his due.

Dekker's good women emerge from their trials too often, like some perfect machine, guaranteed mechanically perfect under all conditions. To yoke their pathos with the noisy fun and violent brutalities of a rake's progress is fatally incongruous. Grissel, almost completely medieval in conception, is set off by a termagant Welsh widow and her henpecked second husband, and by the Lady Julia, who prefers the freedom of virginity. If either were less natural, it might pass; only because he cannot devise perspectives of artifice Dekker, in his easy pity and boundless tolerance, appears something of a moral sloven, and Jonson's rasping judgements more than railing. Dekker writes at his best when he collaborates with someone who will stiffen the plot and provide him with clear outlines of character upon which he can impress his own lyric tenderness or gaiety. In his most considerable work, **The Honest Whore,** he worked with the satirist Middleton. The repentant whore, her father and her wild husband are joined with an Italianate revenge story, and with 'the humours of the patient man' Candido, a linen-draper from Cheapside. Scenes in Bedlam and Bridewell, ruffling humours and the fights of 'prentices are interspersed with tremendous moral tirades. Bellafront, careless and gay and sluttish, is more engaging in her unregenerate state: she has not the brilliant horror of Marston's Franceschina, who appeared in the following season in a Blackfriars play, but her conversion leads to a deal of dreary sermonizing, and she ends, with all the other characters, in 'Bethlem Monastery', which has transported itself from London to Milan with remarkably little change of character. In a scene of savage farce, between three of the real madmen, Dekker seems to be recalling *Hamlet* as he does elsewhere in this play: the sweeper of Bethlem moralizes on his charges in the very accents of the grave-digger.

> *Duke:* And how long is't till you recover any of
> these?

> *Sweeper:* . . . An alderman's son will be mad a
> great while, a very great while, especially if his
> friends left him well: a whore will hardly come

to her wits again: a puritan, there's no hope of him. . . .

A broken merchant and two men who have run mad for love are displayed to the visitors by their doctor with the observation:

> They must be used like children, pleased with toys,
> And anon whipped for their unruliness.

This is the formula by which all the characters in the play are brought to felicity. Bellafront is deprived of Hippolito, and married by the Duke to the man who first seduced her; the Duke himself is cheated of his revenge by the doctor-friar who helps the two young lovers to steal a marriage. The final exposition of a cure is given with the sudden transformation of Candido, the linen-draper. He has displayed his humour of patience in a series of appalling situations which his wife has devised in the longing to put him out of humour, and ends also in Bethlem, where she has committed him, after he has accepted and even improved on all her stratagems. When, thoroughly remorseful, she comes to procure his release, he coolly throws up his role, telling her that the only lunatic is herself, and that he had swallowed all the indignities she heaped on him simply to cure her perverse longing. This novel and strikingly up-to-date method of taming a shrew is much more convincing than the moral objurgations with which Hippolito converts Bellafront; but it requires that Candido should be played in a manner far from guileless. No doubt to the City, the Draper who attended the Mansion House in a tablecloth with a hole cut for his head because his wife had locked up his livery was simply a farcical innocent; while the naïve pieties of his final sermon on patience endeared him to the admirers of Patient Grissel. Candido is an 'open' character in the Shakespearean mode: he could be played in several ways and is complex enough to be inconsistent, like the play in which he appears. He was revived for Part II and given a second wife, whom he tames by the much simpler expedient of a threatened taste of the stick. The sequel is in general a poor copy of Part I: but a procession of Bridewell whores which concludes Part II achieves true dramatic objectivity, and is in the sharpest contrast with the conventional speeches of the reformed Bellafront. The women are displayed in a procession, beating hemp, pounding chalk, and going to a whipping at the cart's tail.

> *Enter Doll Termagent, brave.*
>
> *Infelice:* Dost thou not weep now thou art here?
>
> *Doll:* Say ye? weep? yes, forsooth, as you did when you lost your maiden-head: do you not hear how I weep? (*sings*).
>
> *Lodowick:* Farewell, Doll.
>
> *Doll:* Farewell, dog . . .
>
> *Enter Penelope Whorehound.*
>
> *Penelope:* I never was in this pickle before: yet if I go among citizens' wives, they jeer at me: if I go among the loose bodied gowns, they cry a pox on me, because I go civilly attired, and swear their trade was a good trade till such as

> I took it out of their hands. Good Lieutenant Bots, speak to these captains to bail me.

Seen against the fate of Penelope (dressed like a citizen's wife), the cheating game of easy virtue played in Dekker's city comedies, *Westward Ho!* and its very inferior sequel, *Northward Ho!,* becomes more savage than farcical. Jaunts to the Three Pigeons at Brentford, to Staines, Ware and Hoxton are the occasions for gallants to press their suits, and for punks and thieves to ply their trades. The city husbands themselves frequent bawdy houses, and have their garden retreats in Moorfields; but at the end, adultery is avoided, the citizens' wives remain honest, and a general Act of Oblivion covers all faults. The sardonic judgement which the plays evoke is never delivered, for these are not true satires, but only 'domestic' comedy. Well-known scenes and occasions must have given them almost the air of an impromptu and could easily have suggested individual portraits. In two of his more successful collaborations, *The Roaring Girl* and *The Witch of Edmonton,* Dekker depicted living persons as the heroines, and it is likely that Moll Frith, the Roaring Girl, made a personal appearance on the stage. In each case the story is built round the figure of a woman who is cut off from her kind. The paradoxical character of Moll or the desperate wretchedness of old Mother Sawyer could not perhaps have been achieved by Dekker alone, but the sympathy and warmth of tone are his.

Both the revelling plays and the moral *Honest Whore* depend upon popular traditions, but modify them to the taste of the day. The Prodigal Son, the hero of many mid-century moral plays, came back to general favour in the early seventeenth century. The novelty of Dekker's treatment lies in the fact that the roles of tempting harlot and faithful wife, opposed in such plays as *How a Man May Choose a Good Wife* and *The Fair Maid of Bristowe,* are combined by Dekker. Bellafront is the centre of interest rather than her prodigal husband. In all the plays of the prodigal which appear between 1602 and 1607 (except *Eastward Ho!* which burlesques the whole tradition) the sinner is let off very lightly. When he sinks to crime, it is often laid at his father's door. The shift from moral examination of the prodigal to his portrayal as a sympathetic social figure is part of the general movement from a drama based on ethics to one based on the study of man in society; but an additional cause may have been an appeal to the sympathy of the young gallants in the audience. They would not wish to see their own kind too harshly treated. After the prodigal and the clown, the curst wife was probably the most familiar figure in the old comedy. Candido's first and second wives come of distinguished company; but no full-scale treatment of married affliction by Dekker survives, though a lost play entitled *Medicine for a Cursed Wife* indicates that he did not neglect it. In *Westward Ho!* and *Northward Ho!,* as in *The Merry Wives of Windsor,* the cheating tricks which knaves put upon gulls are turned back by the virtuous city wives upon would-be seducers, and thus bitter comedy on the Jonsonian model is converted to somewhat wry-faced revelry.

If the violent moral condemnation of the traitors in *The Whore of Babylon* be excepted, Dekker reserves his denunciation for those who prey upon others: for usurers, brokers and bawds. A boundless charity and willingness to comply with all comers characterize such different figures as Candido and Jacomo Gentilli, the linen-draper and the lord. Ancient hospitality is praised, and though the subplot of *The Wonder of a Kingdom* might almost be called *A Contention between Liberality and Prodigality,* it is the meanness of the prodigal in refusing alms which condemns him, and not his riots.

On the other hand, Dekker never omits the traditional moral element; witness his masque, *The Sun's Darling,* which survives only in a late form refashioned by Ford, but is probably based on the lost *Phaethon* of 1598. This masque has something in common with Nashe's *Summer's Last Will and Testament:* its real subject is the enchantment of spring and the riches of autumn: the exquisite songs distil the best of the scenes into a few stanzas. Nevertheless its fable purports to show the progress of a celestial Prodigal Son through the realms of the four seasons. Raybright, child of the sun, is accompanied through his progress by the whore Humour and the clown Folly, and attended by such figures as Delight and Health at the same time as he is waited upon by a French tailor, an Italian dancing master and a Spanish pastry-cook. The play, though it includes some social satire, celebrates the rites of Nature rather than the judgement of Man. This is Dekker's most complete gallimaufrey, saved by its lyrical naïvety and the freshness of the songs.

It is significant that Dekker's finest work is either in lyric form or in prose. His generous and unforced humanity and his deep vein of piety show up best in his pamphlets, which are incomparably superior to anything he wrote for the stage. His style has always the merits of easiness and simplicity, but the blank verse lacks pulse and power. His range is so wide that no one consistent impression remains. The prose speech of his clowns is the most distinctive of all; this was generally true, of course, and is well marked in the early Shakespeare. From the antithetical wit of Shadow in *Old Fortunatus* (a style roughly equivalent to that of Speed in Shakespeare's *Two Gentlemen of Verona*) Dekker steadily progresses towards colloquial ease. Shadow defines hunger like a scholar:

> Hunger is made of gunpowder or gunpowder of hunger, for they both eat through stone walls: hunger is a grindstone, it sharpens wit: hunger is fuller of love than Cupid, for it makes a man eat himself: hunger was the first that ever opened a cookshop, cooks the first that ever made sauce, sauce being liquorish, licks up good meat; good meat preserves life: hunger therefore preserves life.

This parody of school declamation might well end with a *Sic Probo.* But Cuddy Banks, the clown of one of the latest plays, *The Witch of Edmonton,* speaks in very different accents:

> Prithee look but in the lover's almanac: when he has been but three days absent, 'O' says he, 'I have not seen my love these seven years': there's a long cut! When he comes to her again and embraces her 'O', says he 'now methinks I am in Heaven' and that's a pretty step. He that gets up to Heaven in ten days need not repent his jour-

ney: you may ride a hundred days in a carouche, and be further off than when you set forth.

As his early plays echo Marlowe and Greene, Dekker's middle verse reflects Shakespeare. For formal passages he is addicted to couplets: his imagery is always unobtrusive. His is precisely that simple, lucid, unplanned style which was essential to establish a norm. He is interested in proverbs and in the contrast of foreign speech with English, but language is a tool that has grown into his hand: he does not seek, like Jonson, to polish it.

The delicate fancy and rough vitality of Dekker were quenched by six years' imprisonment in the King's Bench (1613-1619), after which he wrote but little. His pamphlets and pageants continued to appear, but his final comedies are sorry affairs. *The Witch of Edmonton,* a tender and barbarous story, has nothing of comedy in it but Cuddy Banks's jests.

Dekker could not achieve formal structure. The simple contrast of Maid, Wife and Widow in *Patient Grissel* is a traditional one. In *Westward Ho!* and *Northward Ho!* with the aid of Webster he had tried symmetrical grouping of characters, and had speeded up the love-intrigue. In his last plays, *The Wonder of a Kingdom* and *Match Me in London,* he allows three or four pairs of lovers to a play: the method is explained in the epilogue to *The Wonder of a Kingdom:*

> . . . All these changes and these marriages
> Both how they shuffled, cut and dealt about,
> What cards are best, after the trumps were out,
> Who played false play, who true, who sought to save
> An ace i' the bottom and turned up a knave.
> For love is but a card play and all's lost
> Unless you cog: he that packs best, wins most.

The card-play of love had already been summed up unfavourably by Ben Jonson: it is curious that as Dekker in his old age overcrowded his intrigues and multiplied plots in an attempt to follow the style of Jonson and his 'sons', Jonson himself turned back to those old moralities which Dekker had drawn on in his youth. Jonson's failure infuriated him; but his old rival, with characteristic gentleness, appealed to youth to bear with age's infirmity.

> I have been a priest in Apollo's temple many years, my voice is decaying with my age: yet yours being clear and above mine, shall much honour me, if you but listen to my old tunes. Are they ill? pardon them: well? then receive them.

Long before this, the original Elizabethan audience which brought forth the best in the old writer had disintegrated. The later work commanded a much narrower public than that which he enjoyed in the old days when he wrote for Henslowe and Alleyn at the Fortune. The form of the drama too had set, and the inchoate comedies of the nineties were now left far behind. Yet Dekker still aspired to be one who could

> Call the banish'd auditor home, and tie
> His ear with golden chain to his melody. . . .
> Can draw with adamantine pen even creatures
> Forg'd out of the hammer, on tiptoe to reach up

And from rare silence, clap their brawny hands
    T'applaud what their charm'd soul scarce un-
        derstands.

The power to magnetize the London artisan—an instinctive and unstudied sympathy with simple people in a comedy not merely spectacular—was the secret of Dekker's early success and of his slow alienation from the stage. Dekker was essentially an Elizabethan, and his free extemporizing style belonged to the age when comic form was still fluid. Like Drayton, his ancient collaborator, he lived on into bleaker times, when only the Lord Mayor's Show allowed him a chance to revive the 'old Elizabeth fashion' in all its glory. He died, as he had lived, in poverty, yet still keeping friendship with younger poets; his last poem is a commendatory verse for a play by a 'son' of Jonson—Dick Brome. His incorrigible cheerfulness and unteachable simplicity recall the merry old men of his own plays. Throughout his prolific, disorganized career, a clear piping note of the earlier music arises. In spite of his Dutch painting of Bedlam and Bridewell, a countrified innocence and sweetness cling to the Cockney poet. (pp. 121-3)

> M. C. Bradbrook, "Pastime and Good Company: Dekker and Heywood," in her The Growth and Structure of Elizabethan Comedy, *Chatto & Windus, 1955, pp. 119-37.*

Donald G. Mitchell on Dekker's versatility:

There is good meat in what Dekker wrote: he had humor; he had pluck; he had gift for using words—to sting or to praise—or to beguile one. There are traces not only of a Dickens flavor in him, but of a Lamb flavor as well; and there is reason to believe that, like both these later humorists, he made his conquests without the support of a university training. Swinburne characterizes him as a "modest, shiftless, careless nature": but he was keen to thrust a pin into one who had offended his sensibilities; in his plays he warmed into pretty lyrical outbreaks, but never seriously measured out a work of large proportions, or entered upon execution of such with a calm, persevering temper. He was many-sided, not only literary-wise, but also conscience-wise. It seems incredible that one who should write the coarse things which appear in his **Bachelor's Banquet** should also have elaborated, with a pious unction (that reminds of Jeremy Taylor) the saintly invocations of the **Foure Birds of Noah's Ark:** and as for his **Dreame** it shows in parts a luridness of color which reminds of our own Wigglesworth—as if this New England poet of fifty years later may have dipped his brush into the same paint-pot.

> Donald G. Mitchell, in his English Lands, Letters, and Kings: From Celt to Tudor, *1889.*

Harold E. Toliver   (essay date 1961)

[*An American educator and critic, Toliver is particularly concerned with issues of structure in literature. In this excerpt, he finds* The Shoemaker's Holiday *unified around thematic patterns concerning love, honor, and*

money, all three of which, he argues, achieve resolution in the festive atmosphere of holiday at the play's close.]

Thomas Dekker will not likely share the lot of rediscovered minor figures. **The Shoemaker's Holiday,** to be sure, frequently appears in selections of Elizabethan comedy; but Dekker had the misfortune of being overmatched by Jonson in satire and overshadowed by Shakespeare in romantic comedy. An uncertain canon sprinkled with collaborations has made him more attractive to textual studies than to criticism. Like the rest of Dekker's comedies, **The Shoemakers' Holiday** is occasionally commended for its delightful realism, or in Mary Leland Hunt's words, for being "the most attractive picture of citizen life presented on the Elizabethan stage, and perhaps . . . the truest," and for manifesting Dekkers' "sane, sweet, and democratic mind" [*Thomas Dekker: A Study,* 1911]. But the implication is that the "picture" is spontaneous, untidy, and without enduring significance for an age which does not turn excitedly to a drama of sweetness and sanity.

I think, however, that the play's vagabond madness has a method and that its lighthearted "democracy" has a shape and coherence which might tend to raise our estimation of Dekker's craftsmanship if observed. The thematic goal of the play is not to exalt one segment of Elizabethan society above others, to be a trade manual for shoemaker apprentices, or to offer a guidebook to late fifteenth-century London; rather, it is to show that the deficiencies of various social levels are symptomatic of enduring human faults, faults which may be remedied by the right kind of discipline and the right kind of holiday freedom. The special areas of deficiency and their remedies may be divided into a few imagistic and thematic categories. The shoemakers, especially Firk, are addicted to sensual 'feasting' while those of higher standing entertain at a falsely civil and arid table; these two are transcended in the ceremonial-sensuous banquet which Simon Eyre, the shoemaker-mayor, serves the King. A false love for position and wealth threatens the two central love affairs from above while poverty threatens them from below; these dangers are dissolved in love matches-with-blessings. Likewise, a false sense of honor seems momentarily to promise rewards while true honor results only in a crippling lameness and a life of hardship. This condition, the world being what it is, cannot be entirely cured, but is set straight as far as possible. And last, in the shoemakers' lives a holiday atmosphere of irresponsible festivity and the crude necessities of life stand opposed; this condition, too, is ameliorated by the power of the King in conjunction with the shoemaker-mayor. If any of these is central, it would seem to be the last, though the opposition might be more broadly phrased as a struggle between the exigencies imposed upon one's free will by a life of commodity and compromise, and the desire to escape these necessities, to be an entirely free and romantic agent perpetually on a "holiday."

Freedom is not entirely dependent upon money: even those with money must learn to compromise and the unpropertied can find a way to direct their own affairs and to have their own means of creating holidays. "Prince am I none," Simon says, "yet am I princely born," receiving his proper inheritance as the "sole" son of a shoemaker. Honor can in fact be gained in a life of commodity: "I am a handicraftsman," he adds, "yet my heart is without craft" (V.v.10). But the conflict between life as it is and life as the romantic spirit would have it be is nevertheless intimately involved in the differences between social and economic levels, as the two contrasting songs which serve as prelude suggest in their own oblique way. The first of the two combines natural harmony and serenity with comic lowness:

"Now the Nightingale, the pretty Nightingale,
The sweetest singer in all the forest's choir,
Entreats thee, sweet Peggy, to hear thy true
    love's tale;
Lo, yonder she sitteth, her breast against a brier.

"But O, I spy the Cuckoo, the Cuckoo, the
    Cuckoo;
See where she sitteth: come away, my joy;
Come away, I prithee, I do not like the Cuckoo
Should sing where my Peggy and I kiss and toy."

O the month of May, the merry month of May,
So frolic, so gay, and so green, so green, so green!
And then did I unto my true love say:
"Sweet Peg, thou shalt be my summer's queen!"

The poetry of the love holiday is thus 'impure.' Merely setting a romantic "true-love's tale" in the context of the "brier" would not in itself make it so—the holiday atmosphere of romantic comedy is customarily intensified by a token resistance which, it is apparent from the beginning, will be overcome. But romance is confronted also by the formidable challenge of the cuckoo, which, unlike the aristocratic "sweetest singer" of the forest, is common, bourgeois, and a little absurd: love can withstand rich uncles, but can it survive domestication? The singer, at any rate, apparently fears not; he must take his joy "away" from the cuckoo's song. An uncomfortable awareness of creaturely realities impinges itself upon lovers even as they "kiss and toy," which predicts what the play itself will demonstrate, namely, that romantic loves like that of "Rose" and "Lacy" must be considered in the context of the more prosaic life of the shoemakers, especially the marital life of Simon and Margery and the sensual life of Firk.

These two views of love are part of a complex of interrelated class levels and "planes of reality" (in E.M.W. Tillyard's phrase) which the play presents. But other kinds of love besides these two are also possible. The second song resolves the conflict between romantic merriment and disenchanted reality by proposing a spirited resignation and an open-eyed love (reminiscent of Jane's and Ralph's, as we shall see later):

Trowl the bowl, the jolly nut-brown bowl,
    And here, kind mate, to thee:
Let's sing a dirge for Saint Hugh's soul,
    And down it merrily. . . .

Cold's the wind, and wet's the rain,
    Saint Hugh be our good speed:
Ill is the weather that bringeth no gain,
    Nor helps good hearts in need.

If romance is tested by comic realism in the first song, in the second indoor security and warmth contain a measure of sorrow and necessity. Desire for an ideal "summer's queen" and fear of a wife who might make the cuckoos sing are both exchanged for a stable bond with a "kind mate"—an endearing but well-tried love. Likewise, nature's spontaneous tutelary powers are exchanged for society's martyr (Saint Hugh being the patron saint of shoemakers) and the light hearted songs of the May for trowling of the bowl and a "dirge." It is not the best of all possible worlds but festivity is possible—"sing a dirge," but "down it merrily."

The season itself, which is thus a mixture of winter cold and summer merriment, is to be judged partly by what can be "gained" from it. Perhaps the free and light of heart can afford to have the nightingale for a patron, but the shoemakers need Saint Hugh, or as the prologue suggests to the Queen, a goddess who will care for her "meanest vassals," as the King cares for Simon (the implication being that the Elizabethan theater, like Simon's banquet hall, is also a kind of festive meeting place where, "on bended knees," the shoemakers may properly ask for tribute).

The theme of gain is immediately taken up in the first scene by Lincoln and Lord Mayor Oteley, whose feasting together has become a mere outward form, as indeed love and honor have also. Though they are decidedly not "good hearts" in need, money is a commanding power capable of arousing distrust between them. "Poor citizens must not with courtiers wed" (I.i.12) who will spend more in a year on "silks and gay apparel" than the mayor is worth. To make the point sure, Lincoln describes at length the dissolute spending of his nephew, who has become the lowest of the humble, a shoemaker in Wittenberg, "A goodly science for a gentleman / Of such descent!" (I.i.30). Rose, the object of Lacy's love, Lincoln describes as a "gay, wanton, painted citizen" though, as we discover, she presents the only opportunity for Lacy to exchange the bright scarves, the "bunch of feathers," and "the monstrous garters" which characterize his affectation, for the true garland of festivity (I.ii.1). She in turn is enabled by him to be bound "prentice to the Gentle Trade" (III.iii.87). His disguise as a shoemaker is in a sense his own creation of identity; paradoxically, only by becoming a shoemaker can he and Rose share in the "frolic, so gay, and so green, so green. . . ." To this extent, his love takes on the qualities which modify the romantic spirit of the second song—his disguise is a symbolic acquisition of the sturdiness of the lower classes.

The issue is more clearly drawn in Lincoln's instructions to Lacy (I.i.71 f.). The Lord Mayor, "this churl . . . in the height of scorn," according to this Polonius in the height of worldly wisdom, has attempted to "buy" Lacy off. Honor, family position, and the image one puts before the world hinge upon defining love in the "proper" way, not, as the King will tell Lincoln, as that which "respects no blood, / Cares not for difference of birth or state" (V.v.104), but as the essence and achievement of birth and state:

Remember, coz,
What honourable fortunes wait on thee:

Increase the king's love, which so brightly
    shines,
And gilds thy hopes. I have no heir but thee,—
And yet not thee, if with a wayward spirit
Thou start from the true bias of my love.

(I.i.80)

The implications are that a "mixture" of bloods will destroy the social hierarchy rather than bestowing benefits on each level; the King's love functions to "gild" one's personal hopes with an external grace; and "my love" has the "true bias," which cannot be left for the wayward infatuation of romantic love without incurring the risk of disinheritance. As a comparatively free aristocrat, Lincoln misses all the advantages of his station and acquires the disadvantages of those who by necessity must be concerned for "gain." When Lacy falls into the game, Lincoln rewards him with "thirty Portigues" for his fair words of acquiescence. And while Lacy secretly rejects Lincoln's command to seek "fair Honour in her loftiest eminence" in the wars in France, policy is as yet his only remedy for policy. He implicitly endorses a superficial sense of values, while self-flagellation for not living up to them stifles festivity as surely as parental authority and false honor could have. Love is powerful only in changing "High birth to baseness, and a nobler mind / To the mean semblance of a shoemaker!" (I.iii.10). But he also sees another side of things which will develop in the course of the play until the threat of disinheritance ceases to matter:

Then cheer my hoping spirits, be not dismay'd,
Thou canst not want, do Fortune what she can,
The Gentle Craft is living for a man.

Simon Eyre's version of the last line shows "living" to mean not only possessing the minimum necessities but having real life. According to the standards of Lincoln, missing the war in France to become a shoemaker-lover is not to gain a way of living but to kill the real man, the "name": "Lacy, thy name / Liv'd once in honour, now 'tis dead in shame" (II.iv.52). It is to destroy the self and the bank-book, as though identical, in the same fire, "The fire of that love's lunacy" in which Lacy has "burnt up himself, consum'd his credit" (II.iv.41). But Lincoln's economics of love are gradually turned against him. Lacy becomes "surfeit with excess of joy" and is made happy by Rose's "rich perfection," which pays "sweet interest" to his hopes and "redoubles love on love":

let me once more
Like to a bold-fac'd debtor crave of thee,
This night to steal abroad . . .

(IV.iii.12)

Only by the sweet theft of love can important debts be paid. In spite of her father's anger and his uncle's hate ("This traffic of hot love shall yield cold gains," IV.iv.139), trading false honor for love can be consummated in "happy nuptials" blessed by the King himself. As Firk aptly says of this "humble" marriage of the new shoemaker, "They shall be knit like a pair of stockings in matrimony."

The love of Ralph and Jane, on the other hand, is beset more by necessity than by false honor; shoemakers go to France because pressed into service, not to gain a name

but to lose the full use of their limbs. The intercession of Simon is not sufficient to keep the newly married couple together, but even shoemakers can be worthy soldiers if forced to be: "take him, brave men; Hector of Troy was an hackney to him, Hercules and Termagant scoundrels." Simon's advice is somewhat more sound if less delicate than Lincoln's to Lacy; it is not, of course, without its own concern for social class and honor:

> fight for the honour of the Gentle Craft, for the gentlemen shoemakers, the courageous cordwainers, the flower of St. Martin's, the mad knaves of Bedlam, Fleet Street, Tower Street and Whitechapel; crack me the crowns of the French knaves, a pox on them, crack them; fight, by the Lord Ludgate, fight, my fine boy!

(I.i.211)

And as Firk shows, shoemakers can also turn necessity to gain: "God send thee to cram thy slops [pockets] with French crowns, and thy enemies' bellies with bullets," (I.i.221.)

Ralph himself understands clearly the contrast between the poor and the rich as they go to war. Rich men "give their wives rich gifts, / Jewels and rings, to grace their lily hands," while those of his trade make "rings for women's heels." His gift of a pair of shoes, besides being practical, becomes a symbol of fidelity and humbleness. It offers a metaphorical language for the poor to talk about love without ostentation ("These true-love knots I prick'd; I hold my life, / By this old shoe I shall find out my wife"), though to Firk love sentiments are but an "ague-fit of foolishness" (IV.ii.46). And by the shoes Ralph is enabled to find Jane as she is about to accept a counter-gift of Hammon's "rings," which will give her a chance to have "lily hands" of grace rather than the working hands of craft pompously described by Eyre: "Let me see thy hand, Jane. This fine hand, this white hand, these pretty fingers must spin, must card, must work; work, you bombast-cotton-queen; work for your living . . ." (I.i.208).

It is Jane, in fact, who is most clearly faced with the choice between an honorable poverty and a fair name. Her dilemma is this: to choose wealth is to sacrifice romance, but to choose romance is perhaps to destroy it, for it cannot survive without holidays. Hammon would make festivity possible by buying her "hand"; but she finds festivity and necessity incompatible: "I cannot *live* by keeping holiday" (III.iv.31). She would rather, she asserts, be wife of a poor man "than a king's whore" (III.iv.79), and, if her breath will make him "rich," Ralph's death makes her "poor" (III.iv.124). When set between the crippled Ralph and Hammon, like Everyman between vice and virtue, and forced to distinguish between false and true honor, she has little difficulty in choosing, but the choice, considered in context, is not a facile one. "Whom should I choose? Whom should my thoughts affect / But him whom Heaven hath made to be my love?" she asks, turning to Ralph; "Thou art my husband, and these humble weeds / Make thee more beautiful than all his wealth" (V.ii.53). The dilemma is dissolved by submission to a higher order ("for wedding and hanging goes by destiny," Firk remarks) and by a discovery of values in keeping with that order. While it is not possible to achieve an unrestricted self-fulfillment, one can acquiesce in providence and grasp whatever beauty exists in "humble weeds." The original choice lay with heaven, perhaps, but it can be endorsed by an act of free will which, within the limits of contingency, is an act of self-determination. Neither Jane nor Ralph is quite complete until this choice is made, but afterward they alone require no gifts from the King. Hammon is left as he began, requiring the "sunny eyes" of a kind mate to warm a "cold heart" but achieving nothing. His position in the cold street outside Jane's warm (and thoroughly honest) shop in which she sits, "a light burning by her," has revealed symbolically a 'winter' nature which finds love a "lunacy" when it makes a single look "as rich . . . as a king's crown" (III.iv.12 f.).

Hammon's attempt to deter Ralph with "fair gold" offers a way to bring the virtues of the gentle trade into the love-honor-money complex: "dost thou think a shoemaker is so base to be a bawd to his own wife for commodity? Take thy gold, choke with it! Were I not lame, I would make thee eat thy words" (V.ii.82). A choking "feast" of gold and words might be more appropriate for Lincoln, but the point is well made, and properly conditioned by necessity—"were I not lame. . . ." Fidelity and honor, having survived the test, get their reward and the tables are turned upon their false counterparts. Oteley and Lincoln, mistaking appearance for reality, rush in to "unmask" what is, of course, no disguise but the genuine "article." Rather than easing "her blindness," theirs is lifted:

> *Lincoln.*   O base wretch!
> Nay, hide thy face, the horror of thy guilt
> Can hardly be wash'd off. Where are thy powers?
> What battles have you made? O yes, I see,
> Thou fought'st with Shame, and Shame hath
>   conquer'd thee.
> This lameness will not serve.
>
>   (V.ii.121)

Ironically, he speaks more truly than he knows. Real guilt cannot indeed be "washed off " like gilt, and lameness will not "serve" one, though, in another sense, this lameness has served the state, and without a visible entourage of "powers."

In the symmetrical cross-referencing of the two love plots, Jane rejects Hammon for someone lower in the social scale while Rose rejects him for someone higher pretending to be lower; both reject him not because he is personally undesirable—by and large he is sympathetically portrayed to remove that possibility—but because "summer love" cannot be arranged or politic. The democracy of shoemakers, with its levelling of social barriers, would seem to win in both cases. Actually, a countersatire operates throughout which shows that commodity and authority inevitably have their place and that shoemakers as well as courtiers can exalt these things beyond their due. Simon's conveniently quick return on an investment enables him to spread the affectations of the rich thinly over a crude, good-hearted sensuousness. It is significantly a shipload of sweet wares, enough "prunes, almonds, and sugar-candy" to send Firk into raptures and Margery into a French hood, which makes him Lord Mayor. If Margery feels "honour creep upon" her and "a certain rising" in her flesh, meaning a rise in nobility, Firk can correctly interpret it as simply growing fat: "Rising in your flesh do you feel, say you? Ay, you may be with child. . . . But you are such a shrew, you'll soon pull him down" (II.iii.136). While putting on as much finery as the "pishery-pashery" of "those silken fellows, . . . painted beings, outsides, outsides," whose "inner linings are torn," she is quick to reprove Ralph's mourning with a glib morality: "Ralph, why doest thou weep? Thou knowest that naked we came out of our mother's womb, and naked we must return; and, therefore, thank God for all things" (III.ii.91).

Firk himself is not entirely immune to the money-disease, but, like Simon, he is more apt to err on the side of crudity than on that of "finery." True festivity, as we learn from the last scene, should not be entirely without discipline, as he tends to make it: the banquet over which the new mayor and the King preside, like the love of Ralph and Jane, has an appointed order and time. That Simon is both shoemaker and mayor, the King both supreme ruler and "feaster," is significant. And "when all our sports and banquetings are done, / Wars must right wrongs which Frenchmen have begun" (V.v.190): holidays, by the nature of things, cannot last forever. To be sure, both Simon's democracy and his discipline cease when he deals with his wife, and his feast of language is anything but a gourmet's dish: "Away, you Islington whitepot! hence, you hopperarse! you barley-pudding full of maggots! you broil'd carbonado!"; but he is not merely an irresponsible king of misrule designed to carry off subversive and aberrant impulses. Though he is a "wild ruffian," even noblemen praise him as a man "as serious, provident, and wise, / As full of gravity amongst the grave, / As any mayor hath been these many years" (V.iii.7).

Perhaps the nature of the final compromise, which brings out the best in the social hierarchy as well as in love, honor, and the working-festive life of the "gentle craft," can best be seen in the feasting imagery, some examples of which I have already quoted. There have been several false starts towards the final concept of the communal banquet. The only agreement Lincoln and Mayor Oteley can achieve over their "sundry" feasts, as we have seen, is that it is a "shame / To join a Lacy with an Oteley's name." Hammon, the hunter of his "dear," having lost his venison, expects to "find a wife," only to become ironically the prey at Oteley's "hunter's feast." Switching the hunt to Jane, his "poor famish'd eyes do feed on that / Which made them famish" (III.iv.5), but he is finally excluded altogether from the shoemakers' banquet, as he is excluded from the harmony and festivity of love itself (V.ii.91), because he has not been willing to sacrifice station to love. His is a false quest, not without appeal, but clearly misdirected. Before the final banquet a preliminary feast is held during which Eyre dominates and becomes the envy of those who have more money but less gaiety. Margery's suggestion to "put on gravity" (III.iii.11) is found unacceptable and Rose is advised to marry "a grocer," since "grocer is a sweet trade: plums, plums." And so Hodge and Firk, as I have indicated, conceive of the feast of life in sensual terms only:

> *Hodge.* . . . Let's feed and be fat with my lord's
> bounty.

Firk. O musical bell, still! O Hodge, O my brethren! There's cheer for the heavens: venison pasties walk up and down piping hot, like sergeants; beef and brewis comes marching in dry-fats, fritters and pancakes comes trowling in in wheel-barrows; hens and oranges hopping in porters' baskets, collops and eggs in scuttles, and tarts and custards comes quavering in in malt-shovels.

(V.ii.187)

This kind of dream, so full of childlike personification, is, of course, quite different from the aristocratic dream of ideal love, but it, too, rests on the borderline between innocence and irresponsibility. The final shoemakers' banquet, while satisfying these appetites and giving gaiety its due, places controls upon the impulse to take a prolonged vacation. When the pancake bell rings, the shoemakers can be "as free as my lord mayor," shut up their shops, and make holiday, and it may seem that the holiday will "continue for ever"; but in fact it will cease and come again under the cyclical restrictions and discipline of nature and under the sanctions of a social decorum. Except for Ralph, Jane, and Hammon, everyone comes to the banquet to receive his proper reward or retribution. "Care and cold lodgings bring white hairs" (V.v.31), but "mirth lengtheneth long life," as Dekker says in the dedicatory epistle to "all good fellows . . . of the Gentle Craft"; and it causes the King to rule by the promptings of the heart rather than by the promptings of the senior citizens. He perhaps speaks better than he knows when telling Simon that it does him good to see the mayor in a merry mood, as though among his shoemakers (V.v.15). He sends Rose and Lacy to bed and by simple commandment redeems lost honor to one willing to "stoop / To bare necessity," and, forgetting courtly pleasures, to gain love by becoming a shoemaker. As the temporal head of social order, he asserts his power against false divisions. No hand on earth "should dare untie / The sacred knot, knit by God's majesty" which unites unequals "in holy nuptial bands" (V.v.63). God's majesty at the spiritual head of all hierarchies joins with the shoemakers to sustain that democratic union. Not all India's wealth would cause Lacy to forgo his love; for Rose to leave him would be like a separation of body and soul. Festive celebration thus depends upon a harmonious community which fulfills the demands of body and soul through the legal bonds of the "sacred knot," rather than through factitious differences of birth or state, or a sensual indulgence in the feast as such. Finally, even Lincoln and the former mayor are made more or less content in the general harmony.

"Ill is the weather that bringeth no gain," however, and so Simon uses the festive occasion to win a concession from the King allowing the shoemakers to buy and sell leather in the mayor's new hall twice a week. With that gift, the banquet may be concluded. In an exchange of courtesies, Simon asks the King to taste of his "poor banquet" which "stands sweetly waiting" his "sweet presence," served by none but shoemakers:

> Yet add more honour to the Gentle Trade,
> Taste of Eyre's banquet, Simon's happy made.

(V.v.182)

In the semiritualistic mixture of prose and poetry and in the gesture of the King eating from the shoemakers' holiday table, feast and work, nobility and the gentle trade, honor and love, find their festive blessing and their "gain." (pp. 208-18)

> *Harold E. Toliver, " 'The Shoemakers' Holiday': Theme and Image," in* Boston University Studies in English *Vol. V, No. 4, Winter, 1961, pp. 208-18.*

J. J. Jusserand contrasts Dekker's works with those of Thomas Nash:

A marked difference between Dekker and Nash resulted from the fact that Dekker had not only a love of poetry, but a poetical faculty of a high order. He went far beyond the picturesqueness of Nash's word-painting, and reached in his prose as well as in his verse true lyrical emotion and pathos; he had, said Lamb, "poetry enough for anything"; and while Nash's gaiety, true and hearty as it is, takes often and naturally a bitter satirical turn, Dekker's gaiety though sometimes bitter, more usually takes a pretty, graceful, and fanciful turn. . . . Dekker did not write novels properly so called, but his prose works abound with scenes that seem detached from novels, and that were so well fitted for that kind of writing that we find them again in the works of professional novelists of his or of a later time.

> *J. J. Jusserand, in his* The English Novel in the Time of Shakespeare, *1890.*

J. B. Steane (essay date 1965)

[*In this excerpt from the introduction to his edition of* The Shoemaker's Holiday, *Steane examines the play in the contexts of Elizabethan society and Dekker's other writings.*]

In some ways this [*The Shoemaker's Holiday*] is the most approachable of Elizabethan plays. It is quite possible for an intelligent person to go to a performance of *King Lear* and not make head nor tail of what Edgar is doing or exactly how events take shape in the last act. A television production of *The Alchemist* lost half its audience in the first fifteen minutes because the language was so unfamiliar and the pace of speech so fast that people were left behind and gave up the struggle before the action had really begun. This could not happen in *The Shoemaker's Holiday.* Its language is clear and its story easy to follow. Yet there *is* a barrier between us and Dekker's play, and it goes rather deeper than whatever it was that put the television audience off Ben Jonson. For, after all, the humour of *The Alchemist* is remarkably modern: quick-witted, likeable crooks make their fortune and their fun out of fools, but are eventually discomfited themselves. The humour of discomfiture appeals to our age as it did to the Elizabethans. So does the smart, wise-cracking dialogue that is contrasted with the ludicrous, stylised speech of the eccentrics whom the crooks deceive. But *The Shoemaker's Holiday* offers a kindly humour, or rather—and here comes the deadly term—a hearty humour. A 'jocular, back-slapping patriotic piece' it is called by the writer in the Pelican Guide [Pelican Guide to English Literature. Vol. 2. The Age of Shakespeare: D. J. Enright, *Elizabethan and Jacobean Comedy*], and there could hardly be a description less designed to whet the appetite of most modern readers, old or young. For they are unlikely to go to literature as a kind of substitute for a scout camp-fire. From anything back-slapping we tend to flinch; at anything patriotic we tend to smile. And 'hearty' is nowadays a term of abuse; almost as automatic and derogatory as 'suburban', 'middle-class' or the other terrible epithets with which people damn the things they dislike.

But if our sophistication prevents enjoyment of such a comedy as this, the loss is ours. Dekker provides an entertainment; tells a tale, creates characters, hopes to infect an audience with the good-humoured zest of contented workers, ardent lovers, banquets and holidays. He never mocks, rarely satirises. But then, ours is the age which has rediscovered satire: that is the kind of humour to which we have most conspicuously taken. Other kinds of humour still exist: the fantasy of Ionesco, the inconsequential humour of Beckett or Pinter, the irreverent sniping of Kingsley Amis's Lucky Jim, or the sentimental humour of the little man (H. G. Wells and Chaplin providing the prototypes, Thurber's Walter Mitty the archetype). The simple humour of high spirits is not in fashion. But this is what Dekker has to give: innocence (in spite of the bawdry), freshness and energy—characteristics that are valuable in him and the literature of his age in proportion to their rarity in ours.

He takes us, for most of his scenes, to a London very different from that of the present day. We are much aware of the City, through the frequent mention of place-names (Guildhall, Leadenhall, St Paul's, the Savoy, the Conduits, London Stone), through the sense of municipal dignity in the Lord Mayor and Simon, and through the bustle of a populous place with its business transactions and vigorous tradesmen. The Dutch ship which has come in laden with cloths, sugar and spices all going at bargain price is a kind of Elizabethan dream; such good fortune cannot have presented itself often, yet it gives us a picture of the commerce through which middle-class men could become wealthy and influential. With riches would come honour and authority. This meant an important position in one of the trade guilds, then perhaps the rank of Alderman, and possibly even that of Lord Mayor. Such is Simon Eyre's story and as we follow his career it is always with a consciousness of the world in which he rises, the London of great Companies, of masters and prentices, working days and festivals.

Dekker was a great Londoner. London, he says [in *The Seven Deadly Sins of London*], was his cradle: 'from thy womb received I my being, from thy breasts my nourishment'. His feeling for the City was strong throughout his life and is reflected in the liveliness of his observation. He brings the sights and sounds vividly before us in this passage from *The Seven Deadly Sins of London* (1606):

> In every street, carts and coaches make such a thundering as if the world ran upon wheels; at every corner men, women and children meet in such shoals that posts are set up of purpose to strengthen the houses, lest with justling one another they [the people] should shoulder them down. Besides, hammers are beating in one place, tubs hooping in another, pots clinking in a third, water tankards running at tilt in a fourth: here are porters sweating under burdens, there merchants' men bearing bags of money, chapmen (as if they were at leap-frog) skip out of one shop into another, tradesmen (as if they were dancing galliards) are lusty at legs and never stand still. All are as busy as country attornies at an Assises. How then can Idleness think to inhabit here?

This is very much the world of *The Shoemaker's Holiday,* where Eyre and his prentices scurry round from first thing in the morning, and where the words, the banter and cross-talk, come tumbling out at a speed to match. It is the vigorous London that contained Shakespeare's Eastcheap and Jonson's Bartholomew Fair; and in Dekker, probably above all others, we feel a closeness to the day-to-day world of ordinary folk.

Along with the bustle, there was also dignity, and in spite of the congestion a certain spaciousness. The river was still London's main thoroughfare. From the Queen in her royal barge to the folk who paid twopence for the 'common barge' all sorts and conditions would travel by water. They would then see the City much as it appears in the old views of London . . ., a place of fine buildings overlooked by 120 church spires. As Lord Mayor, Simon would have had his own state barge, and as a member of the Company of Shoemakers (Cordwainers) he would probably have used theirs also. The Companies and officials did much to preserve the solid dignity of the town, the sense of its traditions, and the colour of its ceremonies. This too is reflected in the play. (pp. 1-4)

The jollifications of the play all have sound economic justification, and in the joviality of Dekker's entertainment we also gain a vivid and valuable glimpse into City life as it was in his time and as it had been for several centuries before him. For this picture of the workings of a trade, with its own practices and its connection with municipal government, reflects the essential organisation of the towns, as the feudal system embodied that of the country.

Moreover, *The Shoemaker's Holiday* takes us close to the ordinary people of the town in a way that is not common. Simon and Mistress Eyre with their hearty bourgeois liveliness represent a part of London that we meet again in Beaumont and Fletcher's *Knight of the Burning Pestle* but not much elsewhere. For in Elizabethan drama the heroic, 'serious' characters are generally aristocratic, while the lower classes are merely comic or incidental. In this play we are more faithfully introduced to the centre of London life than we are by Shakespeare, or even by the Bartholomew birds of Jonsonian comedy.

This centrality should not be surprising, for Dekker strikes one in most of his writing as a sensible observer, whose feelings and interests correspond reliably with those of the sound, level-headed majority. He is not a profound or original thinker, but that very limitation increases his 'documentary' value. 'He does not draw on popular thought and refine it, like Jonson', says L. C. Knights [in his *Drama and Society in the Age of Jonson,* 1937], 'his thoughts *are* the thoughts of the average Londoner.'

As a social commentator, however, he is very incompletely represented by *The Shoemaker's Holiday,* and it will be necessary if we are to have an understanding of our author to look briefly into some of his other works, particularly the prose pamphlets. In *The Shoemaker's Holiday* the mood is gay, very much as caught in the two 'Three-man songs'. Just occasionally there are darker patches: in Ralph's war-wounds, perhaps, or Jane's grief and perplexity, and the efforts of Mayor and nobleman to thwart the course of true love. But none of these is allowed to shut out the sunshine for very long, and the prevailing tone is set by the high spirits of Eyre and his men. 'A merry cobbler there was, who for joy that he mended men's broken and corrupted soles did continually sing, so that his shop seemed a very bird-cage' [*The Raven's Almanac,* 1609]. Dekker wrote this in another context, but the description (barring the term 'cobbler' of course) suits his own shoe-makers well and suggests the spirit of the play. It is not the spirit of many of his later works, however.

He had, for instance, an intense feeling for the wrongs suffered by the poor. On the title-page of *Work for Armourers* (1609) he wrote the motto: 'God help the poor, the Rich can shift.' The pamphlet contains much sharp analysis of the class struggle and its last words are as biting as its first: 'The rich men feast one another, as they were wont, and the poor were kept poor still, in policy, because they should do no more hurt.' With a similar bitterness several other works set about attacking the 'army of insufferable abuses' that Dekker saw around him. *The Seven Deadly Sins of London* is well worth turning up both as an example of his thought and style, and as a social document. Among the deadly seven is one surprisingly called 'shaving'. This turns out to be what communists might describe as 'capitalist blood-sucking' or hard, extortionate exploitation of the poor. 'Cruel and covetous landlords', he speaks of, 'who for the building up of a chimney, which stands them not above 30s. and for whiting the walls of a tenement, which is scarce worth the daubing, raise the rent presently . . . assessing it three pounds a year more than ever it went for before'. The seventh and worst of the sins is cruelty. Perhaps the most bitter passage here is this:

> Look again over thy walls into thy fields, and thou shalt hear the poor and forsaken wretches lie groaning in ditches, and travailing to seek out Death upon thy common highways. Having found him, he there throws down their infected carcasses, towards which all that pass by look, but (till common shame and common necessity compel) none step in to give them burial. Thou setst up posts to whip them when they are alive—set up an hospital to comfort them being sick! Or purchase ground for them to dwell in when they be well, and that is, when they be dead.

The 'thou' being addressed is the respectable, decent, well-to-do Londoner; and the poor particularly in mind here

are the army of beggars created by enclosures, tormented by the plague, and about to break out into riots, all ruthlessly suppressed, in 1607. Dekker's sympathy is clear; so is the social indignation that burns along with the compassion.

One would very much like that to be a complete account of Dekker's attitude on these problems. It would then be possible to point to him as 'the best democrat of his age' as some have done and leave it at that. But there is a strongly conservative side to him, quite as genuine as the other, and rather hard to reconcile with it. Dr K. L. Gregg [in *Language and Literature* II, No. 2, July 1924] discusses this and quotes from *Four Birds of Noah's Ark* (1609):

> The maid servant prays that, as the Lord has laid upon her the condition of a servant, her mind may be subjected to the state in which she was placed, and the serving man consoles himself in the thought that in the service of the Lord, he has a promotion greater than that due to kings.

This is the perfectly traditional acceptance of that condition 'to which the Lord has called us'. The serenity of this, and much else in Dekker, is certainly in key with the mind that created *The Shoemaker's Holiday,* and it is certainly not the mind of a ruthless root-and-branch social critic. Yet that side of Dekker does exist also and it is interesting to inquire how the two could live together in the same man (for they continued to do so, even though the bitterness seems to have grown in later years). Dr Gregg concludes that 'admiration for the theory of the past and contempt for the manner in which it works' is 'typically English' (she is American); so perhaps even in this apparent contradiction within Dekker as a social writer we have another example of his centrality, thinking 'the thoughts of the average Londoner'.

That Dekker's mind did grow more critical as time went on is evident even from the matter of masters and apprentices as dramatised in *The Shoemaker's Holiday.* In this, all is well; Eyre is a good master, his journeymen are good lads. There is a hint of early trade-unionism in II, 3, where Firke takes umbrage, lays down tools and prepares to leave, only to be followed, with a splendid show of class-solidarity, by Hodge: 'Nay, stay, Firke. Thou shalt not go alone.' But it is all part of the comedy, and 'a dozen cans of beer' (or, in reality, two) from 'The Boar's Head' puts all right again. There is never any real discontent or any serious rub of class-feeling. That was in 1599. In 1606, the year of *The Seven Deadly Sins of London,* we find him writing of the relationship between masters and apprentices under the heading of Cruelty. Several companies in the City, he says, are busy cultivating the arts of cruelty which they apply both during the seven years apprenticeship and afterwards. 'When they have fared hardly with you by indenture and, like your beasts which carry you, have patiently borne all labour and all wrongs you could lay upon them', they then 'lay their heads together in conspiracy' to prevent their men becoming masters. So it is 'as if trades, that were ordained to be communities, had lost their first privileges, and were now turned to monopolies'. Perhaps Dekker had created Eyre as a model master and thus as a rebuke to others, but there is no sense in the play of any similar social criticism making itself felt by either explicit or implicit means. It would seem that the evils he denounced seven years later had impressed themselves upon him in the meantime. And it would be surprising if time had not worked in this way, for Dekker's does not seem to have been the most fortunate of lives.

True, it was quite a long one. Only approximate dates are known: he was probably born in 1570 and died in 1637. On very uncertain grounds, he is said to have gone to Merchant Taylors' School, though his name is not in the school register. It may be that he educated himself more effectively than any school managed to do, and that he is speaking on his own behalf in the poem **Dekker His Dream** when he makes a character refer to

> My private readings, which more schooled my
>   soul
> Than tutors, when they sterrniest did control
> With frowns or rods.

He is fond in his plays of introducing foreigners who speak a kind of Dutch, French or Welsh; but this is not enough to assure us either that he travelled a great deal or that he had an advanced education. The likelihood is that he picked up a working knowledge of these languages and was a good observer. Certainly he worked hard. Twenty-four plays and thirteen prose works have survived and there are contemporary references to others. He received a good salary for the earlier plays—we know this from the diary of Phillip Henslowe, the theatre manager. Nevertheless, he spent seven years (1613-20) in prison, probably for debt, and **Dekker His Dream** begins with a poignant reference to the unhappiness of this time:

> the bed on which seven years I lay dreaming was
> filled with thorns instead of feathers; my pillow
> a rugged flint; my chamberfellows (sorrows that
> day and night kept me company) the very or
> worse than the very infernal furies.

In many of his more personal utterances he shows himself fully aware of the frustrations of a writer's life and the bitterness they can produce. 'I am mad to see men scholars in the broker's shop, and dunces in the mercer's', says a character in **Old Fortunatus** (1, 2, 133). 'The labours of writers are as unhappy as the children of a beautiful woman, being spoilt by ill nurses, within a month or two after they come into the world.' So he complained in the Preface to **The Whore of Babylon,** the initial failure of which he blamed on the bad performers. And more bitterly still, he writes: 'To come to the press is more dangerous than to be pressed to death, for the pains of those tortures last but a few minutes, but he that lives upon the rack in print hath his flesh torn off by the teeth of envy and calumny, even when he means nobody any hurt in his grave. . . . Take heed of critics: they bite like fish at anything, especially at books.' Dekker's bitterness or depression never flattens his prose, but the author of **The Shoemaker's Holiday** was, one would say, such a merry fellow that it comes as a surprise to find these complaints in his writing at all.

He is, of course, a far more *complete* writer for having this darker side to him. **The Shoemaker's Holiday** is still his

best-known work, but I do not think that on the knowledge of that play alone, many readers would take Dekker all that seriously as a writer or a man. A light-hearted entertainer, a good observer, a dramatist with a lively command of language, we might say, but hardly a great deal more. As we have seen, his range was greater than that, and there is more to him still. The kindly humour of **The Shoemaker's Holiday,** for example, does not lead one to expect the satirical sharpness of his play **Satiromastix,** with its well-sustained mockery of Ben Jonson; vigorous rather than neat, but still pointed and unsparing enough. Nor would one credit him with the ability to turn the screw of his attack on moneyed meanness with the sort of irony we see here:

> Let the times be dear though the grounds be
> fruitful, and the markets kept empty though
> your barns (like cormorants bellies) break their
> button-holes; and rather than any of Poverty's
> soldiers, who now range up and down the kingdom,
> should have bread to relieve them: I charge
> you upon your allegiance to hoard up your corn
> till it be musty, and then bring it forth to infect
> these needy Barbarians, that the rot, scurvy or
> some other infectious disease may run through
> the most part of their enfeebled army. Or . . .
> let mice and rats rather be feasted by you and
> fare well in your garners, than the least and
> weakest amongst Poverty's starved infantry
> should get but one mouthful. Let them leap at
> crusts, it shall be sport enough for us and our
> wealthy subjects about us, to laugh at them
> whilst they nibble at the bait and yet be choked
> with the hook.
>
>   (**Work for Armourers,** 1609)

This is from a proclamation by the Queen of Gold and Silver, who is leading the rich men's war against the poor. The technique (saying the opposite of what the author really means and feels) plays for ridicule, as well as for the moral condemnation of the decent man.

Perhaps if he had worked a play instead of a pamphlet out of the depth of feeling that went into **Work for Armourers,** Dekker might have written a successful tragedy (and it would have been unique in kind, for the suffering of poor people would have been its subject). As it is, he is essentially a writer of comedies, though sometimes these touch seriousness and just occasionally maintain it with some strength. The best play to sample for this is Part II of **The Honest Whore** (included in the Mermaid edition of Dekker). Here, particularly in the third act, we find a concern with real problems. The comic scenes illustrate the traditional doctrine that a wife must be subject to her husband; but then in a serious scene the other side is presented. The convention which allows a man the sexual licence for which it condemns a woman is attacked with subtlety and feeling. There is a moving passage too in which the sufferings of a woman married to a wastrel are tensely and eloquently dramatised. The play does not rise to tragedy, but it is good enough sometimes to call to mind the Shakespeare of *Measure for Measure.*

In other plays it is the Shakespeare of *The Winter's Tale* that we think of. **Patient Grissil,** in many ways absurd and monstrous in that we are supposed to see the trials imposed on a good woman as somehow justified by the god-like status of the King who devises them, can nevertheless be moving; especially towards the end, where a rare serenity is attained. There is a grace and a graciousness over it all; a sort of dream-like quality which recalls the endings of Shakespeare's last plays: Hermione being reconciled to Leontes in *The Winter's Tale,* or Prospero blessing Miranda and Ferdinand after their trials in *The Tempest.* Sometimes the language rises to it:

> GRISSIL Blessing distil on you like morning dew;
> My soul knit to your souls, knows you are mine.
> MARQUESS They are, and I am thine: Lords, look not strange.
> These two are they, at whose birth envy's tongue
> Darted envenomed stings; these are the fruit
> Of this most virtuous tree . . .
> My Grissil lives, and in the book of fame
> All worlds in gold shall register her name.
>   (V,2,196-201;207-8)

But it is by **The Shoemaker's Holiday** that Dekker has been generally remembered. There are good reasons for its long survival: the vivid background of London life, the fresh tenderness and humour of some of the love scenes, and, lighting up the whole play, the kindly energy of Simon Eyre, protector of lovers, champion of shoemakers, the middle-aged madcap whom age has not withered or high office staled. He must be one of the most likeable characters in literature. From his first appearance to his last we see him coming forward on behalf of others. At the beginning it is to plead for Rafe; at the end it is to ask a royal favour for his fellow-craftsmen. When the plea for Rafe's exemption from the army is refused, he has no resentment, and can use his cheerfulness and wit to keep up the spirits of everyone else. There never was a man with less of a chip on his shoulder; this too is very un-modern, for our present-day literature abounds in resentfulness. Not that Eyre is given to any soft-centred compliancy: his defence of Rose and Lacy illustrates that. He also has an eye to a sharp bit of business, for the bargain which makes his fortune is procured on borrowed money and (after all) false credit. Eyre dresses up in alderman's gown and other finery so as to impress the Skipper and have his 'earnest' accepted. Nor is he such a starry-eyed employer, however free and convivial with his men. He jollies them along most of the time, but does not let them forget what they owe to him:

> Have I not ta'en you from your selling tripes in Eastcheap and set you in my shop, and made you hail-fellow with Simon Eyre the shoemaker?

—all said, of course, in the usual tone of jovial banter. A few lines farther on we have another example of his genial control of the situation. He has made peace with his rebellious journeymen and now orders a dozen cans of beer to celebrate:

> FIRKE A dozen cans? Oh brave! Hodge, now I'll stay.
> EYRE (*aside to the boy*) An the knave fills any more than two, he pays for them.

It is this mixture of generosity and realism that makes a naturally endearing character also a strong one. With liberality goes thrift, with the impulsive and boisterous high spirits go sharpness and authority. His way with his wife is a similar compound of banter and affection. He calls her all sorts of names—'powder-beef quean', 'queen of clubs', 'rubbish' and 'kitchen-stuff'—yet there is no doubt she is his other half, for in all his triumph and excitement he is constantly fussing with his 'Lady Madgy' to make sure that she is sharing it. This is the spirit that fills the play. Eyre is on stage in less than half the scenes, but his goodness and gaiety provide the keynote throughout.

Firke, Hodge and Margery all sing more or less to his tune: they have a similar fund of energy and goodheartedness. Mistress Eyre is at her best in III, 2. We have her, buxom and red-faced, impatient to know what is happening at the Guildhall, and exercising her 'posh' voice and consequential manner when she finds herself addressed as 'Mistress Shrieve'. There is also her touching dialogue with the war-wounded Rafe, her sense of humour and pity being equally stirred, yet with half her mind still on her own affairs and her husband's. This is her best scene. Firke's is probably IV, 4, where he plays a fine old game with the fuming Lord Mayor and Earl of Lincoln. But he is a useful comic throughout, with a style of his own and a liveliness as inexhaustible as his master's.

The play abounds in good secondary acting parts. There is Sybil: too jolly a girl for all tastes but a good foil to the more maidenly Rose; Rafe, whose dazed interview with Hammon's servant is so well caught (IV,2); Hammon himself, who having begun life in the play as an opportunist, a playboy and a nuisance, eventually gains sympathy as luck goes persistently against him, retiring with dignity and in sorrow so that for a moment he nearly overtips the balance and makes us less jubilant about the tough line which the shoemakers have so successfully taken against him. Jane, his intended bride, is also a part for acting, and not merely a fill-in. Her scene with Hammon (III,4) is probably the most affecting in the play, ranging from a rather charming playfulness, through perplexity and distress, to genuine grief. Unhappiness never stays on the stage for long, but while it is there no cheap or false touch disfigures the treatment of it.

Lincoln and Oatley, Lacy and Rose, are perhaps less fully flavoured characters, and their part of the play, the love-plot, certainly has less life than the rest. Even so, the lovers are a pleasant couple and not as insipid as the romantic leads in most modern comedies. Rose is a strong-willed girl who can hold parents and suitors at bay when she wants, and whose wit moves more quickly than her lover's at a critical moment later on (IV,3). Lacy is no conventional hero, for his desertion of class and colours would brand him as a cad in a more conventional play. The King excuses him, quite seeing that love is a very understandable reason for leaving the army to get on as best it can; and Lacy's unsqueamish and spirited adoption of a working-class existence is presented as a good, manly characteristic compared with the niggling class-consciousness of his uncle and father-in-law.

'Class' is probably the nearest thing to a theme in *The*

Shoemaker's Holiday. It is a habit, often a fruitful one, of modern criticism to look beyond the story and characters of a play to find some underlying concern which gives it unity and depth. Sometimes distortion goes on in the process, and it would not be very fruitful to hunt about for 'significant passages' in the sort of entertainment Dekker has written here. But consciousness of class or indifference to it are amongst the attitudes that he most repeatedly dramatises. Lincoln's insistence that Rose is 'too too base' in birth represents no doubt the normal sentiments of someone who has such a name as Lacy to save from contamination. But the Lord Mayor's inverted snobbery is just as marked. He stands for the barricading of his own class as proudly as any aristocrat: he wants a son-in-law who follows a trade, a gentleman-citizen and no 'silken fellow' with a fancy pedigree. Eyre himself has some of this class feeling: 'marry me with a gentleman grocer like my Lord Mayor your father' is his advice to Rose. Mistress Eyre too, when she goes up in the world, becomes very conscious of her station: in dress, speech and manners she will try to 'keep up'. But that is there to be laughed at, and so is most of this awareness of class. Lacy is indifferent to it, and the King speaks out unequivocally against any social exclusiveness where love is concerned:

> Dost thou not know that love respects no blood,
> Cares not for difference of birth or state?
>   (V,5,108-9)

he says to the Earl of Lincoln. Going with this is the essential spirit of the play, embodied in Eyre, who is his true self whether with his King or his apprentices. 'Prince am I none, yet am I princely born' is his cry: this was an old saying of the shoemakers, but Eyre's proud reiteration of it springs from that sense of personal dignity and worth that cuts across classes and makes snobbery barren and absurd.

Still, *The Shoemaker's Holiday* is not a 'problem play' or a social drama with a thesis. It is an entertainment in verse and prose, and criticism of its quality must base itself on that. On recognition, too, of the stagecraft involved, for Dekker is always workmanlike. He develops three plots: the love story of Lacy and Rose, the history of the advancement of Simon Eyre, and the separation and reuniting of Jane and Rafe. All of them are set moving in the first scene, and with a sure touch each is directed towards its climax. The climax of one plot is neatly made to involve that of another (when Rafe finds his Jane, Lacy has won his Rose and the two are about to 'chop up the matter at the Savoy', while their frustrated elders find themselves hindering the wrong couple, only to be defeated afresh at their second attempt when the good fortune of the lovers coincides with the final triumph of Simon Eyre). In the meantime the dramatist has been working resourcefully to keep the entertainment alive and varied. Knockabout is balanced by wit and a kind of verbal brilliance that are delightful in themselves; the earthy zest of Firke and the rest is offset by the more delicate language of Rose. Nor is all the world tediously playing holiday, for the sight of Rafe with his crutch and single leg cannot have been found amusing in any age, nor can the distress of Jane when she sees her Rafe's name on the list of those killed in the wars. Her unhappiness and the wretched pesterings of Hammon

are dramatised with imagination and sympathy; and in actual stage production the episodes are doubly effective. (pp. 6-19)

We began by speaking of the kind of sophistication the play does *not* possess (while we ourselves do); but it now becomes apparent that another kind of sophistication, and a rather better kind (that we do not so evidently have), is precisely what does have to be attributed to it. For the dramatist's skill in blending these several elements and working them together side by side is considerable, and so is the flexibility and responsiveness required of his audience. The story itself (particularly the love story) is very much the conventional assembly of disguises and confusions. Such conventions were readily acceptable to the Elizabethan audiences presumably because, like a pantomime-plot, it was part of the anticipated fun of play-going, and because it was in any case essentially a vehicle, something which allowed spectators to concentrate on the humour—which is mostly verbal. This was in 1599, and the audience had got past the stage of gaping at mere event and being impressed by rant. They had, in other words, achieved very genuine sophistication.

Still, whatever admiration one has for them and their author, it has to be admitted that the quality of writing in *The Shoemaker's Holiday* is not always distinguished. The most noticeable characteristic is probably how the words come to life when blank verse ends and prose takes over. This is generally so with Dekker. As a writer of prose he had few superiors in what was, after all, a great age. His sentences can skip about with an easy colloquial freedom, or they can move with biblical solemnity and splendour. Always he has an ear for the rhythm of a sentence:

> Let us awhile leave kingdoms and enter into cities. Sodom and Gomorrah were burnt to the ground with brimstone that dropped its flakes from heaven: a hot and dreadful vengeance. Jerusalem hath not a stone left upon another of her first glorious foundation: a heavy and fearful downfall. Jerusalem, that was God's own dwelling house, the school where those Hebrew lectures which he himself read were taught, the very nursery where the Prince of heaven was brought up: that Jerusalem whose rulers were princes and whose citizens were like the sons of kings, whose temples were paved with gold and whose houses stood like rows of tall cedars: that Jerusalem is now a desert. It is unhallowed and untrodden; no monument is left to show it was a city, but only the memorial of the Jews' hardheartedness in making away their saviour. It is now a place for barbarous Turks and poor despised Grecians; it is rather now (for the abominations committed in it) no place at all.
> **(*The Seven Deadly Sins of London*)**

His blank verse is generally workmanlike, but he is not a great poet by any means. After a Preface 'To the Reader', written, like the quotation from *The Seven Deadly Sins,* with marvellous grace and dignity, he opens his poem *Dekker His Dream* with a short rhymed introduction:

> When down the Sun his golden beams had laid,
> And at the western inn his journey stayed,
> Thus sleep the eyes of man and beast did seize,

Whilst he gave light to the Antipodes.
I slept with others, but my senses streamed
In frightful forms, for a strange dream I
    dreamed.

One wonders what has happened to his ear. Nothing as crude as this occurs in *The Shoemaker's Holiday,* but the verse is rarely anything more than a serviceable, staple commodity; and it is much more prosaic than the prose. An example would be 1, 3 and 4, where Lacy has a blank-verse speech of twenty-four lines followed by a speech of Eyre's in prose. The verse is graceful enough and perfectly clear, but the movement of the lines is uninteresting and the language lacks colour. The prose by comparison is rhythmical and imaginative:

> Where be these boys, these girls, these drabs, these scoundrels? They wallow in the fat brewis of my bounty and lick up the crumbs of my table, yet will not rise to see my walks cleansed. Come out, you powder-beef queans!
>
> (1, 4, 1-5)

But here, of course, Dekker is in his element. It is not simply that he is better in prose than in verse, but that the verse generally goes to the ladies and gentlemen, and the prose to the working-class entertainers. Eyre's prose is charged with the vitality of his generous character and the energy of colloquial speech which Dekker could draw on through him.

These exactly matching energies of language and good-heartedness make Dekker's comedy the worth-while thing it is. Ultimately, the lightest of entertainments has its influence upon a society for good or bad. There is no matter in *The Shoemaker's Holiday* that is not wholesome, no scene where inner deadness and manufactured cleverness are suspect. There is little subtlety, little irony, or satire: and sometimes we feel this as a limitation to our enjoyment. 'Psha! there's no possibility of being witty without a little ill-nature: the malice of a good thing is the barb that makes it stick.' One part of us says 'Amen' to that. But the speaker is Lady Sneerwell (*School for Scandal, I, 1*) and her character is what her name proclaims it to be. At any rate, *The Shoemaker's Holiday* manages without ill-nature or malice, and if it does not offer Lady Sneerwell's kind of wit, then there are high spirits in plenty, zest and a sense of decent communal fellowship to compensate. Deeper problems and more complicated emotions intervene at critical points in life, but in the meantime these virtues take us a long way. In *His Dream* Dekker says that life is a voyage to the happiness of heaven: 'Books are pilots in such voyages: would mine were but one point of the compass, for any man to steer well by.' It is doubtful whether that particular book, with its vision of judgment and hell-fire as the ultimate deterrent, will help to pilot any man born in our times. But the very simple goodness and energy of Eyre and his shoemakers might. (pp. 20-3)

> *J. B. Steane, in an introduction to* The Shoemaker's Holiday *by Thomas Dekker, edited by J. B. Steane, Cambridge at the University Press, 1965, pp. 1-23.*

Normand Berlin   (essay date 1966)

[*In the following excerpt, Berlin evaluates Dekker as a moralist. Focusing particularly on* The Honest Whore, *the critic repudiates the charge made by some commentators that Dekker was careless in expressing his moral beliefs.*]

Compared to other Elizabethan and Jacobean dramatists, Thomas Dekker has received little critical attention in recent years. It seems that the last word has been said about this prolific dramatist. All the clichés describing him are known and generally accepted by students of the drama. He has become a stereotype—the gentle, tolerant, lovable "moral sloven" who had his hand in too many plays, who occasionally sang a sweet song, who could at times present lively characters. Having been fixed in a formulated phrase, having been pinned, one can hardly see him wriggling on the critical wall. The purpose here is not to demonstrate the falsity of the stereotype, which often hits the truth, but to investigate Dekker's particular qualities of mind and art that produced such a stereotype, and to indicate that Dekker is more angry and more morally earnest than is commonly recognized. The fact is that the epithet "gentle" describes only one side of Dekker's character, and the condemnation of Dekker as a "moral sloven," although basically correct, needs discussion. For Dekker is essentially a stern moralist. Demonstrating this does not make him a better dramatist, but it will set the record straight.

Because M. C. Bradbrook accepts and forcefully transmits the Dekker stereotype in her *Growth and Structure of Elizabethan Comedy,* her clear views can represent the usual reaction to Dekker. Bradbrook finds that Dekker's plays "have moments of tenderness, gleams of pathos, but the general effect is too often amorphous and blurred." She mentions his virtues of "sympathy, tolerance and spontaneity." She states that "Dekker writes at his best when he collaborates with someone who will stiffen the plot and provide him with clear outlines of character upon which he can impress his own lyric tenderness or gaiety." She alludes to his "incorrigible cheerfulness and unteachable simplicity." And she judges that "Dekker, in his easy pity and boundless tolerance, appears something of a moral sloven." Much of his writing, however, seems to belie each of these statements. The general effect of many of his plays, in and out of collaboration, is not blurred. His tolerance is not boundless, nor is his pity easy.

His three rogue pamphlets—*The Belman of London, Lanthorne and Candle-Light,* and *O per se O*—are perhaps the best place to begin a discussion of the "other" Dekker, for they not only display his anger but they also clearly present the clue to understanding Dekker's entire literary output. Most of the material in the rogue pamphlets is plagiarized from Thomas Harman and Robert Greene, but the pamphlets indicate an attitude toward the underworld which is far more condemnatory than any of his contemporaries. He emphasizes that the members of the underworld, whether they be wandering rogues or city sharpers, are "professed foes to the Republic, to honesty, to civility, and to all humanity." They are "savages," "monsters," "ugly . . . in shape and divelish in conditions," "Wilde and Barbarous Rebels . . . in open armes against the Tranquility of the Weale publique." Their only cure is the gallows. To Dekker the underworld is a hell on earth, a source of disorder and confusion in the commonwealth. He is vehement in his denunciation of the underworld, strong in his hatred of the underworld—and always moral. No rogue in a Dekker pamphlet is allowed to repent, although repentance was a common practice in rogue literature. Dekker's anger and hatred stem from the important fact that the citizens of London and England were the victims of the city and country thieves. It is his love for the citizens that puts him closer to the official enemies of the underworld than to the rogue pamphleteers. Whereas Greene, a Bohemian, can see the charm as well as the harm of the underworld, Dekker, a member of the bourgeoisie and a lover of the citizen class, can see only the harm. His love for the citizen world not only makes Dekker an angry man in behalf of the citizens, but is the most revealing focus for understanding his moral bias. His is the traditional strict morality of the middle-class which at times strongly suggests Puritan fervor.

The Shoemakers' Holiday is Dekker's most popular play and is the source for most of the epithets describing him. In it he displays in dramatic action his love for the citizens. Forgiveness and love and patriotism and pride in work are part of the play's atmosphere. Whether these qualities represent the citizen world as Dekker sees it or whether they are idealized—it is often difficult to make this kind of distinction in Dekker's plays—they still point to Dekker's moral seriousness. This play alone seems to justify the belief that the writer himself is "cheery, friendly, lovable" [J. S. P. Tatlock and R. G. Martin, in *Representative English Plays,* 1938]. "Nothing is purposed but mirth," says Dekker, and mirth is what he gives his audience. The joy in life is the keynote of the play, a joy only hinted at in Dekker's other plays. Dekker presents no elements to destroy this joy. The Ralph-Jane story is presented with a sweet kind of sadness, the audience knowing that Jane will always be true to her husband. Jane's display of loyalty for Ralph is unquestionably a Dekkerian ideal for citizen conduct, against which the behavior of citizens' wives of other plays must be measured. Once Lacy becomes an apprentice of Simon Eyre, the audience has no fear that Lacy will get his Rose. An apprentice of Simon Eyre must be happy! A reader of all of Dekker's plays can discern why this is the healthiest and liveliest—Dekker is portraying the people, the world, he loves most, and he is dealing with them exclusively. (The King is absorbed in the Eyre atmosphere and Lacy becomes a shoemaker's apprentice.) The air is clean. The characters are clean. The craftsman-citizen world is clean. But *Shoemakers' Holiday* is only one of seventeen plays that have survived from the forty-two that Dekker wrote. One should not derive all of a playwright's characteristics from a single play.

The Honest Whore presents a less cheery Dekker whose tolerance displays specific bounds. The conversion of a whore, an Elizabethan commonplace in drama and pamphlet, is the play's main concern. Greene had successfully treated the subject in his "The Conversion of an English Courtezan," a first-person narrative about a girl turned wanton, her whorish affairs, and her final conversion. The conversion of this whore is caused by an honest clothier who reminds her that God is forever watching the world and that whores are eternally damned. She is affected by his talk, gives up whoredom, marries the clothier, and lives happily ever after. The conversion of Dekker's whore, Bellafront, is also caused by the speech of the man she loves, but the resemblance ends there, for Bellafront does not marry the man she loves and lives happily never after. Dekker's idea of conversion is far different from Greene's; it forcefully demonstrates Dekker's strong moral bias.

In the beginning of Act II, scene 1, Bellafront is a popular courtesan. At the end of the scene she has become the Honest Whore. That such a sudden conversion is believable is a credit to Dekker's ability to characterize. That the conversion occurs in the second act of a play that will discuss this conversion for eight more acts is an indication of Dekker's purpose. The converted harlots in other plays of the Elizabethan period and in Dekker's later plays announce their conversion in Act V; the play then ends and all's well. The conversion of Bellafront is the *beginning*—it sets off a chain of miseries which Bellafront must suffer. She must pay for the sins she committed in the underworld she rejects. Dekker is too stern a moralist, at least at the writing of this play, to allow for an easy conversion. Dekker, unlike the other rogue pamphleteers, never mentions conversion in his angry exposés of the underworld. This play, coming before the pamphlets, suggests why— the road to cleanliness and moral health is a treacherous one; only the most enduring can traverse it.

Bellafront is an experienced, witty prostitute, who is able to handle men with the assurance of a Meretrix. Her word play with her servant Roger, "a panderly Six-penny Rascall," her talk with the gallants who visit her, and her anger toward Matheo all display a woman set in the ways of harlotry. When she speaks with Hippolito, however, the soft side of her nature becomes evident. She sincerely desires to be loved by one man.

> O my Stars!
> Had I but met with one kind gentleman,
> That would have purchacde sin alone, to him-
>   selfe,
> For his owne private use, although scarce prop-
>   er:
> Indifferent hansome: meetly legd and thyed:
> And my allowance reasonable—yfaith,
> According to my body—by my troth,
> I would have bin as true unto his pleasures,
> Yea, and as loyall to his afternoones,
> As ever a poore gentlewoman could be.
>   (II.i.267-276)

She sees Hippolito as that potential lover. He, aided by his speech against harlotry, causes her to resolve to turn "pure honest." In Hippolito's tirade Dekker is able to present his own hatred for the whore. The speech is too long to quote in full; these excerpts will indicate the gentle Dekker's venom:

> You have no soule,
> That makes you wey so light: heavens treasure
>   bought it,
> And halfe a crowne hath sold it; for your body,

Its like the common shoare, that still receives
All the townes filth. The sin of many men
Is within you, and thus much I suppose,
That if all your committers stood in ranke,
Theide make a lane, (in which your shame might
    dwell)
And with their spaces reach from hence to hell.
Nay, shall I urge it more, there has bene
    knowne,
As many by one harlot, maym'd and dismem-
    bered,
As would ha stuft an Hospitall: this I might
Apply to you, and perhaps do you right:
O y'are as base as any beast that beares,
Your body is ee'ne hirde, and so are theirs.
Me thinks a toad is happier than a whore,
That with one poison swells, with thousands
    more,
The other stocks her veines: harlot? fie! fie,
You are the miserablest Creatures breathing,
The very slaves of nature.

Oh you have damnation without pleasure for it!
Such is the state of Harlots. To conclude,
When you are old, and can well paynt no more,
You turne Bawd, and are then worse then be-
    fore:
Make use of this: farewell.
            (II.i.322-336, 360-364, 419-423)

The whore, for Dekker, is a damned filthy beast, with disease in every vein, and a menace to all who have contact
with her. Despite the vehemence of this speech, Bellafront's first attempt at self-examination, when Hippolito
leaves, brings forth this question:

Yet why should sweet *Hipolito* shun mine eyes:
For whose true love I would become pure-
    honest,
Hate the worlds mixtures, and the smiles of
    gold:
Am I not fayre? Why should he flye me then?
            (II.i.430-433)

The harlot is not so affected by the subject matter and tone
of the tirade as by Hippolito's reaction to her, personally.
Bellafront, reviewing the words of Hippolito in her mind,
seems to *discover* that her harlotry is the cause for Hippolito's disgust.

Hipolito hath spyed some ugly blemish,
Eclipsing all my beauties: I am foule:
Harlot! I, that's the spot that taynts my soule.
            (II.i.441-443)

Her vanity is a strong part of her nature and love is the
impulse for her conversion. With this slight touch Dekker
demonstrates his ability to present an essentially truthful
depiction of character. Bellafront, now aware of her tainted soul, attempts to stab herself, but is stopped by Hippolito. She resolves to win love in some way, and ends the
scene with these words: "Would all the Whores were as
honest now, as I." The rest of Part I and all of Part II demonstrate the truth of this assertion.

From this point on Dekker is able to use Bellafront as his
mouthpiece of morality. From her lips comes his invective
against sin, whores, bawds, panders, and whoremongering
gallants. This speech, chastising her bawd, Mistress

Fingerlock, is typical of her new morality and emphasizes
that she is a forceful enemy of sin.

Hence, thou our sexes monster, poysonous
    Bawd,
Lusts Factor, and damnations Orator,
Gossip of hell, were all the Harlots sinnes
Which the whole world conteynes, numbred to-
    gether,
Thine far exceeds them all; of all the creatures
That ever were created, thou art basest:
What serpent would beguile thee of thy Office?
It is detestable: for thou liv'st
Upon the dregs of Harlots, guard'st the dore,
Whilst couples goe to dauncing: O course devill!
Thou art the bastards curse, thou brandst his
    birth,
The lechers French disease; for thou dry-suckst
    him:
The Harlots poyson, and thine owne confusion.
            (III.ii.30-42)

Indeed, Bellafront has performed, as Matheo states, "one
of *Hercules* labours"—a whore has turned honest.

Bellafront attempts by stratagems to win Hippolito, and
when the play ends in Bethlem Monasterie, she even feigns
madness, but to no avail. Hippolito has his Infelice; Bellafront accepts Matheo, the man that turned her whore,
who claims that he has been "Cony-catcht, guld." Part I
ends. Bellafront's conversion has not been too difficult—
she is abused by the bawd, pander, gallants, and her future
husband; she loses the one man she loves; she accepts the
unscrupulous Matheo for her husband. Dekker must write
another play to test the sincerity of her conversion.

In Part II Bellafront suffers with a worthless husband who
dices, whores, and cheats. He forces Bellafront to beg for
him. Her gown is taken from her back to be pawned. She
is threatened with physical violence. Matheo even asks her
to turn whore again because he needs the money. Bellafront, in misery, exclaims: "A thousand sorrowes strike /
At one poore heart." Her situation is wretched. Orlando
Friscobaldo's appearance causes her additional anguish,
for she must keep her husband and father at peace with
one another. Then a new temptation, the greatest of all,
arises to test her honesty. Hippolito has become a "mut-
tonmonger" and wishes to seduce Bellafront. He argues
for harlotry, just as he argues against it in Part I. The man
who caused her to convert, her savior, is now her tempter.
But she resists and presents a speech against harlotry
equal in moral fervor to his former speech. In short, Dekker makes her new way of life a continuous trial, a trial
which ennobles her nature, a trial in many ways similar
to the trial of the legendary whore, Thais, who also turned
honest and had to suffer greatly before she gained Paradise. However, Dekker's whore remains, at the end of the
play, with her worthless husband, and Dekker gives no indication that Matheo will ever change. No relief of her
misery is in sight.

Dekker puts his main character through the miseries of a
hell on earth. His treatment of Bellafront is influenced by
his strict and severe morality. He makes the audience feel
genuine sympathy for Bellafront's suffering, but the audience at the same time realizes that her being sinned against

has been caused by her sinning. In the course of the two Parts of *The Honest Whore* Bellafront takes on the characteristics of a Jane. Her citizen virtues, especially her conjugal loyalty, make her a heroine, but her trials are not part of a holiday atmosphere. The misery of Bellafront seems everlasting.

Bellafront's acquisition of citizen virtues points to the importance of the play's subplot, which deals with the clean and healthy citizen world, represented by Candido and his circle. Candido is "a grave citizen" and the "mirror of patience." He is "so milde, so affable, so suffering, that nothing indeede can moove him." His wife Viola cannot endure his patience and tries in many ways to vex him—but she cannot. The gallants visit his shop, also attempting to vex him—but they cannot. Viola, as a last manuever, calls in officers to carry Candido to the madhouse—but even in the madhouse, where the complications of Part I are resolved, Candido remains patient. It is in the madhouse that Candido presents his famous speech, in which the sentiments expressed seem very close to Dekker's heart and which has helped to propagate the image of Dekker as the gentle man.

> Patience my Lord; why tis the soule of peace:
> Of all the vertues tis neerst kin to heaven.
> It makes men looke like Gods; the best of men
> That ere wore earth about him, was a sufferer,
> A soft, meeke, patient, humble, tranquill spirit,
> The first true Gentleman that ever breathd;
> The stock of *Patience* then cannot be poore,
> All it desires it has; what Monarch more?
>
> (Vi.ii.489-496)

The Duke, at the end of Part I, praises Candido's patience and says that Candido "shall teach our court to shine." In Part II Candido continues to display his patience. This time he has a new wife, who at first is strong-minded but learns to submit to her husband. The gallants again try to ruffle Candido, and again they are thwarted. When he goes to Matheo's house to see some pieces of lawn he finds that he is in the company of a bawd and pander and that the pieces of lawn are stolen goods. He is apprehended by officers and taken to Bridewell, where the plots of Part II are resolved. Candido again receives the praise of the Duke.

> Thou hast taught the Citty patience, now our Court
> Shall be thy Spheare, where from thy good report,
> Rumours this truth unto the world shall sing,
> A Patient man's a Pattern for a King.
>
> (V.ii.494-497)

The Candido story is the source of most of the play's humor. But it cannot be dismissed merely as a piece of merriment. Candido is, essentially, a Dekker hero. He is the representative of the citizen world, the world to which Dekker is most attached. He displays the qualities of industriousness, generosity, and patience. He is comically patient, to be sure, but Dekker forgets the comedy when Candido presents his speech on Patience and when the Duke considers him "a Patterne for a King." It is the very quality of patience that Bellafront displays in both parts of *The Honest Whore.* She, however, is heroic in her patience. Candido's comment that "the best of men . . . was

a sufferer" applies to Bellafront almost as much as it does to Jesus. Jesus suffered for the sins of the world; Bellafront suffers for her own sins as a member of the underworld. *The Honest Whore* is basically a dramatic study of patience. To dismiss the Candido story with a chuckle is to neglect a significant element in this study.

The Candido subplot clearly demonstrates how stern a moralist Dekker is, how important it is for his beloved citizen world to isolate itself from the corruption of the underworld. In Part I, the citizen world and the underworld make no contact. In Part II, they meet twice, with interesting results. Carolo, a courtier, gives the bawd and pander money to arrange a meeting between Candido's wife and himself. When the pander Bots presents Carolo's proposition to the bride, she emphatically scorns him, calls him "an arrant knave," and leaves his company. The virtuous wife of the citizen Candido utterly rejects the underworld's representative. Just as the play contains a parallel between the patience of Candido and the patience of Bellafront, so too it contains a parallel between the virtue of Candido's wife and the virtue of Bellafront—both cannot be seduced, both display conjugal loyalty, like Jane in *Shoemakers' Holiday.* Candido's bride and the honest whore are one in faithfulness, with Bellafront having the harder trial because she loved her seducer and because her husband is worthless. Bellafront, once a member of the underworld, in her moral recovery gathers to herself qualities of the citizen world.

The second meeting between the two worlds occurs when Candido goes to Matheo's house to see the pieces of lawn. The bawd and pander are there. Candido, not knowing Mistress Horseleech is a bawd, is introduced to her. She politely kisses him, which causes him to mutter, "Sh'as a breath stinkes worse then fifty Polecats. Sir, a word, is she a Lady?" He is able to smell her bawdiness. When he is told that she is a bawd he is ready to leave the house, but is forced to drink healths to her, which thoroughly disgusts him. The aversion of Dekker's citizen to a representative of the underworld is strikingly evident throughout the scene. The two worlds meet, but the citizen world is repelled.

The Honest Whore, Dekker's most conscientious effort, belies not only many of the clichés about Dekker's personality and moral fiber, but also many critical objections to his faulty dramaturgy. He has complete control of his material. Bellafront's story directly affects the Hippolito-Infelice story. One need only mention that the courtier Matheo is married to the converted whore, that the gallants were customers of Bellafront, that Bellafront helps to resolve the Hippolito-Infelice plot. The play's underplot, concerning the trials of the patient Candido, throws a revealing light on the main plot. In *The Honest Whore* the strictness of Dekker's morality seems to dictate a strictness in handling his material. Dekker acquired, at the writing of this play, Candido's patience.

When he put *The Honest Whore* behind him, Dekker left with it his strict adherence to a citizen morality. In *Westward Ho* and *Northward Ho,* both collaborations with Webster and both acted before private-theater audiences, the morality is easy. The plot of *Westward Ho,* like that of *Northward Ho,* deals with the intrigue between gallants and citizens' wives, helped along by the underworld. The underworld, represented by Birdlime, a disgusting bawd, and Luce, an experienced prostitute, provides Dekker with the moral norm for a mildly satiric attack on the citizens, which indicates nothing less than a changed concept of his much-loved bourgeoisie. The three citizens, Honeysuckle, Tenterhook, and Wafer, are customers of Luce, who runs a thriving trade with the help of Birdlime. That they are patrons of an underworld character, one who displays all of the traditional distasteful characteristics of the whore, indicates that Dekker is tampering with the citizen virtues he holds so high. Candido was repelled by the underworld; the citizens in this play wish to embrace it. The stern morality of *The Honest Whore* is slackening. In presenting the citizens' wives, Dekker neglects the moral values of *The Honest Whore.* Throughout the play there are surprising parallels between the bawd, the whore, and the citizens' wives. They all are coarse, but they will not endure coarseness in others. They all affect virtue. They all chastise tobacco-smoking and drunkenness. They all are immoral—the whore and bawd play with men for pay, the wives play with gallants for merriment. Whereas in *The Honest Whore* Bellafront took on the qualities of the play's citizen world, thereby demonstrating a true conversion, in this play the citizen world acquires the qualities of the underworld. This is seen even in the most fleeting lines. Mistress Wafer tells Mistress Tenterhook that she wishes her "the fortune to change thy name often." Her reason: "For theeves and widdowes love to shift many names, and make sweet use of it so." When Justiniano tells his wife that she was lucky to have received the jewels from the lecherous Earl, he exclaims: "Was it ever heard that such tyrings, were brougt away from a Lord by any wench but thee *Moll,* without paying, unlesse the wench connycatcht him?" (IV.ii.190-192). The methods of the underworld are not unknown or repugnant to these citizens.

That citizens visit the house of a whore and that the wives of citizens imitate whores and bawds indicates a decided slackening of the moral pattern found in *The Honest Whore.* It is true that at the play's end the wives display a change of attitude. They cheat the gallants—"They shall know that Cittizens wives have wit enough to out strip twenty such gulls." The wives are merry and wanton, but "pure about the heart." Dekker's love of the bourgeoisie still seems to emerge, but the stern moralist has been corrupted. His late plays, especially *Virgin Martyr* and *Match Me in London,* indicate that Dekker's *basic* citizen morality did not change. One must, therefore, look for other causes for his reversal of the traditional morality. Any or all of three causes are probable—the nature of the audience, Dekker's own hack tendencies, his collaboration with Webster.

Alfred Harbage has *The Honest Whore* and the *Ho* plays specifically in mind when he states [in his *Shakespeare and the Rival Traditions,* 1952] that "the same authors who wrote amiably of commercialized vice for Paul's provide exposés and denunciations for the Fortune." To please was Dekker's constant aim. His desire to entertain the audience at Paul's who would enjoy a satiric attack on the

bourgeoisie and whose moral standards were less exacting than those of the middle class caused Dekker to compromise his moral position.

In addition, his collaboration with Webster may have affected his outlook in the *Ho* plays. Scholars dealing with this collaboration agree that Dekker was the "guiding spirit" in both *Westward Ho* and *Northward Ho.* There is little doubt that Dekker wrote most of each play. But the exact nature of any collaboration cannot be demonstrated, even though a battery of valid tests can assign particular scenes to one dramatist or the other. Although it is logical to assume that Dekker, the older, more experienced, dramatist, influenced Webster, the apprentice, it is possible that the younger Webster gave the satiric impulse to a hack dramatist whose practice it was to compromise in matters of theater. This is in the realm of speculation, not specifically demonstrable, but it is useful in helping to explain Dekker's changed concept of the bourgeoisie. Dekker's attitude often depends upon his collaborator's attitude, as his later collaborations clearly indicate.

Northward Ho conforms to the new moral pattern set up in *Westward Ho.* In it the vociferous and experienced whore Doll Hornet is placed on the road of respectability. Dekker uses a typical Middleton trick of marrying his whore off to an unsympathetic character. He did this in *The Honest Whore* but the difference here indicates a shifting morality. Bellafront's marriage to Matheo was presented as a punishment for the whore, whereas Doll's marriage to Fetherstone is punishment for Fetherstone who marries her thinking she is a rich ward. Doll vows faithfulness to Fetherstone, who reconciles himself to his fate. Doll's conversion is easy. When one considers that the same dramatist who presented Bellafront presented Doll Hornet, only one conclusion can be drawn— Dekker's basically stern morality could be compromised under specific theatrical conditions.

Northward Ho, like *The Honest Whore,* has a scene in Bedlam, where a mad bawd is one of the inmates. She loves aqua vitae, swears by her virginity, and denies ever being in Bridewell. She is, in short, one of Dekker's traditionally disgusting bawds. Her appearance is very brief, but it serves to indicate a less healthy citizen class than appeared in *The Honest Whore* and *Shoemakers' Holiday,* for she voices her preference for "your London Prentice" and "taylors" as customers. The citizen-bawd relationship sheds a disparaging light on the citizens, with the underworld once again providing the moral norm for a satiric thrust. The citizen world in *Northward Ho* has no "hero" like Candido and no outstanding virtues. The citizens still remain Dekker's favorites: "Sfootc ther's neare a Gentleman of them all shall gull a Citizen, and thinke to go scotfree." But his treatment of them has significantly changed. In the *Ho* plays one witnesses a clear breakdown of a traditional stern morality—a striking example of expediency undermining genuine belief.

The Honest Whore and the *Ho* plays present the two poles of Dekker's morality. His other plays find their places within this wide moral range. The morality of *The Roaring Girl* is close to the *Ho* plays. In it the character of Mary Frith, a notorious thief, is completely whitewashed.

Whereas in *The Honest Whore* the underworld was the object of Dekker's abuse, here it is romanticized. But many of his other plays, both early and late, are closer to the moral stance of *The Honest Whore.* In the romantic morality tale *Old Fortunatus* virtue and vice are clearly marked, as they are in *The Whore of Babylon,* in which Dekker ostensibly attacks Roman Catholicism. *Patient Grissil,* where, as in *The Honest Whore,* the patience of a sympathetic character is tested, also clings to a strict citizen morality. *If This Be Not a Good Play, The Devil Is In It* clearly distinguishes between dark and light, between the hellish activities of a Barterville and the purity of the Sub-Prior, who Candido-like must hold his ears when whores sing. In the late tragicomedy *Match Me in London* Dekker deals with intrigue between court and citizens, as he did in the *Ho* plays, but here the citizens emerge completely clean. These plays testify to Dekker's basic moral bias, as does *The Virgin Martyr,* in which the severe morality of *The Honest Whore* is intensified—because, one must suspect, Dekker was working with Massinger, a collaborator whose moral position is close to his own. Forgiveness of sin was possible for a suffering Bellafront, and was implied in the easy conversion of a Doll Hornet, but Hircius and Spungius, a whoremonger and drunkard, are forcefully thrown outside the pale of Christianity.

A reading of all his plays indicates that Dekker ws genuinely moral and often angry. When he displays his love for the citizen world, he is the gentle and tolerant Dekker—but he can also be the angry and intolerant Dekker of the rogue pamphlets, *The Honest Whore,* and *The Virgin Martyr.* When his morality is easy, as in the *Ho* plays, he may be called a "moral sloven"—but the phrase, although it points to a correct evaluation of the easily-corrupted Dekker, too strongly undermines a basically severe moralist. That this strict morality is, indeed, basic can be seen when one examines his dramaturgy. When his stern morality is translated directly into dramatic action Dekker presents his most effective drama. In *Shoemakers' Holiday,* where the citizen world is filled with merriment and moral health, one finds Dekker's most coherent plotting. *The Honest Whore,* where a converted harlot must suffer, where a Candido must avoid a bawd like the plague, presents his most carefully worked-out plot. When Dekker works against his genuine moral beliefs he becomes an awkward craftsman. When he can draw clear moral lines, solidified by a love for the class which originally drew these lines, he presents aesthetically satisfying drama. For Dekker a quality of mind seems to indicate a quality of dramaturgy.

The most valid cliché concerning Dekker is that he was a Henslowe hack. Discussing him in connection with his collaborators, confronting him in the light of scholarship concerning the nature of the audience, seeing him as a traditional middle-class moralist corrupted by the pressures of daily living, is a surer guide to Dekker's quality as man and artist than the epithets of gentle and cheery. Ben Jonson comes closest to the truth, perhaps, when in *Poetaster* he has Demetrius (Dekker) referred to as a "dresser of plays about the town." (pp. 263-77)

Normand Berlin, "Thomas Dekker: A Partial Reappraisal," in Studies in English Literature, 1500-1900, *Vol. VI, No. 2, Spring, 1966, pp. 263-77.*

Frederick M. Burelbach, Jr.   (essay date 1968)

[In the excerpt below, Burelbach examines Dekker's use of the theme of war in The Shoemaker's Holiday.]

Although the unforgettable merriment of Simon Eyre and his journeymen may prevent us from observing it, the background to *The Shoemakers' Holiday* is one of warfare. References to the war with France begin in the first scene and recur frequently throughout the play, with lame Ralph giving us a constant visual reminder of his impressment and its cause. What is more, the last line of the play, "Warres must right wrongs which Frenchmen haue begun," spoken by no less a personage than the King, sends us out of the theatre with the impression that war will outlast even the pancake bell. His words, however, look forward to the end of war, while we are assured that the holiday will be observed forever. These martial references, to be sure, are neither so frequent nor so ponderous as to outweigh the mood of gaiety, frolic, and holiday, the sanity and good-fellowship, that so many critics have noted in the play. Nevertheless, the war is a constant presence and, moreover, unnecessary to the plot. No war is needed to effect the separation of Rose and Lacy, with the requisite disguise of the lover; the parents' ill-will is sufficient. Nor does it require a war to separate Ralph and Jane; a dozen pretexts would have served, such as the merchant voyage that brought the Skipper from Holland. Why, then, does the war with France figure so largely in the play? The reasons may, perhaps, be divided into two categories: theatrical and thematic.

Among the purely theatrical reasons for including the war we should probably place first the warrant provided by the source of the play. Deloney's account of Crispine and Ursula in the second tale of *The Gentle Craft,* whence Dekker derived the Rose-Lacy plot, describes an unlikely war between the Gauls and the Persians. Into this war, Crispianus, like Ralph, is impressed, but there the resemblance between their experiences ends. As M. T. Jones-Davies says [in her *Un Peintre de la Vie Londonienne: Thomas Dekker,* 1958], this impressment explains in part the background of war in Dekker's play. But, as she continues, Dekker has taken the war out of the realm of the mythical and into that of the historical: "au lieu d'une guerre extraordinaire et mythique entre la France et la Perse, les batailles d' Henry VI contre l'ennemi héréditaire sont plus naturelles et doublent l'intérêt réaliste de la comédie d'un intérêt patriotique." History, therefore, provides further justification for including the war and thus, possibly, giving a clearer identification of the actual era of Simon Eyre.

Whether the realism was for the sake of history or not, it must have appealed to Dekker's contemporaries, most of whom could probably remember the Armada. In fact, citizens of London were in 1598 and 1599, the probable time of the composition of the play, experiencing impressments for Essex's war in Ireland, rumors of English losses there, and fears of a new Armada. These current events were part of the reality of Elizabethan life and help to round out

Dekker's picture of the London tradesmen. Londoners were fond of seeing their country displayed as a conqueror on the stage, as the great volume of Elizabethan plays with this theme makes obvious, and a popular dramatist like Dekker would certainly take advantage of this natural chauvinism in his audience. Indeed, the play bristles with patriotism, from Firk's scoffs at Hans's Dutch "yawing" to Sim Eyre's offer of his beard to stuff tennis balls for the King. Dekker glorifies not only the gentle craft, but, by extension, all Englishmen. The French wars clearly advance this purpose.

Finally, the war helps to solve problems of plotting. Not only does it give a single cause for the supposed departure of Lacy, his need for a clever disguise, and the separation of Ralph from Jane, but it provides, in the impressment scene in I, ii, a means of uniting the three plots of the play. There, Simon Eyre, his wife and journeymen, among whom are Ralph with his Jane, meet Lacy and Askew. All of the personages are brought together in a single problem and the audience is quickly familiarized with the character of each. Dekker's early expository scenes are usually very skillful and this is one of his best. Thus the war aids considerably the dramatic economy of the play.

There is, therefore, ample justification for the references to war, whether they derive from Dekker's source, from history, the urge toward realism or toward patriotism, popular demand, plot exigencies, or even from Dekker's obsession with martial metaphors, or from any combination of these reasons. But if we turn from asking why the military references appear and instead consider what effect they have on the mood and theme of the play we will find an entirely different answer.

The mood of *The Shoemakers' Holiday,* designated in the title and set by Simon Eyre and his cohorts, is obviously one of workaday joviality. Neither the Romeo-Juliet plot of Rose and Lacy, nor the threat to Lacy's life and honor by his desertion, nor Ralph's supposed death and actual lameness can dampen the high spirits of the play. On the contrary, these are not only the conventional difficulties out of which arises the triumph of the comedy, they are also a piquant sauce to prevent so much good-fellowship from cloying. The French war acts in the same manner, providing a point of reference by which to judge the success of good-natured industry in conquering its antagonists. For the war is not the only form of hostility in the play. There is class conflict in the relationship between the Earl of Lincoln and Sir Roger Otley, who can only agree that there should be no mingling of merchants with nobility. There is the conflict between youth and age in the attempts by these men to rule their children, resulting in the disobedience of the latter. (That Lacy is Lincoln's nephew, not his son, does not change the principle but merely mitigates the fault of Lacy's disobedience, in keeping with the desired allotment of sympathies.) Love comes into conflict with honor, in the case of Lacy's desertion, and with prosperity, in the case of Jane's final refusal of Hammon. Finally, Dekker introduces conflicts as to personal worth among the characters; Lacy, Ralph, and Hammon are pitched against one another in such a way as to imply a scale of values. The war with France sums up and stands

behind all these minor hostilities, uniting them under a common metaphor and intensifying their significance. If war represents one level of reality, then, so do conflicts of all kinds.

There is another level of reality, however, which both contrasts with and transcends hostilities, and which eventually harmonizes all warring opposites. Some of the songs sung by and about shoemakers in Deloney's *The Gentle Craft* reveal this harmonious view:

> No malice did they beare to any,
> but shew'd great fauour vnto many;
> Offences soone they would forgiue,
> they would not in contention liue.
> Thus in ioy they spent their daies,
> with pleasant songs and roundelaes,
> And God did blesse them with content;
> sufficient for them he sent.
>
> Of Craft and Crafts-men more and lesse,
> The *Gentle Craft* I must commend:
> Whose deeds declare their faithfulnesse,
> And hearty loue vnto their freind:
> The *Gentle Craft* in midst of strife,
> Yeelds comfort to a carefull life.
>
> . . . . .
> Spending my dayes in sweet content,
> With many a pleasant sugred Song:
> Sitting in pleasures complement,
> Whilst we recorded Louers wrong:
> And while the *Gentle Craft* we us'd
> True Loue by vs was not abus'd.

The purport of these songs may be summed up by the words of Saint Winifred, as Deloney presents her in the same tale about to meet death for her Christian faith: "The Loue of earthly creatures is mixed with many miseries, and interlaced with sundrie sorrowes: and here griefe shall abate the pleasures of Loue, but be well assured that ioy shall follow the same." Saint Winifred, of course, is making the conventional distinction between earthly sorrow and celestial bliss. Dekker's achievement is to domesticate this Christian antimony into a dramatic conflict between human sorrows and joys. Dekker has, in fact, written a play about love and its powers to provide mankind joy and peace as long as it is not abused.

Each of three plots in *The Shoemakers' Holiday* takes up one form of love and demonstrates how, when it is sincere, it triumphs over adversities. Romantic love is the province of the plot involving Lacy and Rose. This love is threatened by both class conflict and the war in France, which endangers Lacy's honor. Nevertheless, the sincerity of the love overcomes these hostilities and produces not only a joyful union of the noble and merchant classes, but a truce (if not a harmony) between the Earl of Lincoln and Sir Roger Otley. It is important to observe that Lacy's marriage to Rose is not a serious rupture of social order; the noble husband is still superior to his merchant-class wife. As we shall see, however, the ultimate success of this romantic love is dependent on the form of love developed in the main plot. As a foil to Lacy's sincere romantic love, Hammon's unsuccessful courtship of Rose illustrates the failure of the unfaithful love, despite his knowledge of all the conventional romantic devices.

The unfortunate Hammon also serves as a foil to Ralph, for in his attempt to marry Jane, Hammon is playing the role of the conjugal lover. Ralph, as the true representative of conjugal love, overcomes the conflicts produced by the false report of his death and the seductive advances of the wealthy Hammon. As a result, the fidelity of man and wife is confirmed. The means by which this humble pair are reunited is especially touching, since it is the hand-wrought pair of shoes, Ralph's simple love-offering, that leads the husband to his wife. By contrast, Hammon's inherited wealth is divisive, and useless against this simple faith. Once again, however, conjugal love alone is not enough to produce final success.

The triumph of both pairs of true lovers results from the form of love developed in the main plot, that which gives the play its special quality—fraternal love. The good-fellowship, the joyous sense of human charity and brotherhood that radiates from Sim Eyre's shop on Tower Street or from the Leadenhall, is not only the clearest illustration of the shoemakers' songs, but is the most important power by which war is transformed into peace. Simon Eyre's mirth obviously produces harmony in his shop, and, as Firk observes, it is in this context that the work goes best: "Ha Ha good maister hire him, heele make me laugh so that I shal worke more in mirth, then I can in earnest." There is other evidence that fraternal love is commercially valuable if mingled with discretion. Not only does Eyre retain the loyalty of his journeymen, but they are willing to do him a good turn when it is in their power, as is demonstrated by Hans's bargain with the Dutch Skipper. Such loyalty is especially necessary to a public official, such as a newly elected Lord Mayor of London; Dekker had recent evidence of this political truism in the apprentice riots directed against Sir John Spencer (Lord Mayor in 1594-95), who may have been his model for Sir Roger Otley. This mutual fidelity is, moreover, the means by which the final success of the love relations in the other two plots is achieved. Threatened with a divorce or violent separation engineered by Lincoln and Sir Roger, Rose and Lacy take refuge with Simon Eyre. The new Lord Mayor, in recognition of both the sincerity of their love and the loyalty and good services of Hans-Lacy, intercedes successfully for them with the King. Although Eyre is not personally involved in the conclusion of the Ralph-Jane plot, it is his spirit of playful camaraderie that guides Hodge, Firk, and their fellows to defend the matrimonial rights of their lamed colleague. Love, therefore, brings peace and harmony to all of the minor conflicts within the play.

In what relationship to these minor conflicts, however, stands the war in France? Most obviously, the war serves to give the personal and class conflicts focus and intensity, but it also helps to reveal character. The selfishness of Lincoln and Otley, for instance, is apparent in their attitude toward the war; they regard it as a convenient means for separating Rose and Lacy. Lincoln's prattle of honor is a thin veil, easily pierced by both Lacy and Askew. The shallow, albeit pathetic, Hammon regards "martiall spoile" as merely a hackneyed ploy of lovers, equivalent to playing the rhymer. Simon Eyre considers war unfortunate, but like all life, to be entered into with gusto. The King, whose strong sense of justice is revealed in his treatment of Rose and Lacy, seems to look upon war as an instrument of justice.

Most interesting, however, is the contrast between Ralph and Lacy. Both are confronted with the problem of leaving their loved ones in order to fight for their country. Ralph, constrained to go, returns with honor but is lamed, impoverished, and in danger of losing his wife. Lacy, deserting his post, remains at home to gain not only a bride but knighthood as well. The discrepancy can not be explained by any facile answer such as the requirements of the plot or the specious cause—Lincoln's plot to separate the lovers—that procured Lacy his commission. Dekker's sympathy for wounded soldiers is too well known for there to be any doubt that he was aware of the effect Ralph's injury would have on the audience. Too much can be made, however, of the contrast. Even if Lacy in his own person is a rather unpleasant young man—hypocritical with Lincoln, haughty toward Sibil, unconcerned about his patriotic duty, befuddled by the sudden entrance of Otley, and simpering throughout the last act—in his role as Hans he is thoroughly agreeable. As Hans, taking Ralph's place in the shop, Lacy displays the saving qualities—common to all the shoemakers—of affability, industry, and loyalty. Ralph, on the other hand, although pitiful and endowed by Dekker with some of the most beautiful and affecting poetry in the play, is too frequently a pawn to the bustling Firk, too little inclined to act in his own behalf, to enter deeply into the audience's imagination and concern. Thus Dekker strikes a neat balance of sympathy in the two characters. Ralph and Lacy also balance out, proportionally, in their rewards. Both receive what they want, plus a small bonus, and both are happy; the small cup and the large are both filled.

Although the primary value of Ralph and Lacy is complexly human, not allegorical, the parallelism between the two is perhaps illustrative of the King's statement that "loue respects no bloud . . . , / Cares not for differences of birth, or state" (V, v, 103-104). The point is not that Lacy and Ralph are made social equals by their loves—this is an Elizabethan play and order must be maintained—but that love is common to humanity and, by its power, it harmonizes men into a community of minds equally bent on the good of the whole. The difference between Ralph and Lacy, sharpened by their conduct in war, may illustrate the manifold power of love. Love can not only help a Ralph to endure sorrow and loss with patience; it can also help to atone for the "sins" of a Lacy. Lacy's "apprenticeship" to the Gentle Craft for the love of Rose is an act of humility and of fidelity to what Dekker evidently considers a higher good than "valors fire."

As M. C. Bradbrook has observed [in her *The Growth and Structure of Elizabethan Comedy*, 1955], the denouement of ***The Shoemakers' Holiday*** includes both of the conventional endings of Elizabethan comedy, "both kingly judgement and a wedding march," all performed within the sumptuous ambience of Eyre's feast, which unites all England, from King to watercarriers. The feast itself, as suggested by the second three-man's song "to be sung at the latter end," is the physical representation of the merriment that exists when "kind mates" are true to one another. It is not, I believe, a manifestation of "the desire to escape these necesities [of "the life of commodity and compromise"], to be an entirely free and romantic agent perpetually on a 'holiday'," as Harold Toliver suggests [in *Boston University Studies in English* V, 1961]. . . . Rather, the feasting and gaiety represent both the answer to human hostilities and the reward provided by brotherly love. . . .

Reconciliation in love and joy is the message of Christianity. Dekker, we know, was dedicated to conventional Christian morality, as revealed in such apposite statements as these:

> Wee are moste like to God that made vs when wee shew loue one to another, and doe moste looke like the Diuell that would destroy vs, when wee are one anothers tormentors.
> [*The Seven Deadly Sins of London*]

> [Heaven is] a Kingdom! where there is no change of Kings, no alteration of State, no losse of Peeres, no Warres, no revenges, no *Citizens* flying for feare of infection, none Dying of them that stay, no Prisoners to write petitions to *Conscience*, yet *Conscience* sits there in glory: there is true Majesty, true honour, true peace, true health: there is all life, all happinesse, all immortallity.
> [*Lanthorne and Candle-Light*]

Wars, therefore, though necessary in this imperfect world to "right wrongs" as Dekker's King tells us, are only part of reality. The King's words look forward to a time of peace, a perpetual "holy day." On the realistic level of citizen comedy, Dekker demonstrates this peace to be the result of a universal application of the other, deeper reality—fraternal love. (pp. 99-106)

> Frederick M. Burelbach, Jr., "War and Peace in 'The Shoemakers' Holiday'," in Tennessee Studies in Literature, Vol. XIII, 1968, pp. 99-107.

Larry S. Champion (essay date 1985)

[*Champion is an American drama scholar. In this excerpt from the introduction to his full-length study,* Thomas Dekker and the Traditions of English Drama, *he examines the opinions of other critics concerning Dekker's works and argues that Dekker was an innovative playwright who consistently experimented with Elizabethan stage conventions.*]

Excepting Thomas Heywood, Thomas Dekker was perhaps the most remarkably productive playwright of the Elizabethan-Jacobean period. Heywood's claim in the preface to *The English Traveller* to having had "either an entire hand or at least a main finger" in some two hundred and twenty plays may be an exaggeration and Jonson's sneer through Histrio that Dekker "ha's one of the most over-flowing ranke wits in [London]" (*Poetaster*, III.iv.338-39) is certainly given to satiric hyperbole, but together—according to the count in *Annals of English Drama*—they figure in at least one hundred ten plays and pageants, of which fifty-three plays are extant. For Dekker

alone nineteen of forty-six plays remain—twelve of twenty-one comedies, two of four tragicomedies, one of eight tragedies, four of sixteen histories. Probably only six of these nineteen were written without collaboration. Romantic comedy, satire, citizen comedy, tragicomedy, even a comedy-tragedy (as the lost *The Late Murder in Whitechapel* is described)—he produced all types in a professional career spanning more than thirty years.

The various bits of contemporary evidence suggest that Dekker was a popular and reasonably well-respected playwright in his own day. For one thing, fifteen of his nineteen extant plays were published during his lifetime, and nine speak to at least a moderately successful stage history through reference on the quarto title page to being "diuerse" or "sundrie times plaid" with "great Applause," to being performed in two instances at both public and private houses, and in one instance, according to the printer, of having received "the Stages approbation" as acted and approved." The presence of his name as among the best for tragedy in Francis Meres' *Palladis Tamia* coincides with the first references to him in Henslowe's *Diary* in 1598, a year in which Dekker was involved in the writing of at least fifteen plays. John Webster describes the "right happy and copious industry" that places "Master Dekker" beside "Master Shakespeare," and it is to his credit also that he was chosen by the players, probably with Marston, to respond to Jonson's *Poetaster* and that his *Satiromastix* apparently played so successfully to audiences both at St. Paul's and at the Globe that Jonson withdrew from the skirmish. So, also, his participation in the pageantry for the coronation of King James in 1604 (*The Magnificent Entertainment*) and later his pageants for performance at the inauguration of three Lord Mayors of London (*Troja-Nova Triumphans* for John Swinerton in 1612, *Britannia's Honor* for Richard Deane in 1628, *London's Tempe* for James Campbell in 1629) bespeak both a respectability and a reasonable reputation.

Whatever the degree of contemporary fame, however, it was evidently short-lived. G. E. Bentley [in his *The Jacobean and Caroline Stage,* 1956] finds fewer than a dozen literary allusions to Dekker in later seventeenth-century literature, none to his drama; and he concludes that the playwright's reputation grew increasingly slight. Gerard Langbaine in his *Account of the English Dramatic Poets* in 1691, while admitting that Dekker "wanted not his Admirers, nor his Friends" in his own age, proclaims that now he "know[s] none [of his plays] of much Esteem, except *The Untrussing of the Humorous Poet,* and that chiefly on account of the subject of it, which was the witty *Ben Jonson.*" Charles Gildon's continuation of Langbaine's work in 1699 deletes even this brief editorial commentary.

By the turn of the nineteenth century, as George Saintsbury observes [in his *History of Elizabethan Literature,* 1894], "Thomas Dekker was probably little more than a name to all but professed students of Elizabethan literature." Among those who kept his name before the students were Charles Lamb, William Hazlitt, and Leigh Hunt, all of whom drew excerpts from his plays in highly impressionistic accounts of Shakespeare's contemporaries.

Lamb, for example, in *Specimens of English Dramatic Poets,* declared that Dekker "had poetry enough for anything"; he found the character of Orleans in **Old Fortunatus** "done to the life," talking "pure Biron and Romeo," and he praised the potential "beauty and force" of the scene of Caelestine's presumed poisoning in **Satiromastix** and the "beauties of so very high an order" in **The Virgin Martyr.** Hazlitt, similarly, in *Lectures on the Dramatic Literature of the Age of Elizabeth,* proclaims his great admiration for Dekker, citing especially the "truth of character" in **The Honest Whore** with the ability of "fine art to chisel thought" in Orlando Friscobaldo and the "masterly portrait" of Matheo. The difficulty with such commendation, of course, is that its very concern with particular details and specific figures draws attention from the achievement of the whole play or any effort to assess Dekker's overall dramatic development. And, in this regard, Saintsbury correctly notes that Dekker had to wait "longer than any of his fellows for due recognition of his work in complete form," with R. H. Shepherd's edition of his dramatic works in 1873, A. B. Grosart's edition of the non-dramatic works in 1884-1886, and Ernest Rhys' Mermaid volume including five plays in 1887.

Romantic generalizations continue, to a considerable degree, to plague Dekker criticism. The idea, for example, that he was "a man whose inborn sweetness and gleefulness of soul carried him through vexations which would have crushed a spirit less hopeful, cheerful, and humane" [E. P. Whipple, *The Literature of the Age of Elizabeth,* 1896] is reiterated time and again; his "divine gift of tenderness" [Algernon Charles Swinburne, *The Age of Shakespeare,* 1908], the "warm heartedness, the sincerity, the piety and the patriotism of the man" [Mary Leland Hunt, *Thomas Dekker,* 1911], approximate that of Shakespeare. The "golden hearted dramatist" [J. LeGay Brereton, Introduction to *Lusts Dominion,* 1931] combines the "mental energy and literary facility of Defoe" with "the happy heart of Goldsmith" [W. Macneil Dixon, *The Cambridge History of English Literature,* 1933]. Constantly "temper[ing] his comment on life with a kindly humor" [Thomas Marc Parrott and Robert H. Ball, *A Short View of Elizabethan Drama,* 1943], he "smiles at [the] foibles" of his fellowmen [J. S. P. Tatlock and R. G. Martin, *Representative English Plays,* 1938] and exudes "a sentimentally optimistic view of human nature" [David Daiches, *A Critical History of English Literature,* 1960]. Then, too, his plays continue to be excerpted for illustrations of superb lyrical abilities or individual moments of characterization; both A. W. Ward [in his *A History of English Dramatic Literature to the Death of Queen Anne,* 1899] and W. J. Courthope [in his *History of English Poetry,* 1903] encourage such a practice through their assertions that the excellence of the plays is to be found in their individual parts rather than in the whole work.

Dekker's ready willingness to collaborate, his apparent haste of composition, his failure on certain occasions to conform to present-day dramatic sensibilities of structure or of characterization, his notably high level of productivity even in an age, whose appetite for new productions is a matter of record—all such matters have provoked from

yet other critics mixed—sometimes contradictory—responses. (pp. 1-3)

Even . . . a cursory review of critical pronouncements reflects not only the broad diversity of opinion but also its generally fragmented nature in that not unusually it is only a small handful of plays that are cited either for praise or condemnation. Mary Leland Hunt and others may well lament that evaluating Dekker's work is "at the outset almost paralyzed by the fact that about half of the plays he wrote alone and the great majority of those he wrote with others have been lost." While, admittedly, it is impossible to minimize the loss of at least thirty plays, the great irony is that the considerable body of extant plays has received relatively scant attention. With that in mind M. L. Wine in 1975, in a bibliographical survey of recent studies of Dekker [in *The Popular School: A Survey and Bibliography of Recent Studies in English Renaissance Drama,* edited by Terence P. Logan and Denzell S. Smith, 1975], urged critics to "focus more clearly on the actual craftsmanship of the plays than it has in the past. George Price [in his *Thomas Dekker,* 1969] began to move in that direction, describing much of the negative comment as the consequence of a misunderstanding of Dekker's themes and techniques and concluding, somewhat cautiously, that his "ability to achieve coherence and relevance seems to be about equal to that of most other Elizabethans of the second rank, for instance, George Chapman and John Ford." James Conover's study in the same year [*Thomas Dekker: An Analysis of Dramatic Structure*] aimed frankly "to re-evaluate Thomas Dekker as a play-craftsman, to subject some of his plays to structural analysis." And, at about the same time, Normand Berlin [in *Studies in English Literature 6,* 1966] was challenging "all the cliches" that have "fixed [Dekker] in a formulated phrase." More recently, participants in a special session on Dekker at the Modern Language Association convention in Los Angeles (December, 1982) reiterated the need for fresh critical perceptions. Certainly the resources are now in place to encourage such investigation. Fredson Bowers' edition brings together the extant plays presumed to form the canon and makes them readily available along with excellent critical apparatus. Within the past five years have appeared Cyrus Hoy's companion volumes featuring critical introductions and extensive notes for each of the plays [*Introductions, Notes, and Commentaries to Texts in "The Dramatic Works of Thomas Dekker,"* ed. Fredson Bowers, 4 vols., 1980]. Then, too, M. T. Jones-Davies' encyclopedic study of Dekker's dramatic and non-dramatic work in relation to London life and culture provides a mine of valuable detail [*Un peintre de la vie londienne: Thomas Dekker,* 2 vols., 1958]. (p. 4)

Thomas Dekker genuinely deserves a considerably higher place in the development and maturation of Elizabethan-Jacobean-Caroline drama than most previous critics have been willing to acknowledge. Certainly the plays are not of uniform quality; several [are] relatively unsuccessful in structure, or characterization, or perspective. But . . . it is highly reductionistic to attribute this failure to moral slovenliness, or to an untrained artistic talent, or to the haste of writing necessitated by extreme poverty.

To whatever extent these or similar conditions were involved, the more significant factor is Dekker's persistent determination to experiment in form and, in some instances, to expand the traditions of English drama. More clearly than Shakespeare's early romantic comedies, for example, *Old Fortunatus* and *Patient Grissil* demonstrate something of the inchoate qualities from which romantic comedy emerges; at the same time they exhibit structural features and dramatic techniques that, in the hands of the more practiced playwright, give rise to his richest creations in *The Shoemakers' Holiday* and *2 The Honest Whore.* The fragmented perspective of *If This Be Not a Good Play,* possibly written shortly after *The Roaring Girl,* results, generally, from tragicomic elements that are incongruous with a realistic plot utilizing material from the morality tradition for comic purposes and, specifically, from a confusion in the spectators' reaction to devil figures who at one moment appear to be comically inept in comparison with a pervasively corrupt society of humans and at another seem to be powerful demons of temptation, judgment, and destruction. Similarly ineffective, despite the effort to create epic drama, is the mingling of allegorical elements from the morality with realistic drama in *The Whore of Babylon.* Countering these failures, however, are the experiments that successfully expand the horizons of established dramatic form. *1, 2 The Honest Whore,* for instance, like *All's Well That Ends Well* and *Measure For Measure,* utilize the conventions of romantic comedy; but these stage worlds feature, not the stylized, one-dimensional puppet of situation comedy, but rather a more complex character who is forced to confront a viable force of evil and to make ethical and moral decisions and who—in the course of the action—experiences a credible and significant development. If *Blurt, Master Constable* is less successful, it prefigures in the enigmatic character of Violetta the profoundly conceived Bellafront in *The Honest Whore,* who as a reformed prostitute willing to strain the quality of mercy for the sake of a man who has grossly wronged her, combines the roles of Violetta and Imperia. *The Roaring Girl* interweaves elements of the dominant comic modes of the early seventeenth-century stage in dealing with issues of serious social and personal concern; stylized citizen-comedy strands are combined with a romanticized topical rogue figure to provide a consistent comic perspective for the romantic-comedy frame. Its treatment of male chauvinism, as old as Aristophanes and as current as the ERA struggle, reflects issues of lively concern to King James and the English Parliament. A wide variety of dramatic techniques helps to set the legend of Dorothea to the stage in *The Virgin Martyr*—the morality format, de casibus tragedy, elements of romantic comedy (the psychology of love, the rival wooer, proxy wooing, the motif of friendship versus love), and a quality of anagnorisis unique to Jacobean tragedy. Stage-tested devices lend dramatic life and depth of perspective to a saint's legend that in itself is heavily didactic and lacks both the dynamic characterization and the sustained tension of opposing value-structures vital to tragedy. *Match Me in London* is a quintessential blend of comedy and tragedy, creating and maintaining the mixed tone of tragicomedy with more effective architectonic unity than Fletcher—and just possibly before (or at least contemporaneous with) *Philaster* and *The Faithful Shepherdess.* **The Witch of Edmonton,** technically neither tragicomedy nor tragedy, achieves a surprisingly powerful impact and reflects an apparently conscious striving for a fresh and provocative dramatic form for a generation of spectators who faced increasingly profound moral and social ambiguities in Jacobean England. By doubling the protagonist and presenting them as driven to destruction not only by their individual flaw but also by the machinations of those in society who materially or emotionally profit from their downfall, Dekker helps to create the societal perspective central to the most powerful Jacobean tragedy. And **The Welsh Embassador,** Dekker's elaborate reshaping of **The Noble Spanish Soldier,** literally encapsulates tragedy within comedy. Athelstane, like Orlando Friscobaldo or Shakespeare's Leontes earlier, must suffer the consequences of his moral and ethical decisions in a stage world that does not preclude the power of evil; as in Shakespeare's romances, however, the power of love is also real, and the protagonist, transfigured by suffering, has the rare opportunity to live beyond tragedy.

Equally as significant as the nature of Dekker's persistent experimentation with dramatic form is his ability to interact creatively with his fellow playwrights. The development of his romantic comedy, for instance, is demonstrably related to Shakespeare's work. **Patient Grissil,** though flawed, appears structurally to be a mirror image of *The Taming of the Shrew;* and the more successful **The Shoemakers' Holiday,** with its intricate interlacing of three separate subordinate plot strands that both parody and counterpoint the major action, is highly reminiscent of the elaborate structure of *A Midsummer Night's Dream,* written some two or three years before. Part Two of **The Honest Whore,** structurally far more coherent than Part One, appears to be directly patterned after *Measure For Measure,* and like that play pushes comedy to its generic fringes in its exploration of the transforming powers of human love and sacrifice. Just such crucial differences also distinguish Dekker's two citizen comedies, and again the answer in large part appears to lie in his professional sensitivity to the judgments of quality and fashion reflected in the responses of his fellow playwrights. The blurred comic perspective of **Westward Ho** fragments the moral foundation of the plot, provoking in *Eastward Ho* a rather wryly moralistic response from Chapman, Marston, and Jonson; **Northward Ho,** presumably in turn a response to *Eastward Ho,* is also in a sense a response and corrective to the moral distortions of his own earlier play. Similarly, any evaluation of Dekker's work in the years following these citizen comedies must consider his reaction to fluctuating stage fashions and must recognize the impact he achieves through the genuinely innovative quality of juxtaposing and combining diverse stage elements and themes—whether for comedy, history, epic, or tragedy. Like the essentially baroque directions of metaphysical verse, such experiments represent, in part, an attempt to expand the scope and effect of drama for an age generally in reaction against Elizabethan literary fashion.

At least one critic [Hunt] has suggested an evolutionary development in Dekker's dramaturgy—"that dramatically and psychologically *The Honest Whore* is an advance upon *Old Fortunatus* and *The Shoemakers' Holiday;* that the finest scenes in *The Virgin Martyr* show a more exquisite perception of the power of language to reveal character than any previous work; and that in tragic power *The Witch of Edmonton* surpasses all earlier work. Considering the unevenness of Dekker's writing, the wide variety of his dramatic genres, and the uncertainties of dating, it is difficult and unnecessary to claim a steady and consistent artistic progress from one stage world to the next. Our more significant concern is to assess the dramatic achievement reflected in his entire canon. Such close consideration quite literally mandates a rethinking of critical judgments that "his early plays are in every way superior to his later" [Swinburne], that he "never did anything better [than] or essentially different" from *The Shoemakers' Holiday* [C. F. Tucker Brooke, in *A Literary History of England,* edited by A. C. Baugh, 1948], that "we miss in the plays the technical experiments of Marston" [Una Ellis-Fermor, in her *Jacobean Drama,* 1936]. Dekker's stage world, to the contrary, like the shape of a Renaissance play "refuses to be static"; to recognize the complexity of its multiple variations is to expose riches "no less breathtaking in its achievement than the glories we have recognized when other generations have been our critical cicerones" [I. Cope Jackson, in *Comparative Drama* I, 1967-68].

Such structural analysis, concentrating primarily on the dramaturgical techniques by which Dekker establishes and maintains the perspective of the individual plays, illuminates only one aspect of drama, of course. It does not address authorial intent or the significance of the theme in a broad historical context—whether, for example, a play is overtly or covertly a document of social protest, whether (or why) a playwright is frankly pandering to the Court, whether there is a particular topical significance, whether the play reveals such matters as shifting social allegiances, changing moral or commercial values. In the final analysis structural criticism is relatively narrow in that it focuses closely on particular features of individual stage worlds. The implications, on the other hand, are of central importance in judging the artistic merits of the individual playwright, in tracing the significance of his persistent dramatic experimentation and the manner in which he addresses the ever-altering stage fashions, and in comprehending something of the evolution of the genre, particularly in a period of development so extensive as that of drama during the more than three decades of Dekker's active career. Jonson's caustic comments and the benign neglect of later generations have all too effectively discouraged careful attention to the craftsmanship of a playwright who, despite his share of failures, deserves a far better epitaph than a "dresser of plays about the town here" (*Poetaster,* III.iv.320). More appropriate is C. R. Baskerville's observation [in *Elizabethan and Stuart Plays,* edited by C. R. Baskerville and others, 1934] that Dekker's combination of new elements of commerce with old elements of romance represents the "culmination of Elizabethan drama proper." (pp. 5-9)

> *Larry S. Champion, in his* Thomas Dekker and the Traditions of English Drama, *Peter Lang, 1985, 198 p.*

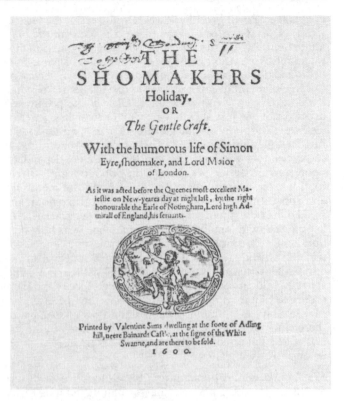

Title page of The Shomakers Holiday.

J. A. Faber   (essay date 1987)

[In this excerpt, Faber analyzes the humor, plot devices, and characters of The Shoemaker's Holiday.*]*

In *The Shoemaker's Holiday,* Thomas Dekker is preeminently a "painter of London life" [M. T. Jones-Davies, *Un peintre de la vie londienne: Thomas Dekker,* 2 vols., 1958], the quality for which he is most consistently praised. Details of the day-to-day life of ordinary people give definiteness to Dekker's drama, which retreats from the pastoral landscape of earlier comedy into the recognizable locale of the Elizabethan manor house, countryside, and city. Such apparent realism, however, is only the surface of the play. On closer scrutiny, the world of *SH* is not realistic but utterly fantastic, a wished-for world into which to escape. For the shoemakers the realms of work and of play are reconciled; class distinctions—real enough in Dekker's day—all but vanish, so that even the King has a proletarian air about him; there is little spatial or temporal perspective, but instead a striking simultaneity of awareness; and there is enough money for everyone. Both Dekker's contemporaries and modern readers of *SH,* if they perceive the world of the play rightly, find a world too-good-to-be-true and experience a nostalgia approaching Aristotle's *athanatidzein,* the yearning for immorality. This getting beyond man's confinement and limitations is at the heart of *SH.* With a daring inversion of the late medieval *de casibus* formula for tragedy, Dekker created a rhapsodic comedy about the rhythmic inevitability of success in the modern world, for, whereas the older tragedy focused on man's limits, *SH* celebrates man's freedom.

The formal argument which Dekker gives in his dedicatory preface "To all good Fellowes, Professors of the Gentle Craft; of what degree soever" places the focus of the play almost entirely on the romance of Lacie, a young nobleman, and Rose, the Lord Mayor's daughter. Such a conventional focus probably can be explained in terms of Dekker's instinctive conservatism or his sense of what would attract a theatre audience. Clearly the people addressed are not just shoemakers, for Dekker has generalized the salutation to "all good Fellowes" and he adds a further qualifying phrase, "of what degree soever," as if to suggest that goodness and gentleness are not dependent upon rank or status. *SH* is not a play about degree, therefore, but one which breaks the older notion of hierarchy and substitutes the more modern notion of freedom. Instead of anxiety about what a person's proper place is, *SH* is suffused with an impudent confidence which makes questions of decorum or propriety irrelevant. The shoemakers' attitude toward their work may be cited as an example. Threatening twice to quit, they exhibit more the spirit of wildcat-strikers than the subservience of the then customary indentures. Note, however, that precisely in such a play, essentially relativistic and anti-absolutistic, there emerges an ethical dimension which stresses the social consequences of individual acts—a dimension which belongs to significant comedy.

SH flaunts conventional morality, although it is by no means an immoral play. It shares the ungainliness of its central character but, nevertheless, teaches and moves and delights its audience precisely because of Simon Eyre's function within the world of the play. Contrary to what one could expect in a domestic drama, Dekker does not exploit the opposition of social classes or of city versus country; instead, he works with the more basic philosophical antilogies of being and becoming, of nature and art, and of reality and appearance. These antilogies are fundamental, but they are not always sharply differentiable, for they are facets or approximations of each other.

Human solidarity is the keynote of the play. It discusses the problem of freedom in the context of the microcommunity dominated by Simon Eyre, who is both a referent to, and a referee for, its inhabitants. He looms larger than life because he transcends time, taking the contingencies of love and death—the reciprocal poles of comedy and tragedy—in stride as a natural man. Eyre's reputation has even reached the King, who explicitly asks that his unusual subject be himself and not act differently in his royal presence (V.iii). When the King asks him about his age, Eyre at first evades the question with marvelous obliquity. But even when he answers it, he demonstrates an enviable disregard of age as a problem. Eyre has reconciled himself with Time:

> KING. Tell me infaith mad *Eyre,* how old thou art.
>
> EYRE. My Liege a verie boy, a stripling, a yonker, you are not a white haire on my head, not a gray in this beard, everie haire I assure thy majestie that sticks in this beard, *Sim Eyre* values at the king of Babilons ransome, *Tamar Chams* beard was a rubbing brush toot: yet Ile shave it off, and stuffe tennis balls with it to please my bully king.

> KING. But all this while I do not know your age.
>
> EYRE. My Liege, I am sixe and fiftie yeare olde, yet I can crie humpe, with a sound heart for the honour of Saint *Hugh;* marke this olde wench, my king, I dauncde the shaking of the sheetes with her sixe and thirtie yeares agoe, and yet I hope to get two or three yong Lorde Maiors ere I die: I am lustie still, *Sim Eyre* still: care, and colde lodging brings white haires. My sweete Majestie, let care vanish, cast it upon thy Nobles, it will make thee looke alwayes young like *Apollo,* and cry humpe: Prince am I none, yet am I princely borne.

> (V.v.18-34)

Dekker endows Simon Eyre, who is perpetually on the go and becoming more important and wealthier with each spectacular appearance, with a static quality. In a world of change he is above change. His irrepressible torrent of words, spiced with common vulgarities as well as choice invective culled from the language of the Bible and of the stage, is an index of his verbal resourcefulness, his invention, a copiousness that resists change. Eyre cannot put on airs. A prosaic man, he has difficulty speaking in verse even when the occasion demands it, and he is utterly proletarian in addressing everyone in the same familiar way. A comparison of his colorful, good natured invective in I.i.117-70, *passim* (Eyre's first appearance on stage) and his last ranting speech in V.iv, just prior to the ceremonial entrance of the King, shows that he is Simon Eyre yesterday, today, and tomorrow, world without end:

> WIFE. Good my Lord have a care what you speak to his grace.
>
> EYRE. Away you Islington whitepot, hence you happerarse, you barly pudding ful of magots, you broyld carbonado, avaunt, avaunt, avoide Mephostophilus: shall *Sim Eyre* learne to speake of you Ladie *Madgie*? vanish mother Miniver cap, vanish, goe, trip and goe, meddle with your partlets, and your pisherie pasherie, your flewes and whirligigs, go, rub, out of mine alley: *Sim Eyre* knowes how to speake to a Pope, to Sultan *Soliman,* to Tamburlaine and he were here: and shall I melt? shal I droope before my Soveraigne? no, come my Ladie Madgie, follow me Hauns, about your businesse my frolicke freebooters: *Firke,* friske about, and about, and about, for the honour of mad *Simon Eyre* Lord Maior of *London.*

> (V.iv.45-57)

Dekker evidently prepared the context of his most extraordinary character very deliberately. Eyre's flamboyant carefreeness in the foreground of the audience's awareness offsets the melancholy music at the periphery of their existence. Consider, for example, the tension between the two contrasted "Three-mans" songs, originally printed before the play itself without indications when they were to be sung. The first song is usually inserted in III.iii, after Eyre has said to the Lord Mayor, whom he is unwittingly about to succeed, "Why what should I do my Lord? a pound of care paies not a dram of debt: hum lets be merry whiles we are yong, olde age, sacke and sugar will steale upon us ere we be aware" (21-23), and before the mayor asks Eyre's wife to counsel his daughter Rose on marriage. It is a song about spring and summer, about young love, with strong iambic and dactyllic rhythms suggestive of the morris dance or other Mayday pageantry. The dominant tone is joyful, but there is a plaintive note also, for, along with the nightingale, there is a cuckoo in the forest choir. The second song is usually inserted in V.iv, during the feast of the London prentices, and just prior to the announcement that the King has come. It is a song about autumn and winter, about death, with regular inversions from iambic to trochaic rhythms giving the ballad-like stanzas an elegiac effect. The dominant tone is sad, with a note of forced mirth in the reiterated refrain of a drinking song. Here, too, Dekker is explicit in his directions: "At last when all have drinke, this verse."

> Cold's the wind, and wet's the raine,
> Saint Hugh be our good speede:
> Ill is the weather that bringeth no gaine,
> Nor helps good hearts in neede

To counter the melancholy progression of the seasons in these songs, Dekker uses the peculiar time sense in the play itself. Mme. Jones-Davies has correctly remarked, "Dekker sait jongler avec le temps." The curious telescoping of days in *SH* creates a loss of time, a timelessness. Nowhere is there a hint of what one could expect, as a prominent tenet of citizen morality, that time is money. Yet, the culminating focus on Shrove Tuesday is very sharp. The Shrove Tuesday festivities are at once the crowning use of, and the most flagrant disregard for, time. The danger of such a freedom rite is evident when Firk, with his usual hyperbole, expands the day into a year of Jubilee, just as he earlier associated Eyre's bounty with heaven:

> Nay more my hearts, every Shrovetuesday is our yeere of Jubile: and when the pancake bel rings, we are as free as my lord Maior, we may shut up our shops, and make holidays: Ile have it calld, Saint *Hughes* Holiday.
>
> (V.ii.202-05)

When Hodge and Firke hope that the new holiday will "continue for ever" to the "eternall credite . . . of the gentle Craft," they are each expressing their Amen to the new liturgy of the "incomprehensible good fellowship." An allusion to Shrove Tuesday in Dekker's **Lanthorne and Candle-light** ten years later tells us that the prentices made such a ruckus on this holiday that a "hue and cry followes after, some twelve or fourteene miles off, (round about London); which was the farthest of their journey as they gave out," and that the "Constable . . . then runnes up and downe . . . halfe out of his wittes."

Love and marriage, hampered by war abroad and insensitivity at home, is a further theme explored by Dekker. Fittingly, the exposition of courtship is presented in private scenes: for example, the idyllic interlude of Rose alone in her garden (I.ii); but the purity of Rose is accentuated by the noisy sensuality of Sibil, her maid. She is a match for Firk, who shows great interest in her: "*Sib whoore,* welcome to *London*" (IV.i.42), and longs for a perpetual Eve of St. Agnes: "For if ever I sigh when sleepe I shoulde take, / Pray God I may loose my mayden-head when I wake" (I.ii.45-46). The exposition of married love is, ap-

propriately enough, presented in public scenes. Simon Eyre's spectacular blowup of the lovers' aubade (I.iv) is drenched with tenderness though masked as roughness. The tone of this boisterous scene, inevitably shocking to modern student-readers, is carefully determined by the authorial stage direction at the beginning of the scene: "*Enter* Eyre *making himself readie.*" Eyre is not set apart from the action; he is at its center. The extraordinary audio-visual sweep of his first sentence, which is typical, has the same panoramic scope and paradoxical appeal as the detail-saturated tavern scenes of Jan Steen:

> Where be these boyes, these girles, these drabbes, these scoundrels, they wallow in the fat brewisse of my bountie, and licke up the crums of my table, yet will not rise to see my walkes cleansed: come out you powder-beefe-queanes, what *Nan,* what *Madge-mumble-crust,* come out you fatte Midriffe-swag-belly whores, and sweepe me these kennels, that noysome stench offends not the nose of my neighbours: what *Firke* I say, what *Hodge*? open my shop windows, what *Firke* I say. I say.
>
> (I.iv.1-8)

The rhetorical punctuation indicates that Eyre should be appreciated not for his grammatical sense but for his sound, not for the letter but the the spirit.

Eyre's prominence in *SH* is facilitated by the role of his apprentice Firk. Just after the news of Rose's elopement with the disguised Lacie, Lincoln and Otley, two men of the world, are humiliated when Firk toys with them (IV.iii). Although they know what is happening—"this villaine calls us knaves by craft" (67)—Firk talks them out of their money, mocks them with his impudence, and gulls them by directing them to the wrong church. Firk's language is a match for Eyre's; it has the same rambling indirectness, panoramic sweep, and sonorous quality. Obviously, Firk loves to talk. He is also very aware of his audience, asking that Sibil be sent out, probably because she would not be able to keep a straight face:

> FIRKE. Pitchers have eares, and maides have wide mouthes: but for *Hauns* prauns, upon my word to morrow morning, he and young mistress *Rose* goe to this geere, they shall be married together, by this rush, or else tourne *Firke* to a firkin of butter to tanne leather withall.
>
> LORD MAYOR. But art thou sure of this?
>
> FIRKE. Am I sure that Paules steeple is a handfull higher than London stone? or that pissing conduit leakes nothing put [mine: misprint for but] pure mother Bunch? am I sure I am lustie Firke, Gods nailes doe you thinke I am so base to gull you?
>
> LINCOLN. Where are they married? dost thou know the church?
>
> FIRKE. I never goe to church, but I know the name of it, it is a swearing church, stay a while, tis: I by the mas, no, no, tis I by my troth, no nor that, tis I by my faith, that that, tis by my *Faithes* church under *Paules* crosse, there they shall be knit like a paire of stockings in matrimonie,

there theile be in conie.

(103-18)

The last pun, *in conie* for *inconnus,* would probably escape most theater goers in Dekker's day and most readers today; it would probably ingratiate Firk with the court audience. The extraordinary verbal proficiency of Eyre and Firk, and ultimately of Dekker, to make sense out of nonsense (among his contemporaries only Shakespeare matches Dekker in this) because they understand that "the medium is the message," stresses the necessity to differentiate verse and poetry. The division between dramatic prose and blank verse is quite conventional, but in *SH* it is surely the prose that is the poetry.

At the final showdown between the shoemakers and the aristocrats (V.ii), Firk once again mocks Lincoln and Otley. When Lincoln indignantly asks, "Where is my Nephew married?" (102), Firk casually answers: "Is he married? God give him joy, I am glad of it: they have a faire day, and the signe is in a good planet, Mars in Venus" (103-04). The cool efficiency of Firk derives from his confidence that things are under control. A recognizable variant of the crafty slave who manipulates the action in Roman comedy, Firk is sharply contrasted with Dodger. In spite of his credentials,

> This Dodger is mine uncles parasite,
> The arranst varlet that e'er breathd on earth.
> He sets more discord in a noble house,
> By one daies broching of his pickethanke tales,
> Then can be salv'd again in twentie yeares . . .
>
> (I.i.189-93)

Lincoln's "jealous eye" contributes to the failure of the aristocrats, for Dodger does not return with information until after what Lincoln hopes to avoid has happened. Their conspicuous lack of success makes Lincoln and Otley, in spite of their pretensions, disreputable, irresponsible upstarts: their ill-considered bursting in on the King with wild charges of treason (V.v.38) would send tremors through the court audience, for the similar behavior of the earl of Essex in the early autumn of 1599 was too recent a memory.

The major movement of the plot, Eyre's ascent, is worked out with great care. His success is usually accentuated by something potentially or actually bad happening about the same time. A contemporary audience, for whom the painful incongruities of the 1590s were not history but fact, would make their own associations with the slightest hint. The sobering news from France of a victory which cost four thousand English lives sets off Eyre's promotion to alderman and his decision to assume the speculative risk (II.iii); Otley's disappointment at losing Hammon as a son-in-law sets off the rumor that Eyre may become sheriff (III..i); the return of the wounded Rafe and the revelation that Jane has disappeared, the fact that Eyre is the new sheriff (III.ii); an epidemic causing the death of seven alderman, his becoming Lord Mayor of London (IV.i and iii); the intoxication of the prentices threatens the propriety of Eyre's entertaining the King (V.iv); and the charge that he is harboring traitors could undercut the audacious requests he is about to make of the King. Eyre pleads with the King like Abraham with the angel in order to save

Sodom. All his requests are granted because Eyre was not out for personal gain but for the prosperity and preservation of London. The Leadenhall, so named by the King, was a primitive but open exchange. In a time when monopolies were a serious threat to the economy, the shoemakers were guaranteed two days free trade per week. And the King honors his eccentric subject, by accepting the invitation to a banquet which by then had surely become bedlam, because he endorses the loyalty and generosity of Simon Eyre.

Just as the character of Simon is the measure of mankind, so his marriage is the touchstone of *SH.* This tumultuous, rough-and-tumble marriage is the epitome of attainable human freedom. In it the negative aspect of the tension between the male and female sex is resolved. The completeness of sexual freedom (always the most fundamental concern, the *telos,* of comedy) is reflected in the absence of any anxiety about sexual identity and in the complete freedom of speech. Eyre is hugely virtuous to the last hair of his beard; Madge, mildly vicious to the last thread of her petticoat; however, the marvel is that the audience-readers participate in the freedom celebrated in *SH* to the extent they accept the conjunction of virtue and vice as a necessary condition of life.

Simon Eyre is a full character, large enough to measure others against, and certainly not a humor character as the advertisement of the title page of Q1 suggests. Nobody's fool, he is the referent of his servants who want to be like their master. He is also the referee, controlling and directing the action. When he is invited to Old Ford, Otley's country home, Eyre brings his own entertainment. He also matter-of-factly packs Lacie and Rose off with Madge to the Savoy for a dawn wedding. Most noticeable is his affirmative sense of humor. Eyre accepts life and can take the future as it comes because he is not ashamed to reveal his humble past even to the King. The inclusive sweep of Eyre's sentences marks him as a circumspect man, but even his syntax shows that Eyre always adds and never subtracts:

> by the lorde of Ludgate, its a madde life to be a
>   lorde
> Mayor, its a stirring life, a fine life, a velvet life,
> a careful life. Well *Simon Eyre,* yet set a good
>   face on
> it, in the honor of sainct *Hugh.* Soft, the king this
> day comes to dine with me, to see my new build-
>   ings, his
> majesty is welcome, he shall have good cheere,
>   delicate
> cheere, princely cheere. This day my felow pren-
>   tises of
> *London* come to dine with me too, they shall
>   have fine
> cheere, gentlemanlike cheere. I promised the
>   mad Cap-
> pidosians, when we all served at the Conduit to-
>   gether,
> that if ever I came to be Mayor of *London,* I
>   woould
> feast them al, and Ile doot, Ile doot by the life
>   of
> *Pharaoh,* by this beard *Sim Eyre* will be no
>   flincher.

Besides, I have procurd, that upon every Shrove-
tuesday,
at the sound of the pancake bell: my fine Assyri-
an lads,
shall clap up their shop windows, and away, this
is the
day, and this day they shall doot, they shall doot:
Boyes, that day are you free, let masters care,
And prentises shall pray for *Simon Eyre.*

(V.i.36-52)

The rime of the closing couplet indicates that Eyre is the antidote for care. Not a ceremonious man, he puts on ceremonies for others; to someone whose very dreams beget responsibilities, life itself is celebration enough.

If it is true generally that London was for Dekker a symbol of life itself [as Jones-Davies states], it is true more particularly of this elaborate artistic vision which is inseparably rooted in the city where he spent his entire life. *The Shoemaker's Holiday* is not a commentary on London life, but a complex imitation, a *mimesis,* of what that life could be like. The rich allusiveness of Dekker's language, a controlled luxuriance like Shakespeare's in *2 Henry IV* and susceptible to similar misunderstanding, represents a unified mosaic of impressions. At its center stands Simon Eyre, larger than life, and therefore, in no danger of stepping off the stage and over the boundary between art and life.

Indeed, there is good reason to call *SH* a one-man play. The orthographic usage of the plural possessive in the title, now sharing the authority of the standard edition, may well be questioned. Though it has been argued that the plural is more logical, the reasoning is hardly convincing: "Le pluriel est beaucoup plus logique. . . . On assiste en effet, dans la comédie, à la fête de tous les joyeux cordonniers londoniens conviés au Leadenhall" (Jones-Davies); also, there is more involved than number, because the sense also changes, from subjective to objective genitive. The original title page gives no clue—it simply reads *The Shoemakers Holiday*—but theater history does. The chief actor of the Admiral's Men was Edward Alleyn. In all likelihood, therefore, Dekker wrote the part of Simon Eyre for this boisterous titan-actor.

Heroes belong to tragedy, not to comedy. A civic hero who is the center of a community and not egregious is now almost unthinkable. Yet, in the context of London, A.D. 1600, such a hero is possible and even probable. The legendary Simon Eyre was for Dekker's contemporaries also a figure of the past, but paradoxically the power of the play makes the old new, and thus, while the play lasts, the redefined central character is thoroughly believable. To enjoy imaginative literature, and especially drama which depends so largely on illusion, one must not be too literal too long. The important question is not what the play is about but what is about the play. A modern reader, or even audience, cannot fully recapture the experience of Dekker's contemporary audience, for there is blurring in space and time which is not fully reversible. We can recover the facts but not all the associations which made Dekker's play live in the seventeenth century. The contrast between Saint Faith's and the the Savoy has already been pointed out. There are other geographical facts crushed by distance:

the smells of Eastcheap where Madge sold tripe; the bells of Saint Paul's and Saint Mary Overies (Saint Savior's in Southwark); the complex system of water conduits to which Firk refers so irreverently; London Stone, a military landmark dating from Roman times; the archery range and muster ground at Finsbury Field; the proximity of Leadenhall and the Guildhall; the contrast between Tower Street and the Old Change; the location of Ludgate and Paul's Cross; the location of the docks and the Custom House down river from London Bridge—all this, and the unnamed connective tissue of the city as a living organism, are lost and can never be recovered in its multidimensional sensory richness. We have difficulty imagining even the extent of Old London, stretching some two thousand yards inland. To take the fragments of a real world and reintroduce them in footnotes as instances of realism is to miss the point.

What holds for geography holds also for history. Having difficulty imagining the taste of pancakes on Shrove Tuesday, a modern reader obviously has even more difficulty penetrating to the time when "plague and famine were the two Great Evils which stalked England"; when in time of dearth the Mayor and Aldermen controlled the distribution of food and fuel; when England simultaneously experienced the terror of disintegration and the challenge of a new, mobile society; when the excitement of discovering new worlds meant the possibility of easing old problems. Much of this, too, is lost and recoverable only as facts. Consider the impact that one day before the court performance of *SH,* on the very last day of 1599, a royal charter was granted to establish the East India Company. It is bad history to accuse Simon Eyre of making a fortune "by sharp practices of which the modern equivalent would be obtaining credit by false trade references" (H. M. Robertson, *Aspects of the Rise of Economic Individualism,* as cited in Knights [*Drama and Society in the Age of Jonson,* 1962]); it is equally bad literary criticism to state that Dekker "slurs over the issues without thinking very hard about them" (Knights). Eyre's good fortune with the cargo ship is, in terms of *SH,* a fact which, however miraculous, is never an issue. The unusual variety of the cargo and the secrecy and speed with which the deal must be made suggest that the skipper was a freebooter; Eyre incorporates this word into his vocabulary after his ship comes in. Furthermore, the Dutch skipper is obviously disreputable—so drunk that he throws caution to the wind, brags about his cargo, and swears sacrilegiously:

De skip ben in revere: dor be van Sugar, Cyvet,
Almonds, Cambricke, and a towsand towsand
tings, gotz sacrament, nempt it mester, yo sal
heb good copen.

(II.iii.119-21)

And the meaning of his alliterative nickname *Skellum Skanderbag* (II.iii.91) is doubly damaging—No-good Shame-bag. Surely when buccaneers like Drake were heroes, when trade rivalry was intense, and nationalism was heightened by religious wars, no one in Dekker's audience would raise any scruples when an Englishman profited by a cargo some Dutchman plundered from the Spanish or Portuguese, especially when it was expected that very soon the English themselves would be getting such products directly. Moreover, by having these goods, (Otley, his predecessor, was a grocer) Eyre could fulfil his duties as a mayor, who was expected to provide for the needs of his people food as well as entertainment.

In the context of London life around 1600, Simon Eyre was undeniably a man of experience. Yet he is also a man of innocence, akin to Babulo, Dekker's fool in the play *Patient Grissell* (also 1599). Enid Welsford [in her *The Fool, His Social and Literary History*, 1961] has called Babulo, whose philosophy of "light-hearted simplicity" is best described in his own words—"Innocence bears it away in the world to come," a unique kind of fool. Though not a fool, Simon Eyre is similarly unique. Dekker's art comes to its fullest expression in this character, who actively embodies both innocence and experience and, thus, harmonizes the harsh actuality of London with the dreams of Cockayne. The calculated decorousness of his preface should not obscure the magic of his achievement; *The Shoemaker's Holiday* is a *trompe l'oeile* with a deceptively simple aim:

> Take all in good worth that is well intended, for nothing is purposed but mirth, mirth lengthneth long life; which, with all other blessings I heartily wish you.
> Farewell.

During a lifetime in the theater, his best period in one named the Fortune, the first New Year's Day of the seventeenth century was Dekker's finest moment, for he never spoke more directly and in a more personal voice for the people he loved. (pp. 359-70)

J. A. Faber, "Thomas Dekker's Gentle Craft: An Essay on 'The Shoemaker's Holiday'," in Iowa State Journal of Research, *Vol. 61, No. 3, February, 1987, pp. 359-72.*

FURTHER READING

Blow, Suzanne. *Rhetoric in the Plays of Thomas Dekker.* Jacobean Drama Studies 3. Salzburg, Austria: Institut für Englische Sprache und Literatur, 1972, 138 p.
Examines the influence of Renaissance rhetorical theory on Dekker's plays.

Bradford, Gamaliel. "The Women of Dekker." *The Sewanee Review* XXXIII, No. 2 (April 1925): 284-90.
Lauds the characterizations of women in Dekker's dramas, concluding that Bellafront in *The Honest Whore* is the most poignant.

Brown, Arthur. "Citizen Comedy and Domestic Drama." In *Jacobean Theatre*, edited by John Russell Brown and Bernard Harris, pp. 63-83. Stratford-upon-Avon Studies 1. London: Edward Arnold, 1960.
Treats Dekker as representative of a trend in Elizabethan and Jacobean theater which contrasts with the tradition represented by Ben Jonson. Brown concludes that Dekker "wrote in a popular and romantic vein" which

was more concerned with plot than was Jonson's rhetorical and intellectual drama.

Bullen, A. H. "Thomas Dekker." In the *Dictionary of National Biography*, Volume 5, edited by Leslie Stephen and Sidney Lee, pp. 747-50. New York: The Macmillan Company, 1908.
General overview of Dekker's life and major works.

———. "Thomas Dekker." In his *Elizabethans*, pp. 73-94. New York: E. P. Dutton, 1924.
Discusses the historical records of Dekker's activities and gives summaries and brief appraisals of many of his dramas and pamphlets.

Conover, James H. *Thomas Dekker: An Analysis of Dramatic Structure.* The Hague, Netherlands: Mouton, 1969, 250 p.
Evaluates Dekker's handling of plot, characterization, setting, and dramatic action, concluding that while Dekker's plays are in some regards uneven and display a "peculiar lack of development of growth" over the dramatist's career, they also reveal Dekker's distinct "sense of theatre, his ability to 'put on a good show'."

Dawson, Anthony B. "Witchcraft/Bigamy: Cultural Conflict in *The Witch of Edmonton.*" *Renaissance Drama* XX (1989): 77-98.
Discusses *The Witch of Edmonton* in terms of Jacobean social roles and mores.

Ellis-Fermor, Una. "Thomas Dekker." In *Shakespeare's Contemporaries*, edited by Max Bluestone and Norman Rabkin, pp. 157-65. Englewood Cliffs, N. J.: Prentice-Hall, 1961.
Reprints Ellis-Fermor's discussion of Dekker in her *The Jacobean Drama: An Interpretation* (1953), in which she analyzes Dekker's poetry, plot construction, and characterizations in his dramas.

Garber, Marjorie. "The Logic of the Transvestite: *The Roaring Girl (1608).*" In *Staging the Renaissance: Reinterpretations of Elizabethan and Jacobean Drama*, edited by David Scott Kastan and Peter Stallybrass, pp. 221-34. New York: Routledge, Chapman and Hall, 1991.
Treats issues of gender identity and social mores in *The Roaring Girl*, comparing the careers of the historical Mary Frith and other cross-dressers with that of the stage character Moll Cut-purse.

Gerrard, Ernest A. "Thomas Dekker (Play-dresser)." In his *Elizabethan Drama and Dramatists, 1583-1603*, pp. 279-97. Oxford: Oxford University Press, 1928.
Biographical and bibliographical essay that describes Dekker as a gifted playwright and ascribes the sources of several Shakespearean plays to Dekker.

Gregg, Kate L. *Thomas Dekker: A Study in Economic and Social Backgrounds.* Seattle: University of Washington Press, 1924, 112 p.
Considers the evidently contradictory judgments of mercantile capitalism expressed in Dekker's works, which generally laud commerce as the source of many blessings, yet condemn hardships brought about by the inequalities it produced. Gregg concludes that "Dekker's hedging between extremes [of praise and blame] seems to be typically English."

Haselkorn, Anne M. "The Puritan View: Thomas Dekker." In her *Prostitution in Elizabethan and Jacobean Comedy*, pp. 115-39. Troy, N. Y.: The Whitston Publishing Company, 1983.

Analyzes *The Honest Whore* as a record of the Puritan view of prostitution. Haselkorn argues that although the marriage of Matheo and Bellafront represents Dekker's attempt to "deal with the whore's problem in a constructive manner worthy of his Puritan ideals," such a "forced marriage, even to a 'born-again' whore, was not a felicitous solution for the harlot and for the social discard she married."

Hoy, Cyrus. *Introductions, Notes, and Commentaries to texts in 'The Dramatic Works of Thomas Dekker' Edited by Fredson Bowers.* 4 vols. Cambridge: Cambridge University Press, 1980.

Critical introductions and comments to accompany Bowers's 1953-61 collection of *The Dramatic Works of Thomas Dekker,* including plays known to be by Dekker as well as some attributed to him.

MacIntyre, Jeanne. "Shore's Wife and *The Shoemaker's Holiday.*" In *Cahiers Élisabéthains* 39 (April 1991): 17-28.

Discusses the influence of other works, especially dramas about Jane Shore, on *The Shoemaker's Holiday.*

Miller, Edwin Haviland. "Thomas Dekker, Hack Writer." In *Notes and Queries* II, No. 4 (April 1955): 145-50.

Cites earlier works of Elizabethan literature concerning rogues to demonstrate that *The Belman of London* "added little to the revelations of [Dekker's] forerunners," and that *Lanthorne and Candle-Light* "provides . . . only a framework for borrowed material."

Novarr, David. "Dekker's Gentle Craft and the Lord Mayor of London." *Modern Philology* LVII, No. 4 (May 1960): 233-39.

Examines contemporary events which may have influenced the plot of *The Shoemaker's Holiday,* suggesting particularly that the characterization of Sir Roger Otley parodies Sir John Spencer, an unpopular politician who was Lord Mayor of London in 1594-95.

Price, George R. *Thomas Dekker.* New York: Twayne Publishers, 1969, 189 p.

Discusses in detail matters of Dekker's biography and offers critical and historical discussions of his works.

Robbins, Larry M. Introduction to *Thomas Dekker's "A Knights Conjuring" (1607): A Critical Edition,* edited by Larry M. Robbins. The Hague, Netherlands: Mouton, 1974.

Surveys the background and narrative strategies of Dekker's pamphlet *A Knight's Conjuring.*

Shaw, Phillip. "The Position of Thomas Dekker in Jacobean Prison Literature." In *Publications of the Modern Language Association of America* LXII, No. 2 (June 1947): 366-91.

Evaluates Dekker's depiction of prison conditions in his plays and pamphlets. "It is evident," Shaw observes, "that the study of works appearing during the reign of James I in the literary genre of prison writings is principally an examination of the contributions of Thomas Dekker to the category."

Shirley, Peggy Faye. *Serious and Tragic Elements in the Comedy of Thomas Dekker.* Jacobean Dramatic Studies 50. Salzburg, Austria: Institut für Englische Sprache und Literatur, 1975, 132 p.

Examines Dekker's use of non-comic devices in *The Shoemaker's Holiday, Old Fortunatus,* and *If It Be Not Good, the Devil Is in It.*

Small, Roscoe Addison. "Thomas Dekker." In his *The Stage-Quarrel Between Ben Jonson and the So-Called Poetasters,* pp. 118-32. 1899. Reprint. New York: AMS Press, 1966.

Relates Dekker's part in the War of the Theaters.

Thornton, George E. *The Social and Moral Philosophy of Thomas Dekker.* The Emporia State Research Studies 4. Emporia, Kansas: Kansas State Teachers College, 1955. 36 p.

Postulates Dekker's ethical ideas by examining *The Honest Whore* and *The Shoemaker's Holiday.*

Ure, Peter. "Patient Madman and Honest Whore: the Middleton-Dekker Oxymoron." In his *Elizabethan and Jacobean Drama,* edited by J. C. Maxwell, pp. 187-208. New York: Barnes & Noble Books, 1974.

Explores the seeming contradictions exhibited by the characters and plot of *The Honest Whore,* attempting to decide which are meant to reveal essential points and which are unintentional contradictions. Ure concludes that "the coupling of [Dekker's] name with Middleton's is the last oxymoron, and perhaps the most fascinating."

Additional coverage of Dekker's life and career is contained in the following source published by Gale Research: *Dictionary of Literary Biography,* Vol. 62.

Elizabethan Drama

INTRODUCTION

Elizabethan drama specifically refers to works produced during the reign of Elizabeth I (1533-1603), but the term is also commonly applied to plays written during the rule of her two immediate successors, James I and Charles I, up to the time of Parliament's closing of the public theaters in 1642. Christopher Marlowe, John Webster, Ben Jonson, and other playwrights of the period, which is also referred to as the Golden Age of English literature and the English Renaissance, helped create a distinctively English drama by combining classical, medieval, and indigenous elements. In this pantheon of playwrights, William Shakespeare occupies a unique position, revered by scholars and the theater-going public as the most important dramatist in the history of English literature. Critically acclaimed for their poetic language, innovative dramaturgy, and penetrating insight into the human condition, the Elizabethan playwrights produced a corpus that Felix E. Schelling has described as "the most universal and imaginative, the most spontaneous and heterogeneous literature in dramatic form which has yet come from the hand of man."

Elizabethan drama had its origin in the liturgy of the medieval Roman Catholic Church. Town craftsmen, organized in guilds, enacted episodes from the Bible and the lives of the saints to celebrate the sacred festivals of the liturgical year. Originally performed in the church nave, these miracle and mystery plays, as they are commonly known, were eventually moved to platforms outside the church building in order to accommodate large crowds; in time they left the church grounds altogether and toured the streets with movable stages called pageants. Devotional in their inception, the liturgical dramas increasingly became secularized through the introduction of humor, dress, and personages familiar to the contemporary audience. The mystery plays gradually evolved into morality dramas that additionally drew upon traditional English folk legends and allegories replete with knights and national heroes. These didactic pieces were intended to teach the audience Catholic tenets regarding salvation by employing personified abstractions like Mercy, Riches, and Death in their treatment of such issues as the power of evil, the human quest to do good, and the fear of eternal punishment. Though serious in tone, the morality plays were not lacking in humor; the character of Vice, originally a sinister representation of evil, evolved into a humorous figure providing comic relief with his verbal and physical assaults. The appearance of such a roguish character simultaneously met the audience's increasing demand for dramatic action. Morality plays were also enlivened by interludes. These lively discussions of the intellectual interests of the day turned the audience's attention to the physical world and its problems, thus further contributing to the secularization of the drama. In addition to the medi-eval influences, the works of the Latin playwrights Seneca, Terence, and Plautus had a significant impact on the development of Elizabethan drama. As early as 1331, Italian Renaissance writers had composed Senecan tragedies and comedies based on Terence's plays; the period of Latin imitation intensified in 1427 when twelve lost comedies of Plautus were recovered. By 1520 the revival of classical drama had reached England, as evidenced by a production that year of a Plautine comedy performed for Henry VIII. The Elizabethans sometimes leaned heavily on the Roman models, on occasion even going so far as to render English historical themes in Latin, as in Thomas Legge's 1579 production of *Richard Tertius Tragedia*.

Scholars generally divide Elizabethan dramas into history plays, comedies, and tragedies. Distinctly native in form and subject, the histories, or "chronicles," were originally a blending of the medieval mystery and morality plays, as in John Bale's *Kynge Johan* (1538), which combines real historical figures with abstract characters to create a polemical drama criticizing the Roman papacy. While the earliest history plays had little interest in the causes and effects of history, by the end of the sixteenth century, playwrights like Marlowe in *Edward II* (1592-93) began to search out the meaning of scattered historical events and analyze history in terms of personalities and opposing political forces. Marlowe's stress on the importance of character over action as the drama's unifying force was imitated by other Elizabethan playwrights such as John Fletcher, Thomas Heywood, and Webster. Likewise Shakespeare, in such plays as *Richard III* (1592-93), *Richard II* (1595), and *Henry V* (1599), followed Marlowe in uniting character with dramatic action—so much so that, in the words of Fredson Bowers, in Shakespeare's plays "history can no longer be felt as an independent action," separable from character. Immensely popular as expressions of national pride during the reign of Elizabeth, the histories faded into relative obscurity after the accession of James I. They had disappeared entirely from the stage by 1642.

Elizabethan comedy, like the histories, developed in part from native dramatic forms and was equally influenced by folk games and the performances of wandering entertainers, dancers, and jugglers. Amalgamating these traditional elements with the stock characters and motifs of Roman comedy, the Elizabethans inaugurated their own brand of high comedy—humor based on thought rather than horseplay—which is acclaimed for its narrative complexity and provocative moral ambiguity. Furthermore, scholars assert, the success of Elizabethan comedy was due in large part to its use of language, which captured the daily intercourse, foibles, and feelings of ordinary people. Playwrights like John Lyly, Thomas Dekker, and Robert Greene, among others, enriched the form with their protean verse, permitting richly detailed characterization and a high degree of realism. It was Shakespeare, however, who was the most markedly eclectic in his appropriation of stylistic elements, not only from Roman classicism, but from French popular farce and modern Italian drama as well. In the romantic comedies *A Midsummer Night's Dream* (1595-96), *As You Like It* (1599), and *Twelfth Night* (1601-02), he focused on the themes of marriage and courtship, creating imaginary "realms" that provide an escape from societal restraints, allowing for a happy resolution of conflict usually involving marriage and a return to a reinvigorated society. Another form of comedy, the comedy of humors, was formulated by Jonson in his *Every Man in His Humour* (1598). In his masterpieces *Volpone; Or, the Fox* (1606) and *The Alchemist* (1610), he combined comedy with intrigue to expose humanity's villainy, greed, and foolhardiness. Satirizing humankind's failures and absurdities, he mocked Elizabethan society's conventions, thereby paving the way for the comedy of manners associated with Restoration drama. At the same time writers like Webster, Philip Marston, and George Chapman produced popular comedies of the life of the London bourgeoisie, while others such as Fletcher and Francis Beaumont collaborated to create tragi-comedies—serious dramas with surprisingly happy dénouements—like *Philaster, Or Love Lies A-Bleeding* (1608-10), which contrasts the love of a young prince and a gross rival for the daughter of a kingly usurper. Varied and eclectic, the Elizabethan comedy is acknowledged for its imaginative interpretation of human nature and its verisimilitude, leading critics like Ashley H. Thorndike to describe it as "low and high, refined and boisterous, witty and farcical, fantastic and realistic."

Elizabethan tragedy is considered to have attained the highest degree of development of the three major genres of the period. Scholars generally divide the tragedies into three groups. The first, *de casibus* tragedy, typically traces a hero's rise to fame and the eventual fall that results from his overweening ambition and lust for power. Originating in the Senecan tragedies *Troades, Thyestes,* and *Oedipus,* this dramatic type appealed to Renaissance audiences, which typically viewed humanity as genuinely helpless, despite its pretensions to power, before a relentless and inflexible world. Suspenseful and shocking, *de casibus* tragedy often depicts political struggles, particularly those of ancient Rome, as in Chapman's *Caesar and Pompey* (1605-12), Shakespeare's *Antony and Cleopatra* (1606-07), and Heywood's *Rape of Lucrece* (1608). The second type, revenge tragedy, focuses on the turbulent dealings and inhuman cruelty of notable persons, and is characterized by an air of brooding fate. This genre was also influenced by the works of Seneca, as well as by the Italian *novella*—popular Renaissance stories depicting the worst of human behavior—often mixing love, lust, and jealousy with political intrigue. Employing such devices as ghosts, prophecies, and a bloody finale, revenge tragedy is praised for its ability to arouse horror and excitement in the audience. In Thomas Kyd's *The Spanish Tragedy* (1585-90), which critics regard as the prototype of all English revenge tragedies, Hieronimo seeks vengeance for the murder of his son by the heartless and calculating Lorenzo, who emerges as the first Machiavellian villain in modern drama. Other examples include Marlowe's *The Famous Tragedy of the Rich Jew of Malta* (1590?) and Webster's *The Tragedy of*

the Dvtchesse of Malfy (1614); Shakespeare's *Hamlet* (1600-01) is regarded as the highest development of the revenge motif. The third species, domestic tragedy, departs from the historical and foreign themes found in *de casibus* and revenge tragedies. Domestic tragedies relate the troubled affairs and values of ordinary middle-class people; the story line typically centers on a farmer or merchant who commits murder out of love or greed but who in the end feels remorse for the deed and seeks reconciliation with God. Also referred to as "dramas of common life," domestic tragedies, like Heywood's *A Woman Killed with Kindness* (1603), are sometimes considered inferior works, critically censored for their exploitation of sentiment at the expense of ethical analysis. Scholars point out that although *de casibus,* revenge, and domestic tragedies are distinctive genres, they all portray pyramidal rises and falls. This similarity has led critics to suggest that such vividly evoked upheavals reflect a generalized fear among the period's playwrights that underlying social, political, and religious tensions would upset the hierarchical order of the Elizabethan world.

Commentators often attribute the success of the Elizabethan drama to its emphasis on the interplay between stage, playwright, and audience. The structure of the theaters was derived from the arrangement of contemporary courtyards of inns which earlier had proved eminently suited to the presentation of touring plays. The interior of the playhouses featured a hollow square surrounded by balconies from which wealthy patrons looked down; the stage projected out into the open yard in which the poor classes, or groundlings, stood. Some members of the audience even sat on the stage itself; thus in the Elizabethan theater there was little physical separation of actors and spectators. The first permanent playhouse, the Theatre, was constructed in 1576, followed by the Swan in 1595, and the most famous, the Globe, in 1599. Although much debate has been engendered regarding the architecture and the stage arrangements of the Elizabethan theater, historians concur that the pattern was either a circular or many-sided building with a tower to which the audience was summoned by means of a trumpet blast and the flying of a flag. Although the playhouses were vastly popular, Puritans, like T. White, decried them as "a continual monument of London's prodigality and folly," and the City administration prohibited performances within the limits of the City of London; therefore the theaters were constructed on the outskirts. The establishment of permanent structures for the presentations of plays was accompanied by the emergence of professional acting companies like the Queen's Company, the Lord Admiral's Men, and the King's Men, of which Shakespeare was a leader. The companies sought protection and financial support from wealthy aristocratic patrons; Elizabeth I, as well as her successors, actively patronized the companies, regarding the dramatic presentations as nothing more than "harmless spenders of time." Since women could not be professional players, boys assumed the female roles; child actors were recruited from often highly accomplished children's companies like the Children of the Chapel Royal Company.

While Elizabethan drama was in many respects a precursor of Restoration drama, it received little critical attention in the late seventeenth century and throughout the eighteenth. Scholarly interest was awakened in 1808 with the publication of Charles Lamb's laudatory *Specimens of English Dramatic Poets who Lived about the Time of Shakespeare,* followed a decade later by William Hazlitt's *Lectures chiefly on the Dramatic Literature of the Age of Elizabeth* (1820), which offered a sustained critical examination of numerous playwrights of the period, placing them in their cultural and literary contexts. By the early twentieth century, the Elizabethan dramatists as a group stood in high critical repute, as evidenced by Algernon Charles Swinburne's extravagant praise of them as a "generation of giants and gods." Critics like John W. Cunliffe and T. S. Eliot investigated the affinity between Greek, medieval, and Elizabethan theater. In 1923 E. K. Chambers described the theatrical companies, individual playhouses, and Elizabethan court in his four-volume work *The Elizabethan Stage,* which is considered one of the most comprehensive treatments of the historical and technical aspects of the theater. During the latter half of the twentieth century, critical attention has been focused in many directions, including the relationship of drama to Elizabethan politics and culture, the nature of theatrical representation in the period, the function of the audience and its effect on the dramatic production, and many others, including the foreign influences on Elizabethan literature. While some critics, like Brander Matthews, have warned against "indiscriminate praise" of the Elizabethan playwrights by highlighting deficiencies in dramatic unity and structure, most concur with Allardyce Nicoll's evaluation that "Avidly attracted by show, unafraid to display their passions, intensely interested in men, the Elizabethans found their truest artistic expression in the drama." "We are," he adds, "the richer for it."

REPRESENTATIVE WORKS

Chapman, George
    Bussy D'Ambois   1604
    Caesar and Pompey   1605-12
    The Revenge of Bussy D'Ambois   1610-11
Daniel, Samuel
    The Tragedy of Cleopatra   1594
    The Queen's Arcadia: A Pastorall Trage-Comedie
    1605
    Hymen's Triumph   1614
Dekker, Thomas
    The Shomakers Holiday. Or the Gentle Craft
    1599
    The Roaring Girle, or, Moll Cut Purse   1611
Fletcher, John
    The Faithful Shepherdess   1608
    Philaster, Or Love Lies a-Bleeding   [with Francis
    Beaumont] 1608-10
    The Maid's Tragedy   [with Francis Beaumont]
    1609-11
Heywood, Thomas
    The Four Prentices of London   1594-1600
    A Woman Killed with Kindness   1603
    The Rape of Lucrece   1608

Jonson, Ben
    Every Man in His Humour   1598
    Volpone; Or, the Fox   1606
    The Alchemist   1610
Kyd, Thomas
    The Spanish Tragedy   1585-90
Lyly, John
    The Woman in the Moone   1583?
    Sapho and Phao   1584
    Endimion, The Man in the Moone   1588
Marlowe, Christopher
    *Tamburlaine the Great: Divided into two Tragicall
    Discourses*   1587, 1588
    The Famous Tragedy of the Rich Jew of Malta
    1590?
    Edward II   1592-93
    The Tragicall History of the Life and Death of Doctor Faustus   1593?
Massinger, Philip
    The Duke of Milan   1621-22
    A New Way to Pay Old Debts   1625
    The Roman Actor   1629
Shakespeare, William
    A Midsummer Night's Dream   1595-96
    Romeo and Juliet   1595-96
    Much Ado About Nothing   1598-99
    Henry V   1599
    As You Like It   1599
    Julius Caesar   1599
    Hamlet   1600-01
    Twelfth Night   1601-02
    Othello   1604
    Macbeth   1606
Webster, John
    *The White Divel, or, the Tragedy of Paulo Giordano
    Ursini, Duke of Brachiano, With The Life and
    Death of Vittoria Corombona the famous Venetian Curtizan*   1612
    The Tragedy Of The Dvtchesse Of Malfy   1614

ORIGINS AND INFLUENCES

Brander Matthews

[*An American scholar, educator, and novelist, Matthews began his literary career by lecturing, contributing extensively to various periodicals, and writing plays. In 1900 he was appointed professor of dramatic literature at Columbia University, becoming the first person to hold such a title at any American university. His published works, including* The Development of the Drama *(1903),* Shakspere as a Playwright *(1913), and* The Principles of Playmaking *(1919), reflect his interest in the practical as opposed to the theoretical aspects of drama. In the essay below, he attempts to perform a balanced assessment of Elizabethan drama as a whole, giv-*

ing due weight to its shortcomings as well as its merits. He attributes many of the dramas' defects to the pressures imposed by audiences' taste and expectations: "When we consider how rank was the quality [of Elizabethan playgoers], how deficient their education, how harsh their experience of life, how rude their likings, the wonder is not that the play prepared for their pleasure was often violent and arbitrary and coarse, but rather that any play devised to delight them was ever logical and elevated, shapely and refined."]

There is no denying that the dominant characteristic of the English-speaking race is energy, and that this energy never expressed itself in literature more completely than it did in the later years of Elizabeth's reign. There was then the most abundant revelation of the power and passion of this sturdy people, the most magnificent luxuriance of its essential imagination, and a sudden outflowering of the vigor of a hardy and prolific stock. And above all the turmoil of those spacious days there towered aloft the genius of Shakespeare. Small wonder is it that many lovers of literature have been blinded by the effulgence of all this genius and have closed their eyes to all except its glory, unable to perceive anything but absolute perfection. So long have we made a habit of using a megaphone to proclaim its manifest and manifold beauties, that a microphone would suffice for our infrequent and unwilling admissions that all was not equally faultless in this splendid era. I can still recall the shock of surprise with which—when I was yet an undergraduate in college—I came across a passage in one of Matthew Arnold's essays seeming to suggest that there might be weak places in Shakespeare's works, and that even his genius did not always maintain him at the topmost pinnacle of transcendent achievement.

But to adopt an attitude of insistent admiration is to renounce the privilege and the duty of criticism, as Gautier did when he declared that, if ever he found a single line of Hugo's to fall short in any way, he would not confess it to himself alone, in a cellar, on a dark night. We deny ourselves the pleasure of knowing wherein the Elizabethan poets are truly mighty, if we give them all credit for all possible excellence, or if we carelessly fail to see clearly that even the mightiest of them does not always sustain himself at his highest level. The work of the great Elizabethans is what it is; and for that we love it. But also it is not what it is not; and we ought to be honest enough not to claim for it the qualities which it lacks, and which it could not have because they are inconsistent with those it actually has. Largeness of vision it has, and depth of insight, and the gift of life itself, and many another manifestation of the energy of the race. These possessions are beyond question; and yet, because it possesses these qualities, because it has sweep, and penetration, youthful daring and robust vitality, it is often violent, often trivial, often grotesque. Reckless and ill-restrained, it is likely to be wanting in taste and lacking in logic. Energy it has above all things else, and a compelling imaginative fire; but balance and proportion it rarely reveals. Only infrequently do we find symmetry and harmony,—qualities seemingly incompatible with the wastefulness of effort always characteristic of this masterful people.

More than any other group of the Elizabethans, have the dramatists suffered from this practice of indiscriminate praise and from the absence of measured appreciation. Sometimes it seems as though the commentators have chosen wilfully to shut their eyes to everything they would wish away. They have made no effort to free themselves from the spell of Lamb's contagious enthusiasm; and they have not resisted the evil influence of the extravagant eulogy habitual with Mr. Swinburne, whose overpowering rhetoric once bade fair to have as pernicious an effect on literary criticism as Ruskin's overpowering rhetoric had for a while upon pictorial criticism. As Ruskin misled many and discouraged more, who, under wiser guidance, might have learned in time to take keen pleasure in the painter's art, so Swinburne by his indiscriminate over-praise must have repelled many a reader who might have been lured into a liking for the real value of the Elizabethan dramatic poets, if this had been modestly set forth.

Many commentators and critics yield themselves up to be hypnotized by the dramatic poet they are dealing with, crediting him with a host of merits and refusing to counterbalance their commendation by allowing weight even to such demerits as they are compelled to record. An amusing instance of this abdication of the critical function can be found in the introduction to *Old Fortunatus* in the Temple Dramatists, in which the editor is permitted to say that this comedy of Dekker's "though containing numberless faults in construction, in weak and ineffective character-drawing, and in improbable psychological deduction, is nevertheless one of the greatest of Elizabethan dramas." Surely, this is the very negation of criticism, to call a piece containing "numberless faults" one of the "greatest of dramas." Such writing is disheartening, not to term it dishonest. The truth is that *Old Fortunatus* is only a narrative in dialogue, and it has little dramaturgic merit; its character-drawing is mere prentice-work; and it pleases because of its primitive unpretentiousness and its fleeting glimpses of poetry. It has none of the broad humor or of the hearty veracity of character which lends charm to Dekker's *Shoemaker's Holiday,* a brisk comedy of the contemporary life of London which the sturdy author knew so well and relished so keenly.

In considering the lack of play-making skill, abundantly evident in the works of the Elizabethan poets, two points must ever be borne in mind. The first of these is that the literary form which happens to be popular and therefore profitable, in any period, attracts to it many who have little or no native gift for that special art. In the nineteenth century, for example, the vogue of the novel was overwhelming; and many a man of letters, who had but a small share of the narrative faculty, undertook to express himself in fiction. So, at the end of the sixteenth century, the drama was the one field in which an aspiring genius might hope to make money; and it is not surprising, therefore, to find only a few among all the mass of Elizabethan dramatic poets who either were born playwrights, or who took the trouble, by dint of hard work, to master the secrets of the craft. Marlowe, for one, had no natural bent toward the theatre; and Webster, for another, for all his striving after the horrible, does not prove his possession of the native endowment of the instinctive playmaker.

Marlowe and Webster were poets, beyond all question; they were richly endowed with imagination; but they were not born playwrights.

The second point to be kept in memory is that the dramatic art was not highly esteemed in Elizabeth's time. The theatre was a means whereby a poet might earn his living; but plays were not held to be literature; they were devised only to satisfy the three hours' traffic of the stage; they were looked down upon by men of letters, much as journalism is looked down upon today. Accustomed as we are to consider the drama as the chief glory of Elizabethan literature, we do not always remember that the Elizabethans themselves scarcely held it to be literature at all. Nothing is more significant of this contemporary opinion than the fact that Shakespeare corrected the proof of his two narrative poems carefully, while he gave no thought to the printing of his plays, carelessly abandoning the manuscripts to his comrades of the theatre. One result of this contemptuous attitude toward the drama was that the poet was not held to any high standard, and that what was good enough for the rude playgoing public of those turbulent times was often good enough for the playwright himself.

Perhaps it is well also to note a third point, the recalling of which will help us to understand certain of the dramaturgic deficiencies of those days; and this is that the drama had not yet come into its own. It was still imperfectly differentiated; it had not disengaged itself from elements wholly undramatic. Just as the Greek drama in the time of Æschylus retained a lyrical element which often delayed the movement of the play itself, so the English drama in the time of Shakespeare had not purged itself of functions which had nothing to do with the setting of a story on the stage. It needs to be remembered that, in those early days, the theatre was not only the theatre; it was also, to a certain extent, the newspaper, the lecture-hall and even the pulpit. So it is that we find the dramatic poet sometimes halting his plot to deliver a lecture or a sermon, which his audience received gladly, but which clogged the movement of his action, and which is seen now to be a hindrance to the artistic shaping of his plot.

Here we touch the connection between the drama as it was under Elizabeth and the drama as it had been under Henry VIII and his predecessors. There is close kinship between the mysteries and miracle-plays of the Middle Ages and the masterpieces of Marlowe and even of Shakespeare. The outward form of the drama is always conditioned by the actual theatre in which it is performed and to which it has to be adjusted. The unroofed playhouses of London in 1600 were wholly unlike our snug modern theatres; and the conditions of the performances therein were very like those under which the mysteries had been acted. A mod

In every epoch when the drama has flourished,—in Athens in the days of Sophocles, in Madrid in the days of Lope de Vega, in London in the days of Shakespeare and in Paris in the days of Molière,—the dramatists have always adjusted their plays to the special theatre in which these were to be performed and to the special audience before whom these were to be acted. The severe drama of Sophocles is not shaped in closer accord with the conditions of

A portrait of Queen Elizabeth I.

the huge theatre of Dionysos than is the tumultuous drama of Shakespeare fitted to the wholly different conditions of the rude Globe Theatre. And when we consider what were the actual circumstances of performance in the Globe Theatre, our wonder is not that the structure of Shakespeare's plays is often straggling and slovenly, but rather that the great dramatist was ever able to attain to a more seemly conduct of his plot, such as he did achieve in *Othello* and in *Macbeth*. Perhaps, indeed, there is no better proof of the might of Shakespeare's genius than this,—that now and again he was able to overcome conditions which seem to be unconquerable, and to produce a play which endures for all time even though it was originally adjusted adroitly to the circumstances of performance upon a semimediæval stage.

Furthermore, the Elizabethan dramatist not only put his plays together in conformity with the customary methods of representation that obtained in the Elizabethan theatre, he also kept in mind always the audience before which they were to be produced. It was for the playgoer of the present that he exerted himself; it was not for the reader of the future. It was the playgoer he had to please; and for the playwright there is never any appeal from the verdict of the playhouse itself. As those "who live to please, must please to live," the playwright is ever dependent upon the public of his own time and of his own town.

The absence of standards and the contemporary contempt of the acted drama, account for many of the defects of the plays of that renowned period; but the chief cause is ever to be sought in the necessity of pleasing a special public, probably far more brutal in its longings than any other to which a great dramatist has had to appeal. The Athenians, for whom Sophocles built his massive and austere tragedies, and the Parisians, for whom Molière painted the humorous portrait of our common humanity,—these were quite other than the mob before whom Shakespeare had to set his studies from life, a mob stout of stomach for sheer horrors and shrinking from no atrocity. It is the Elizabethan public which is mainly responsible for the fact that the Elizabethan drama, glorious as it is with splendid episodes, taken separately, has only a few masterpieces, only a few plays the conduct of which does not continually disappoint even a cordial reader. As M. Jusserand has pointed out, with the calm sanity which is characteristic of French criticism, it is not difficult to select many "luminous parts, scenes brilliant or tragic, moving passages, characters solidly set on their feet," but it is very rare indeed to find complete wholes sustained as a lofty level of art, "plays entirely satisfactory, strongly conceived, firmly knit together, carried to an inevitable conclusion."

Why take the trouble to knit a story strongly and to deduce its inevitable conclusion, when the public the play had to please cared nothing for this artistic victory? Not only did the playgoers of those days find no fault with the lack of plausibility in the conduct of the story, with sudden and impossibly quick changes in character, with coincidences heaped up and with arbitrary artificialities accumulated; but these, indeed, were the very qualities they most enjoyed. They preferred the unusual, the unexpected, the illogical; and it was to behold startling turns of fortune and to get the utmost of surprise that they went to the theatre. To us in the twentieth century it seems strangely unnatural that the jealousy of Leontes should flame up violently and almost without pretext: but to them in the sixteenth century this was a pleasure. To us there is annoyance in the huddling of two and three several stories into a single play, wholly unconnected, the joyous and the gruesome side by side, and in no wise tied together; but to them this was entirely satisfactory, for it gave them variety, and this was what they were seeking. Where we like to find the finger of fate pointing out the inevitable end, they would rather have the climax brought about by the long arm of coincidence; and this is the reason why we must be ready to "make believe," when we surrender ourselves to the charm of these semimediæval poet playwrights. We must be willing to adventure ourselves in a maze of unreality, in a false world differing widely from the real world in which we live and in which cause must go before effect.

No doubt, there were gallants sitting on the stage who had some tincture of cultivation; and there must have been other men of some education in the rooms of the gallery. But the most of those who stood in the yard below were unable to write or to read. Among them were discharged soldiers home from the wars, sailors from the ships of Frobisher and Drake, runaway apprentices and all the riffraff and rabble of a seaport town which happens also to be the capital of an expanding nation. They were violent in their likings, with a constant longing for horse-play and ribaldry, and with a persistent hankering after scenes of lust and

gore. They were used to cock-fighting and bear-baiting and bull-baiting; and these brutal sports were shown sometimes within the very building where on other occasions there were performances of those raw tragedies-of-blood, the sole plays on the stage which could stir the nerves of such a public. These supporters of the stage were used to battle, murder and sudden death, not only in the theatre, but in daily life, for there were scores of public executions every year; and in those spectacular times the headsman of the Tower was a busy man, with his ghastly trophies frequently renewed on the spikes of the gate.

The pressure of the main body of playgoers upon the playwrights was not unwholesome then, as it is not unwholesome now, in so far as it led the dramatic poets to avoid preciosity and to eschew style-mongering; in so far as it forced them to deal directly with life, and to handle passion boldly and amply. But the playgoers of those days had cruder likings also; they craved constant excitement, both for the eye and for the ear; and the aspiring playwright gave them good measure, pressed down and running over. For the pleasure of the eye, he lavished processions, coronations, funerals, encampments, single combats and serried battles. For the pleasure of the ear, he was prolific of songs, melancholy or smutty; and he never stinted such other sounds as he could command, the roll of the drum, the staccato call of the trumpet, the clangor of loud bells, the rattle of musketry and the long reverberation of thunder. Sheeted ghosts and bloody spectres were sure of their welcome in advance; and the playwright was prompt to produce them whenever he had an excuse. He knew also that these ignorant playgoers had a rough sense of fun and liked to laugh heartily; and so he sprinkled throughout his pieces a variety of ingenious retorts and of obvious repartees, even descending now and again to get his laugh by the more mechanical humor of a practical joke. Furthermore, he was aware that, gross as was the taste of the yardlings, they could enjoy pretty sentiment, sometimes presented with simple truth, and sometimes surcharged with the utmost of lyric exaggeration.

When we consider how rank was the quality of those who stood in the yard of the Globe in those days, how deficient their education, how harsh their experience of life, how rude their likings, the wonder is not that the play prepared for their pleasure was often violent and arbitrary and coarse, but rather that any play devised to delight them was ever logical and elevated, shapely and refined. If the best of Shakespeare is for eternity, the worst of him was frankly for the groundlings who were his contemporaries, and whose interest he had to arouse and to retain as best he could. It is evidence of the intense practicality which ever directed his conduct that he was in the habit of taking over old plays which had already proved their power to attract paying audiences. It is evidence of his strict adaptation of his plays to his semimediæval audiences that he had a total disregard of chronological, historic or geographic accuracy, giving clocks and cannons to the Romans and having the Italians going from Milan to Venice take ship when the tide served, because this was the mode of travel most familiar to the Londoner then. It is evidence of his understanding of his public that he is open in having his villains proclaim their own wickedness, so that the spectator might never be in doubt as to their motives.

In nothing else is the superiority of Shakespeare over his contemporaries more obvious than in the adroit dexterity with which he played upon the prejudices of his audience and made profit out of them. He sought always to give the spectators of his own time what he knew they wanted; and yet, now and again, perhaps a dozen times in the score of years of his play-making, uplifted by his genius and by his love of his craft, he looked above the spectators and beyond them, and he took a trouble they did not require of him. On these occasions, all too few, he made a play, pleasing to them indeed, but also pleasing to himself, and to his own intense artistic enjoyment of technical mastery. So it happens that we have the compact and logical *Othello,* as well as the sprawling and incoherent *Cymbeline,* which came long after.

The most of his contemporaries, brilliant as they were and highly gifted, were incapable of this, and they were unable to profit by the example Shakespeare had set them in those of his plays in which he was himself interested enough to do his best and to put forth his full strength. It is because he is at his best only on occasion, and when the spirit of perfection moved him, that he founded no school. He was not a master to follow unhesitatingly, partly because the mark at which he aimed was not always the best target for others, since he was willing often to let the incomparable felicity of the poet cover up and cloak the careless planning of the playwright; and partly also because no weaker arm could bend the bow of Ulysses. His chief gift was uncommunicable; it was the power of endowing all his creatures with independent life. This power is the test of his work; and it never leaves him. We discover it abundantly even in his most recklessly arbitrary plots, and even in those of his episodes which are based on a childish make-believe. It is not to the credit of critics, like Brandes, that they gloss over the absurdities that abound in Shakespeare's plays because Shakespeare was ready enough to give the spectators of his own time the puerile devices they delighted in,—the pound of flesh and the trial of the caskets in the *Merchant of Venice,* for example, and the test of the affection of Lear's daughter, when that fatherly monarch, unless he was already imbecile, ought to have learned the characters of his children in the long years of their family-life. If a critic does not see these absurdities, if he is blind to the arbitrary and muddled plot of *Cymbeline* and to the shocking callousness of the last act of *Much Ado about Nothing,* then we may well doubt whether he is really able to appreciate the masterly simplicity of *Othello* and the orderly richness of *Romeo and Juliet.*

The significant fact is that Shakespeare was, after all, an Elizabethan; and that, like the others, he had to accept the conditions of a semimediæval theatre and to please a full-blooded public. The others cannot climb with him; but not infrequently he sinks with them. They were ready enough to be satisfied themselves when they had satisfied the playgoers of their own day. They had no hesitation in sacrificing consistency of character to immediate effect on the mass of spectators,—very much as their fellow playwrights in Spain were doing at the same time and for the

same reason. Climbing to impossible heights of honor or sinking to impossible depths of dishonor, abounding in the most romantic reversals of fortune and in the most inexplicable transformations of character, caring little for reality or even for plausibility, disregarding the delicacy of art no less than the veracity of nature, they were fertile in inventing striking episodes; and they failed, as a rule, to combine the several parts into a coherent whole, sustaining itself throughout and gathering power as it proceeded. Capable on occasion of the finest shadings of a subtle psychology, they were content for the most part with a bald daubing of character in the primary colors. In other words, they often proved themselves true poets, but far less frequently did they reveal themselves as real playwrights.

This is the reason why the flamboyant and iridescent eulogy of Swinburne is doing them an ill service to-day, while they gained greatly by the apt selection of Lamb, who artfully singled out the perfect passages. Only too often the parts are far finer than the whole; and Lamb presented the best bits so enticingly that he must have lured to disappointment many readers who went straight from his *Specimens* to the complete works of the several dramatic poets. Here also we may find an excuse for Hazlitt and for Lowell, who have praised these poets more especially as poets to be read in a library, while almost wholly neglecting to consider their plays as plays intended to be performed by actors in a theatre and before an audience. To Hazlitt and Lowell, these dramatic poets appealed primarily as poets; and that the poets were dramatists also rarely arrested the attention of either of these acute critics.

Of a certainty, there must be many other readers who are willing enough to follow the example of Hazlitt and of Lowell and to accept the pure poetry which is abundant in the works of the Elizabethan dramatists without caring to consider whether or not the plays enriched by this poetry are all that they ought to be merely as plays. Some of them may even be inclined to resent any attempt to call attention to the dramaturgic defects of plays possessing a host of splendid passages wherein poetry combines with psychology to give the keenest pleasure. Others there are who are willing to admit the existence of the defects themselves, but who deny the justice of a criticism which gauges the semimediæval playwrights by tests properly applicable only to the modern drama. This protest was voiced most persuasively not long ago by a devout admirer of the old dramatists who insisted on the impropriety of judging Marlowe and Massinger by the standards proper enough in judging Scribe and Ibsen.

There is a certain speciousness in this claim; but analysis shows that it was not valid. It may be unfair to weigh the semimediæval Marlowe and Massinger on the same scales as Scribe and Ibsen, who are moderns; but it is not unfair to measure them by the standards we can derive from the comparison of the greatest dramatists, both ancient and modern. If we find certain principles of the art of play-making exemplified in the best dramas of Æschylus and of Sophocles, of Shakespeare and of Molière, of Calderon and of Racine, of Beaumarchais and of Scribe, of Ibsen, of Sudermann and of Pinero, it is not unfair to consider these as the eternal verities of dramaturgy, and to point out that Marlowe and Massinger fail to achieve an excellence of which we find frequent examples all through the long history of the drama, some of them a score of centuries before Scribe and Ibsen were born.

At its best, the dramatist's art reveals itself as akin to the architect's; and a really good play ought to have a solid framework and a bold simplicity of planning, with a foundation broad enough to sustain the superstructure, however massive or however lofty this may prove to be. It ought to have unity of theme, freedom from all extraneous matter, veracity of motive, contrast of character, clearness of exposition, probability of incident, logical coherence, swift movement and culminating intensity of interest. These qualities can be found in *Agamemnon* and *Œdipus the King,* as well as in *Othello* and in *Tartuffe,* in the *Alcalde of Zalamea* and in *Phèdre,* in the *Barber of Seville* and in the *Ladies Battle,* in *Ghosts,* in *Magda* and in the *Second Mrs. Tanqueray.* But these qualities are not to be found in any large degree in *Doctor Faustus* or in the *Roman Actor;* and they are not often to be found in the plays of any of the Elizabethan dramatists,—far more often in Shakespeare than in any of the others.

And if these deficiencies exist, surely it is unwise to close our eyes to the fact; surely it is unjust to pretend that the Elizabethan drama, as a whole, possesses that which it has not; surely it is safer and honester to admit frankly that the art of building plays solidly and symmetrically was little cultivated by the Elizabethan dramatists, just as it was little considered by the Elizabethan critics. Surely, again, it is wisest to try to see things as they really are and to tell the truth about them, the whole truth, and nothing but the truth. Even in criticism, honesty is the best policy; and the Elizabethan poets are indisputably great enough to make it worth while for us to assure ourselves wherein their true greatness lies. They are none the less great as poets when we have seen clearly that—excepting Shakespeare—they are great as playwrights only occasionally, and almost, as it were, by accident. (pp. 604-15)

> *Brander Matthews, "The Truth About the Elizabethan Playwrights," in* The North American Review, *Vol. CLXXXIV, No. 610, March 1, 1907, pp. 604-15.*

Courthope on the barbarism of Elizabethan drama:

In truth [Marlowe's *The Jew of Malta*] shows that the average taste of Elizabethan audiences was not far raised above that of the Spanish populace at a bull-fight. By the vehemence and vigour of their craving for striking stage effects and strong emotions, they compelled even the greatest dramatists to make their tragic action bloody, and though Shakespeare, by the grandeur of his genius, kept this dramatic tendency on the whole within bounds, it cannot be denied that even in him there are scenes, which it is difficult reasonably to defend from Voltaire's reproach of "barbarism."

> *W. J. Courthope, in his* A History of English Poetry, *Vol. II, Macmillan and Co., 1897.*

Felix E. Schelling

[*An American scholar of English literature, Schelling was an editor, anthologist, and prolific writer whose notable works include* A Book of Elizabethan Lyrics *(1895),* English Literature during the Lifetime of Shakespeare *(1910), and* The English Lyric *(1913). His best known work,* Elizabethan Drama, 1588-1642 *(1908), has been described as a "landmark of comprehensiveness" for its full use of secondary as well as primary material. In the following excerpt taken from that work, Schelling surveys Elizabethan literature, acknowledging its strengths, shortcomings, and impact upon the English-speaking world.*]

Elizabethan literature is a term, employed somewhat loosely to denote the fruitful literary period which extends from the beginning of the reign of the last of the Tudor sovereigns to the Restoration of King Charles II (1558-1660). The term is defensible because, various and manifold as is the literature of this time, it is referable to that single impulse, justly called the Renaissance, which, working in ever-widening circles, transformed the medieval England of Chaucer into the modern England of Shakespeare.

The English drama, like the drama in other countries of Western Europe, began in the service of the Church, and at first was merely symbolic and a part of ceremonial. It later passed through the didactic state, and served as a useful handmaid of religion, as an illustrator of the scriptures, and a censor of morals and conduct. It was not until the reign of Henry VIII that dramatic productions came somewhat to put aside these ulterior aims and ends, frankly to avow the pleasure of their auditors as their purpose, and thus to emerge into existence for an artistic end. With these stages of initial growth behind it, the drama became an art; and more, it grew to be the peculiar art in which the worldly and vigorous yet ideal and poetical age of Elizabeth found its most lasting and characteristic expression. For English drama reached in the days of Shakespeare a diversity of species combined with a rare and pervading quality of literary excellence unsurpassed in the literature of other ages and countries; and it finally subsided into a paucity of form and poverty of content by the Restoration which is surprising in view of its previous history. Save for some rudimentary forms, artistic English drama begins with the reign of Elizabeth. Its first great impulse ends with the closing of the theaters, due to the approaching Commonwealth Wars, in 1642.

In the year 1600 Queen Elizabeth had three years yet to live; and James, practically assured of his succession, was waiting eagerly in the north for the event which was to raise him from the petty kingship of a small and divided realm to the sovereignty of what had already become one of the great powers of Europe. In this year Shakespeare was at the height of his popularity and without a rival. The dramatists, Lyly, Peele, Greene, Kyd, and Marlowe, Shakespeare's immediate predecessors, were all of them either dead or silent; and neither Beaumont, Fletcher, nor Massinger had yet begun to write. In *Henry V,* Shakespeare had recently completed—save for the single play of *Henry VIII*—that great series of English historical dramas in which the deeds of their ancestors, the Talbots, the Percys, the princes of Lancaster and York, conquerors of France and victors in deadly civic feud, had been held up to the applause and admiration of Englishmen. In comedy, too, Shakespeare had achieved as signal a success; and with plays such as *Much Ado About Nothing, As You Like It,* and *Twelfth Night* held complete dominion of the stage. In tragedy alone were Shakespeare's greatest triumphs before him; but here he had given the world the rich promise of *Romeo and Juliet,* and was now pondering *Julius Cæsar* and *Hamlet.* In 1600 Jonson had gained his first dramatic success with *Every Man in His Humor,* and had recently launched his notable excursion into the domain of dramatic satire. At the lesser theaters, controlled by Philip Henslowe, Dekker and Middleton had already begun those long years of bondage, from which Jonson's duel with Gabriel Spenser and the good offices of Shakespeare had relieved him; and from which Marston and Chapman were soon to emerge. We could find no better date than 1600 as a point of departure from which to map out the physical dimensions, so to speak, of our subject. If we mark thirty-seven years backward, we have the date of the birth of Shakespeare, 1564; thirty-seven years forward, and we have the date of the death of Ben Jonson, 1637, Shakespeare's greatest contemporary in his own field. If we add five years, backward and forward, to these two lapses of thirty-seven years, we have the period from the accession of Queen Elizabeth, 1558, to the outbreak of the Civil War in 1642. Indeed, this symmetry of dates—for the statement of which we are indebted to that indefatigable if vexatious scholar, F. G. Fleay [in his *A Chronicle History of the London Stage,* 1890]—extends into other points. The career of Shakespeare stretched, roughly speaking, from 1589 to 1611, eleven years on either side of "the meeting point of the centuries;" and again, the first Elizabethan structure built expressly for dramatic presentations, and called the Theater *par excellence,* was erected in 1576, twenty-four years before our point of departure; while the last theater to be rebuilt, before the advancing tide of Puritanism swept all such landmarks as this before it, was the Fortune, in 1624, the same distance of time onward.

Within these eighty-four years arose and flourished in the city of London, then of a population not exceeding 125,000 souls, over a score of active and enterprising theatrical companies, averaging some four or five performing contemporaneously, and occupying at different times some twenty theaters and inn-yards fitted up for theatrical purposes. Among these actors were Edward Alleyn, who made his repute in the title rôles of *Tamburlaine, The Jew of Malta,* and *Doctor Faustus;* Richard Burbage, the original Richard III and perhaps the first to play Hamlet, Lear, and Othello; John Lowin, the creator of the rôles of Jonson's *Sejanus* and *Volpone,* and of Sir Epicure Mammon; and, of a lesser degree as an actor, though not as a manager, William Shakespeare. Within these eighty-four years wrote and starved, or occasionally acquired competence, a swarm of writers, producing some hundreds of plays, less than half of which are in all probability now extant. Amongst these authors were a score of brilliant playwrights, not one of whom but has added his treasures to that richest of our English inheritances, the literature of our tongue; and at least six of whom have written dramas,

which, judged as dramas, are beyond the achievements of the greatest of their successors. Within these eighty-four years, in short, arose, developed, and declined the most universal and imaginative, the most spontaneous and heterogeneous literature in dramatic form which has yet come from the hand of man.

Elizabethan drama may be described as an artistic graft on the old sacred drama. That drama at first found its subjects in the bible and in the legends of saints and holy martyrs. Its purpose was the teaching of Christian dogma. And whether manifested directly in the form of miracle plays or diverted to the schoolmaster's purposes in moralities or scholastic interludes, this earlier drama had ever its roots in medieval Christian ethics. We may therefore speak of the first main element in the English drama as the religious element. . . . [The] religious element as exemplified in English medieval drama had worked itself out by the coming of the Spanish Armada. It had latterly been failing of effect from the circumstances that, in its eagerness to teach and to edify, it habitually confused the end and aim of art and kept the drama subservient to an ulterior purpose.

But the young graft of Elizabethan drama found its sap in another element which is almost as old as religion itself. Whatever the foreign and symbolic original of the drama, even these religious dramatic productions, with the popular farces and interludes which accompanied and followed them, had become intensely national and English before the reign of Henry VIII. We have thus the second main element affecting the coming drama, the national, the distinctively vernacular or English element. In the earliest time this element manifested itself in a crude and realistic simplicity by which the personages and situations of biblical story were translated into the terms of contemporary conditions, by which Joseph became an awkward, elderly original of Snug the joiner; Herod, a brawling braggart; and Noah's wife, a common village scold. Scenes of comedy drawn from real life enter into the drama of England from its very beginning, and are to be found accompanying it in each of the successive stages of its development. Such is the famous episode of the thievish wastrel, Mak, in the *Secunda Pagina Pastorum* of the *Towneley Plays,* and such is the interlude of Pauper in Sir David Lyndsay's *Satire of the Three Estates,* a production otherwise a political morality. Such, too, are the farces of character of John Heywood, the *Four P's* for example, and the farce of character and situation, *Gammer Gurton's Needle,* the first regular English comedy.

Meanwhile another form of secular drama was arising which had its basis in the growing national spirit and sought to express itself in plays detailing the deeds of the heroes of old ballads and the doings of English nobles and princes. Such were the medieval plays on Robin Hood, dramatic offshoots of popular ballading; and such were later the crude dramatized chronicles like *Jack Straw* and *The Famous Victories of Henry V.* This interest in the past set forth by means of the drama also extended from English themes to those of other lands. Above all, it is to be observed that in all these plays, whether based on fact or fiction, engaged with English or foreign life and history, the old symbolic and didactic purpose had waned to all but extinction, and a new artistic purpose had sprung up to make a great literature possible. As the drama advanced the old farcical scenes were superseded by a higher form of comedy in the plays of Robert Greene and others and diverted to a powerful expression of tragic emotion by the unknown author of *Arden of Feversham;* while history was raised by the hand of Marlowe and Shakespeare to one of the most potent and distinctive forms of Elizabethan literature. In the last decade of the century came Dekker, Heywood, and Middleton, in whose hands the simple, realistic representation of contemporary every-day life reached a height only surpassed by the more highly poetic and ideal representation of the same life by Shakespeare himself. In full-grown Elizabethan dramatic literature, the glory of both chronicle play and vernacular drama lay in their uncompromising realism, the fidelity of which, at large as well as in detail, gives to this body of plays a force, as reflections of contemporary life and manners, which makes them a veritable mirror of the age in which they were written.

The third main element or master influence on the Elizabethan drama is that of Italy. Italy was to the subject of Henry VIII and Elizabeth the land of culture and refinement, and the realm of mystery and enchantment as well. Thence had come the song and the sonnet of Wyatt and Surrey, the pastoral romance of Sidney, the allegorical epic of Spenser, and the stream of popular fiction, translated by Painter and Pettie, and imitated by Lyly and Greene; and thence, too, had come much in the drama. The influence of Italy displayed itself in choice of subject, in mode of treatment, and, above all, in a romantic atmosphere which was cast upon everything. This was not what Italy actually was, but what the poets thought Italy to be; and many a homely English story, viewed through this luminous mist, becomes a thing of new and enchanted beauty. It is that spirit whose quest is beauty in strange and often unpromising materials, the spirit that casts precedent to the winds and seeks to produce the effect of art by novel and untried courses which is the heart and soul of Elizabethan drama. This spirit betrayed itself in various species, in the courtly allegorical plays of Lyly, in the later pastoral drama of Daniel and others, in the masque, and in the extreme form of dramatized heroic romances. But the main current of the romantic influence derived from Italy is that wherein the greatest dramatic literature of the age is found. Here is the early drama of passion, straining the leading strings of Seneca in the powerful plays of Thomas Kyd, and launched into the independence of vigorous young manhood by the strong hand of Marlowe. Here it is that Shakespeare sits enthroned the ruler of this, his capital, and of all outlying provinces. For, however thoroughly English are Shakespeare's themes and his characters in their essentials, he too dwelt in the transforming atmosphere of the Italy of the poets, and owes his supremacy to the fact that he is alike the most realistic of dramatists and the most romantic and ideal of poets as well. Shakespeare's example and his extraordinary popularity in his own age and for generations after fixed the romantic influence as that affecting a main current of the drama in subsequent times. Through Beaumont and Fletcher, Massinger, and Shirley this influence continued down to the closing of the theaters; and, dilated into heroic proportions by a revival in the improbable incidents and impossible personages of the later heroic romance, it continued in the heroic plays of Dryden to manifest vitality which not even the trenchant satire of *The Rehearsal* could destroy.

Lastly, we reach the important influence of the classics. Many of the earlier dramatists were scholarly men, men of the universities; and in those days scholarship came through the classics alone. As is well known, the earliest extant English comedy, *Ralph Roister Doister,* was the composition of a schoolmaster, Nicolas Udall, who was anxious to have his scholars perform an English play on the model of Plautus, instead of the customary Latin original. In the same manner, Sackville wrote our earliest extant tragedy, *Gorboduc,* on models furnished by Seneca; although Sackville went a step beyond Udall in selecting a subject from what was then considered English history. The scholars, who never had more than a qualified success with the populace, developed several varieties of drama out of their Latin originals, although some of these species were short-lived. Such was "the school drama," as Herford calls it [in his *Studies in the Literary Relations of England and Germany in the Sixteenth Century,* 1886], a severely didactic utterance derived from the continental Latin drama of the humanists, of which the best example in English is Gascoigne's *The Glass of Government.* Such, too, is the long and interesting series of satirical college plays, which were addressed to a limited audience and are exemplified in Latin plays such as *Ignoramus,* and in the English *Return from Parnassus.* But these were things apart, for it was usual for this age to treat ancient times romantically. Troilus wears Cressida's glove in his helm, Theseus and his Amazonian bride, Hyppolyta, whether in *A Midsummer-Night's Dream* or in *The Two Kinsmen,* are denizens of knightly medieval days. The happy Elizabethans were little troubled by the eternal fitness of things, and were as innocent of the existence of that monster, anachronism, as they were unaware of that strict code of twentieth century morals whereby a man may not take his own thoughts, if he happen to find them in the works of one of his predecessors. Hence, so far as the popular stage was concerned, the classical spirit exercised a regulative and indirect influence, though there is plainly discernible alongside and parallel to the popular drama a scholarly drama, extending from the early imitations of Plautus to the later Senecan plays of Greville, Daniel, and Alexander which cluster about the end of Elizabeth's reign, and to the later college drama which flourished throughout the reigns of James and Charles.

Returning to earlier times and passing Kyd, with a recognition of the important position which he holds as the link between the earliest practical imitators of Seneca, Sackville and Gascoigne, and the popular drama, we find that a great man arose in this school, with a definite purpose in art, a representative of scholarship applied to the drama, just as Marlowe and Shakespeare were representatives of romantic Italian treatment, and Dekker and Middleton the exponents of popular realism. With Ben Jonson arises what may perhaps not inaptly be termed the school of conscious effort, manifesting itself especially in its admirable and vigorous application of classic methods, and, at times of classic imitations, to existing conditions and demands of the Elizabethan stage. This species of drama also showed itself in various forms; in the classically constructed and scholarly wrought tragedies *Sejanus* and *The Fall of Catiline,* which are distinguishable alike from the severe limitations of Seneca, mentioned above, and from Shakespeare's unscholarly and romantic but altogether masterly treatment of subjects from Roman history. This species of drama showed itself also in dramatic satire of a type plainly referable to an intimate acquaintance with Horace and Juvenal, in the "comedy of humors," as Jonson called it; and in the later outgrowth of this last, the comedy of manners. The dramatic satire of Middleton is of that robust, vernacular type which is exemplified in general literature alike by *The Vision of Piers Plowman* and by Sebastian Brandt's *Ship of Fools.* Its ultimate stock is in the vigorous and often ribald interlude of the miracle play and morality. Jonson's satirical plays, on the other hand, whilst strongly tinged with an English flavor, are plainly referable to a classical impetus. In his hands English drama became for the first time a conscious literary utterance. This brought it as much loss as gain; but historically the performance of Jonson's *Every Man in His Humor,* 1598, in which the comedy of manners for the first time took definite form, is an event of the utmost importance. As time went on these two classes of satirical comedy united and led, in Restoration times, to the later comedy of manners, passing on through Dryden, Congreve, Vanbrugh, and Goldsmith to Sheridan and our own day. The comedy of manners is the most persistent species of drama in the language, and forms, with the romantic drama, one of the two permanent types.

Let us recapitulate. With the weakening of the didactic principle, which had ruled the sacred drama and the humanist interlude, the artistic impulse was set free, and whole plays came for the first time to be written, the appeal of which was that of pure literature. These plays were at first exercised in the bare representation of contemporary life or what was taken to have been the life of the past. But the artistic purpose once born, it failed to content itself with a mere imitation of things familiar, and, stretching after novelty, soon came to be ruled with the spirit of romance. But here as in all ages the counter force existed as well; and the age of Elizabeth was not without the force which conserves as well as the force that impels. We have thus a drama the chief interest of which is artistic and romantic; *i.e.* the purpose of which is to please by means of novelty; and we have also, of less prevalence but of equal potency, a drama which is artistic and classical, *i.e.* the purpose of which is also to please, but to please by means of an appeal to things familiar and hallowed by the associations of the past. The various angles which the resultants of these counter forces take, account for the extraordinary variety of Elizabethan drama in kind and explain its relation to what came after.

Here, then, in the year 1600 were three great and, at times, opposing schools,—the popular school of Dekker, Heywood, and Middleton filling the cheaper theaters, the Fortune, the Bell Savage, the Bull, the Cockpit, or the Swan, with plays written to catch the ears of the groundlings,

dramatizing anything, as in the case of Thomas Heywood, who on one occasion sat down to write, a copy of Ovid's *Metamorphoses* on his left hand, and translated it into five plays, omitting little and extenuating nothing. Secondly, the romantic school, presided over by the calm, the benignant, and healthful genius of Shakespeare, whose company was the best, whose theaters, the familiar Globe and Blackfriars, were the most paying, whose plays enjoyed for years a practical monopoly at court and in the city, and whose reputation, as his emolument, was above that of all other dramatists of his time. Lastly, Jonson, Chapman, and Marston, the scholarly poets of the school of conscious effort, theorizing on art and despising the public, for which they were often as heartily despised in return; but triumphing at times, as in *The Alchemist, The Silent Woman,* or *Eastward Hoe,* by sheer force of genius, and deeply affecting the other two schools from their self-assumed position of independence.

It will be noticed that the tendency up to this point has been towards greater diversity in the species of the drama. We had at first only the sacred drama illustrating the scriptures; then was added the morality, an abstract of life intended to promote righteous living and correctness in dogma; then followed the interlude, devised only to amuse; and finally the regular drama, comedy, tragedy romantically or classically conceived, on subjects drawn from ancient and modern history, legend, and folklore, from times historically remote and foreign, and from episodes English and of the day. The diversity of Elizabethan drama at its height is nowhere better exemplified than in the work of Shakespeare, who tried nearly every dramatic form and variety known to his age. Thus, in his earlier career he imitated the comedy of Plautus, which he adapted to the English stage in *The Comedy of Errors;* he improved the chronicle history of Peele and Marlowe by the infusion of a higher art into these representations in his two parts of *Henry IV* and *Henry V;* he attempted the allegorical comedy of Lyly, which he elevated and rendered truly imaginative in *A Midsummer-Night's Dream.* Later, Shakespeare essayed the passionate tragedy of Marlowe and humanized and rationalized it in *Macbeth* and *Othello;* while, on the suggestion of it by Jonson, he attempted even the comedy of humors, in *Twelfth Night,* but lifted it out of the region of caricature into that of faithful realism and employed it for dramatic relief, not as a method of all work. Even Fletcher was not without his influence on Shakespeare; though that Fletcher disturbed the calm serenity of Shakespeare's romantic art so as to make it a mere matter of scenic show and violent theatrical contrast, and to destroy in it, to the slightest degree, that power in the portraiture of actual men which is everywhere the master dramatist's, there are some at least who will feel unwilling to allow. Towards the end of his dramatic career we find Shakespeare settled in the practice of the romantic drama and infusing into all, whether comedy, tragedy, or "romance," the rich and deep-toned colors of a life of experience and a sympathy with his kind which is unparalleled elsewhere.

And now we have reached the climax, and the descent is shorter and simpler. With the retirement of Shakespeare on his well-earned competence to New Place about 1611, the field was open to the henchmen of Henslowe, to the scholarly writers, and to a new class, the gentlemen dramatists. The last alone claim our attention here, for it is Fletcher who now comes forward to claim and wield the scepter of Shakespeare and to represent, in a new and facile, if restricted form, the earlier romantic drama. Indeed, Fletcher held not only the scepter of Shakespeare, but to him and his followers descended the scholarly gown of Jonson. Beaumont, Fletcher, Ford, Massinger, and Shirley combined competent scholarship with the endowments of the men of the world, and with the experience gained by a study of the masterpieces of their great predecessors. And thus it was that with less complexity as to form, the drama became eclectic, tragedy followed the older romantic methods, but tended, from the popular craving for novelty, to situations strained and unnatural and to the delineation of passions inordinate and of superhuman intensity; tragicomedy was invented to satiate the craving for novelty and yet satisfy the desire for a happy solution of all difficulties of plot; and an infusion of the "heroic" spirit of degenerate French romance followed, to substitute strained sentiment and the lofty platitudes of Platonic love for healthy emotion and lead on logically to the heroic play of the Restoration. On the other hand, comedy went almost wholly over to a form of the drama of manners, refined, save for Brome and some others, as compared with the coarse realism of Middleton, and freed from the ingenuity and didactic satire of Jonson, and yet showing its debt to each of these predecessors while reflecting, as such comedy always must to a large degree, the more frivolous side of contemporary life.

The English drama in the age of Elizabeth has been called above the most universal and imaginative, the most spontaneous and heterogeneous literature in dramatic form which has yet come from the hand of man.

—*Felix E. Schelling*

The English drama in the age of Elizabeth has been called above the most universal and imaginative, the most spontaneous and heterogeneous literature in dramatic form which has yet come from the hand of man. . . . As to these other qualities, Elizabethan drama may claim universality not only because much of it has a literary value to-day little tarnished by the lapse of ages, but also because in its day it appealed to all classes, from the groundling, who stood on the cobbles under the open sky, to the plumed and brocaded knights and gentlemen who formed the most conspicuous and troublesome embellishment of the stage itself. We know that a popular play was often raised and dignified by adaptation to a court performance. On the other hand, the queen herself occasionally condescended to witness a popular performance at the Blackfriars or the Globe, duly disguised and masked, as were all women of reputation who ventured within the public

theaters of the day. In their zeal to preserve the peace and, as far as possible, the health of the city, the civic authorities of London opposed the theater. Their attacks were prompted by the antipathy which thrift always feels for extravagance, and encouraged by the growth of Puritanism, the austerity of which was hostile to the loose and thoughtless lives of many of those who acted plays or witnessed them. But as yet these attacks had assumed no very serious proportions and came from religious zealots like Northbrook and John Field, satirists like Philip Stubbs, or renegade actors such as Stephen Gosson. Adverse criticism of the stage in the earlier years of Elizabeth's reign did not wean any considerable class of the London populace from its traditional pleasure in "shews;" and the drama still claimed the quality of universality in the continued strength of its appeal to the lower orders of society, as well as to those in whose children Puritanism was to beget a lively realization of the vanities of the world and a consequent partial withdrawal from them.

It is easy to overlook the function which the Elizabethan stage actually performed in affording not only that amusement which belongs legitimately to the drama in all ages, but likewise that running comment on current affairs, that supply of news, of gossip, of sensational events, scandals, and crime, which is wont to be furnished us in modern times by our newspapers. In the height of the complexity of the Elizabethan drama the spirit that made men Englishmen responded to scenes representing the careers of adventurers like Stukeley and the three Shirleys, or to breezy dramas of action like *The Fair Maid of the West* or *Fortune by Land and Sea;* or answered more vehemently to rude dramatizing of the repulse of the Spanish Armada, whilst a loftier genius moulded into artistic form the deeds of England's hero-king at Agincourt. The chronicle history flourished until an alien and un-English prince succeeded to Elizabeth's throne and lost to the nation its sense of personal allegiance. In the hey-day of this great national utterance, the Elizabethan drama, no event was too trifling, no personage too august to be represented on the stage, if a matter of public interest. Dramatists, courtiers, and even ambassadors were satirized; the citizen was abused and lampooned, or absurdly glorified; the faults, the whims, and the fashions of the day were represented and misrepresented. Plays had to be stayed and their writers imprisoned for matter of seditious or even of treasonable import. From 1598 for some years, a veritable "war of the theaters" raged, with varying fortunes, in which Jonson, armed with the artillery of the ancients, entered the lists against the long-bows, cross-bows, and blunderbusses of Marston, Dekker, and others. If we are to believe some interpretations of a celebrated passage in the satirical college play, *The Return from Parnassus,* Shakespeare himself was not without his part in these broils. Now all this is the full, bustling vigor of real life; agile, urgent, at times fatiguing, occasionally even disappointing; for the great Elizabethan age had its failures and half successes, its lapses from high ideals and its dullness too; but, none the less, full of hope and aspiration, full of the glory of youth and at times of the radiance of beauty, of the warmth, the glow, and the sincerity of truth.

Lastly, Elizabethan art was supremely imaginative; not introspective with that self-centered omnipresence of the ego which accounts for so much of the strength and the weakness of two such diverse poets as Wordsworth and Byron; nor yet analytic with that intellectualizing tendency which substitutes a mental process for an emotional delight and thus transforms art to the humble handmaiden of philosophy. Elizabethan literature, rightly read, has that rare quality, which may almost be called levity, of raising the reader above the point at which he merely understands, of disarming him of his critical panoply, and restoring to him once more that childlike openness of heart in which to understand is to enjoy.

With these major qualities of universality, imaginativeness, and spontaneity once recognized, we may acknowledge the existence of minor shortcomings. Elizabethan drama as a whole is amateurish and unequal; at times it is scarcely literary. Outside of Jonson it is commonly wanting in design and effective elaboration; outside of Shakespeare its earlier efforts are unsustained and fragmentary; its later triumphs often studied or strained. Indeed, barring a few of the greatest, scarcely a play of the time is not open to criticism on the score of exaggeration, carelessness, improbability, or lack of finish. Nor could it well be otherwise, considering the conditions under which this drama was written. The demand was that of the moment, premeditation was usually impossible. At times a single play was let to two or three authors to be cobbled up in haste and learned by the actors before it was finished. Every acted play of the age was subject to incessant revision, excision, and recasting; and the laws of mine and thine commonly applied less to the authors than to the companies who were the real owners of the plays. With all this before our eyes and the purely temporary occasion of the writing, we cannot but be lost in wonder that so many Elizabethan plays have stood the test of transportation across the centuries. Nor need this remain wholly unexplained. The drama of Shakespeare and his immediate fellows spoke to men by right of their manhood, not by virtue of their gentility. It stirred in its appeal the depths of a large and generous humanity. In the hands of Fletcher and his successors the drama rapidly lost this universal character, and although continuing of high poetic and dramatic worth, began to appeal to a class, a dangerous restriction, in time to become a fatal taint. The drama began to lose, too, that firm foundation in ethics which alone can keep a literary production sweet for ages and tide it over to remain a living power to generations to come. The writings of Fletcher and of Ford are of great literary excellence, but they mark the way step by step from the moral heights of the best Elizabethan plays to the moral depths of Restoration comedy, from the wholesome mirth of Shakespeare and his abiding faith in man to the soulless flippancy of Congreve and Vanbrugh, and the leering skepticism of Wycherley.

Thus it was that in some eighty-five years the English world was changed and with it the stage, its mirror. A history of the Victorian stage would present us with one phase of the multitudinous activity of that reign; a phase at its best scarcely literary, for the greatest plays of that age were either unacted or unactable; and the memorable dramatic names of the times were not those of Shelley, Tennyson, Browning, and Swinburne, but Tom Taylor, Sheridan Knowles, and Bulwer, Lord Lytton. In Shakespeare's time the drama had not separated from literature and poetry; and although it might call in the aid of splendid scenic display, as did the masques, discuss a psychological problem or a problem of conduct, as does Shakespeare's *Hamlet* or Middleton's *A Fair Quarrel,* neither these things nor the claims of great actors could impair the splendid and imperishable literary form in which was conveyed a spirit inherently dramatic. Elizabethan drama is preëminently interesting because it focused the activities of the age in itself and was literally a great national utterance. Modern drama is less interesting because it absorbs more of the individual and less of the time, because it habitually intellectualizes emotion and loses sight of the appeal of art in the zeal of the propagandist, in the curious minutiæ of the psychologist or the perverted mania of the pornographist. In a word, modern drama is less interesting because it reflects a narrower range of ideas, and because, for the most part, it has discarded the sacred raiment of poetry. This is not the place in which to write of contemporary drama, English or other. Neither poetry, literature, nor drama wholly die while man is man; but, as to the last, the once full stream of Shakespeare's art, of Calderon's and Molière's, now flows in the babbling shallows of Sardou, in the dreamy meanderings of Maeter-

---

Swinburne in praise of the Elizabethan dramatists:

If it be true, as we are told on high authority, that the greatest glory of England is her literature and the greatest glory of English literature is its poetry, it is not less true that the greatest glory of English poetry lies rather in its dramatic than its epic or its lyric triumphs. The name of Shakespeare is above the names even of Milton and Coleridge and Shelley: and the names of his comrades in art and their immediate successors are above all but the highest names in any other province of our song. There is such an overflowing life, such a superb exuberance of abounding and exulting strength, in the dramatic poetry of the half-century extending from 1590 to 1640, that all other epochs of English literature seem as it were but half awake and half alive by comparison with this generation of giants and of gods. There is more sap in this than in any other branch of the national bay-tree: it has an energy in fertility which reminds us rather of the forest than the garden or the park. It is true that the weeds and briars of the underwood are but too likely to embarrass and offend the feet of the rangers and the gardeners who trim the level flower-plots or preserve the domestic game of enclosed and ordered lowlands in the tamer demesnes of literature. The sun is strong and the wind sharp in the climate which reared the fellows and the followers of Shakespeare. The extreme inequality and roughness of the ground must also be taken into account when we are disposed, as I for one have often been disposed, to wonder beyond measure at the apathetic ignorance of average students in regard of the abundant treasure to be gathered from this wildest and most fruitful province in the poetic empire of England.

Algernon Charles Swinburne, in his The Age of Shakespeare, *Chatto & Windus, 1908.*

linck, or loses itself in the thirsty realistic sands of Ibsen. In the first, melodrama has absorbed not only poetry but truth. In the second, the poet and the mystic has eclipsed once and for all the dramatist. In the last, inexorable actuality has sunk the poetry of the drama once and for all. And no one of these has written in the English tongue. (pp. xxiii-xliii)

Felix E. Schelling, in an introduction to his Elizabethan Drama: 1558-1642, Vol. 1, *1908. Reprint by Russell & Russell, Inc., 1959, pp. xxiii-xliii.*

Theodore W. Hunt

[*Hunt was an American educator who wrote several works on English literature. In the excerpt that follows, he traces the forces that gave rise to the Elizabethan drama, citing the "natural causes" and "innate aptitudes" which contributed to its formation.*]

The Golden Age of English Letters is made so especially by its distinctive dramatic development. Whatever excellence it may have had along other lines of verse, and in the sphere of prose, it is its dramatic character that at once attracts attention, and puts the student on the search after the causes sufficient to account for it; an age which had, as has been said, "many hundreds of pieces and more than fifty masterpieces." Mr. Taine, the eminent French critic of English Literature, would make an application here of his notable threefold condition of the literary status of a nation—that of race, of epoch, and of environment. While dramatic ability, as general literary ability, may be, in part, assignable to natural causes—to genius, to special talent, and to certain innate aptitudes—Mr. Taine insists that the finally determining agencies are external, and so universally such, that no order of genius is independent of them. Shakespeare, Dante, Homer, and Cervantes are thus as surely influenced by them, though not, perhaps, as fully, as are the inferior authors of a nation.

Thus, on the principle of Race, the drama is more germane to certain peoples than to others. The Greek thus offers us a more excellent dramatic literature than the Latin, and the South European continental nations, as a whole, a more excellent drama than the North European, not only as a matter of literary history, but as a matter of racial instincts, capabilities, and tendency, antecedent to history and quite independent of it. As peoples, the one are more dramatic in spirit and function than the other. Nationally and racially, it is easier for them than for others to express their literary life along such lines and in superior forms. They are constitutionally dramatic, so that they must belie their inherited characteristics if they fail to reach decided results in this direction. In this respect, the English race may be said to stand midway between the North and the South of Europe, evincing some of the salient racial tendencies of each, while having distinctive dramatic capacities of its own.

So, as to the second condition, that of Epoch, as determining both the form and quality of literary product at any given period, Mr. Lowell, in his essay on Shakespeare, lays down a general principle which is here in point, as he says,

"The first demand we make on whatever claims to be a work of art is, that it shall be in keeping"; and, he adds, "this may be either extrinsic or intrinsic." It is this principle of propriety, in its extrinsic form, that is here in place; so that the authorship shall be in "keeping" with the era in which it is produced, a synchronism and not an anachronism, the natural product of the age and the hour. Applying this principle historically, we would not expect to find in the Dark Ages of Europe that dramatic development which we find in later and more enlightened periods; nor, in despotic eras, what we find in those of free thought and general national rule; nor, in the earlier epochs of a literature, what we find in the later, when crude conditions give way to maturity, and experiment, to settled literary habit. The lighter forms of verse, the lyric and descriptive, may flourish in the earlier eras as they have historically done, and poetry appear antecedent to prose. Hence, the drama of England, in the sixteenth century, was timely, as it could not have been in the fifteenth or seventeenth. In fact, in no succeeding century has there been an opportune time for the English drama, even though Dryden, Byron, Robert Browning, and Tennyson have done conspicuous work in that direction. Just why this is so is clear enough as to the seventeenth and eighteenth centuries, but not so clear as to the nineteenth, one of the explanations, however, lying in the fact that the material civilization which prevailed in the last century encouraged the production of prose rather than verse and, in verse itself, the lighter lyric forms.

The most sanguine among us are not rationally looking, at the opening of the twentieth century, for a reappearance of the Miltonic epic or Shakespearian drama. So, as to Environment, one of the most favorite words of modern science and literature, one of those sociological terms which other interests have borrowed by which to express certain forms and measures of influence not otherwise explained. What is the habitat of literature, its homestead, the nature of its vicinage? Is it wholesome or unwholesome, incitive or repressive of that which lies dormant, awaiting expression? Are the surroundings favorable or unfavorable? Here and there, as in the case of Milton's great epic, in the sensuous days of Charles the Second, literature comes to high embodiment despite all adverse conditions, as men of bodily vigor will occasionally be found in the most unsanitary districts. This, however, is not the law of life. Literature, if we may so express it, must have good air and an abundance of it, good soil in which to cast and cultivate its seed, sufficient light and heat to insure its growth. In a word, it must have, in all these particulars, a fair chance in its struggle for existence, if so be the fittest may survive and perpetuate its kind. Here, again, England in the sixteenth century was most fortunate, as Italy, also, was, so that the external aided the internal, and what we may call the topography of the literature was the best possible to enable authors to do their best work. Locality is one of the factors in all national development—educational, literary, and social. We speak correctly of the *genius loci*. There is the spirit of the place as well as of the people and the period, a something in the field itself in which we labor to stimulate or stifle exertion. Such are Mr. Taine's conditions, each having force, and together constituting a most important element in the interpretation of any literature.

A performance of a miracle play on a pageant wagon.

To these, however, must be added a fourth, the Author himself, in the sum total of his personality, above all external conditions, be they as potent as they may. The production of great literary results under the most unfriendly circumstances has been often enough illustrated in the history of literature to teach us that there are times when the author will prove himself superior to his antecedents, his epoch, and his environment, and confirm the priority of all personal factors. The production of *The Faerie Queene* amid the wild wastes and the wilder political disturbances of Ireland, or of *The Pilgrim's Progress* in the Bedford jail amid the civic commotions of the Commonwealth, is quite enough to attest the principle. Though genius is dependent somewhat on conditions, there is a sense in which, because it is genius, it is independent of them, and in the great opportunities of authorship takes them but little into account. Literature is one of the Humanities and the human element is central, so that the best explanation of the Elizabethan dramatic development is the genius of the dramatists. In noting, more specifically, the Reasons for this special development of the drama at this era, we emphasize three or four of marked significance.

The first is seen in the Revival of Classical Learning, in that learning was then embodied more fully in the ancient languages than in any other one department of human investigation. More especially was this true as to the Greek,

consequent on the Fall of Constantinople, in 1453, when the Greek language and literature were disseminated over Europe and the West. Hitherto, in the centuries preceding the Fall of Rome and the Fall of Constantinople, theology and philosophy were the prevailing studies, and the Latin, as the language of Rome and the Romish church, was the dominant language of Europe. When the "new learning" came into prominence, in the days of Elizabeth, theology and philosophy became less and less Romish, and the Greek language, more and more prominent—the language, it is to be noted, in which the best expressions of literature in dramatic form had appeared. These tragedies and comedies were the model of all Europe, so that the revival of Greek was the revival of the classical drama, as a standard form of verse. It was now, naturally, the ambition of the native English dramatists to do for England what Sophocles and Æschylus had done for Greece, to establish the drama as national, and on broad and lasting foundations. In connection with this revival, there came in the best results of Medieval learning, especially as expressed in the great semi-dramatic poem of Dante. The coarser elements of Medievalism were largely disappearing, or were transformed by Bacon and others into more modern and attractive forms; so that, while the essential spirit of scholarship and literary inquiry remained, much of the bondage of the letter had disappeared. Dramatists, actors, and patrons of the stage now understood each other better than in the early days of the Miracle Plays and Mysteries, when religious bigotry so prevailed.

A second reason for this unwonted dramatic development is found in a new awakening of the national mind and spirit, awaiting, as it arose, the pen and voice of those who might be capable of appreciating and interpreting it. It was because of this demand for immediate and fitting interpretation, that it begat and fostered a distinctly dramatic tendency. We may thus call the essential type of this national revival, histrionic, possessed of scenic and delineative elements, needing the playwright and the open stage to embody and portray it. For the first time in its history, the modern English nation may be said to have known itself—what it was, just where it stood in modern history, what was expected of it, and what it could reasonably do. In fact, there had been no Modern England previous to this. Modern English statehood and Protestantism now began, as well as Modern English civilization, and so suddenly and fully that the impression was dramatic in its influence on the national mind. Scores of poets, receiving the new impulse, betook themselves to dramatic writing as the first necessity of the hour.

Hence, an additional reason for the special literary expansion now visible is found in the Emphasis of Life as related to literature. Never had the English nation been so thoroughly alive and so impelled, on every hand, to be what it was and do what it did, in the most vital forms. There was nothing in the line of indifference or an easy-going dependence on the past. It was the unique feature of the time, that the past was to be subordinate to the present, that the era was to be, in reality as well as in name and chronology, the Modern Era. All this, it is to be noted, tended to produce dramatic authorship, on the principle that action is the central element of the drama, the word itself meaning action, which is but another name for life. Hence, the comedy of the time was known, and is now known, as the Comedy of Life and Manners. The tragedy of the time was nothing more nor less than the presentation of life on its serious side. So, the historical plays depicted the story of the diversified life of man. Life itself is essentially dramatic, so that human experience in its manifold phases was the theme and content, as it was the imposing cause, of the Elizabethan Plays.

If to these various reasons we add a fourth, the Comprehensiveness of the Era, including the old and the new, the real and the ideal, the pagan and Christian, the native and foreign, all unified and fused into what we call the Elizabethan Age, we have a sufficient explanation of the age itself, of its fundamental quality as dramatic, and of its undisputed primacy, even, yet, in the sphere of representative verse.

The second question of interest that arises is, The Influence of this Sixteenth-century Drama on other forms of contemporary literature. From the fact that it was central it must have affected, more or less closely, every existent form of literature, and, mostly, those forms which stood nearest to it in type and aim.

Its influence on the Prose of the period is, first of all, noticeable. Despite the fact that certain broad distinctions exist between prose and verse, as respectively metrical and unmetrical, there is an area common to them both, within the sphere, especially, of poetical prose and didactic poetry. Hence, in Shakespeare's drama, as in some of Goethe's, prose is not only found coexistent with the poetry, but, at times, in prominent form, as in *Much Ado about Nothing, As You Like It,* and *The Merry Wives of Windsor,* in which last play Falstaff discourses in prose with Mrs. Page and with Pistol and the other characters. In fact, he mingles prose and verse, as he mingles blank verse and rhyme, when, in accordance with his literary insight, the thought and purpose demand it. So the other dramatists of the time, of whom Jonson, in his *Cynthia's Revels* and *Silent Woman,* is a notable example. So, Marlowe, in his *Doctor Faustus.* Of Lyly's nine dramas, seven are in prose, these facts sufficing to show that the drama is not necessarily, though it is presumably, expressed in verse, and that, when the occasion or sentiment demands it, the poet passes freely into the prose-writer. Herein, lies the excellence of Blank verse, as a poetic form, in that it is a kind of accepted compromise between specific prose and specific verse; being verse, in that it is metrical, and having, yet, a prose type, in that it is rhymeless. Hence, epic and dramatic verse have adopted it as their prevailing form, while the lyric and descriptive are, in the main, in rhyme. So, the Drama and the Epic are related. In each of them, the three historic unities—of time, place, and action—are present, though the last of these is more prominent in the drama. Differing somewhat, in that the epic is mainly narrative and deals with the past, while the dramatic is mainly descriptive, and deals with the present and is given in the form of dialogue, each of them, at times, crosses the border-line that separates them, minimizing all differences between them, so as to present a unified effect. Tragedy has an essentially epic element, on the side of moral sublimity, as the Historical Plays have such an element to the degree

in which they are narrative. Spenser's *Faerie Queene,* though a modified epic poem, has a distinctive dramatic feature; with its incidents, scenes and characters, its seriousness and pleasantry, so as to make upon the reader a semi-dramatic impression. So, as to the Drama and the Lyric, as in the Sonnets of Shakespeare, essentially lyric, but partly dramatic, as in Spenser's *Shepheardes Calendar,* a pastoral poem with dramatic elements, most of the playwrights of this era having done something in the sphere of lyric verse. In the Songs and Choruses of the drama, this relation is especially conspicuous. The emotional element germane to tragedy is the central feature of the lyric. So, Humor and Satire as natural to Comedy are essentially lyric. Hence, it appears that, from whatever point of view we study it, dramatic literature in the Golden Age was central, affecting and affected by every other form of literature. Herein is another proof of the fact that the current opinion of criticism as to the superiority of the epic to all other forms of poetry is to be so far modified as to make it subordinate to the dramatic. Its status is, at least, an open question.

Coming now to a more definite survey of this affluent dramatic era, it is in place to note the individual dramatic poets who served, more or less successfully, to make the era what it was in our history. Shakespeare excepted as the central and immutable exponent of the age, it is the critical habit to classify all other playwrights as Minor Authors, whether his predecessors, immediate contemporaries, or successors. Special care is, therefore, to be taken lest the phrase Minor Elizabethan Dramatists be falsely interpreted. The very fact that they are Elizabethan, giving to the Golden Age something of its excellence, is sufficient to show that they are not to be underrated. So able a critic as Hazlitt devotes one-half of his *Elizabethan Literature* to these so-called secondary poets. Lamb, in his *Specimens of English Dramatic Poets,* writes in a spirit even more decidedly favorable. More recently and, as if to secure a continued interest in these authors, Whipple, in his *Essays and Reviews,* pays them a high eulogium; while substantially the last literary work which Mr. Lowell did consisted of a careful discussion of these poets, whom he calls, "Old English Dramatists," thus anticipating a series now in preparation, under the title *The Best Plays of the Old English Dramatists.* No better proof can be found that the term Minor, as here applied, must be used relatively only, and in view of the unique position of Shakespeare at the time. So high was the standard established, that, in any other age, these secondary dramatists, secondary to Shakespeare only, would have been among the first of their order, as the best of them are, even yet, regarded as far above the intellectual average of any subsequent age. Though their work was not Shakespearian, it was invaluable, in separate instances closely bordering on Shakespearian form; while, as a body of playwrights, their aggregate product was of a distinctive order. It is questionable whether Shakespeare himself would have been the peerless author that he was, apart from these forerunners and contemporaries. It is a well-known fact of literary history, that even Shakespeare's asserted preëminence was contested by contemporary critics, nor was it till a century later, in the days of Dryden, that this preëminence was accepted without question. It was the general representative work of Jonson and Marlowe, and the occasional masterly product of Beaumont and Fletcher, Ford and Webster and Massinger, Lodge and Peele and Chapman, that kept this open question before the English public on to the age of Anne. A few suggestions as to these Minor Dramatists may serve to show the important place that they held in the literature of the time.

First of all, they were the real exponents of their age. This is true both in a literary and a mental sense, and especially true of those half-dozen among them who held the leading place. Particularly is it true of the Marlowe Group, as Shakespeare's immediate predecessors, that they heralded the coming epoch and prepared the way for it, using well what light they had, and marking a definite dramatic advance over all that had, as yet, existed. Though not representative to the same degree that Shakespeare was, they were, still, representative, and thus in line with the general literary progress and the specific dramatic progress of the period. Moreover, as a rule, these dramatists were University men, and, thus, by liberal training, qualified to take their place and play their part in the new and broader economy. Some of them, by way of distinction, were known as "University Wits," and thus connected the literary life of the time with its scholarship and culture. Scarcely too much emphasis can be laid upon the fact that, whatever the failings of these minor poets, they had enjoyed special intellectual training at Oxford and Cambridge, and not infrequently exhibit its good effects in their authorship. Here, again, the mastery of Shakespeare's mind and art is all the more amazing, in that he stood in no wise related to the great literary institutions of the nation.

Their exceptional excellence in Dramatic Art is, also, noteworthy. In the special province of versification or verse-structure they were, in the main, far in advance of their time, using the modern accentual method in preference to the older syllabic method, and thus revealing their independence of classical models. Marlowe, at this point, is held in high repute, his *Tamburlaine* being the first English Play in blank verse, as his *Edward the Second* was the first Historical Play of note. His "mighty line" was always effective, so that the Iambic Pentameter of later English verse became firmly established as the prevailing Heroic measure. This inner harmony between the poetic structure and the sense was truly Shakespearian, and at no point do many of these minor dramatists so closely resemble their master.

It should, also, be noted that these so-called secondary poets were a Coöperative School of Workers, and thus unified and intensified their dramatic power. Thus Beaumont and Fletcher, Chapman and Dekker, Webster and Dekker, Middleton and Rowley, Nash and Marlowe, composed their plays in common. They constituted a real Authors' Club or Guild, working toward common ends and on similar methods, while not surrendering, at all, their individual tastes and aims. They were, for the time, real fellow-craftsmen, partly, of necessity, and, partly, by preference and fraternal feeling. Thus Shakespeare himself worked conjointly with Jonson and Marlowe, his two greatest dramatic contemporaries. Indeed, the measure of

this mutual indebtedness can never be fully determined. That it existed at all is proof in point that there was, in the main, good fellowship between the great master and his colleagues, so that the current criticism to the contrary must be modified. It is a fact of Elizabethan history that Shakespeare, when first in London, devoted most of his effort to the revision of the work of his inferiors.

In fine, the more we study the real character of this great dramatic age, the more distinctly it appears that much of its greatness lay in the fact, that, Shakespeare apart, there were at work a body of playwrights masterful enough to give repute to any age in which they lived, and justly classified in later history as Minors only on the principle that the age was strictly exceptional, and that the imposing presence of the greatest dramatist of all literature overshadowed every lesser light. (pp. 251-62)

Theodore W. Hunt, "The Elizabethan Dramatic Development," in The Bibliotheca Sacra: A Religious and Sociological Quarterly, *Vol. LXVI, April, 1909, pp. 251-66.*

Henry W. Wells

[*Wells was an American educator who wrote extensively on English literature. In the following excerpt from a work originally published in 1939, he offers an overview of the Elizabethan theater, noting the manifold cultural influences which destined it to become "one of the most brilliant creations of the Western World."*]

A theatrical movement commonly regarded as the most brilliant in over two thousand years of Europe's history arose in London during the lifetime of Shakespeare. (p. 3)

The entire movement rose and fell with remarkable rapidity. No plays closely resembling those of the great Elizabethans appeared before the last quarter of the sixteenth century, before the tragedies of Kyd and Marlowe and the comedies of Lyly and Greene. The public theatres began to be erected in 1576; the first powerful plays appeared about 1587. The movement reached maturity a little after the death of Elizabeth in 1603, or in the first decade of the seventeenth century, which witnessed masterpieces by Shakespeare, Jonson, Beaumont and Fletcher, and their associates. Its peak was clearly passed when Shakespeare and Beaumont died in 1616 and Jonson gave evidence that his genius was fully spent. Talented playwrights and inspired actors enabled the playhouses to exist on their powerful momentum for nearly a quarter of a century more but with constantly diminishing glory. Fletcher died in 1625, Middleton two years after. When in 1642 Puritan propaganda closed the public theatres, almost all the eminent playwrights were dead and the few who survived had long finished their important work. Eighteen years thereafter the restoration of the Stuarts to the throne gave new life to the English stage, with new men, new manners, and new dramatic forms. It is true that the Restoration stage evolved from the Cavalier stage as the latter was ornamented by Massinger, Shirley, and Davenant; but it remains none the less clear that the break of nearly two decades is highly important in theatrical history. A continuity runs through the drama of three reigns, those of Elizabeth,

James I, and Charles I, like the work of one mind in youth, maturity, and decline. Literally speaking, one generation witnessed the entire development. Ben Jonson probably saw every playwright from Marlowe to Shirley. Marlowe died prematurely in 1593, and Shirley began play-writing about thirty years later. These are terminal figures. Most of the dramatists enjoyed personal acquaintance with the great majority of their fellow craftsmen. Their relations on the whole seem to have been remarkably cordial and about half their plays were written in collaboration, so that the drama of the period may be described as the product of a circle of friends; romantic fancy has painted them grouped about a table in the Mermaid Tavern. What can have caused the emergence of such a group of men and what fate denied them the power to produce further generations for the theatre?

The English theatre from 1576, when the first popular playhouse was built in London, till about 1611, when Shakespeare retired, represents one of the last artistic movements addressing all classes of society. The medieval theatre had also been communal, its piety and ribaldry enjoyed alike by king and countryman. Richard II witnessed at York in the great mystery cycle of that city the homely pageants representing the Christian story. Circumstances favored the rebirth of a really national theatre in Shakespeare's England, whereas no such theatre was destined to arise on the Continent.

The great cycles of the mystery plays performed in all the larger towns of Europe and England from the fourteenth century to the sixteenth show as warm and popular a love for theatrical entertainment as history anywhere records. It is a drama of, for, and by the people. Notably enough this most catholic form of drama flourished nowhere more lustily than in England. A court theatre is seldom so vital as a popular one. When the princes and nobles of the Renaissance took theatrical entertainment under their patronage in their own houses, they cut off much of the vitality of the older tradition and suffered a repression in their own. The farces and moral interludes played abroad or in England before Cardinal Morton at the close of the fifteenth century and before Henry VIII at the beginning of the sixteenth surpassed the earlier popular drama in wit but not in power or inspiration. The old communal soil was ready in England for one more new crop.

The Renaissance or, more specifically, the sixteenth-century drama in Europe all too frequently evolved into a somewhat bookish following of the none too inspired Seneca or a fairly close imitation of Plautus and Terence, of which the tragedies of Garnier in French and the comedies of Ariosto in Italian were the most influential in England. As a power behind such plays lay the Renaissance mind increasingly weaning itself from religious preoccupations and seeking fresh personal expression. The new drama became noble and intellectual. But the serious plays commonly remained, after the Senecan models, more declamatory than dramatic or even poetic, and the comedies relatively stereotyped and traditional. Very gradually gaining in richness and power, the drama of the Continent ultimately reached its climax during the mid-seventeenth century in the tragedies of Corneille and the comedies of Molière. Had no peculiar factors been at work in England, there is small reason to suppose that any other than the more conservative phases of Restoration drama would ultimately have appeared. Quite without the aid of an Elizabethan tradition English wit and intelligence might have created a Congreve and sheer imitativeness have produced the neoclassical tragedies of James Thomson and William Mason. But happily England had a theatrical inspiration of her own.

A theatrical movement is to be explained as much by the audience as by the actors and playwrights. The English Court under Elizabeth enjoyed, but did not direct, the British theatre. So long as theatrical entertainment remained in the hands of the Crown or of the great nobles and ecclesiastics, it made no progress beyond that attained under similar circumstances abroad. Moral shows were produced in the household of Cardinal Morton, farces in the even wittier household of Sir Thomas More, while the Inns of Court and the Court itself harbored many typical entertainments grave and gay. Play-writing became one of the acknowledged avocations of gentility, befitting a great lady or a privy councilor. Tragedies were commonly on the Senecan model, as *Gorboduc,* by Thomas Norton and Thomas Sackville, who afterwards became Lord Buckhurst. Comedies ranged from medieval farce to Terencian satire. All these types of plays were also produced in the schools and colleges, where the works of Seneca and Terence were acted and original plays based upon them were given not only in English but in Latin. Medieval mystery and morality plays were still being acted during the first half of Elizabeth's reign. Then, in 1576, the first popular theatre was built in London, and a new epoch in drama suddenly arose. The new plays were, of course, at first based upon the old, but rapidly developed along novel lines.

The more self-contained spirit of the Continent was owing in great part to the logical and consistent course of Renaissance thought among the continental scholars and aristocracy. There is little evidence that they were interested in the fantastic doings of the London stage. In England the public and the playwrights were for the most part either innocent of the rigid critical theories abroad or, like Ben Jonson, superior to them. The playwrights used a freedom enjoyed by the authors of the plays on the saints' legends during the Middle Ages but with a subject matter almost wholly secular. Their plays were highly eclectic, half medieval and half modern. The popular English theatre called for much more action and for less moralizing and declamation than the aristocratic continental theatre. Moreover, even the new aristocracy in England proved in most respects far more liberal and experimental than the leaders abroad. The coming of the Tudors and the policy of Henry VIII created a group of new families enriched by the spoils of war and the desecration of the monasteries. The *nouveaux riches* of the Western World, they were the less staid and reactionary in upholding tradition of any sort. Both classical Renaissance and Protestant Reformation burst upon them suddenly and disturbingly, less as an evolution than as a revolution. Such men, already keenly sensitized by changes in thought and life, proved ready for any new adventure, whether at Darien with Drake or at the Globe with Shakespeare. Under Elizabeth Protestant-ism had been successfully established as the religion of state, with a measure of toleration which even invited skepticism. Doubtful as to matters of religion and still religious, although generally persuaded that faith was in any case not the greatest thing in life, the average Elizabethan was ideally poised for new emotional and aesthetic experiences. Old standards in society, belief, education, and conduct were breaking down. Europe itself appeared to the true-born Englishman of the day as a vast, newly opened treasure house of the most varied riches from which he might pick his fill with lavish hand. Whatever might be the ambiguous position of the Anglican Church, the country was still more Catholic in spirit than puritanical in the sense that it was pleasure-loving and aesthetic as England has never been since. Trade had won new freedom and horizons for the enterprising Londoner, but had not as yet frozen into dull commercialism. It was still a merry England, more a land of artists than of shopkeepers. Indeed the very people who kept the shops flocked to the theatres. London was wealthy but hardly sober. While its empire was still a dream it could afford to make its dreams imperial. No deadening weight of hollow and unreal dignity crushed the spirit of those who listened for the first time to plays by the Swan of Avon.

Elizabethan inventiveness is brilliantly reflected in the dynamic language of the dramatists. Blank verse, in which the plays are largely written, was a new medium for English poetry. The poetical language itself, though certainly based upon medieval poetry, was a notable departure from anything which had gone before. The towering images and metaphors of Marlowe and Shakespeare, even the pleasant wit of Lyly and Greene, were new things. So in their turn were the epic style of Chapman, the torrential manner of Jonson, the biting words of Webster, the liquid language of Fletcher, and even the eloquence of Massinger and the lucidity of Shirley. The English language was undergoing a rich series of transformations difficult to parallel in any contemporary tongue. Above all others the dramatists took full advantage of this golden hour for English speech. Shakespeare's language is far more poetical than that of either Chaucer or Congreve, for it is neither immature nor oversophisticated. So inspiring was the instrument of English speech which destiny placed in the playwrights' hands.

The stage is an ideal medium for storytelling. Chaucer had lived in a fine age of storytelling too, but at a time when few tales besides those of the Bible found theatrical expression. Public assembly for other purposes than those of Church or State would doubtless have seemed dangerous and irreligious to the fourteenth century. But London must have been even gayer in Shakespeare's time than in Chaucer's. It passionately loved stories, classical, Italian, and modern, and took a more mature attitude toward storytelling than the English of the fourteenth century. The human spirit and the narrative art reserved in Chaucer for the written page were suddenly released by Shakespeare and his companions for the stage. Our own age attempts to use more complex matter for theatrical purposes with much less confidence of success.

The bold experimentation of the Elizabethan theatre cannot be overemphasized. So long as it kept its freshness and explorative spirit, it was masterly. While it combined on an almost equal footing the medieval and the modern, it remained emancipated and alive. But when Jonson produced a school of realists, when Fletcher succeeded to the laurels of Shakespeare and was followed in turn by Massinger and by Shirley, the period of experimentation had passed and that of decadence and imitativeness arrived. It was not the Puritans who killed the Elizabethan stage, but the want of that free, invigorating, and windswept air that the great dramatists breathed as the birthright of their age. Changing times allayed the winds, weighed the atmosphere with heaviness, and induced the playwrights to copy their predecessors, who had themselves been copyists only in minor matters. The theatre ceased to be national and became aristocratic. Shirley wrote much in the spirit later cultivated in Italy by Goldoni. The sudden glory of an age perished.

The drama of the period affords an ideal ground for study in the continuity and evolution of literary and theatrical tradition. It is continuous because the playwrights and theatrical companies for half a century formed a closely knit society. Many plays were written in collaboration. A group of eminent actors and theatrical leaders stamped their impression upon the stage, so that a large number of well-defined theatrical conventions were established. Although such circumstances as the pestilence or a quiet season in London led the theatrical companies to take to the road, the plays were primarily for a relatively small London audience, long accustomed to seeing and criticizing performances. Some of the earliest of the famous dramas, as Marlowe's *Jew of Malta* and *Doctor Faustus,* Shakespeare's *Romeo and Juliet* and *Midsummer-Night's Dream,* were acted and printed even at the close of the period. *The Jew of Malta,* indeed, survives only in a quarto of 1633. The latest of the playwrights, as James Shirley, were writing plays in 1640 clearly based upon ideas of plot, character, and dramatic language inaugurated in Elizabethan times. (pp. 3-11)

The English of the age . . . were great lovers of music and dress. Many of their plays verge upon the operatic, so prominent are the musical elements. They contain delightful songs, and the original performances were accompanied by much instrumental music before and during the acts. Again, since the age was infatuated with dress, the theatrical spectacles, relatively bare in setting, exploited costume to an extraordinary degree. A large part of the wealth of the theatrical companies lay in their gorgeous wardrobes, to which the Court itself made loans and gifts. A notorious case is in the records of a play which might be supposed to have been one of the most simply and soberly produced, Thomas Heywood's bourgeois and sentimental drama, *A Woman Killed with Kindness.* For writing the play Heywood received only a fraction of the sum spent on the heroine's dress. In short, from the Elizabethans' love of music came naturally their lyrical drama, and from their passion for costume and spectacle their brilliant stage pictures.

London was the city where all the dramatists lived and

many had been born. It was an ideal seat for intellectual and artistic stimulus. Here was the Court with its brilliant life and a patronage neither to be blindly trusted nor despised. Here, too, were the Inns of Court, the sanctuaries of the lawyers, who enjoyed a notable renaissance in their own right and enthusiastically supported the performance of plays. Between the lawyers and the actors a bond naturally arose, each being employed in voluble and vehement contests of words. Here, too, were many prosperous citizens eager for entertainment. The town was small, snug, and sociable, exactly the condition to incubate a robust theatre. Houses were relatively small and simply furnished, the scenes of busy family and commercial life. From them in happy hour the citizens issued forth to amuse each other as they could hardly be amused in their busy homes, too narrow and too much like workshops to harbor much varied entertainment. Tavern life was certainly gayer and more popular than the life in the public houses and restaurants of any Anglo-Saxon city today. In the taverns many of the plays were begotten and some apparently written. There the wits met and talk flowed. This most gregarious and sociable people passed in a step from their intimate taverns and ordinaries to their small and tightly packed theatres, numerous, busy, competitive, and thriving. There humanity crowded together upon the floor and against the walls, leaving only the opening for the heavens and for the fourth wall, which must of necessity become the background for an eminently human though poetic performance. Nursed under such circumstances, the Elizabethan drama was fated to become one of the most brilliant creations of the Western World. (pp. 11-13)

Henry W. Wells, in an introduction to his Elizabethan and Jacobean Playwrights, *1939. Reprint by Greenwood Press, 1975, pp. 3-13.*

J. M. R. Margeson

[*Margeson is a highly regarded Canadian educator and Elizabethan scholar. In the following excerpt, he considers the impact of the "craft," or mystery play, cycles upon Elizabethan tragedy. He particularly focuses on the fifteenth-century playwrights' adaptation of character types, situations, and the conception of a suffering and decadent world from medieval religious drama and morality plays.*]

Medieval religious drama has been restored in recent years to a place of first importance in the development of Elizabethan drama. A number of studies have been built upon the massive foundations laid by Sir Edmund Chambers to show the continuity of the popular stage as a living tradition from the fourteenth to the sixteenth centuries. It is a tradition not so much literary as theatrical, depending upon methods of production, acting, and conventions of staging for its continuity rather than upon a growing body of texts. The popularity of the religious drama, its long life, and its direct influence upon the popular drama of Elizabethan England is no longer in doubt.

However, the influence of this religious drama upon later tragedy has received only qualified acceptance: the morality plays, it is said, had a direct connexion through the moral histories, but the mystery plays are unlikely to have

had much influence of any kind. The fact that every incident with possible tragic connotations is eventually subordinated to the total scheme of redemption and triumph has led to a general rejection of the mystery plays as sources of tragic structure or feeling. By contrast, the connexion of the morality plays with tragedy has long been recognized, partly because of the freedom they displayed to develop away from abstractions toward concrete, historical *exempla,* partly because of what Willard Farnham [in his *The Medieval Heritage of Elizabethan Tragedy*] has described as their increasing severity toward the end of their evolution, with emphasis upon the debasement of human life and upon despair and damnation rather than upon God's total plan of redemption. Nevertheless, it seems to me that the craft cycles [i.e., mystery plays] ought to be considered just as seriously in any account of developing tragedy, even if their total framework is not tragic. Not only do they portray a universe where suffering and evil exists as facts of experience, but they portray them intensely and without consolation, at least in the dramatic moment of the individual play. (p. 1)

[There is a] recurring conflict in tragedy between human will and a superior law which is either antagonistic to human will or remote and difficult to comprehend. The mystery plays are full of such conflict, though it must be admitted at once that the superior law is equated with the will of God, and that this will is assumed to be just in absolute terms. The various embodiments of human will acting in opposition to the divine will are the tyrants, from Pharaoh to Antichrist; the servants and soldiers who act as their agents and yet represent another brand of human iniquity; and thirdly, those who know good and yet choose evil—the great sinners, Lucifer, Cain, Judas, and, in a somewhat different category, Adam and Eve.

The tyrants are the most obvious examples of human will completely at odds with reality and doomed to failure. As they are usually portrayed, they are symbols of all the forces in the world opposed to good, incarnations of evil purpose, agents of God's enemy, Satan or Mahound. Their motives are not analysed except in terms of the pride of the kings of this world and hatred of God. Yet frequently there are signs of the imaginative recognition of an individual, as if to say that evil wears numerous forms and even tyranny is human in its variety. Pharaoh is not at all like Herod, and Herod is unlike Pilate. Moreover, the same tyrants, the Herods for example, differ considerably from one cycle to another. The Pilate of the Wakefield cycle is a forerunner of the cunning, self-announced villains of the chronicle plays, of Richard of Gloucester [Richard III] himself, whereas the Pilate of the York cycle seems almost virtuous by comparison, though he is shrewd and worldly.

How seriously should the tyrants be considered as symbolic figures representing the evil forces of the universe? There is, of course, evidence to suggest that the tyrants were melodramatic stage figures of considerable popularity and that they were sometimes played for comic effect, particularly on first entrance to a scene. Nevertheless, the plays read in sequence suggest that these characters were overwhelmingly serious in their major effect, that they were intended as embodiments of man's inherent evil, his lust for power and his boundless cruelty. They arouse a sense of fear before the enormity of evil. This emotion reaches a high pitch of intensity because of the presence of the victims—the children of Bethlehem and Christ.

Our main problem is the relationship of the tyrant scenes in the craft cycles to the emotional and conceptual patterns of later tragedy. The tyrants are not in themselves tragic characters. There is no hint in their motivation of any aspiration with which an audience could sympathize, nor is there any of the tragic feeling which a broken hope or a savagely reversed aspiration can arouse. Yet the tyrant scenes do represent something quite fundamental to the tragic experience, since they picture in harsh terms the opposition of human will and human pride to a larger force that will inevitably defeat them. Because this human will is completely evil and the divine force completely good, the struggle between them is too directly moral to arouse any of the complex feelings of tragedy, but it remains a nucleus from which other elements can grow. It contains more than a hint of the struggle between human will and an implacable fate which later tragedy was to explore. When the motivation of the tyrant was elaborated in transitional moral histories like *Apius and Virginia* and *Cambises,* sympathy with, or at least interest in, the fate of the tyrant became a possibility, and the way lay open for the growth of tragic feeling in such tyrant plays as *Richard III, Tamburlaine,* and *Macbeth.*

Several of the tyrant scenes in the mystery cycles present the fearful, yet satisfying spectacle of pride and cruelty overwhelmed and punished, and in this spectacle lies some hint of a controlling idea of retribution fashioning and shaping an embryonic plot. The basic plot is an inevitable movement from pride towards failure and defeat. Sometimes this structure is merely suggested by the over-all force of the cycle; sometimes it is explicit within the individual scene itself. Thus it exists in the play of the downfall of Pharaoh, though the tyrant is left comparatively undeveloped.

Two of the Advent plays about Herod present the most complete patterns of retribution to be found in the craft cycles. In the Chester play the slaughter of the infants results in the death of one of Herod's own children, and Herod himself is punished by a horrifying and fatal disease. It is the Hegge play, however, that builds up the greatest contrast between the boastful pride of Herod and his approaching doom. During Herod's feast of celebration the allegorical figure of Mors appears and comments on the folly of the king's pride. Like certain morality plays on the Pride of Life theme, the scene is a dramatized *exemplum,* related to the parable of the man who wished to build greater barns for his rich harvest. But the sermon does not diminish the striking dramatic power of the scene in which Herod eats and drinks at his ease, while the sardonic figure of Death stands in the background, waiting to strike.

As we should expect, there is no complete plot worked out for any tyrant in the sequence of Passion plays, where the double climax must be the Crucifixion and the Resurrection. Retribution is therefore by no means a dominating

idea in the craft cycles as a whole. Slight, and dramatically unexpanded, in the play of Pharaoh, the moral pattern of crime and punishment is worked out thoroughly only in the Chester and Hegge plays of the *Slaughter of the Innocents* and in the York *Judas.* In these plays human will directed in enmity against the divine will is not simply represented as a fact of existence, but becomes part of a significant pattern of events leading to defeat and justified punishment.

It is worth remembering that the scenes we have been considering are focused as much upon the victims as upon the tyrants. The tyrant figures represent merely one half of the tyrant-victim or terror-pity combination. As forces standing out against God and all his works, the tyrants are representations of hideous evil, which attacks goodness in this world and demonstrates its power through torture and death. This is clearly a fallen world that is presented to us, a world where human will is often wrongly directed toward cruelty and destruction and is punished accordingly, but a world where the innocent too must suffer, simply because they are born into it. There will be justice for all eventually, but in the meantime, in the world of historical existence, there are tragic events and suffering that are part of the condition of man.

The tyrants are not the only representatives of human will set in opposition to divine will. In the same scenes we encounter their followers and servants, who portray human depravity at a lower level, without the power and self-conscious purpose of the tyrants, but with as much confidence in evil and joy in inflicting pain. The brutality of Herod's soldiers dragging the babies from the mothers of Bethlehem, the casual hardness of the soldiers of Pilate, Herod, and Caiaphas as they torture Christ—these are portrayed in far greater detail than the desire for pathos would seem to require. There is an attempt in such scenes to give expression to certain very harsh facts of experience. They represent the bestial elements in human nature, perhaps something more frightening than bestial—demonic forces which erupt in human nature in every generation. The wall paintings of the Passion scenes which survive in a few English churches portray similar figures, in which a malicious delight in evil is given a visual representation in coarse and degraded human features, and in a leer of the eye or a turning of the lip which is devilish rather than sub-human. Other examples may be found in medieval windows and tapestries, and particularly in a wide variety of carvings in wood and stone.

As natural to fallen man is the comic element that creeps into some versions of the Slaughter of the Innocents, the boisterous delight in evil of Herod's soldiers, their boasting and their cowardice. But the general picture is a dark one. Here, at a level below that of the tyrants, is human will once more seeking its own way, oblivious of a higher power directing universal destiny. One is made strongly aware of human blindness in the face of a totally different scheme of things, which the participants refuse to recognize. The audience must take an ironic view of their self-confident and utterly human wrongness.

These minor characters, soldiers, servants, and other agents of the great tyrants of the mystery plays, are not important enough to the dramatic scheme to form part of a larger structure of retribution. Even as representatives of crude human will in opposition to providence, they do not play any very important part, and their main function lies in contributing to the atmosphere of a fallen world where brutality and suffering are commonplace. Their most striking descendants are the hired ruffians and murderers who torture gentle innocents and noble patriots in the chronicle plays. But the minor figures in many later tragedies who represent the base metal beneath the façade of human splendour could scarcely have had such a vivid existence without this background in the religious drama.

We have not yet considered the most striking and important examples of conflict between individual will and divine will: these occur mainly at the beginning of each cycle in the Fall of Lucifer, the Fall of Man, and what might be called the Fall of Cain. The only example later in the cycles of a similar conflict lies in the story of Judas. The religious reason for placing these stories at the beginning is obvious. Not only does the Biblical narrative begin in this way, but they serve to explain the necessity for the whole universal drama to follow, of Sin, Incarnation, Redemption, and Last Judgement.

Lucifer, Adam and Eve, Cain, and Judas are alike in setting up their own wills in opposition to God's will. They are all involved in a similar progress of action from a state of blessedness or innocence, with an awareness and experience of the good, to a state of sin, frustration, and despair. Their plays differ from the plays we have been considering heretofore in that they show the whole process of choice, and hence of responsibility, so that the suffering and remorse at the end come as the inevitable consequence of choice. I have no wish to obscure the marked differences between these plays by a series of generalizations, but I believe they have certain features in common which grow out of religious conceptions governing the cycles as a whole. The action of each scene is a temptation and fall, the defeat of the individual will in its struggle with the divine will. Characterization is not developed very far, but far enough to reveal a particular fault or sin which provides the motivating force for the rebellion of the individual: pride, ambition, envy, greed. Because of their knowledge of the good and the warnings they have received against evil, the central characters must accept responsibility for their falls, and in their remorse, blame themselves. Characterization goes far enough, therefore, to permit self-knowledge. The emotional patterns of these plays move from over-confidence and pride (which arouse the ironic sense in an audience) to despair and remorse (which may arouse pity). The endings are completely harsh, set against a background of eternal damnation, with the exception of the Fall of Man plays, where the harshness is modified by hope of eventual forgiveness.

The Fall of Lucifer is the beginning of evil in the universe, and is therefore given considerable stress at the beginning of each cycle. This is the primal example of individual will in opposition to God's will; the conflict is the more awe-inspiring because of Lucifer's greatness before his fall and because of the extent of his blasphemy. One may observe some of the typical elements of medieval tragedy: magnifi-

cence of place, supreme confidence in the face of warnings, and a catastrophic fall into misery and remorse, though it is direct providential intervention rather than fortune which brings about the fall. There are variations upon this basic pattern in the different cycles. In the Hegge play there is no actual moment of temptation: at the end of a hymn of worship and praise Lucifer demands that it be directed to him as the worthiest of all. In the York play, however, Lucifer is not immediately evil but undergoes a process of self-temptation as he meditates upon his own brightness and beauty. It is the Chester play that is the most striking of the four in its portrayal of a dramatic conflict of wills. In the dialogue with Lightborne, one of his followers, and in the debate with the other angels, Lucifer becomes more and more outspoken in his pride, until he utters the final blasphemy, proclaims himself greater than God, and ascends the divine throne. His language now attempts to take on the majesty appropriate to the speech of God, but he is suddenly and swiftly cast down to Hell.

The writers of these plays picture the fall of Lucifer as the greatest of all possible tragic falls, from supreme bliss into the darkest depths of misery and pain. Afterwards there is remorse, despair, recrimination, as the devils curse one another and think of revenge. In the York play it is the loss of his own beauty that afflicts Lucifer most intensely, but in all of them the loss of the bliss of Heaven is important. An unusual note in the Chester play is the expression of God's sorrow at the fall of Lucifer, his complaint against pride, and his disclaimer of any wish that it should have happened in this way.

There is undoubted tragic potentiality in these scenes as the great conflict between aspiration and destiny moves to its inevitable close. The pride of Lucifer is ironically turned into complete defeat, his surpassing beauty into ugliness and darkness. In expressing Lucifer's bitter remorse and sense of loss the writers of the mystery plays were at least in some degree aware of the contrast between aspiration and defeat that later generations were to call tragic. Of course, the theological implications are absolutely clear, and there is no doubt of the justice of God or of the necessity of Lucifer's punishment: one does not expect any intermixture of sympathy or pity in the emotional pattern. But the element of fear and the sense of loss remain important factors that the writers of these plays were endeavouring to express.

A similar conflict between individual will and divine will exists in the Fall of Man plays in all the cycles. Adam and Eve are very different from Lucifer as tragic prototypes: their sin is not so extreme in its blasphemy, nor are they self-tempted to the same degree, since part of the blame must be placed on the wiles of a cunning enemy. Though they cannot be as 'heroic' as Lucifer in their rebellion and though their fall cannot have the same grandeur and terror, they have the advantage (for drama) of their humanity, with all its possibilities for human sympathy.

The Fall of Man plays are remarkably alike, so that it is possible to speak of them as if they were a single play. The process of temptation is longer than in the Fall of Lucifer, and more interesting dramatically, since several characters are involved and there are two stages in the temptation. The nature of the temptation is made very plain: if they eat of the fruit of the tree they will become as gods in their knowledge of good and evil. Yet in the moment of aspiration they are aware of the fact that they are disobeying God's direct command, that they are setting their own wills in opposition to God's will. Recognition and the full awakening to the meaning of sin comes when Adam has eaten the apple: at once they are filled with shame and remorse, before God has spoken to them and before the nature of their punishment has been revealed. The great goal they sought is not only far different from what they expected, but terrifying. The tragic irony of their situation is made explicit in God's words to them in the Chester play:

> Thou wouldeste knowe bouth weale and woe,
> Nowe is yt fallne to thee soe,
> Therfore, hense thou muste goe,
> And thy desyer fulfilled. . . .

There are two points I should like to make about the conclusion of this play within the framework of the larger cycle. First, the suffering which results from the struggle between human will and divine will is not merely a physical punishment imposed upon them by God and enforced by the angels: it is even more strikingly an inward suffering as they realize their great loss and their own responsibility. Secondly, several of the Fall of Man plays end without any direct expression of consolation. The audience is aware of the pattern of the whole cycle, of the Redemption of Man and Christ's removal of the dread punishment of death, but this tremendous hope lies outside the scenes I have been speaking of and they end on a note close to despair.

In the Chester cycle Cain's murder of Abel follows at once as a kind of tragic corollary of the Fall. Adam warns his sons to obey God and tells them of his dream of the Redemption to come. Yet we are now in the world of tragic experience, as the fatal quarrel between Cain and Abel makes evident. Adam and Eve return to the stage to lament the death of one son and the damnation of the other as part of their continuing punishment.

There is, perhaps, a more intense expression of despair in the Hegge play than in any other. Eve in her misery can only beg Adam to kill her:

> Alas! alas! and wele away,
> That evyr towchyd I the tre
> I wende as wrecche in welsom way,
> In blake busshys my boure xal be.
> In paradys is plentē of pleye,
> ffayr frutys ryth gret plentē,
> The gatys be schet with Godys keye,
> My husbond is lost because of me.
>   Leve spowse now thou fonde,
> Now stomble we on stalk and ston,
> My wyt awey is fro me gon,
> Wrythe on to my necke bon
>   With hardnesse of thin honde.

Adam comforts her as best he can and the scene ends on a note of resignation, though without hope or consolation. Here, as in the other examples I have referred to, a fundamental tragic pattern is evident, of human aspiration in conflict with divine law, and leading to defeat, remorse, and suffering. It does not seem possible to me to understand the tension between despair and resignation in Elizabethan tragedy without some awareness of the strength of these qualities in the religious drama. (pp. 2-10)

Though the total dramatic scheme of the mystery cycle is a divine comedy, almost all the scenes take place within a fallen world. In this world, whose nature is quickly revealed to us in *The Fall of Man* and *Cain and Abel,* human will is encouraged by ignorance and sin, a desire for some partial good or false reward, to stand out against divine will. Yet such a struggle leads to eventual damnation in the next world, and frequently to mental anguish and physical suffering in this. The divine will against which man struggles at his peril is more clearly defined and more easily discernible than the background of universal law in Renaissance tragedy: yet they are alike in arousing a sense of tragic inevitability.

The religious certainty that God's universe is a just one and that virtue will eventually be rewarded and vice punished is a basic assumption behind the mystery cycles, since the inevitable conclusion for each cycle is the Last Judgement. However, there is quite a powerful sense of a tragic world in the meantime where prosperity and suffering have little relation to merit. In that world innocents are tortured and murdered and evil men triumph: the suffering of pathetic victims like the mothers of Bethlehem, the children, and Christ himself seems to contradict every conception of the moral law, and outrages human feeling, in spite of the assurances of a higher law which will eventually make everything right. (pp. 13-14)

One other element inherited by Elizabethan tragedy from the medieval drama—from craft cycles and from morality plays alike—should be referred to at this point, since it links emotional effect with metaphysical idea. Critics have for long been aware of the mixture of comic and serious action in the mystery plays and have tried to explain the existence of these sometimes incongruous strains in a variety of ways, though generally in terms of the gradual loss of control over the plays by the ecclesiastical authorities. A. P. Rossiter [in his *English Drama from Early Times to the Elizabethans*] has declared that the 'devilish gusto' of torturers and tyrants, so closely bound up with the agony of their victims, is evidence of two rituals, one of which denies the other—and hence the faith of the cycles as a whole. Allied to the ritual of evil, of cruelty and negation, is a kind of mockery and derision which, Rossiter claims, is descended from the Joculator and the 'comic rejoicings of the folk'. This latter spirit may seem entirely comic, but it is often destructive in its effect, because it is a parody, even a demonic parody, of the serious action.

As a qualification of this point of view something might be said of the medieval craftsman's search for realism and a contact with the world around him, whether it be in sculpture, painting, or drama. Thoroughly aware of the meanness and cruelty of human nature, he did not try to falsify it, nor did his religion ask him to hide it. Though a simple artist, he was probably aware also that the more he stressed the cruelty of those who tortured Christ, the greater would be the pity for the suffering victim. Where we possess early and late versions of the same plays, it is apparent that much of the development has been in this direction or for this purpose.

Yet when this has been said, and when allowance has been made for the playwright's delight in portraying the trivial and comic concerns of human beings, it must be admitted that not everything has been accounted for. There is a strange spirit in this drama, which is reflected also in the wall paintings and stone carvings of the time. It is said to appear strikingly in the religious drama of Germany and Austria. The English craft cycles are never dominated by this Gothic spirit, any more than the parish church at Winchcombe is dominated by its gargoyles, but some clash of tones is evident.

The episode of Garcio and Cain in the Wakefield play, *The Killing of Abel,* adds an incongruous element to the scene of Cain's despair. Cain's tiff with the angel in the York version is comic enough to have a similar result. In the Hegge play, *The Trial of Joseph and Mary,* the Detractors are so lewd and mocking in their jests and accusations that the purity of Mary is nearly forgotten. And in the Digby *Killing of the Children* Herod's timorous knight, Watkyn, destroys utterly the pathos of the scene. By contrast, the various Noah plays are humorous only in a homely and familiar way and the comedy does no great harm to the religious theme. Even the parody of the Nativity in *The Second Shepherds' Play* is comparatively innocent in effect because the spirit of comedy in the play is so genial and so closely related to normal human nature.

Apparently the comic and realistic scenes which undermine the emotional effect and religious meaning of certain parts of the cycles belong to the later enlargement of the cycles; some of them were undoubtedly added for the entertainment they provided and can have no other justification. The devilish gusto of the scenes of cruelty, however, cannot be explained away by such terms as secularization and degeneration. Though perhaps intensified by later redactors (as in the Wakefield cycle), they seem to have formed a part of the cycles from an early period and to represent something essential in the medieval artist's view of humanity. Whether part of the religious vision of the plays or outside it, that dark view of the depths of evil in the human heart, evil easily released and immeasurable in its effect, is one of the most striking products of the medieval mind. The combination of this dark vision with the destructive ridicule of the fool, the rustic, or the evil detractor forms an important contribution to later tragedy.

What is clear from a close study of the mystery cycles is that the medieval dramatists had learned to do certain things most effectively. They were not attempting to write tragedy, but in the process of representing scenes of suffering and despair, always within the total religious structure, they gave to the dramatic tradition scenes which could be imitated and developed in a tragic direction by later secular dramatists. What was once learned well by the medieval stage did not have to be learned again, and this dictum applies not only to the conventions of acting and staging which have been widely discussed in recent years but also to dramatic situation and characterization. I have pointed out certain scenes of quite exceptional emo-

tional power, not far removed from tragic feeling. These scenes influenced later dramatists because they became part of the language of stage representation.

Let us consider the way in which some of these dramatic situations or episodes have relevance for later tragedy. One example is the pathetic struggle of the innocent and weak against brutal power which on the surface appears to rule the world. The three Marys in early liturgical drama, and Abel, the mothers of Bethlehem, and Christ in the craft cycles, express this struggle in different ways. When later writers chose to represent the cruelty of tyrants and the miseries of the weak, they could scarcely avoid the notable models already familiar to wide audiences. The terror, the pathos, and the anger which fill the scene of Cambises' shooting of Praxaspes' young son are close to the emotional power of the *Slaughter of the Innocents.* I am not trying to prove a direct descent through the evidence of verbal echoes, but I think the placing of such scenes side by side will confirm my view that playwrights built on what had already been achieved and did not have to learn certain dramatic lessons over again. In addition, and more important for our purpose, the serious intensity of such scenes was carried over from the religious to the secular drama.

The first two passages from the mystery cycles [*Ludus Coventriae* and XVI, *Towneley Plays*] are direct evocations of misery and despair, strongly arousing the emotion of pity, though there is also anger and a demand for vengeance:

> *Prima faemina.* Longe lullynge have I lorn!
> Alas! qwhy was my baron born?
> With swappynge swerde now is he shorn
>   The heed ryght fro the nekke!
> Shanke and shulderyn is al to-torn,
> Sorwyn I se behyndyn and beforn,
> Both mydnyth, mydday, and at morn,—
>   Of my lyff I ne recke.

> *Secunda faemina.* Serteynly I say the same,
> Gon is alle my good game,
> My lytylle childe lyth alle lame,
>   That lullyd on my pappys!
> My ffourty wekys gronynge
> Hath sent me sefne yere sorwynge,
> Mykyl is my mornynge,
>   And ryght hard arne myn happys!

>   · · · · ·

> Outt! morder! man, I say
> strang tratoure & thefe!
> Out! alas! and waloway!
> my child that was me lefe!
> My luf, my blood, my play
> that neuer dyd man grefe!
> Alas, alas, this day!
> I wold my hart shuld clefe
>   In sonder!
> veniance I cry and call,
> on herode and his knyghtys all!
> veniance, lord, apon thaym fall,
>   And mekyll warldys wonder!

In the following passage from *Cambises* one can see that pathos is aroused by the same means—the joy of the mother turned to grief, the long burden of child-bearing become a mockery—and, once again, the grief is mingled with anger:

> With blubred eies into mine armes from earth I
> wil thee take
> And wrap thee in mine apron white, but oh my
> heauy hart:
> The spiteful pangs ẙ it sustains, wold make it in
> two to part.
> The death of this my Sonne to see, O heuy moth-
> er now:
> That from thy sweet & sugred ioy, to sorrow so
> shouldst bow.
> What greef in womb did I retain, before I did
> thee see?
> Yet at the last when smart was gone, what ioy
> wert thou to me.
> How tender was I of thy food, for to preserue thy
> state?
> How stilled I thy tender hart, at times early and
> late?
> With veluet paps I gaue thee suck, with issue
> from my brest:
> And danced thee vpon my knee, to bring thee
> vnto rest.
> Is this the ioy of thee I reap (O King) of tigers
> brood?
> Oh tigers whelp hadst thou ẙ hart, to see this
> childs hart blood.

The literary elaboration is hardly an improvement upon the intensely dramatic speech of the craft cycle plays, but it is clear that the emotional patterns are intended to be similar.

In later plays, the murder of innocent children and the mourning of mother or father is a familiar situation. That such murders could take place on stage, like young Rutland's murder by Clifford in *3 Henry VI*, is itself an indication of the continuity of the tradition. It is true that the murder of the young princes in *Richard III* takes place off stage, but the vivid report of the murderers is very close to actual representation. In the speeches of mourning, too, one often catches an echo of earlier plays in the same tradition. York's lament for Rutland, for example, suggests the last few lines of the mother's lament in *Cambises*, quoted above:

> O tiger's heart wrapp'd in a woman's hide!
> How couldst thou drain the life-blood of the
> child,
> To bid the father wipe his eyes withal,
> And yet be seen to bear a woman's face?
> (*3 Henry VI*, I. iv. 137-40)

The pathos of suffering and the terror of unlimited power in an evil world are part of the heritage of later drama from the cycle plays. (pp. 15-19)

The scenes of Christ's Passion are the most powerful, both as drama and in doctrinal force, in all the mystery cycles. Though unrepeatable in secular terms by their very nature, these scenes contain separable dramatic elements which could be used by later playwrights. Essentially, the Passion scenes represent an innocent victim with dignity and strength of spirit, suffering at the hands of brutal torturers and murderers who act under the orders of men of worldly power. Although the emphasis on innocence suggests pathos as the dominant emotion, the effect is a little more complex than this, since the victim has chosen a course of action knowing full well that it will bring him into conflict with the world. In his own person and office he gathers upon himself the hatred and antagonism of the world.

It is in the chronicle plays that we encounter characters and situations that remind us of this heritage. Woodstock is the outstanding example of the virtuous man whose loyalty and integrity gather together a storm of abuse and eventually bring about his murder. The last scene of Woodstock's life, in which the ghosts of the Black Prince and Edward III appear to him, may seem quite remote from Christ's agony in the garden, and obviously bears a closer relationship to the appearance of lamenting ghosts in the *Mirror for Magistrates*. Nevertheless, the language is filled with references to innocence and the protecting power of angels and of heaven:

> I here remain
> A poor old man, thrust from my native country
> Kept and imprisoned in a foreign kingdom.
> If I must die, bear record, righteous heaven,
> How I have nightly waked for England's good,
> And yet to right her wrongs would spend my
> blood.
> Send thy sad doom, King Richard: take my life.
> (*Enter* LAPOOLE *and the* MURDERERS)
> I wish my death might ease my country's grief.
> (*Woodstock*, V. i. 121-8)

The murder scene that follows takes us forcibly into the very atmosphere and language of the Crucifixion scenes in the mystery cycles. The contrast between helpless innocence and crude brutality in the pay of sinister, worldly forces could scarcely be more deliberately shocking. So that there can be no mistaking the context in which the deed is done, the murderers call each other names

Humphrey of Gloucester in *2 Henry VI* is a character like Woodstock, though much less is made of his death scene. Shakespeare turns our attention instead to the effect of the murder upon Henry and his court and upon the Commons: a larger pattern has taken precedence. Nevertheless, we cannot escape the vision of 'murderous tyranny' which Henry sees in the eyes of Suffolk immediately after Humphrey's death, nor the effect of Humphrey's piety and innocence upon the murderers as they escape from the death chamber. Henry himself, virtuous yet helpless, the sad commentator upon the evils brought to his kingdom by warring ambition, is murdered in *Part 3* by Richard of Gloucester. Though Richard by this stage has already characterized himself as one who will 'set the murtherous Machiavel to school', and though there is much in him also of the cunning Vice of the moralities who delights in the evil he is able to commit, he is, as the murderer of Henry, related also to the Pilates and Herods of the mystery cycles.

> Rich. Think'st thou I am an executioner?
> K. Hen. A persecutor I am sure thou art.
>   If murthering innocents be executing,
>   Why, then thou art an executioner.
>   (*3 Henry VI*, V. vi. 30-33)

Mr. WILLIAM
SHAKESPEARES
COMEDIES,
HISTORIES, &
TRAGEDIES.
Publiſhed according to the True Originall Copies.

LONDON
Printed by Iſaac Iaggard, and Ed. Blount. 1623.

Title page of the First Folio.

One of the essential threads in the total pattern of these plays is the confrontation between evil, worldly power, and helpless innocence, a confrontation which leads on to the increasing horror of Richard's deeds in *Richard III* and the lamentation of the Queens for the deaths of husbands and children. We are constantly reminded of Henry, Rutland, the young Prince Edward, the Princes in the Tower, in the curses of the Queens upon the tyrant who blasphemes against nature and God in every act:

> A hellhound that doth hunt us all to death.
> That dog, that had his teeth before his eyes,
> To worry lambs and lap their gentle blood,
> That foul defacer of God's handiwork,
> That excellent grand tyrant of the earth
> That reigns in galled eyes of weeping souls. . . .
> (*Richard III*, IV. iv. 48-53)

It is a marvellous enlargement of the lamenting mothers of Bethlehem in their outcry against the cruelty of a fallen world.

Henry VI is both victim of the destructive forces of worldly ambition, and incipient rebel against those forces; although not a saint, he is a man of virtuous impulses with a gift for contemplation rather than action. There is the germ of tragic action in his aspiration and downfall. Edward II and Richard II are less like saints, and both display greater energy of rebellious self-will than Henry VI. Yet each of them is drawn at the end into a scene of very considerable pathos, in which their role as victim is stressed. When Marlowe reaches the penultimate scene of *Edward II,* he has brought the sympathy of the audience strongly to bear upon Edward, and presents his royal victim as one who is enduring outrage and torture with dignity and patience. The murder places the helplessness and relative innocence of the suffering victim in striking opposition to the brutal heartlessness of the ruffians and the power-worshipping worldliness of their master, Mortimer. Like Herod in the Chester cycle, Mortimer suffers a complete fall immediately after.

Shakespeare's portrait of Richard II is a complex one, but it has often been noted how he becomes increasingly the victim of power politics as the play proceeds, and more subtly, the sacrificial victim who must die in order to fulfil the destiny prepared for his country. There are several references in the latter scenes of the play to the Christ-like patience of Richard as he endures the jeers and insults of the mob, to the betrayal by Judas, to the helplessness of Christ before his judges, though these are modified by the interplay of different strands of feeling, since some of the images are Richard's own dramatization of his position and are linked by the audience with earlier, very clear statements of Richard's guilt. Richard is neither pure innocent nor complete sinner, but the more dominant strain toward the end is that of the anointed of God, helpless in terms of worldly power, suffering the cruelty of the world.

Richard's long soliloquy in the dungeon gains much of its force from the audience's awareness of the approach of the murderers. Though there is little connexion with Christ's Passion, the speech forms part of a religious pattern that affects the whole scene: the coming of a humble and loyal follower in secret to see his master's face; the striking down of the anointed king by several murderers; the fear of hell which overcomes Exton as soon as the deed is done; and the curse of Cain placed upon Exton by Henry IV when he comes to claim his reward. I think it must be admitted that the tragic conclusion of this play, as of *Edward II,* depends in some degree upon the emotional force and the structure of meaning of the Passion plays.

Among other scenes from the mystery cycles which had an effect on serious drama of a later date, the tyrant plays were probably the most important. It is not difficult to find evidence that Herod and Pilate lived on in the popular memory as fierce, roaring tyrants, brutal and callous in their power, and impenitent in their crimes. There is a resemblance between these rulers and the King of the World figure who appears in *The Castle of Perseverance* and *Mundus et Infans* in that both are representations of the power in the world opposed to God. The worldly king of the morality plays, however, does not commit any brutal crimes: he is merely the ruler of the world of flesh and temptation.

Apius and Virginia is a product of both traditions, mystery cycle and morality play. In the emotions aroused by the conflict between tyrant and victim, and in the ultimate despair of the tyrant, we can see very clearly dramatic elements from the mysteries. They have been secularized, of course, but they have a religious basis which cannot be denied: the clash between innocence and evil, between helplessness and power, which is futile in a worldly sense and yet of the utmost importance in a transcendent universe. The divine justice which saves Virginius and condemns Apius at the end of the play is in miniature the final Judgement of the craft cycles. The debt to the morality play has long been recognized, particularly in the role of Haphazard, who is a traditional Vice. Bernard Spivack [in his *Shakespeare and the Allegory of Evil*] considers it a 'virtue play', carrying on the homiletic tradition of the morality play, though this has been diverted toward the secular themes of fortune, honour, and fame. All this is true, but the fundamental characters, the dramatic situation, and the emotional pattern of the play are closer to *Abraham and Isaac* and *Herod the Great* than they are to the moralities.

Cambises provides us with an even more clearly defined example of a tyrant in the craft cycle tradition. Once more, elements of the morality play are present, particularly in the figure of Ambidexter and the role he plays throughout. But Cambises himself is much more the tyrant of the mystery plays than a worldly king in the Pride of Life tradition. He is arrogant in his power and in his freedom to do what he likes with his subjects, like Herod the very embodiment of this world's enmity against God. His history is a simple pattern of crime and punishment, and the punishment is God's vengeance rather than man's. As in the Herod plays, there is a polarization of opposite emotions, fear and pathos, the contrast between vicious cruelty and helplessness. Undoubtedly what had already been accomplished so powerfully in religious drama lies behind the emotional effect of this play.

It would be foolish to represent the many tyrants of Elizabethan drama simply as direct descendants of the tyrant figure we have been discussing, even though the dramatic archetype became well established, first in religious plays and then in individual Biblical plays and moral histories on the popular stage. There were too many contributions to tyranny and villainy from too many different sources for a single tradition to retain its purity: from Seneca, Thyestes and Nero; from propagandist treatises and travellers' tales, Machiavelli; from Sir Thomas More and the chronicles, Richard III; from contemporary history and legend, Tamburlaine, Selimus, Muly Mahamet, Alphonsus of Aragon, and other warrior-tyrants. The tyrant was enlarged as a supreme embodiment of cruelty and power, or as a figure of unexampled cunning and treachery, or as a creature of passion and extravagant aspiration. There were even divided characters, tyrants liable to attacks of conscience, like Solyman in *Solyman and Perseda* or King John in *The Death of Robert, Earl of Huntington.* Yet in all these variations upon the theme of tyranny, playwrights, actors, and audiences seem to have moved on reasonably familiar ground among conventions that maintained some degree of continuity from the original craft cycle plays. The tyrant remained a boaster, using hyperbolic language to express his actual power or his aspira-

tions. He was unscrupulous, treacherous, and brutal, careless of the sufferings of others and confident in his refusal to acknowledge any limits to his own will. Above all, he continued to be a representative of rebellious, demonic forces in the universe standing out in complete defiance against providential rule and moral law. The religious background is implicit even in Marlowe's reversal of the convention in *Tamburlaine,* and in other plays that followed it.

One might have expected that the theme of the last group of mystery plays, the rebellion of an individual sinner against God and his eventual despair, would be the most influential of all upon later drama. In a sense it was, but in an indirect way, because this theme was taken over by the moralities and explored in a series of plays that continued well into the Elizabethan period. Adam is the first Everyman or Mankind, standing for the whole race of man and representative also in his proneness to sin. One remembers how Mankind at the beginning of *The Castle of Perseverance* and in *Mundus et Infans* enters as a helpless, naked creature, Adam once more, though suffering from the effects of Adam's fall. Cain, Judas, and Lucifer, the more blasphemous rebels, may not have had any direct dramatic descendants, but they remained the common property of the dramatic imagination and occasionally provided vivid images of despair and remorse. Thus, in Thomas Lupton's play, *All for Money* (1570), when the damned appear out of Hell as a warning to the living, Judas is prominent among them:

> Iudas commeth in like a damned soule, in blacke
> painted with flames of fire, and with a fearful viz-
> ard. . . .

And in *The Conflict of Conscience* (1581), an academic play by Nathaniel Woodes, the Judas theme lies close beneath the surface in the final scenes.

The actual debt of Elizabethan tragedy to the mystery plays was not the result of direct succession. Nevertheless, the debt exists, because the popular drama began to acquire many of its lasting characteristics in the late medieval period. There came into existence a large body of drama, widely played to great audiences, which dealt seriously with themes of tragic implication, such as the constant presence of evil in human life and its power to corrupt and destroy, and the suffering of helpless victims of ruthless power. In this drama one can observe several of the essential elements of tragedy, though enclosed still within a Christian framework of justice and mercy. Individual characters are free to obey or free to rebel against God and the divine law of the universe. But responsibility follows close upon free will, so that those who disobey must take the consequences of their rebellion. The divine law against which the individual human will is prone to rebel is a superior order, not always apparent to the fallen world, but certain in its eventual operation. In the world the order that exists seems to lie under the power of evil. Evil is crude and vigorous with life, sometimes cruelly funny, but it is never explained away: the mystery of its control over life and the mystery of suffering remain potent forces in this drama.

In terms of form, medieval drama supplied a legacy of archetypal characters of general significance—the kings of the world acting as enemies of God, the sinners who deserted God and suffered remorse and punishment, and the innocent victims of the world's evil. Attached to these representative figures were situations, Biblical or legendary, also of doctrinal significance, but capable of generating strong emotions polarized in the directions of pathos and horror. Popular drama had been through these experiences during the fifteenth century, and had discovered means of exploiting them within the strict limits of the religious cycles. In the sixteenth century it was ready to accept wider ranges of experience and new forms of expression. (pp. 21-8)

> *J. M. R. Margeson, "The Conflict with Divine Order," in his* The Origins of English Tragedy, *Oxford at the Clarendon Press, 1967, pp. 1-28.*

CHARACTERISTICS AND CONVENTIONS

William Hazlitt

[*An English critic and journalist, Hazlitt was one of the most important commentators of the Romantic age. He is best known for his descriptive criticism in which he stressed that no motives beyond judgment and analysis are necessary on the part of the critic. Characterized by a tough, independent view of the world, by his political liberalism, and by the influence of Samuel Taylor Coleridge and Charles Lamb, Hazlitt is particularly admired for his wide range of reference and catholicity of interests. Though he wrote on many diverse subjects, Hazlitt's most important critical achievements are his typically Romantic interpretation of characters from William Shakespeare's plays and his revival of interest in such Elizabethan dramatists as John Webster, Thomas Heywood, and Thomas Dekker. In the excerpt below from a lecture originally published in his* Lectures on the Dramatic Literature of the Age of Elizabeth *(1820), Hazlitt outlines the various religious and cultural influences which shaped the Elizabethan period, praising the playwrights of the era as a "bold, vigorous, independent race of thinkers, with prodigious strength and energy, with none but natural grace, and heartfelt and unobtrusive delicacy."*]

The age of Elizabeth was distinguished, beyond, perhaps, any other in our history, by a number of great men, famous in different ways, and whose names have come down to us with unblemished honours; statesmen, warriors, divines, scholars, poets, and philosophers, Raleigh, Drake, Coke, Hooker, and higher and more sounding still, and still more frequent in our mouths, Shakespear, Spenser, Sidney, Bacon, Jonson, Beaumont and Fletcher, men whom fame has eternised in her long and lasting scroll, and who, by their words and acts, were benefactors of their country, and ornaments of human nature. Their attainments of different kinds bore the same general stamp,

and it was sterling: what they did, had the mark of their age and country upon it. Perhaps the genius of Great Britain (if I may so speak without offence or flattery), never shone out fuller or brighter, or looked more like itself, than at this period. Our writers and great men had something in them that savoured of the soil from which they grew: they were not French, they were not Dutch, or German, or Greek, or Latin; they were truly English. They did not look out of themselves to see what they should be; they sought for truth and nature, and found it in themselves. There was no tinsel, and but little art; they were not the spoiled children of affectation and refinement, but a bold, vigorous, independent race of thinkers, with prodigious strength and energy, with none but natural grace, and heartfelt unobtrusive delicacy. They were not at all sophisticated. The mind of their country was great in them, and it prevailed. With their learning and unexampled acquirement, they did not forget that they were men: with all their endeavours after excellence, they did not lay aside the strong original bent and character of their minds. What they performed was chiefly nature's handy-work; and time has claimed it for his own.—To these, however, might be added others not less learned, nor with a scarce less happy vein, but less fortunate in the event, who, though as renowned in their day, have sunk into 'mere oblivion,' and of whom the only record (but that the noblest) is to be found in their works. Their works and their names, 'poor, poor dumb names,' are all that remains of such men as Webster, Deckar, Marston, Marlow, Chapman, Heywood, Middleton, and Rowley! 'How lov'd, how honour'd once, avails them not:' though they were the friends and fellow-labourers of Shakespear, sharing his fame and fortunes with him, the rivals of Jonson, and the masters of Beaumont and Fletcher's well-sung woes! They went out one by one unnoticed, like evening lights; or were swallowed up in the headlong torrent of puritanic zeal which succeeded, and swept away every thing in its unsparing course, throwing up the wrecks of taste and genius at random, and at long fitful intervals, amidst the painted gew-gaws and foreign frippery of the reign of Charles II and from which we are only now recovering the scattered fragments and broken images to erect a temple to true Fame! How long, before it will be completed?

If I can do any thing to rescue some of these writers from hopeless obscurity, and to do them right, without prejudice to well-deserved reputation, I shall have succeeded in what I chiefly propose. I shall not attempt, indeed, to adjust the spelling, or restore the pointing, as if the genius of poetry lay hid in errors of the press, but leaving these weightier matters of criticism to those who are more able and willing to bear the burden, try to bring out their real beauties to the eager sight, 'draw the curtain of Time, and shew the picture of Genius,' restraining my own admiration within reasonable bounds! (pp. 175-76)

It is the present fashion to speak with veneration of old English literature; but the homage we pay to it is more akin to the rites of superstition, than the worship of true religion. Our faith is doubtful; our love cold; our knowledge little or none. We now and then repeat the names of some of the old writers by rote; but we are shy of looking into their works. Though we seem disposed to think highly of them, and to give them every credit for a masculine and original vein of thought, as a matter of literary courtesy and enlargement of taste, we are afraid of coming to the proof, as too great a trial of our candour and patience. We regard the enthusiastic admiration of these obsolete authors, or a desire to make proselytes to a belief in their extraordinary merits, as an amiable weakness, a pleasing delusion; and prepare to listen to some favourite passage, that may be referred to in support of this singular taste, with an incredulous smile; and are in no small pain for the result of the hazardous experiment; feeling much the same awkward condescending disposition to patronise these first crude attempts at poetry and lispings of the Muse, as when a fond parent brings forward a bashful child to make a display of its wit or learning. We hope the best, put a good face on the matter, but are sadly afraid the thing cannot answer.—Dr. Johnson said of these writers generally, that 'they were sought after because they were scarce, and would not have been scarce, had they been much esteemed.' His decision is neither true history nor sound criticism. They were esteemed, and they deserved to be so.

One cause that might be pointed out here, as having contributed to the long-continued neglect of our earlier writers, lies in the very nature of our academic institutions, which unavoidably neutralizes a taste for the productions of native genius, estranges the mind from the history of our own literature, and makes it in each successive age like a book sealed. The Greek and Roman classics are a sort of privileged text-books, the standing order of the day, in a University education, and leave little leisure for a competent acquaintance with, or due admiration of, a whole host of able writers of our own, who are suffered to moulder in obscurity on the shelves of our libraries, with a decent reservation of one or two top-names, that are cried up for form's sake, and to save the national character. Thus we keep a few of these always ready in capitals, and strike off the rest, to prevent the tendency to a superfluous population in the republic of letters; in other words, to prevent the writers from becoming more numerous than the readers. The ancients are become effete in this respect, they no longer increase and multiply; or if they have imitators among us, no one is expected to read, and still less to admire them. It is not possible that the learned professors and the reading public should clash in this way, or necessary for them to use any precautions against each other. But it is not the same with the living languages, where there is danger of being overwhelmed by the crowd of competitors; and pedantry has combined with ignorance to cancel their unsatisfied claims.

We affect to wonder at Shakespear, and one or two more of that period, as solitary instances upon record; whereas it is our own dearth of information that makes the waste; for there is no time more populous of intellect, or more prolific of intellectual wealth, than the one we are speaking of. Shakespear did not look upon himself in this light, as a sort of monster of poetical genius, or on his contemporaries as 'less than smallest dwarfs,' when he speaks with true, not false modesty, of himself and them, and of his wayward thoughts, 'desiring this man's art, and that man's scope.' We fancy that there were no such men, that could either add to or take any thing away from him, but

such there were. He indeed overlooks and commands the admiration of posterity, but he does it from the *tableland* of the age in which he lived. He towered above his fellows, 'in shape and gesture proudly eminent'; but he was one of a race of giants, the tallest, the strongest, the most graceful, and beautiful of them; but it was a common and a noble brood. He was not something sacred and aloof from the vulgar herd of men, but shook hands with nature and the circumstances of the time, and is distinguished from his immediate contemporaries, not in kind, but in degree and greater variety of excellence. He did not form a class or species by himself, but belonged to a class or species. His age was necessary to him; nor could he have been wrenched from his place in the edifice of which he was so conspicuous a part, without equal injury to himself and it. Mr. Wordsworth says of Milton, 'that his soul was like a star, and dwelt apart.' This cannot be said with any propriety of Shakespear, who certainly moved in a constellation of bright luminaries, and 'drew after him a third part of the heavens.' If we allow, for argument's sake (or for truth's, which is better), that he was in himself equal to all his competitors put together; yet there was more dramatic excellence in that age than in the whole of the period that has elapsed since. If his contemporaries, with their united strength, would hardly make one Shakespear, certain it is that all his successors would not make half a one. With the exception of a single writer, Otway, and of a single play of his (*Venice Preserved*), there is nobody in tragedy and dramatic poetry (I do not here speak of comedy) to be compared to the great men of the age of Shakespear, and immediately after. They are a mighty phalanx of kindred spirits closing him round, moving in the same orbit, and impelled by the same causes in their whirling and eccentric career. They had the same faults and the same excellences; the same strength and depth and richness, the same truth of character, passion, imagination, thought and language, thrown, heaped, massed together without careful polishing or exact method, but poured out in unconcerned profusion from the lap of nature and genius in boundless and unrivalled magnificence. The sweetness of Deckar, the thought of Marston, the gravity of Chapman, the grace of Fletcher and his young-eyed wit, Jonson's learned sock, the flowing vein of Middleton, Heywood's ease, the pathos of Webster, and Marlow's deep designs, add a double lustre to the sweetness, thought, gravity, grace, wit, artless nature, copiousness, ease, pathos, and sublime conceptions of Shakespear's Muse. They are indeed the scale by which we can best ascend to the true knowledge and love of him. Our admiration of them does not lessen our relish for him: but, on the contrary, increases and confirms it.—For such an extraordinary combination and development of fancy and genius many causes may be assigned; and we may seek for the chief of them in religion, in politics, in the circumstances of the time, the recent diffusion of letters, in local situation, and in the character of the men who adorned that period, and availed themselves so nobly of the advantages placed within their reach.

I shall here attempt to give a general sketch of these causes, and of the manner in which they operated to mould and stamp the poetry of the country at the period of which I have to treat; independently of incidental and fortuitous causes, for which there is no accounting, but which, after all, have often the greatest share in determining the most important results.

The first cause I shall mention, as contributing to this general effect, was the Reformation, which had just then taken place. This event gave a mighty impulse and increased activity to thought and inquiry, and agitated the inert mass of accumulated prejudices throughout Europe. The effect of the concussion was general; but the shock was greatest in this country. It toppled down the fullgrown, intolerable abuses of centuries at a blow; heaved the ground from under the feet of bigotted faith and slavish obedience; and the roar and dashing of opinions, loosened from their accustomed hold, might be heard like the noise of an angry sea, and has never yet subsided. Germany first broke the spell of misbegotten fear, and gave the watch-word; but England joined the shout, and echoed it back with her island voice, from her thousand cliffs and craggy shores, in a longer and a louder strain. With that cry, the genius of Great Britain rose, and threw down the gauntlet to the nations. There was a mighty fermentation: the waters were out; public opinion was in a state of projection. Liberty was held out to all to think and speak the truth. Men's brains were busy; their spirits stirring; their hearts full; and their hands not idle. Their eyes were opened to expect the greatest things, and their ears burned with curiosity and zeal to know the truth, that the truth might make them free. The death-blow which had been struck at scarlet vice and bloated hypocrisy, loosened their tongues, and made the talismans and love-tokens of Popish superstition, with which she had beguiled her followers and committed abominations with the people, fall harmless from their necks.

The translation of the Bible was the chief engine in the great work. It threw open, by a secret spring, the rich treasures of religion and morality, which had been there locked up as in a shrine. It revealed the visions of the prophets, and conveyed the lessons of inspired teachers (such they were thought) to the meanest of the people. It gave them a common interest in the common cause. Their hearts burnt within them as they read. It gave a *mind* to the people, by giving them common subjects of thought and feeling. It cemented their union of character and sentiment: it created endless diversity and collision of opinion. They found objects to employ their faculties, and a motive in the magnitude of the consequences attached to them, to exert the utmost eagerness in the pursuit of truth, and the most daring intrepidity in maintaining it. Religious controversy sharpens the understanding by the subtlety and remoteness of the topics it discusses, and braces the will by their infinite importance. We perceive in the history of this period a nervous masculine intellect. No levity, no feebleness, no indifference; or if there were, it is a relaxation from the intense activity which gives a tone to its general character. But there is a gravity approaching to piety; a seriousness of impression, a conscientious severity of argument, an habitual fervour and enthusiasm in their mode of handling almost every subject. The debates of the schoolmen were sharp and subtle enough; but they wanted interest and grandeur, and were besides confined to a few: they did not affect the general mass of the community. But

the Bible was thrown open to all ranks and conditions 'to run and read,' with its wonderful table of contents from Genesis to the Revelations. Every village in England would present the scene so well described in Burns's 'Cotter's Saturday Night.' I cannot think that all this variety and weight of knowledge could be thrown in all at once upon the mind of a people, and not make some impressions upon it, the traces of which might be discerned in the manners and literature of the age. For to leave more disputable points, and take only the historical parts of the Old Testament, or the moral sentiments of the New, there is nothing like them in the power of exciting awe and admiration, or of rivetting sympathy. We see what Milton has made of the account of the Creation, from the manner in which he has treated it, imbued and impregnated with the spirit of the time of which we speak. Or what is there equal (in that romantic interest and patriarchal simplicity which goes to the heart of a country, and rouses it, as it were, from its lair in wastes and wildernesses) equal to the story of Joseph and his Brethren, of Rachael and Laban, of Jacob's Dream, of Ruth and Boaz, the descriptions in the book of Job, the deliverance of the Jews out of Egypt, or the account of their captivity and return from Babylon? There is in all these parts of the Scripture, and numberless more of the same kind, to pass over the Orphic hymns of David, the prophetic denunciations of Isaiah, or the gorgeous visions of Ezekiel, an originality, a vastness of conception, a depth and tenderness of feeling, and a touching simplicity in the mode of narration, which he who does not feel, need be made of no 'penetrable stuff.' There is something in the character of Christ too (leaving religious faith quite out of the question) of more sweetness and majesty, and more likely to work a change in the mind of man, by the contemplation of its idea alone, than any to be found in history, whether actual or feigned. This character is that of a sublime humanity, such as was never seen on earth before, nor since. This shone manifestly both in his words and actions. We see it in his washing the Disciples' feet the night before his death, that unspeakable instance of humility and love, above all art, all meanness, and all pride, and in the leave he took of them on that occasion, 'My peace I give unto you, that peace which the world cannot give, give I unto you'; and in his last commandment, that 'they should love one another.' Who can read the account of his behaviour on the cross, when turning to his mother he said, 'Woman, behold thy son,' and to the Disciple John, 'Behold thy mother,' and 'from that hour that Disciple took her to his own home,' without having his heart smote within him! We see it in his treatment of the woman taken in adultery, and in his excuse for the woman who poured precious ointment on his garment as an offering of devotion and love, which is here all in all. His religion was the religion of the heart. We see it in his discourse with the Disciples as they walked together towards Emmaus, when their hearts burned within them; in his sermon from the Mount, in his parable of the good Samaritan, and in that of the Prodigal Son—in every act and word of his life, a grace, a mildness, a dignity and love, a patience and wisdom worthy of the Son of God. His whole life and being were imbued, steeped in this word, *charity;* it was the spring, the well-head from which every thought and feeling gushed into act; and it was this that breathed a mild glory from his face in that last agony upon the cross, 'when the meek Saviour bowed his head and died,' praying for his enemies. He was the first true teacher of morality; for he alone conceived the idea of a pure humanity. He redeemed man from the worship of that idol, self, and instructed him by precept and example to love his neighbour as himself, to forgive our enemies, to do good to those that curse us and despitefully use us. He taught the love of good for the sake of good, without regard to personal or sinister views, and made the affections of the heart the sole seat of morality, instead of the pride of the understanding or the sternness of the will. In answering the question, 'who is our neighbour?' as one who stands in need of our assistance, and whose wounds we can bind up, he has done more to humanize the thoughts and tame the unruly passions, than all who have tried to reform and benefit mankind. The very idea of abstract benevolence, of the desire to do good because another wants our services, and of regarding the human race as one family, the off-spring of one common parent, is hardly to be found in any other code or system. It was 'to the Jews a stumbling block, and to the Greeks foolishness.' The Greeks and Romans never thought of considering others, but as they were Greeks or Romans, as they were bound to them by certain positive ties, or, on the other hand, as separated from them by fiercer antipathies. Their virtues were the virtues of political machines, their vices were the vices of demons, ready to inflict or to endure pain with obdurate and remorseless inflexibility of purpose. But in the Christian religion, 'we perceive a softness coming over the heart of a nation, and the iron scales that fence and harden it, melt and drop off.' It becomes malleable, capable of pity, of forgiveness, of relaxing in its claims, and remitting its power. We strike it, and it does not hurt us: it is not steel or marble, but flesh and blood, clay tempered with tears, and 'soft as sinews of the new-born babe.' The gospel was first preached to the poor, for it consulted their wants and interests, not its own pride and arrogance. It first promulgated the equality of mankind in the community of duties and benefits. It denounced the iniquities of the chief Priests and Pharisees, and declared itself at variance with principalities and powers, for it sympathizes not with the oppressor, but the oppressed. It first abolished slavery, for it did not consider the power of the will to inflict injury, as clothing it with a right to do so. Its law is good, not power. It at the same time tended to wean the mind from the grossness of sense, and a particle of its divine flame was lent to brighten and purify the lamp of love!

There have been persons who, being sceptics as to the divine mission of Christ, have taken an unaccountable prejudice to his doctrines, and have been disposed to deny the merit of his character; but this was not the feeling of the great men in the age of Elizabeth (whatever might be their belief) one of whom says of him, with a boldness equal to its piety:

> The best of men
> That e'er wore earth about him, was a sufferer;
> A soft, meek, patient, humble, tranquil spirit;
> The first true gentleman that ever breathed.

This was old honest Deckar, and the lines ought to embalm his memory to every one who has sense either of religion, or philosophy, or humanity, or true genius. Nor can I help thinking, that we may discern the traces of the influence exerted by religious faith in the spirit of the poetry of the age of Elizabeth, in the means of exciting terror and pity, in the delineation of the passions of grief, remorse, love, sympathy, the sense of shame, in the fond desires, the longings after immortality, in the heaven of hope, and the abyss of despair it lays open to us.

The literature of this age then, I would say, was strongly influenced (among other causes), first by the spirit of Christianity, and secondly by the spirit of Protestantism.

The effects of the Reformation on politics and philosophy may be seen in the writings and history of the next and of the following ages. They are still at work, and will continue to be so. The effects on the poetry of the time were chiefly confined to the moulding of the character, and giving a powerful impulse to the intellect of the country. The immediate use or application that was made of religion to subjects of imagination and fiction was not (from an obvious ground of separation) so direct or frequent, as that which was made of the classical and romantic literature.

For much about the same time, the rich and fascinating stores of the Greek and Roman mythology, and those of the romantic poetry of Spain and Italy, were eagerly explored by the curious, and thrown open in translations to the admiring gaze of the vulgar. This last circumstance could hardly have afforded so much advantage to the poets of that day, who were themselves, in fact, the translators, as it shews the general curiosity and increasing interest in such subjects, as a prevailing feature of the times. There were translations of Tasso by Fairfax, and of Ariosto by Harrington, of Homer and Hesiod by Chapman, and of Virgil long before, and Ovid soon after; there was Sir Thomas North's translation of Plutarch, of which Shakespear has made such admirable use in his *Coriolanus* and *Julius Cæsar:* and Ben Jonson's tragedies of *Catiline* and *Sejanus* may themselves be considered as almost literal translations into verse, of Tacitus, Sallust, and Cicero's Orations in his consulship. Boccacio, the divine Boccacio, Petrarch, Dante, the satirist Aretine, Machiavel, Castiglione, and others, were familiar to our writers, and they make occasional mention of some few French authors, as Ronsard and Du Bartas; for the French literature had not at this stage arrived at its Augustan period, and it was the imitation of their literature a century afterwards, when it had arrived at its greatest height (itself copied from the Greek and Latin), that enfeebled and impoverished our own. But of the time that we are considering, it might be said, without much extravagance, that every breath that blew, that every wave that rolled to our shores, brought with it some accession to our knowledge, which was engrafted on the national genius. In fact, all the disposeable materials that had been accumulating for a long period of time, either in our own, or in foreign countries, were now brought together, and required nothing more than to be wrought up, polished, or arranged in striking forms, for ornament and use. To this every inducement prompted, the novelty of the acquisition of knowledge in many cases, the emulation of foreign wits, and of immortal works, the want and the expectation of such works among ourselves, the opportunity and encouragement afforded for their production by leisure and affluence; and, above all, the insatiable desire of the mind to beget its own image, and to construct out of itself, and for the delight and admiration of the world and posterity, that excellence of which the idea exists hitherto only in its own breast, and the impression of which it would make as universal as the eye of heaven, the benefit as common as the air we breathe. The first impulse of genius is to create what never existed before: the contemplation of that, which is so created, is sufficient to satisfy the demands of taste; and it is the habitual study and imitation of the original models that takes away the power, and even wish to do the like. Taste limps after genius, and from copying the artificial models, we lose sight of the living principle of nature. It is the effort we make, and the impulse we acquire, in overcoming the first obstacles, that projects us forward; it is the necessity for exertion that makes us conscious of our strength; but this necessity and this impulse once removed, the tide of fancy and enthusiasm, which is at first a running stream, soon settles and crusts into the standing pool of dulness, criticism, and *virtù*.

What also gave an unusual *impetus* to the mind of man at this period, was the discovery of the New World, and the reading of voyages and travels. Green islands and golden sands seemed to arise, as by enchantment, out of the bosom of the watery waste, and invite the cupidity, or wing the imagination of the dreaming speculator. Fairy land was realised in new and unknown worlds. 'Fortunate fields and groves and flowery vales, thrice happy isles,' were found floating 'like those Hesperian gardens famed of old,' beyond Atlantic seas, as dropt from the zenith. The people, the soil, the clime, everything gave unlimited scope to the curiosity of the traveller and reader. Other manners might be said to enlarge the bounds of knowledge, and new mines of wealth were tumbled at our feet. It is from a voyage to the Straits of Magellan [*Voyage to the Straits of Magellan,* 1594] that Shakespear has taken the hint of Prospero's Enchanted Island, and of the savage Caliban with his god Setebos [in *The Tempest*]. Spenser seems to have had the same feeling in his mind in the production of his *Faery Queen,* and vindicates his poetic fiction on this very ground of analogy.

> Right well I wrote, most mighty sovereign,
> That all this famous antique history
> Of some the abundance of an idle brain
> Will judged be, and painted forgery,
> Rather than matter of just memory:
> Since none that breatheth living air, doth know
> Where is that happy land of faery
> Which I so much do vaunt, but no where show,
> But vouch antiquities, which nobody can know.

> But let that man with better sense avise,
> That of the world least part to us is read:
> And daily how through hardly enterprize
> Many great regions are discovered,
> Which to late age were never mentioned.
> Who ever heard of th' Indian Peru?
> Or who in venturous vessel measured
> The Amazons' huge river, now found true?
> Or fruitfullest Virginia who did ever view?

> Yet all these were when no man did them know,
> Yet have from wisest ages hidden been:
> And later times things more unknown shall show.
> Why then should witless man so much misween
> That nothing is but that which he hath seen?
> What if within the moon's fair shining sphere,
> What if in every other star unseen,
> Of other worlds he happily should hear,
> He wonder would much more; yet such to some appear.

Fancy's air-drawn pictures after history's waking dream shewed like clouds over mountains; and from the romance of real life to the idlest fiction, the transition seemed easy.—Shakespear, as well as others of his time, availed himself of the old Chronicles, and of the traditions or fabulous inventions contained in them in such ample measure, and which had not yet been appropriated to the purposes of poetry or the drama. The stage was a new thing; and those who had to supply its demands laid their hands upon whatever came within their reach: they were not particular as to the means, so that they gained the end. *Lear* is founded upon an old ballad; *Othello* on an Italian novel; *Hamlet* on a Danish, and *Macbeth* on a Scotch tradition: one of which is to be found in Saxo-Grammaticus, and the last in Hollingshed. The Ghost-scenes and the Witches in each, are authenticated in the old Gothic history. There was also this connecting link between the poetry of this age and the supernatural traditions of a former one, that the belief in them was still extant, and in full force and visible operation among the vulgar (to say no more) in the time of our authors. The appalling and wild chimeras of superstition and ignorance, 'those bodiless creations that ecstacy is very cunning in,' were inwoven with existing manners and opinions, and all their effects on the passions of terror or pity might be gathered from common and actual observation—might be discerned in the workings of the face, the expressions of the tongue, the writhings of a troubled conscience. 'Your face, my Thane, is as a book where men may read strange matters.' Midnight and secret murders too, from the imperfect state of the police, were more common; and the ferocious and brutal manners that would stamp the brow of the hardened ruffian or hired assassin, more incorrigible and undisguised. The portraits of Tyrrel and Forrest were, no doubt, done from the life. We find that the ravages of the plague, the destructive rage of fire, the poisoned chalice, lean famine, the serpent's mortal sting, and the fury of wild beasts, were the common topics of their poetry, as they were common occurrences in more remote periods of history. They were the strong ingredients thrown into the cauldron of tragedy, to make it 'thick and slab.' Man's life was (as it appears to me) more full of traps and pit-falls; of hair-breadth accidents by flood and field; more way-laid by sudden and startling evils; it trod on the brink of hope and fear; stumbled upon fate unawares; while the imagination, close behind it, caught at and clung to the shape of danger, or 'snatched a wild and fearful joy' from its escape. The accidents of nature were less provided against; the excesses of the passions and of lawless power were less regulated, and produced more strange and desperate catastrophes. The tales of Boccacio are founded on the great pestilence of

Florence, Fletcher the poet died of the plague, and Marlow was stabbed in a tavern quarrel. The strict authority of parents, the inequality of ranks, or the hereditary feuds between different families, made more unhappy loves or matches.

> The course of true love never did run even.

Again, the heroic and martial spirit which breathes in our elder writers, was yet in considerable activity in the reign of Elizabeth. 'The age of chivalry was not then quite gone, nor the glory of Europe extinguished for ever.' Jousts and tournaments were still common with the nobility in England and in foreign countries: Sir Philip Sidney was particularly distinguished for his proficiency in these exercises (and indeed fell a martyr to his ambition as a soldier)—and the gentle Surrey was still more famous, on the same account, just before him. It is true, the general use of firearms gradually superseded the necessity of skill in the sword, or bravery in the person: and as a symptom of the rapid degeneracy in this respect, we find Sir John Suckling soon after boasting of himself as one—

> Who prized black eyes, and a lucky hit
> At bowls, above all the trophies of wit.

It was comparatively an age of peace,

> Like strength reposing on his own right arm;

but the sound of civil combat might still be heard in the distance, the spear glittered to the eye of memory, or the clashing of armour struck on the imagination of the ardent and the young. They were borderers on the savage state, on the times of war and bigotry, though in the lap of arts, of luxury, and knowledge. They stood on the shore and saw the billows rolling after the storm: 'they heard the tumult, and were still.' The manners and out-of-door amusements were more tinctured with a spirit of adventure and romance. The war with wild beasts, &c. was more strenuously kept up in country sports. I do not think we could get from sedentary poets, who had never mingled in the vicissitudes, the dangers, or excitements of the chase, such descriptions of hunting and other athletic games, as are to be found in Shakespear's *Midsummer Night's Dream,* or Fletcher's *Noble Kinsmen.*

With respect to the good cheer and hospitable living of those times, I cannot agree with an ingenious and agreeable writer of the present day, that it was general or frequent. The very stress laid upon certain holidays and festivals, shews that they did not keep up the same Saturnalian licence and open house all the year round. They reserved themselves for great occasions, and made the best amends they could, for a year of abstinence and toil by a week of merriment and convivial indulgence. Persons in middle life at this day, who can afford a good dinner every day, do not look forward to it as any particular subject of exultation: the poor peasant, who can only contrive to treat himself to a joint of meat on a Sunday, considers it as an event in the week. So, in the old Cambridge comedy of the *Returne from Parnassus,* we find this indignant description of the progress of luxury in those days, put into the mouth of one of the speakers.

> Why is't not strange to see a ragged clerke,

> Some stammell weaver, or some butcher's
> sonne,
> That scrubb'd a late within a sleeveless gowne,
> When the commencement, like a morrice dance,
> Hath put a bell or two about his legges,
> Created him a sweet cleane gentleman:
> How then he 'gins to follow fashions.
> He whose thin sire dwelt in a smokye roofe,
> Must take tobacco, and must wear a locke.
> His thirsty dad drinkes in a wooden bowle,
> But his sweet self is served in silver plate.
> His hungry sire will scrape you twenty legges
> For one good Christmas meal on new year's day,
> But his mawe must be capon cramm'd each day.
> Act III. Scene 2

This does not look as if in those days 'it snowed of meat and drink' as a matter of course throughout the year!—The distinctions of dress, the badges of different professions, the very signs of the shops, which we have set aside for written inscriptions over the doors, were, as Mr. Lamb observes, a sort of visible language to the imagination, and hints for thought. Like the costume of different foreign nations, they had an immediate striking and picturesque effect, giving scope to the fancy. The surface of society was embossed with hieroglyphics, and poetry existed 'in act and complement extern.' The poetry of former times might be directly taken from real life, as our poetry is taken from the poetry of former times. Finally, the face of nature, which was the same glorious object then that it is now, was open to them; and coming first, they gathered her fairest flowers to live for ever in their verse:—the movements of the human heart were not hid from them, for they had the same passions as we, only less disguised, and less subject to controul. Deckar has given an admirable description of a mad-house in one of his plays. But it might be perhaps objected, that it was only a literal account taken from Bedlam at that time: and it might be answered, that the old poets took the same method of describing the passions and fancies of men whom they met at large, which forms the point of communion between us: for the title of the old play, *A Mad World, my Masters,* is hardly yet obsolete; and we are pretty much the same Bedlam still, perhaps a little better managed, like the real one, and with more care and humanity shewn to the patients!

Lastly, to conclude this account; what gave a unity and common direction to all these causes, was the natural genius of the country, which was strong in these writers in proportion to their strength. We are a nation of islanders, and we cannot help it; nor mend ourselves if we would. We are something in ourselves, nothing when we try to ape others. Music and painting are not our *forte:* for what we have done in that way has been little, and that borrowed from others with great difficulty. But we may boast of our poets and philosophers. That's something. We have had strong heads and sound hearts among us. Thrown on one side of the world, and left to bustle for ourselves, we have fought out many a battle for truth and freedom. That is our natural style; and it were to be wished we had in no instance departed from it. Our situation has given us a certain cast of thought and character; and our liberty has enabled us to make the most of it. We are of a stiff clay, not moulded into every fashion, with stubborn joints not easily bent. We are slow to think, and therefore impressions do not work upon us till they act in masses. We are not forward to express our feelings, and therefore they do not come from us till they force their way in the most impetuous eloquence. Our language is, as it were, to begin anew, and we make use of the most singular and boldest combinations to explain ourselves. Our wit comes from us, 'like birdlime, brains and all.' We pay too little attention to form and method, leave our works in an unfinished state, but still the materials we work in are solid and of nature's mint; we do not deal in counterfeits. We both under and over-do, but we keep an eye to the prominent features, the main chance. We are more for weight than show; care only about what interests ourselves, instead of trying to impose upon others by plausible appearances, and are obstinate and intractable in not conforming to common rules, by which many arrive at their ends with half the real waste of thought and trouble. We neglect all but the principal object, gather our force to make a great blow, bring it down, and relapse into sluggishness and indifference again. *Materiam superabat opus,* cannot be said of us. We may be accused of grossness, but not of flimsiness; of extravagance, but not of affectation; of want of art and refinement, but not of a want of truth and nature. Our literature, in a word, is Gothic and grotesque; unequal and irregular; not cast in a previous mould, nor of one uniform texture, but of great weight in the whole, and of incomparable value in the best parts. It aims at an excess of beauty or power, hits or misses, and is either very good indeed, or absolutely good for nothing. This character applies in particular to our literature in the age of Elizabeth, which is its best period, before the introduction of a rage for French rules and French models; for whatever may be the value of our own original style of composition, there can be neither offence nor presumption in saying, that it is at least better than our second-hand imitations of others. Our understanding (such as it is, and must remain to be good for any thing) is not a thoroughfare for common places, smooth as the palm of one's hand, but full of knotty points and jutting excrescences, rough, uneven, overgrown with brambles; and I like this aspect of the mind (as some one said of the country), where nature keeps a good deal of the soil in her own hands. Perhaps the genius of our poetry has more of Pan than of Apollo; 'but Pan is a God, Apollo is no more!' (pp. 179-92)

> *William Hazlitt, "Lecture I," in his* The Complete Works of William Hazlitt, Vol. 6, *edited P. P. Howe, J. M. Dent and Sons, Ltd., 1931, pp. 175-92.*

M. C. Bradbrook

[*An English scholar, Bradbrook is noted for her commentary on the development of Elizabethan drama and poetry as well as for her particular attention to the stage conventions of the Elizabethan and earlier periods. In the following excerpt, she examines how the conventions of locality, time, costuming, staging, and grouping were employed in Elizabethan productions.*]

I. LOCALITY

The Elizabethan public theatre had a projecting main stage, with a small discovery space, closed by a curtain. Above was an upper space, sometimes with practicable windows. There were three doors at least to the main stage, with windows over the doors; and a third storey, the 'top' or 'turret', where the playhouse flag was hoisted. The stage was provided with several traps, and with means of descent from above, the 'thrones'.

The chief characteristic of the Elizabethan stage was its neutrality and its corresponding virtue, flexibility. There was no inevitable scenic background, or any other localising factor, such as a chorus provides.

It followed that far more weight attached itself to the persons and movements of the actors. In short or unimportant scenes no indication of place is given, either by properties or by the speech of the actors, and no place need be assumed. It is the result of oversight rather than a deliberate device: the author was not compelled to locate his characters and, for a short scene between first and second gentlemen, there was no need to do so.

The scenes of a comedy were often located vaguely within a given town; and the short scenes of battle plays could all be covered by a general label. It is uncertain whether the entrance of a fresh set of combatants meant a change of place or not.

Vestiges of the older method of 'houses' set round the stage remain in a few plays of Lyly and Peele, such as *The Arraignment of Paris* and *The Old Wives' Tale.* Marston apologises for the 'entrances' in *Sophonisba* because 'it was given after the fashion of the private stages'. This might explain how in the fourth act the characters go from a bedroom to a wood and back again without in each case leaving the stage.

The private and the common stages could not have been very different, from the ease with which they pirated one another's plays. But the indoor stage gradually imposed itself in Jacobean times.

In the 'split' scene properties were set behind the arras to indicate a fixed locality, and when the curtains were drawn the characters remaining on the main stage from the last scene were attracted into the new setting. Conversely, if the curtains were closed the characters left on the forestage were delocalised. The first kind of split scene occurs in *Bussy D'Ambois,* IV. ii, and *The White Devil,* IV. iii; the second in *The Massacre at Paris,* scene V, and *Othello,* I. iii.

It is clear that the actors were the really important means of locating the scene. They were not set against a background real or imaginary; the audience did not visualise a setting for them. Shakespeare is misleading in this respect because he nearly always suggests a background for his characters, but no other writer did it with such consistency.

It was quite permissible for a character to bring his locality with him. In *The Devil's Charter* Lucrezia Borgia brings in her chair and sets it down like any humbler character: there are the notorious directions about thrusting out beds, though the idea that the royal chair of state was lowered by a pulley on to the stage has been dispelled.

There is one definite method of showing that the place is changed by the movement of the actors. When a character announces his intention of going somewhere, and then goes out at one side of the stage and comes in at the other, it is assumed that he has finished his journey. The two doors often indicated two localities.

Besides the split scene, there are reminiscences of continuous setting in processional scenes and extended scenes. In processional scenes the characters walk about the stage, and are imagined to be travelling for quite a distance. Instances are *The Play of Stukeley,* scene i; *Romeo and Juliet,* I. iv; *Merchant of Venice,* V. i; *Arden of Feversham,* III. v; *A Warning for Fair Women,* act II, lines 476-96; *The Witch of Edmonton,* III. ii. The march of the army round the stage is one of the commonest spectacles.

Processional scenes merge into extended scenes. In Roman plays the senate often sit above while the lower stage represents the street. In *Titus Andronicus,* I. i, the tomb of the Andronici is shown below and the senate sit on the upper stage. Places further apart may be shown, such as a street with several houses or two opposing camps. In *Eastward Hoe,* IV. i, the butcher climbs a post and describes a distant scene of shipwreck offstage, and there is a similar scene in *The Captives.* The most notorious case occurs in a dumb show at the end of *The Three English Brothers.*

The sense of exact place is blurred in early plays by the figures of the induction. The presenters were in one definite locality, in *The Taming of the Shrew* (the Lord's house); the play was in another (Padua and the country round), but also in the Lord's house where it was being witnessed as a play. Conjuring produced something of the same effect, when Friar Bacon showed the Oxford scholars their fathers in Fressingfield or the Conjuror revealed the death of his wife to Brachiano.

The presence of allegorical figures, for whom time and place are irrelevant, and the confusion between induction and play in *The Old Wives' Tale, James IV* and other early dramas, even though they were not consciously felt by authors or audience, would help to establish a vague and unlocated scene. Of course these devices were rejected later, but not for their effects upon localisation.

It is also doubtful how far each scene was a unit. If there were no scenic pauses, the transference from one scene to another would be very much slurred over. In the second act of *Charlemagne,* the place shifts from Paris to Ganelon's country house during a series of short unlocated scenes, so that it is impossible to say exactly at what point the change is effected.

It was not the habit of the audience to visualise precisely (as the choruses to *Henry V* rather suggest), or unlocated and split scenes would have puzzled them. The author was not always conscious of implications of locality. In *King Leir,* scene xxiv, and *The Blind Beggar of Alexandria,* scene iii, banquets are brought on in the middle of an open desert. This could hardly have happened if the audience filled in the background for themselves.

On the early stage title boards were used with the name of the place painted on them. This custom may have survived in the private theatres for a short time. A scene will often begin with some flat declaration of place, such as 'Well, this is the forest of Arden.'

There were certain properties which localised both generally and particularly. Tables, stools and a 'state' indicated a hall; a bed, a chamber; a tomb, or altar (which may have amounted to the same thing), a church. For country scenes there were a bank of flowers and a river bank. As characters sometimes leap into the river, a painted board before an open trap seems the likeliest method of representation. There was an arbour which could rise through a trap, though the discovery space also served as a bower or cave.

In the histories, particularly for the fulfilment of omens, a very definite locality was often needed. The scene is frequently a familiar one as when Cade strikes his staff on London stone, or Queen Eleanor sinks into the earth at Charing Cross and rises at Potter's Hithe.

The two most popular scenes were the orchard or wood-

Frontispiece to The Wits *(1662), an anthology of dramatic pieces. Various characters from the book perform on a deep, rectangular stage with spectators beside it and above the curtained entrance. Lighting comes from candelabra and a row of candles in front.*

land scene and the city gates. The orchard scene must have been more realistic than most, though the exact nature of the trees is uncertain, and the method by which they were disposed on the stage has been much disputed. But they were solid and practicable trees on which verse, or more tragically, corpses, could be suspended (*The Massacre at Paris,* scene viii; *Hoffman,* I. i, v. i). The woodland set was sometimes used for battle scenes, and as late as Shirley it was used to locate a scene out of doors when trees were not really needed.

The city gates were represented by the central door of the stage, the upper stage being the ramparts, and the main stage the surrounding fields. Sieges were the most popular episodes in chronicles: *2 Henry VI,* contains thirteen. The two levels of the stage were the most effective means of securing theatrical grouping, and were an equivalent, if not a substitute, for more realistic settings. Shakespeare's use of the monument in *Antony and Cleopatra* may be cited. It is clear that the stage was not the 'bare board' that Coleridge thought, and certainly not a bare board from choice. Both writers and audience enjoyed spectacle, but there was no consistence in the degree of realism, and therefore there could have been no complete and permanent illusion. The introduction of elaborate spectacle did not prevent unlocated scenes, and the lack of a background did not prevent realism of detail.

II. TIME

The sense of time is partly dependent on the sense of place, and so it is not remarkable that in Elizabethan drama it is frequently disordered, and more frequently omitted. In split scenes, where characters are instantaneously transported from one locality to another, time is telescoped; while unlocated scenes are divorced from the clock.

Some shortening of time, or rather, acceleration of the pace of action, is necessary even in the most realistic plays; the degree of obtrusiveness determines whether the reader passes it over unconsciously or accepts it as an overt dramatic convention.

A simple departure from the actual time sequence is shown in the final scene of *Faustus* which is supposed to take exactly an hour, but requires about seven minutes. There is a similar scene at the opening of the fifth act of *The Changeling. Cymbeline,* II. ii, opens at 'near midnight' and ends at 3 a.m. Orders and journeys are executed with the speed of Puck. In *Appius and Virginia,* a late play, Icilius goes several miles to fetch the body of Virginia while a few lines are spoken: the trick is much commoner in the earlier drama.

In these cases, the telescoping is inevitable on any stage, and could be paralleled from any period. The instantaneous conception of very elaborate schemes of action is less natural. Barabas plans his revenge in a moment or so: the Duchess of Malfi evolves the plan to accuse Antonio of theft on the spur of the moment. Such a situation, however, is dependent on conventions of character rather than of staging, and is related to instantaneous conversions and love at first sight.

In the early plays there are very few references to the passage of time. There is not one in *Alphonsus of Aragon, The Battle of Alcazar* or *Locrine,* so that no time scheme is possible. It was only with the introduction of a close-knit story that the definite time scheme was necessary, and so it did not appear in the chronicle plays as a rule.

Marlowe was acutely aware of its possibilities. In *Faustus* he used a simple one, but in *The Jew of Malta* his intrigue is more complicated and less satisfactory. The manner in which characters come on to inform the audience that something has just happened when in fact it was the last thing enacted is awkward and calls attention to the lack of the time gap (*The Jew of Malta,* I. ii, III. iv; *Edward II,* I. ii, I. iii).

The phenomenon of double time can be found in many plays of the period if they are examined sufficiently closely. Sometimes it is only a matter of a scene or two (*Richard II,* I. iii, II. i) but many plays have two time sequences throughout. There is a striking case in *The Atheist's Tragedy,* when Borachio orders his disguise at the end of the scene in which Charlemont departs for the war, and appears wearing it the same evening to report Charlemont's death at the siege of Ostend.

The combination of plot and subplot often leads to double time sequences, for the subplot may be only an anecdote, and yet it is interwoven with a long story; but as the passage of time is not important, these discrepancies are not noticed. The writer often slips through a desire to link up his scenes neatly. He might connect up the actions by a reference backwards or forwards to 'last Tuesday' or 'next Wednesday' while in the interval some action of a greater length has occurred, or the total action may require more or less time than the sum of the intervening acts. Thus in *Charlemagne,* between the dispatch of Didier to poison Orlando and his decision not to do it, so much has happened that he must have lingered for about a year on the journey.

The use of dumb shows and inductions also helped to confuse the time sequence. Lengthy acts were presented in dumb show symbolically (*Antonio's Revenge,* III. i, ii; *A Warning for Fair Women,* act II (Prologue); *The Changeling,* IV. i). The figures of the inductions, when they were allegorical, were outside time or space: moreover, they could predict the action which is to follow.

The Elizabethan audiences were not trained to put two and two together in the matter of clock time and so these difficulties did not exist for them. The rapidity of decision and quick movement from plan to action so characteristic of this drama was not a matter of hurried time, but only of increasing the speed of the narrative and of heightening suspense and attention. The excitement justifies the logical contradictions, and the well-knit appearance of a play like *Othello* is its own explanation.

In some tragedies flexibility of time and space provides the very structure of the play. This is so in *King Lear,* where things stop during the storm, *Antony and Cleopatra* with its forty-two scenes, and *The Duchess of Malfi* where, in the fourth act, things also stop.

In the late Jacobean and Caroline drama time references

again become scarce. There are few in Fletcher or Massinger. In *Valentinian,* for instance, the general impression is that everything happens in a short time, but there are no indications in the text.

III. COSTUME AND STAGE EFFECTS

The costume and make-up of the actors are what might be expected from the method of setting. Clothes were as gorgeous as possible: a cloak might cost £19, and a gown to be worn in *A Woman Killed with Kindness* £7 13s, which was not an unheard of price for the text of a play. Curiosities of dress were much sought after, especially in the early period, when for instance Peele's Edward I appears in a 'suit of glass'. Later, exactitude conquered novelty, and for *The White Devil* the collars of six noble orders were copied.

Although there were few attempts at historic accuracy, Cleopatra appearing in a farthingale and Cassius in a doublet, there was some geographic differentiation. In *Hoffman* the lovers are disguised as Greeks; in *Caesar and Pompey* Pompey as a Thessalian. Most countries had peculiarities of dress: Englishmen, according to the Lady of Belmont, wore them all in turn. It is probable that a Dutchman's slops or a Spaniard's cloak would be given them on the stage. There was certainly a Turkish costume (*A Very Woman,* IV. i).

Costume was also conventional. There were 'robes to go invisible' [Henslowe's *Diary*] and Faustus would need one at the Papal court. Ghosts could wear leather, though some wore armour; but Snuffe in *The Atheist's Tragedy* disguises as a ghost in 'a sheet, a hair, and a beard'. The ghost's face, according to *The Rebellion,* V. i, was whitened with flour.

The Prologue wore a long black cloak, but no distinctive costume was given to the Epilogue, who was usually one of the dramatis personae. It caused a sensation, however, when spoken in armour at the end of the comedy of *Antonio and Mellida.*

Costume might indicate character, if Lodge may be taken seriously, when in his *Defence of Plays* he observes:

> The Romans had also gay clothing and every man's apparel was applicable to his part and person. The old men in white, the rich men in purple, the parasite disguisedly, the young men in gorgeous colours, there wanted no device nor good judgment of the comedy, whence I suppose our players both drew their plays and forms of garments.

In *The Gentleman Usher,* II. i. 109, there is the direction 'Sarpego puts on his parasite's costume'.

The symbolic use of black and white is very noticeable. The fiendish ancestors of *The Courageous Turk* appear 'all in black', and the doomed favourite in *The Raging Turk* is condemned by the Sultan 'casting a gown of black velvet upon him, called the mantle of death'. The stage was hung with black for tragedies: it was used for mourning and funerals, and, in *The Custom of the Country,* I. ii, there is a bride-bed in black for the tyrant who claims the *droit de seigneur.*

White symbolised innocence and purity; it was worn by angels and good spirits: there are funerals in white in *Mulleasses the Turk,* I. ii, and *The Broken Heart,* V. iii, when a bride and bridegroom are buried.

Perhaps the most interesting use of black and white colour is in the final scene of *The Devil's Law Case.* The chaste heroine Jolenta enters with her face 'coloured like a Moor' and the wanton nun Angelica in the white robes of a Poor Clare. There are also two doctors, one in the robes of his merciful calling, the other disguised as the typical figure of cruelty, a Jew. Jolenta says:

> Like or dislike me, choose you whether.
> The down upon the raven's feather
> Is as gentle and as sleek
> As the mole on Venus' cheek.
> Hence, vain shows: I only care
> To preserve my soul most fair.
> Never mind the outward skin,
> But the jewel that's within,
> And though I want the crimson blood
> Angels boast my sisterhood . . .

It is like a scene from a morality play. The tradition was probably helped by the vogue of the masque: in Middleton's *Masque of the Inner Temple* there is a direction for three Good Days to appear in white, three Bad Days in black, and three Indifferent Days with striped clothes and streaked faces. In *A Game at Chess* Middleton produced the only play where all the characters were dressed in black or white with morals to correspond.

Disguise was so popular in both comedy and tragedy that there are very few plays without at least one instance of it. Sometimes it was donned on the stage: a false beard was enough. When the characters were not assuming any particular rôle but just disguised, like Malevole or Vindice, they probably wore a long cloak and a slouch hat.

Disguise was sometimes used allegorically, as when Bosola brings the news of her death to the Duchess of Malfi in the guise of an old man. It was fully recognised by the sophisticated as an ingenious device. Chapman, who was very prone to it himself, writes in *May Day,* II. iv, of

> those miserable poets [who try] by change of a hat or a cloak to alter the whole state of a comedy, so as the father must not know his own child forsooth, nor the wife her husband, yet you must not think they do it in earnest to carry it away so . . . If I am able to see your face I am able to say This is Signior Lorenzo, and therefore unless your disguise be such as your face may bear as great a part in it as the rest, the rest is nothing.

When one character disguises as another, it is only the garments which are copied: this happens in Chapman's own *Bussy D'Ambois.* Sometimes in the later drama the face was scarred or stained; in *The London Prodigal* the father has only to 'pull off his scar' to reveal himself.

Stage effects were mainly spectacular. Since there was no scenic background, they were of necessity intermittent and striking. The earliest were different kinds of shows and conjuring: trees which shot up through trap doors and signs in the Heavens, particularly the Blazing Star. The effect could not have been natural; by the time the Blazing Star had appeared for the seventh or eighth time the audience must have grown familiar with it and accepted it as a conventional stage property. The properties of spectacle were in fact so limited that its value would soon cease to be purely spectacular, though the groundlings still demanded it, as the well-known passage in the Induction to *Every Man in His Humour* testifies.

Pageants and dumb shows depended more upon the rest of the play, and could be very subtly co-ordinated. The later and more complex uses of the play within the play and the treacherous revels are discussed elsewhere, but they would always have their decorative appeal also.

The most powerful stage effects were connected with the ghost, at least in the early plays. It rose from the cellarage or cried from it: in *Antonio's Revenge* the ghosts cried in chorus from above and beneath; in other plays it rose from a tomb. Unlike the devil, it was always a serious character.

There was a dumb show of particular horror known as 'the bloody banquet' (*The Battle of Alcazar,* act IV, Prologue; *A Warning for Fair Women,* act II, Prologue; *The Bloody Banquet,* act V, Prologue). It was rather like the Thyestean feast: the table was set with black candles, drink set out in skulls and the Furies served it up. The tradition of these diabolical suppers might be behind the cauldron scene in *Macbeth.* A great deal of painstaking and elaborate work went to the staging of atrocities. The realism of the mutilations was helped by bladders of red ink and the use of animal's blood. The property head was very overworked: Henslowe also had property hands which would be required in *Selimus, Titus Andronicus* and *The Duchess of Malfi.* The private theatres were not behind the public ones in this respect: *The Insatiate Countess,* a Whitefriars' play, is almost entirely given up to unpleasant spectacle, though the record for murders is held by *Selimus* with eleven. Vindice's words 'When the bad bleed, then is the tragedy good' might have more than one interpretation. It has to be recognised that a great many scenes were on the level of Madame Tussaud's: the horridly realistic murders in *Two Lamentable Tragedies* were staged only six years before Shakespeare wrote *King Lear.* In this respect, as in others, Shakespeare was not absolutely independent of his age but so modified what it gave that he is often judged in isolation from it.

Small details, which could be given with exactitude, had great attention: Belimperia's letter, written in her blood, was in 'red incke'. The company were ready to utilise any piece of suitable property, and so when, in *Believe as You List,* II. ii, the records of state are called for, there is a prompter's note, 'the great book of accompt', which Sir Walter Greg explains as the company's ledger. This anxious ingenuity suggests how popular realism was. The players were prepared to endure some discomfort as the frequent directions 'Enter wet' after shipwrecks will testify.

Noises of all kinds were most important. The directly stimulating effect of music must have been much greater than anything but the wildest jazz nowadays, to judge from the way in which characters responded. It regularly

charmed and controlled the insane; it accompanied all the most emotional passages, solemn meditations, religious ceremonies, dumb shows, tableaux, love scenes. This is a typical funeral procession:

> Enter at one door, recorders dolefully playing, the coffin of Touchwood Junior . . . at the other door the coffin of Moll . . . While all the company seem to weep and moan there is a sad song in the music room. (*A Chaste Maid in Cheapside,* IV. v)

The descent of the gods was commonly indicated by music or by thunder. Thunder also accompanied their judgments and had always an effect of the supernatural.

A feeling of suspense is often heightened by the striking of a clock or a bell. The clock at the end of *Faustus* is similar to the 'little bell' which, in *Macbeth,* summons Duncan 'to Heaven or to Hell' and Macbeth to a living hell of the mind, while the alarum bell which Macduff commands to ring at the discovery is a 'dreadful trumpet' which rouses up the speakers 'as from their graves' to see 'the great doom's image' itself.

The alarum bell in *Othello* gives a feeling of horror when it is heard, which is supported by Othello's speech:

> Silence that dreadful bell, it frights the isle . . .

It is the signal that the tragedy has begun, for Cassio is doomed by it, and it breaks in on Othello's marriage night like a tocsin.

There was some specially diabolical arrangement of bells which is referred to in *The Battle of Alcazar,* I. i. 115, *Edward II,* IV. vi. 88 ('Let Pluto's bells ring out my fatal knell'), *A Warning for Fair Women,* act II, Prologue ('Strange solemn music like bells' accompanies the Furies) and the Induction to *The Merry Devil of Edmonton.* Bosola brings her coffin to the Duchess of Malfi to the sound of the bell rung for condemned prisoners at Newgate. (pp. 8-21)

IV. GESTURE AND DELIVERY

The London companies were well known to their audience, and Kempe, Burbage and the rest were public figures. There was more lamenting for Burbage's death than for Anne of Denmark's. Even the tireman was a familiar figure: Jonson put him into the Induction to *Bartholomew Fair.*

In a repertory company, which played with spectators on the stage and in broad daylight, it would be very difficult to sink the actor in his part, especially if he were alone on the forestage and soliloquising. The audience's eyes would not be concentrated automatically as they are in a darkened theatre, and hearing would be more difficult in the open air. To maintain attention it would be necessary to exaggerate movement or statuesqueness, to use inflated delivery and conventional posture. The Miracle plays had been very sensationally acted, and a tradition of some strength established. At all events, the acting was probably nearer to that of the modern political platform or revivalist pulpit than that of the modern stage.

There are many references to the actor's strut. Shakespeare speaks of the

> strutting player, whose conceit
> Lies in his hamstring and does think it rich
> To hear the wooden dialogue and sound
> 'Twixt his stretched footing and the scaffold-
> age—
>
> (*Troilus and Cressida,* I. iii. 153-6)

Middleton of spiders 'stalking over the ceiling' like Tamburlaine.

Dekker called Jonson 'a poor honest face-maker', i.e. actor. In *Cynthia's Revels,* II. ii, there is an exhibition of face-making. 'Your courtier theoric is he that hath arrived at his furthest and doth now know the court by speculation rather than practice, this is his face: a fastidious and oblique face, that looks as it went with a vice and were screwed thus.' Kempe's powers of making scurvy faces through a curtain was one of his principal accomplishments, and he gives an exhibition of it in *The Return from Parnassus,* IV. iii. But the tragic hero had equally mobile features. Hamlet's 'Pox, leave thy damnable faces and begin' and Lady Macbeth's 'Why do you make such faces?' are suggestive of much.

The 'eagle eye' was also well known. In *The Spanish Tragedy,* III. xiii, there is the direction 'Bazulto remains till Hieronimo enters again, who, staring him in the face, speaks'. In *Antonio's Revenge,* II. iii, there is the direction 'Piero, going out, looks back' evidently for a prolonged and malignant stare at the hero. As late as Shirley, the noble soldier, confronted by the villain, 'stares upon him in his exit' (*The Cardinal,* IV. ii). The nature of this glance of defiance is easily deduced.

The method of expressing grief which seems most common is for the actor to throw himself to the ground, or in milder cases to sit there. Again, in *Antonio's Revenge,* the hero has a lengthy soliloquy lying on his back. Romeo's behavior in Friar Lawrence's cell was not extravagant by the standards of the time. In *The English Traveller,* III. i, a respectable old gentleman does as much.

Joy was expressed by cutting capers. In *Charlemagne,* when Ganelon the Senecal man is banished, he receives the news with a caper to show how little it affects him. Two more messages of unfortunate news are brought and each one elicits another caper. The tradition of such violent action is behind the most celebrated scene of *The Broken Heart.*

When natural action is required in early plays it is mentioned as though it could not be taken for granted. In *Alphonsus of Aragon,* V. iii, 'Albinus spies Alphonsus and shows him to Belimus . . . Laelius gazes upon Alphonsus . . . Alphonsus talks to Albinus'. A play of Chapman suggests the development of the action, where one of the characters speaks scornfully of behaving

> like a king in an old fashioned play, having his
> wife, his council, his children and his fool about
> him, to whom he will sit and point very learned-
> ly, as followeth,
>
> 'My council grave, and you, my noble peers,

My tender wife, and you, my children's dear,
And thou, my fool'

> thus will I sit as it were and point out all my hu-
> morous acquaintance. (*A Humorous Day's
> Mirth,* I. i)

This presumably refers to something of Greene's period. Later, however, the same character enters with his arm in a sling, and when he is asked to recount something, he says:

> Bear with my rudeness in telling it then, for alas,
> you see, I can but act it with the left hand: this
> is my gesture now.

It is like the 'lamentable action of old Titus with his one arm'.

The torture scenes would need to be acted very violently. In early plays characters were flayed; in later ones they were racked or scourged. Henslowe paid for a sheep's gather for *The Battle of Alcazar,* and it is disquieting to reflect what an audience accustomed to bear-baiting might have got from *The Virgin Martyr.*

The individual actor had to be something of a gymnast. Leaps from the walls or into the trap were not easy. He had also to be a swordsman, for duels were popular and the audience critical. There is a direction in *The Devil's Law Case,* V. ii, for continuing a duel 'a good length'.

On the other hand long speeches required no action at all. It is impossible to play the Nuntius. The other actors could not engage in business while a long speech was given; they would remain stiffly grouped. They could not drop into the background for there was no background in the Elizabethan theatre.

The actors' chief difficulty was to maintain their statuesque pose, particularly since they might be the object of very audible jesting or ridicule. Nashe has a passage which lists their shortcomings:

> Actors, you rogues, come away, cleanse your
> throats, blow your noses, and wipe your mouths
> ere you enter that you may have no occasion to
> spit or cough when you are non-plus. And this
> I bar, over and besides, that none of you stroke
> your beards to make action, play with your cod-
> piece points or stand fumbling on your buttons
> when you know not how to bestow yourself:
> serve God, and act cleanly. (Prologue, *Summer's
> Last Will and Testament*)

The delivery must have been stentorian. It was Burbage's enunciation which made lines like 'A horse, a horse, my kingdom for a horse' into catchwords. Lodge compared the ghost which 'cried so miserably: Hamlet, Revenge' to an oyster wife, which hints at its pitch and volume. Of course there were different fashions in this: Alleyn was prone to Ercles' vein and only parody of this sort could have happened in the children's companies. There is much more opportunity for tearing a passion to tatters in soliloquy than in dialogue: the necessity for exchange produces an inevitable modulation. It may therefore be possible to relate the decline of rant to the decline of the soliloquy and the long speech, as well as to the movement into the roofed private theatres.

In the 1580s, when drama was still close to the courtly recitation or the academic oration, gesture may well have been formal; if gradually the professional troupes evolved particular styles of their own, the constant change of the repertory must have meant that they had to concentrate on verbal memorising. The blank verse had not at first a speech cadence, though later writers used a more colloquial movement, and presumably the enunciation changed in consequence. Perhaps the modification of blank verse was the most important controlling factor of the delivery.

It has always to be remembered that in real life action was so much more violent, that the kick bestowed upon the patient wife, or a frenzied foaming at the mouth, might only mean that the actor was holding the mirror up to nature. Elizabeth's manners are well known to have had as many shades as her vocabulary. As the English actors were apparently considered very natural in Germany when they toured there: what appears formal now was then capable of producing the illusion of reality.

V. GROUPING

The individual actor had large opportunities on the Elizabethan stage, through the popularity of the soliloquy, but the kind of team work expected of him was correspondingly strenuous, and demanded a high degree of self effacement.

The battle scenes of the chronicle plays were often staged formally. The 'army' marched round the stage and went off; the principals came on and fought a series of single combats. The trumpets sounded from the side supposed to have the victory, or, as in Goffe's *Courageous Turk,* 'a token of victory on the Turk's side' was hung out.

The sieges to the music room also allowed of a conventional grouping: the actual attack was often of less importance than the parleys where insults were bandied and defiances hurled.

The processional entries of princes were made as formal as possible, though sometimes their suite was not much greater than the Duke of Plaza-Toro's. In *Antonio and Mellida* the fool is pressed into the guard of honour who form a rank for Piero. The procession merges into the dumb show and the tableau. In *Every Man out of His Humour,* III. i, there is a scene in Paul's walk with

> Orange and Clove: Puntavolo and Carlo: Fastidioso, Deliro and Matalente: Sogliano. They walk up and down and salute as they meet in the walk. They shift: Fastidioso mixes with Puntavolo: Carlo with Sogliano: Deliro and Matalente: Clove and Orange: four couple.

This sounds almost like the direction for a dance.

The Revengers especially used patterned action. They go off the stage linked together, 'If not to Heaven, then hand in hand to Hell', or they come on with joined hands. It is usual to swear revenge in some very ceremonious manner: in *Hoffman* they circle round one of the group who kneels in the middle; in *Antonio's Revenge* they swear on the body

of the murdered Feliche, but this body is laid across the chest of the hero who has just finished his soliloquy on his back.

The movements of the Revengers are always remarkably simultaneous. In *Antonio's Revenge* 'they offer to run all at Piero (with their daggers drawn) and on a sudden stop' to prolong his agony. Before which 'they pluck out his tongue and triumph over him' in dumb show, which must have been a bloody and fantastic spectacle.

The dance was often used significantly. During the changes of the dance in *Satiromastix* the king reveals his love for the bride: the common end of the Revenge play was a dance by masked Revengers who suddenly threw off their vizards and ended the revels with a murder. Their hidden excitement must have been conveyed through the rapid movement most effectively. The ghosts also danced in a sinister way in Revenge plays; so did the Furies.

A formal grouping was especially necessary at the end of a play. Tragedies often ended with the funeral march; comedies with a dance. Kempe, in *The Return from Parnassus,* speaks on the necessity of breaking the lengthy walk down-stage:

> It is good sport in a part to see them never speak in their walk but at the end of the stage, just as though in walking with a fellow we should never speak but at a stile, a gate or a ditch where a man can go no further.

This kind of formality was the result of the stage conditions; but the drama of the treacherous revels and other patterned movements affected the quality of the feeling in the action, making it nearer to the impersonal feeling of ballet.

Early plays seem to divide into passages of declaimed speech, and passages of action of a violent and conventional kind. The effect of this is to underline action where it does occur and to make it portentous. This is especially so with allegorical persons, who are not separated from ordinary characters. Tamora and her sons, disguised as Revenge, Rapine and Murder, move among the characters of *Titus Andronicus* and, in the dumb shows of *A Warning for Fair Women,* Chastity and Lust appear with Mrs Saunders and Browne. Whether the action of these figures was formalised it is impossible to decide.

The action in the dumb shows must certainly have been inflated. At its worst it was purely spectacular, and this use persisted. In *The Revenge of Bussy D'Ambois,* III. ii, there is the direction 'Enter a gentleman usher before Clermont, Renal and Charlotte, two women attendants and others: shows having passed within'. These quite irrelevant shows might have taken up many minutes' action.

By this time, however, the dumb show had also become an integral part of the play, just as the songs had. The famous 'Helen passes over the stage' in *Faustus* meant that such an effect must have been expected that Faust's speech would seem inevitable. The duel in *Friar Bacon and Friar Bungay* is the most tragic action in the play, and it is given in dumb show so that it can be shadowed by another duel. The effect is parallel to the double pathos of 'Enter a father that has killed his son' and 'a son that has killed his father' (*3 Henry VI,* II. v; imitated in *Caesar's Revenge*), which in turn is linked to the use of similar plots and subplots, as in *King Lear.*

The action is often symbolic in these shows. Thus in *Antonio's Revenge,* when Piero woos Maria, she 'flies to the tomb of Andrugio, kneeleth by it and kisseth it'. In the dumb show in *The White Devil* the direction 'Sorrow expressed in Giovanni and Lodovico' calls for formal action.

A tableau may provide the setting for a long lyrical monologue; as it does in *The Devil's Law Case,* where Romelio, having been presented with his own coffin in the manner of the Duchess of Malfi, recites a long set meditation on death, a friar kneeling on one side, the bellman and his mother telling her beads on the other. Sometimes the stage was set for a solemn meditation with a table bearing a death's head, a book and a candle.

Darkness had a suggestion of evil and of the supernatural: it might be directly used in tragedy, as in *Macbeth,* or slightly even in comedies like *A Midsummer Night's Dream, The Faithful Shepherdess* and other nocturnals.

The audiences were trained by their whole dramatic tradition to feel an allegorical significance behind a formal or rhythmic grouping. The influence of the masque and of shows helped to support it; and such passages as those between the Painter and Hieronimo in *The Spanish Tragedy* are sufficient reminder that the paintings of the period were often allegorical too. 'Presentational imagery' or the emblematic grouping of characters has now become a familiar concept. Hamlet standing with drawn sword behind the praying King, as Pyrrhus stood over Priam in the player's speech; Lear with the dead Cordelia in his arms as a secular *Pietà,* belong to the tradition which, in terms of speech, produces impersonal self-dramatisation. (pp. 21-8)

Rossiter on Elizabethan dramatic conventions:

Between this miscellaneous audience and the dramatist there grew up a body of unwritten conventions: a communicative code which often seems to us naïve or silly because we are not used to it. The convention of black-and-white 'realistic' appearances in the cinema is one we do not notice until we are jogged into observing that it is a convention. The Elizabethans plainly found the conventions of the long soliloquy, the unlikely or impossible messenger's speech, and the aside no more troublesome than we cinema-goers find a colourless world where all the persons apparently speak through tin trumpets or out of water-tanks. Nor were they disturbed at what strikes us as an abrupt change of technique, or even of type of play, when morality personages mingle with or interrupt the realistic action. This is where a knowledge of the earlier Elizabethan or Tudor drama is of great value.

A. P. Rossiter, in his English Drama from Early Times to the Elizabethans, *Hutchinsons's University Library, 1950.*

M. C. Bradbrook, "Conventions of Presentation and Acting," in her Theme and Conventions of Elizabethan Tragedy, *second edition, Cambridge University Press, 1980, pp. 8-28.*

Jonas A. Barish

[*Barish is an American educator, editor, and author. In the following essay, comprising the text of a lecture he delivered in 1976, he argues that Elizabethan drama is characteristically multifarious, incorporating a great variety of characters, complex and multiple plots, and a diversity of language and verse forms.*]

Elizabethan drama might be considered to be unique in a number of ways, but I should like to speak only of a single familiar way, the full uniqueness of which may perhaps be easy to overlook. I refer to its multiplicity or comprehensiveness, and I would contrast it rapidly in that respect with three of its main rivals in the theater of Western Europe: the drama of the Greeks, that of neoclassical France toward the end of the seventeenth century, and that of modern Europe in its first or naturalistic phase as pioneered by Ibsen, Strindberg, and Chekhov.

We can start with the physical stage. Whether the Elizabethan theater derives from pageant wagons, or the trestle stages of traveling fairs, or from gaming houses, or innyards, or architectural structures like city gates and funerary monuments, or from the baldachinos and pavilions in Renaissance paintings, what evolves is a complex playing area, with a central platform, an alcove or discovery space at the rear, flanked by doors, a trap door leading to a cellerage below, a balcony or balustraded space above, with possibly a second level above that, and on the platform itself a pair of great columns that divide the stage. We have a versatile, multiple playing space which can represent locales such as a field, a castle, a city wall, a ship's deck, a forest, a desert, a cave, a cell, a tavern, a hall of state, or a street, in free alternation or succession. Characters can wander in from one door and out another, lean out of windows or emerge from the alcove, skulk behind pillars or peer from over arrases, and they may occupy two or more parts of the stage simultaneously. One of the most striking effects in Elizabethan drama comes from this last-named feature, as in the parley scenes in historical plays, when besieging armies stationed on the platform challenge the defenders of a town or castle situated above, or scenes of overhearing, in which characters lurking above, or behind pillars, eavesdrop on others—perhaps, as in Act V of *Troilus and Cressida,* being themselves eavesdropped on in turn—or scenes in which something is going on below stage as well as at platform level, like the cellerage sequence in *Hamlet.*

If we compare all this with the fixed scene, or *skaena,* of the Greek theater, often representing a palace door, as in *Oedipus,* or with the fixed scene of the French neoclassic stage, usually an antechamber of the palace, as in *Britannicus* or *Bérénice* or *Phèdre,* into which come and go only those characters who have essential business there, or with the tasteless bourgeois parlor of Ibsen, with its expressive clutter, perhaps permitting a bare glimpse of some world beyond—a fjord, a mill-stream, a townscape with steeple—we can see that in these other cases the fixed stage creates a sense of high focus. The action with which we are concerned is locked to the place on which our gaze is fixed, and whatever occurs elsewhere will have to be reported by messenger or some similar device of secondary narration.

On the Elizabethan stage, even when the action takes place entirely on a single island, as in *The Tempest,* it still suggests fluidity and dispersal rather than concentration. It moves us hither and yon over the island, refusing to fasten itself to one spot. Probably *The Alchemist* comes closest, of Elizabethan plays, to confining itself to a fixed site, yet it does so for a special and highly eccentric purpose: to create a sense of abnormal pressure, of something bursting at the seams and threatening to explode. The rascally alchemists use the stage doors as places into which they can thrust inopportune clients, so as to make room for new arrivals who cannot be put off, so that what we see is not so much the confinement of a story to its natural locus in a single room as a multiple action deliberately *crammed* into a smaller space than it can naturally occupy, with the result that at length, like the overheated furnace and burning retorts themselves, the whole plot goes up *in fumo,* in a terrific cataclysm, after which the outside world at length comes pouring in, taking its comical revenge on the absurdity of the unity of place.

Spatial restriction, on the Greek and French and modern stages, entails (or imposes) severe temporal restriction. As the action unfolds before the single palace door, or in the palace peristyle, or the bourgeois parlor, it tends to limit itself sharply in time to what can be presented as a more or less continuous process, unfolding before our eyes with a minimum of gaps. This produces the brevity and intensity of what we may call Aristotelian drama. We start close to the climax. We learn about the past through devices of recapitulation and retrospection. We encounter the action only when it has become white-hot. There is no time left for digression or excursion, only for the swift completion of what is already in motion, the speeding of an arrow, long since shot from its bow, into its target—only the few hours in which the fate of Oedipus is decided, or that of Antigone or Philoctetes, or in which Britannicus or Phèdre meet their dooms, or the few days in which Nora Helmer or Mrs. Alving or Hedda Gabler come to terms with their lives and take their resolutions for the future. We need hardly recall Sidney's whimsical lament over the geographical licentiousness of the theater of his day and its promiscuous ways with time, or Ben Jonson's raillery about York and Lancaster's long jars, or Shakespeare's apology for the temerity of his epic enterprise in *Henry V.* What is plain, when we compare Elizabethan habits with those of other stages and other epochs, is that the shameless Elizabethan stage tries to do everything. It refuses to recognize anything as beyond its powers. It crushes decades into minutes and shrinks great empires to a few feet of square board with godlike casualness.

It must be partly this voracious appetite for space and time that gives it such a striking affinity for magic, as in *Friar Bacon and Friar Bungay,* or *Doctor Faustus,* or *Old Fortunatus,* or *Macbeth.* With the literalizing of dreams of flight, of fantasies of transformation, of clairvoyance and clairaudience, and of invisibility, with the annulment of time through the conjuring up of past and future, the whole spatial and temporal universe is brought within the compass of the playhouse. The spectators are invited to share, along with the characters, the dizzying exhilaration of traversing the cosmos in a matter of seconds, of visiting the remote past and journeying into the indiscernible future from a position of absolute security. The other theaters aim at compression and selectivity, at making a little stand for a lot. The Elizabethans wish to drag the whole lot bodily onto the stage. The other theaters hedge themselves about with exclusions and taboos. The really exciting actions, the violence, the sensationalism, the amorous encounters, the magical occurrences, all happen, as Victor Hugo complained [in his Preface to *Cromwell,* in *Oeuvres complètes,* edited by Jeanlouis Cornluz, vol. XI, 1967], frustratingly offstage. Only the Elizabethans, with their split-level stage, their dumb shows, gods, and ghosts, their gluttony for spectacular effects, try to make everything at once visible, audible, and palpable.

Their plays tend, in consequence, to use large casts of characters. An average Greek tragedy will contain half a dozen or so speaking parts plus a chorus. Racinian tragedy rarely exceeds seven personages—three principals, three confidants, and a slave or servant or messenger. In the modern theater, Strindberg's *The Father* contains eight characters, *Miss Julie* three. *Hedda Gabler* has six, *Uncle Vanya* nine. *Henry VI, Part II,* by contrast, includes somewhere in the neighborhood of forty-five designated roles plus a bewildering array of supernumeraries: lords, ladies, attendants, petitioners, aldermen, herald, beadle, sheriff, officers, citizens, prentices, falconers, guards, soldiers, rebels, and messengers. The Elizabethan stage specializes in crowd scenes. The choruses of Greek or Senecan drama can hardly be said to constitute a crowd, such as we find at the Capulets' ball or at the court of Denmark. Still less do they compose a mob, such as we find in the street scenes of *Julius Caesar* or *Coriolanus.* Crowds and mobs, interestingly enough, in Elizabethan plays tend to individuate themselves, to decompose into Hob and Dick, First and Second Citizen, so that we feel them both as a horde, with an almost oppressive group identity, and also as collections of discrete individuals, each with his own passions and idiosyncrasies. When Racine needs a crowd, as in *Bérénice,* or Ibsen, as in *An Enemy of the People,* they keep them as severely off-stage as would Sophocles or Seneca.

The craving for completeness leads Elizabethan playwrights to differentiate their characters not only temperamentally but also socially, to make a practice of including representatives of every social level and mingling them freely on the stage. Final scenes in Shakespearean comedy bring the whole community, from king to commoner, together for some climactic recognition or some communal festivity, while in tragedy the society is likely to be gathered together at some point to witness or perform some painful, crucial rite, as in the forum scene of *Julius Caesar* or the play scene in *Hamlet.* Jonson's comic endings involve the community in a judgment scene, in which rewards and penalties are meted out by some high tribunal before which the rest of the cast is assembled, while in Jacobean tragedy it becomes nearly formulaic for an authority figure such as a Duke or a newly crowned heir to march in and restore order at the end. The effect at such moments is always to enlarge the focus, to expand the vision, to create a sense of plenitude and inclusiveness, whereas in the other kind of play the tendency is for the focus to narrow to only those characters who are central and indispensable to the story: Prometheus alone on his rock, Thésée bending over the lifeless body of Phèdre, Mrs. Alving staring helplessly into space as Osvald demands the sun, or Chekhov's three sisters clinging in desperation to one another as the regiment marches off to its new quarters.

The copious cast of an Elizabethan play, moreover, spanning the social spectrum as it does, is characteristically set to performing actions both numerous and complicated, to the point where after 1600 a play without a double plot becomes almost anomalous. Even when one cannot find a multiple plot according to strict definition, one nevertheless finds a play to be loaded with incident, swollen with episode and subsidiary scene and secondary characters. And again we can set this alongside the tight, spare construction of classical plays, with their preference for the single line, their avoidance of episodes that don't grow inevitably out of each other, or of French plays, with their even closer concatenation of events, or of Ibsenian drama, with its unrelenting pressure of passion and revelation. Most traditional drama, indeed, works by trying to maintain and step up the pressure. Elizabethan drama deliberately throws itself let-up punches, interrupts linear movement in order to go off on tangents, interferes with the single mood by introducing not only the social mixtures deplored by Sidney, the mingle of kings and clowns, but also the mixture of tones, the mingle of hornpipes and funerals which more Aristotelian kinds of drama will not tolerate.

Now this multiplicity of plot and character and stage space, of times and tones and conditions—the mixture of genres, also, which produces the hybrids and crossbreeds catalogued by Polonius—is reflected in the verbal medium. Greek tragedy utilizes its hexameters, varying the long speeches from time to time with bouts of stychomathy, and punctuating the dialogue at regular intervals with choric odes. French neoclassic drama adheres with singleminded fierceness to the Alexandrine couplet. Ibsen, once past his youthful days of experiment with poetic drama, adopts a realistic prose as his standard idiom. But in the Elizabethan drama every kind of verbal style jostles every other. We have both prose and verse: a prose ranging from the most unkempt and colloquial to the most loftily ceremonial, from the most syntactically disordered to the most artfully symmetrical, and a verse which, along with the staple, blank verse, includes rhymed pentameter couplets, octosyllabic couplets, doggerel couplets, lyric and stanzaic and strophic forms, all combined and recombined in endless permutation—as, for example, in *A Midsummer Night's Dream,* with the blank verse of Theseus and Hippolyta, the pentameter couplets of the lovers, the octosyllabic couplets of Robin Goodfellow, the songs and lullabies of the attendant faeries, the clownish prose of Bottom and his associates, and the even more clownish stanzaic verses they recite in their playlet of Pyramus and Thisbe.

Elizabethan dramatic language, moreover, runs heavily to wordplay, and more particularly, to puns. Puns involve precisely the exploiting of the mutiplicities in language, the unlocking of two or more meanings imprisoned in a single word. One could compile a lexicon of words that nearly always contain a punning sense in Elizabethan dramatic dialogue—like crown, royal, noble, angel, cross, face, grace, kind—and a goodly number also that along with the explicator of ambiguity, William Empson, we would designate as complex—like blood, sense, honest, or fool—which cover a range of meanings too wide to be easily schematized. The verbal medium is a kind of three-piled texture, and the dramatists are constantly seeking to unravel the weave, to hold the words up to the light so as to discover the strands of sense woven into them. Racine, by contrast, works with a notoriously tiny vocabulary, where the words sometimes acquire a high expressive charge, and attain the status of symbols, but never the unstable, skittish, multiform identities of their Elizabethan counterparts. In this sphere as in others, where the non-Elizabethan drama presses toward clarity and economy, the Elizabethans long for total inclusiveness. They try to jam a whole linguistic universe into a word or a phrase or a line, bewildering us with the treasures they have to offer, until we are tempted to follow M. M. Mahood's advice [in her *Shakespeare's Wordplay,* 1957], who, after distinguishing four equally valid possible readings of a line in *Romeo and Juliet,* ends by recommending that with "cormorant delight" we simply "swallow the lot." The Elizabethan mode, in all of its manifestations, approaches surfeit, prompting not only cormorant appetites like Miss Mahood's but also fastidious shrinkings like that of Edmund Wilson, who [in his *Triple Thinkers,* 1948] complained of *Bartholomew Fair* that there is in it "so much too much of everything that the whole thing becomes rather a wallow of which the Pig-woman and her pigs are all too truly the symbol."

As a final consideration one might mention the dialectical and open-ended nature of Elizabethan drama, as expounded by critics like Norman Rabkin [in his *Shakespeare and the Common Understanding,* 1967], who sees Shakespeare's plays as marked by "complementarity"—which is to say that they are multiple in meaning and irreducible to a single formulable argument. Shakespeare, in this view—and, I would add, often the other Elizabethans as well—does not encourage us to assign a final interpretation to the events of his plots, does not opt for one among two or more conflicting points of view, but presents them all pitted against each other, each with its own irrefutable force and weight, requiring us to hold them in suspension in our minds as unresolved simultaneities.

Now, obviously, any of the features I have pointed to may be found outside the Elizabethan drama, but it is only there that one finds them in such dense conjunction. Restoration drama, for example, uses the double plot relentlessly, almost mechanically, but shows little of the multiple stagecraft, and less still of the linguistic multiplicity, of the Elizabethans. Words, in the Restoration, are being programmatically stripped of their richness, puns downgraded as "clenches" and disapproved for serious purposes. In the craft cycles of the Middle Ages, to revert to the origins of the Elizabethan stage, one finds a high degree of inclusiveness, but of a relatively linear kind. One hallmark of Elizabethan multiplicity is simultaneity: the contrapuntal effects achieved when two or more plots interlock with each other and interinanimate each other, when two or more areas of the stage are occupied at the same time so as to cast ironic cross-lights on each other, or when two or more meanings spring unexpectedly from a single word. The mediaeval drama tends by contrast to be agglutinative, compound rather than complex.

One hallmark of Elizabethan multiplicity is simultaneity: the contrapuntal effects achieved when two or more plots interlock with each other and interinanimate each other, when two or more areas of the stage are occupied at the same time so as to cast ironic cross-lights on each other, or when two or more meanings spring unexpectedly from a single word.

—*Jonas A. Barish*

It may perhaps be objected that I have been using as a control group a neo-Aristotelian form of drama that has prevailed only for relatively limited periods in the history of the European theater, and that especially since the Romantic revolution the stage has fallen heir to an abundance of just such loose and baggy monsters as the Elizabethans specialized in, engulfing vast tracts of time and space, employing panoramic techniques, and so forth. But this phenomenon is itself inspired by Elizabethan example. With the early Goethe, in *Götz von Berlichingen* (1771), with Victor Hugo in *Cromwell* (1827) or *Hernani* (1830), with Pushkin, in *Boris Godunov* (1836), or Büchner, in *Danton's Death* (1835), or Hebbel, in *Agnes Bernauer* (1852), we find a self-conscious return to the methods of the Elizabethans. These authors all grasp the fact that to free themselves from the tyranny of classical form, with its simple, mythic, monodirectional plot, is to embrace precisely the multifariousness of Shakespeare and his associates. Even so, they tend to avoid double plots and most of the other devices of simultaneity I have been trying to signal. What they capture of the earlier drama, especially of the historical drama, is its power to suggest large-scale historical processes working through individual lives. Their plots bulge with subsidiary characters and digressive incidents, and speeches that enrich the texture without advancing the story, but they rarely display the kind of inner intricacy we find in plays like *King Lear* or *The Silent Woman* or *A Chaste Maid in Cheapside*. The effect is often more mediaeval than Elizabethan. It suggests a series of pageant wagons rather than the image of a complex, intricately ordered cosmos.

When we turn to the Elizabethan stage revival at the end of the nineteenth century, we find a clear though unacknowledged retreat to classical principles. William Poel, its pioneer, understood that you could not properly perform an Elizabethan play except on some variety of platform stage, that it was necessary to dispense with movable scenery, proscenium arch, and the other staples of nineteenth-century theatercraft. But he did not see that the older stage went hand in hand with a certain kind of dramaturgy, and precisely with the expansive, multiple, discontinuous, spatially and temporally stretched-out kind of play we have been describing. He thought of Elizabethan dramatic technique as barbaric, reflecting the incapacity of untutored playwrights to construct a well-knit plot. And so, for his own production of *Arden of Feversham,* he simply rewrote the entire text, gave it a new title, *Lilies that Fester,* and remade it into a snug one-acter, set from beginning to end in the manor parlor and consisting of action made continuous in the best neoclassic manner. If leisure served, one could demonstrate that something very similar happened when Maeterlinck, in France, adapted *'Tis Pity She's A Whore,* and later, *Macbeth,* for performance, or when Jacques Copeau mounted his famed production of *A Woman Killed with Kindness* to inaugurate the Vieux Colombier in 1913. In every case we have either the outright suppression of a second plot or else the removal of a host of subsidiary incidents that are thought to be "doubtful, obscure, and parasitic," to borrow Maeterlinck's terms for the portions of *Macbeth* he deleted from his acting version, a peeling away of the layers of complexity, a stripping off of the alleged excrescencies and redundancies that we have no reason to think did not, for their original creators, belong to the very heart of their inspiration.

The same would apply, *a fortiori,* to the hundreds of closet dramas written throughout the nineteenth century in antiquarian imitation of Elizabethan models. The authors of them are interested in the psychology of violence, in crimes of passion and politics and revenge, in thunderous confrontations between legendary historical personages, but they show little concern for the density of texture that makes the older drama what it is. Ruskin, in *The Stones of Venice,* finds one cardinal feature of Gothic architecture to be its redundancy—the tendency for the creative impulse to spill over in a torrent of expressive detail, repeated and varied in carved capitals and wrought drain spouts, in painted altars and ornamental pulpits, in stained-glass windows and sculptured choir stalls. Some such tendency seems to be at work in the Elizabethan drama, giving it the massive and exuberant character we all recognize in it. Through repetition, through simultaneity, through its insistence on doing everything at once, it tries to keep us in touch not with a limited and local reality, but with the totality—with everything that is, everything that has been, and everything that can be imagined to be, all at one and the same time. (pp. 103-11)

Jonas A. Barish, "The Uniqueness of Elizabethan Drama," in Comparative Drama, *Vol. 11, No. 2, Summer, 1977, pp. 103-12.*

THEATRICAL PRODUCTION

Thomas Marc Parrott and Robert Hamilton Ball

[American educators Parrott and Ball were respected authorities on Shakespearean and Elizabethan drama. In the excerpt that follows, they explore the dynamic interplay between playwright, actor, audience, and stage, which, they assert, accounts for the Elizabethan theater's ultimate success.]

Medieval drama was essentially an amateur affair presented first by the clergy and later by trade guilds. Elizabethan drama, while it retained its amateur standing in academic performances at schools and colleges and Inns of Court, and in the participation of lords and ladies in masques and entertainments, was, in its public aspects, almost wholly professional. In Chaucer's time, while large sums of money were spent on pageant performances and one craft vied with another in sumptuous expenditure, there was no direct charge to the audience for witnessing the performance. Actors, it is true, were paid for their exertions, but the performer was really a fisherman or a butcher, a tailor or a goldsmith, not a professional entertainer. By Shakespeare's time, audiences paid to witness plays in public theatres which earned ample incomes for managers and share-holders, and the business and art of acting had become a profession providing an adequate livelihood. Moreover, since during the transitional period plays changed as well as the theatrical conditions under which they were produced, the methods of staging and presentation also underwent a transformation. Any study of Elizabethan drama which did not take into account the circumstances under which its plays were presented would be not only misleading but fruitless. If we must guard against divorcing plays from the theatre, we must be equally wary not to interpret the work of the great Elizabethan playwrights in the light of our acquaintance with the modern drama or our knowledge of the circumstances under which plays are now presented on Broadway.

The transition from amateur to professional may most easily be marked by considering the rise of the professional actor. It [is known] that local players of Miracles, as in the case of the late *Ludus Coventriae,* sometimes presented their cycle away from home and became thereby an embryonic stock-company, amateur but paid for their services. When it grew apparent to them that there was a conflict between their acting and their local trade duties, that it was possible to earn a living wage and in a new and uncrowded activity, the step to professionalism was easy. Moreover, once a general interest had been aroused in the drama and the presentation of plays became profitable, the ever-present minstrels, mountebanks, and acrobats were quick to turn from juggling, jesting, and gymnastics to acting. Rivalry between amateur and paid entertainers or combinations for mutual assistance stimulated the process of professionalism. . . . *The Castle of Perseverance, ca.* 1450, was carried from place to place by a troupe of travelling players who drummed up trade by announcing performances a week in advance. A little later the actors of *Mankind* felt no compunction in interrupting their play

to pass the hat, and professional comedians were assisting in the banquet-interlude, *Fulgens and Lucres, ca.* 1497.

This development of acting nevertheless exposed the early groups of players to a new danger, as is shown by an Act of 1545. Since the strollers had deserted their regular trades and were no longer members of craft guilds, they were listed as vagabonds and masterless men and hence were subject to arrest and imprisonment. The more fortunate escaped this precarious position by putting themselves like the minstrels under the patronage of important personages, which made them automatically "servants" and freed them from the stigma and the perils of vagabondage. This process was accelerated by later statutes of 1572 and 1596. It had begun a century earlier, for we hear of companies protected by the Earl of Essex, and Richard, Duke of Gloucester, later Richard III, in 1482; and the earls of Northumberland, Oxford, Derby, Shrewsbury, and Lord Arundel had actors in their service before the fifteenth century closed. Henry VI had "pleyars of the Kyngs enterluds" at his Court as early as 1494 and paid them an annual wage, and similar royal patronage was granted by his successors as late as the reign of Elizabeth.

Since the connection between patron and company was partly nominal, it was natural that the acting groups when they were not on duty as members of a household should eke out their income by travelling. In 1559 Robert Dudley, later the Earl of Leicester, wrote a fellow-nobleman requesting his friend's license for "my servants" to play in Yorkshire, and fifteen years later he secured from the Queen permission for them to act in London and elsewhere, despite local rules to the contrary, so long as their plays met the approval of the Master of the Revels. Other noblemen who had companies followed suit, so that by the end of the century there were always two or three groups playing in London and a number of less distinguished companies touring through the country. They presented their plays in great halls and banquet chambers, on village greens, and, most important of all, in inn-yards.

The inn-yard had proved from early times a most satisfactory place for the presentation of plays. The restrictions of a room were absent; there was no chance for the audience to scatter when it came time to levy contributions. It is interesting, for example, that *Mankind,* which includes in its dialogue directions for gathering money, had its stage set in the courtyard of an inn. It is hardly necessary to point out that since the inn was a center of social life as well as a haven for travellers, it made its own contribution to the audience and the festive atmosphere of the theatre. As time went on, certain inns—in London, the Bell, the Cross Keys, the Bull, the Bel Savage, and the Boar's Head (not, however, Falstaff's Boar's Head in Eastcheap)—were specifically dedicated to dramatic purposes, partially reconstructed, and even, somewhat misleadingly, referred to as theatres. Three were destroyed in the London fire of 1666, but in 1668 Samuel Pepys visited the Bull, and the Boar's Head Yard may still be reviewed by the curious in Whitechapel.

Those Elizabethan inns in which actors' companies presented plays were usually made up of a collection of buildings grouped around a hollow square, which formed the court-yard, entered from the street by a single archway. Inside around the yard ran a series of galleries opening on the adjacent rooms of the inn. Opposite the entrance the players set up a scaffold projecting from the building into the yard, and backed by a curtain hung from the gallery immediately over it, which could be utilized for balcony scenes or the walls of a beleaguered city. Behind the curtain was "behind-the-scenes"; in other words, actors came on stage through the curtains from their dressing and property room in the inn. At the entering archway stood a "gatherer" who collected the admission fee, usually a penny, to the flagged quadrangle where the "groundlings" stood. No doubt other "gatherers" within the court pointed out the advantage of paying further pennies for particularly desirable positions. Members of the audience who had the money for more commodious arrangements hired rooms in the inn and sat on benches or stools in the galleries, whence they could look down on groundlings and the stage. The Elizabethan theatre was anything but aristocratic. Class distinctions were certainly important, but all classes were there from nobles and sober citizens and their wives to prentices, pickpockets, and harlots; and the wide scope and variety of Elizabethan drama is mainly due to the heterogeneity of the enthusiastic playgoers at these professional performances in inn-yard or theatre.

In 1575 London had no regular theatres, that is, no buildings designed and constructed primarily for the presentation of plays. Nothing shows more clearly the growth of the professional drama than the fact that eight playhouses rose within the next thirty years, some of them so large and handsome as to evoke the unqualified admiration of travellers from the Continent. The first was built by James Burbage for his fellow actors of Leicester's company in 1576, and was called simply the Theatre; the site chosen was in Shoreditch, outside the city limits to the north, advantageous because of its proximity to the public playground, Finsbury Fields, yet not within the jurisdiction of the Common Council. The city officials from the beginning, unlike the Queen and her court, were chary of public play-acting, partly on moral grounds, more definitely for fear of three menaces: fire, sedition, and the plague. These were no idle fears. Fire was a constant danger to old London, which was at last almost wiped out by the great fire of 1666. The two largest theatres, the Globe and the Fortune, were burnt to the ground in 1613 and 1621. Plague was endemic in London; the deaths from this source averaged forty to fifty a week. When they rose above this number, the theatres were closed until it seemed safe to reopen them. The disorderly groundlings sometimes stormed the stage or indulged in rioting among themselves. One theatre, the Phoenix, was almost destroyed by rioting apprentices in 1617. The Curtain, so called from the estate on which it was erected close to the Theatre, was built in 1577. Soon after another structure was opened at Newington Butts, marking a shift of locality to the south of the Thames; but this was never a popular theatre, since it was an uncomfortable mile beyond the river. The Rose, built in 1587 by Philip Henslowe, who became the most important theatrical proprietor of the age; the Swan, 1595, of whose stage we have a somewhat puzzling picture; and the Globe, erected in 1599 from the timbers of the demolished Theatre by the sons of James Burbage, Cuthbert and the

famous actor, Richard, with five members of their company—Shakespeare among them—as share-holders, were all situated on the south side of the Thames in the district known as the Bankside, also beyond city jurisdiction. Later public theatres were the Fortune, 1600, and the Red Bull, *ca.* 1605, north of the city limits, and the Hope, 1613, once more on the Bankside.

Besides the public theatres, there were so-called private theatres, a somewhat misleading designation since they housed professional actors and were open to the public. The term was apparently chosen mainly to appease the London authorities, for some of these theatres, unlike the public ones, were within the city limits. Moreover, the distinction attached to the word "private" no doubt attracted a more select and higher paying clientele. Used first by children, they came to serve as winter quarters for adult actors. In 1596, for example, James Burbage purchased certain rooms in a building in Blackfriars, once the property of the Dominican monks, and made them over into a theatre. The Privy Council promptly forbade the public use of Blackfriars, but, after the death of James, Richard Burbage leased it to the manager of the Children of the Chapel. It was not until 1608 that Burbage's company was able to use it as a winter home. Other important indoor theatres were in a building near St. Paul's Cathedral, another at Whitefriars, the Cockpit or Phoenix in Drury Lane, and the Salisbury Court Playhouse; all but the first were west of the city walls and north of the Thames.

The companies who played in the Elizabethan theatres are too many and various to discuss in detail, but it will be useful to sketch briefly the development and organization of two of them, and the names of the Burbages and Henslowe suggest the delimitation. With the Burbages we naturally associate Shakespeare; with Henslowe, Christopher Marlowe and a large group of later playwrights. The company of which Shakespeare was a member bore various names at different times as the patron, his rank, or his office changed. It may have begun as the Earl of Leicester's Men; after his death in 1588 its principal actors joined a group under the patronage of Lord Strange and for a time acted at Henslowe's theatre, the Rose. In 1593 Lord Strange became the Earl of Derby, and for a short time the company took over the new title, but he died the next year, and another patron had to be found. This was Elizabeth's cousin, the Lord Chamberlain, Henry Carey, and it is as the Lord Chamberlain's Company that until 1603 it is best known, for though Carey died in 1596, his son, Lord Hunsdon, shortly succeeded to his office. In 1603 the theatrical companies came under the direct patronage of the royal family, and the Lord Chamberlain's Men became the King's Majesty's Servants, a title which they retained until the closing of the theatres in 1642. The principal playwrights associated with this company were Shakespeare, Jonson, Beaumont and Fletcher, Massinger, and Davenant; its best known actor was Richard Burbage, who interpreted the principal roles in Shakespeare's plays, both comedies and tragedies.

The other major group was that controlled by Philip Henslowe, in association with his son-in-law, Edward Alleyn, who rivalled Burbage as the star of the day. Besides

The frontispiece of Paul Scarron's 1676 Comical Romance of a Company of Stage Players *shows the arrival of a group of strolling players at an inn and their later performance on a platform stage in the village square.*

the Rose, built and leased out by Henslowe, they controlled the Fortune and the Hope, and managed the companies under the patronage of the Lord Admiral and the Earl of Worcester; these became respectively after 1603 Prince Henry's and Queen Anne's Men. Alleyn played the principal characters in Marlowe's tragedies, and later dramatists associated with Henslowe's companies included Chapman, Dekker, Middleton, and Thomas Heywood. Much of our knowledge of Elizabethan theatrical conditions derives from the valuable records kept by Philip Henslowe.

The Elizabethan theatrical company, especially such a group as the Lord Chamberlain's, was co-operative, self-governing, and self-perpetuating. It consisted of a certain number of full members who owned shares and divided profits, and leased, or, as in the case of the Globe, built a theatre; hired men paid a fixed salary to play minor parts; and apprentices, notably the boys who played all the female roles on the Elizabethan stage—there were no professional actresses until Restoration times—trained in the routine, as they would be in trade, by their individual masters, who hired them out to the company. The important members of the company played more or less definite "lines." Burbage, as a star, interpreted, we know, such roles as Richard III and the title-parts of Shakespeare's great tragedies; Shakespeare, as an actor, we principally associate with old men or kingly parts; Will Kemp and Armin were comedians. Playwrights were, as a rule, much more definitely associated with particular companies than is the case today. Plays were written for a particular troupe and frequently at their direction. A playwright often read the first acts of a projected play to the leading members of a company at a supper after their afternoon performance. He would listen to their criticism, accept suggestions, and promise to complete his work at a certain date. Surviving manuscripts show that plays were often revised in or after production. All in all, the major adult companies were strong organizations, which so long as they submitted to the rigorous restrictions by which the Master of the Revels forbade plays meddling with matters of Church and State, were free to produce what they pleased as they pleased.

With the children's companies who presented plays at Paul's or Blackfriars it was an entirely different matter. These companies grew out of the choir-schools of the Chapel Royal, of Windsor, and of St. Paul's, and were under the direct control of a master who had the right to impress children for singing and acting. The master supported and trained them, produced the plays, and received the money from performances. For a time the "little eyases," as Shakespeare makes plain in *Hamlet,* acting largely at the private theatres and at Court, vied in popularity with their elders; they must have been unusually competent, for they elicited the charming courtly comedies of Lyly, and performed such tragedies as Chapman's *Bussy* and Marston's *Sophonisba.* Some of these children, Nat. Field for instance, later became leading actors in adult companies.

We may now turn to a consideration of the physical structure of the theatre itself. The public playhouses were by no means alike in size or shape; yet there is substantial agreement about the basic plan of a typical public theatre. Since it is vastly different from anything we have today, since the methods of staging vary substantially from ours, and since both theatre and staging exerted a strong influence on the art of the playwright, it is essential to have a clear picture of the most important features.

The Elizabethan theatre evolved from those structures which had previously served most often and conveniently for the presentation of plays, the inns. Except for the Fortune, however, they did not retain the square or rectangular courtyard or pit, but were roughly circular or polygonal. The alteration was no doubt suggested by the bear- and bull-baiting rings on the Bankside, and assisted the hearing and vision of spectators in pit and gallery by bringing them nearer to the stage. As pictured in contemporary London maps the typical theatre justifies Shakespeare's description (*Henry V,* Prologue) of "this wooden O." Around the inside were three tiers of galleries, roofed over with thatch or tile; the center was uncovered and open to the weather. As in the inn court-yard, the audience entered through a door opposite the stage, except, perhaps, for a few especially favored who might use the players' entrance to the tiring-house or dressing rooms at the rear. A penny to a "gatherer" allowed the groundling to stand in the pit; and an additional charge of a penny or two permitted the more select spectator to climb stairs and sit on stool or bench in one of the galleries.

Halfway into the pit there projected a platform upon which most of the action of the play was presented. It is important to realize that the spectators were not only in front of the stage as in a modern theatre but actually on three sides of it. At the rear of the platform was an inner, or alcove, stage separated from the front by a traverse, or draw-curtain, and flanked by doors which allowed the actors to enter directly onto the platform from the tiring-house. Over the alcove-stage was an upper stage; it also had a curtain which could cut it off from the view of the audience when it was not in use, and in front of the curtain a balcony or "tarras" projected slightly over the platform. Occasionally it may have served as a music room, or for spectators presumably more interested in being seen than in seeing what went on in all sections of the playing space. Other spectators were sometimes allowed to sit on the platform-stage itself and must have been an unholy nuisance both to actors and audience. It is a pity there is no evidence that they ever fell through the various traps in the floors of all the stages. The upper stage, including curtained space and balcony windows on each side of it, over the doors to the main stage, was reached by interior stairs. Projecting from above the balcony-stage over a large part of the platform was a roof variously called the "heavens" or the "shadow" and on part of it a garret or "hut," which extended back over the third story of the tiring-house. The "shadow," usually supported by pillars, served in part to protect from the elements actors on the main stage. Moreover, through it heavy properties or even an actor impersonating a god—the ancient *deus ex machina*—might be let down to the platform. From the "hut" flew a flag on fair days to indicate, along with frequent trumpet blasts, that a play was to be given that afternoon. Sunday performances, though intermittently prohibited, continued till 1603.

The earliest private playhouses were apparently mere adaptations of rooms for the presentation of plays by the Children of the Royal Chapel or by Paul's Boys; there was a platform-stage backed by a curtain and artificially lighted, and seats in the hall, rather than standing-room, accommodated the more luxurious auditors. Beginning with Burbage's Blackfriars, however, the reconstruction included galleries, and no doubt alcove and balcony-stages not essentially different from those in the public theatres, though the galleries may have been less in number and the "interior" stages larger. The ceiling, of course, supplied the function of the "shadow," and an upper room that of the "hut." The public and the later private stages were therefore not essentially different; after 1608 the same plays were frequently given both outdoors and in, and there does not seem to be evidence of necessary adaptation because of the transfer. Performances at Court, of course, were given indoors. There dramatic entertainment was of two kinds: elaborate disguisings and pageantry emphasizing music, dancing, and spectacle for which special settings and properties were devised for the amateur participants; and more regular plays presented by professionals ranging from simple Interludes on simple platforms to more complicated drama with ornate multiple settings. After about 1580, when the regular theatres and their practices had become established, theatricals at Court were more and more dominated by professionals called in to give special performances on variable temporary stages much resembling those in the private playhouses though with more expensive decoration, furnishings, and properties.

No one has ever been more aware than Shakespeare, actor and poet-playwright, with his constant contrasts between seeming and being, illusion and reality, that the theatre is "of imagination all compact."

    If we shadows have offended,

says Robin Goodfellow [in *A Midsummer Night's Dream*]

    Think but this, and all is mended,
    That you have but slumber'd here,
    While these visions did appear.

Fifteen years later, "these our actors" are still "spirits," and the "insubstantial" pageant of *The Tempest* has faded, leaving "not a rack behind," except perhaps the memory of a dream. It was natural that the Elizabethans should emphasize the illusory quality of the drama, for its whole tradition had been one which demanded and evoked the willing suspension of disbelief. Actors and playwrights could count on audiences willing to use their imaginations, to "eke out our performance with your mind"; to help build "cloud-capp'd towers" from the suggestions which they offered. We are still alive to this spell, but not often as yielding. "Show me," says the recalcitrant modern spectator; "convince me in spite of myself!" And so we try to make a play as much as possible like life, our actors must appear natural, and we put both action and actors within a picture-frame to be sufficiently confined. The Elizabethans were different. They said to the playwright,

"Start us off; tell us a story"; to the actor, "Indicate grief; we know what grief is; we'll do the rest." Instead of demanding a designer to realize on the stage a room or a forest, they said to playwright and actor and the theatre itself, "Suggest it; a table is a room, a tree a forest." It is often the realer way. "Scenery," say the Chinese, "is as large as your imagination."

Primitive medieval drama demanded no more than two things of a stage: a neutral playing-space if the action was clear enough to require no localization and, if necessary, certain definite sections of the stage set up to represent specific places. When these are added, the stage, still retaining the neutral space, becomes multiple by the simultaneous presentation of various localities, no matter how far apart they were in actuality. The simple Interludes needed nothing but a platform; the dialogue of the actors did the rest. The elaborate Miracle play, presenting the Bible story from the Fall to the Last Judgment, with its shift from hell to earth to heaven, needed localization. On the fixed stages were various "mansions," as many as the cycle required, symbolically represented in a line or semicircle as a standing scene, hell a gigantic mouth at one end, heaven a raised portion with perhaps a throne for the Trinity at the other. In between were all the necessary "mansions" representing various places on earth, Rome, Jerusalem, the Sea of Galilee. Actors went from one "mansion" to another as the play demanded. Down-stage was still neutral for unlocalized incidents or comic interpolations. When Miracles were acted on a series of pageant-wagons, this meant merely that each pageant had its separate "mansion" and neutral space; in other words the standing scene was divided into its components, and each section was mounted on wheels. Properties, costumes, and action could be realistic, conventional, or symbolic.

As the drama became professional, as actors ceased to be butchers and bakers and chose to earn their living by acting, the neutral tended to supersede the simultaneous stage. Of course the Miracles continued to be presented with standing scenes or pageants well into Shakespeare's lifetime and were even moved ponderously to adjacent towns, but itinerant companies could not carry about the elaborate paraphernalia necessary for simultaneous presentation and not sufficiently adaptable to the conditions or places in which they were to play. At Court where more spectacular drama was possible, and in the early private theatres where children presented courtly plays, multiple setting might linger longer, and it did not entirely disappear from the public stage, but for the simplicity required by strollers the neutral stage with easily portable properties was more practical. The platform erected in inn-yards was a neutral stage. And as this process continued, the curtain became more and more important.

It is essential for any understanding of Elizabethan staging to remember that the curtain used by inn-yard players was not a front curtain but at the rear of the platform and that it served at first merely to screen the actors' dressing-room and to provide a place for their entrance onto the stage. It was the curtain and the inn-yard which gradually transformed the method of staging. The inns were permanent structures, and the section back of the platform served as a permanent façade. The balcony over the curtain could represent the upper room of a house. It was not long before the curtain itself could be drawn to reveal a lower room. And these back-stages were not neutral; they could represent *different* places, but they represented *definite* places. When the public theatres were built, the inner and upper stages, cut off from platform and from the spectators' view by curtains, became permanent features.

Nothing more clearly shows the difference between the Elizabethan and the modern stage than the position and use of the curtain. Most of our plays are presented behind drawn up curtains; the Elizabethan plays were acted largely in front of curtains, either closed or drawn aside. Most modern plays are punctuated by curtains lowered in front of them to indicate structural units, to allow for scene changes, or to provide intermissions; in Elizabethan plays the act unit is relatively unimportant, the "two hours traffic of our stage" was almost continuous, and the curtain was used during the action itself to increase the playing space, to allow dramatic disclosure, or to designate a specific locality. The Elizabethan stage, then, is not ours, nor is it with certain exceptions simultaneous. It is basically a combination of open unlocalized stage, and permanent localizable recesses. It is unlike the multiple stage in that it represents one place at a time; it is unlike our picture-frame stage in being able to represent at any one time whatever place the playwright suggests and the imagination of the audience can accept. The places may be definite or indefinite and in either case are quickly and easily transferable. In short the Elizabethan is the most free and fluid stage that has ever been devised.

If the Elizabethan stage was free and fluid, one must be wary of thinking of it as bare. In our sense of the word, it had little or no scenery, but to assist the imagination, elaborate and expensive properties were used: Tamburlaine's chariot, Don Horatio's arbor, fountains, trees, and thrones. Costuming was extravagant. Plays were acted, with certain adaptations, in contemporary dress, and Elizabethan garments were gorgeous in color and fantastic in cut. Henslowe, who seldom spent more than £8 for a play, squandered £20 for one cloak. Properties and costumes combined to make effective spectacular shows and splendid processions; and masques became a feature of some plays, dancing and music of many. Battles and trial scenes, royal audiences and mob scenes were played on an open platform but they did not leave it bare. Elizabethan drama is full of noise and bustle, of constantly moving and colorful action.

Most of this action took place on the front stage which was neutral ground; localizations in modern texts—a street, the Senate House, etc.—are the work of modern editors. The playwright could, of course, by the nature of the action or properties, or by allusions in the dialogue, immediately localize neutral ground; if he did not, it could be any place, indoors or out. The alcove and balcony-stages, and their adjacent doors and windows could more easily become definite places. The alcove, since it was concealed by a curtain, could be set with properties to indicate indoors, a study, a bed-chamber or prison, a cell for Prospero, a tomb for Juliet. When the curtain was drawn aside, the ac-

tion could remain within the alcove, or could spread to the main stage, which then immediately took on the new locality. As soon as the curtain closed and the actors left the stage, it again became neutral ground. Most of the heavy properties, unless easily removable in full view of the audience, had to be within the curtained sections of the stage. Moreover, the inner stage could be used for discoveries, disclosures, tableaux, and stage-pictures. The doors from tiring-house to main stage were local if the stage was local; otherwise they served merely as entrances and exits for the actors. Upper windows were almost necessarily local, the upper stage usually so, representing upper rooms or balconies, monuments or towers or city walls. All parts of two stories became the playing space for Elizabethan drama and constituted the stage proper. Indeed, gods descending from the "shadow" and ghosts rising from traps added heavens and the subterranean. Over the diverse and shifting playing space, with scene changes indicated by exits and entrances, the Elizabethan play swept smoothly, swiftly, and practically continuously to its conclusion.

Acted on such a stage by companies so constituted, the Elizabethan play was naturally conditioned by its theatrical environment. It was the playwright's task to compose for this stage and these actors, and the conditions under which his play was to be presented determined in part his dramatic technique. How was he affected in his plan and writing by this kind of theatre and company?

Certain features are immediately obvious. He could have as many scenes in his plays as he wished, and he could place them wherever he wished, even on the sea-coast of Bohemia, which has no sea-coast. Action could still be fluid and continuous, no matter how many times he shifted places, no matter whether places were localized or not, real or imaginary. He did assist the audience by indicating in his dialogue where the action was taking place if it was a matter of importance, and he usually ended scenes with rhymed tag-lines, after which the stage would be momentarily bare. He could not, like a modern playwright, work up to a "curtain" because the greater part of the action was preferably on the main stage, close to the audience which surrounded it. Moreover he had to provide for proper exits. For example, characters in Elizabethan tragedy have a high death-rate, especially at the end of the play; bodies on the front stage must be removed; usually there is a funeral procession. Comedies, especially those with marriage-endings, frequently conclude with an exit dance.

It is not remarkable that Elizabethan drama is on the whole a poetic drama. Elizabethans—it is typical of the Renaissance everywhere—had fallen in love with language, with words, with speech of all kinds, homely and conceited, old words and new words, short words and long words, poor words and rich words. The young student of Elizabethan drama, having learned that the pun is the lowest form of humor, is often bothered by the plays on words he discovers there. The pun to an Elizabethan was not merely a joke; it was a rhetorical device by which he managed to say two or three things at once. Wit combats, badinage, thrust and parry are everywhere in Elizabethan drama. So are orations, elaborate descriptions, delicate sentiments, philosophical discussions. But if love of words and of their rhythms is a part of the inheritance of the English Renaissance, it was also fostered by the stage. Here were actors not cut off from the audience by orchestra-pit and proscenium-arch, but in the midst of a word-loving audience. All eyes were on them; all ears strained to hear. They were not puppets seen through a picture-frame but in intimate physical contact. Words accompanied by easily visible gestures and expression went home with extraordinary force and directness, whether they were high astounding terms or mere gags. And so Elizabethan drama is in its best sense a wordy drama. The playwright was not afraid of soliloquies; soliloquies properly used told the audience what was going on inside of a character, what he would not or could not say to anyone else. This was not a realistic stage; an aside was perfectly acceptable. Moreover, a speaker might very well be nearer to his audience than to the actor who was supposed not to overhear him. The variety and scope of the language, the emotional rhythms of poetic speech of the Elizabethan drama were partly the result of the Elizabethan theatre.

One other point may well be made. The Elizabethans loved stories, and their stage was ideally equipped to tell them in action. Since the scene could be shifted at will, and action was swift and continuous, it was not necessary to stick to one story. The playwright could tell two or three. If he was a poor craftsman, he could amuse his audience even if his method was entirely episodic. If he was an artist, he would carefully preserve cause and effect in his handling of multiple plots, and connect the stories to each other by the inter-relationship of characters, and by parallel and contrast. This was a stage which cried out for the narrative method, and the stories became the more real and effective because the characters were seen literally in the round.

If the stage played a vital part in determining the dramatic method of the playwright, he was also strongly influenced by the company for which he was writing. We shall never know how widely this influence operated, but there is no doubt of its force. A dramatist working for a definite group cannot compose in a vacuum; his play must fit his actors. The lovely lyrics scattered through Lyly's plays were written for singing children. How much are Marlowe's supermen due to the titanic Alleyn? Certainly Shakespeare knew his tragic heroes were to be played by Burbage. It is important to remember that while Will Kemp was a member of the company, Shakespeare created for him such parts as Costard, Bottom, and Dogberry; rustic, blundering, unlearned characters at which Kemp was adept. When Robert Armin took his place, however, the comedy role changed. Armin was brilliant, witty, himself a man of letters; as a result we have Touchstone and Feste, court-jesters, "not altogether fool." Do we owe the Fool in *Lear* to Armin's expressed dissatisfaction with the very minor Clown in *Othello*? Moreover, these companies were fairly stable in size; the number of characters in a play was in part determined by the number of actors in the company. No doubt many characters in Elizabethan plays, absent in the sources, owe their origin to the need for utilizing the full talents of the company. The personnel may well have forced the playwright into minor stories

and plot complications which structurally seem unnecessary or superfluous, simply to provide them all with opportunities.

All these forces interact. The companies produced the theatre; the kind of stage affects the work of the playwright. The playwright, conditioned by both theatre and company, may by the nature of his art modify both stage and acting. The Elizabethan audience played its part in creating Elizabethan drama. It is a complex problem. Unless we bear in mind these interactions; unless, more specifically, we understand the theatrical conditions under which Elizabethan playwrights worked, we have no basis for the assumption that we understand their plays. The freedom, the swift variety, the boundless scope in matter and manner, the universality of thought and expression which characterize the dramatic art of the English Renaissance and make it vital, vivid, and moving today stem alike from actor and theatre and poet-playwright. (pp. 45-62)

The freedom, the swift variety, the boundless scope in matter and manner, the universality of thought and expression which characterize the dramatic art of the English Renaissance and make it vital, vivid, and moving today stem alike from actor and theatre and poet-playwright.

—Thomas Marc Parrott and Robert Hamilton Ball

Thomas Marc Parrott and Robert Hamilton Ball, "Actors and Theatres," in their A Short View of Elizabethan Drama, 1943. Reprint by Charles Scribner's Sons, 1958, pp. 45-62.

Michael Hattaway

[A New Zealand educator, author, and editor of Elizabethan literature, Hattaway has been praised for his insightful commentary on the theatricalism of Elizabethan drama. His study, Elizabethan Popular Theatre: Plays in Performance *(1982) is cited by scholars as an "admirable synthesis" of the period's literature. In the following excerpt taken from that work, Hattaway identifies various elements of Elizabethan production. After noting the opposition of the civil authorities to the performances, he attempts to account for their popularity among the general populace, contending that technical innovations in set design, the employment of dumb shows, set pieces, jigs, and the incorporation of music and dance, were effective in heightening audience interest.]*

City and Court

Although . . . foreign tourists numbered the playhouses among the glories of London, the City authorities engaged in almost constant skirmishes through the last decades of the sixteenth century to have them suppressed and plucked down. The players lost the final battle in 1642 when the playhouses were finally closed, but this was merely the final coup in a war that for decades had cast official disrepute on the very men who were building the most enduring cultural monuments of the age. The reasons for this conflict are complex, involve both questions of religious doctrine and considerations of law and order, and reflect wider tussles between rival centres of power in the Church, the City, and the Court.

Because their profession demanded that they wander from town to town in search of audiences, the first troupes of players had appeared to local and civic authorities to fall into the same category as vagrants whose anomalous status had demanded regularisation during feudal times. In the sixteenth century the Tudors found it convenient to consolidate this legislation against such unstable elements of the population with the result that numerous statutes were passed against rogues, vagrants, and 'masterless men', or, as the Lord Mayor of 1580 called them, 'a very superfluous sort of men'. These statutes compelled players to seek protection from the law by taking nominal service with an aristocratic protector—the reason that most of the sixteenth-century acting troupes bear the names of their noble patrons. This legal fiction generally afforded players protection against summary punishments of whipping, branding, and imprisonment, but just as they were achieving some economic security at the time that the first playhouses were being constructed, they were subjected to further threats to their livelihood from the strengthening power of the City. For this feudal relationship between aristocrats and players was a conspicuous anachronism in the new economic structures of London. Players both offended the religious sensibilities and threatened the commercial order of the City fathers. Although sixteenth-century reformers had used drama for polemical purposes—Bale's historical morality *King John* (1538), for example, is a piece of forceful protestant propaganda—the public playhouses soon proved their ability to distract the citizenry from afternoon church-going, and the habits of players and audiences increasingly offended the more fundamentalist members of the reform movement. Players appeared to be sinners because they would perform on the sabbath and during Lent, making profit out of recreation, because, contrary to biblical injunction, they donned women's attire, because their dialogue might be obscene and scurrilous and their gestures lewd, and because the enthusiasm they generated seemed to be a species of idolatry. (Zeal-of-the-Land Busy enters in V. v. of *Bartholomew Fair* to pluck down the 'heathenish idols' of the Fair, Leatherhead's puppets.) The sumptuousness of the playhouses and of the players' costumes offended too against puritan advocacy of simplicity and plainness. Arguments like these as well as traditional humanist topics that date from ancient diatribes against the decadence of Roman theatrical entertainments appeared in several pamphlets of the 1570s and 1580s and were wheeled out when the collapse of scaffolding and the deaths of spectators provided occasions for preachers to point to Providential punishment on the frequenters of bear-baitings, cockfights, and plays.

This was one kind of attack: others came from the City fathers because they felt that the playhouses were sinks of idleness, that they drew 'apprentices and other servants from their ordinary works'. Considerations of holiness and profit combine in the petition of the corporation to the Privy Council in about 1582 to ban all performances in the suburbs—performances in the City had already been suppressed:

> For as much as the playing of interludes, and the resort to the same are very dangerous for the infection of the plague, whereby infinite burdens and losses to the City may increase; and are very hurtful in corruption of youth with incontinence and lewdness, and also great wasting both of the time and thrift of many poor people and great provoking of the wrath of God, the ground of all plagues; great withdrawing of the people from public prayer and from the service of God; and daily cried out against by the grave and earnest admonitions of the preachers of the word of God; Therefore be it ordered that all such interludes in public places, and the resort to the same shall wholly be prohibited as ungodly, and humble suit be made to the Lords that like prohibition be in places near unto the City.

Other petitions were provoked by specific and inevitable disturbances caused by the crowds that attended the playhouses. . . . [Plays] had been frequently performed in inns, including certain inns within the City itself. Experience of these occasions, the hindrances to traffic caused by the crowds attending and the accompanying frays and incitements to petty crime and vice, made the corporation determined to have no permanent and regular playhouses within the City limits. Accordingly we find that except for the short-lived first Blackfriars, no playhouse was built within the City of London in the sixteenth century. Finally the fear of the plague, alluded to in the petition quoted above, gave the City further cause for concern. Performances were allowed only when the weekly bill of plague victims fell below fifty for three weeks and then thirty a week, with the result that Henslowe's diary and other sources reveal that the playhouses were frequently closed for months on end and the players compelled to seek their living in the provinces.

If they were under attack from the City, the players had protectors at Court. Their patrons . . . were aristocrats, and playing had long been at the centre of Court revels, particularly the long feast of Christmas. Men who served on the very body, therefore, that was receiving petitions from the City for the suppression of playing, were also engaged in choosing the entertainments to please the monarch from among the competing troupes. It is not surprising that no action was actually taken when the City prevailed upon the Privy Council to write on 28 July 1597 to the Justices of Middlesex and Surrey ordering them to 'pluck down quite the stages, galleries and rooms that are made for people to stand in, and so to deface the same as they may not be employed again to such use'. If the Privy Council, however, chose to exercise only desultory control over the playhouses, it chose to increase its control over the plays that were presented in them. Proclamations as early as 1559 had required the licensing of plays, and in

1581 the Master of the Revels who had previously served as a kind of dramatic impresario, was commissioned to cause the players to appear before him 'with all such plays, tragedies, comedies, or shows, as they shall have in readiness, or mean to set forth, and them to present and recite before our said servant'. Players who put on satires or political propaganda unpleasing to the government could be imprisoned for sedition, and the texts of plays that had been performed sometimes bear the marks of censorship: the deposition scene in *Richard II* (1595), for example, is missing from the first three quartos that were published.

Audiences

Because a lot of our descriptions of playhouse audiences derive from puritan pamphlets, City petitions, criminal court records, satirical poems, and the invectives of disappointed playwrights, it is easy to get the impression that playhouse yards were filled with an illiterate rabble containing a large proportion of cutpurses, pickpockets, and whores, and that their galleries were crammed with inattentive 'plush and velvet men' paying court to their mistresses or appearing at the play only to be seen themselves. It would be easy to put that construction upon the following letter of 25 February 1592, from the Lord Mayor to the Archbishop of Canterbury, for example:

> Our most humble duties to your Grace remembered. Whereas by the daily and disorderly exercise of a number of players and playing houses erected within this City, the youth thereof is greatly corrupted and their manners infected with many evil and ungodly qualities by reason of the wanton and profane devices represented on the stages by the said players, the prentices and servants withdrawn from their works, and all sorts in general from the daily resort unto sermons and other Christian exercises, to the great hindrance of the trades and traders of this City and profanation of the good and godly religion established amongst us. To which places also do usually resort great numbers of light and lewd disposed persons, as harlots, cutpurses, cozeners, pilferers, and such like, and there, under the colour of resort of those places to hear the plays, devise divers evil and ungodly matches, confederacies, and conspiracies, which by means of the opportunity of the place cannot be prevented nor discovered, as otherwise they might be.

Yet it is important to remember that the Lord Mayor's description was scarcely disinterested and that in the nature of things it was the disorderly performances that were recorded and not the peaceable ones. Although there is a cutpurse visible in a description of a Fortune audience, its authors, Dekker and Middleton, insist on the attentiveness and prosperity of the spectators:

> Nay, when you look into my galleries,
> How bravely they're trimmed up, you all shall swear
> You're highly pleased to see what's set down there:
> Storeys of men and women, mixed together,

> Fair ones with foul, like sunshine in wet weather;
> Within one square a thousand heads are laid,
> So close that all of heads the room seems made;
> As many faces there, filled with blithe looks,
> Show like the promising titles of new books
> Writ merrily, the readers being their own eyes,
> Which seem to move and to give plaudities;
> And here and there, whilst with obsequious ears
> Thronged heaps do listen, a cut-purse thrusts and leers
> With hawk's eyes for his prey; I need not show him;
> By a hanging villainous look yourselves may know him,
> The face is drawn so rarely: then, sir, below,
> The very floor, as't were, waves to and fro,
> And, like a floating island, seems to move
> Upon a sea bound in with shores above.

This suggests that if a few depraved spectators were there for the lewdness of the players' words and gestures, others paid their admission prices to hear fine poetry and enjoy the rich spectacle. Like Pistol in *Henry V,* some may have made themselves ridiculous by imitating in their own speech the high style they heard there, but the Pistols in the audience would at least have been attentive.

The audience was not, therefore, as some early scholars would have us believe, an unruly, ignorant mob. Nor is it likely, however, that it attended to the play in hushed reverence as a modern audience might do. The mere fact that public playhouse performances generally took place by daylight meant that the spectators were on show to one another. Gallants took tobacco as they sat conspicuously on the stage (the habit was established by 1596), orange- and beer-sellers plied their trade before the play began and possibly during the performance; and certainly complaints about the distractions of nut-cracking among the audience are fairly common in the plays. Books and pamphlets were also hawked in the auditoria. There were few if any reserved seats and the passage quoted above bears testimony to the pushing and swaying in the yard when it was full. Although plays were advertised by playbills posted around the town and, occasionally for a new play, a procession, it is possible that some attended performances without a certain knowledge of what would be played. On carnival days the playhouses might be taken over and the programme changed at the demand of the mob: Chambers [in *R.E.S.* I, 1925] prints a letter from a Florentine describing how an audience discontented with the day's offering demanded an impromptu performance of, probably, *Friar Bacon and Friar Bungay.* Such reports are exceptions that prove the rule, but Beaumont was able to use the device of audience taking over the play as the basis of the structure of *The Knight of the Burning Pestle.* In some respects then the atmosphere in an Elizabethan public playhouse must have been more like that of a funfair than of a modern theatre. The players had to draw attention to themselves and could not count on reverent silence. In *A Midsummer Night's Dream* and *Love's Labour's Lost* Shakespeare with great sympathy presents common players whose performances were 'dashed' by frivolous aristocrats and the morose Ben Jonson more in seriousness than in fun felt it necessary to draw up a contract of attention for the audience of *Bartholomew Fair* at the Hope.

Descriptions of the behaviour of Elizabethan audiences have infected descriptions of the types of people who attended the playhouses. Besides mentioning harlots and cutpurses the Lord Mayor in his letter to the Archbishop stated that 'all sorts in general' frequented the playhouses. And yet it has been common among theatre historians to argue that the public playhouses were frequented for the most part by members of the 'lower orders' or 'the working class'. It is in fact extremely difficult if not impossible to ascertain the composition of Elizabethan audiences. The basic demographic information is exceedingly scanty and there are grave dangers of distortion if we allow modern demographic categories to settle on the period. Certainly the Elizabethan distinction between nobility and commoners, a distinction based on caste, cannot be simply translated into modern gradations of class defined as much by income as by birth. Too often the label 'working class' has been applied to Elizabethans who belonged to a spectrum defined by porters and mechanicals at its bottom end, apprentices, artisans, and shopkeepers at its middle, and craftsmen and merchants at its top. Elizabethan society was a pre-industrial society. So too it is naive to postulate a correlation between literacy, taste, or sophistication and social rank: an aristocrat could be depraved or discriminating in judgment, a water-carrier as fond of high rhetoric as inexplicable dumb shows and noise. The academically educated were fascinated by the native wit of the illiterate as the profusion of underworld pamphlets, by Greene and others, reveals. Any generalizations risk foundering on our knowledge that they may hold true for only one playhouse at one period or even for one performance. There does, however, seem to have been a growing distinction between the fare offered and therefore presumably the audience at the playhouses to the north of the City, the Fortune and the Red Bull, which offered a diet of heroic spectacles, and the diet of the Bankside houses which served up plays of intrigue and love. William Turner's *Dish of Lenten Stuff* (unfortunately undatable) puts it thus:

> The players of the Bankside,
>   The round Globe and the Swan,
> Will teach you idle tricks of love
>   But the Bull will play the man.

In his account of his visit to London in 1599 Thomas Platter describes how one paid for admission to the playhouses:

> And thus every day at two o'clock in the afternoon in the city of London two and sometimes three comedies are performed, at separate places, wherewith folk make merry together, and whichever does best gets the greatest audience. The places are so built, that they play on a raised platform, and every one can well see it all. There are, however, separate galleries and there one stands more comfortably and moreover can sit, but one pays more for it. Thus anyone who remains on the level standing pays only one English penny: but if he wants to sit, he is let in at a further door, and there he gives another penny. If he desires to sit on a cushion in the most comfortable place of all, where he not only sees everything well, but can also be seen, then he gives yet another English penny at another door. And in the pauses of the comedy food and drink are carried round amongst the people, and one can thus refresh himself at his own cost.

Now although Platter's account makes it clear that one could see a play for only one penny, it does not follow that the majority of the audience was made up of illiterate 'groundlings'. Artisans earned about a shilling a day throughout the period, while soldiers were provided with a daily ration of food that cost about sixpence. This indicates that half the income of, say, a mason might go on food alone and if he had a family to support there would have been little left over for entertainment. Of course some people whose earned income was low might, then as now, have been prepared to spend a large sum on admission to a popular entertainment, but it is unlikely that they could have gone often. Other factors confirm our speculation that the number of poorer people in the audience must have been comparatively small. Harbage [in his *Shakespeare's Audience,* 1941] deduced that the galleries which were more expensive to enter held in fact twice as many people as the yards and, most important, as Platter noted, plays were performed in the afternoon, a time when wage-earners, the self-employed, apprentices, and purveyors of goods and services would have been labouring at their vocations. Tradesmen as opposed to craftsmen are conspicuously absent from Gosson's invective (in *Plays Confuted,* 1582) against 'the common people which resort to theatres [who are] but an assembly of tailors, tinkers, cordwainers, sailors, old men, young men, women, boys, girls, and such like'. Tailors, like cordwainers (shoemakers), were members of a craft guild, although they were common objects of disdain in proverbs (*v. OED,* 1b). It was probably therefore invective rather than observation that led Gosson to include tinkers in his list. Nor, of course, was admission the only expense in attending the play. To cross the river by boat, the normal manner of reaching the Bankside playhouses, probably cost threepence each way, and if a servant, say, chose to walk out to Shoreditch or round over London Bridge he would have had to take that much more time from his employment. Only on holidays and Sundays, and only then at times when the bans on sabbath performances were not enforced, could such people attend. It seems therefore that the character in *Jack Drum's Entertainment* played by the Children of Paul's in 1600 who praises the private houses because there 'a man shall not be choked with the stench of garlic, or be pasted to the barmy jacket of a beer-brewer' is displaying his own squeamish snobbery and not giving an accurate description of a public playhouse yard. (Admission to Paul's ranged from only twopence to sixpence, which may indicate that admission was regulated there by caste and not by price.)

Nor can we argue easily about audience behaviour from what we know of the social habits of particular groups of the lower orders. It used to be argued that apprentices represented a large and especially unruly part of the audience. Certainly there are records of frays and riots, but these were often associated with Shrove Tuesday, a customary day of licence when it was the practice of the apprentices to prepare for Lent by dousing bawds under water-pumps and taking over and sometimes sacking playhouses. There is a graphic description of the habit in Gayton's *Festivous Notes upon Don Quixote* (1654):

> I have known upon one of these festivals, but especially at Shrove-tide, where the players have been appointed, notwithstanding their bills to the contrary, to act what the major part of the company had a mind to. Sometimes *Tamerlane*, sometimes *Jugurtha* [a lost play of about 1600 by William Boyle?], sometimes *The Jew of Malta*, and sometimes parts of all these; and at last, none of the three taking, they were forced to undress and put off their tragic habits, and conclude the day with *The Merry Milkmaids* [unknown]. And unless this were done, and the popular humour satisfied (as sometimes it so fortuned that the players were refractory), the benches, the tiles, the laths, the stones, oranges, apples, nuts, flew about most liberally; and as there were mechanics of all professions, who fell every one to his trade, and dissolved a house in an instant, and made a ruin of a stately fabric.

What is important to remember, however, is that aspects of these revels reveal puritanical rather than lawless impulses; these ritual cessations of order implicitly assert the normal rule of law. Nor were apprentices riotous adolescents of the lowest caste: as Harbage points out, men were not released from apprenticeship until they had reached the age of twenty-four, 'the sons of unskilled labourers and husbandmen were generally barred from apprenticeship, and certain guilds insisted upon property qualifications in the parents and educational qualifications in the boy'. Apprentices therefore were not 'working class' necessarily. Moreover their working hours would have kept them from the playhouses except on these special occasions, and as they were given only lodgings and board without wages it is unlikely that any poor boys from the group could have afforded admission.

It seems therefore that the majority of the audience was, as Ann Jennalie Cook has argued recently [in her *The Privileged Playgoers of Shakespeare's London*, 1981], 'privileged'. Thomas Nashe suggested as much in *Pierce Penilesse* (1592):

> For whereas the afternoon being the idlest time of the day; wherein men that are their own masters (as Gentlemen of the Court, the Inns of the Court, and the number of captains and soldiers about London) do wholly bestow themselves upon pleasure, and that pleasure they divide (how virtuously it skills not) either into gaming, following of harlots, drinking or seeing a play: is it not then better (since of four extremes all the world cannot keep them but they will choose one) that they should betake them to the least, which is plays?

Allowance has to be made here for satirical licence; a more objective account occurs in a letter of one Philip Gawdy who reports that when the Privy Council ordered the press gangs into the 'playhouses, bowling-alleys, and dicing-houses' 'they did not only press gentlemen and serving-men, but lawyers, clerks, countrymen that had law-causes, aye the Queen's men, knights, and, as it was credibly reported, one earl.' We are reminded of how it was increasingly important for men of position to gravitate about the Court (Harbage refers to 1,500 courtiers in attendance on the Queen), to maintain houses in London, or to spend long times there attending to business or legal affairs. We are reminded too that the Bankside playhouses were almost opposite the Inns of Court where there were approximately 1,000 students in residence, drawn from the more moneyed groups in the land. These 'young gentlemen who have . . . small regard of credit or conscience', as the Lord Mayor complained in 1593, were probably the most influential group in an audience where young adult males were in a majority. Playhouses were therefore obviously a good place for prostitutes to solicit, but it is important to remember that women of quality, masked perhaps, were no less important a group than the whores. In 1580 the Lord Mayor lamented that the Theatre had attracted 'assemblies of citizens and their families', and several travellers remark on how in London it was possible for women to attend the playhouses in safety. In the first Quarto of *Hamlet* (1603), 'Gilderstone' implies that audiences at public and private playhouses were in fact similar if not identical: 'For the principal public audience that, Came to them, are turned to private plays, And to the humour of children'. (pp. 42-50)

Scene building

Given the comparatively brief time that was available for rehearsal it is probable that the companies agreed on only the boldest of effects, which doors to use for entrances and exits, basic blockings for the most important moments of the scenes, cues for the introduction of properties or for flourishes. Many scenes depended on the construction of symmetrical tableaux: the Folio's (Shakespeare's) stage direction to *3 Henry VI*, IV. i. 6, reads: '*Flourish. Enter King Edward [attended]; Lady Grey [as Queen]; Pembroke, Stafford, Hastings, [and others]. Four stand on one side and four on the other.*' Similarly formal groupings are indicated by stage directions in two Rose plays, *Edward I* (1591) and *Look about You* (1599):

> *the Queen Mother being set on the one side, and Queene Elinor on the other, the King sitteth in the middest mounted highest, and at his feet the ensign underneath him.*

> *Sound Trumpets; enter with a Herald on the one side, Henry the Second crowned, after him Lancaster, Chester, Sir Richard Faukenbridge; on the other part, King Henry the son crowned, Herald after him; after him Prince John, Leicester; being set, enters fantastical Robert of Gloucester in a gown girt; walks up and down.*

As the leading players swept down the stage (the mere size of the stage demanded bold moves and large gestures) or took up poses for scenes where they threatened or wooed, the players with smaller parts must have possessed the skills or the sense to find positions or gestures which completed the composition of the scene. There were no spot-lights to highlight a leading player: this must have been done by grouping the players in such a way as to focus the audience's attention where it was required. There can have been few productions which were able to 'shake down' in the way modern productions do, but Elizabethan performances must have had a compensating freshness. A common phrase meaning to perform a role was to 'discharge a part'. Besides giving an opportunity for bawdy, the words suggest an actor releasing his nervous energy in words and gestures as a weapon releases a missile, even if his talents were channelled with what might seem to us restricting conventions. There were obviously conventions for distraction as is indicated by a stage direction from *Richard III* (II. ii. 33): *'Enter the Queen with her hair about her ears'*, and in Marston's *The Insatiate Countess* (1610) we find the bald direction: *'Isabella falls in love with Massino'*.

If we approach the plays of Marlowe or Shakespeare's chronicle of Henry VI from this direction rather than looking in them for patterns of imagery or nice indications of 'character' we can see that they depend on scenes that follow one another with a strong architectonic rhythm, on moments that must have been realised by bold visual effects, formal groupings that tend towards tableaux, archetypal personages, frozen moments that would lodge in the spectators' minds. The final sequence of Heywood's *The Silver Age* opens with a direction that shows how important grouping was, in that the playwright was prepared to sacrifice his knowledge of divine hierarchies to visual effect: *'Sound. Enter Saturn, Jupiter, Juno, Mars, Phoebus, Venus and Mercury: they take their place as they are in height'*. For a more extended analysis we might choose I. ii of *Tamburlaine,* the scene in which we first see the hero. The scene has three such moments, what Brecht was later to call *Gestus* (which I shall translate as 'gest'), a word that means both 'gist' and 'gesture', moments when the visual elements of the scene combine with the dialogue in a significant form that reveals the condition of life in the play. In fact the word 'gesture' has almost this meaning in Elizabethan times. It was a technical term for 'the employment of bodily movements, attitudes, expression of countenance, etc., as a means of giving effect to oratory' (*OED*, 3a). The printer's epistle to the 1590 Quarto of *I Tamburlaine* notes that he has 'omitted and left out some fond and frivolous gestures, digressing (and in my poor opinion) far unmeet for the matter'—these comic scenes presumably were either written by Marlowe himself or developed with his cognizance. The first gest in this scene is established by the opening stage direction: *'[Enter] Tamburlaine leading Zenocrate, Techelles, Usumcasane, [Agydas, Magnetes], other Lords and Soldiers loaden with treasure.'* It would seem appropriate for Tamburlaine to have made his

> You shall have honours as your merits be;
> Or else you shall be forced with slavery
>
> (255-6)

and it is tempting to conjecture that Tamburlaine's soldiers had moved around the stage so that they in fact surrounded both Zenocrate and later Theridamus. This provides a visual frame for the second gest of the scene when Tamburlaine divests himself of his shepherd's weeds (ei-

The first Globe theater, which burned to the ground on 29 June 1613 (from J. C. Visscher's View of London, 1616).

ther a costume of sheepskins or the 'white sheepen cloak' listed in Henslowe's inventory) and dons his 'complete armour and this curtle-axe' (l. 42). The moment is one that lodged in the spectators' imaginations: his preceding line 'Lie here, ye weeds that I disdain to wear!' became a catch phrase and was parodied by Jonson who gave it to Juniper the cobbler in the first scene of *The Case is Altered* (1597). It is the visual enactment of the player becoming his part and draws attention to the art of impersonation. It would be appropriate, therefore, for the soldier who bore in the armour to have taken up his position down-stage from where Tamburlaine can move back to deliver his first great declamation:

> Zenocrate, lovelier than the love of Jove,
> Brighter than is the silver Rhodope,
> Fairer than whitest snow on Scythian hills,
> Thy person is more worth to Tamburlaine
> Than the possession of the Persian crown,
> Which gracious stars have promised at my
>   birth . . .
>
> (87-92)

Like the previous gest in which Alleyn put on his costume before the spectators there is no attempt at illusion here: rather Marlowe draws attention to his own art by deliberate bathos. After Tamburlaine has delivered his mighty lines Techelles demolishes the moment:

TECHELLES. What now! In love?

TAMBURLAINE. Techelles, women must be flat-
tered:
But this is she with whom I am in love.

(106-8)

This suggests that the wooing scene must have been done
with formality; the grouping must have matched the dialogue's switch from ceremony to comedy.

The second part of the scene is a parallel wooing scene as
Tamburlaine wins Theridamus over to his side. Again it
is prepared for by a visual device as the soldiers flip open
the treasure chests to display 'the golden wedges' to the
view of Mycetes' emissary. Theridamus and his followers
are magnificently dressed:

Their plumed helms are wrought with beaten
gold,
Their swords enamelled, and about their necks
Hangs massy chains of gold down to the waist;
In every part exceeding brave and rich.

(124-7)

Tamburlaine being dressed only in steel armour obviously
felt that their richness must be visibly matched. There is
a second long declamation which ends with demonstration of its own artifice:

And when my name and honour shall be spread
As far as Boreas claps his brazen wings,
Or fair Boötes sends his cheerful light,
Then shalt thou be competitor with me,
And sit with Tamburlaine in all his majesty.
THERIDAMUS: Not Hermes, prolocutor to the
gods,
Could use persuasions more pathetical.

(206-11)

Possibly the parallels between the two declamations were
reinforced by quoting the grouping of the first in the second.

What emerges from this kind of analysis—its details of
course can be merely conjectural—is that plays of this sort
moved from set piece, or from one gest or formal dramatic
image, to another. There are important implications in
that once we have realized that the set piece or formal
group is a basic element of the Elizabethan play, we are
in less danger of the moral reductivism that comes with
a concentration on plot, on end-directed action, which deduces a play's meaning simply in moral terms from its resolution. Nor are we tempted to regard the dumb shows,
songs, masques, etc., found in the plays as excrescences or
'insets' but rather we recognize them as evidence of the
basic mode of Elizabethan drama. As late as 1625 Heywood could write in the prologue to *The English Traveller:*

A strange play you are like to have, for know
We use no drum, nor trumpet, nor dumbshow,
No combat, marriage, not so much today
As song, dance, masque, to bombast out a play.
Yet these all good, and still in frequent use
With our best poets.

In plays with conventions like these there can simply have
been no time for the actors to develop the kind of relationship with one another through their roles that allows for

naturalistic character portrayal, nor can their energies
have been devoted to the collective sustaining of illusion.
Rather they must have had a sense of the pattern of their
scenes and the non-representational nature of their art
meant that the dramatic images they created were organized from concepts rather than being pictures of the real
world.

Our hypothesis that Elizabethan drama tended towards
the emblematic rather than the realistic is confirmed when
we consider that the plays consisted of far more than is
represented by the printed words that alone have survived.
The rise of the modern intensive study of Renaissance
plays coincided with the rise of a kind of drama that is
closely related to the novel—the plays, say, of Ibsen and
Chekhov. Such works were set in realist milieux that were
established by naturalistic scenery, and their excellence
depends largely on the credibility, psychological or social,
of their characters. Most educated people find it easy to
imagine the kinds of setting these plays require and also
find that the plays give up much of their meaning when
they are read. Perhaps as a consequence many who have
written about the plays of the Renaissance in this century
have concentrated their energies on what might be read:
stage directions derived from playhouse copy drop into
the small print of textual collation . . . and few editors do
much to kindle the visual imagination of their readers although they may reprint the music for the songs. So too
one often finds an unconscious prejudice against any delight in the visual. The habit of thought, implanted in the
European mind by Aristotle's incidental remarks on spectacle, was further cultivated in England at least by puritan
attitudes towards the theatre. In 1582 Gosson lamented
in *Playes Confuted in Five Actions* that 'the stateliness of
the preparation drowns the delight which the matter affords' and claimed that it was the devil himself that made
plays alluring: 'For the eye, beside the beauty of the houses
and the stages, he sendeth in garish apparel, masks, vault-
ing, tumbling, dancing of jigs, galliards, moriscos, hobby-
horses, showing of juggling casts.' Merely reading the
words, therefore, does not do justice to a body of drama
that, as contemporaries put it, had its life in its 'action' and
depended for its effect on the 'impurity' of its art. In fact
it must have been sometimes very difficult to separate
what was 'drama' from other forms of popular entertainment. In 1584 Lupold von Wedel described the bear-
baiting in Southwark adjacent to the playhouses thus:

There is a round building three storeys high, in
which are kept about a hundred large English
dogs, with separate wooden kennels for each of
them. These dogs were made to fight singly with
three bears, the second bear being larger than
the first and the third larger than the second.
After this a horse was brought in and chased by
the dogs, and at last a bull, who defended himself bravely. The next was that a number of men
and women came forward from a separate com-
partment, dancing, conversing and fighting with
each other: also a man who threw some white
bread among the crowd, that scrambled for it.
Right over the middle of the place a rose was
fixed, this rose being set on fire by a rocket: suddenly lots of apples and pears fell out of it down
upon the people standing below. Whilst the peo-

ple were scrambling for the apples, some rockets were made to fall down upon them out of the rose, which caused a great fright but amused the spectators. After this, rockets and other fireworks came flying out of all corners, and that was the end of the play.

The bear-baiting proper was followed by fireworks and entertainment which, if not arguably a 'play', was in the nature of a jig.

Music and dancing

We might begin our examination of the non-verbal elements of the plays by considering the evidence that survives for the kinds of music that accompanied performances. Music was not 'incidental', expressive of the emotions portrayed, heard by the audience but not by the characters, but provided a dramatic frame and mediating perspective for the action. Plays began with three soundings of a trumpet to herald in many plays the entrance of the black-cloaked Prologue who bowed deeply to the auditory. Trumpets or cornets sounded the flourishes that announced and the 'sennets' that accompanied ceremonial entrances, or the 'tuckets' that were the signals for mounted soldiers to advance, as in I. iii. of *Richard II,* set in the lists at Coventry. Horns were blown to announce messengers as in I. i. of *Edward III* and II. i. of *1 Henry VI.* Many battle sequences were built around these sounds. Drums were sounded for marches, hautboys for the entertainment of guests, pipes for clowns, and the winding of horns established the frequent hunting scenes. Music was a convenient form of dramatic shorthand: III. iii. of *1 Henry VI* provides a good example where Joan Pucelle describes the manoeuvres as the Duke of Burgundy abandons his allegiance to the English Talbot:

> PUCELLE: Your honours shall perceive how I will work
> To bring this matter to the wished end.
> *Drum sounds afar off.*
> Hark! by the sound of drum you may perceive
> Their powers are marching unto Paris-ward.
> *Here sound an English march.*
> There goes the Talbot, with his colours spread,
> And all the troops of English after him.
> *French* [a slow] *march.*
> Now in the rearward comes the Duke and his:
> Fortune in favour makes him lag behind.
> Summon a parley; we will talk with him.
> *Trumpets sound a parley.*
>
>   (27-35)

Three of the first four entrances of *2 Tamburlaine* specify that characters enter *'with drums and trumpets',* a form of words that indicates that musicians accompanied the players onto the stage. (In *Edward I* we find *'Enter the Mayoress of London . . . music before her.'*) A dead march was sounded at the end of tragedies like *The Massacre at Paris* and *Hamlet* ('soldiers' music'), and *Coriolanus* (a play full of music), at the funeral of Zenocrate (*2 Tamburlaine,* III. ii.), and at the openings of *Titus Andronicus* and *1 Henry VI.*

Songs of course were frequent although they can easily be overlooked as they were not always printed with the dialogue and their presence can be inferred only from a terse *'song'* or from an allusion in a character's speech. Often authors did not themselves write the words for them but were content to use a well-known air—or else they set their own words to an existing tune. Many players must have been able to sing music in parts: certainly catches and group songs figure large in interludes and there is no reason to suspect that this talent was missing from the commercial playhouses. II. iii. of *Twelfth Night* is improved if Sir Toby and Sir Andrew can sing their catches in tune. Songs could themselves have visual settings as elaborate as one in Heywood's *The Golden Age:*

> *Enter with music (before Diana) six Satyrs, after them all their Nymphs, garlands on their heads, and javelins in their hands, their bows and quivers. The Satyrs sing:*
>
> Hail, beauteous Dian, Queen of shades,
> That dwells beneath these shadowy glades . . .

In Renaissance theory music was held to be an emblem of the harmonic structures of the universe and was often used as a realisation of the relationship between macrocosm and microcosm, a way of portraying mental torment or social disorder. So it is used in the prison sequence just before Richard II's death and in IV. iv. of *Richard III,* where the newly-crowned tyrant enters with a cacophony of drums and trumpets to interrupt the ceremony of the wailing queens. Later in the private playhouses music was commonly played between the acts. Performances in public playhouses seem to have run almost continuously, possibly with pauses between the acts, although two plays of 1590, *James IV* and *The Dead Man's Fortune,* stipulate songs or dances between the acts. In one rather unlikely public playhouse play, *Sejanus* (1603), Jonson stipulates a chorus of musicians after each act—a feature that is suppressed, incidentally, in the Everyman and World's Classics texts of the play. Music in the public playhouses was generally provided by wind and percussion instruments although Henslowe owned, as well as "iij tymbrells" [tambourine-like instruments], 'iij trumpettes and a drum', 'a trebel viall, a basse viall, a bandore, a sytteren [or cithern, like the bandore which supplied its bass, a guitar-like instrument]'. They may have been used to accompany dumb shows—viols, citherns, and bandores are the instruments used for the first dumb show of *Jocasta* (1566). Musicians and players had separate organisations—they had separate licences from the Revels Office—and it is possible that particular bands or the municipally-paid 'waits' were hired for particular performances. So we hear in *Sir Thomas More* (1595), 'Where are the waits? Go bid them play to spend the time a while' (l. 944).

Dancing too was often incorporated into the plays. When the Devils enter to present Faustus with crowns and rich apparel they dance to delight his mind before they depart; Joan Pucelle witnesses an elaborate mime of devils that signals her end in *1 Henry VI,* V. iii, and Heywood's *A Woman Killed with Kindness,* a Rose play of 1603, calls for a dance of country wenches in its second scene. Then the music changes to the winding of horns to signal the hunting scene that follows. Dances were useful for wooing scenes, and Shakespeare used them thus in *Love's Labour's Lost, Romeo and Juliet,* and *Much Ado about Nothing.* Players in Shakespeare's histories (but significantly not in Marlowe's more pageant-like plays) had also to perform fights before spectators, of whom many would have been keen amateurs of the sport. In 1587 the principal comedian of the Queen's Men, Richard Tarlton, was allowed as a Master of Fence. The outcome of *Hamlet* depends upon the outcome of an elaborate fencing-match—some good modern productions have made the 'action' of the fight mirror the action of the play as a whole.

Dumb shows, set pieces, and jigs

It had been the practice in academic drama performed at the universities, the inns of court, and at Court before the public playhouses opened to begin each act of a play with a dumb show. In the case of *Gorboduc,* the first of these plays to use this device, the dumb shows prefigured the action of the ensuing act:

> First, the music of violins began to play, during which came in upon the stage six wild men, clothed in leaves. Of whom the first bare in his neck a fagot of small sticks, which they all, both severally and together, assayed with all their strength to break; but it could not be broken by them. At the length, one of them plucked out one of the sticks, and brake it: and the rest plucking out all the other sticks, one after another, did easily break them, the same being severed; which being conjoined, they had before attempted in vain. After they had this done, they departed the stage, and the music ceased. Hereby was signified, that a state knit in unity doth continue strong against all force, but being divided, is easily destroyed; as befell upon Duke Gorboduc dividing his land to his two sons, which he before held in monarchy; and upon the dissension of the brethren, to whom it was divided.

This description is fuller though no different in kind from those found in public playhouse plays like Peele's *The Battle of Alcazar* (1589). These allegorical devices were related to the religious and civic shows of the late Middle Ages, to Royal Entries, City pageants, and Lord Mayor's processions. They were obvious occasions for spectacular moments in plays and provided another kind of dramatic shorthand as dramatists could draw upon the moral learning of iconological encyclopaedias and emblem books as well as on the familiar devices of English heraldry. Certain dramatists, notably Jonson and Chapman, did not use the form, but it is a mistake to assume that Shakespeare was parodying this 'pantomimic' (silent) action in the dumb show in *Hamlet* or that the convention was antiquated by the turn of the century. Shakespeare used a kind of dumb show to open Acts I and III of *1 Henry VI* and also in his last plays; they were used extensively in Heywood's *Ages,* and are found in plays by Jonson's protégé, Richard Brome, in the 1630s. They may have sometimes served as sops to the groundlings: they are so described by Puttenham in 1589, whose description of classical practice was probably based on contemporary knowledge (witness his reference to the non-classical 'vices'):

> between the acts when the players went to make ready for another, there was great silence, and the people waxed weary, then came in these manner of counterfeit vices, they were called *Pantomimi,* and all that had before been said, or great part of it, they gave a cross construction to it very ridiculously.

Perhaps these were the kinds of 'graced deformities' that the printer said he had excised from *Tamburlaine.* Inferior dramatists found them useful for compressing their often rambling narratives. Marlowe like others often called for elaborate dumb show entrances. III. i. of *2 Tamburlaine,* for example, begins thus:

> Enter the Kings of Trebizon and Soria, one bringing a sword and another a sceptre; next Natolia [Orcanes] and Jerusalem with the imperial crown; after Callapine, and after him [Almeda and] other lords. Orcanes and Jerusalem crown him and the other give him the sceptre.

Music probably accompanied the entrance and the procession may have passed two or three times about the stage, as was common in the classical tragedies. The moment comes after another emblematic scene, that of the death of Zenocrate:

> The arras is drawn, and Zenocrate lies in her bed of state; Tamburlaine sitting by her; three Physicians about her bed, tempering potions; Theridamus, Techelles, Usumcasane, and the three sons [Calyphas, Amyras, and Celebinus].

The tableau thus discovered is a mute emblem of pathos as Tamburlaine moves forward to join the lords and deliver his lament before his queen dies to the sound of music. The scene ends with Tamburlaine re-entering the discovery space and the arras drawn closed. Marlowe may well have drawn directly on the allegoric conventions of the dumb show for some of his most famous scenes. The chariot drawn by kings, for example, may have been inspired by the first dumb show in *Jocasta* which had been reprinted in 1575 and 1587, although it could equally derive from Italian *trionfi.* The animals listed in Henslowe's inventory may have been employed to draw chariots in triumphant entries. It has been suggested that Tamburlaine's chariot may have entered into the yard of the playhouse and that he here represents the Triumph of Fortune; when he comes in in V. iii., again in his king-drawn chariot, however, he shows the pain-wracked body of the dying man that he is, signifying the Triumph of Death. After alighting from the chariot he may have turned to point to his vacant seat:

> See where my slave, the ugly Monster Death,
> Shaking and quivering, pale and wan for fear,
> Stands aiming at me with his murdering dart,
> Who flies away at every glance I give,
> And when I look away, comes stealing on.
> Villain, away, and hie thee to the field!
>
> (V. iii. 67-72)

It is a simple but most effective piece of visual irony.

Dumb shows are simply extended examples of the visual emblems that are so important in Elizabethan drama. Entrances in particular often established an informing image for the ensuing scene. Stock properties such as torches had two functions when carried on to the stage: to reveal to the audience that the action is taking place by night, but also to suggest that the bearer is in the dark, uncognizant of his fate. So Hieronimo is shown bearing a long torch in the engraving of the titlepage of the 1615 edition of *The Spanish Tragedy* (see Plate 12), which shows the opening of II. v., the moment when Hieronimo discovers the body of his murdered son (the stage direction reads *'Enter Hieronimo in his shirt etc.'*). Similarly Othello enters 'with a light' to strangle Desdemona. The moment 'quotes' Iago's entrance eighty lines before; both men wittingly and unwittingly are turning light and order to darkness and chaos. Earlier in *3 Henry VI*, Keepers enter in III. i. with crossbows to hunt the driven deer, the fleeing King himself. The entrance of players in masks often prefigures confusion as in *Romeo and Juliet* and *Much Ado about Nothing*. A final example of this kind of 'visual metonym' is provided by those scenes in which devils offer men daggers or halters to tempt them to the sin of sins, despair: Macbeth's dagger is a late instance of this. (pp. 56-65)

The dumb shows and set-pieces I have described are those for which there is evidence in the printed texts of the plays that are extant. It is probable, however, that printed stage directions record only a fraction of the spectacular business in Elizabethan performances, for there is considerable evidence outside the printed texts that audiences enjoyed many dances, songs, farcical and satiric routines which have simply not survived. These entertaining interludes which often had little or nothing to do with the story of the play were often referred to by contemporaries as 'jigs'. The word is almost impossible to define: a jig could be a song, a ballad in dialogue form, a burlesque of tradesmen or women, or a dance performed to drum or music. We find a description of such an insert in *The Pilgrimage to Parnassus* (1599):

> *Enter Dromo, drawing a clown in with a rope*
> CLOWN: What now, thrust a man into the commonwealth, whether he will or no? What the devil should I do here?
> DROMO: Why, what an ass art thou? Dost thou not know a play cannot be without a clown? Clowns have been thrust into plays by head and shoulders ever since Kempe could make a scurvy face, and therefore reason thou shouldst be drawn in with a cart rope.
> CLOWN: But what must I do now?
> DROMO: Why if thou canst but draw thy mouth awry, lay thy leg over thy staff, saw a piece of cheese asunder with thy dagger, lap up drink on the earth, I warrant thee, they'll laugh mightily. Well, I'll turn thee loose to them, either say somewhat for thyself, or hang and be *non plus*.
> CLOWN: This is fine in faith: now, when they have nobody to leave on the stage, they bring me up, and which is worse tell me not what I should say. Gentles, I dare say you look for a fit of mirth, I'll therefore

present unto you a proper new love letter of mine to the tune of 'Put on the smock a Monday', which in the heat of my charity I penned, and thus it begins: 'O my lovely Nigra, pity the pain of my liver: that little gallows Cupid hath lately pricked me in the breech with his great pin, and almost killed me thy woodcock with his birdbolt. Thou hast a pretty furrowed forehead, a fine leacherous eye, methinks I see the bawd Venus keeping a bawdy house in thy looks, Cupid standing like a Pander at the door of thy lips.'—How like you masters, has any young man a desire to copy this, that he may have *forma epistolae conscribendae*? Now if I could but make a fine scurvy face I were a king. O nature, why did'st thou give me so good a look?

> [*Re-enter Dromo, with Philomusus and Studioso*]
> DROMO: Give us a voider here for the fool. Sirrah, you must begone, here are other men that will supply the room.
> CLOWN: Why, shall I not whistle out my whistle? Then farewell gentle auditors, and the next time you see me I'll make you better sport.

Texts reveal how such set pieces were inserted into plays: what they seldom record is the habit of ending performances with a jig. English players in Europe were particularly famous for their singing and dancing skills and one of the things that most impressed the Swiss traveller, Thomas Platter, during his visit in autumn 1599 were the jigs that followed a performance of a Julius Caesar play at the Globe:

> After dinner on the 21st September, at about two o'clock, I went with my companions over the water, and in the straw-thatched house [*streü-wine Dachhaus*] saw the tragedy of the first Emperor Julius with at least fifteen characters very well acted. At the end of the comedy they danced according to their custom with extreme elegance, two in each group dressed in men's and two in women's apparel.

Most accounts of the jigs, however, derive either from the puritan enemies of the playhouses and so stress their lewdness or were written by playwrights who, while striving to create refined and academically respectable forms of drama, were forced to admit the popularity of such entertainments—even in the private playhouses and right until the middle of the seventeenth century. In 1615 'I.H.' in his *This World's Folly* inveighed against the 'squeaking out of those . . . obscene and light jigs, stuffed with loathsome and unheard-of ribaldry, sucked from the poisonous dugs of sin-swelled Theatres . . . I will not particularise those . . . Fortune-fatted fools . . . whose garb is the toothache of wit, the plague-sore of judgement . . . who are fain to produce blind Impudence [in margin, 'Garlicke'—a popular actor] to personate himself upon their stage, behung with chains of garlic, as an antidote against their own infectious breaths, lest it should kill their oyster-crying audience.' In the famous prologue to *Tamburlaine*,

Marlowe repudiates the 'jigging veins of rhyming mother wits' and yet the printer's epistle reveals that in performance the play contained episodes of this kind. Even in 1632 one of the characters in Shirley's *Changes* notes that many gentlemen:

> Are not, as in the days of understanding,
> Now satisfied without a jig, which since
> They cannot, with their honour, call for after
> The play, they look to be served up in the middle.

Sometimes the habit of ending a play's action with a dance or a song as in *Much Ado, Twelfth Night* (did Feste's song accompany a dance by the company?) or the Bergomask dance at the conclusion of Pyramus and Thisbe gives some intimation of this convention of a terminal jig, perhaps refined on these occasions; on other occasions the evidence is more difficult to uncover. Despite its several complex textual problems, the epilogue to *2 Henry IV* indicates that that play ended with a dance. Dekker's satirical passage in *A Strange Horse Race* (1613) is therefore supported by more dispassionate testimony:

> As I have often seen, after the finishing of some worthy tragedy or catastrophe in the open theatres that the scene after the epilogue hath been more black (about a nasty bawdy jig) than the most horrid scene in the play was: the stinkards speaking all things, yet no man understanding any thing.

It is even conceivable, therefore, that at the conclusion of *King Lear* the King's Men performed a jig.

There may have been further 'action' after the jig in that it seems that some of the most verbally dextrous clowns, Tarlton and Wilson among others, were in the habit of giving improvised verses or 'themes', based on some idea tossed to them from the audience. There may have then been an announcement of what the next performance was to be, after which the company may have knelt in prayer for their patron or more probably for the sovereign and the estates.

In his prologue for *Midas* (1589), admittedly a Paul's play, Lyly seems therefore to speak for all dramatists: 'If we present a mingle-mangle, our fault is to be excused, because the whole world is become an hodge-podge'. (pp. 66-9)

> Michael Hattaway, "Performances," in his Elizabethan Popular Theatre: Plays in Performance, *Routledge & Kegan Paul*, 1982, pp. 42-69.

HISTORIES

Irving Ribner

[*An American Shakespearean scholar and educator,*

Ribner wrote and edited several works on Elizabethan drama. In the following excerpt, he attempts to distinguish history plays from other Elizabethan dramatic forms, defining histories "as those which use . . . material drawn from national chronicles and assumed by the dramatist to be true." Ribner closely examines what the Elizabethans considered the "legitimate purposes of history," such as the nationalistic glorification of their country or the demonstration of God's providence in human affairs, ideas which derive from classical, humanist, and medieval Christian philosophies.]

The type of history play which flourished in the age of Shakespeare was particularly an expression of the English Renaissance. Although its roots are deep in the medieval drama, it reached its full development in the last years of the reign of Elizabeth. (p. 1)

To define the Renaissance history play as a distinct dramatic genre, however, has not been easy, although many attempts have been made. It is now, more than ever, necessary to so define it, for in the half century that has gone by since the appearance of Professor Felix E. Schelling's pioneer study [*The English Chronicle Play,* 1902], our knowledge both of Elizabethan drama and of Renaissance historiography has increased vastly, and the time has come for a re-examination of the entire field of Elizabethan drama. But before we can begin to write of the English history play, we must decide by what specific standards we may distinguish history plays from other plays of the Elizabethan era. The special use of the term 'histories' in the Shakespeare folio of 1623 is, as we shall see, of little help in this respect. We must further bear in mind that those plays whose theme is the presently authenticated history of England do not comprise the whole of the dramatic genre we may call the history play. (pp. 1-2)

The great age of the history play comes as perhaps the final distinctive manifestation of a new birth of historical writing in England. It may thus be well for us to have clearly in mind the particular historical works which served as the sources of Elizabethan and Jacobean history plays, and which, together with the historical drama and the widely current historical non-dramatic poetry, make up the historical literature of the age of Shakespeare. The Middle Ages had produced its great chroniclers: Matthew Paris, Thomas of Walsingham, Ranulph Higden, and others; but the coming of Henry VII to the English throne in 1485 gave a new impetus to historical writing, for among other things the right of the Tudors to the throne had to be demonstrated. The new English historical writings carried on much of the tradition of the medieval chronicles, but, as we shall see, they were profoundly influenced also by the new historical schools of Renaissance Italy. They were predominantly secular works, intensely nationalistic in their dedication to the greater glory of England, and deliberately propagandistic in their use of history to support the right of the Tudors to the throne and to preach political doctrine particularly dear to the Tudors. Although medieval chroniclers like Geoffrey of Monmouth were also sometimes drawn upon by the historical dramatists of the age of Shakespeare, it was chiefly the writings of these Renaissance English historians which furnished the sources of the history plays with which we shall be concerned.

The new Renaissance history had its birth in England when Duke Humphrey of Gloucester commissioned Tito Livio of Ferrara to write the history of Henry V. But the new historiography begins in earnest with the arrival in England of Polydore Vergil in about 1501. Vergil was commissioned by Henry VII to write a history of England which would, among other things, establish the right of the Tudors to the throne. The *Anglica Historia* was not published, however, until 1534, and in attacking the authenticity of Arthurian legend it did not accomplish the ends Henry VII had envisioned. In 1516, in the meantime, had been published Robert Fabyan's *The New Chronicles of England and France,* essentially a medieval work, but one to be used by Elizabethan writers of history plays. It was to go through three more editions by 1559.

In 1543 appeared Richard Grafton's edition of a verse chronicle of England by John Hardyng, who had recorded English events down to 1436. Grafton continued Hardyng's chronicle down to his own time, and in his book he included also the *Historie of Kyng Rycharde the Thirde,* usually attributed to Sir Thomas More, there printed for the first time. In 1548 Grafton printed posthumously the important work of Edward Hall, a barrister at Gray's Inn. This was *The Union of the two Noble and Illustre Famelies of Lancastre and Yorke,* which . . . did so much to shape the philosophy of history in the plays of Shakespeare. Hall had based his work upon Polydore Vergil, and by writing in English he gave wide currency to Vergil's particular propagandistic view of English history. Hall's was probably the most influential of all Elizabethan accounts of the period from Richard II to the coming of Henry VII. In 1562 Grafton further brought out *An Abridgement of the Chronicles of England* which went through five editions by 1572.

In 1563 John Foxe produced his *Actes and Monuments* or *The Book of Martyrs,* as it was commonly called, which gave to the history he recorded the strong imprint of his own Reformation prejudices. This work was to be a source for historical plays dealing with the Tudor period, and particularly the biographical plays. In 1565 John Stow published *A Summarie of Englyshe Chronicles,* which went through ten editions by 1611 and was probably the most important short history of England of its age.

But the most important work of all, in so far as the history play is concerned, appeared in 1577, when Raphael Holinshed published his monumental *Chronicles of England, Scotlande and Irelande.* This work was prefaced by a *Description of England,* written by William Harrison, and the history of Ireland was written by Richard Stanyhurst, who used materials collected earlier by the Jesuit, Edmund Campion. Holinshed had little imagination and little historical insight, but he was a careful compiler of all that was available to him, and, what is particularly important for the period from Richard II to Henry VII, he used the earlier work of Edward Hall. It was probably through Holinshed that Hall's view of history received its widest currency. A second edition of Holinshed, greatly altered, appeared in 1587, and it was to this edition that Shakespeare and his contemporaries went for the greater part of the Elizabethan and Jacobean historical drama. Holinshed himself had died around 1580, and the additions and expansions in the 1587 volume are the work of John Hooker, Francis Thynne, John Stow, William Harrison, and Abraham Fleming under whose editorial direction the others seem to have worked.

Drama was, of course, not the only literary art in the Elizabethan age which went to the chronicles of England for its inspiration. There is also a long and vital tradition of historical non-dramatic poetry, of which the most significant exemplar, for its influence upon the history play, is *A Mirror for Magistrates*— begun by William Baldwin as a continuation of John Lydgate's *Fall of Princes*— first printed in 1559 after having been suppressed by Queen Mary and enlarged and re-edited six more times by 1587. *The Mirror,* moreover, was widely imitated. Other poetic historics of England include William Warner's *Albion's England,* four books of which were published in 1586 and two more in 1589; Samuel Daniel's *First Foure Bookes of the Civile Wars between the Two Houses of Lancaster and Yorke,* published in 1595, with a fifth book to follow in 1596, a sixth in 1601, and the complete work in 1609. Michael Drayton was the author of several historical poems. His *Piers Gaveston* was printed in 1593, and his *Matilda* followed in 1594. These were both reprinted in 1596, along with *The Tragical Legend of Robert Duke of Normandy.* In that year also Drayton published his *Mortimeriados,* which he was later to rewrite and republish in 1603 as *The Barons Warres.* A related work, although not entirely historical, is Drayton's *Poly-Olbion,* a long topographical poem inspired by Camden's *Britannia.* This was first published in 1612 and then in an enlarged edition in 1622. The age was one of deep interest in history, manifest in prose, poetry, and the drama, and it was to the same preoccupations and tastes as the others that the historical drama catered.

Much confusion has resulted, I believe, from the use of the term 'chronicle play' to refer to the large body of extant plays which take as their subject matter the history of England. The term is always used with the unstated implication that a chronicle play somehow differs from a history play, although what a history is and just how a 'chronicle' may differ from it is never made clear. *Henry V* is labelled a 'chronicle play' and *Julius Caesar* a history, but the only generic difference between the two plays is that the one is drawn from English history and the other from Roman; and although Roman history could never have the same significance as English history to the Elizabethans, both are parts of the great sphere of history, and it is ridiculous to make generic distinctions on the basis of the national origin of subject matter. The term 'chronicle' is used, moreover, to refer to a kind of formless, episodic drama, and the implication is usually that this was the only kind of drama in which the history of England was ever treated. The inadequacy of this notion I shall attempt to demonstrate below. Since a meaningful distinction between 'chronicle' and history is impossible, we had best abandon the term 'chronicle' entirely. Plays which deal with the history of any country are history plays, and no other critical term is needed.

The Elizabethans themselves have left us little of value in so far as a definition of the history play is concerned. The famous induction to *A Warning for Fair Women* (1599), in which History appears upon the stage with Tragedy and Comedy, tells us something about tragedy but does nothing to define the history play. The editors of the Shakespeare folio of 1623 divided his plays into tragedies, comedies, and histories; but it is not likely that Heminges and Condell approached their task with fine critical distinctions, as we know, for instance, from their inclusion of *Cymbeline* among the tragedies. Under histories, they included only Shakespeare's plays on recent British history, but certainly no Elizabethan would have questioned the historicity of such plays as *Julius Caesar* and *Antony and Cleopatra,* to say nothing of *King Lear* and *Macbeth.* It seems likely that the editors of the folio were most interested in presenting Shakespeare's plays on recent English history in chronological order. This they did, labelling the group histories. All other plays they grouped as either comedies or tragedies—except for *Troilus and Cressida,* about which there was apparently some confusion—ignoring whether they were histories as well. The designations on the title-pages of quartos are equally useless, for the term 'history' was applied to almost anything.

Schelling called the history play a distinctively English product which sprang suddenly into being with the great tide of British nationalism and patriotism that accompanied the defeat of the Spanish armada in 1588, and he held that it was more closely related to non-dramatic literature than to other forms of the drama. Schelling made little attempt to fix the limits of the history play as a genre, and in separating it from the general course of Elizabethan drama he was, if anything, misleading. William Dinsmore Briggs [in his edition of *Marlowe's Edward II,* 1914], on the other hand, defined the history play in a more arbitrary manner:

> Let us define the chronicle history as a dramatic composition purporting to draw its materials from the chronicles (or from an equivalent source), treating these materials in a way to bring out their accidental (particularly chronological) relations, recognizing as a rule no other principle of connection than that of personality, and having the general character of a survey of a more or less arbitrarily limited period.

The limitations of such a definition are obvious. Even in so far as form alone is concerned, it will fit only the crudest specimens of the history play. Its inadequacy is implicit in that it cannot apply to such plays as *Woodstock, Edward II,* or *Richard II,* where we find well-knit dramatic structure and integrating forces far more important than the chronological. There is, moreover, in the greatest history plays a distinct political purpose which Briggs ignored. The history play cannot be defined on the basis of dramatic form, for the forms in which we find it are many. Far more important than form is the dramatist's artistic intention. Schelling and Briggs merely perpetuated what A. P. Rossiter has termed [in his *Woodstock, A Moral History,* 1946], 'an academic myth raised by last century aversion to morals and politics, with the resulting failure to estimate aright the shaping influence of the Morality in par-

ticular and allegory in general' on the mature Elizabethan history play. This is the critical myth, still widely accepted, which would define the Tudor history play as an episodic, disintegrated, non-didactic pageant.

A more realistic distinction has been drawn by Professor Alfred B. Harbage [in his *As They Liked It,* 1947] in his separation of Shakespeare's plays into history and fable. Among the histories he would include the ten English and three Roman history plays and *Troilus and Cressida;* all others he would call fables. The primary distinction between the two groups, he holds, is that in fable, 'the relationship among the characters is mainly personal and domestic, not political; and vice and virtue operate on individuals directly, not through the intermediary of national programs or party platforms'; in histories, on the other hand, moral choices are determined by national and political, rather than personal, concerns. The matter of fable, he holds, could be altered freely to suit the dramatist's purposes, whereas the authors of history plays were more closely restricted to their sources.

Professor Harbage is correct in pointing to the political motivation of history, and his distinction is essentially a valid one, although one might question his categorization of Shakespeare's plays, particularly since it is based upon a rigid distinction between history and tragedy which would deny to plays like *Coriolanus* and *Antony and Cleopatra* the status of tragedy. But as a means of defining the history play Harbage's distinction does not go far enough. One wonders whether, in actual analysis of a play, the line between private and political conduct can be clearly drawn. The political and the personal are often inseparable, and it is perhaps inevitably so in a dramatist such as Shakespeare who saw the problems of state in terms of the personality of the ruler and who conceived of society as a dynamic organism in which the goodness of individual men and women was indispensable to the health of the political whole.

The freedom with which a dramatist treats his sources depends largely upon personal attitudes and purposes. Robert Greene in his *Alphonsus of Aragon* could take a widely celebrated historical figure out of Bartolommeo Fazio's history of Naples and involve him in a mosaic of imaginary battles and romance situations, without any concern for historical truth whatsoever. When Shakespeare used Plutarch, he followed his sources much more faithfully than he did when he used Holinshed. To assume that there was in England before the middle of the seventeenth century any great concern for historical accuracy as an end in itself is unwarranted. The purpose of a history, as I shall explain below, was not to present truth about the past for its own sake; it was to use the past for didactic purposes, and writers of history, both non-dramatic and dramatic, altered their material freely in order better to achieve their didactic aims. The King John story furnishes an excellent example. The chronicles through Polydore Vergil had all treated John harshly and from a Catholic point of view, but Reformation writers, from John Bale through Shakespeare, freely adapted the account to serve their own Protestant purposes.

Harbage's distinction, although useful and pertinent, will

thus not give us all that we need in order to isolate the history play as a distinct dramatic genre. Another significant contribution to a definition of the history play, has been that of Professor Lily B. Campbell. She has recognized [in her *Shakespeare's 'Histories': Mirrors of Elizabethan Policy*, 1964] that the historical dramatist attempted to fulfil the purposes of the historian as he and his contemporaries saw those purposes. But the actual criteria Miss Campbell offers are too narrow to be meaningful. The historical dramatist, she holds, deals with politics as opposed to ethics, with the public rather than the private virtues:

> . . . it is to this distinction between private and public morals that we must look for the distinction between tragedy and history. Tragedy is concerned with the doings of men which in philosophy are discussed under *ethics;* history with the doings of men which in philosophy are discussed under *politics.*

Like Harbage's distinction, to which it is closely allied, this is of course true. But as a definition of the history play it is too narrow, for all works which concentrate on the public virtues are not histories. And, as Miss Campbell recognizes, the public and private virtues are so completely interwoven in general Renaissance concepts of kingship that it is almost impossible for a dramatist to deal with the one to the exclusion of the other. No definition which places history and tragedy in mutually exclusive categories will stand the test of close examination. Miss Campbell has recognized, however, serious historical purpose as the distinguishing feature of the history play, and she has also recognized the political bases of Shakespeare's histories.

This historical purpose has also been recognized by E. M. W. Tillyard, who [in his *Shakespeare's History Plays*, 1947] regards Shakespeare's history plays as designed to express a providential view of history in terms of the official Tudor interpretation of earlier events, particularly as expounded by Edward Hall. Tillyard feels that Shakespeare, in his use of Hall, asserts order, degree, and divine providence in the world. He sees Hall's 'Tudor myth', as presenting 'a scheme fundamentally religious, by which events evolve under a law of justice and the ruling of God's providence, and of which Elizabeth's England was the acknowledged outcome.' And what he interprets as Shakespeare's conception of history, Tillyard calls the general Elizabethan conception and the doctrine which all of the best history plays embody.

What Tillyard says of Shakespeare is largely true, but by limiting the goals of the serious history play within the narrow framework of Hall's particular view, he compresses the wide range of Elizabethan historical drama into entirely too narrow a compass. There were other schools of historiography in Elizabethan England. The providential history of Hall, in fact, represents a tradition which, when Shakespeare was writing, was already in decline. To dismiss, for instance, as Tillyard does, Machiavelli and all that he brought to historical method as lying 'outside the main sixteenth-century interest' is clearly short-sighted. In historiography, as in other intellectual areas, the Elizabethan age was one of flux and uncertainty, with new and heretical notions competing in men's minds against old established ideas which could no longer be accepted without doubt and questioning. Both the old and the new notions of history may be found reflected in Tudor history plays. There is room for Marlowe as well as Shakespeare. We cannot consider the history play outside the scope of Elizabethan historiography, as both Tillyard and Miss Campbell have wisely perceived, but we must have a more adequate conception of Elizabethan historical purpose and method than Tillyard has offered.

To understand the history play, we must return to an Elizabethan point of view with regard to subject matter. We cannot limit our analysis to plays on known British history, as is usually done. For instance, how much of the story of King Brute and his descendants, which we today relegate to the realm of myth, was considered actual history by Shakespeare and his contemporaries? And what of that vast body of romantic and apocryphal legend which attaches to every great historical figure and to every historical era, and which was so perpetuated in folk legendry that to Elizabethan chroniclers it was usually indistinguishable from actual historical fact? The body of plays drawn from such matter is a vast one. To what extent must they be included in any concept of the history play as a distinct dramatic genre? We must attempt to see the limits of history as the Elizabethans saw them; yet we cannot fall into the morass which Tucker Brooke so clearly saw [in his *The Tudor Drama*, 1911] when he warned that any discussion of the subject is in danger of 'losing itself hopelessly in the attempt to follow such quasi-historical will-o'-the-wisps as *George a Greene* and *James IV*'. Tucker Brooke saw clearly the need for a definition of the history play, but he could find none which fitted all he chose to call histories. He finally contented himself with grouping all Elizabethan plays dealing with historical or pseudo-historical subjects into five general categories. The relations between these categories are often very vague; what makes all of them history plays is not clear.

The problem is a complex one, and there will always be some plays which defy classification. I believe, however, that we can establish certain general principles which will aid us in definition. We must recognize, to begin with, that any definition of a literary genre is essentially an abstract ideal, and that no conceivable definition will apply equally well to every play we choose to call a history play. Our definition must describe an ideal to which only some history plays will conform fully; the others fall within the genre by virtue of their striving for this ideal, whether or not they achieve it to any appreciable degree. Our concept of the history play is necessarily a twentieth-century construct which we impose upon a relatively homogeneous body of drama which the Elizabethans themselves made no attempt to define but which by its very homogeneity constitutes a separate dramatic genre, whether or not the Elizabethans so conceived of it.

As our principal distinguishing feature, we may assume with Lily B. Campbell that a history play was one which fulfilled what Elizabethans considered the purposes of history. This does not mean that the historical intention was necessarily more important than the dramatic one; a dramatist's primary concern is always to create drama. It implies merely that when a dramatist went to history for his subject matter he could do so with an understanding of the meaning and implications of the historical genre, and the purposes of history would thus naturally become the purposes of his play. To determine whether he first decided to write history or first decided to write a play is like asking whether the chicken preceded the egg, or vice versa. In the history play the dramatic and the historical intentions are inseparable. The dramatist's first objective is to entertain a group of people in a theatre. When he goes to history for his subject matter, however, he assumes the functions of the historian as well.

With this in mind, we must determine, if necessarily only in broad and general terms, what to an Elizabethan was a purpose of history and what was not. We must remember that Elizabethan historical purposes were many and that, as the Renaissance reached maturity in England, particularly in the early seventeenth century, historical purposes were modified and changed. The legendary British history of *Gorboduc* and the Roman history of *Sejanus* are both history plays, although the truth of the events related and the purpose of each play may be far apart. It was not until the seventeenth century that anything approaching a modern conception of history began to evolve in England. We must further try to determine what, to people of the historical era with which we are dealing, was historical subject matter and what was not. This also is difficult, for the age of the English Renaissance is a long one and it embraced many cultural and historical events and points of view. Gorboduc was a real king for John Caius, but a mythical one for Edmund Bolton.

A portrait of Edward Alleyn (1566-1626), a leading Elizabethan actor.

What then was an historical purpose in Renaissance England? Wallace K. Ferguson [in his *The Renaissance in Historical Thought,* 1948] has written that an Italian humanist historian would have offered three reasons for the writing of history: 'that it is a form of literature, highly regarded by the ancients and presenting attractive opportunities for the exercise of style; that it has great practical value since it teaches moral, ethical, and political lessons; and finally, that his history celebrated the past and present glories of his native land or of the state to which it was dedicated.' (pp. 2-13)

[The] most important feature of Italian humanist history, and the one which perhaps most strongly affected Elizabethan historical drama, was its particular moral and didactic purpose. Humanist history, of course, was not unique in its didacticism. In this it was merely following the model of Greek and Roman history; medieval history had been fully as didactic, although its didacticism had been of a different sort. [Italian humanist Leonardo] Bruni regarded history, as B. L. Ullman points out [in *Medievalia et Humanistica* V (1946)], as the 'guide of life', one of the surest means of solving contemporary problems. One of the greatest of French humanists, Isaac Casaubon, called history, 'nothing else but a kind of philosophy using examples'. The events of the past were to be studied for the light which they might throw upon the problems of the present and thus serve as a guide to political behaviour. There was in this an important Renaissance assumption: that man had some measure of control over his own destiny, that by his reason and strength he might determine political success or failure. This had been a basic principle of Greco-Roman historiography, but it had been obscured during the Christian Middle Ages with their *de contemptu mundi* emphasis upon the insignificance of human affairs and their doctrine of the helplessness of man in the face of God's will and the power of divine providence as the governing force of the universe. 'At the Renaissance,' writes Reese [in his *The Cease of Majesty,* 1961], 'classical didacticism, never wholly extinguished in the Middle Ages and newly invigorated as the control of the Church weakened, joined hands with the medieval belief in providence to produce a highly specialized and tendentious form of historical writing that has no exact parallels in any other century.'

This didactic purpose of the humanist historians is in the greatest of Elizabethan history plays. As Lily B. Campbell has pointed out in her study of Shakespeare, historical eras were chosen for dramatization particularly because they offered direct parallels with the events of the dramatists' own times. It was in part for this reason, as well as because it was perhaps the most recent period which censorship permitted dramatists freely to treat, that the period from Richard II to Henry VII was so popular with Shakespeare and his contemporaries.

In the sixteenth century Niccolò Machiavelli and Francesco Guicciardini, the direct descendants of the fifteenth-century humanists, extended this didactic function of history into a new area. The age was full of speculation about the nature of government. The expulsion of the Medici from Florence, the establishment of the republic and then its collapse and the return of the Medici, had led to a concern with types of government, problems of sovereignty, and abstract questions of political theory. The sixteenth-century Florentine historians became political theorists, and history was the device with which they supported their political theories. Francesco Guicciardini, in this respect, was much more of a scientific historian than was Machiavelli. Although he had his own strong prejudices, and although he was concerned with problems less universal than Machiavelli's, he may ultimately be more important as a scientific analyst of history. Guicciardini examined the history of his native city, and he attempted to find in it the causes of political events and thus derive theories of political causation which would be universally applicable. He did not generally warp history to support his preconceived theories.

When Machiavelli came to write his *History of Florence,* however, his political doctrines were already well formulated; he had expressed them in the *Prince* and the *Discorsi.* Rather than derive his political theory from the facts of history as he found them, Machiavelli selected from history what would prove his preconceived notions, and when necessary he deliberately warped history to serve his purposes. This is particularly evident in his *Life of Castruccio Castracani,* in which he transformed the rather contemptible petty tyrant of Lucca into a great statesman such as could unify Italy and repel her foreign invaders. Actually, he drew most of his material from Diodorus Siculus' portrait of Agathocles, the tyrant of Syracuse, using merely the name of Castruccio and such events from his life as suited his doctrinaire purposes. Historical truth for Machiavelli became a matter of relatively small importance. The importance of history was for the support it might lend to political theory. Thus the warping of history so that it may more effectively support political doctrine, such as we find in English history plays from *Kynge Johan* through *Woodstock* and Shakespeare's *Henry IV* plays, had its precedent in the work of one of the most influential historical thinkers of Renaissance Europe.

A word must be said here about the general influence of Machiavelli in Elizabethan England, a subject about which much has been written, but about which there is still widespread confusion. The important intellectual current represented by Machiavelli was not foreign to Elizabethan thought, as so many writers have argued, and as I have sought to disprove in a series of studies. That Machiavelli was misunderstood by many Elizabethans is certain, but it is equally certain that there were many—and for our purposes, most significantly, Christopher Marlowe—who understood him well. We must remember that the popular stage 'Machiavel', the villain who delights in his own villainy and gloats over his successes in lengthy soliloquies, is more surely descended from the Senecan villain-hero and the morality play Vice than from anything in Machiavelli's writings, and that the 'Machiavel' was a stage device used primarily for dramatic rather than political purposes. The idea of the 'Machiavel' has a life and history of its own, related only obliquely to the history of Machiavelli's actual ideas in England. The 'Machiavel' was subjected to ridicule in *The Jew of Malta* by such a writer as Christopher Marlowe, who we know could also

display a true awareness of Machiavelli's actual ideas in *Tamburlaine* and who shared many of Machiavelli's most fundamental premises. Machiavelli's doctrine came from the same classical sources as much of serious Elizabethan political thought, and it was shaped by many of the same Renaissance forces, both historical and intellectual. His philosophy of history is paralleled in Elizabethan historiography, where we may find the same altering of history for political purposes.

The use of history as documentation for political theory was systematized and popularized by Jean Bodin in his widely influential *Methodus ad facilem historiarum cognitionum,* first published in 1566 and circulated throughout Europe. By 1650 it had appeared in thirteen Latin editions. In 1608 Thomas Heywood, one of the most influential of Elizabethan popularizers of history, translated the fourth chapter of Bodin's treatise and published it in the introduction to an English translation of Sallust. Bodin held that from the objective study of history could be learned universal laws which govern political institutions, and that kings by understanding these laws could rule wisely and well. Machiavelli, Guicciardini, and Bodin furthered a purpose in history which became a part of the general Renaissance cultural heritage and which made itself felt ultimately in the Elizabethan history play. Thus the use of history for the exposition of political theory has its roots distinctly in Italian humanism.

These, then, represent the more important aspects of the Italian humanist influence in Elizabethan historical drama. The humanist influence, however, was far from the only current in Elizabethan historiography. There was an older current which we may find extending from the earliest medieval chronicles well into the seventeenth century. This was the tradition of Christian historiography which, as R. G. Collingwood has pointed out [in his *The Idea of History,* 1946], was universal, providential, apocalyptic and periodized. It was anti-nationalist, emphasized world history, and began usually with the creation of Adam. It treated history as above all the illustration of the working out of God's judgment in human affairs, and thus it tended to ascribe relatively little to the independent judgment or to the will of humanity. And—of great importance—it saw in history an intelligible and rational pattern which was inevitably good and which always affirmed the justice of God. It is just such a pattern which both Lily B. Campbell and E. M. W. Tillyard have found in Shakespeare's history plays. And finally, although this has little significance, for drama, Christian history divided the experience of man on earth into certain distinct epochs, each of which had peculiar characteristics of its own, and each of which came to an end with a cataclysmic event, Noah's flood and the birth of Christ being typical 'epoch-making' events.

This Christian philosophy of history persists throughout the Elizabethan era, although Elizabethans generally conceded that in addition to the will of God, the 'primary cause' of all human events, there were 'secondary causes' which could be found in the will of men. Chroniclers like Edward Hall learned much from the new Italian historiography, but they did not abandon the religious premises of the older Christian historiography. Hall differed from his medieval predecessors in his strong political partisanship. He interpreted the purposes of God to coincide with the purposes of the Tudors; the Wars of the Roses were to him part of a divine plan which would culminate in the accession of Henry VII. His school of historiography made great improvements in historical method, some directly due to Italian humanistic examples, and it was marked by peculiarly sixteenth-century English political prejudices, but the medieval Christian current in it is nevertheless very strong. (pp. 16-20)

Its providential scheme is the most important aspect of medieval historiography which we find in the Elizabethan history play. Neither its universalist bias nor its concept of periodization is particularly significant in this respect. Neither was, in any case, applicable to the requirements of drama. The rational pattern which Christian historians found in human events, however, fitted perfectly the needs of drama, and this aspect of Christian history came to have a large part in the history play. One of the most important historical purposes of many Tudor dramatists was to show the logic and reason in God's control of political affairs.

We thus can isolate two distinct trends which exerted an influence upon Elizabethan historiography: a humanist trend essentially classical in origin, and a medieval trend based upon the premises of Christian belief. We cannot suppose, however, that in the minds of Elizabethans there was any clear distinction between these two lines of influence. Writers like Blundeville [in his *The True Order and Methode of Wryting and Reading Hystories,* 1564] and Bolton [in his *Hypercritica, or Rule of Judgement for Writing or Reading our Histories,* 1622] fuse the two traditions without apparent awareness of any inherent contradiction. Both historical traditions found expression in the drama, and in the greatest history plays of the era we find an easy mingling of the two. In *Richard II, King John,* and the *Henry IV* plays, Shakespeare uses history both to glorify England and to support temporal political doctrine, and at the same time he uses it to assert divine providence in the universe and to illustrate a rational plan in human events. The English Renaissance, in most intellectual areas, shows an easy merging of the medieval and humanist.

There were other currents in Elizabethan historiography, such, for instance, as the antiquarian school of Bale, Leland, and Camden. Only one other historical influence is of any real significance for the drama, however, and that is the historical tradition of classical antiquity, which is embodied most clearly in the Roman histories of Jonson and Chapman. The Italian humanist historians, had, of course, modelled their work upon the classics. Bruni, as Ullman points out [in *Medievalia et Humanistica* IV (1946)], had drawn his philosophy of history largely from Cicero, and Livy was the ideal which all of the humanists hoped to equal. In the later Italian Renaissance, the work of Polybius was an influence of particular importance, and we may find its marks clearly in Machiavelli and his school.

Most of the purposes of Italian humanist history are thus also the purposes of classical history. There are, however,

certain differences between the two. One is the substantialist metaphysics underlying classical history. Another is the strong Stoical trend in classical history, a trend perhaps most notably present in Polybius. The great value of history was for the lessons which the past might teach the present, and of these lessons the most important for Polybius was that of how to bear political misfortune [*Histories,* trans. W. R. Paton, 1922]:

> But all historians, one may say without exception, and in no half-hearted manner, but making this the beginning and end of their labour, have impressed on us that the soundest education and training for a life of active politics is the study of history, and that the surest and indeed the only method of learning how to bear bravely the vicissitudes of fortune, is to recall the calamities of others.

History for Polybius would not necessarily teach a ruler to avoid the disasters of others; it could, however, teach him to bear them with fortitude and thus to attain a victory over self which Polybius considered more important than victory over circumstances. The use of history for the exposition of Stoical philosophy as an answer to political problems became, particularly in the Jacobean drama, an important dramatic purpose. We may find it most notably in George Chapman's *Tragedy of Caesar and Pompey.*

Although medieval chroniclers had sometimes recorded the insignificant private affairs of individuals, and something of this practice is carried over in the work of uncritical compilers like Holinshed, the subject matter of Renaissance history was the life of the state. To borrow Fulke Greville's words written in another context [in his *The Life of Sir Philip Sidney,* edited by Nowell Smith, 1907], it was 'the growth, state and declination of princes, change of government, and laws, vicissitudes of sedition, faction, succession, confederacies, plantations, with all other errors or alterations in public affairs.' We may summarize the purposes for which these matters were treated under two general headings. Those stemming from classical and humanist philosophies of history include (1) a nationalistic glorification of England; (2) an analysis of contemporary affairs, both national and foreign so as to make clear the virtues and the failings of contemporary statesmen; (3) a use of past events as a guide to political behaviour in the present; (4) a use of history as documentation for political theory; and (5) a study of past political disaster as an aid to Stoical fortitude in the present. Those stemming from medieval Christian philosophy of history include: (6) illustration of the providence of God as the ruling force in human—and primarily political—affairs, and (7) exposition of a rational plan in human events which must affirm the wisdom and justice of God.

We may then define history plays as those which use, for any combination of these purposes, material drawn from national chronicles and assumed by the dramatist to be true, whether in the light of our modern knowledge they be true or not. The changing of this material by the dramatist so that it might better serve either his doctrinal or his dramatic purposes did not alter its essential historicity in so far as his Elizabethan or Jacobean audience was concerned. Source thus is an important consideration, but it is secondary to purpose. Plays based upon factual matter which nevertheless do not serve ends which Elizabethans considered to be legitimate purposes of history are thus not history plays. John Webster's *White Devil* and *Duchess of Malfi* might be included among examples of such plays. Whether a dramatist considered certain matter mythical or factual is often impossible now to determine. Ultimately each play must be judged individually with all of our modern knowledge brought to bear upon it, and still there will be plays about which we can never be entirely certain. But if a play appears to fulfill what we know the Elizabethans considered to be the legitimate purposes of history, and if it is drawn from a chronicle source which we know that at least a large part of the contemporary audience accepted as factual, we may call it a history play.

But what of that great body of the world's legendry which, if traced far back enough, has its roots in factual sources? A legend based upon actual fact may, through a passage of time, pass out of history and become folk-lore. This may occur when it is taken out of its historical context and told, modified, and retold as popular literature, with no attempt to fulfill the functions of history. This is true of the *Hamlet* story. Plays based upon such legends, although they may have serious political undertones, as does *Hamlet,* cannot be called history plays, for their political implications are secondary to the dominant purposes of the plays.

We must also remember that there is inherent in history a romantic quality which in every age has had a wide popular appeal, but which seems to have delighted the Elizabethans particularly. This romance is a part of all history plays, but we may find it also in plays which are not history. Dramatists with no historical purpose and little historical sense often used the outer trappings of history in their plays, and thus created a type of historical romance which must not be confused with the true history play. Such a dramatist was Robert Greene, all of whose plays draw upon the romance of history, but accomplish none of the accepted purposes of history. The usual device of the writer of historical romance was to take an Italian novella and to place it in a pseudo-historical setting—as Greene does in his *James IV,* where a tale from Giraldi Cinthio's *Hecatommithi* is placed in the setting of the Scottish court. We may distinguish such plays by an examination of their sources and by the fact that in them the historical setting is used entirely to set off romantic themes which have no relation to the serious purposes of history.

We know that Elizabethans generally distinguished between tragedy and comedy and that they admitted a third form, tragi-comedy, although an early writer like Richard Edwards felt the need to justify it in his preface to *Damon and Pythias.* That they made any distinction between tragedy and history as dramatic forms, however, appears very doubtful, although the author of *A Warning for Fair Women* seems to have had some distinction in mind. Francis Meres in his *Palladis Tamia* listed *Richard II, Richard III, King John,* and *Henry IV* as among 'our best for Tragedy'. History was one of the classes of serious matter suitable for treatment in tragedy. Indeed, as the sixteenth century progressed, history came to be regarded as the most suitable matter for tragedy. Ben Jonson, in a preface to the

1605 edition of *Sejanus,* offers his 'truth of argument' as one of the evidences that he has 'discharged the other offices of a tragic writer', points to his indebtedness to Tacitus, Suetonius and Seneca, and indicates his specific use of these historians in marginal notes throughout the text of his play. (pp. 21-6)

The close inter-relation between history and tragedy has continued through the ages. Not all history plays are tragedies, of course, nor are all tragedies histories, but some of the greatest plays of the Elizabethan era are both: *Edward II, Richard II, Julius Caesar, Sejanus,* and others. A history play as we have defined it is, after all, an adaptation of drama to the purposes of history, and tragedy is merely one form of drama. Aristotle's very attempt to separate history and poetry left room for historical tragedy which is a fusion of both. For when he distinguished between the historian who tells what actually has happened and the poet who tells what might have happened, he added that the poet who puts into poetry what actually happened is still a poet, for what has happened might happen. Here then is historical tragedy.

In so far as the form of the Tudor history play is concerned, we must remember that Elizabethan drama, as the last century of investigation has made clear, has its structural roots in two sources: primitive folk ritual and the medieval religious drama. To these were added in the middle sixteenth century the regularizing influences of classical models . . . , but the classical influence never replaced native English dramatic traditions. We have come to recognize, moreover, that of the two native sources of Elizabethan drama, primitive folk pageantry was by far the less important, and that in so far as the religious drama is concerned, we must distinguish between the influence of the miracle play and that of the morality play. From them came two separate streams of influence which we can trace throughout the later drama, although, as is inevitable, the two streams coalesce and complement one another. Perhaps nowhere may we see this more clearly than in the history play, for it is almost possible to divide extant history plays into two groups, the one embodying a dramatic structure stemming from the miracle play and the other one stemming from the morality.

The miracle play was episodic in structure. It was virtually plotless in its simple presentation of incidents as the author found them in his Biblical or apocryphal sources. There was little attempt to relate one incident to the next; the method was factual, entirely devoid of symbolism or allegory. This episodic structure Briggs called the distinctive form of the Elizabethan history play, but it is obvious that such an unintegrated dramatic form was incapable of fulfilling many of the functions which Elizabethans considered historical. This form does not characterize the Elizabethan history play as a whole, although it continued to be a feature of some history plays throughout the life of the genre. Far more important than this miracle play influence, however, is that of the morality play. The history play in its highest form emerged from the morality, [as can be seen in] *Kynge Johan* and *Gorboduc.* The morality play structure was a perfect vehicle for executing the true historical function, for the morality was didactic and symbolic, designed to communicate idea rather than fact, built upon a plot formula in which every event was related to the others so as to create a meaningful whole. This is so in spite of the extraneous horseplay which came to characterize the later interludes. It was these qualities which the history play had to embody before it could reach its ultimate development. Of the two streams of dramatic influence that of the morality play is by far the more significant. In so far as dramatic form is concerned, we must, unlike Schelling, relate the history play to the general development of Elizabethan drama. We see then that it is not only an entirely representative part of that development, but one which serves to illuminate aspects of it which otherwise might not easily be perceived. (pp. 27-9)

> *Irving Ribner, "History and Drama in the Age of Shakespeare," in his* The English History Play in the Age of Shakespeare, *revised edition Methuen & Co. Ltd, 1965, pp. 1-29.*

G. K. Hunter

[*Hunter is a Scottish educator and Shakespearian scholar who has written several works on Elizabethan drama including* Shakespeare: The Later Comedies *(1962),* John Lyly: The Humanist as Courtier *(1962), and* Dramatic Identities and Cultural Tradition *(1978). In the following excerpt, Hunter explores the "problem of linking historical 'truth' to a seriously unified plot." History plays, he contends, accomplish this by utilizing elements drawn from comedy and tragedy, but unlike these genres, attempt to balance the disorder inherent in real life and "the promise of an order that can only emerge as fiction." As Hunter states: "In comedy and tragedy the knowledge that the life depicted does not exactly fit into the artful pattern, is not resolved by the artful closure, is only a minor though recurrent counterpoint, an enrichment of the dominant harmony. In the history play . . . the awareness that life cannot be resolved by art is much more powerful."*]

Since the First Folio says that Shakespeare wrote history plays I think there is a great deal to be said for assuming not only that he did so but did so in the plays thus designated and no others; let evidence precede definition. It is true of course that the evidence available is mixed; Elizabethan generic vocabulary is notoriously spongy: contemporary title pages give us such hybrids as *The Tragedy of Richard II, The Tragedy of Richard III, The History of Troilus and Cressida, The True Chronicle History of King Lear, A Pleasant Conceited History called The Taming of a Shrew.* The Folio's generic divisions seem to belong, however, to a different mode of discourse: F1 is a company volume, and I have no doubt that its division of plays into Comedies, Histories, and Tragedies reflects company understanding of the repertory, and so, I take it, the understanding of that good company man, William Shakespeare.

Academic critics inevitably prefer definitions to be less blandly empirical, for what space for dazzling reinventions, for pulling rabbits out of hats, not to mention a name in lights, is left available by so preconditioning an acceptance? As professional systematizers we like to be

seen to generate our definitions from general principles and our first chapters from titles such as 'What is a history play? Some problems and answers'. Irving Ribner, for example, in what remains by far the most thorough treatment of the Elizabethan genre, starts by asking how the purposes of history were understood in the period and then calls any play that fulfils any of these purposes a 'history play', and so includes under the rubric such works as *Gorboduc, Cambyses,* and *Tamburlaine*— plays that can make no claim to appear in the Heminges and Condell list.

Heminges and Condell offer us no formal definition; what one can derive from their list is the sense that this genre must be defined, above all, by its subject matter: a history play is a play about English dynastic politics of the feudal and immediately post-feudal period—is, you might say, 'a play about barons'. No doubt they had noticed that the audience in a theatre has a relationship to stories about its own national identity in the intelligible past which is different from its relationship to other stories. Several much-quoted testimonies of the period confirm this view of the role of history plays in the culture of the time. But little attempt has been made to interrelate the emotional effect on the Elizabethan or other self-consciously English audience, thus described, to the aesthetic structures of the plays themselves. The usual point made is that these are plays of patriotism—a patriotism that can be linked historically to a national mood following the defeat of the Armada in 1588. But the point would be more convincing if the plays were more than occasionally jingoistic and xenophobic, were not so largely concerned with the malignities and incompetences of English governments; patriotism is part of the story but it cannot be the whole story. A more satisfactory answer to the problem can be derived, I believe, from the general thought (contemporary and modern) that such historical narratives must be 'true', as against other kinds of plays which can be acknowledged and responded to as feigned or fictive.

The paradoxical idea of an invented true history is one that is difficult to get into focus, and there is some evidence from the sixteenth century of the unease that was generated by a genre that undoubtedly existed but could not be fitted into the categories or vocabulary available. The Induction to the anonymous *A Warning for Fair Women* (printed 1599) shows us Comedy, History, and Tragedy in dispute for the possession of the stage. History enters the scene as if he has a role to perform, armed with the accoutrements of war (a drum and an ensign), but no space is provided in the play for the deployment of these signifiers. The axis of the dispute remains stolidly binary: to Tragedy the opponent is 'slight and childish' Comedy; for Comedy it is extremist and hysterical Tragedy. History is relegated to the unfortunate role of a neuter in a family quarrel; between the alternative trajectories of death and happiness no third possibility is allowed. The one Induction of the period which tackles the status of History in a more positive vein is, unsurprisingly, the one attached to an early history play, the anonymous *True Tragedy of Richard III* (printed 1594). This play begins with a conversation between Poetry and Truth:

POETRY. Truth, well met!

> TRUTH. Thanks, Poetry. What makes thou upon
> a stage?
> POETRY. Shadows
> TRUTH. Then will I add bodies to the shadows.
> Therefore depart and give Truth leave To
> show her pageant.
> POETRY. Why, will Truth be a player?
> TRUTH. No, but Tragedia-like for to present A
> tragedy in England done but late That will re-
> vive the hearts of drooping minds.

What we seem to see here is a degree of self-consciousness about the claim that this history play is a 'true tragedy'. Poetry can only (as in Plato) offer 'shadows', but Truth can give substance to poetic shadows by showing things that actually happened, what 'the Chronicles make manifest' (line 21). As a player or fictionalizer, Truth has to allow herself to appear 'Tragedia-like' in order to secure the effects described in the last line quoted, but the recentness of the events and faithfulness to the chronicles may serve to counteract the danger that poetry necessarily means lies.

The sense, clearly expressed in the Induction to *The True Tragedy of Richard III*, that truth has to be invoked to justify history plays, appears as a recurrent feature of the word as it turns up among Elizabethan play titles. I have discovered thirteen uses of the word 'true' among titles of plays published between 1573 and 1616, four times attached to plays about English history, four times to plays about Ancient British history (always as 'true chronicle history'), three times to plays about Roman history, and twice to plays about recent notorious murders (both called 'lamentable and true'). Of course the word 'true' found in such contexts is, like other words in title pages, a piece of advertising copy, not a scientific description; what I take to be significant is therefore only the fact that *this* was the word found recurrently appropriate for advertising plays about history. The word is significant only because it designates a set of claims against a set of received expectations. 'Truth' in these terms may be said to be a word that indicates the rhetorical precondition or mode of history.

A reader today, given the anti-positivist slant of modern thought, might expect that truth of this kind would require a characteristic formal structure before the plays involved could impose their values on the audience. If the Heminges and Condell implication of a third genre is to be sustained in terms of a particular theatrical effect, then the cause ('truth') of that effect can hardly be left as an inert slice of chronicle subject matter unaffected by the shaping process which alone will allow it to achieve the *telos* proposed. Setting the genre side-by-side with Tragedy and Comedy makes this issue particularly hard to avoid. For these others are genres marked by well-known and recurrent formal characteristics. Can the history play justify its place in this row by its possession of comparable qualities requisite to convey its claim to 'truth', its particular hold on an audience's attention, its mode of catharsis?

Most twentieth-century criticism has sought to deal with such questions by allegorizing both history and the mimetic process. The Tudor understanding of history, we are often told, turned individual reigns and individual successes and failures into exemplary instances of the intervention of God (or of the Capitalist System—God under another name) in the daily affairs of men. In particular, the eight plays of Shakespeare that run a continuous course from *Richard II* to *Richard III* are said to present a pattern of divine punishment for national apostasy in which the Tudor audience could identify itself as the final inheritor of God's forgiveness once the pattern had been completed. Inside the plays of the sequence, consequently, we must look *through* individual lives and personal relations so that we may understand their places on the giant wheel of historical necessity (Jan Kott's 'Grand Mechanism' [in his *Shakespeare Our Contemporary,* 1964]). 'Truth' in these terms is identified as the shape of the divine purpose. That there is something of this in the plays need not be denied; but the experience of seeing or reading Shakespeare's history plays, or (more pertinently) of being deeply moved by them, owes very little to this mode of conceptual organization. And this is not, incidentally, what Elizabethan title pages mean when they use the word 'true', which refers there rather to the 'truth' of factual detail, authenticated by the witness of the Chronicles.

Modern scholars usually tell us that the Chronicles (particularly Edward Hall's) are marked by an overall design that controls their presentation of detail. But to read continuously in the Chronicles is to discover that they exemplify less the grand historical design than the complexity, dispersal, randomness, even incomprehensibility of actual happenings. We are regularly told about the genealogical tree on the title-page to Hall's Chronicle as a kind of aerial map of the dynastic conflict that 'explains' the history of this period. But when we turn over the page and actually begin to read in Hall (or better still in Holinshed) word by word and page by page, then we must descend from the hot-air balloon of theory that floats *above* history and see events from the level of the human eye, share in the bemusement and mistakenness that characterizes the 'truth' of historical experience as here retailed. In his dedication to Burghley Holinshed says that the reading of his volumes will 'daunt the vicious'—I find that the reading daunts nearly everyone—and 'encourage worthy citizens'. But in telling his story Holinshed fails to show that history points a moral in either of these directions. And when he does risk causal moralization, that too appears random and particular rather than generally explanatory. Thus when Edward IV arrives at York and swears on the sacrament that he has invaded England only to claim his rightful dukedom of York, Holinshed comments as follows:

> For this wilful perjury (as has been thought) the
> issue of this king suffered (for the father's
> offence) . . . And it may well be. For it is not
> likely that God, in whose hands is the bestowing
> of all sovereignty, will suffer such an indignity
> to be done to his sacred majesty and will suffer
> the same to pass with impunity.

The tentativeness of the judgement here, as well as the limitation imposed on the connection made, are both entirely characteristic of the author. What Holinshed wrote was, in his own phrase, a 'collection of histories'; the pluralism attaches both to the variety of sources drawn on and to the collaborative effort that went into the production, and both these point away from explanatory clarity. We are much indebted to all these authors for the legal documents that they report *in extenso,* giving the actual statements drawn up for Humphrey of Gloucester or Jack Cade (for example). But the authentic words given represent only what these men wanted to be believed, tendentious opinions contradicted by the equally 'true' or authentic documents prepared in rebuttal by Henry Beaufort or the government of Henry VI. The *wie es eigentlich gewesen ist* is nowhere invoked as a unifying perspective, and indeed one might say that the closer the chroniclers bring us to the documentation of the past the more obscured becomes the overview.

The chroniclers' annalistic method of year-by-year accounting further reinforces the general effect of one-thing-after-another randomness. In this mode the idea of an individual's purposive career is difficult to sustain; even though Holinshed sometimes signals ahead with 'as will hereafter appear' and similar locutions, his 'hereafter' is, like God's, mostly invisible. What is entirely and continuously obvious is that life in feudal England is most adequately represented as a series of individual raids on the inarticulable: a castle is besieged here or there and then retired from when a larger army appears on the horizon; the Scots do their annual thing, try to burn Carlisle or Berwick, drive away cattle, then give up when the weather gets too bad (or too good); the price of wheat rises and falls, a high wind destroys houses, people try to avoid taxes and get hanged, drawn, quartered, beheaded, burned, massacred—random events suffered by individuals continually trying to derandomize them, including Holinshed himself, who offers us the guidance of 'some say', 'others allege', 'it is reported that', but makes little or no sustained effort to assess accuracy or probability. And when the absence of explanatory connection is particularly blatant he throws up his hands in a gesture that might be despair or might be piety, as when he says of the usurpation of Bolingbroke that he cannot make sense of it: 'But . . . the providence of God is to be respected and his secret will to be wondered at . . . For as in His hands standeth the donation of kingdoms, so likewise the disposing of them consisteth in His pleasure.' Or again when, after the second battle of St. Albans, he notes that all the advantages seemed to lie with the Lancastrians: 'But what Man proposeth God disposeth'. In such cases a providential pattern emerges, but not as an overall explanation, only as a justification for the humanly inexplicable.

A dramatist who makes his way through such actual chronicles—and we should remember that Shakespeare could not lay his hands on a copy of *Shakespeare's Holinshed*—has to achieve his design by means of rigorous exclusion and reshaping. But if I am right in assuming that the ideal of truth to the experience of life in the past remains a defining quality of the Elizabethan history play, then the process of streamlining a watertight cause-and-effect kind of structure can easily carry the history play beyond its *telos,* for the demonstration of Art inevitably diminishes our acceptance of Truth. And this takes us back to the comparison between Comedy, History, and Tragedy with which I started. Tragedies and Comedies operate inside efficient and well-tested modes of artful unification. It has sometimes seemed as if the history play could not

achieve such unity unless it fell into the artful mode of one or the other of its siblings. This was an agreed and probably an inevitable view among neoclassical critics, whose respect for Art allowed variations from the canon of Tragedy and Comedy only as consequences of ignorance or boorishness ('common . . . among our rude ancestors', Dr Johnson assumed [in *Selections from Johnson on Shakespeare,* edited by Bertrand Bronson and Jean M. O'Meara, 1986]). The earliest systematic critic of Shakespeare, Charles Gildon, is interestingly specific on this issue [in his "Remarks on the Plays of Shakespeare," in volume 9 of Rowe's edition of Shakespeare, 1710]. He calls history plays 'draughts of the lives of princes, brought into dialogue', and goes on to note that 'since these plays are histories, there can be no manner of Fable or Design in them'. Dr Johnson seems to defend history plays from the full rigour of such neoclassical rules: 'his histories, being neither comedies nor tragedies are not subject to any of their laws'; but by agreeing with the principles of the neoclassical position he leaves little or nothing worth defending. He calls the history plays 'a series of actions with no other than chronological succession and without any tendency to introduce or regulate the conclusion . . . a history might be continued through many plays; as it had no plan it had no limits . . . Nothing more is necessary . . . than that the change of action be so prepared as to be understood . . . no other unity is intended, and therefore none is to be sought.' In the jargon of the Russian Formalists and their acolytes, such plays exhibit *fabula* but no *sjužet:* they are mere transcripts of chronology, and chronology provides the only articulation they possess.

It takes very little reading in Shakespeare's historical sources to learn what nonsense this is. But the general issue is not so easily disposed of. History plays are not shaped by the formal closures of death or marriage; they allow the open-endedness of history itself to appear—when one king dies another king emerges; time and politics grind on with a degree of indifference to the life-cycles of individuals. But to say that *Richard II, Richard III* or *King John* are simply tragedies that are poorly unified because open-ended is clearly inadequate as a description. The dialectical relation between Art and Truth seems central enough to require a further effort to define the conditions of history plays, preferably in their simplest and most unsophisticated forms, whether as Shakespeare employed them or as Shakespeare inherited them.

F. P. Wilson [in his *Marlowe and the Early Shakespeare,* 1953] has famously remarked that 'there is no certain evidence that any popular dramatist before Shakespeare wrote a play based on English history'. If that is to be believed, then *Henry VI* is, however sophisticated in itself, the great originating event in the history of the history play. But should one believe it? There are in fact two extant Elizabethan history plays with a powerful claim to anticipate *Henry VI*—one (Dr Legge's *Richardus Tertius*) clearly dated 1579, the other (the anonymous *Famous Victories of Henry V*) probably to be dated before 1588; and it seems reasonable to argue (I intend to do so) that these plays give us a glimpse of dramaturgical control of history in the process of formation. Legge's play is not, of course, that of a 'popular dramatist' and so by definition may be excluded from Wilson's chronology, but the idea that it cannot therefore tell us anything about popular drama seems much too categorical. As for *The Famous Victories of Henry V,* Wilson does refer to it but seems to be denying it a place in the story by the curious argument that it is too bad a play to count. He calls it 'a play of incredible meanness in the form in which it has come down to us, written in bad prose, one imagines, because the compiler could not rise to bad verse'. Even bad plays, one is bound to respond, can influence good dramatists. And as for 'certain evidence' in the matter of Elizabethan theatrical chronology, if this is our criterion we had better cede the territory as quickly as possible, for there is no 'certain' way of defending it.

My aim here is not, however, to argue for or against chronology or to specify influences on Shakespeare or even to deny Shakespeare's originating power, but only to question his power to originate *ex nihilo*—a question, I note in passing, that even God cannot always avoid. In what follows I wish to use these plays only to illustrate the conditions attached to history playwriting outside the Shakespearian orbit, to exemplify what I have called the central dilemma in the genre—the contradiction (or at least tension) between truth to the experience of the past and the fictional or artful means by which such material can be unified and so given general significance.

Dr Legge, unsurprisingly, given his status as Master of Caius and Vice-Chancellor of Cambridge University, undoubtedly found his material (the reign of Richard III) convenient on at least two counts. The reign of Richard III was one of the few reigns that could be presented in political detail without offending the Queen: and Vice-Chancellors, as we all know, have to be very tender of the susceptibilities of their political mistresses. More important from our point of view is the fact that this material lent itself very easily to the formal literary organization that current scholarly opinion most heartily approved. Tyrant-tragedy provided the staple of the Senecan and Italian Humanist tragic repertory. Both the pseudo-Senecan *Octavia Praetexta* (then accepted as genuine) and the *Ecerinus* of Albertino Mussato (usually called 'the first modern tragedy') deal with the careers of recently dead tyrants (Nero and Ezzelino da Romano) seen from the point of view of the subsequent administration, in modes of formal and political organization that could easily be adapted to fit the case of Richard of Gloucester. Indeed this process of aestheticization or adaptation had begun to be applied to Richard soon after his reign ended. Sir Thomas More, in his Suetonian history of the English Nero copied by all the chroniclers, presents a system of explanation for the events of Richard's kingship that Legge did not have to modify. In More he could find that everything in Richard's reign happened as it did because of the kind of person Richard was. His will, or rather his obsession, his manipulative drive, undiverted by social loyalties to brother, mother, wife, benefactor, comrade-in-arms, can be shown directing the passive world around him to the ends he alone foresees. All the others, Hastings, Brackenbury, the Queen Mother, Buckingham, are cajoled, bribed, terrified, deceived, magnetized into compliance; in themselves they

seem to lack positive aims or understandings and therefore must be destined to be victims. In these terms we have a quasi-Senecan scenario already in place.

Yet in dealing even with so well digested a tract of modern history Legge faced methodological problems. Evidently he found it impossible to ignore the un-Senecan modernity of the political forces present in Richard's reign, the complex of voices, resistances, uncertainties that More reveals. The Senecan form is not only static but also heavily retrospective; it is this that gives emotional density to the exchanges of the small family groups, whose shared life together stretches back through history into myth and legend, accumulating the crimes and resentments that eventually explode in the present. But Legge's history must be prospective. His play cannot end in Senecan mayhem and Stoic acceptance of a malign universe but must carry us through the complex web of English political life and show how it slips out of Richard's manipulative control, so leaving space for Henry Tudor, the Christian deliverer, to descend from the flies and take over the system.

In rendering modern political conditions with a degree of documentary truth Legge is, in fact, obliged to betray the unifying formalism of classical tragedy. The vast extent of his three-part play, the mass of its characters, its geographical range across the English landscape, the continual improvisation the protagonist has to engage in to answer new unexpected resistances—all these factors point away from the form he sought to imitate. The play thus becomes significant in the context I am sketching less as an achievement than as a model of the tensions and contradictions inherent in the genre, especially that contradiction between desire to fulfil the trajectory of the protagonist's plot (in the classical manner) and acceptance of the random points of resistance and diversion that his drive was bound to find in any 'true' picture of modern politics.

My second model play—*The Famous Victories of Henry V*—deals with the same issues from a totally different angle. In *Richardus Tertius* the *chorus civium* is shown as disbelieving, reluctant, sullen, and needing to be manipulated, in this *de haut en bas* treatment, by dazzling displays of rhetoric and chicanery. In *The Famous Victories* on the other hand the ruler's power is seen as operating not from above but from below; it is presented as a natural outgrowth from the life of the Folk, so that his rhetoric is simply their rhetoric played back to them, with appropriate magnification. The Cambridge play invites its audience to a distanced observation and analysis of political techniques. The popular play offers no such distance: it invites *its* audience to identify with a man like themselves, with the same emotions and values, though with more space to deploy them. To make this point the author, in a move that must remind us of Shakespeare, shows us Henry V first of all as a down-to-earth Hal, as a bully-boy gang leader who eventually becomes a bully-boy national leader, not too much change of attitude being required. The famous 'conversion' of Hal into Henry, his embracing of the Lord Chief Justice and turning away his riotous companions suggests that here, as in Shakespeare, the action is divided by a change of viewpoint and a new set of values into two distinct and differentiated parts, and critics often tell us that this is how we ought to look at *The Famous Victories*. But a reading of the play in its own terms rather than those of Shakespeare gives us a different profile. It is true that the newly crowned king turns away his evidently well-born boon companions, Ned, Tom, and Jocky Oldcastle. But these are not the figures who represent the 'true' underworld of *The Famous Victories*, which is carried not by deboshed gentlemen but by the genuine proletariat of Dericke, John Cobler, and Cuthbert Cutter (usually known as 'The Thief'). Ned, Tom, and Jocky disappear from the play after Henry comes to the throne, but for Dericke and company the underworld ethos has never represented a holiday in the slums that can be put behind one, but is life itself. Their inevitable mode of existence is simply transferred, when Henry becomes king, from petty criminality in London to the equally criminal milieu of the private soldier in a foreign war (shades of Brecht!). It is true that the Lord Chief Justice is established in England; but the rest of the cast meanwhile removes to France, and there king and commoners carry on with the old populist pleasure of exploiting the formalistic, the smug and self-satisfied, the self-important, by a witty if brutal realism. The exploitables are now French aristocrats rather than London moneybags, but the attitude of the exploiters remains the same. Dericke and the Cobler end their war by retailing their Schweik-like capacity to minimize fighting while maximizing booty. They share with us their ingenious plan to use the funeral procession of the heroic Duke of York as a foolproof method of getting their stolen goods back home. Clearly we are not meant to be shocked but rather amused by their cynical exploitations of convention. When they get home, they tell us, they will show what they have learned in France by burning down Dericke's house, preferably with his wife inside. At the same time, and in a not altogether different vein, we see a ferociously genial King Henry backslap his 'good brother' the French king, his nobles, and his daughter into surrender and matrimony. This is overhand, not underhand; but the same sense that it all grows out of the anti-formalist or 'realist' English way pervades both social levels.

In spite of the coming and going of its large cast of characters, the indeterminacy of the many social levels it contains, the disjointed and episodic nature of its action, *The Famous Victories of Henry V* is, tonally speaking, a remarkably unified play. We may not like the tone—F. P. Wilson has eloquently registered his distaste for it—but we must allow that by assimilating the king and the national destiny to the life of the Folk this play solves the contradiction that appears in *Richardus Tertius* between the personal career of the monarch (dramatic) and the political life of the nation (historical). For the public life of the country is treated in *The Famous Victories* as a simple extension of the (shared) private life of camp and tavern. On the other hand we may well feel that the unification of *muthos* and *ethos* has been bought here at too high a price. And it is true that political life, as presented in this version, has not enough complexity to challenge our imagination or to represent the problems that a real politician must face.

In their startlingly different ways then, one clinging to the mode of high tragedy, the other to that of low comedy, both *Richardus Tertius* and *The Famous Victories of Henry V* show the problem of linking historical 'truth' to a seriously unified plot, in both cases one controlled by a dominant monarch whose will and ambition create the context within which historical development is to be understood. But neither author can be said to have secured that very delicate balance between such opposites in a history play—a balance that may be as much social as aesthetic—where the potentials for tragedy and comedy are combined in a manner that transcends both. What both plays can convey to the modern reader is rather the nature of the coordinates within which a history play must exist (and will exist), vectors moving on one axis through the 'truth' of content towards formlessness, and on the other axis moving through the necessities of form and order towards unhistorical fictional closure. Like other kinds of art, the history play advances by playing 'true' disorder against the promise of an order that can only emerge as fiction. Where the history play differs from more traditional forms, such as tragedy and comedy, is mainly in the nature of the balance it sets up between these two opposed forces. In comedy and tragedy the knowledge that the life depicted does not exactly fit into the artful pattern, is not resolved by the artful closure, is only a minor though recurrent counterpoint, an enrichment of the dominant harmony. In the history play, however, the awareness that life cannot be resolved by art is much more powerful. Here in consequence the power to control and complete that pattern is held at a much more tentative level; the authorial or interpretative stance must be more heavily infected by irony, as has been pointed out by David Riggs in his admirable account of the *Henry VI* plays [*Shakespeare's Heroical Histories: 'Henry VI' and Its Literary Tradition,* 1971].

And so we reach Shakespeare. What I take to be genuinely creative and originating in the *Henry VI* plays (creative, that is, in generating all the other weak-king plays of the early nineties) is the perception that only by placing an inadequate monarch in the centre of the play can this ironic or detached viewpoint be used to fulfil the tragicomic potential of modern history's indeterminate and destabilized worlds. Only so can an audience enjoy both a detached analysis of political activity (as in *Richardus Tertius*) and the pleasure of participating in the world of *The Famous Victories* where (as a recognizable truth) things are liable to happen without anyone anticipating them.

And having reached Shakespeare it is time to stop. My purpose has been to set out the generic conditions within which the texts that Heminges and Condell call history plays can exist. To show how these conditions are exploited is a larger task which belongs to another time and no doubt to another person. (pp. 15-24)

G. K. Hunter, "Truth and Art in History Plays," in Shakespeare Survey: An Annual Survey of Shakespeare Studies and Production, *Vol. 42, 1990, pp. 15-24.*

COMEDY

Ashley H. Thorndike

[*An American educator and scholar, Thorndike wrote extensively on Elizabethan literature. In the following excerpt, he explores how the pastoral and court masque variously aided the development of Elizabethan comedy. The critic also divides the comedy of the period into five general categories or "classes," including comedies of intrigue, comedies of manners, comedies of character, satire, and problem comedies.*]

Pastoralism . . . was a considerable element in Renaissance literature. It attempted to express man's perennial craving for the simple life in terms of the golden age, following the models of Vergil and Theocritus. It made its way into various forms of literature, into lyrical, descriptive and satirical poetry, into the novel and the drama. Its entrance into the drama was by several doors. Accompanying mythological persons and stories, it early found a place in spectacles and shows, shepherds and nymphs appearing on the stage with the deities of Olympus. Again, it took the stage in the form of dramatized eclogues. Spenser's *Shepherd's Calendar,* which embodied nearly all the themes and modes of pastoral poetry, was published in 1579, and one year earlier came the first English pastoral play, Sidney's *Lady of May.* Again it took the stage through the dramatization of pastoral novels, so Lodge's *Rosalynde* supplied story and shepherds for *As You Like It,* and Sidney's *Arcadia* furnished the themes for several later dramas. Finally, the pastoral was equipped with a special stage of its own. Following the division of Vitruvius of the classical stage into three kinds of scenes for tragedy, comedy and satyr, the last of which was "decorated with trees, caverns, mountains, and other rustic objects delineated in landscape style," Italian humanists felt that the pastoral could be made to fit these specifications of a special setting and of a species distinct from both comedy and tragedy. Guarini's *Pastor Fido* was an elaborate and laborious literary effort to meet this critical demand for a pastoral tragicomedy, and it was imitated most skilfully by Fletcher in his *Faithful Shepherdess.*

Pastoralism was thus enabled to aid comedy from time to time in different ways, supplying spectacle and picturesqueness, song and music, romance and fantasy, sentiment and idealization. The effect of the artificial exaggeration of the amatory emotions such as is found in *The Faithful Shepherdess* can be traced throughout the tragedies and tragicomedies of Beaumont and Fletcher, and indeed on into the heroic plays of a later generation. A good deal of the idealization of love in the earlier drama owes something to the imitation of pastoral idyls; certainly the refinement and delicacy as well as the artificiality of Lyly's comedies are in harmony with their use of pastoral themes and persons. Pastoralism served an injunction on the farce and buffoonery that were always threatening to possess the stage. After the clown, the shepherd was not unwelcome; upon the exits of the low comedians, enter the lovelorn nymph or the pleading swain. Shakespeare indeed carried his clowns to the Forest of Arden and to the sheep-shearing in Bohemia, and in those secure retreats real and

pretended rustics dwelt together. In general, however, the drama did not have much success in depicting a genuine countryside or the humours of country folk. The pastoral tradition encouraged fancifulness rather than observation and linked itself more readily to romantic story than to comic reality.

After *The Faithful Shepherdess* the pastoral was recognized as a distinct form of drama, admired by the cultivated though too delicate for the vulgar stage. Under the patronage of Queen Henrietta Maria it had a revival. Inigo Jones devised scenes for *The Faithful Shepherdess* at court (1633-4) and the queen and her ladies acted in the French pastoral *Florimène* (1635). Of the new pieces composed, Randolph's *Amyntas* used the Italian scheme in a more humorous fashion than had his predecessors, but Fletcher's masterpiece had only one really worthy successor, the unfinished *Sad Shepherd* by Ben Jonson. Drawing on folklore, mingling real and fanciful creatures, aiming at the creation of a distinctively English pastoral, Jonson planned what might have been a literary triumph and a dramatic innovation. But it seems unlikely that Jonson's interesting experiment, if completed, could have availed much to maintain the pastoral as a distinct form of drama.

It may be noted, however, that comedy in later, as in Elizabethan times, has often profited from some form or other of pastoralism. It is ever in danger of becoming too citified, too sophisticated, too ingenious, and it needs the refreshment of country air. Though it may do without sheep and shepherds, song contests and echo dialogues, it needs to return from time to time to the simpler virtues and the quiet life. The drama requires some quiet moments in order to give play for its crises and thrills and movement; and comedy may view the placidities as well as the absurdities of mankind.

Masques are common in the early plays and add the gaiety of dance and the colour of dress to the spectacle of comedy. Pastoral sentiment, the machinery and costumes of the court masque, a romantic love story, and burlesque by the low comedians—this would serve as a sort of recipe for romantic comedy. As the masque developed in the hands of Inigo Jones and Ben Jonson into a very expensive spectacle with music, songs, scenery, and libretto, it passed beyond the reach of the regular theaters. It seems to have stirred the creative fancy of both Fletcher in *The Triumph of Time* and Shakespeare in *The Tempest.* . . . And in particular, the antimasques, grotesque and extravagant dances in costume by professional actors, were repeated or imitated in *The Triumph of Time, The Two Noble Kinsmen, A Winter's Tale,* and *The Tempest.* After Shakespeare's death, masques continued to appear frequently in the regular drama, but they could have been only faint reflections of the court performances, which increased in musical and scenic complexity. Their glories ended with the revolution but not before they had furnished the form for Milton's *Comus* and helped Shakespeare to create the enchantments of *The Tempest.*

Both pastoral and masque continued as recognized species of drama long after the Restoration, but they gave place to a new form, the opera. Henceforth the musical and the spoken drama are constant rivals, though comedy of course never entirely surrenders song, dance and spectacle. The masque was practically absorbed by the opera shortly after the Restoration. The pastoral tradition has never been lost entirely and has reappeared from time to time, sometimes in the spoken but more usually in the musical drama.

Another relationship between species was the use of comic scenes in tragedy. This practice was virtually universal during the Elizabethan period and occasioned the nurse in *Romeo and Juliet,* the porter in *Macbeth,* the grave diggers in *Hamlet* and the fool in *Lear.* Little contribution to comedy as a form of drama was made by such employment of comic relief, but some extension of comic material was provided. The purpose of such scenes was contrast and heightening as well as relief, so the low comedians found themselves performing in strange juxtapositions of tears and laughter, horror and merriment. To modern taste some of the most grotesque combinations arise in the presentation of madness, which may be frankly comic as in Middleton's *Changeling* where two gallants with designs on the keeper's wife become inmates of an asylum, or which may be at the same time tragic and comic, as in *The Duchess of Malfi* and *Lear.* Shakespeare is often suggesting that tears and laughter are close kinsmen, but nowhere does he dramatize this intimacy so powerfully as in the babbling of the fool to Lear.

A far less daring combination is the use of the populace or of menials to afford relief to the tragedies of monarchs, as the citizens in *Julius Caesar* or the insurrectionists in *Philaster.* These contrasts have a certain propriety, and Jonson in *Sejanus* was careful to keep his comic portion closely interwoven in the main plot. But after Shakespeare there are few highly imaginative unions of the tragic and the comic. No one else can create comic grave diggers, to say nothing of the Prince of Denmark. Incidental comic scenes become banal, though they are still numerous in tragedy. In heavy tragicomedy the two principal actions were often supplemented by a little buffoonery, but it is usually lifeless.

The clown had . . . a long career, and though the clown, or fool, as a recognized figure is rarely found after Shakespeare, yet a certain amount of horse-play and buffoonery occurs in comedies of all sorts to the very end of the period. Wit, humour, and romance, as well as tragedy, accepted the relief of a little boisterous fun. In this as in other instances the Elizabethans took the ingredients of their dramatic fare well-mixed. Whatever their other emotions, they enjoyed hearty laughter, and they did not tolerate any form of drama without some clowning. But of course low comedy was not restricted to mere uproariousness; it gave the chance for creating eccentric and whimsical persons and for introducing them into laughable predicaments. It offered a place for the grave diggers, for Dogberry and Autolycus, for the motley denizens of *Bartholomew Fair,* for the grocer and his wife in *The Knight of the Burning Pestle,* for Lopez and Diego in *The Spanish Curate* and for a host of other most comic revelations of human nature.

Elizabethan comedy is low and high, refined and boisterous, witty and farcical, fantastic and realistic. In tracing the formation of types, it has been necessary to remind ourselves that opposite characteristics are often united in the same play and that few pure examples of any type are to be found. Nevertheless, it has not proved difficult to trace the main changes and developments under the convenient though over-used classification of romantic and realistic. Though often confused and indistinct yet the broad line of this distinction persists. Romantic comedies are marked by adventures, improbabilities, foreign scenes, fantasy, poetry, and by the idealization of love and other sentiments and of personality. Realistic comedies are distinguished by reflection of current life and manners, especially of London, by domestic incidents, by unidealized sentiments and personalities, by a slighting of love or a stress on its baser aspects, by a tendency to criticism and satire. Toward the end, the two classes were both somewhat conventionalized; romantic comedy usually keeping to persons of rank, foreign scenes, and verse—realistic comedy to London, to persons of the middle or lower classes, and to prose.

Romantic comedy, [may be] followed from its early origins in storyland and spectacle, through the various contributions of Lyly, Peele and Greene in mingling fancy, sentiment and fun, to Shakespeare's apotheosis of the type in *As You Like It* and *Twelfth Night.* After that the old materials remain and are given a new and brilliant life, though coarsened and theatricalized, by Fletcher and his followers. If these plays lack Shakespeare's woodland fancy wild they still take a cheerful view of life and of virtue; as, for example, in Shirley's *Grateful Servant,* or more light-heartedly in Brome's *Jovial Crew.* Buoyant spirits, lofty sentiment, idealized love, and generous human kindness sweeten verse and action. Their purpose is to take us away from actuality on a delightful or at least an entertaining excursion into romance.

The march of realism [may be] followed from the moralities and Plautus to some of its chief exponents, Jonson, Middleton and Massinger. But here the development is not so consistent as in romance, and the crossings of purposes and methods are more confusing. I wish to attempt a further analysis of these varying forms, one which is not inapplicable to the romantic plays but which I shall apply chiefly to the realistic comedies. I shall take some of the terms that have since then come into general use and inquire how far they will aid in analyzing the dramatic realism of the Elizabethans. How far can the plays that we have been considering be classified as comedies of intrigue, of manners, of character, of satire, of social problems?

When we look for intrigue, it is everywhere. Nearly every comedy, romantic or realistic, is based on tricks, and the discovery of the deception makes the dénouement. This is true of *Twelfth Night* and *The Merchant of Venice* as well as of *The Alchemist* and *A New Way to Pay Old Debts.* These tricks are by no means confined to love-making, they may lead to death or disaster as in the cases of Shylock and Overreach, or may be only a playful gesture like Portia's game with the ring, or a theatrical coup like Estefania's prayerbook for a pistol case. But though tricks are omnipresent, some plays rely almost exclusively for their interest on their plots or intrigues; or at least this plot in-

The inn yard at the White Hart, Southwark, where plays were performed on a temporary platform.

terest overshadows any concern in character, wit or moral. These are the comedies of intrigue.

One or two peculiar groups may be noticed where the relationship is wholly that of a special plot. *Look About You, The Blind Beggar of Bethnal Green* and *The Blind Beggar of Alexandria* are alike in using multiple disguise, one person tricking everyone by quick changes of costume. Another group is defined, though less sharply, by the use of the errors of persons wandering about in the dark. Another group, later in our period, copies the lively hide and seek of Spanish comedies of mistakes. The majority of English plays, however, model their tricks more or less on those of Plautus and Terence, often very closely, as in the case of *The Comedy of Errors,* Lyly's *Mother Bombie,* or Jonson's *Case is Altered.* Very few plays confine the intrigue solely to the pursuit of illicit love, as was so common in Restoration comedy and in modern French farce; and very few employ such extravagant and improbable tricks that they result in mere farce. A great many plays, however, depict manners or character so slightly or so incidentally or so ineffectively that they have little interest beyond the contraptions of their plots. This is true of several by Chapman and a number by Middleton, Fletcher, Massinger and Shirley. Heywood's *Wise Woman of Hogsdon* is an elaborate example. Of Fletcher's comedies, *The Woman's Prize* and *Monsieur Thomas* are perhaps the most farcical; and *The Chances* and *A Wild Goose Chase* are examples of intrigue with some mixture of manners and wit. Of Jonson's plays, *Epicœne,* and of Shakespeare's, *Merry Wives of Windsor* come the nearest to being comedies of intrigue. The six plays last named represent well enough the Elizabethan species and they were all received as admirable examples of comedy after the Restoration.

Our second main class is the comedy of manners, by which I shall mean plays whose chief interest lies in the exhibi-

tion of the habits, manners and customs of the society of the time. Manners is a word which may mean almost anything from fashion to character, but I take it as having less reference to the individual and more to society, less to moral decisions than to habits and modes. Romantic comedy has little direct interest in contemporary life, and during the vogue of romance little attention was paid London society. After the realistic movement about 1600, comedies of manners became numerous. They are rarely presented with a photographic impartiality, they are usually given with a sentimental, satirical, farcical or moral bias, but this bias should not be excessive if the play is to be a true comedy of manners.

Certain plays are devoted frankly to the exploitation of some phase of London life, perhaps a trade, or a sect, or a custom. Of trade plays we hear of *A Shoemaker is a Gentleman* and *Six Clothiers,* and Dekker's *Shoemaker's Holiday* is the masterpiece of this class. Middleton's *Family of Love* is a satirical exposure of a religious sect; his and Dekker's *Roaring Girl* tell of a notorious personage. A larger group is concerned especially with the seamy side of city life, with prostitutes, swindlers and other rogues, and their manners may be presented in humorous travesty or in realistic accuracy without any satire. Such are *Northward Ho* and *Westward Ho* and several of Middleton's. Other plays deal more at large with the manners of the London citizens, as in *Eastward Ho,* which traces the careers of the idle and the industrious, or *A Match at Midnight* or Fletcher's *Wit at Several Weapons* or Massinger's *City Madam.*

Domestic conflicts in family life are the themes of others. The old prodigal son story survives in *The London Prodigal,* but in general the Elizabethans were less interested than are we in the differences between parents and children. Griselda and the shrew still furnish the patterns for a discussion of marital relations; but the sport of taming the shrew is supplanted by that of the scornful lady who refuses all suitors, and the old theme of the lusty juventus by that of the libertine converted or the husband tamed. In the later part of our period, comedy becomes more concerned with the affairs of women and fashion. Shirley's *Hyde Park* and *The Ball* and Fletcher's *Wild Goose Chase* are examples of a growing tendency to depict high life and smart society.

One other group includes plays by Jonson and his imitators which seek a carefully wrought analysis of contemporary manners and typical characters. Such plays may transcend the limits I have placed on "manners" and become genuine comedies of character. But often when they fail really to create human beings, they do succeed in presenting an analysis of manners, as for example, *Every Man Out of His Humour, The Staple of News,* or Brome's *Antipodes. Every Man Out of His Humour* is indeed primarily a comedy of manners, and the interest in the characters is incidental to the study of current habits and follies. I am reserving, however, from this group those plays in which the characterization, or the moral satire or the social implications give a value and interest beyond that of mere manners; but perhaps I should note here that the presentation of contemporary manners usually requires the adornment of wit. Cleverness is not only an ornament but often, rather than morality or desert or fortune, becomes the arbiter of events. In the citizen plays the clever scapegrace fools the shopkeepers, and in the comedies of fashion the witty lady disarms and puts to rout all suitors, or the contest for mastery between the sexes becomes a battle of wits.

The third class includes those plays in which the interest goes beyond intrigue and manners to character. Though the delight in characterization is manifest in almost every Elizabethan comedy, very few develop their plots from the persons. Ben Jonson is almost the only dramatist who consciously endeavours to construct comedies of character in that sense. In his *Alchemist, Bartholomew Fair, Volpone* and to a less degree *Every Man in His Humour,* the complications may be said to spring naturally from the characters of the persons involved. In spite of some extravagances in plot, the same may be said of Massinger's two realistic comedies, or of Middleton's *Fair Quarrel.* But such is never the case in Shakespeare, who begins with story and develops character interest out of the persons of the story; and in most realistic comedy even when imitative of Jonson, the humours are merely additions to a plot of tricks. Under my definition, the personalities depicted are not necessarily the mainsprings of the plot, but they are presented with so much vividness or emphasis that they overshadow all else.

Under such a classification it is often difficult to draw the line. *Eastward Ho,* for example, has a plot of tricks and it is a remarkable picture of London manners, but it also presents well defined characters who excite an interest in themselves apart from plot or manners. In a different way the character interest in Fletcher's *Rule a Wife* certainly surpasses that of the plot. Often the depiction of eccentric or whimsical persons supplies the chief comic force of the piece, as in Chapman's *Monsieur D'Olive,* Fletcher's *Humorous Lieutenant* and *Spanish Curate,* or Brome's *Antipodes.* Again, a number of Elizabethan plays fairly run loose on characterization and crowd the stage with comic personages who are responsible for all the fun. Without counting Falstaff and his crew, it would be difficult to match elsewhere in the drama such freedom and vigour and abundance of comic personalities as we have in *A Chaste Maid in Cheapside* or *The Spanish Curate* or *The Knight of the Burning Pestle* or *Bartholomew Fair.*

My fourth class, comedies of satire, is somewhat aside from the preceding divisions, for manifestly satire does not distinguish itself from intrigue, manners or character. It presents a special purpose on the part of the author which might be compared with other purposes, sentimental, burlesque or idealizing. But I wish merely to call attention to the large part which satire played in Elizabethan realistic comedy. Marston, Massinger and Jonson are the most serious, but Chapman, Middleton and others are vigorous. The objects of satire are usually certain types of persons, gulls, cheats, roaring boys, cast captains, prostitutes, usurers, puritans, parvenus, hypocrites; but often the censure extends to sexual immorality in general or to the demerits of large classes such as merchants or courtiers. For a brief time during the war of the theaters, personal satire and caricature are indulged, and we even hear of a suppressed

play which represented James I intoxicated. Other plays, such as Middleton's *Phœnix,* or any of Jonson's, assumed a serious censorship of the age, presented a lengthy and detailed indictment of the times. Occasionally the purpose of amusement is lost sight of in the fierce indignation which denounces rather than ridicules. Comedy is no longer light-hearted, it must show the course of evil and punish its rascals, as does tragedy, and expose folly as allied to vice. Jonson's *Volpone* is the most striking example, but with it may be grouped Marston's *Malcontent* and Massinger's *New Way to Pay Old Debts.*

Our fifth class introduces another special division not coördinate with the others and comprises plays engaging in the discussion of social and moral problems, not altogether unlike problem and thesis plays of today. The audience is asked not only to be amused and thrilled but also to consider a question and to share in a debate. The Elizabethan dramatists did not go very far toward turning their stage into a forum but they well understood the dramatic value in a question. Should a sister sacrifice her honour to save a brother's life?—is the sensational and casuistical problem proposed in *Measure for Measure* and in the sub-plot of *A Woman Killed with Kindness.* Should a son defend by a duel his mother's honour, if the slander is true?—is the theme of *A Fair Quarrel.* Usually the question proposed concerns the relations of the sexes and involves a realistic study of social conditions; but whether sincere, verbal, casuistical, or sensational, the question is kept to the fore and is of interest to society at large. The issue is not merely as to the conduct of John or Mary, the persons of the play, but rather as to the attitude that society should take on the question. In comedies of character the solution is derived from the individual personalities; in satirical comedies the assumption is that the audience knows what is right and the author is denouncing what is wrong; in problem plays the question is proposed and argued before the audience as a tribunal. Of course the three classes are not mutually exclusive, but *A New Way to Pay Old Debts, A Fair Quarrel, The Honest Whore, The English Traveller* and *A Woman Killed with Kindness* are the Elizabethan comedies which go farthest towards a discussion of serious social problems. Of these *A Woman Killed with Kindness* is most revolutionary both in its social thesis and in its departure from current types. It gives warning of the enormous field open to domestic drama inspired by a reformatory or questioning purpose.

My analysis may suggest the range of experimentation in Elizabethan comedy and the extent to which it anticipated later developments. But all its efforts did not arrive at any consensus of opinion or any critical agreement as to the limits or the form of the species. A division into five acts was about the only rule obeyed, and a very foolish rule. Neither Shakespeare's invention nor Jonson's criticism resulted in any such model of comic method as Molière was to leave the French theater. Shirley's comedies at the close of the period come as near as anyone's to summing up what was acceptable to his own day, but even these do not present a distinct and definable type of drama. After nearly a century of free experimentation comedy was still marked by variety and contradiction, richness and confusion, brilliancy and ineptitude.

This bewildering diversity makes it difficult to assess the merits of the Elizabethan drama. Many a critic or reader on turning back to his first love is confronted by some glaring defect which had been scarcely perceptible in the enthusiasm of his earlier admiration. The dramatic construction, even at its best, is not in accord with modern methods. The wit even in Shakespeare sometimes seems trifling. The invention is a little unregulated. But, whatever its faults and weaknesses, this drama does meet the great test, it does give a highly imaginative interpretation of human nature. In comedy as in tragedy, in the minor authors as well as in Shakespeare, its great merits lie in its poetry and in characterization.

By poetry I do not mean merely those flights of fancy that enliven even the most humdrum passages, nor merely the gracious phrase or the unexpected image that are likely to delight us anywhere. These are but the indications of a spirit that animates prose as well as verse and the dialogues of the clown as well as the lyrics of the lovers. In comedy it seeks beauty in grace, in surprise, in mirth, in an exuberant vitality. It manifests itself in a joy in words, in a quest for images, or in audacious invention. It accompanies pensive thought or quick laughter or moral indignation. Nothing arouses its enthusiasm more than the excitement of human nature. The great adventure of expressing human nature in English words was responsible for much bad verse and defective prose, but it gave all discourse an ambition and daring such as it has rarely possessed in the drama. Standards of style, rules of propriety, the common usages of society offered no fetters to a bold initiative always in search of a wider vocabulary, new comparisons, and melodious phrase. Elizabethan comedy might be of any or all varieties; it always afforded an opportunity for poetry.

In the spirit of imaginative surprise the poets undertook the dramatization of men and women. They were not very critical or analytical. They accepted life as a thing of wonder and the humours of human beings as amazing and stimulating. "What a piece of work is man!" "What a paragon is Elizabeth!" "How despicable is a coward!" Of modern analysis, modern psychology, modern belittling of personal volition, they knew nothing. They tried to depict the stupidities and gaieties of our species truthfully but wonderingly. They marvelled at ugliness as well as at beauty. Jonson's method is more critical and deliberate than Dekker's, but in comparison with moderns, Jonson and Dekker differ only in degree, not in kind. Jonson intended that Sir Epicure Mammon and Bobadill should arouse exclamations of wonder and admiration no less than Friscobaldo or Falstaff. Wit and humour and the invention of comic situation display themselves mainly in the dramatic portraiture. When they wish to make us laugh, these Elizabethans create a man. They are constantly engaged in proving how amazing, how charming, how contemptible, how irresistibly funny is human nature.

In Shakespeare often, and now and then in a lesser man such as Dekker, the imagination reveals how slight is the division between tears and laughter, pity and amusement, and the tenderest tolerance gleams in Comedy's smile. But most of the comic writers are at least open-minded and curious and rarely doctrinaire or intolerant in the probing of human motive. Joy in life, wonder at mankind and zeal for poetry are still abundant in Fletcher and Shirley, and discernible even in Brome and D'Avenant. Comedy continues to be, up to the closing of the theaters, a poetic tribute to the humorous delight furnished by men and women. The nineteenth century novel offers a somewhat similar though more prosaic tribute, but nowhere else in the drama except in this Shakespearian period is there such evoking from human nature "of infinite jest, of most excellent fancy." (pp. 252-66)

Ashley H. Thorndike, "Conclusion to Elizabethan Comedy," in his English Comedy, *The Macmillan Company, 1929, pp. 252-66.*

M. C. Bradbrook

[In the following excerpt, Bradbrook attempts to account for the unique quality of Elizabethan comedy. The "especial greatness of the plays written in the last decade of Elizabeth's reign and the first decade of James's was," she asserts, "dependent on conditions essentially transient—upon the momentary fusion of the popular and learned traditions, the temporary interaction of the two modes which were not permanently compatible with each other." She cites Shakespeare and Jonson as adherents to each of these traditions.]

The development of Elizabethan and Jacobean drama cannot readily be plotted. Too many factors are involved. The older historians, such as F. E. Schelling [in his *History of Elizabethan Drama,* 1908], attempted some classification through the subject-matter of the plays, but only in the most general way. Recently writers have devoted themselves to special forms, such as Revenge Tragedy, the English History Play and the Court Masque, which depend on a new understanding of the poetic principles underlying dramatic composition. This is largely due to a revival of interest in rhetoric, the pivot of the higher education in Elizabethan times. Studies both of drama and of nondramatic poetry have been written on the basis of rhetorical form, by which the special 'kinds' of poetry were distinguished.

At the same time, studies in stage history have revealed more of the popular ties of Elizabethan playwriting, its close connexion with seasonal festivals, with the lively tradition of mumming, with city pageantry and revels. This tradition naturally predominates in comedy, the popular domestic tragedy, with its roots in homily and balladry, being a relatively minor 'kind'.

Comedy has received comparatively little attention from critics, perhaps because its ingredients are more varied and its lines of development less obvious than those of the well-marked forms of tragedy and history. Yet comedies out-number tragedies on the Elizabethan stage by nearly three to one. Sweet and bitter comedy, romantic and satiric comedy, or Shakespearean and Jonsonian comedy have all been used as terms of description for the two main divisions, of which the first may be said to be characteristically Elizabethan, and the second Jacobean. (p. 3)

Behind Elizabethan drama there lay at least two modes of acting—first, the tradition of the revels, whether courtly or popular, and all that these implied of intimate collaboration between actors and audience. The general relation of actors and audience is a subject which has become increasingly prominent in Elizabethan studies. The form of the playhouses, at one time the chief concern of stage historians, is now seen to be important chiefly for the collaboration which it induced between audience and players.

Second, the learned tradition of rhetorical and satiric drama upon moral themes, built up in the schools and universities, found expression in an even more intimate private presentation; but the order and formality of such compositions were in sharpest contrast to the shapeless stories of the popular drama, based often upon the rambling medieval romantic tale. When these two traditions coalesced, the great age of Elizabethan drama began. The main literary tradition in England as elsewhere was a narrative one, inherited from the later Middle Ages. The first problem confronting dramatic poets was that of transforming narrative material and traditions into dramatic form. Not only the stories, but the organization of the stories, was based on narrative. In the miracle plays narrative technique had ruled the dialogue.

Classical theory enlarged less on comedy than tragedy, but the plays of the ancient comic theatre were widely known. The precepts of classical writers were refashioned by critics of the Renaissance to conform with their own presuppositions: Italian critics evolved a rigid set of prescriptions for the writing of plays, which were little calculated to help the practising dramatist. At the same time, the whole bias of education was towards a somewhat naïve belief in the efficacy of such formulæ.

Hence the popular playwrights were confronted with a second problem. The right way of making comedies, as indicated for example by learned friends of the Sidneys, was not likely to be compatible with public entertainment. Yet some deference to the rules of art must be achieved if drama was to attract noble patronage, and the shapeless popular tradition was in need of organization. The learned tradition was equally in need of flexibility.

Fortunately in England, as also in Spain, the strength of native taste was sufficiently powerful to counteract the great prestige of neo-classic form. Literary development was retarded in England by comparison with that of France and Italy; the provincial and outlying position of the country on the fringe of Europe had sheltered it from too rapid an infusion of the new learning. Hence a real amalgamation between native art and the learned tradition was possible, and in the drama, a form where the demands of the unlearned made themselves most clearly felt, it was achieved.

Even such early sixteenth century plays as those of John Heywood show this very special fusion of popular vigour and classic organization. The plays of Lyly were the first successful attempts to transplant and modify Italian eloquence and to make a drama both courtly and pungent. He gave the English drama shape. At the same time, Peele,

working in the more indigenous forms, raised them to the level of conscious though simple art.

Shakespeare finally evolved a stable form of Elizabethan comedy, first modelling himself with some strictness upon learned example, and then rejecting the over-ingenious and over-planned pattern of his earliest attempts for a more popular style. His strength alone was capable of welding the two traditions firmly together, and his rejection of simple learning in favour of complex nature was a decisive step. Between *The Comedy of Errors* and *The Merchant of Venice* there is as great a distance as between *Titus Andronicus* and *Romeo and Juliet.* The development in each case is from a prescribed formula towards organic freedom of growth.

Shakespeare remained in the eyes of his contemporaries a popular writer. His art was personal to himself, although his dramatic language, both verse and prose, laid the foundations for the Jacobean comic writers who succeeded him. It was through the speech of his characters that Shakespeare distinguished without dividing them; and this speech was based on the diction of common life. For him, plays belonged to an oral tradition: they sprang from the special conditions of the Elizabethan public theatre, and were designed to appeal in the greatest possible variety of ways to the widest possible audience.

The untutored and 'Elizabethan quality' of Shakespeare's art was replaced by the conscious and deliberately planned work of Ben Jonson. He absorbed the work of Shakespeare, but, like a cuckoo in the nest, supplanted his fostering elder. Jonson's art was more imitable than Shakespeare's; it did not depend so much upon special insight as upon general standards of decorum, order and hard work. Nevertheless, Jonson was bold in his readiness to modify classical precept, he admired the native tradition, and the form which he evolved was as far removed from the pedantic as it was from the spontaneous.

The War of the Theatres represents the first clash between the older and the newer forms of playwriting. Shakespeare and Dekker stood for the old, and Jonson for the new. Although the traditionalists appear to have triumphed on this occasion, the history of comedy in the seventeenth century is the history of their slow retreat before the advance of Jonsonian art. Dekker and Thomas Heywood, who represented the oral way of writing, gradually sank to a spectacular melodrama, as their plays became more and more dissociated from those of the wits; and as the audience lost its old homogeneity and split up into the noisy 'prentices at the Red Bull and the fine gallants at the New Blackfriars, the possibility of a truly inclusive dramatic form gradually disappeared. Fletcher and Chapman wrote for a sophisticated but narrow group; moreover, they wrote not only for the actor but the reader of books also. Finally, in some of the courtly revels, Jonson recalled almost nostalgically the simpler forms of his youth, as the living tradition disintegrated, and the older form perished.

II. Drama and Society

It has been frequently observed that the comedy of Jonson and Fletcher is closely linked with that of the Restoration theatre, where their plays were often revived. Comedy, unlike tragedy, modified and survived. Yet the especial greatness of the plays written in the last decade of Elizabeth's reign and the first decade of James's was dependent on conditions essentially transient—upon the momentary fusion of the popular and learned traditions, the temporary interaction of two modes which were not permanently compatible with each other.

Out of this tension, the greater Elizabethan and Jacobean comedies were bred. Theatrical and rhetorical, organized and spontaneous, artificial and natural, they reflected a way of life and of speech which were likewise of the hour. Formal manners and violent passions, gravity and brutality, jest and dignity might be exemplified in the lives of the great from Sir Thomas More to Sir Walter Ralegh; these virtues did not equally belong to the generation of Strafford and Laud, Pym and Milton.

The critic cannot hope to recreate the Elizabethan point of view for the modern reader. A work of art, once committed to publication, stands in independence of its author. In the custody of the generations which transmit it, it may acquire a patina of meanings which formed no part of the original design. Yet this very tradition, being partly formed by the works of art themselves, will not develop irresponsibly; and eccentricities of misinterpretation can always be corrected by an appeal to the general understanding, and, where it is ascertainable, to the original intent. (pp. 4-7)

[Elizabethan comedy] should not be read in terms merely verbal; it should be imagined as a living, complex, transitory performance. Many Elizabethan plays which appear shapeless on the printed page acquire complete integrity in the theatre. Middleton's *Changeling* is the outstanding example in tragedy; comedy is in general of a far lower vitality when transplanted to the study, and this perhaps may account for the comparative neglect of it by literary historians. Even in the theatre, it is impossible now to reestablish the atmosphere of the older drama. The Elizabethan audience, rowdy, vocal, sometimes dangerous, far more conscious of its unity, far better acquainted and more unified than the modern audience, was also prepared to be instructed and edified. It came with a very definite set of moral expectations, with which both players and playwrights were familiar. Neither the manners nor the morals of the original audience can be recaptured.

Lesser writers accepted the conditions of the theatre; greater writers transformed and thus transmitted them. Among the great, Ben Jonson and Shakespeare stand so far above all competitors that they may well be called the creators of English drama. They were friends and rivals; their contemporaries and successors were aware of the fact, and throughout the seventeenth century they were contrasted. But whereas 'Shakespeare's magic could not copied be', Jonson provided the succeeding age with a model which was only too acceptable. His influence might be compared with that of Milton on the subsequent writers of heroic verse. The 'Chinese wall' which he built against barbarism remained to divide Elizabethan from all subsequent drama; after Jonson nothing was quite the same again.

His return in old age to the forms of an earlier day is none the less proof of the power which they had for him. He himself, if not, like his sovereign, 'mere English', was rooted in the life of the City, and his crowded stages as hospitable as Shakespeare's to all sorts and conditions of men. Jonson's comedies include however the odd rather than the ordinary, and the idiosyncratic rather than the typical character. Shakespeare's characters 'are not modified by the customs of particular places . . . by the peculiarities of studies or professions . . . or by accidents of transient fashions' as Jonson's are. 'In the writings of other poets a character is too often an individual: in those of Shakespeare it is commonly a species' [Samuel Johnson, in his *Preface to Shakespeare*].

In this, too, Shakespeare relied upon older traditions and native models. English poetry had already known, in Chaucer, a writer whose eye for the 'genuine progeny of common humanity' went with a temper both sympathetic and ironic. The connexions between Chaucer and Shakespeare are not of the kind to be readily and easily demonstrated—unlike Spenser, Shakespeare did not make the mistake of trying to use a Chaucerian vocabulary. But the poet whom Deschamps had called 'the very God of Love in England' was the readiest model for 'sweet Master Shakespeare' whose reputation depended upon *Romeo and Juliet* and *The Merchant of Venice*. In Chaucer's young Squire—

> Embroudered was he, as it were a meede
> Al ful of fresshe floures, whyte and reede.
> Syngynge he was, or floytynge, al the day;
> He was as fresh as is the month of May—

may be seen the original of Master Fenton, the wooer of sweet Anne Page—

> . . . he capers, he dances, he has eyes of youth,
> he writes verses, he speaks holiday, he smells
> April and May . . .

or of Orlando himself. The creator of Harry Bailly and the Wyf of Bath would certainly have recognized in the creator of Falstaff his true heir and successor.

When Jonson wrote of the greenwood, as he did in *The Sad Shepherd,* he produced lovely poetry but indifferent drama. He was a Cockney, and his rogues' gallery was based not only on reading but also on observation. Shakespeare saw all large towns, ancient and modern, as if they were London; each had a tidal river and a populace of small tradesmen, and even in Italy the south suburbs held an Elephant Inn. Jonson on the other hand first set *Every Man in his Humour* in Italy, then in the revised version moved it to London and added local colour. Such immediate reflexion of 'the time's form and pressure' in Elizabethan and Jacobean comedy is the origin of its success and the guarantee of its continuing life; for this comedy of character depended upon social relationships, and the delineation of men in society. Both Shakespeare and Jonson themselves enjoyed that kindled fellowship which is the special glory of the theatre.

Modern sympathy with primitive art and with the symbolic rather than the logical structure of poetry makes it easier to accept the form of a writer like Dekker as a genuine alternative to Jonson's. The surviving relics of popular art have in this generation recovered their significance for a wide public. Among literary critics there is a new appreciation of such asyndetic form as that of *Piers Plowman*. Modern poets themselves have learnt from such sources; on the other hand, they have rehabilitated the art of rhetoric, which often, especially in the later plays of Yeats and Eliot, determines their dramatic structure. The conditions for an understanding of Elizabethan comedy are therefore at present unusually favourable; and even the possibility of stage revivals may now be entertained. (pp. 7-10)

> M. C. Bradbrook, in an introduction to The Growth and Structure of Elizabethan Comedy, *Chatto & Windus, 1955, pp. 3-10.*

TRAGEDY

Hardin Craig

[*An American educator and editor, Craig wrote several works on Elizabethan history and culture. His most noteworthy,* The Enchanted Glass *(1936), was an important contribution to the historical school of criticism for its description of the intellectual background of the Elizabethan age. In the essay below, originally published in 1940, he exposes the classical roots of Elizabethan tragedy, noting, in particular, Shakespeare's reliance on Seneca.*]

The Renaissance was an era in which, in obedience to many complicated influences and motives, the ancient world supplied to the modern an ability to express itself in terms of something to say and in terms of forms and patterns of expression. Perhaps, indeed certainly, the ancient world also supplied to the modern what we call inspiration; that is, desire to express thought and feeling and moving interest in human life and its environment.

The process of gaining ideas and forms was begun in grammar schools by means of the study of school authors. These authors, mainly Latin, were the ones who appealed most to the western Europeans of the fifteenth and sixteenth centuries. They were happily chosen, since they were relatively simple, easily comprehended, and so picturesque and human in quality that they may be said to have suited the society to which they were presented. They were the authors who had, for the most part, been best known in the Middle Ages and those who had inherited the sanction of the schools of rhetoric and logic in the Roman empire. Among the poets were Virgil and Ovid. Among the dramatists were, first, Terence (because of the excellence of his latinity), then Seneca, then Plautus. Cicero, who was a writer on rhetoric as well as a proponent of Latin culture, stood in popularity far ahead of Livy and Sallust, who, however, were also known and read. On the philosophic side Aristotle was supreme and next him perhaps stood Plutarch, who in his philosophic and ethical influence is comparable both to Aristotle and to Cicero.

In the very first rank of influences was Boethius, and next him the Neo-Latin writers (Erasmus, Vives, and others), who were also great disseminators of ancient culture. This list is by no means complete; for, as we shall see if we consider the scholastic habits of the Renaissance, a large body of selected doctrine came because of these habits from the remotest corners of the ancient and the modern worlds.

Renaissance learned culture was aggregative in its practices, and as regards its corpus of study was neither consistent nor systematic. It was moralistic rather than moral, rhetorical rather than literary, and often sentimental rather than sincere. It was, however, reverent toward antiquity and relied upon the ancient world as the source of truth rather than upon its own ability to discover truth. This attitude of mind, it may be said, was in some respects a fortunate one. Both text-books and school methods reflect an attitude which was aspiring as well as docile.

The most elementary book, and possibly the text-book most widely used in the grammar schools of the Renaissance, was the famous *Disticha Moralis,* reputed to be the work of one Dionysius Cato. In the school course it was followed by or accompanied by the *Sententiae Pueriles,* a cento of simple aphoristic materials, which seems to have been used as a basis of Latin speaking; this, in turn, by Æsop's *Fables.* The first two of these books exemplify the *sententia* and the third the *exemplum,* both present in the schools since Roman times. The next layer of instruction seems to have been drawn from Terence, Cicero, or the Latin poets, and seems to have had to do, pedagogically speaking, with the art of Latin phrasing.

The particular instrument used in the schools for the mastery by students of these three fundamentals—*sententia, exemplum,* and *phrasis*—was the commonplace book. Pupils were taught from their earliest appearance in school to keep commonplace books. They were instructed as to what to record in their commonplace books and were required to keep them neatly. There was thus bred in them the habit of keeping notes, of looking out for such bits of wisdom and eloquence, wit and beauty, and for such significant anecdotes, apothegms, and apologues as would later serve their turn as writers and speakers and guide them on the road to wisdom. These commonplace books, both those made in school and in later life, exist to this day by the hundreds. Those which have perished must run into the tens of thousands. The commonplace book, which included besides quotations also translations and original compositions, was the center of the school course and is the symbol of the learned mind of the Renaissance both in its habits and its objectives.

The theory of composition which underlay the commonplace book was this: if a student had gathered the truest, wisest, and most timely things that had ever been said on every appropriate subject and had at the same time noted and memorized the best possible phraseology of every available idea from the Latin writers—Cicero, Terence, Virgil, Lucan, and their Neo-Latin exponents—he would be prepared to write with perfection on anything he chose to write about. Given his subject, he would divide it according to the technical principles of logical definition, and then apply to each division the places or *loca* of rhetoric and logic. He would then search his commonplace book for materials and phraseology. After the fundamentals had thus been accumulated, the writer's task was merely amplification. The principles of amplification were well organized for his use, and his commonplace book would again be in demand. With such a system at its base can it be wondered at that the literature of the Renaissance repeats and repeats again the ideation of the age?

In justification of this rather slavish system the Renaissance was ready to advance its doctrine of imitation. This doctrine is more than a defence of plagiarism. It rests ultimately upon the great doctrine of similitude. The Renaissance looked upon man as a universal being repeating in his life the deeds of all men. If man is a universal being, his conduct will always follow a pattern. Men's actions are always alike because their natures are always the same. Imitation was thus inherent in the fundamental concept of man's origin, nature, and relation to the universe. A modern who absorbed the ancients was rendered like the ancients. By saying their words and thinking their thoughts he became like them. He acquired their virtues. There was no other way than imitation by which he might acquire virtues. Renaissance imitation was, in a universe thus patterned, methodologically inevitable.

In addition to materials, patterns, and forms—facts, phrases, *exempla,* aphorisms, *sententiae,* and figures of speech—there was another significant practice within the same tendency. It is a larger aspect of manner which has not been so fully recognized, because it is harder to formulate and identify. I refer to the practice, particularly in drama and fiction, but also in oratory and history, of handling similar situations in similar ways; that is, of following patterns of thought and style derived from the ancients. Given a real or a fancied resemblance of the modern world to the ancient in an array of social forces, in the current of event, or in the logic of fact, the poets, dramatists, and historians of the Renaissance often tended to modify their modern situations to such a degree that they became actual parallels to those treated in the ancient classics. Polydore Vergil, for example, reshaped the English chronicles to conform them to the principles and significances he found in Plutarch, Suetonius, and Livy. This practice is to be regarded as the result of an accepted belief that life was somewhat narrowly patterned, and the models were in part at least rubrics worked out in ancient times in order to render life intelligible.

The greater authors of the Renaissance from Petrarch to Cervantes habitually began on a level of close imitation both in matters rhetorical and in those which were structural and architectonic; but usually, as their geniuses developed, they emancipated themselves to a greater or less degree, from formalism in style and thought. They thus came, by following the road of rather stupid imitation, to exemplify what we regard as true originality, so that their imitation no longer intruded itself or restricted their freedom. There is little doubt that Shakespeare himself is an example of such an emancipated genius, and in general it must be admitted, in the light of performance, that the practice of imitation worked well.

By means of the commonplace book and the habits which

it engendered, as no doubt also by the practice of deliberate imitation of one author by another, Renaissance literature was permeated by classical literature, particularly by the Latin school authors. Our interest in this paper will be in borrowings and imitations of Seneca, particularly as they appear in Shakespeare. By what various ways these influences of Seneca came to Shakespeare has already been suggested, and we shall not concern ourselves with the question of whether Shakespeare knew Seneca and borrowed from him. Perhaps the greatest number of Senecan features came from Italian, French, and English imitators of Seneca, Shakespeare's predecessors in Renaissance drama. It is at least certain that in treating various subjects Shakespeare followed a Senecan pattern, for Seneca had taught dramatists what to say in certain serious or tragic situations and what tone or style to use.

Seneca was a principal channel through which the wisdom of the past reached the Renaissance. His understanding of the workings of human emotions commended itself to the Renaissance and was the more effective since he showed in his plays a dramatic use of the system of thought and feeling to which the Renaissance adhered. In his tragedies certain lines of action are pretty definitely worked out in accordance with his system of thought. The Renaissance was thus schooled in a method of imitation, schooled also in the belief that human behavior is universal; that is to say, that a particular line of action or a particular affection expresses itself always in accordance with the same pattern, so that the imitation of Seneca and the repetition of his ideas was inevitable.

Many bits of wit and wisdom found their way, no doubt by devious roads, into the plays of Shakespeare. Since this influence in the use of aphoristic idea has been dealt with rather adequately by Cunliffe and others, a very few illustrations will suffice here:

a) *Hercules Furens,* 735 ff.:
   Each for his sins of earth
   Must suffer here; the crime returns to him
   Who did it, and the guilty soul is crushed
   By its own precedents.
   Macbeth, I, vii, 8 ff.:
   . . . we but teach
   Bloody instructions, which, being taught,
      return
   To plague the inventor: this even-handed
      justice
   Commends the ingredients of our poison'd
      chalice
   To our own lips.
   Cf. also *Macbeth,* III, iv, 122:
   It will have blood; they say, blood will have
      blood;
   and *Richard III,* V, i, 20 ff.:
   That high All-Seer that I dallied with
   Hath turn'd my feigned prayer on my head
   And given in earnest what I begg'd in jest.
   Thus doth he force the swords of wicked
      men
   To turn their own points on their masters'
      bosoms.

b) *Phœnissœ,* 664:
   A kingdom is well bought at any price.

3 *Henry VI*, I, ii, 16-17:
> But for a kingdom any oath may be broken:
> I would break a thousand oaths to reign one
>   year.

c) *Agamemnon*, 142 ff.:
> Cly.   Where wrath, where grief, where
>   hope shall bear me on,
>   There will I speed my course; my
>   helmless ship
>   I've given to be the sport of winds
>   and floods.
>   Where reason fails 'tis best to follow
>   chance . . .
>   To stop midway in sin is foolish-
>   ness. . . .
> Nurse.   Yet desperate measures no one
>   first attempts.
> Cly.   The path of sin is headlong from the
>   first.

Hamlet, IV, iii, 9 ff.:
> . . . diseases desperate grown
> By desperate appliance are relieved
> Or not at all.

Richard III, IV, iii, 51 ff.:
> . . . I have heard that fearful comment-
>   ing
> Is leaden servitor to dull delay . . .
> Come, muster men: my counsel is my
>   shield.

King Lear, V, i, 68-69:
> . . . for my state
> Stands on me to defend, not to debate.

More significant as regards extent of influence are many passages in which it is obvious that Shakespeare carried over from Seneca, either directly or indirectly, rhetorical methods of handling situations. There are in Seneca, for example, several cases in which a character emphasizes his personal daring or resolution by setting it against impossibilities in the world of nature:

> And dost thou think that I would touch the
>   hand
> That is besprinkled with my father's gore,
> And my two brothers blood? Oh, sooner far
> Shall day's last beams go out in eastern skies,
> And dawn break in the west; sooner shall peace
> Be made 'twixt snow and flame, and Scylla join
> Sicilia's shores with those of Italy,
> And sooner shall Euripus' rushing waves
> Lap peacefully upon Eubea's shores.
>   (*Hercules Furens*, 373 ff.)

With this exaggerated manner of speaking compare the following:

> You may as well go stand upon the beach
> And bid the main flood bate his usual height;
> You may as well use question with the wolf
> Why he hath made the ewe bleat for the lamb;
> You may as well forbid the mountain pines
> To wag their high tops and to make no noise,
> When they are fretten with the gusts of heav-
>   en. . . .
>   (*Mer. Ven.*, IV, i, 71 ff.)

Seneca is also fond of permitting a character to set up for himself possible tests of endurance:

> And shouldst thou bid me tread the driven
>   snows,
> To walk along high Pindus frozen peaks,
> I'd not refuse; no, not if thou shouldst bid
> Me go through fire, and serried ranks of foes,
> I would not hesitate to bare my breast
> Unto the naked swords.
>   (*Hippolytus*, 613 ff.)

Shakespeare turns speech of this type to account in portraying the courage of characters in perilous situations. Compare the following with the passage from Seneca:

> O, bid me leap, rather than marry Paris,
> From off the battlements of yonder tower;
> Or walk in thievish ways; or bid me lurk
> Where serpents are; chain me with roaring
>   bears; . . .
> And I will do it without fear or doubt. . . .
>   (*R. and J.*, IV, i, 77 ff.)

> Rather a ditch in Egypt
> Be gentle grave unto me! rather on Nilus' mud
> Lay me stark naked, and let the water-flies
> Blow me into abhorring! rather make
> My country's high pyramides my gibbet,
> And hang me up in chains!
>   (*A. and C.*, V, ii, 57 ff.)

From Seneca Shakespeare inherited in one way or another much figurative language, prominent here being images contrasting the cares of high and low estate in terms of mountain peaks and valleys, ships in mid-sea and near the shore, palaces and cottages. Typical use of such imagery appears in the following:

> More soft than Tyrian couch,
> The greensward soothes to fearless sleep;
> But gilded ceilings break our rest,
> And sleepless through the night we lie
> On beds of luxury. . . .
> Not so the poor:
>
> His heart is ever full of peace.
> From shallow beechen cups he drinks,
> But not with trembling hands; his food
> Is cheap and common, but he sees
> No naked sword above his head. . . .
>   (*Hercules Œtœus*, 644 ff.)

> 'Tis not the balm, the sceptre and the ball . . .
> Not all these, laid in bed majestical,
> Can sleep so soundly as the wretched slave,
> Who with a body filled and vacant mind
> Gets him to rest, cramm'd with distressful
>   bread. . . .
>   (*Henry V*, IV, i, 277 ff.)

Compare also these figurative descriptions of the effects of sleep:

Hercules Furens, 1065 ff.:
> O sleep, subduer of our ills,
> The spirit's rest, thou better part
> Of human life, . . .

Macbeth, II, ii, 36 ff.:
> . . . the innocent sleep,
> Sleep that knits up the ravell'd sleave of care,
> The death of each day's life, sore labour's
> bath,

Balm of hurt minds, great nature's second
course,
Chief nourisher in life's feast, . . .

2 Henry IV, III, i, 5 ff.:
        O sleep, O gentle sleep,
Nature's soft nurse, how have I frighted thee,
That thou no more wilt weigh my eyelids down,
And steep my senses in forgetfulness? . . .

One might go on to cite passages in which reaction on the
part of characters follows a similar pattern:

Thyestes, 176 ff.:
    O soul, so sluggish, spiritless and weak,
    And (what in kings I deem the last reproach)
    Still unavenged, after so many crimes,
    Thy brother's treacheries, and every law
    Of nature set at naught, canst vent thy wrath
    In vain and meaningless complaints? By now
    The whole wide world should be in arms . . .

Hamlet, II, ii, 593 ff.:
    Yet I,
    A dull and muddy-mettled rascal, peak
    Like John-a-dreams, unpregnant of my cause,
    And can say nothing; no, not for a king,
    Upon whose property and most dear life
    A damn'd defeat was made. . . .
            it cannot be
    But I am pigeon-liver'd, and lack gall
    To make oppression bitter. . . .

Or one might note the tendency on the part of both dramatists to describe emotion in terms of physiological accompaniment. For example, in *Troades* (488 ff.) Andromache
says as she hides her child in the tomb,

    But at the very thought a chilling sweat
    Invades my trembling limbs, for much I fear
    The gruesome omen of the place of death.

And Juliet when she is about to swallow the potion (*R. &
J.*, IV, iii, 15 ff.) says,

    I have a faint cold fear thrills through my veins,
    That almost freezes up the heat of life: . . .
    Or, if I live, is it not very like,
    The horrible conceit of death and night,
    Together with the terror of the place,—
    As in a vault, an ancient receptacle,
    Where, for this many hundred years, the bones
    Of all my buried ancestors are pack't . . .

Similarity exists here in motivating image also.

There are further parallels in Shakespeare to *Phœnissae*,
295 ff., which deals with discord within a kingdom; to *Troades*, 1 ff., and *Hippolytus*, 488 ff., which praise the humble
life and exalt its happiness above the lot of kings; to *Hippolytus*, 671 ff., in which vengeance is expected from heav-
en and night is called upon to hide the sins of men. We
might mention as typical the famous parallel between *Hercules Furens*, 1325 ff., *Hippolytus*, 715 ff., and *Macbeth*, II,
ii, 60 ff.:

        What Tanais or Nile,
    What Tigris, with the waves of Persia mad, . . .
    Can ever cleanse this right hand of its stains?
    Though chill Maeotis pour its icy floods
    Upon me; though the boundless sea should pour

Its waters o'er my hands; still would they be
Deep dyed with crime.

What Tanais could make me clean again?
Or what Maeotis rushing to the sea,
With its barbaric waves? Not Neptune's self,
With all his ocean's waters could avail
To cleanse so foul a stain.
Will all great Neptune's ocean wash this blood
Clean from my hand? No, this my hand will
    rather
The multitudinous seas incarnadine,
Making the green one red.

In the lines from *Macbeth* there is obvious similarity of
phrasing and situation. Elsewhere Shakespeare seems to
have adapted the basic idea of these Senecan passages to
suit other purposes:

    Not all the water in the rough rude sea
    Can wash the balm off from an annointed king.
                (*Rich. II*, III, ii, 54-5.)

    Is there not rain enough in the sweet heavens
    To wash it white as snow?
                (*Hamlet*, III, iii, 45-6.)

Because of the highly formalized patterns of tragic life as
they appear in Seneca, larger structural resemblances are
actually too numerous to record; a few illustrations are,
however, requisite. In *Œdipus* the father of Œdipus, like
the father of Hamlet, appears as a ghost (625 ff.), reveals
the crime, accuses the murderer, and asks for revenge. Jocasta, like Gertrude, is only secondarily guilty. Œdipus's
sorrow for his own deeds is like that of King Lear. The
blinding of Gloucester recalls the blinding of Œdipus,
even to the tearing of the hollow sockets with the nails.
The motive of incest appears in both *Œdipus* and *Hamlet*.
In *Phœnissae* the relation of Eteocles and Polynices resembles both in general situation and in treatment that between Edmund and Edgar in *King Lear*. Œdipus, like
Gloucester, desires to die by jumping from a high cliff. The
speeches of Œdipus to Antigone are much like those of
Lear to Cordelia. The choice that Jocasta is forced to
make between her sons is like that which Octavia is compelled to make in *Antony and Cleopatra* between her husband Antony and her brother Octavius. Jocasta's plea for
reconciliation between her sons is like that which Volum-
nia makes to Coriolanus. And so on in every Senecan play
in large and in small.

It may, moreover, be possible to carry this discussion into
a still wider realm. It is universally admitted that Seneca
was the preceptor of the tragic writers of the Renaissance.
One may, therefore, also inquire whether he and other stoical writers exercised special influences on the nature of
Elizabethan tragedy, influences profounder than those already considered.

The Greeks had no other conception of tragedy than that
it was the theatrical presentation of calamity and grief.
There is nothing to show that Aristotle thought of tragedy
otherwise, although undoubtedly in following his induc-
tive method he laid special stress on the stories of those
heroes who were the victims of fate. He did not regard
death as a necessary culmination of tragedy. Certainly
Seneca did not. On the other hand, the Elizabethans seem

to have believed that a tragedy must close with death, which becomes for them an inevitable end, a symbol of the final and the terrible. In their philosophy and their morals they set a greater value upon death than did the ancients. One must not be misled by the customary infliction of death, for there are many cases in Elizabethan drama in which death is cheapened.

Seneca himself was the leader of a revival of Greek tragedy. Part of the plays which pass under his name present tragedy in the same moral and philosophic terms in which it was produced by the Greeks. These are merely Greek tragedies written in a new rhetorical style and given a certain stoical coloring. I refer to such plays as *Œdipus* and *Agamemnon*. But others of the Senecan tragedies, particularly the Hercules plays and the plays based closely on Euripides, show a different conception of tribulation and disaster from that which appears in Æschylus and Sophocles. Seneca's consolation for the blows of fate is different from that of Æschylus. It is philosophic instead of religious. The naturalistic submission of Æschylus is gone. Instead of a human behavior controlled and directed within human limits and justified by veneration to the gods, Seneca introduces a stoical remedy against the badness of man's lot, which lot he regarded as inevitably bad. Æschylus did not so regard it. With Æschylus and Sophocles and with Aristotle and wherever and as long as the mighty influence of Aristotle prevailed, man was believed to have some chance for happiness. He had some chance to escape disaster, not always and in all circumstances to be sure; but the fact remains that human life was a possible enterprise normally and for most men. Man could live the life of reason. This Aristotelian doctrine belongs to the *Ethics* rather than to the *Poetics*. According to it man might come out a victor in the struggle. In Seneca man was sure to be beaten, but Seneca proposed to build up something within the heart of man which would enable him to gain a pyrrhic victory over fate. This doctrine is inherent in the stories of Hercules and Prometheus and is closely allied with titanism. The Renaissance had thus a fatalistic theory of tragedy remotely derived from Aristotle and a stoical theory implicit in some of the tragedies of Seneca.

An important conception of tragic fate, a conception arising out of Christianity and in its typical form unknown to the ancient world, is that catastrophe is the result of guilt and is a function of character and conscience. The Renaissance was thus provided with a third way of regarding tragedy. Christianity did not deny the badness of man's lot, but it tended to see the spectacle of human calamity as a result of wrongdoing. Sometimes there are attempts to reconcile the new view with the old, as in the following passage from Daniel's *Cleopatra*:

> For sencelesse sensuality, doth euer
> Accompany felicity and greatnesse,
> A fatall witch, whose charmes do leaue vs neuer,
> Till we leaue all in sorrow for our sweetnesse;
> When yet our selues must be the cause we fall,
> Although the same be first decreed on hie:
> Our errors still must beare the blame of all,
> This must it be; earth, aske not heauen why.

Of the Aristotelian, or Æschylean, kind of tragedy there

are many potent and convincing artistic examples. According to this familiar view human calamity is an irresistible and sometimes inexplicable manifestation of divine order. There is nothing to be done about it. Calamity must be accepted as the will of the gods delivered through the agency of fate. There was even no pattern for its acceptance. Man sustained calamity as best he could according to the strength or weakness of his humanity. If man was sufficiently strong in his fortitude, his endurance might become so heroic as to offset the evils of his lot. It had come to be believed that those in high station were most subject to the onslaughts of evil fate; but this idea, universal though it was, is not inherent in the conception.

With Seneca the very nature of things was disastrous, and calamity was irresistible and inescapable. There was nothing left for man but to endure, and in endurance lay his only hope. He could by learning to be indifferent both to life and death rob fate of its triumph, become a victor in attitude in his ability to resist or meet courageously. There is also a positive way of saying this. If man did acquire this self-dependence, if he became the master of himself, he became the master of himself, he became also the master of his fate.

The third idea was that man is the responsible child of God. His joys are God's gift and his misery is God's punishment. Man's character and his conduct are the sources of his weal or woe, though his disasters need not be purely punitive, for whom the Lord loveth he chasteneth.

Confronted by these three doctrines of tragedy, the Renaissance, particularly the English Renaissance, made no absolutely clear choice. Elements of all three are to be met with throughout the period of the Elizabethan drama. Writers of tragedy never thought the matter through. But in practice Shakespeare and some others gave preference to the third or Christian ideal. Shakespeare invented, or perfected the tragedy of character, and to this the world has given its approval as perhaps the greatest of his achievements. Shakespeare is often said to have established modern tragedy, but nobody would contend that Shakespeare was not influenced by and does not give voice to the doctrines of both Aristotle and Seneca. If this is true of Shakespeare, it is even more true of his contemporaries; for Marston, Chapman, Jonson, Webster, and Ford are much more archaic than is Shakespeare. Senecan conceptions are often more fundamental to them than to Shakespeare. Since Seneca carries with him the Æschylean idea, what these closer followers of Seneca often give us is the spectacle of sheer fate, opposed or unopposed by stoical resistance.

The situation here described recalls the familiar modern contrast between the views of Hegel and those of Schopenhauer. The place of tragedy in Hegel's thought is suggested by Paul Elmer More's dictum, 'Vice is the gymnasium for virtue.' Even so in Hegel tragedy is the gymnasium for happiness. His unity is a unity of integrated opposites, and out of his notion of conflict and tragedy comes triumph. Of the two opposing personages in the true tragic play each is represented as in the right. The protagonist, not being able to realize what he knows to be right without the violation of another power, will and end (equally just), is drawn to commit faults notwithstanding his morality, or rather on account of it. This contradiction must be destroyed and a solution of this conflict brought about. Moral unity must be re-established by the destruction, if need be, of what has troubled its repose. Thus, according to Hegel, the real conflict is not so much between particular interests as between moral reason in its pure idea, on the one hand, and, on the other, moral reason in its concrete manifestations in the real world and in human activity.

'There is,' says Schopenhauer, 'only one inborn error, and that is, that we exist to be happy.' If we exist, he would say, we will; if we will, we are striving to be that which we are not; and if we strive and attain only to seek something more, we cannot be happy. The will is bound to no special organ, but is everywhere present as the basic ingredient of the universe, the soul of the soul, the essence of reality. It constitutes the whole organism, is the metaphysical substratum of the phenomenal world and is not, like the intellect, dependent upon the phenomenon, but the phenomenon depends upon it. Though will scorns happiness, there must be a happiness in the exercise of will. This exaltation of will alines Schopenhauer with the stoics; whereas the longing, the unrest, the strife, the will to unity which is Hegel's absolute presupposes a world in which something can be done, such as Aristotle's world, and offers denial to Schopenhauer's doctrine of the totally evil nature of all things.

This distinction may be made clearer by an examination of the well known rubric for the analysis of tragedy based, or supposed to be based, on Aristotle. It is explained in Freytag's *Technique of the Drama* and in many other works on tragedy. According to this scheme, which is in wide popular use, we are to consider the elements of tragic story in some such terms as these: an inciting force, a rising movement, a turning-point or climax (usually said to be brought about by some form of tragic guilt), a moment of final suspense, and a catastrophe. At the very end, as a final element, there is a return to the *status quo ante,* the re-establishment of a normal *Weltanschauung.* There is no doubt that, not only the majority of tragic plots, but physical action, social event, and human life itself conform themselves well to this orderly series; for we behold action followed by reaction, growth followed by decay, and youth followed by maturity, old age, and death. Consider, for example, how consistently Plutarch's *Lives* and the series of Renaissance tragedies conform to this outline. There is an actual series, beginning, let us say, with the fall of Caius Marius. In such an opening drama the fortunes of Sulla were crescent, those of Marius cadent. In the next drama of the series Pompey was crescent and Sulla was cadent; in the next Julius Caesar was crescent and Pompey was cadent; in the next Julius Caesar fell and Brutus rose; in the next Brutus fell and Antony rose; and in the final episode of the series, Antony went down before a triumphant Octavius.

In spite of the critical and pedagogical utility of the scheme we have been discussing, I confess I have long been dissatisfied with its application to certain great tragedies and tragic heroes of the Elizabethan drama. The

thought underlying the sequence—inciting force, rising action, turning-point, declining action, and catastrophe—is certainly Aristotelian. It fits in well with the tragedy of character and conduct, which is also a tragedy of event. But this scheme can hardly be made to agree with the principles of stoicism, since it moves in the wrong direction and assumes that tragedy is only incidental in a world not normally calamitous. This kind of tragedy ends with calamity, shame, and death; whereas the stoical doctrine begins with these things as the inevitables of human life. The difference is one of degree, but the ideal of stoicism is not the avoidance of these things but the triumph over them. This question might therefore be asked: do any of the tragedies of the Elizabethan age show the dramatist elevating these stoical doctrines into an ideal in such a way as to subordinate change and accident to fortitude and self-command? If so, there will be found in that age two types of tragedy often lumped together under one definition, like the following from A. H. Thorndike's *Tragedy:*

> The action of tragedy should represent a conflict of wills, or of will with circumstance, or will with itself, and should therefore be based on the characters of the persons involved. A typical tragedy is concerned with a great personality engaged in a struggle that ends disastrously.

This definition applies with modifications to the first and larger group, those tragedies in which we behold a man or group of men making a (typically brave) struggle against an evil fate; behold them caught in the toils of an unpropitious destiny, like Œdipus, Agamemnon, Philoctetes, Ajax, or Hecuba; or see them as victims of divine justice following in the wake of their sins, like Faustus, Othello, Macbeth, Vittoria Corambona, or Beatrice Joanna.

But is there not a second kind of tragedy in which we see a man struggling for mastery of himself, struggling in order to achieve indifference to disaster and death, struggling ultimately in order to achieve a philosophic calm? It would not be a tragedy in which event would be the important thing. Indeed, it would minimize calamity and subordinate it to the way in which calamity is borne. Such an element appears in most tragedies, since part of tragic effect comes from our admiration of the heroic fortitude which arises as a concomitant. The difference would, therefore, be one of emphasis. We might illustrate this difference by comparing the Œdipus of *Œdipus Rex* with the Œdipus of the *Œdipus at Colonus.* Aged Lear struggles as does Hamlet to gain mastery over self, and he ultimately also achieves a calm; but in certain plays the development is so marked as to become an artistic principle; so much so that it would seem as if here the dramatist has come close to, if he has not actually achieved, a different type of tragedy.

The admirable spectacle of human courage, brought into tragedy from the earliest times, does not constitute a criterion. But with reference to titanism the problem is somewhat more complicated. *Prometheus* is a drama of titanism, and it is not necessary to resort to later times to find an example. There is *ab initio* no relief for Prometheus; the terms of his contract call for suffering. The same thing seems to be true of such tragedies of heroes and demi-gods as *Hercules Furens* and *Hercules Œtœus*. Hercules presents the case of enforced suffering without surrender. The tragedy of the villain-hero in the Elizabethan age, with the fascination which it exercised and still exercises over audiences, is possibly best explained as a form of the tragedy of titanism. Richard III is committed to a religion of selfish ambition; Vindici to a religion of revenge; and, as we watch their pursuit of these ungodly purposes, we may fairly ask ourselves how our attitude differs in its essence from that of the Greeks as they watched rebellion against the gods. In *Octavia* Seneca presents us with a Nero who is possibly the first example of the villain-hero. Our feelings as we follow the machinations of Iago, fascinated by his adroitness, possibly have in them an element of titanism. Richard Crookback has exalted his evil ambition to a level of as complete and irrational tyranny as the will of Zeus or the jealous rage of Juno. We cannot be said to sympathize with Richard III as he preys on the lives of innocent and guilty alike; but we do, I think, sympathize with Chapman's Bussy d'Ambois. Bussy has drawn his titanism from his own character. His will to live, his passion to enjoy, are ours, and, as we see him crash, it is in some sense ourselves who fall. Since the stoic psychologists had taught Chapman that the passions within the heart of man are mighty forces, he chose to make of Bussy a proponent of passion against reason; so that *Bussy d'Ambois* presents rebellion, not only against Christian morals, but against the fundamental principle of Aristotelian ethics, namely, that reason should rule passion. Bussy d'Ambois is neither merely a villain-hero nor an Aristotelian protagonist. He is, I think, primarily a titan, and there are other such heroes in the later Elizabethan drama. In Jacobean drama Neo-Stoicism perhaps tended to express itself in terms of titanism, but this is not the form I have in mind.

All attempts to apply to *Hamlet* the Aristotelian rubric of tragedy are, to say the least, unsatisfactory. Distinguished critics have seen in Hamlet a man dominated by fate in the form of an extreme weakness of will. To do this is to rob the most representative of all fictional characters of his representative quality. It has even been said that Hamlet's failure to stab the King while at his prayers is a manifestation of tragic weakness, which idea is absurd. Hamlet's primary quality is that he is a normal man. His universal appeal is due to the breadth of his humanity. If he is weak in will, or if he is limited by a conflict between his ideals and his realities, these shortcomings are merely those of all men. He is beset with troubles, and he is a man who cares; but to say that he is abnormal in these matters is to rob him of his universality. All men are immersed in difficulties. Most men care acutely about them, as Hamlet does, and strive to throw off the shackles of grief. Hamlet's problem is merely the greatest and most typical: 'who will deliver me from the body of this death?' Hamlet is an inquiry about the validity of human existence, the fundamental query of stoicism on foot. The representative quality of Hamlet accounts for his failure to be explained away by the numerous attempts that have been made to do so.

Hamlet struggles through an existence, very full of evil and, as regards the future, disastrous. So far as one can see, there is no question of praise or blame. He has merely confronted his life. Ultimately he finds a remedy for its evils.

He says to Horatio, 'I defy that augury which says that there is a special significance in the fall of a sparrow. I tell you that death, which has so long threatened me and caused me dread, has at last lost its terrors for me. It will come, and I have at last arrived at a state of mind in which I do not concern myself any longer about when it comes. "If it be now, 'tis not to come; if it be not to come, it will be now. If it be not now, yet will it come: the readiness is all."' This passage, which marks the end of a long struggle, seems to me to be the key to Hamlet's tragedy. He has reached his goal at last, and it is the end and aim of stoicism.

I was long puzzled by Brutus's statement at the end of *Julius Cæsar:*

> Countrymen,
> My heart doth joy that yet in all my life
> I found no man but he was true to me.

Surely an odd assertion by one who has been fooled by almost everybody in the play! But when I sought a stoical interpretation of Brutus's character, the whole thing became clear to me. Brutus meant to say that, if a man such as Marcus Brutus (or Woodrow Wilson) is true to himself, all men, even his enemies, will be true to him for evermore. It is enough that he has been Brutus.

It has seemed to me also that this doctrine of ultimate self-mastery as an ideal may help us in the interpretation of

---

Cunliffe on Seneca's Influence on Elizabethan Tragedy:

Seneca often loses sight of the individual in the universal; but the tendency of the popular drama in England would have been in the opposite direction, and in correcting this tendency Seneca seems to me to have done good service to the Elizabethan drama, giving it permanent value, for the study as well as for the stage. That Seneca misled English dramatists into violence and exaggeration cannot be denied; but these are faults which have their favourable side. If Elizabethan tragedy is sometimes too sensational, it is very seldom dull; and if its diction is sometimes extravagant, it is rarely inadequate to the needs of the situation, however tremendous the tragic crisis may be. What English tragedy would have been without the example of Seneca, it is hard to imagine; its developement from the miracle plays and moralities must have been exceedingly slow; and if the impulse had come from other European nations, it would only have been the influence of Seneca at second hand, in the case of France with exaggerated artificiality, in the case of Italy with exaggerated horrors. Even the direct imitation of Greek tragedy, in all the perfection of Sophocles, might not have been an unmixed blessing; but, after all, literary criticism is concerned, not with what might have been, but with what was; and that the influence of Seneca was paramount in the origin and developement of Elizabethan tragedy has been proved by the testimony of contemporary critics, and by the still more convincing evidence of the tragedies themselves.

John W. Cunliffe, in his The Influence of Seneca on Elizabethan Tragedy, *1893. Reprint. Archon Books, 1965.*

the character of Cleopatra. All limitations being duly recognized, the fact remains that Shakespeare presents in her in her later hours a tragic greatness comparable to the finest of his achievements. The vain, selfish, and frivolous woman rises to a height of magnanimity which, in spite of all the critics have said, is convincing. It presents the aspect of a movement upwards like that of Hamlet and Brutus, a spiritual triumph in the face of death, which you recall was the Elizabethan symbol of catastrophe:

> We'll bury him; and then, what's brave, what's
> 　noble,
> Let's do it after the high Roman fashion,
> And make death proud to take us. . . .
> My desolation does begin to make
> A better life. 'Tis paltry to be Cæsar;
> Not being Fortune, he's but Fortune's knave,
> A minister of her will: and it is great
> To do that thing that ends all other deeds;
> Which shackles accidents and bolts up change.
> 　　　　　　　　　　　　　　　　　(pp. 22-39)

Hardin Craig, "The Shackling of Accidents: A Study of Elizabethan Tragedy," in Elizabethan Drama: Modern Essays in Criticism, *edited by R. J. Kaufmann, Oxford University Press, Inc., 1961, pp. 22-40.*

Madeleine Doran

[An American educator and author, Doran is a respected scholar whose work Endeavors of Art: A Study of Form in Elizabethan Drama *(1954) is considered one of the most important studies of the subject in the latter half of the twentieth century. In the following excerpt taken from that work, she discusses the chronicle play as the foundation for Elizabethan tragedy then sketches the three main types of tragedy as determined by theme and pattern:* de casibus *tragedy, tragedy of intrigue, and domestic tragedy. She concludes that although Elizabethan drama often modified and adapted forms established by Seneca and the classical Roman school, it remained strongly influenced by these precursors.]*

It will be convenient to begin this [essay] with a brief discussion of the English chronicle play, because though it developed as a form distinct from tragedy it also provided for Marlowe and Shakespeare an important proving-ground for tragedy. The brevity of my treatment of the chronicle play is not to be taken as evidence of its unimportance, only of its relative lack of complexity from the formal point of view and also of the fullness with which other scholars have recently handled it. Important as a class competing for public interest with tragedy and comedy was "history." Tragedy in the Induction to *A Warning for Fair Women* complains that Comedy and History are more popular than she. Awareness of the distinction between history which is tragedy and history which is "chronicle," because it sets down history as such, is shown in titles: *The True Tragedy of Richard III, The Famous Victories of Henry the Fifth, The True Chronicle History of King Leir.* (Remember that this pre-Shakespearean play did not end tragically.) The editors of the Shakespeare Folio, it is true, put *Richard III* and *Richard II* into the category of the histories alongside *Henry IV* and *Henry V;*

but to separate them would have broken a historical scheme which had achieved a kind of epical continuity. The rule, besides, could not be hard and fast, for a play with tragic overtones might yet not fully qualify as tragedy. The Henry VI plays are examples. And plays on recent history, handled with less freedom than subjects from remote times, might easily seem to lie across the dividing line.

In so far as history is viewed selectively and tragically, it meets the traditional conception of tragedy; in so far as it remains merely chronicle, it is a quite different genre and has no critical warrant. Authors might have appealed to ancient authority for it, if they had wished, in the *fabula praetextata* of the Romans, the serious play on historical subjects, not necessarily tragic and generally given in celebration of some religious and patriotic festival. Although the *fabula praetextata* was treated by Diomedes and "Donatus," no specimens of it survived except the *Octavia* attributed to Seneca, and that had a tragic bias. The English chronicle play is evidently of wholly native growth. It could grow because of the combination of a popular theater and an increasing new interest in English history. That interest was partly owing, of course, to the nationalistic feeling which followed the Reformation and which was being intensified by the war with Spain. It was owing likewise to the renaissance emphasis on historical studies as a source of enlightenment about the present. In England this took on special significance because of the memory of the internecine struggles throughout the fifteenth century and the fear that without settlement of the prob-

The Swan Theater.

lem of succession the country would again lapse into civil war. Finally, history could be made to illustrate the view, cultivated by the Tudors, of a hierarchical and fixed social order as part of God's great rational plan of an orderly universe. It is interesting that the only other country which developed nontragic historical drama during the sixteenth century was Spain, a country which, like England, was developing strong national awareness, and in which the stage was even freer than the English of academic dominance.

As might be expected, English chronicle plays are likely to be the most formless of the dramas. They have no dramatic models to follow, no organized narrative plots to borrow, only the abundant and undifferentiated material of history to draw on. One way to secure point and shape is to borrow the methods of motivation and opposition from the morality play; that is what Bale does with his *King John.* Another way is to imitate tragedy: that is what the early academic authors of *Gorboduc* and *The Misfortunes of Arthur* do; what Marlowe does in *Edward II,* without the Senecanism and with deeper awareness of the springs of tragedy in character; and what Shakespeare does in *Richard III* and *Richard II.* Only too often the dramatists do nothing except to select enough striking incidents from a reign to fill up the time of a play and set them down as they come. The only selective point of view is liveliness of event, and the chief shaping attitude is patriotism. A familiar example of this type of play is *The Famous Victories of Henry the Fifth,* exploiting the legend of Henry's wild youth for comic purposes and of his French victories for patriotic ones. Another is Peele's *Edward I*—the wildest hodge-podge of romance, battle, rough comedy, *De casibus* morality (in the death of Elinor), and jingoistic patriotism in commemoration of the birth of the first Prince of Wales that the mind of man could conceive. Sometimes a single historical event provides a certain amoebic cohesion, as in *A Larum for London,* on the seige of Antwerp. But royal love and glorious war are not the only themes of the chronicle plays. Heywood makes an appeal to bourgeois sentiment in his *If You Know Not Me,* Part II, which is primarily a glorification of Sir Thomas Gresham, the wealthy London merchant who founded a school at Bishopsgate, built the Royal Exchange, lent money to the Queen, and qualified for the gallery of famous London citizens alongside Dick Whittington. Just to show what stuff a substantial Londoner is made of, when the news of one business reversal after another is brought to him as he is feasting the Russian ambassador and some lords from the court, he drinks the health of the Queen in wine enriched with a crushed pearl too costly for princes to buy. Such a man is obviously worthy of knighthood. Into the play for good measure are stirred the conspiracy of Dr. Parry, the comedy of Hobson the haberdasher, and the defeat of the Armada. Heywood always knows how to touch the sentimental chord. The First Part of *If You Know Not Me* is a rather sticky representation of the persecutions of the young Elizabeth at the hands of the wicked Mary Tudor and Philip of Spain; she is a saintly innocent over whom in her sleep guardian angels hover.

Shakespeare tried his hand at the nontragical history play with varying results. His solutions to the major problem

of unity vary and he is not always successful. The Henry VI plays remain episodic, *King John* is not very well integrated, *2 Henry IV* falls apart into two separate interests—the Falstaff comedy and the serious history. The more successful union of comedy and history in *1 Henry IV* is one solution; the treatment of history as epic pageantry in *Henry V* is another. But his great contribution is not so much in unifying any single play as in giving an epic sweep to the whole series beginning, in historical time, with *Richard II* and ending with *Richard III.* This plan, as the plays show, was clearly evolved during its execution and was not foreseen at the beginning. Nevertheless, the series completed, a partial design emerges. It is a development of what has been called the Tudor myth: the belief that Henry Bolingbroke's deposition of Richard II, an anointed king, was punished by God with a long train of civil discord that ended only with a providentially appointed savior, Henry Tudor, who could unite the two houses. Although both history and Shakespeare's sympathetic insights into opposing characters get in the way of a consistent design, and although Shakespeare's interest seems to me to be dramatically centered in character caught in political action rather than in a political lesson for its own sake, the plays do have an underlying unity of emotional response to England's fate. In them are implicit the fear of civil war, the danger of rebellion, the necessity, above all things, of authority and order, and a deeply felt patriotism.

So much for the history play as such. But history according to critical opinion, and also according to much Elizabethan practice, formed the matter of tragedy. Two of the plays in his series Shakespeare handled as tragedies, and in so doing taught himself a good deal about the structure and motivation of tragedy. Throughout his life, history, with its recurrent theme of man in a position of power and responsibility, remained the primary source of his tragic material. *Julius Caesar* and the other Roman plays, *King Lear,* and *Macbeth,* are different only in depth and complexity from *Richard III* and *Richard II,* not different in kind. In this respect, Shakespeare, like Marlowe, Chapman, and Jonson, is following the dominant tragic tradition of the sixteenth century. To that tradition we now turn.

Elizabethan tragedy may be roughly divided into three main types. according to theme and pattern: *De casibus* tragedy, or the fall of the mighty, with ambition as a chief motivating force; Italianate intrigue tragedy, with love or jealousy usually the central passion; and domestic tragedy, or the tragedy of crime in the lives of ordinary citizens. The first is derived from the traditional medieval conception of tragedy, and is perfectly consonant with Diomedes and "Donatus." The second, if the persons are of rank, also fits the grammarians' definition. The third has no traditional warrant. (pp. 112-16)

[De Casibus Tragedy]

The notion of tragedy as a fall from greatness lent itself especially well to the treatment of ambition and its consequences. The typical *De casibus* story told of the ascent to power as well as of the loss of it, and so perhaps helped to establish the pyramidal rise and fall structure characteristic of so much Elizabethan tragedy. The shape of such stories is clearly indicated in the image of the hill the Painter and the Poet use to describe the rise and predicted fall of Timon:

> This throne, this Fortune, and this hill, me-
> thinks,
> With one man beckon'd from the rest below,
> Bowing his head against the steepy mount
> To climb his happiness, would be well express'd
> In our condition. . . .
>
> When Fortune in her shift and change of mood
> Spurns down her late belov'd, all his dependants
> Which labour'd after him to the mountain's top
> Even on their knees and hands, let him slip
> down,
> Not one accompanying his declining foot.

We can watch the tragedy of power grow more complex. It starts with the medieval idea that tragedy is a fall from greatness resulting from the instability of all sublunary affairs. Descended from the Stoical pessimism of the late Roman world, this view of tragedy was formed as the *contemptus mundi* theme grew in medieval thought and found literary expression in narrative "tragedies" of the falls of princes. In some of Boccaccio's stories, however, and increasingly in the later Mirror literature, retribution for sin freely willed operated in the tragic fall side by side with unstable fortune. This association is well stated by Puttenham in his account of the origin of tragedy after tyrants came into the world:

> . . . their infamous life and tyrannies were laid open to all the world, their wickedness reproached, their follies and extreme insolencies derided, and their miserable ends painted out in plays and pageants, to shew the mutability of fortune, and the just punishment of God in revenge of a vicious and evil life [reprinted in *Elizabethan Critical Essays*, edited by G. Gregory Smith, 1904].

In the Renaissance the *De casibus* conception took dramatic form after a new infusion of Stoicism from Seneca's tragedies. In them the constant theme is the uncertain stay of worldly power.

> Quicumque regno fidit et magna potens
> dominatur aula nec leves metuit deos
> animumque rebus credulum laetis dedit,
> me videat et te, Troia. non umquam tulit
> documenta fors maiora, quam fragili loco
> starent superbi.
>
> ["Whoever trusts in sovereignty and strongly lords it in his princely hall, who fears not the fickle gods and has given up his trustful soul to joy, on me let him look and on thee, O Troy. Never did fortune give larger proof on how frail ground stand the proud."]

So Hecuba at the opening of *Troades*. But pride is unsafe not only because it stands on the uncertain ground of all things beneath the moon; it is also unsafe because it is the sin of Lucifer, the deadliest of the Seven. These two ways of regarding tragic catastrophe, the Stoic and the Christian, are both to be looked for in Elizabethan tragedy.

Actually, they do not form a simple contradiction. They can be, and sometimes were, reconciled theologically: since it was the sin of our first parents that brought the sway of irrational chance into the world, there is a sense in which even bad fortune is retribution. Fortune is a hampering circumstance of this world that men as children of Adam must live with; yet they have some choice in the degree of their subjection. To follow pride and to seek riches and power is to make themselves the more liable both to evil temptations and to the whims of Fortune; to live quietly and modestly, content with their lot, is to avoid the occasion of sins that accompany greatness and to stay clear of the realms where Fortune is most ready to operate. But we do not expect to find the dramatists often concerned with precise logical reconcilement. What is more important for them as poets is that these two views of tragic catastrophe, one regarding it as unavoidable bad fortune, the other as divine retribution for sin, were as much a matter of emotional response to the world as of philosophy. Both views were components of the Christian tradition; different men and different ages, or sometimes even the same man at different times, reflected more strongly now one, now the other, intuition about the world. In Elizabethan plays, we sometimes find the two views operating crudely, as in *Locrine,* in what seems to us unassimilated juxtaposition. More often we find something more complex, with both views present, but with an emphasis of mood in one direction or the other. These matters of emphasis are very hard to define, and philosophical consistency is not to be looked for. More of this, with illustration, as we go along.

A way to intensify tragedy came by a shift of emphasis in the Christian ethical scheme from its theological to its psychological aspect. Aristotelian-Thomistic ethics saw the attainment of virtue as the active victory of reason over the will, which in turn governed the passions in the interests of reason. Potentiality for tragedy lay in the disruptive force of runaway passion. The more narrowly ethical side of this scheme had been expressed in the morality play, with its contest between the virtues and the vices for the soul of every man. And the forms and terms of the morality play were not to be forgotten in later tragedy. But it was the psychological side of the scheme, the conflict between reason and passion, that widened the possibilities for tragedy in the Elizabethan period. In the highly developed psychological theories of the passions in which there was at the time such great interest, dramatists found means of deepening motivation and of intensifying internal conflict. This making of the conflict personal gave, in turn, new immediacy, poignancy, and subtlety to the moral problem. And the dramatists did not lose sight of the stage upon which this battle was fought. In Marlowe, Jonson, Chapman, and Shakespeare, all heirs of the *De casibus* or "Gothic" tradition, the simple old theme deepened into an awareness of the complex tensions between man's individual desires and the divine order, and hence into an awareness of profound tragic irony.

The central irony in old *De casibus* tragedy is the disproportion between the price man sets on worldly power and its actual worth. As the Elizabethans developed the theme, their sympathies and their moral emphases varied.

Ambition, as the sign of man's aspiring mind, could even be viewed as godlike; yet, however regretfully, it was rarely seen as other than ultimately dangerous. Even Tamburlaine, "the fiery thirster after sovereignty," found that

> The perfect bliss and sole felicity,
> The sweet fruition of an earthly crown

must yield before death. And Faustus'

> world of profit and delight,
> Of power, of honor, of omnipotence,

lasted but twenty-four years, a mere breathing moment before the eternity of suffering that, at the hour his term was up, he foresaw so acutely. But Tamburlaine, stilling our judgment, carrying us along emotionally on his joyous surge of magnificence, is at one extreme of the scale. At the other stands Sejanus, seen from the beginning as evil and dangerous in his arrogant impiety, holding power precariously in a world of cruel intrigue and rotten flattery; at the end, when his body is torn to bits by the mob, we are stunned by a retribution horrifying in its savagery, yet somehow fitting to the vicious and hollow world he helped to make:

> The whole, and all of what was great Sejanus,
> And, next to Caesar, did possess the world,
> Now torn and scattered, as he needs no grave—
> Each little dust covers a little part—
> So lies he nowhere, and yet often buried!

Sometimes, as I have suggested, the moral emphasis is more Stoical, sometimes more Christian. Chapman, not altogether consistently with his moral comment in prologues and speeches, suggests obliquely through the imaginative direction of his plays, that Bussy and Byron are somehow blameless in their passion for greatness—victims, like Seneca's heroes, of a world in which human aspirations count for little. This shift of sympathies is partly owing to Chapman's peculiar variation of the great man theme. His heroes are not clearly motivated by simple ambition for power. They seem to be moved as much or more by an intense ambition to be themselves in their innate greatness; they feel themselves caught in a world where man-made law is not true justice, where crooked policy takes the place of direct and honest action, where the holders of power are not always the great in spirit. But Bussy and Byron never recognize that their desire for an uninhibited exercise of "greatness" is inevitably a thrust at power. Since it is not easy to reconcile this absolute freedom to be great with any system of law and government, much less the authoritarian one Chapman himself allows, his heroes are doomed to bafflement and noble protest. Shakespeare, on the other hand, viewing ambition more traditionally, makes two of his insurgents a Richard III and an Edmund, evil troublers of the poor world's peace. A third, Macbeth, is no less capable of noble greatness than Bussy or Byron, but he is differently judged. He himself knows that he is putting his "eternal jewel" in jeopardy when he murders Duncan to get the power that lures him so fatally. But that danger seems a long way off. He has uneasy premonitions that he cannot trammel up nearer consequence:

> . . . that but this blow

Might be the be-all and the end-all here,
But here, upon this bank and shoal of time,
We'd jump the life to come.

What irony! For he loses both the here and the hereafter. We pity him, not because he cannot free himself from the shackles on his ambition, but that in breaking them he but binds himself to damnation.

Nevertheless, the ancient conception of tragedy as a fall from greatness underlies all these plays and, however differently the responsibility for failure is assessed, and however differently power and greatness are valued, the idea lends a constant irony of its own—to Bussy's tragedy no less than to Macbeth's. Worldly greatness is seen as both a fascination and a fatality. (pp. 119-23)

In a society whose equilibrium was felt to be so precarious, the exercise of power was of the most vital concern. Think how many Elizabethan and Jacobean tragedies have some form of it as a theme—the lust for power, the corrupting effects of power, both on the holders of power and on their followers, the conflict between the drive and insight of a great man and the limitations of authority and of man-made laws. There are the early plays from legendary British history on the dangers of overweening ambition and of civil war (*Gorboduc, Misfortunes of Arthur, King Leir, Locrine*); the biographical Mirror plays on a simple rise and fall pattern (*Cromwell, Stukely,* the Jane Shore story central to Heywood's *Edward IV,* the Queen Elinor story in Peele's *Edward I*); the plays in which the reign of an English king is given a tragic pattern (*Troublesome Reign of King John, True Tragedy of Richard III,* Marlowe's *Edward II,* Shakespeare's *Richard III, Richard II,* and parts of the *Henry VI* plays); the "conqueror" plays owning *Tamburlaine* as a progenitor (*Selimus, Alphonsus of Aragon, Battle of Alcazar*); the many tragedies on Roman history, especially the exciting period of struggle for power at the end of the republic and the beginning of the empire (*Caesar's Revenge, Nero,* Chapman's *Caesar and Pompey,* Shakespeare's *Julius Caesar, Antony and Cleopatra,* and *Coriolanus,* Jonson's *Sejanus* and *Catiline,* Heywood's *Rape of Lucrece*); and the tragedies boldly drawn from the lives of contemporary, or nearly contemporary, historical figures (Marlowe's *Massacre at Paris,* Chapman's *Bussy d'Ambois, Chabot,* and his two Byron plays, the anonymous *Sir John Van Olden Barnavelt*). We must add, too, several plays that do not exactly fit into any of these categories: Marlowe's *Dr. Faustus,* Shakespeare's *Timon, Macbeth, King Lear,* and even, in part, *Hamlet.* Power in a far wider sense than the merely political is the motive of Faustus. *Timon,* though it is not concerned with the exercise of power, states in its barest terms the personal problem of the hollow service that goes with power and wealth—the service of the summer-birds that fly when winter comes; and the play is built on the great man pattern, the rise alluded to and the fall enacted. Though power is not the major issue of *Hamlet,* it is nevertheless a crucial issue, since it is responsible for the state of things that Hamlet must set right; and the play, as I have already suggested, is full of echoes of the *De casibus* theme. *King Lear* is not so clearly recognized at first as of this progeny, for it is at the extreme of complexity from the old simple Mirror tale. Nevertheless, it has power as one of its principal themes and plays on it in different keys, as *Hamlet* does on death. *Macbeth* is the full flowering of *De casibus* tragedy, at the end of a straight line from let us say *Richardus Tertius;* deepened and enriched, but with the old elements clearly marked. Power is even one of the motives of *Titus Andronicus.* Except, then, for *Romeo and Juliet* and *Othello,* and in part *Titus Andronicus* and *Hamlet,* all of Shakespeare's tragedies are to a greater or less degree in the tradition of Gothic tragedy. Like Chapman and Jonson, Shakespeare carries over into a time when the focus in tragedy is shifting elsewhere.

There are two specially interesting things to remark about this tragedy of ambition or power. One is that it is based on history, real or imaginary. The reader will recall the critic's prejudice, ultimately based on Aristotle, in favor of historical subjects for tragedy because they have verisimilitude. The critics reasoned that an audience would expect to have heard of such great misfortunes and would not therefore find an invented story—or at least a story with imaginary names—credible. Since this rule for historical subjects appears in Evanthius, one can expect that it was thoroughly familiar.

The other point to be noted is the very un-Aristotelian conception of many of the tragic heroes in this list. The grammarians had nothing to say about the hero beyond his social position. There is no attempt in many of the plays to make the hero "midway between good and bad." In about a third of those I have listed above he is frankly bad, a dangerous seeker, through means ruthless or cunning, of tyrannous power. He may excite a good deal of admiration for his large imagination of power and for his boldness in going after it (as with Tamburlaine and Richard III), but he can hardly be taken as a good man erring through weakness or a mistake in judgment. There is no true *hamartia* in the Mirror tradition. The tragedy lies in the instability of power in itself. True, a man may commit crimes which provoke retribution and for which he will inevitably pay, but to induce him to commit crimes is only one of the tricks false Fortune plays on him. And the good, moreover, who trust to her fall as well. Very powerful reinforcement to interest in the careers of tyrants came in the horrid fascination to Elizabethans of Machiavellian political doctrine. It gave new vividness of realism to the tragedy of ambition, so long familiar. Judging by the standards of Aristotle, who says there is nothing tragic in the fall of a wicked man, we do not find Muly Morocco, King John or Richard III, Sejanus or Catiline, satisfactory tragic heroes. Macbeth is perhaps the only villain-hero who fully arouses both pity and fear. This is only to say that the Elizabethan tragedy of ambition is not in its conception Aristotelian. For we must, I think, admit that this type of hero had immense fascination for the Elizabethans themselves. Puttenham assumes, in the passage I quoted a few pages back, that tragedy originated in the necessity of reproving the tyrannous abuse of power.

There are, of course, many heroes in this tragedy of power who come near, or actually fit, the Aristotelian pattern—figures like Edward II and Richard II, Cassius, Antony, and Coriolanus, figures whom we sympathize with as well as condemn, and whose ends, exciting pity, as well as fear,

give rise to a more complex irony than do the falls of the merely wicked. But it is necessary to point out the long endurance of a different tradition, and to point out, too, the force of horror its simpler irony might have. Jonson with Sejanus is in this respect closer to medieval tradition than Shakespeare with Macbeth or Coriolanus.

Medieval tradition and the theory of the grammarians (partly by its omissions) combined, then, to produce one of the major types of Elizabethan tragedy, the tragedy concerned with ambition and power. It received reinforcement, too, from revived classical tragedy, at least as understood. The play of Sophocles most widely read—almost certainly because Aristotle had discussed it so fully as a perfect tragedy—was *Oedipus Rex.* To the Renaissance, Oedipus became, in a most un-Greek interpretation, the classic type of dangerously ambitious man, and his fall was read as a lesson to the mighty. The lesson was thought to be clearly seen in his reappearance as old, helpless, and blind in the *Phoenissae* of Euripides and of Seneca. Very rarely do any references occur to the wonderful *Oedipus at Colonus,* in which Oedipus has expiated his unwitting crime and achieves in his death a mysterious power for good. Among the favorite plays of Euripides were *Hecuba* and *Troades,* both on the greatest of all *De casibus* themes, the destruction of Troy; and *Phoenissae,* on the fatal struggle between the sons of Oedipus, Eteocles and Polyneices, for the possession of Thebes. It is perhaps suggestive that the one adaptation of Euripides to be published in England was of the *Phoenissae,* Gascoigne and Kinwelmersh's *Jocasta* (1566). Lodovico Dolce's Italian version of a Latin translation of Euripides had Senecanized the play with gloomy reflections on the instability of Fortune, the dangers of ambition, and the superior desirability of the simple life; the English translators of the Italian further emphasized the same themes. This play, with the theme of ambition centered in civil war, was clearly thought by Elizabethans to have a special relevance to their times. Their own early attempts at classical tragedy—*Gorboduc* and *The Misfortunes of Arthur*—make use of native subject matter to point the same lesson.

I said that Dolce's *Giocasta* was Senecanized. Seneca contributed, of course, the predominant classical influence to *De casibus* tragedy. Of the ten plays generally regarded in the Renaissance as his, one, *Troades,* is a straight tragedy on fallen glory, and four have ambition or tyranny as themes; it is central in *Phoenissae* and *Octavia,* subsidiary in *Oedipus* and *Thyestes.* All ten of the plays make much of the mutability of Fortune. English *De casibus* tragedy does not organize itself in Senecan fashion, but it finds in Senecan tragedy powerful reinforcement of familiar themes. . . . [This] is surely an important reason, among others, why the Renaissance took Seneca rather than the Greek dramatists to its heart. He talked about things Englishmen of the sixteenth century knew from historical experience and long moral discipline to be dangerous and fraught with possible tragic consequences. Moreover, he brought poetical power to the expression of that Stoical pessimism latent in much Christian thought. In a world in which the cards are stacked against men, a man must not look for amelioration in circumstance. His chance for happiness lies in learning to see the world for what it is and in enduring it courageously. This is not quite the way out of Christian asceticism; it was a way more acceptable to the Renaissance. A man may live in the world and yet be superior to its lures and its blows. The way lies in self-knowledge and self-dependence.

The Elizabethans would have found in Seneca, too, a warrant for the villainous hero. His characters are on the whole an unlovely lot. And they are un-Aristotelian, in having no flaw that can be rightly interpreted in Aristotle's sense. Medea, Phaedra, Atreus, and Clytemnaestra are so possessed by furious passion that they are hardly responsible agents. Modern taste finds it hard to respond to them with pity. Yet Seneca probably conceived of them as pitiable in the very helplessness with which they are driven by their passions of jealousy, love, or desire for revenge. The relatively passive Hercules, in *Hercules Oetaeus,* who merely suffers and commits no crime, is instructive. The killing of Lichas in the extremity of torture he suffers from the shirt of Nessus cannot count as a crime. Hercules does arouse pity, yet his case is only an exaggeration of that of the other Senecan heroes in that they are all essentially victims of misfortune, a misfortune which drives them to crime. Professor Craig [in *Philosophical Quarterly* XIX, 1940] points out the element of titanism in the Hercules story and reminds us of the fascination that titanism must have had for the Elizabethans. This titanism is expressed in one mood in frankly villainous heroes like Richard III and Selimus, in another in Chapman's more complicated heroes, whose passionate drives are sympathetically conceived and who, like the mighty Hercules, go down without surrender.

> Prop me, true sword, as thou hast ever done!
> The equal thought I bear of life and death
> Shall make me faint on no side; I am up;
> Here like a Roman statue I will stand
> Till death hath made me marble.

Italianate Tragedy of Intrigue

Besides tyranny, Seneca has another repeated theme in his tragedies, revenge incited by jealousy, and this is a theme which leads us into the second great class of English renaissance tragedy, the Italianate tragedies of intrigue centered about crimes of passion. The revenge theme furnished invaluable dramatic motivation to English dramatists; though they shifted its moral implications, they never let go of it as a dramatic device until the closing of the theaters. They did not have to look to Seneca for it, of course, for it was often a component of narrative Mirror tragedies, it was familiar through their favorite, Ovid, it was a notorious feature of contemporary Italian *mores,* and it evidently had a good deal of vitality in their own turbulent lives. But that Seneca impressed them with its dramatic possibilities is clear enough from the early imitative tragedies like *Gorboduc, The Misfortunes of Arthur, Locrine,* and *Titus Andronicus,* and from the revengeful ghosts that continue to haunt the stage into the seventeenth century. Even in the most thoroughly Senecan of English plays, the imitation of the pattern of action is not close, as it is in continental Senecan tragedy, for Seneca was too narrow in plot, too static for English taste, which liked plenty of action as well as plenty of words. Neverthe-

less, Seneca furnished them with a motive for opposition and counter-action out of which exciting conflict might come.

Many Elizabethan tragedies apply this revenge motive, as Seneca does in *Thyestes,* to the favorite theme of ambition (e.g., the early academic tragedies, *Locrine, True Tragedy of Richard III,* Shakespeare's *Richard III* and *Julius Caesar*); and a few Jacobean tragedies do the same (e.g., *Hamlet,* Jonson's *Sejanus* and *Catiline*). But there is another longer-lived line of revenge play where the central themes are love and jealous hatred, as they are in Seneca's *Medea, Agamemnon, Phaedra,* and the two Hercules plays. With these revenge plays we may associate other plays of passionate crime and intrigue where revenge does not figure at all. I am not, that is, treating "revenge" as a class of tragedy, but as a motive which frequently operates in tragedy of two different sorts, the rise-and-fall tragedy of ambition, and the Italianate tragedy of intrigue. There is recognizable in the latter class a different line of tragic interest, with different emphasis. Professor Farnham [in *The Medieval Heritage of Elizabethan Tragedy,* 1936] makes *The Spanish Tragedy* the father of it. A very early example is the Inns of Court drama of *Gismond of Salerne* (1567-68), later revised by Robert Wilmot, one of the original authors, as *Tancred and Gismund* (1591-92); but *The Spanish Tragedy* appears to have started the new fashion on the public stage.

The Spanish Tragedy is primarily a lively play of intrigue, psychologically motivated, in which there is a love affair (as well as the motive of ambition) and in which revenge within revenge cleverly managed furnishes exciting action. Among Elizabethan plays of its descent I should include Kyd's *Soliman and Perseda,* the early *Hamlet,* Marlowe's *Jew of Malta,* Shakespeare's *Titus Andronicus* and *Hamlet,* Marston's *Antonio's Revenge.* The major Jacobean plays in this line are Shakespeare's *Othello,* Marston's *Insatiate Countess* and perhaps his *Sophonisba,* Tourneur's *Revenger's Tragedy* and *Atheist's Tragedy,* Beaumont and Fletcher's *Maid's Tragedy,* Webster's *White Devil* and *Duchess of Malfi,* Middleton's *Women Beware Women* and *Changeling;* the major Caroline ones, Ford's *Broken Heart* and *'Tis Pity She's a Whore.* Many lesser-known plays, besides, fall into this general class. There are many differences, obviously, among the plays in this list. Some, like *Titus Andronicus, Sophonisba,* and *Hamlet,* cross the lines of the other big class, the tragedy of power. (*Bussy D'Ambois* and the *Revenge of Bussy,* which I put into the other class, might likewise, for the same reason, have been included here.) Political intrigue is not absent from many of these tragedies, especially the earlier ones, yet it is usually only one among other motives, and the movement of the action is not the rise-and-fall pattern. Most of the tragedies in the list have love, lust, or jealousy as the motivating passion; but, though none of these passions is dominant, though present, in *Hamlet* or *The Jew of Malta,* both plays are clearly descendants of *The Spanish Tragedy.* Revenge figures in most of the plays, though not centrally in all. Nevertheless, all these plays belong in this same loosely conceived class because they are all tragedies of intrigue motivated by passion, they nearly all have a romantic interest, and when they achieve tragic irony it is of a different sort from that of the tragedy of ambition centered about the theme of power. One may, with large reservations, include even *Romeo and Juliet,* for though revenge does not figure centrally in it and though it does not issue in crime, it is at least a tragedy of love and intrigue quite unrelated to *De casibus* tragedy.

The type of story on which these plays are based is to be found in the Italian *novelle,* which were turned out in quantities in the Renaissance. . . . In English there were numerous collections—free translations, usually with considerable moralizing additions, of Italian tales or their French versions. . . . There were, besides, lesser collections and single tales. Spanish authors likewise translated and imitated the Italian tales and produced collections of their own, the finest being Cervantes' *Novelas ejemplares* (1613); this added to the Italian and French *novelle* a rich source, on the whole more suitable for romance than for tragedy, to be drawn on by later Jacobean and Caroline dramatists.

Another source of the same type of story was in Italian tragedy. Although Italian poets leaned pretty heavily on Seneca and on Roman history for themes, some, like Giraldi, went to the *novelle* for more up-to-date stories. Seven of Giraldi's nine tragedies (published posthumously in Venice in 1583) are based on his own prose tales. *Epitia,* for instance, is based on his fifth novel of the eighth decade; the story, through Belleforest, reached Whetstone and ultimately Shakespeare, who dramatized it as *Measure for Measure.* There is a probability that Shakespeare knew the Italian tale and even play as well as both the narrative and dramatic versions of Whetstone. Another example is Luigi Groto's *La Hadriana* (1578), recognized as possibly influencing *Romeo and Juliet* through the medium of some intermediate English play. We are not very sure of the channels by which the Italian drama influenced the English. We know that Italian actors visited England; whether they acted anything but *commedie dell'arte* we do not know. But it is perhaps unlikely, since the tragedies and the *commedie erudite* were written for the academies and the courts. There is no reason, however, why some of the plays may not have been available in printed copies brought from Italy. Social and literary commerce with Italy was abundant, and animadversions against the influence, literary or moral, of Italian drama imply that it was widely known. Certainly, a number of English comedies are directly traceable to Italian originals. And many English plays, either tragedy or comedy, have features so like Italian plays that we are tempted to posit for their conception and design some immediate Italian source. On the whole, however, the evidence is more extensive and more convincing for comedy than for tragedy. About the *novelle,* at any rate, we can be sure enough.

Now the *novelle* are particularly suitable for dramatic plundering—for comedy, tragedy, or romance. Any reader of Boccaccio's tales knows that those centered around romantic adventure are told chiefly for their narrative point. Complication leads to some sort of neat unraveling, happy or unhappy. They have, besides, an air of verisimilitude; they are located at a particular place, often at a particular time, and the names appear to be those of real peo-ple. Bandello and Giraldi specialize in tales of passion fit for tragedy, with emphasis on violence and horror, Giraldi especially so. All these things make the *novelle* acceptable to English dramatists. It is easy to see, however, how tragedy based on these stories takes on a different color and tone from the tragedy of ambition, and how it sometimes slips away from even that broad conception of tragedy formulated by the grammarians. For one thing, social position ceases to be so essential to the irony. For another, an invented plot may serve as well as a true one. For still another, a romantic intrigue plot may by a clever turn be brought to a happy conclusion. Indeed, that is the inevitable direction of this sort of tragedy, as seen in the tragicomedies and romances of the later Jacobean and Caroline dramatists. Even revenge comes no longer to insure an unhappy ending; compare Middleton and Rowley's *Fair Quarrel* and Webster's *Devil's Law Case.* A rather verbal, posturing "honor" is often satisfied with something considerably short of killing. But this is at the end of things.

Italianate intrigue tragedy was bloody enough in its heyday in the 90's and early 1600's. And it was, too, generally satisfying to the traditional definition of tragedy in that it dealt with the turbulent affairs of illustrious persons and ended in death. It was also, we must believe, capable of satisfying renaissance notions of classical principle. An illuminating instance of this is found in De Nores' *Poetica.* He is perhaps the most rigidly academic and the least imaginative of all the Italian Aristotelians. He is at once so sure of his correct classicism and actually so imperceptive that one can be certain his departures from classical intention are wholly unconscious; they are especially valuable, therefore, in revealing tastes of his time which he did not recognize but from which he could not escape. For each of the major literary forms, epic, tragedy, and comedy, he chooses a tale from Boccaccio and shows how it might be worked up according to Aristotelian principles. (pp. 124-34)

It is interesting to note that the first tragedy of romantic intrigue in England, *Gismond of Salerne,* borrows a similar story from Boccaccio, the one in which Tancred revenges himself on his daughter's secret love by having her lover murdered and his heart carried to her in a cup; she puts poison in it and drinks the blood. That the authors thought they were writing tragedy in the classical manner is suggested by their giving it a Senecan framework of choruses and a fury and a Senecan tone of moralizing rhetoric. Giraldi's *Orbecche,* enormously influential, is of the same type, a story of secret love and savage revenge appearing first in his *Ecatommithi.* If a renaissance dramatist was well enough read in the Greeks to know that violent deeds rarely appeared on the stage, and if he recalled Horace's prohibition, he could appeal in Seneca to Hercules' slaughter of his children or the piecing together of the mangled remains of Hippolytus. Whether Seneca's plays were written only for declamation or were actually produced is an unsettled academic question of no relevance here, since in any case renaissance authors found example for their own deeds of horror in his. Giraldi was shrewd enough to perceive that Aristotle had not actually prohibited the showing of violent scenes and he used this omission as authority for following modern taste. Horrible deeds, then, were a recognized component of tragedy and the shock of bloody spectacle taken as an equivalent to Aristotle's tragic wonder. Shakespeare's *Titus Andronicus,* though complicated by the theme of ambition and not based on a *novella,* is clearly in this same line of tragedy. It is second to none in horror and perhaps seemed as "classical," except in regard to time and place, as *Orbecche* or *Gismond.*

But the Italianate tragedy of intrigue often fell away from the traditional conception of tragedy. The ways in which it did so may be briefly examined. In the first place, historical truth was of less importance than in the tragedy of ambition with political figures as characters. The prejudice persisted, however, and it is probable that many dramatists borrowing the plots of *novelle* thought they were following true tales when they were not. Giraldi and Bandello both told theirs for true. Bandello, by means of references to places and famous people he had met and of considerable realistic detail, invested his with an air of great verisimilitude. In translating Bandello's stories, Belleforest praised them especially for "la verité de l'histoire." Some few, of course, were based on fact, the story of the Duchess of Malfi, for instance. The interesting thing is that a story like this is indistinguishable from one that is pretty certainly fiction, like that of Romeo and Julietta. The central story of Bianca Capella in *Women Beware Women* is grounded in historical fact; the subplot is from a tale that makes the claim of truth—Alexander Hart's *True History of the Tragic Loves of Hippolito and Isabella, Neapolitans.* Middleton perhaps thought he was also using a true tale for *The Changeling,* borrowed from the story of Alsemero and Beatrice-Joanna in John Reynolds' *The Triumph of God's Revenge against Murder* (1621). Perhaps indeed he was, for the source of Reynolds' story is not known. How can we tell if Giraldi's story of the Moor who at the instigation of his ensign murdered his Venetian wife Disdemona is true or not? If a fictional story can pass for true, then the inhibition against inventing plots for tragedy is removed. Later plays do, indeed, contain more fictional plots than earlier ones. Clearly, standards of verisimilitude are less exacting in the requirement of historical truth for tales of love than for tales of princely ambition.

The second way in which Italianate tragedy modified the traditional conception was in sometimes having heroes of lower rank. When the tragic irony is not centered, as in the tragedy of ambition, in the distance of a man's fall, his rank ceases to be of quite so much importance. Bianca Capella in *Women Beware Women* is a merchant's wife; for this reason Professor Adams [in his *English Domestic or Homiletic Tragedy,* 1943] treats the play as a domestic tragedy. But Bianca's love affair is with Francesco de' Medici, Duke of Florence, and the management and tone of the play put it with other Italianate intrigue plays, e.g., *The White Devil,* where the same duke figures. It is not different in any essential particular of setting or handling of plot from *The Changeling,* where the characters are hardly noble either, but at least military and so outside the range of domestic tragedy. Similar observations about rank and tone might be made of Ford's *'Tis Pity.* I should treat it as somewhat debased romantic tragedy, whereas Mr. Adams treats it as decadent domestic tragedy. Since

these classes are in any case imposed after the fact, there is no reason to quarrel; it all depends from which end one starts. The difference of opinion is testimony to the point I am making, namely that in tragedies of romantic intrigue rank is of less crucial significance than in tragedies of power.

Most important of all is the movement towards the happy ending. An intermediate stage (not necessarily so in time, but so in logic) is the tragedy with the double ending that Aristotle deplores, punishment for the bad, reward for the good. Giraldi justifies it as being pleasing to the taste of his own day. He tries it in at least two of his plays, *Altile* and *Selene;* they are still tragedies because they deal with the lamentable affairs of illustrious persons. In *Epitia* and several other "tragedies" he carries the process a step further and has the evil-doers forgiven; this is possible since no actual crime has been committed. In *Epitia* as in *Measure for Measure,* the heroine's brother, whom the perjured governor has ordered executed, turns out to be not dead after all; the heroine is so overjoyed to find him alive that she pleads for the villain's life and they all live happily ever after. This is instructive. We are in the region where tragedy and comedy are cut out of the same cloth. The major plot of *Much Ado,* for instance, is from a story of Bandello's in which malicious plotting on the part of a rival for the heroine's hand and of his evil accomplice is made to produce only mishap, not irrevocable criminal action, and therefore does not preclude a happy outcome. Romantic plots which put a premium on the strangeness and complication of event for its own sake naturally tend towards this kind of solution. This type of plot had always been known and popular in England, but in the later years of Elizabeth's reign it yielded somewhat to more sharply distinguished tragedy and comedy. However, very early in James's reign, the current set strongly in the direction of tragi-comedy.

But when the Italianate tragedy of intrigue is still tragedy, how does it differ in essential tragic feeling from the rise-and-fall tragedy of ambition? In the early tragedies of romantic intrigue, interests appropriate to the murder mystery—plentiful action, suspense leading up to a deed of horror, shocking crime—are apt to take the place of any deeper questioning about man's destiny. *The Spanish Tragedy, Soliman and Perseda, Tancred and Gismund, The Jew of Malta, Titus Andronicus,* and other Elizabethan tragedies of this sort strike us as primarily lively thrillers, although we sometimes catch glimpses of a deeper purpose, as in the pathos of the distraught Hieronimo or in the mordancy of Barabas. The exciting force in this kind of plot is frequently love or jealous hatred, mixed or not with political intrigue. Bandello's 214 tales contain sixty-six tales of adultery and kindred themes (excluding those involving the clergy) and nineteen tales of the tribulations of love ending unhappily. The largest class in Giraldi's collection is likewise illicit love—twenty-eight out of 110. Here, of course, in the contemplation of the unhappiness that comes upon men and women in their relations with each other, is a chance to deepen tragic feeling, and this was done in the great Jacobean plays. The considerable interest in psychological studies around the turn of the century, especially in pathological mental states, gave dramatists the means of rendering human behavior more richly and subtly. Another line of interest growing strong at the same time, for social and literary reasons that I need not develop here, was the interest in satire; it helped set a tone in the treatment of problems of sex. Moreover, in their French and English versions, the source stories had to be quarried out from layers of moralizing on sin, especially on adultery. The interests in psychology and in satire joined hands in the favorite malcontent type, with his bitter wit exposing all the ugliness of the society around him. The result, at its best, of this amalgam of psychology, satire, and moral gloom is a tragedy of intensely conceived characters—not always attractive and often unbalanced emotionally—caught in an evil world of adultery, incest, and murder.

How are we to take tragedy like this? A tragic flaw will hardly describe what is wrong with heroes and heroines like Vittoria or Evadne or Bianca Capella, not to mention the Insatiate Countess, Brachiano, or Vindici. Nor is the response indicated so often one of pity and fear as of fascination or disgust or both together. These attitudes are most strongly felt in Marston, Tourneur, and Webster, though in Webster with much qualification. Morbid fascination and disgust find their extreme expression in *The Revenger's Tragedy.* (If the tone of disgust at sexual licence is as strong in *Hamlet* as in *The Revenger's Tragedy,* it is less crude, less morbid, not exclusive of pity.) Though Middleton's world is as ugly as Marston's or Tourneur's, he has more emotional detachment than they in regarding it. In Beaumont and Fletcher plentiful statement of attitude takes the place of actual feeling about it. Ford has lost the disgust, but kept the fascination. As with much of the tragedy of power, it is evident that Aristotelian canons, either of the nature of the tragic hero, or of the emotions appropriate to tragedy, do not generally apply. Shakespeare in *Othello,* in the nobility of his hero, and in the catharsis of emotion he effects, is rather the exception than the rule. It is true that we feel a compelling admiration for the boldness and vitality of many of the principal characters in these plays—people like Beatrice Joanna, Evadne, Flamineo, and De Flores—but we should find it hard, I think, to pity many of them; nor are we usually asked to. The Duchess of Malfi, who has goodness and greatness in her as well as intensity, is a significant non-Shakespearean exception, and perhaps Vittoria is, too, in a different way.

Webster, though he is in this line of tragedy, is more complicated and harder to define than the others. His dark world is lit by a splendor that evokes something more than morbid fascination and disgust. Even creatures like Brachiano, Lodovico, and Flamineo shine in darkness. However wicked they may be, there is defiance and a kind of glory in the courage with which they meet death. In this respect Vittoria is akin to the Duchess. If the Duchess is Duchess of Malfi still, Vittoria in her death will not shed one base tear. There is something here, in a different realm of action, like the defiant courage of Chapman's heroes. Simple vitality asserts itself in a world that is doomed. The Duchess of Malfi cries out in justified protest against Ferdinand's jealously revengeful and diseased "honor," which she has supposedly violated by her clandestine marriage:

> Why might not I marry?
> I have not gone about in this to create
> Any new world, or custom. . . .

> Why should only I
> Of all the other princes of the world
> Be cased up, like a holy relic? I have youth
> And a little beauty.

But Vittoria's defense, in so far as she deigns to make any answer to the charges against her of adultery and of complicity in murder, is akin to the Duchess':

> Sum up my faults, I pray, and you shall find
> That beauty and gay clothes, a merry heart,
> And a good stomach to a feast are all,
> All the poor crimes that you can charge me with.

If the world is doomed, then such vitality and such courage must evoke pity, a pity that transcends the lines of good and evil. In Webster, there is a hint, afar off, that all the sons of men are to be pitied. In the tragic wonder he evokes, Webster, with Shakespeare, comes closer than his contemporaries to Aristotelian tragedy; but in his moral and philosophical implications he is far more Stoical than Aristotelian.

Different as these Jacobeans may be in their separate emphases, there is one way in which they can be viewed as part of a common tradition. In their tragedies, Death and the Devil are common symbols. As in the tragedy of power a little grave is the end man's glory comes to, so in the tragedy of sex the foulness of the skeleton is the end of woman's beauty. The ironic contrast is not to power, as in the other tragedy, but to the life of the senses, and, occasionally, to a beauty and love beyond that level. But in any case death opposes a different form of vitality from the energy of ambition. Death is present in the midst of life, and the Devil has taken over the world. There is a significant difference here, however, from the Christian tradition. The symbol opposed to Death in the morality plays (the Virtues in some form, or a Good Angel) and by whose aid man might save himself, has largely disappeared. Man, therefore, in these plays lives "in what a shadow, or deep pit of darkness." If there is to be any assertion of value in such a world, it can only be endurance in life and courage in confronting death. Antony, Cleopatra, Clermont, and Cato in courageous death remove themselves beyond the caprice of Fortune:

> . . . and it is great
> To do that thing that ends all other deeds,
> Which shackles accidents, and bolts up change.

As Clermont puts it:

> Since I could skill of man, I never liv'd
> To please men worldly, and shall I in death,
> Respect their pleasures, making such a jar
> Betwixt my death and life, when death should
>   make
> The consort sweetest, th'end being proof and
>   crown
> To all the skill and worth we truly own?

He will follow his admired master, the Guise:

> Now, then, as a ship
> Touching at strange and far-removed shores,

Her men ashore go, for their several ends,
Fresh water, victuals, precious stones, and pearl,
All yet intentive (when the master calls,
The ship to put off ready) to leave all
Their greediest labours, lest they there be left
To thieves or beasts, or be the country's slaves:
So, now my master calls, my ship, my venture,
All in one bottom put, all quite put off,
All gone under sail, and I left negligent,
To all the horrors of the vicious time,
The far-remov'd shores to all virtuous aims,
None favouring goodness, none but he respect-
    ing
Piety or manhood—shall I here survive,
Not cast me after him into the sea,
Rather than here live, ready every hour
To feed thieves, beasts, and be the slave of
    power?
I come, my lord! Clermont, thy creature, comes.

Cato by his suicide conquers conquering Caesar. Yet if the world is not just one of unhappy circumstance, but one of positive evil, actually the Devil's world, without chance of redemption, then there is hardly even a victory in stoical courage. The noble Pompey, treacherously caught and stabbed, questions eternal justice:

See, heavens, your sufferings! Is my country's
    love,
The justice of an empire, piety,
Worth this end in their leader? Last yet, life,
And bring the gods off fairer: after this
Who will adore or serve the deities?

He hides his face in his robe and submits to his assassins. Middleton's De Flores, in a Christian setting, takes his mistress boldly to Hell.

Make haste, Joanna, by that token to thee [i.e.,
    the wound he had given her],
Canst not forget, so lately put in mind;
I would not go to leave thee far behind.

Alsemero has prepared the way with a grim image:

. . . rehearse again
Your scene of lust, that you may be perfect
When you shall come to act it to the black audi-
    ence,
Where howls and gnashings shall be music to
    you.
Clip your adulteress freely, 'tis the pilot
Will guide you to the *mare mortuum*,
Where you shall sink to bottoms fathomless.

And Webster's Bosola dies in a mist, on a voyage of doom.

Shakespeare uses the same symbols of Death, the Devil, and Hell in *Othello*, and Othello makes a stoical speech of courage in the face of death. But the judgment on himself is without defiance. There is a note of humility in Othello scarcely to be found elsewhere in these plays, unless it is in Bosola. Above all, the play is different in effect from most of the others because in it there is goodness and redemption as well as ruin and death.

To summarize the ironic implications of these two major lines of tragedy we have been considering: The special irony in the tragedy of ambition, where it is fully realized, is in the final helplessness of man, in spite of his godlike aspirations for power, before an inexorable universe. The special irony in the tragedy of sex is in man's betrayal by his passions to a world of evil. A supreme realization of this irony is in *Othello,* where a man rich in all that we most admire in character—emotional depth, integrity, idealism, frankness, and generosity—is led by his very largeness into self-betrayal by the basest of passions, and led by a man who is the epitome of meanness, cynicism, malice, and intelligence directed toward evil ends. A more characteristic realization of the irony, however, is perhaps found in other Jacobeans, where men less good and great are betrayed by vanity or lust or simply a desire for life, as with the Duchess of Malfi, to a world in which death is supreme.

Domestic Tragedy

The third major class of tragedy is domestic tragedy. It has been seen as a direct derivation from the morality play, especially of the Prodigal Son type. The general theme of the Prodigal Son plays—e.g., *Mundus et Infans, Lusty Juventus, Nice Wanton,* Gascoigne's *Glass of Government*—is that the temptations of the world lead to sin, the wages of which are death, but that true repentance and reformation of life may move God to mercy. The hero in the plays is a young man or woman whose social position is not in itself important and whose problem of salvation is intensely personal. He is a descendant, of course, of Everyman, and, in this view, he prepares the way for the tragedy of common men.

Another way to look at domestic tragedy, however, is to see it simply as the dramatization of a class of stories, which, like chronicles, romances, *novelle,* or any other sort of lively story, looked like promising material to be put on the stage. Stories of contemporary crime would have a special appeal as thrillers, and it would have been strange if the popular stage had neglected to exploit them. On this view, the trace in many of these tragedies of a moral play or homiletic scheme of temptation, sin, repentance, and punishment looks less like the original impulse to the plays than like a conventional moral pattern such subjects would attract. This is not to say that domestic tragedy did not owe a good deal to the morality, but only to shift the emphasis in viewing the relationship. One cannot be dogmatic about the matter or make an inclusive statement about all the plays in the class, but certainly some of them, especially *Arden, Woman Killed,* and *The Witch of Edmonton* suffer distortion if viewed as dramatized homilies.

Domestic tragedy deals with the troubled affairs in the private lives of men of less than noble birth—gentlemen, farmers, merchants. It is a small and fairly well-defined class; the action is most frequently a murder, committed for greed or love, the setting is usually English and realistic, the basis for the story is nearly always an actual and fairly recent crime, recorded in a chronicle like Stow's or in ballad, chapbook, or pamphlet. The principal Elizabethan domestic tragedies conforming to this pattern are *Arden of Feversham, A Warning for Fair Women,* and Robert Yarington's *Two Lamentable Tragedies;* the principal Jacobean ones, *A Yorkshire Tragedy,* Heywood's *Woman Killed with Kindness* and *English Traveller,* Heywood and Rowley's *Fortune by Land and Sea*, Dekker, Rowley, and Ford's *Witch of Edmonton*.

That some of the authors of domestic tragedy were conscious of their boldness in attempting it is attested by their deliberate calling attention to its differences from orthodox tragedy. The curious framework of *A Warning for Fair Women* is evidently to be understood as an apology for this type of tragedy. The presenters of the play are Comedy, History, and Tragedy. The first two deride Tragedy with a description of the Senecanized variety:

> How some damn'd tyrant, to obtain a crown,
> Stabs, hangs, impoisons, smothers, cutteth
>   throats,
> And then a Chorus too comes howling in,
> And tells us of the worrying of a cat;
> Then of a filthy whining ghost,
> Lapt in some foul sheet or a leather pilch,
> Comes screaming like a pig half-stickt,
> And cries "*Vindicta!* revenge, revenge!"
> With that a little rosin flasheth forth,
> Like smoke out of a tobacco pipe, or a boy's
>   squib:
> When comes in two or three like to drovers,
> With tailors' bodkins, stabbing one another.
> Is not this trim? is not here goodly things?

The attitude of Tragedy is ambiguous. She appears to take the description as maliciously libelous, not as a true account of an inferior type of tragedy:

> Thus with your loose and idle similes
> You have abused me: but I'll whip you hence,
> I'll scourge and lash you both from off the stage;
> 'Tis you [i.e., History and Comedy] have kept
>   the theaters so long,
> Painted in play-bills upon every post,
> That I am scorned of the multitude,
> My name profaned.

But when the play is done, she describes it in terms that form an unmistakable contrast to the earlier description:

> Perhaps it may seem strange unto you all,
> That one hath not reveng'd another's death
> After the observation of such course:
> The reason is, that now of truth I sing,
> And should I add, or else diminish aught,
> Many of these spectators then could say,
> I have committed error in my play.
> Bear with this true and home-born tragedy,
> Yielding so slender argument and scope
> To build a matter of importance on.

Nevertheless, perhaps to be on the safe side, in the first of the dumb shows between the acts (the division itself a noteworthy concession to classical form) the old standbys, the Senecan Furies, together with Lust and Chastity, appear to motivate the action. Notice of a wedding between Senecan tragedy and native moral play could scarcely be more plainly given.

It was evidently felt, too, that decorum demanded a plain style for these mean and domestic subjects in place of the elevation demanded by great personages and state affairs. The author of *Arden* describes his play as "naked" and without "filed lines." Heywood characterizes *A Woman Killed* as "a barren subject, a bare scene," *The English Traveller* as composed of "bare lines."

> A strange play you are like to have, for know,
> We use no drum, nor trumpet, nor dumb show;
> No combat, marriage; not so much today
> As song, dance, masque, to bombast out a play.

In style, as in theme, domestic tragedy perhaps owed something to the morality play, which had helped establish a tradition of realism in scenes of common life. See the truancy scenes, for instance, in *Nice Wanton,* or the scenes between the young married couple in *The Disobedient Child,* in which, after the borrowed money runs out, bickering and recrimination succeed to the billing and cooing of the honeymoon scenes.

The peculiarity of domestic tragedy to England at this period is an interesting testimony both to the relative freedom of the English stage from critical dominance and to the large middle-class element in its audience. Professor Harbage's revealing study [*Shakespeare's Audience,* 1941] shows that the public theaters must have drawn on a wide cross section of the population of London, excluding normally only the very poor. Domestic tragedy has the characteristics of bourgeois literature in its heavy moral emphasis and in its combination of sensationalism and sentiment.

The ethical pattern of temptation, sin, repentance, and punishment that domestic tragedy inherited from the moral play was one widely familiar to everybody through persistent Christian teaching. It was given precise and elaborate form in the official book of homilies prescribed for weekly reading in every church, and it was echoed everywhere in sermons and moralizing pamphlets, even in the broadside ballads commemorating striking crimes that served in that day in place of sensational journalism.

The type of tragedy making use of this scheme lends itself to excessive emphasis on pathos to the exclusion of more complicated feelings and of reflection. Pathos was a specialty of the writers of domestic tragedy. Their chances to develop it came in three places: the innocence of the victims (e.g., Beech and his boy in one story of *Two Lamentable Tragedies* and Pertillo the child in the other; Bean in *A Warning,* children and wife in *A Yorkshire Tragedy,* Susan in the *Witch of Edmonton*); the Christian forbearance of one of the characters (the young friend of Pertillo in *Two Lamentable Tragedies,* the injured husband in *A Woman Killed,* Geraldine the injured lover in *The English Traveller*); and the repentance of the guilty hero (in all the plays in my first list). While the repentances of Alice Arden and Calverly, both strongly conceived characters, have little of the pathetic in them, the good ends of Geraldine's lady, of Mistress Shore, and of Mistress Frankford are worked for all the pathos they are worth. Other plays range along the scale between these. The stern view of the preachers might be that man is essentially only worthy of damnation and can be saved only by the grace of God. But in the blurring of this view with the tears of innocence, forgiveness, and repentance the writers of domestic tragedy appeal to softer sentiment and lose the harsh edge of tragedy. An easily achieved divine mercy takes the curse off original sin.

The tendency to the sentimental leads, as one would expect, to the happy ending. Heywood's *Woman Killed* and *English Traveller* are tragedies with double endings; only the guilty die. George Wilkins in his *Miseries of Enforced Marriage* takes the same story as in *A Yorkshire Tragedy,* and by omitting the commission of murder makes possible the complete reformation of the hero and a reconciliation with his wife. Dekker's two plays of *The Honest Whore* have affinities with domestic tragedy in this respect, though their courtiers, their love affairs, and their intrigues link them with Italianate romantic drama. But Bellafront is certainly less than noble in social position; and her repentance, together with her persistence in the reformed state despite all the pressure on her to break down, is a declaration of possible goodness, even in a fallen woman. Although both plays end happily, Dekker's firm hold on character, his satiric humor, and his vivid realism in the portrayal of his rogues keep out sentimentalism.

We may conclude our examination of the major types of tragedy by remarking on a traditional idea about Elizabethan drama, the idea that it was wholly free in its development, wholly scornful of critical theory. Free as compared with the Italian and later French drama it certainly was, and running ahead of criticism rather than behind it. But the dramatists were certainly not working in critical darkness. Whether or not they ever went to Aristotle or the Italian critics, they could not have avoided the traditional concepts of tragedy and comedy as formulated by the grammarians, and they could not have avoided acquaintance with Senecan tragedy and Roman comedy. We are often misled in comparing their tragedy with classical tragedy as we understand it by not seeing clearly enough how they understood it. They were sometimes imitating it according to their lights when they seem to us not to be. When they were actually trying to do something different, I believe they knew what they were doing. (pp. 135-47)

> Madeleine Doran, "History and Tragedy," in her *Endeavors of Art: A Study of Form in Elizabethan Drama, University of Wisconsin Press, 1954, pp. 112-47.*

FURTHER READING

I. Historical Overviews

Archer, William. *The Old Drama and the New.* Boston: Small, Maynard, and Co., 1923, 396 p.
    Outlines the course of theatrical history, paying particular attention to the Elizabethan period, in order to account for the twentieth century's revitalized interest in the drama as literature.

Briggs, Julia. *This Stage-Play World: English Literature and Its Background 1580-1625.* Oxford: Oxford University Press, 1983, 225 p.

Surveys Elizabethan literature within its historical setting.

Chambers, E. K. *The Elizabethan Stage.* 4 vols. 1923. Reprint. Oxford: Clarendon Press, 1945.
    Comprehensive overview of the Elizabethan theater, describing the court apparatus regulating productions, theatrical companies, individual playhouses, and various dramatic works.

Courthope, W. J. "The Infancy of the Romantic Drama: Greene, Peele, Marlowe, Kyd." In his *A History of English Poetry,* Vol. II, pp. 379-429. London: Macmillan and Co., 1897.
    Studies the historical background and classical influences which gave rise to the Elizabethan drama.

Edwards, Philip. "Shakespeare's England." In his *Threshold of a Nation: A Study in English and Irish Drama,* Part I, pp. 17-190. London: Cambridge University Press, 1979.
    Discusses how the English national spirit was instrumental in the rise of Elizabethan drama.

Farnham, Willard. *The Medieval Heritage of Elizabethan Tragedy.* 1936. Reprint. Oxford: Basil Blackwell, 1956, 487 p.
    Examines the Elizabethan theater as an "heir of the medieval stage." Farnham asserts that the tragic spirit found in English Renaissance drama was inherited from both Gothic and Greco-Roman culture.

Gassner, John. "Playwrights of the Church and the Guild." In his *Masters of the Drama,* pp. 139-59. New York: Dover Publications, 1940.
    Elucidates the theatrical activity of the early Middle Ages, citing the impact of the miracle and mystery plays upon Elizabethan drama.

Jones, Marion. "The Court and the Dramatists." In *Elizabethan Theatre,* edited by John Russell Brown and Bernard Harris, Stratford-Upon-Avon Studies 9, pp. 169-95. London: Edward Arnold, 1966.
    Argues that Queen Elizabeth I provided the catalyst for the artistic innovations of the English Renaissance.

Nicoll, Allardyce. *The Elizabethans.* Cambridge: Cambridge University Press, 1957, 174 p.
    Presents the Elizabethan period through the words and pictures of those who lived during the epoch.

Ringler, William. "The First Phase of the Elizabethan Attack on the Stage, 1558-1579." *The Huntington Library Quarterly* V, No. 4 (July 1942): 391-418.
    Analyzes the social, economic, and religious forces which eventually led to the closing of the theaters in 1642.

Rossiter, A. P. *English Drama from Early Times to the Elizabethans: Its Background, Origins, and Developments.* London: Hutchinson's University Library, 1950, 176 p.
    Scrutinizes the cultural continuities between medieval and Elizabethan drama.

Wallace, Charles William. *The Evolution of the English Drama up to Shakespeare.* Berlin: George Reimer, 1912, 246 p.
    Presents the origins and development of the Elizabethan drama with particular emphasis on the ramifying influ-

ence of the children's companies on the drama itself and on the men's companies from 1485 to the Restoration.

Wasson, John. "The Morality Play: Ancestor of Elizabethan Drama?" *Comparative Drama* 13, No. 3 (Fall 1979): 210-21.
    Challenges the assumption that English Renaissance drama was derived from the medieval morality play. Admitting that even though parallels can be found between the two, Wasson judges that traditional folk and miracle plays of the Middle Ages were greater influences.

II. Critical Studies

Bevington, David M. *From* Mankind *to* Marlowe: Growth of Structure in the Popular Drama of Tudor England. Cambridge, Mass.: Harvard University Press, 1962, 310 p.
    Considers the popular and national character of Elizabethan drama, exploring how its themes and forms of expression were derived from its "own native tradition."

Bowers, Fredson. *Elizabethan Revenge Tragedy 1587-1642.* Princeton, N. J.: Princeton University Press, 1940, 258 p.
    Investigates the background, origin, and historical development of revenge tragedy, tracing the various influences which affected the Elizabethan dramatists who composed such works.

Boyer, Clarence Valentine. *The Villain as Hero in Elizabethan Tragedy.* London: George Routledge and Sons, 1914, 264 p.
    Discusses the influence of the Senecan character-type on the dramatic construction of Elizabethan tragedy.

Brodwin, Leonora Leet. *Elizabethan Love Tragedy 1587-1625.* New York: New York University Press, 1971, 404 p.
    Analyzes three categories of Elizabethan love tragedies—those of courtly love, of false romantic love, and of worldly love—noting their common dramatic patterns and history.

Cunliffe, John W. *Early English Classical Tragedies.* Oxford: Clarendon Press, 1912, 349 p.
    Investigates the affinity between classical, medieval, and Elizabethan theater. Cunliffe contends that the early English tragedies incorporated elements of the earlier dramatic forms.

————. *The Influence of Seneca on Elizabethan Tragedy,* 1893. Reprint. Hamden, Conn.: Archon Books, 1965, 155 p.
    Seminal study of Seneca's impact on Elizabethan drama.

Eliot, T. S. *Elizabethan Essays.* London: Faber and Faber, 1934, 195 p.
    Collection of essays exploring a variety of related topics such as the influence of Seneca and Stoicism on Shakespeare. Eliot also offers commentary on several other dramatists, including Ben Jonson, Christopher Marlowe, and Thomas Heywood.

Fansler, Harriott Ely. *The Evolution of Technic in Elizabethan Tragedy.* 1914. Reprint. New York: Phaeton Press, 1968, 283 p.
    Traces the development of Elizabethan dramatic technique, particularly in the works of Shakespeare, in an effort to determine what constitutes a "well-built tragedy."

Hellenga, Robert R. "Elizabethan Dramatic Conventions and Elizabethan Reality." *Renaissance Drama* XII (1987): 27-49.
    Attempts to account for interpretive differences as arising from the discrepancy between who characters are and what they do, particularly in Shakespearean dramas. Hellenga maintains that since Elizabethan reality was different from our own, dramatic conventions of a more "capacious" nature were employed.

Herrington, H. W. "Witchcraft and Magic in the Elizabethan Drama." *The Journal of American Folk-lore* 32, No. 126 (October-December 1919): 447-85.
    Examines how witchcraft and magic were represented in Elizabethan literature. Herrington concludes: "The appearance and popularity of the [occult] themes in the drama are to be explained, not by any shifts in public interest, but by the history of dramatic vogue."

Hillman, Richard W. "Meaning and Mortality in Some Renaissance Revenge Plays." *University of Toronto Quarterly* XLIX, No. 1 (Fall 1979): 1-17.
    Suggests that dramatists used the revenge convention to probe the human psyche and force human beings to face their own mortality.

Hunter, G. K. "The Beginnings of Elizabethan Drama: Revolution and Continuity." *Renaissance Drama* XVII (1986): 29-52.
    Asserts that Renaissance playwrights, while remaining faithful to traditional popular forms, sought to revolutionize dramatic writing so as "to impose their literary values on the extant institutions."

Johnson, S. F. "The Tragic Hero in Early Elizabethan Drama." In *Studies in the English Renaissance Drama,* edited by Josephine W. Bennett, et al., pp. 157-71. New York: New York University Press, 1959.
    Acknowledges that the conventions found in later Elizabethan drama concerning the depiction of the tragic hero had already been employed in earlier tragedies such as *Kynge Johan* and *Gorboduc.*

Kaufmann, R. J., ed. *Elizabethan Drama: Modern Essays in Criticism.* New York: Oxford University Press, 1961, 372 p.
    Collection of essays by such scholars as G. Wilson Knight, William Empson, L. C. Knights, Muriel Bradbrook, and T. S. Eliot, dealing with a variety of topics relevant to Elizabethan drama.

Knight, G. Wilson. "Elizabethan." In his *The Golden Labyrinth: A Study of British Drama,* pp. 43-65. London: Phoenix House, 1962.
    Surveys Elizabethan literature, noting, in particular, the contributions of dramatists John Lyly, Thomas Kyd, and Christopher Marlowe.

Knoll, Robert E. "Drama of Fulfillment and Drama of Choice: A Note on Greek and Elizabethan Drama." *Western Humanities Review* XI, No. 4 (Autumn 1957): 371-76.
    Compares Greek classical to Elizabethan drama, arguing that the former is "metaphysical" whereas the latter is "psychological."

Lamb, Charles. *Specimens of English Dramatic Poets Who Lived about the Time of Shakespeare,* edited by Israel Gollancz. 2 vols. 1808. Reprint. New York: Johnson Reprint Corporation, 1970.

> Extracts from the works of such major dramatists as John Lyly, Christopher Marlowe, Ben Jonson, and George Chapman. This work, critics concur, was the impetus for a revitalization of interest in Elizabethan plays.

Russell, H. K. "Elizabethan Dramatic Poetry in the Light of Natural and Moral Philosophy." *Philological Quarterly* XII, No. 2 (April 1933): 187-95.

> Asserts that an understanding of the natural and moral philosophy of the Elizabethan period is necessary to appreciate the poetry of the Renaissance dramatists. Russell states that, "Science and poetry are fused in the rich and human drama of the Elizabethans."

Simpson, Percy. *Studies in Elizabethan Drama.* Oxford: Clarendon Press, 1955, 265 p.

> Collection of essays on a variety of related topics, including considerations of works by William Shakespeare, Ben Jonson, and Christopher Marlowe, as well as a discussion of the revenge theme in Elizabethan tragedy.

Smith, Winifred. "Italian and Elizabethan Comedy." *Modern Philology* V, No. 4 (April 1908): 555-67.

> Explores the Italian influence on Elizabethan comedy, contending that its impact was both "fundamental and far-reaching."

Southern, Richard. "The Mystery of the Elizabethan Stage." *The Listener* LXIII, No. 1617 (24 March 1960): 533-35.

> Recreates the physical Elizabethan stage based on the historical research of such scholars as Leslie Hotson and Richard Hosley.

Spencer, Theodore. *Death and Elizabethan Tragedy: A Study of Convention and Opinion in the Elizabethan Drama.* Cambridge, Mass.: Harvard University Press, 1936, 288 p.

> Identifies the impact of medieval teaching and Elizabethan attitudes on the treatment of death in the dramatic poetry of the sixteenth century.

Stroup, Thomas B. "The Characters: Orders and Degrees."

In his *Microcosmos: The Shape of the Elizabethan Play,* pp. 147-78. Lexington: University of Kentucky Press, 1965.

> Studies the characters in several Elizabethan dramas, contending that the playwrights "generally attempted to put into each play, whether comedy or tragedy, representatives of a sufficient number of the orders of society to suggest, at least, that the [dramatic] action was representative of the whole."

Swinburne, Algernon Charles. *The Age of Shakespeare.* London: Chatto and Windus, 1909, 286 p.

> Highly regarded commentary on some of the principal Elizabethan dramatists, including Christopher Marlowe, Thomas Dekker, Thomas Heywood, and George Chapman.

Talbert, Ernest William. *Elizabethan Drama and Shakespeare's Early Works: An Essay in Historical Criticism.* Chapel Hill: University of North Carolina Press, 1963, 410 p.

> Analysis of the dramatic structure, characterization, and conventional situations in the works of Shakespeare and his early contemporaries.

Ure, Peter. *Elizabethan and Jacobean Drama: Critical Essays by Peter Ure,* edited by J. C. Maxwell. New York: Barnes & Noble Books, 1974, 258 p.

> Collection of essays on Shakespeare and other Elizabethan and Jacobean playwrights, treating various aspects of the period's literature.

Williamson, George. "Elizabethan Drama and Its Classical Rival." *University of California Chronicle* 31, No. 3 (July 1929): 251-56.

> Argues that Elizabethan drama is a unique blending of native and Greco-Roman influences.

Wright, Louis B. "The Scriptures and the Elizabethan Stage." *Modern Philology* XXVI, No. 1 (August 1928): 47-56.

> Discusses the dramatists' employment of sacred scripture, concluding that "the Bible was more useful in the theaters than we have been accustomed to believe."

Thomas Kyd

1558-1594

English playwright and translator.

INTRODUCTION

Primarily known for *The Spanish Tragedy,* Kyd is recognized as an innovative and transitional figure in Elizabethan drama. In *The Spanish Tragedy,* Kyd developed previously unrefined dramatic devices and conventions to a new level of sophistication, and his masterful use of classical tragic models far surpassed the efforts of preceding dramatists. Kyd was the first playwright in English literature to feature revenge as the central focus of a tragedy, introducing to the popular stage a literary genre which has become known as the revenge tragedy and which has been characterized by Deborah Rubin as "the most perfect vehicle for the portrayal of man's struggle to harmonize his spontaneous need for retribution with his religious and ethical beliefs." Kyd's form was widely imitated throughout the Elizabethan era and the theatrical success of *The Spanish Tragedy* lasted well into the seventeenth century. Moody E. Prior has credited Kyd with "greatly [advancing] the art of verse drama," claiming that with *The Spanish Tragedy,* "English tragedy had been clearly started in the direction of its artistic destiny."

Kyd was born in London in 1558. A record of his baptism on November sixth of that year still exists, identifying him as the son of Francis Kyd, a scrivener of good standing. Francis Kyd enrolled his son in the newly established Merchant Taylors' school in 1565, where he was a classmate of Edmund Spenser. Kyd's later life and career are not well documented. There is no evidence that he pursued a university education and some scholars have speculated that he may have temporarily practiced his father's trade before he began writing for the stage. It is known that Kyd entered the service of a lord in some capacity in 1587 and that he was released in 1593. According to London records, Kyd was arrested that year in a city-wide search for the author of discriminatory threats against foreigners residing in London. Authorities who searched Kyd's room for proof of his involvement in this matter instead found papers that they considered atheistic and sacrilegious. During his imprisonment, Kyd was subjected to what he described in a letter to his previous employer as "paines and undeserved tortures," but he would not confess to writing the heretical essays. In fact, Kyd attributed them to his friend and fellow playwright, Christopher Marlowe, with whom he had shared the searched quarters. Before this accusation could be fully investigated, however, Marlowe was murdered. Although Kyd was eventually freed from prison, he was never wholly cleared of the charges, and he died destitute little more than a year later at the age of thirty-six.

Although Kyd's reputation is based solely on *The Spanish Tragedy,* the play was not published under his name until several centuries after it was written. Literary historians have assigned the work to Kyd in large measure because Thomas Heywood attributed it to him in his 1612 *Apology for Actors.* The date of the tragedy's composition, however, is the subject of much debate. Scholars have generally agreed that the tragedy may have been written as early as 1582, when published material alluded to in *The Spanish Tragedy* was first printed, or as late as 1592, the year in which the play was staged for the first time. Frederick S. Boas concluded that *The Spanish Tragedy* was written around 1586 or 1587 based on apparent references to its subject matter by Thomas Nashe in his preface to Robert Greene's *Menaphon* (1589). Arthur Freeman has seconded Boas's opinion for similar reasons and because he believes that Kyd's treatment of the Spanish milieu in his tragedy indicates that it was written before the destruction of the Spanish Armada in 1588. Philip Edwards, however, has disagreed with both Boas and Freeman, positing that 1590 is a more accurate composition date based on the work's thematic and stylistic parallels with other dramas from that period.

Kyd's *Cornelia* is the only play that has been definitely ascribed to him and that has a precise composition date. A translation of Robert Garnier's *Cornélie* (1585), Kyd's play was registered for publication in early 1594 under his name. Scholars have characterized *Cornelia* as an attempt by Kyd to compose a tragedy for academia, rather than for the popular stage. They also believe that Kyd translated Torquato Tasso's *Il Padre di Famiglia* (1583) as *The Housholder's Philosophie,* a small pamphlet espousing rural wisdom and offering strategies for running a successful household. This work was published in 1588 under the initials T. K. and resembles Kyd's *Cornelia* in its method of translation and certain peculiarities of style. Literary historians have also posited that Kyd is the author of *Soliman and Perseda,* a play that was anonymously registered for publication in 1592 but was most likely written earlier. The attribution of *Soliman and Perseda* to Kyd primarily rests on the appearance of a virtually identical story in the play-within-the-play of *The Spanish Tragedy* also entitled *Soliman and Perseda.* Similarities in dramatic technique, melodramatic elements, and dramatic irony in these two works have led many critics to conclude that they were both written by the same playwright.

Many commentators have further speculated that Kyd produced a dramatic work, now lost, of significance equal to or greater than that of *The Spanish Tragedy.* Several references in Elizabethan literature suggest that Kyd may have created a well-known version of the Hamlet story at least a decade before Shakespeare's great tragedy. The probable source for this drama was Saxo Grammaticus's *Historiae Danicae* (c. 1200), a rendering of the Norse legend of *Amloth.* In the above-mentioned preface to Greene's *Menaphon,* Nashe alluded to "the Kidde in Aesop" who would "affoord you whole *Hamlets,* I should say handfulls of tragical speeches." This and other vague comments in Nashe's preface have led critics to ascribe the so-called *Ur-Hamlet* to Kyd. They also cite parallels in dramatic style and plot between *The Spanish Tragedy* and Shakespeare's early quarto of *Hamlet* as proof of Kyd's authorship of the *Ur-Hamlet.* Literary scholars have refuted, however, the long-accepted theory that Kyd penned *The First Part of Jeronimo,* a prequel to *The Spanish Tragedy. The First Part of Jeronimo,* which relates the events leading up to the action in *The Spanish Tragedy,* was not published until after Kyd's death in the early 1600s and commentators contend that it is the work of an imitator hoping to profit from the success of Kyd's play.

As the first significant tragedy on the Elizabethan stage in which the central action is linked to the progression of revenge, Kyd's *Spanish Tragedy* introduced a new dramatic genre to the English theater. The so-called revenge tragedy is generally characterized by a son seeking revenge for the death of a father or vice versa, sensational brutality, intrigue, the occurrence of insanity and suicide, a scheming villain, and the ghost of a murdered man who urges vengeance. *The Spanish Tragedy* centers on the character of Hieronimo, who seeks to avenge the death of his son Horatio, who has been murdered by Lorenzo, nephew to the King of Spain, and Balthazar, son of the Viceroy of Portugal. The murder was committed to end Horatio's affair with Bel-Imperia, Lorenzo's sister, who is loved by Balthazar. At various points in the play, the ghost of the nobleman Andrea—who had earlier been killed by Balthazar—appears, acting as a "chorus" figure, commenting on the action and promoting the idea of revenge. The tragedy is particularly memorable for its enactment of great horrors; by the end of the play, nearly every one of the main characters has been violently killed onstage. Kyd's focus on violence and bloodshed in *The Spanish Tragedy* has further led scholars to classify the play as a tragedy of blood, an intensely morbid version of the revenge tragedy in which retribution is achieved through murder, assassination, and mutilation. In addition, because Hieronimo avenges the death of a blood relative, Kyd introduces yet another motif, identified as blood-revenge, into *The Spanish Tragedy.*

The plays of Seneca—a first century Roman dramatist, philosopher, prose writer, and statesman—are considered among the leading sources for *The Spanish Tragedy.* Kyd's drama exhibits many characteristics of Senecan tragedy, including the use of a chorus, stock characters such as the ghost and the tyrannical villain, sensational themes and the explicit depiction of horrors, and a highly rhetorical style marked by both sharp dialogue and tragic soliloquies. Imitations of Seneca's themes and techniques were prevalent in the English theater in the decades before *The Spanish Tragedy* was composed, and Senecan tragedy became the subject of great academic and popular interest throughout the Elizabethan era. However, while revenge had appeared in Seneca as an important vehicle for the culmination of tragedy, it was never exploited in his plays as fully as in Kyd's *Spanish Tragedy.* Some scholars have

suggested that Kyd adopted this added emphasis from popular Italian tragedy: Italian theater as well as Italian and French novellas often treated vengeance and horror as central plot concerns. Furthermore, ruthless Machiavellian villains resembling Kyd's Lorenzo and revengeful female characters similar to Bel-Imperia in *The Spanish Tragedy* were common features in French and Italian fiction. Perhaps most importantly, however, critics have claimed that the carnage associated with the vendetta tradition in Italian tragedy could easily have enhanced Kyd's principal theme. Other commentators have presumed that Kyd may have borrowed the blood-revenge motif in *The Spanish Tragedy* from the source for his *Ur-Hamlet,* asserting that the two works treat a markedly similar theme.

Critics have speculated that Renaissance audiences probably relished the bloody spectacle of *The Spanish Tragedy* since they had a decided fondness for such entertainment as bear-baiting and public executions. Nevertheless, a decade after its appearance on the stage, Philip Henslowe commissioned another dramatist to revise Kyd's tragedy, presumably to make the play conform to the audience's changing tastes. Ben Jonson has generally been acknowledged as the author of these additions, although John Webster and even Shakespeare have been suggested as well. This version inspired a great number of enlarged and amended editions of *The Spanish Tragedy,* although Kyd's original text still survives. Later generations of theatergoers were less attracted to the overt melodrama and violence of Kyd's tragedy of blood, and *The Spanish Tragedy* became the object of parody and ridicule by subsequent playwrights. It has rarely been produced on stage since the seventeenth century, but Kyd's play has not failed to receive a great deal of scholarly interest. In fact, it is the only work attributed to Kyd that has uniformly received substantial critical attention. Until the late nineteenth century, Kyd's celebrity depended mostly on the originality and exceptional theatrical appeal of *The Spanish Tragedy,* although some scholars also praised *The First Part of Jeronimo* as a worthy prequel to his masterpiece, believing it to be one of his works. By the turn of the century, however, critics began to reexamine early attributions of dramas to Kyd; they dismissed *The First Part of Jeronimo* from Kyd's canon and questioned the evidence supporting Kyd's association with *Soliman and Perseda* and the *Ur-Hamlet.* While critical debate still exists over this issue, many commentators have come to accept his authorship of these works. Boas and Fredson Bowers, in particular, have given special attention to the *Ur-Hamlet,* analyzing the textual relationship between the hypothetical work, its source story by Saxo Grammaticus, *The Spanish Tragedy,* and the first quarto version of Shakespeare's *Hamlet.*

As critical interest in these attributions has waned, literary scholars have turned almost exclusively to *The Spanish Tragedy* in their studies of Kyd. Yet while so much attention has been devoted to Kyd's impact on the development of English tragedy, commentators have often neglected to assess the artistic value of his dramaturgy. Some critics have concentrated on Kyd's sources as well as how his adaptation of Senecan themes influenced later Elizabethan dramas. Other scholars have examined *The Spanish Tragedy* in the historical context of early dramatic composition, identifying the advances Kyd made in plot and character development, but asserting, like G. Gregory Smith, that while his play reveals "new possibilities and [offers] a model in technique," it "does not make a second claim upon us as great literature." Recent critics have stressed that Kyd exhibited a masterful dramatic technique, however, asserting that in *The Spanish Tragedy* he presents a coherent and carefully constructed plot as well as a complex and various use of rhetoric and blank verse. These commentators have lauded Kyd's ability to interweave plot and counterplot and to develop and accentuate the dramatic action through the use of imagery and rhetorical models.

These innovations notwithstanding, Kyd's work has often been appraised as technically immature by scholars who maintain that *The Spanish Tragedy* suffers from his failure to justify Hieronimo's motives for exacting private revenge rather than obtaining public justice. Furthermore, some commentators have contended that the dislocation of the play's action and its seemingly extraneous episodes are also signs of Kyd's crude dramatic technique. Fredson Bowers has voiced both of these complaints, asserting that the diffusion of the various subplots in *The Spanish Tragedy* detracts from the central theme of revenge and thus deprives the tragedy of unity. He has further claimed that because Hieronimo does not seek justice through the proper channels, but instead deceitfully satisfies his need for retribution through private revenge, the protagonist was interpreted as a villain in the eyes of Elizabethan audiences. Many critics have strongly disagreed with Bowers's reading of *The Spanish Tragedy,* suggesting that if Kyd's main concern was justice, rather than revenge, these perceived faults could be reconciled. According to these scholars, Hieronimo does in fact attempt to secure justice for Horatio's murder, but Lorenzo successfully outmaneuvers him in each of his efforts to approach the king. Commentators have also attempted to deflect accusations of Hieronimo's villainy by emphasizing Kyd's rationalization of the protagonist's actions through the *vindicta mihi* speech and by showing how Kyd dramatized the gradual deterioration of Hieronimo's judgment to the point that he lapses into insanity toward the end of the play. William Empson and other scholars have provided another perspective on the theme of revenge and justice in *The Spanish Tragedy.* They suggest that the ghost of Andrea's desire for vengeance is triggered by the Duke of Castile and his son Lorenzo's engineering of Andrea's murder in a scheme to arrange a marriage between Bel-Imperia and Balthazar. However, the vast majority of critics have dismissed this interpretation of *The Spanish Tragedy* as textually unfounded. Other commentators who have given particular attention to the ghost of Andrea episodes in the play contend that the principal theme of *The Spanish Tragedy* is divine justice, focusing on Kyd's use of dramatic irony in depicting the absolute metaphysical control of pagan deities over the destiny of each character. These critics underscore the portrayal of Hieronimo as a sympathetic character, arguing that he is merely used as an instrument of divine justice to carry out Andrea's revenge.

While critics continue to debate over the ambiguous nature of Kyd's plot and character development in *The*

Spanish Tragedy, they generally concede his skill in creating an exciting and absorbing theatrical spectacle. Kyd's dramatic achievement has largely been overshadowed by that of his contemporaries, Marlowe and Shakespeare, but he is nevertheless accorded a significant place in the history of English drama. *The Spanish Tragedy* remains a testament to Kyd's innovative cultivation of dramatic technique, representing, as Philip Edwards has summarized, "a most ingenious and successful blending of the old and the new in drama."

PRINCIPAL WORKS

* *Ur-Hamlet* (drama) 1587?
† *The Housholder's Philosophie* [translator; of Torquato Tasso's *Il Padre di Famiglia*] (essay) 1588
‡ *The Spanish Tragedy* (drama) 1590?
§ *Soliman and Perseda* (drama) 1592?
Cornelia [translator; of the play *Cornélie* by Robert Garnier] (drama) 1594
The Works of Thomas Kyd (dramas and essays) 1901
The Tudor Facsimile Texts: Solimon and Perseda (drama) 1912
The Spanish Tragedy (drama) 1959

---

* The hypothetical *Ur-Hamlet* is not extant. Its existence and date have been inferred from several contemporary essays, poems, and dramas, most notably Thomas Nashe's prose preface to Robert Greene's *Menaphon* (1589). The work has been attributed to Kyd on the basis of these references and on parallels between *The Spanish Tragedy* and Shakespeare's first quarto version of *Hamlet.*

† Although scholars have not been able to attribute this work to Kyd with absolute certainty, it bore the initials T. K. when it was first published in 1588. *The Housholder's Philosophie* has also been ascribed to Kyd because the style of translation closely resembles that of Kyd's *Cornelia.*

‡ This date is based on Philip Edward's estimate in his 1959 edition of *The Spanish Tragedy.* Most scholars agree that *The Spanish Tragedy* was written between 1582 and 1592. This ten-year range is inferred from the appearance in 1582 of material alluded to in Kyd's famous tragedy and on the first recorded performance of *The Spanish Tragedy* in 1592. Although *The Spanish Tragedy* was published anonymously, Thomas Heywood ascribed it to Kyd in his *Apology for Actors* (1612).

§ *Soliman and Perseda* was entered in the Stationer's Register in 1592 as *The Tragedye of Solyman and Perseda.* The date above is derived from that entry, although the play may have been written earlier. Kyd's possible authorship of this play has been suggested by similarities in dialogue, plot, and style between *Soliman and Perseda* and both *The Spanish Tragedy* and its play-within-the-play also entitled *Soliman and Perseda.*

Thomas Nash   (essay date 1589)

[*In the following excerpt from his 1589 introduction to Robert Greene's* Menaphon, *Nash censures the work of English authors and translators influenced by Seneca in a passage believed to refer to Kyd and his writings.*]

It is a cõmon practise now a daies amongst a sort of shifting companions, that runne through euery arte and thriue by none, to leaue the trade of *Nouerint* whereto they were borne, and busie themselues with the indeuors of Art, that could scarcelie latinize their necke-verse if they should haue neede; yet English *Seneca* read by candle light yeeldes manie good sentences, as *Bloud is a begger,* and so foorth: and if you intreate him faire in a frostie morning, he will affoord you whole *Hamlets,* I should say handfulls of tragical speaches. But ô griefe! *tempus edax rerum,* what's that will last alwaies? The sea exhaled by droppes will in continuance be drie, and *Seneca* let bloud line by line and page by page, at length must needes die to our stage: which makes his famisht followers to imitate the Kidde in *Æsop,* who enamored with the Foxes new fangles, forsooke all hopes of life to leape into a new occupation; and these men renowncing all possibilities of credit or estimation, to intermeddle with Italian translations: wherein how poorelie they haue plodded, (as those that are neither prouenzall men, nor are able to distinguish of Articles,) let all indifferent Gentlemen that haue trauailed in that tongue, discerne by their twopenie pamphlets: and no meruaile though their home-born mediocritie be such in this matter; for what can be hoped of those, that thrust *Elisium* into hell, and haue not learned so long as they haue liued in the spheares, the iust measure of the Horizon without an hexameter. Sufficeth them to bodge vp a blanke verse with ifs and ands, and other while for recreation after their candle stuffe, hauing starched their beardes most curiouslie, to make a peripateticall path into the inner parts of the Citie, and spend two or three howers in turning ouer French *Doudie,* where they attract more infection in one minute, than they can do eloquence all dayes of their life, by conuersing with anie Authors of like argument. But least in this declamatorie vaine, I should condemne all and commend none. (pp. 8-9)

Thomas Nash, "To the Gentlemen Students of Both Universities," in Menaphon *by Robert Greene and A Margarite of America by Thomas Lodge, edited by G. B. Harrison, Basil Blackwell, 1927, pp. 4-18.*

J. Payne Collier   (essay date 1831)

[*In the excerpt below, Collier briefly examines the technical and thematic elements of Kyd's major works.*]

Thomas Kyd was an author of great celebrity, and his **Spanish Tragedy** went through more editions than perhaps any play of the time: it is to be recollected, however, that after 1602, the impressions were accompanied by the supplemental scenes and speeches of Ben Jonson, which added so much to the force and beauty of the play, that Kyd's portion of the tragedy is read to some disadvantage. Ben Jonson was paid for some of them in September, 1601, and for others in June, 1602; but it is clear, from a passage in his *Cynthia's Revels,* played in 1600, that at that date *The Spanish Tragedy* was not in its original shape, as it came from the hands of Kyd: 'Another swears down all that sit about him, that the *old* Hieronimo, *as it was first acted,* was the only best and judiciously penned play of Europe.' Besides the *Jeronimo* and **The Spanish Tragedy,** Kyd was the translator of **Cornelia,** from the French of Garnier. Whether he was older or younger than Marlow, we are without the means of determining; but it seems likely that he was older, and that before he adopted blank-

verse, in pursuance of Marlow's example, he had written some plays either in rhyme or prose. His oldest extant play, *The First Part of Jeronimo,* (not published until 1605,) has about as much rhyme in it as blank-verse, and Kyd does not seem to have ventured then to run the risk of relinquishing a popular attraction. It is to be gathered from another passage in *Cynthia's Revels,* that *The First Part of Jeronimo* was brought upon the stage about the year 1588.

Kyd was a poet of very considerable mind, and deserves, in some respects, to be ranked above more notorious contemporaries: his thoughts are often both new and natural; and if in his plays he dealt largely in blood and death, he only partook of the habit of the time, in which good sense and discretion were often outraged for the purpose of gratifying the crowd. In taste he is inferior to Peele, but in force and character he is his superior; and if Kyd's blankverse be not quite so smooth, it has decidedly more spirit, vigour, and variety. As a writer of blank-verse, I am inclined, among the predecessors of Shakespeare, to give Kyd the next place to Marlow.

The First Part of Jeronimo was only once printed, and certainly never attracted half the attention that was directed to **The Spanish Tragedy.** It is the first play upon record that bears evidence of having been written for a particular performer, a man of unusually small stature, and in many places this circumstance is brought forward. The story is wanting in incident, the love of Don Andrea and Bellimperia, and the death of the first, forming the principal features of it: the scene, however, rapidly changes from Spain to Portugal, and the deficiency in events is in some degree made up for by the bustle and show of hostility between the two kingdoms, in consequence of the refusal of its annual tribute by the latter. As a dramatic production, *Jeronimo* is in every respect below **The Spanish Tragedy,** but the language is often striking and the thoughts bold: thus, when Andrea is about to proceed to Lisbon to demand the tribute withheld, Bellimperia expresses her fears that a conflict must ensue between her lover and the young courageous Prince of Portugal. She tells Andrea—

> Ye'll meet like thunder—each imperious
> Over other's spleen; you both have proud spirits,
> And both will strive to aspire:
> When two vex'd clouds justle, they strike out
> fire.

In this tragedy there is an attempt at character, and not without success: that of the hero, who gives it name, is not so fully made out as in **The Spanish Tragedy;** but Andrea, and Bathezar his rival, are drawn with decision and force, and the unsuspecting generosity of the former is well opposed to the wily intricacies of Lorenzo, the nephew of the King, and the heir to the Spanish crown. As a specimen of the blank-verse in this play, the subsequent may be taken, and it shows no little command of language. It is from the speech of Balthezar, before he leads the Portuguese army to the field against Spain.

> Come, valiant spirits, you peers of Portugal,
> That owe your lives, your faiths, and services,
> To set you free from base captivity.
> Oh, let our fathers' scandal ne'er be seen

As a base blush upon our freeborn cheeks.
Let all the tribute that proud Spain received
Of those all captive Portugals deceased,
Turn into chaff and choke their insolence.
Methinks no memory, not one little thought
Of them whose servile acts live in their graves,
But should raise spleens big as a cannon bullet
Within your bosoms. Oh, for honour,
Your country's reputation, your lives' freedom,
Indeed your all that may be term'd revenge!
Now let your bloods be liberal as the sea,
And all those wounds that you receive of Spain,
Let theirs be equal to quite yours again.

Here we see trochees used at the ends of the lines, and the pauses are even artfully managed; while redundant syllables are inserted, and lines left defective still farther to add to the variety.

Too strong an epithet is not applied to **The Spanish Tragedy** (or, as it may be fitly termed, *The Second Part of Jeronimo*), if we call it a very powerful performance. The story has many incongruities and absurdities, and various passages and situations were made the laughing-stocks of subsequent dramatists; but parts of it are in the highest degree pathetic and interesting. It turns upon the love of Horatio, the son of Hieronimo (so he is now called, perhaps because Kyd found in the interval, that Jeronimo was rather Italian than Spanish) and Belimperia, who, after the death of Andrea, had turned the full tide of her affections upon his young, faithful, and noble friend. Horatio is hanged upon the stage, in the garden of his father, by his rival, the Prince of Portugal, and Lorenzo, the brother of Belimperia, in the commencement of the second act: during the rest of the play, Hieronimo, in a state of distraction, is seeking revenge, and finds it only at last in the chance-medley, as it were, of a play represented before the King and nobility of Spain. The old father is always meditating the punishment of the guilty, and always postponing the execution of his project; so that, in this respect, his character in some degree resembles that of *Hamlet:* the insertion of a play within a play, gives the whole tragedy a still greater appearance of similarity to that of Shakespeare. In the fourth Act, Hieronimo comes before the King and Court of Spain to demand justice upon the murderers of Horatio, and is put aside by the interference of Lorenzo, one of the guilty parties, almost without a struggle for a hearing: soon afterwards, the Spanish Ambassador speaks of a ransom due from the Prince of Portugal to Horatio, and at the unexpected mention of his dear son's name, the old man starts from a melancholy abstraction and exclaims,

Horatio! Who calls Horatio? . . . .
Justice! Oh, justice! justice, gentle king!
King. Who is that? Hieronimo?
Hier. Justice! Oh, justice! O my son, my son!
Lorenzo. Hieronimo, you are not well advis'd.
Hier. Away, Lorenzo! hinder me no more,
For thou hast made me bankrupt of my bliss.
Give me my son! you shall not ransom him.

He sees nothing but Horatio in every face he looks upon, and all objects take their colour and appearance from his sorrows. His grief is not as sublime, but it is as intense as that of Lear; and he dwells upon the image of his lost Ho-

ratio, with not less doating agony than Constance, when she exclaims

Grief fills the room up of my absent child, &c.

The other characters are all far inferior to that of Hieronimo. Whole passages of this play are in rhyme, but the jingle is less frequent towards the close, after the author thought he had sufficiently engaged the interest and attention of his hearers. The blank-verse can hardly be said to be any improvement upon that of *The First Part of Jeronimo:* one short extract from a speech of Belimperia, to her brother Lorenzo, who had confined her in a tower after the murder of Horatio, will be sufficient.

What means this outrage that is offered me?
Why am I thus sequester'd from the Court?
No notice? Shall I not know the cause
Of these my secret and suspicious ills?
Accursed brother! unkind murderer!
Why bend'st thou thus thy mind to martyr me?
Hieronimo, why writ I of thy wrongs,
Or, why art thou so slack in thy revenge?
Andrea! Oh Andrea! that thou sawest
Me for thy friend Horatio handled thus,
And him for me thus causeless murdered!
Well, force perforce, I must constrain myself
To patience, and apply me to the time,
'Till heaven, as I have hop'd, shall set me free.

Kyd's **Cornelia** merely requires notice as a very successful translation for the time at which it appeared: it was printed in 1594, but it was not intended for the stage; and it was so much liked, that in the following year it arrived at a second impression.

I will insert a short specimen from the chorus to Act iv., in order to show the facility with which Kyd wrote in lyrical measure.

He only lives most happily
That, free and far from majesty,
Can live content, although unknown;
He fearing none, none fearing him,
Meddling with nothing but his own,
While gazing eyes at crowns grow dim.

(pp. 205-12)

J. Payne Collier, "Review of Thomas Kyd's Dramatic Works," in his The History of English Dramatic Poetry to the Times of Shakespeare and Annals of the Stage to the Restoration, Vol. 3, *1831. Reprint by AMS Press, Inc., 1970, pp. 205-12.*

Adolphus William Ward   (essay date 1899)

[*In the following excerpt, Ward provides a general overview of Kyd's principal works, as well as those attributed to him.*]

Thomas Kyd, the author of **The Spanish Tragedy,** has the honour of being ranked by Ben Jonson, with Lyly and Marlowe, among the dramatists whom Shakspere 'outshone.' Jonson calls him 'Sporting Kyd'—manifestly by way of nothing more than a facile, and probably familiar, pun. There is sufficient reason for supposing him to have been trained for the profession (paternal, it would seem) of a law scrivener, before he diverged into literary activity. He published in 1588 a translation of one of Tasso's prose tractates, and followed it up by at least one pamphlet narrating a contemporary case of 'secret' murder—a theme entirely in agreement with the tastes of the period, and, one may venture to add, of the writer himself. His authorship of *The Spanish Tragedy,* which was licensed in 1592, and printed at all events as early as 1594, is established on sufficient authority; but he published nothing with his name except a translation of Robert Garnier's tragedy of *Cornélie,* printed in 1594, and reprinted in the following year under the title of **Pompey the Great, his faire Cornelias Tragedie, effected by her Father and Husbandes downe-cast, death and fortune.** Whether or not because in the latter part of his career Kyd's personal repute suffered, as it seems to have done, from reports as to his participation in the recently dead Marlowe's vagaries of opinion, he was manifestly anxious to establish a sort of literary orthodoxy, undertaking in the Dedication of his *Cornelia* to the Countess of Sussex to 'assure her his next summer's better travel with the tragedy of *Portia,'* a version of the *Julius Caesar* theme which is thought to surpass the *Cornelia* in power. For Kyd is said to have died in 1595. His *Cornelia* carries us back, like all the earlier of Garnier's tragedies, to a phase of the drama antecedent to that which is represented by Kyd himself as an original poet. Not only is Seneca, with his ghosts and the rest of his machinery, still master of the method, but the drama, with its endless speeches and generally retrospective procedure, is still in the embrace of the epos. Kyd seems here to be doing penance for the spasmodic extravagances as well as for the freer movement of his earlier efforts.

Among these it seems to me imperative to mention first the famous **Spanish Tragedy, or, Hieronimo is mad again,** not because of its fame, but because of the fact that on the evidence contained in it rests the argument as to Kyd's claim to the authorship of any other plays. The exceptional popularity of this piece is attested by the frequency with which it was performed after its first appearance on the stage in 1588, or a year or two earlier. It was, moreover, frequently reprinted after the first extant edition, which itself refers to an earlier impression. The edition of 1602 purports to have received 'new additions of the Painter's part and others,' with which it had been of late several times performed; and Henslowe's *Diary* contains two entries of sums paid to 'Bengemen Johnson,' *alias* 'Bengemy Johnsone,' for 'additions' and for 'new additions' to this play. Charles Lamb is sceptical as to Ben Jonson's authorship of certain of the additions, which he terms [in his *Specimens of English Dramatic Poetry,* 1893] 'the salt of the old play'—an expression that appears rather too strong, although Lamb's extracts no doubt comprise the most highly-wrought passages, especially in the great scene which another critic of rare insight agrees in thinking beyond Ben Jonson's powers. Jonson himself was at no pains to conceal his opinion of the value of the additions; for in the *Induction* to his *Cynthia's Revels* he ridicules the man who, 'furnished with more beard than wit,' 'prunes his mustachio, lisps and swears "that the old **Hieronimo,** as it was first acted, was the only best and judiciously penned play of Europe." ' For the rest, although perhaps no other play received so ample a recognition as

The Spanish Tragedy in the way of quotation by dramatists contemporary with its author or belonging to the generation next ensuing, yet it is obvious that they largely regarded it as the type of antiquated extravagance. They may be excused for having overlooked the notable advance which **The Spanish Tragedy,** with its direct and forcible, if excessive, presentment of human passions, represents in comparison with our earlier English tragedies modelled on Seneca, and as yet lacking the impulse towards freedom of movement which is unmistakeably present in Kyd's work. Its influence, I may add, was by no means confined to our own national drama.

A notion of the plot of *The Spanish Tragedy* will perhaps be most easily gathered from a ballad which must have been composed after the production of the play, and which thus adds one more to the many testimonies to its popularity. A terrific woodcut depicts the most sensational situation in the story. In the play itself the introductory speech of the *Ghost of Andrea* and the narrative of the *General* briefly explain what may be called the antecedents of the action; but inasmuch as these antecedents themselves form the action of another and shorter play, now usually called *The First Part of Jeronimo,* but apparently referred to by Henslowe under the title of *Jeronimo* pure and simple, the relation between this and **The Spanish Tragedy** becomes a problem of interest. Was the shorter as well as the longer play the work of Kyd, and if so, which of the two was the earlier in date of composition? *The First Part* is unmistakeably slighter in construction (so much so that it has been actually conjectured to have merely formed the first act of **The Spanish Tragedy**) as well as less forcible in diction, and altogether less characteristic of Kyd's special manner than the more important work. That manner is not easily described, since so many reminiscences of an earlier form of tragic writing still adhere to it. But as is justly observed by Schlegel [in his *Lectures on Dramatic Art and Literature,* 1846], when comparing the whole of **The Spanish Tragedy** to the drawings of children, scribbled down by an uncertain hand without regard to perspective or proportion, the tone of the dialogue, notwithstanding the large quantity of bombast, possesses a certain naturalness, and the changes of scene impart to the action an attractive lightness of movement. Thus, no clogging influence upon the action is exercised even by the superhuman machinery of the *Ghost of Andrea* (the first lover of the heroine, enamoured in **The Spanish Tragedy** of Horatio, the son of Hieronimo) and the abstraction of *Revenge,* who reappear at the end of Acts i. and iv. and at the close of the play, and accordingly, in the words of *Revenge,* serve 'for Chorus' in this tragedy, and during its course we feel ourselves transplanted into the region of real human emotion, powerfully and on occasion even pathetically depicted. The sensuous charm of the love-scene between Belimperia and Horatio (written in rimed couplets of no ordinary beauty) cannot be gainsaid, although the author's chief effort (heightened by the later additions) is reserved for what ensues. After Horatio has been hanged on the stage by his enemies, the body is discovered by his father, the brave old Marshal Hieronimo, whose desperate grief and craving for revenge become the keynote of the climax and catastrophe of the action at large. Here is introduced the striking device of the play within the play,—

in its main features the same as that employed in *Hamlet,* although in Kyd's tragedy it is more directly interwoven with the action. And, indeed, the whole dramatic idea of **The Spanish Tragedy** needs nothing but inversion to resemble that of *Hamlet* itself; for the main theme of the former is the effect of the murder of a son upon the mind of his father, whose slowly prepared revenge at last wreaks itself as a Nemesis upon the authors of the original wrong, as well as upon the contrivers of the actual process of retaliation.

The First Part of Jeronimo, which, as already observed, is a far slighter production, and while not wanting in vehemence and even extravagance of diction, lacks both the peculiar *afflatus* and a certain flacidity of style, aided by a tendency to 'return' word or phrase, characteristic of **The Spanish Tragedy,** may or may not have been the work of the same hand; to me it seems on the whole most probable that it was a play of rather earlier date, written perhaps under the effects of the first appearance of Marlowe's *Tamburlaine,* i.e. about the year 1587; and that its subsequent popularity was due to the continuation of its theme in **The Spanish Tragedy,** whence it became customary to perform the two plays on successive days. It is in *Jeronimo,* and not in the longer play, that occur the repeated allusions to the small size of the hero, from which it may be inferred that the part was originally written for a particular actor. The tradition that Ben Jonson 'took mad Jeronymo's part' (which would have been in **The Spanish Tragedy**) ill accords with this particular association.

The authorship of the tragedy of **Solyman and Perseda** is, as it seems to me, a much more interesting question than that of a production which can in no case be regarded as more than an adjunct of **The Spanish Tragedy,** its nominal continuation. The 'play within the play,' introduced in the last act of Kyd's famous tragedy, treats the story of Erastus and Perseda, which is that of the piece now in question; but it merely follows in abstract, so to speak, the general course of the action which in **Solyman and Perseda** fills a larger canvas, while diverging from the latter in details of incident, and only occasionally recalling its actual diction. **Solyman and Perseda,** which was first printed in 1599, though licensed as early as 1592, is itself founded in plot upon a story forming part of a collection published in 1578 by Sir Henry Wotton, under the title of *A Courtlie Controversie of Cupid's Cautels;* a noteworthy passage in it, descriptive of the beauty of Perseda, is partly borrowed from a sonnet in Watson's *Ecatompathia* (1582). It is a tale containing varied ingredients—a chivalrous opening, an episode of sheer chance put to base use by intriguing guile (the episode of the gold chain given by Perseda to Erastus, that finds its way into the possession of Lucina), a romantic developement which places the fate of the lovers in the hands of Sultan Solyman, and a tragic catastrophe which involves their doom, together with that of Christian Rhodes. This story is modified, while the characters are partly elaborated, partly altered, in the play, where an allegorical element is introduced in the personages of Love, Fortune, and Death, who prologise and 'serve as chorus,' and a comic element is added to meet the demands of the groundlings. The action is full of interest, and the indebt-edness of Shakspere to this drama is by no means limited to reminiscences of particular passages.

The question as to Kyd's authorship of this remarkable work cannot be determined by inferences drawn from the fact that the 'play within the play' in **The Spanish Tragedy** was derived from the same source as **Solyman and Perseda,** more especially as that drama and the abstract differ in the contrivance of the final catastrophe. The answer depends on the general evidence as to agreement in construction and style between the two tragedies; and this evidence must be allowed to be strong, though not overwhelming. The use made in both plays of the abstract figures that 'serve as chorus,' though not precisely peculiar to these two dramas, is yet somewhat different from the employment of similar impersonations in any earlier drama; possibly, as will be seen, the suggestion may be due to a third play, of which the framework bears a general resemblance to that of the two plays in question, and which has likewise been attributed to Kyd. Of more importance are the very striking similarities of style. Not only is there in the two plays an undeniably frequent recurrence of the same sorts of quotations and allusions, and a remarkable parallelism—at times an actual identity—of more or less unusual phrases and collocations of words; but in both we find mannerisms such as it is not usual for two authors to share in common—such as the usage, indulged in so largely as to become a characteristic feature, of repeating a catch-word from the line preceding, and of bandying back as it were the half or the whole of a line from speaker to speaker. Both plays were unmistakeably written by the hand of a Euphuist, and on the whole I am inclined to think that hand, in the case of **Solyman and Perseda** as well as in that of **The Spanish Tragedy,** to have been Thomas Kyd's.

There appears to me to be no sufficient reason for accepting the supposition that the curious old play entitled *The Rare Triumphs of Love and Fortune,* printed in 1589, but doubtless performed several years earlier, was written by Kyd. The Induction is occupied with a 'debate' or 'mutiny' among the divinities of Olympus, due to the endeavour of Venus to destroy the power of Fortune, in order to assert her own supreme authority. At the bidding of Jupiter, Mercury hereupon exhibits a series of dumb-shows of persons slain by Love or Fortune; after which the action of the play itself begins, accompanied by musical demonstrations of the alternating successes of the two contending deities in aiding or defeating the purposes of the lovers Hermione and Fidelia, with whose story it is concerned. In the body of the play, of which the greater part is written in a rimed twelve-syllable measure, there seems nothing to connect it with a writer so comparatively advanced in manner as Kyd; of the Induction part is in blank verse, but rimes are here also frequent.

Other early plays have been attributed to Kyd by Mr. Fleay and earlier writers, among them the *Taming of a Shrew* (1594), on which Shakspere founded his comedy, *Titus Andronicus,* which similarity of theme and treatment naturally associated with **The Spanish Tragedy,** and (on the evidence of a few parallel passages) *Arden of Feversham.* Of more interest, and supported by certain specious considerations partaking of the nature of both external and internal evidence, is the hypothesis, first offered by Malone and since adopted by Widgery, Fleay, and others, that Kyd was the author of an early tragedy of *Hamlet*, lost to us but known to Shakspere. The extent and depth of the interest which such a hypothesis involves may be illustrated by the statement of one of its more recent supporters, that 'whatever in *Hamlet* is relatively out of harmony with Shakspere's taste, may be more or less interpreted to be due to Kyd.' But to examine from such a point of view the conjecture in question would be foreign to the purpose of a historical sketch. . . . Resemblance—or let us say cognateness—of theme furnishes no proof of identity of authorship—still less is the latter demonstrated by incidental similarities of treatment. For my part, I am unable, in dealing with a lost *caput,* to reach conviction except by way of external evidence, which in this instance appears to me inadequate.

The author of **The Spanish Tragedy** was a contemporary of dramatists who were greater than himself, in whatever degree he may have directly or indirectly influenced their endeavours. But, to whatever extent he may in his turn have profited from the productions of his fellow-playwrights, he was himself a dramatic poet of high and original capacity for dealing with both the matter and the form of the branch of literature to which he devoted his labours. He proved himself capable of presenting, without servile adherence to Senecan models,

> *Tragoedia cothurnata,* fitting kings,
> Containing matter, and not common things;
> [**The Spanish Tragedy,** V]

and he was at the same time able to exhibit with natural force the operation of incidents upon character, and to make a direct and irresistible appeal to the passions that move all men, and are felt by generation after generation. Herein lies the great difference between him and the authors of *Gorboduc;* nor will he, because of the ridicule which was his recompense from some of those to whom he had helped to point the way, be refused the tribute due to original power. (pp. 303-13)

> *Adolphus William Ward, "Thomas Kyd (1557 c.-1595 c.)," in his* A History of English Dramatic Literature to the Death of Queen Anne, *Vol. I, revised edition, 1899. Reprint by Octagon Books, Inc., 1966, pp. 303-13.*

Frederick S. Boas   (essay date 1901)

[*In the excerpt below, Boas attributes the* Ur-Hamlet *and* Soliman and Perseda *to Kyd, citing contemporary references and stylistic similarities to Shakespeare's early quarto version of* Hamlet *for the former and stylistic and textual likenesses to* The Spanish Tragedie *for the latter.*]

[Kyd's biographer has a difficult, if] alluring task in vindicating his claim to be the first playwright who put the story of Hamlet upon the stage. There is only one piece of external evidence in support of this claim, but it is very strong in itself, and is rendered practically conclusive by arguments from analogy. The external evidence is contained in the passage from Nash's prefatory Epistle to

Menaphon. . . . [Unless] we are misled by a wellnigh incredible conspiracy of coincidences, Kyd must be the object of Nash's attack, and, consequently, the author of the early Hamlet-tragedy to which he derisively alludes.

One point only in Nash's invective, which has been somewhat overlooked, raises a difficulty. He talks of his enemy as being scarcely able to 'latinize' his neck-verse, and then continues: 'yet English Seneca read by candle-light yeeldes manie good sentences, as "bloud is a begger," and so forth: and if you intreate him faire in a frostie morning, he will affoord you whole *Hamlets,* I should say handfulls of tragical speeches.' It must be admitted that to say of Kyd that he could scarcely latinize his neck-verse is stretching a satirist's licence to its limits. The *alumnus* of Merchant Taylors' had . . . a fairly wide, if not very accurate knowledge of classical literature, and he knew his Seneca thoroughly in the original. But in a passage like Act III. i. 1-11 of **The Spanish Tragedie,** where lines 57-73 of the Roman dramatist's *Agamemnon* are adapted into English, an unfriendly eye might see the influence of a translation, and the **Ur-Hamlet** may have contained a number of these borrowings. In any case, the charge against its author of 'bleeding' English Seneca line by line, and page by page, must be exaggerated, for the play seems to have been in blank verse, while the translations of the 'Ten tragedies' were chiefly in rhymed fourteeners. Moreover, with a reckless disregard of consistency in his eagerness to make damaging hits, Nash, having first taunted his enemy with his lack of Latinity, afterwards accuses him of borrowing his description of the lower world from Virgil, for this is what is evidently meant by his learning 'the measure of the Horizon' from 'an hexameter.' Thus the satirist's scurrilous depreciation of his rival's classical attainments may be largely discounted, and cannot outweigh the cumulative argument from the entire passage for identifying Kyd and the author of the **Ur-Hamlet.**

Can this identification be supported on other grounds, and can we form any definite idea of the nature of the lost play? To answer these questions, with their far-reaching consequences, we must glance first at the Hamlet-story in its undramatized form. As freely rendered by Belleforest in his *Histoires Tragiques,* 1571 (Bk. V.), from the Latin of Saxo Grammaticus, it is a primitive tale of lust, blood-feuds, and revenge. It embraces the marriage of Horvvendille, governor of Diethmarsen, with Geruthe, daughter of the King of Denmark, and the birth of their son Amleth; the murder of Horvvendille by his brother Fengon, and the latter's union with Geruthe, whom he had previously seduced; Amleth's pretence of madness to compass his revenge on his uncle; his interview with his mother in a closet, and the murder of an eaves-dropping councillor; his dispatch by Fengon to England with secret instructions for his assassination; his discovery of the plot and return, followed by the execution of his long-delayed vengeance; his ascent afterwards of the Danish throne, his double marriage, and his death in battle at the hands of his maternal uncle Wiglere.

The dramatization of this story was doubtless prompted by the visit of English actors to the Court of Helsingör (Elsinore) in 1586. The troupe returned in the autumn of

1587, and it was probably in the latter part of this year, or in 1588, that the piece ridiculed by Nash was written. From his allusions we gather that this first Hamlet-play was in Senecan style, and that it contained elaborate 'tragi-call speeches,' and phrases like 'bloud is a begger,' which caught the popular ear. In all these points its technique corresponded to that of *The Spanish Tragedie.* One of its Senecan features was evidently the introduction of the Ghost of Hamlet's father—of whom Belleforest knows nothing—for Lodge in his *Wit's Miserie,* 1596, speaks of 'the ghost which cried so miserally at the Theator like an oister-wife, *Hamlet, reuenge.*' The parallelism with the Ghost of Andrea is obvious, but these bloodthirsty *Umbrae* haunt early Elizabethan Tragedy so assiduously that the presence of one of them does not count for much in deciding claims of authorship.

What is far more significant is the transformation in other, more unique, features which Belleforest's story seems to have undergone as soon as it was put upon the stage. For the First Quarto of the Shakespearean *Hamlet,* whatever view be taken of the problems which it raises in other ways, reproduces, it may be reasonably inferred, at least the broad outlines of the earlier play on the subject. And in it we find the original saga developed into a complex dramatic structure curiously analogous to *The Spanish Tragedie.* For as in that play the *Leitmotif* of Hieronimo's revenge is interwoven with a political intrigue and a love-romance, so the First Quarto contains a tripartite plot, on exactly parallel lines. Belleforest does not mention Norway except to say that Collere, its king, was killed in a duel with Horvvendille. But as in *The Spanish Tragedie* ambassadors pass to and fro, between Spain and Portugal, with 'articles' relating to the Viceroy's son, so in the First Quarto they come and go between Denmark and Norway with articles concerning the Norwegian king's nephew. Belleforest represents Hamlet, before his coronation, as indifferent to women. But as the Portuguese prince Balthazar has an ill-starred love for Bel-imperia, so Hamlet in the Quarto is found similarly circumstanced towards a lady, Ofelia. And as Bel-imperia's father and brother lecture her in turn on her behaviour, so Ofelia is treated in like manner by Leartes and Corambis. The parallel between the two brothers Leartes and Lorenzo is strikingly close, and it is noticeable that the latter, as well as the former, is represented as having been for a time in Paris (*Sp. Tr.* IV. i. 166-7). The contrast between Hamlet and Leartes in their pursuit of vengeance for a murdered father is akin to that between Hieronimo and Bazulto in their endeavours to obtain justice for a murdered son. Hamlet, like Hieronimo, makes use of a theatrical performance as a factor in his plan of revenge. This 'play-scene' in the Quarto, it is true, does not, as in *The Spanish Tragedie,* bring about the catastrophe of the piece. But the final episode of the fencing-match between Hamlet and Leartes, when (as the stage-direction puts it) they 'play' before the King, Queen, and Court, and when an apparently harmless diversion turns abruptly into a tragic *mêlée* involving performers and spectators in a common doom—does not all this, of which there is no hint in Belleforest, exactly reproduce the crowning situation at the close of *The Spanish Tragedie?*

Thus if the First Quarto of *Hamlet* preserves even the

broadest outlines of the *Ur-Hamlet,* the strong external evidence in favour of Kyd's authorship thereof is confirmed by practically irresistible internal tests. But can we go even further and find in the First Quarto, or elsewhere, something more than mere outlines—actual traces of the early play? In the German piece *Der Bestrafte Brudermord,* known from a MS. dated 1710, and first printed by Reichard in 1781, critics like Latham (*Two Dissertations on Hamlet,* 1872) and Widgery (*Harness Prize Essay,* 1880) have seen an adaptation of the *Ur-Hamlet,* preserving features of it otherwise lost. But Tanger [in his article *Der bestrafte Brudermord oder Prinz Hamlet aus Dänemark und sein Verhältniss zu Shakespeare's Hamlet* in the *Shakespeare-Jahrbuch*] has, I consider, conclusively proved that this piece is nothing more than a version of the First Quarto, with probably a few later additions due to actors familiar with Shakespeare's play in its later form. Its unique passages, instead of being survivals from a vanished original, are simply such accretions to the text as would naturally arise after its acclimatization on the German stage. Thus the poetical Prologue in which Night summons the Furies and dispatches them to their fell work might, with little change, be prefixed to any tragedy of lust and murder. Hamlet's anecdote (II. iv) of the cavalier in Anion who at night found his seemingly lovely bride a mere patchwork of paint and false features is met with in other German plays of the period. His reproof to the actors (II. vii), who call themselves *hochteutsche Comödianten,* exactly hits off the weak points in the German travelling companies of the time. His tale in the same Scene of the woman in Strassburg who, after murdering her husband, was moved to confess her crime by seeing a similar tragedy represented on the stage, is suggested by the lines,

> I have heard that guilty creatures sitting at a
> play
> Hath, by the very cunning of the scene, confest
> a murder.

There is only one of his utterances that presents difficulty. When the King tells him (III. 10) that he is going to send him to England he retorts, 'Ja, ja, König, schickt mich nur nach Portugall, auf dass ich nimmer wieder komme, das ist das beste.' Latham has detected here an allusion, retained from the *Ur-Hamlet,* to the disastrous English expedition to Portugal in 1589. But apart from the fact that the *Ur-Hamlet* was written probably in 1587 or 1588, the words blurted out by the Prince in a dialogue, where he talks arrant nonsense throughout, probably contain no historical reference whatever.

Thus, if traces of the old play survive at all, it is in the First Quarto only that they are to be found. It is needless to labour here the universally accepted conclusion that the text of this Quarto, however mutilated and imperfect, represents an earlier version of the tragedy than the definitive Quarto of 1604. The two Quartos diverge mainly in the later three Acts, and Messrs. Clark and Aldis Wright in their Clarendon Press edition of *Hamlet* (1871) conjectured that there was an old play in the story of Hamlet, some portions of which are still preserved in the Quarto of 1603; that about the year 1603 Shakespeare took this, and began to remodel it for the stage, as he had done with other plays; that the Quarto of 1603 represents the play after it had been retouched by him to a certain extent, but before his alterations were complete; and that in the Quarto of 1604 we have for the first time the *Hamlet* of Shakespeare. Since these words were written, the existence of the old play has been proved beyond dispute, and the evidences of Kyd's authorship of it have become practically conclusive. If then the First Quarto 'preserves portions' of the *Ur-Hamlet,* traces of Kyd's style should be found in it; and this, I hold, is the case. The bulk of the blank verse in the three later Acts is, in my opinion, unmistakably pre-Shakespearean. The vocabulary and the rhythm are not those of the master-dramatist at any stage of his career, while in Kyd's works they may be frequently paralleled.

Thus (First Quarto, III. 2) after the play-scene Hamlet cries:

> And if the King like not the tragedy,
> Why then, belike, he likes it not, perdy.

So (*Sp. Tr.* IV. i. 196-7) shortly before the play-scene, Hieronimo cries:

> And if the world like not this Tragedie,
> Hard is the hap of olde *Hieronimo.*

When Hamlet proposes to his mother to help him in his revenge, she answers (First Quarto, III. 4):

> I will conceale, consent, and doe my best,
> What strategem soere thou shalt deuise.

Compare the dialogue in a similar situation between Bel-imperia and Hieronimo:

> *Bel. Hieronimo,* I will consent, conceale,
> And ought that may effect for thine auaile,
> Ioyne with thee to reuenge Horatioes death.
> *Hier.* On then; whatsoeuer I deuise,
> Let me entreat you, grace my practises.

After the King has sought to restrain Leartes' rage at his father's death, the young nobleman declares (First Quarto, IV. 5):

> You have preuailed, my Lord: a while Ile striue
> To bury grief within a tombe of wrath.

So when Horatio calms Bel-imperia's agitation, she murmurs (*Sp. Tr.* II. iv. 20)

> Thou hast preuailde; ile conquer my misdoubt,
> And in thy loue and councell drowne my feare.

The King, later, when proposing to Leartes the strategem of the fencing-match, tells him that Hamlet has often wished (First Quarto, IV. 7)

> He might be once tasked for to try your cunning.

When Hieronimo suggests to Bel-imperia that she should act the part of Perseda in French, she replies in almost identical words (*Sp. Tr.* IV. i. 178):

> You meane to try my cunning then, Hieronimo.

Leartes, not understanding the purport of the King's suggestion, asks, 'And how for this?' and the latter begins his explanation with 'Marry, Leartes, thus.' Precisely in the same way, Lorenzo asks Hieronimo, when he is leading up to the mention of his 'tragedy' (*Sp. Tr.* IV. i. 74), 'And

how for that?' to which the Marshal answers, 'Marrie, my good Lord thus,' and then discloses his project. And in either case, at the end of the explanation, there comes the applauding cry, ' 'Tis excellent' from Leartes, and 'O excellent' from Lorenzo.

Immediately after Leartes' ejaculation the Queen enters with the news of Ofelia's death by drowning, whereupon her brother exclaims:

> Too much of water hast thou, Ofelia,
> Therefore I will not drowne thee in my teares,
> Reuenge it is must yeeld this heart releefe
> For woe begets woe, and griefe hangs on griefe.

Hieronimo, gazing upon his murdered son, yearns 'to drowne' him 'with an ocean of' his 'teares' (*Sp. Tr.* II. v. 23), and cries fiercely:

> To know the author were some ease of greife,
> For in reuenge my hart would find releife.

And as Ofelia has 'A Dirge sung for her maiden soul' (First Quarto, V. 1), so over Horatio his father says his dirge, as 'singing fits not this case.'

Hamlet, in the same Scene, after asking Leartes why he wrongs him, protests, 'I neuer gaue you cause'; Lorenzo uses exactly the same words to the Marshal (*Sp. Tr.* III. xiv. 148). And as the King thereupon exclaims to Gertred:

> Wee'l haue Leartes and our sonne
> Made friends and Louers, as befittes them both;

so Castile cries to his son and to Hieronimo:

> But heere, before Prince Balthazar and me,
> Embrace each other, and be perfect freends.

In both cases, it may be added, the scene of feigned reconciliation is the prelude to the final catastrophe.

In Kyd's other works further parallels with the First Quarto occur. One of the most remarkable features of the plot in the Quarto, as contrasted with Belleforest's story, is the prominence given to the question of second marriage—a question in which Shakespeare nowhere else shows any interest. In the play-scene, especially, the dialogue on the topic is striking (First Quarto, III. 2):

> *Duke.* . . . Therefore, sweete, Nature must pay
>   his due,
> To heauen must I, and leaue the earth with you.
> *Dutchesse.* O say not so, lest that you kill my
>   heart,
> When death takes you, let life from me depart.
> *Duke.* Content thy selfe, when ended is my date,
> Thou maist (perchance) haue a more noble
>   mate . . .
> *Dutchesse.* O speake no more, for then I am ac-
>   curst,
> None weds the second, but she kils the first:
> A second time, I kill my Lord that's dead,
> When second husband kisses me in bed.
> *Duke.* I doe beleeue you, sweete, what now you
>   speake,
> But what we doe determine oft we breake. . . .
> *Dutchesse.* Both here and there pursue me last-
>   ing strife,
> If once a widdow, euer I be wife.

Duke. 'Tis deepely sworne, sweete, leaue me
here a while.

With the thought and, to a slighter degree, the phraseology of this passage, may be compared Cornelia's self-reproaches for having taken a second husband (*Corn.* II. 31-54). The same topic is discussed in *The Housholders Philosophie* . . . where second marriage is permitted only as a concession to human weakness. So, too, the King of Denmark's moralizings to Hamlet on the loss of fathers as a general law of nature (First Quarto, I. 2) are paralleled by Cicero's similar reflections addressed to Cornelia (*Corn.* II. 214-6 and 252-7). And his outburst of remorse after the play-scene (First Quarto, III. 3):

> The earth doth still crie out vpon my fact,
> Pay me the murder of a brother and a king.

recalls *The Murder of Iohn Brewen* . . . where of the first fratricidal sin it is said: 'Albeit there was none in the world to accuse *Caine* for so fowle a fact . . . yet the blood of the iust *Abel* cried most shrill in the eares of the righteous God for vengeance, and reuenge on the murderer.'

Even when we remember that Elizabethan writers were fond of ringing the changes on a stock of current phrases, and that verbal coincidences here and there may be purely accidental, the series of parallels quoted above point to the survival in the First Quarto of traces of Kyd's play. But it must be admitted, on the other hand, that we do not find in the Quarto some features of style characteristic of the author of *The Spanish Tragedie*. We miss the passages of semi-lyrical dialogue, the flights of rhetorical imagination, the 'handfuls of tragical speeches' which, as we know from Nash, must have been prominent in the *Ur-Hamlet*.

For so complex a problem, no short and simple solution is to be found. But the following theory of the evolution of the Hamlet-tragedy is the one I would propose as covering most satisfactorily all the known *data*. The *Ur-Hamlet* was written by Kyd, probably in the latter part of 1587, and resembled *The Spanish Tragedie* in style and technique. It did not, however, become as popular as its sister play. There is no record of its having been printed; and when it was revived by Henslowe on June 9, 1594, at Newington Butts, it brought in only eight shillings, and was not repeated under his management. But Lodge's allusion, quoted above, suggests a performance of it at the 'Theater' in 1596, and it would appear to have been brought out again about 1602 at Paris Garden, for Tucca in *Satiromastix* exclaims, 'My name's *Hamlet revenge:*—thou hast been at Parris garden, hast not?'

We thus see the play keeping the stage in somewhat fitful fashion for fifteen years before Shakespeare began to handle it. During this period it probably underwent, in manuscript form, a certain amount of adaptation to suit the rapid changes of popular taste, or the circumstances of different companies. Thus, when Shakespeare, possibly stirred to emulation by the extraordinary success of Ben Jonson's expanded version of *The Spanish Tragedie,* began in 1602 to remodel the kindred *Ur-Hamlet,* he would appear to have had as his basis, not Kyd's play in its primitive form, but a popularized stage version of it. Shakespeare himself, in his first revision, kept in the three

last Acts considerable portions of this version. Evidences of Kyd's hand, though partly overlaid, are, as I have tried to show, scattered sufficiently through the text to vindicate his share in the creation of the modern world's most wonderful tragedy. Nor is there anything presumptuous or paradoxical in making such a claim on his behalf. Kyd, be it repeated, was not a great poet nor thinker, but he was a brilliant playwright. The elaboration of a complicated plot, the invention of striking situations and effective dialogue, the portraiture of aristocratic social types—all were well within his range. In so far as *Hamlet* still fascinates us by virtue of these qualities, the credit, I believe, belongs primarily to him. But, if untouched by Shakespeare, it would have remained a well-wrought stage-play, and nothing more. The master-dramatist transformed what was probably a flamboyant presentment of the Prince of Denmark's irresolution into the subtle study of diseased emotion and palsied will with which the world is familiar. He filled in the outlines of the other figures at the Court of Elsinore, till they formed a matchless picture of a corrupt, artificial society. He replaced monotonous and lack-lustre verse by dialogue, both in prose and poetry, so vivid and inexhaustibly suggestive, that *Hamlet* in its final form holds its unique position less as a play, in the strict sense, than as a marvellous literary creation thrown into dramatic form. Generations of critics have sought to find a completely satisfying interpretation of the work. They have failed to do so—even the greatest of them—and failed inevitably. For the *Hamlet* that we know is not a homogeneous product of genius. It is—unless evidences external and internal combine to mislead us—a fusion, with the intermediate stages in the process still partly recognizable, of the inventive dramatic craftsmanship of Thomas Kyd, and the majestic imagination, penetrating psychology, and rich verbal music of William Shakespeare. (pp. xlv-liv)

. . . . .

Soliman and Perseda is anonymous in all three [of its published] editions, and there is no external evidence to indicate its author. But there are weighty grounds for attributing it to Kyd, and, even if these are not accepted as conclusive, it still stands in unique relation to his dramatic work. For the story of Soliman and Perseda is the subject of Hieronimo's play in Act IV of *The Spanish Tragedie.* It must, therefore, have deeply interested Kyd, and been looked upon by him as suitable material for the stage. Could we be certain that the Marshal's words (*Sp. Tr.* IV. i. 76-7):

> When in *Tolledo* there I studied
> It was my chance to write a Tragedie . . .
> Which long forgot, I found this other daie.

were thinly veiled autobiography, we should conclude that Kyd, while at one of the Universities, had composed a piece on this pathetic theme. But this is a very doubtful assumption and even if the tragic 'interlude' introduced into *The Spanish Tragedie* was a youthful production of Kyd's, it was little more than a skilful *tour de force* 'in vnknowne languages,' each of the characters speaking a different tongue. It is far more likely to have been written expressly for its function in *The Spanish Tragedie,* as the plot of the tale is modified to suit the peculiar exigencies of the situation in the main play. Wotton's *Courtlie Controuersie* was probably the source of the Marshal's piece; though in narrating its 'argument' he cites the 'Chronicles of Spaine,' and calls Perseda 'an Italian Dame,' though Wotton speaks of her as 'borne in the Isle of Rhodes.' But its *dénouement* is arranged to accomplish Hieronimo's purpose of revenge. Therefore Erastus (Lorenzo), instead of being beheaded on a false charge of treason, is stabbed by the Bashaw (Hieronimo); and Perseda (Bel-imperia), instead of being slain by Turkish bullets, and buried by Soliman (Balthazar) in a magnificent tomb, kills the Sultan and afterwards herself. The Bashaw, too, instead of being hanged by Soliman, is the last survivor, because it was necessary for Hieronimo to address an *apologia* to the Court. Hence I cannot accept Sarrazin's theory [in his "Der Verfasser von *Soliman & Perseda,*" Englische Studien, 1891] that Kyd had written a youthful piece in English on the subject of Soliman and Perseda before *The Spanish Tragedie;* that he drew upon this for Hieronimo's play; and that, in a later revised form, this is the drama licensed for the press in 1592, and known to us in the Quartos described above. Kyd is much more likely to have first introduced the story episodically into *The Spanish Tragedie,* and afterwards to have elaborated it in an independent work. And the extant play in its metrical characteristics, such as the comparative frequency of double endings and run-on lines, and in its proportion of blank verse to rhyme, is more akin to *Cornelia* than *The Spanish Tragedie.* It was, we may conclude, written between the two, either towards the close of Kyd's chief dramatic period, about 1588, or possibly a few years later, when he had entered the service of his powerful patron.

The play, especially in the first three Acts, follows the lines of Wotton's novel very closely, at times borrowing even from its phraseology. But it makes additions and changes which recall the technique of *The Spanish Tragedie,* and which, coupled with Kyd's known interest in the story, go far to prove his authorship of *Soliman and Perseda.* The introduction of a chorus consisting of the allegorical figures, Fortune, Love, and Death, is not in itself very significant; but it is noteworthy that the trio argue and quarrel at the end of each Act, like the Ghost of Andrea and Revenge in *The Spanish Tragedie,* and that, when all is over, the Ghost and Death respectively count up exultingly the numbers of the slain. Erastus' description to Perseda (I. ii. 53-61) of the combatants who have assembled for the tournament, is closely akin to the similar enumeration of national types in *Cornelia,* I. 59-63, and IV. ii. 44-51; while the next Scene, wherein the Prince of Cipris questions the knights about their exploits and mottoes, and they reply in turns, resembles *The Spanish Tragedie,* I. v. 13-56, where the King questions Hieronimo concerning the knights with their 'scutchions,' introduced into his masque, and he recounts the achievements of each of the three.

But more significant in its bearing on the problem of authorship is Act I, sc. v, to which there is nothing parallel in the novel. In this Scene Soliman is introduced with his two brothers Amurath and Haleb, of whom the former kills the latter as a traitor, for protesting against an attack on Rhodes, and is slain in retribution by Soliman himself.

The episode has little relation to the main plot, and serves mainly to keep a balance between the scenes at Constantinople and on the island of Rhodes. It thus is remarkably parallel to Act I, sc. iii of *The Spanish Tragedie,* where, on similar grounds, the action is abruptly shifted from Spain to Portugal, and the Viceroy appears between two lords, one of whom, by a charge of treachery, nearly brings the other to his doom. As this Scene is followed by the first tender interview between Horatio and Bel-imperia, so the similar one at Constantinople precedes the opening love-dialogue between Ferdinando and Lucina, which is also an invention of the playwright's. Here Ferdinando's greeting—

> As fits the time, so now well fits the place,
> To coole affection with our words and lookes,
> If in our thoughts be semblant simpathie.

recalls Horatio's address to his mistress (*Sp. Tr.* II. ii. 1-4)—

> Now, Madame, since by fauour of your loue
> Our hidden smoke is turned to open flame,
> And that with lookes and words we feed our
>   thoughts,
> (Two chiefe contents, where more cannot be
>   had).

And the dialogue between Erastus and Perseda (*Sol. and Pers.* II. i. 153-66), where the latter gives a mocking twist to her apparently faithless lover's pleadings, is akin in spirit and structure to that in which Bel-imperia parries ironically the addresses of Balthazar (*Sp. Tr.* I. iv. 77-89). Perseda again displays her powers of repartee, under graver circumstances, in her first interview with Soliman (*Sol. and Pers.* IV. i. 91-110). The episode that follows, where she is doomed to execution and delivered on the very stroke of death, is not found in the novel; but it has a counterpart in *The Spanish Tragedie,* III. i, where Alexandro similarly makes ready for martyrdom upon the stage, and is saved as if by miracle. The whole process, too, of Alexandro's condemnation on a false charge is paralleled by the arraignment of Erastus on perjured evidence, of which the novel gives only the barest hint (*Sol. and Pers.* V. ii). And the last interview between Soliman and Perseda, where the heroine, in man's disguise, declares (V. iv. 31):

> Then will I yeeld *Perseda* to thy hands,
> If that thy strength shall ouer match my right,
> To vse as to thy liking shall seeme best;

her death in single combat with the amorous Sultan, and her crafty revenge upon him by granting him a kiss from her poisoned lips—all this is in the mingled vein of tragic irony and of crude melodrama, which marks the close of *The Spanish Tragedie.*

It is in these final episodes that the play diverges chiefly from the novel—where Perseda, as mentioned above, is slain by a volley of shot, and not by Soliman, who survives to mourn her loss and bury her and Erastus in a magnificent tomb. This, though appropriate in a sentimental tale, would have been an anti-climax on the boards, and is rightly altered by the dramatist. Nor are the differences between the finale here and in Hieronimo's play a proof of different authorship. For in the latter case the peculiar conditions made it inevitable that Perseda should kill Soliman, and then take her own life, and that the last survivor should be the Bashaw (Brusor). But in the independent drama the Sultan, not Brusor, is the dominant figure, and the *dénouement* had to be so managed that he should be the last left of the personages in the story, and utter the closing speech.

It has been objected, however, that the comic underplot of *Soliman and Perseda,* introducing Piston and Basilisco, is not in Kyd's manner. But the interweaving of humorous relief with the graver issues of the main theme is an essential feature of *The Spanish Tragedie,* though less prominent than in the present play. Thus the grimly jocular episode of the trial and execution of Pedringano, with its subordinate figures of the Hangman and the Boy, is elaborated into almost an independent little comedy. In *Soliman and Perseda* Piston, who, like Pedringano, is the servant of one of the principal characters, is a leading comic figure; and, though he is more of the conventional 'clown' than his fellow in *The Spanish Tragedie,* he might easily have been drawn by the same hand. Basilisco has no counterpart in Kyd's chief play, but the type of *miles gloriosus,* of which he is a notable variation, must have been so familiar to a man of the dramatist's classical attainments that its introduction into one of his works would be in no way surprising. Basilisco, of whom Wotton's tale knows nothing, owes his birth in a double sense to Latin comedy, for with the coxcombry of the braggart he unites much of the inflated verbiage of the pedant.

The recognition of Kyd as the author of *Soliman and Perseda* would certainly give us a higher estimate of his humorous powers; but to deny his claim as Schroer has done [in his *Über Titus Andronicus*], on the ground that it is a work of far greater merit than *The Spanish Tragedie,* is strangely uncritical. Though with more of lyrical grace and charm, and more even in workmanship, it has not the same stamp of genius as the more popular play. It contains no such titanic figure as Hieronimo, nor so strongly individualized a group of subordinate characters. It is less closely knit in structure, and has nothing to rival the wonderful situation of tragic 'suspense,' which precedes the performance of the Marshal's interlude. Nevertheless, it would be well worthy of Kyd. It transforms, as has been already partly shown, an over-sentimental and diffuse love-story into a well-balanced drama of diversified interest, and is particularly skilful in linking together the earlier and later episodes which in the novel are very loosely connected. Thus Brusor is introduced among the knights who take part in the tournament at Rhodes, and are overthrown by Erastus (I. iii). At the beginning of Act I. v, Soliman is eagerly expecting his return with the news 'how Rhodes is fenc'd'; and his account (III. i. 17-24) of Erastus' exploits on the tilting-field fittingly preludes the Knight's sudden entrance as a fugitive from his native isle. From this point Brusor plays much the same part as in the novel, but Lucina is made his accomplice in the betrayal of Erastus. Wotton only mentions her in the earlier part of the story as receiving from 'a gentleman of the town' the lost chain, which had been Perseda's gift to Erastus, and thereby producing the breach between the heroine and her lover. After the death of her suitor in a duel with Erastus she disappears from the tale. But in the drama she is brought with Perseda a prisoner to Constantinople, and for her share in Brusor's treachery towards the Rhodian knight his infuriated mistress stabs her dead. Thus her fortunes, instead of being merely an episode, are woven skilfully into the entire fabric of the plot.

In the characterization of the principal figures less advance upon the novel is shown. In fact, consistency is somewhat sacrificed for the sake of heightened effect. Erastus remains the type of chivalrous love and gallantry, crushed by adverse fate. But a needless stain is thrown upon his honour by making him win back the chain from Lucina by the use of false dice (II. i. 201-43). Perseda is more markedly changed. In the novel she is a tender maiden, sentimentally impulsive, and quick to seek suicide as a refuge from her woes. In Acts I-III of the play she alters little, but when she is transported to Constantinople she rises to tragic height. Instead of frantically attempting her own life, she faces with heroic calm and fortitude the doom with which Soliman threatens her. Better perhaps had she fallen beneath his stroke then than later; for her hypocritical method of vengeance on him, more repellent far than her stabbing of Lucina, blurs disastrously at the close the fair image of her womanhood. Yet the Sultan's fate is the needful expiation of his crimes. For though the drama borrows from the novel some of his traits of quick sensibility and generous temper, it reveals much more fully the barbarian nature underneath. Victim after victim, beginning with his own brother, falls by his order or by his hand; in his crowning outburst of homicidal fury he kills, over Perseda's body, Basilisco and Piston, and sends his faithful henchman, Brusor, to the block. It is almost a repetition of the orgie of bloodshed that ends *The Spanish Tragedie,* where Hieronimo extends his vengeance to his well-wisher, the Duke of Castile. And though internal evidence alone cannot establish beyond dispute the authorship of an anonymous play, it may be affirmed without doubt that *Soliman and Perseda* was either written by Kyd himself, or—a less probably supposition—by some disciple who elaborated in the master's manner a theme already handled by him in brief upon the stage. (pp. lvi-lxi)

> *Frederick S. Boas, in an introduction to* The Works of Thomas Kyd *edited by Frederick S. Boas, Oxford at the Clarendon Press, 1901, pp. xiii-cvii.*

G. Gregory Smith   (essay date 1910)

[*In the following excerpt, Smith discusses Kyd's authorship of the major dramatic works attributed to him, and emphasizes the influence of his dramatic technique on such playwrights as Ben Jonson and William Shakespeare.*]

The earliest known dated work ascribed to Kyd is *The Householders Philosophie,* a version of Tasso's *Padre di Famiglia.* This volume, by "T. K.," printed in 1588, probably represents the "twopenny pamphlet" work from the Italian to which Nashe refers towards the close of his depreciation. The French enterprise, also amiably described by the same hand, may remain to us in **Pompey the Great, his faire Corneliaes Tragedie,** which appeared under Kyd's name in 1595 as a translation of Garnier's *Cornélie,* and in the record of his intention to follow with a rendering of that author's *Porcie.* [The critic adds in a footnote that an anonymous text of *Cornelia* appeared in 1594.] This intimation of Kyd's interest in the French Senecan brings him into immediate touch with lady Pembroke and her coterie, and gives point to Nashe's double-sensed gibe that the translators "for recreation after their candle-stuffe, having starched their beardes most curiously" made "a peripateticall path into the inner parts of the Citie" and spent "two or three howers in turning over French *Doudie.*" The translation of *Cornélie,* a pamphlet on *The Murthering of John Brewen, Goldsmith,* and perhaps another on *The Poisoninge of Thomas Elliot, Tailor* (both printed by his brother John Kyd in 1592), appear to be the latest efforts of Kyd's short career, which came to an end about December, 1594. In the short interval anterior to this hackwork, between 1585 and the publication of Nashe's attack in 1589, the public were probably in possession of the works on which his reputation rests, his **Hamlet, The Spanish Tragedie,** and **The Tragedie of Solimon and Perseda.** These, and the discredited *First Part of Jeronimo,* still supply some of the thorniest problems to Elizabethan scholarship. Here, only a partial statement can be attempted.

We know that in 1592 **The Spanish Tragedie** was enjoying the fullest popular favour. None of the earliest quartos—Allde's undated print, Jeffes's in 1594, White's in 1599—gives a clue to the authorship. The entry of the licence for **The Spanishe tragedie of Don Horatio and Bellmipeia** (Bellimperia) on 6 October, 1592, is silent; so, too, the later editions, and the notes in Henslowe of Ben Jonson's additions in 1601 and 1602. It is not till we come to the casual reference by Thomas Heywood [in his *Apology for Actors,* 1612] to "M. Kid" as the author that what might have proved another bibliographical crux is fully determined. We may assume, from the hints in the inductions to *Cynthia's Revels* and *Bartholomew Fayre,* that the play was written between 1585 and 1587. Not only are there no direct references to the great events of 1588, such as could hardly be absent from a "Spanish" tragedy—but the deliberate allusion to older conflicts with England shows that the opportunity which Kyd, as a popular writer, could not have missed had not yet come.

The theme of **The Spanish Tragedie** is the revenge of "old Hieronimo" for the undoing of his son Don Horatio and the "pittiful death" of the former in accomplishing his purpose. Though contemporary satire fixed upon the play, and made it out-Seneca Seneca in passion for blood, the essence of the drama lies in the slow carrying-out of the revenge. In this, rather than in the mere inversion of the *roles* of father and son, is there analogy with the Shakespearean *Hamlet*; as there is, also, in certain details of construction, such as the device of the play within the play, the presence of the ghost (with all allowance for Senecan and early Elizabethan habit), and, generally, the co-ordination of three stories in one plot. Consideration of this analogy helps us to define Kyd's position in regard to both the English Senecan tragedy and the Shakespearean:

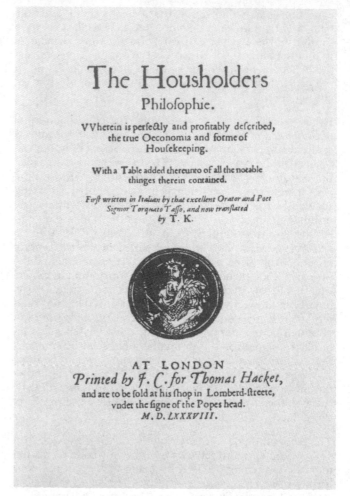

Title page of the 1588 quarto edition of The Housholders Philosophie, *a translation of Tasso's* Il Padre de Famiglia *that has been attributed to Kyd.*

the more immediate matter is that Kyd's interest in this "variant" of the Hamlet story supports, rather than condemns, the conjecture that he had already been engaged on the tragedy of the son's revenge. Such recasting by one hand of a single and simple dramatic *motif* is credible; and, in Kyd's case, likely, when we recall the alleged relationship of **Solimon and Perseda** with **The Spanish Tragedie.** There are few authors of Kyd's repute whose work suggests more clearly a development from within, a re-elaboration of its own limited material. For this reason, it is hard to disbelieve that he wrote a "first part" to his **Spanish Tragedie,** even if we be persuaded that the extant text of the *First Part of Jeronimo* is not from his pen.

Kyd's authorship of a **Hamlet** which served as the basis for the Shakespearean *Hamlet* is more than a plausible inference. As the arguments in support of this are too lengthy for discussion in this place, only a general statement may be made. In regard to the date, we conclude, from the passage in Nashe, that the Saxo-Belleforest story had been dramatised before 1589. As there is no evidence that it had attracted attention in England before the tour of English actors on the continent, and, as they returned from Elsinore towards the close of 1587, we may very reasonably fix the date of production in 1587 or 1588. The assumption that Kyd is the author rests on these main bases: that the first quarto of the Shakespearean *Hamlet* (1603) carries over some sections of an original play, and that there are many parallelisms between the Shakespearean play and *The Spanish Tragedie,* in construction, in phrase and even in metre, and between it and Kyd's other works, in respect of sentiment. The likenesses in construction already hinted at make up, with the textual data, a body of circumstantial evidence which the most cautious criticism, fully conscious of the risks of interpreting the re-echoed expressions of the spirit of the age as deliberate plagiarism, is not willing to throw aside. Indeed, the cumulative force of the evidence would appear to convert the assumption into a certainty. If, as no one will doubt, Shakespeare worked over, and reworked over, some *Hamlet* which had already secured popular favour, why should we, with Nashe and the comparative testimony before us, seek for another than Kyd as the author of the lost, perhaps unprinted, play? We are left with the regret that, having Shakespeare's revisions, we are denied the details of the master's transformation of the original copy. The lesson of this sequence would have told us more of Shakespeare's "mind and art" than we could learn from the unravelling of all his collaborated plays.

That Kyd, following his "serial" habit of production, wrote a "first part" for his "tragedy" is, as we have said, possible, but not a tittle of evidence is forthcoming: that he wrote *The First Part of Jeronimo. With the Warres of Portugall, and the life and death of Don Andrœa,* which we have in the quarto edition of 1605, is, despite the authority lent in support of the ascription to him, wholly untenable. The problem of Kyd's association with a first part may be resolved into two main questions. In the first place, did he write, or could he have written, the extant text of 1605? In the second place, is this piece to be identified with the play entitled "Done oracio" *alias* "The Comedy of Jeronymo," *alias* "Spanes Comodye donne oracoe," which appears seven times in Henslowe's list of the performances, in 1592, of *The Spanish Tragedie?* A rapid reading of the *First Part* will show that, far from there being "adequate internal evidence" for assigning the play to Kyd, there is proof that it must be by another hand. To maintain the ascription of Kyd, we should have to adduce very solid testimony, external as well as internal, that Kyd was capable of burlesque, was a veritable "sporting Kyd," and was Puck enough to make havoc of his art and popular triumph. For, from beginning to end, the piece is nothing but a tissue of rhetorical mockery, a satire of "tragical speeches" and of intermeddling ghosts; often, on closer inspection, a direct quizzing of *The Spanish Tragedie* itself. By no access of literary devilry could the author of old Jeronimo transform that hero to the speaker of such intentional fustian as

> Now I remember too (O sweet rememberance)
> This day my years strike fiftie, and in Rome
> They call the fifty year the year of Jubily,
> The merry yeare, the peacefull yeare, the jocond
>   yeare,
> A yeare of joy, of pleasure, and delight.
> This shall be my yeare of Jubily, for 't is my fifty.

> Age ushers honor; 't is no shame; confesse,
> Beard, thou art fifty full, not a haire lesse.

And it would be hard to believe that Kyd had joined in the raillery of Nashe and the pamphleteers,

> O, for honor,
> Your countries reputation, your lives freedome,
> *Indeed your all that may be termed reveng,*
> Now let your blouds be liberall as the sea;

or could write the ludicrous dialogue between the ghost of Andrea and Revenge at the close. The inevitable conclusion is that this *First Part* cannot have been written by the author of *The Spanish Tragedie;* and further (and almost as certainly), that this burlesque by another hand is not the piece which was interpolated by lord Strange's men in their repertory of 1592. The opportunity for the burlesque came more naturally in the early years of the new century, when *The Spanish Tragedie* had been refurbished by Ben Jonson, and attention had been called to it by his characteristic criticism of the old play. Internal evidence, notably the allusions to the Roman jubilee of 1600 and the acting of the play by the children of the chapel, supports the general conclusion against Kyd's authorship. It should, however, be noted that the argument that the *First Part* does not answer Henslowe's label of "comodey" is irrelevant, if we make allowance for the vague nomenclature of the time and consider that the play makes no pretence to more than the "seriousness" of burlesque. Further, the shortness of the text may be responsible for the view that the play was a "forepiece," presumably to *The Spanish Tragedie.* The Henslowe play (never acted on the same night as the serious *Jeronimo*) might as well be called an afterpiece; but it is hard, in any circumstances, to conjure up an audience of the early nineties, or even of 1605, taking kindly to the two Jeronimos at one sitting.

Though no solid reason has been advanced against the ascription of *Solimon and Perseda* to Kyd, it is only on the slenderest grounds that it has been claimed for him. The story on which it is based appears in Henry Wotton's *Courtlie Controversie of Cupids Cautels* (1578), which also supplies the original of the pseudo-Shakespearean *Faire Em;* the play is entered in the Stationers' register on 22 November, 1592, and is extant in an undated quarto and two quartos of 1599. Its association with Kyd has been assumed from the fact that he uses the same plot in the interpolated play which Jeronimo and Bellimperia present in *The Spanish Tragedie.* If we assume that one author is responsible for both renderings, the question remains as to which play was the earlier. Decision on this point is more difficult because of the long popularity of Wotton's translation, and of Jacques Yver's original, *Le Printemps d'Iver*—as shown in the successive references, from Greene's *Mamillia* (1583), to Shakespeare's *King John* and *Henry IV.* Shakespeare's pointed allusions to Basilisco—the captain Bobadil of *Solimon and Perseda*—imply an immediate and current popularity of the play; and for this reason we incline to dispute Sarrazin's conclusion that it was an early effort, and antecedent to *The Spanish Tragedie.* It appears, on the whole, reasonable to fix the date of composition between the appearance of *The Spanish Tragedie* and the entry in the Stationers' register in

1592, and to consider it, if it be given to Kyd, as a fuller handling of the sketch for Jeronimo and Bellimperia. Certain similarities in *motif,* construction and phrase are tempting aids to the finding of a single author for both plays. On the other hand, the closer we find the likeness, the harder is it to reckon with the difficulty of believing that an author would thus repeat himself. If, as Kyd's most recent editor maintains, **Solimon** lacks the show of genius of **The Spanish Tragedie,** and if, as is also admitted, there is a close family likeness (on which, indeed, the argument of one parentage is based), we are in danger of being forced, contrary to this critic's view and our own (as already stated), to the conclusion that the inferior play must be the earlier. The problem is further complicated by the presence of a strange element of comedy in **Solimon.** This, and, especially, the transcript of the *miles gloriosus* type in the braggart Basilisco, introduces us, if not to a new author, to a new phase of Kyd's art. And so we float, rudderless and anchorless, on the sea of speculation.

The difficulty of determining the authentic work of Kyd makes any general estimate of his quality and historical place more or less tentative; yet the least uncertain of these uncertainties and the acknowledged work in translation give us some critical foothold. Kyd, in the words of his Hieronimo, proclaims his artistic fellowship with the author of *Tamburlaine:*

> Give me a stately written tragedie;
> *Tragedia cothurnata* fitting Kings,
> Containing matter, and not common things.

Even if we allow, on the most liberal interpretation of the claims set up by his editors, that he shows a subtler sense of humour than is to be found in Marlowe, we are never distracted from the sombre purpose of his art. A closer student of Seneca than was his brother dramatist, he transfers, with direct touch, the "tragical" rhetoric, the ghostly personages, the revel in stage massacre; yet never in the intimate fashion of the *Tenne Tragedies* or of his own version of Garnier. We have probably exaggerated his love of "blood." Despite the sensationalism of Horatio's death, Kyd never reaches to the depths of horror satirised in the induction of *A warning for Faire Women,* or disclosed in *Titus Andronicus . . .*; and though, like Webster, whose career as a dramatist began after Kyd's had ended, he deals rawly with the story of revenge, we observe that his zest for the terrible is losing force. Popular opinion neglects these hints of approximation to the gentler mood of Shakespearean tragedy, as it chooses, also, to forget the contributory usefulness of his and Marlowe's extravagance in the making of that tragedy.

The interest of Kyd's work is almost exclusively historical. Like Marlowe's, it takes its place in the development of English tragedy by revealing new possibilities and offering a model in technique; unlike Marlowe's, it does not make a second claim upon us as great literature. The historical interest lies in the advance which Kyd's plays show in construction, in the manipulation of plot, and in effective situation. Kyd is the first to discover the bearing of episode and of the "movement" of the story on characterisation, and the first to give the audience and reader the hint of the development of character which follows from this interac-

tion. In other words, he is the first English dramatist who writes dramatically. In this respect he was well served by his instinct for realism. The dialogue of his "stately written tragedy" is more human and probable than anything which had gone before, or was being done by Marlowe. In the working out of his plot, he escapes from the dangers of rhetoric by ingenious turns in the situation. In such a scene as that where Pedringano bandies words with the hangman when the boy brings in the empty box, or in Bellimperia's dropping of her glove, we are parting company with the older tragedy, with the English Senecans, with *Tamburlaine* and *Faustus* and even *Edward II,* and we are nearer Shakespeare. When we add to this talent for dramatic surprise the talent for displaying character, as it were, rooted in the plot, and growing in it—not strewn on the path of a hero who is little more than the embodiment of a simple idea—we describe Kyd's gift to English tragedy, and, more particularly, to Shakespeare himself. Direct references in Shakespeare and his contemporaries, though they be many, count for little beyond proving the popularity of **The Spanish Tragedie.** The indebtedness must be sought in the persistent reminiscence of Kyd's stagecraft throughout the Shakespearean plays, of devices which could not come from any earlier source, and, because of their frequency, could not come by chance. We reflect on the fact that he, who may have been the young author making trial of Kyd's manner in *Titus Andronicus,* found more than a theatre hack's task in working and re-working upon the early *Hamlet.* From the straggling data, we surmise, not only that Shakespeare knew and was associated

---

Symonds on *The Spanish Tragedy* as a tragedy of blood:

[An] outline of **The Spanish Tragedy** will give a fair notion of the stock ingredients of a Tragedy of Blood. There is a ghost in it—the ghost of Andrea—crying out, 'Revenge! Vindicta!' as it stalks about the stage. There is a noble and courageous lover, young Horatio, traitorously murdered. There is a generous open-hearted gentleman, old Hieronymo, forced to work out his plot of vengeance by craft, and crazy with intolerable wrongs. There is a consummate villain, Lorenzo, who uses paid assassins, broken courtiers, needy men-at-arms, as instruments in schemes of secret malice. There is a beautiful and injured lady, Bellimperia, whose part is one romantic tissue of love, passion, pathos, and unmerited suffering. There is a play within the play, used to facilitate the bloody climax. There are scenes of extravagant insanity, relieved by scenes of euphuistic love-making in sequestered gardens; scenes of martial conflict, followed by pompous shows at Court; kings, generals, clowns, cutthroats, chamberlains, jostling together in a masquerade medley, a carnival of swiftly moving puppets. There are, at least, five murders, two suicides, two judicial executions, and one death in duel. The principal personage, Hieronymo, bites out his tongue and flings it on the stage; stabs his enemy with a stiletto, and pierces his own heart. Few of the characters survive to bury the dead, and these few are of secondary importance in the action.

John Addington Symonds, in his Shakspere's Predecessors in the English Drama, *1900. Reprint. Cooper Square Publishers, Inc., 1967.*

with Kyd's work, but that the association was more to him than a chance meeting in the day's round. Jonson with his "additions"—even with the Painter's Part placed to his credit—supplies an instructive contrast; he intrudes as a censor, and will not be on terms. Yet the fact is worth record in the story of Kyd's influence, that his work is found in direct touch with that of Shakespeare and Jonson. We want to know more of this association, above all of the early *Hamlet* which Shakespeare used; and, wishing thus, we are driven to vain speculation, till the Jonsonian Hieronimo stays us (as he may well do elsewhere in the "quest of enquirie" into Elizabethan authorship):

'T is neither as you think, nor as you thinke,
Nor as you thinke; you'r wide all;
These slippers are not mine; they were my sonne
   Horatio's.

(pp. 177-85)

G. Gregory Smith, "Marlowe and Kyd: Chronicle Histories," in The Cambridge History of English Literature: The Drama to 1642, Part One, Vol. V, *edited by A. W. Ward and A. R. Waller, G. P. Putnam's Sons, 1910, pp. 160-85.*

C. F. Tucker Brooke (essay date 1911)

[*In the following excerpt, Brooke identifies several aspects of Kyd's skillful reworking of the Senecan model in* The Spanish Tragedy *and records the play's influence on later Elizabethan dramatists. The critic also compares* The Spanish Tragedy *to* Soliman and Perseda, *finding that latter play more refined, albeit less inspired, than the former.*]

One of the first popular English tragedies may well be *Locrine,* though the revised version in which the play is preserved can hardly antedate 1591. This drama, the obvious work of a scholar, is formed upon the general lines of the academic Senecan tragedy, but it is developed in harmony with the tastes of a democratic rather than a learned audience. . . . It combines in its loose and tangled structure all the salient features of the native and the imported methods. It displays a healthy desire to present life frankly and freely, without exclusion either of comic or tragic incident, and in the way most impressive to the general spectator. It gives evidence of the availability of the materials of tragedy and indicates the existence of an untrained taste for tragic entertainment. To make of it a tragedy in the true sense there was lacking only the selective and refining power of individual genius.

This genius appeared in Thomas Kyd, by all odds the greatest benefactor of Senecan tragedy in England. Kyd found tragic drama an undomesticated stray, on the one hand barely keeping up a precarious existence in the fashionable shows produced at court and college; on the other hand waging a blind and losing battle on the popular stage against the vigorous comic tradition of the time. Since the first production of *The Spanish Tragedy,* about 1587, the English equivalent of Senecan melodrama has never lost its hold on vulgar audiences. This play is in many ways a much truer representative of Seneca than confessed imitations like *Ferrex and Porrex.* Kyd's dramatic eye seized at once the strong point of the Senecan type,—its power of arousing horror and excitement. By abandoning altogether the conventional practice of indicating action at second hand through the mouths of messengers, and by supplanting the archaic mythological plot, which Norton and Hughes had endeavored vainly to resuscitate, by a modern theme of love and political intrigue, Kyd was enabled to approach the nearer to the actual spirit of Latin tragedy. The chorus, the ghost, and the spectacular peculiarities of Senecan plot remain; but they are vitalized by Kyd's manipulations till they reveal dramatic powers far beyond the vision of antiquarian reactionaries like Hughes,—far even beyond what Seneca himself perceived. The progeny of *The Spanish Tragedy* is infinite. *The Jew of Malta, Titus Andronicus,* and *Hamlet* are all, on one side, at least, its direct descendants; and what each of these owes to Kyd's play is precisely what the latter had derived from the judicious imitation of Seneca.

The "Tragedy of Blood," thus inaugurated by Kyd, depends for success upon the presentation of sensational action in the development of a more or less consecutive plot. To this sensational interest—the characteristic feature of melodrama—all ethical and psychological aims are subordinated. The promise made by Revenge at the beginning of *The Spanish Tragedy* to the ghost of Andrea,—

Thou shalt see the author of thy death,
Don Balthazar, the Prince of Portingale,
Depriu'd of life by Bel-imperia,—

is recalled to the memory of the spectators at the end of each act; and it is the prosecution of this action, together with the parallel vengeance of Hieronimo for Horatio's murder, that furnishes the play with purpose and continuous interest through its four otherwise wandering acts. Moral import is entirely without the scope of this type of drama; there is no thought of picturing the avengers as more amiable or more noble-minded than their victims. The tone of the play is frankly that of the vendetta, and the author accepts savage conditions as he finds them without essaying any interpretation of life's problems.

Nor does *The Spanish Tragedy* seriously attempt the portrayal of individual character. With two exceptions, the delineation of the figures is not only crude, but obviously careless and perfunctory,—the work of a man absorbed entirely in action and devoid of sympathy with the actors. Two characters in the play have, however, received Kyd's attention and possess distinctive traits, because in each case their portrayal offered opportunity for melodramatic effect. The treatment of Hieronimo's madness, glaringly unnatural as it is, made excellent stage business, and impressed itself ineradicably upon the contemporary public, furnishing the sub-title of the play in later printed editions, and the subject of the extensive interpolations ascribed to the pen of Jonson. The exploitation of insanity became, indeed, one of the marked features of Kydian tragedy, even outvaluing as a theatrical asset the inherited Senecan ghost.

In his portrayal of Lorenzo, Kyd manifests again an apparent interest in character, founded not upon psychological discernment, but upon his recognition of the spectacular possibilities of the type. Lorenzo is the first of a long line of Machiavellian villains, whose popularity with a sensation-loving public was in no degree impaired by the palpable improbabilities and limitations in their presentment. He is the original progenitor of the villain of modern melodrama. In contrast with the great tragic heroes of Shakespeare, the species lost prestige; but when first introduced upon the stage, there was a zest hitherto inspired by no dramatic figure about this ardent devotee of policy who could "smile and smile and be a villain,"—who, utterly soulless and heartless, could composedly intrigue out of his way the innocent obstacles to his ends, and, if necessary, could meet his own fate with a like egotistical composure. This is, of course, a low ideal of tragic character, born of the primitive philosophy that makes *sang-froid* and remorseless efficiency the justification of all guile; but its rich potentialities for thrilling action gave it on the untutored tragic stage an irresistible vogue. Its influence was strong enough to cause Marlowe, who knew well a higher form of tragedy, to sacrifice the great psychological and poetic opportunity of his *Jew of Malta;* and in the figure of Young Mortimer it again introduced a coarse thread into the delicate characterization of the same author's *Edward II.* It was one of the determining factors that moulded the youthful work of Shakespeare, inspiring his Aaron in *Titus Andronicus,* his Richard III, and Margaret of Anjou, and coloring deeply his whole idea of tragic character, till Marlowe's example and the experience of life taught him a purer art. Traces of the same conception of the hero-villain show themselves in *Hamlet,* probably as a heritage from Kyd rather than from Shakespeare; and the type continues unchanged in the main characters of Chettle's *Hoffman,* of Barnes's *Devil's Charter,* of *Lust's Dominion,* and *Alphonsus of Germany.*

Lorenzo indicates his character and that of the species to which he belongs in the words of his soliloquy concerning his servant-accomplices, Pedringano and Serberine (III, iii, 111-119):—

> As for my selfe, I know my secret fault,
> And so doe they; but I have dealt for them.
> They that for coine their soules endangered,
> To saue my life, for coyne shall venture theirs:
> And better its that base companions dye,
> Then by their life to hazard our good haps.
> Nor shall they liue, for me to feare their faith:
> Ile trust my selfe, my selfe shall be my friend;
> For dye they shall, slaues are ordeined to no
>   other end.

The source of this crude conception of life and character, which Kyd made one of the assets of cheap tragedy, is to be found in the contemporary attitude toward the works of Machiavelli, one of the most talked of writers of the age, and a particularly well-known figure on the stage. It has been shown that the tenets of the Italian policist were most familiar in the exaggerated form in which they were represented by a French opponent, Innocent Gentillet. Gentillet's work, which by attacking the Satanic shrewdness and egotism of Machiavelli's doctrine, gave an enormous notoriety to the philosophy of the latter, was translated by Simon Patericke as early as 1577, and several times published under the title: "A discourse upon the Meanes of

Well Governing and Maintaining in good Peace, a Kingdom, or other Principality—Against Nicholas Machiavell the Florentine." A passage from Patericke's Epistle Dedicatory will indicate the conception of Machiavellianism which this work disseminated:

> For then Sathan being a disguised person amongst the French, in the likenesse of a merry ieaster [*i. e.,* Rabelais] acted a Comœdie, but shortly ensued a wofull Tragedie. When our countriemens minds were sick, and corrupted with these pestilent diseases, and that discipline waxed stale; then came forth the books of Machiavell, a most pernicious writer, which began not in secret and stealing manner (as did those former vices) but by open meanes, and as it were a continuall assault, utterly destroyed, not this or that vertue, but even all vertues at once: Insomuch as it tooke Faith from the princes; authoritie and maiestie from lawes; libertie from the people, and peace and concord from all persons.

The frank diabolism here attributed to the Florentine provided Kyd with an effective ready-made character for his intriguing prince, Lorenzo; and, in consequence of Kyd's successful employment, created a permanent stage type which long retained its popularity in the face of all efforts at psychological truth.

The Spanish Tragedy virtually created a great deal of Elizabethan stage business. Depending altogether upon spectacular effect, in entire indifference to moral purpose and truth of characterization, Kyd raised tragedy at a single bound to a position decidedly higher in vulgar favor than that occupied by the previously dominant comedy. *The Spanish Tragedy* received and merited more both of popularity and of derision than any other play, probably, which the sixteenth century produced; and it was everywhere imitated. Besides his clever adaptation of Senecan convention to the taste of his time, and his creation of the stock types already referred to, Kyd inaugurated in this play a greater variety of plot devices which persisted in the later drama than can easily be enumerated. The idyllic garden scene between Horatio and Bel-Imperia, setting off the tragedy that environs it; the play within the play of the last act; the employment of the dumb-show, no longer as a mere prelude, but as an integral part of the drama; the dialogue of Andrea and Revenge, encompassing and interpreting the entire course of events; the carefully articulated sub-plot of Serberine and Pedringano, filling out and relieving with its grim humor the bleak horror of the main tragedy: each of these elements—the result of Kyd's quick sense of striking effect—passed into the common stock of the theatre, and repeated itself in numerous variations in the plays of Shakespeare and his contemporaries.

The enormous success of *The Spanish Tragedy* inspired two other plays, which courted popularity by a treatment of the same themes. *The First Part of Jeronimo, With the Warre of Portugall, and the life and death of Don Andrœa* (1605) is a crude sketch of the antecedent history of the Spanish and Portuguese courts. The general appearance of plagiarism about this piece and the many contradictions in the presentation of the main figures of the two plays show *Jeronimo* to be almost certainly the effort of a theatrical hack to deck himself in borrowed glory.

The Tragedy of Solyman and Perseda (1592?), though published anonymously, and lacking decisive evidence of authorship, is now more generally accepted as Kyd's. It is an amplification into a five-act tragedy of the same story which had previously furnished the material for Hieronimo's interpolated play; and it possesses considerable interest as showing how the innovations of **The Spanish Tragedy** fared in later practice. **Soliman and Perseda** is a work of greater polish and much less originality than the earlier play, but it shows the same general characteristics. It is not at all surprising that Kyd should have exhausted his imagination in the prodigality of intrigue and incident which mark his first play. The later effort has little of the uncouth energy of language and action which made **The Spanish Tragedy** ridiculous to critics, but enormously influential. None of the serious characters in **Soliman and Perseda** possesses the interest which attaches to Hieronimo and Lorenzo; yet the later play is obviously better balanced and maturer. Equally with the other it depends for its appeal upon the portrayal of physical action of a bloody and surprising nature; and its plot, though neatly worked out, is even more entirely a narrative of consecutive events, closely following its novelistic source, and lacking the unity which the figures of Andrea and Revenge give to **The Spanish Tragedy.** The main superiority of **Soliman and Perseda** lies in the comic scenes, where the humors of Piston and Basilisco, though quite conventional, are well handled; and in an increased sanity throughout. By most rules, **Soliman and Perseda** should be a better play than its predecessor; but, in fact, it has hardly a tithe of the interest of **The Spanish Tragedy,** either for the critic or the reader. It is an instructive failure, marking clearly the superficiality and insipidity which were inherent in the melodrama, but which the very fault of **The Spanish Tragedy**—its violent excess—served largely to disguise. Along the path which Kyd had outlined, no true advance in tragedy was possible. His first play, struck out wildly in the flush of invention, remained the best of its type; and in spite of its immense vogue and the enormous gain in dramatic technique which it accomplished, it proved to its closest imitators a very misleading guide.

The reason for this is simple. Kyd brought within the range of tragedy all the forces by which an audience might be moved, except only the portrayal of human character. That he entirely ignored. In consequence, the plays of Kyd's type betray their lack of this fundamental requisite of all healthy drama only the more clearly in proportion as they grow saner in other respects. The tragic form which Kyd, with genius almost creative, had evolved from the Senecan tradition was for the present little more than an empty shell. In the case of **The Spanish Tragedy,** the author tempered the barren coldness of his imaginary world by the artificial heat of lurid incident; but the human warmth which he did not find in Seneca he was not able to impart. It was only after Marlowe had breathed into tragedy the vital spirit of psychological truth that the English theatre was prepared to develop effectively the technical form which Kyd had invented. (pp. 207-17)

C. F. Tucker Brooke, "Classical Influence in Tragedy," in his The Tudor Drama: A History of English National Drama to the Retirement of Shakespeare, *Houghton Mifflin Company, 1911, pp. 188-229.*

Donald Clive Stuart   (essay date 1928)

[*In the excerpt below, Stuart examines the significance of Kyd's artistic advances over previous English playwrights in* The Spanish Tragedy, *focusing especially on his skillful development of dramatic tension and a complex plot.*]

About 1587, Kyd composed **The Spanish Tragedy.** It achieved a deserved success, for it is the best example of theatrical art in England up to the time of Shakespeare, who was indebted to Kyd for much of his technique. The plot is based upon the Senecan motive of revenge represented by an abstract character which enters with the ghost of Andrea in a prologue inspired by *Thyestes.* These two characters act as a chorus; and, at the end of the play, they pronounce an epilogue. Their presence gives the whole series of scenes a kind of fictitious unity, for the plot purports to represent the retribution for the death of Andrea in a battle which has already occurred before the play begins. Unfortunately for the dramatic value of the device, the spectator has little interest in the death of Andrea and cares not at all whether his death on the field of battle is avenged or not. Andrea was loved by Bel-Imperia, the heroine; but she, immediately and with no artistic motivation, turns her affections to Horatio who monopolizes the sympathy of the audience, so far as the character of the young lover is concerned. His murder at the hands of Lorenzo, Bel-Imperia's brother, is the death which the spectators wish to see avenged by his father Hieronimo. The motive of revenge in the case of Andrea is purely external. In regard to Horatio, it springs from the father's heart. The theatrical Senecan motive thus becomes dramatic. Kyd wished to open the play with a ghost. He could have chosen the ghost of Horatio; but he also wished to place many events on the stage in conformity to English taste. He therefore selected an early point of attack and introduced the ghost of Andrea. But the point of attack is too late, if we are to be interested in Andrea, and too early, if our sympathy for Horatio is to be the point of departure. The interest of the spectator in the dramatic possibilities is fully assured when Bel-Imperia has fallen in love with Horatio and is loved by the captured prince, Balthazar, who is seconded in his unrequited passion by Lorenzo.

These circumstances cause the spectator to look forward, at least; and when Horatio is murdered, Hieronimo's vow to discover and punish the assassins of his son arouses suspense in a manner and to a degree hitherto unknown in English drama. The vengeance is delayed; but as Professor Boas points out [in his introduction to *The Works of Thomas Kyd,* 1901]: "The cardinal weakness in the play which prevents it ranking among dramatic masterpieces, is Kyd's failure in an adequate psychological analysis of the Marshal's motives for this delay. Inaction only becomes dramatic material when, as in the case of the Shakespearean *Hamlet,* it is shown to be rooted in some disease of character or will." But the delay is theatrically effective. At first it is caused by the fact that Hieronimo does not know, hardly suspects the identity of the murderers. Then he distrusts Bel-Imperia's letter in which she denounces the guilty men. When the intercepted letter from one of the accomplices confirms his suspicions, he is on the point of demanding justice in plain terms, but is evidently cowed by Lorenzo. At last come sickness of heart and mind and self-upbraiding for his delay. It is a first sketch of the original portrait of Hamlet, drawn probably by Kyd, to which Shakespeare added the strokes of dramatic genius. In these progressive steps there is a sweep of climactic action which culminates in the play within the play. Kyd foreshadows the tragedy but does not anticipate the successive *coups de théâtre* in which the feigned avenging murders and suicide turn out to be real.

Although much of the exposition is in narrative form and the battle in which Andrea was killed is described in classical fashion, most of the action is represented. There are several scenes—notably those at the Portuguese court—which do not even deserve reporting, much less actual representation. But in the succession of scenes, there are many situations handled with deftness and melodramatic power. The love scene between Bel-Imperia and Horatio in the bower shows that Lyly's graceful dialogue was not falling in vain upon Kyd's ears. It is a scene in which sympathy goes out to innocent lovers—a rare situation in tragedy up to that time, be it Greek or Senecan, English or French. The ensuing murder of the lover in the presence of his mistress by her brother and her jealous admirer, the finding of the body of his son by Hieronimo plucked from his "naked bed," the entrance of the mother, form a series of effective scenes. Throughout the rest of the play there are too many surprising *coups de théâtre;* Hieronimo takes a handkerchief from his pocket and finds it to be a cloth stained with Horatio's blood; he suddenly discloses the body of his son to show why he has slain the prince and Lorenzo; he makes a sign for a knife to mend his pen when he has bitten out his tongue, and stabs the Duke and himself with the weapon. Theatrical and sensational as they may be, it was from such striking tricks that Shakespeare learned to handle such dramatic actions as the suicide of Othello.

Kyd skilfully combined a secondary action with the main plot. Pedringano, Bel-Imperia's servant, betrays to Lorenzo the secret of her love and her tryst with Horatio. He also is an accomplice, together with Serberine, in the murder. Lest these wretches betray him, Lorenzo incites Pedringano to slay Serberine; Pedringano does so, is captured and condemned to die by Hieronimo himself. Lorenzo has no desire to save him but pretends to send him a pardon in a box. The grisly jesting on the part of Pedringano, who thinks his life is safe just before he is hanged, foreshadows such scenes as the Porter's ghastly joking in *Macbeth.* The effect is not comic relief but grotesque intensification of horror. Finally, the letter of Pedringano to Lorenzo discloses the truth. In no serious play up to this time had such artistry been employed. The sub-plot in Lyly's plays had only a tenuous connection, if any, with the main story. The moralities and chronicles were most inept in this respect. To Kyd belongs the credit of showing

future playwrights how to handle striking situations and construct a plot which arouses suspense and sympathy.

His depiction of characters is not so successful; yet even in this respect he shows an advance over his predecessors. The hero is Hieronimo. He becomes prominent too late in the play; but he is a real personality in comparison to the stock characters of earlier plays. He develops into a different being through a crisis which he himself directs and plans. He suffers, where other heroes merely wail or rage. He is opposed by a somewhat Machiavellian villain in the person of Lorenzo and a lesser villain in Balthazar, neither of whom is drawn with the subtlety of Iago. However, they serve their purpose of actively opposing the protagonist in obligatory scenes, not developed to the utmost, but of a kind rarely represented in Senecan drama. Bel-Imperia and Horatio enlist our sympathy, not merely pity. The mother of Horatio is only sketched. Kyd did not realize the finer shades of psychology inherent in these rôles nor did he make character the keystone of his dramatic structure. (pp. 210-13)

> *Donald Clive Stuart, "English Medieval Drama: Kyd, Marlowe, Shakespeare," in his* The Development of Dramatic Art, *1928. Reprint by Dover Publications, Inc., 1960, pp. 187-240.*

Henry W. Wells (essay date 1939)

[*Wells, an American educator and literary critic who wrote primarily on English-language authors, has also written several essays on Chinese, Japanese, and Sanskrit literature. In the following excerpt from his* Elizabethan and Jacobean Playwrights, *the critic briefly comments on Kyd's masterful plot construction, characterization, and use of language in* The Spanish Tragedy *and emphasizes his influence on later Elizabethan dramatists.*]

The ancestor of [a] long line of satirical and moralizing melodramas of revenge is Kyd's celebrated **Spanish Tragedy,** printed in 1594, one of the most successful of all English plays upon the stage and one of the most influential in the history of the theatre. It is probably the only original play by Kyd which has survived. While it cannot be held equal to the mature work of Webster, Jonson, and the playwrights of the golden age of the theatre, it has no place in the ranks of mediocrity. For at least a quarter of a century it was frequently played and continually revised. For the first time with complete success it introduced to the English stage love, lust, honor, murder, madness, and revenge as themes for tragedy. Far more rapid and lively and essentially medieval in its theatrical style and tempo than the French, Italian, or earlier English plays based on the poetic or declamatory works of Seneca, it set the most popular model for the serious Elizabethan drama. Marlowe's poetry could be parodied but not imitated; Shakespeare was destined for achievements too subtle for reduplication; but Kyd in one stroke determined the technique and the temper of most of the representative tragedies of the period.

The considerable merits of the work are unescapable. It

is both a better constructed and more dignified drama than *Titus Andronicus* or *Hoffman*. The chorus of Ghost and Revenge brilliantly focuses the attitude of reader or audience. The impressive antecedent action gives depth to the theatrical perspective. Major and minor plots are artfully drawn together. Thus at the same moment that the Viceroy of Portugal discovers that he has not, as he has believed, lost a beloved son, Hieronimo finds himself a wrongfully bereaved father. A network of relations between the various characters is firmly knit. Almost all the persons are of some interest, as may be instanced in such secondary figures as Pedringano, who jests so diabolically at death, and Hieronimo's wife, who cries in vain for justice. The relation of brother and sister is successfully studied in the roles of Bel-Imperia and Lorenzo, affording a suggestion for Ophelia and Laertes. Lorenzo and Balthazar, seeking love through secret murder and wealth through conspiracy, are perfect types of the theatrical villain. Hieronimo madly crying for justice in an unjust world and attaining his end only by wide-embracing and bloody murders becomes a type for one of the most important characters repeated throughout Elizabethan drama. He is conceived of as both hero and villain: an unjustly injured man seeking retaliation and a bold individualist breaking the laws of society to effect his primitive and violent justice. Revenge is an even sweeter sin than lust. A much more sinister and less idealized figure than Hamlet, Hieronimo stands somewhere between Shakespeare's noble prince and Tourneur's too savage Vendice in *The Revenger's Tragedy*. Repeatedly the play points the way to later, more mature and more brilliant work. We have foreshadowings of characters and situations, of thoughts and words, in *Hamlet, King Lear*, and *Macbeth*. The use of a play within the play to end the tragedy and serve the conspirators as a cloak for murder gives a stately conclusion not only to this tragedy but to nearly a score of notable plays to follow.

The verse has the quality of an art movement in its lusty youth, the strength and glamour which connoisseurs commonly term "primitive." Though stiff, over-formal, and derivative from earlier English neo-Senecan drama, it is nervous, vigorous, and expressive. Kyd's language seems entirely adequate to voice the sturdy and elementary feelings which he seeks to convey. The unknown hands who contributed the additional passages found in the later quartos enriched the play without marring Kyd's original spirit and design. He obviously writes as a brilliant apprentice in his craft, not as yet free from verbal imitation. Thus he freely quotes or translates passages from Seneca, especially the *Thyestes,* and uses those rhetorical devices which Lyly and his Elizabethan contemporaries loved and which Jonson and the Jacobeans shortly put to tireless ridicule. "O eyes, no eyes" is neither the worst nor the purest style. But the writing becomes an integral part of Kyd's feeling for his art and of the design and sinews of his play. He gives us that first pleasure which we derive from any work aesthetically sound: the joy of encountering a mind which knows thoroughly where it is going. So however we may value his work, we must at least acknowledge it to be unfaltering. His dialogue, based on end-stopped lines, balanced phrases, and frequent rhyme, lacks the flexibility and ease of verse-conversations in the later playwrights

and yet has the measured firmness of a truly lyrical and artificial style. The famous opening speech of the Ghost, the soliloquies of Hieronimo, and the last love scene between Bel-Imperia and Horatio exhibit his style at its typical best. It sounds like clear bells booming over water. Poetry in a measure it undeniably is, though it never reaches the heights attained by any of Kyd's greater successors. Even Ben Jonson in the last stages of his career spoke with apparent sympathy for the old play which he had so often parodied yet to which he had himself made repeated additions.

So far was Kyd in advance of his age that the most faithful and distinguished of his followers in the drama wrote a considerable time after he had come to his own tragic end. Nearly a score of years had passed before it became apparent that Kyd had discovered the richest single vein in the drama of the period. A bloody revenge in which honor exacts the price of lust became the formula for many an Elizabethan masterpiece. (pp. 21-4)

> *Henry W. Wells, "The Tragedy of Evil," in his* Elizabethan and Jacobean Playwrights, *1939. Reprint by Greenwood Press, Publishers, 1975, pp. 14-58.*

Fredson Bowers (essay date 1940)

[*Bowers was an American scholar and educator whose works include* Elizabethan Revenge Tragedy *(1940) and* Hamlet: A Guide to the Play *(1965). In the following excerpt, he argues that* The Spanish Tragedy *"is far from a perfect working out of the revenge theme." In Bowers's opinion, the Andrea-Revenge episodes bear little significance on the rest of the tragedy, Kyd fails to unify the numerous revenge plots in the play, and Elizabethan audiences would have perceived Hieronimo as a villain for exacting lawless, private revenge on Lorenzo and Balthazar. The critic further concludes that Kyd wrote an early version of the Hamlet story, the so-called* Ur-Hamlet, *that preceded* The Spanish Tragedy *and that included themes which Kyd more fully developed in the later drama.*]

With the production of ***The Spanish Tragedy*** Elizabethan tragedy received its first great impetus. The immediate and long-lasting popularity of the play stamped it as a type, a form to be imitated. Thus it is of the highest significance that ***The Spanish Tragedy*** first popularized revenge as a tragic motive on the Elizabethan popular stage by using blood-vengeance as the core of its dramatic action. True, earlier English tragedies, leaning heavily on Seneca, had utilized revenge to a certain extent for dramatic motivation. But in *Gorboduc* (1562) any incipient interest in the characters' motives of revenge is stifled under the emphasis on the political theme and the general classical decorum, and the ancient classical story of revenge in John Pikeryng's *Horestes* (1567) is so medievalized that it loses all significance except as a basis for comedy and pageantry. *Gismond of Salerne*, acted at the Inner Temple in 1567/8, borrows various revenge trappings from Seneca and the Italians but the pathetic love story usurps the main interest.

Elizabethan revenge tragedy properly begins with Thomas Kyd's extant masterpiece, *The Spanish Tragedy* (1587-1589) which presented revenge in kind—blood-revenge, the sacred duty of the father to avenge the murder of his son—and from that sensational theme derived its popularity. Sensational though the central motive proved, it was a universal one, appealing to all classes of people and to all time. As in the law-abiding Athens of Aeschylus, the Greek audience saw enacted in the Orestes trilogy events of a more turbulent past but now outmoded, so the English spectators viewed dramatic action at once somewhat foreign to their present state of society yet still within their range of sympathy and understanding. The realism was clinched when the scene was laid in another country where, to their knowledge, the people were crueler and more revengeful, and where, as in Italy, the individualistic spirit still flourished among the nobility in despite of the law.

The Spanish Tragedy is far from a perfect working-out of a revenge theme. Kyd started to make a Senecan imitation adapted to the popular stage. Someone has been killed, and the slayer is to suffer the revenge of the ghost, presumably by becoming tangled in his own misdeeds as in *Hercules Furens,* or, as in *Thyestes,* through the malign influence of the supernatural chorus. Curiously, this Senecan ghost's reason for revenge is extraordinarily weak as seen through English eyes. The parallel with the ghost of Achilles in *Troades* which rises to demand vengeance for death in battle is obvious, but an English popular audience could not become excited over a ghost seeking vengeance for a fair death in the field. No very personal interest can be aroused in the early action of the play if it proceeds solely from the point of view of an alien ghost, and with Horatio as the successful avenger of his friend.

The first human note is struck when Bel-Imperia resolves to use second love, in the person of Horatio, to revenge the death of her first lover. If this resolution had furnished the plot, the sequence of events would still have revolved about the ghost but with greater logic. Bel-Imperia is more closely connected with Andrea than Horatio, and some semblance of justification is added when Balthazar begins his suit, for the audience can visualize a forced marriage with the slayer of her lover, an impossible situation. Furthermore, at the moment she was the logical revenger since women were noted for their revengefulness in Elizabethan life and the Italian *novelle.* The whole first act is devoted to the exposition and to the resolution of the beloved to revenge the death of her lover. The rising action is begun when Bel-Imperia starts to charm Horatio, her chosen instrument for the revenge, and some hint is given of an opposing force in the person of her brother Lorenzo who has sided with Balthazar's suit.

Still the situation is dramatically almost impossible. Horatio has no thought that Andrea's death requires vengeance; consequently, if he is intended for the revenger of blood, he will prove no more than the weak tool of Bel-Imperia, who, by her insistence in driving him to the deed, will become a villainess. And if Horatio is not to be made this anomalous revenger, Bel-Imperia's only course would be so to set Balthazar and Horatio at odds over her love

that one or the other is killed. If Balthazar falls, the play is no tragedy. If, on the other hand, Horatio is killed, his position as Bel-Imperia's tool precludes the sympathy of the audience, and forces Bel-Imperia herself to kill Balthazar, a course she might have followed in the beginning without causing the death of an innocent man. If Horatio is not conceived as a mere instrument for the unscrupulous Bel-Imperia but as a real and requited lover, his position as revenger for a preceding lover grows even more anomalous, and the revenge for Andrea loses all ethical dignity.

The only solution lies in developing the strength of the opposing force. The second act, therefore, is given over entirely to showing the ascendancy of Lorenzo. Necessarily the revenge theme lies dormant while Kyd devotes himself to painting an idyllic picture of the love of Horatio and Bel-Imperia, and its fatal end. Bel-Imperia is ostensibly carrying out her avowed intention to love Horatio and thus spite Balthazar, but since her passion for Horatio (which has rapidly passed from pretense to reality) seems to have replaced her desire to revenge Andrea, the central theme of revenge is dropped in the emphasis on the happy lovers. Balthazar now has a tangible reason for a revenge: first, because Horatio took him prisoner in battle, and second because Horatio has preempted his intended bride. With Lorenzo as the guiding spirit, the two slay Horatio. The deed is presumably the revenge of Balthazar, but Lorenzo's cold determination to brush aside all obstacles to his sister's royal marriage makes him the real murderer.

At this point the tragedy has strayed its farthest from the main theme as announced by the chorus composed of Revenge and the ghost of Andrea. This time, however, a real revenger of blood appears. Hieronimo does not know the murderers of his son, but he plans to dissemble until he learns and then to strike. At the finish of the second act, with Bel-Imperia imprisoned, and a new revenger for a new crime appearing, the play actually disregards the revenge for Andrea and settles down to dramatize a revenge among men for a crime already seen and appreciated by the audience, no longer a revenge for an unreasonable ghost. From this point the ghost and his theme, which was to be the core of the play, are superfluous; and, indeed, need never have been introduced.

The third act, which begins the second half of the play, works out two lines of action: the progress made by the revenger Hieronimo, and the efforts of the murderer Lorenzo to consolidate his position in order to escape detection. The difficulty of appropriate dramatic action for the revenger posed a nice problem for Kyd. A revenger with no knowledge and no possible clues to investigate is a static figure since action is impossible. Yet a revenger with complete knowledge would normally act at once, and the play would be over. Kyd solved the problem brilliantly. The note from Bel-Imperia which gives him the names of the murderers is so startling that Hieronimo suspects a trap, for he knows of no motive why Lorenzo and the foreign prince should have killed his son. He must therefore assure himself of the truth before he acts, and since Bel-Imperia has been removed from court a delay is unavoidable. At one stroke Kyd has given the necessary information to the revenger, and then tied his hands until the plot has further unfolded.

Hieronimo's projected investigation has provided him with some dramatic action, particularly when the course of his inquiries sets the opposing force once more in motion. Lorenzo, believing his secret revealed, endeavors to destroy all proof by ridding himself of his accomplices Serberine and Pedringano. Ironically, it is this deed which finally gives the revenger his necessary corroboration in the incriminating letter found on Pedringano's dead body. The doubts of Bel-Imperia's letter are now resolved; his delay ended, Hieronimo rushes to the king for justice. It is important to note that Hieronimo first endeavors to secure his legal rights before taking the law into his own hands. Again a problem in plotting occurs. Hieronimo with his proof will gain the king's ear; Bel-Imperia will second Pedringano's letter; the murderers will be executed. Another impossible dramatic situation looms, for there would be no conflict of forces and no tragedy except of the most accidental sort.

It is evident that the revenger must be made to delay once more. Fear of deception cannot be employed again, and clearly the only possible means is either to delay Hieronimo's interview with the king or else to introduce some motive that would lead the king to discredit him. Once again Kyd brilliantly solved the problem by introducing the motive of madness. Isabella, Hieronimo's wife, runs mad, and Hieronimo next appears so stunned by grief for her and for his son that his own wits have been unsettled. He answers a request for information so wildly that his questioners think him wholly insane. Realizing that his madness has made him impotent, he meditates suicide but thrusts the thought aside before the reviving sense of his duty to revenge. His distraction, however, keeps him from gaining the king's ear, and when he recovers his senses he realizes that he can never find legal justice but must act as the executioner himself.

At this point the reasons for delay, previously logical, break down. Hieronimo says simply that he will revenge Horatio's death, but

> not as the vulgare wits of men,
> With open, but ineuitable ils,
> As by a secret, yet a certaine meane,
> Which vnder kindeship wilbe cloked best.
> Wise men will take their opportunitie,
> Closely and safely fitting things to time.
> But in extreames aduantage hath no time;
> And therefore all times fit not for reuenge. . . .
> *Remedium malorum iners est.*
> Nor ought auailes it me to menace them
> Who as a wintrie storme vpon a plaine,
> Will beare me downe with their nobilitie.
>   (III, xiii, 21-38)

These are scarcely valid reasons for delay in the execution of his private justice, since he admits that open and inevitable ills exist (without the necessity for delay) by which he could overthrow his enemies. Of course, his intention to dissemble patiently and to wait until he can consummate his vengeance at the right time and place heightens the interest in the inevitable catastrophe. The speech, in its entirety, would nevertheless irretrievably weaken the logic of the plot and the conception of Hieronimo's character were it not that it marks the turning point from Hieronimo the hero to Hieronimo the villain.

The fourth and last act opens with Bel-Imperia, now entirely forgetful of Andrea, swearing that if Hieronimo neglects his duty to revenge Horatio she herself will kill the murderers. Hieronimo presumably has a plan in mind, for the manuscript of the tragedy is ready when Lorenzo asks for an entertainment. Isabella, tortured by the thought of the unrevenged death of her son, kills herself in a fit of madness. Hieronimo braces himself for his revenge, and the fatal play is enacted. Even with Lorenzo and Balthazar slain and Bel-Imperia a suicide, the Viceroy, Balthazar's father, interposes for Hieronimo. Then occurs a scene which is useless except as it leads to the final culmination of horrors and the eventual conception of Hieronimo as a dangerous, blood-thirsy maniac. Hieronimo from the stage has already rehearsed his reasons for the murders, but the king orders him captured and inexplicably tries to wring from him the causes (already explained) for the deed, and the names of the confederates (already revealed as Bel-Imperia alone). Without this senseless action Hieronimo would have had no opportunity to tear out his tongue or to stab the duke, Lorenzo's father. His own suicide closes the play.

An analysis of the play reveals the basic Kydian formula for the tragedy of revenge:

(1) The fundamental motive for the tragic action is revenge, although the actual vengeance of Hieronimo is not conceived until midway in the play. This revenge is by a father for the murder of his son, and extends not only to the murderers but also to their innocent kindred. The revenger is aided by a revenger accomplice, and both commit suicide after achieving their vengeance.

(2) Hieronimo's revenge is called forth by the successful revenge, conceived for a supposed injury, of the villains on his son.

(3) The ghost of the slain Andrea watches the revenge on the person who killed him and on those who hindered his love, but the action of the latter half of the play does not spring from the motive of a revenge for him nor is this revenge directed chiefly at his slayer. Consequently the ghost has no real connection with the play. This loose use of a vengeance-seeking ghost was not repeated in later plays.

(4) An important dramatic device is the justifiable hesitation of the revenger, who requires much proof, and, on the failure of legal justice, supposedly lacks a suitable opportunity for straight-forward action. Hieronimo finds his task difficult; he is burdened with doubt and human weakness and delayed by his madness. The letter from Bel-Imperia, Pedringano's posthumous confession, the exhortations of Bel-Imperia and her offers of assistance, and the death of his wife, are all required to spur his resolution to the deed.

(5) Madness is an important dramatic device. Hieronimo is afflicted with passing fits of genuine madness brought on by his overwhelming grief and the overwhelming sense

of his obligation and his helplessness to revenge which saps his will. It is not probably that in Kyd's original version Hieronimo ever pretended madness. There are two scenes in which his words are too glib and flighty (the reconciliation with Lorenzo and the plans for the play-within-a-play), but in both his nerves are under pressure owing to the rôle he is acting, and his wild talk shows the intense strain on a mind already somewhat weakened rather than a pretense to lure his opponents into false security.

(6) Intrigue used against and by the revenger is an important element. Lorenzo's machinations fill a considerable portion of the play. Hieronimo secures his revenge by elaborate trickery.

(7) The action is bloody and deaths are scattered through the play. Ten characters are killed, eight of these on-stage.

(8) The contrast and enforcement of the main situation are achieved by parallels. Andrea requires revenging, as does Horatio. Hieronimo's grief for his son is reenforced by the grief of the Viceroy for the supposed death of Balthazar and later for his actual slaying. More particularly, Hieronimo is paralleled by the petitioner whose son has been killed. His madness finds a counterpart in Isabella's, and his hesitation is contrasted to Bel-Imperia's desire for action.

(9) The accomplices on both sides are killed. Bel-Imperia falls a suicide, and the villain with keen irony destroys Serberine and Pedringano in order to protect himself.

(10) Lorenzo, the villain, is an almost complete Machiavellian, as full of villainous devices as he is free from scruples.

(11) The revenge is accomplished terribly, fittingly, with irony and deceit. Once his resolution is screwed to the point, the revenger becomes exceedingly cunning, dissembles with the murderers, and adroitly plans their downfall.

(12) Minor characteristics are: the exhibition of Horatio's body; the wearing of black; reading in a book before a philosophical soliloquy; a letter written in blood and a handkerchief dipped in blood and kept as a memento to revenge; the melancholy of the revenger, who struggles with the problems of revenge, fortune, justice, and death; the sentimental but desperately revengeful woman.

A specific source is customarily presupposed for *The Spanish Tragedy,* but it has never been found, and very probably no detailed source for the entire story ever existed; for if this hypothetical source be disregarded, the roots of the play are found in Seneca's tragedies, the Italian and French *novelle,* possibly in the Renaissance Italian tragedy, and certainly in the old Teutonic story of Hamlet as told by Saxo Grammaticus and translated by Belleforest.

Senecan influence there is undoubtedly in the penning of the lines. The machinery of the ghost of Andrea and Revenge is also Senecan in construction, although the function of the two as chorus is not classical. The Spirit of Revenge is presumably influencing the actions of the characters in much the same fashion in which the ghost of Tantalus casts his malign influence over the house of Pelops in

Thyestes. Such a pulling of the strings from without, therefore, is wholly Senecan, as is the parallel to *Thyestes* where a particular revenge enacted on the stage satisfies the debt to an unrelated crime from the past. Senecan, too, are the bloodshed and horrors, though typically Renaissance in their form. Seneca usually emphasizes one great passion; *The Spanish Tragedy* is a study of the overwhelming passion of revenge. Revenge either moderately forthright, as in *Agamemnon,* or else by secret, deceitful means, as in *Thyestes,* had already appeared in Seneca as a proper subject for tragedy.

To a certain extent, however, the debt to Seneca has been exaggerated. Actual insanity in Seneca is limited to the madness sent by Juno upon Hercules, a situation which has no possible parallel in *The Spanish Tragedy.* Somewhat closer to Kyd's conception are the divine "madnesses" of Medea and Deïanira, but the origin of Hieronimo's insanity does not actually come from the Roman tragedian. The hesitation of the revenger had appeared momentarily when Medea once falters in her resolve and when Clytemnestra requires the goading of Aegisthus. Neither of these plays, however, utilized the motive of hesitation to prolong the plot, as does Kyd, but instead merely to fillip the interest of the audience for a moment with the possibility that the revenge might be abandoned. The true source for Hieronimo's dramatically important hesitation is not there. Again, the suicides of Bel-Imperia and Hieronimo have no relation to the expiatory suicides of Seneca's characters who have caused the death of some beloved person. The most specific contribution of Seneca to the dramatic form of *The Spanish Tragedy* is the ghost; yet it has been noted how Kyd was gradually led away from the Senecan construction so that his supernatural chorus became superfluous and even intrusive. The interest in the play is on the revenge on Lorenzo (and only incidentally on Balthazar) for a Horatio murdered in plain view of the audience, not the revenge on Balthazar for the ghost of Andrea, with whom Hieronimo is entirely unconnected.

Yet the general influence of Seneca on the writing and the original conception of the play cannot be denied, for such an influence was unavoidable at the time. Classical tragedy had gained an enormous prestige in England because of the great value set on classical learning, of which tragedy was supposed to be the highest expression; and knowing little of the Greeks the Elizabethans came to regard Seneca as the most tragic, the most perfect of ancient writers. Senecan tragedy was dominant on the Continent; Seneca was read freely in the English schools and universities where his plays were acted, as were Latin imitations. His methods of treating tragic situations were akin to Elizabethan temperament, for the men of the time were well equipped to understand his philosophy, which held that man, the individual, was more than the puppet of medieval scholasticism and was, indeed, to some extent the master of his fate. Even the fatalistic Senecan passages found a ready echo in the breasts of Englishmen already afflicted with the melancholia which sometimes turned them to practising malcontents. Seneca's cosmopolitanism was near to the Elizabethans, who were starting an empire and were beginning to cast off their insular provincialism.

The crudity hidden beneath the superficial polish of the Elizabethans made them less sensitive to the fundamental emptiness of much of Seneca. They were delighted with his rhetoric, for they were still so intellectually young as to be impressed by bombast and flamboyance. Introspection had become a national trait, and fed agreeably on the elaborate Senecan philosophizing, with its spice of stoicism suitable to a hard-bitten age. The long Senecan descriptions were suited for imitation on the bare English stage. Finally, Seneca's emphasis on sensationalism, on physical horrors to stimulate emotion, appealed to the English taste, for blood and horror on the stage could not be offensive to the spectators at cruel executions. Ghosts were accepted as fact, and forewarnings were everyday affairs, as with Ben Jonson's on the death of his son. Except for his classical subject-matter and his rigid classical form involving the use of choruses, there was no single element of Seneca that could not be accepted immediately by the spectator in the pit.

With such a tradition it was inevitable that *The Spanish Tragedy* should ring with Seneca in its rhetoric. Kyd, however, was no humble slave in his dramatic craftmanship. Admitting freely that it would be difficult to conceive *The Spanish Tragedy* without Seneca, we find, when details are sought for specific sources of plot and characterization, that the way leads beyond Seneca. It is highly probable that Kyd, uninfluenced specifically save by Belleforest's story of Hamlet, drew his main inspiration for the working out first of Lorenzo's and then of Hieronimo's and Bel-Imperia's revenges not from Seneca but from the ethics and incidents in the Italian and French stories and from English ideas about the Italian character.

So closely allied with the villainous characters of the Italian novels that the two cannot be separated is the Elizabethan's creation of the Italian villain based on Machiavelli's principles. Lorenzo in *The Spanish Tragedy* is the first of the long line of Elizabethan villains who owe their sole inspiration to Machiavelli. Although Lorenzo is not the protagonist of the play, he is so extremely active as the opposing force that he is almost as prominent as Hieronimo, and just as necessary to the extension of the dramatic action. Except that he is not a prince relying upon the doctrines of Machiavelli to rule and hold his state, every one of Lorenzo's actions reads like a exemplum of Machiavellian "policy." Even though the boundless Machiavellian ambition which produced the bloody Italian despot is absent, yet the ambition to raise his house by a royal marriage for his sister is the motivating spring of his murder of Horatio. His fundamental likeness to the Machiavellian comes in his ruthlessness toward all who stand in the way of his plans, in his perfect indifference to the sufferings he causes others, in his mania for secrecy and willingness to employ other men as catspaws, and in the tortuous and deceitful means he uses to attain his ends. Lorenzo is fundamentally cold-blooded and unsentimental, a practical man after Machiavelli's own heart. What lends particular interest to his character is the weighty evidence for believing that he was partly drawn from scandalous accounts of the Earl of Leicester, who was naîvely believed by his enemies to be the foremost exponent in England of the hated Machiavellian doctrines.

Although several are found in the French, the Italian *novelle* contain few stories of actual blood-revenge. Terrible revenges for other reasons are plentiful, however, and these influenced *The Spanish Tragedy* not only in incident but also in character and motivation. The type of revengeful woman exemplified by Bel-Imperia is a commonplace in Italian and French fiction, as is the brutal intriguing Lorenzo. In particular, his disposal of accomplices is partly drawn from the forty-fifth novel of the first part of Bandello. Balthazar, swearing revenge the moment he learns Horatio has won Bel-Imperia's love, fits the conception of touchy Italian pride which motivated so many tragic *novelle*. Above all, the atmosphere of the vendetta was unassailably Italian.

It is, indeed, the carrying-out of the vendetta tradition which turns Hieronimo from a hero to an Italianate villain. So long as he is pitiful in his grief for Horatio and in search of his murderers, so long the English audience would give him full sympathy. When, at last spurred to action by complete knowledge, he rushes to the king for legal justice, he would still be the hero whose actions, according to the best Elizabethan ethics, were those of an honorable man. But when Lorenzo foils him in his attempt at legal redress and he consciously gives up an open revenge in favor of a secret, treacherous device, according to English standards he inevitably becomes a villain. Indeed, so transparently weak is his sophistry and so open-eyed his turning from God's to the devil's means in the soliloquy opening Act III, scene xiii, that it is evident Kyd is deliberately veering his audience against Hieronimo.

Hieronimo begins,

> *Vindicta mihi,*

and, pursuing this promise from the Bible, consoles himself with the thought that Heaven never leaves murder unatoned; therefore he will await Heaven's decree. A quotation from Seneca then comes to his mind, and, swayed by the materialistic Senecan philosophy, he reflects that one crime opens the way for another, and he should repay wrong with wrong, for death ends both the resolute and the patient man and the end of destiny for each is merely the grave. Fortified by this un-Christian sophistry, he determines to anticipate Heaven's slow justice and to revenge for himself at his own appointed hour. Having decided to cast off Heaven, he cannot now expect a divinely awarded opportunity and so must carve the occasion for himself. He scorns acting

> as the vulgare wits of men,
> With open, but ineuitable ils,

(the only formula with which his "vulgar" audience could sympathize) and therefore, from his Machiavellian superiority to common humanity, he chooses a secret, albeit certain, plan, which he will conceal under the cloak of pretended friendship with Lorenzo. Since his project is of so great weight, he cannot hasten the hour but must bide the proper time for his revenge; delay, and dissemble his true feelings, hoping by his feigned ignorance to deceive his wary opponents. He then weakly excuses his planned hypocrisy by arguing that, even if he revealed his true feelings, he is too helpless to prevail merely with threats against his enemies' high position. Therefore he must deceive until opportunity offers revenge.

Since the next scene with Bazulto shows Hieronimo led by his grief into a fresh fit of insanity, it might be held that he is not responsible for his actions, that his weakened mind has forced him into the winding channels of his soliloquy, and that the subsequent scenes of deceit leading to the final slaughter are the actions of an insane person holding himself so rigidly in check that his madness is not visible. Such a view might, to the Elizabethans, mitigate his deed, but it would not release him from the consequences of his blood-guilt, since he would then be merely a villainous madman. Whether Kyd had enough psychological subtlety to portray Hieronimo's conversion according to this line of thought may well be a matter of opinion. A careful examination of the text leads to the view that, except for certain well defined scenes, Hieronimo is entirely sane in his revengeful plans—as sane certainly as Shakespeare's Hamlet when he stabs Claudius—although the actor may well have chosen to play him as unbalanced.

"With the production of *The Spanish Tragedy* Elizabethan tragedy received its first great impetus. The immediate and long-lasting popularity of the play stamped it as a type, a form to be imitated. Thus it is of the highest significance that *The Spanish Tragedy* first popularized revenge as a tragic motive on the Elizabethan popular stage by using blood-vengeance as the core of its dramatic action."

—*Fredson Bowers*

This change marked by the soliloquy from open to dissembling action was forced upon Hieronimo by the absolute necessity for Kyd to evolve a final reason for delay, and also, one may suspect, by Kyd's leaning toward the Italianate, the sensational, for the dramatic catastrophe. Once Hieronimo adopted the Italianate Machiavellian tactics, he immediately lost the absolute admiration of his audience. The English insistence on straightforward action by open assault or formal duel, which they would be inclined to view as manslaughter, refused to tolerate treacherous Italian plots. The Bible said, "Cursed is he that smiteth his neighbour secretly," and they heartily agreed. The Machiavellian breach of faith was not to be endured, for it led only to the total destruction of the breaker, and Hieronimo's pretended reconciliation with Lorenzo, with its reminiscence of Judas's kiss, was branded with the brand of Cain and of Machiavelli. With all allowance for the fact that, owing to Kyd's delight in wholesale slaughter, it was unlikely even an innocent Hieronimo would have survived the play, the fact that he was guilty of murder made it absolutely necessary for him to die. No slayer in Elizabethan drama escaped some penalty, and that penalty was usually death.

If the means by which Hieronimo ensnared and killed Lorenzo and Balthazar were not sufficient to label him a villain, the débâcle which ends the play (when, after promises of immunity if his cause has been just, he refuses all questions and wilfully stabs Lorenzo's father) certainly transported him beyond the pale. While collective revenge was understood in Elizabethan times, it was universally decried:

> "Farre be the first from God, farther be this; to strike the godly sonne for the godlesse Sire, to punish innocencie for Iniquitie. . . . Man is so just, *Amagias* slew the men, that kill'd his Father: but their children he slew not, 2 *Chron.* 14. and mans law provides for it, that *factum unius* doe not *nocere alteri,* one mans fact hurt another, saith old *Vlpian*" [Richard Clerke, *Sermons*, 1647].

The act would have been serious enough if Hieronimo had wreaked his revenge on the duke alone, according to the primitive custom where, in a state of family solidarity, any member of a family is as acceptable as the criminal; but when, after killing Lorenzo, Hieronimo refuses a pardon and stabs the duke also, he is departing so far from the English sense of justice as finally to withdraw all sympathy. (pp. 65-81)

Hieronimo's act is . . . either the culmination of his villainy (mad or sane), or else Kyd, swept away by a passion for violence, wrote the scene with no motive in mind but the wish to portray more bloody deeds. It is faintly possible that the duke's death satisfies in some roundabout manner the justice demanded by the ghost of Andrea—long since forgotten in the play's action—for the duke had apparently discouraged with considerable emphasis Andrea's love-affair with Bel-Imperia. It might be argued that Kyd was possibly following too closely his hypothetical source with its different morality, and so confused the ethics of the play. But the theory that Kyd followed one main source is very uncertain, and there is hardly a doubt that, mad or sane, Hieronimo was a villain to the English audience at the end and was forced to commit suicide to satisfy the stern doctrine that murder, no matter what the motive, was never successful.

Bel-Imperia shares the blood-guilt with Hieronimo, but the audience probably viewed her with a more lenient eye. Her suicide, thus, was not so necessary to satisfy morality as it was the usual move of the woman in romantic fiction who refused to outlive her slain lover after seeing vengeance done. The women of Elizabethan drama did not bear the guilt of blood, as did the men, unless they were portrayed as unmistakable villainesses from their position in the plot. That they, too, often perished after staining their hands with blood or assisting in the revenge, is owing more to their refusal to live after their slain lovers than to the demands of contemporary ethics. When the reason for their revenge is not romantic, they customarily enter a convent to purge themselves.

The characters of Lorenzo, Hieronimo, and Bel-Imperia, the whole atmosphere of brutal and Machiavellian vendetta, together with part of the Pedringano incident, thus were the outgrowth of the Italian and French *novelle* and the Elizabethan's hostile view of Machiavelli and the Italian character. (pp. 81-3)

There is no definite proof that Kyd had ever read an Italian tragedy. Indeed, with the exception of the translation of *Jocasta* from Dolce by Gascoigne and Kinwelmarsh, and some borrowings by the author of *Gismond of Salerne* from Dolce's *Didone* (not omitting the debt to the Italian of the academic *Progne* and *Roxana*), no direct relationship between Italian and English tragedy has been established. Dubious parallels there are, to be sure, to indicate that early Elizabethan tragedy was perhaps following Italianate Seneca more than Seneca himself in the elaborate use of dumb shows, the rejection of the traditional Latin and Greek stories, and the extension of the scope of the action and of the list of characters. The motive of sexual love, the intensification of physical horrors and their performance on the stage, all had been paralleled in Italian tragedy; and in *Gismond of Salerne* and its later revision had been deliberately adopted from the Italian. With *The Spanish Tragedy* and *Locrine* the mingling of classical and popular traditions ended with the fixation of the English form of tragedy. The most suitable elements of Seneca were completely naturalized by incorporation with the main stream of popular drama, and henceforth Seneca or his Italian and French derivatives had really nothing more to teach.

Moreover, even the few early parallels were all the work of men of the Inner Temple or of the universities, and, being learned performances, were no true indication of a diffused knowledge of the Italian tragic art. In Italy itself Neo-Senecan tragedy was not a popular form, and there is no evidence that more than a handful of Englishmen were at all familiar with Italian tragedies. Certainly the typical sixteenth century Italian tragedies were not of a type to exercise any especial influence on *The Spanish Tragedy,* although certain rough parallels may be drawn. The Italian tragedy interested itself chiefly in the depiction of villainy and horrors. Horrors are emphasized in *The Spanish Tragedy* and Lorenzo is extremely important as a villain. The sources for Lorenzo's character, however, have been noted, and he bears little relation to the bloody tyrants of Italian tragedy. Furthermore, the horrors of *The Spanish Tragedy* are honest English horrors based on the copiousness with which blood is shed and the resulting emotional response of the audience, and have little to do with the unnaturalness of the crude Thyestean banquets and elaborate dissection and poisoning scenes of the Italian.

The most important point of similarity to Italian tragedy lies in the ghosts. In none of Seneca's plays does the ghost of the recent dead rise to demand vengeance for his own murder, as Andrea does, although such a demand is common in Italian tragedies like Cinthio's *Orbecche* (1541) and Decio da Orte's *Acripanda* (1591). The rather important parallel between the spirit of Revenge in *The Spanish Tragedy* and the spirit of Suspicion in Groto's *La Dalida* must be noticed, and there may possibly be an authentic borrowing here. For the rest, Seneca's tragedies, while bloody, are not the slaughter-houses of the Italian, where

hardly a character remains alive. In this respect Italian tragedy is paralleled in Kyd.

Here the general resemblance ceases, for the action of Italian tragedy and *The Spanish Tragedy* is vitally dissimilar. No Italian play depends for its plot, like *The Spanish Tragedy,* upon blood-revenge for a person slain on the stage. The Italian usually revolves about a villain protagonist and a heroine, with lust ever in the foreground. This villain is usually a tyrannous king, who is portrayed in some incident of his private life (like a love-affair where he is either the lover or the father of the lover) in which he exercises the powers of his kingship for a terrible revenge. "Tragic error" is expanded to include even the ordering of a Thyestean banquet. There is little in common between such a type and *The Spanish Tragedy.* Possibly a detail or two in Kyd came from the Italian, but there is no argument for any general, thoroughgoing influence.

The chief foreign influence on *The Spanish Tragedy,* rivalling and probably even surpassing Seneca in the importance of its details, is the story of Hamlet which Kyd found in Belleforest, who had borrowed it from Saxo Grammaticus. To the Senecan, Italian, and French, is now added a primitive Teutonic influence on the nascent revenge tragedy.

Without going into the various arguments for and against, the belief may be stated that a play by Kyd, written on the subject of Hamlet's revenge, was in existence at some time before 1589. This play is not extant, and there is no reason to believe that it was ever printed. The first quarto of Shakespeare's *Hamlet* was entered on July 26, 1602, and published in 1603. This is a vulgarized memorial version, put together for pirated acting, of an original that is represented substantially by the second quarto of 1604/5, and it cannot be trusted to offer evidence about an earlier state of the play. Another text which must be considered is a German play, *Der Bestrafte Brudermord,* which bears obvious relations to the two quartos of *Hamlet.* Although the manuscript cannot be traced farther back than the early eighteenth century, the play is always thought to be of considerably earlier date.

In order to evaluate Kyd's *Ur-Hamlet* properly the major features of the plot and characterization must be surmised, and, if the connection with *The Spanish Tragedy* is to be of benefit, the date must be conjectured. The only clues to these questions can be sought in Shakespeare's *Hamlet* in its two quarto editions and in *Der Bestrafte Brudermord. Alphonsus, Emperor of Germany,* an anonymous tragedy of about 1597, may perhaps be included. A vast amount of learning and much ingenious conjecture have been brought to bear on the problem of the exact relation between the *Ur-Hamlet, Der Bestrafte Brudermord,* and *Hamlet.* There is little reason here to venture into the conflicting theories of this criticism. For the purposes of this [essay] it is postulated that *Der Bestrafte Brudermord* was drawn from the *Ur-Hamlet* either in its original form or in a somewhat revised version of 1594-1595, and that the *Ur-Hamlet* did not differ materially from the main outline of the story as represented in the German play and in the second quarto of Shakespeare.

Belleforest's account in *Les Histoires Tragiques,* from which Kyd drew, follows in the main the incidents as narrated by Saxo Grammaticus with the omission of the more primitive portions as in the details of the attempt to seduce Amleth, and with a considerable expansion of the speeches. Some few incidents are altered. Thus in Belleforest, Fengon has committed incest with Geruthe before the murder of Horwendille, and the murderer bolsters his excuses for the deed by the assertion that Horwendille had threatened her life. Furthermore, he procures false witnesses to prove it, and so convinces the court. Belleforest, accordingly, paints Geruthe as a deep-dyed, lascivious villainess, and emphasizes her evil character by having her deliberately abandon Amleth to his fate. Still, the ground is prepared for her repentance when he (where Saxo is vague) makes clear that she knew nothing of the scheme to conceal the courtier under the quilt to overhear her conversation with Amleth. Whereas in Saxo the repentance of Geruthe comes only after Amleth's reproaches and is baldly described, in Belleforest the shock of the slaying brings her to remorse while Amleth is disposing of the body. Consequently, instead of being greeted at his return, as in Saxo, with reproaches for his folly, he finds her in a mood to listen to his harangue, and she afterwards promises to help him with his revenge. The course of Amleth's revenge follows that in Saxo except for the addition of a long speech after the slaying in which Amleth consigns Fengon to hell, there to tell his brother's spirit "que c'est son fils qui te faict faire ce message, à fin que soulagé par ceste memoire, son ombre s'appaise parmy les esprits bienheureux, et me quitte de celle obligation qui m'astraignoit à pursuivre ceste vengeance sur mon sang."

The difference in spirit between the two narratives, however, is distinct. Saxo, telling his primitive tale, is never in doubt about the justness of the revenge, or, indeed, of any other revenge in his history. Belleforest, not at all influenced by the pagan Scandinavian tradition, is divided between his Renaissance French appreciation of a *bella vendetta* and the Christian doctrine that all revenge must be left to God. Moreover, he is apprehensive lest his tale of tyrannicide be censured as treasonable. At the start he grafts Christianity on revenge by asserting a moral purpose for his story and placing Amleth in the position of an agent of God, so that the long delay is explained in a sidenote as owing to "la tardiue vengeance de Dieu." After some quibbling over the ethics of feigning madness to procure revenge, Belleforest in Amleth's speech over the body of Fengon writes a final justification for the particular revenge, which is solely for the murder of a father, prefaced by the sidenote, "Vengeance juste, ou est ce que doit estre consideree." Amleth, after praising himself for his well considered and courageous plan of revenge, cries: "Si jamais la vengeance sembla avoir quelque face et forme de justice, il est hors de doute, que la pieté et affection qui nous lie à la souvenance de nos peres, pursuivis injustement, est celle qui nous dispence à cercher les moyens de ne laisser impunie une trahison, et effort outrageux et proditoire." Thus Belleforest follows Christian ethics on the one hand in denouncing private revenge for injuries, except that he is in perfect accord, on the other, with the pagan classical belief in the duty of the son to revenge the murder of a father. In his opinion such a crime exempts the revenger from following honorable means of revenge and justifies any mode of procedure, such as Amleth's trickery. Only king-killing is barred to the just revenger of a father's murder. Here Amleth's act is justified as no treason since Amleth is the rightful heir, and Fengon then, properly, his subject.

Kyd, with Belleforest's narrative for a source, was forced to make wide changes to adapt the action to the stage and to the tragic form. First of all, to be suitably tragic the play must end with death to the avenger as well as to the victim, and they must drag down with them all other guilty persons concerned. As the first step, the incidents following Hamlet's revenge must be omitted, as well as those occurring during his first stay in Britain. At this stage the story would be: Hamlet's father has been killed and his mother incestuously married to the murderer, who now occupies the vacant office of prince-governor. Hamlet is bent on revenge and pretends madness in order to preserve his life. This madness is suspected by the prince-governor and his courtiers, who test him by tempting him with a young girl and eavesdropping at an interview with his mother, during which Hamlet kills the spy. His mother repents and promises to aid Hamlet in his revenge. He declares he will meet trickery with trickery. The prince sends him to England with false messages intending his death which Hamlet discovers and rewrites to apply to his companions sent to guard him. He returns to Denmark to find the court celebrating his funeral feast, fires the hall and burns his enemies, and then kills the prince with his sword.

With this simple story Kyd begins the dramatization. At the very start, however, he confronts the most serious problem of the play. For there to be any play at all, the revenger must delay. The reasons for delay must also fulfil two requirements: they must be dramatic, and they must not prejudice the character of the revenger either by imputation of cowardice or of Machiavellism. The audience can have no sympathy for a craven in the most desperate situation that can well face a man. On the other hand, luring a victim to destruction by deceit is not the rôle of a hero, for it carried with it the imputation of Machiavellism. For this reason delay cannot be caused by a long and elaborate plot against the king. Belleforest was of little help. His Amleth delays, it is true, but only for the undramatic reason that he is awaiting the best opportunity.

Kyd, as is shown by *The Spanish Tragedy,* was a brilliant inventor of dramatic incident. He realized that the solution for his problem lay in the contrivance of positive obstacles through which Hamlet must cut for his revenge. And as the primary obstacle, Hamlet must find his path barred not by a hostile court in full possession of the fact of his father's murder, but by a court which had never dreamed that his father had been murdered. Since proof is completely lacking, Hamlet must act alone and in constant danger.

But if the murder is unrecognized, the problem arises how to introduce Hamlet to the truth. Kyd, the everspectacular, broke wide with tradition and introduced into the action of the play itself a ghost who acquaints his son with the true facts of his death. The classical drama had employed ghosts as omens of disaster and, as in *Agamemnon* and *Troades,* to demand vengeance; but, it must be emphasized, never as actors to reveal the murder to the unsuspecting revenger-to-be.

Amleth's pretense of madness in Belleforest is the real starting-point for the story, and, indeed, its most integral feature. It was the common Scandinavian practice for a murderer to endeavor to wipe out all possible revengers as well, and Amleth, rightly fearing for his life, pretends insanity only to preserve himself by lulling Fengon into the belief that no revenger for Horwendille will appear. The secrecy of the murder in the *Ur-Hamlet* automatically disposes of any reason for Hamlet's instant plan to play the madman, since Claudius, believing the murder unknown, can have no strong motive for slaying Hamlet also. Indeed, it turns out ironically that Hamlet's madness is the very thing that excites Claudius's fatal suspicions. Whether Kyd realized the logical uselessness of the device is impossible to determine. What we do know is that he retained Hamlet's feigned madness, for to discard it would have been to ruin the play.

The Elizabethan audience would instantly recognize Hamlet's revenge as just, for a revenge for murder either by legal or extra-legal means was still felt as a bounden duty. That Hamlet cannot secure legal justice forces him to rely on personal justice; this distinction would be recognized by the audience which would thereupon approve his ends and await with interest his procedure. The feigning of madness was a clever trick but the audience would reserve judgment on Hamlet's character until it was shown he did not intend to use treachery and hypocrisy, or the hated Italianate devices, to secure vengeance.

As the first scenes close Kyd has provided for dramatic effects by the madness motif and has introduced the first step in the necessary delay in Hamlet's search for an opportunity. The strict guard kept about Claudius discourages Hamlet as the play proceeds and his emotional frustration drives him to thoughts of suicide. It is impossible for him to make a direct assault on Claudius. Such a disclosure of his secret means the end of the play. From Hamlet's own point of view, it is a poor revenge which leads to the death of the revenger; since he wishes to ascend the throne himself, he must take proper precautions for his own safety, and so continue his delay. But this delay very shortly ceases to be dramatic, and additional reasons must be sought which yet will mark some sort of forward step. This problem was ingeniously solved by the doubt of the ghost, necessitating the play-within-a-play. Simultaneously the opposing action—which becomes of increasing importance as the play progresses—is started when Claudius takes steps to discover the reasons for Hamlet's madness. From this point the future action is indicated as a stirring duel of wits between Hamlet and the king.

The rising action, with Hamlet on the offensive, sweeps through the mousetrap play and into the prayer scene. The meeting of the two under such conditions is a daring though necessary move. Hamlet has lamented that he can never find the king without his guards. Yet the king must have some private life, and the audience may well begin to wonder why Hamlet cannot find an accidental opportunity. Kyd daringly presents this opportunity but under such circumstances that Hamlet cannot accept it. Probability of incident has been affirmed, a little crisis has developed and subsided, and the audience has been momentarily put upon edge. The religious scruples Hamlet advances combine ill with his bloodthirsty thoughts, but actions speak louder than words and the audience has been assured that Hamlet is no villain.

It is obvious from *The Spanish Tragedy* that Kyd had a fondness for balancing incident. The crisis of the tragedy has been cleverly formed from an elaboration of the relatively unimportant murder of the eavesdropper in Belleforest. Now the strength of the opposing action forces delay on Hamlet. The English voyage affords a period of rest, and on Hamlet's return he is met by a parallel revenger seeking his life. For this device Kyd is directly indebted to the maxims of Machiavelli which advised a prince to give the performance of cruel acts to another in order to escape the blame. One peg was best to drive out another, and enemies should be set at odds to destroy themselves. The primitive revenge of the Belleforest story was unsuitable for the stage since it contained no real conflict, and also since it offered no means of drawing the play to a close with the death of Hamlet. Kyd therefore plans to create his catastrophe in the meeting of revenge and counter-revenge which will engulf all the principals in disaster.

The poisonings which end the play are interesting as showing how Kyd drew on the gossip of the period for a catastrophe which would involve the king. The backfiring of a poison upon the poisoner, the method by which Leonhardus is killed and the queen poisoned, is of considerable antiquity. Occurring as early as the ancient tale of Deïanira and the centaur's poison, it is also found in romances, as in the Tristram story, and was a standard piece of Renaissance gossip. Kyd may have drawn on a scandalous tale current about the Earl of Leicester (one of his alleged practices was used in *The Spanish Tragedy*) which recounted that Leicester prepared a poisoned draught for his wife Lettice which she was to drink whenever she felt faint. She, not suspecting its properties, gave him the drink a short time later when he returned from a fatiguing journey. But two other famous examples were at hand in the stories about the death of Pope Alexander VI and the accidental poisoning of her husband by Bianca Capello.

Since, legally, the king was guilty of the murder of his wife as well as of Hamlet, his death was not only the culmination of a just revenge for a past murder but also a judgment for two present ones. Leonhardus, too, must die, for he has been the knowing agent in a murder by particularly treacherous means. He was not so culpable as the king, however, because his motive was purer and he was merely the agent, not the principal on whom the chief guilt lay. It is significant that Hamlet, realizing the dupe the king has made of Leonhardus, forgives the unlucky revenger of Corambis. The queen, only doubtfully innocent of the murder of her first husband, is stained with the guilt of incest.

If, as seems probable, the catastrophe of *Der Bestrafte Brudermord* is roughly that of the *Ur-Hamlet,* the slaughter of Phantasmo by Hamlet is at first sight a particularly brutal and unnecessary piece of business; but Hamlet at the time does not know that he himself is doomed and in his royal capacity he is meting swift justice to an accessory before the fact to the poisoning of his mother.

The lengths to which Kyd went to maintain the audience's sympathy for his protagonist make Hamlet one of the least guilty of all Elizabethan stage revengers. Because he was no Machiavellian, Hamlet's sole actions toward revenge had consisted only in the play-within-a-play to establish the king's guilt, his refusal to murder a man at prayer, and the mistaken slaying of Corambis. His dissimulation had never overstepped the allowable bounds of "policy" and if ever a revenger were blameless in his plots it is Hamlet.

It is probably true that Kyd's Hamlet was a more blood-thirsty person in his speeches than Shakespeare's. It is also true that a certain amount of brutality is shown in the stabbing of Phantasmo who might better have been left to his certain legal execution, as was usually the practice with guilty minor characters in later plays. But what puts Hamlet definitely over the borderline is the killing of Corambis. Kyd had probably taken some pains to make Corambis innocent of the plot laid by the king against Hamlet, and his slaying, no matter what the circumstances of ironical mistaken identity, seals Hamlet's eventual doom, for the religious teaching of the day held that revenge by murder was never allowable: "That vengeance appertaineth vnto God only. . . . Therefore it followeth, that whosoeuer doth reuenge himselfe, committeth sacrilege. . . . That seeing the wrong that our neighbour doth, happeneth not without the prudence of God, it is not lawful for vs to resist and withstand it by oblique and sinister meanes, and such as displease God" [John Eliot, *Discourses of Warre and Single Combat, by B. De Loque*, 1591]. Hamlet cannot even plead manslaughter, for his intent was to kill the king, and it is still murder if he mistakes Corambis for his intended victim.

The Elizabethan audience always insisted on seeing eventual justice, and one who stained his hands with blood had to pay the penalty. That no revenger, no matter how just, ever wholly escapes the penalty for shedding blood even in error, is borne out by subsequent plays and is emphasized especially in Thomas Rawlins's *Rebellion*. Very likely Kyd would have killed off Hamlet anyway in order to end with a holocaust of pity and terror; but it seems probable that, as with later playwrights, he subscribed to the doctrine that a shedder of blood should not live.

One can imagine an Elizabethan sympathizer pointing out that Hamlet was justified since he could not appeal to legal justice. But the inevitable and unanswerable reply would come that Hamlet must therefore await God's justice. If he anticipates divine vengeance, he must pay the penalty: given his sympathetic characterization he is a hero, but he must die. But God sometimes uses human instruments as the agents for the heavenly vengeance. If Hamlet is such an agent, does he not operate under God's favor? That question was answered in such later plays as *The Atheist's Tragedy, The Maid's Tragedy,* and *The Unnatural Combat.* Heaven may be using Hamlet—and even Hieroni-

mo—as its agent, but that does not remove guilt, for, as *The Maid's Tragedy* states,

> Unlooked-for sudden deaths from Heaven are
> sent;
> But cursed is he that is their instrument.

This question outlines in sharp relief the fundamental problem facing every writer of a revenge tragedy whose protagonist is a hero. The audience is sympathetic to his revenger so long as he does not become an Italianate intriguer, and so long as he does not revenge. At the conclusion the audience admits its sentimental satisfaction with the act of personal justice but its ethical sense demands the penalty for the infraction of divine command.

It seems most probable that the *Ur-Hamlet* preceded *The Spanish Tragedy,* chiefly because the parallels between the two plays would originate more logically in the *Ur-Hamlet* to be copied in *The Spanish Tragedy.* A major parallel is the play-within-a-play. The idea for this device in the *Ur-Hamlet* without question came from current stories of the involuntary fear of criminals at the playhouse when viewing their crimes acted on the stage, and as such it has a vital and apposite part in the plot. Such an origin is not possible in *The Spanish Tragedy* where there is no source but a vague resemblance to the diversions of the Emperor Nero. The device for the final bloodshed in each play seems to have originated in the *Ur-Hamlet.* Hamlet's stabbing of Phantasmo was partially warranted as the disposal of the last of the conspirators, but in *The Spanish Tragedy* the unwarranted stabbing of the Duke of Castile seems merely a reminiscence of the earlier scene.

If the *Ur-Hamlet* came afterwards it is most surprising that the German play does not give any indication that Hamlet is actually insane, a part of Hieronimo's success which Kyd would have been sure to emphasize after its first proved popularity. This is not to say that Kyd's Hamlet could not have been slightly unbalanced on occasion. It seems very possible that Hieronimo's more complete emotional insanity, so extremely original if *The Spanish Tragedy* preceded the *Ur-Hamlet,* was an expansion of hints in Hamlet. Burton the Anatomist wrote [in *The Anatomy of Melancholy*], "Many lose their wits by *the sudden sight of some spectrum or divil, a thing very common in all ages,* saith *Lavater part* I. *cap.* 9. as *Orestes* did at the sight of the *Furies,* which appeared to him in black." Given the precedent of Orestes and the popular belief, it seems almost inevitable that Kyd with his dramatic genius portrayed Hamlet's feigned madness as at times merging into real distraction, not only from excessive grief and frustration but from the effect of the ghost's appearance. On the evidence of *Der Bestrafte Brudermord,* as well as the evidence of the relative unpopularity of the early *Hamlet,* one may infer that this characterization was not emphasized as was Hieronimo's, and that it was not until he came to write *The Spanish Tragedy* that Kyd realized the full latent possibilities in such a dramatic device. Even this emphasis was insufficient for Elizabethan taste, for another dramatist had to be employed subsequently to expand the mad scenes.

The two chief breaks with Senecan tragedy in *The Spanish Tragedy* involve the madness of the revenger and his delay. To believe that Kyd conjured these important points out of his imagination without a source, wrote *The Spanish Tragedy,* and then stumbled on them as an integral part of the Amleth story in Belleforest and later wrote his *Hamlet,* is asking too much of coincidence. The view must be accepted that Kyd at least knew Belleforest's account before he wrote *The Spanish Tragedy.* But if Kyd knew Belleforest's account beforehand, it is curious he should abstract the two best dramatic features to create an original plot instead of dramatizing Belleforest's story where they were native. It must be emphasized that Kyd was forced to invent certain dramatic conventions by the very exigencies of dramatizing the Amleth story, and that these are also found in *The Spanish Tragedy.* Merely to have known Belleforest cannot explain them; they could have been evolved only by a person transferring the Amleth material to the stage, and the lessons learned thereupon being transferred in turn to *The Spanish Tragedy.* Again, the seeming lack of popularity of Kyd's *Hamlet,* with its superior plot and more intrinsic interest of character and situation, is difficult to explain unless it were a first crude attempt at tragedy which was bettered in *The Spanish Tragedy.*

Lastly, the Belleforest narrative as it stood, even without its tragic ending, bore a nearer relation to the standard elements of Seneca's dramas than *The Spanish Tragedy:* fratricide as in *Thyestes* with a parallel to the husband-murder in *Agamemnon;* cunning revenge as in *Agamemnon, Thyestes,* and *Medea;* and the conflict between revenge and the forces that would put it down as in *Medea.* Slight and obvious changes made the play even more Senecan, such as the creation of the confidant Horatio and the actual appearance of a speaking ghost demanding vengeance as in *Agamemnon.* The likeness of Belleforest's story to the Orestes legend, the first part of which was dramatized by Seneca, must have been apparent to Kyd. Horwendille was Agamemnon; Geruthe, Clytemnestra; the king, Aegisthus; Hamlet, Orestes. The revenge of a son for his father was nearer the classical tradition than Hieronimo's revenge for a son.

With these considerations the date of the *Ur-Hamlet* may be set with fair certainty as approximately 1587, with *The Spanish Tragedy* following in 1587-1588, prompted by the increasing interest in Spanish affairs at the threat of a Spanish invasion. If one accepts the priority of the *Ur-Hamlet,* the material from which Kyd built *The Spanish Tragedy* becomes so evident that it is likely Kyd had few other sources than his earlier Hamlet play and various pieces of information about Spain and Spanish affairs. The story of a father's revenge for a son is merely the reversal of Hamlet's for his father. That it is prefaced by the Andrea story is only an indication that Kyd, realizing from his experience in *Hamlet* the difficulty of filling a play with the simple revenge theme, endeavored to avoid repetition by substituting a full account of the prior action. In addition, since Kyd was still to a certain extent under the influence of Seneca, the ghost of some previously murdered man was essential to start the action of revenge.

Hamlet's reasons for delay are only two: his doubt of the ghost, and his inability to conceive a plan for a safe revenge on a guarded enemy. There are indications that Hamlet becomes extremely discouraged and blames himself unjustly for his delay. Just as Hamlet doubts the ghost, so Hieronimo doubts Bel-Imperia's letter. As Hamlet is not certain that he has grounds for revenge until after the mousetrap play, so Hieronimo needs Pedringano's letter to fortify his conviction.

After a delay caused by Hieronimo's distraction arising from an over-burdening yet impotent sense of wrong, he is next balked by his failure to secure legal justice. Thereupon his character changes, for he attempts to excuse the treacherous acts which are to follow by the statement that he is otherwise unable to revenge himself on men in superior stations. This excuse is modelled on Hamlet's real problem, for Hamlet knows the king is suspicious, but Lorenzo does not realize that his guilt has been revealed to Hieronimo. Thus when Lorenzo thwarts Hieronimo's attempts to gain the king's ear, his sole motive is to hush the fact that Horatio has been murdered. It has been indicated how this excuse and the actions to which it led finally turned Hieronimo into villainous courses. His reconciliation with Lorenzo is a Machiavellian extension of Hamlet's with the king before the fencing match. His double-edged remarks are drawn from Hamlet's, which in turn came direct from Belleforest. The play scene utilizes Hamlet's mousetrap but with a gory conclusion, and finally the murder of Castile parallels senselessly that of Phantasmo.

The weak points in Hamlet's revenge have been strengthened. Hamlet, despite his firm purpose, is actually helpless except for the contrivance of the play to reveal the king's guilt, and so, without the saving genius of Shakespeare's philosophical characterization, tends to be too static a figure. Only the faith of the audience that a scheme for revenge will eventually come to him, and their confidence in his personal character—largely gained from the daring of his supposedly mad remarks—keep him a figure strong enough to balance the rising force of the opposing action. Since he is portrayed sympathetically throughout, he cannot be given too much to do, and yet he cannot be given too little. Circumstances force him unwittingly to slay an innocent man, but these are so arranged as not to alienate the sympathy of the audience, although the tragic error is recorded and must later receive payment. Fate provides the dénouement in *Hamlet;* conversely, in *The Spanish Tragedy* a change of character, through which the driving necessity for revenge corrupts the hero, affects the action more materially. The difference enabled Hieronimo to give the audience more positive action for its money, but by that action he became a faulty character.

As for the rest, Lorenzo is a villainous extension of the king: both are villains who oppose the revenger by Machiavellian sleights. Isabella's largely spectacular madness and suicide is based on Ofelia's, which was more essential to the plot. In like manner, Bazulto's demand for justice is only of emotional significance, whereas Leonhardus's is rooted in the action. Each of these minor parallels, owing to the derivative nature of the simpler story of *The Spanish Tragedy,* is not so closely linked to the main plot as in *Hamlet.* Finally, from the hints of Machiavelli and Gentillet, from Italian and French *novelle,* from Seneca, and—as with the action between Lorenzo and Pedringano—from contemporary English life, Kyd built up, in a timely setting, the framework of incidents for *The Spanish Tragedy*. (pp. 83-100)

Fredson Bowers, "The Spanish Tragedy and the Ur-Hamlet," in his Elizabethan Revenge Tragedy, 1587-1642, 1940. Reprint by Princeton University Press, 1966, pp. 62-100.

Wolfgang Clemen (essay date 1955)

[*A German Shakespearean scholar, Clemen was among the first critics to consider Shakespeare's imagery an integral part of the development of his dramatic art. John Dover Wilson described Clemen's method as focusing on "the form and significance of particular images or groups of images in their context of the passages, speech, or play in which they occur." Clemen was also greatly interested in the development of Shakespeare's dramatic technique and in the playwright's use of sixteenth-century theatrical conventions. In the excerpt below from his* English Tragedy Before Shakespeare, *first published in German in 1955, the critic praises Kyd's technical virtuosity in* The Spanish Tragedy.]

That Kyd was . . . successful in his attempt to reconcile the classical and the native styles of drama is obvious in *The Spanish Tragedy.* In this play we see how a gifted playwright with a strongly marked sense of theatre managed to fuse the heterogeneous and discordant elements of earlier types of play, and from them produced a striking and original composition of his own. With its skilful exploitation and combination of different stylistic levels and different kinds of dramatic artifice and stage-effect, *The Spanish Tragedy* was bound to be a success; moreover, Kyd sensibly took into account the various tendencies of contemporary taste. However, his mastery is grounded in matters of technique rather than in any dramatic urge that took its rise from his own personal experience, and as a result *The Spanish Tragedy* fails to move us today; furthermore, we are offended by the lapses in taste which Schlegel deplored. However, the prodigious success of the play on the Elizabethan stage is evidence that Kyd's contemporaries must have felt otherwise. Its exaggerated theatricality and its combination of a highly emotional rhetoric with an intricate and exciting plot are the very qualities which are likely to have roused their admiration, the qualities which gave the play its exceptional appeal.

What effect has this new skill in the techniques of dramatic composition on the handling of the set speech? Kyd knew how to pull out all the stops, how to exploit every linguistic and theatrical trick at his disposal in the theatre of the day; naturally he also recognized the potentialities of the declamatory set speech, and he showed some skill in adapting it to his purposes as a whole. In contrast to *Locrine, The Spanish Tragedy* offers us a coherent and artistically constructed plot in which the threads of the action are skilfully interwoven and complicated. Although a number of subsidiary episodes are introduced, the course of the main plot remains perfectly clear; with all his tricks of mystification and delayed action and contrast, Kyd shows a conscious virtuosity in his handling of plot, and

steadily advances the action through its various stages. Within this framework, the set speeches which periodically occur are strategically placed. Even when, as often happens, their subject-matter goes beyond the requirements of the immediate context, the mere fact that they are part of a coherent plot prevents them from losing touch with the action of the play.

Furthermore, even the *visible* structure of the work, the distribution of the longer speeches through its pages, shows the skill and the conscious artistry with which they have been introduced. There are no longer any scenes in which a number of long set speeches just follow one another without variation. Equally striking is the fact that situations which in the earlier tradition would have been represented entirely by means of long set speeches are now dealt with in other ways. For example, the second part of the second scene (I. ii) corresponds in its outlines to the familiar 'tribunal scene'; it is a scene in which a dispute between two nobles is arbitrated and settled by the King. This settlement is brought about, not by means of long-drawn statements, but in rapid, dramatically exciting dialogue. Where the longer set speeches or monologues do occur, they are generally placed next to passages of stichomythia—concise, quickly-changing single-line dialogue that moves at a great pace. Thus the tempo of the play is speeded up, and by a situation's being consciously worked up to a climax, the relevant phase of the action is advanced. In the set speeches and monologues, however, this forward movement is checked, and by means of the deliberation upon a course of conduct or the declamatory set piece we are transported to a higher, more universal level, and thus lose contact with the specific situation that is being presented. This rise and fall in the dramatic tempo, and the diversity in the method of presentation—with its claims alike upon the eye and the ear—give rise to a structural pattern which far surpasses anything with a similar tendency up to that time found in English drama.

Even in the structure of the individual scene we may observe, in the distribution of the longer speeches, the deliberate application of a structural principle. In Act II, Scene i, for instance, the two long speeches of Balthazar are placed at the beginning and the end; these are the speeches in which, in his highly rhetorical and antithetic style, he discusses the objects respectively of his love and his hate, Bellimperia and Horatio. The first speech is devoted entirely to Bellimperia; the second, after Pedringano's disclosure of the love-affair between Horatio and Bellimperia, concerns itself with Horatio alone. Thus the two goals of Balthazar's future endeavours are brought into sharp relief, not only in dialogue enlivened by action, but also through the rhetorical emphasis of the set speeches; and the significant new turn given to events in the central part of the scene, in the disclosures made in the exciting, fast-moving dialogue of Lorenzo and Pedringano, is shown for what it is by means of the two corner-posts of the scene, that is, the two set speeches of Balthazar. Comparable corner-posts in Act III, Scene ii, are the long soliloquy of Hieronimo at the beginning of the scene, and the closing soliloquy in which Lorenzo reveals his purposes; by their means we find out all about the two contending forces which, in the course of the ensuing scenes, are to be engaged in intrigue and conflict against each other.

A structural device of another kind may be seen in Act I, Scene iv. In the first part of this scene the meeting between Horatio and Bellimperia takes place. On this occasion Horatio has once more to tell the story of Don Andrea's death. There follows, together with Bellimperia's symbolic action in bestowing Don Andrea's scarf on Horatio, an ambiguous conversation, which is rounded off, on Horatio's departure, with a soliloquy by Bellimperia. In this first section of the scene the longer speeches impose a slower tempo, and this is in keeping with the situation, in which the recapitulated account of Don Andrea's death gradually draws Horatio and Bellimperia together. Now comes some dialogue employing a very different technique. The encounter between Bellimperia and her future adversaries Lorenzo and Balthazar—shortly to be broken in upon by Horatio—is conducted in a rapid exchange of polished, witty, single-line questions and answers. By means of this rapid cross-fire of questions asked and countered, these tactics of evasion and pointed rejoinder, tension is raised, and the main lines of the conflict are sketched in, its significance being emphasized by the by-play with the glove which Bellimperia drops and Horatio picks up. Both times, therefore, the outward form and the tempo of the dialogue are adapted to the situation, and an impressive sense of contrast is produced by the clash of the two different techniques. As far as concerns the distribution of long and short speeches, of duologue and colloquy divided between several speakers, the same observations might be applied to a number of other scenes.

Even when the speeches disconcert us by their length, as in Act I, Scene ii, suggesting a reversion to the technique of detailed narrative report characteristic of the earlier classical plays, we find on closer study that the long-drawn recapitulation serves a definite dramatic purpose in the complication of the plot. *The Spanish Tragedy* is a tragedy of revenge; it is introduced by an Induction in which Don Andrea appears in the company of Revenge. What Andrea here discloses about his death was not sufficient, however, to establish an urgent revenge-motif; this motif had to be forcibly impressed on the audience by means of a detailed report of the battle in which, at the same time, the true circumstances of Balthazar's capture could be related. As a contrast to this dispassionate report, presented by the Spanish General, the next scene (I. iii) gives us the distortions and misrepresentations of Villuppo, and these are followed again (I. iv) by Horatio's corrective account of the facts. According to the convention hitherto followed, any report-speech in a play had to be accepted as an objective account of what had happened, and it would have been superfluous to give more than one version of the same event. Here, however, we have reports given from several different points of view, and their relative value is of dramatic significance; among them there is even one wholly false report. These varying reports all have their consequences in the events of later scenes; they become mainsprings in the action of the play. Moreover, the retrospective narration in them is to some extent woven into the texture of the plot. Of course Kyd could not have drawn out to such a length the Spanish General's account of the bat-

tle, which indeed in its earlier part (up to 1. 45) has no real relevance to the plot, had not his audience expected showy and elaborately rhetorical report-speeches of this kind, and valued them as 'good theatre' and as the peculiar glory of a play.

That the set speeches are more closely integrated with the structure of the plot than had up till then been the case does not mean that their speakers are brought into a close relationship with each other. Where the longer speeches are concerned, even in *The Spanish Tragedy* the characters are much more prone to talk at cross purposes than to make contact with one anothers' minds. Only in the genuine dialogue-passages does any interplay develop in which the speakers are delicately attuned to one another and establish a real contact. When the device of 'speaking past one another' is employed in such a context, it is usually done as a deliberate dramatic artifice; understanding and misunderstanding are by this means deftly and ironically played off against each other, and in such a way as to bring out more subtle contrasts between the speakers. However, scarcely a single one of the longer speeches is fully attuned to the person addressed, except in those few instances where it is a matter of giving instructions or of announcing a decision (e.g., I. ii. 179 ff.); and in any case these are not rhetorical set speeches as we have been using the term. In fact there are no long speeches that could be classified as conventional 'conversion-speeches', 'dissuasion-speeches', or 'instigation-speeches'; where an attempt is made to influence a person, it is done in dialogue. The inference may be drawn that Kyd found the long set speech inappropriate for the development of close personal relationships; he assigned this function to his dialogue.

From the early classical tragedies we are familiar with the two ends normally and chiefly served by the long set speech: those of moralizing self-revelation and dissection of the emotions. The novelty of Kyd's method may be illustrated by a couple of examples. The two speeches of the Viceroy at the beginning of Act I, Scene iii, and Act III, Scene i, are not essentially different in theme from that of Gorboduc at the beginning of Act III in *Gorboduc*. The main difference lies in the stronger dramatic quality imparted to the Viceroy's speeches, especially the first one (I. iii), where his throwing himself on the ground and the gesture with which he offers to give away his crown are intended to add to the theatricality. There is a further difference in the effective way in which the climax is worked up in the Viceroy's speech, with all its rhetorical figures and its pointedly antithetic phraseology; for in the place of Gorboduc's dispassionate reflections he gives us an impassioned display of a man reasoning with himself. We get the impression of a mind-probing self-communion, a quasi-psychological soliloquy, as the Viceroy enters into judgement with himself and with the goddess Fortune.

We find the same tendency to break up the thought into antitheses, and to analyse a situation by means of argument and counter-argument, in Balthazar's first speech in Act II, Scene i (ll. 9-28). This speech is actually intended as an answer to Lorenzo's attempt to allay his despair at his repulse by Bellimperia. However, finding a self-sufficing pleasure in the rhetorical development of his theme, he draws out through twenty lines of ingenious antitheses his contrast between his wooing of Bellimperia and her rejection of his advances, as well as his examination of his prospects as a lover. The rhetorical 'type' underlying this effusion is the Senecan 'deliberation-speech'. In Seneca, however, in spite of of all the rhetorical colouring, a continuous train of thought emerges, whereas here the thought is split up into a series of symmetrically ordered antitheses for the sake of the rhetorical pattern. By this procedure, which Kyd also follows in other passages, thought and feeling are trimmed and shaped in such a way as to adapt them to the rationalistic see-saw of argument and counter-argument.

Balthazar's speech at the end of the scene (II. i. 113-35), in which all his thoughts are concentrated on Horatio, shows us another form of this verbal ingenuity by means of which the facts of a case are 'dressed up' for the sake of a rhetorical pattern. In this case Horatio's fight with him and his fate as a lover are, by the rhetorical devices of epiploke and climax, given the appearance of a logical chain of cause and effect in which the one circumstance is a necessary consequence of the other. But this logic is of the most superficial kind, and moreover it is only one component of the ingenious verbal byplay which is at this point being carried on. Certainly it cannot have been by accident that Kyd here allows Balthazar in particular to indulge in a pointed, rhetorical turn of speech of just this nature (cf. his speeches at I. ii. 138-44, 161-5; I. iv. 93-7). For the lack of substance in this repetitive style of his, tediously amplified by antithesis and other rhetorical figures, is exactly in keeping with the irresolute, dependent, puppet-like role that Balthazar is to sustain in the play. The replies and retorts that his words receive from Lorenzo and Bellimperia seem to provide some hint as to the way in which his manner of speech is to be understood (I. iv. 90, 'Tush, tush, my lord! let goe these ambages'; I. iv. 98, 'Alas, my Lord, these are but words of course'; II. i. 29, 'My Lord, for my sake leaue this extasie'). Although this technique of characterizing a person by his habits of speech is not consistently followed (see, e.g., III. xiv. 95 ff.), the passages that have been referred to may be taken as an attempt to indicate character by the use of overworked or misused rhetorical tricks. This dramatic contrivance was later considerably developed by Shakespeare.

Much more significant of course are Hieronimo's soliloquies and set speeches, which to a large degree determine the peculiar character of *The Spanish Tragedy,* and which helped to give to the famous role of Hieronimo its outstanding success. Not only are they the pith and marrow of this play itself; they also form a kind of core for the whole body of drama that immediately preceded Shakespeare, for they were imitated by many playwrights; and by a few playwrights somewhat later they were also burlesqued. By means of these soliloquies, and of other speeches that are virtually soliloquies, Kyd added to a play already abounding in action and intrigue something which was designed to provide a complement, as it were, to the theatrically effective world of outward event and action, of underhand conspiracies, murders, and tangled enmities; he added the inward drama which is played out in the soul of the protagonist, Hieronimo, and which causes

him to lead a solitary existence in the midst of the affairs of this world and drives him to the verge of madness. Hieronimo's emotional and declamatory set speeches, therefore, though they remain strongly indebted to the style of Seneca, acquire a new significance. In the classical tragedies all the leading characters as a rule delivered set speeches and soliloquies in which their deepest thoughts and feelings were brought to the surface and laid bare. In *The Spanish Tragedy* it is especially Hieronimo who does this; only the soliloquy of Isabella which ends in her suicide (IV. ii), and which is to be regarded as a kind of prelude to what is yet to come, might also be named in this connexion. Lorenzo's soliloquies are of a different order; they are not soliloquies in which his deepest feelings are involved, but the self-revelatory soliloquies of a villain in which his scheming is disclosed, together with the explanation of his motives.

In Hieronimo, on the other hand, Kyd has created a figure who, by his singular and eccentric nature, his brooding over his sorrow, his mistrust and vacillation and procrastination, is set apart in a very marked fashion from the other characters. Hieronimo becomes a solitary. He is forced into a lonely isolation by the terrible suffering that falls upon him. He has to keep his own plans secret, and in his reflections on the murder, his tactics of delay, and his investigation of the outrage, he has to act quite alone. Hieronimo's part in the play is therefore planned in terms of soliloquy, and Kyd has thus given his numerous soliloquies a new basis in their function of revealing a type of character and establishing its role in the plot. Already in Seneca, of course, there were the beginnings of such a process, and these might have served as a model; yet Kyd appears to have been the first playwright in the history of English drama who from these beginnings succeeded in creating a convincing character by means of soliloquy.

In spite of the rhetorical commonplaces of classical origin in Hieronimo's utterances of grief and despair, and in spite of Kyd's obvious endeavour wherever possible to out-Seneca Seneca within the framework of classical conventions of rhetoric, a whole range of new qualities emerged in his work. Let us glance at Hieronimo's first soliloquy (II. v. 1-33). As Schücking has shown with some probability, the second part of this speech, with its conventional apostrophes of lament, may well have been replaced in the later version of the play by the expanded form of it which occurs in lines 46-98. The first part, however, is not in the manner of the soliloquies with which we have so far been familiar:

> What out-cries pluck me from my naked bed,
> And chill my throbbing hart with trembling
>   feare,
> Which neuer danger yet could daunt before?
> Who cals *Hieronimo?* speak, heere I am.
> I did not slumber; therefore twas no dreame.
> No, no, it was some woman cride for helpe;
> And heere within this garden did she crie;
> And in this garden must I rescue her.
> But stay, what murdrous spectacle is this?
> A man hangd vp and all the murderers gone:
> And in my bower, to lay the guilt on me.
> This place was made for pleasure, not for death.
>
>   (II. v. 1-12)

This is a soliloquy which is not only spoken, but also acted. Hieronimo comes running into the garden in his night-shirt, Bellimperia's screams still ringing in his ears, so that they cannot have been a dream or a figment of his imagination. In the darkness of the garden he searches for this woman who has cried out for help, and comes upon the body of a dead man hanging from a tree. Up to this point the soliloquy is not a mere passage of emotional rhetoric unaccompanied by action; it is a speech which accurately reflects what Hieronimo is experiencing, at the same time indicating his actions by means of internal stage-directions. We still find this technique used by Shakespeare, though by him it is as a rule more subtly and more covertly managed.

Hieronimo's soliloquies are on several occasions, though not invariably, attended by stage-business; they demand properties or appropriate gesture. At such times we see the hand of the true man of the theatre; declamatory as it may be, the soliloquy is made an integral part of the plot, and at the same time turned into a piece of good theatre. That great cry of grief, 'Oh eies, no eies . . .' (III. ii. 1 ff.), one of the most famous pieces of rhetoric in Elizabethan drama, is given actuality on the stage by the direction, *A Letter falleth*. From this point onwards the soliloquy is carried on in much less rhetorical language, for Hieronimo picks up the letter, reads it, and from its contents draws deductions as to his future course of conduct. In the same way, his soliloquy at the end of Act III, Scene vii, is largely taken up by the reading of the letter handed to him by the Hangman, the information it gives him about the circumstances of Horatio's murder, and the deliberations to which it gives rise. Even the outbursts of grief, 'Woe to the cause of these constrained warres . . .' etc., are associated with direct references to action; only the soliloquy with which the scene opens consists of unmixed lamentation. Similarly, the soliloquy at the beginning of Act III, Scene xii, when Hieronimo enters with a dagger in one hand and a rope in the other to await the arrival of the King, is an 'acted' soliloquy. It is true that it contains that lurid image of the fiery tower of judgement beside the lake of hell; but immediately after this it is again linked with the action, and Hieronimo engages in some stage-business with the properties:

> Downe by the dale that flowes with purple gore,
> Standeth a firie Tower; there sits a iudge
> Vpon a seat of steele and molten brasse,
> And twixt his teeth he holds a fire-brand,
> That leades vnto the lake where hell doth stand.
> Away, *Hieronimo;* to him be gone:
> Heele doe thee iustice for *Horatios* death.
> Turne downe this path: thou shalt be with him
>   straite;
> Or this, and then thou needst not take thy breth:
> This way, or that way:—soft and faire, not so:
> For if I hang or kill my selfe, lets know
> Who will reuenge *Horatios* murther then?
> No, no; fie, no: pardon me, ile none of that.
> *He flings away the dagger and halter.*
>
> (III. xii. 7-19)

There is nothing of this kind in Seneca. The histrionic quality of the popular drama has here forced its way into the static, declamatory monologue of the classical tradi-tion. Only with regard to the lament at the beginning of Act III, Scene vii, can it be said that the conventional form of the rhetorical lament has been preserved in its entirety. On all other occasions the action of the play is advanced in one way or another in the course of the soliloquies, and the speaking is accompanied by gesture or by stage-business. Even in Isabella's final soliloquy (IV. ii) this histrionic and theatrically effective quality is manifested; for in the form of a soliloquy we are given what is essentially a short 'action-scene', in the course of which Isabella tears down the leaves and branches of the tree on which Horatio was hanged, lays her curse on the garden in which the tree is growing, and finally stabs herself.

What is to be said of the speeches of Hieronimo that are not soliloquies, those which occur in dialogue-scenes? In these scenes his speeches for the most part tend to deviate into monologue, and the use of this type of speech is particularly effective in reinforcing the sense of isolation in Hieronimo's mind. In *Gorboduc* and the tragedies that succeeded it the speech that veers away into monologue had been employed because the playwright needed it as a vehicle for moral reflections or passionate lament. Kyd, however, makes Hieronimo address his words to himself in a fashion that is wholly appropriate to his spiritual condition; he consciously and deliberately isolates him from the other characters present in these dialogues. The grief-stricken old man, who is obsessed by thoughts which remain hidden from the other characters, and who appears distracted (and indeed wants to appear so), must with his very strange manner and speech have produced an uncanny effect on the stage. The set speech deviating into monologue, a mere convention with Kyd's predecessors, is now well on the way to becoming an organic and dramatically significant form of expression, even if it is not yet so on all occasions. Other good examples occur in the twelfth and thirteenth scenes of Act III; both times Hieronimo breaks up a dialogue-sequence. He is so strongly reminded of his grief by a catch-word—'Horatio' at III. xii. 58, and the Old Man's petition 'for his murdred Sonne' at III. xiii. 78—that he lets the despair he has with difficulty been holding in check break out into wild and whirling words.

The calculated failure to understand, the talking at cross-purposes, the breaking away from a dialogue-sequence: all these devices, up till now the peculiar property of comic drama, have in this exhibition of Hieronimo's pretended madness been given a new function, which is dramatically effective, and at the same time sound psychology. Here, too, Kyd reveals himself as a master craftsman, one who knew how to make dramatic capital out of the greatest variety of dramatic artifices.

The remaining plays of Kyd, **Soliman and Perseda** and **Cornelia** (a translation of Garnier's *Cornélie*), may in this context be disregarded. On a few occasions, indeed, the speeches in **Soliman and Perseda** show a noticeably stronger tendency to establish and maintain contact with the person addressed (e.g., I. ii. 1 ff.), and the rigidity of the set-speech pattern is relaxed by making the longer speeches part of the dialogue. The style of the work as a whole, however, the method of presentation, and the general dramatic technique, are weaker and less original than those of *The Spanish Tragedy,* where Kyd was quite obviously writing at the height of his powers. (pp. 100-12)

Wolfgang Clemen, "Kyd," in his English Tragedy before Shakespeare: The Development of Dramatic Speech, *translated by T. S. Dorsch, Methuen & Co. Ltd., 1961, pp. 100-12.*

William Empson   (essay date 1956)

[*Empson was an English critic, poet, and editor who is best known for* Seven Types of Ambiguity *(1930), his seminal contribution to the formalist school of New Criticism. His critical theory is based on the assumption that all great poetic works are ambiguous and that this ambiguity can often be traced to the multiple meanings of words. Empson analyzes a text by enumerating and discussing these various meanings and examining how they fit together to communicate the poem's ideas and emotions. While he is almost unanimously respected for his ingenuity and exhaustive readings of a text, Empson has been faulted for the limitations of his approach. In the following essay, which was originally published in* Nimbus *in 1956, he argues that the central concern of* The Spanish Tragedy *is the fulfillment of the Ghost of Andrea's revenge against Balthazar and the Castile family for arranging his murder. Empson also attempts to vindicate Hieronimo's retributive actions, maintaining that he is merely an instrument of Andrea's revenge and that "only great and prolonged forces would have driven such a character to such a crime."*]

It seems to me that *The Spanish Tragedy* of Kyd has been underrated through misunderstanding, as I shall try to show in this [essay]. The question may seem remote, but the play is commonly regarded as the surviving analogue to the *Ur-Hamlet* of Kyd, so has a considerable bearing on Shakespeare's *Hamlet;* or at least on what the first audience thought Shakespeare was doing when he rewrote the old favourite, a thing which they had laughed at even before they decided it was out of date.

So far as I have seen, critics always take for granted that the Ghost of Andrea has no point; Kyd was crude, and anyhow he was copying Seneca. I think the point was obvious at the time, so obvious that it did not get stated in the text. Andrea has suffered the fate of Uriah; the father and brother of Belimperia, that is, the Duke of Castile and Lorenzo, had arranged to have him killed in battle so that they could marry her to Balthazar the Prince of Portugal. Presumably they informed the enemy Prince, who killed him in the battle, where he was going to be sent and how he could be recognized. There is a reason for not mentioning this (though I agree that one would expect the Ghost to say it at the end) because the Ghost is part of the audience, and it has been arranged by the Queen of Hades that he must discover what happened to him, without being told. The culprits themselves, of course, have no occasion to mention it. If this is assumed, the audience has the interest of keeping half an eye on the Ghost, to see whether he has guessed the point yet, while the Ghost watches the actors and the actors watch the play-within-the-play. I do not think this bold conception has been given its due.

The Ghost opens the play by entering with Revenge, and makes clear at once that he knows of no reason for revenging himself. His coolness all round, indeed, compared to Hamlet's Father for example, is very refreshing. (However, we cannot suppose that the Ur-Father-Hamlet was cool, since the only thing we hear about him is that he was pale and cried Revenge miserably like an oyster-wife; this would at least prevent the two plays from being absurdly similar.) When alive he was at the Spanish Court, he says, and was accepted as a lover by a lady above his social position, not that his position was bad; then he happened to get killed in a war with Portugal. The puzzle began when he got to the classical Hades; the officials there couldn't decide whether he was a lover or a soldier, so he was referred up in the administrative machine to the King and Queen. Proserpina smiled, and asked Pluto to let her settle it; then she whispered in the ear of Revenge, and the two have arrived back on earth. Revenge says Andrea will see his Belimperia kill the man who killed himself (Andrea); 'here sit we down to see the mystery.' But on the face of it there is no mystery, and no reason why the administration of Hades should be disturbed, let alone why Proserpina should grin and whisper. The Ghost also sees something else, which he is not told beforehand; Belimperia chooses another lover, Horatio, and Horatio is killed by her brother Lorenzo, so that there will again be no obstacle to her marrying the Prince of Portugal. Surely all this has only one possible point; Andrea is to guess that her family had previously arranged, in the same way, to kill himself.

We may pause at 'Here sit we down' to ask where they sit. The text as we have it seems planned for a full Elizabethan stage, and it looks as if the play-within-the-play was done on the inner stage, with the courtly audience on the balcony, rather absurdly pretending that the spectacle was in front of them. In any case, human listeners appear 'above' at II. ii, the imprisoned Belimperia appears 'at a window' in III. ix, and before the play-within-the-play Hieronymo asks the Duke to throw him down the key after the audience has gone up (this gives him a bit of time to harangue them before they 'break down the doors'). Thus Ghost and Revenge can't be 'above'; I take it they sit right out in front, each of them leaning against one of the pillars which held up the Heavens. This puts them on a rather homely footing, and makes clear that they are part of the audience, except that most of the time Revenge is asleep.

At I. iv, Belimperia hears about Andrea's death from Horatio, who captured Balthazar just after he had killed Andrea. Andrea, he says, had fought long with Balthazar, but then Fate took a hand and 'brought a fresh supply of halberdiers, Which paunched his horse and dinged him to the ground'; then Balthazar 'finished' him, 'taking advantage of his foe's distress.' Belimperia, after Horatio has gone, finds this sufficient reason to want revenge on Balthazar, and to make Horatio her lover for the purpose:

> But how can love find harbour in my breast
> Till I revenge the death of my beloved?
> Yes, second love shall further my revenge.
> I'll love Horatio, my Andrea's friend,
> The more to spite the prince that wrought his
>   end;

And where Don Balthazar, that slew my love,
Himself now pleads for favour at my hands,
He shall, in rigour of my just disdain,
Reap long repentance for his murderous deed.
For what was't else but murderous cowardice
So many to oppress one valiant knight
Without respect of honour in the fight?

However, she clearly doesn't mean to kill him for his unsporting behaviour—she assumes he will have 'long repentance'; nor would the audience think it an adequate reason for the Ghost to be sent back by Proserpina. The audience can however notice that the halberdiers arrived very opportunely; maybe they weren't sent only by Fate. By the way, on the stage Belimperia has not yet met Balthazar; it is assumed that for dynastic reasons he is already her suitor, not that he fell in love with her on meeting her after his capture. At II. i. 45, when Lorenzo is extracting the secret of Belimperia's love for Horatio from her servant Pedringano, we learn that her father was angry at her love for Andrea, and that the watchful Lorenzo then saved Pedringano from being punished as a go-between, apparently to use him later; it all helps to make the fate of Andrea look suspicious. The nearest we get to an admission of the murder is in the evasive language which Lorenzo uses to Belimperia when he is explaining why he locked her up (III. x). He says it is essential for her honour that he should protect her from herself, so when he happened to find her with Horatio—

Why then, remembering that old disgrace
Which you for Don Andrea had endured
And now were likely longer to sustain
By being found so meanly companied
Thought rather—for I knew no readier means—
To thrust Horatio forth my father's way.

We learn nothing about how she interprets this; she is behaving with fierce dignity, especially because of the presence of Balthazar. We do not see her again for some time, apart from two riddling answers in public, till IV. i. where she upbraids Hieronymo for not having done his revenge, threatens to do it herself, and promises to help him (prefiguring Lady Macbeth and the Queen of *Hamlet* Q1). One might think that her brother's remark had some geographical meaning, that Horatio was banished from the town by a private gate; but she would know this to be a lie; she saw the murder, said so at the time, and told about it in her letter afterwards. Thus there seems no meaning for 'I thrust him forth my father's way' except 'I killed him, as my father did Andrea.' It is meant of course to be the more thrilling because obscure.

The idea that the Duke is guilty appears again prominently at the end, though he has always kept up an innocent appearance. The last act of Hieronymo before he kills himself is to kill the Duke; this might be merely a sign of madness, or might give him a complete revenge against the son, but I do not think the audience would find that satisfying. In any case, the Ghost of Andrea is then allowed by Revenge to arrange punishments for the villains; he starts the list cheerfully with the Duke, and it is clear that Revenge thinks this proper. The reason must be (though poor Hieronymo may not have been told by Belimperia, and the audience only know it from the phrase 'my fa-

ther's way') that the Duke had arranged the death of Andrea.

The reason why we have this Duke in the caste, brother to a childless King, is I take it simply to avoid revenge against a King, which would be too wicked on the separate ground of Divine Right; the King has then to be childless to make the proposed marriage of Belimperia dynastic. We gather from III. xiv. that Lorenzo has hidden his murder of Horatio from the Duke, which seems unnecessary as he must know the Duke would approve; but it adds to the mystery to make the Duke a complete hypocrite, and no doubt Lorenzo himself is merely keeping to his principles:

no man knows it was my fetching reach.
Tis hard to trust unto a multitude,
Or any one, in mine opinion,
When men themselves their secrets will reveal.

The effect of the speech (III. iv. 45) is a challenge to the audience to discover further secrets.

Going back to the scene of Lorenzo with his sister, the actors need to make clear that he is trying to break her spirit. Soon after the riddle about 'my father's way,' which she ought to receive as a horrible flash of light, she asks with her usual firm dignity whether her father has not inquired for her while Lorenzo kept her imprisoned, and he breaks the formality of their dialogue (Balthazar being present) by saying he must whisper in her ear. We heard about this before she entered; Balthazar remarked that she had better be released soon because her father was asking for her, and Lorenzo said jauntily:

Lor. Why, and my lord, I hope you heard me say
Sufficient reason why she kept away.
But that's all one. My lord, you love her?
Bal. Ay.
Lor. Then in your love beware; deal cunningly

and so forth; 'jest with her gently,' which in view of the other jokes in the play may be expected to mean something appalling. He might simply have told her father that she was prostrated by the murder of her lover, but why need such a story be whispered to her? I take it the audience presumed him to whisper, perhaps falsely, that he had told her father she was procuring an abortion. She could make this clear by a flash of horror and disgust, though she must recover at once her contemptuous grandeur towards both of them:

Too politic for me, past all compare,
Since last I saw you; but content yourself,
The prince is meditating higher things.

(i.e. 'Balthazar is too holy to have overheard you'). The play should be rather like an opera, with the end-stopped lines pronounced next door to song, so this break is a strong dramatic effect; what had to be whispered, presumably, was what could not be said in the high language of the Honour of Spain. She ends the scene with a riddle about fear in Latin, and no doubt this would easily suggest Seneca and a determination to revenge.

I think, then, that the play could be produced so as to make pretty clear to the audience that Andrea had been

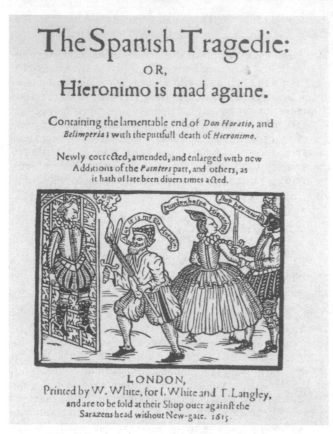

Title page of the 1615 edition of The Spanish Tragedy.

murdered for love, but I admit that it is peculiar for the text never to say it. A mystery is dramatic, but you expect to have an answer at the end of the play, and the Ghost could give it in one line. Perhaps he did, and it got dropped from the printed text. But there were several editions, the first probably earlier than the first dated one of 1594, and you might argue that even the Elizabethans would want to restore such an important omission. However, though the answer would need to be made clear to the first audiences (if only by the production), the first readers would know it already, not buy the quarto to find it. In any case, the Ghost at the end could not say much about himself, because the audience has rather lost interest in his story compared to what they have seen; he settles down contentedly to the administrative work of giving the villains suitable torments in his classical Hades. He is an unusual type of Ghost, and one may imagine that from the first he didn't bother to draw the moral about himself; thus perhaps recovering some of the mystery which he had otherwise so frankly thrown away.

Another peculiar thing about him is that he is entirely unjealous; to watch Belimperia giving herself to Horatio excites no complaint. He does indeed complain at the end of Act I that he is only shown 'league, love, and banqueting' instead of revenge as expected (Revenge gives him a brief appalling reassurance), but presumably he would mention the infidelity of Belimperia if he felt it as such; and at the end of Act II he combines their names without the smallest resentment:

Broughtst thou me hither to increase my pain?
I looked that Balthazar should have been slain.
But 'tis my friend Horatio that is slain;
And they abuse fair Belimperia
On whom I doted more than all the world
Because she loved me more than all the world.

(Revenge gives him a brief appalling reassurance). For that matter, Belimperia while imprisoned (III. ix. 9) herself appeals to the Ghost of Andrea, taking for granted that he would not mind her change to Horatio:

Andrea, oh Andrea! That thou sawest
Me for thy friend Horatio handled thus,
And him for me thus causeless murdered!

By the way, this almost necessitates some reaction from the Ghost, so he may be presumed to have reacted elsewhere; I think Revenge ought to have to hush him, both here and at the words 'my father's way.' The appeal seems to get him worked up, though in a stupid manner, because after Act III (there are only four acts) he needs a longer interlude. He is distressed at finding all quarrels apparently quieted, and Belimperia agreeing to marry the prince of Portugal. The audience are to think the poor creature rather dull, because the agreement of Hieronymo is patently false, and we only hear from Belimperia three and a half lines of harsh double-talk. Revenge while trying to reassure him uses an exact echo of the riddling talk of Hieronymo in III. xiii, and prepares us for more of it in IV. i:

Nor dies Revenge, although he sleeps a while,
For in unquiet, quietness is feigned,
And slumbering is a common worldly wile.

This proves to the audience that Hieronymo is a correct Revenger; and indeed a Revenger always wants to be somehow Revenge in person. It is inadequate to calm the Ghost, who is only made to shut up ('argue not') by being given a separate Dumb Show with an explanation of it. He then says

Sufficeth me: thy meaning's understood;
And thanks to thee, and those infernal powers
That will not tolerate a lover's woe.

Now the combination of this grand phrase with his complete friendship to Horatio cuts out all but one interpretation; the Lover's Woe has to be the Arranged Marriage. I understand that this custom was almost universal, at least in the sense that the families were expected to come to an agreement about the money affairs of a young couple; but the theatre was always in favour of the lovers as against the Arranged Marriage, and no doubt it was echoing a state of sentiment which often avoided harshness in borderline cases. Now, if you wanted to have a play against the Arranged Marriage, the royal marriages of Spain and Portugal gave the most impressive example you could find. It is clear that dynastic importance attaches to the marriage of Belimperia and Balthazar; as early as II. iii. 20, by way of settling the war, the King says to the Portuguese Ambassador (after referring to the dowry from the lady's father),

in case this match go forward
The tribute which you pay shall be released;

> And if by Balthazar she have a son
> He will enjoy the kingdom after us.

One might assume that this meant giving Spain itself to the royal family of Portugal, but he never speaks of excluding his nephew Lorenzo, and Portugal is only ruled by a Viceroy, whose failure to pay tribute has caused the war. He means that Portugal would be allowed to recover its independent sovereignty in favour of a son of this marriage. The only problem is that, if Lorenzo is the heir to both Spain and Portugal, he can hardly want to commit all these murders merely in order to make his sister produce an independent heir to Portugal. He might conceivably argue, in a statesmanlike manner, that Portugal is getting too hard to hold under the present system. Presumably the audience wouldn't bother much; they would only feel sure that the marriage somehow mattered a great deal.

The question of course was a major one of current politics. Spain and Portugal had acquired the first maritime empires, and the Pope had divided America between them. For England, the great enemy was Spain, and Spain when the play was new had recently acquired by inheritance the whole empire of Portugal. That is, Philip II took it in 1580 and made a reasonable hereditary claim; he had to send an army to Lisbon, and I gather had other grounds such as that the Portuguese had been trying to take Morocco, but the hereditary claim was an essential part. One could hardly say that he got Portugal by marriage; he got it because the more direct male heirs of that house had become too holy to produce children; but he got it by an earlier royal marriage, and that is the kind of thing the play envisages. Emanuel the Fortunate, I learn from the encyclopaedia, in whose reign the Portuguese Empire was founded, 'had pursued the traditional policy of intermarriage with royal families of Castile and Aragon, hoping to weld together the Spanish and Portuguese dominions'; as indeed he did, though sexually the wrong way round for his purpose. (The arrangement, with Portugal technically independent but happening to have as its King the King of Spain, lasted till 1640.) One might think the first audiences would be in favour of Belimperia for liking brave native lovers and refusing to unite Spain with Portugal, but politically they would have to be in favour of this marriage, because it might separate Spain from Portugal. Presumably they would also be rather shocked by her because it is made so clear that she goes to bed with her lovers (among the first words of the play are 'In secret I possessed a worthy dame.') One would assume that all the characters were a bit wicked, but the main sentiment would be against these oppressively important royal marriages (which the Queen of England had been quite right to refuse); one would take for granted that any amount of murder would be done before such a thing was arranged.

A slight suggestion that all these characters are wicked no doubt helps to bring in the idea of Fate, which gets rather unusual treatment. Some critics have called the Ghost a clumsy and undramatic device because, not only pointless, he has no effect on the action. In any case, it is dramatic to be able to glance at the Ghost in the audience, as you might at one of your friends, and wonder whether he has got on to the point yet. But I also think it is symbolically

good as expressing a moral truth. Swinburne wrote about the *Hamlet* of Shakespeare that the characters 'veer sideways to their doom'; this is true in general about the Elizabethan Revenge Play, rather than making as he supposed a contrast between the First and Second Quarto. May I express here my impatience with 'Fate'; it seems both logical nonsense and harmful in its historical effects. But in the story before us we can give the word a reasonable interpretation; if this family keeps on killing the daughter's suitors, one after another, to make a grand marriage, then it does seem likely to run into trouble some time. Persephone might intelligibly smile when she told Andrea to go and see what happened next. Revengers indeed are usually presented as acting in a roundabout manner, chiefly perhaps because they dislike what they are trying to approach; and the catastrophe is usually arranged to come as much from the nature of the villains as from the loony though fascinating calculations of the Revenger. In this play, for example, Lorenzo is only discovered because he is so vainly ingenious about getting his tools to kill each other off. However, though this gives us a tolerable meaning for Fate, I must admit it is not one that a Revenger while in mental turmoil would accept. He wants to take part in Fate; he wants to show that he is acting *as* or *like* Fate, which itself evidently works in a roundabout way. Such is the doom of Old Hieronymo, but the Ghost is spared it; he sits among the audience listening with some impatience while the Revenger babbles about how clever and useful it is for him to be mad. I have come to think that this early play gave a more profound treatment of Revenge than the later ones.

It can be presumed, I think, that the **Ur-Hamlet,** with its handfuls of speeches and the Ghost crying miserably like an oyster-wife, had been written before **The Spanish Tragedy.** The French of Belleforest was an easily accessible source for Hamlet, and likely to be combed for material—it was a big collection of moral tales; whereas for **The Spanish Tragedy** no source has ever been found. None could be, if it was simply an attempt to apply the technique and atmosphere of the **Ur-Hamlet** to the highly topical theme of the royal marriages of Spain. The basic idea would be 'Take a woman who revolted against one of these shocking royal marriages, and you would get a similar case of madness and revenge.' Like so many previous critics, I am putting a lot of weight on the **Ur-Hamlet** for conjectural arguments, but to do that one need not assume it was very good (indeed, it seems plausible as well as comforting to suppose that no very good Elizabethan play failed to hit print). It was a decisively important foundation, or piece of basic engineering, for the Elizabethan drama, because it showed them how to express something they wanted to (if you like, how to adapt their Seneca to the Christian conscience and the Renaissance code of honour); but Kyd would have learned a bit by experience, the year after his initial success, when he entirely transposed his material into **The Spanish Tragedy.** This would be a good reason why only the second play got printed, though no doubt there were accidental causes as well.

I am assuming that the audiences of the first period of Elizabethan drama thought revenge wicked, and that a dramatist trying to present a revenger had to reckon with the weight of that feeling. This is handled by the structure of the play, before it advances on the serious case of Hieronymo; such is the only purpose of the rather absurd sub-plot, about events at the court of Portugal. The first time human characters speak of revenge is when the Viceroy is brooding over the fate of his son if captured in the battle; a courtier suggests that the Spaniards would not make 'a breach of common law of arms,' but he answers, in the first of the grand echoing lines of which the play is so full,

> They reck no laws that meditate revenge.

A courtier in reply calls revenge 'foul.' We then see the captured son insisting with high rhetoric (II. i. 111-133) that revenge is essential to his nature if the woman refuses the marriage which his plans demand;

> Yet I must take revenge, or die myself,

he says, if she has another lover. The dramatic irony is heightened if we already suspect that he had been tipped off to kill her previous lover in the battle. In any case, he is presented early as the admittedly wicked type of man who takes revenge for granted, therefore as very unlike the final revenger Hieronymo.

Some critics have said that in a crude play like *The Spanish Tragedy* the revenger is simply mad, whereas the whole subtlety and profundity of Shakespeare consisted in introducing doubt as to whether the hero was mad or not. This sounds likely, but I believe it is now generally admitted to be wrong. It underrates the general moral background of the audience, apart from their native wits; and the questions which were being discussed in the theatre, in a theatrical manner as one might expect, had a good deal of practical importance. I want now to advance on a rather lengthy attempt to prove that Hieronymo is just like Hamlet in being both mad and not mad, both wise and not wise, and so forth.

The last action of Hieronymo, before the trick by which he secures a knife to kill the Duke and himself, is to bite out his tongue lest tortures force him to confess his secret. Many critics have complained at the 'sensationalism' of this, particularly as he seems to have no secret to tell. I think they would have discovered the point if they had allowed themselves to speak with less restraint; the incident is wildly absurd, as it was meant to be, because Hieronymo has just told the bereaved fathers everything he possibly could.

> And to this end the bashaw I became
> That might revenge me on Lorenzo's life,
> Who therefore was appointed to the part
> And was to represent the knight of Rhodes
> That I might kill him more conveniently.
> So, Viceroy, was this Balthazar, thy son,
> That Soliman which Belimperia,
> In person of Perseda, murdered,
> Solely appointed to that tragic part
> That she might slay him who offended her.
> Poor Belimperia missed her part in this
> For though the story saith she should have died
> Yet I of kindness, and of care to her,
> Did otherwise determine of her end;
> But love of him whom they did hate too much

> Did urge her resolution to be such.

Nothing could seem madder than this professorial tone, patiently explaining at length what is already obvious, with a pedantic satisfaction in making clear where there were little errors of detail. But at last, when he has finished telling everything, a great wave of revulsion comes over him; there is something he must never tell, at all costs; so he bites out his tongue. This is very imaginative, I think, and the whole point of it is that he is now completely mad. The reason why critics have not found this obvious, I suspect, is that they were ready to assume the old play would commit any absurdity, just to have some more blood splashing about, and also ready to let the development of the character be obscured by Jonson's additions. Jonson removed the incident of biting out the tongue and put in some poetical mad talk instead; no doubt it had come to seem too absurd altogether, *too* un-life-like, by 1600. But really his additions, as a whole, made the old play much *more* un-life-like, because he was going all out to satisfy 'the modern convention' of the Revenge Play. He makes Hieronymo raging mad as soon as he finds his son dead, and from then on another splendid bout of madness is inserted at each convenient point; then each time we return to the old text and find him sane enough to carry on his plot. But in the crude old play he is only gradually pushed into madness, just as he is only gradually pushed into revenge; he disapproves of both, but cannot keep them from him; a long period of grizzling over his wrong and puzzling over his duty has to be gone through, and all this time he is getting madder. Just before he gets to the deed of blood his wife kills herself because he hasn't yet done it; this ought to be enough to show that he is assumed to feel powerful resistances against it. And after he at last has done it, instead of being 'pleased and eased' as he boasts, he is for the first time completely off his rocker. Presumably the audience knew that a man would be unable to bite out his tongue unless in a highly abnormal condition. All this makes a much more human and sensible picture of revenge and its madness than you get from the play with Jonson's additions, though I confess that the old version would be very hard to put over on a modern audience, as no doubt Jonson felt about his own audience. The theatre of Kyd was presumably very formalized both in acting style and in the way the audience was meant to interpret; they were to feel that biting out the tongue symbolized something true, rather than that this individual had already convinced them he had a character likely to do it.

The contrast between the periods looks rather more definite if one considers Jonson himself. We know from Henslowe's accounts that he was twice paid to write Additions to Hieronymo, in 1601 and 1602, and it seems clear that this marks an attempt by the Admiral's Company to offer an adequate counter to Shakespeare's *Hamlet* (incidentally I think Shakespeare was also offering further 'additions' in the second year). Some critics carry their reverence for style so far that even with the accounts in front of them they refuse to believe Jonson wrote the existing Additions, because they aren't 'in Jonson's style'; so Henslowe must have paid somebody else for better Additions than Jonson's, and these are what got printed. From what we know of Henslowe it is extremely unlikely that he tossed money about in this manner, and I don't think it at all unlikely that Jonson could write in a different style if he was challenged and paid to. He was then 29, rather struggling for his position, and a very clever man. It does him great credit that he could write so wonderfully in the high Elizabethan romantic manner:

> Confusion, mischief, torment, death and hell
> Drop all your stings at once in my cold bosom
> That now is stiff with horror: kill me quickly.
> Be gracious to me, thou infective night,
> And drop this deed of murder down on me;
> Gird in my waste of grief with thy large darkness
> And let me not survive to see the light
> May put me in the mind I had a son.

(this is Hieronymo when he has just discovered the corpse); but one can understand that he did not want to print it in his collected edition. No doubt he didn't himself know quite how far his tongue was in his cheek; but in any case he was trying to satisfy a demand, he was writing to a very clear-cut 'convention.' Whereas, when Kyd wrote the old version, the convention had not yet been established; he needed to make his basic development of character much more reasonable and in accordance with serious moral opinion, even though the incidents he used could be less realistic. This view, I submit, gives a consistent explanation of the difficulties of the texts.

I must admit that Hieronymo speaks of revenge soon after he has discovered the body. He has twenty lines of lament before his wife enters, then:

> *Isabella.* What world of grief! My son Horatio!
> O, where's the author of this endless woe?
> *Hier.* To know the author were some ease of grief;
> For in revenge my heart must find relief.

He tells her that he will keep the bloody handkerchief till he takes revenge, and tells her to dissemble her sorrow for the present: 'so shall we sooner find the practice out.' It seems to be the lament of the mother which puts this practical idea into his head. Even so, they both appear to be thinking in terms of law; as when Isabella says 'The heavens are just; murder cannot be hid.' It is only when the heir to the throne is found to be implicated that normal justice is assumed to be impossible. The discovery of the body is at the end of Act II; in Act III. i. we are taken away to see the Viceroy of Portugal doing injustice because of the false witness of a villain, and the victim says

> Nor discontents it me to leave the world
> With whom there nothing can prevail but wrong

Then sc. ii. begins with the famous soliloquy of Hieronymo denouncing all the world, as

> Confused and filled with murder and misdeeds.

The whole scene is darkening. He feels he is being dragged into revenge; both night and day, he says, are driving him to seek the murderer, and

> The ugly fiends do sally forth of Hell
> And frame my steps to unfrequented paths
> And fear my heart with fierce inflamed thoughts.

These lines can only mean that he partly suspects the whole process of revenge to be a bad one. Next the letter falls, written by the imprisoned Belimperia in her blood to accuse her brother. Hieronymo like Hamlet is suspicious of this first evidence, and warns himself that it may only be intended to prevent his revenge by inducing him to make a false accusation against Lorenzo, which would endanger his life. In spite of this caution to himself, he immediately does excite the suspicion of Lorenzo, who enters at once, and Lorenzo therefore sets to work to cover his tracks by killing both his accomplices. This is done by getting one of them, Pedringano, to kill the other, and then having him hanged for it; Pedringano believes till the last moment that Lorenzo will get him off. We next see Hieronymo in sc. vi, acting in his function as judge; he begins by bemoaning that 'neither gods nor men be just to *me*.' The refusal of Pedringano to pray before he is hanged (actually because he can see the boy holding the box which he believes to contain his pardon) draws from Hieronymo his most splendid sentence against the revengeful mind.

> I have not seen a wretch so impudent.
> O monstrous times, where murder's set so light,
> And where the soul, that should be shrined in
>   heaven,
> Solely delights in interdicted things,
> Still wandering in the thorny passages
> That intercept itself of happiness.
> Murder! O bloody monster! God forbid
> A fault so foul should scape unpunished.
> Despatch, and see this execution done!
> This makes me to remember thee, my son.

In a way it is dramatic irony against Hieronymo, who fails to apply this reflection to himself. But it is not heavily against him; he is speaking as a judge, and we are not meant to think him wrong for wanting justice to be done. By the way, there is evidence here that our text at any rate leaves out stage directions, because no use is made of the boy standing by with the box. When Pedringano demands life 'by my pardon from the king,' and the hangman replies

> Stand you on that? Then you shall off with this.
> *Turns him off.*

it is clear that Pedringano must point at the boy with the box, who opens it with hearty laughter showing it to be empty, before the hangman dare proceed. A critic may reasonably impute other omitted 'business' elsewhere, such as might clear up the mystery about Andrea.

In sc. vii. Hieronymo in soliloquy is a noticeable degree crazier; he has

> Made mountains marsh with spring-tides of my
>   tears
> And broken through the brazen gates of hell,
> Yet still tormented is my tortured soul . . .

Then the Hangman brings a letter written by Pedringano in prison, begging Lorenzo to hurry up, and pleading for himself 'I holp to murder Don Horatio too.' Hieronymo is now convinced that the letter written in blood was true; and by the way he hasn't learned it by any of the subtlety he proposed—the prison letter is merely handed on to him as the officiating judge. For that matter, Hamlet's pretence of madness in Saxo does not let him find out who the murderer is (a thing universally known), and even in Shakespeare it at most only makes the king act suspiciously—what convinces Hamlet is the play-within-the-play. Hamlet in Saxo has superfine senses (like the fairy-story princess who was black and blue from the pea under the nineteen mattresses), and Belleforest makes this 'rational' by explaining he was a magician. Shakespeare may have been drawing on this tradition for the piercing and testing quality of the mad talk of his Hamlet, but I don't suppose it was much use to the Hamlet of Kyd. The main thrill about his talk was that he could tell the truth without being believed.

Hieronymo deduces from this accident that Heaven is arranging to punish the murderer by letting out the truth (II. 50 and 58). He is still thinking as a judge, and can say as such that 'nought but blood can satisfy my woes'; indeed, not only does he still hope to get this blood lawfully, but he noticeably refuses to threaten that he will otherwise get it unlawfully.

> I will go plain me to my lord the king
> And cry aloud for justice through the court
> Wearing the flints with these my withered feet;
> And either purchase justice by entreats
> Or tire them all with my revenging threats.

There should I suppose be a dramatic pause after 'Or.' We next see him, after three more scenes, on his way to the Court for this procedure; and he is now, perhaps from reflecting on the difficulty of it, at a stage where passers-by call him mad. He goes out and comes back (a mark of folly on the stage used by Hamlet in talking both to Ophelia and the Queen). The passers-by ask him the way to Lorenzo's house, and he describes it as going to hell; this appears simply to denounce Lorenzo, but also means that his own going there puts him on the path of wickedness.

> A darksome place, and dangerous to pass;
> There shall you meet with melancholy thoughts
> Whose baleful humours if you but uphold
> It will conduct you to despair and death.

He begins the next scene by rejecting two methods of suicide as an unreliable source of revenge—this is not as stagey as it may appear, because many suicides actually are done to punish other people (institutionally among the Japanese); and it was a necessary partial justification of the Revenger that he should be willing to die. In his appearance before the king (this is sc. xii) he is too easily shuffled aside by Lorenzo; one would think the letter of Pedringano need only be shown. It would be fussy to deny that Kyd is unskilful at this crucial point of the play, unless our text has been curtailed. But the story is not absurd; Hieronymo's nervous condition might well prevent him from making his accusation except in so violent a form as to sound mad, and the first audiences might recognize more easily than we do that he had a practical danger—if he produced at once his evidence against the heir to the throne, it could simply be taken from him and destroyed. He does win the sympathy of the King, who proposes to look into his case later (l. 99). As the chief object of Hieronymo is to speak to the king away from the brother and nephew, this means that his choice of mad behaviour nearly succeeded. (Of course, in one way he can't help being peculiar, but in another way he is trying to make use

of it.) But the King only says this after he has gone, and then refers the matter to the Duke, who has Lorenzo at the interview; so that Hieronymo again feels that his case is hopeless.

He next comes in (sc. xiii) 'with a book in his hand' like Hamlet, because he is grappling with the theory of revenge. I want to maintain that his arguments were meant to seem mad to the audience, or at least tragically deluded; such is the point of development he ought to have reached, and he is at least very confused about the well-known difficulties of his topic. But you may say that the audience was confused too, and I confess that there is at least one point in the play where we are inclined to think both author and audience very simple. It is at the end of Act I; to establish the position of Hieronymo as court playwright, we have him showing a masque to the King and the Portuguese Ambassador, consisting of three English knights who capture two Portuguese kings and one Spanish king. Both dignitaries accept this with high chivalry, saying that, as even little England can win, one ought to accept calmly the fortunes of war. This seems childlike unreality, but I suppose any members of the audience who thought so would be content to take it as charming; in any case, it comes early, before the play is too serious for it. I do not think we need impute the same careless effrontery to the discussion of Hieronymo about revenge. He begins with the Scripture text 'Vindicta mihi' (I will repay, saith the Lord), which meant that men must *not* do this work of God, and contrives to twist it into meaning only that a revenger ought to delay until God gives him a good opportunity. Having used Latin for this Bible text, he can move smoothly over to Seneca as if the two had equal moral authority; but his next bit of Latin has to be twisted equally violently before it will suit his purpose. The line became a stock one for the Elizabethan drama, either in quotation or in echo, but I doubt whether it was ever again so starkly misused.

> *Per scelus semper tutum est sceleribus iter;*
> Strike, and strike home, when wrong is offered
>   thee.

Clytemnestra says this when nerving herself to kill Agamemnon, and has just remarked that her chance of taking 'the better way' has already gone; she has already behaved so badly that her only chance of safety lies in further crime. Nobody but Hieronymo ever took it to mean that a good man, when a crime is done against him, ought to commit an immediate crime in reply. Even so, his interpretation contradicts the one he has just made from the Bible text; he deduces now that he ought to revenge at once, instead of waiting till God gives him a good opportunity. He encourages this view by a baffling argument that the duty of 'patience,' which of course was prominent in medieval thought, was really a recommendation to suicide. This is supported by a third Latin quotation, about Fate; this time from the *Troiades,* when poor little Astyanax is hidden in a tomb and told that, even if the Greeks catch him there, he has at least got his tomb handy. Hieronymo manages to deduce:

> let this thy comfort be;
> Heaven covereth him that hath no burial.
> And, to conclude, I will revenge his death!

But how? Not as the vulgar wits of men,
With open, but inevitable ills,
As by a secret, yet a certain mean,
Which under kindship will be cloaked best.

'Not with open injuries, as men do, but with inevitable ones, as Fate does'—such has to be the grammar, and the effect is that he proposes to become Fate in person, so he must act by roundabout and unexpected methods, as one must agree that Fate appears to do. The lines go straight on to a solution of the problem whether to delay, and here I think the audience *must* have been meant to realize that he is talking nonsense, even if they were meant to be rather stunned by the bits of Latin.

Wise men will take their opportunity
Closely and safely fitting things to time.
But in extremes advantage hath no time;
And therefore all times fit not for revenge.
Thus therefore will I rest me in unrest,
Dissembling quiet in unquietness,
Not seeming that I know their villainies,
That my simplicity may make them think
That ignorantly I will let all slip;
For ignorance, I wot, and well they know
Remedium malorum iners est.

In extremes advantage hath no time can only mean, I submit, 'in such a hard case as mine waiting is useless, because there will never be a safe opportunity'; and indeed all cases suited to revenge plays are 'extreme' like this, because the revenger is so desperate that he is ready to die as soon as he has succeeded—this is necessary, to make the audience respect him however much they think him wrong. But this created a difficulty for the other requirement of the theatre, that he is needed to argue and delay; and here the knot is cut (by a complete contradiction in the next line) with a bold absurdity intended to make the audience realize that he is mad. Now that he has settled his problem the poetry sounds very contented; he enjoys thinking how subtle he will be, and manages to extract a kind of cosy gloating out of a third tag from Seneca, which is again off the point. Oedipus was saying, with courageous public spirit, that the reason for the plague must necessarily be found, whatever its unpleasantness to himself; this is very remote from the idea of hiding by flattery an intention of private revenge. After thus consistently showing the informed spectator that he is hopelessly confused, he ends the speech with the one argument that the audience would respect; that he cannot work in any other way, because if he showed any 'menace' to his enemies they would 'bear him down with their nobility.'

Some petitioners now enter to see the judge, and for the first time he is violently crazy, as the speech has prepared us to find him; he rips up their expensive documents, and then patters away saying 'catch me' (Shakespeare copied this twice, separating the two elements of the madness of the revenger; we get the grim humour of the pretence in Hamlet—'Hide fox, and all after'—and the pathos of its reality in Lear, waving his boots in his hands). It is in the next scene that we see Hieronymo fail in his last chance of getting public justice, the interview with the Duke of Castile (the audience thinks he is right in suspecting the Duke to be a hypocrite, but also that a saner man would

have made some attempt); then we advance on the final Act, where he agrees on revenge with Belimperia and has only to plan the method with a lunatic and presumably unnecessary cunning.

I hope this is enough to show that the old play gives a graduated advance towards madness and revenge, taking for granted that only great and prolonged forces would have driven such a character into such a crime. It might not seem to need much proof, but a rival theory has been growing up, of a kind which I call 'neo-Christian,' that the Elizabethans considered their theology to be in favor of revenge, and that we would too if we weren't rotted with 'humanitarianism.' I find something rather alarming in this fashion for savagery among dons. Actually, I take it, the clergy regularly said that revenge was very wicked, but the soldiers tended to say that a man's honour might require it; an audience would not have only one opinion, but would broadly agree on feeling that, while revenge was nearly always very wicked, a point might come where it was almost inevitable. Indeed, so far as we still find the plays good, we do so because they reflect this breadth of feeling. As for Hieronymo, who has worried about it as much as he ought to have done, the pretence of a classical next world might leave room for doubt, but still he is definitely not damned at the end of the play by the supernatural characters who distribute punishments in Hades; indeed the Ghost calls him 'good Hieronymo.'

It could be said, however, that the second crop of Elizabethan Revenge Plays, around 1600, was itself a rather similar fashion; Marston makes a pet of a hero in a monstrous fit of sulks, in some way that Kyd does not. Shakespeare in re-writing *Hamlet* seems to have been following a trend, and, though he certainly didn't abandon himself to it, I rather suspect he cut out the 'moral' of the old play, in the course of bringing it up to date. The obvious moral, from the surviving plot, is that Hamlet ought not to have spared Claudius at prayer, at least for the reason he gave; being the rightful King, it was his duty to kill a criminal usurper, but even a King had no right to try to send a man to Hell (as by refusing absolution before he was executed). Hamlet went too far about revenge, and this was fatal to him. He is already an alarmingly tricky character in the sources, and Kyd needed to invent some crisis which would turn his story into a tragedy. If you admit that **The Spanish Tragedy** is not pointless, this moral for *Hamlet* seems one which Kyd might well have invented. Shakespeare of course would assume it to be well known, so that the chief effect of not mentioning it in his version was to raise a further mystery about the real motives of the character. Many critics of the last century, including Bernard Shaw, thought that Shakespeare couldn't say plainly what he thought about revenge because he was morally so much in advance of his coarse audience; and I should fancy they were right, except that he was about ten years behind it. (pp. 60-80)

William Empson, "The Spanish Tragedy," in Elizabethan Drama: Modern Essays in Criticism, *edited by R. J. Kaufmann, Oxford University Press, Inc., 1961, pp. 60-80.*

An excerpt from *The Spanish Tragedy:*

HIERONIMO

O eyes, no eyes, but fountains fraught with tears;

O life, no life, but lively form of death;

O world, no world, but mass of public wrongs,

Confused and filled with murder and misdeeds!

O sacred heavens! if this unhallowed deed,

If this inhuman and barbarous attempt,

If this incomparable murder thus

Of mine, but now no more my son,

Shall unrevealed and unrevengéd pass,

How should we term your dealings to be just,

If you unjustly deal with those that in your justice trust?

The night, sad secretary to my moans,

With direful visions wake my vexed soul,

And with the wounds of my distressful son

Solicit me for notice of his death.

The ugly fiends do sally forth of hell,

And frame my steps to unfrequented paths,

And fear my heart with fierce inflamed thoughts.

The cloudy day my discontents records,

Early begins to register my dreams

And drive me forth to seek the murderer.

Thomas Kyd, in his The Spanish Tragedy, *edited by
J. R. Mulryne, Hill and Wang, 1970.*

John D. Ratliff (essay date 1957)

[*In the excerpt below, Ratliff asserts that Hieronimo's
"vindicta mihi" speech not only explains to the audience
his motives for taking private revenge, but it also justifies
his actions as those of an honorable revenger.*]

Perhaps the most important speech in **The Spanish Tragedy** is Hieronimo's soliloquy at III. xiii. 1-45. In it Hieronimo, having discovered who murdered his son and having
failed to obtain legal redress from the king, explains to the
audience why and how he must take private revenge.

While previous students have recognized the importance
of the passage, their interpretations have run counter to
certain strong evidence in the play which has been unnoticed. Boas, for example, [in his introduction to *The Works*

of *Thomas Kyd*, 1901] bases his interpretation on the following lines:

> *Per scelus semper tutum est sceleribus iter.*
> Strike, and strike home, where wrong is offred
>   thee;
> For euils vnto ils conductors be.
>
> (III. xiii. 6-8)

Here the third line is of course a free rendering of the first.
As Boas reads it, Hieronimo is arguing that the villains'
crime against him opens the way for a counter-crime of
his own. This would seem to lower Hieronimo to his enemies' level and to rob him of all dignity if not of all righ-
teousness.

Bowers' discussion of the soliloquy [in his *Elizabethan Revenge Tragedy*, 1940] carries the condemnation of
Hieronimo much farther. The speech is built around several Latin apothegms together with Hieronimo's reflections on them as they apply to his situation. These apothegms Boas identifies as from Seneca and suggests therefore that it is a volume of his works which Hieronimo
bears in his hand while speaking. But Bowers rightly objects that the first saying, with which the speech begins,
is simply the well-known Biblical prohibition of revenge
from Romans xii. 19. His argument is substantiated by the
second line of the speech, which provides a religious context wholly lacking in the Senecan source suggested by
Boas:

> *Vindicta mihi!*
> I, heauen will be reuenged of euery ill.

Bowers finds this a very significant identification, for a few
lines further on, consideration of an indubitably Senecan
quotation leads Hieronimo to decide to "Strike, and strike
home," regardless of the divine command. Bowers argues
that Hieronimo has deliberately rejected the Christian injunction in order to embrace the advice of a pagan. Holding that nothing could more clearly underline Hieronimo's unrighteousness, he takes the speech to mark the
transition from Hieronimo the hero to Hieronimo the
deep-dyed villain. He adds that Hieronimo's character is
further blackened later in the speech when the means by
which he intends to consummate this pagan revenge are
revealed. Hieronimo intends to revenge

> by a secret, yet a certaine meane,
> Which vnder kindeship will be cloked best.
>
> (III. xiii. 23-24)

This is open to the imputation of Machiavellianism, which
Bowers makes. He admits that Hieronimo argues that
such a course is necessary in the following lines:

> Nor ought auailes it me to menace them
> Who, as a wintrie storme vpon a plaine,
> Will beare me downe with their nobilitie.
>
> (III. xiii. 36-38)

But he rejects this as mere casuistry and concludes that the
dramatic purpose of the soliloquy is to make Hieronimo's
villainy unmistakable.

If we consider only the soliloquy, Bowers' view seems reasonable. But since there is much evidence in the rest of the
play that Kyd did *not* consider Hieronimo a villain, it is

worth seeing if these lines will not bear another interpretation. It seems to me that they will—and one directly contrary to that usually given. In fact there is good evidence that the real purpose of the scene is to explain Hieronimo's behavior carefully so as to keep any suspicion of villainy from him. It is easy to see why such an explanation might have been necessary, for private revenge was a ticklish subject which required defense and delicate handling. And that such an explanation is indeed intended is suggested by the carefully contrived situation in which Hieronimo finds himself at the beginning of the scene, by his remarks in the soliloquy as seen in that light, and by the interpretation of those remarks provided in later passages. These may be surveyed in turn.

Hieronimo's situation at the beginning of the scene is not of his choosing and was beyond his power to avoid. He is in a tangle into which the dramatist carefully put him. First there is the matter of his rank: Hieronimo is no prince like his enemies but merely a retainer who holds his station at the sufferance of his sovereign. The play makes this point clear. Second there is the secrecy of the murder: the court does not even know that a crime has taken place, and it is up to Hieronimo to announce the murder and reveal the murderers if he can overcome the handicap of his inferior rank to do so.

Hieronimo makes the attempt in III. xii. In accord with the obvious ethical requirement that a civilized man must prefer to leave the punishment of criminals to constituted authority rather than to himself, it is justice he seeks, not revenge. What makes the play a revenge play is the simple fact that his enemies are so powerful and he so low-born that they prevent him from reaching constituted authority—in the person of the King—with his plea. Legal redress is impossible, and revenge is up to Hieronimo—or, as Kyd notes in deference to a widely held view of his time, to heaven.

Hieronimo's failure in III. xii is so clumsy that it is easily misinterpreted. He approaches the King at a moment when the latter, unfortunately for his purpose, is in conference with the Portuguese ambassador and in no mood to suffer the prattle of favor seekers. His cry for justice is heard not by the King but by Lorenzo, who brusquely orders him away. Hieronimo retreats in confusion and, having failed, falls to digging distractedly at the stage floor with his dagger.

Hieronimo's acceptance of this rebuff as a final defeat seems to Bowers the lame excuse of a villain bent on murder. But Hieronimo's insistence that his enemies "Will beare me downe with their nobilitie" is substantiated by another important personage wholly neutral to the situation. Castile, who does not even know of the crime and is therefore surely disinterested, roundly berates his son Lorenzo for preventing Hieronimo's suit to the King:

It is suspected, and reported too,
That thou, *Lorenzo*, wrongst *Hieronimo*,
And in his sutes towards his Maiestie
Still keepst him back, and seeks to crosse his sute.

(III. xiv. 53-56)

This is unimpeachable testimony which makes it clear that Hieronimo has been confronted with an external difficulty he cannot surmount. The lines bear a further implication that he has made more than one attempt to reach the King and that Lorenzo's behavior has become a scandal. It seems clear that Hieronimo's discomfiture is intended to demonstrate the impossibility of legal redress.

It will be observed, then, that when Hieronimo enters for the soliloquy, Kyd has placed him in the very position in which his audience's natural sympathy with revenge would be highest. Hieronimo has been flagrantly wronged by a corrupt aristocrat who uses his position to prevent punishment; yet the wanton brutality of the crime shrieks for requital. Even so, revenge was a ticklish subject, for Kyd's audience, or at least his critics, desired that stage heroes should act as nearly as possible in accord with the ethics of Elizabethan gentlemen, and the Biblical prohibition of revenge weighed heavily in their minds. What Kyd needed now was a final argument to allay their qualms and to state clearly the view of the play that the revenge upon which Hieronimo was embarking was just and necessary. This the soliloquy at III. xiii was designed to provide.

Kyd begins this task with characteristic directness. If the Biblical prohibition of revenge may prevent sympathy with Hieronimo, it must be explained away. Kyd might more wisely have left it unmentioned, as did the authors of succeeding revenge plays, but he did not. He at least deserves credit for grasping the bull firmly by the horns. Hieronimo opens his soliloquy by quoting the Biblical injunction and interpreting it:

Vindicta mihi.
I, heauen will be reuenged of euery ill;
Nor will they suffer murder vnrepaide.
Then stay, *Hieronimo*, attend their will:
For mortall men may not appoint their time.

(III. xiii. 1-5)

But at this point a highly practical consideration occurs to him as he reflects on this earlier-quoted passage in his Seneca:

Per scelus semper tutum est sceleribus iter.
Strike, and strike home, where wrong is offred thee;
For euils vnto ils conductors be.

(III. xiii. 6-8)

Boas treats the Latin line as equivalent to *vim vi repellere licit;* but that is certainly not its meaning in Seneca. When Clytemnestra says it [in Seneca's *Agamemnon*], it is one of a series of remarks with which she goads herself into a frenzy adequate for the murder of her husband. Her argument throughout the passage is that she is too far gone in crimes against Agamemnon to turn back. She realizes that if she does not kill Agamemnon, Agamemnon will kill her for what she has already done. Her safety lies in committing a new crime to remove the person who would otherwise revenge the old one. When she speaks the line in question, that is precisely her meaning—"through crime is ever the safe way for crime." Then, most significantly, she adds, "*scelus occupandum est*"—"revenge must be forestalled." It is noteworthy, too, that the *per scelera* quotation has its Senecan force when it appears in a later revenge play. Mendoza, the usurper of [John Marston's] *The Malcontent,* uses it to justify the murder of Malevole's wife—a possible revenger—and provides the following translation: "Black deed only through black deed safely flies."

There is no sound reason for believing that Hieronimo is twisting Seneca's meaning. If we give him credit for reading intelligently and quoting appropriately, the explanation of the passage is obvious. Clytemnestra's example is a warning that a criminal may seek safety by killing anyone who could threaten him—that he may seek to forestall revenge. Hieronimo sees that since he is the potential revenger, the men who killed his son are all too likely to go further and attack him just as Clytemnestra attacked Agamemnon. He sees also that he cannot behave like an ostrich and expect the evil somehow to miss him,

> For he that thinks with patience to contend
> To quiet life, his life shall easily end.
>
> (III, xiii, 10-11)

It follows that he must "Strike, and strike home," or be slain himself.

Hieronimo's argument is intended to answer the Biblical objection to revenge and is indeed the obvious answer, however secular. He does not call into question the belief that heaven would revenge Horatio's murder in time. He merely expresses his conviction that if he waits, heaven will have to revenge his own murder too; and he quotes and interprets a well-known maxim from Seneca to convince the audience as well. His revenge is presented as a matter of simple self-preservation, something in which even the moral Elizabethans no doubt believed. Whether Kyd satisfied all of his audience with this argument is uncertain, but it seems clear that he satisfied himself.

Self-preservation also dictates the method of Hieronimo's revenge and rescues it from the imputation of Machiavellianism. Hieronimo is unable to overcome his enemies in open confrontation; he has already tried that and failed. He therefore has no choice but to bide his time until he can take them by surprise. It seems wholly unnecessary to read anything sinister into this. When he observes that

> Wise men will take their opportunitie,
> Closely and safely fitting things to time
>
> (III. xiii. 25-26)

he is not deliberately affording himself a period of gloating anticipation; instead he is bowing to the fact that his weakness may force a delay. And when he speaks of

> a secret, yet a certaine meane,
> Which vnder kindeship wilbe cloked best
>
> (III. xiii. 23-24)

he is not resorting to hypocrisy; instead he is bowing to the fact that his enemies will not hesitate to kill him if they find reason to. In fact Hieronimo is here justifying his course for the audience and preparing them for the dramatically necessary delay in his revenge. He is not revealing himself as a villain: on the contrary, by explaining his conduct he is making the charge of villainy impossible.

Such seems to be the only interpretation of Hieronimo's soliloquy that fits the facts of the play. There is one additional important passage in support of it which appears at the very end of the play and which strangely enough has gone unmentioned in interpretations of Hieronimo's character. The play closes with the re-entry of the Ghost and Revenge. The Ghost has been granted the right to assign the slaughtered agonists to their fates in the Hereafter. He assigns Hieronimo's victims all to the direct torment, but he explicitly refers to the aged revenger as "good Hieronimo" (IV. v. 11) and awards him the following fate:

> Ile lead *Hieronimo* where *Orpheus* plaies,
> Adding sweet pleasure to eternall daies.
>
> (IV. v. 23-24)

It is hard to see why Kyd would insert such a passage in this crucial spot unless he looked upon Hieronimo as an honorable, justified revenger, however much he may have blurred his execution through carelessness and lack of taste. The passage is therefore further evidence that Hieronimo was so and that in III. xiii he explained himself as such in order that there would be no mistake about it. (pp. 112-18)

> *John D. Ratliff, "Hieronimo Explains Himself," in* Studies in Philology, *Vol. LIV, No. 2, April, 1957, pp. 112-18.*

Anne Righter   (essay date 1962)

[*In the following excerpt, Righter maintains that Kyd's use of a chorus and the play-within-the-play in* The Spanish Tragedy *emphasizes "the idea of the world as a stage" and demonstrates the relationship between illusion and reality. According to the critic, these innovations helped English drama advance to a new level of sophistication.*]

Fredson Bowers, writing about *The Spanish Tragedy,* has remarked that after the close of Act II, "the ghost and his theme, which was to be the core of the play, are superfluous; and indeed, need never have been introduced" [*Elizabethan Revenge Tragedy,* 1940]. Certainly, the murder of Horatio alters the entire nature of the action, leading it away from its original preoccupation with Andrea's death. The usefulness of the ghost, however, does not really depend upon its intimate connection with Hieronimo's revenge. Andrea serves Kyd primarily as an intermediary. He is a link between the two worlds of audience and actors, combining within himself certain elements drawn from each. As such, he helps to define the relationship of reality and illusion.

Before *The Spanish Tragedy,* English experiments with the play within the play seem to have been limited to *Fulgens and Lucres* and, with less certainty, the anonymous *Rare Triumphs of Love and Fortune* (1582?). Medwall's two servants A and B, however, relinquishing their initial position as spectators, had quickly become extempore actors in the illusion they introduced. As soon as they plunged themselves into the affairs of Lucres and her suitors, they became indistinguishable from the other characters of the comedy. Jocular, but a little embarrassed, they lavished upon Cardinal Morton's guests the same haphazard but unremitting attention characteristic of the play as a whole. *The Rare Triumphs,* like *Fulgens and Lucres,* is filled with random, extra-dramatic address, and also handles its spectator figures in a rather uncertain manner. Throughout most of the play, Venus and Fortune, the rivals for power, go unnoticed by the other characters. Silently, they control the destinies of Hermione and Fidelia from a position on "the battlements" high above the stage. Only the theatre audience is party to their controversy. Then, suddenly, in the last act of the comedy, the two goddesses cease to be onlookers. They discover themselves to the mortals in King Phizanties' court and set about undoing the spells and misunderstandings created by their former strife. The frame dissolves bewilderingly into the illusion it had once set off.

Kyd's Don Andrea, on the other hand, is a far more consistent figure than Venus and Fortune or Medwall's A and B. He maintains throughout **The Spanish Tragedy** precisely that equilibrium between involvement and distance which marked his first appearance. Never stirring from his place above the stage, never meddling with the action, he remains from beginning to end a figure associated with and yet distinct from the play world. His relationship with this world is defined clearly by Revenge in the first moments of the drama. For this latter character, the plots and vengeances accumulating in the court of Spain are playlike in quality.

> Heere sit we downe to see the misterie,
> And serve for Chorus in this Tragedie.

The words of Revenge operate in two ways. Viewed objectively, Andrea and his savage companion quite literally represent the Chorus in Kyd's play. It must be remembered, however, that this is a fact of which they themselves are not aware. For Don Andrea, . . . the events occurring on the stage below are painfully real, in no sense a rehearsal at second-hand. As he watches, Horatio is murdered, Bel-Imperia proves her loyalty, and Hieronymo exacts his terrible revenge for the first and only time. It is the symmetry and violence of these events, together with the position of himself and his companion, which suggest to Revenge the comparison with tragedy. Knowing what is to come, in all its complexity and horror, he implies that in these particular happenings, at least, life appears to imitate the drama.

Like *Damon and Pithias,* but in a fashion which is both more complicated and more assured, **The Spanish Tragedy** deliberately builds upon the idea of the world as a stage. Here, for the first time, that new attitude towards the audience upon which Shakespearean drama was to rely can be seen fully worked out. Pre-eminently a man of the theatre, profoundly aware of its unexplored potentialities, Kyd was even more successful than Richard Edwardes in uniting that mediaeval sense of contact with the audience with the concept of the self-sufficient play. There is no extra-dramatic address in **The Spanish Tragedy.** It is as self-contained as the Senecan tragedies on which it was modelled. Through the actor-spectator Don Andrea, through certain deliberate uses of the world as a stage image in the form both of simple statement and of plays within the play, the relation of illusion to reality, actors to audience, is constantly being examined and re-defined.

For Don Andrea and Revenge, sitting a little apart from the action, **The Spanish Tragedy** seems playlike. Within the illusion itself, other characters also betray a consciousness of the way in which life borrows from the theatre. For old Hieronymo, the murder of Horatio is a deed somehow larger than life, a monstrous exaggeration of reality which calls to mind the violence and excesses of the tragic stage.

> And actors in th' accursed tragedy
> Wast thou, Lorenzo? Balthazar, and thou?

A little earlier in the drama, Lorenzo himself invokes the idea of tragedy to lend an added sense of horror to his threatening of Pedringano.

It is upon the play within the play, however, that Kyd chiefly depends. Here, the image of the world as a stage presents itself in an extended, three-dimensional form. As the "reality" of the play world opens out into a further level of illusion, the audience in the theatre is confronted with an image of itself in the persons of those actors who sit as spectators within the play. The real and the fictitious audiences are drawn together, the world of sixteenth-century London and the imaginary court of Spain. The first of these plays within the play, the masque which Hieronymo presents before the King and the Portuguese Ambassador, prepares the way for the second, fatal spectacle, the means of Hieronymo's revenge. In the masque, the elements of illusion declare themselves honestly; they are what they seem. Yet beyond the Marshal's innocent show of knights and kings stretch further, more sinister levels of pretence. The grim presenters sit above, and for them the audience in the court of Spain is composed of actors in a larger, predestined drama. Revenge and Don Andrea watch a play within a play, unconscious of the fact that they themselves represent, for that theatre audience which they cannot see, simply the first in a series of three illusions receding into depth.

Kyd's concern with the interpenetration of life and the drama works itself out most vividly, of course, in the second of Hieronymo's productions, the tragedy of Soliman and Perseda. Here, everything that seems illusory is in fact real. Hieronymo truly is the murderer he plays; the daggers drawn, apparently in jest, pierce the hearts of Lorenzo, Balthazar and Bel-Imperia. Most fatally real of all is the "spectacle" with which the performance concludes, the sudden, masque-like discovery of Hieronymo's dead son. Life has fitted itself into the formal pattern of art, and so skilfully that Hieronymo, the chief actor, must abandon his rôle and explain the true nature of the action before his courtly audience stiffens, and understands.

In **The Spanish Tragedy,** after more than a century of subservience to the inhibiting demands of the banqueting hall, English drama at last regained a power equal to, if altogether different in quality from, that which it possessed in the ritual theatre of the Middle Ages. It is no accident that Hieronymo prefaces his tragedy with assertions of the dignity and worth of the actor's profession, a profession exercised in the past even by emperors and kings. As the Elizabethan theatre matured, creating imaginary worlds of increasing naturalism and depth, its adherents came to believe quite firmly in the power which illusion could exercise over reality. (pp. 77-81)

Anne Righter, "The World and the Stage," in her Shakespeare and the Idea of the Play, 1962. Reprint by Greenwood Press, Publishers, 1977, pp. 64-88.

Ernest William Talbert   (essay date 1963)

[*In the excerpt below, Talbert examines Kyd's usage of dramatic conventions in* The Spanish Tragedy, *focusing on such elements as the chorus, the play-within-the-play, Hieronimo's madness, and Lorenzo's Machiavellianism.*]

Although Kyd's [**Spanish Tragedy**] (ca. 1584-88) does not mark the introduction of sensationalism to the English stage, no previous Elizabethan drama had so emphasized the horrific character of events while preserving a Senecan effect and an over-all control of melodramatic materials. In writing **The Spanish Tragedy,** Kyd obviously remembered *Agamemnon* and *Thyestes;* indeed, it has been demonstrated that he also knew the eight other tragedies assigned to Seneca. Although both of the plays to which he seems particularly indebted would confirm the popular revenge motif, Kyd modifies his representation of a conflict between protagonist and antagonist so that only the antagonist is vicious—in contrast, for example, with *Thyestes.* With the eight deaths that occur throughout the play, as well as other sensational events, with both Horatio and Hieronimo suffering from the designs of Lorenzo and Balthazar, with a minor congruous movement turning upon the viciously plotting Villuppo, Kyd also shows his acceptance of a Renaissance multiplicity as he develops the major movement of suffering protagonist becoming active and effecting his revenge against a viciously intriguing opponent.

This major movement points to an interesting division that seems to control Kyd's multiplicity and that is underlined by the choruses. Throughout the first 856 lines, the revenge motif arises in a naïve context of chivalry and courtly love. Its culmination in the murder of Horatio leads to a development double in length (some 1746 lines). The first portion of this later development represents the vicious antagonist and the suffering hero and might well be called the mid-portion of the play (some 1218 lines). The latter portion represents the effectively plotting hero (some 528 lines). The long mid-portion at first emphasizes the plotting of the antagonist and then the resulting passion of the protagonist. Such a shift in emphasis, consequently, makes its parts correspond more nearly in length to the introductory and the final portions of the drama. Although the introductory unit, usually printed as the first two acts, effects a tangential beginning in that Hieronimo appears therein only as a subsidiary figure, it nevertheless clearly indicates the nature of what is to come. As it closes, Hieronimo emerges as the protagonist, and the course of the action has been developed by a brief plot and counterplot.

There is structural precision in the play. Indeed, the main features of the preceding development are signalled by what must have impressed itself on any spectator. In what is usually printed as Act II, scene ii, Kyd effects upon the

stage three concentric circles of attention: Bel-imperia and Horatio, with their stichomythia and love-rhetoric; the watching Balthazar and Lorenzo, with their despairing love and villainous foreboding; the hovering ghost of Andrea and Revenge. Such a theatrical situation is then represented even more strikingly in the different circumstances of the catastrophe: the play-within-the-play; the main play-world; and Andrea and Revenge. One theatrical feature of the approach to the ending of a dramatic introduction is thus repeated in the approach to the ending of the play. Similarly, Hieronimo's reading of two letters (III, ii, 24 ff.; III, vii, 19 ff.) frames Kyd's emphasis upon Lorenzo's concatenated plots and may well have been conceived of as a structural device.

In the introductory development, however, Kyd avoids some potential thematic conflicts. When, for example, Balthazar learns that his captor is Bel-imperia's lover, no chivalric regard for Horatio (e.g., I, ii, 192-94) is balanced against Balthazar's thwarted love. In answer to Lorenzo's question as to how pleased he is with the revelation, Balthazar replies:

> Both well and ill; it makes me glad and sad:
> Glad, that I know the hinderer of my love;
> Sad, that I fear she hates me whom I love:
> Glad, that I know on whom to be reveng'd;
> Sad, that she'll fly me, if I take revenge.
> Yet must I take revenge, or die myself,
> For love resisted grows inpatient.
> I think Horatio be my destin'd plague:
> First, in his hand he brandished a sword,
> And with that sword he fiercely waged war,
> And in that war he gave me dangerous wounds,
> And by those wounds he forced me to yield,
> And by my yielding I became his slave.
> Now in his mouth he carries pleasing words,
> Which pleasing words do harbour sweet conceits,
> Which sweet conceits are lim'd with sly deceits,
> Which sly deceits smooth Bel-imperia's ears,
> And through her ears dive down into her heart,
> And in her heart set him, where I should stand.
> Thus hath he ta'en my body by his force,
> And now by sleight would captivate my soul. . . .

> (II, i, 111-31)

Like the use of *gradatio* in the preceding speech (a word at the end of one line reappearing early in the next), the theatrical effectiveness of revenge is its own excuse. "They reck no laws that meditate revenge" (I, iii, 48). Yet even though the motif is not developed as part of an explicit thematic nexus, such an attitude is censured; for by embodying it in the figures of Lorenzo and Balthazar, the major and the minor villains, Kyd develops a situation at the end of the second act that makes Hieronimo, the father of the murdered Horatio, a character worthy of pathos. As it has been noted, this feature of the drama departs from Seneca's portrayal of Thyestes. Seen in the light of moralities, it moves Hieronimo toward the position of Mankind. This favorable aspect of the protagonist's portrayal will be stressed subsequently by the king's regard for Hieronimo and by lines about his public justice. This last development, consequently, builds upon the horrific representation of Horatio's death at the hands of Lorenzo and Balthazar.

At the same time, the emergence of Hieronimo as the protagonist would arouse anticipations of further bloodshed. In Act II, scene iv, when a repetition of love-rhetoric is broken by the seizure, hanging, and stabbing of Horatio, and as the cries of Bel-imperia introduce the lamenting passion of Hieronimo and his wife, an audience would witness the cutting down of Horatio's body and the display of a handkerchief smeared with blood. They would hear a vow that the handkerchief shall remain with Hieronimo until the murder is avenged, and they would see the bloody body of Horatio carried off stage. Thereby the spectators would be prepared for the larger sequence of plotting and counterplotting that also will involve the hero's tragic passion and his turn from an essentially passive figure to an active one.

Although the later additions quickly move the representation of the tragic hero to a frantic, even laughing, madness (II, v, 70 ff.), Kyd moves much more gradually in that direction. With Hieronimo's first appearance in the third act, Kyd strikes only the note, conventional since at least the days of Seneca, that the heavens cannot be called just if a villainous deed, such as the murder of Horatio, goes unpunished (III, ii, 1-23). The appearance of the first letter then motivates the further plots of the antagonist; and although that letter also motivates the hero's search for confirmation, Hieronimo is given only some slightly distraught action (ll. 54-66). The idea of justice is returned to with relative restraint on his next appearance (III, vi). At that time, Hieronimo balances his public justice against the fact that "neither gods nor men be just" to him (ll. 10). His subsequent appearance follows logically (III, vii): his introductory lines (1-18) develop the idea just mentioned; the remaining lines are concerned with the fact that the second letter confirms the first and with some rhetorical, but still relatively restrained, vituperation of Lorenzo and Balthazar.

Frantic speech and action are emphasized, however, during the last 634 of the 1218 lines in the long mid-portion of the drama (III, viii, through the final scene of Act III). And the popularity of this franticness is attested by the fact that it was elaborated in all of the additions. Isabella's madness (III, viii) is reinforced by the rhetoric of Bel-imperia's lamenting speech (III, ix, 1-14) and anticipates the scene of Hieronimo with the Portuguese, who laugh at this man they believe to be "passing lunatic" or doting from the "imperfection of his age" (III, xi). The emphasis is continued in Hieronimo's next scene but intensified. Witness, for example, the business with the halter and especially with the dagger (III, xii, 16-20, 70 ff.). Frustrated by the villain in attempting to secure justice from the ruler, the hero shows a "fury" (l. 79) that is falsely interpreted, first by Lorenzo, as resulting from extreme pride and covetousness, and then, quite sympathetically, by the king, as a melancholy to be cured (ll. 84-100). This portrayal of a pathetic distraction is then enlarged by the madness of the parallelism between Hieronimo and Don Bazulto (III, xiii, 46-173).

In spite of his emphasis upon the passion of his hero, and

immediately before the parallelism just noted, Kyd, nevertheless, gives to Hieronimo a speech that is once more relatively restrained (III, xiii, 1-45). From the Latin tags of a book, Hieronimo weighs alternate lines of action, defends the one chosen, and emphasizes patience. This last thought agrees, for example, with lines in earlier scenes between the appearance of the two letters (III, ii, to III, vii). The topic also had been stated explicitly in Bel-imperia's speech of Act III, scene ix (ll. 1-14); and in the varying circumstances of the Portuguese court, patience had been referred to as the only remedy against the wrongs of an infected earth until justice be achieved (III, i, 31-37). By giving such a speech to Hieronimo, Kyd reinforces the relationship between the latter part of Act III and its earlier portions; but he also adumbrates the resolution of the drama. Relatively restrained rhetoric in a soliloquy is what one might expect of a figure who, in spite of a present emphasis upon his "madness," will become effectively active.

Kyd's emphasis, however, almost obscures the first movement of Hieronimo from a passive to an active figure, even though that development had been called explicitly to an audience's attention:

> But wherefore waste I mine unfruitful words,
> When naught but blood will satisfy my woes?
> I will go plain me to my lord the king,
> And cry aloud for justice through the court,
> Wearing the flints with these my wither'd feet;
> And either purchase justice by entreats,
> Or tire them all with my revenging threats.
>   (III, vii, 69-75)

As has been indicated, the antagonist's success in stopping Hieronimo's complaints to the king led to the protagonist's intensified distraction and to a line both famous and infamous to Elizabethans:

> *Lor.* Back! see'st thou not the king is busy?
> *Hier.* O, is he so?
> *King.* Who is he that interrupts our business?
> *Hier.* Not I. Hieronimo, beware! go by, go by!
>   (III, xii, 28-30)

The situation was then repeated:

> *Hier.* Justice, O, justice! O my son, my son!
>   My son, whom naught can ransom or redeem!
> *Lor.* Hieronimo, you are not well-advis'd.
> *Hier.* Away, Lorenzo, hinder me no more;
>   For thou hast made me bankrupt of my bliss.
>   Give me my son! you shall not ransom him!
>   Away! I'll rip the bowels of the earth,
>   *He diggeth with his dagger.*
>   And ferry over to th' Elysian plains,
>   And bring my son to show his deadly wounds.
>   Stand from about me!
>   I'll make a pickaxe of my poniard,
>   And here surrender up my marshalship;
>   For I'll go marshal up the fiends in hell,
>   To be avenged on you all for this.
> *King.* What means this outrage?
>   Will none of you restrain his fury?
> *Hier.* Nay, soft and fair! you shall not need to
>   strive.
>   Needs must he go that the devils drive.

Exit.

(ll. 64-81)

Granted that these incidents were memorable in the theater, their franticness probably overrode any realization that Hieronimo was becoming an active figure. Although he is more nearly successful in his second attempt than in his first, the consequence of this digging episode is that any effective action by the hero is left for the catastrophe.

For that matter, Kyd's theatrical emphases, achieved in part by his multiplicity—by such incidents as those involving Don Bazulto, the Portuguese, and the women connected with the hero—obscure the appearance of *sententiœ* even more easily than they obscure the first representation of retaliatory action by the protagonist. And again, the ideas expressed by those maxims are not developed thematically. In the middle, as in the first, portion of the drama, what is melodramatic dominates any thematic interest a situation might have had in the theater. Kyd has created, however, a memorable protagonist, with a minor parallel in Bazulto and pathetic women.

Certain features of the portrayal of Lorenzo, who is the vicious antagonist, have been noted already. Although he is connected with the court and with important events, political power is not the objective of his villainy; nor is his plotting motivated explicitly by any desire to clear a touchy "honor," blemished, for example, by the rivalry of Horatio. Only Lorenzo's association with Balthazar and his position as confidant to the rejected lover explicitly motivate the action that causes Hieronimo to become a suffering hero. Even then, there is no mention, let alone any development, of the idea of friendship, that exceedingly popular Renaissance topic. The situation accords with what has just been noted. In this portrayal, Kyd apparently considered a villainous secrecy and melodramatic actions to be a theatrically sufficient point of interest.

The soliloquies given Lorenzo and their repetitive pattern, however, may well have engraved upon a theater-goer's memory the impression that he was a man of intellectual virtuosity. The quick, skillful, and successful way in which he knits up the loose ends from an initial deed of villainy must have been theatrically obvious. Hieronimo's question about Bel-imperia leads to Lorenzo's plot with Pedringano against Serberine. This is followed by Lorenzo's soliloquy about his plans for Pedringano (III, ii, 53-129). The successful execution of the plot against Serberine follows immediately (III, iii). It leads to Lorenzo's fear of betrayal and to his plot with Balthazar against Pedringano (III, iv, 1-34). This leads to another soliloquy (ll. 35-46). The appearance of a messenger then leads to the plot using the page. Lorenzo is then given his third soliloquy (ll. 74-84). The accomplishment of the last plot follows immediately and is developed . . . with a grim ironic humor that shows Kyd's variation upon a conventionally comic development (III, v, vi). With increasing complexity, in the two deaths following from the murder of Horatio, there has appeared a triple representation of cause, plotting dialogue, and soliloquy, and a double representation of the plotter's success. Such a development is clearly capable of visual, repetitive stage-groupings; while the concatenation of incidents would be pointed out constantly, and the suc-

cessful duping "policy" of the villain's manipulating secrecy would be constantly apparent:

> Why so, this fits our former policy,
> And thus experience bids the wise to deal.
> I lay the plot; he prosecutes the point:
> I set the trap; he breaks the worthless twigs,
> And sees not that wherewith the bird was lim'd.
> Thus hopeful men, that mean to hold their own,
> Must look like fowlers to their dearest friends.
> He runs to kill whom I have holp to catch,
> And no man knows it was my reaching fatch.

(III, iv, 35-43)

Another situation characteristic of the vicious plotter should also be noted. It appears when Lorenzo protests that all he has done to Bel-imperia has been to protect her honor (III, x). This aspect of a witty hypocrisy that with rhetoric would effect its purpose with a woman is thoroughly compatible with the Elizabethan's belief in the power of the spoken word and with the intellectual aura given to Lorenzo. Similarly, in accordance with Lorenzo's earlier virtuosity, and even as Hieronimo's franticness and Isabella's madness dominate the stage, this villain continues to exhibit a quick ingenuity. He stops Hieronimo's approach to the king and then capitalizes upon it; and in Lorenzo's next scene, Kyd represents his villain as again seizing upon the immediate to suggest, with the pose of an honest man, that

> 'Twere good, my lord, that Hieronimo and I
> Were reconcil'd, if he misconster me.

(III, xiv, 91-92)

The success of this last stratagem of Lorenzo's is handled, however, with a dramatic irony that makes the catastrophe possible.

In brief, Kyd skillfully elaborates with a Renaissance fullness, but with precision, the old motif of protagonist and vicious antagonist. Lorenzo's clever but fearsome villainy makes the world one in which patience is man's only remedy—unless he is willing to sacrifice himself and achieve a just vengeance by an equally clever and bloody stratagem (IV, iv). The melodrama of *The Spanish Tragedy,* however, overpowers even this reflective consideration as theatrically memorable figures perform their parts in a conventional structural movement, the elaboration of which provided the age with its conventions for the tragedy of blood. (pp. 72-9)

Ernest William Talbert, "Aspects of Structure and Serious Character-Types," in his Elizabethan Drama and Shakespeare's Early Plays: An Essay in Historical Criticism, *1963. Reprint by Gordian Press Inc., 1973, pp. 61-131.*

Michael Henry Levin   (essay date 1964)

[*In the essay below, Levin discusses the morality and motivation of Kyd's characters in* The Spanish Tragedy. *He claims that "the positions of the central characters with respect to the morality of vengeance pinpoint the question which is the thematic keystone of the play: Is revenge justifiable in the name of goodness, right, and truth?"*]

As a pioneering attempt at a drama of action, Kyd's *Spanish Tragedy* could hardly fail to be flawed. It opens with a ghost who seeks a niche in the underworld, then abandons his quest to assume an entirely different role. Its transparent subplot sacrifices characterization to morality. Its characters spout rhetoric, occasionally maunder, and sometimes appear to be puppets of the plot rather than fully-realized people in an autonomous world. The catastrophe contains more sensation than motivation: there is no justification for the death of Castile, and the Viceroy's credulity in giving Hieronimo the fatal knife is as questionable as the moral necessity of the use to which that knife is put. And Andrea's ghost and Revenge are neither large nor awful enough to conjure up the inexorable forces which rule a tragic universe.

Critics have traditionally grown fat by battening on these weaknesses, but they have done so by refusing to recognize the play's central strengths. Kyd was a more-than-competent dramatist; as the first English tragedian to write dramatically, he could not help making mistakes, but those he makes pale to insignificance beside the exciting swirl of action and emotion that encloses them. It is the contention of this article that Kyd, far from imitating the Senecan revenge play per se, consciously translated it into the idiom of the young Elizabethan stage; that the characters he created can stand as living people both within and without the dramatic pattern; that almost nothing in the play is gratuitous; and that *The Spanish Tragedy,* which has often been blasted as a disorganized amalgam of Senecan convention and cheap sensationalism, is in fact unified by triple threads of meaning, morality, and motivation which bind its disparate parts into a comprehensible and effective dramatic whole.

Kyd's drama is simple, and in that simplicity openly bares the furies that drive his characters. As a hero bent on vengeance, Hieronimo is superficially similar to Shakespeare's Hamlet, and doubtless resembles the Kydian prototype from which the Prince of Denmark was later drawn. Like Hamlet, he exhibits overpowering love for a member of his immediate family, although his love is guided by a clear-headed sense of perspective:

> That was my son, my gracious sovereign;
> Of whom though from his tender infancy
> My loving thoughts did never hope full well,
> He never pleased his father's eyes till now,
> Nor filled my heart with overcloying joys.
>
> (I. i. 116-120)

Like Hamlet, Hieronimo is torn by grief and rage at the revelation of his loved one's undeserved death:

> O poor Horatio, what hadst thou misdone,
> To lose thy life ere life was new begun?
> O wicked butcher, whatsoe'er thou wert,
> How could thou strangle virtue and desert?
> Ay me most wretched, that have lost my joy,
> In losing my Horatio, my sweet boy!
>
> (II. v. 28-33)

Like Hamlet, he is thrust by circumstance into the role of the avenger, and, like Hamlet, he channels his emotions into what becomes the duty of revenge:

> Seest thou this handkercher besmeared with
>   blood?
> It shall not from me till I take revenge.
> Seest thou these wounds that yet are bleeding
>   fresh?
> I'll not entomb them till I have revenged.
> Then will I joy amidst my discontent,
> Till then my sorrow never shall be spent.
>
> (II. v. 105-110)

But Hieronimo's position and personality differ fundamentally from the Dane's. In the first place, he is not informed of the murderer's identity as Hamlet is; he must discover the proper objects of vengeance before he can avenge. Thus, his immediate hesitation is more logical than psychological. Secondly, Hieronimo has a preternaturally acute sense of right and wrong (III. vi. et passim); he is Chief Magistrate of Spain, and his life has been devoted to administering the law. He is inclined by temperament to public justice; unlike Hamlet, he wants compensation for his wrongs by due process, and, unlike Hamlet, he firmly believes that such compensation may be attained:

> I will go plain me to my lord the King,
> And cry aloud for justice through the Court,
> Wearing the flints with these my withered feet.
>
> (III. vii. 69-71)

Thirdly, Hieronimo has a constant purpose; he may momentarily weary of life (IV. v. 6-15), but he is never plunged into melancholic apathy for long. Revenge, not suicide, is always uppermost in his mind:

> This way or that way? Soft and fair, not so.
> For if I hang or kill myself, let's know
> Who will revenge Horatio's murther then?
>
> (IV. v. 16-18)

Finally, despite the incipient madness that springs from frustration (IV. vi. 170-206, 305-330, et passim), Hieronimo remains master of his emotions until his vengeance is complete. "Dissembling quiet in unquietness" (IV. vi. 198), he is a much better actor than Hamlet; he is never rash enough to alarm his intended victims, and he eventually deceives them so thoroughly that they embrace him as a friend. He never convinces himself that he is acting when his actions do nothing to further his revenge, and this is perhaps where he differs from Hamlet most.

Hamlet acts sporadically, often in tangents to his avowed purpose; his self-criticisms are seldom triggered by inner motivation, and it takes external objects (the Player, *Ham.* II. ii. 545-603; the Ghost, III. iv.; Fortinbras, IV. iv.) to rouse him from the gloomy lassitude which is his normal state of being in the play. His actions move him no closer to his goal; at best, they merely maintain the *status quo* (the pirate ship, IV. vi.; the commission to England, V. ii. 4-55), and at worst they are worse than useless (the play-within-the-play), yet he feels he has accomplished a great deal when they are completed. His purpose is not just blunted; he often forgets it entirely in the course of philosophic musings on life, death, and corruption. Hamlet's revenge is ultimately consummated because Claudius forces the issue, not by Hamlet's own volition, and his lack of concerted action ends by costing him his life.

Hieronimo is more the man of action in revenge. His resolution is immediate and binding, influenced by an innate
sense of justice rather than a ghost. He is acutely conscious
of his initial helplessness, lamenting first his failure to
identify Horatio's murderers (III. iii. 1-23), then the impossibility of bringing them to trial:

> Nor aught avails it me to menace them,
> Who, as a wintry storm upon a plain,
> Will bear me down with their nobility.
>
> (IV. vi. 204-206)

Unlike Hamlet, he undergoes a genuine moral crisis—as
well as a psychological one—over the prospect of personal
revenge; his faith in the law implies a feeling that no single
man has the right to play God by judging and executing
his fellows. To act as a judge in court is to function as the
representative of society, but to become judge, jury, and
executioner is to assume a responsibility no mortal is large
enough to bear.

Caught in this gap between vengeance and public justice,
Hieronimo hesitates also, but during hesitation continues
to gather the information that will enable him to act.
Whether attempting to gain access to Bel-imperia (III. ii.
50-76), comparing her letter to Pedringano's (III. vii. 29-
60), or seeking redress from a preoccupied King (IV. v. 20-
82), his sights are fixed on a single goal. When his faith in
the law is shattered by Lorenzo's machinations, it takes
an external object in the person of Bazulto to shock him
into undertaking a personal revenge:

> See, see, O see thy shame, Hieronimo!
> See here a loving father to his son;
> Behold the sorrows and the sad laments
> That he delivreth for his son's decease.
> If love's effects so strives in lesser things, . . .
> Then shamest thou not, Hieronimo, to neglect
> The sweet revenge of thy Horatio?
>
> (IV. vi. 268 f.)

Yet Bazulto, in contrast to Hamlet's external stimuli, mar-
shals Hieronimo the way he is already going. When the
Knight-Marshal's vengeful momentum is augmented by
Bel-imperia's (V. i. 1-50), the avenger begins to act in earnest, and his acts are not, like Hamlet's, subconscious excuses for delaying a larger action. Hieronimo may have
briefly resigned himself to the "divinity that shapes men's
ends":

> Ay, heaven will be revenged of every ill,
> Nor will they suffer murder unrepaid.
> Then stay, Hieronimo, attend their will,
> For mortal men may not appoint their time.
>
> (IV. vi. 170-173)

but he is now absolute master of the situation, and he
guides the murderers skilfully to their destruction.

Like Hamlet, Hieronimo stages an ironic play-within-the-
play whose plot and characters correspond to the dramatic reality within which his own tragedy takes place (V. i.
106-124; read "Horatio" for "Erastus," "Bel-imperia" for
"Perseda," "Balthazar" for "Soliman," "Lorenzo" for
"Bashaw," "lover" for "husband," "bedded" for "wedded"). He even has a speech to the Players:

> Fie! comedies are fit for common wits;

> But to present a kingly troop withal,
> Give me a stately written tragedy;
> *Tragedia cothurnata,* fitting kings,
> Containing matter, and not common
> things. . . .
> And all shall be concluded in one scene,
> For there's no pleasure tane in tediousness.
>
> (V. i. 153 f.)

Hieronimo's play, however, is the rational culmination of
his previous acts. Its verisimilitude is carefully established,
even to details of costume (V. i. 140-150), language (V. i.
168-174), and theatrical abstracts of the parts to be played
(V. i. 137-139). It is neither a momentary inspiration
prompted by the arrival of some strolling players, nor the
result of an agonized realization of neglected duty, but the
product of a magistrate's mind still bent on doing justice.
It is planned to prevent external interference:

> Let me entreat your grace
> That, when the train are passed into the gallery,
> You would vouchsafe to throw me down the
>   key.
>
> (V. iii. 11-13)

and engineered to give the avengers the greatest satisfaction in their victim's deaths. Its aim is justice through vengeance, not information or delay, and it is so arranged that
it cannot but succeed.

In the failure of public redress, Hieronimo appears to find
a greater justice of the spirit:

> My guiltless son was by Lorenzo slain,
> And by Lorenzo and that Balthazar
> Am I at least revenged thoroughly,
> Upon whose souls may heavens be yet avenged,
> With greater far than these afflictions.
>
> (V. iii. 200-204)

Yet while this thought is doubtless some measure of comfort to a bereaved father, it provides no incentive to go on
living. With vengeance complete, Hieronimo's life is
ended; his son, his wife, and his faith in man's justice have
all been destroyed:

> Here lay my hope, and here my hope hath end.
> Here lay my heart, and here my heart was slain.
> Here lay my treasure, here my treasure lost.
> Here lay my bliss, and here my bliss bereft.
> But hope, heart, treasure, joy, and bliss,
> All fled, failed, died, yea, all decayed with this.
>
> (V. iii. 119-124)

The closing action is more than sensational; Hieronimo's
existence has been framed with words—words of law,
words of grief, words of vengeance, the ironic words of the
play-within-the-play itself—and the biting-out of the
tongue signifies that both words and existence have run
their course. Hieronimo's audience would have seen this
truth as something to be accepted as *ding an sich* rather
than as an incident to be probed for deeper motivation; his
self-destruction enables him to exit with dignity when a
dignified exit is all he now demands of his world.

Lorenzo is perhaps the most interesting of the other characters in *The Spanish Tragedy.* The dramatic potential of
Elizabethan Machiavellism is realized for the first time

with his creation; as the essence of absolute villainy, he is the seed from which Iagos, Bosolas, and Vasqueses will spring. Lorenzo is proud and imperious, a man born to rule; for him, as for his cohort Balthazar, the forms of honor are more valuable than honor itself, and chivalry is only a convenience to be shed when his machinations are in danger of being forestalled. His most characteristic trait is his belief that truth is something to be shaped to his personal specifications; he acknowledges no rights larger than his own. He quashes his sister's liaison with Andrea (II. i. 43-49), appropriates Horatio's honor (I. i. 152-160), engineers the dynastic union of Balthazar and Bel-imperia (q.v.), removes Horatio when Horatio disrupts his designs (II. iv), and liquidates his accomplices (III. ii-vi)—all to remake reality in his own image. He thwarts Hieronimo's quest for justice at every turn, barring access to Bel-imperia (III. ii. 51-56) and the King (IV. v. 20-31), and attributing the Knight-Marshal's disturbed state to simple greed:

> My gracious lord, he is with extreme pride,
> Conceived of young Horatio, his son,
> And covetous of having to himself
> The ransom of the young Prince Balthazar,
> Distract, and in a manner lunatic.
>
> (IV. v. 85-89)

Lorenzo cannot remove Hieronimo as he eradicated Horatio, Serberine, and Pedringano (q.v.); the King is too fond of his Knight-Marshal to remain ignorant of his death or allow it to go unpunished (IV. v. 90-101 et passim). But Lorenzo can attempt to render Hieronimo's actions ineffective, and in this he appears to succeed admirably throughout much of the play.

Lorenzo, like many Machiavellians, has a bit of the paranoid in him: he fixes on ideas with unshakeable tenacity and attempts to impose them on the external world. Whether guiding Balthazar's affair with Bel-imperia:

> Some cause there is that lets you not be loved;
> First that must needs be known and then removed. . . .
> My lord, for once you shall be ruled by me;
> Hinder me not, what'er you hear or see.
>
> (II. i. 31 f.)

demanding Horatio's death:

> Let's go, my lord; your staying stays revenge.
> Do you but follow me, and gain your love;
> Her favor must be won by his remove.
>
> (II. i. 134-136)

or destroying the witnesses to his crime:

> They that for coin their souls endangered,
> To save my life for coin shall venture theirs;
> And better it's that base companions die
> Than by their life to hazard our good haps.
> Nor shall they live, for me to fear their faith.
> I'll trust myself, myself shall be my friend;
> For die they shall; slaves are ordained to no other end.
>
> (III. ii. 122-128)

Lorenzo is not to be denied. His desires become laws unto themselves, those who hinder them, obstacles to be swept out of the way. Lorenzo is devoid of any saving grace of morality; he believes that he exists *sui generis,* that he has a divine right to determine events, and that others cannot but agree with the patterns of destiny he shapes. He is incapable of feeling guilt, never repents, and goes to his death convinced of his moral and physical invulnerability.

Lorenzo's need to pile plot upon plot stems not from any real fear of punishment—he is too noble to be brought to trial—but from a colossal vanity which demands continual proof of his superiority to mankind as a whole. This is really why he removes Pedringano and Serberine. Hieronimo's inquiry (III. ii. 48-90) is a mere pretext for what would have been effected anyway; feigned suspicion (III. ii. 79-89) notwithstanding, Lorenzo knows that neither of the servants would dare betray him. He eliminates them largely for the esthetic satisfaction of a job well done, and it is no accident that their deaths—Lorenzo's most gratuitous murders—provide the letter (III. vii. 19-73) that marks the beginning of his doom.

Lorenzo is so concerned with tying up the loose ends of his plots that he is unable to visualize the possibility of their overall failure. This is why he releases Bel-imperia when he knows she is the only hostile witness to his crime:

> And if she hap to stand on terms with us,
> As for her sweetheart and concealment so,
> Jest with her gently; under feignèd jest
> Are things concealed that else would breed unrest.
>
> (IV. iii. 21-24)

And this, above all, is why he readily participates in Hieronimo's little tragedy. Lorenzo was momentarily shaken by the fury of Hieronimo's attempt to seek justice from the King (cf. IV. v., IV. vii. 119). When the Knight-Marshal greets him with loyalty and devotion (IV. vii. 130-155), and even with a hint of villainous comradeship:

> Friends, quoth he? See, I'll be friends with you all,
> Specially with you, my lovely lord;
> For divers causes it is fit for us
> That we be friends; the world is suspicious,
> And men may think what we imagine not.
>
> (IV. vii. 157-161)

he is so pleased that Hieronimo has been put off the scent that he forgets to suspect this radical reversal of affection. He accepts Hieronimo's words at face value, and his acceptance opens the way for his participation in the play-within-the-play. In the end, Lorenzo, despite his conviction that he is a free agent, is no less a prisoner of personality than the other people in the play. Ironically, he is betrayed by his love of betrayal, trapped by the intriguing nature of intrigue.

Balthazar deserves few compliments. He is weak, hypocritical, shallow, inconstant, and thoroughly unappetizing. He is, in short, exactly what he should be in the context of the play—the venal foil for Lorenzo's towering villainy, the jackal to round out the tiger's world. He appears in the guise of a national hero, as a ruthless warrior in battle and a gracious diplomat in defeat. He even lavishes praise on his captors (I.i.161-194). Yet as soon as he ar-

rives we find him both in love with Bel-imperia and lugu-
briously despairing of that love:

> No, she is wilder and more hard withal
> Than beast, or bird, or tree, or stony wall.
> But wherefore blot I Bel-imperia's name?
> It is my fault, not she, that merits blame.
> My feature is not to content her sight;
> My words are rude and work her no delight.
> The lines I send her are but harsh and ill,
> Such as do drop from Pan and Marsyas'
>   quill. . . .
>
> (II. i. 9-16)

And at once the "national hero" sets about the assassination of the man he has previously praised:

> Yet must I take revenge, or die myself,
> For love resisted grows impatient.
> I think Horatio be my destined plague: . . .
> But in his fall I'll tempt the destinies,
> And either lose my life or win my love.
>
> (II. i. 116 f.)

Balthazar's mawkish sentimentalizing of the rigors of
courtly love:

> Led by the loadstar of her heavenly looks,
> Wends poor oppressèd Balthazar,
> As o'er the mountains walks the wanderer,
> Incertain to effect his pilgrimage.
>
> (IV. iii. 106-109)

is characterization as well as convention; he lacks faith in
his abilities, and depends on Lorenzo's initiative to aug-
ment his fortunes. He is as evil as his leader because he
shares in Horatio's murder and its aftermath, but he does
not possess the awesome self-assurance that makes Lorenzo larger than life. Lorenzo lives by a rigid code—the
pseudo-Machiavellian principle that desirable ends justify
foul means—and, morally repellent as this code may seem
in the pattern of the play, he sticks to it. He guides himself
consistently by his own lights, advances in perfect accord
with his conception of his position and power. By proceeding methodically from goal to goal, he becomes an active
force in his world, a determiner of events who always
knows (or thinks he knows) where he is going before he
starts. Balthazar, on the other hand, is an unprincipled opportunist. He lives by no code, maintains no goals, but
functions by taking advantage of people as the opportunity arises (I. iii. 10-26 et passim). He leaves others to lay
the foundations for his skulduggery, and never embarks
on a decisive action unless the odds are unchivalrously in
his favor (loc. cit.). Compared to Lorenzo's frightening efficiency, Balthazar's is a purely vegetative evil; if he were
not dragged along by Lorenzo's momentum, he might become so enmeshed in ornate declamation:

> . . . it makes me glad and sad:
> Glad, that I know the hinderer of my love,
> Sad, that I fear she hates me whom I love;
> Glad, that I know on whom to be revenged,
> Sad, that she'll fly me if I take revenge.
>
> (II. i. 111-115)

that he would never act at all. By Act III, he has become
Lorenzo's tool:

> I lay the plot; he prosecutes the point.
> I set the trap; he breaks the worthless twigs,
> And sees not that wherewith the bird was
>   limed. . . .
> He runs to kill whom I have holpe to catch,
> And no man knows it was my reaching fatch.
>
> (III. iv. 40 f.)

and he blindly follows Lorenzo to destruction.

Lorenzo's deeds contradict the moral scheme of the
play—the belief in universal justice established by the supernatural elements—and so he is doomed. But his desire
to unite Balthazar and Bel-imperia can be partially justified on grounds of political expediency. Balthazar, however, is not even motivated by politics; he commits murder
in pursuit of a "love" which appears to be a whim. Now,
it is true that instant love is an Elizabethan convention;
Horatio's inheritance of his late friend's mistress (I. iii. 40-
57) would not have been questioned by the original audience. But Balthazar's emotions are marked by a shallow-
ness that passes beyond romantic stylization and would be
obvious on the stage. A brief comparison of the tone of
Horatio's remarks to Bel-imperia:

> Now, madam, since by favor of your love
> Our hidden smoke is turned to open flame,
> And that with looks and words we feed our
>   thoughts,
> Two chief contents, where more cannot be had.
> Thus in the midst of love's fair blandishments,
> Why show you sign of inward languishments?
>
> (II. ii. 1-6)

and the tone of Balthazar's:

> Yes, to your gracious self I must complain,
> In whose fair answer lies my remedy,
> On whose perfection all my thoughts attend,
> On whose aspect mine eyes find beauty's bower,
> In whose translucent breast my heart is lodged.
>
> (I. iii. 93-97)

reveals sufficient reason for the latter's failure quite apart
from Bel-imperia's a priori vow (I. iii. 66-72). Horatio
scarcely mentions Bel-imperia's beauty, but speaks of humility and service (I. iii. 53-56), content and fulfillment
(II. ii), pleasure and peace (II. iv). His words are backed
by tender solicitude; he cares about Bel-imperia as a
human being. Balthazar's admiration, however, is that of
a man for an inanimate object he wants to possess; he
makes no attempt to know Bel-imperia as a person, and
his chivalrous speeches ring flatulent and false. The affection Balthazar exhibits may be as much as he can muster,
but it is a bloodless passion at its best; it is not enough to
justify murder, and it is not enough to enable him to escape the retribution which that murder invokes.

Bel-imperia, as a hot-headed individualist who delights in
flouting convention, properly assumes a high place in the
retributive hierarchy of her world. Bel-imperia is as imperious as her brother—she chooses her lovers, woos them,
and sleeps with them regardless of their social position—
but she reveals a depth of feeling that Lorenzo never
shows. She blows a refreshing breath into the atmosphere
of the play; whether loving:

Speak thou fair words, I'll cross them with fair
    words;
Send thou sweet looks, I'll meet them with sweet
    looks;
Write loving lines, I'll answer loving lines;
Give me a kiss, I'll countercheck thy kiss:
Be this our warring peace, or peaceful war.

(II. ii. 34-38)

or avenging:

Hieronimo, for shame, Hieronimo,
Be not a history to after times
Of such ingratitude unto thy son. . . .
For here I swear, in sight of heaven and earth,
Shouldst thou neglect the love thou shouldst re-
    tain,
And give it over and devise no more,
Myself should send their hateful souls to hell,
That wrought his downfall with extremest
    death.

(V. i. 13 f.)

she always becomes passionately involved in the matter at
hand. Her constancy dwarfs Hieronimo's frequently
checkmated resolution; when she loves, she will not relin-
quish love (the secret meetings with Andrea, Induction 5-
11), and when she avenges, she is dedicated to vengeance
with an intensity that refuses to be denied. She may begin
the Horatio affair with a calculating desire to use it in fur-
thering her ends:

But how can love find harbor in my breast,
'Till I revenge the death of my beloved?
Yes, second love shall further my revenge;
I'll love Horatio, my Andrea's friend,
The more to spite the Prince that wrought his
    end.

(I. iii. 62-68)

but she finishes with a passion so strong that we are forced
to give her the benefit of the doubt.

As Lorenzo's sister, Bel-imperia is under surveillance, and
her actions are necessarily limited, but she does everything
in her power to gain redress (the letter to Hieronimo, III.
ii. 23-52), and she does it immediately, instinctively, without hesitation, doubt, or fear. Mercurial and melancholic,
amorous, clever, coy, and scornful by turns, she is the eternal female—and her femininity has iron in its soul. It must
never be forgotten that her demand for retribution, not
Hieronimo's, activates the supernatural machinery of the
play; Andrea has been summoned to witness:

. . . the author of [his] death,
Don Balthazar, the prince of Portingale,
Deprived of life by Bel-imperia.

(Induction, 87-89)

rather than Hieronimo's vengeance on Lorenzo. It is Bel-
imperia who scorns Andrea's slayer (q.v.), Bel-imperia
who is quick-witted enough to utter the only words which
might save Horatio's life:

O save him brother; save him, Balthazar!
I loved Horatio but he loved not me.

(II. iv. 57-58)

and Bel-imperia whose second love prompts the chain of

events that enables her to avenge her first. It is Bel-imperia
whose presence drives the moral balance of good and evil
towards a reestablishment of justice on earth. And, ironically enough, it is Bel-imperia whose thirst for vengeance
renders morally questionable the dramatic movement
which it begins.

We never really know whether Andrea's death in battle requires revenge. His ghost does not initially say so; it appears to regard its demise as a basic fact of existence:

For in the late conflict with Portingale,
My valor drew me into danger's mouth
Till life to death made passage through my
    wounds.

(Induction, 15-17)

And when Horatio relates the event to Bel-imperia, he sees
no need for vengeance:

But wrathful Nemesis, that wicked power,
Envying at Andrea's praise and worth,
Cut short his life to end his praise and worth.
She, she herself, disguised in armor's mask
(As Pallas was before proud Pergamus)
Brought in a fresh supply of halberdiers,
Which paunched his horse and dinged him to
    the ground.
Then young Don Balthazar, with ruthless rage
Taking advantage of his foe's distress,
Did finish what his halberdiers begun,
And left not till Andrea's life was done.

(I. iii. 16-26)

The circumstances are admittedly suspicious, and Balthazar's actions are consistent with his back-biting personality. But can the victorious warrior be condemned for the
nature of his victory? Isn't common morality suspended
during battle? For Bel-imperia, it is not; she immediately
brands Balthazar a murderer:

He shall, in rigor of my just disdain,
Reap long repentance for his murderous deed.
For what was't else but murderous cowardice,
So many to oppress one valiant knight,
Without respect of honor in the fight?

(I. iii. 71-75)

There are two separate moral schemes in these views of
Andrea's death: (1) the flexible chivalry of Andrea and
Horatio, which varies with the situation at hand and rejects the need for reckoning, and (2) Bel-imperia's instinctive morality, which sees life subjectively and decries what
it thinks unjust regardless of the extenuating circumstances in which injustice takes place. Of the two, Bel-
imperia's would seem to be at a disadvantage, for her attitude is obviously influenced by her love for Andrea. But
Bel-imperia's morality is congruent with that of the play
itself; her implicit faith in the rightness of retribution is the
human translation of the tragic assumption that a greater
power supervises the feeble deeds of men. Because the
drama's moral significance rests on our acceptance of Bel-
imperia's motivation to revenge, we must take it on faith
if *The Spanish Tragedy* is to work for us without distortion. When we do so, Bel-imperia is identified as the hammer of God, her desire for vengeance becomes right, and,
in tandem with Hieronimo's, it ends by restoring justice

to a world "confused and filled with murder and misdeeds" (III. ii. 4).

The positions of the central characters with respect to the morality of vengeance pinpoint the question which is the thematic keystone of the play. Is revenge justifiable in the name of goodness, right, and truth? Can there be extenuating circumstances for a man who assumes the awful responsibility of playing God? It is relatively easy to observe that Lorenzo and Balthazar are morally in the wrong. For them, there is no question of public justice; they carry out their designs without recourse to conscience, and are destroyed because they violate the tragic dictum that no man is large enough to judge and execute his fellows on his own authority. What is not usually noticed is that Bel-imperia and Hieronimo are nearly as guilty, in an absolute sense, as the villains upon whom they are avenged. Bel-imperia questions the morality of personal vengeance no more than her brother, and possesses no more conscience than he. It never occurs to her that revenge might be a mortal sin, that only the Lord can repay. Only Hieronimo seems to realize that personal revenge is a footpath to damnation:

> There is a path upon your left-hand side
> That leadeth from a guilty conscience
> Unto a forest of distrust and fear,
> A darksome place and dangerous to pass.
> There shall you meet with melancholy thoughts,
> Whose baleful humors if you but uphold,
> It will conduct you to despair and death.
>
> (IV. iv. 60-66)

Only Hieronimo attempts to circumvent disaster by appeals to public law. And Hieronimo is forced to take the same path as his feminine accomplice. It does not matter that the traumatic experiences of Pedringano's execution, Bazulto's supplication, and Isabella's suicide (q.v.) push him into vengeance, that he kills only after all other avenues have been exhausted, or even that supernatural forces absolve him of responsibility by appointing him their agent (q.v.). Hieronimo cannot know what transpires in the underworld, cannot know that he is in the right and that his cause has been blessed. The fact remains that he has taken human lives, and that no supernatural sanction can cancel the payment his actions demand. He may be absolved in heaven, but he must die on earth, and his death is required by the same rules which require Bel-imperia's. They die because the avenger can never really be right, because murder, whatever its motivation, is a fatal violation of an unwritten and a higher law.

However, to say that Kyd's "message" is that there are no absolutes, that we are all guilty, is to warp the moral vision that is the backbone of the *Tragedy*'s world. And to say, without qualification, that Hieronimo and Bel-imperia are guilty is to regard them without respect to their meaning in the pattern of the play. We cannot condemn them as we condemn Lorenzo and Balthazar; they are far too sympathetic. Furthermore, the infernal powers remind us that they *are* good; they are endorsed by Revenge (q.v.), and since we see them from his viewpoint as well as ours, we do not seriously challenge the judgment that places them in Elysium at the close.

Their guilt, nevertheless, remains. It remains in Bel-imperia's slightly calculating use of Horatio, in the avengers' utilization of deception, in their murder of Lorenzo, Balthazar, and Castile, and in Hieronimo's insistence on calling it just that:

> O, that will I, my lords; make no doubt of it:
> I'll play the murderer, I warrant you,
> For I already have conceited that.
>
> (V. i. 130-133)

It remains necessarily, for in a pitched battle between good and evil, good will lose if it plays by the rules of goodness, and good cannot be defeated here if the justice established by the supernatural powers is to be preserved. Granted, it is a special guilt which differs from the overt culpability of a Lorenzo. Granted, it is the guilt of the human predicament, the guilt of those who must upset the applecart in their quest for meaning and order in existence. Kyd recognizes this on a universal plane by sending the avengers to his supernatural heaven (V. iii. Epilogue, 21-24). But he also realizes that on the human plane—the concrete level at which we emphasize most directly—there can be no contact with the supernatural and no salvation from the penalty that murder entails. Because Kyd sees this duality and dares to pose doubts around it, *The Spanish Tragedy* assumes the outlines of a searching examination of the morality of revenge. There are no answers to the questions his characters raise; he has given us a dramatic exposition of vengeance, not an explanation. And in the end we can do nothing but accept.

The Spanish Tragedy is many things. It is a theatrically conceived essay on the moral dilemma of the avenger. It is a study of Machiavellism in action. It is a treatise to the effect that nobility confers obligations, not exemptions from moral responsibility. It is a superbly handled exercise in dramatic irony. Finally, it is an object lesson in the imperishability of justice. For even as Hieronimo bewails his impotence and Bel-imperia chafes in forced inaction, the mills of the gods are grinding towards moral resolution. They are grinding in the subplot, where Villuppo, a two-dimensional villain who incorporates the worst traits of Balthazar and Lorenzo, is exposed and condemned (I. ii.; III. i.). And they are grinding in the underworld, where a ghost is being educated in the immutable justice of the forces that rule the universe:

> *Ghost* I looked that Balthazar should have been
> slain;
> But 'tis my friend Horatio that is slain,
> And they abuse fair Bel-imperia. . . .
> *Revenge* Thou talkest of harvest, when the corn
> is green:
> The end is crown of every work well done;
> The sickle comes not till the corn be ripe.
> Be still, and ere I take thee from this place,
> I'll show thee Balthazar in heavy case.
> (II. v. 136 f.)
> *Ghost* Awake, Revenge; if love—as love hath
> had—
> Have yet the power or prevalence in hell.
> Hieronimo with Lorenzo is joined in league,
> And intercepts our passage to revenge. . . .
> *Revenge* Content thyself, Andrea; though I
> sleep,

Yet is my mood soliciting their souls.
Sufficeth thee that poor Hieronimo
Cannot forget his son Horatio.

(IV. Epilogue, 11 f.)

Andrea's ghost is more than an expository device to arrest attention; it is part of the audience, and as it becomes cognizant of the justice working through the events onstage, the spectator becomes cognizant of it also. The ghost and Revenge guide the audience in its reaction to the play; with the Portuguese subplot, they ensure the triumph of Hieronimo and Bel-imperia even when the prospects for vengeance appear most bleak. They establish a superhuman and overriding scheme of justice, and thus give the *Tragedy* the moral stability which forms the foundations for its chaotic, grandiose, and eternal world. (pp. 307-24)

Michael Henry Levin, "'Vindicta mihi!': Meaning, Morality, and Motivation in 'The Spanish Tragedy'," in Studies in English Literature, 1500-1900, Vol. IV, 1964, pp. 307-24.

Prior on Kyd's variations in dramatic style:

[Kyd's] variations in style seem to conform to some vague principle of appropriateness to the speaker or the kind of situation involved. Thus, the Induction, spoken by the Ghost, is done in the style of the imitations of the Virgilian descent to hell common to the metrical tragedy, of which Sackville's Induction to *The Mirror for Magistrates* is the best known example. The reports of battles are rendered with an epic stateliness combined with the turgid sensationalism of reference to broken bodies and bloodshed which had become the characteristic manner of the conventional Nuntius, and was retained for such accounts in later plays. . . . The speeches of Balthazar are almost invariably marked by greater artifice than those, for instance, of his Machiavellian companion Lorenzo. Certain of the speeches in which a character is represented as probing for himself the personal aspects of some situation are . . . marked by a patterned formality. It appears as though Kyd, confronted by the need of introducing a wholly new style to satisfy the special demands of his plot and characters, and at the same time of retaining the established artifices of manner which were features of the tragic pieces up to his time, solved the problem by admitting a variety of styles through a kind of principle of decorum which suited the style to person or occasion.

Moody E. Prior, in his The Language of Tragedy, Indiana University Press, 1947.

T. B. Tomlinson (essay date 1964)

[*An Australian editor and scholar of English literature, Tomlinson is primarily known for his* A Study of Elizabethan and Jacobean Tragedy (1964). *In the following excerpt from the above-mentioned work, the critic appraises the simplicity and clarity of the revenge theme in Kyd's* Spanish Tragedy *as compared to the complexity of later revenge plays.*]

[Kyd's] revengers—principally Hieronymo, Lorenzo, Bellimperia, Villuppo—like his play as a whole, have compar-

atively simple motives. In *The Spanish Tragedy* (c. 1589), . . . Revenge is most clearly allied with motives of worldly gain (Villuppo, Balthazar, Lorenzo) or the eye-for-an-eye attitude summed up by the Ghost of Andrea at the end:

Let me be judge, and doom them to unrest.
Let loose poor Tityus from the vulture's gripe,
And let Don Cyprian supply his room;
Place Don Lorenzo on Ixion's wheel,
And let the lover's endless pains surcease . . .

Similarly, in the wider context of the play as a whole, when issues like Hieronymo's concern for justice come in, they are clearly defined and limited. Whatever its limitations and crudenesses, Kyd's play has at any rate the characteristic advantages of the beginning of a literary convention. Obviously it does not range as widely as Webster; it has not the close-knit thickness of texture of Tourneur's verse; in sum, it cannot really be placed beside the best of the later Revenge plays. What it does have is simply the advantages of limitation. When it does manage to raise interesting or serious issues, they are clearly and sharply put. The best of the later Revenge writers, Tourneur, manages extraordinary clarity only in the face of mounting difficulty and complexity.

In a completely un-naturalistic context, this gives Kyd tremendous advantages. He can sketch in a 'motivation'—in the Elizabethan sense . . . —for Villuppo, the Portuguese Machiavel, and a reader accepts this without protest, despite the fact that it must occur to everybody to wonder how on earth Villuppo could have imagined he could get away with claiming Balthazar was dead when he obviously wasn't! Again, Kyd (with the help of his collaborator) stage-managers the business of Hieronymo biting out his tongue—and doing so for no very obvious reason—simply so that he can finalize his picture of the revenger pleased with his own art, for its own sake. The closest scrutiny of the text doesn't seem to reveal anything further in the way of information that could have been got out of Hieronymo at this stage. And generally speaking, where Tourneur, and the far more individualistic Webster, dwell on and depend on the more intangible aspects of the Revenge idea, Kyd, by virtue of his position in the convention, is able to base his play more consistently on clear-cut issues. When dealing with Hieronymo, of course, he reaches out sometimes into the difficult and the intangible, but even here, and even if one includes the additions attributed to Jonson, the madness has a pre-Shakespearean simplicity about it. The rest of the play is resolutely un-Jacobean. Balthazar, Lorenzo, Bellimperia, Villuppo—all these are people more concerned with worldly gain or revenge in its most primitive and clear-cut form than with the groping after difficulty and complexity that fascinated Tourneur, Webster and their characters. Even when, as with Balthazar, Bellimperia and the rulers of Spain and Portugal, the business of revenge is based on contracted marriages, alliances between states, and revenge for the deaths of Andrea and Horatio (as Bellimperia's two lovers), Kyd is untroubled to keep the lines of intrigue, if not exactly simple, then at least clear-cut. There is as yet little tendency or temptation to involve a reader in dangerous complexities of the kind that arise out of speeches like Vendice's on similar topics.

The kinds of verse and dialogue Kyd uses define both the limitations and the interest of his attempt to deal with these matters at the beginning of what was to be a comparatively short but certainly important literary convention. In the first place, Kyd is obviously experimenting widely. Stichomythia and patterned, near-Petrarchan verse stand out as the basis for a lot of the early acts at least. Often, the effect is ridiculous and poorly managed:

> *Bellimperia* Why stands Horatio speechless all
>   this while?
> *Horatio* The less I speak, the more I meditate.
>
> II, ii, 24-5

(Who was it suggested Hieronymo bit out his tongue because he was sick of stichomythia?) But it is probably a mistake to take this sort of writing as Kyd's main aim, or the basis of the play as a whole. He relies more on using whatever comes to hand than on any one or two main lines of attack. He is prepared at times to use the couplet form, or else the kind of balance that draws on but does not copy exactly sixteenth-century couplet writing. War, for instance, is often a matter of the picturesque, the neatly and, to us, rather amusingly dispassionate observation enclosed in stiffly moving, puppet-like images which remind one inevitably of early couplet writing (particularly translations):

> Here falls a body sund'red from his head,
> There legs and arms lie bleeding on the grass,
> Mingled with weapons and unbowell'd steeds,
> That scattering overspread the purple plain . . .
>
> I, i, 59 ff.

At other times, Kyd converts Elizabethan pastoral writing to grimmer uses. Compare, for instance, the following from Hieronymo:

> The blust'ring winds, conspiring with my words,
> At my lament have mov'd the leafless trees,
> Disrob'd the meadows of their flower'd green,
> Made mountains marsh with spring-tides of my
>   tears,
> And broken through the brazen gates of hell.
>
> III, vii, 5-9

Or, again, he may decide that a Spenserian morality might be useful:

> There is a path upon your left-hand side
> That leadeth from a guilty conscience
> Unto a forest of distrust and fear,
> A darksome place, and dangerous to pass.
> There shall you meet with melancholy
>   thoughts . . .
>
> IV, iv, 60 ff.

Much of this, of course, a reader dismisses as immaturity or conscious experiment, but the presence of so many kinds of verse is a sign at least that Kyd is not to be judged by first impressions and that he may possibly be performing a useful function, both for his own play and for others, in investigations of this kind. At his best, he has a surprisingly light hand at writing dramatic dialogue and there is life even in the extensive borrowings.

What of more consequence the play has to say than this must depend on how Kyd manages the two or three important sections where he does move away from more or less deliberate experimentation, or at any rate where he uses the experiments and the borrowings for wider ends. One of the first important signs of a widening and tightening of the play's field of reference is Act II, scene iv, the wooing of Bellimperia and the death of Horatio. The dialogue here is still almost embarrassingly patterned and self-conscious; but it also both reaches out towards the sort of pointed irony which will increasingly inform Revenge plays, and at the same time exhibits a clarity of outline denied to Webster, and even Tourneur. Horatio, we notice, is given lines the significance of which he cannot possibly realize because Kyd is using the mannered love-talk, which Horatio takes at face-value, for quite other ends:

> Now that the night begins with sable wings
> To overcloud the brightness of the sun,
> And that in darkness pleasures may be done,
> Come, Bellimperia, let us to the bower,
> And there in safety pass a pleasant hour.
>
> II, iv, 1-5

Consistently, Horatio himself takes this as a sort of development of the sonneteer's approach to love. To him 'safety', 'pleasant hour', are merely polite compliments necessary in a romantic situation:

> Sweet, say not so; fair fortune is our friend,
> And heavens have shut up day to pleasure us.
> The stars, thou seest, hold back their twinkling
>   shine,
> And Luna hides herself to pleasure us.
>
> II, iv, 16-19

Actually, as the dramatic irony rather heavily but very clearly points out, Horatio is being made to say precisely the wrong sort of thing for this stage of the play. As Hieronymo and others later make quite clear, and as indeed is clear on the face of it even here, references to night, darkness, the action of the heavenly bodies in carefully providing concealment for the two lovers—all these things point to disaster, not happiness. As in much of the writing for the Masque, for instance, darkness works here as a manifestation, embodiment, symbol of the opportunity nature gives to tragedy and evil. Horatio's blindness in not seeing the real import of his remarks, while not exactly causing or even actively contributing to his own downfall, is foolish because not sufficiently aware of the presence of forces of evil and destruction. His actions in courting Bellimperia in this way, and his speeches, are the trigger-action which, however well-meant, releases a destruction that was waiting for him anyway. The character of the world as Kyd sees it is pointed by the fact that Horatio must contribute, in however small degree, to his own murder by being unaware of the grimmer meaning inherent in what he is saying. On the discovery of the body, Hieronymo points the meaning again:

> O Heavens, why made you night to cover sin?
> By day this deed of darkness had not been.
>
> II, iv, 86-87

'Sin' here means, literally, the murder, but I think Kyd is

sufficient of an Elizabethan to welcome the obvious echo of poor Horatio's own words and actions. In a conventional sense, at least, it was 'sin' that he and Bellimperia were flirting with, the more so as it was qualified by Horatio's dangerous insensitivity to the possibilities suggested by his love speeches. It is certainly no accident that Hieronymo here picks up the talk of day and night and makes specifically the point that Horatio failed to see consciously earlier on, though making it in fact by implication even then.

No-one could pretend that this was great dramatic verse. Some of it is downright childish:

> Ay me most wretched, that have lost my joy,
> In leesing my Horatio, my sweet boy!
>
> II, iv, 94-95

But *The Spanish Tragedy,* as well as being an interesting play, is a portent, and the fact that already the Revenge convention is using conventional writing for wider ends plays a significant part in one's vision of the whole range of Elizabethan writing. In the central acts, Hieronymo and others stretch the limits of the play beyond anything that could have been expected from earlier, surface impressions. Act III, scene ii, for instance, opens with the famous soliloquy 'O eyes! no eyes, but fountains fraught with tears . . . ' Immediately, and largely, this is quaintly patterned verse of historical interest only. It even does its best to bury the perfectly valid complaint it is in fact making under the mass of patterning that culminates triumphantly in

> Eyes, life, world, Heav'ns, hell, night, and day,
> See, search, show, send some man, some mean,
>   that may— (A letter falleth)

From beneath poetical exhibitionism of this kind, however, the point that the play is trying to make does finally emerge:

> O world! no world, but mass of public
>   wrongs . . .

Characteristically, when the point is made, it is allowed a simplicity and a clarity of outline later writers simply had to sacrifice in favour of a richer complexity of meaning.

More interesting, however, than the famous speech itself is the extent to which the play as a whole does manage to make something of this embryonic tragic complaint. Immediately before this scene, the sub-plot—if that is what it can be called—has made the same point in a quietly effective way. Alexandro's trials are in fact happily ended by the arrival of the Portuguese Ambassador from Spain, but he too is very nearly destroyed by the workings of Machiavellian intrigue which blandly disregards natural justice and the innocence of individuals. With considerable imaginative insight, Kyd has used the limited, conventional plot of Villuppo to show how easily and how unjustly slander will stick, and the texture of the play is thickened by the parallels between Alexandro's complaints and Hieronymo's:

> *Alexandro* But in extremes what patience shall
>   I use?
> Nor discontents it me to leave the world,

With whom there nothing can prevail but
    wrong . . .
As for the earth, it is too much infect
To yield me hope of any of her mold.

> III, i, 32-37

Already the Shakespearean tragic complaint is overshadowing the unstinted vigour of *Tamburlaine!*

More impressively—and even discounting the additions attributed to Jonson—Hieronymo, stilted though much of his dialogue and speeches are, focuses a complaint which later tragedy will develop more intricately but not always more rewardingly. Kyd's version, put largely through Hieronymo, is clumsy, but has the interest of freshness, forthrightness and clarity of outline that often characterizes the beginning of a literary theme:

> *Hieronymo* [*as the magistrate deciding others'
>   causes*]:
> Thus must we toil in other men's extremes,
> That know not how to remedy our own,
> And do them justice, when unjustly we,
> For all our wrongs, can compass no redress . . .
> This toils my body, this consumeth age,
> That only I to all men just must be,
> And neither gods nor men be just to me.
>
> III, vi, I ff.

Kyd's verse, though not at this point literally in couplet form, is still bound to the couplet mentality which gives it, at its best, directness and point. Act III, scene vii develops this kind of attitude and hints broadly at the quizzical attitude to the justice of the heavens which Shakespeare, Tourneur and Webster later developed. Here, again, the outlines of the imagery are sharper and more uncompromisingly devoted to an obvious single point than in later writers, but by the same token Kyd's attitude is remarkably fresh and forthright. It's not that he's doubting the existence of the heavens, or that he's saying divine justice doesn't exist; only that in these circumstances it's difficult if not impossible to see anything rational or humane in it. The heavens are strikingly beautiful but unintelligibly aloof:

> Yet still tormented is my tortured soul
> With broken sighs and restless passions,
> That, winged, mount and, hovering in the air,
> Beat at the windows of the brightest Heavens,
> Soliciting for justice and revenge.
> But they are plac'd in those empyreal heights,
> Where, countermur'd with walls of diamond,
> I find the place impregnable . . .
>
> III, vii, 10 ff.

This is the best of Hieronymo, and of Kyd. The play here is asking the impertinent questions that great tragedy constantly asks, but with Kyd they have a singleness of impact possible only to the writer who does not see complications beyond the questions asked. Thus Shakespeare is obviously an infinitely more complex writer than Kyd, but on a simple level Hieronymo's concern with justice is related to Lear's and is in any case impressive in its own right. In particular, the personal directness of his final protest, with only the faintest echo now of the affectations of 'O eyes! no eyes', is admirable:

I find the place impregnable; and they
Resist my woes, and give my words no way.

Compared with the extreme patterning of many of Hieronymo's more famous speeches the 'woes . . . words' balance here is barely detectable and almost all a reader's attention is taken up with the directness and frankness of his complaint.

The 'additions' develop both this and, of course, the questioning madness which follows from it. Whether or not they are Jonson's, they clearly represent both a more truly dramatic dialogue and a freer and more flexible verse generally. Certainly, whoever wrote them had his eye firmly on questions raised by Kyd himself:

> *Hieronymo* Light me your torches at the mid of
>   noon,
> Whenas the sun god rides in all his glory;
> Light me your torches then . . .
>
> . . . Night is a murderous slut,
> That would not have her treasons to be seen.
>   IV, vi, 28-32

And later there is a wilder version of Hieronymo's old point about the justice of the heavens:

> *Hieronymo* O ambitious beggar,
> Wouldest thou have that that lives not in the
>   world?
> Why, all the undelved mines cannot buy
> An ounce of justice, 'tis a jewel so inestimable.
> I tell thee, God hath engrossed all justice in his
>   hands,
> And there is none but what comes from him.
>   IV, vi, 82-87

But clearly the Kyd of the main text could not compete with verse of this competence. The interest we have in his verse is of a more limited—and for the most part academic—kind. The additions, by keeping firmly to questions precisely raised by the original, give the play imaginative depth; at the same time they illustrate some of the directions in which the revenge play will be modified as writing closer to Shakespeare's in tone and idiom takes command. In particular, the idiomatic vigour of 'Night is a murderous slut . . . ', and the almost Shakespearean ring of Pedringano's

> So that with extreme grief and cutting sorrow
> There is not left in him one inch of man.
> See, where he comes.
>   IV, vi, 14-16

—together with the more responsive, less patterned dialogue in the shorter exchanges between characters, all point away from Kyd towards the extreme flexibility of Jacobean and later Elizabethan writing. The uniqueness of Kyd's own section of the play is that it stands firmly off—often quite successfully—from this more mature writing and yet clearly provides the impetus and some of the cast of mind for later plays. It has the virtues of clarity and at the same time it is more representative and suggestive of future needs than, for instance, Marlowe's *Tamburlaine.* (pp. 75-85)

T. B. Tomlinson, "The Morality of Revenge:

Kyd and Marlowe," in his A Study of Elizabethan and Jacobean Tragedy, *Cambridge at the University Press, 1964, pp. 73-94.*

Jonas A. Barish   (essay date 1966)

[*Barish is an American scholar and critic who has written numerous studies on the English Renaissance and Restoration drama. He is perhaps best known for* Ben Jonson and the Language of Prose Comedy *(1960) and the monograph* The Antitheatrical Prejudice *(1981). In the excerpt below, Barish analyzes Kyd's use of rhetorical models to accentuate the action and themes of* The Spanish Tragedy, *particularly focusing on how the symmetrical speech patterns balance the actions of the characters.*]

The Spanish Tragedy is, as has long been recognised, a repository of 'patterned' speech. What has perhaps been less well recognised is that this speech derives, for the most part, not so much from the dramatic as from the nondramatic verse of Kyd's predecessors and contemporaries among the poets. Specifically, it seems to represent Kyd's adaptation of the rhetoric of the 'middle style', the rhetoric of the schemes, tropes and figures, as enshrined in the poetical miscellanies of the later sixteenth century and codified in the manuals of style. The figures had as their purpose simply to please, 'to avoyd sacietie [sic], and cause delight: to refresh with pleasure, and quicken with grace the dulnesse of mans braine' (Wilson's *Art of Rhetoric*), and thus to assist the poet in his aim of persuasion. Doubtless it was the acknowledged delightfulness of the figures that led Kyd to employ them so bountifully in **The Spanish Tragedy** that the play might almost have served, like Sidney's *Arcadia,* as a text on which to base a rhetorical lexicon, but it was wholly a consequence of his feeling for the connection between language and gesture that he was able to take devices that had often proved intractable in the hands of other playwrights, and turn them into vital constructive elements. Unlike his predecessors, Kyd used the figures of rhetoric not simply to decorate the action but to articulate it. (p. 59)

It was playwrights like Kyd who helped bring into being our present sense of the dramatic. What Kyd does is to make functional the schemes and tropes of the figured style. He pares away the fatty amplification that writers like Mundy [in his *Fidele and Fortunio*] did not even recognize as encumbering, and what remains he remanages so as to fit it for its new context. When he borrows directly, he improves. Lorenzo's notorious echoing of a sonnet by Thomas Watson [*The Hekatompathia, or Passionate Century of Love,* 1582] represents, simply on the level of versification, a distinct advance:

> My lord, though Bel-imperia seem thus coy,
> Let reason hold you in your wonted joy:
> In time the savage bull sustains the yoke,
> In time all haggard hawks will stoop to lure,
> In time small wedges cleave the hardest oak,
> In time the flint is pierc'd with softest shower,
> And she in time will fall from her disdain,
> And rue the sufferance of your friendly pain.

BALTHAZAR. No, she is wilder, and more hard
  withal,
Than beast, or bird, or tree, or stony wall.
                                              (II. i. 1)

Watson's version ran thus:

  In time the Bull is brought to weare the yoake;
  In time all haggred Haukes will stoope the
    Lures;
  In time small wedge will cleave the sturdiest
    Oake;
  In time the Marble weares with weakest she-
    wres:
    More fierce is my sweet *love,* more hard wi-
      thall,
    Then Beast, or Birde, then Tree, or Stony
      wall.

'The oftener it is read of him that is no great clarke', declares Watson patronisingly in his headnote to the sonnet, 'the more pleasure he shall have in it', thus emphasising the auricular drubbing to which he will subject his vulgar readers. Kyd provides dramatic context for the lines, and uses them to score a dramatic point. The familiar conflict in the mind of the Petrarchan lover, between the spectacle of his mistress' cruelty and the hope that she may relent, turns into a lively interchange between the confident Lorenzo, unimpressed by the genuineness of his sister's indifference toward Balthazar, and the despairing Balthazar, already daunted by the conviction of his own worthlessness. Kyd resists the temptation to shovel a complete poem, with its own beginning, middle and end, into his play; where Mundy, following Watson, would have spun twelve lines more of schematic parallels on the properties of bulls, hawks, oaks and flints, Kyd cuts short the amplification, makes the quatrain a vivid moment of persuasion in Lorenzo's speech and allots only the despondent rejoinder to Balthazar. In addition, he confers a new compactness and energy on the familiar images by curbing the stream of monosyllables, reducing the shower of sibilants and practising other small but significant metrical improvements.

When, in short, we turn from the sporadic and halting attempts of earlier playwrights to *The Spanish Tragedy,* we find that the figures have ceased being mere aimless embroidery. They no longer represent self-indulgence on the playwright's part, nor do they suggest a flagging imagination. They now work actively to order the materials of the play. In addition to being 'auricular' and 'rhetorical', they have conceptual force. They help articulate the relationships among the characters; they aid the plot to incarnate itself as a physical event on a physical stage. At the same time, they gradually serve the playwright to turn a critical eye on language itself. Words come to oppose physical events as well as to buttress them, and in the tension between speech and act lies much of the tragic force of the plot.

The tendency for most of the schemes of antithesis, parallel, and balance to carve experience into dualities, triads, tetrads, and the like—in short, to impose a symmetrical patterning on phenomena—pervades the language of *The Spanish Tragedy* from the start, long before the figures, as figures, begin to press themselves on our notice. The sol-

emn periphrasis with which the ghost of Don Andrea makes his entry lodges us at once in a realm of precise distinctions and complementary rejunctions:

  When this eternal substance of my *soul*
  Did live imprison'd in my wanton *flesh,*
  Each in their function *serving other's* need, . . .
                                       (I. i. 1, my italics)

Andrea elaborates the body-soul dualism in two successive lines, and then in a third reunites the separated halves into a mutually co-operative union. The use of the word 'flesh' rather than 'body', in contrast to 'soul', slightly mutes the rhetorical emphasis of the opposition, without affecting its conceptual import. Death is next viewed as a divisive power that cleaves in sunder not the body and soul, as we might expect, but the speaker and his mistress:

  But in the harvest of my summer joys
  Death's winter nipp'd the blossoms of my bliss,
  Forcing divorce betwixt my love and me.
                                              (I. i. 12)

Here a new series of antitheses—between summer and winter, harvest and frost, life and death—runs obliquely against the earlier opposition of flesh and soul and the splintered unity of the lovers arrived at in the final line. The mode of thinking is continuously antithetical and disjunctive, but the disjunctions at this moment remain slightly out of phase with one another, so that they do not crystallise into obvious patterns.

Andrea's description of his visit to the underworld, based on the voyage in Book VI of the *Aeneid,* condenses and abridges Virgil's account; it also regularises and patterns it. At the threshold of Hades, Aeneas meets only Minos among the infernal judges; Rhadamanth appears further on, in Tartarus; and Aeacus is not mentioned at all. Kyd makes Andrea's arrival in Hades the occasion of a ceremonious debate in which all three judges, sitting as a high tribunal, ponder the fate of their new charge. They comprise a perfect trinity of thesis, antithesis and synthesis. Aeacus recommends that Andrea, a lover, be sent to the fields of love; Rhadamanth proposes to send him, as a soldier, to dwell with martialists; Minos, finally, arbitrates the difference by referring the question to Pluto. The journey toward Pluto deals in a like manner with infernal geography; on the right, the path leading to the fields of lovers and warriors; on the left, the steep descent to hell; in between, the entrance to the Elysian fields, where Pluto holds court. The arrangement revises Virgil's plan of the region so as to satisfy Kyd's liking for symmetrical patterns and the reconciliation of opposites.

The epic narrative of the victory of Spain over Portugal is conducted along similar lines. When, in the account of the Spanish general, the opposing armies set forth, they confront each other in a six-fold sequence of identical gestures:

  Both furnish'd well, both full of hope and fear,
  Both menacing alike with daring shows,
  Both vaunting sundry colours of device, . . .
    [etc.]
                                              (I. ii. 25)

The battle itself proceeds like a tournament. Each aggressive move made by one side is countered by an equivalent defensive manœuvre from the other:

> I brought a squadron of our readiest shot
> From out our rearward to begin the fight:
> They brought another wing to encounter us.
> Meanwhile our ordnance play'd on either side,
> And captains strove to have their valours tried.
>
> (I. ii. 35)

First the assault from the rear of one army, then the riposte from the flank of the other. First the challenge and answer of the ordnance, then the striving of the anonymous captains. When the smoke clears enough to enable us to discern and identify individual combatants, the same arrangement prevails. First,

> Don Pedro, their chief horseman's colonel,
> Did with his cornet bravely make attempt
> To break the order of our battle ranks.
> But Don Rogero, worthy man of war,
> March'd forth against him with our musketeers,
> And stopp'd the malice of his fell approach.
>
> (I. ii. 40)

So, Don Pedro with his cavalry must oppose Don Rogero with his musketry; the first launches an attack which is repulsed by the energy of the second. Kyd allots three lines to each opponent: the first gives the identity of the officer, the second indicates the nature of the troops in his command, the third specifies the purpose of his mission.

And so with the rest of the description; group is pitted against group in symmetrical antagonism. Kyd has done more than 'straighten out' Grimald's contorted lines in 'The Death of Zoroas' on which he may have based his narrative [Howard Baker, *Induction to Tragedy,* 1939]; he has nearly reimagined the scene. Instead of an impenetrable confusion, he visualises a battle of nearly heraldic formality. Even the description of a field strewn with the dead acquires an ordered clarity:

> On every side drop captains to the ground,
> And soldiers, some ill-maim'd, some slain out-
>   right:
> Here falls a body scinder'd from his head,
> There legs and arms lie bleeding on the grass,
> Mingled with weapons and unbowell'd steeds,
> That scattering overspread the purple plain.
>
> (I. ii. 57)

There is no gainsaying the total effect of horror, but it is a controlled and lucid horror, achieved by the patient laying on of apposite details, like bricks, usually in pairs: first the captains, then the soldiers; first the maimed, then the slain; first the decapitated bodies, then the disembodied limbs; first the weapons, then the steeds. Turmoil and hubbub are rendered with a certain pictorial sharpness of outline by the antithetic rhetoric, as in a tapestry, while the free play of detail helps keep the symmetries unobtrusive.

After the battle the antitheses and oppositions surge more insistently into view, and begin to mesh more closely with the stage action. As the king finishes hearing the reports from the campaign, the victorious Spanish army crosses the stage, with Balthazar led between Lorenzo and Horatio. The two Spanish warriors, flanking their prisoner,

provide a visual image of their rivalry for the honour of his capture. The king inquires into the circumstances of the capture:

> KING. But tell me, for their holding makes me
>   doubt,
> To which of these twain art thou prisoner?
> LORENZO. To me, my liege.
> HORATIO. To me, my sovereign.
> LORENZO. This hand first took his courser by the
>   reins.
> HORATIO. But first my hand did put him from
>   his horse.
> LORENZO. I seiz'd his weapon and enjoy'd it
>   first.
> HORATIO. But first I forc'd him lay his weapons
>   down.
> KING. Let go his arm, upon our privilege.
>
> (I. ii. 152)

The plot here involves a symmetrical antagonism, mimed simultaneously in the language and in the stage action. At the king's bidding, the Spanish knights release their captive, who now explains his position for himself:

> KING. Say, worthy prince, to whether didst thou
>   yield?
> BALTHAZAR. To him in courtesy, to this per-
>   force:
> He spake me fair, this other gave me strokes:
> He promis'd life, this other threaten'd death:
> He wan my love, this other conquer'd me:
> And truth to say I yield myself to both.
>
> (I. ii. 160)

Again the antitheses in the language are mirrored by the antithetic gestures with which Balthazar designates his captors, as he particularises by turns their treatment of him. His final line, surprisingly, collapses the vivid contrast back into a noncommittal unity. Here we meet one of the perils of rhetoric. It is true that Balthazar is merely answering the king's question, and that he has, in fact, surrendered to both Horatio and Lorenzo. It hardly follows, however, from the opposition between courteous and peremptory treatment elaborated in the first four lines, that he should end by casually abandoning the distinction. The sharply registered preference for the one who offered gentle usage cannot be so limply disowned without making retrospective nonsense of the rest of the speech. Kyd's penchant for the reconciliation of opposites seems to have led him to enfeeble the force of his own disjunction at a crucial moment. And this leads to the further suspicion that the odd ascription of harsh behaviour to Horatio and generous behaviour to Lorenzo springs itself from the passion for disjunctions.

The king next mediates the contention by awarding Balthazar's weapon and horse to Lorenzo, but his ransom to Horatio; the custody of him to Lorenzo, but his armour to Horatio. All claims are scrupulously adjudicated, both the rights and rewards arising from the combat itself, and the larger issues arising from the unequal social rank of the rivals. The latter, in fact, interfere with the former, and prevent true justice; the king awards the armour to Horatio as a compensation for depriving him of the prisoner himself. The competing claims of the two knights, then, can be regulated only in part, even by a king renowned for his equity. When conflicts arise in a situation more resistant to justice, such as the rivalry between Horatio and Balthazar for the favours of Bel-imperia, tragedy ensues, and justice flees to heaven.

For the moment, however, justice is done as it was in Hades: competing extremes are moderated by compromise. The patterning in the language, clearly, is more than a perfunctory verbal manœuvre; it reflects the patterning in the plot, and helps to delineate it. In the episodes leading up to the murder, the patterns become more pronounced; Kyd uses them to reinforce the relationships on the stage, to intensify the mood, and to underline the varying temperaments of the *dramatis personae.* When Bel-imperia finishes her first frank avowal of love to Horatio in II. ii, our attention shifts to Lorenzo and Balthazar, hidden, by pre-arrangement, above, to spy on the lovers:

> BALTHAZAR. O sleep mine eyes, see not my love profan'd,
> Be deaf my ears, hear not my discontent,
> Die heart, another joys what thou deserv'st.
> LORENZO. Watch still mine eyes, to see this love disjoin'd,
> Hear still mine ears, to hear them both lament,
> Live heart, to joy at fond Horatio's fall.
>
> (II. ii. 18)

Balthazar's speech and Lorenzo's belong to the kind of 'conceited verse' that Fraunce praised in Sidney, where the same grammatical scheme recurs a number of times in sequence, with its key words—subject, verb, object—shifted like interchangeable blocks. Each speaker pursues a formula of systematic invocation, directing his eyes, ears and heart in turn to react to love, to sorrow, and to joy. But the two speeches are also antithetical, and Lorenzo's forms an answer to Balthazar's. Balthazar invites his faculties to abandon their function, to wrap him in insensibility and death. Lorenzo, following the same grammatical scheme, instructs *his* senses to redouble their activity. The first speech expresses defeatism and passivity, the second violence and aggression; so that while the symmetry reflects the close partnership between the two eavesdroppers, the antitheses reflect the contrast in their dispositions, the self-abandon of the one and the vindictive energy of the other.

These speeches, perhaps, should be spoken like incantations. During the speaking of them, there is nothing for Horatio and Bel-imperia to do but remain silent and motionless below. When they resume their interrupted duet, Kyd capitalises brilliantly on the interval of enforced silence. Bel-imperia is still waiting for an answer to her declaration of love; Horatio is still lost in his own thoughts.

> BEL-IMPERIA. Why stands Horatio speechless all this while?
> HORATIO. The less I speak, the more I meditate.
> BEL-IMPERIA. But whereon dost thou chiefly meditate?
> HORATIO. On dangers past, and pleasures to ensue.
> BALTHAZAR. On pleasures past, and dangers to ensue.

> BEL-IMPERIA. What dangers and what pleasures dost thou mean?
> HORATIO. Dangers of war, and pleasures of our love.
> LORENZO. Dangers of death, but pleasures none at all.
> BEL-IMPERIA. Let dangers go, thy war shall be with me.
>
> (II. ii. 24)

Even more strikingly than before, the patterned language here, with its intricacies of repetition and echo, translates itself into stage rhetoric. Balthazar and Lorenzo, unseen, unheard, give the reply to Horatio and Bel-imperia, grimly converting each cheerful presage into a menacing one. The repetitions bind the two levels of the stage together into a unity, and charge the love dialogue with heavy irony. Caught up as we are in the vigorous rhythm of the patterning, we scarcely notice such blemishes as the fatuousness of Bel-imperia's question, 'What dangers and what pleasures dost thou mean?'

In the wooing scene in the arbour, the intimate reciprocity between word and stage gesture becomes even closer:

> BEL-IMPERIA. If I be Venus, thou must needs be Mars,
> And where Mars reigneth there must needs be wars.
> HORATIO. Then thus begin our wars: put forth thy hand,
> That it may combat with my ruder hand.
> BEL-IMPERIA. Set forth thy foot to try the push of mine.
> HORATIO. But first my looks shall combat against thine.
> BEL-IMPERIA. Then ward thyself, I dart this kiss at thee.
> HORATIO. Thus I retort the dart thou threw'st at me.
> BEL-IMPERIA. Nay then, to gain the glory of the field,
> My twining arms shall yoke and make thee yield.
> HORATIO. Nay then, my arms are large and strong withal:
> Thus elms by vines are compass'd till they fall.
> BEL-IMPERIA. O let me go, for in my troubled eyes
> Now may'st thou read that life in passion dies.
> HORATIO. O stay awhile and I will die with thee,
> So shalt thou yield and yet have conquer'd me.
>
> (II. iv. 34)

Here the language dictates physical gesture nearly line by line; the governing analogy between love and war completes itself in a series of bodily movements. The hand, the foot, the lips, the glance of each lover advance with ceremonious gravity, to be parried by their counterparts from the other, just as the sallies of the Portingale troops were repulsed by the counter-assaults of the Spaniards. As with infernal justice, as with the campaign between the neighbouring kingdoms, as with the dispute over the capture of Balthazar, initial oppositions are here more than ready to merge into a dialectal unity, when the killers rush in with drawn swords and rend the fabric of reconciliation for good. Open antagonisms can be mediated and compromised; stealth cannot. From this point on the dialectic retreats into the inner spirit of Hieronimo, as he wrestles to reconcile his impulse toward revenge with the sanctions against it.

In all these cases we find Kyd using imaginatively and incisively the same rhetorical materials used so inanely and ineffectively by Mundy and the author of *The Rare Triumphs*. Sometimes, however, the use of the figures involves Kyd in the sort of decorative writing in which the decorativeness obscures narrative clarity instead of sustaining it. Balthazar's celebrated Euphuistic lament in II. i, though it establishes him as a despairing Petrarchan wooer, does so at some strain to the known facts of the plot; most of its details have the air of having been improvised hastily, and none too accurately, for the occasion. A more damaging illogicality creeps into the symmetrical flourish at the end of the same scene, when Balthazar expresses his fury with Horatio:

> I think Horatio be my destin'd plague:
> First in his hand he brandished a sword,
> And with that sword he fiercely waged war,
> And in that war he gave me dangerous wounds,
> And by those wounds he forced me to yield,
> And by my yielding I became his slave.
> Now in his mouth he carries pleasing words,
> Which pleasing words do harbour sweet conceits,
> Which sweet conceits are lim'd with sly deceits,
> Which sly deceits smooth Bel-imperia's ears,
> And through her ears dive down into her heart,
> And in her heart set him where I should stand.
> Thus hath he ta'en my body by his force,
> And now by sleight would captivate my soul: . . .
>
> (II. i. 118)

It is of at least passing interest to notice Kyd's especial fondness for this figure of climax, or 'Marching figure', as Puttenham terms it [in his *Art of English Poesy*, 1589]. Its propulsive forward motion makes it in a sense intrinsically dramatic, lends it particular power to create sequences of cause and effect. Kyd ordinarily uses it as he does here, to forge a chain in which A brings about B brings about C, each effect becoming in turn a new cause. His partiality to the figure reflects the causality ingrained in his thinking, his penchant for intrigue and concern for motivation, and the densely sequential texture of his language in general.

A chain, however, is no stronger than its weakest link, and the present ladder contains a number of shaky rungs, offences against the facts of Kyd's own story. We know that Horatio gave no dangerous wounds to Balthazar. Had he done so, we should have heard about them earlier, and, strictly speaking, they would have made it impossible for Balthazar to appear before the king to explain the circumstances of his capture. If Horatio did not dangerously wound Balthazar, by the same token he did not, with those wounds, force Balthazar to yield. And least of all did he, by the alleged wounds, make Balthazar his 'slave'; he has not even acquired nominal custody, much less privilege of restraint over him.

Of the second half of the dyptych, lines 124-9 may be allowed as the resentful fantasies of an envious rival, though

we may notice that they are founded on mere conjecture; Balthazar has no information about what prompted Belimperia to love Horatio. It is the concluding couplet, however, that effects a final divorce between sound and sense: 'Thus hath he ta'en my body by his force, / And now by sleight would captivate my soul'. Here the pressure of the antithetic patterning requires attributing 'sleight' to Horatio in his wooing, to match the 'force' of his soldiership, and it requires, even more bizarrely, charging him with the aim of enslaving Balthazar's 'soul', to correspond to his previous capture of his 'body'. At the moment of the ringing final rhyme on 'soul', the rhetorical pattern thus reaches its satisfying auricular conclusion, and the plain prose sense of the speech, as a reflection of the humble facts of the narrative, collapses into absurdity.

The failure here, if it is not to be ascribed to a deliberate attempt to show Balthazar as the victim of his own words, as I think it is not, illustrates the tendency of figural rhetoric to strew hidden reefs in the path of its own smooth sailing. The figures develop an impetus of their own, which can carry them athwart the dramatic current as well as along with it. The danger lies not, as an older school of critics might have said, in the fact that 'passion runs not after' exact schemes and tropical symmetries, but in the tendency of the schemes and symmetries to coerce thought. They bend somewhat reluctantly to quick shifts in feeling; they pursue a statelier, more galleon-like course; they tend to promote an effect of ritualized abstraction, so that it takes a sure hand to keep them obedient to all the particulars of a given dramatic context. Perhaps there is some justice in Moody Prior's charge that 'ostentatiously rhetorical art of any sort endows almost any sentiments with an academic, generalised quality' [*The Language of Tragedy*, 1947].

Kyd is nevertheless often strikingly successful in projecting even extreme emotion within the bristling geometry of the figures. Hieronimo's much parodied outburst in III. ii brings to the stage, for a moment of clamorous passion, a scheme derived ultimately from Petrarch, which Sidney had already used, or would shortly use, in *Astrophil and Stella*:

> O teares, no teares, but raine from beautie's skies,
>   Making those Lillies and those Roses grow,
>   Which ay most faire, now more then most faire show,
> While gracefull pitty beauty beautifies.
> O honied sighs, which from that breast do rise, . . .
>   O plaints conserv'd in such a sugred phraise,
>   That eloquence it selfe envies your praise,
> While sobd out words a perfect Musike give.
>   Such teares, sighs, plaints, no sorrow is, but joy:
>   Or if such heavenly signes must prove annoy,
> All mirth farewell, let me in sorrow live.
>   (*Poems*, ed. W. A. Ringler (1962), p. 231)

Sidney's use of the figure creates a sense of majestic calm. Each quatrain, through a spacious suspension, elaborates on one of the beloved's attributes of sorrow—her tears, her sighs, her plaints—and all three are made to converge at length under the sign of joy rather than sorrow. The theme of the poem is the transformation of apparent sorrow into pleasure through the beloved's beauty. Kyd, by packing the three successive apostrophes into three successive lines, and stressing the correspondences between them, achieves an effect of swollen passion breaking loose:

> O eyes, no eyes, but fountains fraught with tears;
> O life, no life, but lively form of death;
> O world, no world, but mass of public wrongs,
> Confus'd and fill'd with murder and misdeeds;
> O sacred heavens! If this unhallow'd deed . . .
>
> (III. ii. 1)

In Sidney, the lady's manifestations of sorrow remain on the same level of importance and intensity; they do not evolve, except perhaps in the direction of increasing articulateness. Kyd proceeds climactically, through circles of widening significance: eyes, life, world, heavens—organ, organism, social milieu, cosmos. The theme is the progressive perversion of all order and health into disease and disorder through the murder of Horatio. Each of the first three members of the series represents a realm felt to be deranged by the murder. In the case of the final realm, the heavens, the question is left open—left, indeed, for the heavens themselves to answer.

Hieronimo's sense of cosmic dislocation leads him to a second series, in which he enumerates forces that spur him to revenge: the night, the ugly fiends, the cloudy day. Finally, in a recapitulation—what Puttenham would term a 'collection'—of the sort adopted by Sidney in line 12 of his sonnet, Hieronimo gathers together all the phenomena he has discoursed upon, and appeals to them for aid in the discovery of the identities of his son's killers:

> Eyes, life, world, heavens, hell, night, and day,
> See, search, shew, send, some man, some mean,
>   that may—
>
> (III. ii. 22)

At which point, the stage direction informs us, '*A letter falleth*'. Hieronimo's recapitulation thus serves a dramatic as well as a rhetorical purpose. It constitutes a plea for action, and it leads up to a significant bit of stage business, the dropping of Bel-imperia's letter with its disclosure about the murderers. What is remarkable is that Kyd has worked out the schematism of the speech with a high degree of precision—no rhetorical treatise of the day would have had to apologise for offering it in illustration of the figures it uses—yet with enough flexibility in detail, especially prosodic detail, to make it convincing as an expression of Hieronimo's grief. What Elizabethan audiences found exciting and memorable in the language of **The Spanish Tragedy** was precisely such moments of high artifice as these. The numerous parodies of Hieronimo's lament, and of Balthazar's complaints, testify to the auricular impact of Kyd's theatrical tropes—testify, that is, to the pleasures of rhetoric, as well as, by their scorn, to its perils.

One problem faced by the bereaved Hieronimo throughout is how to find adequate expression for his feelings. When we meet him first, after the battle in Act I, he only with difficulty refrains from pleading his son's cause against Lorenzo. He refrains not out of any mistrust of his own eloquence, but because the king's well-known wisdom makes eloquence unnecessary; the king can be counted on to decide justly. Despite its evident scrupulosity, however, the king's justice, bending as it does to the pressure of the world's prejudices, inspires little confidence. Hieronimo, along with the rest, accepts it without protest, but it is not long before he is plunged into a situation in which he can find neither justice nor relief for his anguished feelings. The latter, indeed, becomes as cardinal a necessity as the former, and a main spur to revenge; revenge alone can provide a satisfactory outlet for his grief and outrage. 'Where shall I run to breathe abroad my woes', he cries, entering distractedly shortly after the murder,

> My woes, whose weight hath wearied the earth?
> Or mine exclaims, that have surcharg'd the air
> With ceaseless plaints for my deceased son?
>
> (III. vii. 1)

The immensity of Hieronimo's desolation demands cosmic scope for its utterance. Even his adjutants, the compassionate winds, who have vexed nature in his behalf, have wrought too feebly, for 'still tormented is my tortur'd soul / With broken sighs and restless passions'. Words, even when they denote extremest woe, remain words. Even when reinforced by the eloquence of the blustering winds, verbal plaints remain insufficient to express the fullness of grief. Still less can they bring about justice or revenge. Words, indeed, as Hieronimo comes to feel, are 'unfruitful', and yet, they are all he has.

> But wherefore waste I mine unfruitful words,
> When naught but blood will satisfy my woes?
> I will go plain me to my lord the king,
> And cry aloud for justice through the court,
> Wearing the flints with these my wither'd feet,
> And either purchase justice by entreats
> Or tire them all with my revenging threats.
>
> (III. vii. 67)

If language cannot be made to relieve his feelings, or accomplish justice, at least it can be turned into a weapon of harassment, and used to disturb the peace of mind of his foes.

The fact that his cries go unheard—partly through his own imprudence, partly through Lorenzo's cunning—deepens Hieronimo's skepticism toward the efficacy of speech. The decision to revenge, which crystallises in the *Vindicta mihi* soliloquy (III. xiii. 1), carries with it the realisation that henceforth, in order to combat those who have violated the natural current between speech and feeling, he must tamper with it himself. Having been driven, by abnormal circumstances, to adopt a course of action abhorrent to him, he must embrace the unnatural methods that will enable him to accomplish his purpose. He must enjoin his eye to 'observation', and his tongue 'To milder speeches than [his] spirit affords' (III. xiii. 40). From this moment on, he must turn language into something opaque and deceptive, instead of revelatory and transparent.

The apparition of Don Bazulto, the forlorn *senex* who stands mutely by at the sessions, proffering the humble supplication for his murdered son, acquaints Hieronimo with a kind of silent eloquence that he recognises as more potent than mere speech. Convinced of the futility of spoken words, Don Bazulto refuses to give voice to his distress. Instead, he presents the supplication. Ink must 'bewray', he explains, what blood began; passion must be reduced to formal writ, to documentary petition, to visible emblem. As the writ serves Bazulto, so the bloody napkin dipped in Horatio's wounds serves Hieronimo, as a mute testimony or dumb significant, helping to express the inexpressible. The old man himself, returning to the stage to confront Hieronimo alone, suddenly becomes an image in a hallucination, the ghost of Horatio, until Hieronimo awakens to the realisation that he is staring at a simulacrum of himself. The scene bears fresh witness to Kyd's power to make figured rhetoric convey intensity of feeling:

> Ay, now I know thee, now thou nam'st thy son,
> Thou art the lively image of my grief:
> Within thy face, my sorrows I may see.
> Thy eyes are gumm'd with tears, thy cheeks are
> wan,
> Thy forehead troubl'd, and thy mutt'ring lips
> Murmur sad words abruptly broken off,
> By force of windy sighs thy spirit breathes,
> And all this sorrow riseth for thy son:
> And selfsame sorrow feel I for my son.
>
> (III. xiii. 161)

Gazing at the old man gradually becomes, for Hieronimo, a process of self-discovery, an act of mirror-gazing. As on previous occasions, the patterned rhetoric participates deeply in the configuration of action: the anaphora, the repetitions, the near-identity of the two last lines, all express the growing identity felt by Hieronimo between himself and Bazulto. Bazulto is his semblable, as the audience already knows. The patterning in the language allows Hieronimo to make the discovery himself, as the two bereft old fathers stare hopelessly into each other's faces.

By this time, words scarcely avail Hieronimo at all, either as vehicles of woe, or vessels of truth. Like Lorenzo, he will henceforth keep his own counsel: 'pocas palabras, mild as the lamb' becomes the motto (III. xiv. 118); a distrust of all language replaces his former fluent security with it. When asked to contribute some 'pleasing motion' to entertain the visiting Portingales, he answers with a bit of autobiography:

> When I was young, I gave my mind
> And plied myself to fruitless poetry:
> Which though it profit the professor naught,
> Yet is it passing pleasing to the world.
>
> (IV. i. 71)

Hieronimo may arraign the fruitlessness of poetry out of bitter experience. His skill has in fact already diverted the court once before, in the show of knights and scutcheons in Act I, but it has not enabled him to give proper utterance to his grief, or to secure justice, earthly, celestial or infernal. The play commanded for the visiting monarch will allow him, at last, to validate his poetical talent by translating it into action—reprehensible action, to be sure, but action none the less. For once, fruitless poetry will bear fruit. And it will do so in terms suitable both to the distracted poet and to the ceremonious audience. Suitable to the distracted poet in being an incomprehensible medley of tongues, expressive of the chaos in Hieronimo's spirit; suitable to the court in being 'tragedia cothurnata, fitting kings' (IV. i. 160)—appropriate in stateliness and style to the pompous occasion it is intended to honour.

In view of the sustained emphasis in **The Spanish Tragedy** on verbal artifice, it seems reasonable to think that the original audience did indeed hear the play within a play spoken 'in sundry languages'. An audience that had already listened to various miscellaneous scraps of Latin, Italian, and Spanish in the course of the afternoon, including Hieronimo's 14-line dirge recited over the bleeding body of Horatio, would not have been likely to balk at the brief polyglot interlude of *Soliman and Perseda*. Even if the original script, in its sundry languages, ran to the same length as its English translation, the plot had already been fully explained in advance; it would twice be interrupted for further explanation while in progress, would be interrupted a third time for a spectacular stabbing and was capable of being mimed vividly throughout so as to heighten and clarify its essential gestures.

The effect, perhaps, would have been to suggest the extremes to which language can evolve, the lengths to which verbal ingenuity can be carried and how unintelligible

Title page of the 1592(?) edition of Soliman and Perseda, *a play that has been attributed to Kyd on the basis of its similarities to* The Spanish Tragedy.

words can become when they lose their moorings in the realities they are meant to express. The jabbering in four languages turns the whole phenomenon of speech under a strange phosphorescent glare, revealing it as a kind of disembodied incantation, a surrealistic dance of abstractions, divorced from roots in lived existence. Hieronimo's experience has involved a progressive alienation of language, a breakdown of the links between rhetoric and reality. To this alienation the playlet forms a fitting climax. It acts out the insubstantiality of words, sets them at loggerheads with motives and at cross-purposes with each other, shows them as the fantasms they threaten to become, and cancels them out, finally, by a stroke of the sword. The disclosure of Horatio's mutilated body provides a more devastating climax, a silent spectacle of woe for which words serve humbly as interpreters again:

> See here my show, look on this spectacle:
> Here lay my hope, and here my hope hath end:
> Here lay my heart, and here my heart was slain:
> Here lay my treasure, here my treasure lost:
> Here lay my bliss, and here my bliss bereft:
> But hope, heart, treasure, joy and bliss,
> All fled, fail'd, died, yea, all decay'd with this.
>
> (IV. iv. 89)

The patterned litany, with its insistent anaphora on the adverb 'here', pins us relentlessly to this moment in time and this point in space. It enforces repeatedly on us the reality of the visible, palpable fact and so, momentarily, restores the wholeness of the fractured image.

Having thus published to the world what heretofore he confided only to the winds, the night, and the churlish heavens, Hieronimo ends with the declared determination to 'as resolute conclude his part / As any of the actors gone before'. When, at the king's command, the guards bar his flight, he concludes his long agony by biting out his tongue. The final lunatic gesture betrays the final despair at the uselessness of talk, the berserk resolve to have done with language forever. And not spoken language only—the knife he is given to mend his pen he plunges into his heart; the last instrument available to facilitate expression he uses savagely to annul all further possibility of expression.

The Spanish Tragedy, then, with its thickets of figural rhetoric, is also to some degree a critique of rhetoric, an assessment of the limits of impassioned speech. We might term it a theatrical digression on a familiar Senecan text: *Curae leves loquuntur; ingentes stupent.* Language, including the patterned language borrowed from the sonneteers, proves able to meet the expressive requirements of epic narration in Act I, and the portrayals of love and hate in Act II. With the murder of Horatio, the world's equilibrium is upset; justice goes awry, and language with it. An unnatural state of divorce sets in between thought and word, word and deed; speech deteriorates as an instrument of reality and an agent of truth. In the distracted climax, it horribly apes the confusions of the world, sending them back magnified and further deformed as from a distorting mirror. The Babel-Babylon playlet does not so much reflect the visible ceremony of the Spanish court as its inner ethical chaos.

Action, in nondramatic poetry, remains of necessity verbal action. The poet, rebuffed by his mistress or the world, withdraws, perhaps, into frustration, or comes to terms with his plight rhetorically—through argument or retort, through objurgation, defiance, or self-inflicted melancholy. In the drama, words must be affirmed or denied by other acts—coupled with blows, or mingled with kisses. Under normal conditions, words and acts complete and complement each other: a half-angry, half-submissive Balthazar displays both anger and submissiveness to his captors and his captor king, and yields himself to both; a proud Hieronimo beguiles the triumphant court with vignettes of an earlier epoch when England invaded the Iberian peninsula. When the healthy reciprocity between words and acts is fractured, they develop independent and dangerous lives of their own; instead of confirming and corroborating each other, they delude and destroy. When the divorce becomes chronic, it leads, ultimately, to the splintering, shattering finale of *The Spanish Tragedy,* in which all communication breaks down, the community collapses in horror, and the stage is left littered with silent corpses for whom there is nearly no-one alive to mourn. (pp. 65-83)

Jonas A. Barish, " 'The Spanish Tragedy', or The Pleasures and Perils of Rhetoric," in Elizabethan Theatre, edited by John Russell Brown and Bernard Harris, Edward Arnold (Publishers) Ltd., 1966, pp. 59-85.

Margaret Lamb   (essay date 1975)

[*In the essay below, Lamb disagrees with the conclusions of previous scholars of* The Spanish Tragedy, *maintaining that " 'what happens' must account, more than given ideas of justice or the frequently parodied language, for the tremendous impression this play made on its time." She then assesses the play as a radical departure from the tradition of English drama up to that time, particularly examining Kyd's ironic treatment of Senecan models and his dramatic innovations.*]

In both philosophy and form *The Spanish Tragedy* represents a great innovation in English drama. It tries out and rejects both Senecan and Christian concepts of revenge and justice; its great moments are more often embodied in stage pictures and actions than in poetry. Its peculiar virtues have often caused it to be underrated because the shape of the play, and the meaning of this pattern, aren't so much studied; literary critics working in the period have traditionally concentrated on language, influences, historical significance, and—perhaps unfortunately—moral judgment. Yet the picture of "what happens" must account, more than given ideas of justice or the frequently parodied language, for the tremendous impression this play made on its time. *The Spanish Tragedy* had such an impact because it was a radical departure, not an imitation or a link.

Critics sometimes forget that a creative mind works by friction. But if Euripides and Seneca and modern French playwrights can use Greek myths and classical devices to throw a startling light, a kind of red-shift time-measurement, on the story, why can't Kyd? Perhaps

Kyd's Ghost is not so much a tribute to Seneca as it is a challenge to him on native ground. The literary and historical frames of reference are important as a starting point; but Hieronimo, like Hamlet, falls out of his frame of reference. The revenge theme changes and Hieronimo goes into new territory beyond revenge. Most critics have not tried to follow him there. Yet this is the territory of the greatest English tragedies.

In the beginning, Andrea and Revenge have obviously just arrived from somewhere. Most critics agree they come from Seneca. There is, however, wide disagreement on the function of these frame figures in the play. They have been seen as the useless borrowings of an apprentice playwright; as representatives of a higher world which can guarantee the just revenger Hieronimo "ease" among the shades at the end; or a device which unifies the main plot with previous action, through identification of Andrea and Horatio. Such explanations consider the play as a puzzle text for readers, to be studied at leisure. The philological approach invites legalistic and moral speculations of a kind that may be irrelevant to the work in the form in which it was created. But what is the meaning (*i.e.,* effect) of the Chorus in the unfolding nonstop sequence of the action? For Boas [in his edition of Kyd's *Works,* 1901], the language justifies the Chorus: seventeen lines of pure Seneca, followed by vivid descriptions which give "a sense of the unseen world enfolding the solid earth, on which men hated, loved, slew and were slain." This sombre description is particularly striking when one considers the stage picture. The Chorus is always onstage. The play begins and ends with this underworld, and Revenge even falls asleep before the last act—an indication that the borrowings from Seneca are not taken straight.

Kyd's Chorus performs a heavily ironic function, like Euripides' gods—or like the Asylum director's family who sit near the edge of the stage to watch the madmen in *Marat / Sade.* In such plays as *Alcestis, The Trojan Women* and *Hippolytus,* gods with usually petty motives provide a prologue and tell the audience why they've got it in for the human characters. William Arrowsmith has brilliantly argued that Euripides' use of such devices is ironic, showing "the widening gulf between reality and tradition." ["Euripides' Theatre of Ideas," in *Euripides: A Collection of Critical Essays,* ed. Erich Segal, 1968]. Euripides was the only Greek dramatist the Elizabethans knew, and Kyd's contemporaries seemed to prefer problem plays like *Orestes* and *Alcestis* to the more tightly structured and unmixedly tragic works. Kyd's final Chorus makes a direct claim that modern villains are worthy to replace classical figures:

> Place Don Lorenzo on Ixion's wheel . . .
> Hang Balthazar about Chimaera's neck,
> And let him there bewail his bloody love,
> Repining at our joys that are above;
> Let Serberine go roll the fatal stone,
> And take from Sisyphus his endless moan . . .
> (V. Ch. 33, 36-40)

The notorious sluggishness of the classical representatives—first of Andrea, then of sleepy Revenge—contrasts with the force and vigor of Kyd's characters in the realm of living sufferers. The comparison is deliberate.

Another contrast that has been noted, especially by critics interested in Kyd's language, concerns the heavy concentration of rhetorical speeches early on—"as though Kyd *began* to write a literary Senecan play" [*The Spanish Tragedy,* ed. Philip Edwards, 1959]. Barish remarks [in *Elizabethan Theatre,* ed. by John Russell Brown and Bernard Harris, 1966] on the patterned speech of Andrea and Balthazar (the two characters whose announced motives sound feeblest) and observes that after Horatio's murder "the dialectic retreats into the inner spirit of Hieronimo." Is it that Kyd is learning how to write dialogue as he goes along? Considered in theatrical terms, in connection with the early actions, this very formal verse is not only adequate but most appropriate to the formal feudal world of Act I.

In the first Chorus, Andrea's problem is whether he belongs in the part of the underworld reserved for lovers or the part for warriors. This rigid duality is echoed in the long description of opposing armies (I, 1). As in Uccello's paintings, the battle is reduced by geometrical precision to a tournament. (The slain Spaniards are casually dismissed in line two, while Andrea's Ghost sits watching). In this unreal world of war-with-honor, love is emblematic: the lady transfers her love and favors—the scarf, the glove—to her new champion. Hieronimo's dumb show of kings in Act I is a perfect picture of painless chivalric warfare. Royalty's complacent patriotic "interpretation" of the dumb show (I. iii. 140-170) is, like the injustice done Alexander at the Portuguese court, completely in harmony here. Diplomats speak. Etiquette rules. Situations described in the three scenes of Act I are perfunctorily attributed to Justice (Spanish victory, 1. 10-11), to Fortune (Balthazar's reported death, ii. 10-20), and to Nemesis (Andrea's death, iii. 16). This is the world as Hieronimo believes it to be. A Polonius in appearance, he hangs about the King and cautiously tries to advance his son's career. Only Bel-Imperia with her double passion threatens the smooth surface.

The enamelled picture is sometimes dull to look at; like O'Neill, another pioneer, Kyd often uses awkward means toward a great cumulative end. Shakespeare learned to present and dismiss a world in miniature, in a few lines. Kyd takes his time, but he is clearly showing the audience that the ideal medieval world, like the Senecan classical world, is not the real one.

Act II presents betrayal, jealousy, sexual love, murder and uncomprehending grief. Horatio hanging in the bower is the new "dumb show" of what the world is like. The bloody handkerchief replaces the scarf as the standard of love and revenge. (One critic ingeniously suggests the same stage property was used for both, thus further identifying the two young victims, Andrea and Horatio [Ejner Jensen, in "Kyd's *Spanish Tragedy:* The Play Explains Itself," *Journal of English and Germanic Philology* (1965)]. The language does not change entirely with catastrophe; Balthazar fittingly employs a feeble sonneteer's style throughout the play. But there are constant exclamations, eruptions from the underworld of feeling up to the surface of logical speech.

Kyd's gift for "stage business" and dramatic innovation is acknowledged by critics who consider him inferior as a poet and character creator. But such bits of business as those mentioned above can vividly present and then shatter a world-picture. Consider the further dumb shows of Pedringano's hanging and the empty box, or Isabella's hacking at the tree: all preludes to the final public show. [In his "The Figure of Silence in *The Spanish Tragedy*," *ELH* (1972),] McMillin traces the extraordinary sequence of Hieronimo advancing toward the King with halter and dagger in hand, justice on his lips—the combined image "of the antithetical terms of the play"; then Hieronimo's frustrated digging into the ground with the dagger, when the King does not understand. This sort of creative gift is as rare as the poetic gift, of which it is a form (the Greek *poeta* being "maker"). The pattern of tragic "dumb show" Kyd created may be obscured now by our familiarity with it through the later variations of greater poets.

One of Kyd's great innovations in English drama is to change the theme. That is, he changes the moral or metaphysical frame of reference.

In both the English medieval drama and in Seneca, values assumed at the beginning are proved to endure at the end. This is to be expected in Christian drama. *Everyman* may enlarge the viewer's understanding but does not jolt it. Nero's tutor knew the worst about the world—and so do his important characters, right from the start. Thyestes discovers what he had feared; Atreus enjoys his revenge as he knew he would. But Hieronimo learns what he had never dreamed, and the world turns upside down. Some Jacobean tragedy has the claustrophobic atmosphere of Senecan drama; world-weary revengers, doomed from the start, work from a blueprint. They do not, like Hieronimo or the great Shakespearean tragic heroes, fall from innocence into a void.

The *finis* of the closed-system plays is Q.E.D. Other plays familiar in England in 1585 would have been Tudor or Latin comedies, classical models which do not change terms in the middle. So *The Spanish Tragedy* really was new and shocking on the largest scale. (*Tamburlaine I,* the next important English play produced, is a confident demonstration in which the hero's views are triumphantly confirmed).

The Greek tragic dramatists, Ibsen and Shakespeare, present characters who change as profoundly as Kyd's. In *The Spanish Tragedy* part of the difficulty in understanding character motivation may be due to the wrenching violence with which these changes are effected. The Bel-Imperia who switches love-objects in Act I is not the woman who *sees* her new lover killed in Act II. Character need not be consistent in Elizabethan drama, just as point of view need not be consistent in Picasso's paintings. Subplots and anecdotes which may seem extraneous are treated by Kyd in the same bold way. Such plot strands as Villuppo's treachery are used contrapuntally; they complete the picture of a world of plots in which Hieronimo finds himself.

Radical changes in theme and world-picture are not looked for by critics who operate from fixed moral premises. Hieronimo's motives for delay, and his degree of madness, worry scholars who expect the *quid pro quo* of conventional revenge. For one writer the play cannot be great because there is no "adequate psychological analysis" of Hieronimo's reasons for delay; for another, the delay is "logical" so long as Hieronimo is searching for the murderer's motive [Boas; Fredson Bowers, in his *Elizabethan Revenge Tragedy 1587-1642,* 1940]. Suggesting "some disease of character or will," Boas is casting a backward glance from Coleridge's Hamlet. The critics who become caught up in the horrible events of the play are more likely to see "the tragic dilemma of the officially appointed minister of justice who is forced by circumstances to take justice into his own hands" [S. F. Johnson, "*The Spanish Tragedy,* Or Babylon Revisited," in *Essays on Shakespeare and Elizabethan Drama,* ed. Richard Hosley, 1962]. Here is "Hieronimo's occupation gone!" The scene with the Citizens and Old Man (III. vi) is the Marshal's farewell.

> To say that Hieronimo is obsessed by his son's murder or that he becomes mad under this pressure is to set the problem in poor focus; both statements imply that he could have acted in some normal and approvable manner. [McMillin]

Such views relate to what happens in *The Spanish Tragedy* rather than to ethical standards which are irrelevant to the nightmare unfolding. In performance, the pressure can be made clear and the ambivalence kept. Here as in *Hamlet,* the counterfeiting of a state close to what one actually feels is not only prudent for plot's sake but a *relief* to the constantly suffering character. The pretense of madness takes up the excess of feeling and furnishes Hamlet and Hieronimo that patience denied Ophelia and Isabella. Hieronimo is at his wit's end—playing. . . . Also, Hieronimo feels unique in his suffering, so it must be private. Horatio represents to him the perfection that Hamlet's father was to Hamlet. Of course Kyd is trying to express elusive emotional states without Shakespeare's supple and intimate language.

The question of madness is related to the difficulties of language and to predilections toward judgment on the end of the play. (Madness would be an extenuating circumstance in the view of some who want Act V to be a meting out of right ends.) Now that *Titus Andronicus* and *The Revenger's Tragedy* are regularly produced, critical reactions exclaiming at Kyd's bad taste—or expressing satisfaction at the triumph of justice—seem to relate particularly to closet reading.

The tongue-biting is a "superfluous horror" to a critic [Boas] who condemns the final murder and suicide and the "note of sheer savagery" prolonged in Andrea's epilogue; to another critic [Bowers], the *play* condemns Hieronimo for "his planned hypocrisy" in not taking revenge aboveboard. The Marshal is chastised for offering the King "not the slightest proof of the guilt of the victims," though through a legalistic "proper horror of oath-breaking" (his vow of silence to Bel-Imperia) he performs what is delicately called "autoglossatomy" [Johnson]. Yet here the ending is considered acceptable because Andrea is dispensing the judgment of God. Several critics have given Hieronimo a dispensation, based on his *Vindicta mihi* speech and various revenge concepts. In one view "the scheme of divine justice which governs the action" proves that "god is not dead" [D. J. Palmer, "Elizabethan Tragic Heroes," in *Elizabethan Theatre,* ed. John Russell Brown and Bernard Harris, 1966].

Another critical solution is to avoid moral problems by calling **The Spanish Tragedy** a "swinging revenge play" which lets the audience forget its daily docility and disapproval of extra-legal killing.

> If its moral attitudes are mistaken for the 'real life' attitudes of the dramatist, then the play has an appalling message. But if the play is seen as a thing of great—and skillful—artificiality, with standards of values which we accept while we are in the theatre, there is no problem at all about sympathizing with the hero. [Edwards]

A more subtle variation of this view presents Hieronimo as an artificer who allows us to see the killings with esthetic satisfaction through the "double response" of the audience to a play-within-a-play [Barry B. Adams, "The Audiences of **The Spanish Tragedy,**" *JEGP,* 68 (1969)]. Such critics urge us not to take it seriously. But a work of truly original power like **The Spanish Tragedy** gets that power from "real life" pressures in the artist. This play *does* have "an appalling message." The critic who rejects it acknowledges that even Marlowe never wrote "a less Christian play" [Edwards].

Why doesn't he discuss it then? The Tragic Flaw belongs not to drama but to criticism. The Elizabethan definitions of tragedy quoted by Doran suggest "horrors" and pity, not concepts of *hamartia* or justice [Madeleine Doran, in her *Endeavors of Art,* 1963]. Conservative or Christian critics like Dryden and Dr. Johnson were sometimes appalled by the barbaric lack of morality in the old English tragedy, but they did not try to blur the issue.

Edwards implies that one may consider the play as either instruction or entertainment. Doran's more interesting categories are artistic and ethical. (She calls the Horatian tradition of poetry for instruction "utilitarian.") Baker says tragic form "can be looked at from two important angles . . . craftsmanship or technique; and ethical or moral significance [*Induction to Tragedy,* 1939].

A false choice is set up here. The primary impact of a play is not moral or esthetic but metaphysical. The message is an image of the world: it is so. The final Babel, the play in a medley of tongues is—whether produced by the Elizabethans in English or "divers" languages—"suitable to the chaos" in Hieronimo's spirit. Barish goes on to describe speech as coming in the end "under a strange phosphorescent glare," becoming "surrealistic." But this chaos is not only inside Hieronimo. He makes the entire court feel what he feels. Then they know, at last. Then he need not bother to speak. Words express moral ideas and so are useless. Kyd shows the unspeakable. If the Marshal's "show trial" is a travesty of justice, that is because justice is a travesty.

The long recapitulation with the King's questions may represent overlapping alternate endings. But perhaps these unnecessary questions just mean "why? why?" What explanations could satisfy the bereaved King and Viceroy? As for Castile's death, it is in effect pathetic, a waste, like Paris' in Juliet's tomb. If more specific motives and effects are needed, Castile's questions anger the frenzied Hieronimo—and his death makes the King a mourner too.

This is the first English tragedy to go beyond good and evil. Royalty sits watching death and can't recognize it. The Viceroy will take his dead son on a "ship unmanned" (V, iii, 292)—an appropriate description of the state in chaos. Shakespeare never left such a mess. The gloating Ghost plans to dispense reward and punishment in the underworld. This final chorus is meant to show how inadequate the revenge concept is to what has occurred.

One of the most interesting critics of **The Spanish Tragedy** is the playwright who did the Additions of 1602. Whoever he was, he makes the Painter Scene a preview of the terrible end. Hieronimo demands the impossible of art:

> . . . and draw me five years younger than I am—do you see, sir, let five years go, let them go—like the Marshal of Spain, my wife Isabella standing by me, with a speaking look to my son Horatio . . . and my hand leaning upon his head . . .
>
> Canst paint a doleful cry?

Stein on Kyd's treatment of justice and revenge in *The Spanish Tragedy*:

To argue that Kyd distinguishes justice from revenge and that in doing so he may reflect the Elizabethan condemnation of private revenge is not to account for the power of **The Spanish Tragedy** or to determine the extent of its didacticism. Though the play may suggest that revenge is morally condemnable, it certainly emphasizes that the impulse toward revenge is terrifyingly human. Some, like Bel-imperia, may embrace the initial impulse and never sway from the bloody course of vengeance. Others, like Hieronimo, may serve the ideal of justice and (as they perceive they ought) pursue justice in place of revenge. But even the strongest may not be able to endure the frustration of their pursuit.

Hieronimo is the heart of the matter because he embodies both an ideal commitment to justice and a human impulse toward revenge. Because a Lorenzo can keep him from a source of justice, and because the pull toward revenge may be strengthened as justice is frustrated, Hieronimo can be driven to despair of all earthly justice and, consequently, to embrace revenge. In its separation of justice and revenge, Kyd's drama stands forth as a tragedy of Hieronimo's painful disintegration rather than a testament to the immutability of justice.

Charles H. Stein, in his "Justice and Revenge in The Spanish Tragedy," *Iowa State Journal of Research, August 1981.*

Well, sir, then bring me forth, bring me through
alley and alley, still with a distracted countenance going along. . . . Make me curse, make
me rave, make me cry, make me mad, make me
well again.

(IV, vi, 117 ff)

He wants first the impossible happy past and then the moment of horror repeated. Plainly, he wants a *moving* picture—the play.

His second wish is granted. The whole court shares the
horror. They are instructed when it happens to *them*. The
play-doctor of 1602—Webster or Shakespeare or another—knew that *The Spanish Tragedy* does not end in se-
rene acceptance or a moral lesson but in static horror:

O no, there is no end; the end is death and madness.

(IV, vi, 162-163)
(pp. 33-40)

*Margaret Lumb, "Beyond Revenge: 'The
Spanish Tragedy',"* in Mosaic: A Journal for
the Comparative Study of Literature and
Ideas, *Vol. IX, No. 1, Fall, 1975, pp. 33-40.*

Roger Stilling   (essay date 1976)

[*In the following excerpt, Stilling examines Kyd's use of
the love-death antithesis in* The Spanish Tragedy, *asserting that due consideration of the play's elements of
love is necessary to appreciate fully Kyd's emphasis on
hatred in the drama.*]

Of *The Spanish Tragedy* one could say that its distinctive
characteristic is the incorporation of love into a powerful
story of hatred. Indeed, in his treatment of the tale Kyd
seems to insist that this doubleness is a necessary part of
his dramatic strategy. The opening section, with its Hades
and ghosts, is built around ironies of eros and thanatos.
Don Andrea explains his own predicament in just these
terms:

For there in prime and pride of all my years,
By duteous service and deserving love,
In secret I possess'd a worthy dame,
Which hight sweet Bel-imperia by name.
But in the harvest of my summer joys
Death's winter nipp'd the blossoms of my bliss,
Forcing divorce betwixt my love and me.

(I. i. 8-14)

Such was his earthly situation. Because of it the rulers of
the underworld send him to act as Chorus to the play of
love and death that springs out of his own ambiguous situation.

The surface whimsy of this opening exchange masks its seriousness. Kyd is announcing that he has two themes in
mind and that they are interrelated in art as in life. This
remark of Philip Edwards [from his introduction to the
1959 edition of *The Spanish Tragedy*] points the direction
to be followed. With the meeting of Bel-imperia and Horatio, "character and plot are married, and the action drives
forward on its twin pistons of love and revenge." This interplay of love and revenge also organizes the symbolism
and moral values of the play. Kyd criticism has been pre-

dominantly one-sided, stressing mainly the death motive—the revenge plot and the character and moral status
of the avengers. But to judge the hatred, the lust for revenge, without its complicating and complementing opposite is to lose an influential source of richness in the play,
for it is more in Kyd's complex sense of the dramatic and
emotional potential of his material and his ability to exploit that material than in any pioneering of themes or
subject matter that we see his distinctive genius. The critical problem is, therefore, to show how Kyd works with
great care to establish a coherent framework for the study
of hatred by establishing in the midst of hate a sense of
love.

The forward action of *The Spanish Tragedy* falls into two
major parts: the first concerns the love of Bel-imperia and
Horatio and the jealousy and machinations that lead to
Horatio's death, the second mainly Hieronimo's madness,
his alliance with Bel-imperia and their bloody vengeance.
In both parts, the conflict of love and death exists as a a
theme and a source of metaphor, although in each the
manifestations differ. In the first part Kyd develops the
theme of love in terms of love's beauty, love's healing qualities, love's place and value as creator of human bonds; in
the second we see how the violent frustration and negation
of love lead in turn to more violence, though so complex
is Kyd's handling of his themes that one line of development hardly exists without the other.

In this [essay] I deal with the first part of the play, which
for clarity can be divided into three major scenes or groups
of scenes: (a) the long and complicated Act I. iv in which
the male rivals are set in patterns of opposition around
Bel-imperia; (b) the counterpointed first and second scenes
of Act II, in which flawed ideas of love are set against a
natural and beautiful one; and (c) Act II. iv—the brilliantly orchestrated murder of Horatio in the bower.

The focus of Act I. iv is unquestionably Bel-imperia, and
one could argue that she is the first genuinely seductive
heroine to take the Elizabethan stage. In her, the bold presentation of female sexuality is established early. We have
learned already that she had been enjoying a sexual relationship with Andrea before his death. The point is made
stronger by the nature of her first appearance, which—
coming as it does after three scenes devoted mainly to public pomp and splendor—has a certain quiet provocative-
ness. She is seen alone with Don Horatio; they talk of her
dead lover; the two on stage are united by their temporary
isolation where previously all had been bustle and crowds.
They are further united by their mutual love for Don Andrea. No words of love pass between them at this first
meeting, but a token does change hands; Bel-imperia gives
Horatio the scarf which Andrea had worn to battle. The
mantle of the dead man passes by means of one of the great
Romance symbols to the one most worthy to succeed him.

The tone of this exchange is decorous and calm, much
more melancholy than sensual. Bel-imperia keeps well
within the limits of courtly respectfulness:

For 'twas my favour at his last depart.
But now wear thou it both for him and me,
For after him thou hast deserv'd it best.
But for thy kindness in his life and death,

Be sure while Bel-imperia's life endures,
She will be Don Horatio's thankful friend.

(I. iv. 47-52)

And Horatio's answer is pitched to the same key: "And, Madam, Don Horatio will not slack / Humbly to serve fair Bel-imperia" (I. iv. 53-54). The two are linked therefore by this poetic unity, the unity of souls being suggested by the consistency of tone, the impression of unspoken communication residing in the spoken. I stress this aspect for two reasons. First, exchanges such as this and later ones demonstrate how far the dramatists had come since *Gismond* in their ability to depict close personal relationships, to write poetry that is also genuine dialogue. The second reason springs from the first. Bel-imperia is also being courted by the captured Portuguese prince who in dubious circumstances killed her first lover. The gulf between Prince Balthazar and Bel-imperia is created first of all from this fact, but it is maintained, made dramatically alive, by a radical shift in the tone of conversation when the two are together. Where Horatio had spoken the language of courtly service with obvious sincerity and honesty, Balthazar speaks it in a way which empties it of meaning. The result is the kind of distancing effect pointed out by Wolfgang Clemen [in his *English Tragedy Before Shakespeare*, 1961] and demonstrated by such a dialogue as the following:

LOR: But here the prince is come to visit you.
BEL: That argues that he lives in liberty.
BAL: No madam, but in pleasing servitude.
BEL: Your prison then belike is your conceit.
BAL: Ay, by conceit my freedom is enthrall'd.
BEL: Then with conceit enlarge yourself again.

(I. iv. 79-84)

The stichomythia . . . underlines a lack of contact which later becomes aggravated into open enmity.

The scene ends with a piece of stage action that reinforces the effects made in the first part. Bel-imperia drops a glove in leaving. A contest ensues between the male rivals, a duel reduced to social proportions which Horatio wins by retrieving the glove. He then receives it as a further token of favor. Five quick lines complete the action:

HOR: Madam, your glove.
BEL: Thanks good Horatio, take it for thy pains.
BAL: Signior Horatio stoop'd in happy time.
HOR: I reap'd more grace than I deserv'd or hop'd.
LOR: My lord, be not dismay'd for what is past, . . .

(I. iv. 100-104)

The very briskness of it, the quickness with which Bel-imperia and Horatio respond to each other and exclude the other two, the first hint in Balthazar's line of his looming jealous reaction indicate that with Kyd, English tragedy was as ready to deal dramatically with the subtleties of love as the comedies of Lyly and his followers.

The gulf opened in Act I. iv widens rapidly in the first two scenes of Act II. On one hand we have Bel-imperia and Horatio coming closer together and on the other the closer alliance of Balthazar and Bel-imperia's brother Lorenzo.

From the start Kyd draws Balthazar as a courtly fool. The questionable nature of his triumph over Andrea and the exaggerated quality of his courtly rhetoric mark him as one even before we learn that he has fallen in love with Bel-imperia. His first conversation with her (a part of which has already been quoted) confirms the first impression. Kyd gives him language which can be nothing else than a parody of the abuses of customary Romance speech and emphasizes this by having the other characters intensely conscious of his absurdity. His keynote is unreality, embodied in a ridiculous, transcendental love rhetoric which seems all the more nonsensical in comparison with the earthy realism and calm lyricism of Bel-imperia and Horatio. With the latter, Kyd penetrates to what is true and beautiful in courtly language. He gives Balthazar what is patently false and untrue. The answer Balthazar makes to Bel-imperia's witticism—"A heartless man and live? A miracle!" (I. iv. 88)—is typical: "Ay lady, love can work such miracles" (I. iv. 89). His final plea is another example:

Yes, to your gracious self must I complain,
In whose fair answer lies my remedy,
On whose perfection all my thoughts attend,
On whose aspect mine eyes find beauty's bower,
In whose translucent breast my heart is lodg'd.

(I. iv. 93-97)

All the cliché terms—"gracious self," "complain," "fair answer," "remedy," "perfection," "beauty's bower," "translucent breast"—are dutifully and stiffly trotted out. Bel-imperia calls them "words of course" (I. iv. 98), and just before this speech of Balthazar's, Lorenzo has told him to "let go these ambages" (I. iv. 90). Both characters point to the fact that Balthazar's love language has no roots in profound emotion.

Balthazar's emotional facility is not at this point dangerous, but the doggedness with which Kyd keeps Balthazar talking as he does dramatizes the relationship between shallow, self-regarding language and shallow, self-regarding emotions and the potential danger of the combination of the two. That Balthazar is self-obsessed is shown by the luxuriant self-humiliation of the speech which opens Act II:

Yet might she love me for my valiancy,
Ay, but that's slander'd by captivity.
Yet might she love me to content her sire,
Ay, but her reason masters his desire.

(II. i. 19-22)

When Kyd moves Balthazar into the more serious realms of love and death, his stiff jog-trot rhythms express perfectly the facile and superficial logic by which he moves to his very dangerous decision:

Both well, and ill: it makes me glad and sad:
Glad, that I know the hinderer of my love,
Sad, that I fear she hates me whom I love.
Glad, that I know on whom to be reveng'd,
Sad, that she'll fly me if I take revenge.
Yet must I take revenge or die myself,
For love resisted grows impatient.

(II. i. 111-17)

In other words, Kyd uses Balthazar here to suggest that

a man with so limited a feeling for love and the language of love will have a similarly superficial understanding of the meaning of death. Diction points to morality, and the study of one becomes the study of the other.

These comments apply as well to Lorenzo's very different style; his speech is direct and vivid, but its very precision indicates a kind of moral insufficiency. He is supremely confident and seems supremely knowledgeable:

> Let's go my lord, your staying stays revenge.
> Do you but follow me and gain your love:
> Her favour must be won by his remove.
> (II. i. 134-36)

But the third line above marks him an ignoramus about the nature of love, as the story proves. Like Balthazar he is profoundly egocentric, and his egocentrism finds outlet in the need to manipulate and dominate. This trait dominates his concept of love:

> My lord, though Bel-imperia seem thus coy,
> Let reason hold you in your wonted joy:
> In time the savage bull sustains the yoke,
> In time all haggard hawks will stoop to lure,
> In time small wedges cleave the hardest oak, . . .
> (II. i. 1-5)

To him love is a process of humbling the loved one, bringing her to heel; but this combination of brutality and pragmatism results in a self-defeating blindness to the irrational strength of the bond that love can form. The Lorenzo point of view has its local victories (with Iago, for instance), but—in Elizabethan romantic tragedy—no staying power, no lasting value.

Set against the obtuse self-love of these two, Horatio and Bel-imperia seem ideal lovers. The chief note of their relationship is quiet but sensuous decorum. The result is some poetry of quiet, beautiful joy. After war and loss come the still moments of calm and happiness, expressed in images of the sea and of music. Bel-imperia says:

> My heart, sweet friend, is like a ship at sea:
> She wisheth port, where riding all at ease,
> She may repair what stormy times have worn,
> And learning on the shore, may sing with joy. . . .
> (II. ii. 7-10)

They arrange to meet in Hieronimo's bower, a place which is itself a stage metaphor carrying all the Elizabethan connotations of pastoral peace and safety ("The court were dangerous, that place is safe" [II. ii. 44].) and Edenic love and sexuality. Kyd seems very much involved in his writing here, for the verse is natural and limpid enough to approach the Shakespearean:

> Our hour shall be when Vesper gins to rise
> That summons home distressful travellers.
> There none shall hear us but the harmless birds:
> Happily the gentle nightingale
> Shall carol us asleep ere we be ware,
> And singing with the prickle at her breast,
> Tell our delight and mirthful dalliance.
> Till then each hour will seem a year and more.
> (II. ii. 45-52)

Such details as the "distressful travellers" and the gentle nightingale "singing with the prickle at her breast" complicate and give resonance to the calm lyricism of Bel-imperia's description by hinting that their love is not (and is not to be) unalloyed happiness.

This point is made in a much stronger manner by the brilliant staging of the scene. Shortly before the lovers speak the lines just quoted, Lorenzo and the rejected Balthazar have been shown creeping into a secret vantage place above the lovers. As Bel-imperia and Horatio speak of love, the two watchers—death personified—are driven . . . into a state of revengeful fury. Their unheard threats counterpoint the lovers' exchanges, enveloping them in a miasma of morbid, sadistic hatred. As the lovers speak, Lorenzo intones his curses:

> Watch still mine eyes, to see this love disjoin'd,
> Hear still mine ears, to hear them both lament,
> Live heart, to joy at fond Horatio's fall.
> (II. ii. 21-23)

Kyd thus makes a powerful theater image out of what was a nondramatic voyeur scene in *Gismond*. The gain by this kind of stagecraft is multifold. In this context I would list three main ones . . .: the direct visual involvement of the audience; the emphasis on the frustration felt by Balthazar, who can only see, while Horatio and Bel-imperia touch; and the impressiveness of the audience's realization (they being able to see and hear both killers and lovers) that the expectations of love are to be balked by death.

The first part of the play comes to its climax in the very powerful murder scene in the bower. In this scene Kyd merges all the possible implications and ironies of the love-death antithesis. He first induces a sense of foreboding and mystery which arises naturally out of the precarious secrecy of the lovers' affair and the tension which attends the anticipation of lovemaking, as well as any premonition of danger:

> BEL: I follow thee my love, and will not back,
> Although my fainting heart controls my soul.
> (II. iv. 6-7)

Then references to the song of the nightingale lead us into the gentle ambiguities of the love-war relationship, of the relationship between Mars and Venus, of darting kisses like spears, and finally the doubleness of the idea contained in the word *yield* :

> BEL: Nay then, to gain the glory of the field,
> My twining arms shall yoke and make thee yield.
> (II. iv. 42-43)

All this would, of course, be acted out as it is spoken, thus bringing the ever-increasing intimacy of physical contact between the lovers to its penultimate moment. This moment itself is graced by the sensitive, dramatic use of the most fundamental of all the loving versions of the love-death antithesis, the death of the ego in the moment of passion:

> BEL: O let me go, for in my troubled eyes
> Now may'st thou read that life in passion dies.
> HOR: O stay awhile and I will die with thee,

So shalt thou yield and yet have conquer'd me.

(II. iv. 46-49)

Kyd exploits all the bitterly ironic poetic and dramatic paradoxes of the situation. It is at this moment that the lovers make their shocked discovery of the murderers and the murder itself is executed. Appropriately enough it is staged as a deliberate and gross verbal and physical parody of the act of love. As Lorenzo thrusts home he says: "Ay, thus, and thus, these are the fruits of love" (II. iv. 55). This is a crowded moment but a very important one, for . . . the moment of death is the moment when each character reveals himself fully in relation to the idea of love. The final words of Bel-imperia, for instance, put the stamp of authenticity on her love by showing its essential selflessness:

O save his life and let me die for him!
O save him brother, save him Balthazar:
I lov'd Horatio but he lov'd not me.

(II. iv. 56-58)

One cannot help but think of Coleridge's cryptic lecture note on love [in his *Shakespearean Criticism*, Vol. 1]: "With love, pure love, the anxiety for the safety of the object—the disinterestedness by which it is distinguished from the counterfeits of its name." By the same token, Lorenzo's and Balthazar's responses reveal the full egocentrism of their natures: Lorenzo in terms of his preoccupation with status—"Although his life were still ambitious proud, / Yet is he at the highest now he is dead" (II. iv. 60-61)—and Balthazar (wildly imagining that his deed demonstrates profound affection) in terms of his lunatic insensitivity. He insists to the end: "But Balthazar loves Bel-imperia" (II. iv. 59).

The remainder of the play is dominated by Hieronimo's revenge, but the reverberations of the first part are never lost, particularly since Hieronimo's revenge has its robots in the first part and the revenge theme itself proceeds side by side with another version of the love theme, that of the Enforced or Arranged Marriage. It is primarily to this latter theme that I now turn.

The "enforced marriage" (to use the term given the practice by George Wilkins, the author of a seventeenth-century tragicomedy on the subject [*The Miseries of Enforced Marriage*]) or the "arranged marriage" (the term used by William Empson [in his *"The Spanish Tragedy,"* Nimbus (1956)] becomes with Kyd's play one of the leading minor motifs in Elizabethan and Jacobean tragedy. The central characteristic of this convention (in society and in drama) is that such a marriage normally victimizes the woman involved, and, indeed, the practice could probably not have arisen without a widespread feeling among males that women were chattel. Therefore, any betterment in the status of women would undermine the conventions of male dominance; certainly the idea of romantic love would do so, since love implies the acceptance and celebration of the beloved's individual humanity. Furthermore, the marriage for financial, social, or political reasons is a direct denial of the romantic marriage, the marriage for love. . . . In essence the Arranged Marriage in **The Spanish Tragedy** stands in the same relation to the lovers as Tancred's denial of his daughter's desire to wed

did to Gismond and Guishard, since both actions are negative, frustrate a very powerful natural force, and end in disaster.

In **The Spanish Tragedy** the Arranged Marriage motif is muted but very powerful, particularly since it has its roots in the very peace treaty which ends the war between Spain and Portugal and its end at the instant of Hieronimo's and Bel-imperia's vengeance. The first scene in which it is explicitly mentioned (it is implicit in Balthazar's early protestations of love) is Act II. iii, where it is significantly sandwiched between the scene in which Prince Balthazar and Lorenzo murderously observe Bel-imperia and Horatio exchanging their first love vows and that in which they murder Horatio. The ironic implication of the juxtaposition is clear: that the Arranged Marriage, carried on at a high diplomatic level, is to be closely associated with the murder of Horatio. Nor is this just a symbolic association; whether Castile or the king knew about the murder or not (and there is nothing in the text to suggest they do), it is a necessary step in the progress which will end in a state wedding. The actions of Lorenzo—the most dedicated, self-conscious *politician* of the group—make it clear that he realizes this fact; his downfall is that he expects no trouble in bringing his sister to his way of thinking, his same high valuation of political advancement.

In any case, although Castile and the king cannot be convicted of premeditated murder (as William Empson would convict Castile), they are implicated in it by their casual acceptance of the clichés of male dominance. Their colossal sense of their own importance makes it impossible for them to take Bel-imperia seriously as a free agent with her own mind and heart. Castile's complacency on the matter is almost amusing; the repeated *I* and the verb *stoop* give him away in this passage:

Although she coy it as becomes her kind,
And yet dissemble that she loves the prince,
I doubt not, I, but she will stoop in time.
And were she froward, which she will not be,
Yet herein shall she follow my advice,
Which is to love him or forgo my love.

(II. iii. 3-8)

The final threat is more serious, however, because it betrays the superficiality of his idea of love. Castile never considers the possibility that his daughter could not love Prince Balthazar and neither does the king, who on the spot commits her to the marriage. Their ignorance of the power of love, combined with the unthinking exercise of their own self-will over the fortunes of a daughter, puts them in the same category as Tancred and Shakespeare's old Capulet. Indeed, so often do the Elizabethans use this character type as an agent of death in love tragedies that one can only conclude that it is at least partly intended as a foil to the ever-increasing belief in the sanctity of personal affairs, particularly for women. Such must be the conclusion here at any rate. The ironies are too strong to suggest otherwise. How ominous, for instance, the king's innocent words sound in the larger context in which Kyd has placed them:

Now brother, you must take some little pains
To win fair Bel-imperia from her will:

Young virgins must be ruled by their friends.
The prince is amiable and loves her well,
If she neglect him and forgo his love,
She both will wrong her own estate and
    ours: . . .

                                        (II. iii. 41-46)

The king's philosophy is Lorenzo's philosophy precisely, and the vigorous Lorenzo pushes the idea of "some little pains" to its ultimate logical conclusion. Lorenzo says as much to Bel-imperia in explaining why he killed Horatio and spirited her into seclusion; he had, he says falsely, been sent ahead of the king and Castile to Hieronimo and found Bel-imperia with Horatio:

Why then, remembering that old disgrace
Which you for Don Andrea had endur'd,
And now were likely longer to sustain,
By being found so meanly accompanied,
Thought rather, for I knew no readier mean,
To thrust Horatio forth my father's way.

                                        (III. x. 54-59)

The patronizing tone, the heavy implication that the name of honor is worth more than a human life, the inability or unwillingness to imagine that her lovemaking is anything more than transient lust, the expectation that she will calm down and see things his way: all these are present in this short speech as in the whole scene. Bel-imperia gulls her brother fatally by seeming to fall in with his stereotype of woman, by playing the ironist and appearing to acquiesce in the political marriage. Hieronimo, fighting down bouts of madness, plays the same kind of game and the two come together to subvert the marriage feast and, in so doing, orchestrate the final love-death ironies.

There is a definite implication that the last acts of this play are meant to represent the paradoxical triumph of love over death, through revenge. In the first two acts, Lorenzo and Balthazar were the hunters, pouncing at a climactic moment to substitute a death act for a love act. In the last half of the play, Horatio's lover and his father, drawn into conjunction by their mutual love for the murdered man, are the hunters, coming together over a series of carefully counterpointed scenes to substitute a second death for a second act of love, the expected marriage of Bel-imperia and Balthazar. The symmetry of the design is striking and—particularly when we consider how many times in Elizabethan tragedy this reversal occurs—requires a name, if only to acknowledge that the motif exists as a repeated complement to the Arranged Marriage theme. My suggestion would be the Fatal Wedding or Deadly Nuptial.

Kyd's use of Deadly Nuptial symbolism is vivid. Act III ends in a prophetic dumb-show (staged by Revenge for Andrea's benefit) in which the symbolic qualities of red and black, of light and dark, and of marriage and murder are used to effect a deepening of the dramatic mood within the context of the love-death theme:

The two first, the nuptial torches bore,
As brightly burning as the mid-day's sun:
But after them doth Hymen hie as fast,
Clothed in sable, and a saffron robe,

And blows them out and quencheth them with
    blood,
As discontent that things continue so.

                                        (III. xv. 30-35)

Andrea's gloss introduces the idea of the triumph of love:

Sufficeth me, thy meaning's understood,
And thanks to thee and those infernal powers
That will not tolerate a lover's woe.

                                        (III. xv. 36-38)

Taken together these lines could be seen as the author's commentary on the whole action of the play.

For his final turn on the theme, Kyd uses the special conventions of his own trade and of this evolving genre of love tragedy. He makes Hieronimo the author, director, and star of a play of passion and death—the tragedy of Soliman and Perseda—wherein Balthazar plays a part that parallels his role in **The Spanish Tragedy** and Hieronimo plays one not unlike that of Lorenzo:

HIER: *Let not Erasto live to grieve great Soliman.*
BAL: *Dear is Erasto in our princely eye.*
HIER: *But if he be your rival, let him die.*
BAL: *Why, let him die, so love commandeth me.*

                                        (IV. iv. 45-48)

The conclusion of the play finds both Balthazar and Lorenzo murdered, Bel-imperia dead by suicide, and Hieronimo explaining the meaning of his revenge in terms of the love-death relationship:

The cause was love, whence grew this mortal
    hate,
The hate, Lorenzo and young Balthazar,
The love, my son to Bel-imperia.

                                        (IV. iv. 98-100)

This is baldly stated, and it presents in outline the thematic structure which gives the play's ironic, deadly ending its considerable resonance. Hieronimo's play of love and death is ostensibly an ornament to a royal marriage. It proves to be no gesture of love, however, but an act of death revenging the death of love. Already then, in this the second of the plays on love and death, we find the dramatist seeking fresh levels of significance in the opposition of these two great ultimates and the genre itself finding its basic formal and intellectual principles.

I would put forward two final points as a means of moving to a larger interpretation. First, there is one line of imagery which connects Andrea, Horatio, Bel-imperia, Horatio's mother Isabella, and Hieronimo and excludes—except as enemies—all the others. This is nature or pastoral imagery. I have already mentioned its intimate connection with the love poetry of Bel-imperia and Horatio. It is also the imagery of the "fields of love" (I. i. 42) which Don Andrea sees after death, with their "green myrtle trees and cypress shades" (I. i. 44). These are linked with the earthly field of love, the love bower in which Horatio and Bel-imperia meet and Horatio dies. Hieronimo's wild laments associate the bower with life and pleasure, and he refers to his son as "Sweet lovely rose, ill-pluck'd before thy time" (II. v. 46). Somewhat later he makes reference to the participation of nature in his own mourning:

The blust'ring winds, conspiring with my words,
At my lament have mov'd the leaveless trees,
Disrob'd the meadows of their flower'd green,
Made mountains marsh with spring-tides of my
    tears, . . .

(III. vii. 5–8)

The mad Isabella's frenzy takes the ironic form of vengeance upon nature itself. Cutting down the arbor, she says:

Down with these branches and these loathsome
    boughs
Of this unfortunate and fatal pine: . . .
I will not leave a root, a stalk, a tree,
A bough, a branch, a blossom, nor a leaf,
No, not an herb within this garden plot—
Accursed complot of my misery.
Fruitless for ever may this garden be, . . .

(IV. ii. 6-7, 10-14)

The full relationship of all these symbols is made clear through her frenzied identification of herself and her son (and by implication Hieronimo and Bel-imperia) with nature through the larger idea of sexual love as a creative force:

And as I curse this tree from further fruit,
So shall my womb be cursed for his sake,
And with this weapon will I wound the breast,
    She stabs herself
The hapless breast, that gave Horatio suck.

(IV. ii. 35-38)

Her suicidal madness points up the power of her love for her son, and her self-inflicted death identifies her still more closely with those others who have lost their taste for life because of the violent loss of a loved one.

In other words, all the sympathetic characters are unified by the bond of love, whether it be erotic or familial, and by the imagery of nature. . . . Such a grouping also helps make one final puzzle reasonably clear; Castile's death and his relegation to eternal torture find their logic in the fact that he is a man who attempted to meddle for extrapersonal reasons in an area of his daughter's life which was her own closest concern. This made him one of the forces of death, and it is this that he pays for with his life.

My final point concerns the wider application of these ideas in terms of the development of the revenge play. Most critics have tended to treat the idea of vengeance in a vacuum, as if it arose from emotional nullity, a zero degree of feeling. The result has been that arguments about the moral emphasis of the revenge drama often have been sidetracked into somewhat sterile, abstract discussions of Elizabethan ideas of revenge divorced from a full response to the whole of the dramatic poetry and action. This passage from Fredson Bowers's *Elizabethan Revenge Tragedy* shows how tenuous the connection between abstract theory and emotional response really is:

Under these circumstances—and the evidence of the tragedies bears out the theory—the revenger of the drama started with the sympathy of the audience if his cause were good and if he acted according to the typically English notions of straightforward fair play. It was only, as with

Hieronimo (although this example may seem the most debatable of the many available), when he turned to "Machiavellian" treacherous intrigues that the audience began to veer against him.

This seems very shaky to me, as anything resting on so fragile a moral foundation as "typically English notions of straightforward fair play" must inevitably be. This is one reason why love must have a part in any discussion of plays about hate. It is only love which makes hatred meaningful, whether it is set in opposition to hatred or shown in the process of becoming hatred. In *The Spanish Tragedy,* . . . love and hate are seen in both of these contexts. Acknowledgment of this brings us down on the side of those critics for whom Hieronimo remains a compelling, sympathetic figure. Professor Edwards puts it perfectly [in his *Thomas Kyd and Early Elizabethan Tragedy,* 1966]:

There can be no doubt that the audience is on his side, whatever the Elizabethan preachers and moralists said about private revenge. We are in a different place from the preacher's auditory. . . . Hieronimo's voice is the voice of protest against criminal cruelty, the voice of real sorrow and love.

What is said here of Hieronimo is equally true of all his associates, and it is these associations, these bonds, that make it true of Hieronimo. (pp. 26-40)

Roger Stilling, "The Spanish Tragedy," in his Love and Death in Renaissance Tragedy, *Louisiana State University Press, 1976, pp. 26-40.*

Peter Sacks   (essay date 1982)

[*Sacks, a South-African born American poet and scholar, is best known for* The English Elegy: Studies in the Genre From Spenser to Yeats *(1985). In the excerpt below, Sacks examines* The Spanish Tragedy *as a new kind of literature that was preoccupied with grief and remorse due to the prevalence of suffering and death in England at that time. According to the critic, the revengeful characters of Kyd's play reflect a "moving dramatization of the dilemmas that ensue when man's need for consolation or redress is obstructed by his loss of faith in the power of art's reply."*]

Where words prevail not, violence prevails.
    The Spanish Tragedy II. 1. 110

    The mere word's a slave,
Debauch'd on every tomb, on every grave
A lying trophy; and as oft is dumb
Where dust and damn'd oblivion is the tomb
Of honour'd bones indeed. What should be said?
    All's Well That Ends Well II. 3. 135-39

Toward the end of the sixteenth century, the question of "what should be said" in the face of suffering and death had become particularly vexing. For when supposedly immutable principles of divine, human, and natural order were increasingly suspected of being no more than figural impositions on an essentially intractable reality, the traditional means of consolation were robbed of their protec-

316

tive charm. As Thomas Nashe spelled it out in 1592 [in his "A Litany in Time of Plague"], "Hell's executioner / Hath no ears for to hear / What vain art can reply."

Many poems of the time offer moving testimony to this predicament. But it is in such plays as *The Spanish Trage-dy, Titus Andronicus,* and *Hamlet* that one finds the most moving dramatization of the dilemmas that ensue when man's need for consolation or redress is obstructed by his loss of faith in the power of art's reply. By "art" I here understand not only such fictions as those of pastoral elegy, but also the no less artificial mediations of justice and the law. These plays reveal that no work of mourning can be successfully completed without positive recourse to various forms of such mediation; and while they offer penetrating views of melancholics and revengers, they invite us to study these failed mourners not as pure phenomena, but rather in their inescapable and unhappy relation to such artful fabrics as those of language and the law. (p. 576)

The Spanish Tragedy begins with a shuffle of judgment in the next world, implying that even there justice may be a problem. The three-fold judge pronounces conflicting opinions as to whether the ghost of Andrea should be committed to the afterworld of lovers, or of soldiers. In a referral to another court, so typical of the late Elizabethan age, Andrea's case is presented to Pluto, who in turn allows Proserpine to summon Revenge. Revenge leads Andrea through the gates of horn ("Where dreams have passage in the silent night"), to view the ensuing action on earth. The suggestion is, therefore, that the entire play to come is but a dead man's dream.

We move to the court of Spain, to hear the King rejoicing over his victory against Portugal: "Then blessed be heaven and guider of the heavens, / From whose fair influence such justice flows" (I. 2. 9-10). His words, echoing the traditional view of justice, will of course be ironized throughout the play, as the heavenly source of influence is shown to be in fact a diamond-hard wall, impervious to the words or needs of man. As though to introduce the problem, the king is immediately embroiled in a scene of judgment where he must decide between the claims of Horatio and Lorenzo, rival captors of the Portuguese prince Balthazar, who had slain Andrea. His words, "Then, by my judgment, thus your strife shall end," will also be ironized by the following conflict.

It is probably unnecessary to rehearse the plot, except to notice the persistent slighting of language at crucial moments of its development. Bellimperia, in love now with Horatio, rejects Balthazar's suit: "these are but words of course." And her brother, Lorenzo, in league with Balthazar, bribes Pedringano "not with fair words, but store of golden coin" to assist in the murder of Horatio. Lorenzo has, after all, decided that "where words prevail not, violence prevails."

The murder of Horatio is a vicious rupture and perversion of a miniature pastoral world. "The court were dangerous, that place is safe," said Bellimperia, referring as a rendezvous to "the pleasant bow'r the field" of Horatio's father. Yet it is in this allegedly idyllic spot, "made for pleasure, not for death," that Horatio is hung up in the trees and

stabbed to death: " 'What, will you murder me?' 'Ay, thus and thus: these are the fruits of love.' " This perverse substitution of death for fruit is echoed much later by one of Hieronimo's laments for his son:

> This was the tree; I set it of a kernel: . . .
> It grew a gallows, and did bear our son
> It bore thy fruit and mine—O wicked, wicked
>   plant!
>
> (III. 12. 64-72)

And the motif culminates in the extraordinary scene in which Isabella, insane with grief, destroys the remnants of this pastoral world.

Isabella's rampage is a literal *enactment* of the elegiac verbal curse against nature, or of the pathetic fallacy which asserts nature's suffering. For Isabella has none of the elegist's necessary trust in words. She has heard and said enough:

> Tell me no more!
> Since neither piety nor pity moves
> The king to justice or compassion,
> I will revenge myself upon this place
> Where thus they murder'd my beloved son.
> [She cuts down the arbour.]
>
> (IV. 2. 1-5)

We notice the "thus" of the revenger. She destroys the trees "in the same way as" the murderer had killed her son.

> Down with them Isabella; rent them up,
> And burn the roots from whence the rest is
>   sprung.
> I will not leave a root, a stalk, a tree,
> A bough, a branch, a blossom, nor a leaf,
> No, not an herb within this garden-plot—:
> Accursed complot of my misery.
> Fruitless for ever may this garden be.
>
> (IV. 2. 10-16)

Isabella's literalization of the language of elegy, her inability to rest content with the mere words, will of course be matched by her husband's similar refusal to allow theatrical pretense to remain mere pretense. Her destruction of the pastoral setting is followed by her own suicide, another actual performance of the kind of "breast-wounding" or "piercing" that we encounter only figuratively in elegies.

It is, however, Hieronimo who most claims our attention, for it is he who most suffers from a sense of the inadequacy of language and from an attendant loss of faith in justice:

> O sacred heav'ns! if this unhallow'd deed, . . .
> Shall unreveal'd and unrevenged pass,
> How should we term your dealings to be just,
> If you unjustly deal with those that in your jus-
>   tice trust?
>
> (III. 2. 5-11)

> Yet still tormented is my tortur'd soul
> With broken sighs and restless passions,
> That winged mount; and, hov'ring in the air,
> Beat at the windows of the brightest heavens,
> Soliciting for justice and revenge:
> But they are plac'd in those empyreal heights,
> Where, countermur'd with walls of diamond,

I find the place impregnable; and they
Resist my woes, and give my words no way.

(III. 7. 10-19)

Here then, for Hieronimo, is the essential failure of language to serve as an intermediary agent of justice or compensation. The human court is equally impregnable, leaving him to circle desperately, calling for "Justice, O, Justice to Hieronimo . . . Justice, O, justice, justice, gentle king." By its very repetition, the word is losing valency, becoming a mere sound.

In a crucial scene Hieronimo receives the petition of an old man seeking redress for the murder of a son. Declaring that "on this earth justice will not be found," Hieronimo proposes a quest in which the old man will act as his Orphic courier:

> I'll down to hell, and in this passion
> Knock at the dismal gates of Pluto's court, . . .
> Yet lest the triple-headed porter should
> Deny my passage to the slimy strand,
> The Thracian poet thou shalt counterfeit:
> Come on, old father, be my Orpheus,
> And if thou canst no notes upon the harp,
> Then sound the burden of thy sore heart's-grief,
> Till we do gain that Proserpine may grant
> Revenge on them that murdered my son.
> Then will I rent and tear them, thus and thus,
> Shiv'ring their limbs in pieces with my teeth.
> [Tears the papers.]

(III. 13. 108-22)

Since Moschus' elegy for Bion, the figure of Orpheus has been close to the consciousness of many mourners, but that closeness is by no means unequivocal. On the one hand, Orpheus is an attractive figure, having the power to enchant not only the natural world, but also the guardians of the threshold to the world of death. On the other hand, as Ovid emphasizes, he is also a negative model for the mourner. For Orpheus insists on rescuing his *actual* wife from death, rather than a figure or substitute for her. His looking back, and her subsequent return to the underworld are proof that she herself can never be revived. And it is Orpheus' failure to reattach his affections elsewhere that brings about his martyrdom. The resentful women tear him apart precisely because of his refusal to turn away from the dead.

Like Orpheus, Hieronimo will die for his refusal to accept what might be considered the mediated forms of consolation. His final transgression will be to literalize the actions of what is supposed to be a play within the play, to kill *in fact* the victims whose "killing" he might only have *represented* in theater. In the light of this association of Hieronimo with Orpheus, we understand more fully, perhaps, why it is that he is finally led in the next world to the fields "where Orpheus plays." For the moment, however, we are left with the image of Hieronimo, in his role as Chief Justice of Spain, literally ripping apart what represents the fabric of language and the law, in fact avenging himself against it with the same "thus and thus" equation that his wife makes in the arbor. (pp. 580-84)

At Hieronimo's insistence, the play within the play is enacted in various languages, as though to emphasize his

sense of the opacity of *any* language, and to "breed confusion," an impossibility of interpretation such that action itself will seem to have the only meaning. After the killings, he disabuses the audience by explaining how the mediate has in fact been made immediate ("Haply you think—but bootless are your thoughts—/ That this is fabulously counterfeit"). Significantly, Hieronimo concludes his entire war against language, expressing the "rupture of [his] part," by biting out his tongue. And as if this were not yet sufficient proof of how consistently his violence has been assaulting language itself, he makes signs for a knife to mend his pen, but instead uses the knife to stab the Duke of Castile and at last to kill himself.

One cannot forget that Kyd has framed his play by the suggestion of its being Andrea's dream, and by the fact that it is viewed by Andrea and Revenge as audience, like ourselves. Kyd thus implies that, although imperceptible to the benighted Hieronimo, there *is* contact between the diamantine heavens and the fallen world. Hieronimo's words do penetrate above, and the principle of Revenge does watch over events. But this is paradoxical, for there would have been no revenge had not Hieronimo felt the absence of justly enforced retribution and had he not felt compelled to take justice into his own hands. However much one may invoke theories about the so-called "scourge of god" attitude, Hieronimo is plagued by his very *separation* from an impersonal or transcendent authority. Indeed, by having Hieronimo become insanely violent, killing even the innocent Duke, Kyd suggests that the instruments of revenge are themselves always imperfect, and that there may be some flaw in the actual embodiment or vehicle of this now dubious principle we see personified as leaning over the play.

Critics have nevertheless argued that Kyd is deliberately portraying the aberrations of a man who loses faith in justice, and who abandons spiritual hope. But the hapless, mournfully secular nature of the action and language of the play nevertheless goes a long way towards shaking our belief that there *is* another, "higher" level other than merely that which is shared by the dramatist and spectator. Indeed, when we recall that Revenge is the usher of Andrea's dream, we see these two inhabitants of that "upper" realm as little more than versions of the playwright and his audience. (pp. 584-85)

Peter Sacks, "Where Words Prevail Not: Grief, Revenge, and Language in Kyd and Shakespeare," in ELH, Vol. 49, No. 3, Fall, 1982, pp. 576-601.

Philip Edwards   (essay date 1990)

[*Edwards, an English scholar and educator, is the author of several critical studies on drama of the Elizabethan period and the editor of various works from that era. In the following excerpt, he discusses Kyd's use of pagan deities and the question of divine justice as a central concern of* The Spanish Tragedy.]

It is, surely, remarkable that Thomas Kyd should provide a pagan context for his story of a modern Christian Spain. Though *The Spanish Tragedy* is not an historical play, its fictional events have a sixteenth-century appearance. Andrea, an officer in the Spanish army, has met his death fighting the Portuguese, and his corpse travels back 1500 years on a journey through an elaborately-described Virgilian underworld and the gloomy realm of Pluto. As the play opens, his spirit has arrived in his own Spain to observe the events which are to follow his death; to observe events in his own Christian Spain as they will be relentlessly controlled and directed by "those infernal powers" dwelling in an ancient pagan underworld from which he has been temporarily released.

> Imagine thou
> What 'tis to be subject to destiny! (3. 15. 27-28)

All the passionate effort of the characters, Bel-Imperia, Lorenzo, Balthazar, Hieronimo, the Spanish King and the Portuguese Viceroy, is exploited by the forces of destiny and deflected from its intended or wished-for result in order to achieve a single objective, the death of Balthazar at the hands of Bel-Imperia. Here is a sixteenth-century play written for a sixteenth-century audience; and in it everything that men and women do is seen as a contribution to the fulfilment of purposes which have been decreed by a refurbished set of pagan deities.

We have to be very precise about these deities and their decree. Those who are responsible in the underworld for assigning souls to their eternal home, Aeacus, Rhadamanthus and Minos, cannot agree what category Don Andrea comes into. He is like a book that is difficult to classify: is he to go with the lovers or with the martialists? They send him to Pluto, the gloomy king of the dead, to solve the problem, but Proserpine intervenes and becomes responsible for Andrea's "doom" (71). She whispers something to a being called Revenge, who transports Andrea back to middle-earth—

> Where thou shalt see the author of thy death,
> Don Balthazar the prince of Portingale,
> Deprived of life by Bel-Imperia. (1. 1. 87-89)

By her intervention, Proserpine assumes control not only of the destination of Andrea's soul—which was the only matter at issue—but of the fate of those who are still living. They have become "subject to destiny" as a result of a whisper by Proserpine who wants, it seems, to do a favour to Andrea.

It has often been noted that Andrea himself has not demanded vengeance on Balthazar, and that in any case his death was part of the fortune of war rather than the result of a criminal act on Balthazar's part.

Kyd has given total control over the living to the wife of the king of the dead, and has made an unalterable decree out of her grant of a favour that has not been asked for. What on earth has Andrea done to attract the special notice and favour of the gods? One is accustomed in Seneca's tragedies to the inscrutability of the gods and their purposes, but Seneca offers us inscrutability of a different order from Kyd's. In Seneca "the deep truth is imageless." What conceivable purpose can be served by heaping up crime upon crime? So asks Thyestes at the terrible end of the play concerning him. *"Scelere quis pensat scelus?"* (1103) Tantalus has been released from the torments of

hell in order, under duress, to incite his grandson to commit unspeakable deeds; this office is an extension of his punishment, and he protests helplessly about it. What dark forces seek to perpetuate sin in the name of punishing sin? This is the question which Seneca asks in the tragedy of *Thyestes* and to which he makes no attempt at an answer. But in Kyd the gods in charge are clearly described, and a rather cheerful lot they are. It is then that the darkness descends. In Seneca there is a dreadful logic in the involvement of Tantalus in the chain of crimes which scourges his family from generation to generation. In Kyd, Andrea stands out as insignificant and irrelevant to the sufferings of Horatio and Hieronimo and Isabella. Meaninglessness falls with a different accent; in Kyd it is not a question of a "dreadful logic" emanating from an unknown source. The source is named, but the logic is wholly wanting.

For a mere whim of Proserpine, kindly meant, Hieronimo and his family are wiped out along with "the whole succeeding hope" of the royal households of Spain and Portugal. Andrea is of the opinion that these well-disposed gods "will not tolerate a lover's woe" (3. 15. 38). Bel-Imperia is eventually reunited with Andrea in the Elysian fields. Is it the case then that the gods wish to foster and encourage the sexual relations between Andrea and Bel-Imperia which we are told society refused to tolerate and which Balthazar (unwittingly) put an end to? The price seems excessive.

Or is it—it must pass through the spectator's mind—is it a gigantic joke? If we take the whole human mess so faithfully portrayed in *The Spanish Tragedy*—

> O world, no world, but mass of public wrongs,
> Confused and filled with murder and misdeeds
>   (3. 2. 3-4)

and, looking back over the misery and the suffering, say, "Ah, it's all the plan of the gods to restore Bel-Imperia to her Andrea," would it not be very black humour, a deeply ironical impiety, a fatuous and insufficient explanation, a very bad joke? That is to say, if the black humour does not belong to the gods, who "kill us for their sport," does it belong to Kyd, satirically inventing a metaphysical machinery as a way of labelling the vindictive lusts of the human heart which so dominate this play? What seriousness is the theology of *The Spanish Tragedy* meant to have?

In confining the control of the human world to the "infernal powers" Kyd has gone far beyond the precedent of his two main influences, Virgil and Seneca. He has however allowed to his characters the traditional belief that there were both supernal and infernal deities. Jupiter was lord of the sky, Neptune of the sea, Pluto of the underworld. The archetype of turning for help from the heavenly gods to the infernal powers is Juno in *Aeneid,* Book VII, furious that the Trojans have safely landed in Italy: "If I cannot move the gods above, I shall bestir Acheron" (*flectere si nequeo superos, Acheronta movebo*). So Seneca's Medea, to assist her vindictive hate, calls on "the realms remote from heaven" (*aversa superis regna*) (10), on Pluto and Proserpine and the Furies. Jason, on the other hand, appeals to the celestial goddess Justice—"if in heaven thou dwellest"—

> sancta si caelum incolis
> Iustitia, numen invoco ac testor tuum. (439-40)

Kyd's infernal deities, whose "real" existence is vouched for in the narrative, are pagan deities; his supernal deities, whose existence lies in the suppositions of his characters, are Christian (or thereabouts). It always comes as a surprise, when we return in the second scene from Andrea's account of the underworld where the future of Spain has just been fixed, to hear the bland words of the Spanish King:

> Then blest be heaven, and guider of the heavens,
> From whose fair influence such justice flows. (1. 2. 10-11)

Kyd's generosity with names for concealed metaphysical forces, such as Nemesis and Fortune, as well as the absence of direct references to Christ, blurs our reception of a clear distinction between a pagan and a Christian system. Kyd's characters seem to share with Seneca's a tendency to call on any divinity in a very large pantheon as it may seem appropriate or effective at the time. Nevertheless, there *is* a distinction, and it is of fundamental importance.

Like the Spanish King, Hieronimo believes (very nervously and querulously, it is true) in the existence of a watchful and concerned providence in the upper air that we may fairly call Christian.

> O sacred heavens! if this unhallowed deed, . . .
> Shall unrevealed and unrevengèd pass,
> How should we term your dealings to be just,
> If you unjustly deal with those that in your justice trust? (3. 2. 5, 9-11)

> Yet still tormented is my tortured soul
> With broken sighs and restless passions,
> That winged mount, and, hovering in the air,
> Beat at the windows of the brightest heavens,
> Soliciting for justice and revenge:
> But they are placed in those empyreal heights
> Where, countermured with walls of diamond,
> I find the place impregnable, and they
> Resist my woes, and give my words no way. (3. 7. 10-18)

As his mind cracks under the strain of his suffering and his feeling of injustice, Hieronimo begins to indulge in demented geographical fantasizing about metaphysical forces. By a kind of accident, as it were, the rhetoric of his crazed imagination veers toward what the play's induction showed as the real location of cosmic power, Pluto's infernal court.

> There sits a judge
> Upon a seat of steel and molten brass. . . .
> Away, Hieronimo, to him be gone:
> He'll do thee justice for Horatio's death. (3. 12. 8-9, 12-13)

> Though on this earth justice will not be found,
> I'll down to hell, and in this passion
> Knock at the dismal gates of Pluto's court. . . .
> Then sound the burden of thy sore heart's grief,

> Till we do gain that Proserpine may grant
> Revenge on them that murderèd my son. (3. 13. 108-10, 119-21)

In his madness, the contending maxims of philosophy and religion, chiefly from Seneca and the Old Testament, swirl around in his mind. Sometimes he thinks he is prompted by hell, and sometimes by heaven. All that emerges is that if he is to obtain the retaliatory satisfaction which he defines as justice, he will have to carry out the punishment himself.

It doesn't matter whom Hieronimo believes in or whom he calls on. No one is listening. It has all been decided beforehand what is to happen.

In what is probably the most important essay written on the play in this century, "Ironies of Justice in *The Spanish Tragedy*," [reprinted in *Dramatic Identities and Cultural Tradition,* 1978], G. K. Hunter, emphasizing the wholeness of the action of the play, rightly argued that its central concern was not the enactment of revenge but the question of justice. He wrote powerfully of the blindness and ineffectuality of those who sought to achieve their own ideas of justice in a predetermined world. But I have never agreed with his equation of Proserpine's decree with "the process of heavenly justice," with speaking of the play as "an allegory of justice" and "a parable of perfect recompense." Hunter did indeed stress that such an idea of justice is strange: "the absorption of the human into the divine justice machine means the destruction of the human"; "humanity has been sacrificed so that justice can be fulfilled." Martin Luther somewhere said that if human beings could *recognize* divine justice it would not be divine. It is only in terms of such a sentiment that the divine order in *The Spanish Tragedy* can be called just; namely that it violates every human conception of what justice might mean. Is it just that Bel-Imperia should take her own life? Is it just that Hieronimo should go raving mad? Is it just that Castile should be killed? That Isabella should die as she does? Even Serberine?

Of course many of us (those who do not live in the shadow of Bowers and Prosser) are on Hieronimo's side; we are deeply sympathetic with him in his shocking bereavement; we share his anxiety to discover and denounce the criminals; we are encouraged when the identity of the killers is revealed; we understand when in the loneliness of his frustration he decides to exact punishment on his own; we feel all this, but we cannot conceivably accept that Kyd is telling us that the revealing and punishing of the crimes of Lorenzo, Balthazar and Pedringano is the way he sees divine justice working. Quite the contrary. If something recognizable as justice gets done in the working out of Hieronimo's revenge, it is not to the credit of the gods. The gods of Kyd's play are supremely unconcerned with justice of any kind, supremely unconcerned with Hieronimo and his welfare or with Lorenzo and his punishment. Hieronimo's belief that the sacred heavens will not permit murder to remain concealed and unpunished can only move them to laughter in Pluto's hall. The death of Lorenzo may bring satisfaction to whom it will; the only concern of the gods is the death of Balthazar and the reunion of Andrea and Bel-Imperia.

Of course, as in every Elizabethan play, the characters will interpret straws blowing in the wind as evidence of a caring providence. Kyd is no more interested in validating such interpretations than was Marlowe. The letter that Bel-Imperia drops in Hieronimo's path is greeted by him as "this unexpected miracle." The events of the strange Portuguese sub-plot seem designed as a satire on the operations of human justice and divine intervention. The fortuitous arrival of the Ambassador, seconds before Alexander is to be unjustly executed for causing Balthazar's death, with the news that Balthazar is actually alive and well in Spain is a close shave indeed. But critics have been known to surpass the characters in seeing it as an excellent example of the way God cares for man. Kyd's capacity for Marlovian irony must not be underestimated.

Kyd's play is a denial of God's care for man. And it is in this aspect that it is most deeply Senecan. By "Senecan," I mean the Seneca of the plays, "Seneca Tragicus," whom the Renaissance (understandably) had difficulty in equating with "Seneca Philosophus." It is as well to keep the two Senecas apart, initially at least. To read the plays without importing into them the theodicies and consolations of Stoicism is a powerful experience. Beneath all the violence and the outrage and the impetuous rhetoric there is a sombre silence which is the only response made to the never-ending questions about evil and suffering. Continually the characters try to make sense of the painfulness of their lot by postulating a divine pattern. Even the ubiquitous sense of fate may be a consolatory attempt to impose pattern and meaning. But no explaining voice is privileged: nothing is certain concerning the gods but their remoteness, indifference, absence.

> sed cur idem qui tanta regis,
> sub quo vasti pondera mundi
> librata suos ducunt orbes,
> hominum nimium securus abes,
> non sollicitus prodesse bonis,
> nocuisse malis?
>
>   Res humanas ordine nullo
>
> Fortuna regit sparsitque manu
> munera caeca, peiora fovens;
> vincit sanctos dira libido,
> fraus sublimi regnat in aula. (Chorus from *Hippolytus*, 972-82)

[But why, again, art thou, who holdest such wide sway, and by whose hands the ponderous masses of the vast universe are poised and wheel their appointed courses—why dost thou dwell afar, all too indifferent to men, not anxious to bring blessing to the good, and to the evil, bane? Fortune without order rules the affairs of men, scatters her gifts with unseeing hands, fostering the worse; dire lust prevails against pure men, and crime is enthroned in the lofty palace.]

The ravages of Fortune, which in orthodox Stoicism the philosopher learns to distinguish as the inessential contortions and contrarieties embossed on the deep structure of nature and fate, are in Seneca's tragedies the ineradicable norms of existence, though few will admit or accept them.

There is a dramatic moment in the *Agamemnon* when Cly-temnestra contemptuously repudiates the conventional cosmetics of divine control. In a bitter mood at what her association with Aegistheus has led her to, she taunts him with being the fruit of his father's incest. Aegistheus blandly palliates his father's sin: "Auctore Phoebo gignor; haud generis pudet" (294). [Phoebus was the source of my begetting; my birth shames me not.] To which Clytemnestra retorts: "quid deos probro addimus?" [Why attribute shameful deeds to the gods?.] Why do men and women pass on the blame for their own weakness and criminality? "This is the excellent foppery of the world . . . as if we were villains by necessity, fools by heavenly compulsion."

A more renowned moment is at the end of *Medea*, when, as the heroine escapes on her winged car, Jason shouts after her: "testare nullos esse, qua veheris, deos" (1027). [Bear witness, wherever you ride, that there are no gods] In Jason's view evil of Medea's kind is not compatible with any credible scheme of divine concern.

It seems to me unlikely that because sixteenth-century England was nominally a Christian country the dramatists, who used Seneca widely, did not notice the radical doubt and the impious protests of Seneca's characters. It was G. K. Hunter's view, in his influential essay "Seneca and the Elizabethans" (1967) [reprinted in *Dramatic Identities and Cultural Tradition*], that they were not prepared to take account of it.

> As Christians they could hardly endorse his resolute sense of divine malevolence, and in their adherence to the idea of 'the Christian Ethnicke Seneca' as Studley, the first translator of the *Medea*, learned from Erasmus to call him, they probably did not observe it. Studley's well-known mistranslation of the last line of the *Medea*
>
> testare nullos esse, qua veheris, deos
>
>   into
>
> Bear witness, grace of God is none in place of they repayre
>
> may serve as a paradigm of this easy distortion. [*Dramatic Identities and Cultural Tradition*]

What goes for Studley does not necessarily go for Kyd, Marlowe and Shakespeare, all of whom, incidentally, were quite capable of reading Seneca in the original and had not the least need to depend on the stumbling obtuseness of English Seneca (whatever Nashe said). It is not by reading *Thyestes* in the Elizabethan translation that one can perceive its profound influence on *King Lear*. (pp. 117-25)

The Spanish Tragedy, *Titus Andronicus, The Jew of Malta* and *Tamburlaine,* all seem to me to be deeply speculative, ruminating with unbelievable freedom, considering the restraints of the time, on the relation of the willed activities of men and women to divine intervention and control. ***The Spanish Tragedy*** differs from the other plays in not being agnostic. It sets up a rather horrifying and totally un-Christian cosmic machinery in which metaphysical control is absolute and "justice" an irrelevance. I now return to the question I raised earlier, how far the theology of ***The Spanish Tragedy*** is seriously meant. In the first place, the cosmic machinery of the play is a decisive repudiation of the idea of Christian providence. But, as an alternative to a Christian view of divine control, what status do Pluto, Prosperpine and Revenge have? It is certainly an attractive notion that they are merely ways of naming the forces within individuals which, as they entangle in a complex of personal relationships, bring those individuals to unforeseen and unwanted ends. I don't think that is enough. The sense of supernatural control is far too strong. Yet to take Kyd's supernatural creatures and their activities literally would be absurd. He took advantage of mythologies made available by Virgil and Seneca, and with extraordinary audacity worked into them the whim of Proserpine as a sufficient explanation of all that happens to the characters in his play. Positively then, **The Spanish Tragedy** argues no more (and no less) than that men and women *are* subject to destiny, and that what has been mapped out for them is ultimately inexplicable in any rational scheme of things, though it is clear that anything a human being can accept as justice is no part of the divine plan. This *may* be what Nashe meant when he spoke of "those that thrust *Elisium* into hell," in his preface to Green's *Menaphon*. (pp. 131-32)

> *Philip Edwards, "Thrusting Elysium into Hell: The Originality of 'The Spanish Tragedy'," in* The Elizabethan Theatre XI, *edited by A. L. Magnusson and C. E. McGee, P. D. Meany, 1990, pp. 117-32.*

FURTHER READING

BIBLIOGRAPHY

Tannenbaum, Samuel A. *Elizabethan Bibliographies Number 18: Thomas Kyd (A Concise Bibliography).* New York: Samuel A. Tannenbaum, 1941, 34 p.
> Bibliography of the Kyd canon and the body of criticism surrounding it.

OVERVIEWS AND GENERAL STUDIES

Boas, Frederick S. Introduction to *The Works of Thomas Kyd,* by Thomas Kyd, edited by Frederick S. Boas, pp. xiii-cvii. Oxford: Clarendon Press, 1901.
> Seminal study of Kyd's life and works, outlining the major issues regarding his career and his influence on Elizabethan drama.

Edwards, Philip. *Thomas Kyd and Early Elizabethan Tragedy.* London: Longmans, Green & Co., 1966, 48 p.
> Briefly discusses Kyd's biography and the minor works attributed to him, but primarily "concentrates on *The Spanish Tragedy,* and places it in the perspective of the development of Elizabethan tragedy."

Farnham, Willard. "The Establishment of Tragedy upon the Elizabethan Stage (Continued)." In his *The Medieval Heritage of Elizabethan Tragedy,* pp. 368-420. 1936. Reprint. Oxford: Basil Blackwell, 1963.
> Describes the influence of the *De casibus* story and Senecan themes on Kyd's dramas and observes that the pop-

ularity of romantic intrigue in Elizabethan tragedy began with *The Spanish Tragedy.*

Fleay, Frederick Gard. "Kyd." In his *A Biographical Chronicle of the English Drama 1559-1642,* Vol. II, pp. 26-35. London: Reeves and Turner, 1891.
> General commentary on Kyd's plays and others that have been attributed to him.

Freeman, Arthur. *Thomas Kyd: Facts and Problems.* London: Oxford University Press, 1967, 200 p.
> Exhaustive study of Kyd's life and career, attempting to clarify the uncertainties surrounding *The Spanish Tragedy* and other works ascribed to him.

THE SPANISH TRAGEDY

Adams, Barry B. "The Audiences of *The Spanish Tragedy.*" *Journal of English and German Philology* LXVIII, No. 2 (April 1962): 221-36.
> Defines and analyzes audience response to *The Spanish Tragedy.*

Ardolino, Frank R. *Thomas Kyd's Mystery Play: Myth and Ritual in 'The Spanish Tragedy.'* New York: Peter Lang, 1985, 189 p.
> Examines the elements of mystery and ritual in *The Spanish Tragedy.*

Baker, Howard. "*The Spanish Tragedy, Titus Andronicus,* and Senecanism." In his *Induction to Tragedy: A Study in a Development of form in 'Gorboduc,' 'The Spanish Tragedy,' and 'Titus Andronicus,'* pp. 106-53. 1939. Reprint. New York: Russell & Russell, 1956.
> Attempts to show that the Ghost of Andrea and Revenge in *The Spanish Tragedy* are characters adapted from medieval metrical tragedies rather than Senecan figures.

Barber, C. L. "Unbroken Passion: Social Piety and Outrage in *The Spanish Tragedy.*" In his *Creating Elizabethan Tragedy: The Theater of Marlowe and Kyd,* edited by Richard P. Wheeler, pp. 131-63. Chicago and London: University of Chicago Press, 1988.
> Discusses the elements of social drama, religious outrage, and theatrical vengeance in *The Spanish Tragedy.*

Coursen, Herbert R., Jr. "The Unity of *The Spanish Tragedy.*" *Studies in Philology* LXV, No. 5 (October 1968): 768-82.
> Maintains that Hieronimo's actions are not the central focus of *The Spanish Tragedy,* rather it is Andrea's revenge for the crimes and ambitious machinations of the House of Castile.

Cunliffe, John W. *The Influence of Seneca on Elizabethan Tragedy.* 1893. Reprint. Hamden, Conn.: Archon Books, 1965, 155 p.
> Provides brief commentary on the Senecan themes in *The Spanish Tragedy.*

Daalder, Joost. "The Role of 'Senex' in Kyd's *The Spanish Tragedy.*" *Compartive Drama* 20, No. 3 (Fall 1986): 247-60.
> Examines how Senecan dramas influenced *The Spanish Tragedy* and poses the theory that the appearance of a character named Senex in the play demonstrates Kyd's belief that Seneca would approve of Hieronimo's actions.

De Chickera, Ernst. "Divine Justice and Private Revenge in

The Spanish Tragedy." *Modern Language Review* LVII, No. 2 (April 1962): 228-32.

Asserts that the theme of revenge in *The Spanish Tragedy* reflects the Elizabethan conception of private revenge as an instrument of divine justice.

Edwards, Philip, ed. Introduction to *The Spanish Tragedy,* by Thomas Kyd, pp. xvii-lxviii. Cambridge, Mass.: Harvard University Press, 1959.

Discusses the issues regarding the authorship, date, and sources for *The Spanish Tragedy* and briefly examines its themes and structure.

Harbage, Alfred. "Intrigue in Elizabethan Tragedy." In *Essays on Shakespeare and Elizabethan Drama in Honor of Hardin Craig,* edited by Richard Hosley, pp. 37-44. Columbia: University of Missouri Press, 1962.

Maintains that Kyd dealt with the difficulties of introducing the element of intrigue into *The Spanish Tragedy* by using comic methods, "thus creating a species of comitragedy."

Heilman, Robert B., ed. Introduction to *An Anthology of English Drama Before Shakespeare,* pp. v-xvii. New York: Holt, Rinehart and Winston, 1952.

Defines Kyd's historical role as an Elizabethan dramatist and predecessor of Shakespeare, but questions the artistic value of *The Spanish Tragedy.*

Henke, James T. "Politics and Politicians in *The Spanish Tragedy.*" *Studies in Philology* LXXVIII, No. 4 (Fall 1981): 353-69.

Contends that Hieronimo's own distrust of legal and divine justice leads him to pursue private revenge.

Horwich, Richard. "The Settings of *The Spanish Tragedy.*" *The CEA Critic: An Official Journal of the College English Association* 49, Nos. 2, 3, 4 (Winter 1986-Summer 1987): 33-6.

Maintains that Kyd endeavored throughout *The Spanish Tragedy* to remind the audience that it was witnessing a play rather than actual events.

Hunter, G. K. "Ironies of Justice in *The Spanish Tragedy.*" In his *Dramatic Identities and Cultural Tradition: Studies in Shakespeare and his Contemporaries,* pp. 214-29. Liverpool: Liverpool University Press, 1978.

Asserts that the question of justice, rather than revenge, is the central concern of *The Spanish Tragedy.*

Jensen, Ejner J. "Kyd's *Spanish Tragedy:* The Play Explains Itself." *Journal of English and German Philology* LXIV, No. 1 (January 1965): 7-16.

Objects to Fredson Bowers's interpretation of *The Spanish Tragedy* (see excerpt dated 1940) and argues that if the play is viewed as an exploration of "the problem of justice" rather than as a revenge tragedy, its various disparate themes and elements combine to create a skillful dramatic unity.

Johnson, S. F. "*The Spanish Tragedy,* or Babylon Revisited." In *Essays on Shakespeare and Elizabethan Drama in Honor of Hardin Craig,* edited by Richard Hosley, pp. 23-36. Columbia: University of Missouri Press, 1962.

Posits that Hieronimo's play-within-the-play was meant to recall the biblical fall of Babylon.

Justice, Steven. "Spain, Tragedy, and *The Spanish Tragedy.*" *Studies in English Literature* 25, No. 2 (Spring 1985): 271-88.

Analyzes the religious influence behind Kyd's moral perspective in *The Spanish Tragedy.*

Laird, David. "Hieronimo's Dilemma." *Studies in Philology* LXII, No. 2 (April 1965): 137-46.

Maintains that the *vindicta mihi* speech in *The Spanish Tragedy* serves to explain Hieronimo's dilemma. The critic claims that Hieronimo, unable to "accomplish his revenge within the framework of the law," must choose between two alternatives: wait for divine justice or regain his honor through private revenge.

Leggatt, Alexander. "The Three Worlds of *The Spanish Tragedy.*" *Southern Review* VI, No. 1 (March 1973): 35-47.

Contends that the structure of *The Spanish Tragedy,* consisting of three interrelating levels of reality, is a key element to Kyd's presentation of the themes of justice and revenge.

McAlindon, Thomas. "*Tamburlaine the Great* and *The Spanish Tragedy:* the Genesis of a Tradition." *The Huntington Library Quarterly* 45, No. 1 (Winter 1982): 59-81.

Examines the contributions of Kyd's *Spanish Tragedy* to the development of English Renaissance tragedy in contrast to those of Christopher Marlowe's *Tamburlaine.*

McMillin, Scott. "The Figure of Silence in *The Spanish Tragedy.*" *ELH* 39, No. 1 (March 1972): 27-48.

Discusses the significance of the character of Senex in *The Spanish Tragedy,* focusing on his silence and the images seen in his face by Hieronimo.

Maslen, Elizabeth. "The Dynamics of Kyd's 'Spanish Tragedy'." *English* XXXII, No. 143 (Summer 1983): 111-25.

Asserts that Kyd establishes a distrust of verbal communication in *The Spanish Tragedy* which justifies Hieronimo's final actions.

Mulryne, J. R., ed. Introduction to *The Spanish Tragedy,* by Thomas Kyd, pp. xiii-xxxii. New York: Hill and Wang, 1970.

Offers a general overview of the theme, structure, and characterization in *The Spanish Tragedy* and maintains that "the securing of justice . . . might be named the play's central preoccupation."

Murray, Peter B. *Thomas Kyd.* New York: Twayne Publishers, 1969, 170 p.

In-depth study of Kyd's development of action, character, and theme in *The Spanish Tragedy* as a whole and in individual scenes.

Prior, Moody E. "The Elizabethan Tradition." In his *The Language of Tragedy,* rev. ed., pp. 16-153. Bloomington: Indiana University Press, 1966.

Maintains that Kyd varied the rhythm and style of his language according to the character or scene and used imagery to accentuate the action in *The Spanish Tragedy.*

Rubin, Deborah. "Justice, Revenge and Villainy in Kyd's *Spanish Tragedy.*" *Thoth: Syracuse University Graduate Studies in English* 16, No. 2 (Spring 1976): 3-13.

Assesses Hieronimo's conception of justice and revenge in relation to other characters in *The Spanish Tragedy* in an attempt to establish a moral perspective for the play.

Spriet, Pierre. "Antisocial Behaviour and the Code of Love

in Kyd's *The Spanish Tragedy." Cahiers Élisabéthains,* No. 17 (April 1980): 1-9.

> Posits that Kyd meant to punish the characters who opposed the code of love in *The Spanish Tragedy.*

Stein, Charles H. "Justice and Revenge in *The Spanish Tragedy." Iowa State Journal of Research* 56, No. 1 (August 1981): 97-104.

> Discusses "the ideal commitment to justice and a human impulse toward revenge" in Kyd's characters in *The Spanish Tragedy.*

Stockholder, Kay. " 'Yet can he write': Reading the Silences in *The Spanish Tragedy." American Imago* 47, No. 2 (Summer 1990): 93-124.

> Psychoanalytical study of identity, romance and honor, and relationships between fathers and sons in *The Spanish Tragedy.*

Willbern, David P. "Thomas Kyd's *The Spanish Tragedy:* Inverted Vengeance." *American Imago* 28, No. 3 (Fall 1971): 247-67.

> Contends that "the true subject of *The Spanish Tragedy* . . . is as much sex and marriage as death and revenge."

Additional coverage of Kyd's life and career is contained in the following sources published by Gale Research: *Dictionary of Literary Biography*, Vol. 62 2nd *Drama Criticism*, Vol. 3.

Christopher Marlowe

1564-1593

(Also Kit; also Marlow, Marlo, Merling, Merlin, Marlin, Marley, and Morley) English dramatist and poet.

INTRODUCTION

Marlowe is the author of such renowned plays as *Doctor Faustus; Tamburlaine, Parts I* and *II; The Jew of Malta;* and *Edward II.* Scholars recognize him as the first English dramatist to reveal the full potential of blank verse poetry, and as one who made significant advances in the genre of English tragedy through keen examinations of Renaissance morality. Although his achievements have been generally overshadowed by his exact contemporary William Shakespeare, many critics contend that had he not died young, Marlowe's reputation would certainly have rivaled that of the more famous playwright.

Marlowe was born the son of a prosperous shoemaker in Canterbury. He received his early education at the King's School in Canterbury and at age seventeen was awarded a scholarship to study for the ministry at Cambridge. He obtained his Bachelor of Arts degree in 1584, but controversy surrounded his attempt to graduate with a Master of Arts degree three years later. Scholars have learned that Cambridge officials attempted to withhold Marlowe's degree based on reports that he had visited a Catholic seminary at Rheims, France, and that he was planning to be ordained a Catholic priest upon graduation. Queen Elizabeth's Privy Council intervened, however, and declared that Marlowe had in fact been sent to Rheims on matters related to national security. Some modern critics interpret this remarkable occurrence as evidence that Marlowe served as a spy for the government on this occasion and perhaps others as well. Ultimately, the Cambridge officials relented and awarded him his degree, but controversy continued to follow him. Contemporary accounts indicate that, after taking up residence in London, he adopted a bohemian lifestyle and continually abused social norms. During this time Marlowe was implicated in a murder and spent two weeks in jail until he was acquitted after it was determined that he had acted in self-defense. In other clashes with the law, he was accused of atheism and blasphemy and was awaiting a trial verdict on such charges when he was killed in 1593. The circumstances surrounding his death puzzled scholars for centuries until records discovered in the early twentieth century revealed that Marlowe died of a stab wound received during a brawl with a dinner companion with whom he had been arguing over the tavern bill. A critical dispute remains, however, over the question of whether Marlowe's death was really inadvertent or if he was in fact assassinated.

Marlowe wrote during the Elizabethan period, a time of change and uncertainty. The spirit of the age was marked

Portrait of a young man, possibly Christopher Marlowe. No authenticated portrait of the author exists.

by both the Renaissance and the Reformation. Society had begun to loose itself from medieval institutions and to celebrate the ascendancy of the individual. Marlowe witnessed these developments first-hand and began to explore the potential consequences of this newfound freedom. In his dramas, Marlowe often created distinctively Renaissance characters, providing them with such attributes as great strength, wealth, or knowledge. These virtues initially appear to give them unlimited potential, but as events unfold the characters are inevitably consumed by pride and ultimately corrupted. The dangers of excessive ambition and the apparent compulsion to strive for more than one already has forms a major theme in Marlowe's plays. The philosophy of Machiavellianism constitutes another important—and related—theme for Marlowe, for his characters commonly strive to achieve their ambitions with the single-minded, ruthless, and amoral cunning described by Niccolò Machiavelli in his controversial political treatise *The Prince* (1532).

Scholars speculate that Marlowe wrote his first play in 1586, just seven years before his death. In this brief period, he composed all his dramas and began the narrative poem *Hero and Leander,* a project left incomplete at the time of his death. Because Marlowe's literary career was so brief yet prolific, scholars have found the accurate dating of many of his works extremely difficult.

While a critical consensus on the dating of Marlowe's works is lacking, some scholars maintain that *Dido Queen of Carthage* is his first play. Although *Dido* was not published until 1594, these critics assert that it was composed perhaps as early as 1586, when Marlowe was still a student at Cambridge. The title page of the first edition states that the play had already been performed by the company of boy actors known as the "Children of Her Majesties Chappell." The first of Marlowe's plays to appear on the London stage was most likely Part I of *Tamburlaine,* which was probably presented around 1587. It was a great success among Elizabethan theatergoers and in fact was so popular that Marlowe produced a sequel a year later. As the Prologue to Part II states, "The generall welcomes *Tamburlain* receiv'd, / When arrived last upon our stage, / Hath made our Poet pen his second part."

Marlowe wrote *Tamburlaine* as a direct challenge to his audience to rise above the "jigging veins of riming mother wits / And such conceits as clownage keeps in pay" often found in early Elizabethan drama. Marlowe thus introduces the Scythian shepherd Tamburlaine, a figure of heroic dimensions who epitomizes "Renaissance man" and who single-handedly orchestrates the forging of an empire. According to Gāmini Salgādo, *Tamburlaine* represents "the saga of the self-made man, triumphing through no advantages of birth or inheritance, but entirely through qualities of character." As such, the play reflects transitions in Marlowe's society, in which the dependence of personal advancement upon matters of birthright was gradually giving way to advancement earned through individual achievement. Tamburlaine accomplishes an unbroken series of military and political triumphs by sheer strength—not just physical power as demonstrated by his military prowess, but also by his forceful and eloquent rhetoric. These traits combined with his ruthless will to dominate identify him as a consummate Machiavellian, one who is able to assume and sustain leadership by sheer force of personality. In Part I, Marlowe defies theatergoers' expectations, for Tamburlaine pays no tragic retribution for his overweening pride. The dramatist follows a more classical approach in Part II, however, which is pervaded by the theme of death and decay. With the defeat of all human opposition and his massive consolidation of power, Tamburlaine gradually succumbs to megalomania and attempts to defy Death, his last and most significant adversary. Death slowly erodes Tamburlaine's resolve, first by taking his beloved wife, Zenocrate, and finally by claiming Tamburlaine himself. Marlowe thus demonstrates that for all the hero's striving and accomplishment, he is nevertheless human; ultimately even he must face death.

As already noted, the two parts of *Tamburlaine* were first staged around 1587-88. Their first publication was in a 1590 edition containing both parts, here called "two Tragicall Discourses." Interestingly, although this edition represents the only known printing of any of Marlowe's plays in his lifetime, his name is nowhere given. His next play may have been *The Jew of Malta,* perhaps performed around 1590, though not published until 1633, long after the dramatist's death. The title page of the first edition of *The Jew of Malta* designates the play a tragedy, but critics have often described it as a black comedy or, in the words of T. S. Eliot, a "savage farce."

As he does in *Tamburlaine,* Marlowe explores the implications of Machiavellianism in *The Jew of Malta;* but while Barabas, the central figure of the latter drama, shares Tamburlaine's ruthlessness, he manifests none of the earlier character's heroic grandeur. Indeed, nearly all the characters in this bitterly ironic piece are remarkable for their meanness. In *The Jew of Malta,* according to Eric Rothstein, Marlowe creates a world where "all values are inverted by a central diabolism in grotesque form, expressing itself through materialism . . . and a Machiavellian ethic." The inversion of values and the "diabolism" of the play are evident in the confrontation between the wealthy Jew Barabas and his antagonists, the Roman Catholic rulers of Malta. (Significantly, both groups, Jews and Catholics, were objects of fear and distrust in Elizabethan England.) The Governor of Malta, Ferneze, in financial straits, hypocritically denounces Barabas and confiscates his wealth, depriving him not only of his money but also of the love and mercy which Christianity represents. Barabas seeks revenge with unnerving viciousness, and a profusion of brutal murders ensues until, caught in one of his own traps, he dies cursing. Critics maintain that although there is tragedy inherent in Barabas's fall, his overreaching himself in his quest for revenge, his ignoble motives, and his cruel conduct preclude sympathy for him and therefore deprive him of tragic definition.

The Massacre at Paris is similar in tone and style to *The Jew of Malta* and was perhaps written around the same time. Although it is known to have been performed in 1593, it could not have been composed until after 1589, since it depicts the death of Henry III of France, who died in August of that yeàr. This play survives in an undated octavo edition that provides what critics commonly regard as a corrupt and unreliable text.

Many scholars consider *Edward II*—probably written during the winter of 1592-93, but not published until 1594—the first great English history play, and possibly Marlowe's most accomplished drama in any genre. George L. Geckle maintains that of Marlowe's major plays, "*Edward II* stands out as the most coherent in terms of structure and as the most complex in terms of the interrelationship between theme and character." Although *Edward II* is not one of Marlowe's best-known plays, critics have identified numerous factors contributing to what they regard as its remarkable literary success. Marlowe's sensitive construction of the relationships between this play's chief characters marks a significant advance over his earlier work, in which a play's most important motifs are typically centered around one dominant figure. Marlowe's merging of such elements as the selfish, hedonistic relationship between Edward and Gaveston, with its subtle suggestion of homosexuality, and Mortimer's Machiavellian ambition, commentators agree, gives *Edward II* unprecedented dimension. Marlowe's eloquent dramatic verse, variously lyrical, comedic, and tragic, additionally draws the play's many elements into a cohesive whole. Commentators have also praised Marlowe's masterful compression of twenty-three years of history into a five-act drama. It is commonly held that Shakespeare himself was aware of the exceptional literary achievement of *Edward II,* for his *Richard II* (1595) displays marked similarities to Marlowe's drama.

Although *Doctor Faustus* was not widely popular with Elizabethan audiences, today it is generally considered Marlowe's greatest drama. Written in the tradition of medieval morality plays, *Doctor Faustus* explores the implications of one man's pact to sell his soul to the devil for twenty-four years of power and knowledge. Salgādo observes that "built into the very bones of the story is the element of the cautionary tale, with Faustus as the horrible example of what happens when creatures rebel against their lot and aspire to the condition of their Creator." Critics agree that Faustus represents a Renaissance man whose intellectual ambitions cause him to overstep his human bounds. Marlowe masterfully illustrates how Faustus, although he aspires to divinity, is gradually debased throughout the play by the devil Mephistophilis. Succumbing to pride, avarice, and physical gratification, Faustus never realizes he has been duped into trading his soul for a life of triviality, and he refuses to avail himself of numerous chances to repent. The explicitly religious theme of *Doctor Faustus* continues to perplex critics, for many consider it uncharacteristic of Marlowe to treat theological issues in his works. Whether or not *Doctor Faustus* is meant to convey a particular religious message, it nevertheless presents a penetrating philosophical analysis of the consequences of human aspiration.

Marlowe's dramatic works are suffused with the spirit of the Elizabethan age, clearly reflecting the intellectual enlightenment of the Renaissance as well as the profound political impact of Machiavellianism. In play after play, Marlowe examines various aspects of these revolutionary cultural changes in an effort to better understand their influence on the human condition. In addition, Marlowe's verse greatly improves upon the crude style of his predecessors and vastly expands the scope and power of dramatic representation. Michael Drayton, the eminent English man of letters, paid tribute to his contemporary's literary genius in the poem entitled "Of Poets and Poesie." He wrote, "Neat *Marlow* bathed in the *Thespian* springs / Had in him those brave translunary things, / That the first Poets had, his raptures were, / All ayre, and fire, / which made his verses cleere, / For that fine madness still did he retaine, / Which rightly should possesse a Poets braine." Similarly, Ben Jonson hailed the force and beauty of "Marlowe's mighty line."

Marlowe's poetic genius, which inspired lyrical sections of great beauty in his dramas, shines most brightly in *Hero and Leander,* his most important non-dramatic work. This unfinished poem was based on a love epyllion (short epic poem), derived from the Hellenistic story of two lovers by the Greek poet Musaeus Grammaticus (fl. 500

A.D.). Completed by George Chapman, who divided Marlowe's poem into two sestiads and added four of his own, *Hero and Leander* is esteemed as a remarkable formal and aesthetic accomplishment. "In clear mastery of narrative and presentation," Swinburne wrote, "in melodious ease and simplicity of strength, it is not less preeminent than in the adorable beauty and impeccable perfection of separate lines or passages." In particular, critics have praised Marlowe's extraordinary mastery of the narrative decasyllabic couplet, as well as the powerful eroticism of his descriptions. C. S. Lewis, who characterized Marlowe's poetic sensibility as perfectly suited for the erotic epyllion, remarked that Marlowe "does not see beyond the erotic frenzy, but writes from within it." In Lewis's view, it is in his poetry that Marlowe attains greatness.

During his brief career, Marlowe created poetic works of great power and originality while helping to guide English drama to an unprecedented level of artistic maturity. His poetic audacity, imaginatively stated pessimism, and psychological insight have earned him the critical reputation as the only poet and dramatist of the Elizabethan age to approach the accomplishment of Shakespeare.

PRINCIPAL WORKS

The Tragedy of Dido Queen of Carthage (drama) 1586? [published 1594]

Tamburlaine the Great: Divided into two Tragicall Discourses (drama) 1587, 1588 [published 1590]

The Famous Tragedy of the Rich Jew of Malta (drama) 1590? [published 1633]

The Massacre at Paris: with the Death of the Duke of Guise (drama) 1590? [published 1594?]

The Troublesome Raigne and Lamentable Death of Edward the Second, King of England (drama) 1592-93 [published 1594]

The Tragicall History of the Life and Death of Doctor Faustus (drama) 1593? [published 1604, 1616]

Hero and Leander (poetry) 1593? [incomplete; published 1598]

The Works and Life of Christopher Marlowe. 6 vols. (dramas and poetry) 1930-33

William Hazlitt   (lecture date 1820?)

[*Hazlitt is considered a leading critic of the English Romantic movement. A prolific essayist and commentator on a wide variety of subjects, he emphasized character studies. Hazlitt's works include* Lectures on English Philosophy *(1812),* Characters of Shakespeare's Plays *(1817), and* Table Talk *(1821-22). In the following excerpt from a lecture delivered in approximately 1820, Hazlitt praises Marlowe as a seminal dramatic genius who matched, and sometimes exceeded, Shakespeare's powers of characterization. In Hazlitt's view, Marlowe's Faustus "may be considered as a personification of the pride of will and eagerness of curiosity, sublimed beyond the reach of fear and remorse.''*]

Marlowe is a name that stands high, and almost first [among the dramatic worthies of his time]. He was a little before Shakspeare's time, and has a marked character both from him and the rest. There is a lust of power in his writings, a hunger and thirst after unrighteousness, a glow of the imagination, unhallowed by any thing but its own energies. His thoughts burn within him like a furnace with bickering flames; or throwing out black smoke and mists that hide the dawn of genius, or, like a poisonous mineral, corrode the heart. His *Tragical History of Doctor Faustus,* though an imperfect and unequal performance, is his greatest work. Faustus himself is a rude sketch, but it is a gigantic one. This character may be considered as a personification of the pride of will and eagerness of curiosity, sublimed beyond the reach of fear and remorse. He is hurried away, and, as it were, devoured by a tormenting desire to enlarge his knowledge to the utmost bounds of nature and art, and to extend his power with his knowledge. He would realise all the fictions of a lawless imagination, would solve the most subtle speculations of abstract reason; and for this purpose, sets at defiance all mortal consequences, and leagues himself with demoniacal power, with "fate and metaphysical aid." The idea of witchcraft and necromancy, once the dread of the vulgar and the darling of the visionary recluse, seems to have had its origin in the restless tendency of the human mind to conceive of and aspire to more than it can achieve by natural means, and in the obscure apprehension that the gratification of this extravagant and unauthorised desire can only be attained by the sacrifice of all our ordinary hopes and better prospects to the infernal agents that lend themselves to its accomplishment. Such is the foundation of the present story. Faustus, in his impatience to fulfil at once and for a moment, for a few short years, all the desires and conceptions of his soul, is willing to give in exchange his soul and body to the great enemy of mankind. Whatever he fancies becomes by this means present to his sense; whatever he commands is done. He calls back time past, and anticipates the future: the visions of antiquity pass before him, Babylon in all its glory, Paris and Œnone; all the projects of philosophers or creations of the poet pay tribute at his feet; all the delights of fortune, of ambition, of pleasure, and of learning, are centered in his person; and from a short-lived dream of supreme felicity and drunken power, he sinks into an abyss of darkness and perdition. This is the alternative to which he submits; the bond which he signs with his blood! As the outline of the character is grand and daring, the execution is abrupt and fearful. The thoughts are vast and irregular; and the style halts and staggers under them, "with uneasy steps;"—"such footing found the sole of unblest feet." (pp. 43-4)

Perhaps the finest *trait* in the whole play, and that which softens and subdues the horror of it, is the interest taken by the two scholars in the fate of their master, and their unavailing attempts to dissuade him from his relentless career. The regard to learning is the ruling passion of this drama; and its indications are as mild and amiable in them as its ungoverned pursuit has been fatal to Faustus:

> Yet, for he was a scholar once admir'd

> For wondrous knowledge in our German schools,
> We'll give his mangled limbs due burial;
> And all the students, cloth'd in mourning black,
> Shall wait upon his heavy funeral.

So the chorus:

> Cut is the branch that might have grown full straight,
> And burned is Apollo's laurel bough,
> That sometime grew within this learned man.

And still more affecting are his own conflicts of mind and agonising doubts on this subject just before, when he exclaims to his friends:

> Oh, gentlemen! Hear me with patience, and tremble not at my speeches. Though my heart pant and quiver to remember that I have been a student here these thirty years; oh! would I had never seen Wertenberg, never read book!

A finer compliment was never paid, nor a finer lesson ever read to the pride of learning. The intermediate comic parts, in which Faustus is not directly concerned, are mean and grovelling to the last degree. One of the clowns says to another: "Snails! what hast got there? A book? Why thou canst not tell ne'er a word on't." Indeed, the ignorance and barbarism of the time, as here described, might almost justify Faustus' overstrained admiration of learning, and turn the heads of those who possessed it, from novelty and unaccustomed excitement, as the Indians are made drunk with wine! Goëthe, the German poet, has written a drama on this tradition of his country, which is considered a masterpiece. I cannot find, in Marlowe's play, any proofs of the atheism or impiety attributed to him, unless the belief in witchcraft and the Devil can be regarded as such; and at the time he wrote, not to have believed in both, would have been construed into the rankest atheism and irreligion. There is a delight, as Mr. Lamb says, "in dallying with interdicted subjects;" but that does not, by any means, imply either a practical or speculative disbelief of them. (pp. 48-9)

I do not think *The Rich Jew of Malta* so characteristic a specimen of this writer's powers. It has not the same fierce glow of passion or expression. It is extreme in act, and outrageous in plot and catastrophe; but it has not the same vigorous filling up. The author seems to have relied on the horror inspired by the subject, and the national disgust excited against the principal character, to rouse the feelings of the audience: for the rest, it is a tissue of gratuitous, unprovoked, and incredible atrocities, which are committed, one upon the back of the other, by the parties concerned, without motive, passion, or object. There are, notwithstanding, some striking passages in it, as Barabas' description of the bravo, Philia Borzo; the relation of his own unaccountable villanies to Ithamore; his rejoicing over his recovered jewels "as the morning lark sings over her young;" and the backwardness he declares in himself to forgive the Christian injuries that are offered him, which may have given the idea of one of Shylock's speeches, where he ironically disclaims any enmity to the merchants on the same account. It is perhaps hardly fair to compare the *Jew of Malta* with the *Merchant of Venice;* for it is evident, that Shakspeare's genius shows to as much advantage in knowledge of character, in variety and stage effect, as it does in point of general humanity.

Edward II. is, according to the modern standard of composition, Marlowe's best play. It is written with few offences against the common rules, and in a succession of smooth and flowing lines. The poet, however, succeeds less in the voluptuous and effeminate descriptions which he here attempts, than in the more dreadful and violent bursts of passion. *Edward II.* is drawn with historic truth, but without much dramatic effect. The management of the plot is feeble and desultory; little interest is excited in the various turns of fate; the characters are too worthless, have too little energy, and their punishment is, in general, too well deserved, to excite our commiseration; so that this play will bear, on the whole, but a distant comparison with Shakspeare's *Richard II.* in conduct, power, or effect. But the death of Edward II., in Marlowe's tragedy, is certainly superior to that of Shakspeare's King; and in heart-breaking distress, and the sense of human weakness, claiming pity from utter helplessness and conscious misery, is not surpassed by any writer whatever. . . . (pp. 52-5)

> *William Hazlitt, in an excerpt from* Lectures on the Literature of the Age of Elizabeth and Characters of Shakespear's Plays, *Bell & Daldy, 1870, pp. 43-55.*

James Russell Lowell   (essay date 1892)

[*A celebrated nineteenth-century American poet, critic, and essayist, Lowell was the first editor of the* Atlantic Monthly, *and co-editor, with Charles Eliot Norton, of the influential* North American Review. *His writings include the satirical poem* A Fable for Critics *(1848), as well as two volumes of essays,* Among My Books *(1870), and* My Study Windows *(1871). In the following excerpt from an essay published a year after his death, Lowell defines Marlowe as a great precursor, a poet and dramatist of genius who "has an importance less for what he accomplished than for what he suggested to others."*]

Goethe tells us that the first thing needful to the critic, as indeed it is to the wise man generally, is to see the thing as it really is; this is the most precious result of all culture, the surest warrant of happiness, or at least of composure. But he also bids us, in judging any work, seek first to discover its beauties, and then its blemishes or defects. Now there are two poets whom I feel that I can never judge without a favorable bias. One is Spenser, who was the first poet I ever read as a boy, not drawn to him by any enchantment of his matter or style, but simply because the first verse of his great poem was,

A gentle knight was pricking on the plain,

and I followed gladly, wishful of adventure. Of course I understood nothing of the allegory, never suspected it, fortunately for me, and am surprised to think how much of the language I understood. At any rate, I grew fond of him, and whenever I see the little brown folio in which I read, my heart warms to it as to a friend of my childhood.

With Marlowe it was otherwise. With him I grew acquainted during the most impressible and receptive period of my youth. He was the first man of genius I had ever really known, and he naturally bewitched me. What cared I that they said he was a deboshed fellow? nay, an atheist? To me he was the voice of one singing in the desert, of one who had found the water of life for which I was painting, and was at rest under the palms. How can he ever become to me as other poets are? But I shall try to be lenient in my admiration. (p. 196)

[Marlowe] was taxed with atheism, but on inadequate grounds, as it appears to me. That he was said to have written a tract against the Trinity, for which a license to print was refused on the ground of blasphemy, might easily have led to the greater charge. That he had some opinions of a kind unusual then, may be inferred, perhaps, from a passage in his *Faust.* Faust asks Mephistopheles how, being damned, he is out of hell. And Mephistopheles answers, "Why, this is hell, nor am I out of it." And a little farther on he explains himself thus:

> Hell hath no limits, nor is circumscribed
> In one self place; for where we are is hell,
> And where hell is there must we ever be;
> And, to conclude, when all the earth dissolves,
> And every creature shall be purified,
> All places shall be hell that are not heaven.

Milton remembered the first passage I have quoted, and puts nearly the same words into the mouth of his Lucifer. If Marlowe was a liberal thinker, it is not strange that in that intolerant age he should have incurred the stigma of general unbelief. Men are apt to blacken opinions which are distasteful to them, and along with them the character of him who holds them.

This at least may be said of him without risk of violating the rule of *ne quid nimis,* that he is one of the most masculine and fecundating natures in the long line of British poets. Perhaps his energy was even in excess. There is in him an Oriental lavishness. He will impoverish a province for a simile, and pour the revenues of a kingdom into the lap of a description. In that delightful story in the book of Esdras, King Darius, who has just dismissed all his captains and governors of cities and satraps, after a royal feast, sends couriers galloping after them to order them all back again because he has found a riddle under his pillow, and wishes their aid in solving it. Marlowe in like manner calls in help from every the remotest corner of earth and heaven for what seems to us as trivial an occasion. I will not say that he is bombastic, but he constantly pushes grandiosity to the verge of bombast. His contemporaries thought he passed it in his *Tamburlaine.* His imagination flames and flares, consuming what it should caress, as Jupiter did Semele. That exquisite phrase of Hamlet, "the modesty of nature," would never have occurred to him. Yet in the midst of the hurly-burly there will fall a sudden hush, and we come upon passages calm and pellucid as mountain tarns filled to the brim with the purest distillations of heaven. And, again, there are single verses that open silently as roses, and surprise us with that seemingly accidental perfection, which there is no use in talking about because itself says all that is to be said and more.

There is a passage in *Tamburlaine* which I remember reading in the first course of lectures I ever delivered, thirty-four years ago, as a poet's feeling of the inadequacy of the word to the idea:

> If all the pens that ever poets held
> Had fed the feeling of their masters' thoughts,
> And every sweetness that inspired their hearts,
> Their minds, and muses on admired themes;
> If all the heavenly quintessence they still
> From their immortal flowers of poesy,
> Wherein, as in a mirror, we perceive
> The highest reaches of a human wit;—
> If these had made one poem's period,
> And all combined in beauty's worthiness,
> Yet should there hover in their restless heads
> One thought, one grace, one wonder, at the least,
> Which into words no virtue can digest.

Marlowe made snatches at this forbidden fruit with vigorous leaps, and not without bringing away a prize now and then such as only the fewest have been able to reach. Of fine single verses I give a few as instances of this:

> Sometimes a lovely boy in Dian's shape,
> *With hair that gilds the water as it glides,*
> Shall bathe him in a spring.

Here is a couplet notable for dignity of poise describing Tamburlaine:

> Of stature tall and straightly fashionèd,
> Like his desire, lift upward and divine.

> For every street like to a firmament
> Glistered with breathing stars.

> Unwedded maids
> Shadowing more beauty in their airy brows
> Than have the white breasts of the queen of
> Love.

This, from *Tamburlaine,* is particularly characteristic:

> Nature
> Doth teach us all to have aspiring minds.
> Our souls, whose faculties can comprehend
> The wondrous architecture of the world,
> And measure every wandering planet's course,
> Still climbing after knowledge infinite,
> And always moving as the restless spheres,
> Will us to wear ourselves and never rest
> Until we reach the ripest fruit of all.

One of these verses reminds us of that exquisite one of Shakespeare where he says that Love is

> Still climbing trees in the Hesperides.

But Shakespeare puts a complexity of meaning into his chance sayings, and lures the fancy to excursions of which Marlowe never dreamt.

But, alas, a voice will not illustrate like a stereopticon, and this tearing away of fragments that seem to bleed with the avulsion is like breaking off a finger from a statue as a specimen.

The impression he made upon the men of his time was uniform; it was that of something new and strange; it was that of genius, in short. Drayton says of him, kindling to an un-

wonted warmth, as if he loosened himself for a moment from the choking coils of his Polyolbion for a larger breath:

> Next Marlowe bathèd in the Thespian springs
> Had in him those brave translunary things
> That the first poets had; his raptures were
> All air and fire, which made his verses clear;
> For that fine madness still he did retain
> Which rightly should possess a poet's brain.

And Chapman, taking up and continuing Marlowe's half-told story of Hero and Leander, breaks forth suddenly into this enthusiasm of invocation:

> Then, ho! most strangely intellectual fire
> That, proper to my soul, hast power to inspire
> Her burning faculties, and with the wings
> Of thy unspherèd flame visit'st the springs
> Of spirits immortal, now (as swift as Time
> Doth follow motion) find the eternal clime
> Of his free soul whose living subject stood
> Up to the chin in the Pierian flood.

Surely Chapman would have sent his soul on no such errand had he believed that the soul of Marlowe was in torment, as his accusers did not scruple to say that it was, sent thither by the manifestly Divine judgment of his violent death.

Yes, Drayton was right in classing him with "the first poets," for he was indeed such, and so continues—that is, he was that most indefinable thing, an original man, and therefore as fresh and contemporaneous to-day as he was three hundred years ago. Most of us are more or less hampered by our own individuality, nor can shake ourselves free of that chrysalis of consciousness and give our "souls a loose," as Dryden calls it in his vigorous way. And yet it seems to me that there is something even finer than that fine madness, and I think I see it in the imperturbable sanity of Shakespeare, which made him so much an artist that his new work still bettered his old. I think I see it even in the almost irritating calm of Goethe, which, if it did not quite make him an artist, enabled him to see what an artist should be, and to come as near to being one as his nature allowed. Marlowe was certainly not an artist in the larger sense, but he was cunning in words and periods and the musical modulation of them. And even this is a very rare gift. But his mind could never submit itself to a controlling purpose, and renounce all other things for the sake of that. His plays, with the single exception of *Edward II.,* have no organic unity, and such unity as is here is more apparent than real. Passages in them stir us deeply and thrill us to the marrow, but each play as a whole is ineffectual. Even his *Edward II.* is regular only to the eye by a more orderly arrangement of scenes and acts, and Marlowe evidently felt the drag of this restraint, for we miss the uncontrollable energy, the eruptive fire, and the feeling that he was happy in his work. Yet Lamb was hardly extravagant in saying that "the death scene of Marlowe's king moves pity and terror beyond any scene, ancient or modern, with which I am acquainted." His tragedy of *Dido, Queen of Carthage,* is also regularly plotted out, and is also somewhat tedious. Yet there are many touches that betray his burning hand. There is one passage illustrating that luxury of description into which Marlowe is always glad to escape from the business in hand. Dido tells Æneas:

> Æneas, I'll repair thy Trojan ships
> Conditionally that thou wilt stay with me,
> And let Achates sail to Italy;
> I'll give thee tackling made of rivelled gold,
> Wound on the barks of odoriferous trees;
> Oars of massy ivory, full of holes
> Through which the water shall delight to play;
> Thy anchors shall be hewed from crystal rocks
> Which, if thou lose, shall shine above the waves;
> The masts whereon thy swelling sails shall hang
> Hollow pyramides of silver plate;
> The sails of folded lawn, where shall be wrought
> The wars of Troy, but not Troy's overthrow;
> For ballast, empty Dido's treasury;
> Take what ye will, but leave Æneas here.
> Achates, thou shalt be so seemly clad
> As sea-born nymphs shall swarm about thy
> 　　ships
> And wanton mermaids court thee with sweet
> 　　songs,
> Flinging in favors of more sovereign worth
> Than Thetis hangs about Apollo's neck,
> So that Æneas may but stay with me.

But far finer than this, in the same costly way, is the speech of Barabas in *The Jew of Malta,* ending with a line that has incorporated itself in the language with the familiarity of a proverb:

> Give me the merchants of the Indian mines
> That trade in metal of the purest mould;
> The wealthy Moor that in the Eastern rocks
> Without control can pick his riches up,
> And in his house heap pearl like pebble-stones,
> Receive them free, and sell them by the weight;
> Bags of fiery opals, sapphires, amethysts,
> Jacynths, hard topaz, grass-green emeralds,
> Beauteous rubies, sparkling diamonds,
> And seld-seen costly stones of so great price
> As one of them, indifferently rated,
> 　. 　. 　. 　. 　. 　.
> May serve in peril of calamity
> To ransom great kings from captivity.
> This is the ware wherein consists my wealth:
> 　. 　. 　. 　. 　. 　.
> Infinite riches in a little room.

This is the very poetry of avarice.

Let us now look a little more closely at Marlowe as a dramatist. Here also he has an importance less for what he accomplished than for what he suggested to others. Not only do I think that Shakespeare's verse caught some hints from his, but there are certain descriptive passages and similes of the greater poet which, whenever I read them, instantly bring Marlowe to my mind. This is an impression I might find it hard to convey to another, or even to make definite to myself; but it is an old one, and constantly repeats itself, so that I put some confidence in it. Marlowe's *Edward II.* certainly served Shakespeare as a model for his earlier historical plays. Of course he surpassed his model, but Marlowe might have said of him as Oderisi, with pathetic modesty, said to Dante of his rival and surpasser, Franco of Bologna, "The praise is now all his, yet mine in part." But it is always thus. The path-finder is for-

gotten when the track is once blazed out. It was in Shakespeare's *Richard II.* that Lamb detected the influence of Marlowe, saying that "the reluctant pangs of abdicating royalty in Edward furnished hints which Shakespeare has scarce improved upon in Richard." In the parallel scenes of both plays the sentiment is rather elegiac than dramatic, but there is a deeper pathos, I think, in Richard, and his grief rises at times to a passion which is wholly wanting in Edward. Let me read Marlowe's abdication scene. The irresolute nature of the king is finely indicated. The Bishop of Winchester has come to demand the crown; Edward takes it off, and says:

> Here, take my crown; the life of Edward too:
> Two kings of England cannot reign at once.
> But stay awhile: let me be king till night,
> That I may gaze upon this glittering crown;
> So shall my eyes receive their last content,
> My head the latest honor due to it,
> And jointly both yield up their wishèd right.
> Continue ever, thou celestial sun;
> Let never silent night possess this clime;
> Stand still, you watches of the element;
> All times and seasons, rest you at a stay—
> That Edward may be still fair England's king!
> But day's bright beam doth vanish fast away,
> And needs I must resign my wishèd crown.
> Inhuman creatures, nursed with tiger's milk,
> Why gape you for your sovereign's over-
> 　　throw?—
> My diadem, I mean, and guiltless life.
> See, monsters, see, I'll wear my crown again.
> What, fear you not the fury of your king?
> 　. 　. 　. 　. 　. 　.
> I'll not resign, but whilst I live be king!

Then, after a short further parley:

> 　　　Here, receive my crown.
> Receive it? No; these innocent hands of mine
> Shall not be guilty of so foul a crime:
> He of you all that most desires my blood,
> And will be called the murderer of a king,
> Take it. What, are you moved? Pity you me?
> Then send for unrelenting Mortimer,
> And Isabel, whose eyes, being turned to steel,
> Will sooner sparkle fire than shed a tear.
> Yet stay, for rather than I'll look on them,
> Here, here!—Now, sweet God of Heaven,
> Make me despise this transitory pomp,
> And sit for aye enthronizèd in Heaven!
> Come, Death, and with thy fingers close my
> 　　eyes,
> Or, if I live, let me forget myself.

Surely one might fancy that to be from the prentice hand of Shakespeare. It is no small distinction that this can be said of Marlowe, for it can be said of no other. What follows is still finer. The ruffian who is to murder Edward, in order to evade his distrust, pretends to weep. The king exclaims:

> Weep'st thou already? List awhile to me,
> And then thy heart, were it as Gurney's is,
> Or as Matrevis', hewn from the Caucasus,
> Yet will it melt ere I have done my tale.
> This dungeon where they keep me is the sink
> Wherein the filth of all the castle falls,

And there in mire and puddle have I stood
This ten days' space; and, lest that I should
      sleep,
One plays continually upon a drum;
They give me bread and water, being a king;
So that, for want of sleep and sustenance,
My mind's distempered and my body numbed,
And whether I have limbs or no I know not.
O, would my blood dropt out from every vein,
As doth this water from my tattered robes!
Tell Isabel the queen I looked not thus,
When, for her sake, I ran at tilt in France,
And there unhorsed the Duke of Clerëmont.

This is even more in Shakespeare's early manner than the other, and it is not ungrateful to our feeling of his immeasurable supremacy to think that even he had been helped in his schooling. There is a truly royal pathos in "They give me bread and water"; and "Tell Isabel the queen," instead of "Isabel my queen," is the most vividly dramatic touch that I remember anywhere in Marlowe. And that vision of the brilliant tournament, not more natural than it is artistic, how does it not deepen by contrast the gloom of all that went before! But you will observe that the verse is rather epic than dramatic. I mean by this that its every pause and every movement are regularly cadenced. There is a kingly composure in it, perhaps, but were the passage not so finely pathetic as it is, or the diction less naturally simple, it would seem stiff. Nothing is more peculiarly characteristic of the mature Shakespeare than the way in which his verses curve and wind themselves with the fluctuating emotion or passion of the speaker and echo his mood. Let me illustrate this by a speech of Imogen when Pisanio gives her a letter from her husband bidding her meet him at Milford-Haven [Cymbeline]. The words seem to waver to and fro, or huddle together before the hurrying thought, like sheep when the collie chases them.

O, for a horse with wings!—Hear'st thou, Pi-
      sanio?
He is at Milford-Haven: Read, and tell me
How far 'tis thither. If one of mean affairs
May plod it in a week, why may not I
Glide thither in a day?—Then, true Pisanio
(Who long'st like me to see thy lord; who
      long'st—
O, let me 'bate—but not like me—yet long'st—
But in a fainter kind:—O, not like me;
For mine's beyond beyond)—say, and speak
      thick
(Love's counsellor should fill the bores of hear-
      ing,
To the smothering of the sense), how far it is
To this same blessed Milford: and, by the way,
Tell me how Wales was made so happy as
To inherit such a haven: but, first of all,
How we may steal from hence.

The whole speech is breathless with haste, and is in keeping not only with the feeling of the moment, but with what we already know of the impulsive character of Imogen. Marlowe did not, for he could not, teach Shakespeare this secret, nor has anybody else ever learned it.

There are, properly speaking, no characters in the plays of Marlowe—but personages and interlocutors. We do not get to know them, but only to know what they do and say.

The nearest approach to a character is Barabas, in *The Jew of Malta,* and he is but the incarnation of the popular hatred of the Jew. There is really nothing human in him. He seems a bugaboo rather than a man. Here is his own account of himself:

As for myself, I walk abroad o' nights,
And kill sick people groaning under walls;
Sometimes I go about and poison wells;
And now and then, to cherish Christian thieves,
I am content to lose some of my crowns,
That I may, walking in my gallery,
See 'em go pinioned by my door along;
Being young, I studied physic, and began
To practise first upon the Italian;
There I enriched the priests with burials,
And always kept the sexton's arms in ure
With digging graves and ringing dead men's
      knells;
And, after that, was I an engineer,
And in the wars 'twixt France and Germany,
Under pretence of helping Charles the Fifth,
Slew friend and enemy with my stratagems.
Then, after that, was I an usurer,
And with extorting, cozening, forfeiting,
And tricks belonging unto brokery,
I filled the jails with bankrupts in a year,
And with young orphans planted hospitals;
And every moon made some or other mad,
And now and then one hang himself for grief,
Pinning upon his breast a long great scroll
How I with interest tormented him.
But mark how I am blest for plaguing them—
I have as much coin as will buy the town.

Here is nothing left for sympathy. This is the mere lunacy of distempered imagination. It is shocking, and not terrible. Shakespeare makes no such mistake with Shylock. His passions are those of a man, though of a man depraved by oppression and contumely; and he shows sentiment, as when he says of the ring that Jessica had given for a monkey: "It was my turquoise. I had it of Leah when I was a bachelor." And yet, observe the profound humor with which Shakespeare makes him think first of its dearness as a precious stone and then as a keepsake. In letting him exact his pound of flesh, he but follows the story as he found it in Giraldi Cinthio, and is careful to let us know that this Jew had good reason, or thought he had, to hate Christians. At the end, I think he meant us to pity Shylock, and we do pity him. And with what a smiling background of love and poetry does he give relief to the sombre figure of the Jew! In Marlowe's play there is no respite. And yet it comes nearer to having a connected plot, in which one event draws on another, than any other of his plays. I do not think Milman right in saying that the interest falls off after the first two acts. I find enough to carry me on to the end, where the defiant death of Barabas in a caldron of boiling oil he had arranged for another victim does something to make a man of him. But there is no controlling reason in the piece. Nothing happens because it must, but because the author wills it so. The conception of life is purely arbitrary, and as far from nature as that of an imaginative child. It is curious, however, that here, too, Marlowe should have pointed the way to Shakespeare. There is no resemblance, however, between the Jew of Malta and the Jew of Venice, except that both have daughters whom they love. Nor is the analogy close even here. The love which Barabas professes for his child fails to humanize him to us, because it does not prevent him from making her the abhorrent instrument of his wanton malice in the death of her lover, and because we cannot believe him capable of loving anything but gold and vengeance. There is always something extravagant in the imagination of Marlowe, but here it is the extravagance of absurdity. Generally he gives us an impression of power, of vastness, though it be the vastness of chaos, where elemental forces hurtle blindly one against the other. But they are elemental forces, and not mere stage properties. Even in Tamburlaine, if we see in him—as Marlowe, I think, meant that we should see—the embodiment of brute force, without reason and without conscience, he ceases to be a blusterer, and becomes, indeed, as he asserts himself, the scourge of God. There is an exultation of strength in this play that seems to add a cubit to our stature. Marlowe had found the way that leads to style, and helped others to find it, but he never arrived there. He had not self-denial enough. He can refuse nothing to his fancy. He fails of his effect by over-emphasis, heaping upon a slender thought a burthen of expression too heavy for it to carry. But it is not with fagots, but with priceless Oriental stuffs, that he breaks their backs.

Marlowe's **Dr. Faustus** interests us in another way. Here he again shows himself as a precursor. There is no attempt at profound philosophy in this play, and in the conduct of it Marlowe has followed the prose history of Dr. Faustus closely, even in its scenes of mere buffoonery. Disengaged from these, the figure of the protagonist is not without grandeur. It is not avarice or lust that tempts him at first, but power. Weary of his studies in law, medicine, and divinity, which have failed to bring him what he seeks, he turns to necromancy.

> These metaphysics of magicians (he says)
> And necromantic books are heavenly.
>
> . . . . . .
>
> Oh, what a world of profit and delight,
> Of power, of honor, of omnipotence,
> Is promised to the studious artizan!
> All things that move between the quiet poles
> Shall be at my command. Emperors and kings
> Are but obeyèd in their several provinces;
> Nor can they raise the winds or rend the clouds;
> But his dominion that exceeds in this
> Stretcheth as far as doth the mind of man.
> A sound magician is a mighty god.
> Here, Faustus, tire thy brains to gain a deity.

His good angel intervenes, but the evil spirit at the other ear tempts him with power again:

> Be thou on earth as Jove is in the sky,
> Lord and commander of these elements.

Erelong Faustus begins to think of power for baser uses:

> How am I glutted with conceit of this!
> Shall I make spirits fetch me what I please,
> Resolve me of all ambiguities,
> Perform what desperate enterprise I will?
> I'll have them fly to India for gold,
> Ransack the ocean for Orient pearl,
> And search all corners of the new-found world

> For pleasant fruits and princely delicates;
> I'll have them read me strange philosophy,
> And tell the secrets of all foreign kings.

And yet it is always to the pleasures of the intellect that he returns. It is when the good and evil spirits come to him for the second time that wealth is offered as a bait, and after Faustus has signed away his soul to Lucifer, he is tempted even by more sensual baits. I may be reading into the book what is not there, but I cannot help thinking that Marlowe intended in this to typify the inevitably continuous degradation of a soul that has renounced its ideal, and the drawing on of one vice by another, for they go hand in hand like the Hours. But even in his degradation the pleasures of Faustus are mainly of the mind, or at worst of a sensuous and not sensual kind. No doubt in this Marlowe is unwittingly betraying his own tastes. Faustus is made to say:

> And long ere this I should have slain myself
> Had not sweet pleasure conquered deep despair.
> Have I not made blind Homer sing to me
> Of Alexander's love and Œnon's death?
> And hath not he that built the walls of Thebes
> With ravishing sound of his melodious harp
> Made music with my Mephistophilis?
> Why should I die, then? basely why despair?

This employment of the devil in a duet seems odd. I remember no other instance of his appearing as a musician except in Burns's "Tam o'Shanter." The last wish of Faustus was Helen of Troy. Mephistophilis fetches her, and Faustus exclaims:

> Was this the face that launched a thousand
>   ships,
> And burned the topless towers of Ilium?
> Sweet Helen, make me immortal with a kiss!
> . . . . . .
> Here will I dwell, for Heaven is in these lips,
> And all is dross that is not Helena:
>
> Oh, thou art fairer than the evening air
> Clad in the beauty of a thousand stars.

No such verses had ever been heard on the English stage before, and this was one of the great debts our language owes to Marlowe. He first taught it what passion and fire were in its veins. The last scene of the play, in which the bond with Lucifer becomes payable, is nobly conceived. Here the verse rises to the true dramatic sympathy of which I spoke. It is swept into the vortex of Faust's eddying thought, and seems to writhe and gasp in that agony of hopeless despair.

> Ah, Faustus,
> Now hast thou but one bare hour to live,
> And then thou must be damned perpetually.
> Stand still, ye ever-moving spheres of Heaven,
> That time may cease and midnight never come;
> Fair Nature's eye, rise, rise again, and make
> Perpetual day; or let this hour be but
> A year, a month, a week, a natural day,
> That Faustus may repent and save his soul!
> The stars move still, time runs, the clock will
>   strike,
> The devil will come, and Faustus must be
>   damned.

Oh, I'll leap up to my God! Who pulls me down?
See, see, where Christ's blood streams in the fir-
   mament!
One drop would save my soul—half a drop; ah,
   my Christ!
Ah, rend not my heart for naming of my Christ!
Yet will I call on Him. Oh, spare me, Lucifer!
Where is it now? 'Tis gone; and see where God
Stretcheth out His arm and bends His ireful
   brows!
Mountains and hills, come, come and fall on me,
And hide me from the heavy wrath of God!
No? No?
Then will I headlong run into the earth.
Earth, gape! Oh no, it will not harbour me!

        .   .   .   .   .   .

Ah! half the hour is past; 'twill all be past anon.
O God,
If Thou wilt not have mercy on my soul,
Yet, for Christ's sake, whose blood hath ran-
   somed me,
Impose some end to my incessant pain;
Let Faustus live in hell a thousand years—
A hundred thousand—and at last be saved!
Oh, no end's limited to damnèd souls.
Why wert thou not a creature wanting soul?
Or why was this immortal that thou hast?
Ah, Pythagoras' metempsychosis, were that
   true,
This soul should fly from me, and I be changed
Unto some brutish beast! All beasts are happy,
For when they die
Their souls are soon dissolved in elements;
But mine must live still to be plagued in Hell!
Cursed be the parents that engendered me!
No, Faustus, curse thyself, curse Lucifer,
That hath deprived thee of the joys of Heaven.
Oh, it strikes! it strikes! Now, body, turn to air,
Or Lucifer will bear thee quick to Hell.
O soul, be changed to little waterdrops
And fall into the ocean; ne'er be found!
My God, my God, look not so fierce on me!
Adders and serpents, let me breathe awhile.
Ugly Hell, gape not. Come not, Lucifer!
I'll burn my books. Ah, Mephistophilis!

It remains to say a few words of Marlowe's poem of **"Hero and Leander,"** for in translating it from Musæus he made it his own. It has great ease and fluency of versification, and many lines as perfect in their concinnity as those of Pope, but infused with a warmer coloring and a more poetic fancy. Here is found the verse that Shakespeare quotes somewhere. The second verse of the following couplet has precisely Pope's cadence:

Unto her was he led, or rather drawn,
By those white limbs that sparkled through the
   lawn.

It was from this poem that Keats caught the inspiration for his "Endymion." A single passage will serve to prove this:

So fair a church as this had Venus none;
The walls were of discolored jasper stone,
Wherein was Proteus carved, and overhead
A lively vine of green sea-agate spread,
Where by one hand light-headed Bacchus hung,
And with the other wine from grapes outwrung.

Milton, too, learned from Marlowe the charm of those long sequences of musical proper names of which he made such effective use. Here are two passages which Milton surely had read and pondered:

So from the East unto the furthest West
Shall Tamburlaine extend his puissant arm;
The galleys and those pilling brigantines
That yearly sail to the Venetian gulf,
And hover in the straits for Christians' wreck,
Shall lie at anchor in the isle Asant,
Until the Persian fleet and men of war
Sailing along the Oriental sea
Have fetched about the Indian continent,
Even from Persepolis to Mexico,
And thence unto the straits of Jubaltar."

This is still more Miltonic:

As when the seaman sees the Hyades
Gather an army of Cimmerian clouds,
Auster and Aquilon with winged steeds,

        .   .   .   .   .   .

All fearful folds his sails and sounds the main

Spenser, too, loved this luxury of sound, as he shows in such passages as this:

Now was Aldebaran uplifted high
Above the starry Cassiopeia's chair.

And I fancy he would have put him there to make music, even had it been astronomically impossible, but he never strung such names in long necklaces as Marlowe and Milton were fond of doing.

Was Marlowe, then, a great poet? For such a title he had hardly range enough of power, hardly reach enough of thought. But surely he had some of the finest qualities that go to the making of a great poet; and his poetic instinct, when he had time to give himself wholly over to its guidance, was unerring. I say when he had time enough, for he, too, like his fellows, was forced to make the daily task bring in the daily bread. We have seen how fruitful his influence has been, and perhaps his genius could have no surer warrant than that the charm of it lingered in the memory of poets, for theirs is the memory of mankind. If we allow him genius, what need to ask for more? And perhaps it would be only to him among the group of dramatists who surrounded Shakespeare that we should allow it. He was the herald that dropped dead in announcing the victory in whose fruits he was not to share. (pp. 196-203)

James Russell Lowell, "Marlowe," in Harper's New Monthly Magazine, *Vol. LXXXV, No. DVI, July, 1892, pp. 194-203.*

Algernon Charles Swinburne (essay date 1908)

[*Swinburne was an English poet, dramatist, novelist, and essayist whose dedication to the ideal of beauty openly challenged the dominant Victorian morality of his time. In his poetry, which is esteemed for its rich sonority, Swinburne did not hesitate to treat erotic themes, suggesting an atmosphere of pagan sensuality. In the following excerpt from his* Age of Shakespeare, *he characterizes Marlowe as a tremendous literary force, declar-*

ing him the "first great English poet" and "the father of English tragedy and the creator of English blank verse."]

The first great English poet was the father of English tragedy and the creator of English blank verse. Chaucer and Spenser were great writers and great men: they shared between them every gift which goes to the making of a poet except the one which alone can make a poet, in the proper sense of the word, great. Neither pathos nor humour nor fancy nor invention will suffice for that: no poet is great as a poet whom no one could ever pretend to recognise as sublime. Sublimity is the test of imagination as distinguished from invention or from fancy: and the first English poet whose powers can be called sublime was Christopher Marlowe.

The majestic and exquisite excellence of various lines and passages in Marlowe's first play must be admitted to relieve, if it cannot be allowed to redeem, the stormy monotony of Titanic truculence which blusters like a simoom through the noisy course of its ten fierce acts. With many and heavy faults, there is something of genuine greatness in *Tamburlaine the Great;* and for two grave reasons it must always be remembered with distinction and mentioned with honour. It is the first poem ever written in English blank verse, as distinguished from mere rhymeless decasyllabics; and it contains one of the noblest passages, perhaps indeed the noblest in the literature of the world, ever written by one of the greatest masters of poetry in loving praise of the glorious delights and sublime submission to the everlasting limits of his art. In its highest and most distinctive qualities, in unfaltering and infallible command of the right note of music and the proper tone of colour for the finest touches of poetic execution, no poet of the most elaborate modern school, working at ease upon every consummate resource of luxurious learning and leisurely refinement, has ever excelled the best and most representative work of a man who had literally no models before him, and probably or evidently was often, if not always, compelled to write against time for his living.

The just and generous judgment passed by Goethe on the *Faustus* of his English predecessor in tragic treatment of the same subject is somewhat more than sufficient to counterbalance the slighting or the sneering references to that magnificent poem which might have been expected from the ignorance of Byron or the incompetence of Hallam. And the particular note of merit observed, the special point of the praise conferred, by the great German poet should be no less sufficient to dispose of the vulgar misconception yet lingering among sciolists and pretenders to criticism, which regards a writer than whom no man was ever born with a finer or a stronger instinct for perfection of excellence in execution as a mere noble savage of letters, a rough self-taught sketcher or scribbler of crude and rude genius, whose unhewn blocks of verse had in them some veins of rare enough metal to be quarried and polished by Shakespeare. What most impressed the author of 'Faust' in the work of Marlowe was a quality the want of which in the author of 'Manfred' is proof enough to consign his best work to the second or third class at most. 'How greatly it is all planned!' the first requisite of all great work, and one of which the highest genius possible to a greatly gifted

barbarian could by no possibility understand the nature or conceive the existence. That Goethe 'had thought of translating it' is perhaps hardly less precious a tribute to its greatness than the fact that it has been actually and admirably translated by the matchless translator of Shakespeare—the son of Victor Hugo; whose labour of love may thus be said to have made another point in common, and forged as it were another link of union, between Shakespeare and the young master of Shakespeare's youth. Of all great poems in dramatic form it is perhaps the most remarkable for absolute singleness of aim and simplicity of construction; yet is it wholly free from all possible imputation of monotony or aridity. *Tamburlaine* is monotonous in the general roll and flow of its stately and sonorous verse through a noisy wilderness of perpetual bluster and slaughter; but the unity of tone and purpose in *Doctor Faustus* is not unrelieved by change of manner and variety of incident. The comic scenes, written evidently with as little of labour as of relish, are for the most part scarcely more than transcripts, thrown into the form of dialogue, from a popular prose 'History of Doctor Faustus'; and therefore should be set down as little to the discredit as to the credit of the poet. Few masterpieces of any age in any language can stand beside this tragic poem—it has hardly the structure of a play—for the qualities of terror and splendour, for intensity of purpose and sublimity of note. In the vision of Helen, for example, the intense perception of loveliness gives actual sublimity to the sweetness and radiance of mere beauty in the passionate and spontaneous selection of words the most choice and perfect; and in like manner the sublimity of simplicity in Marlowe's conception and expression of the agonies endured by Faustus under the immediate imminence of his doom gives the highest note of beauty, the quality of absolute fitness and propriety, to the sheer straightforwardness of speech in which his agonising horror finds vent ever more and more terrible from the first to the last equally beautiful and fearful verse of that tremendous monologue which has no parallel in all the range of tragedy.

It is now a commonplace of criticism to observe and regret the decline of power and interest after the opening acts of *The Jew of Malta.* This decline is undeniable, though even the latter part of the play is not wanting in rough energy and a coarse kind of interest; but the first two acts would be sufficient foundation for the durable fame of a dramatic poet. In the blank verse of Milton alone, who perhaps was hardly less indebted than Shakespeare was before him to Marlowe as the first English master of word-music in its grander forms, has the glory or the melody of passages in the opening soliloquy of Barabas been possibly surpassed. The figure of the hero before it degenerates into caricature is as finely touched as the poetic execution is excellent; and the rude and rapid sketches of the minor characters show at least some vigour and vivacity of touch.

In *Edward the Second* the interest rises and the execution improves as visibly and as greatly with the course of the advancing story as they decline in *The Jew of Malta.* The scene of the king's deposition at Kenilworth is almost as much finer in tragic effect and poetic quality as it is shorter and less elaborate than the corresponding scene in Shakespeare's *King Richard II.* The terror of the death-scene undoubtedly rises into horror; but this horror is with skilful simplicity of treatment preserved from passing into disgust. In pure poetry, in sublime and splendid imagination, this tragedy is excelled by *Doctor Faustus;* in dramatic power and positive impression of natural effect it is as certainly the masterpiece of Marlowe. It was almost inevitable, in the hands of any poet but Shakespeare, that none of the characters represented should be capable of securing or even exciting any finer sympathy or more serious interest than attends on the mere evolution of successive events or the mere display of emotions (except always in the great scene of the deposition) rather animal than spiritual in their expression of rage or tenderness or suffering. The exact balance of mutual effect, the final note of scenic harmony between ideal conception and realistic execution, is not yet struck with perfect accuracy of touch and security of hand; but on this point also Marlowe has here come nearer by many degrees to Shakespeare than any of his other predecessors have ever come near to Marlowe.

Of *The Massacre at Paris* it is impossible to judge fairly from the garbled fragment of its genuine text which is all that has come down to us. To Mr. Collier, among numberless other obligations, we owe the discovery of a striking passage excised in the piratical edition which gives us the only version extant of this unlucky play; and which, it must be allowed, contains nothing of quite equal value. This is obviously an occasional and polemical work, and being as it is overcharged with the anti-Catholic passion of the time, has a typical quality which gives it some empirical significance and interest. That antipapal ardour is indeed the only note of unity in a rough and ragged chronicle which shambles and stumbles onward from the death of Queen Jeanne of Navarre to the murder of the last Valois. It is possible to conjecture what it would be fruitless to affirm, that it gave a hint in the next century to Nathaniel Lee for his far superior and really admirable tragedy on the same subject, issued ninety-seven years after the death of Marlowe.

The tragedy of *Dido, Queen of Carthage,* was probably completed for the stage after that irreparable and incalculable loss to English letters by Thomas Nash, the worthiest English precursor of Swift in vivid, pure, and passionate prose, embodying the most terrible and splendid qualities of a personal and social satirist; a man gifted also with some fair faculty of elegiac and even lyric verse, but in no wise qualified to put on the buskin left behind him by the 'famous gracer of tragedians,' as Marlowe had already been designated by their common friend Greene from among the worthiest of his fellows. In this somewhat thinspun and evidently hasty play a servile fidelity to the text of Virgil's narrative has naturally resulted in the failure which might have been expected from an attempt at once to transcribe what is essentially inimitable and to reproduce it under the hopelessly alien conditions of dramatic adaptation. The one really noble passage in a generally feeble and incomposite piece of work is, however, uninspired by the unattainable model to which the dramatists have been only too obsequious in their subservience.

It is as nearly certain as anything can be which depends chiefly upon cumulative and collateral evidence that the better part of what is best in the serious scenes of *King Henry VI.* is mainly the work of Marlowe. That he is, at any rate, the principal author of the second and third plays passing under that name among the works of Shakespeare, but first and imperfectly printed as 'The Contention between the two Famous Houses of York and Lancaster,' can hardly be now a matter of debate among competent judges. The crucial difficulty of criticism in this matter is to determine, if indeed we should not rather say to conjecture, the authorship of the humorous scenes in prose, showing as they generally do a power of comparatively high and pure comic realism to which nothing in the acknowledged works of any pre-Shakespearean dramatist is even remotely comparable. Yet, especially in the original text of these scenes as they stand unpurified by the ultimate revision of Shakespeare, there are tones and touches which recall rather the clownish horseplay and homely ribaldry of his predecessors than anything in the lighter interludes of his very earliest plays. We find the same sort of thing which we find in their writings, only better done than they usually do it, rather than such work as Shakespeare's a little worse done than usual. And even in the final text of the tragic or metrical scenes the highest note struck is always, with one magnificent and unquestionable exception, rather in the key of Marlowe at his best than of Shakespeare while yet in great measure his disciple.

It is another commonplace of criticism to affirm that Marlowe had not a touch of comic genius, not a gleam of wit in him or a twinkle of humour: but it is an indisputable fact that he had. In *The Massacre at Paris,* the soliloquy of the soldier lying in wait for the minion of Henri III. has the same very rough but very real humour as a passage in the 'Contention' which was cancelled by the reviser. The same hand is unmistakable in both these broad and boyish outbreaks of unseemly but undeniable fun: and if we might wish it rather less indecorous, we must admit that the tradition which denies all sense of humour and all instinct of wit to the first great poet of England is no less unworthy of serious notice or elaborate refutation than the charges and calumnies of an informer who was duly hanged the year after Marlowe's death. For if the same note of humour is struck in an undoubted play of Marlowe's and in a play of disputed authorship, it is evident that the rest of the scene in the latter play must also be Marlowe's. And in that unquestionable case the superb and savage humour of the terribly comic scenes which represent with such rough magnificence of realism the riot of Jack Cade and his ruffians through the ravaged streets of London must be recognisable as no other man's than his. It is a pity we have not before us for comparison the comic scenes or burlesque interludes of *Tamburlaine* which the printer or publisher, as he had the impudence to avow in his prefatory note, purposely omitted and left out.

The author of *A Study of Shakespeare* was therefore wrong, and utterly wrong, when in a book issued some quarter of a century ago he followed the lead of Mr. Dyce in assuming that because the author of *Doctor Faustus* and *The Jew of Malta* was as certainly—and certainly it is difficult to deny that whether as a mere transcriber or as an original dealer in pleasantry he sometimes was— 'one of the least and worst among jesters as he was one of the best and greatest among poets,' he could not have had a hand in the admirable comic scenes of *The Taming of a Shrew.* For it is now, I should hope, unnecessary to insist that the able and conscientious editor to whom his fame and his readers owe so great a debt was over hasty in assuming and asserting that he was a poet 'to whom, we have reason to believe, nature had denied even a moderate talent for the humorous.' The serious or would-be poetical scenes of the play are as unmistakably the work of an imitator as are most of the better passages in *Titus Andronicus* and *King Edward III.* Greene or Peele may be responsible for the bad poetry, but there is no reason to suppose that the great poet whose mannerisms he imitated with so stupid a servility was incapable of the good fun.

Had every copy of Marlowe's boyish version or perversion of Ovid's *Elegies* deservedly perished in the flames to which it was judicially condemned by the sentence of a brace of prelates, it is possible that an occasional bookworm, it is certain that no poetical student, would have deplored its destruction, if its demerits—hardly relieved, as his first competent editor has happily remarked, by the occasional incidence of a fine and felicitous couplet—could in that case have been imagined. His translation of the first book of [Lucan's *Pharsalia*] alternately rises above the original and falls short of it; often inferior to the Latin in point and weight of expressive rhetoric, now and then brightened by a clearer note of poetry and lifted into a higher mood of verse. Its terseness, vigour, and purity of style would in any case have been praiseworthy, but are nothing less than admirable, if not wonderful, when we consider how close the translator has on the whole (in spite of occasional slips into inaccuracy) kept himself to the most rigid limit of literal representation, phrase by phrase and often line by line. The really startling force and felicity of occasional verses are worthier of remark than the inevitable stiffness and heaviness of others, when the technical difficulty of such a task is duly taken into account.

One of the most faultless lyrics and one of the loveliest fragments in the whole range of descriptive and fanciful poetry would have secured a place for Marlowe among the memorable men of his epoch, even if his plays had perished with himself. His **'Passionate Shepherd'** remains ever since unrivalled in its way—a way of pure fancy and radiant melody without break or lapse. The untitled fragment, on the other hand, has been very closely rivalled, perhaps very happily imitated, but only by the greatest lyric poet of England—by Shelley alone. Marlowe's poem of **Hero and Leander,** closing with the sunrise which closes the night of the lovers' union, stands alone in its age, and far ahead of the work of any possible competitor between the death of Spenser and the dawn of Milton. In clear mastery of narrative and presentation, in melodious ease and simplicity of strength, it is not less pre-eminent than in the adorable beauty and impeccable perfection of separate lines of passages.

The place and the value of Christopher Marlowe as a leader among English poets it would be almost impossible for historical criticism to over-estimate. To none of them all, perhaps, have so many of the greatest among them been so deeply and so directly indebted. Nor was ever any great writer's influence upon his fellows more utterly and unmixedly an influence for good. He first, and he alone, guided Shakespeare into the right way of work; his music, in which there is no echo of any man's before him, found its own echo in the more prolonged but hardly more exalted harmony of Milton's. He is the greatest discoverer, the most daring and inspired pioneer, in all our poetic literature. Before him there was neither genuine blank verse nor genuine tragedy in our language. After his arrival the way was prepared, the paths were made straight, for Shakespeare. (pp. 1-14)

> *Algernon Charles Swinburne, "Christopher Marlowe," in his* The Age of Shakespeare, *Chatto & Windus, 1908, pp. 1-14.*

Émile Legouis   (essay date 1924)

[*Legouis was an eminent French historian of English literature whose books include* Geoffroy Chaucer *(1910;* Geoffrey Chaucer, *1913),* Edmund Spenser *(1923;* Spenser, *1926); and the acclaimed* Histoire de la litterature anglaise *(1924;* A History of English Literature, *1926), written with Louis Cazamian. In the following excerpt from the last-named work, Legouis surveys the works of Marlowe, defining him as "a great poet whose extravagance was justified because it expressed his nature."*]

Tamburlaine, in its two parts, of which the first appeared in 1587 and the second in 1588, astonished the public for quite other reasons than the *Spanish Tragedie.* Its author was . . . , a young man of twenty-three, who had just left Cambridge. He was entirely without experience of the stage, but he compensated for this lack by the extraordinary spirit of defiance and revolt which animated his dramatic work. Novel though *Arden of Feversham* and the *Spanish Tragedie* were, they were plays which bore the imprint of the traditional morality. From end to end they denounced and condemned crime; their murders cried out for vengeance. But the new playwright dared to claim admiration for the most bloodthirsty of men, to make of him a sort of demigod.

Nothing is more characteristic of Marlowe than his choice of his first hero. He had read a translation of Tamerlane's life by the Spaniard Pedro Mexia and another life of him by Perondinus of Florence. His imagination was inflamed by the story of the career of this unmatched adventurer who from a mere shepherd became the most powerful man in all the world. There was no need to invent: to follow history, or legend in the guise of authentic history, was enough. What were Alexander and Cæsar beside this fourteenth-century Tartar, the conqueror of Persia and Muscovy who laid Hindustan and Syria waste, vanquished the Ottomans, and died at last as he was flinging himself upon China at the head of two hundred thousand warriors? What cruelty did not seem mildness beside his, who strangled a hundred thousand captives before the walls of Delhi, and set up before Bagdad an obelisk built of ninety thousand severed heads? What symbol could strike more terror than the white tents and banners which stood, in sign of friendship, before a town on the first day of one of

Tamerlane's sieges, the red tents and red flags which were there on the second day, in sign of pillage, and the banners and tents, all black, which beset it on the third day, in sign of extermination?

All this was so grandiose that Marlowe was dazzled. The man capable of so prodigious a destiny, of such unbridled contempt for human life, seemed to him a superior being, a superman to whom the petty rules of morality did not apply. His Tamburlaine massacres wholesale, women and children as well as men, laughs at the blood he sheds, imprisons the vanquished Emperor Bajazet in a cage, has his chariot drawn by kings whom he insults, burns a town in honour of the funeral of his wife, Zenocrate, and all the while remains entirely admirable, outside and above human judgment. He is the despiser of men and gods. Marlowe endows him with the boundless arrogance of an emancipated virtuoso and philosopher of the Renascence. Tamburlaine is the great victor, the conqueror of the world. Therefore he is in the right.

Marlowe transfigures him, not by omitting or weakening any of his atrocities, but by exalting them. He sees in him the triumph of the will to power and thinks that nothing could be finer. To glorify his Tamburlaine he goes to the romances of chivalry in search of heroes moved by an unbridled appetite for glory, and there finds the poetry a mere exterminator would lack. Like those extravagant knights, Tamburlaine is capable of extraordinary love. He lays the earth at the feet of his Zenocrate and when death takes her from him he threatens Heaven with his rage.

This play, which is simply Tamburlaine's life divided into scenes, expresses the strange ardours of a young scholar who had cut himself irrevocably adrift from all restraint. A libertine in both senses of the word, Marlowe prided himself on his paganism, his rebellion, not against the dogma of the Trinity only, but against the very spirit of Christianity. His ideal was the man freed from all morality who seeks the maximum of strength and enjoyment by way of impiety, sensuality and crime. What he could not declare to the public directly, he makes his Tamburlaine proclaim upon the stage. It was to the quest of the impossible that he himself aspired, and Tamburlaine is vowed to it at his first meeting with Zenocrate. She has come to him, all dishevelled and disconsolate, to ask him to pardon her father, the Sultan of Egypt. At this moment the man who had, an instant before, slaughtered the suppliant virgins of Damascus and had their corpses hoisted on pikes, utters the most lyrical of appeals to absolute beauty, a cry of grief because he knows and declares that what he calls upon is beyond his reach.

The like exaltation had already been felt by Tamburlaine at the thought of being king. On the precedent of Jupiter, who ousted his father Saturn from the throne in order to reign himself, Tamburlaine regards ambition as the spontaneous act of human nature:

> Still climbing after knowledge infinite,
> And always moving as the restless spheres.

The same wild rapture is sustained through ten acts, for two dramas are consecrated to this one hero Tamburlaine, who is almost always on the stage and by himself is nearly

the whole of either play. It is appalling to reflect on the task of Alleyn, the actor who created the part and who had to utter all this character's declamatory violence and repeated lyrical tirades. Nothing could be less dramatic or more monotonous: the same theme and same tone of passionate emphasis recur endlessly. It is true that, to captivate the sight, there are some scenes which haunted men's memories: Bajazet dying of hunger in his cage while a banquet is served to Tamburlaine, who tenders him a mouthful or two on the point of his sword; Bajazet, at the end of his endurance, braining himself against the iron bars which imprison him; his wife, Zabina, seized by madness when she sees him dead and taking her own life; above all that famous spectacle of Tamburlaine, whip in hand, drawn by two kings harnessed to his chariot to whom he cries:

> Holla, ye pamper'd jades of Asia!
> What, can ye draw but twenty miles a day?

It was never necessary to parody *Tamburlaine:* to mention it was enough. On the whole, its spectacular extravagances are dispersed, but the declamation is continuous. That men listened to this play from end to end can be explained only by supposing that the fire in the heart of the young poet caught his audience. They too must have been in a state of half-delirious exaltation. The distraught rhetoric is sustained by verse of which the unfailing sonority was as new as the subject. Marlowe began his career with a superb contempt for the popular rhymesters. He makes blank verse, hitherto without brightness or ring, thunder and echo through his play like a drum that never ceases. Other heroes, from the Herod of the mysteries downwards, had already uttered fearful blasphemies and unending rodomontade, but they had had to express them in slight stanzas or frail couplets. The verse for which men had been waiting, completely formed verse, now sounded on the stage for the first time. It was a thing too prestigious to be withstood. The wits might mock at this "spacious volubilitie of a drumming decasyllabon," at this "bragging blank verse," but, whether they would or no, they had soon, in deference to the public, themselves to beat the drum as well as they could.

The madcap was in truth a great poet whose very extravagance was justified because it expressed his nature. He produced play after play, all continuations of his first. They were perhaps less purely the expression of his temperament, but they gained by his increasing knowledge of the stage, which did not prevent them from being still mainly lyrical and oratorical. He was, however, leading a life of intense dissipation which hardly ever left him time to produce a complete work like *Tamburlaine.* He became the improviser who flings a couple of powerful scenes into a botched play.

Such was the composition of the *Tragical History of Doctor Faustus* (1588), for which he drew on one of the most fruitful of legends, but merely built an admirable framework about scenes hardly written, and clowning which reads as though the actors had been invited to fill it in as they chose.

Once more faithful to the custom of his country's stage, Marlowe divided the German legend of Faust, as he had read it, into scenes. His forceful egoism is projected into the character of the necromancer who vows himself to the devil in return for sovereign knowledge and sovereign power, and who is thus able for twenty-four years to satisfy his appetites. They are poor and coarse enough in the legend, leading him mainly to play practical jokes on the great ones of his day, the pope and the cardinals, and to make poor wretches the butt of his magic. Marlowe takes little interest in these distractions, which he barely outlines. But when Faustus evokes the spirits of the past and obtains a vision of the Greek Helen, the poet, imagining her supreme beauty, is rapt to incomparable lyricism.

Retribution follows: Faustus has to keep his bargain with Lucifer, and tremblingly awaits death and hell. Marlowe, the atheist, alone in a Christian world, must also, at times, have felt to the full the horror of his denials and his blasphemies. He was too near faith to be indifferent. The very vehemence of his professions of impiety was a sign that his emancipation was incomplete. He shook his fist at Heaven and feared at the same moment that Heaven might fall and crush him. The last scenes of *Faustus* are among the most pathetic and most grandiose in Renascence drama. They stand by themselves, distinct from all the rest of this drama. They are unsurpassable, even by Shakespeare. Marlowe, incapable of a whole masterpiece, yet had genius to reach, here and there, the sublime beauty which has no degrees. When Goethe took the same legend for the basis of one of the chief accomplishments of modern poetry, he could not eclipse the poignant greatness of his forerunner's scenes. He, who did not know how the impious tremble, could not recapture that anguish of horror.

Marlowe never again found a plot which gave him so much scope, but even in the *Jew of Malta* (1589) he sometimes reveals his lyrical power. He was doubtless led to write this melodrama by the success of the *Spanish Tragedie* and other tragedies of atrocious vengeance. His Jew, Barabas, is unjustly deprived of his goods by Christians, and by an extraordinary series of crimes avenges himself on them, and also, becoming a monomaniac, on mankind in general. Obliged to use cunning to attain his object, he is Machiavellism incarnate. His crimes must have made the hair of audiences stand on end. They accumulate until, having first delivered Malta to the Turks and then the Turks to the Christians, he falls into a cauldron of boiling water into which he had schemed to throw his last enemies.

There is only one other character who counts in this play, and he is yet more terrible, the Moorish slave Ithamore who is Barabas's tool and an incarnation of the lust of extreme cruelty.

This melodrama opens grandly, and before the Jew becomes a criminal maniac he has, like Tamburlaine, dignity and greatness. Enormously rich, we see him first in his counting-house, with heaps of gold before him, a poet intoxicated by the immensity of his own wealth and the immerse power which is its consequence. As he enumerates the countries whence his treasures come, his exaltation has a mystical greatness. Something of this remains to him when he hears the governor's order that half his estate and that of the other Jews shall be confiscated to pay the trib-

ute to the Turks, and when only he of all his co-religionists keeps his pride, remaining indignant and inflexible. It has often been said that Shakespeare dared to defy contemporary prejudice by attracting sympathy intermittently to Shylock. Yet Shakespeare's Shylock is as avaricious as he is cruel, and ridiculous through his avarice. The only true rehabilitation of the Jew is that which Marlowe attempted in his first act, where the haughty, intrepid Barabas, facing the hypocritical governor, is really a splendid figure. That he subsequently appears as a frenzied wretch is of little consequence. For a time the poet identified himself with the Jew, who may even, by the very enormity of his later crimes, have retained the strange sympathy of his creator.

Besides an unfinished play, the *Massacre at Paris,* on the massacre of St. Bartholomew, a subject which gave Marlowe his fill of horrors and attracted him by the boundless ambition of the Duke of Guise whom he made his hero, he wrote a *Dido,* which was finished by Nashe and in which he dramatised the Fourth Book of the Æneid. This play is less sombre in colour than his earlier work, but is marred in places by the worst lapses of taste. Marlowe was also able, before he died at the age of twenty-nine, to write the best of the tragedies on national history which preceded Shakespeare's, his *Edward the Second,* first acted in 1592.

Whether because Marlowe's genius had developed, or because the exigencies of historical drama obliged him to self-effacement, this play has qualities which are properly dramatic and are found in none of its predecessors. The lyrical declamation is under a new restraint. The tirades are shorter and the dialogue is better distributed in speeches. The blank verse is less strained and more pliable, nearer to the tones of the human voice. Progress in character-study is also evinced, over a numerous and diversified cast.

The subject is the truthful history of a king who is dominated by his favourites, first Gaveston and then young Mortimer. Mortimer reaches an understanding with Queen Isabella, who becomes his mistress. The betrayed king is cast into prison and put to death by the order of the two accomplices, who are in their turn executed by their victim's son.

Edward II. stands for sentimental weakness, the royal baseness which cowardice can make bloodthirsty. In Mortimer, with his unbridled ambition, Marlowe returned to one of his favourite types, and it is Mortimer who connects this play with its predecessors.

Except the death of Faustus, nothing in Marlowe's plays is more poignantly pathetic than the scene of the murder of Edward II. in Killingworth Castle by two ruffians. The end of the bad king is so miserable that he becomes an object of pity.

Edward the Second is better constructed than Marlowe's other plays, free from his habitual extravagance, humanised and less removed from contemporary drama at its average. But it shows the author's dramatic weakness the more clearly because of its very merits. This tragedy has not the lucidity necessary to character-drawing, to the weaving of a plot and to the distribution of sympathy. It also lacks variety and dramatic progression. Of the plays devoted to national history, it was, until Shakespeare, the most artistic, but a long distance separates it from the least of Shakespeare's historical dramas. The spirit of patriotism necessary to a work of the kind does not breathe in it, possibly because Marlowe, a rebel against the religion and morality of his fellow-countrymen, did not share their political passions either. Again in this play, he shows himself in revolt against the common morality, when, with lyrical exaltation, he paints the unnatural love of Edward II. for his favourite Piers Gaveston.

Marlowe added nothing to dramatic technique saving that he determined the victory of blank verse. His merit is that in his short career he set the stage on fire with the flame of his passion. Less versatile than the other prominent playwrights of his day, less able than they to conceive of multitudinous feelings distinct from his own emotions, less quick than some to catch the scenic side of things, surpassed not only by the masters, but also by mediocre playwrights, as an architect of drama and constructor of pliable and nimble dialogue, without any sense of the comic or sense of humour or any aptitude to draw a woman, Marlowe yet possessed a supreme quality which enabled him at once to lift drama into the sphere of high literature. He was a great poet, a lyrical, personal, violently egoistical poet, who carried with him his own unique conception of man and life. In spite of his atheism, he foreshadowed Milton from afar; a little of him was in the Byron who wrote *Cain,* a little in Shelley. His exclusiveness produced intensity, and the English stage was in great need of intensity. Grace, wit and fancy had been scattered on it, mingled indeed with faults of every kind, but never hitherto had it known this dash, this vehemence, animating a whole play, this rapid march, as to victory, by which drama inspires the conviction that thus to move is to be alive.

It is, after all, a mistake to suppose that every work written for the stage must have specially dramatic qualities. To give an audience an impression of greatness, to cause them to tremble with enthusiasm and feel the rush towards an end—any end: this does as well. The fact is proved by Marlowe's work as by part of Corneille's. His immediate success and his powerful influence are unquestionable. Even when his plays had come to seem extravagant they remained popular. They first made the English public feel the pride of strength, and persuaded or deluded English drama into the belief that it equalled the sublimity of the ancients. As did the *Cid,* Marlowe's plays, for all their lack of patriotism, made hearts swell with a new national pride. His characters, out of scale and unnatural as they are, can dispense with probability because they have the breath of life. Their passionate declaiming, as well as the triumph over the Armada, one year after Marlowe's first play, and the pride in distant conquests, made English hearts drunk and giddy with triumphant strength. Together with the discoveries of the great seafarers, these figures on the stage enlarged, in men's minds, the bounds of the possible. These plays were a pæan to the infinity of military power, of knowledge and of wealth. The subjects Marlowe borrowed, the heroes he moulded, were no more than his mouthpieces, voicing his exorbitant dreams. Like him

they sought the infinite and like him were never sated. (pp. 413-21)

Émile Legouis, "The Drama Until Shakespeare, From 1580 to 1592," in History of English Literature: The Middle Ages and the Renascence (650-1660) *by Émile Legouis, translated by Helen Douglas Irvine,* Modern Times (1660-1914) *by Louis Cazamian, translated by W. D. MacInnes and Louis Cazamian, revised edition, 1929, pp. 391-424.*

C. S. Lewis   (essay date 1954)

[*Lewis is considered one of the foremost Christian and mythopoeic writers of the twentieth century. An acknowledged master of fantasy literature, he was also an authority on Medieval and Renaissance literature. In the following excerpt from his* English Literature in the Sixteenth Century, *he describes* Hero and Leander *as the greatest expression of Marlowe's poetic genius. Marlowe, according to Lewis, "is our great master of the material imagination."*]

Marlowe's greatest poetical achievement is the two sestiads of his unfinished ***Hero and Leander.*** This is a more perfect work than any of his plays, not because their poetry is always inferior to it but because in it the poetry and the theme are at one. Here, and here only, he found matter to which his genius was entirely adequate. For Marlowe is our great master of the material imagination; he writes best about flesh, gold, gems, stone, fire, clothes, water, snow, and air. It is only in such concretes that his imagination can fix itself. Dramatic necessity, born of economic necessity, often drove him into alien fields and he failed to crystallize in passions proper to his characters the heady exuberance of his own emotion. The monotonous megalomania of his heroes argues as much penury as depravity in the poet. They utter screaming follies very largely because he cannot think of anything more relevant or probable for them to say. But what incapacitated him as a tragedian qualified him magnificently as a writer of erotic epyllion. This was the work he was born to do. In this form his sole business was to make holiday from all facts and all morals in a world of imagined deliciousness where all beauty was sensuous and all sensuality was beautiful. The honey-sweetness which appears as one element among many in the *Faerie Queene* or the *Arcadia* was to be the substance of the whole poem. Nothing could be simpler or more obvious than such a project, but this does not mean that it was easy to execute. Most attempts of the sort have been failures: Shakespeare himself . . . largely failed in *Venus and Adonis.* For the poet has to be continuously sweet yet never cloy us. He must be realistic enough to keep us in touch with the senses (for his theme is the flesh) yet never so realistic as to awake disgust or incredulity. Nor our sense of humour: laughter at the wrong moment is as fatal in this kind as in tragedy. Sneers at 'a pretty piece of Paganism' are inadmissible. We may, no doubt, condemn the whole genre on moral grounds: but if it is to be written at all it demands powers which hardly any poet possesses.

Marlowe's success is particularly instructive because it depends on the continual presence of a quality which would at first sight appear to be wholly inappropriate to his design: the quality of hardness. Marlowe chose for his epyllion a ringing, predominantly end-stopped couplet. He also excluded all tenderness. Love, in this poem, is not 'full of pittie' but 'deafe and cruell'. Leander woos like 'a bold sharpe sophister'. The temple of Love is decorated not with scenes of pathos and gentleness but with insolent grotesques:

> the gods in sundry shapes
> Committing headdie ryots, incest, rapes.

A male and immortal lover tries first to ravish Leander and then to murder him. The effect of all this is to dehumanize the story and thus, in one sense, to disinfect it. The mawkishness which (as Keats knew) frequently disfigures "Endymion" can win no entry. We do not think of Hero and Leander as a girl and a boy who have fallen in love; they are nothing but lovers and have no existence apart from their desires. It is as if we were allowed to share in the erotic experience of two daemons or two wild animals. And the word 'share' is here important. We do not see their frenzy from outside as we see that of Shakespeare's Venus. We are at the centre and see the rest of the universe transfigured by the hard, brittle splendour of erotic vision. That is the real function of Marlowe's preposterous, yet wholly successful, hyperboles. Hero has been offered Apollo's throne. A necklace of pebbles shines like diamonds with the light reflected from her throat. When the ladies of Sestos walk in procession the street becomes a firmament of breathing stars. In that world there are boys so beautiful that they never dare to drink at a fountain: naiads would pull them under. These hyperboles are not, even if Marlowe thought they were, mere rhetoric. They build up something like the world as the world appears at a moment of wholly unrestrained passion. In *Venus and Adonis* we are the spectators of such a passion, and it sometimes sickens us. In Marlowe's poem we see not the passion but what the passion thinks it sees. His very limitations here come to his aid. Shakespeare was even in youth too full and ripe a man to keep all reality and humanity (one thing excepted) out of his poem. Marlowe had no such difficulty: his difficulty had always been to bring them in, and this time he did not need them. We bid goodbye to the world of sober experience at the very outset. Hence the integrity, in a sense one might almost say the purity, of his poem. There is no nonsense about it, no pitiful pretence that appetite is anything other than appetite. I do not know that any other poet has rivalled its peculiar excellence. (pp. 486-88)

> *C. S. Lewis, "Verse in the 'Golden' Period," in his* English Literature in the Sixteenth Century, Excluding Drama, *Oxford at the Clarendon Press, 1954, pp. 464-535.*

Wolfgang Clemen   (essay date 1955)

[*A distinguished German Shakespearean scholar, Clemen is known for his studies on various aspects of Elizabethan drama, particularly imagery and dramatic technique. His writings include* The Development of Shakespeare's Imagery *(1951) and* Die Tragödie von Shake-

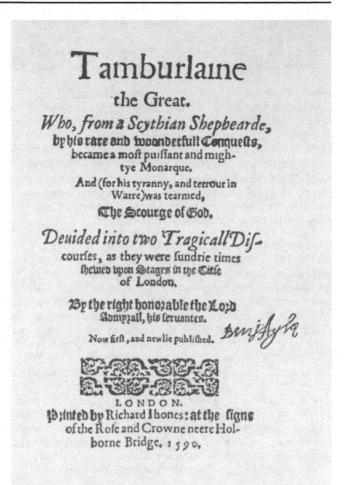

Title page for the 1590 octavo edition of Tamburlaine.

speare: ihre Entwicklung im Spiegel der dramatischen Rede *(1955;* English Tragedy before Shakespeare: The Development of Dramatic Speech, *1961). In the following excerpt from the latter work, he analyzes dramatic speech in Marlowe's major plays. In Clemen's view, the function of dramatic speech is to enable the protagonist to express the central idea of the tragedy.*]

What distinguishes the treatment of the set speech in Marlowe's ***Tamburlaine*** (c. 1587) from all that came before it will be best understood from a consideration of the play as a whole. In the classical tragedy up to this time such unity as a play possessed was a matter of outward qualities alone; in most of Marlowe's plays, on the other hand, there is an unmistakable focal point, a central issue, to which all subsidiary issues are related. In [the early English tragedy] *Gorboduc* the plot was designed to exemplify a political and moral doctrine, to which there were repeated references, and the central interest of the play is therefore communicated only in a very diluted form. In Marlowe, however, the focal point of the play is an *idea*. This idea impresses itself on us the more insistently because its representative and embodiment is the hero himself, the protagonist, round whom the whole action and all the other characters revolve. ***Tamburlaine*** represents the earliest stage of this type of drama, for here the central figure, having no one of comparable magnitude to balance him, too powerfully dominates the play and too exclusively determines its plot; he is, moreover, the only unifying factor in a work which is still clumsy and jerky in structure, and in which the same course of events is worked over again and again, climax following upon climax in a series of episodes not greatly differing from one another. For this central figure 'great and thundering speech' is the entirely appropriate medium of expression—and of existence; indeed it is the one and only form in which he does exist. When *Tamburlaine* the play is mentioned, we immediately think of Tamburlaine's speeches; they are what remains most vividly and enduringly in the memory, and the play would be unthinkable without them.

This in itself is an indication that these speeches are no longer mere 'declamatory insertions', mere purple patches introduced for the sake of immediate effect. Furthermore, the long set speech no longer appears so much a thing apart from the more fast-moving dialogue which occurs with it; on the contrary, some kind of balance is beginning to be struck, so that there are frequent transitions from long to short speeches, and from short speeches to brisk dialogue. As was becoming apparent already in *The Spanish Tragedy,* and in a cruder form even earlier in *Locrine,* speech-drama is gradually being transformed into the drama of action. However, whereas in *The Spanish Tragedy* the longer set speeches for the most part lacked any clear connexion with the passages of dialogue, even when they were immediately next to them, in *Tamburlaine* the disparity has been still further reduced, as is obvious even to the eye if we turn over the pages of the two works.

The characters of the earlier plays gave the impression that they would seize every suitable opportunity for turning a given situation into an occasion for long-winded declamation and the delivery of a set speech. This can no longer be said with regard to Tamburlaine. For Tamburlaine the set speech is a necessary and constant condition of his existence; it is the very stuff and substance of his role in the play. It follows therefore that where Tamburlaine is concerned there is a very much closer relationship between the speaker and his speeches, and that they are very much more characteristic of him personally than had been the case with any previous figure in English drama. However, even with him, it must be admitted, there is not yet any question of the creation of a real *character;* rather we have here the conception of 'a dramatic figure symbolising certain qualities' [M. C. Bradbrook, *Themes and Conventions of Elizabethan Tragedy,* 1935], and this conception is so powerful that it colours every one of Tamburlaine's speeches, and stamps it with the unmistakable hall-mark of his utterance. If Elizabethan drama more than the drama of any other time takes its life from speech, from the spoken word, if in a larger measure than any other drama it gains its power from the language it employs, then Marlowe's *Tamburlaine* marks a fresh stage of development, a stage at which this language at last becomes a genuinely dramatic medium of expression and of character-portrayal. For this is the really novel function assumed by Tamburlaine's speeches, that they are self-expression and self-portrayal of an exceptional and dynamic type;

and it is this that marks the play, for all its weaknesses, as a work of amazing genius.

Self-portrayal of the kind illustrated in Tamburlaine's speeches is something very different from the 'self-introduction' and 'self-explanation' that were regularly employed as a dramatic convention on the first entry of the characters or personified abstractions in the Miracle and Morality plays. Marlowe has made something entirely new of this device. Instead of the neutral, more or less colourless account of the character's origin, name, and nature, instead of the recital of plans and purposes, he has in Tamburlaine given us a unique self-representation which is informed in every line by the individuality of this mighty figure. In the drama before this time the monologue had usually combined its expository function with that of reinforcing the moral of the whole play; it is now in a much fuller sense a means of self-expression, and for the reason that the 'moral' in *Tamburlaine* is identified with the feelings and desires of the protagonist. Thus the earlier conventions of self-portrayal have in the person of Tamburlaine been turned to new purposes. What had been straightforward self-introduction becomes on his lips self-glorification on the grand scale; what had been the mere statement of purposes becomes the daring anticipation of all future contingencies; and the disclosure of wishes for the future becomes a voluptuous surrender to wishful thinking. All these attitudes, which find their expression in the set speeches of the play, are in a new fashion rooted in Tamburlaine's unique and remarkable personality, in his presumptuous, superhuman aspirations. His hyperbolical way of speaking, for example, his ostentatious boastfulness, fantastic and exaggerated as it may appear, does not, as Miss Una Ellis-Fermor has pointed out [in *Christopher Marlowe,* 1927], strike us as absurd. It is not just a mode of behaviour imposed on him as a dramatic type, but a personal style that is in proportion to the man himself.

This style of Tamburlaine's, well as it serves for the expression of a variety of motifs, is remarkably uniform. It is partly achieved by the grandiloquence of the blank verse; however, it is also permeated and coloured throughout by a rich metaphorical quality, and is marked by distinctive syntactical and stylistic patterns and by a distinctive vocabulary. The poetry of Tamburlaine flashes and sparkles and reverberates with sound, as though to dazzle us with its lightnings and deafen us with its thunders; it rings with the names of precious metals and other things of price; immeasurable distances and vast unplumbed depths open before us; the whole universe seems to whirl about us. It is this highly individual quality in Marlowe's imagery that fuses the heterogeneous elements of the poetry into a close harmony; it is this which, together with the dynamic character of the blank verse, constitutes the most important unifying principle of the speeches.

The most characteristic attitude that is revealed in Tamburlaine's speeches is his anticipation of the future. This comes out not only when he is unfolding his plans for the future, and in his threats and his promises, his curses and his protestations, but even in his self-glorification. For the most part this future of his has no existence in the real world, but only in a dream-world of his imagination. Accordingly it is his aspiring imagination which is the true driving force behind Tamburlaine's speeches. It flares up in every picture he gives of the future, and transmutes it into a golden vision. In consequence his plans for the future lose all concreteness and precision; they become vague, and out of touch with reality. It could hardly have been otherwise. Had Marlowe made his hero in declaring his aims for the future confine himself strictly to ideas based on reality, the intrinsic contradiction between wish and fulfilment, between the superhuman, godlike figure, as Marlowe had conceived it, and its inevitable human limitations, would have struck us as grotesque.

In these speeches of Tamburlaine, with their fanciful visions of the future, Marlowe has at the same time tried to give expression to the indomitable will of man. No playwright before Marlowe felt so intensely this power of the human will, or was able to voice it as convincingly as he did in the mighty sweep of his self-conscious, boldly individual blank verse. Practically all of Tamburlaine's utterances are manifestations of a gigantic will which, combining with his fantastic anticipations, is invested with a dynamic quality not previously found in English dramatic speech. His speeches give the impression of having an immense driving-power behind them; for all their lack of touch with reality, they have been transformed into action, and they are like blows from a club—though it must be admitted that some of these blows fall upon the empty air. The deeds which Tamburlaine in fact performs are also essentially lacking in reality, for there is no opposition, no counterforce, such as every kind of reality must give rise to.

This new passion and drive in Tamburlaine's speeches had the effect of thoroughly disrupting the static pattern of the old rhetorical structure and the old methods of rationalistic analysis. The procedure of piling up phrase upon phrase, motif upon motif, balancing verse-paragraph against verse-paragraph in an attempt to build up an obvious symmetry, is resorted to comparatively seldom, indeed only in a handful of the set speeches. Such a formal rhetorical pattern as often occurs in Kyd is certainly very rare. In its place Marlowe, true artist in language as he was, with his new blank verse introduced a new dynamic principle into the dramatic set speech, one which clearly made a profound impression on his contemporaries, and not least on Shakespeare. In his use of language form and content entered upon a new alliance. The following lines will serve as an example; they are from one of the many passages in which Tamburlaine announces his future intentions:

> Our quivering lances shaking in the air
> And bullets like Jove's dreadful thunderbolts
> Enrolled in flames and fiery smouldering mists
> Shall threat the gods more than Cyclopian wars;
> And with our sun-bright armour, as we march,
> We'll chase the stars from heaven and dim their eyes
> That stand and muse at our admired arms.
>
> (II. iii. 18-24)

The succeeding line, spoken by Theridamas, 'You see, my lord, what working words he hath', no doubt represents the impression that language of this kind made on Marlowe's contemporaries.

Such highly metaphorical language, no less than his habit of working his imagination up to the pitch of a wishful thinking that is utterly remote from reality, is characteristic of the majority of Tamburlaine's speeches, even where there is no question of threats or of warlike projects. When he is wooing Zenocrate, he does so by means of just such promises for the future, promises which develop into increasingly unreal wish-fulfilment dreams:

> Thy garments shall be made of Median silk,
> Enchas'd with precious jewels of mine own,
> More rich and valurous than Zenocrate's.
> With milk-white harts upon an ivory sled
> Thou shalt be drawn amidst the frozen pools,
> And scale the icy mountains' lofty tops,
> Which with thy beauty will be soon resolv'd.
>
> (I. ii 95-101)

What we find illustrated in this and in many other passages is a new principle of structure in the dramatic set speech, one which is no longer based on rhetoric and the rationalization of the subject-matter, but is essentially poetic in character. The imagination of the poet, darting forward to what is remote and in the future, is set aflame by the first idea it seizes upon—often it need only be a name—and bodies forth images which become progressively less tangible until they reach the realms of unreality. The structural principle in this case, therefore, is no longer that of a preconceived rhetorical 'disposition', in which every motif is treated according to the circumscribed conventions laid down for it; on the contrary, Tamburlaine's speeches are actually growing while they are being spoken. They also show, of course, the same fundamental tendency that was apparent in the classical plays, the tendency, that is, towards heightened effects, and towards *amplificatio*. The heightening and the amplification are no longer, however, achieved by the stringing together of rhetorical devices—apostrophes, questions, and the like—but by the process of enlarging on a vision; that is, it is no longer mere rhetoric which is responsible for the heightening effect, but imagination. Even when Tamburlaine speaks to Zenocrate merely to tell her to sit down on the throne beside Zabina, her name and her beauty at once conjure up in his imagination those increasingly fantastic images with which he so voluptuously invests her:

> Zenocrate, the loveliest maid alive,
> Fairer than rocks of pearl and precious stone,
> The only paragon of Tamburlaine;
> Whose eyes are brighter than the lamps of heaven,
> And speech more pleasant than sweet harmony;
> That with thy looks canst clear the darkened sky,
> And calm the rage of thundering Jupiter;
> Sit down by her.
>
> (III. iii. 117-24)

If we ran through all of Tamburlaine's speeches, we should find that the greatest amount of space in them is taken up by wish-fulfilment images of this kind. These images find their most appropriate and characteristic form of expression in Tamburlaine's many formulas of protestation, especially in the more hyperbolical protestations; it is a form of expression which Marlowe nowhere else employs as often as in this play. At the same time, these wish-fulfilment imaginings have a part to play in Tamburlaine's self-portrayal. When he sets his feet on the back of the conquered Turkish emperor Bajazeth, making a footstool of him, and triumphantly proclaims:

> For I, the chiefest lamp of all the earth,
> First rising in the east with mild aspect,
> But fixed now in the meridian line,
> Will send up fire to your turning spheres,
> And cause the sun to borrow light of you;
> (IV. ii. 36-40)

this mixture of self-glorification and vision of the future is typical of what occurs in many other passages. Indeed, even when Tamburlaine knows that his fortunes are at their highest point, expressly avowing this knowledge, even then he cannot bear to remain in the present moment, but at once turns his thoughts to new plans of conquest.

How then does it come about that this constant preoccupation with an imagined future in Tamburlaine's wishes, threats, promises, and protestations does not give the impression of wearisome rhodomontade or mere attitudinizing? The answer to this question is that, especially in Part I, Tamburlaine is impelled by more than merely a naked lust for material conquest and kingly power. As Miss Ellis-Fermor has so convincingly show, there stands behind this superhuman will the idea of the omnipotence of the human spirit, of the transfiguring power of the aspiring soul of man which can bring the unattainable within his grasp. It is this idea of the youthful Marlowe, typical of the Renaissance in its lofty conception of the human will, and at the same time romantic in its preoccupation with the remote and unattainable, that governs the speeches of Tamburlaine. It is this that sublimates the crude boasting of the bloodthirsty world-conqueror, so that the objects touched by the verse are transmuted into true poetry.

The question of the relationship between the set speech and the person addressed in it has been glanced at only in passing. Tamburlaine himself often begins a speech by addressing some other person, but within a few lines is talking about himself. This happens even in the 'conversion-speeches'. For instance, when Theridamas takes the field against him with a large army and appears before him for a parley, Tamburlaine succeeds by the persuasive power of his tongue in shaking his loyalty to his king and enticing him over to his own side. Yet the core of his speech here is self-portrayal, in the shape of a vision of the future. Again, when he addresses the captive Soldan in order to restore him, as the father of Zenocrate, to his kingly power, it is only a few moments before he goes on to speak of his own power, and the speech develops into a fresh example of his self-glorification (V. ii. 423 ff.). Even in his wooing of Zenocrate, Tamburlaine makes no attempt to attune himself to her and respond to her feelings; his courtship takes the form of boastful promises which, in that they concern solely his own purposes, once again amount to self-glorification (I. ii. 34 ff., 83 ff.). This practice of disregarding the other participant in a dialogue—a frequent practice in the earlier drama, as we have seen—

finds its dramatic justification in *Tamburlaine* in the nature of the protagonist. For in his monomania he has eyes for himself alone; he is Marlowe's first sketch of the egocentric attitude to life, an attitude which must in some ways have been that of Marlowe himself.

There are only a few speeches of Tamburlaine to which these remarks do not apply. Among them are his panegyric on Zenocrate as she lies dying and his lament for her (*2 Tam.,* II. iv. 1 ff.), the lecture on fortification to which he treats his sons (*2 Tamb.,* III. ii. 53 ff.), the long retrospective account of his life that he gives just before he himself dies (*2 Tamb.,* V. iii. 126 ff.), and his actual dying speech (*2 Tamb.,* V. iii. 224 ff.).

The panegyric on Zenocrate shows close affinities with Elizabethan poetic conventions in its structure, in the repetition of the metrically regular lines in which Zenocrate's name is introduced, and in its imagery. It is a highly lyrical description—it is indeed a formal lyric in the style of the contemporary epithalamium. It opens with references to nature's participation in Tamburlaine's feelings, and goes on to speak of Zenocrate's imminent death; it ends with five parallel visions in which we are shown the loving sympathy and grief in turn of the angels, of the heavenly bodies, of nature, and of God himself. This panegyric exemplifies the ease and naturalness with which lyrical forms could be absorbed by the drama; it shows too that Marlowe the playwright is inseparable from Marlowe the poet. Marlowe had the skill, however, to harmonize the lyricism of this passage with the dramatic style of his death-bed scene, and to make it effective in the dramatic sense; this point will be developed later. For the rest, this speech, as are all the speeches addressed to Zenocrate, is an expression of that passionate delight in beauty by which Marlowe himself was moved, and which he wished to bring out also in Tamburlaine, together with his aspirations towards infinite power. This duality might be regarded as an inconsistency by any one who, thinking in terms of psychological types, wanted to look on Tamburlaine as a real-life character, which of course he is not. As for the lecture to his sons and the account of his past life, they are both rather uncharacteristic of the way in which the set speech is normally used in *Tamburlaine;* like a number of passages in *Faustus* and other later plays of Marlowe, they are examples of traditional set-speech types introduced into a play which otherwise is striking out in new directions in the handling of the set speech. (pp. 113-23)

So far only Tamburlaine's speeches have been discussed. The other characters, who are only conventionally portrayed, and who could easily be interchanged like puppets, appear to derive their manner of speech from Tamburlaine; they give us the same boasts and threats, the same curses, and the same vehement protestations. Moreover, the same formulas occur in their speeches as in his. Bajazeth's dark threats and maledictions are in essence nothing more than a reduplication of Tamburlaine's threats with the speech-headings changed (e.g., V. ii. 151 ff.). However, the speeches of the subsidiary figures do more than those of Tamburlaine in the way of exposition, that is to say, it is they who supply the narrative element of the play. Yet it is important that the impression of Tamburlaine's greatness and might should be constantly kept before us in the speeches of these other characters, so that we may hear about him almost without intermission. This represents a further step in the direction of dramatic unity, and it is at the same time an example of that dramatic device of character-portrayal through the words of other *dramatis personae* which Shakespeare was later to develop in so masterly a fashion. There is, however, less art in the way in which this 'presence' of Tamburlaine in scenes where he does not appear in person is brought out than there is in the sense we have of Richard III's presence in every scene of the play that bears his name. Like everything else in Marlowe's play, this aspect of the hero's portrayal is obvious and obtrusive. In Act II, Scene i, for instance, there is a straightforward *descriptio* devoted to his appearance in the form of a set speech by Menaphon (II. 7-30). Such a concentrated treatment of set 'themes' by means of set speeches, not yet broken up into looser units, is typical of the pre-Shakespearian drama. These character-descriptions—and to them we might add the portrayal of Zenocrate in Tamburlaine's speeches—are also typical of the way in which Marlowe himself experienced concrete reality and gave it verbal expression. For we get no precise or concrete impressions from these speeches, and there is nothing in them of the conventional way of describing characters. Anything concrete resolves itself into comparatives and superlatives which rather obscure than clarify the picture; reality is heightened to the point where it ceases to be real. We are given, not the portrait of a person whom it would be possible to imagine, but a dynamic impression which is intended to reflect and enhance the splendour and might of the person described.

It was in the nature of Marlowe that he should thus bypass concreteness and reality and move about in worlds of ideas and fantasies, and that in his ardent, youthful aspiration towards the highest he should transcend the limitations of the immediately present and actual. This natural bent he imparted to his characters, and gave it expression in the style of their speeches. What we find in an especially pronounced degree in Tamburlaine is in a lesser degree a characteristic of all the Marlovian heroes; for all of them language is, so to speak, a means of existing in another dimension, in that it carries them beyond the bounds of their own real existence and enables them constantly to soar beyond what is actual and present. In the language they use they are able to bring to realization what they 'will' and 'desire', but would not be able to accomplish in a real existence. It is in their language that they have a foretaste and an illusion of things which happen in dreams that never come true.

Tamburlaine's 'great and thundering speech' made a tremendous impression on Marlowe's contemporaries. Obviously it reflected pretty accurately some latent ideal cherished by the men of the English Renaissance. What modern critics may feel to be insufferable bombast must at that time have seemed like a trumpet-call sounding the advent of an age that was conscious and proud of its own power. For the Elizabethans, who so persistently aimed at strong and vivid effects, quietness and restraint, the subtle point and the veiled hint, had to give place to the blatant and the forceful, to uninhibited emotion and the full-voiced assertion. It would have been easier in any other age than this to tone down the fortissimo of Tamburlaine's speeches. Shakespeare's great achievement must be seen against this background. For although parodies of this bombastic style began to appear soon after Tamburlaine became so well known a figure, Shakespeare is nevertheless the first to have toned down this forcefulness of utterance; he was the first to bring out shades of meaning, and to speak in a quiet voice capable of expressing nuances and half-tones.

The significance attached to the more considerable speeches in *Tamburlaine* might easily mislead us into overlooking the connexion between these speeches and the staging of the play as a whole. Yet the two things go hand in hand. In the classical plays the presentation of an argument by means of a set speech and its explanation in mime ran side by side, but no relationship was established between them; in *Tamburlaine* Marlowe created a highly individual dramatic style in which stage-tableau and stage business combined with the long speeches to produce a new kind of unity. A good example of this is the scene of Zenocrate's death, the scene that opens with the panegyric on Zenocrate already referred to. The stage-direction reads:

> *The arras is drawn, and* ZENOCRATE *lies in her bed of state;* TAMBURLAINE *sitting by her; three Physicians about her bed, tempering potions;* THERIDAMAS, TECHELLES, USUMCASANE *and the three sons.*
>
> (*2 Tamb.,* II. iv)

When the curtain of the inner stage is drawn a living picture is disclosed, a tableau, the stylized and symbolical grouping of which lends it a peculiar expressiveness and power. In this picture we see three sets of three characters positioned round the central group, which consists of the grief-stricken Tamburlaine and the dying Zenocrate; apart from one of the Physicians, who speaks two lines at the end of the panegyric, and Theridamas, who speaks six lines near the end of the scene, they stand there in complete silence, like a group of statuary. Marlowe has repeatedly used a three-fold arrangement of this kind in *Tamburlaine,* not only in the construction of individual scenes, but in the composition as a whole, embracing both the first and the second parts. The purely episodic type of structure appears thus to have been replaced by a closely knit, consciously stylized method of construction which aims at a clear system of character-grouping.

In Zenocrate's death-bed scene this set tableau of mutes provides a fitting background for the solemn measure of the deeply moving panegyric and lament, the second half of which also observes the tripartite principle, in that it is divided into six sections, each consisting of three lines followed by a refrain closing with Zenocrate's name. This speech ends abruptly with Tamburlaine's single-line question to the Physicians, which opens the way to dialogue; and a further question to Zenocrate, similarly a single-line question, leads to the final exchange between Zenocrate and her beloved, which again consists of three speeches. Then in Zenocrate's last words,

> Some music, and my fit will cease, my lord,
>
> (*2 Tamb.,* II. iv. 77)

we have an indirect stage-direction, which is given effect by the formal stage-direction, *They call music.* The three succeeding speeches in which Tamburlaine gives way to his grief and despair are set like frames about the death of Zenocrate, which occurs during a short pause, to the sound of music. The last of these three speeches, ending with the name of the dearly-loved Zenocrate, brings the whole scene to a close, and at its conclusion there is the final stage-direction, *The arras is drawn.* The scene is built up as a strictly organized dramatic sequence, where the speeches, like massive pillars, both frame and support the statuesque tableau, in which meanwhile only a single slight movement takes place. The grand, monumental style of the speeches, with their lyricism and their strong appeal to the emotions, has found its counterpart in a stage-tableau and a stage-action which are attended by the same ritual solemnity and grandeur. Thus the question asked earlier, whether the set speech is a mere 'insertion', leading us away from the action proper and holding it up, is not here to the point.

The last scene of the Second Part of *Tamburlaine* is also a death-bed scene, at the end of which the protagonist himself dies. In its construction this scene again illustrates Marlowe's development of a 'monumental' style of presentation, a style which no longer leaves the set speech in a vacuum, but relates it organically to the scene pictured on the stage, to the economical yet expressive and symbolic use of properties, and not least of all to the significance of the action. The solemn introductory passage is shared out between the three viceroys with their choric lament on the imminent death of Tamburlaine; and then comes Tamburlaine's triumphal entry on the ceremonial car drawn by the captive kings. The episode that follows, with its more vigorous action, is cut short and brought to a standstill by Tamburlaine's long retrospect over his past life, which stands at the mid-point of the scene. With the help of a map of the world that is brought to him, Tamburlaine describes the course of his extensive conquests, and thus at the very end of his life he at last leaves the vague realms of wishful thinking and makes contact with reality by the exactness of his topographical references. There follows the crowning of the prince Amyras, set between a speech by Tamburlaine and the answer from his newly crowned son, which develops into a lament. After a final exchange of dialogue between Tamburlaine and his trusty lieutenants, there comes the great dying speech of the world-conqueror, symbolically introduced by the bringing in of the hearse holding the body of Zenocrate. Thus in this scene all the more substantial speeches are placed at important focal points and are appropriately supported by stage-tableau or stage-business—for to all intents and purposes the group of the three mourning viceroys at the beginning is a tableau. In the main speeches the action is continually being held up or brought to a standstill, but this process is consciously and deliberately integrated with the slow forward movement of the plot, relaxed only at carefully regulated intervals.

Finally, while we are dealing with scenes of mourning and death, we should consider the way in which, in the last scene of Part I, the mourning and dying speeches of Bajazeth and Zabina and Zenocrate's contribution are made to form a natural sequence, and in which they are set off against one another and contrasted, and adjusted to the action taking place on the stage. First there is the exchange, once again divided into three pairs of speeches, between Bajazeth and Zabina, the climax of which is the two parallel speeches of execration uttered by the two as 'pendants', so to speak (V. ii. 176 ff., 192 ff.). Then, as the first part of a second trilogy, comes the dying speech of Bajazeth. This ends with his self-destruction, and it is both contrasted and outdone by its successor, which, tailing off into prose, presents the madness and death of Zabina. Both kill themselves by dashing out their brains against the iron bars of Bajazeth's cage. Hard upon this follows Zenocrate's lament, in which the blank verse is resumed, and which with Bajazeth's speech frames Zabina's prose speech and 'spotlights' it as the climax of the whole episode. This speech of Zenocrate's harks back to the bloody execution of the virgins of Damascus, and thus is made to achieve a carefully designed cumulative effect in that, to the reasons for grief that we have just beheld with our own eyes, it adds a third reason which is merely reported. Only at the very end does Zenocrate's lament refer to the calamity which has taken place a few moments earlier and which her eyes all at once take in. Thus the third of this series of laments works up a remarkable dramatic suspense. For while the spectators are every moment expecting Zenocrate to catch sight of the two bodies, the disaster that has just occurred is outweighed in her speech by her grief for an outrage that was committed earlier. Anippe's short speech of three lines which follows once more concentrates the interest of the audience directly upon the scene on the stage; and now Zenocrate embarks on another long speech in which this last frightful deed is anathematized and its ruthless author Tamburlaine is apostrophized.

If we examine this series of important speeches at the end of Part I of *Tamburlaine* solely from the point of view of the language they employ, we cannot avoid the conclusion that here, as in other episodes, Marlowe's starting-point was the epic style, and not the dramatic. However, he always succeeded in combining these epic forms of expression with a dramatic setting. Indeed he created for himself a dramatic style of presentation which was capable of absorbing a very large proportion of epic language.

In Tamburlaine's showy parades, in the set tableaux, and in the impressive way in which symbolic gesture, stage-business and properties are brought into prominence, it is quite easy to point to the various influences operating on the play: those of the pageants, of the spectacular elements in the masques, and of the Italian *trionfi*—just as, on the other side, the 'Renaissance style' of the sixteenth-century Continental theatre exhibits many features corresponding to those of *Tamburlaine,* as may be illustrated from the style of production of the Rederijke Drama in Holland, which also employed tableaux logically correlated with the grand style of declamation.

That Marlowe in his *Tamburlaine* consciously coordinated the set speech and the stage-tableau, the spoken word and stage-business, can, it is true, be maintained only with regard to a few scenes. For in many other episodes sudden alarums and battles are scattered indiscriminately among passages of speech, or are introduced by means of awkwardly explanatory lines of prose. The scuffling and the running hither and thither that are designed to cater for the eyes remain, as it were, self-contained; they are not yet related to an artistic control of language. It is with a full knowledge of this fact that the scenes in which Marlowe achieved a successful combination of language, stage-tableau, and action have been singled out for special comment. (pp. 113-29)

The Jew of Malta belongs, with *Doctor Faustus* and *Dido,* to those plays of Marlowe which, in W. W. Greg's words, 'are or appear to be only in part Marlowe's' [*Marlowe's Doctor Faustus, 1604-1616,* 1950]. The state of their texts makes it difficult to criticize these plays satisfactorily, and comment on their style and artistry must therefore be somewhat tentative. However, if we are to trace the development of Marlowe's dramatic art in general and of his handling of dramatic speech in particular, such important plays as *The Jew of Malta* and *Doctor Faustus* can certainly not be left out of account.

Even if we could assume that *The Jew of Malta* originally contained more long set speeches than the three to be found in the extant version, there can be no doubt that it has a very great deal more in the way of short dialogue than *Tamburlaine,* and that it represents an entirely different method of dramatic composition. Our safest way of approaching the play will be to begin by comparing its structure and plot with those of *Tamburlaine,* for these are the things least likely to have been affected by any cuts or alterations that may have taken place during the transmission of the text.

Tamburlaine is made up of a series of clearly defined episodes in the course of which single groups of characters appear and exchange speeches. *The Jew of Malta,* on the other hand, has a plot which is full of incident, and which includes a variety of swiftly developing and skilfully interwoven subsidiary episodes. This plot is no longer, like that of *Tamburlaine,* entirely dependent on the protagonist, nor does it, like that of *Faustus,* mirror symbolically the temptations and spiritual conflicts of the principal character. It is much more like a piece of everyday life in that it unfolds independently of its hero Barabas; it reacts on him and obliges him too to act and react, and with its constant interchange of movement and countermovement, stroke and counterstroke, it makes possible a new kind of dramatic interplay in which the hero is set against a background of continually changing situations, these situations being what determines whether he is to resolve upon action or refrain from it. In many respects, therefore, the architecture of the plot is reminiscent of Kyd's *Spanish Tragedy.* However, in spite of Kyd's greater virtuosity in the handling of the intrigue, the plot of *The Spanish Tragedy* has something contrived and artificial about it; the strings on which the puppets are made to dance are all too obviously visible. The highly melodramatic tone produced in *The Spanish Tragedy* by the declamatory character of the set speeches reappears in *The Jew of Malta* only as an undercurrent. In its place we catch, even in Barabas's long soliloquies, a new note which is much closer to the idiom of everyday speech—an unusually well modulated poetic diction, constantly varying its tempo, and capable of being adapted with a dramatic vividness to the changing subject-matter.

Marlowe's play contains no such emotional set-piece or lament, detaching us altogether from the concrete circumstances of the plot, as we find, for instance, at the beginning of Act III, Scene vii, in *The Spanish Tragedy.* Only on rare occasions does the language make us lose touch with the reality and immediacy of the events that are taking place. Nevertheless, even in *The Jew of Malta* we are still faced by the familiar discrepancy between the lyricism of the emotional outbursts and the prosaic realism with which the events of the play are reported, whether in the speeches or in the dialogue. For although these passages of lyrical emotionalism have become both shorter and fewer than those of *Tamburlaine,* they are not yet so perfectly fused with the structure and the overall stylistic impression of the play that the transition from the one level of style to the other is not perceptible. However, generally speaking this is true of Elizabethan drama as a whole, and even of the early plays of Shakespeare. Thus, for example, in Barabas's long soliloquy at the beginning of Act II, Scene i, the simile of 'the sad presaging raven, that . . . in the shadow of the silent night Doth shake contagion from her sable wings', creates a lyrical atmosphere, which forms a curious contrast with the cool and calculating terms in which Barabas elsewhere lays bare his policy. The language of the *dramatis personae* is not yet in any consistent fashion determined by their characters; this is to be found for the first time in Shakespeare.

We have seen that Marlowe was already well on the way to writing 'character-drama' in *Tamburlaine* (as also later in *Doctor Faustus*), in that he used the set speech for the self-portrayal of his characters and the reflection of their spiritual processes. Following up this side of his dramatic development, we find that in *The Jew of Malta* Barabas's longer speeches and soliloquies also serve this purpose of establishing his character; his character and personality are revealed to at least the same extent, however, in the dialogue, in the plots he devises, and in his actions and reactions generally. This method of characterization plays but a small part in *Tamburlaine* and *Doctor Faustus;* it is more finely developed here, and gives an impression of greater richness, especially in the earlier acts. In the second half of the play, which is evidently only a crude, unpolished draft, Marlowe again neglects this means of portraying character, in the third and fourth acts in particular.

While Faustus's longer speeches and soliloquies are intended to reflect his intellectual and spiritual conflicts, in Barabas's self-portrayal the emphasis is to a very large extent laid on the unfolding of his stratagems and descriptions of the circumstances in which he finds himself. Yet this self-characterization of his has a thoroughly original ring, with its thrillingly dramatic use of language and the vividness with which it conveys his actions and environment, continually intermingling the stately dignity of the poetry with the idiom of everyday speech, and even including a certain amount of colloquialism.

This form of self-revelation is the more necessary in establishing the figure of Barabas because Marlowe has endowed him with a duplicity which to a large extent derives from the fact that he is here giving dramatic embodiment to the 'policy' of the English perversions of Machiavelli. The Prologue, which is spoken by Machiavelli in person, puts the connexion beyond dispute. The extent of Machiavelli's influence on the composition, the subject-matter and the action of *The Jew of Malta* and *The Massacre at Paris* has with reason been judged so considerable, that these two plays are often spoken of as the 'Machiavellian plays' [Michel Poirer, *Christopher Marlowe,* 1951] or the 'plays of policy' [Una Ellis-Fermor, *Christopher Marlowe,* 1927]. The role of Barabas consists in this, that he almost constantly practises dissimulation towards his fellows and is a very different person from what he appears to be, and that, with a view to securing his rights or encompassing vengeance or gaining his nefarious ends, he devises dark intrigues, sets unsuspecting persons at one another's throats, and, calling 'policy' to his aid, stealthily lays traps in which his opponents, and finally even his own daughter, are to be brought to their downfall.

Barabas's numerous soliloquies are continually used to throw light on this duplicity of his. The two soliloquies at the very beginning of the play have the function of revealing to the audience the peculiar nature of the man which would account for such behaviour. The first, spoken by Barabas in his counting-house as he tells over his riches, is intended with its highly-coloured enumeration of precious stones and distant lands to give us a picture of the wealthy Jewish merchant wallowing among his treasures and awaiting the return of his argosies. The second brings into close relationship the blessings represented by this wealth and the lot of the Jew in a Christian world:

> Rather had I, a Jew, be hated thus,
> Than pitied in a Christian poverty.
>
> (I. i. 112-13)

Thus both soliloquies have a purely expository purpose. They furnish no glimpses of an inner life, nor do they represent philosophic self-questioning or disclose what the speaker's plans are for the future; in a thoroughly concrete fashion, and without any details of what has gone before, they give a picture of the present and as yet unthreatened standing of Barabas, bringing into relief the two leading motifs that are to be so important in the future action, that is, his riches and his situation as a member of the Jewish nation. No longer are these two soliloquies mere 'footlight-soliloquies'; the first in particular is attended by visible activity—the counting of the money and the stowing away of the treasures—which has a dramatic effect much more to the purpose than the passionate gestures by which soliloquies were accompanied in the earlier drama. Equally remarkable is the extent to which both soliloquies derive their substance solely from the present moment, reducing to a minimum the retrospect which elsewhere is drawn out to such great length.

However, this technique by which so much of the expository material is packed into two long soliloquies is later in the play replaced by a form of representation which makes increasingly greater use of carefully organized dialogue. All the soliloquies that follow these two are shorter; very often they are nothing more than indications of action that is going forward, combined with a brief account of the present state of affairs and intended to prepare us for future events by showing us the speaker's motives and designs. In these soliloquies, therefore, it is much less important that depth should be added to the character-study than that the audience should be provided with pointers to what is going on; thus they will not misunderstand the double game being played by Barabas, but will get some idea how his future intrigues are to be carried on. This type of soliloquy, which is very common in pre-Shakespearian drama, is almost always associated with villains and schemers. Lorenzo's soliloquies in *The Spanish Tragedy* are of the same kind, and those of Shakespeare's Richard III and Iago are also in this tradition. It is a part of the convention that the principles which are at issue should be clearly expounded, and this is illustrated in one of Barabas's soliloquies in the fifth act:

> Thus hast thou gotten, by thy policy,
> No simple place, no small authority;
> I now am governor of Malta; true,
> But Malta hates me, and, in hating me,
> My life's in danger; and what boots it thee,
> Poor Barabas, to be the governor,
> Whenas thy life shall be at their command?
> No, Barabas, this must be look'd into;
> And, since by wrong thou gott'st authority,
> Maintain it bravely by firm policy;
> At least, unprofitably lose it not:
> For he that liveth by authority,
> And neither gets him friends, nor fills his bags,
> Lives like the ass that Aesop speaketh of,
> That labours with a load of bread and wine,
> And leaves it off to snap on thistle tops:
> But Barabas will be more circumspect.
> Begin betimes; Occasion's bald behind:
> Slip not thine opportunity, for fear too late
> Thou seek'st for much, but canst not compass it.
>
> (V. ii. 27-46)

At the same time remarks dropped in dialogue are taking over the functions of self-characterization and self-explanation. The various structural forms of the play are no longer sharply differentiated, therefore, like those of earlier days; they can be interchanged, and a balance between them is beginning to be struck.

Only once in *The Jew of Malta* is there a set speech which, by reason both of its length and its subject-matter, quite obviously falls outside the bounds of dialogue; this is when Barabas tells his newly-acquired slave Ithamore about his criminal dealings (II. iii. 175 ff.). And this speech happens to be one of the weakest and least convincingly motivated in the whole play; it shows clearly the break in the portrayal of Barabas which becomes so strongly evident in the third and fourth acts.

In *The Massacre at Paris,* which has come down to us in a badly mutilated text offering little satisfactory basis for criticism, there is nothing that can be called a real set speech, although at the beginning Guise delivers a rather long expository and self-revelatory soliloquy to which the comments just made might well be applied. Quite apart from the poor state of its text, the whole play was obviously written hastily and without care, and moreover without any particular inspiration. Not only is the plot muddled, obscure, and entirely lacking in urgency; even the vigour of the language, the weight and energy of expression which are so noteworthy in all of Marlowe's other plays, has deteriorated so much that Marlowe's authorship seems to be assured only for parts of the work, and it may therefore be left out of account in the present study.

Marlowe's *Doctor Faustus* signalizes a new stage in the history of English drama in so far as here for the first time a playwright embodied in dramatic form a symbolic representation of his own spiritual wrestlings. A spiritual conflict had, it is true, been dramatized in the Morality Plays—in *Everyman,* for example. There, however, it had been the universal human conflict between good and evil, entirely divorced from the individual standpoint of the playwright. In contrast to this, although to some extent he employs the same technique as the Moralities, Marlowe endows Faustus with his own personal problems, and dramatizes his own conflicting ideas about the fundamental issues of human life. Thus *Doctor Faustus* develops into a spiritual tragedy, in the sense that the external circumstances and events of the play no longer have any intrinsic value, but are significant only in so far as they enable us to understand Faustus's spiritual state and to see what goes on inside his mind. In this context we may disregard the interpolated episodes, which were provided partly as comic relief and partly to pander to the audience's fondness for spectacle; Marlowe's authorship of these episodes is very questionable, and in any case they do not represent the core of the play. *Doctor Faustus* is, like *Tamburlaine,* a single-character play, in that the action proceeds entirely from the central figure and is entirely dependent on him; with the difference, however, that this action is not kept in motion, as in *Tamburlaine,* by the 'acting' and willing of the hero, but represents, as in *Everyman,* the temptations, conflicts, and inner struggles by which Faustus himself is beset. The other characters have therefore very little existence of their own; Faustus's antagonists are not human beings, but ultimately supernatural powers which ally themselves with the forces in his own soul.

This specific pattern is responsible for some of the essential qualities in Faustus's speeches. Although his soliloquies and longer speeches do not by any means take up the greatest amount of space in the play, for it abounds in dialogue, they are nevertheless its lifeblood, and the most important part of what it has to say.

These speeches are the natural vehicle for the expression of the spiritual warfare and the conflicts of ideas that take place in Faustus himself, the successive stages of which also determine the external structure of the play. This no longer takes the form of parallel scenes presenting contrasts or variations on a theme, but is a true sequence of scenes which have their basis entirely in Faustus's own development. Thus Marlowe in this play advances a further step towards dramatic unity, towards a full internal coherence in the dramatic structure. Not only is Faustus himself on the stage during the greater part of the play, not only does he sustain its spirit from beginning to end, but his

speeches and soliloquies open before us a path of spiritual experience the different stages of which are organically related to one another. This was not the case in *Tamburlaine.* There the longer speeches merely represented variously stated expressions of the same mental attitude and of the same determination on the protagonist's part to impose his will on others; they cannot be said to give us any feeling of development in him.

The internal conflict which we see going on through all of Faustus's speeches and soliloquies may affect their structure and diction. This is to be seen happening already in the opening soliloquy, with which Goethe's presentation of Faust has so often been compared. Here is a short excerpt:

> '*Stipendium peccati mors est.'* Ha! *'Stipendium,'*
>   etc.
> The reward of sin is death· that's hard. [*Reads*]
> '*Si pecasse negamus, fallimur*
> *Et nulla est in nobis veritas.'*
> If we say that we have no sin,
> We deceive ourselves, and there is no truth in us.
> Why, then, belike we must sin,
> And so consequently die;
> Ay, we must die an everlasting death.
>   (I. i. 39-47)

In this, as in many other passages, Latin or English sayings in the form of moral maxims and *dicta* are introduced, and at first sight it might seem that the same thing is being done here as was done by Seneca and his direct imitators in England, namely, that epigrams and sententious maxims are being dragged in at every conceivable opportunity. But in *Faustus* these sayings have an entirely different function, both in the text of the play and in the train of thought. They are not just rhetorical adornments imposed on the speeches; they are judgements that Faustus arrives at for himself, truths that he lays out before himself for examination, and which call out in him new questions or contradictions. There is serious meaning in these maxims of his; they represent for him the heads round which his thoughts revolve.

Analysis of this soliloquy as a whole, as of the majority of Faustus's speeches and soliloquies, shows that in this play we have got away from the form of set speech which deals successively, according to a plan prescribed in advance, with stereotyped themes and motifs; in its place we have self-communion, which evolves according to the promptings of the moment. Up till this time the practice of systematizing the set speech and tricking it out with rhetorical devices had stifled and deadened the processes of real thought and feeling. Here, however, Faustus is actually thinking at the same time as he is speaking; the speech grows step by step, keeping pace with the progress of his thoughts, and this is a very significant fact for the future development of dramatic speech. The voicing of genuine doubt and irresolution has taken the place here of the old see-saw of argument and counter-argument, and instead of a character talking to himself, using his speech as a means of self-revelation for the benefit of the audience, we have true soliloquy; instead of quotations and maxims with a purely decorative function, we have personal judgements which the speaker has painfully arrived at by puzzling them out for himself.

There are some exceptions, of course. A few of Faustus's speeches follow the earlier method of providing internal directions for stage-business (e.g., I. iii. 1-15) or merely reporting action (e.g., III. i. 1-24). Others again are reminiscent of the wishful thinking that was so characteristic of Tamburlaine's speeches, for Faustus shares with Tamburlaine his aspirations towards the remote, the fabulous, and the unattainable. In a good many passages, however, it is evident that a new language has been created to express hesitation and irresolution and the fluctuations of a mind torn by changing moods—for the expression, in short, of spiritual conflict. Thus the handling of the soliloquy in such a way that for the first time in English drama it reproduces the actual inner experience of a soliloquy has led in this play to the development of a new type of speech, and one that is unmistakably different from anything that had been heard before. This is illustrated in the following two short soliloquies, neither of which expresses any particular 'point of view', any 'plan', any *ad hoc* form of self-revelation; on the other hand, they both mirror exactly what goes on in Faustus's mind in those moments when he is alone:

> Now, Faustus, must
> Thou needs be damn'd, and canst thou not be
>   sav'd.
> What boots it, then, to think on God or heaven?
> Away with such vain fancies, and despair;
> Despair in God, and trust in Belzebub:
> Now go not backward; Faustus, be resolute:
> Why waver'st thou? O, something soundeth in
>   mine ear,
> 'Abjure this magic, turn to God again!'
> Ay, and Faustus will turn to God again.
> To God? he loves thee not;
> The God thou serv'st is thine own appetite,
> Wherein is fix'd the love of Belzebub:
> To him I'll build an altar and a church,
> And offer lukewarm blood of new-born babes.
>   (II. i. 1-14)

> What might the staying of my blood portend?
> Is it unwilling I should write this bill?
> Why streams it not, that I may write afresh?
> *Faustus gives to thee his soul:* oh, there it stay'd!
> Why shouldst thou not? is not thy soul thine
>   own?
> Then write again, *Faustus gives to thee his soul.*
>   (II. i. 64-9)

It is not only in the soliloquies that we are made aware of these fluctuations and conflicts in Faustus's mind; this also happens in some of the speeches that he utters in the presence of others. These often have a passionate intensity which must suggest that Marlowe was translating into dramatic speech his own personal and most deeply experienced spiritual struggles (cf. II. ii. 18-32). And this is a very remarkable, indeed astonishing, thing to find in the drama of this period, not excluding Shakespeare's.

Faustus's famous last soliloquy shows how these processes of thought and feeling may be given a setting in time, and here too the irrevocability of the fleeting time is emphasized by the stage-device of the clock that strikes the half-

hours from eleven o'clock to midnight. This is one of the outstanding passages of pre-Shakespearian drama; [in *Marlowe's Doctor Faustus, 1604-1616*] W. W. Greg describes it as 'spiritual drama keyed to its highest pitch'. Here are the first twenty lines or so:

> [*The clock strikes eleven*]
>
> Ah, Faustus,
> Now hast thou but one bare hour to live,
> And then thou must be damn'd perpetually.
> Stand still, you ever moving spheres of heaven,
> That time may cease, and midnight never come;
> Fair Nature's eye, rise, rise again, and make
> Perpetual day; or let this hour be but
> A year, a month, a week, a natural day,
> That Faustus may repent and save his soul!
> *O lente, lente currite, noctis equi!*
> The stars move still, time runs, the clock will
>   strike,
> The devil will come, and Faustus must be
>   damn'd.
> O, I'll leap up to my God!—Who pulls me
>   down?—
> See, see, where Christ's blood streams in the firmament!
> One drop would save my soul, half a drop: ah,
>   my Christ!—
> Ah, rend not my heart for naming of my Christ!
> Yet will I call on him: O, spare me, Lucifer!—
> Where is it now? 'tis gone: and see, where God
> Stretcheth out his arm, and bends his ireful
>   brows!
> Mountains and hills, come, come, and fall on
>   me,
> And hide me from the heavy wrath of God!
> No, no!
> Then will I headlong run into the earth:
> Earth, gape! O, no, it will not harbour me!
>   (V. ii. 136-60)

It is a very long way from this to the rhetorical rant of the common run of pre-Shakespearian tragic heroes when they are at the point of death. Here it is deep spiritual experience that is being transmuted into drama, reproduced with unexampled immediacy and verisimilitude in the diction and imagery, and, too, in the exclamatory character of the soliloquy. This is a true soliloquy, the utterance of a tragic hero who is overcome by a sense of desertion in the agony of his returning self-knowledge and his realization that he must carry on his struggle completely unaided. The tendency towards abstract thinking which elsewhere marks Faustus's speeches has been replaced here by the capacity to see spiritual abstractions in concrete terms as visible figures and actions, so that the spiritual conflict is transformed into something that happens before our eyes. It impresses itself on us so strongly as 'happening' for the further reason that here, probably for the first time in pre-Shakespearian drama, time is made a part of the very substance of the speech; the swift and irresistible passing of that final hour before midnight is conveyed by the unrealistic but in the dramatic sense unusually effective compression of this period of time into a speech of fifty-eight lines. It is true that the soliloquy opens with the conventional apostrophe to the heavenly spheres to stand still and the appeal to the sun to go on shining through the night. However, in this instance both appeals have their rise in Faustus's horror at the unstayable passing of time. They are not just dragged in from outside, and then immediately forgotten; the image is kept alive, so that a few lines later we read, 'The stars move still . . . ' The same is true of the later invocation to the stars (II. 160 ff.) and the images of heaven and the clouds, which are instinct with the agonized impotence of the soul that is shut off from all hope of salvation and is 'damn'd perpetually'. Desire and the frustration of desire, aspiration and its violent disappointment, here affect the character of the language itself, down to the very movement of the sentence and the choice of diction. The thrusting together within a single line of two short statements, the second of which negatives the first and despairingly acknowledges it as something impossible of fulfilment, may be classed as a form of antithesis, but it is antithesis which has ceased to be a mere rhetorical trick, because in this case it has been overlaid with reality. The tendency in the language towards a lapidary conciseness and direct simplicity, already apparent in a few of the dialogue-passages, but also to the fore in the present speech, suggests that a new type of subject-matter and a remarkable intenstification of experience have forced the playwright to seek out new forms of expression and style. In passages like this we find Marlowe's most mature dramatic writing, and the power with which Faustus's spiritual experience is conveyed in certain scenes of the play places **Doctor Faustus,** for all its deficiencies, at the very summit of Marlowe's achievement. (pp. 141-54)

Wolfgang Clemen, in his English Tragedy before Shakespeare: The Development of Dramatic Speech, *translated by T. S. Dorsch, Methuen & Co. Ltd., 1961, 301 p.*

David Daiches   (lecture date 1961)

[*Daiches is a scholar and writer whose books include* Two Worlds *(1957),* A Critical History of English Literature *(1960), and* More Literary Essays *(1968). In the following lecture originally delivered in 1961 and published in the last-named book, he praises Marlowe's extraordinary command of poetic language in his dramas, adding, nevertheless, that "we feel that, in plays as in men, virtuosity is not enough."*]

The greatest drama demands poetry rather than prose, and the reason is not far to seek. In drama the total meaning must be carried by the speech of the characters; the author cannot, as he can in the more discursive form of the novel, allow himself to comment or explain or moralise or in any other way to comment on or interpret the action. The author disappears behind his characters, whose speech and action constitute the play. The novel, which allows of every variety of author's direct and indirect comment and manipulation, does not require a language rich enough to be capable of satisfying simultaneously both the needs of the plot and the full range of awareness of the author's imaginative understanding of all its implications and suggestions. There the author can always speak in his own person. But the drama needs poetry because it needs an extra dimension of meaning built in to the speech of the characters. Modern dramatists of any stature who have

used prose have tended to insert bits of novels under the guise of stage directions, as Bernard Shaw did, giving detailed biographical and psychological information in explanatory prose before allowing any character to come on to the stage. But we could hardly imagine Shakespeare inserting a long stage direction before Hamlet's first appearance telling us that he was a sensitive young man who had recently had a severe shock and discussing the implications of his childhood relations with his dead father, his adored mother, and his smooth and resourceful uncle. In *Hamlet* all this comes out in the speech of the characters, in the language they use, in the overtones, associations, suggestions, and explorations achieved by poetic dialogue and soliloquy.

If, then, drama always tends towards poetic speech—even when, as often in Ibsen, it is formally written in prose—because it is only through poetic speech that the dramatist can make us aware of the full implications of the action, we surely do right to seek for the dramatist's meaning, his personal sense of the significance of the action he is showing us, in patterns of imagery and other characteristically poetical aspects of his use of language. To put it crudely, one might say that it is the way in which the characters talk about the actions in which they are involved that shows us what those actions mean both to the characters and to the author. In Shakespeare we often find a most suggestive counterpointing between those aspects of the language which suggest a character's own view of the significance of his actions and those which suggest if not the author's then at least some more objective or inclusive vision. In Marlowe, especially in the early Marlowe (and though the chronology of Marlowe's plays is largely a matter of inference, there can be little real doubt as to which are the earlier plays), the situation is rather different: the poetry is used not so much to interpret the action as to embody it. In **Tamburlaine** particularly there is a kind of relationship between language and action which is not easily paralleled in other poetic drama and which clearly reflects something of Marlowe's own temperament and approach to the subject. Before developing this point, let me try and illustrate it by some examples.

The Prologue, as has often been noted, shows Marlowe repudiating the more popular modes of drama of his time: he announces that he will eschew equally the "jigging veins of riming mother wits" and "such conceits as clownage keeps in pay"—that is, jog-trot rhyming verse and rough-and-tumble comic scenes. Instead

> We'll lead you to the stately tent of war
> Where you shall hear the Scythian Tamburlaine
> Threatening the world with high astounding terms
> And scourging kingdoms with his conquering sword.

We are going to see Tamburlaine in action, and that action involves, first, his "threatening the world in high astounding terms" and then "scourging kingdoms with his conquering sword". His action, that is, involves his way of talking, and indeed we might almost say that in view of the way it is put here language and action are actually equated: threatening with words and scourging with swords are parallel and even equivalent activities. The high imagination that leads to the desire for great actions must always first prove itself in rhetoric. Rhetoric, indeed, is shown in this play to be itself a form of action. We move immediately from the Prologue to the opening scene, where we find the weak Persian king Mycetes expressing to his brother his incapacity to express in words what the occasion demands:

> Brother Cosroe, I find myself agriev'd;
> Yet insufficient to express the same,
> For it requires a great and thundering speech:
> Good brother, tell the cause unto my lords;
> I know you have a better with than I.

It seems clear from these few lines that Marlowe is implying that the ability to take appropriate action is bound up with the ability to express forcibly in "a great and thundering speech" the nature of the action proposed and of the situation which provokes it. Cosroe, the stronger brother, replies to the weaker in a speech which attempts to recover in language something of the lost might and glory of Persia:

> Unhappy Persia, that in former age
> Hast been the seat of mighty conquerors,
> That, in their prowess and their policies,
> Have triumphed over Afric, and the bounds
> Of Europe where the sun dares scarce appear
> For freezing meteors and congealed cold.

This is Marlowe's first introduction of the vocabulary of power which so dominates the play. "Might", "conquerors", "prowess", "triumphed", "dares"—these potent words rise in the beat of the blank verse with a martial clang. Their force is feeble compared to the force of Tamburlaine's own speeches, but at this opening moment in the play they sufficiently express the difference between the two brothers—just as Tamburlaine's even more soaring speech will express *his* martial superiority to Cosroe.

Now this is not simply a question of Marlowe's realising the limitations of the stage, as Professor Harry Levin suggests. "Driven by an impetus towards infinity and faced with the limitations of the stage", Professor Levin writes, "the basic convention of the Marlovian drama is to take the word for the deed". This is true, and the point is acutely made, yet is seems to me wrong to suggest that "the limitations of the stage" represent a significant cause of this characteristic of Marlovian drama. It is not as though Marlowe were saying, "I cannot show you their actions, the limitations of the stage being what they are; I shall therefore have to content myself by letting you listen to them talking about their actions". It is made clear in innumerable ways that for Marlowe the proper kind of talk is both the precondition for and in a sense the equivalent of action. Soaring talk is the sign of the soaring mind, and only the soaring mind can achieve spectacularly successful action. I am not altogether happy, either, about the other cause which Professor Levin gives for Marlowe's characters taking the word for the deed—"an impetus towards infinity". One needs to be more specific about what is involved here. The infinite ambitions which spur on the Marlovian hero represent the impulse to do something more than can ever be achieved or even defined, but which

at best can only be suggested by a particular kind of poetic imagery and rhetorical splendour. There is never an objective correlative in action to the ambitions of such a hero. When Dr Faustus exclaims

> O what a world of profit and delight,
> Of power, of honour, of omnipotence
> Is promised to the studious artisan!

he is not merely giving expression to the Baconian concept of knowledge as power, as control over one's environment; both the abstractness and the variety of the words he chooses—"profit", "delight", "power", "honour", "omnipotence"—suggests that he seeks something greater than could be represented by any practical example. True, Faustus' trivial use of the power which he gets—playing practical jokes on the Pope and similar pranks—suggests the fatuity which overcomes man once he has achieved power through infernal help, and this is an important moral point: but it is also true that any given example of power in action must be trivial beside the exalted human imagination that aspires after it. The disparity between desire and achievement is for Marlowe part of the human condition, and, this being so, it is in the expression of the desire rather than in accomplishing the achievement that man reveals his most striking qualities.

To return to the opening scene of *Tamburlaine.* The first mention of the hero's name is deliberately reductive: the Persians are trying to diminish him by reducing his stature verbally, by denying his claims to a grand description. The initial description of him is as a highway robber, compared to a fox in harvest time:

> . . . that Tamburlaine,
> That, like a fox in midst of harvest-time,
> Doth prey upon my flocks of passengers, . . .

And Meander follows this up by describing him as

> that sturdy Scythian thief,
> That robs your merchants of Persepolis
> Trading by land unto the Western Isles,
> And in your confines with his lawless train
> Daily commits incivil outrages, . . .

Marlowe wants to give Tamburlaine a chance to build himself up from the lowest possible position. What could be more lowering than "sturdy Scythian thief" and "lawless train", and what a contemptuous and reductive phrase we have in "incivil outrages" when applied to Tamburlaine's deeds! When we first see Tamburlaine in the following scene, he does not immediately proceed to build himself up by magnificent rhetoric. When the Medean lords tell him that

> Besides rich presents from the puissant Cham
> We have his highness' letters to command
> Aid and assistance, if we stand in need,

he vaults over all intermediate ranks in a single quiet sentence:

> But now you see these letters and commands
> Are countermanded by a greater man.

Tamburlaine excels in the expression of the consciousness

of superiority, and this is in fact one important reason why he *is* superior.

Consciousness and acceptance of mortality limits both speech and action. The weak Mycetes charges his captain Theridamas to destroy Tamburlaine and return swiftly:

> Return with speed, time passeth swift away,
> Our life is frail, and we may die to-day.

Like Tamburlaine, he can imagine destruction, but not with the intoxicating sense of being the "scourge of God" and acting in the spirit of divine wrath, rather merely as a more passive observer of his dead enemies:

> I long to see thee back return from thence,
> That I may view these milk-white steeds of mine
> All loaden with the heads of killed men, . . .

No sooner is Mycetes off the stage than his brother Cosroe asserts his power and is crowned king by Ortygius and Cencus. The rhetoric begins to rise:

> Magnificent and mighty prince Cosroe,
> We, in the name of other Persian states
> And commons of this mighty monarchy,
> Present thee with th' imperial diadem.

This is followed shortly afterwards by the first of many speeches in which exotic geographical names sound trumpet-like, proclaiming pomp and power:

> We here do crown thee monarch of the East,
> Emperor of Asia and of Persia,
> Great lord of Media and Armenia,
> Duke of Africa and Albania,
> Mesopotamia and of Parthia,
> East India and the late discovered isles,
> Chief lord of all the wide vast Euxine Sea,
> And of the ever raging Caspian Lake.
> Long live Cosroe, mighty emperor!

Eventually, of course, Tamburlaine's trumpets out-blow all others; his rhetoric soars to heights unequalled by any other speaker in the play. But his first appearance, following immediately on Cosroe's magniloquence and Ortygius' cry, "Sound up the trumpets, then. God save the king!", shows him as relatively subdued. He is still merely the robber-shepherd, leading in his captured treasure and his fair captive Zenocrate, to whom he speaks at first rather as Comus speaks to the Lady in Milton's Masque:

> Come lady, let not this appal your thoughts;
> The jewels and the treasure we have ta'en
> Shall be reserv'd, and you in better state
> Than if you were arriv'd in Syria.

Zenocrate addresses him as "shepherd". Then, after Tamburlaine's second speech to Zenocrate, in which, as I have noted, he quietly raises himself above the "puissant Cham", Zenocrate addresses him as "my lord", adding significantly "for so you do import". Tamburlaine accepts the title, adding the characteristically Marlovian remark that it is his deeds rather than his birth that will prove him so. (It should be noted, in passing, that Marlowe was a rebel against a hereditary social hierarchy, and though his imagination revelled in all the ritual of power and rank—he several times makes great play, for example, with subordinate kings receiving their crowns from the chief of them all—he accepted it only when it was the reward of achievement rather than merely of birth. Thus Faustus was born of "parents base of stock" and Tamburlaine vaunts rather than denies his humble origin. The poverty of the University Wits bred a special kind of pride, which in Marlowe's case merged with one current of Renaissance humanism to produce a non-hereditary view of aristocracy.) Zenocrate's third address to Tamburlaine appeals to him as one who

> hop'st to be eternised
> By living Asia's mighty emperor.

It is an interesting and rapid progression—from "shepherd", to "my lord", to "mighty emperor"—and is produced entirely by Tamburlaine's way of speech.

It is perhaps surprising that Tamburlaine's first appearance should show him less as the warrior than as the lover. After all, the chief interest of the play centres on his power, whether of language or of action, and falling in love is a kind of submission rather than an exercise of power. But it is significant that Tamburlaine regards Zenocrate as someone precious whose possession signifies power. As the daughter of the Soldan of Egypt she represents a high and ancient lineage, as the betrothed of the King of Arabia she represents a challenge, and as having supreme beauty she is, like a supremely precious stone, of inestimable *value*. Tamburlaine manifests his growing power by talking about and by achieving the conquest of inexpressibly rich treasures and of kingdoms. Competitive speeches promising wealth and pomp to your favourites or to those who come over to your side, represent one of the recurring features of the play, one of Marlowe's ways of establishing relative greatness of character. In his wooing of Zenocrate Tamburlaine is outbidding all other kings and princes in the wealth and glory he can promise her and at the same time he is winning for himself something infinitely precious. His first speech of courtship both expresses his sense of Zenocrate's enormous value and promises her the highest possible style of living. Rhetoric is the art of persuasion: in putting a blazing rhetoric into Tamburlaine's mouth Marlowe expressly recognises that one of the roads to power is the ability to *win people over*. Great speech is not only both the guarantor and even the equivalent of great action; it is also in itself a means to power which takes precedence of naked physical aggression. On several occasions Tamburlaine is shown as using it first, as trying to seduce his enemies into his service or into unconditional surrender. Action, we are sometimes made to feel, is only to be resorted to when speech meets with stubbornness or deafness. Or rather, to make the point yet again, speech is presented as being the primary form of action, that form which corresponds most closely to man's actual ambitions.

We first hear the full sound of Tamburlaine's rhetoric when he encounters Theridamas, the Persian captain sent against him by Mycetes. Before Theridamas' arrival, Tamburlaine has his soldiers lay out in public view their captured gold treasure, "that their reflexions may amaze the Persians". Surrounded by this spectacular wealth, he is found by Theridamas and greets him with a huge elemental dignity:

Whom seeks thou, Persian? I am Tamburlaine.

Theridamas is impressed by Tamburlaine's appearance, and takes fire from it to speak in Tamburlaine-like tones:

> His looks do menace heaven and dare the gods,
> His fiery eyes are fixed upon the earth,
> As if he now devis'd some stratagem,
> Or meant to pierce Avernas' darksome vaults
> To pull the triple headed dog from hell.

Tamburlaine responds at once to this kind of rhetoric: this is his way of talking, and he appreciates it. We may wonder perhaps why he takes it as a sign that Theridamas is "noble and mild", but I should think that we are to regard these adjectives as a general sign of approval of his worthiness on the one hand and his capacity for being won over on the other. Tamburlaine then returns the compliment paid by Theridamas to his appearance:

> With what majesty he rears his looks!

He then embarks on the greatest of all the several speeches of competitive promising in the play. The increasing abstractness of Tamburlaine's imagery in the opening lines is the measure of his rapidly soaring imagination. The difference between being "but captain of a thousand horse" and triumphing "over all the world" is more than a difference in degree; it is the difference between the paltriness of a realisable kind of power and the magnificence of an ambition too tremendous to be capable of concrete definition. The contrast is immediate:

> Art thou but captain of a thousand horse,
> That by characters graven in thy brows,
> And by thy martial face and stout aspect,
> Deserv'st to have the leading of an host?
> Forsake thy king and do but join with me,
> And we will triumph over all the world.

From this point—as though he has intoxicated himself with the phrase "And we will triumph over all the world"—Tamburlaine's speech moves into its full grandiloquence:

> I hold the Fates bound fast in iron chains,
> And with my hand turn Fortune's wheel about,
> And sooner shall the sun fall from his sphere
> Than Tamburlaine be slain or overcome.
> Draw forth thy sword, thou mighty man at
>   arms,
> Intending but to raze my charmed skin,
> And Jove himself will stretch his hand from
>   heaven
> To ward the blow, and shield me safe from
>   harm.
> See how he rains down heaps of gold in showers,
> As if he meant to give my soldiers pay,
> And as a sure and grounded argument
> That I shall be the monarch of the East,
> He sends this Soldan's daughter rich and brave,
> To be my queen and portly emperess.
> If thou wilt stay with me, renowned man,
> And lead thy thousand horse with my conduct,
> Besides thy share of this Egyptian prize,
> Those thousand horse shall sweat with martial
>   spoil
> Of conquered kingdoms and of cities sacked.
> Both we will walk upon the lofty clifts,

> And Christian merchants, that with Russian
>   stems
> Plough up huge furrows in the Caspian Sea,
> Shall vail to us as lords of all the lake.
> Both we will reign as consuls of the earth,
> And mighty kings shall be our senators;
> Jove sometimes masked in a shepherd's weed,
> And by those steps that he hath scal'd the heav-
>   ens,
> May we become immortal like the gods.
> Join with me now in this my mean estate,
> (I call it mean, because, being yet obscure,
> The nations far remov'd admire me not,)
> And when my name and honour shall be spread,
> As far as Boreas claps his brazen wings,
> Or fair Bootes sends his cheerful light,
> Then shalt thou be competitor with me,
> And sit with Tamburlaine in all his majesty.

One has the feeling, here as elsewhere, that when Marlowe uses classical mythology it is not for decorative purposes or to make literary capital out of references to known legends, but in order to give the myths new meaning by showing their usefulness in illustrating the limitless nature of human ambition at its most magnificent:

> Jove sometimes masked in a shepherd's weed,
> And by those steps that he hath scal'd the heav-
>   ens,
> May we become immortal like the gods.

It is as though Marlowe is showing us for the first time what classical mythology is all about, what it is *for:* it helps to provide symbols for the undefinable ambitions of the unfettered human imagination. Similarly, the monstrous extravagance of

> I hold the Fates bound fast in iron chains,
> And with my hand turn Fortune's wheel about,

is not to be glossed simply by reference to the medieval notion of Fortune's wheel, though of course Marlowe depends here for his shock effect on his readers' and hearers' realising that this is a frontal attack on the common idea of the fickleness of fortune. That attack is not, however, as it has sometimes been taken to be, a sign of an almost blasphemous arrogance on Tamburlaine's or on Marlowe's part; it is a way of expressing what it feels like to have limitless ambition and limitless self-confidence. Once again one might say that the use of this kind of language is a kind of action: to be able to talk that way is half the battle. Marlowe does not present this kind of talk as *boasting,* and the actual boasting of lesser figures, such as Bajazeth, is clearly differentiated from this particular kind of abstract extravagance. Tamburlaine, when he speaks like this, has gone far beyond boasting: he is in an almost trance-like condition of relishing the significance of his own highest imaginings. Such talk carries its own conviction: a man who can talk like that is the man on whose side we want to be. Theridamas makes this quite clear:

> Not Hermes, prolocutor to the gods,
> Could use persuasions more pathetical.

This scene ends with Tamburlaine's creating around him an atmosphere of total loyalty and mutual trust. Here Tamburlaine is at his most attractive. Service on the one hand and protection on the other are subsumed in a common notion of soldierly friendship and faithfulness which has its own simpler eloquence:

> THERIDAMAS: But shall I prove a traitor to my king?
>
> TAMBURLAINE: No, but the trusty friend of Tamburlaine.
>
> THERIDAMAS: Won with thy words, and conquered with thy looks,
> I yield myself, my men, and horse to thee:
> To be partaker of thy good or ill,
> As long as life maintains Theridamas.
>
> TAMBURLAINE: Theridamas, my friend, take here my hand.
> Which is as much as if I swore by heaven,
> And call'd the gods to witness of my vow,
> Thus shall my heart be still combined with thine,
> Until our bodies turn to elements,
> And both our souls aspire celestial thrones.
> Techelles, and Casane, welcome him.
>
> TECHELLES: Welcome renowned Persian to us all.
>
> USUMCASANE: Long may Theridamas remain with us.
>
> TAMBURLAINE: These are my friends in whom I more rejoice,
> Than doth the king of Persia in his crown: . . .

The next scene shows us Cosroe being swung round to Tamburlaine by Menaphon's description of his appearance. Like Shakespeare's Cleopatra, whose beauty is symbolised by its ability to inspire eloquence in hard-bitten military men when they describe it, so Tamburlaine's greatness lies partly in its capacity for being eloquently talked about. The language here has not Tamburlaine's passion of grandeur, his commitment through language to the genuineness of his own enormous ambitions, but it strikes effectively the note of compelled admiration:

> Of stature tall, and straightly fashioned,
> Like his desire, lift upwards and divine,
> So large of limbs, his joints so strongly knot,
> Such breadth of shoulders as might mainly bear
> Old Atlas' burthen; 'twixt his manly pitch,
> A pearl more worth than all the world is placed,
> Wherein by curious sovereignty of art
> Are fixed his piercing instruments of sight,
> Whose fiery circles bear encompassed
> A heaven of heavenly bodies in their spheres,
> That guides his steps and actions to the throne
> Where honour sits invested royally:
> Pale of complexion, wrought in him with passion,
> Thirsting with sovereignty and love of arms,
> His lofty brows in folds do figure death,
> And in their smoothness amity and life:
> About them hangs a knot of amber hair,
> Wrapped in curls, as fierce Achilles' was,
> On which the breath of heaven delights to play,
> Making it dance with wanton majesty:
> His arms and fingers long and sinewy,
> Betokening valour and excess of strength:
> In every part proportioned like the man

> Should make the world subdued to Tamburlaine.

This mediated persuasion does not work as effectively as the words of Tamburlaine himself work directly on Theridamas. Cosroe does not yield to Tamburlaine as a preliminary to gaining his true friendship; he tries to make the best of both worlds by asserting that Tamburlaine will be his regent in Persia. Where Cosroe goes wrong is made abundantly clear in a later scene, where he patronises Tamburlaine and indicates that he is using him to further his own ambitions. He addresses Tamburlaine jovially as 'worthy Tamburlaine' and asks, in the tone of a squire addressing a farm labourer,

> What thinkst thou, man, shall come of our attempts?

In answer to Tamburlaine's speech of boundless confidence, Cosroe simply reiterates that he expects that the efforts of Tamburlaine and his friends

> Shall make me solely emperor of Asia,

and proceeds to dole out promises of advancement in language that sounds very tame beside that of Tamburlaine in his promising mood:

> Then shall your meeds and valours be advanced
> To rooms of honour and nobility.

Tamburlaine replies with an irony of which Cosroe is totally oblivious:

> Then haste, Cosroe, to be king alone, . . .

We are prepared for Cosroe's ultimate rejection and destruction by Tamburlaine: he has not made the right response to Tamburlaine's language.

The scene in which the timid Mycetes, caught by Tamburlaine in the act of trying to hide the crown, is contemptuously given back the crown by Tamburlaine and then runs away, will be misconstrued by the modern reader if he reads Mycetes' opening line

> Accursed be he that first invented war!

as a serious pacifist argument. Those critics who see Marlowe here as showing a humanitarian feeling and voicing a proper horror of war, or as adding some subtle touches to his portrait of Mycetes, are not reading the play that Marlowe wrote. The point about Mycetes—one is tempted to add, the only relevant point—is that he can find neither language nor gesture to correspond to his royal state, and therefore his royal state is forfeit. A crown is a symbol of human aspiration; in great spirits it provokes to eloquence of speech and magnificence of action, or at least to some behaviour correlative to the symbol's significance. All that Mycetes can think of doing with it is to hide it, to prevent himself from being known as king:

> So shall not I be known; or if I be,
> They cannot take away my crown from me.
> Here will I hide it in this simple hole.

This is anti-rhetoric, one might say. To say of a crown "Here will I hide it in this simple hole" is the ultimate lack of response to the challenge of the symbol. Tamburlaine's words, "The thirst of reign and sweetness of a crown", spoken later, show the approved response. Mycetes tends to speak in monosyllables, "For kings are clouts that every man shoots at", "And far from any man that is a fool", and when he encounters Tamburlaine he is quite incapable of rising to the occasion. Even Tamburlaine in his presence speaks with an unwonted and contemptuous simplicity:

> Well, I mean you shall have it again.
> Here, take it for a while; I lend it thee,
> Till I may see thee hemm'd with armed men.
> Then shalt thou see me pull it from thy head;
> Thou are no match for mighty Tamburlaine.

And when Mycetes discovers that it was Tamburlaine himself speaking, he records the fact in the most deflating language possible:

> O gods, is this Tamburlaine the thief?
> I marvel much he stole it not away.

Everywhere it is language that provides the clue. Compare, for example, the Persian Meander cheering up his army, with Tamburlaine's speaking to *his* men. Here is Meander:

> Therefore cheer up your minds; prepare to fight.
> He that can take or slaughter Tamburlaine,
> Shall rule the province of Albania.
> Who brings that traitor's head, Theridamas,
> Shall have a government in Media,
> Beside the spoil of him and all his train.

The province of Albania or a government in Media is tame indeed beside the vaguer but infinitely more eloquent

> We'll chase the stars from heaven and dim their
>   eyes
> That stand and muse at our admired arms.

Again, we find that for Marlowe what is realisable in precise terms cannot be the product of a truly inspired imagination. The greatest ambitions are undefinable save in terms of abstraction, mythology, or cosmic metaphor. The best that Meander can promise his soldiers is that they shall

> Share equally the gold that bought their lives,
> And live like gentlemen in Persia.

Live like gentlemen indeed! Tamburlaine's soldiers will live like gods:

> For fates and oracles of heaven have sworn
> To royalise the deeds of Tamburlaine,
> And make them blest that share in his attempts.

That Tamburlaine cannot enjoy his power unless he is talking about it or indulging in a gesture symbolical of it is not to be explained simply by the limitations of the stage: it is a paradox inherent in Marlowe's conception of human ambition. It is only after he has crowned Cosroe as emperor that Tamburlaine allows his imagination to batten on the thought of kingship. Menaphon promises Cosroe that he will "ride in triumph through Persepolis", and after he and Cosroe have gone out, leaving Tamburlaine, Theridamas, Techelles, and Usumcasane on the

stage—that is, Tamburlaine and his most faithful officers—Tamburlaine repeats and savours the words:

> And ride in triumph through Persepolis!
> Is it not brave to be a king, Techelles?
> Usumcasane and Theridamas,
> Is is not passing brave to be a king,
> And ride in triumph through Persepolis?

Here for the first time we hear the note of pure incantation in Tamburlaine's language. What is in fact involved in being a king? If we think of it, limited things—limited functions, limited powers, above all, limited length of life. The idea of kingship as it kindles the aspiring mind is more significant than a king's actual rights and duties. The word suggests power and glory—"for Thine is the kingdom, the power and the glory"—of a kind more absolute than any given example of human power and glory can be. Human beings have the power of responding to this suggestion, and in this lies their especial capacity for tragedy. Macbeth and Lady Macbeth, captivated by the magic of the idea of kingship, destroyed themselves in order to obtain it and learned at the very moment of obtaining it that their imagination of it had had nothing to do with the reality. *Tamburlaine* however is not a tragedy: Marlowe is not concerned with the disparity between the magic of names and the true nature of things, between the imagination and the reality, or with the corruption of noble minds to which this disparity can lead. To this extent the play lacks a moral pattern, lacks any real core of meaning. There is no sense of the pity of it or the waste of it or even of the ambiguity of it, though Marlowe does show some awareness of some of the paradoxes involved in the relation between words and actions. Tamburlaine is held up to our admiration in the literal Latin sense of *admirari*. His cruelty, which can be appalling, has no real moral significance one way or the other; it is simply a mode of action appropriate to a soaring ambition, and to Marlowe a soaring ambition is a mode of feeling appropriate to man's restless desire to break out of the limiting bounds within which any given actions of his must be confined. The slaughtering of the virgins and the other inhabitants of Damascus is a *gesture,* like the change of Tamburlaine's colours from white to red to black, and gestures are attempts to find actions which, though inevitably limited, are at least symbolic of something larger than themselves. I am not here concerned with Part II, which raises some different questions, but I would remark that Tamburlaine's insistence on courage to bear wounds and so on, in his discussion with his sons in Part II, and the somewhat confused picture of Calyphas as part coward, part sensualist, part realist, and part pacifist, lead us into other realms altogether. Part I is the original play, and complete in itself: in continuing it Marlowe had to modify the purity of his original conception and introduce elements which if examined closely take us far from the essential play as first conceived and written.

Tamburlaine, then, in repeating the phrase about riding in triumph through Persepolis and building up from it into an incantatory speech on the joys of kingship, is demonstrating his superiority to more mundane imaginations and his capacity for enjoying speech as a mode of action. What a king actually does, how a king actually employs and enjoys his power, is not inquired into. The idea of kingly power is itself intoxicating. When he sounds the names of his followers in a litany of invoked kingship, he is trying to carry them with him in his imaginative conception of the sweets of power. But they are not Tamburlaine. All that Techelles can say is

> O, my lord, 'tis sweet and full of pomp!

Usumcasane tries to go one better with

> To be a king, is half to be a god.

But Tamburlaine brushes these tame expressions away impatiently:

> A god is not so glorious as a king:
> I think the pleasure they enjoy in heaven,
> Cannot compare with kingly joys in earth;
> To wear a crown enchas'd with pearl and gold,
> Whose virtues carry with it life and death;
> To ask and have, command and be obeyed;
> When looks breed love, with looks to gain the
>   prize,
> Such power attractive shines in princes' eyes.

From now on he is to be chasing his language in his actions, and, in the nature of things, never catching up. I have said that the spectacle is not tragic. Tamburlaine's imagination vents itself in rhetoric which in turn rekindles his imagination to still greater ambitions, and this process is shown as guaranteeing military success. But it is an amoral process. We get the point about the restless, limitless nature of human ambition and the impossibility of its being able to find any single correlative in action. But what does it all add up to in the end?

It is no use saying that it adds up to great poetry, even if not always great dramatic poetry, for the point at issue is just how great is this kind of poetry and why. Consider the speech in which Tamburlaine most fully equates kingship with limitless human aspiration:

> The thirst of reign and sweetness of a crown
> That caused the eldest son of heavenly Ops
> To thrust his doting father from his chair,
> And place himself in the imperial heaven,
> Mov'd me to manage arms against thy state.
> What better precedent than mighty Jove?
> Nature, that fram'd us of four elements
> Warring within our breasts for regiment,
> Doth teach us all to have aspiring minds:
> Our souls, whose faculties can comprehend
> The wondrous architecture of the world,
> And measure every wandering planet's course,
> Still climbing after knowledge infinite,
> And always moving as the restless spheres,
> Wills us to wear ourselves and never rest,
> Until we reach the ripest fruit of all,
> That perfect bliss and sole felicity,
> The sweet fruition of an earthly crown.

Critics have differed as to whether the conclusion of this passage is an anti-climax or a supreme climax. At the beginning of the speech, characteristically, Marlowe presses a new meaning on a Greek myth to make it serve as an illustration and an illumination of the inevitability of continuously aspiring ambition among men. The line "What better precedent than mighty Jove?" rings out as an arrogant challenge. He next goes on to say that the four ele-

ments of which man's physical nature is composed (according to medieval and Aristotelian physiology), since they are in continual conflict with each other, teach us all to have aspiring minds. We might say that the relation between conflict and aspiration is not made clear and there seems to be no reason why the former should suggest the latter, but there is a suppressed middle term, emulation, which might bridge the logical gap here. In any case the argument is not essentially rational, but rhetorical: Tamburlaine is seeking mythological, cosmic, and natural sanctions for human aspiration: human ambition forms part of the total wonder of nature. The Faustian lines

> Our souls, whose faculties can comprehend
> The wondrous architecture of the world,
> And measure every wandering planet's course,
> Still climbing after knowledge infinite,

are very impressive in their rising eloquence and the fine, steady abstraction of "Still climbing after knowledge infinite". We are made to feel the *insatiable* nature of human curiosity. The search is never-ending—

> Until we reach the ripest fruit of all,
> That perfect bliss and sole felicity,
> The sweet fruition of an earthly crown.

The play itself, of course, belies this. Tamburlaine collects crowns as a philatelist collects stamps and remains unsatisfied. The extraordinary force of the abstract words "perfect bliss and sole felicity", suggesting a theological conception of heavenly beatitude, and, reminding us of Milton's "When everything that is sincerely good and perfectly divine", hardly prepares us for what they are leading up to, "the sweet fruition of an earthly crown". Yet I do not think the passage ends in anti-climax. The *ripest fruit* of all, that *perfect bliss* and *sole felicity,* turns out to be the *sweet fruition* of an earthly crown. The crown in this context is made, by its culminating position, into a symbol of ultimate human ambition. *This is what Tamburlaine (and Marlowe) mean, then, when they talk of a crown.* It is not the usual meaning of the word "crown" that limits the totality of meaning achieved by these lines; on the contrary, it is the meaning set up by the preceding lines that determines in what sense we are to take the word "crown" when we come to it in its climactic position. Contemplated by the imagination, an earthly crown seems to be the guarantee of what a heavenly crown is conventionally assumed to promise—"perfect bliss and sole felicity". It is the imagination which invests words and objects with symbolic meaning. The word "crown" literally "means" a circle placed on the head of a king. But the word, like the word "king", can be used to contain an idea or an emotion. This is what Shakespeare does with the words in *Richard II.* But with Marlowe the idea and the emotion are larger than any practice of kingship would warrant. Acting out kingship in language or in coronation ceremony thus becomes a way of pointing to the nature of human aspiration. Indeed, language and gesture become the best kind of action because they can bear all that the imagination puts into them and are therefore not limited as even the greatest ordinary actions are bound to be. A coronation ceremony is always more moving than a king giving laws or in any other way exhibiting his power. And in the last resort it is in the ceremony of language that human aspiration finds fullest satisfaction. This is the point so splendidly made by—or rather embodied in—the passage quoted.

What, then, does it all add up to in the end? *Tamburlaine* is a play in which the virtuosity of the actor is more important than the moral nature of his actions. The hero tells us what he is going to do before he does it; tells us what he is doing when he is doing it, and after he has done it tells us what he has done—and all in language whose grandiloquence makes almost every speech a ritual of aspiration. Successful action follows on the speech almost automatically, for speech of this kind can only spring from an irrepressible energy, a perpetual hunger for always going further and doing more, which *must* be satisfied. Those who fail are those with limited aims—contrary to the vulgar view that to limit one's aim is to make success more probable. Tamburlaine's antagonists are not only those with pettier minds; they are also those—like Bajazeth, his most formidable opponent—whose aim is complacently to maintain their achieved power, which they take for granted as part of the permanent state of things. The language of Bajazeth is not unlike that of Tamburlaine: he must be an opponent to challenge Tamburlaine's imagination and also one whose overthrow marks a significant step in Tamburlaine's pursuit of his words by his actions. One difference between the language of Bajazeth and that of Tamburlaine is that Tamburlaine's tends to be directed towards the future—what he wills to do and what he therefore will do, "For Will and Shall best fitteth Tamburlaine"—whereas the language of Bajazeth is more a complacent vaunting of what he is. When Bajazeth does talk of the future, it is in terms of intention—

> —We *mean to* take his morning's next arise
> For messenger he will not be reclaim'd,
> And *mean to* fetch thee in despite of him—

which sounds tentative beside Tamburlaine's

> I that am term'd the Scourge and Wrath of God,
> The only fear and terror of the world,
> Will first subdue the Turk, and then enlarge
> Those Christian captives which you keep as slaves.

In the verbal duel between Bajazeth and Tamburlaine this difference disappears, and both speak in terms of "will" and "shall". The event shows which is the boaster. It is however worth noting that Bajazeth projects his images of power in terms of number and quantity rather than in the cosmic and mythological imagery characteristic of Tamburlaine.

The scene immediately preceding the exchange of words between Tamburlaine and Bajazeth shows us Zenocrate, now deeply in love with Tamburlaine, being urged by Agydas to give up Tamburlaine in favour of her original Arabian king. Agydas, significantly, has no appreciation of Tamburlaine's language. When Zenocrate looks for "amorous discourse", he tells her, Tamburlaine

> Will rattle forth his facts of war and blood.

Marlowe is deliberately playing a dangerous game here, allowing us to hear this brilliantly contemptuous descrip-

tion of Tamburlaine's speech in the very middle of the play. But he is confident that once we hear Tamburlaine's voice sounding again we shall dismiss this belittling description. Even before this, he has Zenocrate reply, in language that echoes Tamburlaine's own,

> As looks the sun through Nilus' flowing stream,
> Or when the Morning holds him in her arms,
> So looks my lordly love, fair Tamburlaine;
> His talk much sweeter than the Muses' song
> They sung for honour 'gainst Pierides,
> Or when Minerva did with Neptune strive;
> And higher would I rear my estimate
> Than Juno, sister to the highest god,
> If I were matched with mighty Tamburlaine.

Tamburlaine discovers Agydas trying to tempt Zenocrate away from him, and to this man who belittles his language he addresses no words but only sends a dagger as an invitation to him to kill himself. Agydas gets the point:

> He needed not with words confirm my fear,
> For words are vain when working tools present
> The naked action of my threatened end.

There is a fine irony in Tamburlaine's refusal to use words to the man who cannot appreciate them. One is reminded of a dialogue, earlier in the play, between Mycetes and Meander.

> MYCETES: Was there such brethren, sweet Meander, say,
> That sprung of teeth of dragons venomous?
>
> MEANDER: So poets say, my lord.
>
> MYCETES: And 'tis a pretty toy to be a poet.

Miss Ellis-Fermor, in her note on this line in her edition, drew attention to what she considered its "biting irony", seeing it as a bitter comment by Marlowe on the reputation and fate of poets. But surely the irony does not lie here at all, but in the man who can neither speak nor act both doubting mythology and despising poetry. Mythology is the very stuff of much of Tamburlaine's speech, and his poetic utterance is bound up with his aspiration and thus with his capacity for action. Mycetes, incapable of poetic utterance and equally of effective action, shows his lack of understanding of the relation between language and action by his contemptuous remark about poets.

The slanging match between Zenocrate and the Turkish empress Zabina is a rather crude acting out of this same correlation between speech and action that is so important in the play: while their husbands fight it out on the field, they "manage words" in mutual taunting. Tamburlaine's humiliation and degradation of Bajazeth and Zabina and his complete victory over the Turkish forces is another acting out of his soaring ambition, yet it cannot be denied that there is an element of sadism in the detailed presentation of this cruel treatment. Bajazeth has counted on Mahomet to save him, and appeals desperately to the prophet for succour: but none comes. Man stands alone in Marlowe's universe and draws his strength from his own aspiring imagination. When Tamburlaine uses Bajazeth as a footstool and mounts on him to his throne, the gesture itself is striking—a gesture of overweening ambition and aspiration; he is not content, however, to leave it at that, but breaks out into a speech whose rhetorical extravagance gives full meaning to his symbolic act:

> Now clear the triple region of the air,
> And let the majesty of heaven behold
> Their scourge and terror tread on emperors.
> Smile, stars that reign'd at my nativity,
> And dim the brightness of their neighbour
>   lamps;
> Disdain to borrow light of Cynthia,
> For I, the chiefest lamp of all the earth,
> First rising in the east with mild aspect,
> But fixed now in the meridian line,
> Will send up fire to your turning spheres,
> And cause the sun to borrow light of you.
> My sword struck fire from his coat of steel,
> Even in Bithynia, when I took this Turk;
> As when a fiery exhalation,
> Wrapt in the bowels of a freezing cloud,
> Fighting for passage, makes the welkin crack,
> And casts a flash of lightning to the earth.
> But ere I march to wealthy Persia,
> Or leave Damascus and th' Egyptian fields,
> As was the fame of Clymene's brainsick son
> That almost brent the axletree of heaven,
> So shall our swords, our lances and our shot
> Fill all the air with fiery meteors;
> Then, when the sky shall wax as red as blood,
> It shall be said I made it red myself,
> To make me think of naught but blood and war.

In any other kind of tragedy such a speech would represent the ultimate *hubris*. But, as I have insisted, Tamburlaine is not a true tragedy and is a wholly amoral play. This is inordinate aspiration in action: it is offered to us for our admiration, not necessarily for our approval.

There is an element not only of sadism but at times of sheer sensationalism in the later scenes with Bajazeth and Zabrina, which are carefully spaced so as to suggest a crescendo of humiliation to its ultimate point. The contrast between what these two were and what they have now become is not pointed, as it would be in a medieval tragedy, with the lesson of the uncertainty of fortune and the other usual accompaniments of accounts of the falls of princes, nor, after a certain stage, does it serve any more to symbolise Tamburlaine's achievement in overcoming the great Turkish emperor. An independent psychological interest comes in, and the scene in which, after Bajazeth has brained himself against his cage, Zabina goes mad and in a whirl of lunatic words follows his example, exist for its own sake; it had many successors in Elizabethan drama.

Meanwhile, we have had the destruction of Damascus, with all its histronic accompaniments, and the defeat, and liberation for Zenocrate's sake, of Zenocrate's father, the Soldan of Egypt. As I have already argued, Tamburlaine's behaviour at Damascus is to be interpreted as showing him applying the appropriate rituals of destruction which are in turn the appropriate accompaniments of the rituals of his rise to ever increasing power. Zenocrate is unhappy, because these are her fellow Egyptians who have been slaughtered and she has not yet been reassured about her father. But we are not to see a genuine conflict here. Marlowe is not presenting Tamburlaine as torn between desire

for military glory on the one hand and love of Zenocrate on the other; there is no suggestion either of any sort of conflict between love and honour. Marlowe was no Corneille, and no Dryden. True, he shows us Zenocrate troubled about her father, and Tamburlaine troubled because Zenocrate is troubled. And Tamburlaine's distress produces one of the most admired speeches in the play. What he says in this speech is that his appreciation of female beauty is one thing which cannot be adequately represented in words. Hitherto, as we know, he has never had any difficulty in giving verbal embodiment to his ambitions, and he has not been able to savour them until he has given them verbal embodiment. Zenocrate, whom he had earlier described in language suggesting her value and preciousness, is now seen to be the possessor of a quality which troubles because the expression of it in words lies beyond "the highest reaches of human wit". The passage is a set piece—I cannot help feeling that it may have been written earlier as a separate poem and then incorporated into the play at this point—and the point it makes is not developed, nor is it related to any other pattern of meaning in the play. Further, the latter part of the speech is textually confused and in parts difficult to interpret. It almost looks as though Marlowe did not know what to do with his speech on beauty after he had introduced it. Here is the passage:

> What is beauty, saith my sufferings, then?
> If all the pens that ever poets held
> Had fed the feeling of their master's thoughts,
> And every sweetness that inspir'd their hearts,
> Their minds and muses on admired themes;
> If all the heavenly quintessence they still
> From their immortal flowers of poesy,
> Wherein as in a mirror we perceive
> The highest reaches of a human wit—
> If these had made one poem's period,
> And all combin'd in beauty's worthiness,
> Yet should there hover in their restless heads
> One thought, one grace, one wonder, at the least,
> Which into words no virtue can digest.
> But how unseemly is it for my sex,
> My discipline of arms and chivalry,
> My nature, and the terror of my name,
> To harbour thoughts effeminate and faint!
> Save only that in beauty's just applause,
> With whose instinct the soul of man is touched,
> And every warrior that is rapt with love
> Of fame, of valour, and of victory,
> Must needs have beauty beat on his conceits,
> I thus conceiving, and subduing both,
> That which hath stopt the tempest of the gods,
> Even from the fiery spangled veil of heaven,
> To feel the lovely warmth of shepherds' flames,
> And march in cottages of strowed weeds,
> Shall give the world to note, for all my birth,
> That virtue solely is the sum of glory,
> And fashions men with true nobility.

The first fourteen lines constitute a poem on the mystery and inexpressibility of beauty, very Elizabethan in feeling and imagery and conventional in movement and diction. Then Tamburlaine reproaches himself for harbouring effeminate thoughts, but goes on to defend himself by making the point that it is the working of beauty on the human imagination which leads men to their highest exploits. He ends by saying that he, who both responds to beauty and knows how to keep it in its proper place—that beauty which has led the gods to assume humble disguises—will announce to the world that it is the proper response to beauty which enables men to achieve true glory and nobility. It is difficult to feel that this speech really belongs to the play. How is this consistent with

> Nature, that fram'd us of four elements
> Warring within our breast for regiment,
> Doth teach us all to have aspiring minds

and the rest of that great vindication of the perpetually aspiring mind? Further, the conflict suggested here is not developed dramatically at all. Immediately after the speech he briefly baits Bejazeth, announces that for Zenocrate's sake he will spare her father, and goes off to win another victory. Then comes the spectacular scene of the suicide of both Bajazeth and Zabina, followed by a speech by Zenocrate in which we really see her with a divided mind. She is unhappy at the slaughter of the citizens of Damascus, and she is shaken to see the dead bodies of Bajazeth and Zabina. The sight leads her to fear for Tamburlaine: he has defied Fortune, and may in the end come to a sudden fall like "the Turk and his great empress". She asks both Jove and Mahomet to pardon Tamburlaine's "contempt of earthly fortune" and then—and this is the first and only touch of this in the whole play—shows some pity for Bajazeth and Zabina and regret that she "was not moved with ruth", for which she also asks pardon. Her main fear seems to be that Tamburlaine's contempt of fortune threatens them both. Immediately after this, the King of Arabia, mortally wounded, comes in to die at Zenocrate's feet, and Tamburlaine enters bringing in the captured and now liberated Soldan of Egypt, Zenocrate's father. Tamburlaine's worry about beauty and Zenocrate's about her husband's temerity receive no further mention. Indeed, Tamburlaine now breaks into one of his most thundering speeches, abounding in high images of power, in which he sees the multitude of those dead by his hand, including the culminating sight of the dead Bajazeth and Zabina and the dead king of Arabia, as "sights of power to grace my victory". For the first time we feel Tamburlaine's speech almost horrible, indeed inhuman, in its expression of limitless lust for power and his intoxication with the bare notion of triumphing and overcoming:

> The god of war resigns his room to me,
> Meaning to make me general of the world;
> Jove, viewing me in arms, looks pale and wan,
> Fearing my power should pull him from his throne;
> Where'er I come the fatal sisters sweat,
> And grisly death, by running to and fro
> To do their ceaseless homage to my sword;
> And here in Afric, where it seldom rains,
> Since I arriv'd with my triumphant host,
> Have swelling clouds, drawn from wide gasping wounds,
> Been oft resolv'd in bloody purple showers,
> A meteor that might terrify the earth,
> And makes it quake at every drop it drinks;
> Millions of souls sit on the banks of Styx,
> Waiting the back return of Charon's boat;
> Hell and Elysium swarm with ghosts of men

> That I have sent from sundry foughten fields
> To spread my fame through hell and up to heaven;
> And see, my lord, a sight of strange import
> Emperors and kings lie breathless at my feet;
> The Turk and his great empress, as it seems,
> Left to themselves while we were at the fight,
> Have desperately despatched their slavish lives;
> With them Arabia too hath left his life:
> All sights of power to grace my victory.
> And such are objects fit for Tamburlaine,
> Wherein, as in a mirror, may be seen
> His honour, that consists in shedding blood
> When men presume to manage arms with him.

It is immediately after this speech that the play ends with the crowning of Zenocrate and promise of her immediate marriage to Tamburlaine.

Tamburlaine is essentially a play about human aspiration, which is presented as something admirable, to be wondered at, and as something which can be fully rendered only in a special kind of rhetorical poetry in which, and only in which, the proper vehicle for the expression of this aspiration can be found. Action takes second place; it is often either perfunctory, or the casual implementation of previous and succeeding speech about it, or stylised into a ritual which removes from it all moral implication. Human nature in its less strenuous aspects breaks in on occasion, but this forms no part of the grand design of the play but is the inevitable consequence of the dramatist's inability to sustain in a state of continuous excitement his vision of man as purely *homo ambitiosus* (in his translation of Ovid's *Elegies*, Marlowe renders *ambitiosus amor* of Elegy IV Book II as "my ambitious ranging mind"). It is indeed impossible to keep going a whole play without paying some attention to the more domestic elements in human nature. The dialogue between Bajazeth and Zabina in their extremity of torment and humiliation has a kind of affectionate sweetness which threatens the whole fabric of the play:

> Sweet Bajazeth, I will prolong thy life
> As long as any blood or spark of breath
> Can quench or cool the torments of my grief.

Zabina, who is here speaking, never falters in her tone of loving courtesy towards her degraded husband, so long as he is alive. This suggests a world of values in the light of which the value of aspiration as such demands to be judged with a moral judgment. But the whole point of *Tamburlaine* is that moral judgments are irrelevant. Aspiring man is for Marlowe man at his most impressive, and impressiveness of this sort has no relation at all to morality: it is *virtù*, not virtue in the present English sense of the word, that matters. But though aspiration does certainly represent an important and captivating aspect of man, and though the picture of the great conqueror as representing one mode of man "still climbing after knowledge infinite" is presented by Marlowe with extraordinary brilliance, the glare of naked and continuous desire for power, however that desire may be presented so as to symbolise a central aspect of the human condition, becomes in the end too unrelieved a light by which to look at human nature. There are moments when we feel that Marlowe himself realised this, but because at such moments Marlowe is deflected away from his grand design, it is difficult to integrate them into the play as a whole. To take up such moments and discuss them as though they represent a genuine psychological sophistication in the presentation of the characters seems to me to be quite unrealistic. To attempt to see subtleties in the development of Zenocrate's character or to find profound moral conflict implied in Tamburlaine's "What is beauty, saith my sufferings then" speech is to try to read the play for something other than it is, and this is not profitable. *Tamburlaine* is a dramatic poem about man as an aspiring animal, and so far as a play can be made out of this limited theme Marlowe has made one. The greatest drama does not, however, push a single viewpoint so relentlessly. However much we call into service our knowledge and appreciation of the way in which Renaissance humanism developed a new and exciting view of the significance of human aspiration, the fact remains that *homo umbitiosus* is in the end a bit of a bore. For all its splendour, *Tamburlaine* tires us before we have done with it.

"I put", wrote Thomas Hobbes in his *Leviathan,* "I put for a general inclination of all mankind, a perpetual and restless desire of power after power, that ceaseth only in death". Hobbes thought that this notion was his own sadly realistic discovery. But Marlowe had been there before him, noting the same fact not with sadness but triumphantly. In spite of the sustained note of triumph, however, even in Marlowe the sadness is there. What in the end is this fury of ambition, this boundless appetite for power, this high frenzy of rhetorical expression of lust for perpetually exceeding? It divides man from his fellows (in spite of Tamburlaine's capacity for loyalty and friendship), damps down the more valuable human responses, and rides roughshod over reason and morality. Marlowe cannot, in spite of all his endeavours, prevent a sense of this from breaking into his play, though it never becomes really part of it. *Tamburlaine* the play, like Tamburlaine the character, exhibits astonishing virtuosity: but in the end we feel that, in plays as in men, virtuosity is not enough. (pp. 42-69)

> *David Daiches, "Language and Action in Marlowe's 'Tamburlaine'," in his* More Literary Essays, *The University of Chicago Press, 1968, pp. 42-69.*

Douglas Cole   (essay date 1962)

[*Cole is a literary scholar whose writings include* Suffering and Evil in the Plays of Christopher Marlowe. *In the following excerpt from that work, he discusses Marlowe's artistic vision of evil, pain, and despair. As Cole concludes, although Marlowe's "dramatic universe is humanistically oriented, it remains a world where one must say with Mephostophilis: 'Why this is Hell: nor am I out of it'."*]

In trying to define the characteristic dramaturgical and ideological dimensions of Marlowe's portrayal of suffering and evil, one is struck at first by the sheer diversity of technique and attitude exhibited in such a small body of work. The exploitation of staged physical violence ranges from the wholesale slaughter of *The Massacre at Paris* to the

single "hellish fall" of Doctor Faustus; the focus of suffering which in Part I of *Tamburlaine* falls solely on the protagonist's victims is confined in *Edward* II to the victimized protagonist; the isolable evil of *The Jew of Malta* and *The Massacre at Paris,* incarnated in an external villain, becomes inextricably part of human nature—the "enemy within"—in *Doctor Faustus;* the tableau-like formality of the death scenes of Zenocrate and Tamburlaine gives way to the grotesquely violent but symbolic character that marks the ends of Barabas and Edward; the psychological effects of grief range from pathetic illusion to malicious cursing, from madness and wild rage to passive self-pity, from Stoic resolution to Christian resignation, from despair to hateful revenge. It is evident, too, that Marlowe's diverse treatment of suffering and evil is in part a result of his dramatic eclecticism; for he has made use of the full range of the dramatic traditions and conceptions of tragedy available to him.

Marlowe's plays, in the minor scenes in *Dido* and *Faustus,* carry over from the mysteries and moralities the quality of the comedy of evil; in the behavior of Barabas, Ithamore, and Lightborn, reminiscent of the Vice, that quality is given a new twist of mordant irony. The allegorical dimension of evil in the Vice figure of the moralities is not altogether lost in Barabas, the human symbol of the ava-

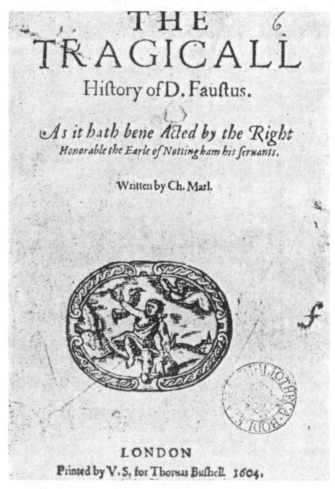

Title page for the unique copy of the 1604 quarto edition of Doctor Faustus.

rice and egoism which infect every level of action in *The Jew of Malta.* The morality conflict between spiritual good and evil lies at the heart of *Doctor Faustus,* while the more particular devices associated with this dramatic form are often reversed in the play in order to focus attention on the moral energies, choices, and blindness within Faustus himself. The characteristic emotions of the suffering wicked in the mystery-cycles, wrath and despair, are carried over into Marlowe's usage, but in an entirely new context. The element of Herodian rage in Tamburlaine's fury is undercut, not by the familiar elements of the Christian myth which provide for the ultimate defeat of evil, but by the ironic helplessness of even the mightiest of conquerors in the face of disease and death. Faustus' despair is indeed the despair of the spiritually damned, but it is a condition of his being which springs from the dramatic pattern of his repeated actions and choices throughout the play; it is not the despair *ex machina* of the older religious plays. It also functions as an operative force in the persistent tension generated by the uncertain state of Faustus' soul.

The sense of retributive justice that pervades the handling of suffering in the morality plays and the plays which borrow from that tradition is also felt in Marlowe. Suffering and destruction brought on by the character's own action or perversity is at work in one degree or another in the fates of Barabas, Guise, Edward, Mortimer, and Faustus, affording one major means of making their suffering intelligible. The "hybrid" plays, *Cambises, Horestes,* and the like, also provided Marlowe with dramatic precedent for the secularization of the Vice figure: in characters like Barabas and Lightborn, physical rather than spiritual destruction becomes the prime object of professional pride.

The motif of the inevitable fall from material prosperity which characterized *De Casibus* tragedy is given sensational embodiment in the deaths of Cosroe, Bajazeth, Zabina, and Tamburlaine himself in the two parts of *Tamburlaine;* it is epitomized in the rise and fall of Mortimer, and reaches its most subtly modulated expression in the histrionic suffering of the deposed Edward II. The *Mirror for Magistrates'* persistent urging of the responsible will rather than Fortune as the determining cause of tragic downfall is also converted into dramatic terms in Marlovian tragedy, where the network of evil is always traced to its source in the willful desires and ambitions of human agents; the careers of Barabas, Guise, Mortimer, Edward, and Faustus are effective demonstrations of this principle.

The confluence of non-dramatic *De Casibus* tragedy with the morality tradition and with the Elizabethan theoretic view of tragedy provided Marlowe with a major structural pattern: the parading of a character with a morally shocking nature through a series of incidents which demonstrate dramatically his destructive or evil quality. The Jew of Malta and the Duke of Guise are the most obvious examples; there is more procession than plot involved in the exhibition of their villainies. The same can be said of the career of Faustus, though here the moral nature of the protagonist is more complex, and the incidents which lead him to his tragic destruction are ranged in order of increasing intensity and deepening ironic significance. Tam-

burlaine's career is equally pageant-like; as his victories and ambitions swell to greater and greater proportions, the violence and destruction wrought in their wake become more and more evident; his honor is mirrored in blood, and the irony of his accomplishment is reflected in the gold coffin of Zenocrate. *The Tragedy of Dido* represents a variant of this essential framework; Cupid, representing love, provides the motive force behind the exhibition of destruction. *Edward II* is more complex; its structure is clearly divided into two parts with different aims, but the pattern in each part is roughly equivalent to the pattern of repetitive, illustrative incident which is basic in the other plays. In the first part, the object of demonstration is Edward's failure to give proper attention to either his kingdom or his wife; in the second, every scene involving Edward develops his suffering over his lost kingship, while each of the other scenes puts Mortimer's tyrannical ambition on display in the blackest of terms. It is, by the way, this characteristic tendency of Marlovian tragedy to put evil on exhibition—a tendency derived ultimately from medieval traditions—that impedes any critical approach which operates either on an Aristotelian theory of tragedy, with its demands for an admirable hero, or on a romantic-humanist theory, which exalts and values the rebel and the individualist. Although most of Marlowe's major figures are indeed individualists, one of the persistent measures of their distinction is a whole-hearted indulgence in thought and action which to the Elizabethan audience was patently evil and reprehensible. In Marlovian tragedy it is not the universe that is destructive, but the heart of man.

Unlike many *De Casibus* tragedies, Marlowe's plays do not demand the psychological punishment of remorse for those whose deeds are so clearly evil and destructive. With the great exception of Faustus, Marlowe's protagonists exhibit no sign of self-condemnation, no matter how guilty they may appear to the audience. Their lack of conventional conscience is notorious, and it cannot always be attributed to the heritage of the conscienceless Vice or Senecan tyrant. Edward II, whose torment is so closely allied to the *De Casibus* theme of lost glory, is not allowed by Marlowe to exhibit awareness of his own partial responsibility for his fall that the chronicle sources are so careful to point out. This omission achieves a measure of ironic detachment from the final plight of the king, and such ironic distance seems to be Marlowe's goal with other characters as well. The fearful dreams of Shakespeare's Richard III or the agonies of Lady Macbeth, both of which embody dramatically the conventional idea of retributive remorse, have no counterpart in Marlowe's representation of suffering. One may interpret this lack as an index of Marlowe's own contempt for conventional moralizing devices, but it would be more consistent with Marlowe's general dramatic technique to attribute it to his concern for establishing and maintaining ironic distance. Marlowe's Jew is less human than Shakespeare's Richard, though both bear the hereditary marks of the Vice; Marlowe's Guise and Mortimer, and even Tamburlaine, are less human than Macbeth, though all become bloody tyrants. At least one measure of the difference in Marlowe's figures lies in their total lack of human fear. To the degree that they lack such humanity they also lack dramatic sympathy; and thus the physical retributions that finally destroy them come with a greater sense of justice.

Marlowe's representation of suffering and evil owes less to Seneca and to English classical drama than to native tragic traditions of medieval origin. In the most "classical" and academically oriented of his plays, ***Dido Queen of Carthage,*** there is little Senecan flavor, except perhaps in the lurid quality of Aeneas' narration of the fall of Troy; Virgil and Ovid provide the predominant themes and bases of expression. ***Tamburlaine*** remains the most Senecan of Marlowe's works, but only in occasional parallels of character conception and expression, such as the physiological description of physical pain, the Stoicism of Agydas and Olympia, and the Herculean fury of the stricken Tamburlaine. Although Marlowe shares in the general debt which Elizabethan tragic drama owes to Seneca for the use of classical allusion, hyperbolic imagery, the five-act structure, and carefully elaborated rhetoric, neither of the ***Tamburlaine*** plays bears much resemblance to the conscious imitations of Senecan style found in the academic tragedies. For all ***Tamburlaine's*** emphasis on eloquence, there is more dramatized action involving suffering and death in the play than in any of the academic efforts, just as there is an obvious lack of sententiousness or explicit moral comment by a chorus. Though the theme of ambition makes a startling appearance in Marlowe's plays, it has little to do with the political contexts of evil established in the English classical drama. Marlowe has even less to do with the basic Senecan situations of the sufferer tormented by overpowering passion, or by the suicidal wish to inflict punishment upon himself for some semi-voluntary or involuntary crime, and actual suicide is conspicuously absent from the plays except for ***Tamburlaine*** and ***Dido.*** Finally, the fundamental Senecan theme of Stoical resistance to an inevitably hostile universe is also conspicuous for its absence in Marlovian tragedy; in Marlowe's tragic vision the root of hostility, evil, and destruction lies in the will of man.

Marlowe shares with Kyd the wholesale exhibition of violence and death on stage, but the most tragic of his plays—***Faustus*** and ***Edward II***—do not depend primarily on such sensational exploitation of external suffering. The motive of revenge, vital in Kyd's *Spanish Tragedy,* is used by Marlowe chiefly in **The Jew of Malta,** but with differences greater than any similarities: in *The Spanish Tragedy,* revenge is an obsession which drives the distraught but innocent parents of Horatio to frenzy and insanity; in ***The Jew,*** revenge is but one of the fine arts of destruction practiced with cold and ingenious calculation by the malicious Barabas—the difference is that between the impassioned Senecan revenger and the inhuman morality Vice. The kind of mental suffering Kyd exploits is in a long tradition of domestic pathos: the lament of a father or mother for a lost child—a stock situation in both the native and Senecan dramatic traditions. Kyd gives it poetic and dramatic elaboration and makes it part of the motive force of his play; Marlowe, on the contrary, hardly ever touches it. Where Kyd and Marlowe are most alike is in turning poetry into drama, the verbal image into the visual image, metaphor into action. The sorrow of their characters is given more than precise poetic articulation; it is dramatically activat-

ed. Though there are still traces of the self-contained, set lament in both ***Tamburlaine*** and *The Spanish Tragedy,* one can see new life breaking out in dramatic gesture, such as the mourning Tamburlaine's splintering his lance on the ground in the effort to free the furies who might bring back Zenocrate, or Isabella's cutting down the arbor in which her son was slain. Marlowe's dramatic articulation of suffering is most effectively realized in the last scenes of ***Edward II*** and ***Faustus:*** the hell of grief that the deposed king feels is mirrored in his physical situation—helplessness before his diabolic torturers; similarly, when the aspiring Faustus tries to leap up to his God, he falls, Icarus-like, back to earth—the earth that will not harbor him.

Despite all that is diverse and derivative in Marlowe's dramatic depiction of suffering and evil, there emerge from his plays certain central preoccupations and techniques which are the true measure of his originality. At the heart of Marlovian tragedy one finds the persistent expression of the sense of loss, the persistent dimension of irony in human aspiration and destruction, and persistent emphasis on human responsibility for suffering and evil.

It has been truly said that in the development of English tragedy Marlowe's heroes were "the first to die dramatically, significantly, revealing in their deaths the deepest meaning of their lives" [Herbert J. Muller, The Spirit of Tragedy, 1956]. It might be more accurate to say that they reveal in their greatest sufferings the deepest meaning of their lives, and the greatest suffering in each case is not always death. Dido's deepest grief is the cause of her death, but it is not the prospect of death that causes her deepest grief—it is the loss of her lover. Tamburlaine's greatest fury—his way of expressing suffering—is sparked by the death of Zenocrate, and by the temporary loss of his own convictions of superhumanity. The Jew of Malta is struck most severely by the loss of his gold; Guise, by the frustration of his ambition. Edward's most extravagant sorrow results from separation from his unworthy favorites, and especially from the loss of his crown. In **Doctor Faustus,** the greatest suffering of hell is revealed as what theology calls the pain of loss: the pain that Faustus will not credit until he feels it for himself, until he experiences its foreshadowing during his last terrible hour on earth; for him it is not death, but the loss beyond death, that is most tormenting. Essentially, it is the pain of loss, either in its precise theological definition or in an analogous form, which constitutes the greatest anguish for each of Marlowe's protagonists; the pain of loss is central to the Marlovian vision of suffering.

If Marlowe's theological training entered into his view of human experience, as I think **Doctor Faustus** demonstrates, it provided him with a conception of the causes of pain in the human soul which could be fruitfully developed in dramatic tragedy. The pain of loss is the greatest of all known sufferings because it represents the alienation of the creature from the Creator, the interminable separation of the human soul from the one Being in which it could have found perfect fulfillment. The nature of the suffering is defined by the nature of the sufferer. This principle can be transposed by analogy to human experience which does not involve the supernatural, and to any human relationship grounded in love or desire, in which the object of love or desire promises a certain fulfillment and the privation of that object results in frustration or pain. The soul is weighed in the balance by what delights her, as St. Augustine put it, which is another way of saying that what a man loves tells most about what that man *is*. The converse is equally true: what makes a man most acutely suffer reveals his nature—his own particular nature is defined by the nature of his suffering. Here is a principle rich in potential for dramatic characterization. The suffering of a dramatic figure can define the precise nature of his character, if what makes him suffer most is distinct from what makes others suffer most. In Marlowe's handling of suffering, the limiting and distinguishing factors are the nature of the loss which causes his characters' greatest pain, and the mode of reaction to that loss.

Marlowe's handling of the suffering of loss functions not only in the definition of character, but also in the definition of dramatic theme. His protagonists' deepest griefs reveal their greatest values, and in each case these values constitute the central thematic significance of the play. In Dido's case, the love of Aeneas is all-important; the play is concerned with the winning and losing of that love—in it centers the dramatic interest and dramatic irony. Tamburlaine's greatest affliction is the sickness which proves him to be a man; his whole career has been a series of stupendous efforts to prove himself lord above all men—his audacious ambition is the theme of the play. When the gold which is Barabas' god is taken from him, the Jew weeps and rages in torment; but practically everyone else in the play worships at the same altar. The ambition of the Duke of Guise is less infectious; the propagandistic nature of the drama keeps the disease from spreading to the "good side." Nevertheless, his pitiless climb to power constitutes the center of the play, and his fatal stumbling *en route* causes him the most agony. Edward's favorites and Edward's crown are the foci of dramatic interest in *Edward II;* the struggle for Faustus' soul is the central conflict of *Doctor Faustus*. Over and over again, that which is lost represents the central thematic issue.

The pain of loss helps to define the character of Marlowe's protagonists insofar as they are the victims of suffering. But figures like Tamburlaine, Barabas, Guise, and Mortimer are also defined by another kind of suffering, the suffering they inflict on others. Aside from Barabas, whose Jewishness, Machiavellianism, and resemblance to a Vice automatically define his destructive and malicious nature, the driving force behind these figures is material ambition, the material ambition which critics have singled out as the quintessence of the Renaissance spirit and the burning thirst of Marlowe himself. If an examination of Marlowe's plays from the perspective of suffering and evil accomplishes anything, it should certainly help to point out the inadequacies of this characterization. If one considers only the words on the printed page, it is perhaps understandable that one should be swept away by the grand poetry and rhetoric which express the desires of the characters. But there is a rhetoric of action in the drama which must be heeded as well; in a wider context which includes awareness of that rhetoric, the theme of ambition takes on

a different note. As Tamburlaine soars to the heights of aspiration he plunges a dagger into the heart of his cowardly but curiously rational son; his march to fame leaves kings and queens in bloody heaps behind him; it terrorizes mothers into slaying their own sons, leaves riddled corpses on city walls, and disposes of conquered kings as so many beasts of burden that have outlived their usefulness. The ambition of the Duke of Guise leaves an even more congested wake of bloody corpses, all good pious Protestants, defenseless and innocent. Mortimer's rise is established by the subjection of Edward to pitiful torments, and confirmed by one of the most gruesome executions of the Elizabethan theater. This is suffering with dramatic point, suffering that pricks the bubble of ambition's enchantment, suffering which does more to underscore the destructive fruits of ambition than the most sententious of moralizing choruses. It is the tool of a dramatist with an eye for irony rather than a concern for moralizing; but it is no less moral for all that.

It has become something of a commonplace to seize upon Marlowe as the symbol of the "pagan Renaissance," or as one writer puts it, a dramatist who "beat the drum for that kind of self-reliance and autonomous glory that permitted one to rise above both good luck and disaster to achieve the complete realization of personality" [Herschel Baker, *The Dignity of Man: Studies in the Persistence of an Idea,* 1947]. How well does this judgment fit the dramatic spectacle of human destruction that Marlowe's aspiring heroes leave behind them? Does the rhetoric of his dramatic action permit one to rest in admiration of the self-reliance of a Mortimer or a Barabas? Or does anything in *The Massacre at Paris* point to the author's beating a drum for the Duke of Guise? It seems to me that no one who takes into account the full dramatic experience of Marlowe's plays, and the historical context of their original presentation, can give an affirmative answer to these questions. On the contrary, Marlowe's staged suffering clearly underlines the irony of the kind of human "fulfillment" to which his major characters aspire.

Marlowe's sense of irony is at work in more ways than one in his treatment of suffering and evil. It is nowhere more evident than in the dramatic shape he gives to the catastrophic downfalls of his major characters. I fail to see the "self-reliance and autonomous glory," the rising above good luck or disaster, or "the complete realization of personality" in Dido's pitiful grief and suicide, in the vengeful curses of the dying Guise, in the spectacle of Barabas thrashing about in his caldron, hurling his invectives and boasts of malicious deeds at those around him, in the ragged and tormented Edward's last moments with the grim and mocking Lightborn, or in the desperately fearful end of Faustus as he pleads with the elements to hide him from the dreadful wrath of God. The final suffering of these characters does not embody that victory of the spirit or that sublime sense of the transcendent human individual upon which rests the romantic or heroic humanist theory of tragedy; Marlowe is not wont to stress the splendor of defeat, but the deep ironies of defeat.

In *The Massacre at Paris* and *The Jew of Malta,* the ironic appropriateness of the traitor betrayed is effective, though somewhat mechanically contrived. In *Dido,* the suicidal catastrophe is foreknown, and Marlowe depends on that foreknowledge when he inserts the imagery of fiery destruction into the love-pleadings of Dido, thereby stressing the irony of her particular destructive aspiration. By introducing the element of illusion into the sufferings of both Aeneas and Dido, Marlowe again emphasizes the irony of their situations, revealing their pitiful helplessness, rather than any spiritual resilience, in the face of affliction. And finally, Dido's pain of loss is given its most agonizing twist by her recognition of her own measure of responsibility for it.

Illusion is a mark of Tamburlaine's suffering, too, and once more it is used to stress his helplessness in the face of death, his unwillingness to accept the conditions of mortality even when they press closely upon him. His response to pain is indeed extraordinarily audacious, but the very fantasy of his daring and of his extravagant action is its own ironic comment on the little even the strongest of men can accomplish against inevitable human limitations. He "overcomes" the pain of loss by pretending the loss does not exist.

In *Edward II* and *Doctor Faustus,* Marlowe's irony cuts deepest of all. The suffering of the damned, with its inherent ironies, is at work in both plays, at a spiritual level in *Faustus,* and at the analogical material level in *Edward.* In the aspiring pride that leads him to repudiate his humanity, Doctor Faustus, like Lucifer, brings on his own damnation and is himself the cause of his worst suffering. His career, which begins in the flush of superhuman desires, progresses through the satisfaction of strictly mundane requests and the exhibition of illusory pranks, and ends in the inevitable reality of eternal loss. The grand dream is reduced to limited and spiritually destructive accomplishment; the inflated aspiration sputters out in the cravings of *cupiditas.* There is cupidity in Edward's "sin" as well: in the indulgence of his flattering and self-seeking favorites, he repudiates his kingship. Like the repudiation of Faustus, Edward's bears the seed of his own punishment: after his fall from power, it is the loss of the very thing he repudiated—his kingship—which torments him most. Like Faustus, too, he engages in a pitiful fight against time, because his closest links are with the temporal rather than the timeless. His final aspiration is as ironic as the aspirations of all the others; he yearns for what is essentially unattainable.

The ironic dimensions of Marlowe's representation of suffering and evil reveal the underlying reality beneath the fanciful aspirations of man. Marlowe's tragic vision is defined, not so much by awe for the powerful and rebellious individual, as by the trenchantly ironic display of the limitations, frustrations, and destructive effects of aspiration and power. The theme itself is neither original nor heterodox in the history of English tragedy, but the *mode* of its elaboration and communication is. No English dramatist before Marlowe had demonstrated with such spectacular effect the ironic force of the rhetoric of action in counterpoint with the rhetoric of language; the dream of the poetic word is consistently confronted with the reality of the dramatic action. No earlier playwright had ever put dramatic irony to such remarkable and responsible work in English tragedy.

To reveal the ironies of human aspiration is not to discount the naked forcefulness of will inherent in Marlowe's protagonists. His heroes are defined by the strength of both their sufferings and their desires. But within the total context of each play, the revelation is clear that it is just this force of will that explains and makes intelligible the panorama of calamity, destruction, and evil exhibited upon the stage. The root of tragedy is in the will of man. Here lies the dramatically intelligible cause of evil in Marlovian drama.

"It is of the essence of tragedy," writes Helen Gardner, "that it forces us to look at what we normally do not care to look at, and have not invented for ourselves" ["Milton's 'Satan' and the Theme of Damnation in Elizabethan Tragedy," *English Studies,* 1948]. Yet the suffering and the evil that Marlowe's drama forces us to look at are above all examples of what man *has* invented for himself, for here the human will is always the observable agent of destruction and pain. The problem of suffering is resolved in the mystery of iniquity; there is a Barabas here, but no Job. The guiltless sufferer is never the primary subject of Marlowe's concern; wherever there are innocent sufferers, there too is the human agent. And yet, not Barabas but Faustus is the most significant embodiment of the mystery of iniquity in Marlowe's plays; he is his own afflicter; the complexity of his moral nature is more like that of every man, and out of it he spins the thread of his tragic fate. In Faustus' career Marlowe has best fused two characteristic elements which appear throughout the plays: the irony of self-destruction and the sense of retributive justice. They are united dramatically much as they are united conceptually in the theological formulation of damnation. One major reason that we accept the justice by which Marlowe's tragic protagonists are destroyed is the dramatist's careful working out of human self-will as the cause of human catastrophe.

Once again, Marlowe's essential view of the causes of evil in human experience is no different from the orthodox Christian one; his distinction lies in the dramatic skill in converting his theoretical knowledge into effective theater. Unlike the tragic figures of the *Mirror for Magistrates,* his characters do not talk about free will and human responsibility as the determining forces in life; instead they demonstrate the idea by acting. The total action of Marlowe's dramas reveals his conception of tragic fate, a conception that he shares ultimately with both Dante and Shakespeare. It is the conception, as Hardin Craig describes it, "arising out of Christianity and in its typical form unknown to the ancient world, [which holds] that catastrophe is the result of guilt and is a function of character and conscience" ["The Shackling of Accidents: A Study of Elizabethan Tragedy," *Philological Quarterly,* 1940]. Craig contrasts this view with the Greek formulation of human calamity as an irresistible and sometimes inexplicable manifestation of divine order, which calls for a response of heroic acceptance; and with the Senecan view that disaster lies in the very nature of things, so that man can be victorious only in attitude, in his ability to meet fate with courage. There is an inkling of the Senecan attitude in Marlowe, but it crops up in the least admirable of his figures, Barabas, Guise, and Mortimer. Their final posturings of "resolution," however, do not find justification in the context of any hostile universe—their catastrophes are wrought in an ordered universe in which evil of its very nature works toward its own destruction. The Christian conception of tragic fate remains predominant.

In Marlovian tragedy evil erupts into dramatic action through personality, and the suffering that it produces is nearly always deeply personal and individually felt. The tragedy in Marlowe's plays is always the tragedy of individuals; it does not reach cataclysmic proportions, as Shakespeare's does. Bernard Spivack has characterized the Shakespearean vision of tragedy as one in which "evil in its greatest magnitude expresses division and disorder." The tragic deeds of Shakespeare's great tragedies, he notes, all have social, metaphysical, and cosmic overtones: "They violate the nature of man, the nature of society, the nature of the universe. It is in this deep sense that they all receive their great condemnation as *unnatural* acts," [*Shakespeare and the Allegory of Evil,* 1958]. Marlowe does not share the breadth and scope of this vision; his emphasis is largely, if not wholly, on personal aberration. But there is a sense in which he tries to give a dimension of universality to the personal crimes and weaknesses of his characters. Dido's self-destructive yearning for an unattainable love is echoed in Anna and Iarbas, so that she becomes a symbol for the destructive effects of love, the central theme of the play. Tamburlaine, as one of the greatest conquerors, becomes, as Theodore Spencer points out [in *Death and Elizabethan Tragedy*], "a type of all conquerors," whose march to fame must lie through fields of blood. Barabas is himself a dramatic emblem of the self-seeking greed that pervades *The Jew of Malta.* In *Edward II* Gaveston, Baldock, and Spencer are all cast in the same mold of the flatterer, while Mortimer and ambition become practically synonymous. And Faustus, of course, is framed in the shadow of Lucifer but shaped with the fuller dimensions of Everyman. Marlowe's characters, in other words, are often fashioned as concrete universals: for all their unarguable individuality they still hint at an allegorical dimension and the dramaturgical heritage of the morality tradition.

When we have acknowledged the fact that in Marlowe's plays suffering and evil are the result of human responsibility, that Marlowe's tragic characters, unlike those of the Greeks, knowingly push themselves and others into disaster by their own driving wills and desires, we are left with an important question: does Marlovian tragedy as a whole imply or assert a faith in man? When Tamburlaine's soaring words are matched against his deeds and Faustus' godlike aspirations with the illusion and sensuality of his career, when the powerful and individual wills of Barabas and Guise result in wholesale treachery and slaughter, and the dissensions, cruelties, and betrayals of the world of *Edward II* are spread upon the stage, how can one characterize Marlowe as the Elizabethan herald of romantic humanism? Is not his vision of human tragedy more akin to the judgment of the Earl of Gloucester in Shakespeare's *Lear?*—"Machinations, hollowness, treachery, and all ru-

inous disorders, follow us disquietly to our graves." But there is a difference: Marlowe stresses above all the human habit of cloaking these manifestations of disorder and perversity in eloquently expressed "ideals" and high-sounding language. Faustus' speech to Helen is the masterpiece of this kind of irony. For Marlowe, the tragedy lies, not in the inevitable falling off of human achievement from the ideal, but in the travesty of the ideal that the deeds of men so often represent, and in the illusory aura of nobility with which man persistently invests his base desires. It is the tragic view of the ironist who sees in man the responsible cause of his own undoing, who presents man as a destructive agent who, by the abuse of freedom and will, persistently betrays others and inevitably betrays himself. One of the few characters in Marlowe's plays whose suffering brings new insight or deepened wisdom makes a relevant judgment: " . . . experience, purchased with griefe, / Has made me see the difference of things," says Abigail [in *The Jew of Malta*], "I perceiue there is no loue on earth." Marlowe's image of man may have heroic proportions, but the giant's deeds inspire neither faith nor optimism. Inwardly and inherently, it is the image of a fallen giant.

All three of the central components of Marlowe's vision of suffering and evil—the pain of loss, the irony of human aspiration, the root of evil in the will of man—are conceptions which were essential elements in the Christian theological formulation of the nature and destiny of man. Whatever Marlowe may personally have felt about Christianity, he clearly drew from its doctrines the ideological bases for his portrayal of the dark side of human existence. Whether or not he found the formulations of Christian theology ratified in human experience is a matter of speculation, but there is little doubt that he found in them the potentially effective themes for creating vital dramatic experience. By his dramatic genius for transforming thought into action, by his poetic genius for the formulation of functional blank verse, and by his highly developed sense of irony, he succeeded in bringing these themes to theatrical fruition in tragic drama which, though rooted in tradition, was unmistakably powerful and original. This tragic power was greatest in the plays which most clearly compressed and explicated all three themes: *Edward II* and *Doctor Faustus.*

To say that Marlowe gave dramatic life to conceptions involved in Christian theology is not to say that he wrote as a theologian, nor even that he dramatized the Christian view of human suffering in its entirety. There are few "fortunate falls" in Marlowe's plays, few examples of the suffering that clears and deepens human perception and insight, or of the suffering that redeems. One finds in Marlovian tragedy a clearly definable vision of evil, but little vision of good. Marlowe may share with Dante the Christian conception of tragic fate, and the idea that sin and its punishment are essentially identical, but there is little inclination in his work to move beyond the circles of the inferno. For Marlowe the inferno extended into the world of men; although his dramatic universe is humanistically oriented, it remains a world where one must say with Mephostophilis: "Why this is hell: nor am I out of it." In the end, Peele's judgment is still the fitting final word:

Christopher Marlowe's unique province was to give undying dramatic voice to the sufferings of "the soules below." (pp. 247-64)

> *Douglas Cole, in his* Suffering and Evil in the Plays of Christopher Marlowe, *Princeton University Press, 1962. 274 p.*

L. C. Knights   (lecture date 1964)

[*An eminent Shakespearean critic, Knights is known for his 1933 essay* "How Many Children Had Lady Macbeth," *a seminal reaction to the traditional emphasis on plot and character in Shakespearean criticism. His other writings include* Drama and Society in the Age of Jonson *(1937),* Some Shakespearean Themes *(1959), and* Further Explorations *(1965). In the following excerpt from a 1964 lecture, Knights interprets Marlowe's oeuvre as an imaginative reaction to the vicissitudes of life in Elizabethan England.* "What we find in Marlowe's work, . . . besides great verbal power," *he concludes,* "is a critical intelligence almost, but not quite, of the first order, combined with unruly and conflicting emotions that were never fully clarified in a compelling dramatic image."]

Marlowe's life and works together present one of the strangest puzzles in our literary history. Of his life we know enough to make the blanks and uncertainties tantalizing. We cannot even trace with certainty the development of his thought and art; for although it is probable that **Tamburlaine** was Marlowe's first work for the London stage the chronological order of the other plays is still open to dispute. **Dr Faustus,** which some regard as the culmination of his short career, is placed by others near its beginning. The text of that play, as is well known, exists in two versions, and although it seems likely that the later of the two is nearer to the original, we do not know how much of the original was Marlowe's, or who—if anyone—collaborated with him. Even more important, critical opinion concerning the nature and the value of the plays is sharply divided.

> Sunrise and thunder fired and shook the skies
> That saw the sun-god Marlowe's opening eyes.

If there are none today to share Swinburne's raptures about Marlowe as the herald of a new humanism, it is still possible to present him, in a sober study, as a serious and impassioned proponent of free thought and rational disbelief—'an heir of all the ages of protest against Christianity and a voice for the inarticulate and nameless of his own day'. On the other hand there are equally sober, equally well documented studies that tell us the precise opposite: however much Marlowe may have sympathized with the arrogant individualism of his heroes, the sequence of plays traces, with increasing objectivity, 'the inevitable impoverishment of Renaissance humanism'. Such differences of opinion do more than reflect conflicting attitudes towards the Renaissance; they spring from radically opposed critical judgments concerning the nature of Marlowe's achievement. And when we put the critics on one side and try once more to make a personal estimate of the plays—asking ourselves what kind of thing they are and how they

demand to be taken, how they stand in relation to other works of literature and what nourishment for the imagination they contain—then, unless we have a very strong *parti pris,* we are likely to find ourselves veering with each fresh reconsideration of the major plays. (pp. 75-6)

Marlowe was in some ways an outsider, one who did not easily find a place in the established society of his day. But how did that society appear to the man who experienced it in his living consciousness? There is evidence enough that he regarded much of what he saw with exasperation and contempt; and before we turn to the plays we may dwell for a moment on some features of that complex and remote Elizabethan world. It is doubtful whether Cambridge did much for Marlowe beyond giving him access to a good library. Ruled by an oligarchy, divided into factions, remote from the world of action yet offering a foothold for worldly corruption, it was not a great home of learning, nor a place where exceptional talent could be sure of reward. Scholarship had suffered from the religious strife of the mid-century; Roman Catholic and Protestant scholars alike had been compelled to go abroad, and much energy was expended in petty controversy. What a contemporary referred to as 'these fanatical contests about the surplice and the cap' (amid which 'the time once bestowed upon the arts and sciences' was 'frittered away in frivolous disputes') had died down by 1580. But theology, narrow and intolerant, remained the dominant study; and although rhetoric and logic retained their medieval preeminence, the mathematical sciences had no place in the formal curriculum, such knowledge as there was of cosmography and astronomy had no relation to contemporary discovery, history and linguistic studies were at a low ebb. By the end of the century, according to [James Bass Mullinger's work *The University of Cambridge,* Vol. II, *From the Royal Injunctions of 1535 to the Accession of Charles I*], 'the enquiring spirit of the Renaissance had again given place to something like medieval credulity'. It is hard to resist the conclusion that Arnold's 'national glow of life and thought'—which, he said, made possible the literary achievement of the Elizabethan age—was somewhat dimly reflected in Marlowe's Cambridge, where, it must be remembered, he spent rather more than half his adult life.

As for the greater world that Marlowe saw when he 'cast the scholar off' and rejected a clerical career, there is only one aspect of it that can be touched on here. In **Edward II,** Spencer Junior advises the ambitious ex-scholar Baldock:

> 'Tis not a black coat and a little band,
> A velvet-cap'd cloak, faced before with serge,
> And smelling to a nosegay all the day . . .
> Or looking downward with your eyelids close,
> And saying, 'Truly, an't may please your honour',
> Can get you any favour with great men;
> You must be proud, bold, pleasant, resolute,
> And now and then stab, as occasion serves.

This, besides providing an example of the dramatist's best laconic manner, opens a window on Marlowe's world. To trace the ramifications of Sir Francis Walsingham's activities as head of the secret service (with which Marlowe was perhaps connected) is to learn something of the devious violence with which Elizabethan state power was underpinned. Violence less devious was enacted at the Tower and Tyburn and elsewhere; and although much of this could be defended on grounds of national security, a similar ruthlessness inspired both the struggle for wealth and power of Elizabeth's courtiers at home and the mercantile struggle to exploit the new sources of wealth abroad. It was with some restraint that Marx described the methods of that phase of capitalist activity as 'anything but idyllic' [*Das Kapital*]. It was Shakespeare's Faulconbridge [in *King John*] who jauntily supplied a motto for the age:

> Since kings break faith upon commodity,
> Gain be my lord, for I will worship thee.

This thumb-nail sketch is of course grossly oversimplified; and rapacity is not peculiar to any age. My point however is not only that these were in fact obtrusive features of the world that Marlowe knew, but that a ruthless self-seeking was linked by complex gradations to an official piety altogether too deficient in self-questioning. It was not Marx but an unusually well-qualified literary scholar who said, 'Religion is soon shaped to fit the peculiar wishes of a rising capitalist nation. Protestantism, particularly in its Calvinist branches, develops into a faith supporting property and the prudential virtues. Christ and the New Testament become the bulwarks of trade and commerce' [Louis B. Wright, *Middle-Class Culture in Elizabethan England*]. If I may put it so, there was a large element of the Victorian in the Elizabethan mind. The self-righteous self-assurance of a world that offered small resistance to drives for power and riches might well provoke exasperation in a mind that was not afraid of asking radical questions:—'What right had Caesar to the empery?' In these circumstances the intelligent outsider who was also a born writer might do one of two things. He might identify himself with the expansive drives of his contemporaries, magnifying them and stripping them of any conventional protective justifications. Or he might—and by the same process of stripping—expose them for what they were.

> Now tell me, worldlings, underneath the sun
> If greater falsehood ever has bin done?

My reading of the plays is that Marlowe attempted to do both, and that for the most part he was never quite clear about his own purposes.

Marlowe's plays deal with power and pride and individual self-assertion. What, as an artist, has he to say of these matters? Does he simply endorse, or does he probe and clarify, that 'unrestrained individualism' which is rightly regarded as his main, his obsessive, theme? I have already indicated my own opinion; but the question is too complicated to admit an easy answer, and I propose to approach it indirectly. Since in art 'substance' only exists in and through 'form', we may obtain some illumination by considering a particular feature of Marlowe's blank verse. In *The Massacre at Paris* the Guise reveals his ambitions:

> Now Guise begins those deep-engender'd
>   thoughts
> To burst abroad those never-dying flames

> Which cannot be extinguished but by blood.
> Oft have I levell'd, and at last have learn'd
> That peril is the chiefest way to happiness,
> And resolution honour's fairest aim.
> What glory is there in a common good,
> That hangs for every peasant to achieve?
> That like I best, that flies beyond my reach.
> Set me to scale the high Pyramides,
> And thereon set the diadem of France;
> I'll either rend it with my nails to naught,
> Or mount the top with my aspiring wings,
> Although my downfall be the deepest hell.
> For this I wake, when others think I sleep,
> For this I wait, that scorns attendance else;
> For this, my quenchless thirst, whereon I build,
> Hath often pleaded kindred to the King;
> For this, this head, this heart, this hand, and
>   sword,
> Contrives, imagines, and fully executes,
> Matters of import aimed at by many,
> Yet understood by none;
> For this, hath heaven engender'd me of earth;
> For this, this earth sustains my body's weight,
> And with this weight I'll counterpoise a crown,
> Or with seditions weary all the world. . . .

The Massacre is, admittedly, a very bad play; but—to misquote Coleridge—if you met these lines running wild in the deserts of Arabia, you would instantly exclaim 'Marlowe'. It is not only that the Guise provides a motto for so many of Marlowe's heroes ('That like I best that flies beyond my reach'), the verse itself—with its constant superlatives, over-emphasis, and hyperbole—is characteristically Marlovian. The exaggeration and expansiveness are not in the least critical—as you can see by putting the passage beside comparable speeches of Ben Jonson's *Sejanus*: it simply flows with the minimum of control. Marlowe, as we shall see, had other ways of writing, and what he achieved in blank verse, at his best, has been rightly praised; but the passage quoted does fairly represent a quality found in almost all his plays—a free-flowing impetuousness that somehow fails to be transformed into the energies of art.

It was a valuable remark of T. S. Eliot's that 'no artist produces great art by a deliberate attempt to express his personality. He expresses his personality indirectly through concentrating upon a task . . .'. What I have called the energies of art spring from a disciplined concentration: they do their work most effectively when the artist's primary impulses are subject to a certain resistance—a resistance that may indeed be assimilated and overcome, but that is in some ways similar to the resistance offered to the sculptor by the intrinsic nature of wood and stone. The analogy is suggestive rather than exact, and different poets find different formal disciplines. They may practise their art by imitating chosen masters. Dante and Shakespeare were skilled in the rhetorical arts of language of their times. (The figure of Beatrice begins her ever-growing symbolic life in the *Vita Nuova*, which to modern eyes can seem, at times, an almost pedantic exercise; and of Shakespeare's Sonnets Keats said, 'They seem to be full of fine things said unintentionally—in the intensity of working out conceits'.) The Metaphysical poets carried into poetry some of the sternly patterned techniques of religious meditation. Emily Dickinson hammered out her concentrated expressive forms with the help of a manual of hymnbook metrics. In great works of art, therefore, there is a certain doubleness. They extend the area of consciousness, but in such a way that their symbolic forms activate a wider area of experience than their authors, or anyone else, could express in conceptual, non-symbolic language. But it is by the way of artifice that they enlist what is pre-conscious and inarticulate, drawing—as Dryden has it—'the sleeping images of things *towards the light'* (my italics). In Marlowe this subtle balance between 'reason', deliberate craftsmanship or formal artifice and the unconscious or partly conscious affective life from which reason springs, is upset. His work does not only enlist, it is partly at the mercy of, unconscious drives. That is why Symonds could say of Marlowe's 'colossal personifications' that 'we feel them to be day-dreams of their maker's deep desires' [*Shakespeare's Predecessors*].

It is important to be clear on this point, for the issues are sometimes clouded by the assumption that these 'embodiments of a craving for illimitable power', whether or not they are meant to be admired, are in fact heroic. It is a questionable assumption; how questionable we are unlikely to know so long as we continue to see these figures exclusively in relation to some Herculean prototype or to the Renaissance quest for power and knowledge in the real world of thought and action. In the curious prologue to the action in ***Dido, Queen of Carthage,*** Marlowe embroiders freely on a hint from Virgil. Jupiter is dandling upon his knee the youthful Ganymede.

> What is't, sweet wag, I should deny thy
>   youth? . . .
> Sit on my knee, and call for thy content,
> Control proud Fate, and cut the thread of Time:
> Why, are not all the gods at thy command,
> And heaven and earth the bounds of thy delight?
> Vulcan shall dance to make thee laughing sport,
> And my nine daughters sing when thou art sad;
> From Juno's bird I'll pluck her spotted pride,
> To make thee fans wherewith to cool thy face;
> And Venus' swans shall shed their silver down,
> To sweeten out the slumbers of thy bed. . . .

It is with unmistakeable—and characteristic—gusto that Marlowe paints his picture of indulged infancy. And what is promised to the baby-figure Ganymede ('that wanton female boy') is precisely the unlimited power, gained without effort—'To ask and have, command and be obeyed'—that enters so largely into the enormous fantasy of ***Tamburlaine the Great.***

The element of fantasy, of day-dream, in ***Tamburlaine*** is recognized in most accounts of Marlowe's work, but perhaps not the nature and significance of the fantasy. The scenes of violence, presented or described, with which Marlowe indulges himself and his audience—Bajazeth and his empress in the cage, Bajazeth as Tamburlaine's footstool, the kings drawing the chariot—are not only exaggerated, they bear no relation to the cruelty that men actually inflict on each other, as the blinding of Gloucester in *Lear* brings to a head all the latent cruelty of the world. They are spectacular, and their function—crudely enough—is to say. 'Look at me, doing this!'

> TECHELLES: Methinks I see kings kneeling at his
>   feet,
>   And he with frowning brows and fiery looks
>   Spurning their crowns from off their captive heads. . . .
> TAMBURLAINE: Nobly resolv'd, sweet friends
>   and followers!

Tamburlaine, it seems, can never have enough of being looked at.

> And with our sun-bright armour, as we march,
> We'll chase the stars from heaven and dim their
>   eyes
> That stand and muse at our admired arms.
>
> Then in my coach, like Saturn's royal son
> Mounted his shining chariot gilt with fire,
> And drawn with princely eagles through the
>   path
> Pav'd with bright crystal and enchas'd with
>   stars,
> When all the gods stand gazing at his pomp,
> So will I ride through Samarcanda streets. . . .

For the gazing gods we may substitute parents and other grown-ups whose favours can be won for the powerless and demanding child by almost magical means:

> To ask and have, command and be obeyed;
> When looks breed love, with looks to gain the
>   prize.

The power that is expressed through Tamburlaine has no gradations; it knows no obstacles, and it is immediate in effect.

> Draw forth thy sword, thou mighty man at
>   arms,
> Intending but to raze my charmed skin,
> And Jove himself will stretch his hand from
>   heaven
> To ward the blow, and shield me safe from
>   harm.
>
> . . . such a star hath influence in his sword
> As rules the skies and countermands the
>   gods. . . .
>
> I speak it, and my words are oracles.

None of this has any relation to the real extension of human capacity in the sixteenth century; it is simply the regressive craving for effortless and unlimited power. Tamburlaine's titanic boast—

> I hold the Fates bound fast in iron chains,
> And with my hand turn Fortune's wheel about

—is a precise echo of what was promised to the obviously infantile Ganymede.

Clearly if this were all that Marlowe had to offer we should not be bothering with him four hundred years after his birth, and I must now face directly what seems to me the central puzzle of his plays. For Marlowe, with all his limitations, does have a creative energy that keeps his plays alive as something other than pieces in the Elizabethan museum. He is important, moreover, not only because of the unusual vigour with which he pursues his day-dreams, but because with part of his mind he knew those day-dreams for what they were.

I have commented on the free-flow of much of Marlowe's verse. But besides the note of unresisted self-indulgence there is, almost from the first, another note, which Dr Bradbrook has defined so well in relation to *Hero and Leander* [in *Scrutiny,* June, 1933]: it is the note of dry and sardonic detachment and irony that blends with and qualifies the exuberance.

> Where'er I come the fatal sisters sweat,
> And grisly death, by running to and fro
> To do their ceaseless homage to my sword. . . .

That flicker of caricature comes from the last scene of the first Part of *Tamburlaine,* and together with Zenocrate's moving lament for 'the Turk and his great emperess'—

> Ah, mighty Jove and holy Mahomet,
> Pardon my love! O pardon his contempt
> Of earthly fortune and respect of pity—

it perhaps does something to put in a sane perspective the prevailing megalomania. In Part II, as is well known, there is rather more to qualify Tamburlaine's own view of himself. The cowardly son, Calyphas, has a glimmer of not quite Falstaffian realism:

> The bullets fly at random where they list;
> And should I go and kill a thousand men,
> I were as soon rewarded with a shot,
> And sooner far than he that never fights.

And the death of Zenocrate—'I fare, my lord, as other empresses'—does act as a touchstone of reality: as Theridamas is allowed to comment, 'All [Tamburlaine's] raging cannot make her live'—just as it cannot prevent his own death. Instances of an increasing objectivity and critical detachment are undoubtedly there, in the play: it may be doubted however whether they do more than offer a temporary check to the underlying emotional drive. Miss Mahood says of Tamburlaine's death that it is 'the last in a series of events which have shown him that man cannot usurp power over life and death for his own ends'. Maybe; but to me the imaginative effect of the last Act cannot be reduced to that stark reality. Tamburlaine's savage cruelty towards the Governor and inhabitants of Babylon is perhaps commented on by the verse—'hesitating on the edge of caricature'—in which the mass drowning is described—

> fishes, fed by human carcasses,
> Amazed, swim up and down upon the waves—

as well as by Tamburlaine's sudden distemper. But the final scene opens with a long formal lament by the devoted followers—'Blush, heaven, to lose the honour of thy name' etc.—which is obviously intended to be taken seriously. And although in Tamburlaine's defiance of fate hyperbole is, it seems, deliberately deflated—

> Come let us march against the powers of heaven,
> And set black streamers in the firmament,
> To signify the slaughter of the gods.
> Ah, friends, what shall I do? I cannot stand.
> Come, carry me to war against the gods—

that is not the end. Tamburlaine is allowed to win one more effortless victory, to describe at length (with the aid of an impressive map) his career of conquest, and to make a noble departure from the scene.

> Meet heaven and earth, and here let all things
>   end,
> For earth hath spent the pride of all her fruit,
> And heaven consum'd his choicest living fire!

It may be an exaggeration to say, as Kocher does, that 'all is sympathy, adoration and grief'; but what we find at the climax is surely alternation of attitude rather than any real growth of understanding.

If I have spent what may seem a disproportionate amount of time on *Tamburlaine* it is because that play gives us the clue to Marlowe's failure ever to bring his gifts to fruition in a coherent 'criticism of life'—for 'criticism of life' is what the plays are, in part, directed towards. The material of the plays that succeed *Tamburlaine* is the behaviour of men in sixteenth-century England—their greed for power and money, their violence, falsehood and (in the Elizabethan sense) 'policy', all summed up in Machiavel's scornful prologue to *The Jew of Malta.*

> Albeit the world think Machiavel is dead,
> Yet was his soul but flown beyond the Alps;
> And, now the Guise is dead, is come from
>   France,
> To view this land, and frolic with his friends.
> To some perhaps my name is odious,
> But such as love me, guard me from their
>   tongues,
> And let them know that I am Machiavel,
> And weigh not men, and therefore not men's
>   words.
> Admir'd I am of those that hate me most:
> Though some speak openly against my books,
> Yet will they read me, and thereby attain
> To Peter's chair; and, when they cast me off,
> Are poison'd by my climbing followers,
> I count religion but a childish toy,
> And hold there is no sin but ignorance.
> Birds of the air will tell of murders past:
> I am asham'd to hear such fooleries.
> Many will talk of title to a crown:
> What right had Caesar to the empery?
> Might first made kings, and laws were then most
>   sure
> When, like the Draco's, they were writ in
>   blood. . . .

Marlowe's overt attitude towards this behaviour, and the hypocrisy and stupidity that so often accompanied it, is one of contempt; and to express his own peculiar blend of exasperation and irony he develops a manner that, as T. S. Eliot noted long ago, points forward to Ben Jonson. In the process he is impelled to a radical questioning of what seem to have been his own fundamental assumptions—a labour of intelligence that shows in the cutting-edge of some of his best verse. It may be doubted, however, whether he ever succeeded in understanding, and so mastering, his own fantasies. That, at all events, seems to me the only explanation for the lapses and uncertainty of purpose that prevent even his best work from being completely satisfying. There are emotional entanglements at the roots of his conscious attitudes, and he is too heavily committed to what his intelligence condemns.

Both *The Jew of Malta* and *The Tragical History of Dr Faustus* demand full and serious attention; each, in different ways, alternately rewards and frustrates the attention it demands. One would need to be obstinately dull not to enjoy large stretches of *The Jew.* Marlowe's sardonic intelligence is genuinely engaged with what actually goes on in his world—a world where either you eat or are eaten, and where unction is a sure sign of corrupt purpose. When the rulers of Malta have swindled Barabas out of all his possessions, it would be difficult to improve on the almost Dickensian command of speech inflexions through which the hypocrisy of the whole affair is exposed.

> BARABAS: Will you, then, steal my goods?
>   Is theft the ground of your religion?
>
> FERNEZE: No, Jew; we take particularly thine,
>   To save the ruin of a multitude:
>   And better one want for a common good,
>   Than many perish for a private man:
>   Yet, Barabas, we will not banish thee,
>   But here in Malta, where thou gott'st thy wealth,
>   Live still; and, if thou canst, get more.
>
> BARABAS: Christians, what, or how can I multiply?
>   Of naught is nothing made.
>
> FIRST KNIGHT: From naught at first thou cam'st to little wealth,
>   From little unto more, from more to most:
>   If your first curse fall heavy on thy head,
>   And make thee poor and scorn'd of all the world,
>   'Tis not our fault, but thy inherent sin.
>
> BARABAS: What, bring you scripture to confirm your wrongs?
>   Preach me not out of my possessions.
>   Some Jews are wicked, as all Christians are;
>   But say the tribe that I descended of
>   Were all in general cast away for sin,
>   Shall I be tried by their transgression?
>   The man that dealeth righteously shall live:
>   And which of you can charge me otherwise?
>
> FERNEZE: Out, wretched Barabas!
>   Sham'st thou not thus to justify theyself,
>   As if we knew not thy profession?
>   If thou rely upon thy righteousness,
>   Be patient, and thy riches will increase.
>   Excess of wealth is cause of covetousness:
>   And covetousness, O, 'tis a monstrous sin!

Christians are hypocrites: this is the message of the action between Barabas and his adversaries.

> Rather had I, a Jew, be hated thus,
> Than pitied in a Christian poverty:
> For I can see no fruits in all their faith,
> But malice, falsehood, and excessive pride,
> Which methinks fits not their profession.

And if the Jew is a greedy monster he only embodies without disguise that 'desire of gold' which is 'the wind that bloweth all the world besides'. It is through a half-complicity with him that we see how wicked the world is. But it is the nature of that complicity, and the uses to which Marlowe puts his central figure, that we find ourselves questioning. Great merchant, comic monster, master of policy, whining victim—these transformations we could perhaps assimilate if we felt that Marlowe, as deliberate artist, were sure of his tone—of his attitude towards his audience, and towards his subject. I for one cannot believe that he is; and a play that at times deserves the description of 'serious farce' at others becomes something like an undergraduate parody of a play that had yet to be written. The success, in short, is local and sporadic. I spoke earlier of the energies of art, and clearly, when the work is true, these spring not only from the immediate verbal organization but from the interaction of part with part, held steadily in one focus. In *The Jew of Malta* there is no focus; there is no unseen spectator—as there is, say, in *Volpone*—effectively disposing our attitudes to manipulator and victim alike. There are no standards, and by way of contempt alone there is no escape.

Is there—it now remains to ask—a way out in what must be regarded as Marlowe's greatest play? To what extent is *Dr Faustus* a product of the liberated imagination? To this question also there is no clear answer. Criticism, we know, should beware of interpreting particular works in the light of general notions imputed, on various grounds, to their author. *Dr Faustus* is important for what it is—a work of art in which the desire for effortless and unlimited power is subjected to the scrutiny of a powerful mind—and not merely as a document in the history of Marlowe's religious beliefs. In attempting a total estimate of the dramatist, however, it is impossible not to be puzzled by the relation between the orthodoxy so emphatically asserted in the play and the opinions attributed to Marlowe both by Kyd and Baines. And the fact that there *is* a puzzle may throw some light on the play itself.

Marlowe's persistent concern with religion was certainly not confined to exposing the gulf between the beliefs and the practices of professing Christians, and Kocher is right to insist on that fundamental aspect of Marlowe's thought. It is doubtful, however, whether he was the dedicated rationalist that Kocher makes him out to be. In the documents to which I have referred there are strictly rational arguments and objections to the fundamentalist strain in contemporary Christian thought, but there are also merely exasperated assertions of anti-Christian attitudes. And although the latter may be explained in part by the failure of his Christian contemporaries to meet him—as a Hooker could have met him—with more than dogmatic assertions, there is a residue of what seems like mere obsessive blasphemy. Referring to some of Marlowe's more outrageous statements, Kyd said, 'he would so suddenly take slight occasion to slip [them] out'. 'Almost into every company he cometh,' said Baines, 'he persuades men to atheism.' In both statements there is the suggestion of a compulsive need; and although it would be useless and impertinent to try to trace this compulsion to its sources, it may nevertheless offer a clue to the ambivalent effect of *Dr Faustus.*

No one who studies the play with any care can subscribe to the view that Marlowe damns Faustus unwillingly, either as a concession to orthodoxy or because of a final failure of nerve. [As James Smith wrote in "Marlowe's *Dr Faustus*," *Scrutiny,* June, 1939, no] one writes poetry of the order of Faustus's last terrible soliloquy without being wholly engaged, and more than in any other of his plays Marlowe shows that he knows what he is doing. From the superbly presented disingenuousness of the opening soliloquy, in which Faustus dismisses the traditional sciences with a series of quibbles, Marlowe is making a sustained attempt to present as it really is the perverse and infantile desire for enormous power and immediate gratifications.

> O what a world of profit and delight,
> Of power, of honour and omnipotence,
> Is promis'd to the studious artizan!
> All things that move between the quiet poles
> Shall be at my command.

However deeply Marlowe may have been versed in demonology it is unlikely that he took very seriously the business of 'Lines, circles, letters and characters'. Baudelaire says somewhere, *'Tout homme qui n' accepte pas les conditions de la vie vend son âme'* [quoted by Enid Starkie, *Rimbaud*]; and a modern writer, James Baldwin, 'Everything in a life depends on how that life accepts its limits' [*Nobody Knows my Name: More Notes of a Native Son*]. It is in the light of such remarks that we should see the pact with the devil and the magic: they serve as dramatic representations of the desire to ignore that 'rightness of limitation', which, according to Whitehead, 'is essential for growth of reality' [*Religion in the Making*]. Marlowe—the overreacher—was only too familiar with that desire, and the turning on himself—on the self of *Tamburlaine,* Part I—is a measure of his genius.

Some such intention as I have described, the intention of coming to terms with a corrupting day-dream, determines the main structural lines and the great passages of *Dr Faustus.* But few even of the play's warmest admirers claim that it lives in the imagination as an entirely satisfying and consistent whole. Interest flags and is fitfully revived. And although the scenes in which Faustus's power is exhibited in such imbecile ways may be defended as presenting the gross stupidity of sin, this always feels to me, in the reading, as an explanation that has been thought up. With one or two exceptions, Faustus's capers represent an escape from seriousness and full realization—not simply on Faustus's part but on Marlowe's: and what they pad out is a crucial gap in the play's imaginative structure. For where, we may ask, are the contrasting positives against which Faustus's misdirection of his energies could be measured?

With this we return once more to the unresolved conflicts, the intrusive subjectivity, in terms of which it seems necessary to explain this remarkable play, as they are necessary to explain the obvious failures. It is not merely that—unlike Macbeth—Faustus has no vision of the life-giving values against which he has offended: Marlowe doesn't grasp them either. And you have the uneasy feeling that Faustus's panic fear of hell is not only the inevitable result of a wilful, self-centred denial of life. It is as though Mar-

lowe himself felt guilt about *any* of his assertive drives (understandably enough, since they were tied up with his regressions), and conceived of religion not in terms of a growth into freedom and reality but as binding and oppressing.

We may put this in another way. I have said that in some important respects Marlowe's creative fantasy did not meet sufficient resistance—the kind of resistance that is necessary for the production of the highest kind of energy, which is at once affirmation, growth and understanding. In *Dr Faustus* the resistance is, as it were, externalized. The anarchic impulse (the Ganymede-Tamburlaine fantasy) collides with a prohibition. Because what is prohibited and rebuked in this play is indeed a denial of life, and because the rebuke is charged with the full force of that other self of Marlowe's which appears so fitfully in the other plays, the result is poetry of very great power indeed. But even in the last great despairing speech, where almost overpowering feeling moulds the language in a way in which it had never been moulded before, the reader's submission is, I suggest, of a different order from the submission one gives to the greatest art, where a sense of freedom is the concomitant of acceptance of reality, however painful this may be.

If this is indeed so, it does something to explain how the orthodoxy of *Dr Faustus* and the animus against religion in the Baines document and elsewhere could be harboured simultaneously. It also helps to explain the diametrically opposed views to be found among the critics of the play. It seems to me that those who see the final soliloquy as the logical culmination of the play's action are right; and that those who see a more or less deliberate suppression of Marlowe's sympathy for his hero, in order to bring about an orthodox dénouement, are wrong. But the latter are in fact responding to an unresolved emotional quality that lies behind the rational structure of the play.

What we find in Marlowe's work therefore, besides great verbal power, is a critical intelligence almost, but not quite, of the first order, combined with unruly and conflicting emotions that were never fully clarified in a compelling dramatic image. But on this occasion it is proper for the critic—whose abilities are of a quite different order from those of the poet—to conclude by reflecting that Marlowe's great powers were at least struggling towards clarification. And he would be a foolhardy critic who, contemplating *Dr Faustus* and *The Jew of Malta,* would deny the quality of greatness in such diverse achievement. (pp. 78-98)

> *L. C. Knights, "The Strange Case of Christopher Marlowe," in his* Further Explorations, *Chatto & Windus, 1965, pp. 75-98.*

Cleanth Brooks   (lecture date 1965)

[*Brooks is a noted proponent of New Criticism, an influential American critical movement which viewed the literary work as as independent object open to interpretation through a close analysis of symbol, image, and metaphor. His writings include* The Well Wrought Urn: Studies in the Structure of Poetry *(1947,* Modern Rhetoric *(1949, written with Robert Penn Warren,* Literary Criticism: A Short History *(1957), written with William Wimsatt, and* A Shaping of Joy: Studies in the Writer's Craft *(1971). In the following lecture, originally delivered in 1965 and published in the last-named work, Brooks analyzes the subtle interplay of formal structure and psychological insight in* Doctor Faustus.]

In his *Poetics,* Aristotle observed that a tragedy should have a beginning, a middle, and an end. The statement makes a point that seems obvious, and many a reader of our time must have dismissed it as one of more tedious remarks of the Stagirite, or indeed put it down to one of the duller notes taken by the student whom some suppose to have heard Aristotle's lectures and preserved the substance of them for us. Yet the play without a middle does occur, and in at least three signal instances that I can think of in English literature, we have a play that lacks a proper middle or at least a play that *seems* to lack a middle. Milton's *Samson Agonistes* is one of them; Eliot's *Murder in the Cathedral,* another; and Marlowe's ***Doctor Faustus,*** the third. Milton presents us with Samson, in the hands of his enemies, blind, grinding at the mill with other slaves, yet in only a little while he has Samson pull down the temple roof upon his enemies. There is a beginning and there is an end, but in the interval between them has anything of real consequence happened? *Murder in the Cathedral* may seem an even more flagrant instance of an end jammed on to a beginning quite directly and without any intervening dramatic substance. Thomas has come back out of exile to assume his proper place in his cathedral and act as shepherd to his people. He is already aware of the consequences of his return, and that in all probability the decisive act has been taken that will quickly lead to his martyrdom and death.

Marlowe's ***Doctor Faustus*** may seem to show the same defect, for very early in the play the learned doctor makes his decision to sell his soul to the devil, and after that there seems little to do except to fill in the time before the mortgage falls due and the devil comes to collect the forfeited soul. If the consequence of Faustus's bargain is inevitable, and if nothing can be done to alter it, then it doesn't much matter what one puts in as filler. Hence one can stuff in comedy and farce more or less *ad libitum,* the taste of the audience and its patience in sitting through the play being the only limiting factors.

In what I shall say here, I do not propose to do more than touch upon the vexed problem of the authorship of ***Doctor Faustus*** in either the A or B version. But I think that it is significant that the principal scenes that are confidently assigned to Marlowe turn out to be the scenes that open and close the play. To other hands is assigned the basic responsibility for supplying the comedy or sheer wonder-working or farce that makes up much of the play and is the very staple of Acts III and IV.

For their effectiveness, ***Doctor Faustus,*** *Samson Agonistes* and *Murder in the Cathedral,* all three, depend heavily upon their poetry. One could go further: the poetry tends to be intensely lyrical and in the play with which we are concerned arises from the depths of the character of Faustus himself; it expresses his aspirations, his dreams, his fears, his agonies, and his intense awareness of the conflicting feelings within himself. The poetry, it ought to be observed, is not a kind of superficial gilding, but an expression—and perhaps the inevitable expression—of the emotions of the central character. If there is indeed a "middle" in this play—that is, a part of the play concerned with complication and development in which the character of Faustus becomes something quite different from the man whom we first meet—then the "middle" of the play has to be sought in this area of personal self-examination and inner conflict, and the poetry will prove its most dramatic expression. One observes that something of this sort is true of *Samson Agonistes.* The Samson whom we meet at the beginning of the play is obviously incapable of undertaking the action that he performs so gloriously at the end. Something very important, I should argue, does happen to Samson in the course of the play, and his awareness of some "rousing motions" after Harapha has left him is no accident—that is, the rousing motions did not simply happen to occur at the propitious moment. I should argue that the encounter between Samson and his father, his wife, and the giant, all have had their part in transforming the quality of his response to the world about him, and that the sensitive auditor or reader will, if he attends to the poetry with which Milton has invested the play, come to see that this is true.

I think that a similar case can be made for Eliot's *Murder in the Cathedral,* though I must concede that Eliot has cut it very fine. An attentive reading or a good production of the play will make the reader aware that the Thomas who is presented early in the play is not yet ready for martyrdom. True, Thomas thinks he has prepared himself. He has foreseen the three tempters. But the Fourth Tempter is indeed, as he tells us, unexpected, and Thomas himself is clearly shaken by the encounter and does not experience *his* rousing motions until after a further conflict.

But before attempting to get deeper into the problem of whether ***Doctor Faustus*** has a proper middle, it will be useful to make one or two general observations about the play. ***Doctor Faustus*** is a play about knowledge, about the relation of one's knowledge of the world to his knowledge of himself—about knowledge of means and its relation to knowledge of ends. It is a play, thus, that reflects the interests of the Renaissance and indeed that looks forward to the issues of the modern day. There is even an anticipation in the play, I should suppose, of the problem of the 'two cultures'. Faustus is dissatisfied and even bored with the study of ethics and divinity and metaphysics. What has captured his imagination is magic, but we must not be misled by the associations that that term now carries for most of us. The knowledge that Faustus wants to attain is knowledge that can be put to use—what Bertrand Russell long ago called power knowledge—the knowledge that allows one to effect changes in the world around him. When Faustus rejects philosophy and divinity for magic, he chooses magic because, as he says, the pursuit of magic promises "a world of profit and delight, / Of power, of honour, of omnipotence." He sums it up in saying: "A sound Magician is a mighty god." But if one does manage to acquire the technical knowledge that will allow one to "Wall all Germany with brass" or to beat a modern jet plane's time in flying in fresh grapes from the tropics, for what purpose is that technical knowledge to be used? How does this knowledge of means relate to one's knowledge of ends? Marlowe is too honest a dramatist to allow Faustus to escape such questions.

This last comment must not, however, be taken to imply that Marlowe has written a moral tract rather than a drama, or that he has been less than skilful in making Faustus's experiments with power-knowledge bring him, again and again, up against knowledge of a more ultimate kind. Marlowe makes the process seem natural and inevitable. For example, as soon as Faustus has signed the contract with the devil and has, by giving himself to hell, gained his new knowledge, his first question to Mephistopheles, rather naturally, has to do with the nature of the place to which he has consigned himself. He says: "First will I question with thee about hell, / Tell me, where is the place that men call hell?" In his reply, Mephistopheles explodes any notion of a local hell, and defines hell as a state of mind; but Faustus cannot believe his ears, and though getting his information from an impeccable source, indeed from the very horse's mouth, he refuses to accept the first fruits of his new knowledge. He had already come to the decision that stories of hell were merely "old wives' tales"—one supposes that this decision was a factor in his resolution to sell his soul. Yet when Mephistopheles says that he is an instance to prove the contrary since he is damned, and is even now in hell, Faustus cannot take in the notion. "How? Now in hell? / Nay and this be hell, I'll willingly be damned here. . . . "

The new knowledge that Faustus has acquired proves curiously unsatisfactory in other ways. For instance, Faustus demands a book in which the motions and characters of the planets are so truly set forth that, knowing these motions, he can raise up spirits directly and without the intervention of Mephistopheles. Mephistopheles at once produces the book, only to have Faustus say: "When I behold the heavens, then I repent / . . . Because thou has deprived me of those joys." Mephistopheles manages to distract Faustus from notions of repentance, but soon Faustus is once more making inquiries that touch upon the heavens, this time about astrology; and again, almost before he knows it, Faustus has been moved by his contemplation of the revolution of the spheres to a more ultimate question. "Tell me who made the world," he suddenly asks Mephistopheles, and this thought of the Creator once more wracks Faustus with a reminder of his damnation. Marlowe has throughout the play used the words *heaven* and *heavenly* in a tantalizingly double sense. *Heavenly* refers to the structure of the cosmos as seen from the earth, but it also has associations with the divine—the sphere from which Faustus has cut himself off.

Thus, technical questions about how nature works have a tendency to raise the larger questions of the Creator and the purposes of the creation. Faustus cannot be content—such is the education of a lifetime—or such was Marlowe's education, if you prefer—cannot be content with the mere workings of the machinery of the universe: he must push on to ask about ultimate purposes. Knowledge of means cannot be sealed off from knowledge of ends, and here

Faustus's newly acquired knowledge cannot give him answers different from those he already knew before he forfeited his soul. The new knowledge can only forbid Faustus to dwell upon the answers to troubling questions that persist, the answers to which he knows all too well.

To come at matters in a different way, Faustus is the man who is all dressed up with no place to go. His plight is that he cannot find anything to do really worthy of the supernatural powers that he has come to possess. Faustus never carries out in practice his dreams of great accomplishments. He evidently doesn't want to wall all Germany with brass, or make the swift Rhine circle fair Wittenberg. Nor does he chase the Prince of Parma from Germany. Instead, he plays tricks on the Pope, or courts favour with the Emperor by staging magical shows for him. When he summons up at the Emperor's request Alexander the Great and his paramour, Faustus is careful to explain— Faustus in some sense remains to the end an honest man— that the Emperor will not be seeing "the true substantial bodies of those two deceased princes which long since are consumed to dust." The illusion is certainly life-like. Faustus has gone beyond a mere cinematic presentation to the feelings of Aldous Huxley—the Emperor is invited to go up and touch the wart on the Grecian paramour's neck— but even so, Alexander and his paramour are not more than apparitions. This magical world lacks substance.

With reference to the quality of Faustus's exploitations of his magical power, one may point out that Marlowe is scarcely answerable for some of the stuff that was worked into the middle of the play. Yet to judge only from the scenes acknowledged to be Marlowe's and from the ending that Marlowe devised for the play, it is inconceivable that Faustus should ever have carried out the grandiose plans which he mentions in Scene iii—such matters as making a bridge through the moving air so that bands of men can pass over the ocean, or joining the hills that bind the African shore to those of Spain. Faustus's basic motivation—his yearning for self-aggrandisement—ensures that the power he has gained will be used for what are finally frivolous purposes.

I have been stressing the author's distinction between the different kinds of knowledge that Faustus craves, and his careful pointing up of the inner contradictions that exist among these kinds of knowledge. I think that these matters are important for the meaning of the play, but some of you may feel that in themselves they scarcely serve to establish the requisite middle for the play. To note the confusions and contradictions in Faustus's quest for knowledge may make Faustus appear a more human figure and even a more modern figure. (I am entirely aware that my own perspective may be such as to make the play more "modern" than it is.) Yet, if Faustus is indeed doomed, the moment he signs, with his own blood, his contract with the devil, then there is no further significant action that he can take, and the rest of the play will be not so much dramatic as elegiac, as Faustus comes to lament the course that he has taken, or simply clinical, as we watch the writhings and inner torment of a character whose case is hopeless. Whether the case of Faustus becomes hopeless early in the play is, then, a matter of real consequence.

On a purely legalistic basis, of course, Faustus's case *is* hopeless. He has made a contract and he has to abide by it. This is the point that the devils insist on relentlessly. Yet there are plenty of indications that Faustus was not the prisoner of one fatal act. Before Faustus signs the bond, the good angel twice appears to him, first to beg him to lay his "Damned book aside" and later to implore him to beware of the 'execrable art' of magic. But even after Faustus has signed the bond, the good angel appears. In Scene vi he adjures Faustus to repent, saying: "Repent, yet God will pity thee." The bad angel, it is true, appears along with him to insist that "God cannot pity thee". But then the bad angel had appeared along with the good in all the early appearances too.

There are other indications that Faustus is not yet beyond the possibility of redemption. The devils, in spite of the contract, are evidently not at all sure of the soul of Faustus. They find it again and again necessary to argue with him, to bully him, and to threaten him. Mephistopheles evidently believes that it is very important to try to distract Faustus from his doleful thoughts. The assumption of the play is surely that the devils are anxious, and Mephistopheles in particular goes to a great deal of trouble to keep Faustus under control. There is never any assumption that the bond itself, signed with Faustus's blood, is quite sufficient to preserve him safe for hell. At least once, Lucifer himself has to be called in to ensure that Faustus will not escape. Lucifer appeals to Faustus's sense of logic by telling him that "Christ cannot save thy soul, for he is just, / There's none but I have interest in the same." But Lucifer employs an even more potent weapon: he terrifies Faustus, and as we shall see in Scene xiii, a crucial scene that occurs late in the play, Faustus has little defence against terror.

In Scene xiii, a new character appears, one simply called "an Old Man". He comes just in the nick of time, for Faustus, in his despair, is on the point of committing suicide, and Mephistopheles, apparently happy to make sure of Faustus's damnation, hands him a dagger. But the Old Man persuades Faustus to desist, telling him: "I see an angel hovers o'er thy head, / And with a vial full of precious grace, / Offers to pour the same into thy soul: / Then call for mercy, and avoid despair".

The Old Man has faith that Faustus can still be saved, and testifies to the presence of his good angel, waiting to pour out the necessary grace. But Faustus has indeed despaired. It may be significant that Faustus apparently does not see the angel now. At this crisis when, as Faustus says, "hell strives with grace for conquest in my breast", Mephistopheles accuses him of disobedience, and threatens to tear his flesh piecemeal. The threat is sufficient. A moment before, Faustus had addressed the Old Man as "my sweet friend". Now, in a sudden reversal, he calls Mephistopheles sweet—"Sweet Mephistopheles, intreat thy lord / To pardon my unjust presumption, / And with my blood again I will confirm / My former vow I made to Lucifer." The answer of Mephistopheles is interesting and even shocking. He tells Faustus: "Do it then quickly, with un-

feigned heart, / Lest greater danger do attend thy drift." There is honour among thieves, among devils the appeal to loyalty and sincerity. "Unfeigned heart" carries ironically the very accent of Christian piety.

Faustus, for his part, shows himself, now perhaps for the first time, to be truly a lost soul. For he suddenly rounds upon the Old Man and beseeches Mephistopheles to inflict on him the "greatest torments that our hell affords". The pronoun is significant. Faustus now thinks of hell as "our hell", and the acceptance of it as part of himself and his desire to see the Old Man suffer mark surely a new stage in his development or deterioration. The shift-over may seem abrupt, but I find it credible in the total context, and I am reminded of what William Butler Yeats said about *his* Faustian play, *The Countess Cathleen.* The Countess, as you will remember, redeemed the souls of her people from the demons to whom they had sold their souls by selling her own. Many years after he had written the play, Yeats remarked that he had made a mistake, he felt, in his treatment of the Countess. As he put it in his *Autobiography:* "The Countess sells her soul, but [in the play] she is not transformed. If I were to think out that scene to-day, she would, the moment her hand has signed, burst into loud laughter, mock at all she has held holy, horrify the peasants in the midst of their temptations." Thus Yeats would have dramatized the commitments she had made. The comment is a valid one, and I think is relevant here. Yeats, in making the signing of the bond the decisive and effective act, is of course being more legalistic than is Marlowe, but he vindicates the psychology of the *volte face.* When Faustus does indeed become irrecoverably damned, he shows it in his conduct, and the change in conduct is startling. Faustus has now become a member of the devil's party in a sense in which he has not been before.

I think too that it is a sound psychology that makes Faustus demand at this point greater distractions and more powerful narcotics than he had earlier required. In the scene before this, it was enough for Faustus to call up the vision of Helen. Now he needs to possess her. And if this final abandonment to sensual delight calls forth the most celebrated poetry in the play, the poetry is ominously fitting. Indeed, the poetry here, for all of its passion, is instinct with the desperation of Faustus's plight. Helen's was the face "that launched a thousand ships and burnt the topless towers of Ilium". If the wonderful lines insist upon the transcendent power of a beauty that could command the allegiance of thousands, they also refer to the destructive fire that she set alight, and perhaps hint at the hell-fire that now burns for Faustus. After this magnificent invocation, Faustus implores Helen to make his soul immortal with a kiss, but his soul is already immortal, with an immortality that he would gladly—as he says in the last scene—lose if he could.

It may be worth pointing out that the sharpest inner contradictions in Faustus's thinking are manifest in the passage that we have just discussed. Faustus is so much terrified by Mephistopheles's threat to tear his flesh piecemeal that he hysterically courts the favour of Mephistopheles by begging him to tear the flesh of the Old Man. Yet Mephistopheles in his reply actually deflates the terror by remarking of the Old Man that "His faith is great, I cannot touch his soul". He promises to try to afflict the Old Man's body, but he observes with business-like candour that this kind of affliction amounts to little—it "is but little worth".

Perhaps the most powerful testimony in the play against any shallow legalistic interpretation of Faustus's damnation occurs in one of the earlier speeches of Mephistopheles. If Mephistopheles later in the play sees to it, by using distractions, by appealing to Faustus's sense of justice, by invoking terror, that Faustus shall not escape, it is notable that early in the play he testifies to the folly of what Faustus is proposing to do with his life.

When Faustus asks Mephistopheles why it was that Lucifer fell, Mephistopheles replies with complete orthodoxy and with even Christian eloquence: "Oh, by aspiring pride and insolence," When Faustus asks him "What are you that live with Lucifer?" Mephistopheles answers that he is one of the "unhappy spirits that fell with Lucifer", and that with Lucifer he is damned forever. It is at this point that Faustus, obsessed with the notion that hell is a place, expresses his astonishment that Mephistopheles can be said at this very moment to be in hell. Mephistopheles's answer deserves to be quoted in full:

> Why, this is hell, nor am I out of it:
> Think'st thou that I who saw the face of God,
> And tasted the eternal joys of Heaven,
> Am not tormented with ten thousand hells,
> In being deprived of everlasting bliss?
> Oh Faustus, leave these frivolous demands,
> Which strike a terror to my fainting soul.

Faustus is surprised that great Mephistopheles should be, as he puts it, "so passionate" on this subject, and the reader of the play may himself wonder that Mephistopheles can be so eloquent on the side of the angels—of the good angels, that is. But Marlowe has not been careless nor is he absent-minded. The psychology is ultimately sound. In this connection, two points ought to be observed. Though there is good reason to believe that Marlowe expected his audience to accept his devils as actual beings with an objective reality of their own and not merely as projections of Faustus's state of mind, in this play—as in any other sound and believable use of ghosts, spirits, and other such supernatural beings—the devils do have a very real relation to the minds of the persons to whom they appear. Though not necessarily merely projections of the characters' emotions, they are always in some sense mirrors of the inner states of the persons to whom they appear.

The second point to be observed is this: Faustus does learn something in the course of the play, and in learning it suffers change and becomes a different man. At the beginning of the play, he does seem somewhat naïve and jejune. He is fascinated by the new possibilities that his traffic with magic may open to him. Mephistopheles's use of the phrase "these frivolous demands" is quite justified. But in a sense, the very jauntiness with which he talks to Mephistopheles is proof that he is not yet fully damned, has not involved himself completely with the agents of evil. As the play goes on, he will lose his frivolousness: he will learn to take more and more seriously the loss of heaven. Yet

at the same time, this very experience of deeper involvement in evil will make more and more difficult any return to the joys of heaven.

At any rate, there is a tremendous honesty as the play is worked out. Faustus may appear at times frivolous, but he is honest with himself. With all of his yearning for the state of grace that he has lost, he always acknowledges the strength of his desire for illicit pleasures and powers. At one point in the play, before he signed the fatal bond. Faustus says to himself that he will turn to God again. But immediately he dismisses the notion: "To God?" he asks incredulously, and then replies to himself: "He loves thee not, / The God thou servest is thine own appetite."

Most of all, however, Faustus is the prisoner of his own conceptions and indeed preconceptions. It is not so much that God has damned him as that he has damned himself. Faustus is trapped in his own legalism. The emphasis on such legalism seems to be a constant element in all treatments of the Faustian compact. It occurs in Yeats's *The Countess Cathleen,* when the devils, trusting in the letter of the law, are defeated and at the end find they have no power over the soul of the Countess. Legalism is also a feature of one of the most brilliant recent treatments of the story, that given by William Faulkner in *The Hamlet.*

Faustus's entrapment in legalism is easily illustrated. If the devils insist that a promise is a promise and a bond is a bond that has to be honoured—though it is plain that they are far from sure that the mere signing of the bond has effectively put Faustus's soul in their possession—Faustus himself is all too easily convinced that this is true. Apparently, he can believe in and understand a God of justice, but not a God of mercy. If Faustus's self-knowledge makes him say in Scene vi: "My heart's so hardened, I cannot repent," his sense of legal obligation makes him say in Scene xiii: "Hell calls for right, and with a roaring voice / Says, Faustus come, thine hour is come / And Faustus will come to do thee right." Even at this point the Old Man thinks that Faustus can still be saved. The good angel has reiterated that he might be saved. The devils themselves would seem to fear that Faustus even at the last might escape them: but Faustus himself is convinced that he cannot be saved and his despair effectually prevents any action which would allow him a way out.

In one sense, then, this play is a study in despair. But the despair does not paralyze the imagination of Faustus. He knows constantly what is happening to him. He reports on his state of mind with relentless honesty. And at the end of the play, in tremendous poetry, he dramatizes for us what it is to feel the inexorable movement towards the abyss, not numbed, not dulled with apathy, but with every sense quickened and alert. (Kurtz, in Conrad's *Heart of Darkness,* shows these qualities. He is damned, knows that he's damned, indeed flees from redemption, but never deceives himself about what is happening, and mutters, "The horror, the horror.")

One may still ask, however, whether these changes that occur in Faustus's soul are sufficient to constitute a middle. Does Faustus act? Is there a sufficient conflict? Is

Faustus so incapacitated for choice that he is a helpless victim and not a conscious re-agent with circumstance?

Yet, one must not be doctrinaire and pedantic in considering this concept of decisive action. As T. S. Eliot put it in *Murder in the Cathedral,* suffering is action and action is suffering. Faustus's suffering is not merely passive: he is constantly reaffirming at deeper and deeper levels his original rash tender of his soul to Lucifer. Moreover, if Faustus's action amounts in the end to suffering, the suffering is not meaningless. It leads to knowledge—knowledge of very much the same sort as that which Milton's Adam acquired in *Paradise Lost*—"Knowledge of good bought dear by knowing ill"—and through something of the same process. Early in the play, Mephistopheles told him: "Think so still till experience change thy mind." Perhaps this is the best way in which to describe the "middle" of the play: the middle consists of the experiences that do change Faustus's mind so that in the end he knows what hell is and has become accommodated to it, now truly damned.

My own view is that the play does have a sufficient middle, but this is not to say that it is not a play of a rather special sort—and that its dependence upon its poetry—though a legitimate dependence, I would insist—is very great.

There is no need to praise the poetry of the wonderful last scene, but I should like to make one or two brief observations about it. The drama depends, of course, upon Faustus's obsession with the clock and his sense of time's moving on inexorably, pushing him so swiftly to the final event. But this final scene really grows integrally out of the play. The agonized and eloquent clock-watching matches perfectly the legalism which has dominated Faustus from the beginning of the play. What Faustus in effect tries to do is to hold back the hand of the clock, not to change his relation to God. Incidentally, what Faustus does not notice is that like Mephistopheles earlier, he himself is now already in hell. The coming of the hour of twelve can hardly bring him into greater torment than that which now possesses him and which the poetry he utters so powerfully bodies forth.

Everybody has commented on Marlowe's brilliant use of the quotation from Ovid: "O lente, lente, currite noctis equi," in the *Amores* words murmured by the lover to his mistress in his wish that the night of passion might be prolonged, in this context so jarringly ironic. But the irony is not at all factitious. The scholar who now quotes the lines from Ovid in so different a context is the same man who a little earlier had begged the phantasm of Helen to make his soul immortal with a kiss. Now, in his agony, he demands of himself: "Why wert thou not a creature wanting soul? / Or, why is this immortal that thou hast?"

Again, the great line, "See, see where Christ's blood streams in the firmament," echoes a significant passage much earlier in the play. (I do not insist that the reader has to notice it, or that Marlowe's audience would have necessarily been aware of the echo, but I see no reason why we should not admire it if we happen upon it ourselves or if someone calls it to our attention.) When Faustus prepares to sign the document that will consign his soul to the devil, he finds that he must sign in blood, and he pierces his arm to procure the sanguine ink. But his blood will hardly trickle from his arm, and he interprets his blood's unwillingness to flow as follows: "What might the staying of my blood portend? / Is it unwilling I should write this bill? / Why streams it not, that I might write afresh?" His own blood, in an instinctive horror, refuses to stream for his damnation. Now, as he waits for the clock to strike twelve, he has a vision of Christ's blood *streaming* in the firmament for man's salvation. But in his despair he is certain that Christ's blood does not stream for his salvation.

In short, the magnificent passage in the final scene bodies forth the experience of Faustus in a kind of personal *dies irae,* but it is not a purple patch tacked on to the end of a rather amorphous play. Rather, the great outburst of poetry finds in the play a supporting context. It sums up the knowledge that Faustus has bought at so dear a price, and if it is the expression of a creature fascinated with, and made eloquent by, horror, it is still the speech of a man who, for all of his terror, somehow preserves his dignity. Faustus at the end is still a man, not a cringing wretch. The poetry saves him from abjectness. If he wishes to escape from himself, to be changed into little water drops, to be swallowed up in the great ocean of being, he maintains to the end—in spite of himself, in spite of his desire to blot out his personal being—his individuality of mind, the special quality of the restless spirit that aspired. This retention of his individuality is at once his glory and his damnation. (pp. 367-80)

> *Cleanth Brooks, "The Unity of Marlowe's 'Doctor Faustus'," in his* A Shaping of Joy: Studies in the Writer's Craft, *1971. Reprint by Harcourt Brace Jovanovich, 1972, pp. 367-80.*

Jan Kott (essay date 1967)

[*Kott is a distinguished Polish critic and professor of English and comparative literature known for his influential analyses of Shakespeare's plays. In his acclaimed study* Szkice o Szekspirze *(1961;* Shakespeare Our Contemporary, *1964), he interprets several of the plays as presenting a profoundly tragic, even nihilistic, vision of history. Kott's other publications include* The Bottom Translation: Marlowe and Shakespeare and the Carnival Tradition *(1987), as well as essays on Polish, French, and English literature. In the following essay from the second-named work, Kott discusses* Dr. Faustus *in the context of European literary, historical, spiritual, and occult traditions. Describing Marlowe's play as a "polytheatrical" work including a variety of voices and styles, he concludes that in* Doctor Faustus *we "get—as in none of the other masterpieces of the Renaissance and Baroque drama except perhaps Shakespeare's* Hamlet, *Tirso de Molina's* El Burlador de Sevilla, *and Calderon's* Life Is a Dream—*a sense of man's predicament at the threshold of the seventeenth century."*]

I

In one of Rembrandt's etchings (probably done between 1651 and 1653), Faust is depicted in his study. In the lower right-hand corner, there is an early Renaissance astrolabe fixed to a wooden ring. Faust wears a wide, loose coat and has a nightcap or white turban on his head, much like those worn by the Jewish elders of Amsterdam in other paintings. It is daybreak, and Faust is gazing at the first rays of sunlight. The rectangular window is made up of smaller panes, as in stained-glass windows finished with soldered arches in older German colleges. Under the window is a radiant illuminated shield, with three circles bearing signs. In the middle circle is Christ's monogram. On the outer circle are the letters AGLA (written in reverse order), the old Hebrew blessing. [In the *Occult Philosophy in the Elizabethan Age,* 1979] Frances Yates has speculated that this Faust-sage in the Rembrandt etching, the embodiment of inspired melancholy, is immersed in the mysteries of the Christian Cabala.

On the title page of the 1616 edition of Christopher Marlowe's *The Tragicall History of the Life and Death of Doctor Faustus,* a Magus is shown in his study. A spherical cage with a bird inside, a clock, and a crucifix hang on the wall. Faustus wears a beret and formal gown trimmed in fur. He has a moustache twisted up at the ends and is somewhat chubby. No shade of melancholy is in his face. He holds a rod in his right hand and points it at the circle of tiles bearing magical signs: Arabic and Hebrew letters joined with symbols of the sun, moon, and planets. In his left hand he holds a book from which he reads incantations. In Marlowe's drama, the most evocative line is the last one in the Prologue: "And this the man that in his study sits." Faustus' study is at the University of Wittenberg.

[Mikhail] Bakhtin introduces the concept of the chronotope in *Dialogic Imagination.* The joining of time and space in one category, used by Bakhtin in his analyses of the novel, seems to be even more useful for the interpretation of drama. The stage is a perfect image of this blending of time and space. Onstage every time has its particular setting, and within this setting a time is almost a protagonist of the drama.

Perhaps the most revealing aspect of Marlowe's dramaturgy is his choice of setting. In *The Jew of Malta,* the first place of action is a counting-house, where a moneylender inspects his treasury—"Infinite riches in a little room" [I. i. 37]. To Karl Marx, this scene would have provided an excellent image of "the first era of capitalist accumulation." Barabas sits "in his counting house, with heaps of gold before him": his riches were not notes, checks, or bills but gold coins—"crowns," so called because of the royal stamp depicting a crown.

A chronotope even more revealing than the Renaissance counting-house of the moneylender is the study of the Renaissance magus at Wittenberg University. Before Protestant orthodoxy curtailed the free study of nature and the range of theological and philosophical disputes, Wittenberg was a center of Renaissance art and science dominating all of Germany. If we allow ourselves a certain freedom of chronology, we can situate Hamlet and Faust in Wittenberg during the same time span. This would produce a beautiful literary chronotope. The first "real" Faust, a self-invested conjurer and astrologer, sodomite and globetrotter, was expelled from all the universities, but probably stayed in Wittenberg on more than one occa-

sion. In addition to casting horoscopes, he practiced necromancy and could have told Hamlet, over a glass of sack in a local tavern, how he summoned the ghosts of the dead. Perhaps this is why the Prince of Denmark was not a little incredulous when he saw the ghost of his father walking along the castle platform at midnight. The play *Faust and Hamlet in Wittenberg* is still awaiting its author.

And this the man that in his study sits.

Offstage lie the real world, the university, and the city; then come Germany, France, and Italy; "And from America the golden fleece" [I. ii. 130]; and further, in the now half-mythical geography, "Lapland giants." The globe had been traversed all round. Both Magellan and Columbus were contemporaries of the first Faust.

Faustus' study, like Prospero's "uninhabited isle," is a new "theater of the world." The *axis mundi* passes through his Wittenberg study; on it lie Heaven and Hell. The heavens invite transgression. Leonardo, Faustus' contemporary, drew models of airships that were flawless in construction and had astounding equilibrium, but the wood and metal which he used were too heavy; human muscles could not lift the wings of this Renaissance Icarus.

> His waxen wings did mount above his reach,
> And melting, heavens conspired his overthrow.
>
> (Prologue 31-2)

II

In the German *Faustbuch* (its English translation, published in 1592, was the main source for Marlowe's *Faustus*), the pact with Mephistophilis had guaranteed that "the spirit should tell nothing but that which is true." The devil is not allowed to lie. Nor is science. The pact with darkness inspires both fascination and horror. It horrified even Thomas Mann: "Here try the brains to get a deity!" exclaims Marlowe's Faustus in his Wittenberg cell.

Not until Romanticism does Faust demand the gift of eternal youth from the devil. The Renaissance Faust did not prize youth very highly—with power one can have any man and any woman. Even Helen. Eternal youth was not the price Faustus exacted in exchange for his soul. He had other, far more serious ambitions.

> Oh, what a world of profit and delight,
> Of power, of honour, of omnipotence,
> Is promised to the studious artisan!
> All things that move between the quiet poles
> Shall be at my command.
>
> [I. i. 53-7]

In no other great Renaissance text is the fascination with hermetic knowledge more apparent than in Pico della Mirandola's *Oration on the Dignity of Man,* written in 1486, when the first German Faust was not much more than five years old.

> . . . magic has two forms, one of which depends
> entirely on the work and authority of demons,
> a thing to be abhorred, so help me God of truth,
> and a monstrous thing: the other, when it is
> rightly pursued, is nothing else than the utter
> perfection of natural philosophy . . .

The distinction between the experiments with elements and magical spells was far from clear. Numerical conjurations with the images of little angels and Arabic and Hebrew letters were discovered even in Newton's manuscripts. Hermetic speculation has accompanied astrology for centuries, representing perhaps the prescientific intuition that matter and energy are interrelated in a mathematical formula.

There were two heavens over Doctor Faustus' study: the heaven of astrology and the heaven of astronomy. The planets moved in conjunction with the signs of the zodiac and forecast victory or defeat in battle, happy or disastrous events. Seven movable spheres rotated around the unmoving Earth: the moon, Mercury, Venus, the Sun, Mars, Jupiter, and Saturn. Above them was the firmament, or the "eighth" sphere of fixed stars. But who moved the moving stars? Doctor Faustus of Renaissance Wittenberg no longer believed in the angels, called "dominions" or *"intelligentia,"* which, according to [St. Thomas] Aquinas' *Summa Theologica,* moved the planets. As to who did move them—the devil knew only what he had heard at Oxford or Cambridge, where he was taught nothing but skepticism of the Ptolemaic tradition. The heaven of the astronomers at Corpus Christi College, Cambridge, where Kit Marlowe was reading for his degree in 1583, was still preCopernican. It was Giordano Bruno who first spoke of Copernicus' doctrine in England in that same year. He defended the heliocentric view because the sun was more important than the earth, as Zoroaster and the Assyrians had been preaching for centuries. "There is the Magus announcing the Copernican theory in the context of the astral magic and sun worship of the *De Vita Coelitus Comparanda*" [Frances Yates, *Giordano Bruno and the Hermetic Tradition,* 1969]. The first great Magus of the Renaissance was Ficino.

These two heavens of the astrologers and astronomers over Cambridge and Wittenberg would not allow themselves to be separated for a long time. Two hells also hung over Cambridge and Wittenberg for quite a while.

> First will I question with thee about hell.

The German Faust was called "the insatiable speculator." Marlowe's **Faustus** was also most curious about the mysteries of heaven and hell.

> FAUSTUS: How many heavens or spheres are there?
>
> MEPHISTOPHILIS: Nine: the seven planets, the firmament, and the empyreal heaven:
>
> FAUSTUS: But is there not *coelum igneum? et crystallinum?*
>
> MEPHISTOPHILIS: No, Faustus, they be but fables.
>
> [II. ii. 58-62]

III

On the same title page of **The Tragicall History,** the devil extends a hairy paw to Faustus. He has a goatee, horns, black wings, and a corkscrew tail. He bears an uncanny resemblance to the Lucifer in *Queen Mary's Psalter,* and to the devil who tempts Christ in the thirteenth-century *Bible moralisée.* Lucifer appears in the same shape in the fourteenth- and fifteenth-century York plays. Among the props belonging to the Admiral's Men was a "dragon in fostes." But Faustus quickly chases this "dragon" from the medieval stage and tells the devil to change into monk's robes:

> Go, and return an old Franciscan friar.
> That holy shape becomes a devil best.
>
> [I. iii. 25-6]

In the German *Faustbuch,* Mephistophilis appears to Faustus as "a gray Friar." Luther believed in the devil. He had even seen him peering over his shoulder when he translated the Scripture into German in Wartburg Castle. And it was a devil in a frock. Protestants and even the great Melanchthon depicted the Catholic clergy as the devil's priests, and even saw a diable with a tail and cloven feet behind the Pope in Rome. "Why had not the Devil made a Pope of me?" wonders Faust in his Lutheran biography.

Marlowe borrowed the devil's monk's robes from the German *Faustbuch,* but his own dramatic discovery was to disguise the tempter as a Franciscan friar on stage. The "conjuror laureate," who attracts the "flowering pride of Wittenberg" to his lectures, disputes with a devil wearing monk's attire about the existence of hell.

> This word "damnation" terrifies me not,
> For I confound hell in elysium.
> My ghost be with the old philosophers.
>
> [I. iii. 58-60]

What an astonishing intellectual drama, utterly lost by modern directors, who like to depict Marlowe's Mephistophilis in the skimpy dress coat of Goethe's *Faust* or the red cape from the opera. The devil always appears in disguise, because otherwise he could frighten but not tempt. Even in the Garden of Eden, he took the guise of a serpent with a female head, according to an old and respectable tradition. But this pious disguise is the most sardonic. An unorthodox Doctor of Divinity convinces an orthodox devil that there is no hell: "Come, I think hell's a fable" [I. V. 130]. But who, if not the devil, would know that hell exists?

For a while it might seem that we are watching one of Shaw's comedies. But this Mephistophilis belongs to the late Renaissance, and this is the first tragic devil in the history of theater. "Why this is hell, nor am I out of it" [I. iii. 130]. For the first time, hell is existential and there is "no exit" from its inner darkness. This is the hell which both Pascal and Kierkegaard will know well.

> But where we are is hell,
> And where hell is there must we ever be.
>
> [I. v. 125-26]

But this is not the only hell in **Doctor Faustus.** "Enter Devils, giving crowns and rich apparel to Faustus; they dance and then depart" (stage direction [I. v. 81]). The spectators at early seventeenth-century performances well remembered the "shaggehayr'd Devills . . . roaring ouer the stage with Squibs in their mouthes, while Drummers make Thunder in the Tyringhouse, and the twelve-penny Hirelings make artificiall Lightning in their Heavens" [John Melton (1620), cited in John Bakeless, *The Tragicall History of Christopher Marlowe,* 1964]. They were the same old demons who in the fourteenth-century York *Creation of Heaven and Earth* ran around whacking each other with sticks.

This masque with its heavenly—or rather, infernal—fireworks with "thunder" and "lightning bolts" could be called the theater of Mephistophilis, just as the three spectacles in *The Tempest*—the initial storm, the banquet scene with disappearing food, and the last masque—might be called Ariel's shows. Interpreters have persistently defended Prospero against charges of black sorcery and have drawn subtle theological distinctions between the white magic of the exiled Duke of Milan and Faustus' conjuring of the devil. Faustus himself wants to be a "spirit in form and substance" in the pact to which Mephistophilis in turn must swear. "Thou art a spirit. God cannot pity thee" [II. ii. 13]. But who is Ariel? Also "a spirit." Black as well as white magic, the manipulation of ways and means, seeks power through unlimited knowledge. The difference, if any, is not in the means, but only in the goals.

In *De civitate dei,* Augustine believes in demons, but these are not Socrates' *daemonion* who mediates between gods and men but ordinary devils or "wicked spirits." Ariel in *The Tempest* would have been a "demon" in the hermetic tradition to the Neo-platonists, and one of the honest "spirits" to whom Pico turned for help, a mask for the devil to Augustine. In this theology, Caliban is, of course, an "evil spirit"—his father being a devil, his mother a witch. On his uninhabited isle, Prospero has only the good and evil spirits for company. But whether they are good or evil, all spirits are supposed to be obedient. Mephistophilis must execute Faustus' commands without objection, just as Ariel must be Prospero's obedient "slave" until he is freed.

> PROSPERO: Hast, thou, spirit
>   perform'd to point the tempest that I bade
>   thee?
>
> ARIEL: To every article.
>
> [I. ii. 193-95]

The word "perform" is a theatrical term. In both plays, one hears it quite often. Mephistophilis and Ariel are the directors and main actors at the service of their masters. In *The Tempest* and *Doctor Faustus,* there is a theater within a theater with *two* separate audiences. Prospero attentively watches the spectacular storm which Ariel performs "to every article." He sits at "the top" watching as Ariel/Harpy performs tricks and snatches food and drink. In the last mythological masque, Prospero and the young couple sit in the first row of spectators.

Mephistophilis' circus is shown with full consciousness of the dramatic strategy as theater within a theater.

> FAUSTUS: What means this show? Speak, Mephistophilis.
>
> MEPHISTOPHILIS: Nothing, Faustus, but to delight thy mind.

And let thee see what magic can perform.
[II. i. 83-5]

At the next show of the diableries, Beelzebub himself will clearly announce: "Faustus, we are come from hell in person to show thee some pastime. Sit down . . ." [II. ii. 103-4].

The most perverse, ingenious, and still astonishing novelty of Marlowe was to show the Renaissance scholar as a spectator of the old morality play in which the medieval warlock, torn between good and evil angels, is tempted by the devils on his road to the grave. What a challenge for the directors; this alienated hell in the parody and reenactment of the medieval mystery play by the devil.

When Faustus demands that "the fairest maid in Germany" be brought to him, Mephistophilis is clearly enraged: "Marriage is but a ceremonial toy" [II. i. 150]. But in the cast of that diabolical performance, there is also a role for a "wife": "Enter a Devil dressed like a woman, with fireworks" (pyrotechnics are Mephistophilis' directorial specialty).

> MEPHISTOPHILIS: Now Faustus, how dost thou like thy wife?
> FAUSTUS: Here's a hot whore, indeed!
>
> [II. i. 148-49]

The next show is the parade of the Seven Deadly Sins, "led by a Piper," as in the morality plays from the lost *Ludus de Pater Noster* of the end of the fourteenth century to the best known, the *Castle of Perseveraunce.* They were well presented in the windows of gothic churches and in the allegorical wall paintings. Pride was shown at Ingatestone/Essex as "a richly dressed woman wearing a low-cut dress, seated upon a bench, or a coffer, while an attendant offered her a mirror" [M. D. Anderson, Drama and Imagery in English Medieval Churches, 1963]. In hell's pageant of *Doctor Faustus,* Pride is more ludicrous: "I can creep into every corner of a wench. Sometimes like a perevig I sit upon her brow. Next, like a necklace I hang about her neck. Then, like a fan of feathers, I kiss her . . ." [II. i. 116ff.].

At Ingatestone as well as in Mephistophilis' show, the Sins recall the ludicrous stories from sermons on the Devil's tricks and wiles. The Seven Deadly Sins are malicious and didactic. Envy, black and malodorous, "begotten of a chimneysweeper and an oyster wife," learned her jokes from Erasmus: "I cannot read and therefore wish all books were burnt" (lines 132 ff.). "Illiterate must dictate," wrote Stanislaw Jerzy Lec, the most brilliant of modern Polish aphorists three hundred years after Marlowe. The Sins giggle, boast, and make obscene gestures almost as masques or costumed figures which could be seen in Polish villages during Shrovetide, or in New England during Halloween. Once again the pageant of the Seven Deadly Sins in *Faustus* comes from the carnival tradition. "O, how this sight doth delight my soul!" [III. ii. 163].

The protagonist of the first hell in *The Tragicall History* is a bitter and sad Mephistophilis, a sophisticated dialectician with the awareness of man in the twilight of the Renaissance. The protagonist of the second hell is the indefatigable and resourceful director, costume designer, and pyrotechnics expert. The two hells of *Doctor Faustus* are two different theaters. The first hell, with its soliloquies and rhetorical and poetic tropes, marks the beginning of a tense and mature Elizabethan drama. The second is, at the same time, a parody and ingenious repetition of the medieval interludes, during which the folk devils tear the crown off Herod's head and drag him away. The first hell is discourse, the second is only a spectacle. The first hell is tragic, the second is farce, or, in terms closer to Marlowe's age, a burlesque and "mummery."

But to which of these two theaters does the scene with the selling of the soul and the signing of the pact with the devil belong? These would seem to be the most pathetic events in *The Tragicall History of Doctor Faustus.* The blood from the cut in Faustus' hand coagulates before he is able to sign with it. But Mephistophilis, taking care of everything, returns "with the chafer of fire." Faustus signs the pact with his own blood: "*consummatum est:* the bill is ended" [II. i. 73].

Christ's last words on the cross, "It is finished," sound blasphemous on the lips of a man who has just signed a pact with the devil. And, undoubtedly, this is "blasphemy," but blasphemy with an old and respectable tradition. Religious hymns, the words of the Gospel, and liturgical tropes had been parodied from the early Middle Ages by monks and clerics. *Parodia sacra* and *risus paschalis* spared no hallowed text or sacred gesture. It was an old and time-honored custom, especially in the abbeys and parishes in the country. *Sacrum* and *profanum* were not divided, either in everyday life or on holy days. The Renaissance took over the parody of *sacra* from the Middle Ages. The greatest master of travesty of liturgical, legal, or medical texts was Rabelais. And it is not mere coincidence that Faustus' "blasphemy" appeared first in *Gargantua and Pantagruel:* in *Rabelais and His World*, Bakhtin wrote:

> Rabelais' Friar John is the incarnation of the mighty realm of travesty of the low clergy. He is a connoisseur of all that concerns the breviary (*en matière de brevière*): this means that he can reinterpret any sacred text in the sense of eating, drinking, and eroticism, and transpose it from the Lenten to the carnival "obscene" level . . . For instance, Christ's last words on the cross, *sitio*, "I thirst," and *consummatum est*, "it is consummated," are travestied into terms of eating and overindulgence. *Venite apotemus,* come and have a drink, replaced *venite adoremus.*

The scene with the "chafer of fire" in which "the learned Faustus, fame of Wittenberg," signs the pact with the devil, belongs to the popular theater of a comic hell and immediately after the selling of the soul, which outwardly seems tragic and pathetic, a devilish circus takes place.

In the first scene of *The Tragicall History,* even before Mephistophilis is summoned, *serio* is mixed with *buffo.* Faustus sits and settles accounts with the books in his university study. First with Aristotle: "Sweet Analytics, 'tis thou has ravished me. / *Bene disserere est finish logices*" [I. i. 6-7]. In the following verses the quotation turns openly ironic: "Is to dispute well logic's chiefest end? / Affords

this art no greater miracle?" And again, in Greek: "Bid *on cai me on* farewell." A farewell to Aristotle's "being and non-being."

After philosophy comes the attack on medicine. Galen, famous in antiquity, is summoned: "*Summum bonum medicinae sanitas:* / The end of physic is our body's health." But medicine will not raise the dead and so is worth nothing. "Physic, farewell." Justinian is summoned after Galen. But Faustus has nothing but a mocking contempt for Roman law and its Latin maxims memorized at trivia:

> This study fits a mercenary drudge.
> Who aims at nothing but external trash.
> Too servile and illiberal for me.
> [I. i. 33-5]

This violent repudiation of the traditional learning in the first soliloquy of Faustus was repeated after Cornelius Agrippa's *De vanitate scientiarum* (1526). Agrippa is present in *Doctor Faustus* at three different levels: as a character in drama under the name Cornelius who with Valdes (who may also have been a real person) visits Faustus in his study and encourages his black magic; as a historical person evoked in the dialogue ("I . . . will be as cunning as Agrippa was" [I. i. 111, 116]); and, what is most important, as a model or double for Faustus himself.

One of the last Renaissance magic in the tradition of Ficino and Pico della Mirandola, Agrippa cultivated hermetic knowledge with a profound study of nature. After *De vanitate*, he wrote *De occulta philosophia.* Both treatises, translated in their day into Italian, French, and German, were published in several editions and widely read. In *De occulta*, Agrippa distinguished between natural magic, which was empirical science; mathematical magic, which operated in the planetary world; and a conjuration, sometimes called "ceremonial," which reached the supercelestial heaven, the realm of the spirits. With the power of the mind and through the secret incantations, one could not only draw forth feelings of love or hate at will, but one could also detect thieves, confuse columns of enemy armies, and summon storms, gales, and downpours. Prospero could have had Agrippa's *De occulta* in his Milanese library. But while writing *The Tempest*, Shakespeare knew that the "carpenter" Inigo Jones was capable of producing tempests in the Blackfriars theater more spectacular than any magician's.

In *De vanitate* both knowledge and magic were futile and empty. Agrippa ridicules in their turn grammar and dialectics, arithmetic and geometry, cosmography and astronomy, lullism or the art of remembering, poetry and music. Everything outside of the Divine Scripture was nothing but *vanitas vanitatum.* But Faustus ends his reenactment of Agrippa's *De vanitate* with an unexpected sneer: "Divinity, adieu!" Faustus' first great soliloquy, or rather the dialogue of the Renaissance scholar with old books, seems to belong, as Agrippa's *De vanitate*, to the long tradition of *serio ludere* almost as much as does the other contemporary masterpiece of mockery, *The Praise of Folly.* And that is how it was interpreted since the beginning.

In his *Defense of Poetry* (1595), Philip Sidney writes:

"Agrippa will be as merry in showing the vanity of science as Erasmus was in the defending of folly. Neither shall any man or matter escape some touch of these smiling railers . . . " Faustus' contempt for the dead knowledge ends in the blasphemous challenge: *"Che serà, serà: / What will be, shall be"* (47-8). This first great soliloquy, studded with quotations and phrases in four languages, is a striking example of the *heteroglossia* of clowns and jesters described in Bakhtin as the source of the medieval and Renaissance fabliaux and street songs, "Where all 'languages' were masks and where no language could claim to be an authentic, incontestable face. . . . It was parodic, and aimed sharply and polemically against the official languages of its time: It was *heteroglossia* that had been dialogised" [*The Dialogic Imagination: Four Essays,* 1981].

"Bid *on cai me on* farewell." "Physic, farewell." "Divinity, adieu!" To whom is Faustus bidding farewell in his university study? The *gay sciencia* of the Renaissance? No. He is saying adieu to the rubble of medieval disciplines and the theology which condemns all joy as a sad heritage of the Fall. Faustus sneers, as will Molière once again in the seventeenth century, at the arrogance of scholars, the ignorance of doctors, and the guile and subversion of lawyers.

The first teachers of this "sacred drôlerie" were Rabelais and Erasmus. both, another chronological surprise, are contemporaries of the first German Fausts. One hears their sonorous laughter in this monologue, which neither interpreters from the Academia nor stage producers of *Doctor Faustus* seemed to have understood and praised.

Throughout the entire *Tragicall History,* at least from the first through fourth acts, *buffo* follows *serio.* After Faustus' incantations and the summoning of Mephistophilis, Wagner, Faustus' servant and pupil, threatens to change Clown, his hungry colleague, into a dog, cat, mouse, or rat. This poor fellow is always ready to sell his soul for "a shoulder of mutton . . . well roasted." But like Pride of the Seven Deadly Sins, Clown prefers to "tickle the pretty wenches' placket." In the interludes, "all he-devils has horns and all the she-devils has cliffs and cloven feet." Clown steals one of the magic books and, imitating his master, traces a magic circle. He does not know how to read and so spells the words, but even so he is efficient enough in his conjuring to summon Mephistophilis all the way from Constantinople.

In *serio ludere,* whose patrons in antiquity are Apuleius and Lucian, *serio* is *buffo* and *buffo* is *serio.* There is seriousness in the laughter and laughter in the seriousness. The high and the low, pedantry and superstition, the inflated and the shriveled, the dogma and the prejudice, the face and the mask, the refined and the vulgar, the learned and the rude, reflect and ape each other as in a funhouse mirror.

This medieval hell and the vulgar adventures of a folk magus have never been read from the perspective of carnival laughter and popular wisdom. Literary historians often express distaste for the lower genres. The scenes unworthy of the great dramaturge are gladly attributed to lesser writers. It is possible that many of the lines in the

middle acts of *Faustus* are not from Marlowe's pen, but even if they are just hasty imitations of the *Faustbuch,* they are gold ore. *Doctor Faustus* remained an alive folk spectacle in innumerable ornate adaptations throughout Europe almost until the beginning of the nineteenth century. There must have been something powerful in this vulgar and naive spectacle. The young Goethe had seen his first *Faust* in the German puppet theater.

IV

Mephistophilis knew all the devils and subterfuges of the stage from the medieval interludes to the *commedia dell'arte* and the emergent Elizabethan theater. When Faustus decided to sneer at the Pope in Rome, Mephistophilis found him "a robe for to goo invisible" in the old prop room. Ariel dons the same "invisible-dress" when dispatched by Prospero on a special mission. The "invisible" Faustus has his irreverent jokes with the Pope, just as in *The Tempest* Ariel will play with Caliban and the drunken Stephano and Trinculo. Mephistophilis also finds a "false head" [IV. iii. 37] in the old prop room, so that Benvolio, who seeks revenge, can "kill" Faustus. But the greatest "miracle" occurs when he summons the dead to the court of the German emperor. Faustus begins with a warning:

> My lord, I must forewarn your majesty
> That when my spirits present the royal shapes
> Of Alexander and his paramour.
> Your grace demand no question of the king,
> But in dumb silence let them come and go.
> [IV. ii. 44-8]

When the fascinated emperor tears himself away from his seat to embrace Alexander's apparition, Faustus blocks his way and warns again, "These are but shadows, not substantial" (line 54). Mephistophilis advised Faustus to conjure up "spirits" by using the well-known device of the dumb show. But perhaps the master of all devilry knew a more modern method of conjuring. In the first scene of act 1, Faustus predicts:

> And I . . .
> Will be as cunning as Agrippa was,
> Whose shadows made all Europe honour him.

What were these "shadows" which amazed the whole world? The narrator in Thomas Nashe's *The Unfortunate Traveler* (1594) had traversed Europe and met in Wittenberg "that abundant scholar," Agrippa, who was reputed "to be the greatest conjuror in Christendom." Agrippa then appears at the court of the emperor where he conjures up the destruction of Troy "in a dream," which is followed by the appearance of David, Gideon, and Solomon "in that similitude and likeness that they lived upon earth." The next night Agrippa showed Henry VIII and his lords hunting in Windsor forest "in a perspective glass."

What is this "perspective glass"? Undoubtedly a magic lantern with which Leonardo was apparently the first to experiment and whose striking effects were well known to sixteenth- and seventeenth-century magicians and conjurors. Ariel in *The Tempest* had knowledge of the more subtle and sophisticated stage effects; the devilish director in **Doctor Faustus** with unquenched ambitions had to content himself with an old pantomime: "Music Sounds. Mephistophilis brings in Helen; she passeth over the stage" (stage direction [V. i. 26]).

The first apparition of Helen is to be viewed in fear: "Be silent then, for danger is in words" [V. i. 25]. In a similar manner, Prospero warns Ferdinand and Miranda at the start of the masque in *The Tempest:* "No tongue! all eyes! be silent" [IV. i. 59]. But the Helen who appears for the second time in **Doctor Faustus** is no longer a shadow without substance. Faustus holds her in his arms. In a modern theater where the traditions and conventions of the pre-Elizabethan and Elizabethan stage have been lost, Marlowe's astonishing ingenuity can be entirely overlooked. The convention of the "dumb show" is violated. The apparition has become flesh. And it is then that Faustus speaks two lines which will forever remain in English poetry:

> Was this the face that launched a thousand ships
> And burnt the topless towers of Ilium?
> > [V. i. 99-100]

The classical source of these lines is Lucian's *Dialogues of the Dead*—one of the most amazing incidents in the whole history of literature is Lucian's co-authorship with Marlowe and Shakespeare. The same few lines are also the source of another scene, one of the most memorable in Renaissance drama:

> Alexander died, Alexander was buried, Alexander
> returneth to dust, is earth, of earth we make him
> loam.
> and why of that loam whereto he was converted
> might
> they not stop a beer-barrel?
> > [*Hamlet*, V. i. 194-98]

Lucian's *Dialogues of the Dead* take place in hell. Hermes shows the newly arrived Menippus around Hades.

> MENIPPUS: Hermes, where are all the handsome men and
> beautiful women? Show me the sights: I've just arrived.
>
> HERMES: I am busy now, Menippus. Just look over there, on
> the right. You'll find Hyacinth, Narcissus, Nireus, Achilles,
> Tyro, Helen, Leda—in short, all the great beauties of long
> ago.
>
> MENIPPUS: All I can see are bones and skulls without any flesh
> on them. Most of them look alike.
>
> HERMES: Well, these bones that you seem to look down your
> nose at are what all the poets have been raving about.
>
> MENIPPUS: Show me Helen's head anyway. I could hardly pick
> it out by myself.
>
> HERMES: This one is Helen.

> MENIPPUS: Well! Is this what launched a thousand ships from
> every part of Greece, and was responsible for slaughtering
> so many Greeks and Trojans and destroying so many cities?
>
> HERMES: Ah, Menippus, you never saw her in the flesh.

In this Greek Hades, the skulls and bones lie scattered in a common ditch. Lucian's hell, hallucinating and horrifying, imprinted itself on the memories of both Shakespeare and Marlowe, who had read *Dialogues of the Dead* as schoolboys. From ancient times to the late Renaissance, Alexander was the image of human greatness, while Helen personified beauty. In the mass grave history remains nameless, the bones cannot be distinguished, and nothing remains but the stench.

> HAMLET: Dost thou think Alexander looked o' this fashion i'
> the earth?
>
> HORATIO: E'en so.
>
> HAMLET: And smelt so? puh!
> > [V.i. 184-86]

Faustus conjures Alexander's shadow for the German emperor, for himself "to glut the longing of my heart's desire" [V. i. 6] asks Mephistophilis to conjure Helen. But "heavenly Helen," who Faustus holds in his arms and kisses, in this blend of the concrete and the symbolic, is at the same time an apparition and flesh, a ghost and a succubus, as much pagan myth as Christian nightmare.

> Her lips suck forth my soul: see where it flies
> Come, Helen, come . . .
> > [I. i. 100-01]

Helen of sex and metaphysics sucks out both the marrow and the soul. And she will never return the body and soul she comes to possess. Her immortality is the ashes of cities. All Troys burn in Marlowe and Shakespeare, just as they burned in Homer and Virgil. And in each new Troy, there is a new face of Helen:

> I will be Paris and for love of thee
> Instead of Troy shall Wittenberg be sack'd.
> > [I. i. 106-07]

Once again one can hear this rare voice of an undisguised and penetrating confession: "And all is dross that is not Helena" (line 103). All of us who are old enough know: life with Helen is a disaster, but life without Helen is a void.

This deadly Helen appears, almost at the same time, in the final stanzas of Thomas Nashe's *Summer's Last Will and Testament*. Summer dies, but this is a summer of impending plague.

> The plague full swift goes by;
> I am sick, I must die;
> > Lord, have mercy on us.
>
> Beauty is but a flower,
> Which wrinkles will devour,
> Brithness falls from the air.

Queens have died young and fair,
Dust hath clos'd Helen's eye.
I am sick, I must die;
   Lord, have mercy on us.

At the close of the Renaissance, Helen is a sign and omen of doom.

V

In a moment the clock will strike eleven. Faustus has but one hour left before he dies. Out of the theatrical "heavens" there is "Music while the throne descends" (stage direction [V. ii. 108]). In one moment later "the jaws of hell" (line 126), breathing fire, emerge from the trap room. In Elizabethan theater, the "throne" from the heavens descended only one more time in a now-forgotten play [*A Looking Glass for London and England*], and no other source mentions "the jaws of hell' again after *Doctor Faustus.*

For the Elizabethan spectator, these two anachronistic emblems were not the imagining and summoning of Heaven and Hell, but of the medieval "heaven" and the medieval "hell" of the old, almost forgotten theater. From the early medieval York cycle to the late medieval *Everyman,* the theology and dramatic action of all the mystery and morality plays is the path from damnation to salvation in the history of mankind and the life of everyman. Christ, the second Adam, leads the first Adam out of purgatory, as in *The Harrowing of Hell.* There are only two exceptions to this theological and dramatic rule: Cain, whose "synne it passis al mercie," and later Judas [in *Sacrificium Cayme and Abell* from the Chester cycle]. The morality play always ends with the salvation of the sinner. *The Tragicall History of Doctor Faustus* ends with eternal damnation.

Damned art thou, Faustus, damned: despair and
   die!
Hell claims his right . . .

               [V. i. 56-7]

The morality play became an anti-morality play. The message of the Christian morality play is inverted and negated in *Doctor Faustus.* Despair—*desperatio*—signifies loss of hope, even in the root of the word. Despair, a sin against the Holy Spirit, a lack of faith in God's mercy, and a lack of faith in salvation, is the consciousness of death everlasting in desperation. "Despair and die!"

Marlowe's *Faustus* has often been called a tragedy of despair. The words "despair" and "desperate" appear thirteen times in this play. Even before Faustus summons Mephistophilis, we hear of a "desperate maladie" and "desperate enterprise." Later there are "desperate thoughts" and "desperate steps," and, the most modern, "desperate lunacy."

The first great magus of Renaissance tragedy is Faustus. The last is Prospero. In *The Tempest,* the word "despair" appears at the very end, in the sixth verse before the last line, in that farewell monologue of Prospero's spoken directly to the spectators: "And my ending is despair, / Unless I be reliev'd by prayer." But Marlowe's Faustus knows that no prayers will be able to keep the yawning gates of hell at bay: "I do repent and yet I do despair" [V. i. 71]. Man must die; there is no getting around it. "What art thou, Faustus, but a man condemned to die?" [IV. v. 22]. Faustus dies in despair.

I'll burn my books!" are his last words. The other great conjurer also renounces his art:

          I'll break my staff,
Bury in certain fathoms in the earth,
And deeper than did ever plummet sound
I'll drown my book.

              [V. ii. 61-4]

The bitterness of both of these late Renaissance magi is the loss of hope. All hope. Neither Art, nor Magic, nor Knowledge is capable of changing the world. The serpent in Paradise imposed an illusion of hope: "ye shall be as gods." This late Renaissance Satan is a teacher of despair. The despair in *Faustus* and the despair of Faustus are not simply Christian, but only a Christian despair has created a language rich enough in emotional tension and metaphysics to express the despair of unbelievers as well. It is not just a Christian hell that contains no hope. Marlowe knew this as perhaps none of his contemporaries did. Nor is this hell just a personal, private one. It is a hell of history without hope or salvation. Marlowe's hell may be our hell, too.

Mephistophilis carries hell within himself. This was Marlowe's greatest dramatic discovery, even if he did borrow it from Aquinas. But this is not merely a hell of despair. It is also a hell of transgression and rebellion. Faustus rejects God who had rejected him. "To God? He loves thee not." The message of the medieval mystery play is once again inverted.

The only mythical figures of the new epoch, which began with the Renaissance, are Faust and Don Juan. They have a different darkness within themselves and carry various hells, but both have eaten the forbidden fruit from the tree of knowledge. The price of cognition is hell, but the price of delight is another hell.

In Thomas Kyd's *Spanish Tragedy,* staged in 1592, the same year as *Doctor Faustus,* the avenger tells of "monstrous times" when "the soul delights in interdicted things." Faustus and Don Juan know by the senses and by intellect the delight of transgression. The great teacher of this delight is ever Lucifer. He discloses a truth, one which twentieth-century literature will repeatedly rediscover: "But Faustus, in hell is all manner of delight." Marlowe himself must have been acquainted with this truth or even more with this experience, as Faustus' lines have a personal tone not found in any of his other plays, nor even in any of Shakespeare's dramas, except *The Tempest.* In a strange way, both Faust and Don Juan from the end of the Renaissance, who know so well that hell is the price of knowledge and joy, do not cease being contemporary heroes from at least the second half of the eighteenth century to the end of our own.

"The Renaissance magus turned into Faust," suggested Frances Yates. But into what kind of Faust? Into the folk sorcerer who advertised himself as a "fountain of necromancers, astrologer, magus secundus, chiromancer, aromancer, pyromancer, second in hydromancy" [Frank Baron, *Doctor Faustus: From History to Legend*, 1978], and whom, shortly after his death, the Lutherans and Jesuits alternately joined to Agrippa and accused of being "ignoble conjurers," whom the devil always accompanied in the shape of a black dog? (This "black poodle [*der schwarze Pudel*]" was to reappear in Goethe's *Faust.*) Or perhaps into that rotund and complacent astrologer from the title page of **The Tragicall History,** to whom an old-fashioned dragon extends his hairy paw? Or maybe into the Faust from Rembrandt's etching which depicts him as the personification of the new Melancholy? But what sort of face does Marlowe's Faustus have?

Marlowe, one of the most radical and independent minds of his day, believed neither in guardian angels nor in the conjuring of spirits, and that is why Faustus sells his soul among the "diableries" of the devils' comic theater. But this comic theater is just one part of **The Tragicall History of the Life and Death of Doctor Faustus.**

Bakhtin has often written about the dialogic nature of thought and truth, which appeared most fully in the literature which stemmed from the Saturnalia and the carnival tradition. The linguistic expression of this dialogue is polyphony, Bakhtin's *heteroglossia*—meetings and matings at the marketplace, where idiolects and idioms, slang and dialects, the most various social tongues, each bring a different experience, different beliefs and customs, different vision and understanding.

"Dialogue" and "dialogization" are the basic principles, indeed the essence, of a novel. But not of drama. For Bakhtin, a dramatic dialogue does not have the "carnival polyphony," the multiple voices, the encounter between various experiences in "their own" separate tongues. But polyphony, the meeting of various experiences, of various "ways of speaking," may appear not in the dialogue of characters but in the "dialogue" of various "theaters," of various theatrical forms in one play. "Polyphony" is then "polytheatricality," polymorphics are stage polygraphics.

In this sense, Marlowe's **Faustus** is a great "polytheatrical" drama. Theaters and spectacles appear in it as dramatis personae, who speak with their own, various and independent "voices": tragic discourse in blank verse; the anachronistic morality of the late Middle Ages; interludes with ribald jokes and coarse humor; the masques and antimasques; the dumbshow; Italian *lazzi* from the *commedia dell'arte,* the parody of liturgical rites and exorcisms; and even metaphysical poetry, as in Faustus' last soliloquy, the tension of whose religious horror, its *tremendum,* can challenge that in Donne's poems.

In all these stages, not only are all of Faustus' fascinating and repugnant faces shown, but we also get—as in none of the other masterpieces of the Renaissance and Baroque drama except perhaps Shakespeare's *Hamlet,* Tirso de Molina's *El Burlador de Sevilla,* and Calderón's *Life Is a Dream*—a sense of man's predicament at the threshold of the seventeenth century. This bitter vision could not be arranged into a harmonious whole because of its violent internal contradictions. The Renaissance magus' hopes of penetrating the mysteries of the heavens turned out to be

illusory, and even more illusory were the philosophers' hopes for the coming of a kingdom of reason and freedom. Giordano Bruno was thrown into the dungeons of the Holy Office in 1592, the same year in which Marlowe wrote **Doctor Faustus.**

"O, would I had never seen Wittenberg, never read a book" [V. ii. 46]. This was not a victory for Mephistophilis but for the small, envious, and hateful devils in the hoods of the Holy Inquisition.

The Tragicall History of the Life and Death of Doctor Faustus has two endings. In the first, Faustus is found lying on the floor, his limbs mangled, "all torn asunder by the hand of death" [V. iii. 7]: an old warning not "to practice more than heavenly power permits" (epilogue, line 8). But there is also another ending:

> Yet, for he was a scholar, once admir'd
> For wondrous knowledge in our German
>   schools,
> We'll give his mangled limbs due burial;
> And all the students, clothed in mourning black,
> Shall wait upon his heavy funeral.

This is the first lay funeral in the entire history of drama. Hamlet's body was carried on the shoulders of soldiers. The performance of **Tragicall History** should end with a procession of Faustus' friends and students bearing his body from his study in Wittenberg.

Marlowe did not have such a funeral. On May 30, 1593, he was stabbed "over his right eye" with a dagger. Like Faustus, he lay face down on the floor. The murder had been ordered by the powerful of that world. Embroiled in many sordid affairs, Marlowe was too well known to be a blasphemer and atheist.

Seven years later a pamphlet appeared which claimed that the death of Marlowe, just like that of Faustus, was divine punishment: "Thus did God the true executioner of divine justice, invoke the end of an impious atheist" [Irving Ribner, *The Complete Plays of Christopher Marlowe*, 1963].

That same year, Hamlet's words to the two royal spies, Rosencrantz and Guildenstern, rang from the Elizabethan stage:

> What a piece of work is man! how noble in reason! how infinite in faculties! in form and moving, how express and admirable! in actions, how like an angel! in apprehension, how like a god! the beauty of the world; the paragon of the animals! And yet to me what is this quintessence of dust? Man delights not me—not, nor woman neither . . .
>
> [II. ii. 319-24]
> (pp. 1-23)

Jan Kott, "The Two Hells of Doctor Faustus: A Polytheatrical Vision," translated by Lillian Vallee, in his The Bottom Translation: Marlowe and Shakespeare and the Carnival Tradition, *translated by Daniela Miedzyrzecka and Lillian Vallee, Northwestern University Press, 1987, pp. 1-27.*

Title page of the 1628 edition Doctor Faustus.

C. L. Barber   (essay date 1980?)

[*A noted American scholar, Barber was one of the most important contemporary critics of Shakespearean comedy. His influential study* Shakespeare's Festive Comedy (1959) *examines the parallels between Elizabethan holiday celebrations and Shakespeare's comedies. His other writings include* Poetry in English (1983), The Theme of Honor's Tongue, *and* Creating Elizabethan Tragedy: The Theater of Marlowe and Kyd (1988). *In the following excerpt from a revised and updated version, completed some time before his death in 1980, of a 1964 essay, he offers an exhaustive analysis of* Doctor Faustus, *examining the religious context and psychological consequences of the protagonist's revolt against the human condition. After the opening scene, Barber writes, we miss the principal character's "heroic commitment to the motive at the base of his identity. Instead we are shown his frantic efforts to escape identity."*]

From Bloody to Black Magic

Faustus in the opening scenes outdoes Tamburlaine in pronouncing omnipotent prospects:

> Ile be great Emprour of the world,
> And make a bridge through the moouing ayre,
> To passe the *Ocean* with a band of men,
> Ile ioyne the hils that binde the *Affricke* shore,
> And make that land continent to *Spaine,*

And both contributory to my crowne:
The Emprour shal not liue but by my leaue.
>   (340-46)

But here, of course, the omnipotence is overtly *magical* and *only* expectation. The rhapsody begins, moreover, with

> Had I as many soules as there be starres,
> Ide giue them al for *Mephastophilis:*
> By him Ile be . . .
>   (337-40)

In magic and the figure of the magus, Marlowe found a social activity outside the theater that embodied what he had earlier done with his poetry in the theater. By putting Faustus's pact with the devil inside the tragedy, he found an objective correlative for his own dependent relationship to a figure of cruel power unacknowledged in **Tamburlaine.** In dramatizing Faustus's motives for the pact and his subservience to it, he brings to bear a profound understanding, including bodily understanding, of the predicaments of Protestant theology and of tensions involved in Protestant worship, especially in the service of Holy Communion.

Despite the Christian framing, it is of course too simple to see the play as a retraction. It resituates motives active in **Tamburlaine** in a way which is irreducibly dramatic. Where **Tamburlaine** can be viewed as an unacknowledged blasphemy, **Doctor Faustus** dramatizes blasphemy. But not with the single perspective of religion: it dramatizes blasphemy also as heroic endeavor. Here again Renaissance and Reformation are both present: Protestant religious perspectives are brought to bear on, and also questioned by, magical expectation which at high moments is Promethean. Caught up to an astonishing degree in the violent cross-currents of Renaissance experience, the play tends to fall apart in paraphrase. Faustus's search for magical dominion can be turned into a fable of modern man seeking to break out of religious limitations. When one retells the story in religious terms, it tends to come out as though it were Marlowe's source, *The History of the Damnable Life and Deserved Death of Doctor John Faustus.* But by the *novum organum* of the poetic drama, Marlowe can convey experience with its own integrity, beyond categories: he can "performe, / The forme of *Faustus* fortunes good or bad" (7-8).

A combination of detachment from and involvement in both magic and religion clearly goes with this control. Marlowe was certainly no believer in literalistic or vulgar magic. "Why Madam, think ye to mocke me thus palpably?" (**2 Tam.** 3948) is Theridamas's response to Olympia's magic ointment for invulnerability. This could be Jonson's Surly in *The Alchemist.* About the learned magical expectations of the Hermetic philosophy Marlowe's complete silence is striking. Faustus as a figure of the magus commands in some ways the prestige achieved by the English Hermetic magus John Dee in the early years of Elizabeth at least, or again, precariously, by Giordano Bruno during his stay in England while Marlowe was at Cambridge. He could not have been ignorant of this tradition; his neglect of it, *as such,* fits with his rigorous university education (Bruno got short shrift at Oxford). Hermes, until the seventeenth century, was believed to have written his works in Egypt before Moses (whereas in fact they were late classical elaborations of gnostic Neo-platonism, capitalizing on the reputation of ancient Egypt for a divine wisdom—a place to go alternative to the early Christians' Palestine). For Marlowe, filtered to be sure through the informer Baines, Moses himself "was but a juggler."

As Frances Yates's studies have made clear, there were students of the Hermetic books, from Ficino and Pico on down to the anonymous authors of the Rosicrucian manifestos in Germany and Robert Fludd in Jacobean England, for whom the power they promised was not clearly distinguished from science or piety. Dee's contributions to cosmography and the design of navigational instruments were substantial, though he ended his life, poverty-stricken, still trying to bring down angelic spirits by drawing the right diagrams (Jonson mocks him by the anagram DEE in the "magical" sign for Drugger's shop). As for piety, Bruno put his life in the Pope's hands (and lost it at the stake) through conviction that he had arrived at an understanding of man's relation to God which could reconcile Christendom. It was piety, however, which involved becoming, in effect, God, according to a Neoplatonic mode of relationship turned so as to include climbing up into deity as well as receiving divine energy streaming down.

One way to look at Marlowe's relation to the Hermetic strain is to see the Tamburlaine plays as his bloody-minded version of it. There is a moment in the second part when deity is described in a way exactly consistent with Hermetic Neoplatonism:

> he that sits on high and neuer sleeps,
> Nor in one place is circumscriptible,
> But euery where fils euery Continent,
> With strange infusion of his sacred vigor.
>
> (2906-9)

In *NOUS to Hermes,* or *Corpus Hermeticum XI* [quoted in Peter J. French, *John Dee: The World of an Elizabethan Magus,* 1972], we get assertions of human omnipotence of mind that parallel Faustus's expectations at the outset:

> Command your soul to take itself to India, and there, sooner than your order, it will be. Command it to pass over the ocean, and in an instant it will be there, not as if it had to voyage from one place to another, but as if it had always been there. Command it to fly to heaven, it has no need of wings: nothing can obstruct it, neither the fire of the sun, nor the air, nor the revolution of the heavens, nor the other celestial bodies.

We have Tamburlaine's "still climing after knowledge infinite, / And alwaies moouing as the restles Spheares," but his way of realizing divine potential is by rapid marches and his conquering sword. Yet Marlowe's poetic expression of what he achieves involves violent equivalents of the intellectual power Nous promises Hermes: "to crack the vault of the universe itself and contemplate that which is beyond (at least if there is anything beyond the world)."

I have quoted above one of Tamburlaine's accounts of the identity of his own spirit with Jove's, and so his need to "leuie power against thy throne, / That I might mooue the turning Spheares of heauen" (3791-92). Nous argues that God must be conceived according to the swiftness and power that man commands. Of God, he says, "all that is, he contains within himself *like thoughts,* the world, himself, the All. If in that event you do not make yourself equal to God, you cannot know God: because like is intelligible only to like" (my italics). The Hermetic enterprise is phrased in gnostic, spiritual modes. But it could be intoxicating to the point of megalomania: Bruno especially was as self-made, self-determining, and manic as Tamburlaine, who proposes as action what Hermetic magic envisages quasi-mystically. Marlowe will not traffic in the pious imperialism of the Hermeticists; he likes his imperialism straight. But then he has an equivalent of omnipotence of *mind* by poetry in the theater.

Faustus's first description of his expectations from magic could be Hermetic:

> These Metaphisickes of Magicians,
> And Negromantike bookes are heauenly:
> Lines, circles, sceanes, letters and characters:
> I, these are those that *Faustus* most desires.
> O what a world of profit and delight,
> Of power, of honor, of omnipotence
> Is promised to the studious Artizan?
> All things that mooue betweene the quiet poles
> Shalbe at my commaund, Emperours and Kings
> Are but obeyd in their seuerall prouinces:
> Nor can they raise the winde, or rend the cloudes:
> But his dominion that exceedes in this,
> Stretcheth as farre as doth the minde of man.
> A sound Magician is a mighty god:
> Heere *Faustus* trie thy braines to gaine a deitie.
>
> (77-91)

The overt emphasis on power is emphatically secular—but similar expectations peer out from behind Hermetic gnosticism's noble and moral language. Faustus the scholar, trying on professional identities after "hauing commencde," clearly projects a version of the situation Marlowe had been in, on a scholarship intended for students planning to become divines (as his roommates did). The decision in favor of magic had an equivalent, as I have been stressing, in the decision to use poetry in the theater to write *Tamburlaine!* (And also, almost certainly, to enter the *secret* service—and know perhaps "the secrets of all forraine kings" [*Faus.* 115]).

The decision to dramatize the Faustus story, with its pact, carried with it black magic, "Negromantike," not white; it made the Christian Devil his servant, not the good demons intermediate to deity in Hermetic Neoplatonism. But Marlowe holds back the realization of this dark dependency so that Faustus can find it out for himself, in a superb dramatic double take. There is no mention of devil or pact in the opening chorus as it summarizes Faustus's career. In the opening soliloquy the "heavenly" necromantic books, with their figures, seem to be all that the studious artisan needs—with the instruction of Valdes and Cornelius. So too when they appear: "*Faustus,* / These bookes, thy wit and our experience / Shall make all nations to canonize us" (147-49). The evil angel also promises an independent dominion: "Be thou on earth as *loue* is in the skie, / Lord and commanunder of these Elements" (104-05). When Valdes says that "the subiects of euery element" will be "alwaies seruiceable" (151-52), they can be assumed to be spirits of white magic, such as Prospero commands in airy Ariel and earthy Caliban. It is only after the conjuring in "some lustie groue" (180) that Mephostophilis appears in a coup de theatre. He obeys Faustus's first command to disguise himself as a Friar (how on top Faustus feels with his "That holy shape becomes a diuell best" [261]). But when Mephostophilis returns, he is far from "servile"—his civilized courtesy makes him a social equal.

And it is *he,* in this very great moment of dramatic literature, who has the wit and the experience. Without realizing it, Faustus moves into the dependent position as he asks the questions and Mephostophilis gives the answers—and not the answers he expects.

> FAUSTUS: Was not that *Lucifer* an Angell once?
>
> MEPHOSTOPHILIS: Yes *Faustus,* and most dearely lou'd of God.
>
> FAUSTUS: How comes it then that he is prince of diuels?
>
> MEPHOSTOPHILIS: O by aspiring pride and insolence,
>   For which God threw him from the face of heauen.
>
> (300-04)

Or again, "Why, this is hel, nor am I out of it" (312). Faustus does not recognize the import of the double take as it happens: "This word damnation terrifies not him, / For he confounds hell in *Elizium*. . . . " "Learne thou of *Faustus* manly fortitude, / And scorne those ioyes thou neuer shalt possesse" (294-95, 321-22).

One can hardly admire too much the understanding Marlowe has brought to bear on the delusory side of the hopes of the Renaissance magus. (He never, so far as I am aware, did justice even by implication to the scientific side, except as it could contribute to the creation of "stranger engines for the brunt of warre" [123]. Probably he lacked the patience, in view of his need to conceive and subdue at once. And he had his own instruments and situation in the theater.) Equally stunning is the exposure, or better exposition, of the suffering sense of alienation and loss underlying the diabolic:

> Vnhappy spirits that fell with *Lucifer,*
> Conspir'd against our God with *Lucifer,*
> And are for euer damnd with *Lucifer.*
> . . . .
> Thinks thou that I who saw the face of God,
> And tasted the eternal ioyes of heauen,
> Am not tormented with ten thousand hels,
> In being depriv'd of euerlasting blisse?
>
> (306-08, 313-16)

The repetition of "Lucifer" as the doom unfolds is on the level of Shakespeare at his best.

In the excellent comic scene which follows, Wagner with the clown is a burlesque of Faustus in his conjuring, complete with an academic servant's tags of Latin: "Ile make thee go like *Qui mihi discipulus*" (366-67). Our theatrical taste by now surely can handle the literal implausibility of his raising actual devils—and using them with a mastery already crucially disappointed in his master's conjuring. The interval gives Faustus time to begin to take in what he has learned from the devil's own mouth: "Now Faustus must thou needes be damnd, / And canst thou not be saued?" (433-34). In the next encounters, he becomes in effect "discipulus" to Mephostophilis, and a rather slow pupil at that: "and this be hell, Ile willingly be damnd here: what walking, disputing, ¢." (570-71). The plot's program requires that the pact work on a narrative level, so Faustus is given magic books, taken by dragons to Rome; he can be invisible and box the pope's ear; he can have his spirits produce the royal shape of Alexander. It is hard to know how to take much of this outward action. Many critics make much of its triviality as heavily ironic. There is certainly much that lets us down, or is irrelevant—much more in the 1616 version than in the 1604. The triviality is never noted as such, however, by Faustus or anybody else—even the horning of the knight and gulling of the horse courser are presented straight. Of course both texts are corrupt and include, probably even in the 1604 version, matter improvised by the acting company. It seems to me best to regret the bad text and also recognize that problems limiting what could be enacted were partly insoluble.

It is quite another matter as Mephostophilis brings Faustus up short again and again. As he refuses to provide a wife or to name God, the sense grows of Faustus being closed in on. That Faustus learns nothing now is underscored: "these slender trifles *Wagner* can decide" (661). The sweeping outreach of "Tel me, are there many heauens above the Moone?" (646)—which moves toward the plurality of worlds that Bruno asserted—is answered with a summary of the Ptolemaic universe as an enclosure: "As are the elements, such are the spheares, / Mutually folded in each others orbe" (649-50). [In *Marlowe's Theater: The Limits of Possibility,* 1979] Thomas P. Cartelli has pointed out that at one point in the Faust-book the geocentric conception is challenged, a cosmological opening up which Marlowe ignores. The closing in on mind and spirit in these scenes anticipates the final enclosure, alone, in his study. And Faustus slips more and more into the propitiatory mode next door to surrender, which finally becomes "Vgly hell gape not, come not *Lucifer,* / Ile burne my bookes, ah *Mephastophilis*" (1476-77). Empson's telling observation [in *Seven Types of Ambiguity,* 1947] bears repeating, that the stresses on "gape" and "come" make the line almost ask for hell and Lucifer. "Loe *Mephastophilis,* for loue of thee, / I cut mine arme," (485-86) he had said as he set out. The love is never returned, except as desire "to obtaine his soule" (505). His final "ah *Mephastophilis*" still makes an appeal, even as it accepts destruction as consummation.

"to glut the longing"

The striving for endlessness and the need for an end are worked into the texture of the play with rigor and complexity that prove astonishing, as Edward Snow has shown [in "Marlowe's *Doctor Faustus* and the Ends of Desire," *Two Renaissance Mythmakers: Christopher Marlowe and Ben Jonsen,* ed. Alvin Kernan, 1977]. The centrality of Faustus's insatiable longing and its radiations reflect at once the strategic historical moment when the drama was written, the strategic mastery of the author, and the desperate psychological predicament he brings to the play. My own explorations have come to center on how the longing in the work is expressed in a way that might have been satisfied by the ritual of the Holy Communion, and, more broadly, on the stresses that made Communion problematic for Protestant thought and sensibility.

Kuriyama's excellent psychological study [*Hammer or Anvil: Psychological Patterns in Christopher Marlowe's Plays,* 1980] appropriately brings into high focus a latent family constellation in which salvation is equivalent to an unattainable "loving and harmonious relationship with the father" and damnation means "perpetual alienation from the father's love and, on a more primitive level, the castration and death which follow as a consequence of the father's hatred." But, as she herself emphasizes, the psychoanalytic perspective isolates this family-derived core from its social matrix. Each of Marlowe's plays moves out from a core of feelings grounded in family relationships and into possible modes of action, successive *theaters* of action, each different. [In "Marlowe and Renaissance Self-Fashioning," *Two Renaissance Mythmakers: Christopher Marlowe and Ben Jonson,* 1977, Stephen J.] Greenblatt emphasizes how this always moving, restless exploration of possibilities exhibits destructiveness actually in the Renaissance and Reformation world; after Tamburlaine, each successive hero self-destructs according to the pattern of the violent mode of action by which he seeks mastery. In *Doctor Faustus,* the social action involves blasphemy and dependence on an alternative figure of power to God. That dependence is consummated by a black mass, alternative to Holy Communion. By performing it, Faustus seeks to serve a hunger that Communion might satisfy were it not beyond his reach.

After the opening fantasies of omnipotence, where "phallic" aggression is prominent, imagery of appetite reaching toward equivalents for Communion becomes more and more prominent. In psychoanalytic terms, this is recourse from phallic to oral modes of satisfaction and mastery, and also to a physical way of relating to worshipful figures. Such regression is explicitly central to the Communion experience of eating the body and drinking the blood of Christ; there regression can be transformed, for the successful worshiper, into reconciliation with God and community. Before we consider how this strain develops with astonishing poetic and psychological consistency in the play, it will be useful to step back and consider the tensions involved in this sacrament for the Reformation and in particular for the Elizabethan church.

Lily B. Campbell related *Doctor Faustus* to fundamental tensions in Reformation religious experience in an essay which considers Marlowe's hero, against the background of Protestant casuistry, as "a case of conscience" ["*Doctor Faustus:* A Case of Conscience," *PMLA* 67, 1952]. She fo-

cuses on Faustus's sin of despair, his inability to believe in his own salvation, a sin to which Protestants, particularly Calvinistic Protestants, were especially subject. They had to cope with the immense distance of Calvin's God from the worshiper and with God's terrifying, inclusive justice, just alike to the predestined elect and the predestined reprobate. And they had to do without much of the intercession provided by the Roman church. Faustus's entrance into magic is grounded in despair. He quotes crucial texts, regularly heard as part of the Anglican service:

> When all is done, Diuinitie is best.
> *Ieromes* Bible, *Faustus,* view it well.
> *Stipendium peccati mors est:* ha, *Stipendium,* .
> The reward of sinne is death: thats hard.
> *Si peccasse negamus, fallimur, & nulla est in nobis veritas.*
> If we say that we haue no sinne,
> We deceiue our selues, and theres no truth in vs.
> Why then belike
> We must sinne, and so consequently die.
> I, we must die an euerlasting death:
> What doctrine call you this, *Che sera, sera,*
> What wil be, shall be? Diuinitie, adieu,
> These Metaphisickes of Magicians,
> And Negromantike bookes are heauenly:
> (65-78)

Faustus leaves out the promises of divine grace which in the service go with "the reward of sin is death"; here, as always, he is unable to believe in God's love for him. But he does believe, throughout, in God's justice.

Campbell observes that it was peculiarly the God-fearing man who was vulnerable to despair, dragged down, like Spenser's Red Cross Knight in the Cave of Despair, by a sense of his sins. What Despair in his cave makes Spenser's knight forget, by insisting on his sinfulness, is God's love: as Una tells him in snatching away the dagger: "Where Justice grows, there grows eke greater Grace." Faustus forgets this too: vivid as is his sense of the lost joys of heaven, he never once expresses any sense that God could love him in spite of his sins. "Faustus wil turne to God againe. / To God? he loues thee not" (441-42). Lucifer himself points to divine justice: "Christ cannot save thy soule, for he is iust" (697).

Campbell parallels Faustus as Marlowe presents him with the experience of Francis Spira, a historical case of conscience which became an exemplar of despair for Protestants. This Italian lawyer, who in 1548 died of no outward cause, surrounded by counseling Catholic doctors but miserably certain of his own damnation, had recanted Protestant views under Catholic pressure. Earlier he had been enthusiastic in his conviction of the truth of justification by faith. In his last weeks, Spira was tormented by a burning physical sensation of thirst which no drink could assuage. Dying in terror, Spira could no longer believe in the efficacy of the Roman rites. Faustus embraces magical rituals—they are something he can *do*—though their efficacy expires with the pact, and he too dies in terror.

It is striking that Marlowe does not make a conviction of predestinate reprobation the basis for Faustus's despair, as it often was historically. Wilbur Sanders, in a discussion of the play [in *The Dramatist and The Received Idea,*

1968] and the Calvinist doctrine of reprobation, sees it as "a death-struggle with Calvin's God." He surveys doctrinal formulations and popular tracts dealing with predestination, which he brilliantly terms "the basilisk eye of Christianity" (p. 228), to conclude that Faustus is held under its gaze "by the umbilical cord of a terror-which-is-still faith" (p. 229). Certainly he is right that the quality of Faustus's despair, his conviction that he cannot be saved, is like the anguished conviction of reprobation so many felt. But repeatedly, especially in the latter part of the play, the good angel, Faustus himself, and, most emphatically, the old man insist that grace is there. "Neuer too late, if Faustus can repent" (692).

> Ah stay good Faustus, stay thy desperate steps,
> I see an Angell houers ore thy head,
> and with a violl full of precious grace,
> Offers to powre the same into thy soule,
> Then call for mercie and auoyd dispaire.
>
> (1290-94)

And though these appeals sound hollow to Sanders—as they do not to me—there is the further objection that Faustus never once refers to the possibility that he is reprobate by predestination. Instead, it is what he has actively done that dooms him: "Seeing *Faustus* hath incurrd eternall death, / By desprate thoughts against *Ioues* deitie" (324-25). God's justice, not his inscrutable decision, before all time, condemns Faustus—as is appropriate as Marlowe turns from alliance with a hero who alternately defies and claims sanction from "a God full of reuenging wrath" (*2 Tamb.* 4294) to the fear and despair attending desperate thoughts against such a god.

Near the end, Faustus expresses his longing for communion in imagery which reflects tensions that were involved, for the Elizabethan church, in the use and understanding of Holy Communion:

> O Ile leape vp to my God: who pulles me downe?
> See see where Christs blood streames in the firmament.
> One drop would saue my soule, halfe a drop, ah my Christ.
> Ah rend not my heart for naming of my Christ,
> Yet wil I call on him: oh spare me *Lucifer!*
> Where is it now? tis gone: And see where God Stretcheth out his arme, and bends his irefull browes.
>
> (1431-37)

The immense distance away that the blood is, streaming in the sky like the Milky Way, embodies the helplessness of the Protestant who lacks faith in his own salvation. Calvin taught that communion could come by the lifting up of the soul to heaven, that it was not necessary that the essence of the flesh descend from heaven. But Faustus must try to leap up by himself, without the aid of grace. His focus on the one drop, half a drop, that he feels would save his soul, expresses the Reformation's tendency to isolate the individual in his act of communion and to conceive of his participation, as Dom Gregory Dix underscores in his great history, *The Shape of the Liturgy* [1945], "as something *passive,* as a 'reception.' " At the same time, the cosmological immensity of the imagery embodies Marlowe's characteristic sense of the vastness of the universe and, here, of the tremendousness of the God who rules it and yet concerns himself with every life, stretching out his arm and bending his ireful brows.

The piety of the late Middle Ages had dwelt on miracles where a host dripped actual blood and had depicted scenes where blood streamed down directly from Christ's wounds into the chalice on the altar. The Counter-Reformation, in its own way, pursued such physical imagery and literal conceptions, which remained viable for the Roman Catholic world as embodiments of grace. A hunger for this kind of physical resource appears in the way that Faustus envisages Christ's blood, visibly streaming, in drops to be drunk. But for the Elizabethan church, such thinking about Communion was "but to dreame a grosse carnall feeding," in the words of the homily "Of the worthy receiving of the Sacraments" [quoted by C. W. Dugmore in *The Mass and the English Reformers,* 1958]. We have good reason to think that Marlowe had encountered Catholic ceremony during his absences from Cambridge, when the reasonable assumption is that he was working at intervals as a secret agent among Catholic English exiles and students on the Continent. The letter from the Privy Council which secured him his degree is best explained on that hypothesis, since it denies a rumor that he is "determined to have gone beyond the seas to Reames and there to remaine" (as secret Catholics were doing after graduation) and speaks of his having been employed "in matters touching the benefitt of his Countrie" [quoted in John Bakeless, *The Tragicall History of Christopher Marlowe,* 1942]. To have acted the part of a possible student convert would have involved understanding the Catholic point of view. And we have Marlowe the scorner's talk, again filtered through [the informer Richard Baines, as quoted by C. F. T. Brooker, *Life of Marlowe*], "that if there be any god or any good Religion, then it is in the papistes because the service of god is performed with more Cerimonies, as Elevation of the mass, organs, singing men, Shaven Crowns, & cta. That all protestantes are Hypocriticall asses . . . . "

What concerns us here is the way *Doctor Faustus* reflects the tension involved in the Protestant world's denying itself miracle in a central area of experience. Things that had seemed supernatural events, and were still felt as such in Rheims, were superstition or magic from the standpoint of the new Protestant focus on individual experience. . . . Yet the Anglican church kept the basic physical gestures of the Mass, with a service and words of administration which leave open the question of how Christ's body and blood are consumed. And Anglican divines, though occasionally going all the way to the Zwinglian view of the service as simply a memorial, characteristically maintained a real presence, insisting, in Bishop Jewell's words, that "we feed not the people of God with bare signs and figures" [quoted in *The Mass and the English Reformers*]. Semantic tensions were involved in this position: the whole great controversy centered on fundamental issues about the nature of signs and acts, through which the age pursued its new sense of reality.

In the church of the Elizabethan settlement, there was still, along with the Reformation's insistence that

"Christ's Gospel is not a ceremonial law . . . but it is a religion to serve God, not in bondage of the figure or shadow," an ingrained assumption that the crucial physical acts of worship had, or should have, independent meaning. This was supported by the doctrine of a real though not physical presence of Christ. But for many worshipers the physical elements themselves tended to keep a sacred or taboo quality in line with the old need for physical embodiment.

The Prayer Book's admonition about the abuse of Holy Communion strikingly illuminates Marlowe's dramatization of blasphemy:

> Dearly beloved in the Lord: yet that mind to come to the holy Communion of the body and blood of our Savior Christ, must consider what S. Paul writeth to the Corinthians, how he exhorteth all persons diligently to try and examine themselves, before they presume to eat of that bread, and drink of that cup: for as the benefit is great, if with a truly penitent heart and lively faith we receive that holy sacrament (for then we spiritually eat the flesh of Christ, and drink his blood, then we dwell in Christ and Christ in us, we be one with Christ, and Christ with us:) so is the danger great, if we receive the same unworthily. For then we be guilty of the body and blood of Christ our Savior. We eat and drink our own damnation not considering the Lord's body.

To eat and drink damnation describes not only Faustus's attitude, but the physical embodiment of it, as we shall see in considering the ramifications of gluttony in the play.

Blasphemy implies belief of some sort, as T. S. Eliot observed in pointing, in his seminal 1918 essay, to blasphemy as crucial in Marlowe's work: blasphemy involves also, consciously or unconsciously, the magical assumption that signs can be identified with what they signify. Ministers were warned by several rubrics in the Tudor Prayer Books against allowing parishioners to convey the bread of the sacrament secretly away, lest they "abuse it to superstition and wickedness." Such abuse depends on believing or feeling that, regardless of its context, the bread is God, so that by appropriating it one can magically take advantage of God. Spelled out in this way, the magical thinking which identifies sign and significance seems so implausible as to be trivial. But for the sort of experience expressed in **Doctor Faustus,** the identifications and displacements that matter take place at the levels where desire seeks half blindly to discover or recover its objects. Faustus repeatedly moves through a circular pattern, from thinking of the joys of heaven, through despairing of ever possessing them, to embracing magical dominion as a blasphemous substitute. The blasphemous pleasures lead back, by an involuntary logic, to a renewed sense of the lost heavenly joys for which blasphemy comes to seem a hollow substitute—like a stolen Host found to be only bread after all. And so the unsatisfied need starts his Ixion's wheel on another cycle.

The irony which attends Faustus's use of religious language to describe magic enforces an awareness of this circular dramatic movement. "Diuinitie, adieu, / These . . .

Negromantike bookes are heauenly" (76-8). What seems to be a departure is betrayed by "heavenly" to be also an effort to return. "Come," Faustus says to Valdes and Cornelius, "make me blest with your sage conference" (126-27). And Valdes answers that their combined skill in magic will "make all nations to canonize vs" (149). In repeatedly using such expressions, which often "come naturally" in the colloquial language of a Christian society, the rebels seem to stumble uncannily upon words which condemn them by the logic of a situation larger than they are. So Mephostophilis, when he wants to praise the beauty of the courtesans whom he can give to Faustus, falls into saying:

> As wise as *Saba,* or as beautiful
> As was bright *Lucifer* before his fall.
>
> (589-90)

The auditor can experience a qualm of awe in recognizing how Mephostophilis has undercut himself by this allusion to Lucifer when he was still star of the morning, bright with an altitude and innocence now lost.

The last and largest of these revolutions is the one that begins with showing Helen to the students, moves through the Old Man's effort to guide Faustus's steps "vnto the way of life" (1274), and ends with Helen. In urging the reality of grace, the old man performs the role of Spenser's Una in the Cave of Despair, but Faustus can only think "Hell calls for right" (1287). Mephostophilis, like Spenser's Despair, is ready with a dagger for suicide; Marlowe at this point is almost dramatizing Spenser. Faustus asks for "heauenly *Helen*" "To glut the longing of my hearts desire" and "extinguish cleane / Those thoughts that do disswade me from my vow" (1320-24). The speech to Helen is a wonderful poetic fusion of many elements, combining chivalric worship of a mistress with humanist intoxication over the project of recovering antiquity. In characteristic Renaissance fashion, Faustus proposes to relive classical myth in a medieval way: "I wil be *Paris* . . . weare thy colours" (1335, 1338). But these secular elements do not account for the peculiar power of the speech: the full awe and beauty of it depend on hoping to find the holy in the profane.

The prose source can provide a useful contrast here; Helen is described there so as to emphasize a forthright sexual appeal: "her hair hanged down loose as fair as the beaten Gold, and of such length that it reached down to her hams, with amorous coal-black eyes, a sweet and pleasant round face, her lips red as a Cherry, her cheeks of rose all colour, her mouth small, her neck white as the Swan, tall and slender of personage. . . . she looked round about her with a rolling Hawk's eye, a smiling and wanton countenance." On the stage, of course, a full description was not necessary; but Marlowe in any case was after a different kind of meaning. He gives us nothing of the sort of enjoyment that the Faust-book describes in saying that Helen was "so beautiful and delightful a piece" that Faustus "made her his common Concubine and bed-fellow" and "could not be one hour from her, . . . and to his seeming, in time she was with child". There is nothing sublime about this account, but it has its own kind of strength—an easy, open-eyed relishing which implies that sensual fulfillment is possible and satisfying in its place within a larger whole. The writer of the Faust-book looked at Helen with his own eyes and his own assumption that the profane and the holy are separate. But for Marlowe—it was his great, transforming contribution to the Faust myth—magical dominion ambiguously mingles the divine and the human, giving to the temporal world a wonder and excitement appropriated, daringly and precariously, from the supernatural.

The famous lines are so familiar, out of context, as an apotheosis of love, that one needs to blink to see them as they fit into the play's motion, with the play's ironies. (Eartha Kitt, telling *Life* magazine about playing Helen opposite Orson Welles, ignored all irony, saying simply "I made him immortal with a kiss.") By contrast with the Helen of the source, who has legs, Marlowe's Helen is described only in terms of her face and lips; and her beauty is *power:*

> Was this the face that lancht a thousand ship-
> pes?
> And burnt the toplesse Towres of *Ilium?*
> (1328-29)

The kiss which follows is a way of reaching this source of power: it goes with a prayer, "make me immortall with a kisse," and the action is like taking Communion, promising, like Communion, a way to immortality. It leads immediately to an ecstasy, parallel to the one Tamburlaine envisaged to join Zenocrate in heaven. The soul seems to leave the body: "Her lips suckes forth my soule, see where it flies." The speech ends with a series of worshiping gestures expressing wonder, awe, and a yearning towards encountering a fatal power. It is striking that Helen comes to be compared to Jupiter, god of power, rather than to a goddess:

> O thou art fairer than the euening aire,
> Clad in the beauty of a thousand starres,
> Brighter art thou then flaming *Iupiter,*
> When he appeared to haplesse *Semele,*
> More louely then the monarke of the skie
> In wanton *Arethusaes* azurde armes,
> And none but thou shalt be my paramour.
> (1341-47)

Upward gestures are suggested by "the euening aire" and "the monarke of the skie"; Faustus's attitude towards Helen is linked to that of hapless Semele when Jupiter descended as a flame, and to that of the fountain nymph Arethusa when she embraced Jupiter in her spraylike, watery, and sky-reflecting arms. Consummation with the power first described in Helen's face is envisaged as dissolution in fire or water. There is no suggestion, here, that she might be an intercessor, even such as we get when Tamburlaine first describes God welcoming Zenocrate, just before he turns to resentment against her possession by amorous Jove.

I can imagine a commonsense objection at this point to the effect that after all Faustus's encounter with Helen is a sexual rhapsody, and that all this talk about it does not alter the fact: a kiss is a kiss. Mistresses, it could be added, are constantly compared to heaven and to gods, and lovers often feel, without being blasphemers, that a kiss makes mortality cease to matter. But it is just here that, at the

risk of laboring the obvious, I want to insist that Marlowe's art gives the encounter meaning both as a peculiar kind of sexual experience *and* as blasphemy.

The stage directions of the 1604 text bring the old man back just at the moment when Faustus in so many words is making Helen into heaven:

> Here wil I dwel, for heauen be in these lips,
> And all is drosse that is not *Helena:*
>   Enter old man
>   (1333-34)

This figure of piety is a presence during the rest of the speech; his perspective is summarized after its close: "Accursed *Faustus,* miserable man, / That from thy soule excludst the grace of heauen" (1348-49).

Another perspective comes from the earlier scenes in the play where the nature of heaven and the relation to it of man and devil are established in conversations between Mephostophilis and Faustus. For example, the large and final line before the old man's entrance in the later scene, "And all is drosse that is not *Helena,*" has almost exactly the same movement as an earlier line of Mephostophilis's which ends in "heauen":

> And to conclude, when all the world dissolues,
> And euery creature shalbe purified,
> All places shall be hell that is not heauen.
> (556-58)

One does not need to assume a conscious recognition by the audience of this parallel, wonderfully ironic as it is when we come to hear it as an echo. What matters is the recurrence of similar gestures in language about heaven and its substitutes, so that a meaning of heaven and postures toward it are established.

The most striking element in this poetic complex is a series of passages involving a face:

> Why this is hel, nor am I out of it:
> Thinkst thou that I who saw the face of God,
> And tasted the eternal ioyes of heauen,
> Am not tormented with ten thousand hels,
> In being depriv'd of euerlasting blisse?
> (312-16)

Just as Faustus's rapt look at Helen's face is followed by his kiss, so in the lines of Mephostophilis, "saw the face of God" is followed by "tasted the eternal ioyes of heauen."

Both face and taste are of course traditional religious imagery, as is motion upward and downward. Marlowe's shaping power composes traditional elements into a single complex gesture and imaginative situation which appears repeatedly. The face is always high, something above to look up to, reach or leap up to, or to be thrown down from:

> FAUSTUS: Was not that *Lucifer* and Angell once?
>
> MEPHOSTOPHILIS: Yes *Faustus,* and most dearely lou'd of God.
>
> FAUSTUS: How comes it then that he is prince of diuels?

MEPHOSTOPHILIS: O by aspiring pride and insolence,
    For which God threw him from the face of
heauen.

(300-04)

A leaping-up complementary to this throwing-down, with
a related sense of guilt, is expressed in Faustus's lines as
he enters at midnight, about to conjure and eagerly hoping
to have "these ioyes in full possession":

Now that the gloomy shadow of the earth,
Longing to view *Orions* drisling looke,
Leapes from th' antartike world vnto the skie,
And dimmes the welkin with her pitchy breath:
Faustus, begin thine incantations.

(235-39)

Here the reaching upward in *leaps* is dramatized by the
word's position as a heavy stress at the opening of the line.
There is a guilty suggestion in *gloomy* both discontented
and dark—linked with *longing to view.* An open-mouthed
panting is suggested by *pitchy breath,* again with dark associations of guilt which carry through to Faustus's own
breath as he says his *incantations.* The whole passage has
a grotesque, contorted quality appropriate to the expression of an almost unutterable desire, at the same time that
it magnificently affirms this desire by throwing its shadow
up across the heavens.

A more benign vision appears in the preceding scene,
where the magician Valdes promises Faustus that "serviceable" spirits will attend:

Sometimes like women, or vnwedded maides,
Shadowing more beautie in their ayrie browes,
Then has the white breasts of the queene of
Loue.

(156-58)

Here we get an association of the breast with the face corresponding to the linkage elsewhere of tasting power and
joy with seeing a face. The lines suggest by "ayrie browes"
that the faces are high (as well as that the women are unsubstantial spirits).

The complex we have been following gets its fullest and
most intense expression in a passage of Faustus's final
speech, where the imagery of communion with which we
began is one element. To present it in this fuller context,
I quote again:

The starres mooue stil, time runs, the clocke wil
strike,
The diuel wil come, and Faustus must be
damnd.
O Ile leape vp to my God: who pulles me downe?
See see where Christs blood streames in the fir-
mament.
One drop would saue my soule, halfe a drop, ah
my Christ.
Ah rend not my heart for naming of my Christ,
Yet wil I call on him: oh spare me *Lucifer!*
Where is it now? tis gone: And see where God
Stretcheth out his arme, and bends his irefull
browes.

(1429-37)

Here the leap is discovered to be unrealizable. Faustus's

blasphemous vision of his own soul with Helen—"see
where it flies"—is matched now by "See, see where Christs
blood streames." It is "in the firmament," as was Orion's
drizzling look. A paroxysm of choking tension at once
overtakes Faustus when he actually envisages drinking
Christ's blood. And yet—"one drop would saue my
soule." Such communion is denied by the companion vision of the face, now dreadful, "irefull browes" instead of
"ayrie browes," above and bending down in overwhelming anger, "the heauy wrath of God" (1439).

"A surffet of deadly sinne"

When we turn to consider the presentation of the underside of Faustus's motive, complementary to his exalted
longings, the Prayer Book again can help us understand
Marlowe. The seventeenth of the Thirty-Nine Articles
contains a warning remarkably applicable to Faustus:

As the godly consyderation of predestination,
and our election in Christe, is full of sweete,
pleasaunt, and vnspeakeable comfort to godly
persons . . . : So, for curious and carnal persons, lacking the spirite of Christe, to haue continually before their eyes the sentence of Gods
predestination, is a most daungerous downefall,
whereby the deuyll doth thrust them either into
desperation, or into rechelesnesse of most vncleane liuing, no lesse perilous then desperation.

Faustus is certainly a "curious and carnal person." And
though he does not have "the sentence of God's predestination," as such, continually before his eyes, he has an
equally devastating conviction of his own unworthiness
and God's anger at him. The article relates this characteristically Calvinist predicament to the effort to use the body
to escape despair: *rechelesnesse* (or *wretchlesness*) seems to
combine wretchedness and recklessness; the phrase "most
vncleane liuing" suggests that the appetites become both
inordinate and perverse.

The psychoanalytic understanding of the genesis of perversions can help us to understand how, as the article says,
such unclean living is spiritually motivated—like blasphemy, with which it is closely associated. We have noticed
how blasphemy involves a magical identification of action
with meaning, of sign with significance. A similar identification appears in perversion as Freud has described it.
Freud sees in perversions a continuation of the secondary
sexual satisfactions dominant in childhood. The pervert,
in this view, is attempting, by repeating a way of using the
body in relation to a certain limited sexual object, to recover or continue in adult life the meaning of a relationship
fixed on this action and object in childhood. So, for example, the sucking perversions may seek to establish a relationship of dependence by eating someone more powerful.
Faustus lives for twenty-four years "in al voluptuous-
nesse" (328), in "rechelesnesse of most vncleane liuing":
it is the meanings that he seeks in sensation that make his
pleasures unclean, violations of taboo. We have seen how
what he seeks from Orion or from Helen is an equivalent
for Christ's blood, how the voluptuousness which is born
of his despair is an effort to find in carnal satisfactions an
incarnation. Perversion can thus be equivalent to a striving for a blasphemous communion.

In the same period that Eliot wrote the essay in which he pointed to the importance of blasphemy in Marlowe's work, his poem "Gerontion" expressed a vision of people in the modern world reduced to seeking spiritual experience in perverse sensuality and aestheticism:

> In the juvescence of the year
> Came Christ the tiger
>
> In depraved May, dogwood and chestnut,
>   flowering judas
> To be eaten, to be divided, to be drunk
> Among whispers; by Mr. Silvero,
> With caressing hands, at Limoges
> Who walked all night in the next room;
>
> By Hakagawa, bowing among the Titians;
> By Madame de Tornquist, in the dark room
> Shifting the candles; Fräulein von Kulp
> Who turned in the hall, one hand on the door.

As I read the elusive chronology of Eliot's poem, Marlowe would have envisaged Helen in the luxuriance of a "depraved May" associated with the Renaissance, from which we come down, through a characteristically telescoped syntax, to the meaner modern versions of a black mass. What immediately concerns us here is the seeking of incarnation in carnal and aesthetic satisfactions. The perverse has an element of worship in it.

When we consider the imagery in *Doctor Faustus* in psychoanalytic terms, an oral emphasis is very marked, both in the expression of longings that reach towards the sublime and in the gluttony which pervades the play and tends toward the comic, the grotesque, and the terrible. It is perhaps not fanciful to link the recurrent need to leap up which we have seen in the play's imagery with an infant's reaching upward to mother or breast, as this becomes fused in later life with desire for women as sources of intoxicating strength: the face as a source of power, to be obliviously kissed, "ayrie browes" linked to "the white breasts of the queene of Loue." Such imagery neighbors directly religious images, Christ's streaming blood, the taste of heavenly joys.

It is because Faustus has the same fundamentally acquisitive attitude toward both secular and religious objects that the religious joys are unreachable. The ground of the attitude that sustenance must be gained by special knowledge or an illicit bargain with an ultimately hostile power is the deep conviction that sustenance will not be given freely, that life and power must come from a being who condemns and rejects Faustus. From her psychoanalytic perspective, Kuriyama emphasizes fear of castration in *Doctor Faustus,* as in the prospect, finally realized, of being torn to pieces. Certainly Lucifer is a "father substitute," an alternative to a vengeful God, who proves to be equally cruel. And the devils make phallic threats as they overawe Faustus at moments of his hesitating. But Faustus's situation is not shaped by open oedipal confrontation that runs the risk of provoking paternal rejection or retaliation. Faustus's insistent hunger for satisfaction is a more deeply regressive effort that sustains desire in the face of an unalterable rejection that has already taken place. We can see Faustus's blasphemous need, in psychoanalytic terms, as fixation or regression to infantile objects and attitudes,

verging toward perverse developments of the infantile pursued and avoided in obscure images of sexual degradation. When the Arethusa image merges Helen with Jupiter, the longing for the taste of heavenly joys, for the breasts of Venus, moves across to suggestions of fellatio. Faustus's longing confuses or identifies the two parents, reducing each to an object to feed on, so that the need appears in fantasies of somehow eating the father, of panting for Orion's drizzling look, or, later, of desperately craving the inaccessible drop of Christ's blood. We have at such moments a shift from whole-person relationship to the search for satisfaction in "part objects" which W. R. D. Fairbairn has described [in *An Object Relations Theory of Personality,* 1954].

But to keep the experience in the perspective with which Marlowe's culture saw it, we must recognize that Faustus's despair and obsessive hunger go with his inability to take part in Holy Communion. In Holy Communion, he would, in the words of the Prayer Book, "spiritually eat the flesh of Christ, and drink his blood . . . dwell in Christ . . . be one with Christ." In the Lord's Supper, the very actions toward which the infantile, potentially disruptive motive tends are transformed for the successful communicant into a way of reconciliation with society and the ultimate source and sanction of society. But communion can only be reached by "a truly penitent heart" which recognizes human finitude, and with "a lively faith" in the possibility of God's love. Psychoanalytic interpretation can easily lead to the misconception that when we encounter infantile or potentially perverse imagery in a traditional culture it indicates, a priori, neurosis or degradation. Frequently, on the contrary, such imagery is enacted in ritual and used in art as a way of controlling what is potentially disruptive.

Ritual is something done in common which validates the individual's membership in society—in the community, the Communion. Tudor rubrics instructed the minister to try to reconcile quarreling parishioners before admitting them to the Lord's Supper—as well as to seek out notorious sinners and try to bring them round to confession and reconciliation. Saint Thomas regarded the Eucharist as the most important sacrament because "the reality of the sacrament is the unity of the mystical body, without which there can be no salvation" [quoted in Sheldon S. Wolin, *Politics and Vision: Continuity and Innovation in Western Political Thought,* 1960]. But the church as a *corpus mysticum* is never even envisaged by Marlowe's protagonist. Faustus's affinities with the individualistic trend in Protestantism come out in the loneliness of his search for equivalents for something "heauenly" to "feede my soule," passively; he does not envisage participating in a *common* sacred meal, even in the blasphemous version of the witches' coven.

Since ritual carries a social and moral meaning spontaneously understood by members of the culture, in tragedy it provides perspective on individual experience. So in *Lear* the audience feels the validity of Cordelia's appeal to the marriage service, or again, recoils at Lear's refusal to provide her with a dower. In *Doctor Faustus,* the Holy Communion has the same central significance as Faustus is swept away by currents of deep aberrant motives associated with it, motives it ordinarily serves to control. This becomes fully conscious, as such, for audience and for protagonist at the moment when Faustus seals his bargain by performing in effect a black mass—by giving his blood and testament instead of receiving Christ's. How deeply the awesome significance we have seen spelled out in the Prayer Book is built into his sensibility appears when he stabs his arm:

> My bloud conieales and I can write no more.
> . . . .
> Faustus giues to thee his soule: ah there it stay-
> de,
> Why shouldst thou not? is not thy soule thine
> owne?
>
> (494, 499-500)

This is the crucial moment, for Faustus imitates Christ in sacrificing himself—but to Satan instead of to God. A moment later he will repeat Christ's last words, *"Consummatum est."* His flesh cringes to close the self-inflicted wound, so deeply is its meaning understood by his body.

The deep assumption that all strength must come from consuming another accounts not only for the desperate need to leap up again to the source of life, but also for the moments of reckless elation in fantasy. Faustus uses the word *fantasy* in exactly its modern psychological sense:

> . . . your words haue woon me at the last,
> To practise Magicke and concealed arts:
> Yet not your words onely, but mine owne fanta-
> sie,
> That will receiue no obiect for my head,
> But ruminates on Negromantique skill.
>
> (129-33)

Here "ruminates" carries on the imagery of gluttony. Moving restlessly around the circle of his desires, Faustus wants more from nature than nature can give, and gluttony is the form his "unclean living" characteristically takes. The verb "glut" recurs: "How am I glutted with conceit of this!" "That heauenly *Helen* . . . to glut the longing . . . " The prologue summarizes his career in the same terms, introducing like an overture the theme of rising up by linking gluttony with a flight of Icarus:

> Till swolne with cunning, of a selfe conceit,
> His waxen wings did mount aboue his reach,
> And melting heauens conspirde his ouerthrow.
> For falling to a diuelish exercise,
> And glutted now with learnings golden gifts,
> He surffets vpon cursed Negromancy.
>
> (20-5)

On the final night, when his fellow scholars try to cheer Faustus, one of them says, "tis but a surffet, neuer feare man." He answers, "A surffet of deadly sinne that hath damnd both body and soule" (1366-68). How accurately this exchange defines the spiritual, blasphemous motivation of his hunger!

Grotesque and perverse versions of hunger appear in the comedy. Like much of Shakespeare's low comedy, the best clowning in **Doctor Faustus** spells out literally what is metaphorical in the poetry. When the comic action is a burlesque that uses imaginative associations present in the poetry, its authenticity is hard to doubt. Commentators are often very patronizing about the scene with the pope, for example; but it carries out the motive of gluttony in a delightful and appropriate way by presenting a pope "whose *summum bonum* is in belly-cheate" (855) and by having Faustus snatch his meat and wine away and render his exorcism ludicrous, baffling magic with magic. Later Wagner tells of Faustus himself carousing and swilling amongst the students with "such belly-cheere, / As *Wagner* nere beheld in his Life" (1243-44). The presentation of the seven deadly sins, though of course traditional, comes back to hunger again and again, in gross and obscene forms; after the show is over, Faustus exclaims "O this feedes my soule" (781). One could go on and on.

Complementary to the active imagery of eating is imagery of being devoured. Such imagery was of course traditional, as for example in cathedral carvings of the Last Judgment and in the Hell's mouth of the stage. With being devoured goes the idea of giving blood, also traditional, but handled, like all the imagery, in a way to bring together deep implications. To give blood is for Faustus a propitiatory substitute for being devoured or torn in pieces. The relation is made explicit when, near the end, Mephostophilis threatens that if he repents, "Ile in peecemeale teare thy flesh" (1306). Faustus collapses at once into propitiation, signaled poignantly by the epithet "sweet" which is always on his hungry lips:

> Sweete *Mephastophilis*, intreate thy Lord
> To pardon my vniust presumption,
> And with my blood againe I wil confirme
> My former vow I made to *Lucifer*.
>
> (1307-10)

By his pact Faustus agrees to be devoured later provided that he can do the devouring in the meantime. Before the signing, he speaks of paying by using other people's blood:

> The god thou seruest is thine owne appetite,
> Wherein is fixt the loue of Belsabub.
> To him Ile build an altare and a church,
> And offer luke warme blood of new borne babes.
>
> (443-46)

But it has to be his own blood. The identification of his blood with his soul (a very common traditional idea) is underscored by the fact that his blood congeals as he is about to write "gives to thee his soule," and by Mephostophilis's vampire-like exclamation, as the blood clears again under the influence of his ominous fire: "O what will not I do to obtaine his soule?" (505)

Faustus's relation to the devil here is expressed in a way that was characteristic of witchcraft—or perhaps one should say, of the fantasies of witch-hunters about witchcraft. Witch lore often embodies the assumption that power can be conveyed by giving and taking the contents of the body, with which the soul is identified, especially the blood. To give blood to the devil—and to various animal familiars—was the ritual expression of submission, for which in return one got special powers. Witches could be detected by the "devil's mark" from which the blood was drawn. In stabbing his arm, Faustus is making a "devil's mark" or "witch's mark" on himself.

The clown contributes to this theme in his role as a commonsense prose foil to the heroic, poetic action of the protagonist. When Wagner buys the ragged but shrewd old "clown" into his service, he counts on hunger:

> . . . The vilaine is bare, and out of seruice, and so hungry, that I know he would giue his soule to the Diuel for a shoulder of mutton, though it were blood rawe.
>
> (358-61)

We have just heard Faustus exclaim:

> Had I as many soules as there be starres,
> Ide giue them al for *Mephastophilis:*
>
> (338-39)

But the clown is not so gullibly willing to pay all:

> How, my soule to the Diuel for a shoulder of mutton though twere blood rawe? not so good friend, burladie I had neede haue it wel roasted, and good sawce to it, if I pay so deere.
>
> (362-65)

After making game of the sturdy old beggar's ignorance of Latin tags, Wagner assumes the role of the all-powerful magician:

> . . . Binde your selfe presently vnto me for seauen yeeres, or Ile turne al the lice about thee into familiars, and they shall teare thee in peeces.
>
> (377-80)

But again the clown's feet are on the ground:

> Doe you heare sir? you may saue that labour, they are too familiar with me already, swowns they are as bolde with my flesh, as if they had payd for my meate and drinke.
>
> (381-84)

Mephostophilis, who is to become the hero's "familiar spirit" (as the emperor calls him later at line 1011), "pays for" his meat and drink, and in due course will "make bold" with his flesh. The old fellow understands such consequences, after his fashion, as the high-flown hero does not.

One final, extraordinarily complex image of surfeit appears in the last soliloquy, when Faustus, frantic to escape from his own greedy identity, conceives of his whole body being swallowed up by a cloud and then vomited away:

> Then wil I headlong runne into the earth:
> Earth gape. O no, it wil not harbour me:
> You starres that raignd at my natiuitie,
> Whose influence hath alotted death and hel,
> Now draw vp Faustus like a foggy mist,
> Into the intrailes of yon labring cloude,
> That when you vomite foorth into the ayre,
> My limbes may issue from your smoaky
>   mouthes,
> So that my soule may but ascend to heauen.
>
> (1441-49)

Taken by themselves, these lines might seem to present a very far-fetched imagery. In relation to the imaginative design we have been tracing, they express self-disgust in terms exactly appropriate to Faustus's earlier efforts at self-aggrandizement. The hero asks to be swallowed and disgorged, anticipating the fate his sin expects and attempting to elude damnation by separating body and soul. Yet the dreadful fact is that these lines envisage death in a way which makes it a consummation of desires expressed earlier. Thus in calling up to the "starres that raigned at my natiuitie," Faustus is still adopting a posture of helpless entreaty toward powers above. He assumes their influence to be hostile but nevertheless inescapable: he is still unable to believe in love. And he asks to be "drawn up," "like a foggy mist," as earlier the "gloomy shadow," with its "pitchy breath," sought to leap up. The whole plea is couched as an eat-or-be-eaten bargain: you may eat my body if you will save my soul.

In the second half of the soliloquy Faustus keeps returning to this effort to distinguish body and soul. As the clock finally strikes, he asks for escape in physical dissolution:

> now body turne to ayre,
> Or *Lucifer* wil beare thee quicke to hel:
> *Thunder and lightning.*
>
> O soule, be changde into little water drops,
> And fal into the *Ocean,* nere be found.
>
> (1470-73)

It is striking that death here is envisaged in a way closely similar to the visions of sexual consummation in the Helen speech. The "body turne to ayre," with the thunder and lightning, can be related to the consummation of hapless Semele with flaming Jupiter; the soul becoming little water drops recalls the showery consummation of Arethusa. Of course the auditor need not notice these relations, which in part spring naturally from a pervasive human tendency to equate sexual release with death. The auditor does feel, however, in these sublime and terrible entreaties, that Faustus is still Faustus. Analysis brings out what we all feel—that Faustus cannot repent. Despite the fact that his attitude toward his motive has changed from exaltation to horror, he is still dominated by the same motive—body and soul are one, as he himself said in the previous scene: "hath damnd both body and soule." The final pleas themselves confirm his despair, shaped as they are by the body's desires and the assumptions those desires carry.

"as farre as doth the minde of man"

After the Marprelate controversy was handled on the stage, the prohibition of religious subject matter obviated the possibility of dealing directly and explicitly with its central act of worship. This gives a special interest to the relationships we have been tracing between religious and dramatic action. We get actions analogous to Holy Communion in Shakespeare, but they are not explicitly related to it. A striking example is in *Julius Caesar*. In Calphurnia's dream, which Shakespeare develops beyond Plutarch, Caesar's statue, "like a fountain with an hundred spouts, / Did run pure blood" (2.2.77-8), in which smiling Romans bathed their hands. Decius interprets it as a happy omen: "from you great Rome shall suck / Reviving blood," "great men shall press / For tinctures, stains, relics, and cognizance" (2.2.87-9). He and the other conspirators do indeed hope to carve up Caesar and share out his spirit among them, reviving republican Rome. After the assassination, Shakespeare makes their dipping their arms in his blood into an effort to do this, with what results the sequel shows after Antony makes the wounds speak to the mob.

Caesar concludes the scene in which his fears are overcome with "Good friends, go in, and taste some wine with me, / And we, like friends, will straightway go together" (2.2.126-27). This invitation to casual social communion wrings from Brutus the aside, "That every like is not the same, O Caesar, / The heart of Brutus earns to think upon!" (2.2.128-29). He knows that he is involved in a sacrifice, and feels anguish that it must be bloody:

> Let's be sacrificers, but not butchers, Caius.
> We all stand up against the spirit of Caesar,
> And in the spirit of men there is no blood;
> O that we then could come by Caesar's spirit,
> And not dismember Caesar! But, alas,
> Caesar must bleed for it! Ah, gentle friends,
> Let's kill him boldly, but not wrathfully;
> Let's carve him as a dish fit for the gods,
> Not hew him as carcas fit for hounds.
>
> (2.1.166-74)

Yet it is Brutus who in their staggered moment after the assassination cries out:

> Stoop, Romans, stoop,
> And let us bathe our hands in Caesar's blood
> Up to the elbows, and besmear our swords.
>
> (3.1.105-07)

I do not think that we need be conscious of the Christian analogies, but clearly the meaning of assassination has been shaped by Christianity. Christian interpretation can understand the play as exhibiting the need for the mystery of Christ's sacrifice leading to butchery—to use Brutus's own word. Eliot observed that Greek tragedy deals with problems whose solution had to wait for the Incarnation. [In a 1917 lecture published in 1954 as *Religious Drama: Medieval and Modern*] The relationship is there to be made for what I have come to think of as Shakespeare's post-Christian art as well as for some pre-Christian Greek art. But Shakespeare does not make it.

Marlowe's *Faustus* does make such relationship explicit—so explicit that in following out the human underside of eucharistic need in the themes of gluttony and blasphemy I have largely ignored their irreducibly dramatic combination with the heroic, "Renaissance" side of the play. Marlowe was able to present blasphemy and gluttony as he did only because he was able to envisage them also as something more or something else: "his dominion that exceedes in this, / Stretcheth as farre as doth the minde of man" (88-9). We have been considering how the play presents a shape of longing and fear which might have lost itself in the fulfillment of the Lord's Supper or become obscene and hateful in the perversions of a witches' sabbath. But in fact Faustus is neither a saint nor a witch—he is Faustus, a particular man whose particular fortunes are defined not by ritual but by drama.

When the good angel tells Faustus to "lay that damned booke aside . . . that is blasphemy" (98, 101), the evil angel can answer in terms that are not moral but heroic:

> Go forward *Faustus* in that famous art,
> Wherein all natures treasury is contained:
> Be thou on earth as *loue* is in the skie.
>
> (102-04)

It is because the alternatives are not simply good or evil that Marlowe has not written a morality play but a tragedy: there is the further, heroic alternative. In dealing with the blasphemy, I have emphasized how the vision of magic joys invests earthly things with divine attributes; but the heroic quality of the magic depends on fusing these divine suggestions with tangible values and resources of the secular world.

This ennobling fusion depends, of course, on the poetry, which brings into play an extraordinary range of contemporary life:

> From *Venice* shall they dregge huge Argoces,
> And from *America* the golden fleece,
> That yearely stuffes olde *Philips* treasury.
>
> (159-61)

Here three lines draw in sixteenth-century classical studies, exploration and commercial adventure, national rivalries, and the stimulating disruptive influence of the new supply of gold bullion. Marlowe's poetry is sublime because it extends desire so as to envisage as objects of passion the larger life of society and nature: "Was this the face that . . ."—that did what? ". . . lancht a thousand shippes?" "Clad in the beauty of . . ."—of what? ". . . a thousand starres." **Doctor Faustus** has sublime dimensions because Marlowe was able to occupy so much actual thought and life by following the form of Faustus's desire. At the same time, it is a remorselessly objective, ironic play because it dramatizes the ground of the desire which needs to ransack the world for objects; and so it expresses the precariousness of the whole enterprise along with its magnificence.

Thus Faustus's gluttonous preoccupation with satisfactions of the mouth and throat is also a delight in the power and beauty of language: "I see theres vertue in my heauenly words" (262). Physical hunger is also hunger for knowledge; his need to depend on others, and to show power by compelling others to depend on him, is also learning and teaching. Academic vices and weaknesses shadow academic virtues: there is a fine, lonely, generous mastery about Faustus when he is with his colleagues and the students; and Mephostophilis too has a moving dignity in expounding unflinchingly the dreadful logic of damnation to Faustus as to a disciple. The inordinate fascination with secrets, with what cannot be named, as Mephostophilis cannot name God, includes the exploring, inquiring attitude of "Tel me, are there many heauens aboue the Moone?" (646). The need to leap up becomes such aspirations as the plan to "make a bridge through the moouing ayre, / To passe the *Ocean* with a band of men" (341-42). Here we have in germ that sense of man's destiny as a vector moving through open space which [Oswald] Spengler described as the Faustian soul form. Faustus's alienation, which we have discussed chiefly as it produces a need for blasphemy, also motivates the readiness to alter and appropriate the created universe—make the moon drop or ocean rise—appropriating them for man instead of for the greater glory of God, because the heavens are "the booke of *loues* hie firmament" (794), and one can hope for nothing from Jove. Perhaps most fundamental of all is the assumption that power is something outside oneself, something one does not become (as a child becomes a man); something beyond and stronger than oneself (as God remains stronger than man); *and yet* something one can capture and ride—by manipulating symbols.

Marlowe of course does not anticipate the kind of manipulation of symbols which actually has, in natural science, produced this sort of power: Mephostophilis answers Faustus with Ptolemy, not Copernicus—let alone the calculus. But Marlowe was able to exemplify the creative function of controlling symbols by the way he has made poetic speech an integral part of drama as a mode of action. Faustus can assert about himself, "This word damnation terrifies not him, / For he confounds hell in *Elizium*" (294-95). The extraordinary pun in "confounds hell in Elizium" suggests that Faustus is able to change the world by the way he names it, to *destroy* or *baffle* hell by *equating* or *mixing* it with Elysium.

Scott Buchanan, in his discussion of tragedy in *Poetry and Mathematics* [1929], suggested that we can see tragedy as an experiment where the protagonist tests reality by trying to live a hypothesis. Elizabethan tragedy, seen in this way, can be set beside the tentatively emerging science of the period. The ritualistic assumptions of alchemy were beginning to be replaced by ideas of observation; a clear-cut conception of the experimental testing of hypothesis had not developed, but Bacon was soon to speak of putting nature on the rack to make her yield up her secrets. Faustus's scientific questions and Mephostophilis's answers are disappointing; but the hero's whole enterprise is an experiment, or "experience" as the Elizabethans would have termed it. We watch as the author puts him on the rack.

> FAUSTUS: Come, I thinke hell's a fable.
>
> MEPHOSTOPHILIS: I, thinke so still, till experience change thy minde.
>
> (559-60)

We can see particularly clearly in *Doctor Faustus* how the new drama was a step in the developing self-consciousness of Western civilization parallel to Protestantism. The restriction of the impulse for physical embodiment in the new Protestant worship connects with a compensatory fascination with magical possibilities for self-realization and the incarnation of meaning in physical gesture and ceremony: the drama carries on, for the most part in secular terms, the preoccupation with a kind of religious meaning which had been curtailed but had not been eliminated in religion. Tamburlaine talks about himself as though from the outside, almost always to aggrandize his identity; we watch to see whether words will become deeds—whether the man will become demigod. The range of relationships expressed between self and world is much wider with Faustus: "Settle thy studies *Faustus,* and beginne . . . " (29); "what shall become of Faustus, being

in hel for euer?" (1382-83). In the opening speech, where Faustus uses his own name seven times in trying on the selves provided by the various arts, he is looking in books for a miracle. When he finally takes up the necromantic works, there is a temporary consummation, calling for a gesture to express the new being which has been seized: "All things that mooue betweene the quiet poles / Shalbe at my commaund" (84-5). At the very end of the play, Faustus's language is still demanding miracles, while the *absence* of corroborating physical actions makes clear that the universe cannot be equated with his self: "Stand stil you euer moouing spheres of heauen" (1422).

Such centering of consciousness, providing a context for the self by naming oneself, runs through all the subsequent major drama. So of course does magical thinking. Elizabeth Sewell, in *The Orphic Muse* [1960], observed that an original artist can make what he is doing widely comprehensible by finding a myth that embodies equivalents of the new art form. Marlowe found such a myth for the Elizabethan theater in magic. The double medium of poetic drama was peculiarly effective to express the struggle for omnipotence and transcendence along with its tragic (and comic) failure. Shakespeare uses and controls the magic in the web of his art from the beginning of his career to its end. King Lear in the storm, at the summit of Elizabethan tragedy, is, like Faustus, trying, and failing, to realize magical omnipotence of mind: "All-shaking thunder, / Strike flat the thick rotundity o' th' world!" (3.2.6-7). . . . [In] Kyd's *Spanish Tragedy*, . . . outrage done to social and family piety leads the protagonist to magical thinking which is madness, and . . . the play ends by going out of control.

Marlowe signified *his* control in *Doctor Faustus* by writing at the end of the text, *"Terminat hora diem, Terminat Author opus."* As my friend the late John Moore remarked, it is as though he finished the play at midnight. The final hour has terminated the work and its hero, but the author is still alive. This is another kind of power than magical dominion, a social power that depends on the resources of art realized in alliance with the "patient judgments" in an audience. Marlowe has earned an identity apart from his hero's—he is the author. In his own life, what was working in the work caught up with him at Deptford. Art, even such austere art as *Doctor Faustus,* did not save the man in the author. But the author did save, within the limits of art, and with art's permanence, much that was in the man, to become part of the evolving culture in which his own place was so precarious.

There is a limitation about *Doctor Faustus* as a tragedy, however, that goes with its ending and the attitude expressed in the author's postscript. The tragedy has turned into something like—too like—a scapegoat ritual: let the hero carry off into death the evil of the motive he has embodied, ridding it from the author-executioner and the participating audience. The final chorus pulls back from the hero to the relief of conventional wisdom:

> *Faustus* is gone, regard his hellish fall,
> Whose fiendful fortune may exhort the wise,
> Onely to wonder at vnlawful things,
> Whose deepenesse doth intise such forward wits,

To practise more than heauenly power permits.
(1481-85)

Beyond the limiting moral perspective of the chorus, we have seen in detail, notably in the final soliloquy, how the fate of the hero is integral with his motive. But it is a motive that, in its dreadful consummation, has lost all connection with the willed heroic alternative that gave it value as a rebellious quest for pleasure, beauty, power.

Faustus's increasing, finally total helplessness in the grip of his motive is part of the play's limitation. Partly this is the effect of his egotism and alienation and the limited realization of a social world around him. The moment of greatest human pathos, as his end approaches, comes when he is with the scholars:

> 1. SCHOLAR: Why did not Faustus tel vs of this before, that Diuines might haue prayed for thee?
>
> FAUSTUS: Oft haue I thought to haue done so, but the diuell threatened to teare mee in peeces, if I namde God, to fetch both body and soule, if I once gaue eare to diuinitie: and now tis too late: Gentlemen away, lest you perish with me.
>
> 2. SCHOLAR: O what shal we do to saue Faustus?
>
> FAUSTUS: Talke not of me, but saue your selues, and depart.
>
> 3. SCHOLAR: God wil strengthen me, I wil stay with Faustus.
>
> 1. SCHOLAR: Tempt not God, sweete friend, but let vs into the next roome, and there pray for him.
>
> FAUSTUS: I, pray for me, pray for me, and what noyse soeuer yee heare, come not vnto me, for nothing can rescue me.
>
> 2. SCHOLAR: Pray thou, and we will pray that God may haue mercy vpon thee.
>
> FAUSTUS: Gentlemen farewel, if I liue til morning, Ile visite you: if not, Faustus is gone to hel.
>
> ALL: Faustus, farewel.
>
> *Exuent Scholars*
> (1400-18)

Here, in some of the most effective writing in the play, is the only moment when Faustus feels the loss not of his own soul, or of heaven for his soul, but of human society: "Ah my sweete chamber-fellow! had I liued with thee, then had I liued stil, but now I die eternally . . . " (1359-60). But it is pathetic rather than tragic: the loss Faustus expresses is for a kind of fulfillment that he has neither sought nor left behind in his heroic enterprise. Compare, by contrast, Macbeth's stark realization that "honor, love, obedience, troops of friends, / I must not look to have" (5.3.25-6), which becomes fully tragic through its relation to the fulfillment he has known and lost in the social world he disrupts.

More full-hearted tragedy presents a protagonist committed to his heroic motive, on terms that he establishes, right through to the end—which in a tragic situation is his end. Bruno in Rome, recanting his recantation, becomes a trag-

ic figure. Coriolanus, in his quest for heroic martial identity, is almost as self-isolating as Faustus, and Shakespeare's play presents him nearly as clinically as Marlowe's does Faustus. But Coriolanus never surrenders the heroic dimension of the motive that has animated his quest, even though Shakespeare ruthlessly dramatizes the self-destructiveness at its psychological core. When, after his mother has persuaded him to spare Rome, Coriolanus is back at Corioli, Aufidius's accusation rests on a shrewd insight into the protagonist's withdrawal: "at his nurse's tears / He whin'd and roar'd away your victory" (5.6.96-7). To Coriolanus's outraged "Hear'st thou, Mars?" Aufidius cunningly answers: "Name not the god, thou boy of tears!" (5.6.99-100). The hero's response is to reassert his driving motive to escape "boy" by martial prowess.

> Measureless liar, thou hast made my heart
> Too great for what contains it. "Boy"? O slave!
> . . . .
> Cut me to pieces, Volsces, men and lads,
> Stain all your edges on me. "Boy," false hound!
> If you have writ your annals true, 'tis there
> That, like an eagle in a dove-coat, I
> Flutter'd your Volscians in Corioles.
> Alone I did it. "Boy"!
> (5.6.102-03; 111-16)

He would rather mean than be—mean what he has made the name Coriolanus mean—even in the impossible situation among Volscians to which his motive has brought him.

At the very end of *Coriolanus* there is a tribute to the protagonist's human achievement. Second Lord tries to intervene in the assassination:

> Peace ho! no outrage, peace!
> The man is noble, and his fame folds in
> This orb o' th' earth. His last offenses
> Shall have judicious hearing.
> (5.6.123-26)

The conspirators cut him down nevertheless, and Aufidius *"stands on him,"* fulfilling *his* motive. But Shakespeare concludes the play with a change of heart, even in Aufidius:

> My rage is gone,
> And I am struck with sorrow. Take him up.
> Help, three a' th' chiefest soldiers; I'll be one.
> Beat thou the drum, that it speak mournfully,
> Trail your steel pikes. Though in this city he
> Hath widowed and unchilded many a one,
> Which to this hour bewail the injury,
> Yet he shall have a noble memory.
> (5.6.146-53)

In *Doctor Faustus,* by contrast, the failure of the final choric judgment to locate the protagonist's heroic significance in a larger human context reflects Faustus's withdrawal from his own endeavor. With Faustus we miss, after the opening scene, heroic commitment to the motive at the base of his identity. Instead we are shown his frantic efforts to escape identity.

There is a devastated feeling at the close of *Doctor Faustus,* in my experience almost shattering. None of the strange feeling *for* life comes through at the end, such as we get in Shakespeare (though perhaps less in *Coriolanus* than in any other major tragedy). Snow has suggested that the center of feeling in **Doctor Faustus** is somehow outside the central conflict, displaced by the gap that opens between "the phenomenological contours of the play" and Faustus's consciousness. Perhaps one can say that it moves more and more away from the protagonist as his helplessness and the play's understanding of it increase. **Tamburlaine** is limited by Marlowe's identification with a protagonist who himself dominates others by "conceiving and subduing both." In the more complex action of **Doctor Faustus,** identification gives way to the ever-widening distance the author puts between himself and what in him animates his protagonist. As Marlowe's Latin postscript boasts, it is another instance of "conceiving and subduing both." (pp. 87-130)

> *C. L. Barber, " 'The forme of Faustus fortunes good or bad',"* in his Creating Elizabethan Tragedy: The Theater of Marlowe and Kyd, *edited by Richard P. Wheeler, The University of Chicago Press, 1988, pp. 87-130.*

FURTHER READING

Overviews and General Studies

Bevington, David M. *From* Mankind *to* Marlowe. Cambridge, Mass.: Harvard University Press, 1962, 310 p.
Includes a detailed discussion of Marlowe's works, particularly *Tamburlaine, The Jew of Malta,* and *Edward II,* in an Elizabethan and Renaissance literary context.

Boas, Frederick S. *Christopher Marlowe: A Biographical and Critical Study.* Oxford: Oxford University Press, 1940, 336 p.
Seminal analysis of Marlowe's life and literary career.

Brooke, Nicholas. "Marlowe the Dramatist." In *Elizabethan Theatre,* edited by John Russell Brown and Bernard Harris, pp. 87-105. London: Edward Arnold, 1966.
Explores Marlowe's use of poetry for dramatic effect and examines the structures of his major plays.

Brooke, Tucker. "Marlowe's Versification and Style." *Studies in Philology* XIX, No. 2 (April 1922): 186-205.
Textual analysis of Marlowe's innovations in blank verse in his most important dramas.

Brown, John Russell. "Marlowe and the Actors." *Tulane Drama Review* 8, No. 4 (Summer 1964): 155-73.
Discusses various technical approaches to producing and acting Marlowe's plays, citing some of the most famous performances in the Marlovian stage history.

Courtney, W. L. "Christopher Marlowe: I and II." *The Fortnightly Review* n.s. LXXVIII, Nos. CCCCLXV and CCCCLXVI (September and October 1905): 467-84, 678-91.

Extensive critical analysis of Marlowe's life and literary career.

Danson, Lawrence. "Christopher Marlowe: The Questioner." *English Literary Renaissance* 12, No. 1 (Winter 1982): 3-29.
Examines the use of various kinds of questioning as a dramatic technique in Marlowe's plays,

Dowden, Edward. "Christopher Marlowe." In *Modern English Essays,* Vol. 1, edited by Ernest Rhys, pp. 216-40. London: J. M. Dent, 1922.
Compares Marlowe's dramatic style to those of Shakespeare and other Elizabethan playwrights, and surveys major themes in his plays.

Ellis-Fermore, U. M. *Christopher Marlowe.* 1927. Reprint. Hamden, Conn.: Archon Books, 1967, 172 p.
Critical analysis of Marlowe's works by a noted scholar.

Friedenreich, Kenneth; Gill, Roma; and Kuriyama, Constance, B., eds. *"A Poet and a filthy Play-maker": New Essays on Christopher Marlowe.* New York: AMS Press, 1988, 376 p.
Anthology of critical essays on Marlowe's works by prominent Elizabethan scholars.

Kocher, Paul. *Christopher Marlowe: A Study of his Thoughts, Learning and Character.* New York: Russell & Russell, 1962, 344 p.
Analyzes Marlowe's world view, with particular emphasis on the playwright's attitudes towards religion. Discerns a Promethean element in Marlowe's atheism.

Leech, Clifford. "Marlowe's Humor." In *Essays on Shakespearean and Elizabethan Drama in Honor of Hardin Craig,* edited by Richard Hosley, pp. 69-81. Columbia: University of Missouri Press, 1962.
Discusses the comedic aspects of Marlowe's plays.

Ribner, Irving. "Marlowe and the Critics." *Tulane Drama Review* 8, No. 4 (Summer 1964): 211-24.
Traces Marlowe scholarship from 1774 to 1962.

Shaw, Bernard. "The Spacious Times." In his *Plays and Players: Essays on the Theatre,* pp. 105-14. London: Oxford University Press, 1952.
Includes an 1896 performance review of *Doctor Faustus,* in which Shaw dismisses Marlowe as "the true Elizabethan blank-verse beast," an unimaginative writer prone to vulgarity.

Steane, J. B. *Marlowe: A Critical Study.* Cambridge: Cambridge University Press, 1964, 381 p.
Comprehensive overview of Marlowe's plays and poetry.

Stroup, Thomas B. "Ritual in Marlowe's Plays." *Drama in the Renaissance: Comparative and Critical Essays,* edited by Clifford Davidson, C. J. Giankarlis, and John H. Stroupe, pp. 21-44. New York: AMS Press, 1986.
Examines Marlowe's use of formal and ceremonial processions in his plays, analyzing their effect on the dramatic actions.

Swinburne, Algernon Charles. "Marlowe, Christopher." In *The Encyclopaedia Britannica,* vol. 17, pp. 741-44. Cambridge: Cambridge University Press, 1910.
Surveys Marlowe's life and literary career. According to

Swinburne, Marlowe's poetic genius paved the way for Shakespeare.

Symonds, John Addington. "Marlowe." In his *Shakespeare's Predecessors in the English Drama,* pp. 465-536. London: Smith, Elder, 1884.
> Includes a broad overview of Marlowe's oeuvre, with emphasis on the playwright's tragic view of life. Maintains that even "in his tragedies it is the poet, rather than the playwright, who commands our admiration."

Weil, Judith. *Christopher Marlowe: Merlin's Prophet.* Cambridge: Cambridge University Press, 1977, 219 p.
> Investigates the influence of Marlowe's ideas on his style.

Tamburlaine, I and II

Battenhouse, Roy W. "Tamburlaine, The 'Scourge of God.' " *PMLA* LVI, No. 2 (June 1941): 337-48.
> Explores the origin of the concept "scourge of God" and how Marlowe used this tradition to portray Tamburlaine as a Renaissance hero.

————. *Marlowe's Tamburlaine: A Study in Renaissance Moral Philosophy.* Nashville, Tenn.: Vanderbilt University Press, 1941, 266 p.
> Influential analysis of Marlowe's play, focusing on its intellectual background, Elizabethan literary context, and dramatic structure.

Brooks, Charles. "*Tamburlaine* and Attitudes toward Women." *ELH: A Journal of English Literary History* 24, No. 1 (March 1957): 1-11.
> Maintains that in keeping with the Renaissance concept that identifies women with "prizes that must be seized" by a "triumphant hero," the women in *Tamburlaine* embody the men's aspirations.

Leech, Clifford. "The Structure of *Tamburlaine.*" *Tulane Drama Review* 8, No. 4 (Summer 1964): 32-46.
> Close examination of the dramatic structure of *Tamburlaine.*

Levin, Richard. "The Contemporary Perception of Marlowe's *Tamburlaine.*" In *Medieval & Renaissance Drama in England: An Annual Gathering of Research, Criticism, and Reviews,* edited by J. Leeds Barroll, III, pp. 51-70. New York: AMS Press, 1984.
> Argues that, contrary to prevailing critical opinion, Marlowe's *Tamburlaine* is an artistic failure because it inadequately conveyed its major themes to its contemporary audiences.

Richards, Susan. "Marlowe's *Tamburlaine II:* A Drama of Death." *Modern Language Quarterly* XXVI, No. 3 (September 1965): 375-87.
> Surveys the effects of Tamburlaine's "death-dealing power" and the results of his own confrontation with death.

The Jew of Malta

Friedenreich, Kenneth. "*The Jew of Malta* and the Critics: A Paradigm for Marlowe Studies." *Papers on Language and Literature* 13, No. 3 (Summer 1977): 318-35.
> Records various critical interpretations of *The Jew of Malta* by prominent Elizabethan scholars.

Rothstein, Eric. "Structure as Meaning in *The Jew of Malta.*"

JEGP: Journal of English and Germanic Philology LXV (1966): 260-73.
> Analyzes Marlowe's parodic technique throughout the dramatic structure of *The Jew of Malta.* The critic asserts that the dramatist has created a grotesque setting in the play where all values are "inverted by a central diabolism."

Edward II

Voss, James. "*Edward II:* Marlowe's Historical Tragedy." *English Studies* 63, No. 6 (December 1982): 517-30.
> Demonstrates how intensely personal and emotional desires precipitate key political crises, which in turn lead to Edward's downfall. This dramatic structure forms a unique literary genre which the critic deems "historical tragedy."

Doctor Faustus

Empson, William. *Faustus and the Censor: The English Faust-book and Marlowe's* Doctor Faustus. London: Basil Blackwell, Ltd, 1987, 226 p.
> Unorthodox interpretation of *Doctor Faustus* that regards the play not as a tragedy, but as a subversive burlesque of the social and religious issues of Marlowe's England.

Heilman, Robert B. "The Tragedy of Knowledge: Marlowe's Treatment of Faustus." *Quarterly Review of Literature* II, No. 4 (1945): 316-32.
> Examines the ramifications of Faustus's quest for knowledge, concluding that the tragedy of knowledge is that it leads to "pride" and "wilfulness," which cause "blindness to the nature and destiny of man."

Hunter, G. K. "Five-Act Structure in *Doctor Faustus.*" *Tulane Drama Review* 8, No. 4 (Summer 1964): 77-91.
> Argues that *Doctor Faustus* possesses a five-act structure, despite the absence of any such divisions in its early editions and the general critical reluctance to apply this framework to the drama.

Kocher, Paul. H. "The Witchcraft Basis in Marlowe's *Faustus.*" *Modern Philology* XXXVIII, No. 1 (August 1940): 9-36.
> Demonstrates that in addition to using the *English Faust-book* as a source for *Doctor Faustus,* Marlowe also drew heavily upon the European witch tradition.

McAlindon, T. "Classical Mythology and Christian Tradition in Marlowe's *Doctor Faustus.*" *PMLA* LXXXI, No. 3 (June 1966): 214-23.
> Describes how in *Doctor Faustus* classical mythology plays more than the merely aesthetic role it assumes in Marlowe's other plays. Here, the critic maintains, mythology acts as an agent for Faustus's demise in that it represents the evil alternative to Christianity.

————. "The Ironic Vision: Diction and Theme in Marlowe's *Doctor Faustus.*" *The Review of English Studies* n.s. XXXII, No. 126 (May 1981): 129-41.
> Focuses on the ways in which Marlowe's use of diction contributes to an overall ironic theme in *Doctor Faustus.*

Morgan, Gerald. "Harlequin Faustus: Marlowe's Comedy of Hell." *The Humanities Association Bulletin* XVIII, No. 1 (Spring 1967): 22-34.
> Views *Doctor Faustus* as a comic satire on Classical and

Medieval myths and traditions surrounding the concept of Hell.

Ornstein, Robert. "The Comic Synthesis in *Doctor Faustus*." *RLH: A Journal of English Literary History* 22, No. 3 (September 1955): 165-72.

Contends that scenes with coarse humor in *Doctor Faustus* "unite with the seemingly fragmented main action to form a subtly ironic tragic design."

Ricks, Christopher. "*Doctor Faustus* and Hell on Earth." *Essays in Criticism* XXXV, No. 2 (April 1985): 101-20.

Analyzes the effect that living in a plague-ridden society may have had on Marlowe's composition of *Doctor Faustus.*

Hero and Leander

Bush, Douglas. "Marlowe: *Hero and Leander.*" In his *Mythology and the Renaissance Tradition in English Poetry,* pp. 121-36. New York: W. W. Norton, 1963.

Provides the mythological and literary background of Marlowe's poem.

Lewis, C. S. "Hero and Leander." In *Selected Literary Essays,* pp. 58-73. Cambridge: Cambridge University Press, 1969.

Extols Marlowe's poem as a work of genius.

For further information on Marlowe's life and career, see *Dictionary of Literary Biography,* Vol 62; and *Drama Criticism,* Vol. 1.

Literature
Criticism from
1400 to 1800
Cumulative Indexes

How to Use This Index

The main references

list all author entries in the following Gale Literary Criticism series:

CLC = Contemporary Literary Criticism
CLR = Children's Literature Review
CMLC = Classical and Medieval Literature Criticism
DC = Drama Criticism
LC = Literature Criticism from 1400 to 1800
NCLC = Nineteenth-Century Literature Criticism
PC = Poetry Criticism
SSC = Short Story Criticism
TCLC = Twentieth-Century Literary Criticism

The cross-references

See also CANR 23; CA 85-88;
obituary CA 116

list all author entries in the following Gale biographical and literary sources:

AAYA = Authors & Artists for Young Adults
AITN = Authors in the News
BLC = Black Literature Criticism
BW = Black Writers
CA = Contemporary Authors
CAAS = Contemporary Authors Autobiography Series
CABS = Contemporary Authors Bibliographical Series
CANR = Contemporary Authors New Revision Series
CAP = Contemporary Authors Permanent Series
CDALB = Concise Dictionary of American Literary Biography
CDBLB = Concise Dictionary of British Literary Biography
DLB = Dictionary of Literary Biography
DLBD = Dictionary of Literary Biography Documentary Series
DLBY = Dictionary of Literary Biography Yearbook
HW = Hispanic Writers
MAICYA = Major Authors and Illustrators for Children and Young Adults
MTCW = Major 20th-Century Writers
SAAS = Something about the Author Autobiography Series
SATA = Something about the Author
WLC = World Literature Criticism, 1500 to the Present
YABC = Yesterday's Authors of Books for Children

Literary Criticism Series
Cumulative Author Index

Aleichem, Sholom . . . . TCLC 1, 35
  See also Rabinovitch, Sholem

Aleixandre, Vicente 1898-1984 . . . CLC 9, 36
  See also CA 85-88; 114; CANR 26;
   DLB 108; HW; MTCW

Alepoudelis, Odysseus
  See Elytis, Odysseus

Aleshkovsky, Joseph 1929-
  See Aleshkovsky, Yuz
  See also CA 121; 128

Aleshkovsky, Yuz . . . . CLC 44
  See also Aleshkovsky, Joseph

Alexander, Lloyd (Chudley) 1924- . . CLC 35
  See also AAYA 1; CA 1-4R; CANR 1, 24,
   38; CLR 1, 5; DLB 52; MAICYA;
   MTCW; SATA 3, 49

Alfau, Felipe 1902- . . . . CLC 66
  See also CA 137

Alger, Horatio Jr. 1832-1899 . . . . . NCLC 8
  See also DLB 42; SATA 16

Algren, Nelson 1909-1981 . . . . CLC 4, 10, 33
  See also CA 13-16R; 103; CANR 20;
   CDALB 1941-1968; DLB 9; DLBY 81,
   82; MTCW

Ali, Ahmed 1910- . . . . CLC 69
  See also CA 25-28R; CANR 15, 34

Alighieri, Dante 1265-1321 . . . . CMLC 3

Allan, John B.
  See Westlake, Donald E(dwin)

Allen, Edward 1948- . . . . CLC 59

Allen, Roland
  See Ayckbourn, Alan

Allen, Woody 1935- . . . . CLC 16, 52
  See also AAYA 10; CA 33-36R; CANR 27,
   38; DLB 44; MTCW

Allende, Isabel 1942- . . . . CLC 39, 57
  See also CA 125; 130; HW; MTCW

Alleyn, Ellen
  See Rossetti, Christina (Georgina)

Allingham, Margery (Louise)
   1904-1966 . . . . CLC 19
  See also CA 5-8R; 25-28R; CANR 4;
   DLB 77; MTCW

Allingham, William 1824-1889 . . . NCLC 25
  See also DLB 35

Allston, Washington 1779-1843 . . . . NCLC 2
  See also DLB 1

Almedingen, E. M. . . . . CLC 12
  See also Almedingen, Martha Edith von
  See also SATA 3

Almedingen, Martha Edith von 1898-1971
  See Almedingen, E. M.
  See also CA 1-4R; CANR 1

Alonso, Damaso 1898-1990 . . . . CLC 14
  See also CA 110; 131; 130; DLB 108; HW

Alta 1942- . . . . CLC 19
  See also CA 57-60

Alter, Robert B(ernard) 1935- . . . . . . CLC 34
  See also CA 49-52; CANR 1

Alther, Lisa 1944- . . . . CLC 7, 41
  See also CA 65-68; CANR 12, 30; MTCW

Altman, Robert 1925- . . . . CLC 16
  See also CA 73-76

Alvarez, A(lfred) 1929- . . . . CLC 5, 13
  See also CA 1-4R; CANR 3, 33; DLB 14,
   40

Alvarez, Alejandro Rodriguez 1903-1965
  See Casona, Alejandro
  See also CA 131; 93-96; HW

Amado, Jorge 1912- . . . . CLC 13, 40
  See also CA 77-80; CANR 35; DLB 113;
   MTCW

Ambler, Eric 1909- . . . . CLC 4, 6, 9
  See also CA 9-12R; CANR 7, 38; DLB 77;
   MTCW

Amichai, Yehuda 1924- . . . . . . CLC 9, 22, 57
  See also CA 85-88; MTCW

Amiel, Henri Frederic 1821-1881 . . NCLC 4

Amis, Kingsley (William)
   1922- . . . . . . CLC 1, 2, 3, 5, 8, 13, 40, 44
  See also AITN 2; CA 9-12R; CANR 8, 28;
   CDBLB 1945-1960; DLB 15, 27, 100;
   MTCW

Amis, Martin (Louis)
   1949- . . . . CLC 4, 9, 38, 62
  See also BEST 90:3; CA 65-68; CANR 8,
   27; DLB 14

Ammons, A(rchie) R(andolph)
   1926- . . . . CLC 2, 3, 5, 8, 9, 25, 57
  See also AITN 1; CA 9-12R; CANR 6, 36;
   DLB 5; MTCW

Amo, Tauraatua i
  See Adams, Henry (Brooks)

Anand, Mulk Raj 1905- . . . . CLC 23
  See also CA 65-68; CANR 32; MTCW

Anatol
  See Schnitzler, Arthur

Anaya, Rudolfo A(lfonso) 1937- . . . . CLC 23
  See also CA 45-48; CAAS 4; CANR 1, 32;
   DLB 82; HW; MTCW

Andersen, Hans Christian
   1805-1875 . . . . NCLC 7; SSC 6
  See also CLR 6; MAICYA; WLC; YABC 1

Anderson, C. Farley
  See Mencken, H(enry) L(ouis); Nathan,
   George Jean

Anderson, Jessica (Margaret) Queale
  . . . . CLC 37
  See also CA 9-12R; CANR 4

Anderson, Jon (Victor) 1940- . . . . CLC 9
  See also CA 25-28R; CANR 20

Anderson, Lindsay (Gordon)
   1923- . . . . CLC 20
  See also CA 125; 128

Anderson, Maxwell 1888-1959 . . . . . TCLC 2
  See also CA 105; DLB 7

Anderson, Poul (William) 1926- . . . . CLC 15
  See also AAYA 5; CA 1-4R; CAAS 2;
   CANR 2, 15, 34; DLB 8; MTCW;
   SATA 39

Anderson, Robert (Woodruff)
   1917- . . . . CLC 23
  See also AITN 1; CA 21-24R; CANR 32;
   DLB 7

Anderson, Sherwood
   1876-1941 . . . . . . TCLC 1, 10, 24; SSC 1
  See also CA 104; 121; CDALB 1917-1929;
   DLB 4, 9, 86; DLBD 1; MTCW; WLC

Andouard
  See Giraudoux, (Hippolyte) Jean

Andrade, Carlos Drummond de . . . . . . CLC 18
  See also Drummond de Andrade, Carlos

Andrade, Mario de 1893-1945 . . . . . TCLC 43

Andrewes, Lancelot 1555-1626 . . . . LC 5

Andrews, Cicily Fairfield
  See West, Rebecca

Andrews, Elton V.
  See Pohl, Frederik

Andreyev, Leonid (Nikolaevich)
   1871-1919 . . . . TCLC 3
  See also CA 104

Andric, Ivo 1892-1975 . . . . CLC 8
  See also CA 81-84; 57-60; MTCW

Angelique, Pierre
  See Bataille, Georges

Angell, Roger 1920- . . . . CLC 26
  See also CA 57-60; CANR 13

Angelou, Maya 1928- . . . . CLC 12, 35, 64
  See also AAYA 7; BLC 1; BW; CA 65-68;
   CANR 19; DLB 38; MTCW; SATA 49

Annensky, Innokenty Fyodorovich
   1856-1909 . . . . TCLC 14
  See also CA 110

Anon, Charles Robert
  See Pessoa, Fernando (Antonio Nogueira)

Anouilh, Jean (Marie Lucien Pierre)
   1910-1987 . . . . . . CLC 1, 3, 8, 13, 40, 50
  See also CA 17-20R; 123; CANR 32;
   MTCW

Anthony, Florence
  See Ai

Anthony, John
  See Ciardi, John (Anthony)

Anthony, Peter
  See Shaffer, Anthony (Joshua); Shaffer,
   Peter (Levin)

Anthony, Piers 1934- . . . . CLC 35
  See also CA 21-24R; CANR 28; DLB 8;
   MTCW

Antoine, Marc
  See Proust,
   (Valentin-Louis-George-Eugene-)Marcel

Antoninus, Brother
  See Everson, William (Oliver)

Antonioni, Michelangelo 1912- . . . . . CLC 20
  See also CA 73-76

Antschel, Paul 1920-1970 . . . . . . CLC 10, 19
  See also Celan, Paul
  See also CA 85-88; CANR 33; MTCW

Anwar, Chairil 1922-1949 . . . . TCLC 22
  See also CA 121

Apollinaire, Guillaume . . . . TCLC 3, 8
  See also Kostrowitzki, Wilhelm Apollinaris
   de

Appelfeld, Aharon 1932- . . . . CLC 23, 47
  See also CA 112; 133

Apple, Max (Isaac) 1941- . . . . CLC 9, 33
  See also CA 81-84; CANR 19; DLB 130

Appleman, Philip (Dean) 1926- . . . . . CLC 51
  See also CA 13-16R; CANR 6, 29

Appleton, Lawrence
See Lovecraft, H(oward) P(hillips)

Apuleius, (Lucius Madaurensis)
125(?)-175(?) . . . . **CMLC 1**

Aquin, Hubert 1929-1977 . . . . **CLC 15**
See also CA 105; DLB 53

Aragon, Louis 1897-1982 . . . . **CLC 3, 22**
See also CA 69-72; 108; CANR 28;
DLB 72; MTCW

Arany, Janos 1817-1882 . . . . **NCLC 34**

Arbuthnot, John 1667-1735 . . . . **LC 1**
See also DLB 101

Archer, Herbert Winslow
See Mencken, H(enry) L(ouis)

Archer, Jeffrey (Howard) 1940- . . . . **CLC 28**
See also BEST 89:3; CA 77-80; CANR 22

Archer, Jules 1915- . . . . **CLC 12**
See also CA 9-12R; CANR 6; SAAS 5;
SATA 4

Archer, Lee
See Ellison, Harlan

Arden, John 1930- . . . . **CLC 6, 13, 15**
See also CA 13-16R; CAAS 4; CANR 31;
DLB 13; MTCW

Arenas, Reinaldo 1943-1990 . . . . **CLC 41**
See also CA 124; 128; 133; HW

Arendt, Hannah 1906-1975 . . . . **CLC 66**
See also CA 17-20R; 61-64; CANR 26;
MTCW

Aretino, Pietro 1492-1556 . . . . **LC 12**

Arguedas, Jose Maria
1911-1969 . . . . **CLC 10, 18**
See also CA 89-92; DLB 113; HW

Argueta, Manlio 1936- . . . . **CLC 31**
See also CA 131; HW

Ariosto, Ludovico 1474-1533 . . . . **LC 6**

Aristides
See Epstein, Joseph

Aristophanes
450B.C.-385B.C. . . . . **CMLC 4; DC 2**

Arlt, Roberto (Godofredo Christophersen)
1900-1942 . . . . **TCLC 29**
See also CA 123; 131; HW

Armah, Ayi Kwei 1939- . . . . **CLC 5, 33**
See also BLC 1; BW; CA 61-64; CANR 21;
DLB 117; MTCW

Armatrading, Joan 1950- . . . . **CLC 17**
See also CA 114

Arnette, Robert
See Silverberg, Robert

**Arnim, Achim von (Ludwig Joachim von
Arnim)** 1781-1831 . . . . **NCLC 5**
See also DLB 90

Arnim, Bettina von 1785-1859 . . . . **NCLC 38**
See also DLB 90

Arnold, Matthew
1822-1888 . . . . **NCLC 6, 29; PC 5**
See also CDBLB 1832-1890; DLB 32, 57;
WLC

Arnold, Thomas 1795-1842 . . . . . . **NCLC 18**
See also DLB 55

Arnow, Harriette (Louisa) Simpson
1908-1986 . . . . **CLC 2, 7, 18**
See also CA 9-12R; 118; CANR 14; DLB 6;
MTCW; SATA 42, 47

Arp, Hans
See Arp, Jean

Arp, Jean 1887-1966 . . . . **CLC 5**
See also CA 81-84; 25-28R

Arrabal
See Arrabal, Fernando

Arrabal, Fernando 1932- . . . **CLC 2, 9, 18, 58**
See also CA 9-12R; CANR 15

Arrick, Fran . . . . **CLC 30**

Artaud, Antonin 1896-1948 . . . . . **TCLC 3, 36**
See also CA 104

Arthur, Ruth M(abel) 1905-1979 . . . . **CLC 12**
See also CA 9-12R; 85-88; CANR 4;
SATA 7, 26

Artsybashev, Mikhail (Petrovich)
1878-1927 . . . . **TCLC 31**

Arundel, Honor (Morfydd)
1919-1973 . . . . **CLC 17**
See also CA 21-22; 41-44R; CAP 2;
SATA 4, 24

Asch, Sholem 1880-1957 . . . . **TCLC 3**
See also CA 105

Ash, Shalom
See Asch, Sholem

Ashbery, John (Lawrence)
1927- . . . **CLC 2, 3, 4, 6, 9, 13, 15, 25, 41**
See also CA 5-8R; CANR 9, 37; DLB 5;
DLBY 81; MTCW

Ashdown, Clifford
See Freeman, R(ichard) Austin

Ashe, Gordon
See Creasey, John

Ashton-Warner, Sylvia (Constance)
1908-1984 . . . . **CLC 19**
See also CA 69-72; 112; CANR 29; MTCW

Asimov, Isaac
1920-1992 . . . . . . **CLC 1, 3, 9, 19, 26, 76**
See also BEST 90:2; CA 1-4R; 137;
CANR 2, 19, 36; CLR 12; DLB 8;
DLBY 92; MAICYA; MTCW; SATA 1,
26

Astley, Thea (Beatrice May)
1925- . . . . **CLC 41**
See also CA 65-68; CANR 11

Aston, James
See White, T(erence) H(anbury)

Asturias, Miguel Angel
1899-1974 . . . . **CLC 3, 8, 13**
See also CA 25-28; 49-52; CANR 32;
CAP 2; DLB 113; HW; MTCW

Atares, Carlos Saura
See Saura (Atares), Carlos

Atheling, William
See Pound, Ezra (Weston Loomis)

Atheling, William Jr.
See Blish, James (Benjamin)

Atherton, Gertrude (Franklin Horn)
1857-1948 . . . . **TCLC 2**
See also CA 104; DLB 9, 78

Atherton, Lucius
See Masters, Edgar Lee

Atkins, Jack
See Harris, Mark

Atticus
See Fleming, Ian (Lancaster)

Atwood, Margaret (Eleanor)
1939- . . . . **CLC 2, 3, 4, 8, 13, 15, 25, 44;
SSC 2**
See also BEST 89:2; CA 49-52; CANR 3,
24, 33; DLB 53; MTCW; SATA 50; WLC

Aubigny, Pierre d'
See Mencken, H(enry) L(ouis)

Aubin, Penelope 1685-1731(?) . . . . **LC 9**
See also DLB 39

Auchincloss, Louis (Stanton)
1917- . . . . **CLC 4, 6, 9, 18, 45**
See also CA 1-4R; CANR 6, 29; DLB 2;
DLBY 80; MTCW

Auden, W(ystan) H(ugh)
1907-1973 . . . . . **CLC 1, 2, 3, 4, 6, 9, 11,
14, 43; PC 1**
See also CA 9-12R; 45-48; CANR 5;
CDBLB 1914-1945; DLB 10, 20; MTCW;
WLC

Audiberti, Jacques 1900-1965 . . . . . . **CLC 38**
See also CA 25-28R

Auel, Jean M(arie) 1936- . . . . **CLC 31**
See also AAYA 7; BEST 90:4; CA 103;
CANR 21

Auerbach, Erich 1892-1957 . . . . **TCLC 43**
See also CA 118

Augier, Emile 1820-1889 . . . . **NCLC 31**

August, John
See De Voto, Bernard (Augustine)

Augustine, St. 354-430 . . . . **CMLC 6**

Aurelius
See Bourne, Randolph S(illiman)

Austen, Jane
1775-1817 . . . . **NCLC 1, 13, 19, 33**
See also CDBLB 1789-1832; DLB 116;
WLC

Auster, Paul 1947- . . . . **CLC 47**
See also CA 69-72; CANR 23

Austin, Frank
See Faust, Frederick (Schiller)

Austin, Mary (Hunter)
1868-1934 . . . . **TCLC 25**
See also CA 109; DLB 9, 78

Autran Dourado, Waldomiro
See Dourado, (Waldomiro Freitas) Autran

Averroes 1126-1198 . . . . **CMLC 7**
See also DLB 115

Avison, Margaret 1918- . . . . **CLC 2, 4**
See also CA 17-20R; DLB 53; MTCW

Ayckbourn, Alan
1939- . . . . **CLC 5, 8, 18, 33, 74**
See also CA 21-24R; CANR 31; DLB 13;
MTCW

Aydy, Catherine
See Tennant, Emma (Christina)

Ayme, Marcel (Andre) 1902-1967 . . . **CLC 11**
See also CA 89-92; CLR 25; DLB 72

Barry, Philip 1896-1949 . . . . TCLC 11
See also CA 109; DLB 7

Bart, Andre Schwarz
See Schwarz-Bart, Andre

Barth, John (Simmons)
1930- . . . . . . **CLC 1, 2, 3, 5, 7, 9, 10, 14,
27, 51; SSC 10**
See also AITN 1, 2; CA 1-4R; CABS 1;
CANR 5, 23; DLB 2; MTCW

Barthelme, Donald
1931-1989 . . . . . **CLC 1, 2, 3, 5, 6, 8, 13,
23, 46, 59; SSC 2**
See also CA 21-24R; 129; CANR 20;
DLB 2; DLBY 80, 89; MTCW; SATA 7,
62

Barthelme, Frederick 1943- . . . . CLC 36
See also CA 114; 122; DLBY 85

Barthes, Roland (Gerard)
1915-1980 . . . . CLC 24
See also CA 130; 97-100; MTCW

Barzun, Jacques (Martin) 1907- . . . . CLC 51
See also CA 61-64; CANR 22

Bashevis, Isaac
See Singer, Isaac Bashevis

Bashkirtseff, Marie 1859-1884 . . . NCLC 27

Basho
See Matsuo Basho

Bass, Kingsley B. Jr.
See Bullins, Ed

Bassani, Giorgio 1916- . . . . CLC 9
See also CA 65-68; CANR 33; DLB 128;
MTCW

Bastos, Augusto (Antonio) Roa
See Roa Bastos, Augusto (Antonio)

Bataille, Georges 1897-1962 . . . . CLC 29
See also CA 101; 89-92

Bates, H(erbert) E(rnest)
1905-1974 . . . . CLC 46; SSC 10
See also CA 93-96; 45-48; CANR 34;
MTCW

Bauchart
See Camus, Albert

Baudelaire, Charles
1821-1867 . . . . NCLC 6, 29; PC 1
See also WLC

Baudrillard, Jean 1929- . . . . CLC 60

Baum, L(yman) Frank 1856-1919 . . . TCLC 7
See also CA 108; 133; CLR 15; DLB 22;
MAICYA; MTCW; SATA 18

Baum, Louis F.
See Baum, L(yman) Frank

Baumbach, Jonathan 1933- . . . . . . CLC 6, 23
See also CA 13-16R; CAAS 5; CANR 12;
DLBY 80; MTCW

Bausch, Richard (Carl) 1945- . . . . . . CLC 51
See also CA 101; CAAS 14; DLB 130

Baxter, Charles 1947- . . . . CLC 45
See also CA 57-60; CANR 40; DLB 130

Baxter, George Owen
See Faust, Frederick (Schiller)

Baxter, James K(eir) 1926-1972 . . . . CLC 14
See also CA 77-80

Baxter, John
See Hunt, E(verette) Howard Jr.

Bayer, Sylvia
See Glassco, John

Beagle, Peter S(oyer) 1939- . . . . CLC 7
See also CA 9-12R; CANR 4; DLBY 80;
SATA 60

Bean, Normal
See Burroughs, Edgar Rice

Beard, Charles A(ustin)
1874-1948 . . . . TCLC 15
See also CA 115; DLB 17; SATA 18

Beardsley, Aubrey 1872-1898 . . . . . NCLC 6

Beattie, Ann
1947- . . . . CLC 8, 13, 18, 40, 63; SSC 11
See also BEST 90:2; CA 81-84; DLBY 82;
MTCW

Beattie, James 1735-1803 . . . . NCLC 25
See also DLB 109

Beauchamp, Kathleen Mansfield 1888-1923
See Mansfield, Katherine
See also CA 104; 134

Beauvoir, Simone (Lucie Ernestine Marie
Bertrand) de
1908-1986 . . . CLC 1, 2, 4, 8, 14, 31, 44,
50, 71
See also CA 9-12R; 118; CANR 28;
DLB 72; DLBY 86; MTCW; WLC

Becker, Jurek 1937- . . . . CLC 7, 19
See also CA 85-88; DLB 75

Becker, Walter 1950- . . . . CLC 26

Beckett, Samuel (Barclay)
1906-1989 . . . . . CLC 1, 2, 3, 4, 6, 9, 10,
11, 14, 18, 29, 57, 59
See also CA 5-8R; 130; CANR 33;
CDBLB 1945-1960; DLB 13, 15;
DLBY 90; MTCW; WLC

Beckford, William 1760-1844 . . . . NCLC 16
See also DLB 39

Beckman, Gunnel 1910- . . . . CLC 26
See also CA 33-36R; CANR 15; CLR 25;
MAICYA; SAAS 9; SATA 6

Becque, Henri 1837-1899 . . . . NCLC 3

Beddoes, Thomas Lovell
1803-1849 . . . . NCLC 3
See also DLB 96

Bedford, Donald F.
See Fearing, Kenneth (Flexner)

Beecher, Catharine Esther
1800-1878 . . . . NCLC 30
See also DLB 1

Beecher, John 1904-1980 . . . . CLC 6
See also AITN 1; CA 5-8R; 105; CANR 8

Beer, Johann 1655-1700 . . . . LC 5

Beer, Patricia 1924- . . . . CLC 58
See also CA 61-64; CANR 13; DLB 40

Beerbohm, Henry Maximilian
1872-1956 . . . . TCLC 1, 24
See also CA 104; DLB 34, 100

Begiebing, Robert J(ohn) 1946- . . . . . CLC 70
See also CA 122; CANR 40

Behan, Brendan
1923-1964 . . . . CLC 1, 8, 11, 15
See also CA 73-76; CANR 33;
CDBLB 1945-1960; DLB 13; MTCW

Behn, Aphra 1640(?)-1689 . . . . LC 1
See also DLB 39, 80; WLC

Behrman, S(amuel) N(athaniel)
1893-1973 . . . . CLC 40
See also CA 13-16; 45-48; CAP 1; DLB 7,
44

Belasco, David 1853-1931 . . . . TCLC 3
See also CA 104; DLB 7

Belcheva, Elisaveta 1893- . . . . CLC 10

Beldone, Phil "Cheech"
See Ellison, Harlan

Beleno
See Azuela, Mariano

Belinski, Vissarion Grigoryevich
1811-1848 . . . . NCLC 5

Belitt, Ben 1911- . . . . CLC 22
See also CA 13-16R; CAAS 4; CANR 7;
DLB 5

Bell, James Madison 1826-1902 . . . TCLC 43
See also BLC 1; BW; CA 122; 124; DLB 50

Bell, Madison (Smartt) 1957- . . . . . . CLC 41
See also CA 111; CANR 28

Bell, Marvin (Hartley) 1937- . . . . . CLC 8, 31
See also CA 21-24R; CAAS 14; DLB 5;
MTCW

Bell, W. L. D.
See Mencken, H(enry) L(ouis)

Bellamy, Atwood C.
See Mencken, H(enry) L(ouis)

Bellamy, Edward 1850-1898 . . . . . . NCLC 4
See also DLB 12

Bellin, Edward J.
See Kuttner, Henry

Belloc, (Joseph) Hilaire (Pierre)
1870-1953 . . . . TCLC 7, 18
See also CA 106; DLB 19, 100; YABC 1

Belloc, Joseph Peter Rene Hilaire
See Belloc, (Joseph) Hilaire (Pierre)

Belloc, Joseph Pierre Hilaire
See Belloc, (Joseph) Hilaire (Pierre)

Belloc, M. A.
See Lowndes, Marie Adelaide (Belloc)

Bellow, Saul
1915- . . . . . CLC 1, 2, 3, 6, 8, 10, 13, 15,
25, 33, 34, 63
See also AITN 2; BEST 89:3; CA 5-8R;
CABS 1; CANR 29; CDALB 1941-1968;
DLB 2, 28; DLBD 3; DLBY 82; MTCW;
WLC

Belser, Reimond Karel Maria de
1929- . . . . CLC 14

Bely, Andrey . . . . TCLC 7
See also Bugayev, Boris Nikolayevich

Benary, Margot
See Benary-Isbert, Margot

Benary-Isbert, Margot 1889-1979 . . . CLC 12
See also CA 5-8R; 89-92; CANR 4;
CLR 12; MAICYA; SATA 2, 21

Benavente (y Martinez), Jacinto
1866-1954 . . . . TCLC 3
See also CA 106; 131; HW; MTCW

Benchley, Peter (Bradford)
1940- .... **CLC 4, 8**
See also AITN 2; CA 17-20R; CANR 12,
35; MTCW; SATA 3

Benchley, Robert (Charles)
1889-1945 .... **TCLC 1**
See also CA 105; DLB 11

Benedikt, Michael 1935- .... **CLC 4, 14**
See also CA 13-16R; CANR 7; DLB 5

Benet, Juan 1927-.............. **CLC 28**

Benet, Stephen Vincent
1898-1943 .... **TCLC 7; SSC 10**
See also CA 104; DLB 4, 48, 102; YABC 1

Benet, William Rose 1886-1950 ... **TCLC 28**
See also CA 118; DLB 45

Benford, Gregory (Albert) 1941-.... **CLC 52**
See also CA 69-72; CANR 12, 24;
DLBY 82

Bengtsson, Frans (Gunnar)
1894-1954 .... **TCLC 48**

Benjamin, Lois
See Gould, Lois

Benjamin, Walter 1892-1940 ..... **TCLC 39**

Benn, Gottfried 1886-1956........ **TCLC 3**
See also CA 106; DLB 56

Bennett, Alan 1934- .... **CLC 45**
See also CA 103; CANR 35; MTCW

Bennett, (Enoch) Arnold
1867-1931 .... **TCLC 5, 20**
See also CA 106; CDBLB 1890-1914;
DLB 10, 34, 98

Bennett, Elizabeth
See Mitchell, Margaret (Munnerlyn)

Bennett, George Harold 1930-
See Bennett, Hal
See also BW; CA 97-100

Bennett, Hal .... **CLC 5**
See also Bennett, George Harold
See also DLB 33

Bennett, Jay 1912-.............. **CLC 35**
See also AAYA 10; CA 69-72; CANR 11;
SAAS 4; SATA 27, 41

Bennett, Louise (Simone) 1919-..... **CLC 28**
See also BLC 1; DLB 117

Benson, E(dward) F(rederic)
1867-1940 .... **TCLC 27**
See also CA 114

Benson, Jackson J. 1930-.......... **CLC 34**
See also CA 25-28R; DLB 111

Benson, Sally 1900-1972 .... **CLC 17**
See also CA 19-20; 37-40R; CAP 1;
SATA 1, 27, 35

Benson, Stella 1892-1933......... **TCLC 17**
See also CA 117; DLB 36

Bentham, Jeremy 1748-1832 ..... **NCLC 38**
See also DLB 107

Bentley, E(dmund) C(lerihew)
1875-1956 .... **TCLC 12**
See also CA 108; DLB 70

Bentley, Eric (Russell) 1916-....... **CLC 24**
See also CA 5-8R; CANR 6

Beranger, Pierre Jean de
1780-1857 .... **NCLC 34**

Berger, Colonel
See Malraux, (Georges-)Andre

Berger, John (Peter) 1926- ...... **CLC 2, 19**
See also CA 81-84; DLB 14

Berger, Melvin H. 1927-.......... **CLC 12**
See also CA 5-8R; CANR 4; SAAS 2;
SATA 5

Berger, Thomas (Louis)
1924- .... **CLC 3, 5, 8, 11, 18, 38**
See also CA 1-4R; CANR 5, 28; DLB 2;
DLBY 80; MTCW

Bergman, (Ernst) Ingmar
1918- .... **CLC 16, 72**
See also CA 81-84; CANR 33

Bergson, Henri 1859-1941 .... **TCLC 32**

Bergstein, Eleanor 1938-.......... **CLC 4**
See also CA 53-56; CANR 5

Berkoff, Steven 1937-............. **CLC 56**
See also CA 104

Bermant, Chaim (Icyk) 1929- ...... **CLC 40**
See also CA 57-60; CANR 6, 31

Bern, Victoria
See Fisher, M(ary) F(rances) K(ennedy)

Bernanos, (Paul Louis) Georges
1888-1948 .... **TCLC 3**
See also CA 104; 130; DLB 72

Bernard, April 1956- .... **CLC 59**
See also CA 131

Bernhard, Thomas
1931-1989 .... **CLC 3, 32, 61**
See also CA 85-88; 127; CANR 32;
DLB 85, 124; MTCW

Berrigan, Daniel 1921-............. **CLC 4**
See also CA 33-36R; CAAS 1; CANR 11;
DLB 5

Berrigan, Edmund Joseph Michael Jr.
1934-1983
See Berrigan, Ted
See also CA 61-64; 110; CANR 14

Berrigan, Ted..................... **CLC 37**
See also Berrigan, Edmund Joseph Michael
Jr.
See also DLB 5

Berry, Charles Edward Anderson 1931-
See Berry, Chuck
See also CA 115

Berry, Chuck.................... **CLC 17**
See also Berry, Charles Edward Anderson

Berry, Jonas
See Ashbery, John (Lawrence)

Berry, Wendell (Erdman)
1934- .... **CLC 4, 6, 8, 27, 46**
See also AITN 1; CA 73-76; DLB 5, 6

Berryman, John
1914-1972 ..... **CLC 1, 2, 3, 4, 6, 8, 10,
13, 25, 62**
See also CA 13-16; 33-36R; CABS 2;
CANR 35; CAP 1; CDALB 1941-1968;
DLB 48; MTCW

Bertolucci, Bernardo 1940- .... **CLC 16**
See also CA 106

Bertrand, Aloysius 1807-1841 .... **NCLC 31**

Bertran de Born c. 1140-1215 ..... **CMLC 5**

Besant, Annie (Wood) 1847-1933 ... **TCLC 9**
See also CA 105

Bessie, Alvah 1904-1985.......... **CLC 23**
See also CA 5-8R; 116; CANR 2; DLB 26

Bethlen, T. D.
See Silverberg, Robert

Beti, Mongo..................... **CLC 27**
See also Biyidi, Alexandre
See also BLC 1

Betjeman, John
1906-1984 .... **CLC 2, 6, 10, 34, 43**
See also CA 9-12R; 112;
CDBLB 1945-1960; DLB 20; DLBY 84;
MTCW

Betti, Ugo 1892-1953............. **TCLC 5**
See also CA 104

Betts, Doris (Waugh) 1932-.... **CLC 3, 6, 28**
See also CA 13-16R; CANR 9; DLBY 82

Bevan, Alistair
See Roberts, Keith (John Kingston)

Beynon, John
See Harris, John (Wyndham Parkes Lucas)
Beynon

Bialik, Chaim Nachman
1873-1934 .... **TCLC 25**

Bickerstaff, Isaac
See Swift, Jonathan

Bidart, Frank 19(?)-.............. **CLC 33**

Bienek, Horst 1930-............. **CLC 7, 11**
See also CA 73-76; DLB 75

Bierce, Ambrose (Gwinett)
1842-1914(?) ..... **TCLC 1, 7, 44; SSC 9**
See also CA 104; 139; CDALB 1865-1917;
DLB 11, 12, 23, 71, 74; WLC

Billings, Josh
See Shaw, Henry Wheeler

Billington, Rachel 1942-.......... **CLC 43**
See also AITN 2; CA 33-36R

Binyon, T(imothy) J(ohn) 1936- .... **CLC 34**
See also CA 111; CANR 28

Bioy Casares, Adolfo 1914-.... **CLC 4, 8, 13**
See also CA 29-32R; CANR 19; DLB 113;
HW; MTCW

Bird, C.
See Ellison, Harlan

Bird, Cordwainer
See Ellison, Harlan

Bird, Robert Montgomery
1806-1854 .... **NCLC 1**

Birney, (Alfred) Earle
1904- ....**CLC 1, 4, 6, 11**
See also CA 1-4R; CANR 5, 20; DLB 88;
MTCW

Bishop, Elizabeth
1911-1979 ..... **CLC 1, 4, 9, 13, 15, 32;
PC 3**
See also CA 5-8R; 89-92; CABS 2;
CANR 26; CDALB 1968-1988; DLB 5;
MTCW; SATA 24

Bishop, John 1935-.............. **CLC 10**
See also CA 105

Bissett, Bill 1939-............... **CLC 18**
See also CA 69-72; CANR 15; DLB 53;
MTCW

Bitov, Andrei (Georgievich) 1937-... **CLC 57**

Biyidi, Alexandre 1932-
See Beti, Mongo
See also BW; CA 114; 124; MTCW

Bjarme, Brynjolf
See Ibsen, Henrik (Johan)

Bjornson, Bjornstjerne (Martinius)
1832-1910 .... **TCLC 7, 37**
See also CA 104

Black, Robert
See Holdstock, Robert P.

Blackburn, Paul 1926-1971 ...... **CLC 9, 43**
See also CA 81-84; 33-36R; CANR 34;
DLB 16; DLBY 81

Black Elk 1863-1950 .... **TCLC 33**

Black Hobart
See Sanders, (James) Ed(ward)

Blacklin, Malcolm
See Chambers, Aidan

Blackmore, R(ichard) D(oddridge)
1825-1900 .... **TCLC 27**
See also CA 120; DLB 18

Blackmur, R(ichard) P(almer)
1904-1965 .... **CLC 2, 24**
See also CA 11-12; 25-28R; CAP 1; DLB 63

Black Tarantula, The
See Acker, Kathy

Blackwood, Algernon (Henry)
1869-1951 .... **TCLC 5**
See also CA 105

Blackwood, Caroline 1931- .... **CLC 6, 9**
See also CA 85-88; CANR 32; DLB 14;
MTCW

Blade, Alexander
See Hamilton, Edmond; Silverberg, Robert

Blaga, Lucian 1895-1961 .... **CLC 75**

Blair, Eric (Arthur) 1903-1950
See Orwell, George
See also CA 104; 132; MTCW; SATA 29

Blais, Marie-Claire
1939- .... **CLC 2, 4, 6, 13, 22**
See also CA 21-24R; CAAS 4; CANR 38;
DLB 53; MTCW

Blaise, Clark 1940- .... **CLC 29**
See also AITN 2; CA 53-56; CAAS 3;
CANR 5; DLB 53

Blake, Nicholas
See Day Lewis, C(ecil)
See also DLB 77

Blake, William 1757-1827 .... **NCLC 13**
See also CDBLB 1789-1832; DLB 93;
MAICYA; SATA 30; WLC

Blasco Ibanez, Vicente
1867-1928 .... **TCLC 12**
See also CA 110; 131; HW; MTCW

Blatty, William Peter 1928-........ **CLC 2**
See also CA 5-8R; CANR 9

Bleeck, Oliver
See Thomas, Ross (Elmore)

Blessing, Lee 1949-............... **CLC 54**

Blish, James (Benjamin)
1921-1975 .... **CLC 14**
See also CA 1-4R; 57-60; CANR 3; DLB 8;
MTCW; SATA 66

Bliss, Reginald
See Wells, H(erbert) G(eorge)

Blixen, Karen (Christentze Dinesen)
1885-1962
See Dinesen, Isak
See also CA 25-28; CANR 22; CAP 2;
MTCW; SATA 44

Bloch, Robert (Albert) 1917-....... **CLC 33**
See also CA 5-8R; CANR 5; DLB 44;
SATA 12

Blok, Alexander (Alexandrovich)
1880-1921 .... **TCLC 5**
See also CA 104

Blom, Jan
See Breytenbach, Breyten

Bloom, Harold 1930- .... **CLC 24**
See also CA 13-16R; CANR 39; DLB 67

Bloomfield, Aurelius
See Bourne, Randolph S(illiman)

Blount, Roy (Alton) Jr. 1941-...... **CLC 38**
See also CA 53-56; CANR 10, 28; MTCW

Bloy, Leon 1846-1917............ **TCLC 22**
See also CA 121; DLB 123

Blume, Judy (Sussman) 1938-... **CLC 12, 30**
See also AAYA 3; CA 29-32R; CANR 13,
37; CLR 2, 15; DLB 52; MAICYA;
MTCW; SATA 2, 31

Blunden, Edmund (Charles)
1896-1974 .... **CLC 2, 56**
See also CA 17-18; 45-48; CAP 2; DLB 20,
100; MTCW

Bly, Robert (Elwood)
1926- .... **CLC 1, 2, 5, 10, 15, 38**
See also CA 5-8R; DLB 5; MTCW

Bobette
See Simenon, Georges (Jacques Christian)

Boccaccio, Giovanni 1313-1375
See also SSC 10

Bochco, Steven 1943-............. **CLC 35**
See also CA 124; 138

Bodenheim, Maxwell 1892-1954 ... **TCLC 44**
See also CA 110; DLB 9, 45

Bodker, Cecil 1927- .... **CLC 21**
See also CA 73-76; CANR 13; CLR 23;
MAICYA; SATA 14

Boell, Heinrich (Theodor) 1917-1985
See Boll, Heinrich (Theodor)
See also CA 21-24R; 116; CANR 24;
DLB 69; DLBY 85; MTCW

Bogan, Louise 1897-1970..... **CLC 4, 39, 46**
See also CA 73-76; 25-28R; CANR 33;
DLB 45; MTCW

Bogarde, Dirk .... **CLC 19**
See also Van Den Bogarde, Derek Jules
Gaspard Ulric Niven
See also DLB 14

Bogosian, Eric 1953- .... **CLC 45**
See also CA 138

Bograd, Larry 1953-.............. **CLC 35**
See also CA 93-96; SATA 33

Boiardo, Matteo Maria 1441-1494 .... **LC 6**

Boileau-Despreaux, Nicolas
1636-1711 .... **LC 3**

Boland, Eavan 1944-.......... **CLC 40, 67**
See also DLB 40

Boll, Heinrich (Theodor)
1917-1985 ... **CLC 2, 3, 6, 9, 11, 15, 27,
39, 72**
See also Boell, Heinrich (Theodor)
See also DLB 69; DLBY 85; WLC

Bolt, Lee
See Faust, Frederick (Schiller)

Bolt, Robert (Oxton) 1924-........ **CLC 14**
See also CA 17-20R; CANR 35; DLB 13;
MTCW

Bomkauf
See Kaufman, Bob (Garnell)

Bonaventura.................... **NCLC 35**
See also DLB 90

Bond, Edward 1934-....... **CLC 4, 6, 13, 23**
See also CA 25-28R; CANR 38; DLB 13;
MTCW

Bonham, Frank 1914-1989......... **CLC 12**
See also AAYA 1; CA 9-12R; CANR 4, 36;
MAICYA; SAAS 3; SATA 1, 49, 62

Bonnefoy, Yves 1923-........ **CLC 9, 15, 58**
See also CA 85-88; CANR 33; MTCW

Bontemps, Arna(ud Wendell)
1902-1973 .... **CLC 1, 18**
See also BLC 1; BW; CA 1-4R; 41-44R;
CANR 4, 35; CLR 6; DLB 48, 51;
MAICYA; MTCW; SATA 2, 24, 44

Booth, Martin 1944-.............. **CLC 13**
See also CA 93-96; CAAS 2

Booth, Philip 1925-............... **CLC 23**
See also CA 5-8R; CANR 5; DLBY 82

Booth, Wayne C(layson) 1921- ..... **CLC 24**
See also CA 1-4R; CAAS 5; CANR 3;
DLB 67

Borchert, Wolfgang 1921-1947 ..... **TCLC 5**
See also CA 104; DLB 69, 124

Borges, Jorge Luis
1899-1986 ... **CLC 1, 2, 3, 4, 6, 8, 9, 10,
13, 19, 44, 48; SSC 4**
See also CA 21-24R; CANR 19, 33;
DLB 113; DLBY 86; HW; MTCW; WLC

Borowski, Tadeusz 1922-1951...... **TCLC 9**
See also CA 106

Borrow, George (Henry)
1803-1881 .... **NCLC 9**
See also DLB 21, 55

Bosman, Herman Charles
1905-1951 .... **TCLC 49**

Bosschere, Jean de 1878(?)-1953... **TCLC 19**
See also CA 115

Boswell, James 1740-1795.......... **LC 4**
See also CDBLB 1660-1789; DLB 104;
WLC

Bottoms, David 1949-............. **CLC 53**
See also CA 105; CANR 22; DLB 120;
DLBY 83

Boucolon, Maryse 1937-
See Conde, Maryse
See also CA 110; CANR 30

Bourget, Paul (Charles Joseph)
1852-1935 .... **TCLC 12**
See also CA 107; DLB 123

Bourjaily, Vance (Nye) 1922- . . . . **CLC 8, 62**
See also CA 1-4R; CAAS 1; CANR 2;
DLB 2

Bourne, Randolph S(illiman)
1886-1918 . . . . **TCLC 16**
See also CA 117; DLB 63

Bova, Ben(jamin William) 1932- . . . . **CLC 45**
See also CA 5-8R; CANR 11; CLR 3;
DLBY 81; MAICYA; MTCW; SATA 6,
68

Bowen, Elizabeth (Dorothea Cole)
1899-1973 . . . . . **CLC 1, 3, 6, 11, 15, 22;**
                                 SSC 3
See also CA 17-18; 41-44R; CANR 35;
CAP 2; CDBLB 1945-1960; DLB 15;
MTCW

Bowering, George 1935- . . . . **CLC 15, 47**
See also CA 21-24R; CAAS 16; CANR 10;
DLB 53

Bowering, Marilyn R(uthe) 1949- . . . **CLC 32**
See also CA 101

Bowers, Edgar 1924- . . . . **CLC 9**
See also CA 5-8R; CANR 24; DLB 5

Bowie, David . . . . **CLC 17**
See also Jones, David Robert

Bowles, Jane (Sydney)
1917-1973 . . . . **CLC 3, 68**
See also CA 19-20; 41-44R; CAP 2

Bowles, Paul (Frederick)
1910- . . . . **CLC 1, 2, 19, 53; SSC 3**
See also CA 1-4R; CAAS 1; CANR 1, 19;
DLB 5, 6; MTCW

Box, Edgar
See Vidal, Gore

Boyd, Nancy
See Millay, Edna St. Vincent

Boyd, William 1952- . . . . **CLC 28, 53, 70**
See also CA 114; 120

Boyle, Kay 1902- . . **CLC 1, 5, 19, 58; SSC 5**
See also CA 13-16R; CAAS 1; CANR 29;
DLB 4, 9, 48, 86; MTCW

Boyle, Mark
See Kienzle, William X(avier)

Boyle, Patrick 1905-1982 . . . . **CLC 19**
See also CA 127

Boyle, T. Coraghessan 1948- . . . . **CLC 36, 55**
See also BEST 90:4; CA 120; DLBY 86

Boz
See Dickens, Charles (John Huffam)

Brackenridge, Hugh Henry
1748-1816 . . . . **NCLC 7**
See also DLB 11, 37

Bradbury, Edward P.
See Moorcock, Michael (John)

Bradbury, Malcolm (Stanley)
1932- . . . . **CLC 32, 61**
See also CA 1-4R; CANR 1, 33; DLB 14;
MTCW

Bradbury, Ray (Douglas)
1920- . . . . **CLC 1, 3, 10, 15, 42**
See also AITN 1, 2; CA 1-4R; CANR 2, 30;
CDALB 1968-1988; DLB 2, 8; MTCW;
SATA 11, 64; WLC

Bradford, Gamaliel 1863-1932 . . . . . **TCLC 36**
See also DLB 17

Bradley, David (Henry Jr.) 1950- . . . **CLC 23**
See also BLC 1; BW; CA 104; CANR 26;
DLB 33

Bradley, John Ed 1959- . . . . **CLC 55**

Bradley, Marion Zimmer 1930- . . . . . **CLC 30**
See also AAYA 9; CA 57-60; CAAS 10;
CANR 7, 31; DLB 8; MTCW

Bradstreet, Anne 1612(?)-1672 . . . . **LC 4**
See also CDALB 1640-1865; DLB 24

Bragg, Melvyn 1939- . . . . **CLC 10**
See also BEST 89:3; CA 57-60; CANR 10;
DLB 14

Braine, John (Gerard)
1922-1986 . . . . **CLC 1, 3, 41**
See also CA 1-4R; 120; CANR 1, 33;
CDBLB 1945-1960; DLB 15; DLBY 86;
MTCW

Brammer, William 1930(?)-1978 . . . . **CLC 31**
See also CA 77-80

Brancati, Vitaliano 1907-1954 . . . . . **TCLC 12**
See also CA 109

Brancato, Robin F(idler) 1936- . . . . . **CLC 35**
See also AAYA 9; CA 69-72; CANR 11;
SAAS 9; SATA 23

Brand, Max
See Faust, Frederick (Schiller)

Brand, Millen 1906-1980 . . . . **CLC 7**
See also CA 21-24R; 97-100

Branden, Barbara . . . . **CLC 44**

Brandes, Georg (Morris Cohen)
1842-1927 . . . . **TCLC 10**
See also CA 105

Brandys, Kazimierz 1916- . . . . **CLC 62**

Branley, Franklyn M(ansfield)
1915- . . . . **CLC 21**
See also CA 33-36R; CANR 14, 39;
CLR 13; MAICYA; SAAS 16; SATA 4,
68

Brathwaite, Edward (Kamau)
1930- . . . . **CLC 11**
See also BW; CA 25-28R; CANR 11, 26;
DLB 125

Brautigan, Richard (Gary)
1935-1984 . . . . **CLC 1, 3, 5, 9, 12, 34, 42**
See also CA 53-56; 113; CANR 34; DLB 2,
5; DLBY 80, 84; MTCW; SATA 56

Braverman, Kate 1950- . . . . **CLC 67**
See also CA 89-92

Brecht, Bertolt
1898-1956 . . . . . **TCLC 1, 6, 13, 35; DC 3**
See also CA 104; 133; DLB 56, 124;
MTCW; WLC

Brecht, Eugen Berthold Friedrich
See Brecht, Bertolt

Bremer, Fredrika 1801-1865 . . . . . **NCLC 11**

Brennan, Christopher John
1870-1932 . . . . **TCLC 17**
See also CA 117

Brennan, Maeve 1917- . . . . **CLC 5**
See also CA 81-84

Brentano, Clemens (Maria)
1778-1842 . . . . **NCLC 1**

Brent of Bin Bin
See Franklin, (Stella Maraia Sarah) Miles

Brenton, Howard 1942- . . . . **CLC 31**
See also CA 69-72; CANR 33; DLB 13;
MTCW

Breslin, James 1930-
See Breslin, Jimmy
See also CA 73-76; CANR 31; MTCW

Breslin, Jimmy . . . . **CLC 4, 43**
See also Breslin, James
See also AITN 1

Bresson, Robert 1907- . . . . **CLC 16**
See also CA 110

Breton, Andre 1896-1966 . . . **CLC 2, 9, 15, 54**
See also CA 19-20; 25-28R; CANR 40;
CAP 2; DLB 65; MTCW

Breytenbach, Breyten 1939(?)- . . **CLC 23, 37**
See also CA 113; 129

Bridgers, Sue Ellen 1942- . . . . **CLC 26**
See also AAYA 8; CA 65-68; CANR 11,
36; CLR 18; DLB 52; MAICYA;
SAAS 1; SATA 22

Bridges, Robert (Seymour)
1844-1930 . . . . **TCLC 1**
See also CA 104; CDBLB 1890-1914;
DLB 19, 98

Bridie, James . . . . **TCLC 3**
See also Mavor, Osborne Henry
See also DLB 10

Brin, David 1950- . . . . **CLC 34**
See also CA 102; CANR 24; SATA 65

Brink, Andre (Philippus)
1935- . . . . **CLC 18, 36**
See also CA 104; CANR 39; MTCW

Brinsmead, H(esba) F(ay) 1922- . . . . **CLC 21**
See also CA 21-24R; CANR 10; MAICYA;
SAAS 5; SATA 18

Brittain, Vera (Mary)
1893(?)-1970 . . . . **CLC 23**
See also CA 13-16; 25-28R; CAP 1; MTCW

Broch, Hermann 1886-1951 . . . . **TCLC 20**
See also CA 117; DLB 85, 124

Brock, Rose
See Hansen, Joseph

Brodkey, Harold 1930- . . . . **CLC 56**
See also CA 111; DLB 130

Brodsky, Iosif Alexandrovich 1940-
See Brodsky, Joseph
See also AITN 1; CA 41-44R; CANR 37;
MTCW

Brodsky, Joseph . . . . **CLC 4, 6, 13, 36, 50**
See also Brodsky, Iosif Alexandrovich

Brodsky, Michael Mark 1948- . . . . . **CLC 19**
See also CA 102; CANR 18

Bromell, Henry 1947- . . . . **CLC 5**
See also CA 53-56; CANR 9

Bromfield, Louis (Brucker)
1896-1956 . . . . **TCLC 11**
See also CA 107; DLB 4, 9, 86

Broner, E(sther) M(asserman)
1930- . . . . **CLC 19**
See also CA 17-20R; CANR 8, 25; DLB 28

Bronk, William 1918- . . . . **CLC 10**
See also CA 89-92; CANR 23

Bronstein, Lev Davidovich
See Trotsky, Leon

Channing, William Ellery
    1780-1842 . . . . NCLC 17
    See also DLB 1, 59

Chaplin, Charles Spencer
    1889-1977 . . . . CLC 16
    See also Chaplin, Charlie
    See also CA 81-84; 73-76

Chaplin, Charlie
    See Chaplin, Charles Spencer
    See also DLB 44

Chapman, George   1559(?)-1634 . . . . . . LC 22
    See also DLB 62, 121

Chapman, Graham   1941-1989 . . . . . . CLC 21
    See also Monty Python
    See also CA 116; 129; CANR 35

Chapman, John Jay   1862-1933 . . . . . TCLC 7
    See also CA 104

Chapman, Walker
    See Silverberg, Robert

Chappell, Fred (Davis)   1936- . . . . CLC 40
    See also CA 5-8R; CAAS 4; CANR 8, 33;
    DLB 6, 105

Char, Rene(-Emile)
    1907-1988 . . . . CLC 9, 11, 14, 55
    See also CA 13-16R; 124; CANR 32;
    MTCW

Charby, Jay
    See Ellison, Harlan

Chardin, Pierre Teilhard de
    See Teilhard de Chardin, (Marie Joseph)
    Pierre

Charles I   1600-1649 . . . . LC 13

Charyn, Jerome   1937- . . . . CLC 5, 8, 18
    See also CA 5-8R; CAAS 1; CANR 7;
    DLBY 83; MTCW

Chase, Mary (Coyle)   1907-1981 . . . . . . DC 1
    See also CA 77-80; 105; SATA 17, 29

Chase, Mary Ellen   1887-1973 . . . . CLC 2
    See also CA 13-16; 41-44R; CAP 1;
    SATA 10

Chase, Nicholas
    See Hyde, Anthony

Chateaubriand, Francois Rene de
    1768-1848 . . . . NCLC 3
    See also DLB 119

Chatterje, Sarat Chandra   1876-1936(?)
    See Chatterji, Saratchandra
    See also CA 109

Chatterji, Bankim Chandra
    1838-1894 . . . . NCLC 19

Chatterji, Saratchandra . . . . TCLC 13
    See also Chatterje, Sarat Chandra

Chatterton, Thomas   1752-1770 . . . . LC 3
    See also DLB 109

Chatwin, (Charles) Bruce
    1940-1989 . . . . CLC 28, 57, 59
    See also AAYA 4; BEST 90:1; CA 85-88;
    127

Chaucer, Daniel
    See Ford, Ford Madox

Chaucer, Geoffrey   1340(?)-1400 . . . . . LC 17
    See also CDBLB Before 1660

Chaviaras, Strates   1935-
    See Haviaras, Stratis
    See also CA 105

Chayefsky, Paddy . . . . CLC 23
    See also Chayefsky, Sidney
    See also DLB 7, 44; DLBY 81

Chayefsky, Sidney   1923-1981
    See Chayefsky, Paddy
    See also CA 9-12R; 104; CANR 18

Chedid, Andree   1920- . . . . CLC 47

Cheever, John
    1912-1982 . . . . . CLC 3, 7, 8, 11, 15, 25,
                                          64; SSC 1
    See also CA 5-8R; 106; CABS 1; CANR 5,
    27; CDALB 1941-1968; DLB 2, 102;
    DLBY 80, 82; MTCW; WLC

Cheever, Susan   1943- . . . . CLC 18, 48
    See also CA 103; CANR 27; DLBY 82

Chekhonte, Antosha
    See Chekhov, Anton (Pavlovich)

Chekhov, Anton (Pavlovich)
    1860-1904 . . . . . . TCLC 3, 10, 31; SSC 2
    See also CA 104; 124; WLC

Chernyshevsky, Nikolay Gavrilovich
    1828-1889 . . . . NCLC 1

Cherry, Carolyn Janice   1942-
    See Cherryh, C. J.
    See also CA 65-68; CANR 10

Cherryh, C. J. . . . . CLC 35
    See also Cherry, Carolyn Janice
    See also DLBY 80

Chesnutt, Charles W(addell)
    1858-1932 . . . . TCLC 5, 39; SSC 7
    See also BLC 1; BW; CA 106; 125; DLB 12,
    50, 78; MTCW

Chester, Alfred   1929(?)-1971 . . . . CLC 49
    See also CA 33-36R; DLB 130

Chesterton, G(ilbert) K(eith)
    1874-1936 . . . . TCLC 1, 6; SSC 1
    See also CA 104; 132; CDBLB 1914-1945;
    DLB 10, 19, 34, 70, 98; MTCW;
    SATA 27

Chiang Pin-chin   1904-1986
    See Ding Ling
    See also CA 118

Ch'ien Chung-shu   1910- . . . . CLC 22
    See also CA 130; MTCW

Child, L. Maria
    See Child, Lydia Maria

Child, Lydia Maria   1802-1880 . . . . NCLC 6
    See also DLB 1, 74; SATA 67

Child, Mrs.
    See Child, Lydia Maria

Child, Philip   1898-1978 . . . . CLC 19, 68
    See also CA 13-14; CAP 1; SATA 47

Childress, Alice   1920- . . . . CLC 12, 15
    See also AAYA 8; BLC 1; BW; CA 45-48;
    CANR 3, 27; CLR 14; DLB 7, 38;
    MAICYA; MTCW; SATA 7, 48

Chislett, (Margaret) Anne   1943- . . . . CLC 34

Chitty, Thomas Willes   1926- . . . . CLC 11
    See also Hinde, Thomas
    See also CA 5-8R

Chomette, Rene Lucien   1898-1981 . . CLC 20
    See also Clair, Rene
    See also CA 103

Chopin, Kate . . . . TCLC 5, 14; SSC 8
    See also Chopin, Katherine
    See also CDALB 1865-1917; DLB 12, 78

Chopin, Katherine   1851-1904
    See Chopin, Kate
    See also CA 104; 122

Chretien de Troyes
    c. 12th cent. - . . . . CMLC 10

Christie
    See Ichikawa, Kon

Christie, Agatha (Mary Clarissa)
    1890-1976 . . . . . . CLC 1, 6, 8, 12, 39, 48
    See also AAYA 9; AITN 1, 2; CA 17-20R;
    61-64; CANR 10, 37; CDBLB 1914-1945;
    DLB 13, 77; MTCW; SATA 36

Christie, (Ann) Philippa
    See Pearce, Philippa
    See also CA 5-8R; CANR 4

Christine de Pizan   1365(?)-1431(?) . . . . LC 9

Chubb, Elmer
    See Masters, Edgar Lee

Chulkov, Mikhail Dmitrievich
    1743-1792 . . . . LC 2

Churchill, Caryl   1938- . . . . CLC 31, 55
    See also CA 102; CANR 22; DLB 13;
    MTCW

Churchill, Charles   1731-1764 . . . . LC 3
    See also DLB 109

Chute, Carolyn   1947- . . . . CLC 39
    See also CA 123

Ciardi, John (Anthony)
    1916-1986 . . . . CLC 10, 40, 44
    See also CA 5-8R; 118; CAAS 2; CANR 5,
    33; CLR 19; DLB 5; DLBY 86;
    MAICYA; MTCW; SATA 1, 46, 65

Cicero, Marcus Tullius
    106B.C.-43B.C. . . . . CMLC 3

Cimino, Michael   1943- . . . . CLC 16
    See also CA 105

Cioran, E(mil) M.   1911- . . . . CLC 64
    See also CA 25-28R

Cisneros, Sandra   1954- . . . . CLC 69
    See also AAYA 9; CA 131; DLB 122; HW

Clair, Rene . . . . CLC 20
    See also Chomette, Rene Lucien

Clampitt, Amy   1920- . . . . CLC 32
    See also CA 110; CANR 29; DLB 105

Clancy, Thomas L. Jr.   1947-
    See Clancy, Tom
    See also CA 125; 131; MTCW

Clancy, Tom . . . . CLC 45
    See also Clancy, Thomas L. Jr.
    See also AAYA 9; BEST 89:1, 90:1

Clare, John   1793-1864 . . . . NCLC 9
    See also DLB 55, 96

Clarin
    See Alas (y Urena), Leopoldo (Enrique
    Garcia)

Clark, (Robert) Brian   1932- . . . . CLC 29
    See also CA 41-44R

Davison, Frank Dalby 1893-1970 ... **CLC 15**
    See also CA 116

Davison, Lawrence H.
    See Lawrence, D(avid) H(erbert Richards)

Davison, Peter 1928- .... **CLC 28**
    See also CA 9-12R; CAAS 4; CANR 3;
    DLB 5

Davys, Mary 1674-1732............ **LC 1**
    See also DLB 39

Dawson, Fielding 1930- .... **CLC 6**
    See also CA 85-88; DLB 130

Dawson, Peter
    See Faust, Frederick (Schiller)

Day, Clarence (Shepard Jr.)
    1874-1935 .... **TCLC 25**
    See also CA 108; DLB 11

Day, Thomas 1748-1789............ **LC 1**
    See also DLB 39; YABC 1

Day Lewis, C(ecil)
    1904-1972 .... **CLC 1, 6, 10**
    See also Blake, Nicholas
    See also CA 13-16; 33-36R; CANR 34;
    CAP 1; DLB 15, 20; MTCW

Dazai, Osamu .... **TCLC 11**
    See also Tsushima, Shuji

de Andrade, Carlos Drummond
    See Drummond de Andrade, Carlos

Deane, Norman
    See Creasey, John

de Beauvoir, Simone (Lucie Ernestine Marie
        Bertrand)
    See Beauvoir, Simone (Lucie Ernestine
    Marie Bertrand) de

de Brissac, Malcolm
    See Dickinson, Peter (Malcolm)

de Chardin, Pierre Teilhard
    See Teilhard de Chardin, (Marie Joseph)
    Pierre

Dee, John 1527-1608 .... **LC 20**

Deer, Sandra 1940-.............. **CLC 45**

De Ferrari, Gabriella .... **CLC 65**

Defoe, Daniel 1660(?)-1731 .... **LC 1**
    See also CDBLB 1660-1789; DLB 39, 95,
    101; MAICYA; SATA 22; WLC

de Gourmont, Remy
    See Gourmont, Remy de

de Hartog, Jan 1914-............ **CLC 19**
    See also CA 1-4R; CANR 1

de Hostos, E. M.
    See Hostos (y Bonilla), Eugenio Maria de

de Hostos, Eugenio M.
    See Hostos (y Bonilla), Eugenio Maria de

Deighton, Len .... **CLC 4, 7, 22, 46**
    See also Deighton, Leonard Cyril
    See also AAYA 6; BEST 89:2;
    CDBLB 1960 to Present; DLB 87

Deighton, Leonard Cyril 1929-
    See Deighton, Len
    See also CA 9-12R; CANR 19, 33; MTCW

Dekker, Thomas 1572(?)-1632...... **LC 22**
    See also CDBLB Before 1660; DLB 62

de la Mare, Walter (John)
    1873-1956 .... **TCLC 4**
    See also CA 110; 137; CDBLB 1914-1945;
    CLR 23; DLB 19; MAICYA; SATA 16;
    WLC

Delaney, Franey
    See O'Hara, John (Henry)

Delaney, Shelagh 1939- .... **CLC 29**
    See also CA 17-20R; CANR 30;
    CDBLB 1960 to Present; DLB 13;
    MTCW

Delany, Mary (Granville Pendarves)
    1700-1788 .... **LC 12**

Delany, Samuel R(ay Jr.)
    1942- .... **CLC 8, 14, 38**
    See also BLC 1; BW; CA 81-84; CANR 27;
    DLB 8, 33; MTCW

Delaporte, Theophile
    See Green, Julian (Hartridge)

De La Ramee, (Marie) Louise 1839-1908
    See Ouida
    See also SATA 20

de la Roche, Mazo 1879-1961...... **CLC 14**
    See also CA 85-88; CANR 30; DLB 68;
    SATA 64

Delbanco, Nicholas (Franklin)
    1942- .... **CLC 6, 13**
    See also CA 17-20R; CAAS 2; CANR 29;
    DLB 6

del Castillo, Michel 1933- .... **CLC 38**
    See also CA 109

Deledda, Grazia (Cosima)
    1875(?)-1936 .... **TCLC 23**
    See also CA 123

Delibes, Miguel .... **CLC 8, 18**
    See also Delibes Setien, Miguel

Delibes Setien, Miguel 1920-
    See Delibes, Miguel
    See also CA 45-48; CANR 1, 32; HW;
    MTCW

DeLillo, Don
    1936- ...... **CLC 8, 10, 13, 27, 39, 54, 76**
    See also BEST 89:1; CA 81-84; CANR 21;
    DLB 6; MTCW

de Lisser, H. G.
    See De Lisser, Herbert George
    See also DLB 117

De Lisser, Herbert George
    1878-1944 .... **TCLC 12**
    See also de Lisser, H. G.
    See also CA 109

Deloria, Vine (Victor) Jr. 1933- .... **CLC 21**
    See also CA 53-56; CANR 5, 20; MTCW;
    SATA 21

Del Vecchio, John M(ichael)
    1947- .... **CLC 29**
    See also CA 110; DLBD 9

de Man, Paul (Adolph Michel)
    1919-1983 .... **CLC 55**
    See also CA 128; 111; DLB 67; MTCW

De Marinis, Rick 1934-........... **CLC 54**
    See also CA 57-60; CANR 9, 25

Demby, William 1922-........... **CLC 53**
    See also BLC 1; BW; CA 81-84; DLB 33

Demijohn, Thom
    See Disch, Thomas M(ichael)

de Montherlant, Henry (Milon)
    See Montherlant, Henry (Milon) de

de Natale, Francine
    See Malzberg, Barry N(athaniel)

Denby, Edwin (Orr) 1903-1983 ..... **CLC 48**
    See also CA 138; 110

Denis, Julio
    See Cortazar, Julio

Denmark, Harrison
    See Zelazny, Roger (Joseph)

Dennis, John 1658-1734............ **LC 11**
    See also DLB 101

Dennis, Nigel (Forbes) 1912-1989.... **CLC 8**
    See also CA 25-28R; 129; DLB 13, 15;
    MTCW

De Palma, Brian (Russell) 1940-.... **CLC 20**
    See also CA 109

De Quincey, Thomas 1785-1859 ... **NCLC 4**
    See also CDBLB 1789-1832; DLB 110

Deren, Eleanora 1908(?)-1961
    See Deren, Maya
    See also CA 111

Deren, Maya .... **CLC 16**
    See also Deren, Eleanora

Derleth, August (William)
    1909-1971 .... **CLC 31**
    See also CA 1-4R; 29-32R; CANR 4;
    DLB 9; SATA 5

de Routisie, Albert
    See Aragon, Louis

Derrida, Jacques 1930-........... **CLC 24**
    See also CA 124; 127

Derry Down Derry
    See Lear, Edward

Dersonnes, Jacques
    See Simenon, Georges (Jacques Christian)

Desai, Anita 1937- .... **CLC 19, 37**
    See also CA 81-84; CANR 33; MTCW;
    SATA 63

de Saint-Luc, Jean
    See Glassco, John

de Saint Roman, Arnaud
    See Aragon, Louis

Descartes, Rene 1596-1650 .... **LC 20**

De Sica, Vittorio 1901(?)-1974 ..... **CLC 20**
    See also CA 117

Desnos, Robert 1900-1945........ **TCLC 22**
    See also CA 121

Destouches, Louis-Ferdinand
    1894-1961 .... **CLC 9, 15**
    See also Celine, Louis-Ferdinand
    See also CA 85-88; CANR 28; MTCW

Deutsch, Babette 1895-1982 .... **CLC 18**
    See also CA 1-4R; 108; CANR 4; DLB 45;
    SATA 1, 33

Devenant, William 1606-1649 ...... **LC 13**

Devkota, Laxmiprasad
    1909-1959 .... **TCLC 23**
    See also CA 123

De Voto, Bernard (Augustine)
1897-1955 .... **TCLC 29**
See also CA 113; DLB 9

De Vries, Peter
1910- .... **CLC 1, 2, 3, 7, 10, 28, 46**
See also CA 17-20R; DLB 6; DLBY 82;
MTCW

Dexter, Martin
See Faust, Frederick (Schiller)

Dexter, Pete 1943- .... **CLC 34, 55**
See also BEST 89:2; CA 127; 131; MTCW

Diamano, Silmang
See Senghor, Leopold Sedar

Diamond, Neil 1941- .... **CLC 30**
See also CA 108

di Bassetto, Corno
See Shaw, George Bernard

Dick, Philip K(indred)
1928-1982 .... **CLC 10, 30, 72**
See also CA 49-52; 106; CANR 2, 16;
DLB 8; MTCW

Dickens, Charles (John Huffam)
1812-1870 .... **NCLC 3, 8, 18, 26**
See also CDBLB 1832-1890; DLB 21, 55,
70; MAICYA; SATA 15

Dickey, James (Lafayette)
1923- .... **CLC 1, 2, 4, 7, 10, 15, 47**
See also AITN 1, 2; CA 9-12R; CABS 2;
CANR 10; CDALB 1968-1988; DLB 5;
DLBD 7; DLBY 82; MTCW

Dickey, William 1928- .... **CLC 3, 28**
See also CA 9-12R; CANR 24; DLB 5

Dickinson, Charles 1951- .... **CLC 49**
See also CA 128

Dickinson, Emily (Elizabeth)
1830-1886 .... **NCLC 21; PC 1**
See also CDALB 1865-1917; DLB 1;
SATA 29; WLC

Dickinson, Peter (Malcolm)
1927- .... **CLC 12, 35**
See also AAYA 9; CA 41-44R; CANR 31;
DLB 87; MAICYA; SATA 5, 62

Dickson, Carr
See Carr, John Dickson

Dickson, Carter
See Carr, John Dickson

Didion, Joan 1934- ..... **CLC 1, 3, 8, 14, 32**
See also AITN 1; CA 5-8R; CANR 14;
CDALB 1968-1988; DLB 2; DLBY 81,
86; MTCW

Dietrich, Robert
See Hunt, E(verette) Howard Jr.

Dillard, Annie 1945- .... **CLC 9, 60**
See also AAYA 6; CA 49-52; CANR 3;
DLBY 80; MTCW; SATA 10

Dillard, R(ichard) H(enry) W(ilde)
1937- .... **CLC 5**
See also CA 21-24R; CAAS 7; CANR 10;
DLB 5

Dillon, Eilis 1920- .... **CLC 17**
See also CA 9-12R; CAAS 3; CANR 4, 38;
CLR 26; MAICYA; SATA 2

Dimont, Penelope
See Mortimer, Penelope (Ruth)

Dinesen, Isak .... **CLC 10, 29; SSC 7**
See also Blixen, Karen (Christentze
Dinesen)

Ding Ling .... **CLC 68**
See also Chiang Pin-chin

Disch, Thomas M(ichael) 1940-... **CLC 7, 36**
See also CA 21-24R; CAAS 4; CANR 17,
36; CLR 18; DLB 8; MAICYA; MTCW;
SAAS 15; SATA 54

Disch, Tom
See Disch, Thomas M(ichael)

d'Isly, Georges
See Simenon, Georges (Jacques Christian)

Disraeli, Benjamin 1804-1881 .. **NCLC 2, 39**
See also DLB 21, 55

Ditcum, Steve
See Crumb, R(obert)

Dixon, Paige
See Corcoran, Barbara

Dixon, Stephen 1936- .... **CLC 52**
See also CA 89-92; CANR 17, 40; DLB 130

Doblin, Alfred .... **TCLC 13**
See also Doeblin, Alfred

Dobrolyubov, Nikolai Alexandrovich
1836-1861 .... **NCLC 5**

Dobyns, Stephen 1941-............. **CLC 37**
See also CA 45-48; CANR 2, 18

Doctorow, E(dgar) L(aurence)
1931- ..... **CLC 6, 11, 15, 18, 37, 44, 65**
See also AITN 2; BEST 89:3; CA 45-48;
CANR 2, 33; CDALB 1968-1988; DLB 2,
28; DLBY 80; MTCW

Dodgson, Charles Lutwidge 1832-1898
See Carroll, Lewis
See also CLR 2; MAICYA; YABC 2

Doeblin, Alfred 1878-1957....... **TCLC 13**
See also Doblin, Alfred
See also CA 110; DLB 66

Doerr, Harriet 1910- .... **CLC 34**
See also CA 117; 122

Domecq, H(onorio) Bustos
See Bioy Casares, Adolfo; Borges, Jorge
Luis

Domini, Rey
See Lorde, Audre (Geraldine)

Dominique
See Proust,
(Valentin-Louis-George-Eugene-)Marcel

Don, A
See Stephen, Leslie

Donaldson, Stephen R. 1947-....... **CLC 46**
See also CA 89-92; CANR 13

Donleavy, J(ames) P(atrick)
1926- .... **CLC 1, 4, 6, 10, 45**
See also AITN 2; CA 9-12R; CANR 24;
DLB 6; MTCW

Donne, John 1572-1631 .... **LC 10; PC 1**
See also CDBLB Before 1660; DLB 121;
WLC

Donnell, David 1939(?)- .... **CLC 34**

Donoso (Yanez), Jose
1924- .... **CLC 4, 8, 11, 32**
See also CA 81-84; CANR 32; DLB 113;
HW; MTCW

Donovan, John 1928-1992 .... **CLC 35**
See also CA 97-100; 137; CLR 3;
MAICYA; SATA 29

Don Roberto
See Cunninghame Graham, R(obert)
B(ontine)

Doolittle, Hilda
1886-1961 .... **CLC 3, 8, 14, 31, 34, 73;
PC 5**
See also H. D.
See also CA 97-100; CANR 35; DLB 4, 45;
MTCW; WLC

Dorfman, Ariel 1942-............. **CLC 48**
See also CA 124; 130; HW

Dorn, Edward (Merton) 1929-... **CLC 10, 18**
See also CA 93-96; DLB 5

Dorsan, Luc
See Simenon, Georges (Jacques Christian)

Dorsange, Jean
See Simenon, Georges (Jacques Christian)

Dos Passos, John (Roderigo)
1896-1970 ... **CLC 1, 4, 8, 11, 15, 25, 34**
See also CA 1-4R; 29-32R; CANR 3;
CDALB 1929-1941; DLB 4, 9; DLBD 1;
MTCW; WLC

Dossage, Jean
See Simenon, Georges (Jacques Christian)

Dostoevsky, Fedor Mikhailovich
1821-1881 .... **NCLC 2, 7, 21, 33; SSC 2**
See also WLC

Doughty, Charles M(ontagu)
1843-1926 .... **TCLC 27**
See also CA 115; DLB 19, 57

Douglas, Ellen
See Haxton, Josephine Ayres

Douglas, Gavin 1475(?)-1522........ **LC 20**

Douglas, Keith 1920-1944 .... **TCLC 40**
See also DLB 27

Douglas, Leonard
See Bradbury, Ray (Douglas)

Douglas, Michael
See Crichton, (John) Michael

Douglass, Frederick 1817(?)-1895.. **NCLC 7**
See also BLC 1; CDALB 1640-1865;
DLB 1, 43, 50, 79; SATA 29; WLC

Dourado, (Waldomiro Freitas) Autran
1926- .... **CLC 23, 60**
See also CA 25-28R; CANR 34

Dourado, Waldomiro Autran
See Dourado, (Waldomiro Freitas) Autran

Dove, Rita (Frances) 1952- ... **CLC 50; PC 6**
See also BW; CA 109; CANR 27; DLB 120

Dowell, Coleman 1925-1985....... **CLC 60**
See also CA 25-28R; 117; CANR 10;
DLB 130

Dowson, Ernest Christopher
1867-1900 .... **TCLC 4**
See also CA 105; DLB 19

Doyle, A. Conan
See Doyle, Arthur Conan

Doyle, Arthur Conan 1859-1930 .... **TCLC 7**
See also CA 104; 122; CDBLB 1890-1914;
DLB 18, 70; MTCW; SATA 24; WLC

Doyle, Conan
See Doyle, Arthur Conan

Doyle, John
See Graves, Robert (von Ranke)

Doyle, Sir A. Conan
See Doyle, Arthur Conan

Doyle, Sir Arthur Conan
See Doyle, Arthur Conan

Dr. A
See Asimov, Isaac; Silverstein, Alvin

Drabble, Margaret
1939- . . . . CLC 2, 3, 5, 8, 10, 22, 53
See also CA 13-16R; CANR 18, 35;
CDBLB 1960 to Present; DLB 14;
MTCW; SATA 48

Drapier, M. B.
See Swift, Jonathan

Drayham, James
See Mencken, H(enry) L(ouis)

Drayton, Michael 1563-1631 . . . . LC 8

Dreadstone, Carl
See Campbell, (John) Ramsey

Dreiser, Theodore (Herman Albert)
1871-1945 . . . . TCLC 10, 18, 35
See also CA 106; 132; CDALB 1865-1917;
DLB 9, 12, 102; DLBD 1; MTCW; WLC

Drexler, Rosalyn 1926- . . . . CLC 2, 6
See also CA 81-84

Dreyer, Carl Theodor 1889-1968. . . . CLC 16
See also CA 116

Drieu la Rochelle, Pierre(-Eugene)
1893-1945 . . . . TCLC 21
See also CA 117; DLB 72

Drop Shot
See Cable, George Washington

Droste-Hulshoff, Annette Freiin von
1797-1848 . . . . NCLC 3

Drummond, Walter
See Silverberg, Robert

Drummond, William Henry
1854-1907 . . . . TCLC 25
See also DLB 92

Drummond de Andrade, Carlos
1902-1987 . . . . CLC 18
See also Andrade, Carlos Drummond de
See also CA 132; 123

Drury, Allen (Stuart) 1918- . . . . CLC 37
See also CA 57-60; CANR 18

Dryden, John 1631-1700 . . . . LC 3, 21; DC 3
See also CDBLB 1660-1789; DLB 80, 101;
WLC

Duberman, Martin 1930- . . . . CLC 8
See also CA 1-4R; CANR 2

Dubie, Norman (Evans) 1945- . . . . . . CLC 36
See also CA 69-72; CANR 12; DLB 120

Du Bois, W(illiam) E(dward) B(urghardt)
1868-1963 . . . . CLC 1, 2, 13, 64
See also BLC 1; BW; CA 85-88; CANR 34;
CDALB 1865-1917; DLB 47, 50, 91;
MTCW; SATA 42; WLC

Dubus, Andre 1936- . . . . CLC 13, 36
See also CA 21-24R; CANR 17; DLB 130

Duca Minimo
See D'Annunzio, Gabriele

Ducharme, Rejean 1941- . . . . CLC 74
See also DLB 60

Duclos, Charles Pinot 1704-1772 . . . . . LC 1

Dudek, Louis 1918- . . . . CLC 11, 19
See also CA 45-48; CAAS 14; CANR 1;
DLB 88

Duerrenmatt, Friedrich
1921-1990 . . . . . . CLC 1, 4, 8, 11, 15, 43
See also Durrenmatt, Friedrich
See also CA 17-20R; CANR 33; DLB 69,
124; MTCW

Duffy, Bruce (?)- . . . . CLC 50

Duffy, Maureen 1933- . . . . CLC 37
See also CA 25-28R; CANR 33; DLB 14;
MTCW

Dugan, Alan 1923- . . . . CLC 2, 6
See also CA 81-84; DLB 5

du Gard, Roger Martin
See Martin du Gard, Roger

Duhamel, Georges 1884-1966 . . . . CLC 8
See also CA 81-84; 25-28R; CANR 35;
DLB 65; MTCW

Dujardin, Edouard (Emile Louis)
1861-1949 . . . . TCLC 13
See also CA 109; DLB 123

Dumas, Alexandre (Davy de la Pailleterie)
1802-1870 . . . . NCLC 11
See also DLB 119; SATA 18; WLC

Dumas, Alexandre
1824-1895 . . . . NCLC 9; DC 1

Dumas, Claudine
See Malzberg, Barry N(athaniel)

Dumas, Henry L. 1934-1968 . . . . . CLC 6, 62
See also BW; CA 85-88; DLB 41

du Maurier, Daphne
1907-1989 . . . . CLC 6, 11, 59
See also CA 5-8R; 128; CANR 6; MTCW;
SATA 27, 60

Dunbar, Paul Laurence
1872-1906 . . . . TCLC 2, 12; PC 5; SSC 8
See also BLC 1; BW; CA 104; 124;
CDALB 1865-1917; DLB 50, 54, 78;
SATA 34; WLC

Dunbar, William 1460(?)-1530(?) . . . . LC 20

Duncan, Lois 1934- . . . . CLC 26
See also AAYA 4; CA 1-4R; CANR 2, 23,
36; MAICYA; SAAS 2; SATA 1, 36

Duncan, Robert (Edward)
1919-1988 . . . CLC 1, 2, 4, 7, 15, 41, 55;
PC 2
See also CA 9-12R; 124; CANR 28; DLB 5,
16; MTCW

Dunlap, William 1766-1839 . . . . NCLC 2
See also DLB 30, 37, 59

Dunn, Douglas (Eaglesham)
1942- . . . . CLC 6, 40
See also CA 45-48; CANR 2, 33; DLB 40;
MTCW

Dunn, Katherine (Karen) 1945- . . . . . CLC 71
See also CA 33-36R

Dunn, Stephen 1939- . . . . CLC 36
See also CA 33-36R; CANR 12; DLB 105

Dunne, Finley Peter 1867-1936. . . . TCLC 28
See also CA 108; DLB 11, 23

Dunne, John Gregory 1932- . . . . CLC 28
See also CA 25-28R; CANR 14; DLBY 80

**Dunsany, Edward John Moreton Drax
Plunkett** 1878-1957
See Dunsany, Lord; Lord Dunsany
See also CA 104; DLB 10

Dunsany, Lord . . . . TCLC 2
See also Dunsany, Edward John Moreton
Drax Plunkett
See also DLB 77

du Perry, Jean
See Simenon, Georges (Jacques Christian)

Durang, Christopher (Ferdinand)
1949- . . . . CLC 27, 38
See also CA 105

Duras, Marguerite
1914- . . . . . . CLC 3, 6, 11, 20, 34, 40, 68
See also CA 25-28R; DLB 83; MTCW

Durban, (Rosa) Pam 1947- . . . . CLC 39
See also CA 123

Durcan, Paul 1944- . . . . CLC 43, 70
See also CA 134

Durrell, Lawrence (George)
1912-1990 . . . . CLC 1, 4, 6, 8, 13, 27, 41
See also CA 9-12R; 132; CANR 40;
CDBLB 1945-1960; DLB 15, 27;
DLBY 90; MTCW

Durrenmatt, Friedrich
. . . . CLC 1, 4, 8, 11, 15, 43
See also Duerrenmatt, Friedrich
See also DLB 69, 124

Dutt, Toru 1856-1877 . . . . NCLC 29

Dwight, Timothy 1752-1817 . . . . . . NCLC 13
See also DLB 37

Dworkin, Andrea 1946- . . . . CLC 43
See also CA 77-80; CANR 16, 39; MTCW

Dylan, Bob 1941- . . . . CLC 3, 4, 6, 12
See also CA 41-44R; DLB 16

Eagleton, Terence (Francis) 1943-
See Eagleton, Terry
See also CA 57-60; CANR 7, 23; MTCW

Eagleton, Terry . . . . CLC 63
See also Eagleton, Terence (Francis)

East, Michael
See West, Morris L(anglo)

Eastaway, Edward
See Thomas, (Philip) Edward

Eastlake, William (Derry) 1917- . . . . . CLC 8
See also CA 5-8R; CAAS 1; CANR 5;
DLB 6

Eberhart, Richard (Ghormley)
1904- . . . . CLC 3, 11, 19, 56
See also CA 1-4R; CANR 2;
CDALB 1941-1968; DLB 48; MTCW

Eberstadt, Fernanda 1960- . . . . CLC 39
See also CA 136

Echegaray (y Eizaguirre), Jose (Maria Waldo)
1832-1916 . . . . TCLC 4
See also CA 104; CANR 32; HW; MTCW

Echeverria, (Jose) Esteban (Antonino)
1805-1851 . . . . NCLC 18

Echo
See Proust,
(Valentin-Louis-George-Eugene-)Marcel

Eckert, Allan W. 1931- . . . . **CLC 17**
See also CA 13-16R; CANR 14; SATA 27, 29

Eckhart, Meister 1260(?)-1328(?) . . **CMLC 9**
See also DLB 115

Eckmar, F. R.
See de Hartog, Jan

Eco, Umberto 1932- . . . . **CLC 28, 60**
See also BEST 90:1; CA 77-80; CANR 12, 33; MTCW

Eddison, E(ric) R(ucker)
1882-1945 . . . . **TCLC 15**
See also CA 109

Edel, (Joseph) Leon 1907- . . . . . . **CLC 29, 34**
See also CA 1-4R; CANR 1, 22; DLB 103

Eden, Emily 1797-1869 . . . . **NCLC 10**

Edgar, David 1948- . . . . **CLC 42**
See also CA 57-60; CANR 12; DLB 13; MTCW

Edgerton, Clyde (Carlyle) 1944- . . . . **CLC 39**
See also CA 118; 134

Edgeworth, Maria 1767-1849 . . . . . . **NCLC 1**
See also DLB 116; SATA 21

Edmonds, Paul
See Kuttner, Henry

Edmonds, Walter D(umaux) 1903- . . **CLC 35**
See also CA 5-8R; CANR 2; DLB 9; MAICYA; SAAS 4; SATA 1, 27

Edmondson, Wallace
See Ellison, Harlan

Edson, Russell . . . . **CLC 13**
See also CA 33-36R

Edwards, G(erald) B(asil)
1899-1976 . . . . **CLC 25**
See also CA 110

Edwards, Gus 1939- . . . . **CLC 43**
See also CA 108

Edwards, Jonathan 1703-1758 . . . . **LC 7**
See also DLB 24

Efron, Marina Ivanovna Tsvetaeva
See Tsvetaeva (Efron), Marina (Ivanovna)

Ehle, John (Marsden Jr.) 1925- . . . . **CLC 27**
See also CA 9-12R

Ehrenbourg, Ilya (Grigoryevich)
See Ehrenburg, Ilya (Grigoryevich)

Ehrenburg, Ilya (Grigoryevich)
1891-1967 . . . . **CLC 18, 34, 62**
See also CA 102; 25-28R

Ehrenburg, Ilyo (Grigoryevich)
See Ehrenburg, Ilya (Grigoryevich)

Eich, Guenter 1907-1972 . . . . **CLC 15**
See also CA 111; 93-96; DLB 69, 124

Eichendorff, Joseph Freiherr von
1788-1857 . . . . **NCLC 8**
See also DLB 90

Eigner, Larry . . . . **CLC 9**
See also Eigner, Laurence (Joel)
See also DLB 5

Eigner, Laurence (Joel) 1927-
See Eigner, Larry
See also CA 9-12R; CANR 6

Eiseley, Loren Corey 1907-1977 . . . . . **CLC 7**
See also AAYA 5; CA 1-4R; 73-76; CANR 6

Eisenstadt, Jill 1963- . . . . **CLC 50**

Eisner, Simon
See Kornbluth, C(yril) M.

Ekeloef, (Bengt) Gunnar
1907-1968 . . . . **CLC 27**
See also Ekelof, (Bengt) Gunnar
See also CA 123; 25-28R

Ekelof, (Bengt) Gunnar . . . . **CLC 27**
See also Ekeloef, (Bengt) Gunnar

Ekwensi, C. O. D.
See Ekwensi, Cyprian (Odiatu Duaka)

Ekwensi, Cyprian (Odiatu Duaka)
1921- . . . . **CLC 4**
See also BLC 1; BW; CA 29-32R; CANR 18; DLB 117; MTCW; SATA 66

Elaine . . . . **TCLC 18**
See also Leverson, Ada

El Crummo
See Crumb, R(obert)

Elia
See Lamb, Charles

Eliade, Mircea 1907-1986 . . . . **CLC 19**
See also CA 65-68; 119; CANR 30; MTCW

Eliot, A. D.
See Jewett, (Theodora) Sarah Orne

Eliot, Alice
See Jewett, (Theodora) Sarah Orne

Eliot, Dan
See Silverberg, Robert

Eliot, George 1819-1880 . . . . **NCLC 4, 13, 23**
See also CDBLB 1832-1890; DLB 21, 35, 55; WLC

Eliot, John 1604-1690 . . . . **LC 5**
See also DLB 24

Eliot, T(homas) S(tearns)
1888-1965 . . . . **CLC 1, 2, 3, 6, 9, 10, 13, 15, 24, 34, 41, 55, 57; PC 5**
See also CA 5-8R; 25-28R; CDALB 1929-1941; DLB 7, 10, 45, 63; DLBY 88; MTCW; WLC 2

Elizabeth 1866-1941 . . . . **TCLC 41**

Elkin, Stanley L(awrence)
1930- . . . . **CLC 4, 6, 9, 14, 27, 51**
See also CA 9-12R; CANR 8; DLB 2, 28; DLBY 80; MTCW

Elledge, Scott . . . . **CLC 34**

Elliott, Don
See Silverberg, Robert

Elliott, George P(aul) 1918-1980 . . . . . **CLC 2**
See also CA 1-4R; 97-100; CANR 2

Elliott, Janice 1931- . . . . **CLC 47**
See also CA 13-16R; CANR 8, 29; DLB 14

Elliott, Sumner Locke 1917-1991 . . . **CLC 38**
See also CA 5-8R; 134; CANR 2, 21

Elliott, William
See Bradbury, Ray (Douglas)

Ellis, A. E. . . . . **CLC 7**

Ellis, Alice Thomas . . . . **CLC 40**
See also Haycraft, Anna

Ellis, Bret Easton 1964- . . . . **CLC 39, 71**
See also AAYA 2; CA 118; 123

Ellis, (Henry) Havelock
1859-1939 . . . . **TCLC 14**
See also CA 109

Ellis, Landon
See Ellison, Harlan

Ellis, Trey 1962- . . . . **CLC 55**

Ellison, Harlan 1934- . . . . **CLC 1, 13, 42**
See also CA 5-8R; CANR 5; DLB 8; MTCW

Ellison, Ralph (Waldo)
1914- . . . . **CLC 1, 3, 11, 54**
See also BLC 1; BW; CA 9-12R; CANR 24; CDALB 1941-1968; DLB 2, 76; MTCW; WLC

Ellmann, Lucy (Elizabeth) 1956- . . . . **CLC 61**
See also CA 128

Ellmann, Richard (David)
1918-1987 . . . . **CLC 50**
See also BEST 89:2; CA 1-4R; 122; CANR 2, 28; DLB 103; DLBY 87; MTCW

Elman, Richard 1934- . . . . **CLC 19**
See also CA 17-20R; CAAS 3

Elron
See Hubbard, L(afayette) Ron(ald)

Eluard, Paul . . . . **TCLC 7, 41**
See also Grindel, Eugene

Elyot, Sir Thomas 1490(?)-1546 . . . . . **LC 11**

Elytis, Odysseus 1911- . . . . **CLC 15, 49**
See also CA 102; MTCW

Emecheta, (Florence Onye) Buchi
1944- . . . . **CLC 14, 48**
See also BLC 2; BW; CA 81-84; CANR 27; DLB 117; MTCW; SATA 66

Emerson, Ralph Waldo
1803-1882 . . . . **NCLC 1, 38**
See also CDALB 1640-1865; DLB 1, 59, 73; WLC

Eminescu, Mihail 1850-1889 . . . . . **NCLC 33**

Empson, William
1906-1984 . . . . **CLC 3, 8, 19, 33, 34**
See also CA 17-20R; 112; CANR 31; DLB 20; MTCW

Enchi Fumiko (Ueda) 1905-1986 . . . . **CLC 31**
See also CA 129; 121

Ende, Michael (Andreas Helmuth)
1929- . . . . **CLC 31**
See also CA 118; 124; CANR 36; CLR 14; DLB 75; MAICYA; SATA 42, 61

Endo, Shusaku 1923- . . . . . **CLC 7, 14, 19, 54**
See also CA 29-32R; CANR 21; MTCW

Engel, Marian 1933-1985 . . . . **CLC 36**
See also CA 25-28R; CANR 12; DLB 53

Engelhardt, Frederick
See Hubbard, L(afayette) Ron(ald)

Enright, D(ennis) J(oseph)
1920- . . . . **CLC 4, 8, 31**
See also CA 1-4R; CANR 1; DLB 27; SATA 25

Enzensberger, Hans Magnus
1929- . . . . **CLC 43**
See also CA 116; 119

Ephron, Nora 1941- . . . . **CLC 17, 31**
See also AITN 2; CA 65-68; CANR 12, 39

Forsyth, Frederick 1938- ...... **CLC 2, 5, 36**
See also BEST 89:4; CA 85-88; CANR 38;
DLB 87; MTCW

Forten, Charlotte L. .... **TCLC 16**
See also Grimke, Charlotte L(ottie) Forten
See also BLC 2; DLB 50

Foscolo, Ugo 1778-1827.......... **NCLC 8**

Fosse, Bob .... **CLC 20**
See also Fosse, Robert Louis

Fosse, Robert Louis 1927-1987
See Fosse, Bob
See also CA 110; 123

Foster, Stephen Collins
1826-1864 .... **NCLC 26**

Foucault, Michel
1926-1984 .... **CLC 31, 34, 69**
See also CA 105; 113; CANR 34; MTCW

Fouque, Friedrich (Heinrich Karl) de la Motte
1777-1843 .... **NCLC 2**
See also DLB 90

Fournier, Henri Alban 1886-1914
See Alain-Fournier
See also CA 104

Fournier, Pierre 1916- .... **CLC 11**
See also Gascar, Pierre
See also CA 89-92; CANR 16, 40

Fowles, John
1926- .... **CLC 1, 2, 3, 4, 6, 9, 10, 15, 33**
See also CA 5-8R; CANR 25; CDBLB 1960
to Present; DLB 14; MTCW; SATA 22

Fox, Paula 1923-................ **CLC 2, 8**
See also AAYA 3; CA 73-76; CANR 20,
36; CLR 1; DLB 52; MAICYA; MTCW;
SATA 17, 60

Fox, William Price (Jr.) 1926- ..... **CLC 22**
See also CA 17-20R; CANR 11; DLB 2;
DLBY 81

Foxe, John 1516(?)-1587 .... **LC 14**

Frame, Janet .... **CLC 2, 3, 6, 22, 66**
See also Clutha, Janet Paterson Frame

France, Anatole................... **TCLC 9**
See also Thibault, Jacques Anatole Francois
See also DLB 123

Francis, Claude 19(?)- .... **CLC 50**

Francis, Dick 1920- ...... **CLC 2, 22, 42**
See also AAYA 5; BEST 89:3; CA 5-8R;
CANR 9; CDBLB 1960 to Present;
DLB 87; MTCW

Francis, Robert (Churchill)
1901-1987 .... **CLC 15**
See also CA 1-4R; 123; CANR 1

Frank, Anne(lies Marie)
1929-1945 .... **TCLC 17**
See also CA 113; 133; MTCW; SATA 42;
WLC

Frank, Elizabeth 1945-............ **CLC 39**
See also CA 121; 126

Franklin, Benjamin
See Hasek, Jaroslav (Matej Frantisek)

Franklin, (Stella Maraia Sarah) Miles
1879-1954 .... **TCLC 7**
See also CA 104

Fraser, Antonia (Pakenham)
1932- .... **CLC 32**
See also CA 85-88; MTCW; SATA 32

Fraser, George MacDonald 1925-.... **CLC 7**
See also CA 45-48; CANR 2

Fraser, Sylvia 1935-.............. **CLC 64**
See also CA 45-48; CANR 1, 16

Frayn, Michael 1933-...... **CLC 3, 7, 31, 47**
See also CA 5-8R; CANR 30; DLB 13, 14;
MTCW

Fraze, Candida (Merrill) 1945- ..... **CLC 50**
See also CA 126

Frazer, J(ames) G(eorge)
1854-1941 .... **TCLC 32**
See also CA 118

Frazer, Robert Caine
See Creasey, John

Frazer, Sir James George
See Frazer, J(ames) G(eorge)

Frazier, Ian 1951-................ **CLC 46**
See also CA 130

Frederic, Harold 1856-1898...... **NCLC 10**
See also DLB 12, 23

Frederick, John
See Faust, Frederick (Schiller)

Frederick the Great 1712-1786 ...... **LC 14**

Fredro, Aleksander 1793-1876..... **NCLC 8**

Freeling, Nicolas 1927- .... **CLC 38**
See also CA 49-52; CAAS 12; CANR 1, 17;
DLB 87

Freeman, Douglas Southall
1886-1953 .... **TCLC 11**
See also CA 109; DLB 17

Freeman, Judith 1946-............ **CLC 55**

Freeman, Mary Eleanor Wilkins
1852-1930 .... **TCLC 9; SSC 1**
See also CA 106; DLB 12, 78

Freeman, R(ichard) Austin
1862-1943 .... **TCLC 21**
See also CA 113; DLB 70

French, Marilyn 1929-...... **CLC 10, 18, 60**
See also CA 69-72; CANR 3, 31; MTCW

French, Paul
See Asimov, Isaac

Freneau, Philip Morin 1752-1832.. **NCLC 1**
See also DLB 37, 43

Friedan, Betty (Naomi) 1921- ...... **CLC 74**
See also CA 65-68; CANR 18; MTCW

Friedman, B(ernard) H(arper)
1926- .... **CLC 7**
See also CA 1-4R; CANR 3

Friedman, Bruce Jay 1930- .... **CLC 3, 5, 56**
See also CA 9-12R; CANR 25; DLB 2, 28

Friel, Brian 1929-........... **CLC 5, 42, 59**
See also CA 21-24R; CANR 33; DLB 13;
MTCW

Friis-Baastad, Babbis Ellinor
1921-1970 .... **CLC 12**
See also CA 17-20R; 134; SATA 7

Frisch, Max (Rudolf)
1911-1991 ..... **CLC 3, 9, 14, 18, 32, 44**
See also CA 85-88; 134; CANR 32;
DLB 69, 124; MTCW

Fromentin, Eugene (Samuel Auguste)
1820-1876 .... **NCLC 10**
See also DLB 123

Frost, Frederick
See Faust, Frederick (Schiller)

Frost, Robert (Lee)
1874-1963 ... **CLC 1, 3, 4, 9, 10, 13, 15,
26, 34, 44; PC 1**
See also CA 89-92; CANR 33;
CDALB 1917-1929; DLB 54; DLBD 7;
MTCW; SATA 14; WLC

Froy, Herald
See Waterhouse, Keith (Spencer)

Fry, Christopher 1907-........ **CLC 2, 10, 14**
See also CA 17-20R; CANR 9, 30; DLB 13;
MTCW; SATA 66

Frye, (Herman) Northrop
1912-1991 .... **CLC 24, 70**
See also CA 5-8R; 133; CANR 8, 37;
DLB 67, 68; MTCW

Fuchs, Daniel 1909- .... **CLC 8, 22**
See also CA 81-84; CAAS 5; CANR 40;
DLB 9, 26, 28

Fuchs, Daniel 1934-............... **CLC 34**
See also CA 37-40R; CANR 14

Fuentes, Carlos
1928- ...... **CLC 3, 8, 10, 13, 22, 41, 60**
See also AAYA 4; AITN 2; CA 69-72;
CANR 10, 32; DLB 113; HW; MTCW;
WLC

Fuentes, Gregorio Lopez y
See Lopez y Fuentes, Gregorio

Fugard, (Harold) Athol
1932- .... **CLC 5, 9, 14, 25, 40; DC 3**
See also CA 85-88; CANR 32; MTCW

Fugard, Sheila 1932- .... **CLC 48**
See also CA 125

Fuller, Charles (H. Jr.)
1939- .... **CLC 25; DC 1**
See also BLC 2; BW; CA 108; 112; DLB 38;
MTCW

Fuller, John (Leopold) 1937-........ **CLC 62**
See also CA 21-24R; CANR 9; DLB 40

Fuller, Margaret .... **NCLC 5**
See also Ossoli, Sarah Margaret (Fuller
marchesa d')

Fuller, Roy (Broadbent)
1912-1991 .... **CLC 4, 28**
See also CA 5-8R; 135; CAAS 10; DLB 15,
20

Fulton, Alice 1952-................ **CLC 52**
See also CA 116

Furphy, Joseph 1843-1912........ **TCLC 25**

Fussell, Paul 1924-................ **CLC 74**
See also BEST 90:1; CA 17-20R; CANR 8,
21, 35; MTCW

Futabatci, Shimei 1864-1909 ...... **TCLC 44**

Futrelle, Jacques 1875-1912 ...... **TCLC 19**
See also CA 113

G. B. S.
See Shaw, George Bernard

Gaboriau, Emile 1835-1873 ...... **NCLC 14**

Gadda, Carlo Emilio 1893-1973 .... **CLC 11**
See also CA 89-92

Gaddis, William
1922-........ **CLC 1, 3, 6, 8, 10, 19, 43**
See also CA 17-20R; CANR 21; DLB 2;
MTCW

Gaines, Ernest J(ames)
1933- .... **CLC 3, 11, 18**
See also AITN 1; BLC 2; BW; CA 9-12R;
CANR 6, 24; CDALB 1968-1988; DLB 2,
33; DLBY 80; MTCW

Gaitskill, Mary 1954-............. **CLC 69**
See also CA 128

Galdos, Benito Perez
See Perez Galdos, Benito

Gale, Zona 1874-1938 .... **TCLC 7**
See also CA 105; DLB 9, 78

Galeano, Eduardo (Hughes) 1940-... **CLC 72**
See also CA 29-32R; CANR 13, 32; HW

Galiano, Juan Valera y Alcala
See Valera y Alcala-Galiano, Juan

Gallagher, Tess 1943-......... **CLC 18, 63**
See also CA 106; DLB 120

Gallant, Mavis
1922- .... **CLC 7, 18, 38; SSC 5**
See also CA 69-72; CANR 29; DLB 53;
MTCW

Gallant, Roy A(rthur) 1924- .... **CLC 17**
See also CA 5-8R; CANR 4, 29; CLR 30;
MAICYA; SATA 4, 68

Gallico, Paul (William) 1897-1976 ... **CLC 2**
See also AITN 1; CA 5-8R; 69-72;
CANR 23; DLB 9; MAICYA; SATA 13

Gallup, Ralph
See Whitemore, Hugh (John)

Galsworthy, John 1867-1933 .... **TCLC 1, 45**
See also CA 104; CDBLB 1890-1914;
DLB 10, 34, 98; WLC 2

Galt, John 1779-1839 .... **NCLC 1**
See also DLB 99, 116

Galvin, James 1951-.............. **CLC 38**
See also CA 108; CANR 26

Gamboa, Federico 1864-1939...... **TCLC 36**

Gann, Ernest Kellogg 1910-1991.... **CLC 23**
See also AITN 1; CA 1-4R; 136; CANR 1

Garcia, Christina 1959- .... **CLC 76**

Garcia Lorca, Federico
1898-1936 .. **TCLC 1, 7, 49; DC 2; PC 3**
See also CA 104; 131; DLB 108; HW;
MTCW; WLC

Garcia Marquez, Gabriel (Jose)
1928-... **CLC 2, 3, 8, 10, 15, 27, 47, 55;**
                                    SSC 8
See also Marquez, Gabriel (Jose) Garcia
See also AAYA 3; BEST 89:1, 90:4;
CA 33-36R; CANR 10, 28; DLB 113;
HW; MTCW; WLC

Gard, Janice
See Latham, Jean Lee

Gard, Roger Martin du
See Martin du Gard, Roger

Gardam, Jane 1928-.............. **CLC 43**
See also CA 49-52; CANR 2, 18, 33;
CLR 12; DLB 14; MAICYA; MTCW;
SAAS 9; SATA 28, 39

Gardner, Herb................... **CLC 44**

Gardner, John (Champlin) Jr.
1933-1982 .... **CLC 2, 3, 5, 7, 8, 10, 18,**
                            28, 34; SSC 7
See also AITN 1; CA 65-68; 107;
CANR 33; DLB 2; DLBY 82; MTCW;
SATA 31, 40

Gardner, John (Edmund) 1926-..... **CLC 30**
See also CA 103; CANR 15; MTCW

Gardner, Noel
See Kuttner, Henry

Gardons, S. S.
See Snodgrass, William D(e Witt)

Garfield, Leon 1921-.............. **CLC 12**
See also AAYA 8; CA 17-20R; CANR 38;
CLR 21; MAICYA; SATA 1, 32

Garland, (Hannibal) Hamlin
1860-1940 .... **TCLC 3**
See also CA 104; DLB 12, 71, 78

Garneau, (Hector de) Saint-Denys
1912-1943 .... **TCLC 13**
See also CA 111; DLB 88

Garner, Alan 1934-............... **CLC 17**
See also CA 73-76; CANR 15; CLR 20;
MAICYA; MTCW; SATA 18, 69

Garner, Hugh 1913-1979 .... **CLC 13**
See also CA 69-72; CANR 31; DLB 68

Garnett, David 1892-1981 .... **CLC 3**
See also CA 5-8R; 103; CANR 17; DLB 34

Garos, Stephanie
See Katz, Steve

Garrett, George (Palmer)
1929- .... **CLC 3, 11, 51**
See also CA 1-4R; CAAS 5; CANR 1;
DLB 2, 5, 130; DLBY 83

Garrick, David 1717-1779 .... **LC 15**
See also DLB 84

Garrigue, Jean 1914-1972 .... **CLC 2, 8**
See also CA 5-8R; 37-40R; CANR 20

Garrison, Frederick
See Sinclair, Upton (Beall)

Garth, Will
See Hamilton, Edmond; Kuttner, Henry

Garvey, Marcus (Moziah Jr.)
1887-1940 .... **TCLC 41**
See also BLC 2; BW; CA 120; 124

Gary, Romain .... **CLC 25**
See also Kacew, Romain
See also DLB 83

Gascar, Pierre .... **CLC 11**
See also Fournier, Pierre

Gascoyne, David (Emery) 1916- .... **CLC 45**
See also CA 65-68; CANR 10, 28; DLB 20;
MTCW

Gaskell, Elizabeth Cleghorn
1810-1865 .... **NCLC 5**
See also CDBLB 1832-1890; DLB 21

Gass, William H(oward)
1924- .... **CLC 1, 2, 8, 11, 15, 39**
See also CA 17-20R; CANR 30; DLB 2;
MTCW

Gasset, Jose Ortega y
See Ortega y Gasset, Jose

Gautier, Theophile 1811-1872 ..... **NCLC 1**
See also DLB 119

Gawsworth, John
See Bates, H(erbert) E(rnest)

Gaye, Marvin (Penze) 1939-1984 ... **CLC 26**
See also CA 112

Gebler, Carlo (Ernest) 1954-....... **CLC 39**
See also CA 119; 133

Gee, Maggie (Mary) 1948-........ **CLC 57**
See also CA 130

Gee, Maurice (Gough) 1931-....... **CLC 29**
See also CA 97-100; SATA 46

Gelbart, Larry (Simon) 1923- ... **CLC 21, 61**
See also CA 73-76

Gelber, Jack 1932-........... **CLC 1, 6, 14**
See also CA 1-4R; CANR 2; DLB 7

Gellhorn, Martha Ellis 1908- ... **CLC 14, 60**
See also CA 77-80; DLBY 82

Genet, Jean
1910-1986 ... **CLC 1, 2, 5, 10, 14, 44, 46**
See also CA 13-16R; CANR 18; DLB 72;
DLBY 86; MTCW

Gent, Peter 1942-................ **CLC 29**
See also AITN 1; CA 89-92; DLBY 82

George, Jean Craighead 1919-...... **CLC 35**
See also AAYA 8; CA 5-8R; CANR 25;
CLR 1; DLB 52; MAICYA; SATA 2, 68

George, Stefan (Anton)
1868-1933 .... **TCLC 2, 14**
See also CA 104

Georges, Georges Martin
See Simenon, Georges (Jacques Christian)

Gerhardi, William Alexander
See Gerhardie, William Alexander

Gerhardie, William Alexander
1895-1977 .... **CLC 5**
See also CA 25-28R; 73-76; CANR 18;
DLB 36

Gerstler, Amy 1956-.............. **CLC 70**

Gertler, T. .... **CLC 34**
See also CA 116; 121

Ghalib 1797-1869 .... **NCLC 39**

Ghelderode, Michel de
1898-1962 .... **CLC 6, 11**
See also CA 85-88; CANR 40

Ghiselin, Brewster 1903- .... **CLC 23**
See also CA 13-16R; CAAS 10; CANR 13

Ghose, Zulfikar 1935-............. **CLC 42**
See also CA 65-68

Ghosh, Amitav 1956- .... **CLC 44**

Giacosa, Giuseppe 1847-1906 ...... **TCLC 7**
See also CA 104

Gibb, Lee
See Waterhouse, Keith (Spencer)

Gibbon, Lewis Grassic .... **TCLC 4**
See also Mitchell, James Leslie

Gibbons, Kaye 1960- .... **CLC 50**

Gibran, Kahlil 1883-1931........ **TCLC 1, 9**
See also CA 104

Gibson, William (Ford) 1948- ... **CLC 39, 63**
See also CA 126; 133

Gibson, William 1914-............. **CLC 23**
See also CA 9-12R; CANR 9; DLB 7;
SATA 66

Gide, Andre (Paul Guillaume)
1869-1951 .... TCLC **5, 12, 36**
See also CA 104; 124; DLB 65; MTCW;
WLC

Gifford, Barry (Colby) 1946- .... CLC **34**
See also CA 65-68; CANR 9, 30, 40

Gilbert, W(illiam) S(chwenck)
1836-1911 .... TCLC **3**
See also CA 104; SATA 36

Gilbreth, Frank B. Jr. 1911- .... CLC **17**
See also CA 9-12R; SATA 2

Gilchrist, Ellen 1935- .... CLC **34, 48**
See also CA 113; 116; DLB 130; MTCW

Giles, Molly 1942- .... CLC **39**
See also CA 126

Gill, Patrick
See Creasey, John

Gilliam, Terry (Vance) 1940- .... CLC **21**
See also Monty Python
See also CA 108; 113; CANR 35

Gillian, Jerry
See Gilliam, Terry (Vance)

Gilliatt, Penelope (Ann Douglass)
1932- .... CLC **2, 10, 13, 53**
See also AITN 2; CA 13-16R; DLB 14

Gilman, Charlotte (Anna) Perkins (Stetson)
1860-1935 .... TCLC **9, 37**
See also CA 106

Gilmour, David 1944- .... CLC **35**
See also Pink Floyd
See also CA 138

Gilpin, William 1724-1804 .... NCLC **30**

Gilray, J. D.
See Mencken, H(enry) L(ouis)

Gilroy, Frank D(aniel) 1925- .... CLC **2**
See also CA 81-84; CANR 32; DLB 7

Ginsberg, Allen
1926- ..... CLC **1, 2, 3, 4, 6, 13, 36, 69;**
PC **4**
See also AITN 1; CA 1-4R; CANR 2;
CDALB 1941-1968; DLB 5, 16; MTCW;
WLC 3

Ginzburg, Natalia
1916-1991 .... CLC **5, 11, 54, 70**
See also CA 85-88; 135; CANR 33; MTCW

Giono, Jean 1895-1970 .... CLC **4, 11**
See also CA 45-48; 29-32R; CANR 2, 35;
DLB 72; MTCW

Giovanni, Nikki 1943- ..... CLC **2, 4, 19, 64**
See also AITN 1; BLC 2; BW; CA 29-32R;
CAAS 6; CANR 18; CLR 6; DLB 5, 41;
MAICYA; MTCW; SATA 24

Giovene, Andrea 1904- .... CLC **7**
See also CA 85-88

Gippius, Zinaida (Nikolayevna) 1869-1945
See Hippius, Zinaida
See also CA 106

Giraudoux, (Hippolyte) Jean
1882-1944 .... TCLC **2, 7**
See also CA 104; DLB 65

Gironella, Jose Maria 1917- .... CLC **11**
See also CA 101

Gissing, George (Robert)
1857-1903 .... TCLC **3, 24, 47**
See also CA 105; DLB 18

Giurlani, Aldo
See Palazzeschi, Aldo

Gladkov, Fyodor (Vasilyevich)
1883-1958 .... TCLC **27**

Glanville, Brian (Lester) 1931- ...... CLC **6**
See also CA 5-8R; CAAS 9; CANR 3;
DLB 15; SATA 42

Glasgow, Ellen (Anderson Gholson)
1873(?)-1945 .... TCLC **2, 7**
See also CA 104; DLB 9, 12

Glassco, John 1909-1981 .... CLC **9**
See also CA 13-16R; 102; CANR 15;
DLB 68

Glasscock, Amnesia
See Steinbeck, John (Ernst)

Glasser, Ronald J. 1940(?)- .... CLC **37**

Glassman, Joyce
See Johnson, Joyce

Glendinning, Victoria 1937- .... CLC **50**
See also CA 120; 127

Glissant, Edouard 1928- .... CLC **10, 68**

Gloag, Julian 1930- .... CLC **40**
See also AITN 1; CA 65-68; CANR 10

Gluck, Louise (Elisabeth)
1943- .... CLC **7, 22, 44**
See also Glueck, Louise
See also CA 33-36R; CANR 40; DLB 5

Glueck, Louise .... CLC **7, 22**
See also Gluck, Louise (Elisabeth)
See also DLB 5

Gobineau, Joseph Arthur (Comte) de
1816-1882 .... NCLC **17**
See also DLB 123

Godard, Jean-Luc 1930- .... CLC **20**
See also CA 93-96

Godden, (Margaret) Rumer 1907- ... CLC **53**
See also AAYA 6; CA 5-8R; CANR 4, 27,
36; CLR 20; MAICYA; SAAS 12;
SATA 3, 36

Godoy Alcayaga, Lucila 1889-1957
See Mistral, Gabriela
See also CA 104; 131; HW; MTCW

Godwin, Gail (Kathleen)
1937- .... CLC **5, 8, 22, 31, 69**
See also CA 29-32R; CANR 15; DLB 6;
MTCW

Godwin, William 1756-1836 ...... NCLC **14**
See also CDBLB 1789-1832; DLB 39, 104

Goethe, Johann Wolfgang von
1749-1832 .... NCLC **4, 22, 34**; PC **5**
See also DLB 94; WLC 3

Gogarty, Oliver St. John
1878-1957 .... TCLC **15**
See also CA 109; DLB 15, 19

Gogol, Nikolai (Vasilyevich)
1809-1852 ..... NCLC **5, 15, 31**; DC **1;**
SSC **4**
See also WLC

Gold, Herbert 1924- .... CLC **4, 7, 14, 42**
See also CA 9-12R; CANR 17; DLB 2;
DLBY 81

Goldbarth, Albert 1948- .... CLC **5, 38**
See also CA 53-56; CANR 6, 40; DLB 120

Goldberg, Anatol 1910-1982 .... CLC **34**
See also CA 131; 117

Goldemberg, Isaac 1945- .... CLC **52**
See also CA 69-72; CAAS 12; CANR 11,
32; HW

Golden Silver
See Storm, Hyemeyohsts

Golding, William (Gerald)
1911- ..... CLC **1, 2, 3, 8, 10, 17, 27, 58**
See also AAYA 5; CA 5-8R; CANR 13, 33;
CDBLB 1945-1960; DLB 15, 100;
MTCW; WLC

Goldman, Emma 1869-1940 ...... TCLC **13**
See also CA 110

Goldman, Francisco 1955- .... CLC **76**

Goldman, William (W.) 1931- .... CLC **1, 48**
See also CA 9-12R; CANR 29; DLB 44

Goldmann, Lucien 1913-1970 ...... CLC **24**
See also CA 25-28; CAP 2

Goldoni, Carlo 1707-1793 .... LC **4**

Goldsberry, Steven 1949- .... CLC **34**
See also CA 131

Goldsmith, Oliver 1728-1774 .... LC **2**
See also CDBLB 1660-1789; DLB 39, 89,
104, 109; SATA 26; WLC

Goldsmith, Peter
See Priestley, J(ohn) B(oynton)

Gombrowicz, Witold
1904-1969 .... CLC **4, 7, 11, 49**
See also CA 19-20; 25-28R; CAP 2

Gomez de la Serna, Ramon
1888-1963 .... CLC **9**
See also CA 116; HW

Goncharov, Ivan Alexandrovich
1812-1891 .... NCLC **1**

Goncourt, Edmond (Louis Antoine Huot) de
1822-1896 .... NCLC **7**
See also DLB 123

Goncourt, Jules (Alfred Huot) de
1830-1870 .... NCLC **7**
See also DLB 123

Gontier, Fernande 19(?)- .... CLC **50**

Goodman, Paul 1911-1972 .... CLC **1, 2, 4, 7**
See also CA 19-20; 37-40R; CANR 34;
CAP 2; DLB 130; MTCW

Gordimer, Nadine
1923- .... CLC **3, 5, 7, 10, 18, 33, 51, 70**
See also CA 5-8R; CANR 3, 28; MTCW

Gordon, Adam Lindsay
1833-1870 .... NCLC **21**

Gordon, Caroline
1895-1981 .... CLC **6, 13, 29**
See also CA 11-12; 103; CANR 36; CAP 1;
DLB 4, 9, 102; DLBY 81; MTCW

Gordon, Charles William 1860-1937
See Connor, Ralph
See also CA 109

Gordon, Mary (Catherine)
1949- .... CLC **13, 22**
See also CA 102; DLB 6; DLBY 81;
MTCW

Gordon, Sol 1923- .... CLC **26**
See also CA 53-56; CANR 4; SATA 11

Gordone, Charles 1925- .... **CLC 1, 4**
See also BW; CA 93-96; DLB 7; MTCW

Gorenko, Anna Andreevna
See Akhmatova, Anna

Gorky, Maxim................... **TCLC 8**
See also Peshkov, Alexei Maximovich
See also WLC

Goryan, Sirak
See Saroyan, William

Gosse, Edmund (William)
1849-1928 .... **TCLC 28**
See also CA 117; DLB 57

Gotlieb, Phyllis Fay (Bloom)
1926- .... **CLC 18**
See also CA 13-16R; CANR 7; DLB 88

Gottesman, S. D.
See Kornbluth, C(yril) M.; Pohl, Frederik

Gottfried von Strassburg
fl. c. 1210- .... **CMLC 10**

Gottschalk, Laura Riding
See Jackson, Laura (Riding)

Gould, Lois .... **CLC 4, 10**
See also CA 77-80; CANR 29; MTCW

Gourmont, Remy de 1858-1915.... **TCLC 17**
See also CA 109

Govier, Katherine 1948-.......... **CLC 51**
See also CA 101; CANR 18, 40

Goyen, (Charles) William
1915-1983 .... **CLC 5, 8, 14, 40**
See also AITN 2; CA 5-8R; 110; CANR 6;
DLB 2; DLBY 83

Goytisolo, Juan 1931- .... **CLC 5, 10, 23**
See also CA 85-88; CANR 32; HW; MTCW

Gozzi, (Conte) Carlo 1720-1806 .. **NCLC 23**

Grabbe, Christian Dietrich
1801-1836 .... **NCLC 2**

Grace, Patricia 1937-............. **CLC 56**

Gracian y Morales, Baltasar
1601-1658 .... **LC 15**

Gracq, Julien................. **CLC 11, 48**
See also Poirier, Louis
See also DLB 83

Grade, Chaim 1910-1982 .... **CLC 10**
See also CA 93-96; 107

Graduate of Oxford, A
See Ruskin, John

Graham, John
See Phillips, David Graham

Graham, Jorie 1951-............. **CLC 48**
See also CA 111; DLB 120

Graham, R(obert) B(ontine) Cunninghame
See Cunninghame Graham, R(obert)
B(ontine)
See also DLB 98

Graham, Robert
See Haldeman, Joe (William)

Graham, Tom
See Lewis, (Harry) Sinclair

Graham, W(illiam) S(ydney)
1918-1986 .... **CLC 29**
See also CA 73-76; 118; DLB 20

Graham, Winston (Mawdsley)
1910- .... **CLC 23**
See also CA 49-52; CANR 2, 22; DLB 77

Grant, Skeeter
See Spiegelman, Art

Granville-Barker, Harley
1877-1946 .... **TCLC 2**
See also Barker, Harley Granville
See also CA 104

Grass, Guenter (Wilhelm)
1927- .. **CLC 1, 2, 4, 6, 11, 15, 22, 32, 49**
See also CA 13-16R; CANR 20; DLB 75,
124; MTCW; WLC

Gratton, Thomas
See Hulme, T(homas) E(rnest)

Grau, Shirley Ann 1929- .... **CLC 4, 9**
See also CA 89-92; CANR 22; DLB 2;
MTCW

Gravel, Fern
See Hall, James Norman

Graver, Elizabeth 1964-........... **CLC 70**
See also CA 135

Graves, Richard Perceval 1945- .... **CLC 44**
See also CA 65-68; CANR 9, 26

Graves, Robert (von Ranke)
1895-1985 ..... **CLC 1, 2, 6, 11, 39, 44,
45; PC 6**
See also CA 5-8R; 117; CANR 5, 36;
CDBLB 1914-1945; DLB 20, 100;
DLBY 85; MTCW; SATA 45

Gray, Alasdair (James) 1934- ...... **CLC 41**
See also CA 126; MTCW

Gray, Amlin 1946- .... **CLC 29**
See also CA 138

Gray, Francine du Plessix 1930-.... **CLC 22**
See also BEST 90:3; CA 61-64; CAAS 2;
CANR 11, 33; MTCW

Gray, John (Henry) 1866-1934 .... **TCLC 19**
See also CA 119

Gray, Simon (James Holliday)
1936- .... **CLC 9, 14, 36**
See also AITN 1; CA 21-24R; CAAS 3;
CANR 32; DLB 13; MTCW

Gray, Spalding 1941-............. **CLC 49**
See also CA 128

Gray, Thomas 1716-1771....... **LC 4; PC 2**
See also CDBLB 1660-1789; DLB 109;
WLC

Grayson, David
See Baker, Ray Stannard

Grayson, Richard (A.) 1951- .... **CLC 38**
See also CA 85-88; CANR 14, 31

Greeley, Andrew M(oran) 1928- .... **CLC 28**
See also CA 5-8R; CAAS 7; CANR 7;
MTCW

Green, Brian
See Card, Orson Scott

Green, Hannah .... **CLC 3**
See also CA 73-76

Green, Hannah
See Greenberg, Joanne (Goldenberg)

Green, Henry .... **CLC 2, 13**
See also Yorke, Henry Vincent
See also DLB 15

Green, Julian (Hartridge)
1900- .... **CLC 3, 11**
See also CA 21-24R; CANR 33; DLB 4, 72;
MTCW

Green, Julien 1900-
See Green, Julian (Hartridge)

Green, Paul (Eliot) 1894-1981...... **CLC 25**
See also AITN 1; CA 5-8R; 103; CANR 3;
DLB 7, 9; DLBY 81

Greenberg, Ivan 1908-1973
See Rahv, Philip
See also CA 85-88

Greenberg, Joanne (Goldenberg)
1932- .... **CLC 7, 30**
See also CA 5-8R; CANR 14, 32; SATA 25

Greenberg, Richard 1959(?)- .... **CLC 57**
See also CA 138

Greene, Bette 1934- .... **CLC 30**
See also AAYA 7, CA 53-56, CANR 4;
CLR 2; MAICYA; SAAS 16; SATA 8

Greene, Gael .... **CLC 8**
See also CA 13-16R; CANR 10

Greene, Graham (Henry)
1904-1991 ... **CLC 1, 3, 6, 9, 14, 18, 27,
37, 70, 72**
See also AITN 2; CA 13-16R; 133;
CANR 35; CDBLB 1945-1960; DLB 13,
15, 77, 100; DLBY 91; MTCW;
SATA 20; WLC

Greer, Richard
See Silverberg, Robert

Greer, Richard
See Silverberg, Robert

Gregor, Arthur 1923-.............. **CLC 9**
See also CA 25-28R; CAAS 10; CANR 11;
SATA 36

Gregor, Lee
See Pohl, Frederik

Gregory, Isabella Augusta (Persse)
1852-1932 .... **TCLC 1**
See also CA 104; DLB 10

Gregory, J. Dennis
See Williams, John A(lfred)

Grendon, Stephen
See Derleth, August (William)

Grenville, Kate 1950-............. **CLC 61**
See also CA 118

Grenville, Pelham
See Wodehouse, P(elham) G(renville)

Greve, Felix Paul (Berthold Friedrich)
1879-1948
See Grove, Frederick Philip
See also CA 104

Grey, Zane 1872-1939 .... **TCLC 6**
See also CA 104; 132; DLB 9; MTCW

Grieg, (Johan) Nordahl (Brun)
1902-1943 .... **TCLC 10**
See also CA 107

Grieve, C(hristopher) M(urray)
1892-1978 .... **CLC 11, 19**
See also MacDiarmid, Hugh
See also CA 5-8R; 85-88; CANR 33;
MTCW

Griffin, Gerald 1803-1840 .... **NCLC 7**

Griffin, John Howard   1920-1980. . . . **CLC 68**
   See also AITN 1; CA 1-4R; 101; CANR 2

Griffin, Peter . . . . **CLC 39**

Griffiths, Trevor   1935- . . . . **CLC 13, 52**
   See also CA 97-100; DLB 13

Grigson, Geoffrey (Edward Harvey)
   1905-1985 . . . . **CLC 7, 39**
   See also CA 25-28R; 118; CANR 20, 33;
   DLB 27; MTCW

Grillparzer, Franz   1791-1872. . . . . . **NCLC 1**

Grimble, Reverend Charles James
   See Eliot, T(homas) S(tearns)

Grimke, Charlotte L(ottie) Forten
   1837(?)-1914
   See Forten, Charlotte L.
   See also BW; CA 117; 124

Grimm, Jacob Ludwig Karl
   1785-1863 . . . . **NCLC 3**
   See also DLB 90; MAICYA; SATA 22

Grimm, Wilhelm Karl   1786-1859 . . **NCLC 3**
   See also DLB 90; MAICYA; SATA 22

Grimmelshausen, Johann Jakob Christoffel
   von   1621-1676 . . . . **LC 6**

Grindel, Eugene   1895-1952
   See Eluard, Paul
   See also CA 104

Grossman, David . . . . **CLC 67**
   See also CA 138

Grossman, Vasily (Semenovich)
   1905-1964 . . . . **CLC 41**
   See also CA 124; 130; MTCW

Grove, Frederick Philip . . . . **TCLC 4**
   See also Greve, Felix Paul (Berthold
   Friedrich)
   See also DLB 92

Grubb
   See Crumb, R(obert)

Grumbach, Doris (Isaac)
   1918- . . . . **CLC 13, 22, 64**
   See also CA 5-8R; CAAS 2; CANR 9

Grundtvig, Nicolai Frederik Severin
   1783-1872 . . . . **NCLC 1**

Grunge
   See Crumb, R(obert)

Grunwald, Lisa   1959- . . . . **CLC 44**
   See also CA 120

Guare, John   1938- . . . . **CLC 8, 14, 29, 67**
   See also CA 73-76; CANR 21; DLB 7;
   MTCW

Gudjonsson, Halldor Kiljan   1902-
   See Laxness, Halldor
   See also CA 103

Guenter, Erich
   See Eich, Guenter

Guest, Barbara   1920- . . . . **CLC 34**
   See also CA 25-28R; CANR 11; DLB 5

Guest, Judith (Ann)   1936- . . . . **CLC 8, 30**
   See also AAYA 7; CA 77-80; CANR 15;
   MTCW

Guild, Nicholas M.   1944- . . . . **CLC 33**
   See also CA 93-96

Guillemin, Jacques
   See Sartre, Jean-Paul

Guillen, Jorge   1893-1984 . . . . **CLC 11**
   See also CA 89-92; 112; DLB 108; HW

Guillen (y Batista), Nicolas (Cristobal)
   1902-1989 . . . . **CLC 48**
   See also BLC 2; BW; CA 116; 125; 129;
   HW

Guillevic, (Eugene)   1907- . . . . **CLC 33**
   See also CA 93-96

Guillois
   See Desnos, Robert

Guiney, Louise Imogen
   1861-1920 . . . . **TCLC 41**
   See also DLB 54

Guiraldes, Ricardo (Guillermo)
   1886-1927 . . . . **TCLC 39**
   See also CA 131; HW; MTCW

Gunn, Bill . . . . **CLC 5**
   See also Gunn, William Harrison
   See also DLB 38

Gunn, Thom(son William)
   1929- . . . . **CLC 3, 6, 18, 32**
   See also CA 17-20R; CANR 9, 33;
   CDBLB 1960 to Present; DLB 27;
   MTCW

Gunn, William Harrison   1934(?)-1989
   See Gunn, Bill
   See also AITN 1; BW; CA 13-16R; 128;
   CANR 12, 25

Gunnars, Kristjana   1948- . . . . **CLC 69**
   See also CA 113; DLB 60

Gurganus, Allan   1947- . . . . **CLC 70**
   See also BEST 90:1; CA 135

Gurney, A(lbert) R(amsdell) Jr.
   1930- . . . . **CLC 32, 50, 54**
   See also CA 77-80; CANR 32

Gurney, Ivor (Bertie)   1890-1937 . . . **TCLC 33**

Gurney, Peter
   See Gurney, A(lbert) R(amsdell) Jr.

Gustafson, Ralph (Barker)   1909- . . . . **CLC 36**
   See also CA 21-24R; CANR 8; DLB 88

Gut, Gom
   See Simenon, Georges (Jacques Christian)

Guthrie, A(lfred) B(ertram) Jr.
   1901-1991 . . . . **CLC 23**
   See also CA 57-60; 134; CANR 24; DLB 6;
   SATA 62; SATO 67

Guthrie, Isobel
   See Grieve, C(hristopher) M(urray)

Guthrie, Woodrow Wilson   1912-1967
   See Guthrie, Woody
   See also CA 113; 93-96

Guthrie, Woody . . . . **CLC 35**
   See also Guthrie, Woodrow Wilson

Guy, Rosa (Cuthbert)   1928- . . . . **CLC 26**
   See also AAYA 4; BW; CA 17-20R;
   CANR 14, 34; CLR 13; DLB 33;
   MAICYA; SATA 14, 62

Gwendolyn
   See Bennett, (Enoch) Arnold

H. D. . . . . **CLC 3, 8, 14, 31, 34, 73; PC 5**
   See also Doolittle, Hilda

Haavikko, Paavo Juhani
   1931- . . . . **CLC 18, 34**
   See also CA 106

Habbema, Koos
   See Heijermans, Herman

Hacker, Marilyn   1942- . . . . **CLC 5, 9, 23, 72**
   See also CA 77-80; DLB 120

Haggard, H(enry) Rider
   1856-1925 . . . . **TCLC 11**
   See also CA 108; DLB 70; SATA 16

Haig, Fenil
   See Ford, Ford Madox

Haig-Brown, Roderick (Langmere)
   1908-1976 . . . . **CLC 21**
   See also CA 5-8R; 69-72; CANR 4, 38;
   DLB 88; MAICYA; SATA 12

Hailey, Arthur   1920- . . . . **CLC 5**
   See also AITN 2; BEST 90:3; CA 1-4R;
   CANR 2, 36; DLB 88; DLBY 82; MTCW

Hailey, Elizabeth Forsythe   1938- . . . **CLC 40**
   See also CA 93-96; CAAS 1; CANR 15

Haines, John (Meade)   1924- . . . . **CLC 58**
   See also CA 17-20R; CANR 13, 34; DLB 5

Haldeman, Joe (William)   1943- . . . . . **CLC 61**
   See also CA 53-56; CANR 6; DLB 8

Haley, Alex(ander Murray Palmer)
   1921-1992 . . . . **CLC 8, 12, 76**
   See also BLC 2; BW; CA 77-80; 136;
   DLB 38; MTCW

Haliburton, Thomas Chandler
   1796-1865 . . . . **NCLC 15**
   See also DLB 11, 99

Hall, Donald (Andrew Jr.)
   1928- . . . . **CLC 1, 13, 37, 59**
   See also CA 5-8R; CAAS 7; CANR 2;
   DLB 5; SATA 23

Hall, Frederic Sauser
   See Sauser-Hall, Frederic

Hall, James
   See Kuttner, Henry

Hall, James Norman   1887-1951 . . . **TCLC 23**
   See also CA 123; SATA 21

Hall, (Marguerite) Radclyffe
   1886(?)-1943 . . . . **TCLC 12**
   See also CA 110

Hall, Rodney   1935- . . . . **CLC 51**
   See also CA 109

Halliday, Michael
   See Creasey, John

Halpern, Daniel   1945- . . . . **CLC 14**
   See also CA 33-36R

Hamburger, Michael (Peter Leopold)
   1924- . . . . **CLC 5, 14**
   See also CA 5-8R; CAAS 4; CANR 2;
   DLB 27

Hamill, Pete   1935- . . . . **CLC 10**
   See also CA 25-28R; CANR 18

Hamilton, Clive
   See Lewis, C(live) S(taples)

Hamilton, Edmond   1904-1977 . . . . . . **CLC 1**
   See also CA 1-4R; CANR 3; DLB 8

Hamilton, Eugene (Jacob) Lee
   See Lee-Hamilton, Eugene (Jacob)

Hamilton, Franklin
   See Silverberg, Robert

Hamilton, Gail
   See Corcoran, Barbara

Hamilton, Mollie
See Kaye, M(ary) M(argaret)

Hamilton, (Anthony Walter) Patrick
1904-1962 . . . . CLC 51
See also CA 113; DLB 10

Hamilton, Virginia 1936- . . . . CLC 26
See also AAYA 2; BW; CA 25-28R;
CANR 20, 37; CLR 1, 11; DLB 33, 52;
MAICYA; MTCW; SATA 4, 56

Hammett, (Samuel) Dashiell
1894-1961 . . . . CLC 3, 5, 10, 19, 47
See also AITN 1; CA 81-84;
CDALB 1929-1941; DLBD 6; MTCW

Hammon, Jupiter 1711(?)-1800(?) . . NCLC 5
See also BLC 2; DLB 31, 50

Hammond, Keith
See Kuttner, Henry

Hamner, Earl (Henry) Jr. 1923- . . . . CLC 12
See also AITN 2; CA 73-76; DLB 6

Hampton, Christopher (James)
1946- . . . . CLC 4
See also CA 25-28R; DLB 13; MTCW

Hamsun, Knut 1859-1952 . . . TCLC 2, 14, 49
See also Pedersen, Knut

Handke, Peter 1942- . . CLC 5, 8, 10, 15, 38
See also CA 77-80; CANR 33; DLB 85,
124; MTCW

Hanley, James 1901-1985 . . . CLC 3, 5, 8, 13
See also CA 73-76; 117; CANR 36; MTCW

Hannah, Barry 1942- . . . . CLC 23, 38
See also CA 108; 110; DLB 6; MTCW

Hannon, Ezra
See Hunter, Evan

Hansberry, Lorraine (Vivian)
1930-1965 . . . . CLC 17, 62; DC 2
See also BLC 2; BW; CA 109; 25-28R;
CABS 3; CDALB 1941-1968; DLB 7, 38;
MTCW

Hansen, Joseph 1923- . . . . CLC 38
See also CA 29-32R; CAAS 17; CANR 16

Hansen, Martin A. 1909-1955 . . . . . TCLC 32

Hanson, Kenneth O(stlin) 1922- . . . . CLC 13
See also CA 53-56; CANR 7

Hardwick, Elizabeth 1916- . . . . CLC 13
See also CA 5-8R; CANR 3, 32; DLB 6;
MTCW

Hardy, Thomas
1840-1928 . . . . . TCLC 4, 10, 18, 32, 48;
SSC 2
See also CA 104; 123; CDBLB 1890-1914;
DLB 18, 19; MTCW; WLC

Hare, David 1947- . . . . CLC 29, 58
See also CA 97-100; CANR 39; DLB 13;
MTCW

Harford, Henry
See Hudson, W(illiam) H(enry)

Hargrave, Leonie
See Disch, Thomas M(ichael)

Harlan, Louis R(udolph) 1922- . . . . . CLC 34
See also CA 21-24R; CANR 25

Harling, Robert 1951(?)- . . . . CLC 53

Harmon, William (Ruth) 1938- . . . . . CLC 38
See also CA 33-36R; CANR 14, 32, 35;
SATA 65

Harper, F. E. W.
See Harper, Frances Ellen Watkins

Harper, Frances E. W.
See Harper, Frances Ellen Watkins

Harper, Frances E. Watkins
See Harper, Frances Ellen Watkins

Harper, Frances Ellen
See Harper, Frances Ellen Watkins

Harper, Frances Ellen Watkins
1825-1911 . . . . TCLC 14
See also BLC 2; BW; CA 111; 125; DLB 50

Harper, Michael S(teven) 1938- . . CLC 7, 22
See also BW; CA 33-36R; CANR 24;
DLB 41

Harper, Mrs. F. E. W.
See Harper, Frances Ellen Watkins

Harris, Christie (Lucy) Irwin
1907- . . . . CLC 12
See also CA 5-8R; CANR 6; DLB 88;
MAICYA; SAAS 10; SATA 6

Harris, Frank 1856(?)-1931 . . . . TCLC 24
See also CA 109

Harris, George Washington
1814-1869 . . . . NCLC 23
See also DLB 3, 11

Harris, Joel Chandler 1848-1908 . . . TCLC 2
See also CA 104; 137; DLB 11, 23, 42, 78,
91; MAICYA; YABC 1

Harris, John (Wyndham Parkes Lucas)
Beynon 1903-1969 . . . . CLC 19
See also CA 102; 89-92

Harris, MacDonald
See Heiney, Donald (William)

Harris, Mark 1922- . . . . CLC 19
See also CA 5-8R; CAAS 3; CANR 2;
DLB 2; DLBY 80

Harris, (Theodore) Wilson 1921- . . . . CLC 25
See also BW; CA 65-68; CAAS 16;
CANR 11, 27; DLB 117; MTCW

Harrison, Elizabeth Cavanna 1909-
See Cavanna, Betty
See also CA 9-12R; CANR 6, 27

Harrison, Harry (Max) 1925- . . . . . . CLC 42
See also CA 1-4R; CANR 5, 21; DLB 8;
SATA 4

Harrison, James (Thomas) 1937-
See Harrison, Jim
See also CA 13-16R; CANR 8

Harrison, Jim . . . . CLC 6, 14, 33, 66
See also Harrison, James (Thomas)
See also DLBY 82

Harrison, Kathryn 1961- . . . . CLC 70

Harrison, Tony 1937- . . . . CLC 43
See also CA 65-68; DLB 40; MTCW

Harriss, Will(ard Irvin) 1922- . . . . . . CLC 34
See also CA 111

Harson, Sley
See Ellison, Harlan

Hart, Ellis
See Ellison, Harlan

Hart, Josephine 1942(?)- . . . . CLC 70
See also CA 138

Hart, Moss 1904-1961 . . . . CLC 66
See also CA 109; 89-92; DLB 7

Harte, (Francis) Bret(t)
1836(?)-1902 . . . . TCLC 1, 25; SSC 8
See also CA 104; CDALB 1865-1917;
DLB 12, 64, 74, 79; SATA 26; WLC

Hartley, L(eslie) P(oles)
1895-1972 . . . . CLC 2, 22
See also CA 45-48; 37-40R; CANR 33;
DLB 15; MTCW

Hartman, Geoffrey H. 1929- . . . . CLC 27
See also CA 117; 125; DLB 67

Haruf, Kent 19(?)- . . . . CLC 34

Harwood, Ronald 1934- . . . . CLC 32
See also CA 1-4R; CANR 4; DLB 13

Hasek, Jaroslav (Matej Frantisek)
1883-1923 . . . . TCLC 4
See also CA 104; 129; MTCW

Hass, Robert 1941- . . . . CLC 18, 39
See also CA 111; CANR 30; DLB 105

Hastings, Hudson
See Kuttner, Henry

Hastings, Selina . . . . CLC 44

Hatteras, Amelia
See Mencken, H(enry) L(ouis)

Hatteras, Owen . . . . TCLC 18
See also Mencken, H(enry) L(ouis); Nathan,
George Jean

Hauptmann, Gerhart (Johann Robert)
1862-1946 . . . . TCLC 4
See also CA 104; DLB 66, 118

Havel, Vaclav 1936- . . . . CLC 25, 58, 65
See also CA 104; CANR 36; MTCW

Haviaras, Stratis . . . . CLC 33
See also Chaviaras, Strates

Hawes, Stephen 1475(?)-1523(?) . . . . . LC 17

Hawkes, John (Clendennin Burne Jr.)
1925- . . . . . . CLC 1, 2, 3, 4, 7, 9, 14, 15,
27, 49
See also CA 1-4R; CANR 2; DLB 2, 7;
DLBY 80; MTCW

Hawking, S. W.
See Hawking, Stephen W(illiam)

Hawking, Stephen W(illiam)
1942- . . . . CLC 63
See also BEST 89:1; CA 126; 129

Hawthorne, Julian 1846-1934 . . . . . TCLC 25

Hawthorne, Nathaniel
1804-1864 . . . . NCLC 39; SSC 3
See also CDALB 1640-1865; DLB 1, 74;
WLC; YABC 2

Haxton, Josephine Ayres 1921- . . . . CLC 73
See also CA 115

Hayaseca y Eizaguirre, Jorge
See Echegaray (y Eizaguirre), Jose (Maria
Waldo)

Hayashi Fumiko 1904-1951 . . . . TCLC 27

Haycraft, Anna
See Ellis, Alice Thomas
See also CA 122

Hayden, Robert E(arl)
1913-1980 . . . . . . CLC 5, 9, 14, 37; PC 6
See also BLC 2; BW; CA 69-72; 97-100;
CABS 2; CANR 24; CDALB 1941-1968;
DLB 5, 76; MTCW; SATA 19, 26

Jensen, Laura (Linnea) 1948- . . . . . . CLC 37
See also CA 103

Jerome, Jerome K(lapka)
1859-1927 . . . . TCLC 23
See also CA 119; DLB 10, 34

Jerrold, Douglas William
1803-1857 . . . . NCLC 2

Jewett, (Theodora) Sarah Orne
1849-1909 . . . . TCLC 1, 22; SSC 6
See also CA 108; 127; DLB 12, 74;
SATA 15

Jewsbury, Geraldine (Endsor)
1812-1880 . . . . NCLC 22
See also DLB 21

Jhabvala, Ruth Prawer
1927- . . . . CLC 4, 8, 29
See also CA 1-4R; CANR 2, 29; MTCW

Jiles, Paulette 1943- . . . . CLC 13, 58
See also CA 101

Jimenez (Mantecon), Juan Ramon
1881-1958 . . . . TCLC 4
See also CA 104; 131; HW; MTCW

Jimenez, Ramon
See Jimenez (Mantecon), Juan Ramon

Jimenez Mantecon, Juan
See Jimenez (Mantecon), Juan Ramon

Joel, Billy . . . . CLC 26
See also Joel, William Martin

Joel, William Martin 1949-
See Joel, Billy
See also CA 108

John of the Cross, St. 1542-1591 . . . . LC 18

Johnson, B(ryan) S(tanley William)
1933-1973 . . . . CLC 6, 9
See also CA 9-12R; 53-56; CANR 9;
DLB 14, 40

Johnson, Charles (Richard)
1948- . . . . CLC 7, 51, 65
See also BLC 2; BW; CA 116; DLB 33

Johnson, Denis 1949- . . . . CLC 52
See also CA 117; 121; DLB 120

Johnson, Diane (Lain)
1934- . . . . CLC 5, 13, 48
See also CA 41-44R; CANR 17, 40;
DLBY 80; MTCW

Johnson, Eyvind (Olof Verner)
1900-1976 . . . . CLC 14
See also CA 73-76; 69-72; CANR 34

Johnson, J. R.
See James, C(yril) L(ionel) R(obert)

Johnson, James Weldon
1871-1938 . . . . TCLC 3, 19
See also BLC 2; BW; CA 104; 125;
CDALB 1917-1929; DLB 51; MTCW;
SATA 31

Johnson, Joyce 1935- . . . . CLC 58
See also CA 125; 129

Johnson, Lionel (Pigot)
1867-1902 . . . . TCLC 19
See also CA 117; DLB 19

Johnson, Mel
See Malzberg, Barry N(athaniel)

Johnson, Pamela Hansford
1912-1981 . . . . CLC 1, 7, 27
See also CA 1-4R; 104; CANR 2, 28;
DLB 15; MTCW

Johnson, Samuel 1709-1784 . . . . LC 15
See also CDBLB 1660-1789; DLB 39, 95,
104; WLC

Johnson, Uwe
1934-1984 . . . . CLC 5, 10, 15, 40
See also CA 1-4R; 112; CANR 1, 39;
DLB 75; MTCW

Johnston, George (Benson) 1913- . . . CLC 51
See also CA 1-4R; CANR 5, 20; DLB 88

Johnston, Jennifer 1930- . . . . CLC 7
See also CA 85-88; DLB 14

Jolley, (Monica) Elizabeth 1923- . . . CLC 46
See also CA 127; CAAS 13

Jones, Arthur Llewellyn 1863-1947
See Machen, Arthur
See also CA 104

Jones, D(ouglas) G(ordon) 1929- . . . . CLC 10
See also CA 29-32R; CANR 13; DLB 53

Jones, David (Michael)
1895-1974 . . . . CLC 2, 4, 7, 13, 42
See also CA 9-12R; 53-56; CANR 28;
CDBLB 1945-1960; DLB 20, 100; MTCW

Jones, David Robert 1947-
See Bowie, David
See also CA 103

Jones, Diana Wynne 1934- . . . . CLC 26
See also CA 49-52; CANR 4, 26; CLR 23;
MAICYA; SAAS 7; SATA 9, 70

Jones, Edward P. 1951- . . . . CLC 76

Jones, Gayl 1949- . . . . CLC 6, 9
See also BLC 2; BW; CA 77-80; CANR 27;
DLB 33; MTCW

Jones, James 1921-1977 . . . . CLC 1, 3, 10, 39
See also AITN 1, 2; CA 1-4R; 69-72;
CANR 6; DLB 2; MTCW

Jones, John J.
See Lovecraft, H(oward) P(hillips)

Jones, LeRoi . . . . CLC 1, 2, 3, 5, 10, 14
See also Baraka, Amiri

Jones, Louis B. . . . . CLC 65

Jones, Madison (Percy Jr.) 1925- . . . . CLC 4
See also CA 13-16R; CAAS 11; CANR 7

Jones, Mervyn 1922- . . . . CLC 10, 52
See also CA 45-48; CAAS 5; CANR 1;
MTCW

Jones, Mick 1956(?)- . . . . CLC 30
See also Clash, The

Jones, Nettie (Pearl) 1941- . . . . CLC 34
See also CA 137

Jones, Preston 1936-1979 . . . . CLC 10
See also CA 73-76; 89-92; DLB 7

Jones, Robert F(rancis) 1934- . . . . CLC 7
See also CA 49-52; CANR 2

Jones, Rod 1953- . . . . CLC 50
See also CA 128

Jones, Terence Graham Parry
1942- . . . . CLC 21
See also Jones, Terry; Monty Python
See also CA 112; 116; CANR 35; SATA 51

Jones, Terry
See Jones, Terence Graham Parry
See also SATA 67

Jong, Erica 1942- . . . . CLC 4, 6, 8, 18
See also AITN 1; BEST 90:2; CA 73-76;
CANR 26; DLB 2, 5, 28; MTCW

Jonson, Ben(jamin) 1572(?)-1637 . . . . . . LC 6
See also CDBLB Before 1660; DLB 62, 121;
WLC

Jordan, June 1936- . . . . CLC 5, 11, 23
See also AAYA 2; BW; CA 33-36R;
CANR 25; CLR 10; DLB 38; MAICYA;
MTCW; SATA 4

Jordan, Pat(rick M.) 1941- . . . . CLC 37
See also CA 33-36R

Jorgensen, Ivar
See Ellison, Harlan

Jorgenson, Ivar
See Silverberg, Robert

Josipovici, Gabriel 1940- . . . . CLC 6, 43
See also CA 37-40R; CAAS 8; DLB 14

Joubert, Joseph 1754-1824 . . . . NCLC 9

Jouve, Pierre Jean 1887-1976 . . . . . . CLC 47
See also CA 65-68

Joyce, James (Augustine Aloysius)
1882-1941 . . . . TCLC 3, 8, 16, 35; SSC 3
See also CA 104; 126; CDBLB 1914-1945;
DLB 10, 19, 36; MTCW; WLC

Jozsef, Attila 1905-1937 . . . . TCLC 22
See also CA 116

Juana Ines de la Cruz 1651(?)-1695 . . . LC 5

Judd, Cyril
See Kornbluth, C(yril) M.; Pohl, Frederik

Julian of Norwich 1342(?)-1416(?) . . . . LC 6

Just, Ward (Swift) 1935- . . . . CLC 4, 27
See also CA 25-28R; CANR 32

Justice, Donald (Rodney) 1925- . . CLC 6, 19
See also CA 5-8R; CANR 26; DLBY 83

Juvenal c. 55-c. 127 . . . . CMLC 8

Juvenis
See Bourne, Randolph S(illiman)

Kacew, Romain 1914-1980
See Gary, Romain
See also CA 108; 102

Kadare, Ismail 1936- . . . . CLC 52

Kadohata, Cynthia . . . . CLC 59

Kafka, Franz
1883-1924 . . . . . . TCLC 2, 6, 13, 29, 47;
SSC 5
See also CA 105; 126; DLB 81; MTCW;
WLC

Kahn, Roger 1927- . . . . CLC 30
See also CA 25-28R; SATA 37

Kain, Saul
See Sassoon, Siegfried (Lorraine)

Kaiser, Georg 1878-1945 . . . . TCLC 9
See also CA 106; DLB 124

Kaletski, Alexander 1946- . . . . CLC 39
See also CA 118

Kalidasa fl. c. 400- . . . . CMLC 9

Kallman, Chester (Simon)
1921-1975 . . . . CLC 2
See also CA 45-48; 53-56; CANR 3

Krasicki, Ignacy 1735-1801 . . . . **NCLC 8**

Krasinski, Zygmunt 1812-1859 . . . . **NCLC 4**

Kraus, Karl 1874-1936 . . . . **TCLC 5**
See also CA 104; DLB 118

Kreve (Mickevicius), Vincas
1882-1954 . . . . **TCLC 27**

Kristofferson, Kris 1936- . . . . **CLC 26**
See also CA 104

Krizanc, John 1956- . . . . **CLC 57**

Krleza, Miroslav 1893-1981 . . . . **CLC 8**
See also CA 97-100; 105

Kroetsch, Robert 1927- . . . . . . **CLC 5, 23, 57**
See also CA 17-20R; CANR 8, 38; DLB 53;
MTCW

Kroetz, Franz
See Kroetz, Franz Xaver

Kroetz, Franz Xaver 1946- . . . . **CLC 41**
See also CA 130

Kropotkin, Peter (Aleksieevich)
1842-1921 . . . . **TCLC 36**
See also CA 119

Krotkov, Yuri 1917- . . . . **CLC 19**
See also CA 102

Krumb
See Crumb, R(obert)

Krumgold, Joseph (Quincy)
1908-1980 . . . . **CLC 12**
See also CA 9-12R; 101; CANR 7;
MAICYA; SATA 1, 23, 48

Krumwitz
See Crumb, R(obert)

Krutch, Joseph Wood 1893-1970 . . . . **CLC 24**
See also CA 1-4R; 25-28R; CANR 4;
DLB 63

Krutzch, Gus
See Eliot, T(homas) S(tearns)

Krylov, Ivan Andreevich
1768(?)-1844 . . . . **NCLC 1**

Kubin, Alfred 1877-1959 . . . . **TCLC 23**
See also CA 112; DLB 81

Kubrick, Stanley 1928- . . . . **CLC 16**
See also CA 81-84; CANR 33; DLB 26

Kumin, Maxine (Winokur)
1925- . . . . **CLC 5, 13, 28**
See also AITN 2; CA 1-4R; CAAS 8;
CANR 1, 21; DLB 5; MTCW; SATA 12

Kundera, Milan
1929- . . . . **CLC 4, 9, 19, 32, 68**
See also AAYA 2; CA 85-88; CANR 19;
MTCW

Kunitz, Stanley (Jasspon)
1905- . . . . **CLC 6, 11, 14**
See also CA 41-44R; CANR 26; DLB 48;
MTCW

Kunze, Reiner 1933- . . . . **CLC 10**
See also CA 93-96; DLB 75

Kuprin, Aleksandr Ivanovich
1870-1938 . . . . **TCLC 5**
See also CA 104

Kureishi, Hanif 1954(?)- . . . . **CLC 64**
See also CA 139

Kurosawa, Akira 1910- . . . . **CLC 16**
See also CA 101

Kuttner, Henry 1915-1958 . . . . **TCLC 10**
See also CA 107; DLB 8

Kuzma, Greg 1944- . . . . **CLC 7**
See also CA 33-36R

Kuzmin, Mikhail 1872(?)-1936 . . . . **TCLC 40**

Kyd, Thomas 1558-1594 . . . . . . **LC 22; DC 3**
See also DLB 62

Kyprianos, Iossif
See Samarakis, Antonis

La Bruyere, Jean de 1645-1696 . . . . . . **LC 17**

Lacan, Jacques (Marie Emile)
1901-1981 . . . . **CLC 75**
See also CA 121; 104

Laclos, Pierre Ambroise Francois Choderlos
de 1741-1803 . . . . **NCLC 4**

La Colere, Francois
See Aragon, Louis

Lacolere, Francois
See Aragon, Louis

La Deshabilleuse
See Simenon, Georges (Jacques Christian)

Lady Gregory
See Gregory, Isabella Augusta (Persse)

Lady of Quality, A
See Bagnold, Enid

La Fayette, Marie (Madelaine Pioche de la
Vergne Comtes 1634-1693 . . . . **LC 2**

Lafayette, Rene
See Hubbard, L(afayette) Ron(ald)

Laforgue, Jules 1860-1887 . . . . **NCLC 5**

Lagerkvist, Paer (Fabian)
1891-1974 . . . . **CLC 7, 10, 13, 54**
See also CA 85-88; 49-52; MTCW

Lagerkvist, Par
See Lagerkvist, Paer (Fabian)

Lagerloef, Selma (Ottiliana Lovisa)
1858-1940 . . . . **TCLC 4, 36**
See also Lagerlof, Selma (Ottiliana Lovisa)
See also CA 108; CLR 7; SATA 15

Lagerlof, Selma (Ottiliana Lovisa)
See Lagerloef, Selma (Ottiliana Lovisa)
See also CLR 7; SATA 15

La Guma, (Justin) Alex(ander)
1925-1985 . . . . **CLC 19**
See also BW; CA 49-52; 118; CANR 25;
DLB 117; MTCW

Laidlaw, A. K.
See Grieve, C(hristopher) M(urray)

Lainez, Manuel Mujica
See Mujica Lainez, Manuel
See also HW

Lamartine, Alphonse (Marie Louis Prat) de
1790-1869 . . . . **NCLC 11**

Lamb, Charles 1775-1834 . . . . **NCLC 10**
See also CDBLB 1789-1832; DLB 93, 107;
SATA 17; WLC

Lamb, Lady Caroline 1785-1828 . . **NCLC 38**
See also DLB 116

Lamming, George (William)
1927- . . . . **CLC 2, 4, 66**
See also BLC 2; BW; CA 85-88; CANR 26;
DLB 125; MTCW

L'Amour, Louis (Dearborn)
1908-1988 . . . . **CLC 25, 55**
See also AITN 2; BEST 89:2; CA 1-4R;
125; CANR 3, 25, 40; DLBY 80; MTCW

Lampedusa, Giuseppe (Tomasi) di . . . **TCLC 13**
See also Tomasi di Lampedusa, Giuseppe

Lampman, Archibald 1861-1899 . . **NCLC 25**
See also DLB 92

Lancaster, Bruce 1896-1963 . . . . **CLC 36**
See also CA 9-10; CAP 1; SATA 9

Landau, Mark Alexandrovich
See Aldanov, Mark (Alexandrovich)

Landau-Aldanov, Mark Alexandrovich
See Aldanov, Mark (Alexandrovich)

Landis, John 1950- . . . . **CLC 26**
See also CA 112; 122

Landolfi, Tommaso 1908-1979 . . . **CLC 11, 49**
See also CA 127; 117

Landon, Letitia Elizabeth
1802-1838 . . . . **NCLC 15**
See also DLB 96

Landor, Walter Savage
1775-1864 . . . . **NCLC 14**
See also DLB 93, 107

Landwirth, Heinz 1927-
See Lind, Jakov
See also CA 9-12R; CANR 7

Lane, Patrick 1939- . . . . **CLC 25**
See also CA 97-100; DLB 53

Lang, Andrew 1844-1912 . . . . **TCLC 16**
See also CA 114; 137; DLB 98; MAICYA;
SATA 16

Lang, Fritz 1890-1976 . . . . **CLC 20**
See also CA 77-80; 69-72; CANR 30

Lange, John
See Crichton, (John) Michael

Langer, Elinor 1939- . . . . **CLC 34**
See also CA 121

Langland, William 1330(?)-1400(?) . . . **LC 19**

Langstaff, Launcelot
See Irving, Washington

Lanier, Sidney 1842-1881 . . . . **NCLC 6**
See also DLB 64; MAICYA; SATA 18

Lanyer, Aemilia 1569-1645 . . . . **LC 10**

Lao Tzu . . . . **CMLC 7**

Lapine, James (Elliot) 1949- . . . . **CLC 39**
See also CA 123; 130

Larbaud, Valery (Nicolas)
1881-1957 . . . . **TCLC 9**
See also CA 106

Lardner, Ring
See Lardner, Ring(gold) W(ilmer)

Lardner, Ring W. Jr.
See Lardner, Ring(gold) W(ilmer)

Lardner, Ring(gold) W(ilmer)
1885-1933 . . . . **TCLC 2, 14**
See also CA 104; 131; CDALB 1917-1929;
DLB 11, 25, 86; MTCW

Laredo, Betty
See Codrescu, Andrei

Larkin, Maia
See Wojciechowska, Maia (Teresa)

Larkin, Philip (Arthur)
1922-1985 ... **CLC 3, 5, 8, 9, 13, 18, 33, 39, 64**
See also CA 5-8R; 117; CANR 24;
CDBLB 1960 to Present; DLB 27;
MTCW

Larra (y Sanchez de Castro), Mariano Jose de
1809-1837 .... **NCLC 17**

Larsen, Eric 1941- .... **CLC 55**
See also CA 132

Larsen, Nella 1891-1964 .... **CLC 37**
See also BLC 2; BW; CA 125; DLB 51

Larson, Charles R(aymond) 1938-... **CLC 31**
See also CA 53-56; CANR 4

Latham, Jean Lee 1902-........... **CLC 12**
See also AITN 1; CA 5-8R; CANR 7;
MAICYA; SATA 2, 68

Latham, Mavis
See Clark, Mavis Thorpe

Lathen, Emma.................... **CLC 2**
See also Hennissart, Martha; Latsis, Mary
J(ane)

Lathrop, Francis
See Leiber, Fritz (Reuter Jr.)

Latsis, Mary J(ane)
See Lathen, Emma
See also CA 85-88

Lattimore, Richmond (Alexander)
1906-1984 .... **CLC 3**
See also CA 1-4R; 112; CANR 1

Laughlin, James 1914-........... **CLC 49**
See also CA 21-24R; CANR 9; DLB 48

Laurence, (Jean) Margaret (Wemyss)
1926-1987 .. **CLC 3, 6, 13, 50, 62; SSC 7**
See also CA 5-8R; 121; CANR 33; DLB 53;
MTCW; SATA 50

Laurent, Antoine 1952- .... **CLC 50**

Lauscher, Hermann
See Hesse, Hermann

Lautreamont, Comte de
1846-1870 .... **NCLC 12**

Laverty, Donald
See Blish, James (Benjamin)

Lavin, Mary 1912-...... **CLC 4, 18; SSC 4**
See also CA 9-12R; CANR 33; DLB 15;
MTCW

Lavond, Paul Dennis
See Kornbluth, C(yril) M.; Pohl, Frederik

Lawler, Raymond Evenor 1922- .... **CLC 58**
See also CA 103

Lawrence, D(avid) H(erbert Richards)
1885-1930 ...... **TCLC 2, 9, 16, 33, 48;
SSC 4**
See also CA 104; 121; CDBLB 1914-1945;
DLB 10, 19, 36, 98; MTCW; WLC

Lawrence, T(homas) E(dward)
1888-1935 .... **TCLC 18**
See also Dale, Colin
See also CA 115

Lawrence Of Arabia
See Lawrence, T(homas) E(dward)

Lawson, Henry (Archibald Hertzberg)
1867-1922 .... **TCLC 27**
See also CA 120

Lawton, Dennis
See Faust, Frederick (Schiller)

Laxness, Halldor.................. **CLC 25**
See also Gudjonsson, Halldor Kiljan

Layamon fl. c. 1200-........... **CMLC 10**

Laye, Camara 1928-1980 .... **CLC 4, 38**
See also BLC 2; BW; CA 85-88; 97-100;
CANR 25; MTCW

Layton, Irving (Peter) 1912-..... **CLC 2, 15**
See also CA 1-4R; CANR 2, 33; DLB 88;
MTCW

Lazarus, Emma 1849-1887........ **NCLC 8**

Lazarus, Felix
See Cable, George Washington

Lea, Joan
See Neufeld, John (Arthur)

Leacock, Stephen (Butler)
1869-1944 .... **TCLC 2**
See also CA 104; DLB 92

Lear, Edward 1812-1888 .... **NCLC 3**
See also CLR 1; DLB 32; MAICYA;
SATA 18

Lear, Norman (Milton) 1922- ...... **CLC 12**
See also CA 73-76

Leavis, F(rank) R(aymond)
1895-1978 .... **CLC 24**
See also CA 21-24R; 77-80; MTCW

Leavitt, David 1961-.............. **CLC 34**
See also CA 116; 122; DLB 130

Leblanc, Maurice (Marie Emile)
1864-1941 .... **TCLC 49**
See also CA 110

Lebowitz, Fran(ces Ann)
1951(?)-................... **CLC 11, 36**
See also CA 81-84; CANR 14; MTCW

le Carre, John .... **CLC 3, 5, 9, 15, 28**
See also Cornwell, David (John Moore)
See also BEST 89:4; CDBLB 1960 to
Present; DLB 87

Le Clezio, J(ean) M(arie) G(ustave)
1940- .... **CLC 31**
See also CA 116; 128; DLB 83

Leconte de Lisle, Charles-Marie-Rene
1818-1894 .... **NCLC 29**

Le Coq, Monsieur
See Simenon, Georges (Jacques Christian)

Leduc, Violette 1907-1972........ **CLC 22**
See also CA 13-14; 33-36R; CAP 1

Ledwidge, Francis 1887(?)-1917 ... **TCLC 23**
See also CA 123; DLB 20

Lee, Andrea 1953- .... **CLC 36**
See also BLC 2; BW; CA 125

Lee, Andrew
See Auchincloss, Louis (Stanton)

Lee, Don L....................... **CLC 2**
See also Madhubuti, Haki R.

Lee, George W(ashington)
1894-1976 .... **CLC 52**
See also BLC 2; BW; CA 125; DLB 51

Lee, (Nelle) Harper 1926- ...... **CLC 12, 60**
See also CA 13-16R; CDALB 1941-1968;
DLB 6; MTCW; SATA 11; WLC

Lee, Julian
See Latham, Jean Lee

Lee, Lawrence 1903- .... **CLC 34**
See also CA 25-28R

Lee, Manfred B(ennington)
1905-1971 .... **CLC 11**
See also Queen, Ellery
See also CA 1-4R; 29-32R; CANR 2

Lee, Stan 1922-................. **CLC 17**
See also AAYA 5; CA 108; 111

Lee, Tanith 1947-............... **CLC 46**
See also CA 37-40R; SATA 8

Lee, Vernon...................... **TCLC 5**
See also Paget, Violet
See also DLB 57

Lee, William
See Burroughs, William S(eward)

Lee, Willy
See Burroughs, William S(eward)

Lee-Hamilton, Eugene (Jacob)
1845-1907 .... **TCLC 22**
See also CA 117

Leet, Judith 1935- .... **CLC 11**

Le Fanu, Joseph Sheridan
1814-1873 .... **NCLC 9**
See also DLB 21, 70

Leffland, Ella 1931- .... **CLC 19**
See also CA 29-32R; CANR 35; DLBY 84;
SATA 65

Leger, (Marie-Rene) Alexis Saint-Leger
1887-1975 .... **CLC 11**
See also Perse, St.-John
See also CA 13-16R; 61-64; MTCW

Leger, Saintleger
See Leger, (Marie-Rene) Alexis Saint-Leger

Le Guin, Ursula K(roeber)
1929- .... **CLC 8, 13, 22, 45, 71**
See also AAYA 9; AITN 1; CA 21-24R;
CANR 9, 32; CDALB 1968-1988; CLR 3,
28; DLB 8, 52; MAICYA; MTCW;
SATA 4, 52

Lehmann, Rosamond (Nina)
1901-1990 .... **CLC 5**
See also CA 77-80; 131; CANR 8; DLB 15

Leiber, Fritz (Reuter Jr.)
1910-1992 .... **CLC 25**
See also CA 45-48; 139; CANR 2, 40;
DLB 8; MTCW; SATA 45; SATO 73

Leimbach, Martha 1963-
See Leimbach, Marti
See also CA 130

Leimbach, Marti .... **CLC 65**
See also Leimbach, Martha

Leino, Eino .... **TCLC 24**
See also Loennbohm, Armas Eino Leopold

Leiris, Michel (Julien) 1901-1990... **CLC 61**
See also CA 119; 128; 132

Leithauser, Brad 1953-............ **CLC 27**
See also CA 107; CANR 27; DLB 120

Lelchuk, Alan 1938-.............. **CLC 5**
See also CA 45-48; CANR 1

Lem, Stanislaw 1921-........ **CLC 8, 15, 40**
See also CA 105; CAAS 1; CANR 32;
MTCW

Lemann, Nancy 1956-............. **CLC 39**
See also CA 118; 136

Mason, Ernst
See Pohl, Frederik

Mason, Lee W.
See Malzberg, Barry N(athaniel)

Mason, Nick   1945- .... CLC 35
See also Pink Floyd

Mason, Tally
See Derleth, August (William)

Mass, William
See Gibson, William

Masters, Edgar Lee
1868-1950 .... TCLC 2, 25; PC 1
See also CA 104; 133; CDALB 1865-1917;
DLB 54; MTCW

Masters, Hilary   1928- .... CLC 48
See also CA 25-28R; CANR 13

Mastrosimone, William   19(?)- ...... CLC 36

Mathe, Albert
See Camus, Albert

Matheson, Richard Burton   1926- ... CLC 37
See also CA 97-100; DLB 8, 44

Mathews, Harry   1930- .... CLC 6, 52
See also CA 21-24R; CAAS 6; CANR 18,
40

Mathias, Roland (Glyn)   1915- ...... CLC 45
See also CA 97-100; CANR 19; DLB 27

Matsuo Basho   1644-1694 .... PC 3

Mattheson, Rodney
See Creasey, John

Matthews, Greg   1949- .... CLC 45
See also CA 135

Matthews, William   1942- .... CLC 40
See also CA 29-32R; CANR 12; DLB 5

Matthias, John (Edward)   1941- ...... CLC 9
See also CA 33-36R

Matthiessen, Peter
1927- .... CLC 5, 7, 11, 32, 64
See also AAYA 6; BEST 90:4; CA 9-12R;
CANR 21; DLB 6; MTCW; SATA 27

Maturin, Charles Robert
1780(?)-1824 .... NCLC 6

Matute (Ausejo), Ana Maria
1925- .... CLC 11
See also CA 89-92; MTCW

Maugham, W. S.
See Maugham, W(illiam) Somerset

Maugham, W(illiam) Somerset
1874-1965 .... CLC 1, 11, 15, 67; SSC 8
See also CA 5-8R; 25-28R; CANR 40;
CDBLB 1914-1945; DLB 10, 36, 77, 100;
MTCW; SATA 54; WLC

Maugham, William Somerset
See Maugham, W(illiam) Somerset

Maupassant, (Henri Rene Albert) Guy de
1850-1893 .... NCLC 1; SSC 1
See also DLB 123; WLC

Maurhut, Richard
See Traven, B.

Mauriac, Claude   1914- .... CLC 9
See also CA 89-92; DLB 83

Mauriac, Francois (Charles)
1885-1970 .... CLC 4, 9, 56
See also CA 25-28; CAP 2; DLB 65;
MTCW

Mavor, Osborne Henry   1888-1951
See Bridie, James
See also CA 104

Maxwell, William (Keepers Jr.)
1908- .... CLC 19
See also CA 93-96; DLBY 80

May, Elaine   1932- .... CLC 16
See also CA 124; DLB 44

Mayakovski, Vladimir (Vladimirovich)
1893-1930 .... TCLC 4, 18
See also CA 104

Mayhew, Henry   1812-1887 ...... NCLC 31
See also DLB 18, 55

Maynard, Joyce   1953- .... CLC 23
See also CA 111; 129

Mayne, William (James Carter)
1928- .... CLC 12
See also CA 9-12R; CANR 37; CLR 25;
MAICYA; SAAS 11; SATA 6, 68

Mayo, Jim
See L'Amour, Louis (Dearborn)

Maysles, Albert   1926- .... CLC 16
See also CA 29-32R

Maysles, David   1932- .... CLC 16

Mazer, Norma Fox   1931- .... CLC 26
See also AAYA 5; CA 69-72; CANR 12,
32; CLR 23; MAICYA; SAAS 1;
SATA 24, 67

Mazzini, Guiseppe   1805-1872 .... NCLC 34

McAuley, James Phillip
1917-1976 .... CLC 45
See also CA 97-100

McBain, Ed
See Hunter, Evan

McBrien, William Augustine
1930- .... CLC 44
See also CA 107

McCaffrey, Anne (Inez)   1926- ...... CLC 17
See also AAYA 6; AITN 2; BEST 89:2;
CA 25-28R; CANR 15, 35; DLB 8;
MAICYA; MTCW; SAAS 11; SATA 8,
70

McCann, Arthur
See Campbell, John W(ood Jr.)

McCann, Edson
See Pohl, Frederik

McCarthy, Cormac   1933- .... CLC 4, 57
See also CA 13-16R; CANR 10; DLB 6

McCarthy, Mary (Therese)
1912-1989 ... CLC 1, 3, 5, 14, 24, 39, 59
See also CA 5-8R; 129; CANR 16; DLB 2;
DLBY 81; MTCW

McCartney, (James) Paul
1942- .... CLC 12, 35

McCauley, Stephen   19(?)- .... CLC 50

McClure, Michael (Thomas)
1932- .... CLC 6, 10
See also CA 21-24R; CANR 17; DLB 16

McCorkle, Jill (Collins)   1958- ...... CLC 51
See also CA 121; DLBY 87

McCourt, James   1941- .... CLC 5
See also CA 57-60

McCoy, Horace (Stanley)
1897-1955 .... TCLC 28
See also CA 108; DLB 9

McCrae, John   1872-1918 .... TCLC 12
See also CA 109; DLB 92

McCreigh, James
See Pohl, Frederik

McCullers, (Lula) Carson (Smith)
1917-1967 .. CLC 1, 4, 10, 12, 48; SSC 9
See also CA 5-8R; 25-28R; CABS 1, 3;
CANR 18; CDALB 1941-1968; DLB 2, 7;
MTCW; SATA 27; WLC

McCulloch, John Tyler
See Burroughs, Edgar Rice

McCullough, Colleen   1938(?)- ...... CLC 27
See also CA 81-84; CANR 17; MTCW

McElroy, Joseph   1930- .... CLC 5, 47
See also CA 17-20R

McEwan, Ian (Russell)   1948- ... CLC 13, 66
See also BEST 90:4; CA 61-64; CANR 14;
DLB 14; MTCW

McFadden, David   1940- .... CLC 48
See also CA 104; DLB 60

McFarland, Dennis   1950- .... CLC 65

McGahern, John   1934- .... CLC 5, 9, 48
See also CA 17-20R; CANR 29; DLB 14;
MTCW

McGinley, Patrick (Anthony)
1937- .... CLC 41
See also CA 120; 127

McGinley, Phyllis   1905-1978 ...... CLC 14
See also CA 9-12R; 77-80; CANR 19;
DLB 11, 48; SATA 2, 24, 44

McGinniss, Joe   1942- .... CLC 32
See also AITN 2; BEST 89:2; CA 25-28R;
CANR 26

McGivern, Maureen Daly
See Daly, Maureen

McGrath, Patrick   1950- .... CLC 55
See also CA 136

McGrath, Thomas (Matthew)
1916-1990 .... CLC 28, 59
See also CA 9-12R; 132; CANR 6, 33;
MTCW; SATA 41; SATO 66

McGuane, Thomas (Francis III)
1939- .... CLC 3, 7, 18, 45
See also AITN 2; CA 49-52; CANR 5, 24;
DLB 2; DLBY 80; MTCW

McGuckian, Medbh   1950- .... CLC 48
See also DLB 40

McHale, Tom   1942(?)-1982 .... CLC 3, 5
See also AITN 1; CA 77-80; 106

McIlvanney, William   1936- .... CLC 42
See also CA 25-28R; DLB 14

McIlwraith, Maureen Mollie Hunter
See Hunter, Mollie
See also SATA 2

McInerney, Jay   1955- .... CLC 34
See also CA 116; 123

McIntyre, Vonda N(eel)   1948- ..... CLC 18
See also CA 81-84; CANR 17, 34; MTCW

McKay, Claude .... TCLC 7, 41; PC 2
See also McKay, Festus Claudius
See also BLC 3; DLB 4, 45, 51, 117

McKay, Festus Claudius   1889-1948
See McKay, Claude
See also BW; CA 104; 124; MTCW; WLC

McKuen, Rod   1933-............ CLC 1, 3
See also AITN 1; CA 41-44R; CANR 40

McLoughlin, R. B.
See Mencken, H(enry) L(ouis)

McLuhan, (Herbert) Marshall
1911-1980 .... CLC 37
See also CA 9-12R; 102; CANR 12, 34;
DLB 88; MTCW

McMillan, Terry   1951- .... CLC 50, 61

McMurtry, Larry (Jeff)
1936- .... CLC 2, 3, 7, 11, 27, 44
See also AITN 2; BEST 89:2; CA 5-8R;
CANR 19; CDALB 1968-1988; DLB 2;
DLBY 80, 87; MTCW

McNally, Terrence   1939-...... CLC 4, 7, 41
See also CA 45-48; CANR 2; DLB 7

McNamer, Deirdre   1950-......... CLC 70

McNeile, Herman Cyril   1888-1937
See Sapper
See also DLB 77

McPhee, John (Angus)   1931- ...... CLC 36
See also BEST 90:1; CA 65-68; CANR 20;
MTCW

McPherson, James Alan   1943- ..... CLC 19
See also BW; CA 25-28R; CAAS 17;
CANR 24; DLB 38; MTCW

McPherson, William (Alexander)
1933- .... CLC 34
See also CA 69-72; CANR 28

McSweeney, Kerry .... CLC 34

Mead, Margaret   1901-1978........ CLC 37
See also AITN 1; CA 1-4R; 81-84;
CANR 4; MTCW; SATA 20

Meaker, Marijane (Agnes)   1927-
See Kerr, M. E.
See also CA 107; CANR 37; MAICYA;
MTCW; SATA 20, 61

Medoff, Mark (Howard)   1940- ... CLC 6, 23
See also AITN 1; CA 53-56; CANR 5;
DLB 7

Meged, Aharon
See Megged, Aharon

Meged, Aron
See Megged, Aharon

Megged, Aharon   1920-............ CLC 9
See also CA 49-52; CAAS 13; CANR 1

Mehta, Ved (Parkash)   1934-....... CLC 37
See also CA 1-4R; CANR 2, 23; MTCW

Melanter
See Blackmore, R(ichard) D(oddridge)

Melikow, Loris
See Hofmannsthal, Hugo von

Melmoth, Sebastian
See Wilde, Oscar (Fingal O'Flahertie Wills)

Meltzer, Milton   1915- .... CLC 26
See also AAYA 8; CA 13-16R; CANR 38;
CLR 13; DLB 61; MAICYA; SAAS 1;
SATA 1, 50

Melville, Herman
1819-1891 ...... NCLC 3, 12, 29; SSC 1
See also CDALB 1640-1865; DLB 3, 74;
SATA 59; WLC

Menander
c. 342B.C.-c. 292B.C.... CMLC 9; DC 3

Mencken, H(enry) L(ouis)
1880-1956 .... TCLC 13
See also CA 105; 125; CDALB 1917-1929;
DLB 11, 29, 63; MTCW

Mercer, David   1928-1980.......... CLC 5
See also CA 9-12R; 102; CANR 23;
DLB 13; MTCW

Merchant, Paul
See Ellison, Harlan

Meredith, George   1828-1909 ... TCLC 17, 43
See also CA 117; CDBLB 1832-1890;
DLB 18, 35, 57

Meredith, William (Morris)
1919- .... CLC 4, 13, 22, 55
See also CA 9-12R; CAAS 14; CANR 6, 40;
DLB 5

Merezhkovsky, Dmitry Sergeyevich
1865-1941 .... TCLC 29

Merimee, Prosper
1803-1870 .... NCLC 6; SSC 7
See also DLB 119

Merkin, Daphne   1954-............ CLC 44
See also CA 123

Merlin, Arthur
See Blish, James (Benjamin)

Merrill, James (Ingram)
1926- .... CLC 2, 3, 6, 8, 13, 18, 34
See also CA 13-16R; CANR 10; DLB 5;
DLBY 85; MTCW

Merriman, Alex
See Silverberg, Robert

Merritt, E. B.
See Waddington, Miriam

Merton, Thomas
1915-1968 .... CLC 1, 3, 11, 34
See also CA 5-8R; 25-28R; CANR 22;
DLB 48; DLBY 81; MTCW

Merwin, W(illiam) S(tanley)
1927- ...... CLC 1, 2, 3, 5, 8, 13, 18, 45
See also CA 13-16R; CANR 15; DLB 5;
MTCW

Metcalf, John   1938-.............. CLC 37
See also CA 113; DLB 60

Metcalf, Suzanne
See Baum, L(yman) Frank

Mew, Charlotte (Mary)
1870-1928 .... TCLC 8
See also CA 105; DLB 19

Mewshaw, Michael   1943-.......... CLC 9
See also CA 53-56; CANR 7; DLBY 80

Meyer, June
See Jordan, June

Meyer-Meyrink, Gustav   1868-1932
See Meyrink, Gustav
See also CA 117

Meyers, Jeffrey   1939- .... CLC 39
See also CA 73-76; DLB 111

Meynell, Alice (Christina Gertrude Thompson)
1847-1922 .... TCLC 6
See also CA 104; DLB 19, 98

Meyrink, Gustav .... TCLC 21
See also Meyer-Meyrink, Gustav
See also DLB 81

Michaels, Leonard   1933-........ CLC 6, 25
See also CA 61-64; CANR 21; DLB 130;
MTCW

Michaux, Henri   1899-1984 ...... CLC 8, 19
See also CA 85-88; 114

Michelangelo   1475-1564............ LC 12

Michelet, Jules   1798-1874....... NCLC 31

Michener, James A(lbert)
1907(?)-.......... CLC 1, 5, 11, 29, 60
See also AITN 1; BEST 90:1; CA 5-8R;
CANR 21; DLB 6; MTCW

Mickiewicz, Adam   1798-1855 ..... NCLC 3

Middleton, Christopher   1926- ...... CLC 13
See also CA 13-16R; CANR 29; DLB 40

Middleton, Stanley   1919-........ CLC 7, 38
See also CA 25-28R; CANR 21; DLB 14

Migueis, Jose Rodrigues   1901-..... CLC 10

Mikszath, Kalman   1847-1910 ..... TCLC 31

Miles, Josephine
1911-1985 .... CLC 1, 2, 14, 34, 39
See also CA 1-4R; 116; CANR 2; DLB 48

Militant
See Sandburg, Carl (August)

Mill, John Stuart   1806-1873..... NCLC 11
See also CDBLB 1832-1890; DLB 55

Millar, Kenneth   1915-1983 .... CLC 14
See also Macdonald, Ross
See also CA 9-12R; 110; CANR 16; DLB 2;
DLBD 6; DLBY 83; MTCW

Millay, E. Vincent
See Millay, Edna St. Vincent

Millay, Edna St. Vincent
1892-1950 .... TCLC 4, 49; PC 6
See also CA 104; 130; CDALB 1917-1929;
DLB 45; MTCW

Miller, Arthur
1915- ...... CLC 1, 2, 6, 10, 15, 26, 47;
DC 1
See also AITN 1; CA 1-4R; CABS 3;
CANR 2, 30; CDALB 1941-1968; DLB 7;
MTCW; WLC

Miller, Henry (Valentine)
1891-1980 .... CLC 1, 2, 4, 9, 14, 43
See also CA 9-12R; 97-100; CANR 33;
CDALB 1929-1941; DLB 4, 9; DLBY 80;
MTCW; WLC

Miller, Jason   1939(?)- .... CLC 2
See also AITN 1; CA 73-76; DLB 7

Miller, Sue   19(?)-................. CLC 44
See also BEST 90:3; CA 139

Miller, Walter M(ichael Jr.)
1923- .... CLC 4, 30
See also CA 85-88; DLB 8

Millett, Kate   1934-............... CLC 67
See also AITN 1; CA 73-76; CANR 32;
MTCW

Millhauser, Steven   1943-....... CLC 21, 54
See also CA 110; 111; DLB 2

Millin, Sarah Gertrude 1889-1968 .. **CLC 49**
See also CA 102; 93-96

Milne, A(lan) A(lexander)
1882-1956 .... **TCLC 6**
See also CA 104; 133; CLR 1, 26; DLB 10, 77, 100; MAICYA; MTCW; YABC 1

Milner, Ron(ald) 1938- .... **CLC 56**
See also AITN 1; BLC 3; BW; CA 73-76; CANR 24; DLB 38; MTCW

Milosz, Czeslaw
1911- .... **CLC 5, 11, 22, 31, 56**
See also CA 81-84; CANR 23; MTCW

Milton, John 1608-1674 .... **LC 9**
See also CDBLB 1660-1789; WLC

Minehaha, Cornelius
See Wedekind, (Benjamin) Frank(lin)

Miner, Valerie 1947- .... **CLC 40**
See also CA 97-100

Minimo, Duca
See D'Annunzio, Gabriele

Minot, Susan 1956- .... **CLC 44**
See also CA 134

Minus, Ed 1938- .... **CLC 39**

Miranda, Javier
See Bioy Casares, Adolfo

Miro (Ferrer), Gabriel (Francisco Victor)
1879-1930 .... **TCLC 5**
See also CA 104

Mishima, Yukio
...... **CLC 2, 4, 6, 9, 27; DC 1; SSC 4**
See also Hiraoka, Kimitake

Mistral, Gabriela .... **TCLC 2**
See also Godoy Alcayaga, Lucila

Mistry, Rohinton 1952- .... **CLC 71**

Mitchell, Clyde
See Ellison, Harlan; Silverberg, Robert

Mitchell, James Leslie 1901-1935
See Gibbon, Lewis Grassic
See also CA 104; DLB 15

Mitchell, Joni 1943- .... **CLC 12**
See also CA 112

Mitchell, Margaret (Munnerlyn)
1900-1949 .... **TCLC 11**
See also CA 109; 125; DLB 9; MTCW

Mitchell, Peggy
See Mitchell, Margaret (Munnerlyn)

Mitchell, S(ilas) Weir 1829-1914 .. **TCLC 36**

Mitchell, W(illiam) O(rmond)
1914- .... **CLC 25**
See also CA 77-80; CANR 15; DLB 88

Mitford, Mary Russell 1787-1855.. **NCLC 4**
See also DLB 110, 116

Mitford, Nancy 1904-1973 .... **CLC 44**
See also CA 9-12R

Miyamoto, Yuriko 1899-1951 ..... **TCLC 37**

Mo, Timothy (Peter) 1950(?)- ...... **CLC 46**
See also CA 117; MTCW

Modarressi, Taghi (M.) 1931- ...... **CLC 44**
See also CA 121; 134

Modiano, Patrick (Jean) 1945- ..... **CLC 18**
See also CA 85-88; CANR 17, 40; DLB 83

Moerck, Paal
See Roelvaag, O(le) E(dvart)

Mofolo, Thomas (Mokopu)
1875(?)-1948 .... **TCLC 22**
See also BLC 3; CA 121

Mohr, Nicholasa 1935- .... **CLC 12**
See also AAYA 8; CA 49-52; CANR 1, 32; CLR 22; HW; SAAS 8; SATA 8

Mojtabai, A(nn) G(race)
1938- .... **CLC 5, 9, 15, 29**
See also CA 85-88

Moliere 1622-1673 .... **LC 10**
See also WLC

Molin, Charles
See Mayne, William (James Carter)

Molnar, Ferenc 1878-1952 .... **TCLC 20**
See also CA 109

Momaday, N(avarre) Scott
1934- .... **CLC 2, 19**
See also CA 25-28R; CANR 14, 34; MTCW; SATA 30, 48

Monroe, Harriet 1860-1936 .... **TCLC 12**
See also CA 109; DLB 54, 91

Monroe, Lyle
See Heinlein, Robert A(nson)

Montagu, Elizabeth 1917- .... **NCLC 7**
See also CA 9-12R

Montagu, Mary (Pierrepont) Wortley
1689-1762 .... **LC 9**
See also DLB 95, 101

Montague, John (Patrick)
1929- .... **CLC 13, 46**
See also CA 9-12R; CANR 9; DLB 40; MTCW

Montaigne, Michel (Eyquem) de
1533-1592 .... **LC 8**
See also WLC

Montale, Eugenio 1896-1981 ... **CLC 7, 9, 18**
See also CA 17-20R; 104; CANR 30; DLB 114; MTCW

Montesquieu, Charles-Louis de Secondat
1689-1755 .... **LC 7**

Montgomery, (Robert) Bruce 1921-1978
See Crispin, Edmund
See also CA 104

Montgomery, Marion H. Jr. 1925-... **CLC 7**
See also AITN 1; CA 1-4R; CANR 3; DLB 6

Montgomery, Max
See Davenport, Guy (Mattison Jr.)

Montherlant, Henry (Milon) de
1896-1972 .... **CLC 8, 19**
See also CA 85-88; 37-40R; DLB 72; MTCW

Monty Python .... **CLC 21**
See also Chapman, Graham; Cleese, John (Marwood); Gilliam, Terry (Vance); Idle, Eric; Jones, Terence Graham Parry; Palin, Michael (Edward)
See also AAYA 7

Moodie, Susanna (Strickland)
1803-1885 .... **NCLC 14**
See also DLB 99

Mooney, Edward 1951- .... **CLC 25**
See also CA 130

Mooney, Ted
See Mooney, Edward

Moorcock, Michael (John)
1939- .... **CLC 5, 27, 58**
See also CA 45-48; CAAS 5; CANR 2, 17, 38; DLB 14; MTCW

Moore, Brian
1921- .... **CLC 1, 3, 5, 7, 8, 19, 32**
See also CA 1-4R; CANR 1, 25; MTCW

Moore, Edward
See Muir, Edwin

Moore, George Augustus
1852-1933 .... **TCLC 7**
See also CA 104; DLB 10, 18, 57

Moore, Lorrie .... **CLC 39, 45, 68**
See also Moore, Marie Lorena

Moore, Marianne (Craig)
1887-1972 ... **CLC 1, 2, 4, 8, 10, 13, 19, 47; PC 4**
See also CA 1-4R; 33-36R; CANR 3; CDALB 1929-1941; DLB 45; DLBD 7; MTCW; SATA 20

Moore, Marie Lorena 1957-
See Moore, Lorrie
See also CA 116; CANR 39

Moore, Thomas 1779-1852 .... **NCLC 6**
See also DLB 96

Morand, Paul 1888-1976 .... **CLC 41**
See also CA 69-72; DLB 65

Morante, Elsa 1918-1985 .... **CLC 8, 47**
See also CA 85-88; 117; CANR 35; MTCW

Moravia, Alberto .... **CLC 2, 7, 11, 27, 46**
See also Pincherle, Alberto

More, Hannah 1745-1833 .... **NCLC 27**
See also DLB 107, 109, 116

More, Henry 1614-1687 .... **LC 9**
See also DLB 126

More, Sir Thomas 1478-1535 .... **LC 10**

Moreas, Jean .... **TCLC 18**
See also Papadiamantopoulos, Johannes

Morgan, Berry 1919- .... **CLC 6**
See also CA 49-52; DLB 6

Morgan, Claire
See Highsmith, (Mary) Patricia

Morgan, Edwin (George) 1920- ..... **CLC 31**
See also CA 5-8R; CANR 3; DLB 27

Morgan, (George) Frederick
1922- .... **CLC 23**
See also CA 17-20R; CANR 21

Morgan, Harriet
See Mencken, H(enry) L(ouis)

Morgan, Jane
See Cooper, James Fenimore

Morgan, Janet 1945- .... **CLC 39**
See also CA 65-68

Morgan, Lady 1776(?)-1859 ...... **NCLC 29**
See also DLB 116

Morgan, Robin 1941- .... **CLC 2**
See also CA 69-72; CANR 29; MTCW

Morgan, Scott
See Kuttner, Henry

Morgan, Seth 1949(?)-1990 .... **CLC 65**
See also CA 132

Morgenstern, Christian
1871-1914 .... **TCLC 8**
See also CA 105

Morgenstern, S.
See Goldman, William (W.)

Moricz, Zsigmond 1879-1942 ..... TCLC 33

Morike, Eduard (Friedrich)
1804-1875 .... NCLC 10

Mori Ogai .... TCLC 14
See also Mori Rintaro

Mori Rintaro 1862-1922
See Mori Ogai
See also CA 110

Moritz, Karl Philipp 1756-1793 ...... LC 2
See also DLB 94

Morland, Peter Henry
See Faust, Frederick (Schiller)

Morren, Theophil
See Hofmannsthal, Hugo von

Morris, Bill 1952-................. CLC 76

Morris, Julian
See West, Morris L(anglo)

Morris, Steveland Judkins 1950(?)-
See Wonder, Stevie
See also CA 111

Morris, William 1834-1896 .... NCLC 4
See also CDBLB 1832-1890; DLB 18, 35, 57

Morris, Wright 1910-... CLC 1, 3, 7, 18, 37
See also CA 9-12R; CANR 21; DLB 2;
DLBY 81; MTCW

Morrison, Chloe Anthony Wofford
See Morrison, Toni

Morrison, James Douglas 1943-1971
See Morrison, Jim
See also CA 73-76; CANR 40

Morrison, Jim..................... CLC 17
See also Morrison, James Douglas

Morrison, Toni 1931-..... CLC 4, 10, 22, 55
See also AAYA 1; BLC 3; BW; CA 29-32R;
CANR 27; CDALB 1968-1988; DLB 6,
33; DLBY 81; MTCW; SATA 57

Morrison, Van 1945- .... CLC 21
See also CA 116

Mortimer, John (Clifford)
1923-.................... CLC 28, 43
See also CA 13-16R; CANR 21;
CDBLB 1960 to Present; DLB 13;
MTCW

Mortimer, Penelope (Ruth) 1918-.... CLC 5
See also CA 57-60

Morton, Anthony
See Creasey, John

Mosher, Howard Frank .... CLC 62
See also CA 139

Mosley, Nicholas 1923-........ CLC 43, 70
See also CA 69-72; DLB 14

Moss, Howard
1922-1987 .... CLC 7, 14, 45, 50
See also CA 1-4R; 123; CANR 1; DLB 5

Motion, Andrew 1952-............ CLC 47
See also DLB 40

Motley, Willard (Francis)
1912-1965 .... CLC 18
See also BW; CA 117; 106; DLB 76

Mott, Michael (Charles Alston)
1930-.................... CLC 15, 34
See also CA 5-8R; CAAS 7; CANR 7, 29

Mowat, Farley (McGill) 1921- ..... CLC 26
See also AAYA 1; CA 1-4R; CANR 4, 24;
CLR 20; DLB 68; MAICYA; MTCW;
SATA 3, 55

Moyers, Bill 1934-............... CLC 74
See also AITN 2; CA 61-64; CANR 31

Mphahlele, Es'kia
See Mphahlele, Ezekiel
See also DLB 125

Mphahlele, Ezekiel 1919-......... CLC 25
See also Mphahlele, Es'kia
See also BLC 3; BW; CA 81-84; CANR 26

Mqhayi, S(amuel) E(dward) K(rune Loliwe)
1875-1945 .... TCLC 25
See also BLC 3

Mr. Martin
See Burroughs, William S(eward)

Mrozek, Slawomir 1930-........ CLC 3, 13
See also CA 13-16R; CAAS 10; CANR 29;
MTCW

Mrs. Belloc-Lowndes
See Lowndes, Marie Adelaide (Belloc)

Mtwa, Percy (?)-................. CLC 47

Mueller, Lisel 1924-........... CLC 13, 51
See also CA 93-96; DLB 105

Muir, Edwin 1887-1959 .... TCLC 2
See also CA 104; DLB 20, 100

Muir, John 1838-1914 .... TCLC 28

Mujica Lainez, Manuel
1910-1984 .... CLC 31
See also Lainez, Manuel Mujica
See also CA 81-84; 112; CANR 32; HW

Mukherjee, Bharati 1940-........ CLC 53
See also BEST 89:2; CA 107; DLB 60;
MTCW

Muldoon, Paul 1951-.......... CLC 32, 72
See also CA 113; 129; DLB 40

Mulisch, Harry 1927-............ CLC 42
See also CA 9-12R; CANR 6, 26

Mull, Martin 1943-............... CLC 17
See also CA 105

Mulock, Dinah Maria
See Craik, Dinah Maria (Mulock)

Munford, Robert 1737(?)-1783 .... LC 5
See also DLB 31

Mungo, Raymond 1946-........... CLC 72
See also CA 49-52; CANR 2

Munro, Alice
1931- .... CLC 6, 10, 19, 50; SSC 3
See also AITN 2; CA 33-36R; CANR 33;
DLB 53; MTCW; SATA 29

Munro, H(ector) H(ugh) 1870-1916
See Saki
See also CA 104; 130; CDBLB 1890-1914;
DLB 34; MTCW; WLC

Murasaki, Lady.................. CMLC 1

Murdoch, (Jean) Iris
1919- ...... CLC 1, 2, 3, 4, 6, 8, 11, 15,
22, 31, 51
See also CA 13-16R; CANR 8;
CDBLB 1960 to Present; DLB 14;
MTCW

Murphy, Richard 1927-.......... CLC 41
See also CA 29-32R; DLB 40

Murphy, Sylvia 1937-............ CLC 34
See also CA 121

Murphy, Thomas (Bernard) 1935-... CLC 51
See also CA 101

Murray, Albert L. 1916- .... CLC 73
See also BW; CA 49-52; CANR 26; DLB 38

Murray, Les(lie) A(llan) 1938- ..... CLC 40
See also CA 21-24R; CANR 11, 27

Murry, J. Middleton
See Murry, John Middleton

Murry, John Middleton
1889-1957 .... TCLC 16
See also CA 118

Musgrave, Susan 1951- .... CLC 13, 54
See also CA 69-72

Musil, Robert (Edler von)
1880-1942 .... TCLC 12
See also CA 109; DLB 81, 124

Musset, (Louis Charles) Alfred de
1810-1857 .... NCLC 7

My Brother's Brother
See Chekhov, Anton (Pavlovich)

Myers, Walter Dean 1937- .... CLC 35
See also AAYA 4; BLC 3; BW; CA 33-36R;
CANR 20; CLR 4, 16; DLB 33;
MAICYA; SAAS 2; SATA 27, 41, 70, 71

Myers, Walter M.
See Myers, Walter Dean

Myles, Symon
See Follett, Ken(neth Martin)

Nabokov, Vladimir (Vladimirovich)
1899-1977 .... CLC 1, 2, 3, 6, 8, 11, 15,
23, 44, 46, 64; SSC 11
See also CA 5-8R; 69-72; CANR 20;
CDALB 1941-1968; DLB 2; DLBD 3;
DLBY 80, 91; MTCW; WLC

Nagy, Laszlo 1925-1978............ CLC 7
See also CA 129; 112

Naipaul, Shiva(dhar Srinivasa)
1945-1985................. CLC 32, 39
See also CA 110; 112; 116; CANR 33;
DLBY 85; MTCW

Naipaul, V(idiadhar) S(urajprasad)
1932-........... CLC 4, 7, 9, 13, 18, 37
See also CA 1-4R; CANR 1, 33;
CDBLB 1960 to Present; DLB 125;
DLBY 85; MTCW

Nakos, Lilika 1899(?)-............. CLC 29

Narayan, R(asipuram) K(rishnaswami)
1906-................... CLC 7, 28, 47
See also CA 81-84; CANR 33; MTCW;
SATA 62

Nash, (Frediric) Ogden 1902-1971 .. CLC 23
See also CA 13-14; 29-32R; CANR 34;
CAP 1; DLB 11; MAICYA; MTCW;
SATA 2, 46

Nathan, Daniel
See Dannay, Frederic

Nathan, George Jean 1882-1958... TCLC 18
See also Hatteras, Owen
See also CA 114

Natsume, Kinnosuke 1867-1916
See Natsume, Soseki
See also CA 104

Natsume, Soseki .... TCLC **2, 10**
See also Natsume, Kinnosuke

Natti, (Mary) Lee   1919-
See Kingman, Lee
See also CA 5-8R; CANR 2

Naylor, Gloria   1950- .... CLC **28, 52**
See also AAYA 6; BLC 3; BW; CA 107;
CANR 27; MTCW

Neihardt, John Gneisenau
1881-1973 .... CLC **32**
See also CA 13-14; CAP 1; DLB 9, 54

Nekrasov, Nikolai Alekseevich
1821-1878 .... NCLC **11**

Nelligan, Emile   1879-1941........ TCLC **14**
See also CA 114; DLB 92

Nelson, Willie   1933-.............. CLC **17**
See also CA 107

Nemerov, Howard (Stanley)
1920-1991............CLC **2, 6, 9, 36**
See also CA 1-4R; 134; CABS 2; CANR 1,
27; DLB 6; DLBY 83; MTCW

Neruda, Pablo
1904-1973 .... CLC **1, 2, 5, 7, 9, 28, 62;**
PC 4
See also CA 19-20; 45-48; CAP 2; HW;
MTCW; WLC

Nerval, Gerard de   1808-1855...... NCLC **1**

Nervo, (Jose) Amado (Ruiz de)
1870-1919 .... TCLC **11**
See also CA 109; 131; HW

Nessi, Pio Baroja y
See Baroja (y Nessi), Pio

Neufeld, John (Arthur)   1938- ...... CLC **17**
See also CA 25-28R; CANR 11, 37;
MAICYA; SAAS 3; SATA 6

Neville, Emily Cheney   1919-....... CLC **12**
See also CA 5-8R; CANR 3, 37; MAICYA;
SAAS 2; SATA 1

Newbound, Bernard Slade   1930-
See Slade, Bernard
See also CA 81-84

Newby, P(ercy) H(oward)
1918- .... CLC **2, 13**
See also CA 5-8R; CANR 32; DLB 15;
MTCW

Newlove, Donald   1928- .... CLC **6**
See also CA 29-32R; CANR 25

Newlove, John (Herbert)   1938-..... CLC **14**
See also CA 21-24R; CANR 9, 25

Newman, Charles   1938- .... CLC **2, 8**
See also CA 21-24R

Newman, Edwin (Harold)   1919- .... CLC **14**
See also AITN 1; CA 69-72; CANR 5

Newman, John Henry
1801-1890 .... NCLC **38**
See also DLB 18, 32, 55

Newton, Suzanne   1936- .... CLC **35**
See also CA 41-44R; CANR 14; SATA 5

Nexo, Martin Andersen
1869-1954 .... TCLC **43**

Nezval, Vitezslav   1900-1958 ...... TCLC **44**
See also CA 123

Ngema, Mbongeni   1955- .... CLC **57**

Ngugi, James T(hiong'o)........ CLC **3, 7, 13**
See also Ngugi wa Thiong'o

Ngugi wa Thiong'o   1938-.......... CLC **36**
See also Ngugi, James T(hiong'o)
See also BLC 3; BW; CA 81-84; CANR 27;
MTCW

Nichol, B(arrie) P(hillip)
1944-1988 .... CLC **18**
See also CA 53-56; DLB 53; SATA 66

Nichols, John (Treadwell)   1940-.... CLC **38**
See also CA 9-12R; CAAS 2; CANR 6;
DLBY 82

Nichols, Peter (Richard)
1927- .... CLC **5, 36, 65**
See also CA 104; CANR 33; DLB 13;
MTCW

Nicolas, F. R. E.
See Freeling, Nicolas

Niedecker, Lorine   1903-1970.... CLC **10, 42**
See also CA 25-28; CAP 2; DLB 48

Nietzsche, Friedrich (Wilhelm)
1844-1900 .... TCLC **10, 18**
See also CA 107; 121; DLB 129

Nievo, Ippolito   1831-1861 .... NCLC **22**

Nightingale, Anne Redmon   1943-
See Redmon, Anne
See also CA 103

Nik.T.O.
See Annensky, Innokenty Fyodorovich

Nin, Anais
1903-1977 ..... CLC **1, 4, 8, 11, 14, 60;**
SSC 10
See also AITN 2; CA 13-16R; 69-72;
CANR 22; DLB 2, 4; MTCW

Nissenson, Hugh   1933-............ CLC **4, 9**
See also CA 17-20R; CANR 27; DLB 28

Niven, Larry .... CLC **8**
See also Niven, Laurence Van Cott
See also DLB 8

Niven, Laurence Van Cott   1938-
See Niven, Larry
See also CA 21-24R; CAAS 12; CANR 14;
MTCW

Nixon, Agnes Eckhardt   1927-...... CLC **21**
See also CA 110

Nizan, Paul   1905-1940........... TCLC **40**
See also DLB 72

Nkosi, Lewis   1936-............... CLC **45**
See also BLC 3; BW; CA 65-68; CANR 27

Nodier, (Jean) Charles (Emmanuel)
1780-1844 .... NCLC **19**
See also DLB 119

Nolan, Christopher   1965-.......... CLC **58**
See also CA 111

Norden, Charles
See Durrell, Lawrence (George)

Nordhoff, Charles (Bernard)
1887-1947 .... TCLC **23**
See also CA 108; DLB 9; SATA 23

Norfolk, Lawrence   1963-.......... CLC **76**

Norman, Marsha   1947- .... CLC **28**
See also CA 105; CABS 3; DLBY 84

Norris, Benjamin Franklin Jr.
1870-1902 .... TCLC **24**
See also Norris, Frank
See also CA 110

Norris, Frank
See Norris, Benjamin Franklin Jr.
See also CDALB 1865-1917; DLB 12, 71

Norris, Leslie   1921-.............. CLC **14**
See also CA 11-12; CANR 14; CAP 1;
DLB 27

North, Andrew
See Norton, Andre

North, Captain George
See Stevenson, Robert Louis (Balfour)

North, Milou
See Erdrich, Louise

Northrup, B. A.
See Hubbard, L(afayette) Ron(ald)

North Staffs
See Hulme, T(homas) E(rnest)

Norton, Alice Mary
See Norton, Andre
See also MAICYA; SATA 1, 43

Norton, Andre   1912- .... CLC **12**
See also Norton, Alice Mary
See also CA 1-4R; CANR 2, 31; DLB 8, 52;
MTCW

Norway, Nevil Shute   1899-1960
See Shute, Nevil
See also CA 102; 93-96

Norwid, Cyprian Kamil
1821-1883 .... NCLC **17**

Nosille, Nabrah
See Ellison, Harlan

Nossack, Hans Erich   1901-1978..... CLC **6**
See also CA 93-96; 85-88; DLB 69

Nosu, Chuji
See Ozu, Yasujiro

Nova, Craig   1945-.............. CLC **7, 31**
See also CA 45-48; CANR 2

Novak, Joseph
See Kosinski, Jerzy (Nikodem)

Novalis   1772-1801 .... NCLC **13**
See also DLB 90

Nowlan, Alden (Albert)   1933-1983 .. CLC **15**
See also CA 9-12R; CANR 5; DLB 53

Noyes, Alfred   1880-1958 .... TCLC **7**
See also CA 104; DLB 20

Nunn, Kem   19(?)-................ CLC **34**

Nye, Robert   1939-............... CLC **13, 42**
See also CA 33-36R; CANR 29; DLB 14;
MTCW; SATA 6

Nyro, Laura   1947-............... CLC **17**

Oates, Joyce Carol
1938- ..... CLC **1, 2, 3, 6, 9, 11, 15, 19,**
33, 52; SSC 6
See also AITN 1; BEST 89:2; CA 5-8R;
CANR 25; CDALB 1968-1988; DLB 2, 5,
130; DLBY 81; MTCW; WLC

O'Brien, E. G.
See Clarke, Arthur C(harles)

Ozick, Cynthia 1928- . . . . . . **CLC 3, 7, 28, 62**
See also BEST 90:1; CA 17-20R; CANR 23;
DLB 28; DLBY 82; MTCW

Ozu, Yasujiro 1903-1963 . . . . **CLC 16**
See also CA 112

Pacheco, C.
See Pessoa, Fernando (Antonio Nogueira)

Pa Chin
See Li Fei-kan

Pack, Robert 1929- . . . . **CLC 13**
See also CA 1-4R; CANR 3; DLB 5

Padgett, Lewis
See Kuttner, Henry

Padilla (Lorenzo), Heberto 1932- . . . **CLC 38**
See also AITN 1; CA 123; 131; HW

Page, Jimmy 1944- . . . . **CLC 12**

Page, Louise 1955- . . . . **CLC 40**

Page, P(atricia) K(athleen)
1916- . . . . **CLC 7, 18**
See also CA 53-56; CANR 4, 22; DLB 68;
MTCW

Paget, Violet 1856-1935
See Lee, Vernon
See also CA 104

Paget-Lowe, Henry
See Lovecraft, H(oward) P(hillips)

Paglia, Camille 1947- . . . . **CLC 68**

Pakenham, Antonia
See Fraser, Antonia (Pakenham)

Palamas, Kostes 1859-1943 . . . . **TCLC 5**
See also CA 105

Palazzeschi, Aldo 1885-1974 . . . . **CLC 11**
See also CA 89-92; 53-56; DLB 114

Paley, Grace 1922- . . . . **CLC 4, 6, 37; SSC 8**
See also CA 25-28R; CANR 13; DLB 28;
MTCW

Palin, Michael (Edward) 1943- . . . . . **CLC 21**
See also Monty Python
See also CA 107; CANR 35; SATA 67

Palliser, Charles 1947- . . . . **CLC 65**
See also CA 136

Palma, Ricardo 1833-1919 . . . . **TCLC 29**

Pancake, Breece Dexter 1952-1979
See Pancake, Breece D'J
See also CA 123; 109

Pancake, Breece D'J . . . . **CLC 29**
See also Pancake, Breece Dexter
See also DLB 130

Papadiamantis, Alexandros
1851-1911 . . . . **TCLC 29**

Papadiamantopoulos, Johannes 1856-1910
See Moreas, Jean
See also CA 117

Papini, Giovanni 1881-1956 . . . . **TCLC 22**
See also CA 121

Paracelsus 1493-1541 . . . . **LC 14**

Parasol, Peter
See Stevens, Wallace

Parfenie, Maria
See Codrescu, Andrei

Parini, Jay (Lee) 1948- . . . . **CLC 54**
See also CA 97-100; CAAS 16; CANR 32

Park, Jordan
See Kornbluth, C(yril) M.; Pohl, Frederik

Parker, Bert
See Ellison, Harlan

Parker, Dorothy (Rothschild)
1893-1967 . . . . **CLC 15, 68; SSC 2**
See also CA 19-20; 25-28R; CAP 2;
DLB 11, 45, 86; MTCW

Parker, Robert B(rown) 1932- . . . . . . **CLC 27**
See also BEST 89:4; CA 49-52; CANR 1,
26; MTCW

Parkes, Lucas
See Harris, John (Wyndham Parkes Lucas)
Beynon

Parkin, Frank 1940- . . . . **CLC 43**

Parkman, Francis Jr. 1823-1893 . . **NCLC 12**
See also DLB 1, 30

Parks, Gordon (Alexander Buchanan)
1912- . . . . **CLC 1, 16**
See also AITN 2; BLC 3; BW; CA 41-44R;
CANR 26; DLB 33; SATA 8

Parnell, Thomas 1679-1718 . . . . **LC 3**
See also DLB 94

Parra, Nicanor 1914- . . . . **CLC 2**
See also CA 85-88; CANR 32; HW; MTCW

Parrish, Mary Frances
See Fisher, M(ary) F(rances) K(ennedy)

Parson Lot
See Kingsley, Charles

Partridge, Anthony
See Oppenheim, E(dward) Phillips

Pascoli, Giovanni 1855-1912 . . . . . . **TCLC 45**

Pasolini, Pier Paolo
1922-1975 . . . . **CLC 20, 37**
See also CA 93-96; 61-64; DLB 128;
MTCW

Pasquini
See Silone, Ignazio

Pastan, Linda (Olenik) 1932- . . . . . . **CLC 27**
See also CA 61-64; CANR 18, 40; DLB 5

Pasternak, Boris (Leonidovich)
1890-1960 . . . . . **CLC 7, 10, 18, 63; PC 6**
See also CA 127; 116; MTCW; WLC

Patchen, Kenneth 1911-1972 . . . **CLC 1, 2, 18**
See also CA 1-4R; 33-36R; CANR 3, 35;
DLB 16, 48; MTCW

Pater, Walter (Horatio)
1839-1894 . . . . **NCLC 7**
See also CDBLB 1832-1890; DLB 57

Paterson, A(ndrew) B(arton)
1864-1941 . . . . **TCLC 32**

Paterson, Katherine (Womeldorf)
1932- . . . . **CLC 12, 30**
See also AAYA 1; CA 21-24R; CANR 28;
CLR 7; DLB 52; MAICYA; MTCW;
SATA 13, 53

Patmore, Coventry Kersey Dighton
1823-1896 . . . . **NCLC 9**
See also DLB 35, 98

Paton, Alan (Stewart)
1903-1988 . . . . **CLC 4, 10, 25, 55**
See also CA 13-16; 125; CANR 22; CAP 1;
MTCW; SATA 11, 56; WLC

Paton Walsh, Gillian 1939-
See Walsh, Jill Paton
See also CANR 38; MAICYA; SAAS 3;
SATA 4, 72

Paulding, James Kirke 1778-1860 . . **NCLC 2**
See also DLB 3, 59, 74

Paulin, Thomas Neilson 1949-
See Paulin, Tom
See also CA 123; 128

Paulin, Tom . . . . **CLC 37**
See also Paulin, Thomas Neilson
See also DLB 40

Paustovsky, Konstantin (Georgievich)
1892-1968 . . . . **CLC 40**
See also CA 93-96; 25-28R

Pavese, Cesare 1908-1950 . . . . **TCLC 3**
See also CA 104; DLB 128

Pavic, Milorad 1929- . . . . **CLC 60**
See also CA 136

Payne, Alan
See Jakes, John (William)

Paz, Gil
See Lugones, Leopoldo

Paz, Octavio
1914- . . . . . . **CLC 3, 4, 6, 10, 19, 51, 65;**
PC 1
See also CA 73-76; CANR 32; DLBY 90;
HW; MTCW; WLC

Peacock, Molly 1947- . . . . **CLC 60**
See also CA 103; DLB 120

Peacock, Thomas Love
1785-1866 . . . . **NCLC 22**
See also DLB 96, 116

Peake, Mervyn 1911-1968 . . . . **CLC 7, 54**
See also CA 5-8R; 25-28R; CANR 3;
DLB 15; MTCW; SATA 23

Pearce, Philippa . . . . **CLC 21**
See also Christie, (Ann) Philippa
See also CLR 9; MAICYA; SATA 1, 67

Pearl, Eric
See Elman, Richard

Pearson, T(homas) R(eid) 1956- . . . . **CLC 39**
See also CA 120; 130

Peck, John 1941- . . . . **CLC 3**
See also CA 49-52; CANR 3

Peck, Richard (Wayne) 1934- . . . . . . **CLC 21**
See also AAYA 1; CA 85-88; CANR 19,
38; MAICYA; SAAS 2; SATA 18, 55

Peck, Robert Newton 1928- . . . . **CLC 17**
See also AAYA 3; CA 81-84; CANR 31;
MAICYA; SAAS 1; SATA 21, 62

Peckinpah, (David) Sam(uel)
1925-1984 . . . . **CLC 20**
See also CA 109; 114

Pedersen, Knut 1859-1952
See Hamsun, Knut
See also CA 104; 119; MTCW

Peeslake, Gaffer
See Durrell, Lawrence (George)

Peguy, Charles Pierre
1873-1914 . . . . **TCLC 10**
See also CA 107

Pena, Ramon del Valle y
See Valle-Inclan, Ramon (Maria) del

Pendennis, Arthur Esquir
See Thackeray, William Makepeace

Pepys, Samuel 1633-1703 . . . . **LC 11**
See also CDBLB 1660-1789; DLB 101;
WLC

Percy, Walker
1916-1990 . . . **CLC 2, 3, 6, 8, 14, 18, 47,**
65
See also CA 1-4R; 131; CANR 1, 23;
DLB 2; DLBY 80, 90; MTCW

Perec, Georges 1936-1982 . . . . **CLC 56**
See also DLB 83

Pereda (y Sanchez de Porrua), Jose Maria de
1833-1906 . . . . **TCLC 16**
See also CA 117

Pereda y Porrua, Jose Maria de
See Pereda (y Sanchez de Porrua), Jose
Maria de

Peregoy, George Weems
See Mencken, H(enry) L(ouis)

Perelman, S(idney) J(oseph)
1904-1979 . . . **CLC 3, 5, 9, 15, 23, 44, 49**
See also AITN 1, 2; CA 73-76; 89-92;
CANR 18; DLB 11, 44; MTCW

Peret, Benjamin 1899-1959 . . . . **TCLC 20**
See also CA 117

Peretz, Isaac Loeb 1851(?)-1915 . . . **TCLC 16**
See also CA 109

Peretz, Yitzkhok Leibush
See Peretz, Isaac Loeb

Perez Galdos, Benito 1843-1920 . . . **TCLC 27**
See also CA 125; HW

Perrault, Charles 1628-1703 . . . . **LC 2**
See also MAICYA; SATA 25

Perry, Brighton
See Sherwood, Robert E(mmet)

Perse, Saint-John
See Leger, (Marie-Rene) Alexis Saint-Leger

Perse, St.-John . . . . **CLC 4, 11, 46**
See also Leger, (Marie-Rene) Alexis
Saint-Leger

Peseenz, Tulio F.
See Lopez y Fuentes, Gregorio

Pesetsky, Bette 1932- . . . . **CLC 28**
See also CA 133; DLB 130

Peshkov, Alexei Maximovich 1868-1936
See Gorky, Maxim
See also CA 105

Pessoa, Fernando (Antonio Nogueira)
1888-1935 . . . . **TCLC 27**
See also CA 125

Peterkin, Julia Mood 1880-1961 . . . . **CLC 31**
See also CA 102; DLB 9

Peters, Joan K. 1945- . . . . **CLC 39**

Peters, Robert L(ouis) 1924- . . . . **CLC 7**
See also CA 13-16R; CAAS 8; DLB 105

Petofi, Sandor 1823-1849 . . . . **NCLC 21**

Petrakis, Harry Mark 1923- . . . . **CLC 3**
See also CA 9-12R; CANR 4, 30

Petrov, Evgeny . . . . **TCLC 21**
See also Kataev, Evgeny Petrovich

Petry, Ann (Lane) 1908- . . . . . . **CLC 1, 7, 18**
See also BW; CA 5-8R; CAAS 6; CANR 4;
CLR 12; DLB 76; MAICYA; MTCW;
SATA 5

Petursson, Halligrimur 1614-1674 . . . . **LC 8**

Philipson, Morris H. 1926- . . . . **CLC 53**
See also CA 1-4R; CANR 4

Phillips, David Graham
1867-1911 . . . . **TCLC 44**
See also CA 108; DLB 9, 12

Phillips, Jack
See Sandburg, Carl (August)

Phillips, Jayne Anne 1952- . . . . . **CLC 15, 33**
See also CA 101; CANR 24; DLBY 80;
MTCW

Phillips, Richard
See Dick, Philip K(indred)

Phillips, Robert (Schaeffer) 1938- . . . **CLC 28**
See also CA 17-20R; CAAS 13; CANR 8;
DLB 105

Phillips, Ward
See Lovecraft, H(oward) P(hillips)

Piccolo, Lucio 1901-1969 . . . . **CLC 13**
See also CA 97-100; DLB 114

Pickthall, Marjorie L(owry) C(hristie)
1883-1922 . . . . **TCLC 21**
See also CA 107; DLB 92

Pico della Mirandola, Giovanni
1463-1494 . . . . **LC 15**

Piercy, Marge
1936- . . . . **CLC 3, 6, 14, 18, 27, 62**
See also CA 21-24R; CAAS 1; CANR 13;
DLB 120; MTCW

Piers, Robert
See Anthony, Piers

Pieyre de Mandiargues, Andre 1909-1991
See Mandiargues, Andre Pieyre de
See also CA 103; 136; CANR 22

Pilnyak, Boris . . . . **TCLC 23**
See also Vogau, Boris Andreyevich

Pincherle, Alberto 1907-1990 . . . **CLC 11, 18**
See also Moravia, Alberto
See also CA 25-28R; 132; CANR 33;
MTCW

Pinckney, Darryl 1953- . . . . **CLC 76**

Pineda, Cecile 1942- . . . . **CLC 39**
See also CA 118

Pinero, Arthur Wing 1855-1934 . . . **TCLC 32**
See also CA 110; DLB 10

Pinero, Miguel (Antonio Gomez)
1946-1988 . . . . **CLC 4, 55**
See also CA 61-64; 125; CANR 29; HW

Pinget, Robert 1919- . . . . **CLC 7, 13, 37**
See also CA 85-88; DLB 83

Pink Floyd . . . . **CLC 35**
See also Barrett, (Roger) Syd; Gilmour,
David; Mason, Nick; Waters, Roger;
Wright, Rick

Pinkney, Edward 1802-1828 . . . . . **NCLC 31**

Pinkwater, Daniel Manus 1941- . . . . **CLC 35**
See also Pinkwater, Manus
See also AAYA 1; CA 29-32R; CANR 12,
38; CLR 4; MAICYA; SAAS 3; SATA 46

Pinkwater, Manus
See Pinkwater, Daniel Manus
See also SATA 8

Pinsky, Robert 1940- . . . . **CLC 9, 19, 38**
See also CA 29-32R; CAAS 4; DLBY 82

Pinta, Harold
See Pinter, Harold

Pinter, Harold
1930- . . **CLC 1, 3, 6, 9, 11, 15, 27, 58, 73**
See also CA 5-8R; CANR 33; CDBLB 1960
to Present; DLB 13; MTCW; WLC

Pirandello, Luigi 1867-1936 . . . . . **TCLC 4, 29**
See also CA 104; WLC

Pirsig, Robert M(aynard)
1928- . . . . **CLC 4, 6, 73**
See also CA 53-56; MTCW; SATA 39

Pisarev, Dmitry Ivanovich
1840-1868 . . . . **NCLC 25**

Pix, Mary (Griffith) 1666-1709 . . . . . . **LC 8**
See also DLB 80

Pixerecourt, Guilbert de
1773-1844 . . . . **NCLC 39**

Plaidy, Jean
See Hibbert, Eleanor Burford

Plant, Robert 1948- . . . . **CLC 12**

Plante, David (Robert)
1940- . . . . **CLC 7, 23, 38**
See also CA 37-40R; CANR 12, 36;
DLBY 83; MTCW

Plath, Sylvia
1932-1963 . . . . **CLC 1, 2, 3, 5, 9, 11, 14,**
17, 50, 51, 62; PC 1
See also CA 19-20; CANR 34; CAP 2;
CDALB 1941-1968; DLB 5, 6; MTCW;
WLC

Plato 428(?)B.C.-348(?)B.C. . . . . **CMLC 8**

Platonov, Andrei . . . . **TCLC 14**
See also Klimentov, Andrei Platonovich

Platt, Kin 1911- . . . . **CLC 26**
See also CA 17-20R; CANR 11; SATA 21

Plick et Plock
See Simenon, Georges (Jacques Christian)

Plimpton, George (Ames) 1927- . . . . . **CLC 36**
See also AITN 1; CA 21-24R; CANR 32;
MTCW; SATA 10

Plomer, William Charles Franklin
1903-1973 . . . . **CLC 4, 8**
See also CA 21-22; CANR 34; CAP 2;
DLB 20; MTCW; SATA 24

Plowman, Piers
See Kavanagh, Patrick (Joseph)

Plum, J.
See Wodehouse, P(elham) G(renville)

Plumly, Stanley (Ross) 1939- . . . . . . **CLC 33**
See also CA 108; 110; DLB 5

Poe, Edgar Allan
1809-1849 . . . **NCLC 1, 16; PC 1; SSC 1**
See also CDALB 1640-1865; DLB 3, 59, 73,
74; SATA 23; WLC

Poet of Titchfield Street, The
See Pound, Ezra (Weston Loomis)

Pohl, Frederik 1919- . . . . **CLC 18**
See also CA 61-64; CAAS 1; CANR 11, 37;
DLB 8; MTCW; SATA 24

Poirier, Louis 1910-
See Gracq, Julien
See also CA 122; 126

Poitier, Sidney 1927-............. **CLC 26**
See also BW; CA 117

Polanski, Roman 1933-............ **CLC 16**
See also CA 77-80

Poliakoff, Stephen 1952-.......... **CLC 38**
See also CA 106; DLB 13

Police, The...................... **CLC 26**
See also Copeland, Stewart (Armstrong);
    Summers, Andrew James; Sumner,
    Gordon Matthew

Pollitt, Katha 1949-.............. **CLC 28**
See also CA 120; 122; MTCW

Pollock, Sharon 1936-............ **CLC 50**
See also DLB 60

Pomerance, Bernard 1940-........ **CLC 13**
See also CA 101

Ponge, Francis (Jean Gaston Alfred)
    1899-1988 .... **CLC 6, 18**
See also CA 85-88; 126; CANR 40

Pontoppidan, Henrik 1857-1943 ... **TCLC 29**

Poole, Josephine .... **CLC 17**
See also Helyar, Jane Penelope Josephine
See also SAAS 2; SATA 5

Popa, Vasko 1922-............... **CLC 19**
See also CA 112

Pope, Alexander 1688-1744.......... **LC 3**
See also CDBLB 1660-1789; DLB 95, 101;
    WLC

Porter, Connie 1960- .... **CLC 70**

Porter, Gene(va Grace) Stratton
    1863(?)-1924 .... **TCLC 21**
See also CA 112

Porter, Katherine Anne
    1890-1980 ..... **CLC 1, 3, 7, 10, 13, 15,**
                              27; SSC 4
See also AITN 2; CA 1-4R; 101; CANR 1;
    DLB 4, 9, 102; DLBY 80; MTCW;
    SATA 23, 39

Porter, Peter (Neville Frederick)
    1929-.................... **CLC 5, 13, 33**
See also CA 85-88; DLB 40

Porter, William Sydney 1862-1910
See Henry, O.
See also CA 104; 131; CDALB 1865-1917;
    DLB 12, 78, 79; MTCW; YABC 2

Portillo (y Pacheco), Jose Lopez
See Lopez Portillo (y Pacheco), Jose

Post, Melville Davisson
    1869-1930 .... **TCLC 39**
See also CA 110

Potok, Chaim 1929-....... **CLC 2, 7, 14, 26**
See also AITN 1, 2; CA 17-20R; CANR 19,
    35; DLB 28; MTCW; SATA 33

Potter, Beatrice
See Webb, (Martha) Beatrice (Potter)
See also MAICYA

Potter, Dennis (Christopher George)
    1935-...................... **CLC 58**
See also CA 107; CANR 33; MTCW

Pound, Ezra (Weston Loomis)
    1885-1972 ..... **CLC 1, 2, 3, 4, 5, 7, 10,**
                     13, 18, 34, 48, 50; PC 4
See also CA 5-8R; 37-40R; CANR 40;
    CDALB 1917-1929; DLB 4, 45, 63;
    MTCW; WLC

Povod, Reinaldo 1959-............. **CLC 44**
See also CA 136

Powell, Anthony (Dymoke)
    1905-........... **CLC 1, 3, 7, 9, 10, 31**
See also CA 1-4R; CANR 1, 32;
    CDBLB 1945-1960; DLB 15; MTCW

Powell, Dawn 1897-1965 .... **CLC 66**
See also CA 5-8R

Powell, Padgett 1952-............. **CLC 34**
See also CA 126

Powers, J(ames) F(arl)
    1917-.......... **CLC 1, 4, 8, 57; SSC 4**
See also CA 1-4R; CANR 2; DLB 130;
    MTCW

Powers, John J(ames) 1945-
See Powers, John R.
See also CA 69-72

Powers, John R. .... **CLC 66**
See also Powers, John J(ames)

Pownall, David 1938-............. **CLC 10**
See also CA 89-92; DLB 14

Powys, John Cowper
    1872-1963 .... **CLC 7, 9, 15, 46**
See also CA 85-88; DLB 15; MTCW

Powys, T(heodore) F(rancis)
    1875-1953 .... **TCLC 9**
See also CA 106; DLB 36

Prager, Emily 1952-.............. **CLC 56**

Pratt, Edwin John 1883-1964 ..... **CLC 19**
See also CA 93-96; DLB 92

Premchand..................... **TCLC 21**
See also Srivastava, Dhanpat Rai

Preussler, Otfried 1923-.......... **CLC 17**
See also CA 77-80; SATA 24

Prevert, Jacques (Henri Marie)
    1900-1977 .... **CLC 15**
See also CA 77-80; 69-72; CANR 29;
    MTCW; SATA 30

Prevost, Abbe (Antoine Francois)
    1697-1763 .... **LC 1**

Price, (Edward) Reynolds
    1933-......... **CLC 3, 6, 13, 43, 50, 63**
See also CA 1-4R; CANR 1, 37; DLB 2

Price, Richard 1949- .... **CLC 6, 12**
See also CA 49-52; CANR 3; DLBY 81

Prichard, Katharine Susannah
    1883-1969 .... **CLC 46**
See also CA 11-12; CANR 33; CAP 1;
    MTCW; SATA 66

Priestley, J(ohn) B(oynton)
    1894-1984 .... **CLC 2, 5, 9, 34**
See also CA 9-12R; 113; CANR 33;
    CDBLB 1914-1945; DLB 10, 34, 77, 100;
    DLBY 84; MTCW

Prince, F(rank) T(empleton) 1912-.. **CLC 22**
See also CA 101; DLB 20

Prince 1958(?)-................... **CLC 35**

Prince Kropotkin
See Kropotkin, Peter (Aleksieevich)

Prior, Matthew 1664-1721.......... **LC 4**
See also DLB 95

Pritchard, William H(arrison)
    1932-...................... **CLC 34**
See also CA 65-68; CANR 23; DLB 111

Pritchett, V(ictor) S(awdon)
    1900-............... **CLC 5, 13, 15, 41**
See also CA 61-64; CANR 31; DLB 15;
    MTCW

Private 19022
See Manning, Frederic

Probst, Mark 1925-.............. **CLC 59**
See also CA 130

Prokosch, Frederic 1908-1989.... **CLC 4, 48**
See also CA 73-76; 128; DLB 48

Prophet, The
See Dreiser, Theodore (Herman Albert)

Prose, Francine 1947-............. **CLC 45**
See also CA 109; 112

Proudhon
See Cunha, Euclides (Rodrigues Pimenta) da

Proust,
    (Valentin-Louis-George-Eugene-)Marcel
    1871-1922 .... **TCLC 7, 13, 33**
See also CA 104; 120; DLB 65; MTCW;
    WLC

Prowler, Harley
See Masters, Edgar Lee

Prus, Boleslaw................... **TCLC 48**
See also Glowacki, Aleksander

Pryor, Richard (Franklin Lenox Thomas)
    1940-...................... **CLC 26**
See also CA 122

Przybyszewski, Stanislaw
    1868-1927 .... **TCLC 36**
See also DLB 66

Pteleon
See Grieve, C(hristopher) M(urray)

Puckett, Lute
See Masters, Edgar Lee

Puig, Manuel
    1932-1990 .... **CLC 3, 5, 10, 28, 65**
See also CA 45-48; CANR 2, 32; DLB 113;
    HW; MTCW

Purdy, A(lfred) W(ellington)
    1918-................. **CLC 3, 6, 14, 50**
See also Purdy, Al
See also CA 81-84

Purdy, Al
See Purdy, A(lfred) W(ellington)
See also CAAS 17; DLB 88

Purdy, James (Amos)
    1923-............ **CLC 2, 4, 10, 28, 52**
See also CA 33-36R; CAAS 1; CANR 19;
    DLB 2; MTCW

Pure, Simon
See Swinnerton, Frank Arthur

Pushkin, Alexander (Sergeyevich)
    1799-1837 .... **NCLC 3, 27**
See also SATA 61; WLC

P'u Sung-ling 1640-1715 .... **LC 3**

Putnam, Arthur Lee
See Alger, Horatio Jr.

Puzo, Mario   1920- . . . . CLC 1, 2, 6, 36
    See also CA 65-68; CANR 4; DLB 6;
    MTCW

Pym, Barbara (Mary Crampton)
    1913-1980 . . . . CLC 13, 19, 37
    See also CA 13-14; 97-100; CANR 13, 34;
    CAP 1; DLB 14; DLBY 87; MTCW

Pynchon, Thomas (Ruggles Jr.)
    1937- . . CLC 2, 3, 6, 9, 11, 18, 33, 62, 72
    See also BEST 90:2; CA 17-20R; CANR 22;
    DLB 2; MTCW; WLC

Qian Zhongshu
    See Ch'ien Chung-shu

Qroll
    See Dagerman, Stig (Halvard)

Quarrington, Paul (Lewis)   1953- . . . . CLC 65
    See also CA 129

Quasimodo, Salvatore   1901-1968 . . . CLC 10
    See also CA 13-16; 25-28R; CAP 1;
    DLB 114; MTCW

Queen, Ellery. . . . . CLC 3, 11
    See also Dannay, Frederic; Davidson,
    Avram; Lee, Manfred B(ennington);
    Sturgeon, Theodore (Hamilton); Vance,
    John Holbrook

Queen, Ellery Jr.
    See Dannay, Frederic; Lee, Manfred
    B(ennington)

Queneau, Raymond
    1903-1976 . . . . CLC 2, 5, 10, 42
    See also CA 77-80; 69-72; CANR 32;
    DLB 72; MTCW

Quin, Ann (Marie)   1936-1973 . . . . CLC 6
    See also CA 9-12R; 45-48; DLB 14

Quinn, Martin
    See Smith, Martin Cruz

Quinn, Simon
    See Smith, Martin Cruz

Quiroga, Horacio (Sylvestre)
    1878-1937 . . . . TCLC 20
    See also CA 117; 131; HW; MTCW

Quoirez, Francoise   1935- . . . . CLC 9
    See also Sagan, Francoise
    See also CA 49-52; CANR 6, 39; MTCW

Raabe, Wilhelm   1831-1910 . . . . TCLC 45
    See also DLB 129

Rabe, David (William)   1940- . . . CLC 4, 8, 33
    See also CA 85-88; CABS 3; DLB 7

Rabelais, Francois   1483-1553 . . . . LC 5
    See also WLC

Rabinovitch, Sholem   1859-1916
    See Aleichem, Sholom
    See also CA 104

Radcliffe, Ann (Ward)   1764-1823 . . NCLC 6
    See also DLB 39

Radiguet, Raymond   1903-1923 . . . . TCLC 29
    See also DLB 65

Radnoti, Miklos   1909-1944 . . . . . . TCLC 16
    See also CA 118

Rado, James   1939- . . . . CLC 17
    See also CA 105

Radvanyi, Netty   1900-1983
    See Seghers, Anna
    See also CA 85-88; 110

Raeburn, John (Hay)   1941- . . . . CLC 34
    See also CA 57-60

Ragni, Gerome   1942-1991 . . . . CLC 17
    See also CA 105; 134

Rahv, Philip. . . . . CLC 24
    See also Greenberg, Ivan

Raine, Craig   1944- . . . . CLC 32
    See also CA 108; CANR 29; DLB 40

Raine, Kathleen (Jessie)   1908- . . . CLC 7, 45
    See also CA 85-88; DLB 20; MTCW

Rainis, Janis   1865-1929 . . . . TCLC 29

Rakosi, Carl. . . . . CLC 47
    See also Rawley, Callman
    See also CAAS 5

Raleigh, Richard
    See Lovecraft, H(oward) P(hillips)

Rallentando, H. P.
    See Sayers, Dorothy L(eigh)

Ramal, Walter
    See de la Mare, Walter (John)

Ramon, Juan
    See Jimenez (Mantecon), Juan Ramon

Ramos, Graciliano   1892-1953 . . . . . TCLC 32

Rampersad, Arnold   1941- . . . . CLC 44
    See also CA 127; 133; DLB 111

Rampling, Anne
    See Rice, Anne

Ramuz, Charles-Ferdinand
    1878-1947 . . . . TCLC 33

Rand, Ayn   1905-1982 . . . . . . CLC 3, 30, 44
    See also AAYA 10; CA 13-16R; 105;
    CANR 27; MTCW; WLC

Randall, Dudley (Felker)   1914- . . . . . . CLC 1
    See also BLC 3; BW; CA 25-28R;
    CANR 23; DLB 41

Randall, Robert
    See Silverberg, Robert

Ranger, Ken
    See Creasey, John

Ransom, John Crowe
    1888-1974 . . . . CLC 2, 4, 5, 11, 24
    See also CA 5-8R; 49-52; CANR 6, 34;
    DLB 45, 63; MTCW

Rao, Raja   1909- . . . . CLC 25, 56
    See also CA 73-76; MTCW

Raphael, Frederic (Michael)
    1931- . . . . CLC 2, 14
    See also CA 1-4R; CANR 1; DLB 14

Ratcliffe, James P.
    See Mencken, H(enry) L(ouis)

Rathbone, Julian   1935- . . . . CLC 41
    See also CA 101; CANR 34

Rattigan, Terence (Mervyn)
    1911-1977 . . . . CLC 7
    See also CA 85-88; 73-76;
    CDBLB 1945-1960; DLB 13; MTCW

Ratushinskaya, Irina   1954- . . . . CLC 54
    See also CA 129

Raven, Simon (Arthur Noel)
    1927- . . . . CLC 14
    See also CA 81-84

Rawley, Callman   1903-
    See Rakosi, Carl
    See also CA 21-24R; CANR 12, 32

Rawlings, Marjorie Kinnan
    1896-1953 . . . . TCLC 4
    See also CA 104; 137; DLB 9, 22, 102;
    MAICYA; YABC 1

Ray, Satyajit   1921-1992 . . . . CLC 16, 76
    See also CA 114; 137

Read, Herbert Edward   1893-1968 . . . . CLC 4
    See also CA 85-88; 25-28R; DLB 20

Read, Piers Paul   1941- . . . . . . CLC 4, 10, 25
    See also CA 21-24R; CANR 38; DLB 14;
    SATA 21

Reade, Charles   1814-1884 . . . . NCLC 2
    See also DLB 21

Reade, Hamish
    See Gray, Simon (James Holliday)

Reading, Peter   1946- . . . . CLC 47
    See also CA 103; DLB 40

Reaney, James   1926- . . . . CLC 13
    See also CA 41-44R; CAAS 15; DLB 68;
    SATA 43

Rebreanu, Liviu   1885-1944 . . . . TCLC 28

Rechy, John (Francisco)
    1934- . . . . CLC 1, 7, 14, 18
    See also CA 5-8R; CAAS 4; CANR 6, 32;
    DLB 122; DLBY 82; HW

Redcam, Tom   1870-1933 . . . . TCLC 25

Reddin, Keith. . . . . CLC 67

Redgrove, Peter (William)
    1932- . . . . CLC 6, 41
    See also CA 1-4R; CANR 3, 39; DLB 40

Redmon, Anne. . . . . CLC 22
    See also Nightingale, Anne Redmon
    See also DLBY 86

Reed, Eliot
    See Ambler, Eric

Reed, Ishmael
    1938- . . . . CLC 2, 3, 5, 6, 13, 32, 60
    See also BLC 3; BW; CA 21-24R;
    CANR 25; DLB 2, 5, 33; DLBD 8;
    MTCW

Reed, John (Silas)   1887-1920 . . . . . . TCLC 9
    See also CA 106

Reed, Lou. . . . . CLC 21
    See also Firbank, Louis

Reeve, Clara   1729-1807 . . . . NCLC 19
    See also DLB 39

Reid, Christopher   1949- . . . . CLC 33
    See also DLB 40

Reid, Desmond
    See Moorcock, Michael (John)

Reid Banks, Lynne   1929-
    See Banks, Lynne Reid
    See also CA 1-4R; CANR 6, 22, 38;
    CLR 24; MAICYA; SATA 22

Reilly, William K.
    See Creasey, John

Reiner, Max
    See Caldwell, (Janet Miriam) Taylor
    (Holland)

Reis, Ricardo
    See Pessoa, Fernando (Antonio Nogueira)

Remarque, Erich Maria
1898-1970 . . . . **CLC 21**
See also CA 77-80; 29-32R; DLB 56;
MTCW

Remizov, A.
See Remizov, Aleksei (Mikhailovich)

Remizov, A. M.
See Remizov, Aleksei (Mikhailovich)

Remizov, Aleksei (Mikhailovich)
1877-1957 . . . . **TCLC 27**
See also CA 125; 133

Renan, Joseph Ernest
1823-1892 . . . . **NCLC 26**

Renard, Jules 1864-1910 . . . . **TCLC 17**
See also CA 117

Renault, Mary . . . . **CLC 3, 11, 17**
See also Challans, Mary
See also DLBY 83

Rendell, Ruth (Barbara) 1930- . . **CLC 28, 48**
See also Vine, Barbara
See also CA 109; CANR 32; DLB 87;
MTCW

Renoir, Jean 1894-1979 . . . . **CLC 20**
See also CA 129; 85-88

Resnais, Alain 1922- . . . . **CLC 16**

Reverdy, Pierre 1889-1960 . . . . **CLC 53**
See also CA 97-100; 89-92

Rexroth, Kenneth
1905-1982 . . . . . . **CLC 1, 2, 6, 11, 22, 49**
See also CA 5-8R; 107; CANR 14, 34;
CDALB 1941-1968; DLB 16, 48;
DLBY 82; MTCW

Reyes, Alfonso 1889-1959 . . . . **TCLC 33**
See also CA 131; HW

Reyes y Basoalto, Ricardo Eliecer Neftali
See Neruda, Pablo

Reymont, Wladyslaw (Stanislaw)
1868(?)-1925 . . . . **TCLC 5**
See also CA 104

Reynolds, Jonathan 1942- . . . . **CLC 6, 38**
See also CA 65-68; CANR 28

Reynolds, Joshua 1723-1792 . . . . **LC 15**
See also DLB 104

Reynolds, Michael Shane 1937- . . . . **CLC 44**
See also CA 65-68; CANR 9

Reznikoff, Charles 1894-1976 . . . . **CLC 9**
See also CA 33-36; 61-64; CAP 2; DLB 28,
45

Rezzori (d'Arezzo), Gregor von
1914- . . . . **CLC 25**
See also CA 122; 136

Rhine, Richard
See Silverstein, Alvin

Rhys, Jean
1890(?)-1979 . . . . **CLC 2, 4, 6, 14, 19, 51**
See also CA 25-28R; 85-88; CANR 35;
CDBLB 1945-1960; DLB 36, 117; MTCW

Ribeiro, Darcy 1922- . . . . **CLC 34**
See also CA 33-36R

Ribeiro, Joao Ubaldo (Osorio Pimentel)
1941- . . . . **CLC 10, 67**
See also CA 81-84

Ribman, Ronald (Burt) 1932- . . . . **CLC 7**
See also CA 21-24R

Ricci, Nino 1959- . . . . **CLC 70**
See also CA 137

Rice, Anne 1941- . . . . **CLC 41**
See also AAYA 9; BEST 89:2; CA 65-68;
CANR 12, 36

Rice, Elmer (Leopold)
1892-1967 . . . . **CLC 7, 49**
See also CA 21-22; 25-28R; CAP 2; DLB 4,
7; MTCW

Rice, Tim 1944- . . . . **CLC 21**
See also CA 103

Rich, Adrienne (Cecile)
1929- . . . **CLC 3, 6, 7, 11, 18, 36, 73, 76;**
PC 5
See also CA 9-12R; CANR 20; DLB 5, 67;
MTCW

Rich, Barbara
See Graves, Robert (von Ranke)

Rich, Robert
See Trumbo, Dalton

Richards, David Adams 1950- . . . . . . **CLC 59**
See also CA 93-96; DLB 53

Richards, I(vor) A(rmstrong)
1893-1979 . . . . **CLC 14, 24**
See also CA 41-44R; 89-92; CANR 34;
DLB 27

Richardson, Anne
See Roiphe, Anne Richardson

Richardson, Dorothy Miller
1873-1957 . . . . **TCLC 3**
See also CA 104; DLB 36

Richardson, Ethel Florence (Lindesay)
1870-1946
See Richardson, Henry Handel
See also CA 105

Richardson, Henry Handel . . . . **TCLC 4**
See also Richardson, Ethel Florence
(Lindesay)

Richardson, Samuel 1689-1761 . . . . **LC 1**
See also CDBLB 1660-1789; DLB 39; WLC

Richler, Mordecai
1931- . . . . **CLC 3, 5, 9, 13, 18, 46, 70**
See also AITN 1; CA 65-68; CANR 31;
CLR 17; DLB 53; MAICYA; MTCW;
SATA 27, 44

Richter, Conrad (Michael)
1890-1968 . . . . **CLC 30**
See also CA 5-8R; 25-28R; CANR 23;
DLB 9; MTCW; SATA 3

Riddell, J. H. 1832-1906 . . . . **TCLC 40**

Riding, Laura . . . . **CLC 3, 7**
See also Jackson, Laura (Riding)

Riefenstahl, Berta Helene Amalia 1902-
See Riefenstahl, Leni
See also CA 108

Riefenstahl, Leni . . . . **CLC 16**
See also Riefenstahl, Berta Helene Amalia

Riffe, Ernest
See Bergman, (Ernst) Ingmar

Riley, Tex
See Creasey, John

Rilke, Rainer Maria
1875-1926 . . . . . . **TCLC 1, 6, 19; PC 2**
See also CA 104; 132; DLB 81; MTCW

Rimbaud, (Jean Nicolas) Arthur
1854-1891 . . . . **NCLC 4, 35; PC 3**
See also WLC

Ringmaster, The
See Mencken, H(enry) L(ouis)

Ringwood, Gwen(dolyn Margaret) Pharis
1910-1984 . . . . **CLC 48**
See also CA 112; DLB 88

Rio, Michel 19(?)- . . . . **CLC 43**

Ritsos, Giannes
See Ritsos, Yannis

Ritsos, Yannis 1909-1990 . . . . . **CLC 6, 13, 31**
See also CA 77-80; 133; CANR 39; MTCW

Ritter, Erika 1948(?)- . . . . **CLC 52**

Rivera, Jose Eustasio 1889-1928 . . . **TCLC 35**
See also HW

Rivers, Conrad Kent 1933-1968 . . . . . . **CLC 1**
See also BW; CA 85-88; DLB 41

Rivers, Elfrida
See Bradley, Marion Zimmer

Riverside, John
See Heinlein, Robert A(nson)

Rizal, Jose 1861-1896 . . . . **NCLC 27**

Roa Bastos, Augusto (Antonio)
1917- . . . . **CLC 45**
See also CA 131; DLB 113; HW

Robbe-Grillet, Alain
1922- . . . . . . **CLC 1, 2, 4, 6, 8, 10, 14, 43**
See also CA 9-12R; CANR 33; DLB 83;
MTCW

Robbins, Harold 1916- . . . . **CLC 5**
See also CA 73-76; CANR 26; MTCW

Robbins, Thomas Eugene 1936-
See Robbins, Tom
See also CA 81-84; CANR 29; MTCW

Robbins, Tom . . . . **CLC 9, 32, 64**
See also Robbins, Thomas Eugene
See also BEST 90:3; DLBY 80

Robbins, Trina 1938- . . . . **CLC 21**
See also CA 128

Roberts, Charles G(eorge) D(ouglas)
1860-1943 . . . . **TCLC 8**
See also CA 105; DLB 92; SATA 29

Roberts, Kate 1891-1985 . . . . **CLC 15**
See also CA 107; 116

Roberts, Keith (John Kingston)
1935- . . . . **CLC 14**
See also CA 25-28R

Roberts, Kenneth (Lewis)
1885-1957 . . . . **TCLC 23**
See also CA 109; DLB 9

Roberts, Michele (B.) 1949- . . . . **CLC 48**
See also CA 115

Robertson, Ellis
See Ellison, Harlan; Silverberg, Robert

Robertson, Thomas William
1829-1871 . . . . **NCLC 35**

Robinson, Edwin Arlington
1869-1935 . . . . **TCLC 5; PC 1**
See also CA 104; 133; CDALB 1865-1917;
DLB 54; MTCW

Robinson, Henry Crabb
1775-1867 . . . . **NCLC 15**
See also DLB 107

Russ, Joanna 1937-.............. **CLC 15**
See also CA 25-28R; CANR 11, 31; DLB 8;
MTCW

Russell, George William 1867-1935
See A. E.
See also CA 104; CDBLB 1890-1914

Russell, (Henry) Ken(neth Alfred)
1927-..................... **CLC 16**
See also CA 105

Russell, Willy 1947-.............. **CLC 60**

Rutherford, Mark .... **TCLC 25**
See also White, William Hale
See also DLB 18

Ruyslinck, Ward
See Belser, Reimond Karel Maria de

Ryan, Cornelius (John) 1920-1974 ... **CLC 7**
See also CA 69-72; 53-56; CANR 38

Ryan, Michael 1946- .... **CLC 65**
See also CA 49-52; DLBY 82

Rybakov, Anatoli (Naumovich)
1911-................... **CLC 23, 53**
See also CA 126; 135

Ryder, Jonathan
See Ludlum, Robert

Ryga, George 1932-1987 .... **CLC 14**
See also CA 101; 124; DLB 60

S. S.
See Sassoon, Siegfried (Lorraine)

Saba, Umberto 1883-1957 .... **TCLC 33**
See also DLB 114

Sabatini, Rafael 1875-1950 ...... **TCLC 47**

Sabato, Ernesto (R.) 1911-..... **CLC 10, 23**
See also CA 97-100; CANR 32; HW;
MTCW

Sacastru, Martin
See Bioy Casares, Adolfo

Sacher-Masoch, Leopold von
1836(?)-1895 .... **NCLC 31**

Sachs, Marilyn (Stickle) 1927-..... **CLC 35**
See also AAYA 2; CA 17-20R; CANR 13;
CLR 2; MAICYA; SAAS 2; SATA 3, 68

Sachs, Nelly 1891-1970 .... **CLC 14**
See also CA 17-18; 25-28R; CAP 2

Sackler, Howard (Oliver)
1929-1982 .... **CLC 14**
See also CA 61-64; 108; CANR 30; DLB 7

Sacks, Oliver (Wolf) 1933- .... **CLC 67**
See also CA 53-56; CANR 28; MTCW

Sade, Donatien Alphonse Francois Comte
1740-1814 .... **NCLC 3**

Sadoff, Ira 1945-................. **CLC 9**
See also CA 53-56; CANR 5, 21; DLB 120

Saetone
See Camus, Albert

Safire, William 1929-.............. **CLC 10**
See also CA 17-20R; CANR 31

Sagan, Carl (Edward) 1934-........ **CLC 30**
See also AAYA 2; CA 25-28R; CANR 11,
36; MTCW; SATA 58

Sagan, Francoise........ **CLC 3, 6, 9, 17, 36**
See also Quoirez, Francoise
See also DLB 83

Sahgal, Nayantara (Pandit) 1927-... **CLC 41**
See also CA 9-12R; CANR 11

Saint, H(arry) F. 1941- .... **CLC 50**
See also CA 127

St. Aubin de Teran, Lisa 1953-
See Teran, Lisa St. Aubin de
See also CA 118; 126

Sainte-Beuve, Charles Augustin
1804-1869 .... **NCLC 5**

Saint-Exupery, Antoine (Jean Baptiste Marie
Roger) de 1900-1944 .... **TCLC 2**
See also CA 108; 132; CLR 10; DLB 72;
MAICYA; MTCW; SATA 20; WLC

St. John, David
See Hunt, E(verette) Howard Jr.

Saint-John Perse
See Leger, (Marie-Rene) Alexis Saint-Leger

Saintsbury, George (Edward Bateman)
1845-1933 .... **TCLC 31**
See also DLB 57

Sait Faik .... **TCLC 23**
See also Abasiyanik, Sait Faik

Saki .... **TCLC 3**
See also Munro, H(ector) H(ugh)

Salama, Hannu 1936-............. **CLC 18**

Salamanca, J(ack) R(ichard)
1922-.................... **CLC 4, 15**
See also CA 25-28R

Sale, J. Kirkpatrick
See Sale, Kirkpatrick

Sale, Kirkpatrick 1937-.......... **CLC 68**
See also CA 13-16R; CANR 10

Salinas (y Serrano), Pedro
1891(?)-1951 .... **TCLC 17**
See also CA 117

Salinger, J(erome) D(avid)
1919-.... **CLC 1, 3, 8, 12, 55, 56; SSC 2**
See also AAYA 2; CA 5-8R; CANR 39;
CDALB 1941-1968; CLR 18; DLB 2, 102;
MAICYA; MTCW; SATA 67; WLC

Salisbury, John
See Caute, David

Salter, James 1925- .... **CLC 7, 52, 59**
See also CA 73-76; DLB 130

Saltus, Edgar (Everton)
1855-1921 .... **TCLC 8**
See also CA 105

Saltykov, Mikhail Evgrafovich
1826-1889 .... **NCLC 16**

Samarakis, Antonis 1919- .... **CLC 5**
See also CA 25-28R; CAAS 16; CANR 36

Sanchez, Florencio 1875-1910..... **TCLC 37**
See also HW

Sanchez, Luis Rafael 1936-........ **CLC 23**
See also CA 128; HW

Sanchez, Sonia 1934-.............. **CLC 5**
See also BLC 3; BW; CA 33-36R;
CANR 24; CLR 18; DLB 41; DLBD 8;
MAICYA; MTCW; SATA 22

Sand, George 1804-1876.......... **NCLC 2**
See also DLB 119; WLC

Sandburg, Carl (August)
1878-1967 ... **CLC 1, 4, 10, 15, 35; PC 2**
See also CA 5-8R; 25-28R; CANR 35;
CDALB 1865-1917; DLB 17, 54;
MAICYA; MTCW; SATA 8; WLC

Sandburg, Charles
See Sandburg, Carl (August)

Sandburg, Charles A.
See Sandburg, Carl (August)

Sanders, (James) Ed(ward) 1939- ... **CLC 53**
See also CA 13-16R; CANR 13; DLB 16

Sanders, Lawrence 1920-.......... **CLC 41**
See also BEST 89:4; CA 81-84; CANR 33;
MTCW

Sanders, Noah
See Blount, Roy (Alton) Jr.

Sanders, Winston P.
See Anderson, Poul (William)

Sandoz, Mari(e Susette)
1896-1966 .... **CLC 28**
See also CA 1-4R; 25-28R; CANR 17;
DLB 9; MTCW; SATA 5

Saner, Reg(inald Anthony) 1931- .... **CLC 9**
See also CA 65-68

Sannazaro, Jacopo 1456(?)-1530...... **LC 8**

Sansom, William 1912-1976....... **CLC 2, 6**
See also CA 5-8R; 65-68; MTCW

Santayana, George 1863-1952..... **TCLC 40**
See also CA 115; DLB 54, 71

Santiago, Danny .... **CLC 33**
See also James, Daniel (Lewis); James,
Daniel (Lewis)
See also DLB 122

Santmyer, Helen Hooven
1895-1986 .... **CLC 33**
See also CA 1-4R; 118; CANR 15, 33;
DLBY 84; MTCW

Santos, Bienvenido N(uqui) 1911-... **CLC 22**
See also CA 101; CANR 19

Sapper .... **TCLC 44**
See also McNeile, Herman Cyril

Sappho fl. 6th cent. B.C.-.... **CMLC 3; PC 5**

Sarduy, Severo 1937-.............. **CLC 6**
See also CA 89-92; DLB 113; HW

Sargeson, Frank 1903-1982 .... **CLC 31**
See also CA 25-28R; 106; CANR 38

Sarmiento, Felix Ruben Garcia 1867-1916
See Dario, Ruben
See also CA 104

Saroyan, William
1908-1981 ..... **CLC 1, 8, 10, 29, 34, 56**
See also CA 5-8R; 103; CANR 30; DLB 7,
9, 86; DLBY 81; MTCW; SATA 23, 24;
WLC

Sarraute, Nathalie
1900- .... **CLC 1, 2, 4, 8, 10, 31**
See also CA 9-12R; CANR 23; DLB 83;
MTCW

Sarton, (Eleanor) May
1912- .... **CLC 4, 14, 49**
See also CA 1-4R; CANR 1, 34; DLB 48;
DLBY 81; MTCW; SATA 36

Sartre, Jean-Paul
1905-1980 ... CLC 1, 4, 7, 9, 13, 18, 24,
44, 50, 52; DC 3
See also CA 9-12R; 97-100; CANR 21;
DLB 72; MTCW; WLC

Sassoon, Siegfried (Lorraine)
1886-1967 .... CLC 36
See also CA 104; 25-28R; CANR 36;
DLB 20; MTCW

Satterfield, Charles
See Pohl, Frederik

Saul, John (W. III) 1942- .... CLC 46
See also AAYA 10; BEST 90:4; CA 81-84;
CANR 16, 40

Saunders, Caleb
See Heinlein, Robert A(nson)

Saura (Atares), Carlos 1932- .... CLC 20
See also CA 114; 131; HW

Sauser-Hall, Frederic 1887-1961.... CLC 18
See also CA 102; 93-96; CANR 36; MTCW

Saussure, Ferdinand de
1857-1913 .... TCLC 49

Savage, Catharine
See Brosman, Catharine Savage

Savage, Thomas 1915- .... CLC 40
See also CA 126; 132; CAAS 15

Savan, Glenn .... CLC 50

Saven, Glenn 19(?)- .... CLC 50

Sayers, Dorothy L(eigh)
1893-1957 .... TCLC 2, 15
See also CA 104; 119; CDBLB 1914-1945;
DLB 10, 36, 77, 100; MTCW

Sayers, Valerie 1952- .... CLC 50
See also CA 134

Sayles, John Thomas 1950- ... CLC 7, 10, 14
See also CA 57-60; DLB 44

Scammell, Michael .... CLC 34

Scannell, Vernon 1922- .... CLC 49
See also CA 5-8R; CANR 8, 24; DLB 27;
SATA 59

Scarlett, Susan
See Streatfeild, (Mary) Noel

Schaeffer, Susan Fromberg
1941- .... CLC 6, 11, 22
See also CA 49-52; CANR 18; DLB 28;
MTCW; SATA 22

Schary, Jill
See Robinson, Jill

Schell, Jonathan 1943- .... CLC 35
See also CA 73-76; CANR 12

Schelling, Friedrich Wilhelm Joseph von
1775-1854 .... NCLC 30
See also DLB 90

Scherer, Jean-Marie Maurice 1920-
See Rohmer, Eric
See also CA 110

Schevill, James (Erwin) 1920- .... CLC 7
See also CA 5-8R; CAAS 12

Schiller, Friedrich 1759-1805 .... NCLC 39
See also DLB 94

Schisgal, Murray (Joseph) 1926- ..... CLC 6
See also CA 21-24R

Schlee, Ann 1934- .... CLC 35
See also CA 101; CANR 29; SATA 36, 44

Schlegel, August Wilhelm von
1767-1845 .... NCLC 15
See also DLB 94

Schlegel, Johann Elias (von)
1719(?)-1749 .... LC 5

Schmidt, Arno (Otto) 1914-1979.... CLC 56
See also CA 128; 109; DLB 69

Schmitz, Aron Hector 1861-1928
See Svevo, Italo
See also CA 104; 122; MTCW

Schnackenberg, Gjertrud 1953-..... CLC 40
See also CA 116; DLB 120

Schneider, Leonard Alfred 1925-1966
See Bruce, Lenny
See also CA 89-92

Schnitzler, Arthur 1862-1931 ...... TCLC 4
See also CA 104; DLB 81, 118

Schor, Sandra (M.) 1932(?)-1990 ... CLC 65
See also CA 132

Schorer, Mark 1908-1977 .... CLC 9
See also CA 5-8R; 73-76; CANR 7;
DLB 103

Schrader, Paul Joseph 1946-....... CLC 26
See also CA 37-40R; DLB 44

Schreiner, Olive (Emilie Albertina)
1855-1920 .... TCLC 9
See also CA 105; DLB 18

Schulberg, Budd (Wilson)
1914- .... CLC 7, 48
See also CA 25-28R; CANR 19; DLB 6, 26,
28; DLBY 81

Schulz, Bruno 1892-1942.......... TCLC 5
See also CA 115; 123

Schulz, Charles M(onroe) 1922- .... CLC 12
See also CA 9-12R; CANR 6; SATA 10

Schuyler, James Marcus
1923-1991 .... CLC 5, 23
See also CA 101; 134; DLB 5

Schwartz, Delmore (David)
1913-1966 .... CLC 2, 4, 10, 45
See also CA 17-18; 25-28R; CANR 35;
CAP 2; DLB 28, 48; MTCW

Schwartz, Ernst
See Ozu, Yasujiro

Schwartz, John Burnham 1965- .... CLC 59
See also CA 132

Schwartz, Lynne Sharon 1939- ..... CLC 31
See also CA 103

Schwartz, Muriel A.
See Eliot, T(homas) S(tearns)

Schwarz-Bart, Andre 1928- .... CLC 2, 4
See also CA 89-92

Schwarz-Bart, Simone 1938-........ CLC 7
See also CA 97-100

Schwob, (Mayer Andre) Marcel
1867-1905 .... TCLC 20
See also CA 117; DLB 123

Sciascia, Leonardo
1921-1989 .... CLC 8, 9, 41
See also CA 85-88; 130; CANR 35; MTCW

Scoppettone, Sandra 1936-........ CLC 26
See also CA 5-8R; SATA 9

Scorsese, Martin 1942- .... CLC 20
See also CA 110; 114

Scotland, Jay
See Jakes, John (William)

Scott, Duncan Campbell
1862-1947 .... TCLC 6
See also CA 104; DLB 92

Scott, Evelyn 1893-1963........... CLC 43
See also CA 104; 112; DLB 9, 48

Scott, F(rancis) R(eginald)
1899-1985 .... CLC 22
See also CA 101; 114; DLB 88

Scott, Frank
See Scott, F(rancis) R(eginald)

Scott, Joanna 1960- .... CLC 50
See also CA 126

Scott, Paul (Mark) 1920-1978.... CLC 9, 60
See also CA 81-84; 77-80; CANR 33;
DLB 14; MTCW

Scott, Walter 1771-1832......... NCLC 15
See also CDBLB 1789-1832; DLB 93, 107,
116; WLC; YABC 2

Scribe, (Augustin) Eugene
1791-1861 .... NCLC 16

Scrum, R.
See Crumb, R(obert)

Scudery, Madeleine de 1607-1701..... LC 2

Scum
See Crumb, R(obert)

Scumbag, Little Bobby
See Crumb, R(obert)

Seabrook, John
See Hubbard, L(afayette) Ron(ald)

Sealy, I. Allan 1951- .... CLC 55

Search, Alexander
See Pessoa, Fernando (Antonio Nogueira)

Sebastian, Lee
See Silverberg, Robert

Sebastian Owl
See Thompson, Hunter S(tockton)

Sebestyen, Ouida 1924- .... CLC 30
See also AAYA 8; CA 107; CANR 40;
CLR 17; MAICYA; SAAS 10; SATA 39

Sedges, John
See Buck, Pearl S(ydenstricker)

Sedgwick, Catharine Maria
1789-1867 .... NCLC 19
See also DLB 1, 74

Seelye, John 1931-................ CLC 7

Seferiades, Giorgos Stylianou 1900-1971
See Seferis, George
See also CA 5-8R; 33-36R; CANR 5, 36;
MTCW

Seferis, George .... CLC 5, 11
See also Seferiades, Giorgos Stylianou

Segal, Erich (Wolf) 1937- .... CLC 3, 10
See also BEST 89:1; CA 25-28R; CANR 20,
36; DLBY 86; MTCW

Seger, Bob 1945-................. CLC 35

Seghers, Anna .... CLC 7
See also Radvanyi, Netty
See also DLB 69

Seidel, Frederick (Lewis) 1936-..... CLC 18
See also CA 13-16R; CANR 8; DLBY 84

Seifert, Jaroslav 1901-1986 . . . . . **CLC 34, 44**
   See also CA 127; MTCW

Sei Shonagon c. 966-1017(?) . . . . . . **CMLC 6**

Selby, Hubert Jr. 1928- . . . . . . **CLC 1, 2, 4, 8**
   See also CA 13-16R; CANR 33; DLB 2

Selzer, Richard 1928- . . . . **CLC 74**
   See also CA 65-68; CANR 14

Sembene, Ousmane
   See Ousmane, Sembene

Senancour, Etienne Pivert de
   1770-1846 . . . . **NCLC 16**
   See also DLB 119

Sender, Ramon (Jose) 1902-1982 . . . . **CLC 8**
   See also CA 5-8R; 105; CANR 8; HW;
   MTCW

Seneca, Lucius Annaeus
   4B.C.-65. . . . . **CMLC 6**

Senghor, Leopold Sedar 1906- . . . . . . **CLC 54**
   See also BLC 3; BW; CA 116; 125; MTCW

Serling, (Edward) Rod(man)
   1924-1975 . . . . **CLC 30**
   See also AITN 1; CA 65-68; 57-60; DLB 26

Serna, Ramon Gomez de la
   See Gomez de la Serna, Ramon

Serpieres
   See Guillevic, (Eugene)

Service, Robert
   See Service, Robert W(illiam)
   See also DLB 92

Service, Robert W(illiam)
   1874(?)-1958 . . . . **TCLC 15**
   See also Service, Robert
   See also CA 115; SATA 20; WLC

Seth, Vikram 1952- . . . . **CLC 43**
   See also CA 121; 127; DLB 120

Seton, Cynthia Propper
   1926-1982 . . . . **CLC 27**
   See also CA 5-8R; 108; CANR 7

Seton, Ernest (Evan) Thompson
   1860-1946 . . . . **TCLC 31**
   See also CA 109; DLB 92; SATA 18

Seton-Thompson, Ernest
   See Seton, Ernest (Evan) Thompson

Settle, Mary Lee 1918- . . . . **CLC 19, 61**
   See also CA 89-92; CAAS 1; DLB 6

Seuphor, Michel
   See Arp, Jean

Sevigne, Marie (de Rabutin-Chantal) Marquise
   de 1626-1696 . . . . **LC 11**

Sexton, Anne (Harvey)
   1928-1974 . . . **CLC 2, 4, 6, 8, 10, 15, 53;**
                                 PC 2
   See also CA 1-4R; 53-56; CABS 2;
   CANR 3, 36; CDALB 1941-1968; DLB 5;
   MTCW; SATA 10; WLC

Shaara, Michael (Joseph Jr.)
   1929-1988 . . . . **CLC 15**
   See also AITN 1; CA 102; DLBY 83

Shackleton, C. C.
   See Aldiss, Brian W(ilson)

Shacochis, Bob . . . . **CLC 39**
   See also Shacochis, Robert G.

Shacochis, Robert G. 1951-
   See Shacochis, Bob
   See also CA 119; 124

Shaffer, Anthony (Joshua) 1926- . . . . **CLC 19**
   See also CA 110; 116; DLB 13

Shaffer, Peter (Levin)
   1926- . . . . **CLC 5, 14, 18, 37, 60**
   See also CA 25-28R; CANR 25;
   CDBLB 1960 to Present; DLB 13;
   MTCW

Shakey, Bernard
   See Young, Neil

Shalamov, Varlam (Tikhonovich)
   1907(?)-1982 . . . . **CLC 18**
   See also CA 129; 105

Shamlu, Ahmad 1925- . . . . **CLC 10**

Shammas, Anton 1951- . . . . **CLC 55**

Shange, Ntozake
   1948- . . . . **CLC 8, 25, 38, 74; DC 3**
   See also AAYA 9; BLC 3; BW; CA 85-88;
   CABS 3; CANR 27; DLB 38; MTCW

Shanley, John Patrick 1950- . . . . **CLC 75**
   See also CA 128; 133

Shapcott, Thomas William 1935- . . . **CLC 38**
   See also CA 69-72

Shapiro, Jane . . . . **CLC 76**

Shapiro, Karl (Jay) 1913- . . **CLC 4, 8, 15, 53**
   See also CA 1-4R; CAAS 6; CANR 1, 36;
   DLB 48; MTCW

Sharp, William 1855-1905 . . . . **TCLC 39**

Sharpe, Thomas Ridley 1928-
   See Sharpe, Tom
   See also CA 114; 122

Sharpe, Tom . . . . **CLC 36**
   See also Sharpe, Thomas Ridley
   See also DLB 14

Shaw, Bernard . . . . **TCLC 45**
   See also Shaw, George Bernard

Shaw, G. Bernard
   See Shaw, George Bernard

Shaw, George Bernard
   1856-1950 . . . . **TCLC 3, 9, 21**
   See also Shaw, Bernard
   See also CA 104; 128; CDBLB 1914-1945;
   DLB 10, 57; MTCW; WLC

Shaw, Henry Wheeler
   1818-1885 . . . . **NCLC 15**
   See also DLB 11

Shaw, Irwin 1913-1984 . . . . . . **CLC 7, 23, 34**
   See also AITN 1; CA 13-16R; 112;
   CANR 21; CDALB 1941-1968; DLB 6,
   102; DLBY 84; MTCW

Shaw, Robert 1927-1978 . . . . **CLC 5**
   See also AITN 1; CA 1-4R; 81-84;
   CANR 4; DLB 13, 14

Shaw, T. E.
   See Lawrence, T(homas) E(dward)

Shawn, Wallace 1943- . . . . **CLC 41**
   See also CA 112

Sheed, Wilfrid (John Joseph)
   1930- . . . . **CLC 2, 4, 10, 53**
   See also CA 65-68; CANR 30; DLB 6;
   MTCW

Sheldon, Alice Hastings Bradley
   1915(?)-1987
   See Tiptree, James Jr.
   See also CA 108; 122; CANR 34; MTCW

Sheldon, John
   See Bloch, Robert (Albert)

Shelley, Mary Wollstonecraft (Godwin)
   1797-1851 . . . . **NCLC 14**
   See also CDBLB 1789-1832; DLB 110, 116;
   SATA 29; WLC

Shelley, Percy Bysshe
   1792-1822 . . . . **NCLC 18**
   See also CDBLB 1789-1832; DLB 96, 110;
   WLC

Shepard, Jim 1956- . . . . **CLC 36**
   See also CA 137

Shepard, Lucius 19(?)- . . . . **CLC 34**
   See also CA 128

Shepard, Sam
   1943- . . . . **CLC 4, 6, 17, 34, 41, 44**
   See also AAYA 1; CA 69-72; CABS 3;
   CANR 22; DLB 7; MTCW

Shepherd, Michael
   See Ludlum, Robert

Sherburne, Zoa (Morin) 1912- . . . . . . **CLC 30**
   See also CA 1-4R; CANR 3, 37; MAICYA;
   SATA 3

Sheridan, Frances 1724-1766 . . . . **LC 7**
   See also DLB 39, 84

Sheridan, Richard Brinsley
   1751-1816 . . . . **NCLC 5; DC 1**
   See also CDBLB 1660-1789; DLB 89; WLC

Sherman, Jonathan Marc . . . . **CLC 55**

Sherman, Martin 1941(?)- . . . . **CLC 19**
   See also CA 116; 123

Sherwin, Judith Johnson 1936- . . . **CLC 7, 15**
   See also CA 25-28R; CANR 34

Sherwood, Robert E(mmet)
   1896-1955 . . . . **TCLC 3**
   See also CA 104; DLB 7, 26

Shiel, M(atthew) P(hipps)
   1865-1947 . . . . **TCLC 8**
   See also CA 106

Shiga, Naoya 1883-1971 . . . . **CLC 33**
   See also CA 101; 33-36R

Shimazaki Haruki 1872-1943
   See Shimazaki Toson
   See also CA 105; 134

Shimazaki Toson . . . . **TCLC 5**
   See also Shimazaki Haruki

Sholokhov, Mikhail (Aleksandrovich)
   1905-1984 . . . . **CLC 7, 15**
   See also CA 101; 112; MTCW; SATA 36

Shone, Patric
   See Hanley, James

Shreve, Susan Richards 1939- . . . . . . **CLC 23**
   See also CA 49-52; CAAS 5; CANR 5, 38;
   MAICYA; SATA 41, 46

Shue, Larry 1946-1985 . . . . **CLC 52**
   See also CA 117

Shu-Jen, Chou 1881-1936
   See Hsun, Lu
   See also CA 104

Smart, Christopher 1722-1771....... **LC 3**
See also DLB 109

Smart, Elizabeth 1913-1986....... **CLC 54**
See also CA 81-84; 118; DLB 88

Smiley, Jane (Graves) 1949- .... **CLC 53, 76**
See also CA 104; CANR 30

Smith, A(rthur) J(ames) M(arshall)
1902-1980 .... **CLC 15**
See also CA 1-4R; 102; CANR 4; DLB 88

Smith, Betty (Wehner) 1896-1972... **CLC 19**
See also CA 5-8R; 33-36R; DLBY 82;
SATA 6

Smith, Charlotte (Turner)
1749-1806 .... **NCLC 23**
See also DLB 39, 109

Smith, Clark Ashton 1893-1961 .... **CLC 43**

Smith, Dave................. **CLC 22, 42**
See also Smith, David (Jeddie)
See also CAAS 7; DLB 5

Smith, David (Jeddie) 1942-
See Smith, Dave
See also CA 49-52; CANR 1

Smith, Florence Margaret
1902-1971 .... **CLC 8**
See also Smith, Stevie
See also CA 17-18; 29-32R; CANR 35;
CAP 2; MTCW

Smith, Iain Crichton 1928- .... **CLC 64**
See also CA 21-24R; DLB 40

Smith, John 1580(?)-1631 .... **LC 9**

Smith, Johnston
See Crane, Stephen (Townley)

Smith, Lee 1944-.............. **CLC 25, 73**
See also CA 114; 119; DLBY 83

Smith, Martin
See Smith, Martin Cruz

Smith, Martin Cruz 1942-........ **CLC 25**
See also BEST 89:4; CA 85-88; CANR 6, 23

Smith, Mary-Ann Tirone 1944-..... **CLC 39**
See also CA 118; 136

Smith, Patti 1946- .... **CLC 12**
See also CA 93-96

Smith, Pauline (Urmson)
1882-1959 .... **TCLC 25**

Smith, Rosamond
See Oates, Joyce Carol

Smith, Sheila Kaye
See Kaye-Smith, Sheila

Smith, Stevie............. **CLC 3, 8, 25, 44**
See also Smith, Florence Margaret
See also DLB 20

Smith, Wilbur A(ddison) 1933-..... **CLC 33**
See also CA 13-16R; CANR 7; MTCW

Smith, William Jay 1918- .... **CLC 6**
See also CA 5-8R; DLB 5; MAICYA;
SATA 2, 68

Smith, Woodrow Wilson
See Kuttner, Henry

Smolenskin, Peretz 1842-1885.... **NCLC 30**

Smollett, Tobias (George) 1721-1771 .. **LC 2**
See also CDBLB 1660-1789; DLB 39, 104

Snodgrass, William D(e Witt)
1926- .... **CLC 2, 6, 10, 18, 68**
See also CA 1-4R; CANR 6, 36; DLB 5;
MTCW

Snow, C(harles) P(ercy)
1905-1980 .... **CLC 1, 4, 6, 9, 13, 19**
See also CA 5-8R; 101; CANR 28;
CDBLB 1945-1960; DLB 15, 77; MTCW

Snow, Frances Compton
See Adams, Henry (Brooks)

Snyder, Gary (Sherman)
1930- .... **CLC 1, 2, 5, 9, 32**
See also CA 17-20R; CANR 30; DLB 5, 16

Snyder, Zilpha Keatley 1927-...... **CLC 17**
See also CA 9-12R; CANR 38; MAICYA;
SAAS 2; SATA 1, 28

Soares, Bernardo
See Pessoa, Fernando (Antonio Nogueira)

Sobh, A.
See Shamlu, Ahmad

Sobol, Joshua................... **CLC 60**

Soderberg, Hjalmar 1869-1941 .... **TCLC 39**

Sodergran, Edith (Irene)
See Soedergran, Edith (Irene)

Soedergran, Edith (Irene)
1892-1923 .... **TCLC 31**

Softly, Edgar
See Lovecraft, H(oward) P(hillips)

Softly, Edward
See Lovecraft, H(oward) P(hillips)

Sokolov, Raymond 1941-.......... **CLC 7**
See also CA 85-88

Solo, Jay
See Ellison, Harlan

Sologub, Fyodor .... **TCLC 9**
See also Teternikov, Fyodor Kuzmich

Solomons, Ikey Esquir
See Thackeray, William Makepeace

Solomos, Dionysios 1798-1857 ... **NCLC 15**

Solwoska, Mara
See French, Marilyn

Solzhenitsyn, Aleksandr I(sayevich)
1918- ... **CLC 1, 2, 4, 7, 9, 10, 18, 26, 34**
See also AITN 1; CA 69-72; CANR 40;
MTCW; WLC

Somers, Jane
See Lessing, Doris (May)

Sommer, Scott 1951- .... **CLC 25**
See also CA 106

Sondheim, Stephen (Joshua)
1930- .... **CLC 30, 39**
See also CA 103

Sontag, Susan 1933-... **CLC 1, 2, 10, 13, 31**
See also CA 17-20R; CANR 25; DLB 2, 67;
MTCW

Sophocles
496(?)B.C.-406(?)B.C.... **CMLC 2; DC 1**

Sorel, Julia
See Drexler, Rosalyn

Sorrentino, Gilbert
1929- .... **CLC 3, 7, 14, 22, 40**
See also CA 77-80; CANR 14, 33; DLB 5;
DLBY 80

Soto, Gary 1952-................. **CLC 32**
See also AAYA 10; CA 119; 125; DLB 82;
HW

Soupault, Philippe 1897-1990 ..... **CLC 68**
See also CA 116; 131

Souster, (Holmes) Raymond
1921- .... **CLC 5, 14**
See also CA 13-16R; CAAS 14; CANR 13,
29; DLB 88; SATA 63

Southern, Terry 1926- .... **CLC 7**
See also CA 1-4R; CANR 1; DLB 2

Southey, Robert 1774-1843 .... **NCLC 8**
See also DLB 93, 107; SATA 54

Southworth, Emma Dorothy Eliza Nevitte
1819-1899 .... **NCLC 26**

Souza, Ernest
See Scott, Evelyn

Soyinka, Wole
1934- .... **CLC 3, 5, 14, 36, 44; DC 2**
See also BLC 3; BW; CA 13-16R;
CANR 27, 39; DLB 125; MTCW; WLC

Spackman, W(illiam) M(ode)
1905-1990 .... **CLC 46**
See also CA 81-84; 132

Spacks, Barry 1931-............... **CLC 14**
See also CA 29-32R; CANR 33; DLB 105

Spanidou, Irini 1946-............. **CLC 44**

Spark, Muriel (Sarah)
1918- .... **CLC 2, 3, 5, 8, 13, 18, 40;
SSC 10**
See also CA 5-8R; CANR 12, 36;
CDBLB 1945-1960; DLB 15; MTCW

Spaulding, Douglas
See Bradbury, Ray (Douglas)

Spaulding, Leonard
See Bradbury, Ray (Douglas)

Spence, J. A. D.
See Eliot, T(homas) S(tearns)

Spencer, Elizabeth 1921-.......... **CLC 22**
See also CA 13-16R; CANR 32; DLB 6;
MTCW; SATA 14

Spencer, Leonard G.
See Silverberg, Robert

Spencer, Scott 1945-.............. **CLC 30**
See also CA 113; DLBY 86

Spender, Stephen (Harold)
1909- .... **CLC 1, 2, 5, 10, 41**
See also CA 9-12R; CANR 31;
CDBLB 1945-1960; DLB 20; MTCW

Spengler, Oswald (Arnold Gottfried)
1880-1936 .... **TCLC 25**
See also CA 118

Spenser, Edmund 1552(?)-1599 .... **LC 5**
See also CDBLB Before 1660; WLC

Spicer, Jack 1925-1965 ...... **CLC 8, 18, 72**
See also CA 85-88; DLB 5, 16

Spiegelman, Art 1948-............ **CLC 76**
See also AAYA 10; CA 125

Spielberg, Peter 1929-............. **CLC 6**
See also CA 5-8R; CANR 4; DLBY 81

Spielberg, Steven 1947-........... **CLC 20**
See also AAYA 8; CA 77-80; CANR 32;
SATA 32

Spillane, Frank Morrison 1918-
See Spillane, Mickey
See also CA 25-28R; CANR 28; MTCW;
SATA 66

Spillane, Mickey .... CLC 3, 13
See also Spillane, Frank Morrison

Spinoza, Benedictus de 1632-1677 .... LC 9

Spinrad, Norman (Richard) 1940-... CLC 46
See also CA 37-40R; CANR 20; DLB 8

Spitteler, Carl (Friedrich Georg)
1845-1924 .... TCLC 12
See also CA 109; DLB 129

Spivack, Kathleen (Romola Drucker)
1938- .... CLC 6
See also CA 49-52

Spoto, Donald 1941-.............. CLC 39
See also CA 65-68; CANR 11

Springsteen, Bruce (F.) 1949- ...... CLC 17
See also CA 111

Spurling, Hilary 1940-............ CLC 34
See also CA 104; CANR 25

Squires, Radcliffe 1917-.......... CLC 51
See also CA 1-4R; CANR 6, 21

Srivastava, Dhanpat Rai 1880(?)-1936
See Premchand
See also CA 118

Stacy, Donald
See Pohl, Frederik

Stael, Germaine de
See Stael-Holstein, Anne Louise Germaine
Necker Baronn
See also DLB 119

Stael-Holstein, Anne Louise Germaine Necker
Baronn 1766-1817 .... NCLC 3
See also Stael, Germaine de

Stafford, Jean 1915-1979... CLC 4, 7, 19, 68
See also CA 1-4R; 85-88; CANR 3; DLB 2;
MTCW; SATA 22

Stafford, William (Edgar)
1914- .... CLC 4, 7, 29
See also CA 5-8R; CAAS 3; CANR 5, 22;
DLB 5

Staines, Trevor
See Brunner, John (Kilian Houston)

Stairs, Gordon
See Austin, Mary (Hunter)

Stannard, Martin................. CLC 44

Stanton, Maura 1946- .... CLC 9
See also CA 89-92; CANR 15; DLB 120

Stanton, Schuyler
See Baum, L(yman) Frank

Stapledon, (William) Olaf
1886-1950 .... TCLC 22
See also CA 111; DLB 15

Starbuck, George (Edwin) 1931-.... CLC 53
See also CA 21-24R; CANR 23

Stark, Richard
See Westlake, Donald E(dwin)

Staunton, Schuyler
See Baum, L(yman) Frank

Stead, Christina (Ellen)
1902-1983 .... CLC 2, 5, 8, 32
See also CA 13-16R; 109; CANR 33, 40;
MTCW

Stead, William Thomas
1849-1912 .... TCLC 48

Steele, Richard 1672-1729 .... LC 18
See also CDBLB 1660-1789; DLB 84, 101

Steele, Timothy (Reid) 1948-....... CLC 45
See also CA 93-96; CANR 16; DLB 120

Steffens, (Joseph) Lincoln
1866-1936 .... TCLC 20
See also CA 117

Stegner, Wallace (Earle) 1909-... CLC 9, 49
See also AITN 1; BEST 90:3; CA 1-4R;
CAAS 9; CANR 1, 21; DLB 9; MTCW

Stein, Gertrude
1874-1946 .... TCLC 1, 6, 28, 48
See also CA 104; 132; CDALB 1917-1929;
DLB 4, 54, 86; MTCW; WLC

Steinbeck, John (Ernst)
1902-1968 ..... CLC 1, 5, 9, 13, 21, 34,
45, 75; SSC 11
See also CA 1-4R; 25-28R; CANR 1, 35;
CDALB 1929-1941; DLB 7, 9; DLBD 2;
MTCW; SATA 9; WLC

Steinem, Gloria 1934-............ CLC 63
See also CA 53-56; CANR 28; MTCW

Steiner, George 1929-............ CLC 24
See also CA 73-76; CANR 31; DLB 67;
MTCW; SATA 62

Steiner, Rudolf 1861-1925........ TCLC 13
See also CA 107

Stendhal 1783-1842............. NCLC 23
See also DLB 119; WLC

Stephen, Leslie 1832-1904........ TCLC 23
See also CA 123; DLB 57

Stephen, Sir Leslie
See Stephen, Leslie

Stephen, Virginia
See Woolf, (Adeline) Virginia

Stephens, James 1882(?)-1950...... TCLC 4
See also CA 104; DLB 19

Stephens, Reed
See Donaldson, Stephen R.

Steptoe, Lydia
See Barnes, Djuna

Sterchi, Beat 1949-.............. CLC 65

Sterling, Brett
See Bradbury, Ray (Douglas); Hamilton,
Edmond

Sterling, Bruce 1954-............ CLC 72
See also CA 119

Sterling, George 1869-1926....... TCLC 20
See also CA 117; DLB 54

Stern, Gerald 1925-............. CLC 40
See also CA 81-84; CANR 28; DLB 105

Stern, Richard (Gustave) 1928-... CLC 4, 39
See also CA 1-4R; CANR 1, 25; DLBY 87

Sternberg, Josef von 1894-1969..... CLC 20
See also CA 81-84

Sterne, Laurence 1713-1768......... LC 2
See also CDBLB 1660-1789; DLB 39; WLC

Sternheim, (William Adolf) Carl
1878-1942 .... TCLC 8
See also CA 105; DLB 56, 118

Stevens, Mark 1951- .... CLC 34
See also CA 122

Stevens, Wallace
1879-1955 .... TCLC 3, 12, 45; PC 6
See also CA 104; 124; CDALB 1929-1941;
DLB 54; MTCW; WLC

Stevenson, Anne (Katharine)
1933- .... CLC 7, 33
See also CA 17-20R; CAAS 9; CANR 9, 33;
DLB 40; MTCW

Stevenson, Robert Louis (Balfour)
1850-1894 .... NCLC 5, 14; SSC 11
See also CDBLB 1890-1914; CLR 10, 11;
DLB 18, 57; MAICYA; WLC; YABC 2

Stewart, J(ohn) I(nnes) M(ackintosh)
1906-................... CLC 7, 14, 32
See also CA 85-88; CAAS 3; MTCW

Stewart, Mary (Florence Elinor)
1916-.................... CLC 7, 35
See also CA 1-4R; CANR 1; SATA 12

Stewart, Mary Rainbow
See Stewart, Mary (Florence Elinor)

Still, James 1906-................ CLC 49
See also CA 65-68; CAAS 17; CANR 10,
26; DLB 9; SATA 29

Sting
See Sumner, Gordon Matthew

Stirling, Arthur
See Sinclair, Upton (Beall)

Stitt, Milan 1941-................ CLC 29
See also CA 69-72

Stockton, Francis Richard 1834-1902
See Stockton, Frank R.
See also CA 108; 137; MAICYA; SATA 44

Stockton, Frank R................ TCLC 47
See also Stockton, Francis Richard
See also DLB 42, 74; SATA 32

Stoddard, Charles
See Kuttner, Henry

Stoker, Abraham 1847-1912
See Stoker, Bram
See also CA 105; SATA 29

Stoker, Bram .... TCLC 8
See also Stoker, Abraham
See also CDBLB 1890-1914; DLB 36, 70;
WLC

Stolz, Mary (Slattery) 1920-....... CLC 12
See also AAYA 8; AITN 1; CA 5-8R;
CANR 13; MAICYA; SAAS 3;
SATA 10, 70, 71

Stone, Irving 1903-1989............ CLC 7
See also AITN 1; CA 1-4R; 129; CAAS 3;
CANR 1, 23; MTCW; SATA 3; SATO 64

Stone, Oliver 1946-............... CLC 73
See also CA 110

Stone, Robert (Anthony)
1937-.................. CLC 5, 23, 42
See also CA 85-88; CANR 23; MTCW

Stone, Zachary
See Follett, Ken(neth Martin)

Stoppard, Tom
1937- ... CLC 1, 3, 4, 5, 8, 15, 29, 34, 63
See also CA 81-84; CANR 39;
CDBLB 1960 to Present; DLB 13;
DLBY 85; MTCW; WLC

Storey, David (Malcolm)
1933- .... CLC **2, 4, 5, 8**
See also CA 81-84; CANR 36; DLB 13, 14;
MTCW

Storm, Hyemeyohsts 1935- .... CLC **3**
See also CA 81-84

Storm, (Hans) Theodor (Woldsen)
1817-1888 .... NCLC **1**

Storni, Alfonsina 1892-1938 .... TCLC **5**
See also CA 104; 131; HW

Stout, Rex (Todhunter) 1886-1975 ... CLC **3**
See also AITN 2; CA 61-64

Stow, (Julian) Randolph 1935- .. CLC **23, 48**
See also CA 13-16R; CANR 33; MTCW

Stowe, Harriet (Elizabeth) Beecher
1811-1896 .... NCLC **3**
See also CDALB 1865-1917; DLB 1, 12, 42,
74; MAICYA; WLC; YABC 1

Strachey, (Giles) Lytton
1880-1932 .... TCLC **12**
See also CA 110; DLBD 10

Strand, Mark 1934- ...... CLC **6, 18, 41, 71**
See also CA 21-24R; CANR 40; DLB 5;
SATA 41

Straub, Peter (Francis) 1943- ...... CLC **28**
See also BEST 89:1; CA 85-88; CANR 28;
DLBY 84; MTCW

Strauss, Botho 1944- .... CLC **22**
See also DLB 124

Streatfeild, (Mary) Noel
1895(?)-1986 .... CLC **21**
See also CA 81-84; 120; CANR 31;
CLR 17; MAICYA; SATA 20, 48

Stribling, T(homas) S(igismund)
1881-1965 .... CLC **23**
See also CA 107; DLB 9

Strindberg, (Johan) August
1849-1912 .... TCLC **1, 8, 21, 47**
See also CA 104; 135; WLC

Stringer, Arthur 1874-1950 .... TCLC **37**
See also DLB 92

Stringer, David
See Roberts, Keith (John Kingston)

Strugatskii, Arkadii (Natanovich)
1925-1991 .... CLC **27**
See also CA 106; 135

Strugatskii, Boris (Natanovich)
1933- .... CLC **27**
See also CA 106

Strummer, Joe 1953(?)- .... CLC **30**
See also Clash, The

Stuart, Don A.
See Campbell, John W(ood Jr.)

Stuart, Ian
See MacLean, Alistair (Stuart)

Stuart, Jesse (Hilton)
1906-1984 .... CLC **1, 8, 11, 14, 34**
See also CA 5-8R; 112; CANR 31; DLB 9,
48, 102; DLBY 84; SATA 2, 36

Sturgeon, Theodore (Hamilton)
1918-1985 .... CLC **22, 39**
See also Queen, Ellery
See also CA 81-84; 116; CANR 32; DLB 8;
DLBY 85; MTCW

Sturges, Preston 1898-1959 .... TCLC **48**
See also CA 114; DLB 26

Styron, William
1925- .... CLC **1, 3, 5, 11, 15, 60**
See also BEST 90:4; CA 5-8R; CANR 6, 33;
CDALB 1968-1988; DLB 2; DLBY 80;
MTCW

Suarez Lynch, B.
See Borges, Jorge Luis

Suarez Lynch, B.
See Bioy Casares, Adolfo; Borges, Jorge
Luis

Su Chien 1884-1918
See Su Man-shu
See also CA 123

Sudermann, Hermann 1857-1928 .. TCLC **15**
See also CA 107; DLB 118

Sue, Eugene 1804-1857 .... NCLC **1**
See also DLB 119

Sueskind, Patrick 1949-........... CLC **44**

Sukenick, Ronald 1932-..... CLC **3, 4, 6, 48**
See also CA 25-28R; CAAS 8; CANR 32;
DLBY 81

Suknaski, Andrew 1942- .... CLC **19**
See also CA 101; DLB 53

Sullivan, Vernon
See Vian, Boris

Sully Prudhomme 1839-1907 ...... TCLC **31**

Su Man-shu .... TCLC **24**
See also Su Chien

Summerforest, Ivy B.
See Kirkup, James

Summers, Andrew James 1942-..... CLC **26**
See also Police, The

Summers, Andy
See Summers, Andrew James

Summers, Hollis (Spurgeon Jr.)
1916- .... CLC **10**
See also CA 5-8R; CANR 3; DLB 6

Summers, (Alphonsus Joseph-Mary Augustus)
Montague 1880-1948 .... TCLC **16**
See also CA 118

Sumner, Gordon Matthew 1951-.... CLC **26**
See also Police, The

Surtees, Robert Smith
1803-1864 .... NCLC **14**
See also DLB 21

Susann, Jacqueline 1921-1974....... CLC **3**
See also AITN 1; CA 65-68; 53-56; MTCW

Suskind, Patrick
See Sueskind, Patrick

Sutcliff, Rosemary 1920-1992 ...... CLC **26**
See also AAYA 10; CA 5-8R; 139;
CANR 37; CLR 1; MAICYA; SATA 6,
44; SATO 73

Sutro, Alfred 1863-1933........... TCLC **6**
See also CA 105; DLB 10

Sutton, Henry
See Slavitt, David R.

Svevo, Italo .... TCLC **2, 35**
See also Schmitz, Aron Hector

Swados, Elizabeth 1951- .... CLC **12**
See also CA 97-100

Swados, Harvey 1920-1972 .... CLC **5**
See also CA 5-8R; 37-40R; CANR 6;
DLB 2

Swan, Gladys 1934- .... CLC **69**
See also CA 101; CANR 17, 39

Swarthout, Glendon (Fred)
1918-1992 .... CLC **35**
See also CA 1-4R; 139; CANR 1; SATA 26

Sweet, Sarah C.
See Jewett, (Theodora) Sarah Orne

Swenson, May 1919-1989..... CLC **4, 14, 61**
See also CA 5-8R; 130; CANR 36; DLB 5;
MTCW; SATA 15

Swift, Augustus
See Lovecraft, H(oward) P(hillips)

Swift, Graham 1949- .... CLC **41**
See also CA 117; 122

Swift, Jonathan 1667-1745.......... LC **1**
See also CDBLB 1660-1789; DLB 39, 95,
101; SATA 19; WLC

Swinburne, Algernon Charles
1837-1909 .... TCLC **8, 36**
See also CA 105; CDBLB 1832-1890;
DLB 35, 57; WLC

Swinfen, Ann .... CLC **34**

Swinnerton, Frank Arthur
1884-1982 .... CLC **31**
See also CA 108; DLB 34

Swithen, John
See King, Stephen (Edwin)

Sylvia
See Ashton-Warner, Sylvia (Constance)

Symmes, Robert Edward
See Duncan, Robert (Edward)

Symonds, John Addington
1840-1893 .... NCLC **34**
See also DLB 57

Symons, Arthur 1865-1945 .... TCLC **11**
See also CA 107; DLB 19, 57

Symons, Julian (Gustave)
1912- .... CLC **2, 14, 32**
See also CA 49-52; CAAS 3; CANR 3, 33;
DLB 87; DLBY 92; MTCW

Synge, (Edmund) J(ohn) M(illington)
1871-1909 .... TCLC **6, 37; DC 2**
See also CA 104; CDBLB 1890-1914;
DLB 10, 19

Syruc, J.
See Milosz, Czeslaw

Szirtes, George 1948-............. CLC **46**
See also CA 109; CANR 27

Tabori, George 1914-............. CLC **19**
See also CA 49-52; CANR 4

Tagore, Rabindranath 1861-1941.... TCLC **3**
See also CA 104; 120; MTCW

Taine, Hippolyte Adolphe
1828-1893 .... NCLC **15**

Talese, Gay 1932-................. CLC **37**
See also AITN 1; CA 1-4R; CANR 9;
MTCW

Tallent, Elizabeth (Ann) 1954- ..... CLC **45**
See also CA 117; DLB 130

Tally, Ted 1952-.................. CLC **42**
See also CA 120; 124

Thurber, James (Grover)
1894-1961 . . . . **CLC 5, 11, 25; SSC 1**
See also CA 73-76; CANR 17, 39;
CDALB 1929-1941; DLB 4, 11, 22, 102;
MAICYA; MTCW; SATA 13

Thurman, Wallace (Henry)
1902-1934 . . . . **TCLC 6**
See also BLC 3; BW; CA 104; 124; DLB 51

Ticheburn, Cheviot
See Ainsworth, William Harrison

Tieck, (Johann) Ludwig
1773-1853 . . . . **NCLC 5**
See also DLB 90

Tiger, Derry
See Ellison, Harlan

Tilghman, Christopher 1948(?)- . . . . . **CLC 65**

Tillinghast, Richard (Williford)
1940- . . . . **CLC 29**
See also CA 29-32R; CANR 26

Timrod, Henry 1828-1867 . . . . **NCLC 25**
See also DLB 3

Tindall, Gillian 1938- . . . . **CLC 7**
See also CA 21-24R; CANR 11

Tiptree, James Jr. . . . . **CLC 48, 50**
See also Sheldon, Alice Hastings Bradley
See also DLB 8

Titmarsh, Michael Angelo
See Thackeray, William Makepeace

**Tocqueville, Alexis (Charles Henri Maurice
Clerel Comte)** 1805-1859 . . . . . **NCLC 7**

Tolkien, J(ohn) R(onald) R(euel)
1892-1973 . . . . **CLC 1, 2, 3, 8, 12, 38**
See also AAYA 10; AITN 1; CA 17-18;
45-48; CANR 36; CAP 2;
CDBLB 1914-1945; DLB 15; MAICYA;
MTCW; SATA 2, 24, 32; WLC

Toller, Ernst 1893-1939 . . . . **TCLC 10**
See also CA 107; DLB 124

Tolson, M. B.
See Tolson, Melvin B(eaunorus)

Tolson, Melvin B(eaunorus)
1898(?)-1966 . . . . **CLC 36**
See also BLC 3; BW; CA 124; 89-92;
DLB 48, 76

Tolstoi, Aleksei Nikolaevich
See Tolstoy, Alexey Nikolaevich

Tolstoy, Alexey Nikolaevich
1882-1945 . . . . **TCLC 18**
See also CA 107

Tolstoy, Count Leo
See Tolstoy, Leo (Nikolaevich)

Tolstoy, Leo (Nikolaevich)
1828-1910 . . . . . **TCLC 4, 11, 17, 28, 44;
SSC 9**
See also CA 104; 123; SATA 26; WLC

Tomasi di Lampedusa, Giuseppe 1896-1957
See Lampedusa, Giuseppe (Tomasi) di
See also CA 111

Tomlin, Lily . . . . **CLC 17**
See also Tomlin, Mary Jean

Tomlin, Mary Jean 1939(?)-
See Tomlin, Lily
See also CA 117

Tomlinson, (Alfred) Charles
1927- . . . . **CLC 2, 4, 6, 13, 45**
See also CA 5-8R; CANR 33; DLB 40

Tonson, Jacob
See Bennett, (Enoch) Arnold

Toole, John Kennedy
1937-1969 . . . . **CLC 19, 64**
See also CA 104; DLBY 81

Toomer, Jean
1894-1967 . . . . . **CLC 1, 4, 13, 22; SSC 1**
See also BLC 3; BW; CA 85-88;
CDALB 1917-1929; DLB 45, 51; MTCW

Torley, Luke
See Blish, James (Benjamin)

Tornimparte, Alessandra
See Ginzburg, Natalia

Torre, Raoul della
See Mencken, H(enry) L(ouis)

Torrey, E(dwin) Fuller 1937- . . . . **CLC 34**
See also CA 119

Torsvan, Ben Traven
See Traven, B.

Torsvan, Benno Traven
See Traven, B.

Torsvan, Berick Traven
See Traven, B.

Torsvan, Berwick Traven
See Traven, B.

Torsvan, Bruno Traven
See Traven, B.

Torsvan, Traven
See Traven, B.

Tournier, Michel (Edouard)
1924- . . . . **CLC 6, 23, 36**
See also CA 49-52; CANR 3, 36; DLB 83;
MTCW; SATA 23

Tournimparte, Alessandra
See Ginzburg, Natalia

Towers, Ivar
See Kornbluth, C(yril) M.

Townsend, Sue 1946- . . . . **CLC 61**
See also CA 119; 127; MTCW; SATA 48,
55

Townshend, Peter (Dennis Blandford)
1945- . . . . **CLC 17, 42**
See also CA 107

Tozzi, Federigo 1883-1920 . . . . **TCLC 31**

Traill, Catharine Parr
1802-1899 . . . . **NCLC 31**
See also DLB 99

Trakl, Georg 1887-1914 . . . . **TCLC 5**
See also CA 104

Transtroemer, Tomas (Goesta)
1931- . . . . **CLC 52, 65**
See also CA 117; 129; CAAS 17

Transtromer, Tomas Gosta
See Transtroemer, Tomas (Goesta)

Traven, B. (?)-1969 . . . . **CLC 8, 11**
See also CA 19-20; 25-28R; CAP 2; DLB 9,
56; MTCW

Treitel, Jonathan 1959- . . . . **CLC 70**

Tremain, Rose 1943- . . . . **CLC 42**
See also CA 97-100; DLB 14

Tremblay, Michel 1942- . . . . **CLC 29**
See also CA 116; 128; DLB 60; MTCW

Trevanian (a pseudonym) 1930(?)- . . . **CLC 29**
See also CA 108

Trevor, Glen
See Hilton, James

Trevor, William
1928- . . . . **CLC 7, 9, 14, 25, 71**
See also Cox, William Trevor
See also DLB 14

Trifonov, Yuri (Valentinovich)
1925-1981 . . . . **CLC 45**
See also CA 126; 103; MTCW

Trilling, Lionel 1905-1975 . . . . **CLC 9, 11, 24**
See also CA 9-12R; 61-64; CANR 10;
DLB 28, 63; MTCW

Trimball, W. H.
See Mencken, H(enry) L(ouis)

Tristan
See Gomez de la Serna, Ramon

Tristram
See Housman, A(lfred) E(dward)

Trogdon, William (Lewis) 1939-
See Heat-Moon, William Least
See also CA 115; 119

Trollope, Anthony 1815-1882 . . **NCLC 6, 33**
See also CDBLB 1832-1890; DLB 21, 57;
SATA 22; WLC

Trollope, Frances 1779-1863 . . . . . **NCLC 30**
See also DLB 21

Trotsky, Leon 1879-1940 . . . . **TCLC 22**
See also CA 118

Trotter (Cockburn), Catharine
1679-1749 . . . . **LC 8**
See also DLB 84

Trout, Kilgore
See Farmer, Philip Jose

Trow, George W. S. 1943- . . . . **CLC 52**
See also CA 126

Troyat, Henri 1911- . . . . **CLC 23**
See also CA 45-48; CANR 2, 33; MTCW

Trudeau, G(arretson) B(eekman) 1948-
See Trudeau, Garry B.
See also CA 81-84; CANR 31; SATA 35

Trudeau, Garry B. . . . . **CLC 12**
See also Trudeau, G(arretson) B(eekman)
See also AAYA 10; AITN 2

Truffaut, Francois 1932-1984 . . . . **CLC 20**
See also CA 81-84; 113; CANR 34

Trumbo, Dalton 1905-1976 . . . . **CLC 19**
See also CA 21-24R; 69-72; CANR 10;
DLB 26

Trumbull, John 1750-1831 . . . . **NCLC 30**
See also DLB 31

Trundlett, Helen B.
See Eliot, T(homas) S(tearns)

Tryon, Thomas 1926-1991 . . . . **CLC 3, 11**
See also AITN 1; CA 29-32R; 135;
CANR 32; MTCW

Tryon, Tom
See Tryon, Thomas

Ts'ao Hsueh-ch'in 1715(?)-1763 . . . . **LC 1**

Walker, Ted...................... CLC 13
See also Walker, Edward Joseph
See also DLB 40

Wallace, David Foster   1962-....... CLC 50
See also CA 132

Wallace, Dexter
See Masters, Edgar Lee

Wallace, Irving   1916-1990...... CLC 7, 13
See also AITN 1; CA 1-4R; 132; CAAS 1;
CANR 1, 27; MTCW

Wallant, Edward Lewis
1926-1962 .... CLC 5, 10
See also CA 1-4R; CANR 22; DLB 2, 28;
MTCW

Walpole, Horace   1717-1797......... LC 2
See also DLB 39, 104

Walpole, Hugh (Seymour)
1884-1941 .... TCLC 5
See also CA 104; DLB 34

Walser, Martin   1927-............ CLC 27
See also CA 57-60; CANR 8; DLB 75, 124

Walser, Robert   1878-1956........ TCLC 18
See also CA 118; DLB 66

Walsh, Jill Paton.................. CLC 35
See also Paton Walsh, Gillian
See also CLR 2; SAAS 3

Walter, Villiam Christian
See Andersen, Hans Christian

Wambaugh, Joseph (Aloysius Jr.)
1937- .... CLC 3, 18
See also AITN 1; BEST 89:3; CA 33-36R;
DLB 6; DLBY 83; MTCW

Ward, Arthur Henry Sarsfield   1883-1959
See Rohmer, Sax
See also CA 108

Ward, Douglas Turner   1930-....... CLC 19
See also BW; CA 81-84; CANR 27; DLB 7,
38

Ward, Peter
See Faust, Frederick (Schiller)

Warhol, Andy   1928(?)-1987........ CLC 20
See also BEST 89:4; CA 89-92; 121;
CANR 34

Warner, Francis (Robert le Plastrier)
1937- .... CLC 14
See also CA 53-56; CANR 11

Warner, Marina   1946-............ CLC 59
See also CA 65-68; CANR 21

Warner, Rex (Ernest)   1905-1986.... CLC 45
See also CA 89-92; 119; DLB 15

Warner, Susan (Bogert)
1819-1885 .... NCLC 31
See also DLB 3, 42

Warner, Sylvia (Constance) Ashton
See Ashton-Warner, Sylvia (Constance)

Warner, Sylvia Townsend
1893-1978 .... CLC 7, 19
See also CA 61-64; 77-80; CANR 16;
DLB 34; MTCW

Warren, Mercy Otis   1728-1814... NCLC 13
See also DLB 31

Warren, Robert Penn
1905-1989 ...   CLC 1, 4, 6, 8, 10, 13, 18,
39, 53, 59; SSC 4
See also AITN 1; CA 13-16R; 129;
CANR 10; CDALB 1968-1988; DLB 2,
48; DLBY 80, 89; MTCW; SATA 46, 63;
WLC

Warshofsky, Isaac
See Singer, Isaac Bashevis

Warton, Thomas   1728-1790........ LC 15
See also DLB 104, 109

Waruk, Kona
See Harris, (Theodore) Wilson

Warung, Price   1855-1911........ TCLC 45

Warwick, Jarvis
See Garner, Hugh

Washington, Alex
See Harris, Mark

Washington, Booker T(aliaferro)
1856-1915 .... TCLC 10
See also BLC 3; BW; CA 114; 125;
SATA 28

Wassermann, (Karl) Jakob
1873-1934 .... TCLC 6
See also CA 104; DLB 66

Wasserstein, Wendy   1950-...... CLC 32, 59
See also CA 121; 129; CABS 3

Waterhouse, Keith (Spencer)
1929- .... CLC 47
See also CA 5-8R; CANR 38; DLB 13, 15;
MTCW

Waters, Roger   1944-............ CLC 35
See also Pink Floyd

Watkins, Frances Ellen
See Harper, Frances Ellen Watkins

Watkins, Gerrold
See Malzberg, Barry N(athaniel)

Watkins, Paul   1964-............ CLC 55
See also CA 132

Watkins, Vernon Phillips
1906-1967 .... CLC 43
See also CA 9-10; 25-28R; CAP 1; DLB 20

Watson, Irving S.
See Mencken, H(enry) L(ouis)

Watson, John H.
See Farmer, Philip Jose

Watson, Richard F.
See Silverberg, Robert

Waugh, Auberon (Alexander)   1939-.. CLC 7
See also CA 45-48; CANR 6, 22; DLB 14

Waugh, Evelyn (Arthur St. John)
1903-1966 ...   CLC 1, 3, 8, 13, 19, 27, 44
See also CA 85-88; 25-28R; CANR 22;
CDBLB 1914-1945; DLB 15; MTCW;
WLC

Waugh, Harriet   1944- .... CLC 6
See also CA 85-88; CANR 22

Ways, C. R.
See Blount, Roy (Alton) Jr.

Waystaff, Simon
See Swift, Jonathan

Webb, (Martha) Beatrice (Potter)
1858-1943 .... TCLC 22
See also Potter, Beatrice
See also CA 117

Webb, Charles (Richard)   1939-...... CLC 7
See also CA 25-28R

Webb, James H(enry) Jr.   1946- .... CLC 22
See also CA 81-84

Webb, Mary (Gladys Meredith)
1881-1927 .... TCLC 24
See also CA 123; DLB 34

Webb, Mrs. Sidney
See Webb, (Martha) Beatrice (Potter)

Webb, Phyllis   1927-.............. CLC 18
See also CA 104; CANR 23; DLB 53

Webb, Sidney (James)
1859-1947 .... TCLC 22
See also CA 117

Webber, Andrew Lloyd............. CLC 21
See also Lloyd Webber, Andrew

Weber, Lenora Mattingly
1895-1971 .... CLC 12
See also CA 19-20; 29-32R; CAP 1;
SATA 2, 26

Webster, John   1579(?)-1634(?) .... DC 2
See also CDBLB Before 1660; DLB 58;
WLC

Webster, Noah   1758-1843 .... NCLC 30

Wedekind, (Benjamin) Frank(lin)
1864-1918 .... TCLC 7
See also CA 104; DLB 118

Weidman, Jerome   1913-........... CLC 7
See also AITN 2; CA 1-4R; CANR 1;
DLB 28

Weil, Simone (Adolphine)
1909-1943 .... TCLC 23
See also CA 117

Weinstein, Nathan
See West, Nathanael

Weinstein, Nathan von Wallenstein
See West, Nathanael

Weir, Peter (Lindsay)   1944- .... CLC 20
See also CA 113; 123

Weiss, Peter (Ulrich)
1916-1982 .... CLC 3, 15, 51
See also CA 45-48; 106; CANR 3; DLB 69,
124

Weiss, Theodore (Russell)
1916- .... CLC 3, 8, 14
See also CA 9-12R; CAAS 2; DLB 5

Welch, (Maurice) Denton
1915-1948 .... TCLC 22
See also CA 121

Welch, James   1940-........ CLC 6, 14, 52
See also CA 85-88

Weldon, Fay
1933(?)-....... CLC 6, 9, 11, 19, 36, 59
See also CA 21-24R; CANR 16;
CDBLB 1960 to Present; DLB 14;
MTCW

Wellek, Rene   1903- .... CLC 28
See also CA 5-8R; CAAS 7; CANR 8;
DLB 63

Weller, Michael   1942-......... CLC 10, 53
See also CA 85-88

Wilde, Oscar (Fingal O'Flahertie Wills)
1854(?)-1900 . . . . . . **TCLC 1, 8, 23, 41;
SSC 11**
See also CA 104; 119; CDBLB 1890-1914;
DLB 10, 19, 34, 57; SATA 24; WLC

Wilder, Billy . . . . **CLC 20**
See also Wilder, Samuel
See also DLB 26

Wilder, Samuel 1906-
See Wilder, Billy
See also CA 89-92

Wilder, Thornton (Niven)
1897-1975 . . . . . **CLC 1, 5, 6, 10, 15, 35;
DC 1**
See also AITN 2; CA 13-16R; 61-64;
CANR 40; DLB 4, 7, 9; MTCW; WLC

Wilding, Michael 1942- . . . . **CLC 73**
See also CA 104; CANR 24

Wiley, Richard 1944- . . . . **CLC 44**
See also CA 121; 129

Wilhelm, Kate . . . . **CLC 7**
See also Wilhelm, Katie Gertrude
See also CAAS 5; DLB 8

Wilhelm, Katie Gertrude 1928-
See Wilhelm, Kate
See also CA 37-40R; CANR 17, 36; MTCW

Wilkins, Mary
See Freeman, Mary Eleanor Wilkins

Willard, Nancy 1936- . . . . **CLC 7, 37**
See also CA 89-92; CANR 10, 39; CLR 5;
DLB 5, 52; MAICYA; MTCW;
SATA 30, 37, 71

Williams, C(harles) K(enneth)
1936- . . . . **CLC 33, 56**
See also CA 37-40R; DLB 5

Williams, Charles
See Collier, James L(incoln)

Williams, Charles (Walter Stansby)
1886-1945 . . . . **TCLC 1, 11**
See also CA 104; DLB 100

Williams, (George) Emlyn
1905-1987 . . . . **CLC 15**
See also CA 104; 123; CANR 36; DLB 10,
77; MTCW

Williams, Hugo 1942- . . . . **CLC 42**
See also CA 17-20R; DLB 40

Williams, J. Walker
See Wodehouse, P(elham) G(renville)

Williams, John A(lfred) 1925- . . . . **CLC 5, 13**
See also BLC 3; BW; CA 53-56; CAAS 3;
CANR 6, 26; DLB 2, 33

Williams, Jonathan (Chamberlain)
1929- . . . . **CLC 13**
See also CA 9-12R; CAAS 12; CANR 8;
DLB 5

Williams, Joy 1944- . . . . **CLC 31**
See also CA 41-44R; CANR 22

Williams, Norman 1952- . . . . **CLC 39**
See also CA 118

Williams, Tennessee
1911-1983 . . . . **CLC 1, 2, 5, 7, 8, 11, 15,
19, 30, 39, 45, 71**
See also AITN 1, 2; CA 5-8R; 108;
CABS 3; CANR 31; CDALB 1941-1968;
DLB 7; DLBD 4; DLBY 83; MTCW;
WLC

Williams, Thomas (Alonzo)
1926-1990 . . . . **CLC 14**
See also CA 1-4R; 132; CANR 2

Williams, William C.
See Williams, William Carlos

Williams, William Carlos
1883-1963 . . . **CLC 1, 2, 5, 9, 13, 22, 42,
67**
See also CA 89-92; CANR 34;
CDALB 1917-1929; DLB 4, 16, 54, 86;
MTCW

Williamson, David Keith 1942- . . . . . **CLC 56**
See also CA 103

Williamson, Jack . . . . **CLC 29**
See also Williamson, John Stewart
See also CAAS 8; DLB 8

Williamson, John Stewart 1908-
See Williamson, Jack
See also CA 17-20R; CANR 23

Willie, Frederick
See Lovecraft, H(oward) P(hillips)

Willingham, Calder (Baynard Jr.)
1922- . . . . **CLC 5, 51**
See also CA 5-8R; CANR 3; DLB 2, 44;
MTCW

Willis, Charles
See Clarke, Arthur C(harles)

Willy
See Colette, (Sidonie-Gabrielle)

Willy, Colette
See Colette, (Sidonie-Gabrielle)

Wilson, A(ndrew) N(orman) 1950- . . **CLC 33**
See also CA 112; 122; DLB 14

Wilson, Angus (Frank Johnstone)
1913-1991 . . . . **CLC 2, 3, 5, 25, 34**
See also CA 5-8R; 134; CANR 21; DLB 15;
MTCW

Wilson, August
1945- . . . . **CLC 39, 50, 63; DC 2**
See also BLC 3; BW; CA 115; 122; MTCW

Wilson, Brian 1942- . . . . **CLC 12**

Wilson, Colin 1931- . . . . **CLC 3, 14**
See also CA 1-4R; CAAS 5; CANR 1, 22,
33; DLB 14; MTCW

Wilson, Dirk
See Pohl, Frederik

Wilson, Edmund
1895-1972 . . . . **CLC 1, 2, 3, 8, 24**
See also CA 1-4R; 37-40R; CANR 1;
DLB 63; MTCW

Wilson, Ethel Davis (Bryant)
1888(?)-1980 . . . . **CLC 13**
See also CA 102; DLB 68; MTCW

Wilson, John (Anthony) Burgess
1917- . . . . **CLC 8, 10, 13**
See also Burgess, Anthony
See also CA 1-4R; CANR 2; MTCW

Wilson, John 1785-1854 . . . . **NCLC 5**

Wilson, Lanford 1937- . . . . **CLC 7, 14, 36**
See also CA 17-20R; CABS 3; DLB 7

Wilson, Robert M. 1944- . . . . **CLC 7, 9**
See also CA 49-52; CANR 2; MTCW

Wilson, Robert McLiam 1964- . . . . . **CLC 59**
See also CA 132

Wilson, Sloan 1920- . . . . **CLC 32**
See also CA 1-4R; CANR 1

Wilson, Snoo 1948- . . . . **CLC 33**
See also CA 69-72

Wilson, William S(mith) 1932- . . . . . **CLC 49**
See also CA 81-84

Winchilsea, Anne (Kingsmill) Finch Counte
1661-1720 . . . . **LC 3**

Windham, Basil
See Wodehouse, P(elham) G(renville)

Wingrove, David (John) 1954- . . . . . . **CLC 68**
See also CA 133

Winters, Janet Lewis . . . . **CLC 41**
See also Lewis, Janet
See also DLBY 87

Winters, (Arthur) Yvor
1900-1968 . . . . **CLC 4, 8, 32**
See also CA 11-12; 25-28R; CAP 1;
DLB 48; MTCW

Winterson, Jeanette 1959- . . . . **CLC 64**
See also CA 136

Wiseman, Frederick 1930- . . . . **CLC 20**

Wister, Owen 1860-1938 . . . . **TCLC 21**
See also CA 108; DLB 9, 78; SATA 62

Witkacy
See Witkiewicz, Stanislaw Ignacy

Witkiewicz, Stanislaw Ignacy
1885-1939 . . . . **TCLC 8**
See also CA 105

Wittig, Monique 1935(?)- . . . . **CLC 22**
See also CA 116; 135; DLB 83

Wittlin, Jozef 1896-1976 . . . . **CLC 25**
See also CA 49-52; 65-68; CANR 3

Wodehouse, P(elham) G(renville)
1881-1975 . . . **CLC 1, 2, 5, 10, 22; SSC 2**
See also AITN 2; CA 45-48; 57-60;
CANR 3, 33; CDBLB 1914-1945;
DLB 34; MTCW; SATA 22

Woiwode, L.
See Woiwode, Larry (Alfred)

Woiwode, Larry (Alfred) 1941- . . . **CLC 6, 10**
See also CA 73-76; CANR 16; DLB 6

Wojciechowska, Maia (Teresa)
1927- . . . . **CLC 26**
See also AAYA 8; CA 9-12R; CANR 4;
CLR 1; MAICYA; SAAS 1; SATA 1, 28

Wolf, Christa 1929- . . . . **CLC 14, 29, 58**
See also CA 85-88; DLB 75; MTCW

Wolfe, Gene (Rodman) 1931- . . . . **CLC 25**
See also CA 57-60; CAAS 9; CANR 6, 32;
DLB 8

Wolfe, George C. 1954- . . . . **CLC 49**

Wolfe, Thomas (Clayton)
1900-1938 . . . . **TCLC 4, 13, 29**
See also CA 104; 132; CDALB 1929-1941;
DLB 9, 102; DLBD 2; DLBY 85;
MTCW; WLC

Wolfe, Thomas Kennerly Jr. 1930-
See Wolfe, Tom
See also CA 13-16R; CANR 9, 33; MTCW

Wolfe, Tom . . . . **CLC 1, 2, 9, 15, 35, 51**
See also Wolfe, Thomas Kennerly Jr.
See also AAYA 8; AITN 2; BEST 89:1

Literary Criticism Series
Cumulative Topic Index

This index lists all topic entries in the Gale Literary Criticism Series *Contemporary Literary Criticism, Literature Criticism from 1400 to 1800, Nineteenth-Century Literature Criticism,* and *Twentieth-Century Literary Criticism.*

LC Cumulative Nationality Index

AFGHAN
Bābur 18

AMERICAN
Bradstreet, Anne 4
Edwards, Jonathan 7
Eliot, John 5
Knight, Sarah Kemble 7
Munford, Robert 5
Taylor, Edward 11
Wheatley, Phillis 3

ANGLO-AFRICAN
Equiano, Olaudah 16

CANADIAN
Marie de l'Incarnation 10

CHINESE
Lo Kuan-chung 12
P'u Sung-ling 3
Ts'ao Hsueh-ch'in 1
Wu Ch'eng-En 7
Wu-Ching-tzu 2

DANO-NORWEGIAN
Holberg, Ludvig 6
Wessel, Johan Herman 7

DUTCH
Erasmus, Desiderius 16
Lipsius, Justus 16
Spinoza, Benedictus de 9

ENGLISH
Addison, Joseph 18
Andrewes, Lancelot 5
Arbuthnot, John 1
Aubin, Penelope 9

Bacon, Sir Francis 18
Behn, Aphra 1
Brooke, Frances 6
Bunyan, John 4
Burke, Edmund 7
Butler, Samuel 16
Carew, Thomas 13
Caxton, William 17
Chapman, George 22
Charles I 13
Chatterton, Thomas 3
Chaucer, Geoffrey 17
Churchill, Charles 3
Cleland, John 2
Collier, Jeremy 6
Collins, William 4
Congreve, William 5, 21
Davenant, William 13
Davys, Mary 1
Day, Thomas 1
Dee, John 20
Defoe, Daniel 1
Dekker, Thomas 22
Delany, Mary 12
Dennis, John 11
Donne, John 10
Drayton, Michael 8
Dryden, John 3, 21
Elyot, Sir Thomas 11
Fanshawe, Anne, Lady 11
Farquhar, George 21
Fielding, Henry 1
Fielding, Sarah 1
Foxe, John 14
Garrick, David 15
Goldsmith, Oliver 2
Gray, Thomas 4
Hawes, Stephen 17
Haywood, Eliza 1

Henry VIII 10
Herrick, Robert 13
Howell, James 13
Hunter, Robert 7
Johnson, Samuel 15
Jonson, Ben 6
Julian of Norwich 6
Kempe, Margery 6
Killegrew, Anne 4
Kyd, Thomas 22
Langland, William 19
Lanyer, Aemilia 10
Locke, John 7
Lyttelton, George 10
Malory, Thomas 11
Manley, Mary Delariviere 1
Marlowe, Christopher 22
Marvell, Andrew 4
Milton, John 9
Montagu, Mary Wortley, Lady 9
More, Henry 9
More, Sir Thomas 10
Parnell, Thomas 3
Pepys, Samuel 11
Pix, Mary 8
Pope, Alexander 3
Prior, Matthew 4
Reynolds, Sir Joshua 15
Richardson, Samuel 1
Roper, William 10
Rowe, Nicholas 8
Sheridan, Frances 7
Sidney, Mary 19
Sidney, Sir Philip 19
Smart, Christopher 3
Smith, John 9
Spenser, Edmund 5
Steele, Sir Richard 18
Sterne, Laurence 2

LC Cumulative Title Index

Title Index

Title Index

See *Moralske fabler*
The Moral Law Expounded (Andrewes) **5**:28
Moral Proverbs (Christine de Pizan)
　See *Prouverbes moraux*
Moral Reflections (Holberg)
　See *Moralske tanker*
Moral Tales (Marmontel)
　See *Contes moraux*
Moral Teachings (Christine de Pizan)
　See *Enseignemens moraux*
Morale universelle (Holbach) **14**:152, 155-56, 160, 168, 175
Moralske fabler (*Moral Fables*) (Holberg) **6**:278
Moralske tanker (*Moral Reflections*) (Holberg) **6**:266, 273, 278
Moria (Erasmus)
　See *Moriae encomium*
Moriae encomium (*Encomium moriae*; *Folly*; *Moria*; *The Praise of Folly*) (Erasmus) **16**:107-17, 127, 130-33, 135-39, 142, 149, 152-55, 157-62, 165-73, 175-76, 181-83, 185-92, 194-95, 202-07
"Morning" (Parnell)
　See "A Hymn for Morning"
"Morning" (Smart) **3**:366
"Morning" (Wheatley)
　See "An Hymn to the Morning"
"Morning. The Author confined to College" (Warton) **15**:440, 463
"La morosophie" (Rousseau) **9**:345
Morte Arthur (Malory)
　See *Morte Darthur*
Morte Arthure (Malory)
　See *Morte Darthur*
Le Morte d'Arthur (Malory)
　See *Morte Darthur*
Morte Darthur (*The Book of King Arthur and His Noble Knights of the Round Table*; *Morte Arthur*, *Morte Arthure*; *Le Morte d'Arthur*, *The Noble and Joyous Book Entytled Le Morte Darthur*, *The Works of Sir Thomas Malory*) (Malory) **11**:113-202
Mortimer His Fall (Jonson) **6**:311
Mortimeriados. The Lamentable Civell Warres of Edward the Second and the Barrons (Drayton) **8**:19-20, 30, 33
"Moses" (Parnell) **3**:255
"Mother Hubberd's Tale" (Spenser)
　See "Prosopopoia; or, Mother Hubberds Tale"
"A Mountebank" (Butler) **16**:50
"Mourning" (Marvell) **4**:397, 408-10, 425, 439
The Mourning Bride (Congreve) **5**:68-9, 72, 74-6, 79, 85, 88, 101-02, 110-11; **21**:10
"Mourning Muses" (Congreve) **5**:75
Movements of Water (Vinci)
　See *On the Motion and Power of Water*
"The Mower against gardens" (Marvell) **4**:403, 410, 441-42
"The Mower to the Glo-Worms" (Marvell) **4**:411, 425, 441-42
"The Mower's Song" (Marvell) **4**:411, 442
Mr. Burke's Speech, on the 1st December 1783, upon the Question for the Speaker's Leaving the Chair, in Order for the House to Resolve Itself into a Committee on Mr. Fox's East Indian Bill (*Speech on the East India Bill*) (Burke) **7**:34
Mr. Collier's Dissuasive from the Playhouse (Collier) **6**:229

Mr. Howell's Poems upon divers Emergent Occasions (Howell) **13**:427, 431
Mr. Limberham (Dryden)
　See *The Kind Keeper; or, Mr. Limberham*
Mr. Smirk; or, The Divine in Mode (*The Divine in Mode*) (Marvell) **4**:394, 399
Mr. Steele's Apology for Himself and His Writings (Steele) **18**:336, 338, 340
Mubayyan (Babur) **18**:89-91
Mubin (Babur) **18**:87
"Muiopotmos" (Spenser) **5**:305, 312, 329-31, 345, 347-49
"The Murder of the Dog" (Wessel) **7**:391
"Les murs de Troie" (Perrault) **2**:274
"The Muse" (Kochanowski)
　See "Muza"
The Muses Elizium, Lately Discovered, by a New Way over Parnassus. The Passages Therein, Being the Subject of Ten Sundry Nymphalls (Drayton) **8**:21, 28, 31, 34, 37, 40-1, 50
"Musicks Empire" (Marvell) **4**:442-43
"Muza" ("The Muse") (Kochanowski) **10**:160
"My ain kind Dearie" (Burns) **3**:71
"My Daughter Hannah Wiggin Her Recovery from a Dangerous Fever" (Bradstreet) **4**:100
"My Heart Was Slaine, and None But You and I" (Drayton)
　See "Sonnet 2"
"My Luve Is Like a Red, Red Rose" ("A Red, Red Rose") (Burns) **3**:76, 78, 83
"My Nanie O" (Burns) **3**:71
"My Noble Lovely Little Peggy" (Prior) **4**:464
"My Picture Left in Scotland" (Jonson) **6**:347
"My Son's Return out of England" (Bradstreet) **4**:100
"My thankful heart with glorying tongue" (Bradstreet) **4**:107
The Mysterious Mother (Walpole) **2**:451, 459-60, 473-75, 486, 488, 501, 505-06
"Mystery of Godliness" (More) **9**:300
"Mystery of Iniquity" (More) **9**:300
"Na lipe" ("To the Linden Tree") (Kochanowski) **10**:161
"Na nabożną" ("The Pious Woman") (Kochanowski) **10**:160
El nacimiento de Montesinos (Castro) **19**:13-15
Nafahát al-uns (*Breaths of Familiarity*) (Jami) **9**:67, 71
"Die Namen" (Lessing) **8**:69
Nanine (Voltaire) **14**:338
"Narcissa" (Young)
　See "The Complaint; or, Night Thoughts: Night the Third"
Narcisse (Rousseau) **14**:309
Narrative (Equiano)
　See *The Interesting Narrative of the Life of Olaudah Equiano, or Gustavus Vassa, the African*
Der Narrenspital (Beer) **5**:53-4
"Narva and Mored" (Chatterton) **3**:123
Nathan der Weise (*Nathan the Wise*) (Lessing) **8**:59, 61-3, 66-9, 71, 77-9, 83-7, 89, 94-100, 106-07, 112, 114-16
Nathan the Wise (Lessing)
　See *Nathan der Weise*
"Nativity Ode" (Milton)
　See "On the Morning of Christ's Nativity"

"The Nativity of Our Lord and Savior Jesus Christ" (Smart)
　See "Hymn on the Nativity of Our Lord and Saviour Jesus Christ"
The Nature of True Virtue (Edwards) **7**:93, 95, 102, 108-09, 118-20, 124, 131
"Naufragium" ("The Shipwreck") (Erasmus) **16**:128, 141, 174, 194
Naval Minutes (Pepys) **11**:239-41
Nay-namá (*Book of the Reed*) (Jami) **9**:66
A Necessary Doctrine and Erudition for any Christen Man, Sette Furthe by the Kynges Majestie of Englande (*King's Book*) (Henry VIII) **10**:131, 133, 135-37, 139, 141
Neck or Nothing (Garrick) **15**:98, 101-02
"Negli anni molti e nelle molte pruove" (Michelangelo) **12**:363, 371
Nemo (*The Nobody*) (Hutten) **16**:224, 230, 232-33, 245
Neptunes Triumph (Jonson) **6**:337-38
Neptuno Alegórico (Juana Ines de la Cruz) **5**:144
"N'ésperons plus, mon âme, aux promesses du monde" (Malherbe) **5**:181
Der neu ausgefertigte Jungfer-Hobel (*Jungfer-Hobel*) (Beer) **5**:53, 56
Ein neu Lied (*A New Song*) (Hutten) **16**:242, 247
Die neue Cecilia (Moritz) **2**:244-45
Neues ABC Buch, welches zugleich eine Anleitung zum Denken für Kinder enthält (Moritz) **2**:246
"Ein neues Lied wir heben an" ("We Raise a New Song") (Luther) **9**:143
La neuvaine de Cythère (Marmontel) **2**:213
"A New Arabian Night's Entertainment" (Walpole) **2**:500
The New Atalantis (*The Lady's Pacquet of Letters Broke Open*; *Memoirs from Europe Towards the Close of the Eighth Century*; *The Secret Memoirs and Manners of Several Persons of Quality*) (Manley) **1**:306-24
New Atlantis (Bacon)
　See *Nova Atlantis*
New Eloise (Rousseau)
　See *La Nouvelle Héloïse*
New Englands Trials (Smith) **9**:352, 355, 358, 383
A New English Grammar Prescribing as certain Rules as the Language will have for Forreners to learn English. There is also another Grammar of the Spanish or Castillian Toung. (Howell) **13**:427
The New House (Goldoni)
　See *La casa nova*
The New Inn (Jonson) **6**:302, 304, 306, 311, 314, 339
"A New Psalm for the Chapel of Kilmarnock" (Burns) **3**:95
A New Song (Hutten)
　See *Ein neu Lied*
A New Voyage Round the World (Defoe) **1**:133, 174, 176
"A New-Yeares Gift sent to Sir Simeon Steward" ("New Year's Gift") (Herrick) **13**:310, 351-52, 365
"A New-yeares gift. To the King" (Carew) **13**:44
"New Year's Gift" (Herrick)
　See "A New-Yeares Gift sent to Sir Simeon Steward"
New Year's Wishes (Hutten) **16**:225

"The Soldier" ("The Soldier and the
Carthusian") (Erasmus) **16**:119, 195
"The Soldier and the Carthusian" (Erasmus)
See "The Soldier"
"The Soldier and the Carthusian" (Erasmus)
See "The Carthusian"
"The Soldier going to the Field" (Davenant)
13:195
The Soldier's Fortune (Behn) **1**:33
Soliloquium animae (Kempis) **11**:410
Soliloquy of a Beauty in the Country
(Lyttelton) **10**:197, 203
Soliman and Perseda (*Hieronimo*) (Kyd)
22:247, 252-256, 259, 275
De solitudine et silentio (Kempis) **11**:411
"Solomon" (Parnell) **3**:255
"Solomon" (Prior)
See "Solomon on the Vanity of the World"
"Solomon on the Vanity of the World"
("Solomon") (Prior) **4**:455-56, 458-62, 464,
466-68, 470-73
"Solving a Difficult Case" (P'u Sung-ling)
3:345
Solyman and Perseda (Kyd)
See *Tragedy*
*Some Considerations on Doctor Kennet's Second
and Third Letters* (Collier) **6**:209
"Some Reflections" (Winchilsea) **3**:451
*Some Sober Inspections Made into the Carriage
and Consults of the Late Long Parliament*
(*Sober Inspections*) (Howell) **13**:419-20
Some Thoughts concerning Education (Locke)
7:271, 280-81
Somnium (Buchanan) **4**:119, 123, 134, 138
"The Son of God" (More) **9**:298
Sonets amoureux (Ronsard) **6**:426
Sonetti Lussuriosi (*Sonnets*) (Aretino) **12**:14,
18, 21-2, 25
"Song" (Herrick)
See "To the Rose. Song"
"A Song" (Prior) **4**:465
"Song 1" (Drayton) **8**:46
"Song III" (Kochanowski) **10**:161
"Song 5" (Drayton) **8**:46
"Song IX" (Kochanowski) **10**:161
"Song 18" (Drayton) **8**:46
"Song 26" (Drayton) **8**:48
"Song 30" (Drayton) **8**:48
"Song. Endymion Porter and Olivia"
(Davenant) **13**:195
"A Song from Cymbeline" ("Dirge for
Cymbeline") (Collins) **4**:214, 217, 224, 230
"Song. 'Goe, and catche a falling starre'"
("Goe, and catche a falling starre") (Donne)
10:50, 52
"Song: My Days Have Been so Wondrous
Free" (Parnell) **3**:255
"Song of Death" (Burns) **3**:81
"The Song of the Spirit" (John of the Cross)
18:209-11
"A Song on a Painting Depicting the God
Êrh-lang Hunting in the Surrounding
Country with His Followers" (Wu Ch'eng-
en)
See "Êrh-lang Sou-shan-t'u Ko"
"Song. 'Sweetest love, I do not goe'"
("Sweetest love, I do not goe") (Donne)
10:12, 26, 31-2, 36, 52, 58, 82, 96
"Song to Celia" ("Drink to Me Only with
Thine Eyes") (Jonson) **6**:304-05, 317, 322-
23, 346, 349

"A Song to David" (Smart) **3**:365, 369-82,
285-89, 391, 393, 395-401, 403
"A Song to the Maskers" (Herrick) **13**:351,
399, 401
"Song, To Two Lovers Condemn'd to Die"
(Davenant) **13**:205
"A Song upon Sylvia" (Herrick) **13**:367
Songs (Kochanowski)
See *Pieśni*
Songs and Sonets (Donne) **10**:32-3, 35-6, 47,
50, 52, 54-5, 57, 63, 66, 81-2, 84, 88, 92-3,
96, 98, 106
"Songs of the Bride" (John of the Cross)
See "Canciones de la Esposa"
"Songs of the Soul" (John of the Cross)
18:216
"Sonnet 2" ("My Heart Was Slaine, and None
But You and I") (Drayton) **8**:39
"Sonnet 7" ("Love, in a Humor, Play'd the
Prodigall") (Drayton) **8**:39
"Sonnet VIII" ("There's Nothing Grieves Me,
But that Age Should Haste") (Drayton)
8:23
"Sonnet 22" ("With Fooles and Children Good
Discretion Beares") (Drayton) **8**:39
"Sonnet 23" ("Love Banish'd Heav'n, in Earth
Was Held in Scorne") (Drayton) **8**:39
"Sonnet 24" ("I Heare Some Say, this Man Is
Not in Love") (Drayton) **8**:38
"Sonnet 31" ("Me Thinks I See Some Crooked
Mimicke Jeere") (Drayton) **8**:38
"Sonnet 36" ("Thou Purblind Boy, since Thou
Hast Beene So Slacke") (Drayton) **8**:39
"Sonnet XLII" (Ronsard) **6**:413
"Sonnet XLIII" (Ronsard) **6**:413
"Sonnet 46" ("Plaine-Path'd Experience,
th'Unlearneds Guide") (Drayton) **8**:39
"Sonnet 48" ("Cupid, I Hate Thee, Which I'de
Have Thee Know") (Drayton) **8**:39
"Sonnet LVII" (Ronsard) **6**:430
"Sonnet LIX" ("As Love and I, Late
Harbour'd in One Inne") (Drayton) **8**:23
"Sonnet 61" ("Idea 61") (Drayton) **8**:39
"Sonnet 62" ("When First I Ended, Then I
First Began") (Drayton) **8**:39
"Sonnet LXVI" (Spenser) **5**:363
"Sonnet LXXVI" (Ronsard) **6**:430
"Sonnet CLXXIV" (Ronsard) **6**:431
"Sonnet CXXVII" (Ronsard) **6**:430
"Sonnet on Bathing" (Warton) **15**:441
"Sonnet on Hope" (Juana Ines de la Cruz)
5:144
"Sonnet on the Death of Mr. Richard West"
("On the Death of Mr. Richard West")
(Gray) **4**:286, 294, 296, 314-15, 322-23
"Sonnet Written after seeing Wilton-House"
(Warton) **15**:444
"Sonnet Written at Winslade in Hampshire"
(Warton) **15**:441
"Sonnet Written in a Blank Leaf of Dugdale's
'Monasticon'" (Warton) **15**:435, 443, 455
Sonnets (Aretino)
See *Sonetti Lussuriosi*
Sonnets (Warton) **15**:435
Sonnets for Hélène (Ronsard)
See *Sonnets pour Hélène*
Sonnets pour Hélène (*Sonnets for Hélène*)
(Ronsard) **6**:413, 417
Sonnets to Idea (Drayton)
See *Idea*
Le Sopha (Crebillon) **1**:75-7, 79, 81, 88-9
Sophonisba (Thomson)

See *The Tragedy of Sophonisba*
Sophonisbas (Thomson) **16**:393, 395
"Sophronyme" (Rousseau) **9**:345
"Sot" (Butler) **16**:50-1
"Les souhaits ridicules" ("The Ridiculous
Wishes") (Perrault) **2**:253-56, 261, 266,
279-80
"The soul is the salt" (Herrick) **13**:341
"The Spanish Doctor" (Kochanowski)
See "O doktorze Hiszpanie"
The Spanish Friar (Behn) **1**:47
The Spanish Friar (*The Spanish Fryar*)
(Dryden) **3**:186, 193, 210, 214, 229-30, 233;
21:55-7
The Spanish Fryar (Dryden)
See *The Spanish Friar*
The Spanish Lovers (Davenant) **13**:176
*The Spanish Tragedie of Don Horatio and
Bellmipeia* (Kyd) **22**:254
Spanish Tragedy; or, Hieronimo is mad again
(Kyd) **22**:246
The Spanish Wives (*Wives*) (Pix) **8**:259-61,
263, 265, 267-69, 271-72, 274-77
Spartam nactus es (Erasmus) **16**:198
"A speach according to Horace" (Jonson)
6:350
Specimen of an Etimological Vocabulary
(Cleland) **2**:53
Le spectateur Français (Marivaux) **4**:358-60,
371-72, 378-80
The Spectator (Addison) **18**:4, 7, 13-15, 20-1,
24, 26-8, 32-7, 39, 42-4, 46-9, 50-1, 53-4, 58,
60, 63-8, 69-71, 72-6, 78
The Spectator (Steele) **18**:313, 318, 320-22,
330-31, 333-37, 340-44, 348, 351-55, 359,
368-70, 372, 376-77, 384-85
The Spectator, 5 (Addison) **18**:51
The Spectator, 10 (Addison) **18**:50, 65
The Spectator, 26 (Addison) **18**:54
The Spectator, 26 (Steele) **18**:324
The Spectator, 35 (Addison) **18**:77
The Spectator, 38 (Addison) **18**:74
The Spectator, 39 (Addison) **18**:8, 39
The Spectator, 40 (Addison) **18**:39, 77
The Spectator, 42 (Addison) **18**:39
The Spectator, 42 (Steele) **18**:326
The Spectator, 44 (Addison) **18**:39
The Spectator, 45 (Addison) **18**:39
The Spectator, 47 (Steele) **18**:372
The Spectator, 58-63 (Addison) **18**:39, 65
The Spectator, 62 (Addison) **18**:56
The Spectator, 65 (Steele) **18**:372, 383
The Spectator, 66 (Steele) **18**:347
The Spectator, 69 (Addison) **18**:35
The Spectator, 70 (Addison) **18**:56
The Spectator, 74 (Addison) **18**:56
The Spectator, 79 (Steele) **18**:318
The Spectator, 84 (Steele) **18**:318
The Spectator, 85 (Addison) **18**:77
The Spectator, 94 (Addison) **18**:57
The Spectator, 120 (Addison) **18**:57
The Spectator, 125 (Addison) **18**:33, 35
The Spectator, 126 (Addison) **18**:55
The Spectator, 144 (Steele) **18**:346
The Spectator, 158 (Addison) **18**:35
The Spectator, 160 (Addison) **18**:57
The Spectator, 219 (Addison) **18**:71
The Spectator, 237 (Addison) **18**:57
The Spectator, 249 (Steele) **18**:372
The Spectator, 259 (Steele) **18**:318
The Spectator, 267 (Addison) **18**:40, 78
The Spectator, 290 (Steele) **18**:318

Title Index

Title Index

Title Index

ISBN 0-8103-7964-3

90000

9 780810 379640